WORLD PRESS ENCYCLOPEDIA

A SURVEY OF PRESS SYSTEMS WORLDWIDE

SECOND EDITION

VOLUME 1

A–M

WORLD PRESS ENCYCLOPEDIA

A SURVEY OF PRESS SYSTEMS WORLDWIDE

SECOND EDITION

VOLUME 1
A–M

AMANDA C. QUICK, PROJECT EDITOR

Detroit • New York • San Diego • San Francisco • Cleveland • New Haven, Conn. • Waterville, Maine • London • Munich

World Press Encyclopedia, Second Edition
A Survey of Press Systems Worldwide

Project Editor
Amanda C. Quick

Editorial
Mary Alampi, Erin E. Braun, Dawn Conzett DesJardins, Kristen A. Dorsch, Grant Eldridge, Andrew J. Homburg, Eric Hoss, Sarah Knox, Paul Lewon, Chris Lopez, Kristin B. Mallegg, Jane A. Malonis, Rebecca Marlow-Ferguson, Erin Nagel, Terry Peck, Tyra Y. Phillips, Chrystal Rozsa, Kathy Sauer, Jennifer Smith, Jeff Sumner, Valerie Webster, Courtney Young, Margaret Zellers

Permissions
Lori Hines

Imaging and Multimedia
Christine O'Bryan

Product Design
Michael Logusz, Jennifer Wahi

Manufacturing
Wendy Blurton

For more information, contact
The Gale Group, Inc.
27500 Drake Rd.
Farmington Hills, MI 48331-3535
Or you can visit our Internet site at
http://www.gale.com

LIBRARY OF CONGRESS CATALOGING-IN-PUBLICATION DATA

Quick, Amanda C.
World press encyclopedia : a survey of press systems worldwide / Amanda C. Quick.-- 2nd ed.
p. cm.
Includes bibliographical references and index.
ISBN 0-7876-5582-1 (set) -- ISBN 0-7876-5583-X (v. 1) -- ISBN 0-7876-5584-8 (v. 2)
1. Press--Encyclopedias. 2. Mass media--Encyclopedias. I. Title.
PN4728 .Q53 2002
070'.03--dc21

2002152063

Printed in the United States of America
10 9 8 7 6 5 4 3 2 1

TABLE OF CONTENTS

VOLUME 2

Y

Z

Appendix 1

Appendix 2

Appendix 3

Contributor Notes

Öyvind Aadland: Director of Research, *Gimlekolen Mediasenter,* Kristiansand, Norway

Binod Agrawal: Ph.D., Director at *TALEEM,* research foundation in Ahmedabad, India

Khalid Al-Jaber: Arab media authority and master's candidate, Department of Communication Arts, *University of West Florida,* Pensacola, Florida

Eduardo Alemán: Doctoral Candidate, Department of Political Science, *University of California,* Los Angeles

William C. Allen: Associate Professor, Journalism and Mass Communications, *Virginia State University,* Petersburg, Virginia

Philip Auter: Ph.D., Assistant Professor, Department of Communication, *University of Louisiana at Lafayette,* Lafayette, Louisiana

Clint B. Thomas Baldwin: Instructor and Ph.D. (candidate), College of Communications & Information Studies, *University of Kentucky,* Lexington, Kentucky

Brigitte H. Bechtold: Professor of Sociology and Director of European Studies, *Central Michigan University,* Mt. Pleasant, Michigan

Richard W. Benfield: Associate Professor, Department of Geography, *Central Connecticut State University,* New Britain, Connecticut

Karima Benremouga: Associate Dean, Fine Arts and Language Arts, *San Jacinto College,* Texas

Mark Browning: Associate Professor of English, *Johnson County Community College,* Overland Park, Kansas

Sandra J. Callaghan: Director of Development, *Alverno College,* Milwaukee, Wisconsin

Alice-Catherine Carls: Professor of History, *University of Tennessee at Martin*

Rafael Chabrán: Associate Dean for Academic Advisement and First Year Experience and Professor of Spanish, *Whittier College,* Whittier, California

Siegfried Christoph: Professor, Modern Languages Department, *University of Wisconsin-Parkside*

William G. Covington, Jr.: Assistant Professor, Department of Speech and Communication Studies, *Edinboro University of Pennsylvania*

Merrilee Cunningham: Associate Professor, *University of Houston Downtown,* Houston, Texas

Jenny B. Davis: Professional writer

Haig Der-Houssikian: Professor of Linguistics, *University of Florida,* Gainesville, Florida

Emily Dial-Driver: Professor, Department of Communications and Fine Arts, *Rogers State University,* Claremore, Oklahoma

Martin DiNatale: Journalist from *La Nación,* Buenos Aires, Argentina

Arina Dmitriyeva: B.A., International Affairs, *The American University*

Grigory Dmitriyev: Professor, College of Education, *Georgia Southern University,* Statesboro, Georgia

Barbara Lakeberg Dridi: Ph.D., Founder and Principal Researcher, *Concordia International Research,* Philadelphia, Pennsylvania

Eric H. du Plessis: Professor, Department of Foreign Languages and Literatures, *Radford University,* Radford, Virginia

Bonnie W. Epstein: Associate Professor, Department of English, *Plymouth State College,* Plymouth, New Hampshire

Mark Fackler: Professor, Department of Communication Arts and Sciences, *Calvin College,* Grand Rapids, Michigan

John P. Ferré: Professor, Department of Communication, *University of Louisville,* Kentucky

Denis Fitzgerald: Correspondent, *World Press Review*

Helen H. Frink: Professor, Department of Modern Languages, *Keene State College,* Keene, New Hampshire

Leon Ginsberg: Ph.D., Interim Dean and Carolina Distinguished Professor, College of Social Work, *University of South Carolina,* Columbia

Roy Neil Graves: Professor, Department of English, *The University of Tennessee at Martin*

Sister/Dr. Pamela M. Gross: Associate Professor of History and Geography, *Adams State College,* Alamosa, Colorado

Mark Hampton: Assistant Professor, Department of History; Director, Honors Program, *Wesleyan College,* Macon, Georgia

Jennifer Hasty: Assistant Professor, Department of Anthropology, *Pacific Lutheran University,* Tacoma, Washington

Joni Hubred: Editor, *Farmington Observer* (Michigan)

Beverly J. Inman: Adjunct Instructor of German, History, and Humanities, *Kirkwood Community College,* Cedar Rapids, Iowa

Mara Iutcovich: Master's candidate Ethics and Peace, *American University*

Lloyd Johnson: Associate Professor, Department of History, *Campbell University,* Buies Creek, North Carolina

Brad Kadrich: Professional writer

Christopher D. Karadjov: Ph.D., Assistant Professor, Communication Studies Department, *State University of New York at Oswego*

Saliwe M. Kawewe: Professor, School of Social Work, *Southern Illinois University at Carbondale,* Carbondale, Illinois

Howard A. Kerner: Professor, Department of English, *Polk Community College,* Winter Haven, Florida

Keith Knutson: Assistant Professor, Department of History, *Viterbo University,* LaCrosse, Wisconsin

Tendayi S. Kumbula: Ph.D., Journalism Department, *Ball State University,* Muncie, Indiana

Jae-won Lee: Professor, Department of Communication, *Cleveland State University,* Ohio

Andrew Lefebvre: M.A. in History

Richard Lyman: Professor Emeritus of History, *Simmons College*; Lecturer in Asian History, *Brandeis University,* Waltham, Massachusetts

Carol Marshall: Professional writer and editor

Leonid Maximenkov: Ph.D., Centre for Russian and East European Studies, *Munk Centre for International Studies,*Toronto, Ontario, Canada

Ritchard Tamba M'Bayo: Professor, Department of Communications, *Bowie State University,* Bowie, Maryland

Kristen McCleary: Visiting Professor, Department of History, *University of California,* Los Angeles

Thomas McPhail: Professor, Department of Communication, *University of Missouri,* St. Louis

Brij Mohan: Professor, School of Social Work, *Louisiana State University*, Baton Rouge

Melanie Moore: Associate Professor, Department of Sociology, *University of Northern Colorado,* Greeley

Suzanne Drapeau Morley: Special Lecturer, Department of Rhetoric, Communication, and Journalism, *Oakland University,* Rochester, Michigan

Bernard E. Morris: Independent Scholar

Aggrey Mugisha: Video producer, *IFES-Africa,* Kampala, Uganda

Gladys Mutangadura: Visiting Assistant Professor of Economics, *Elon University,* Elon, North Carolina

Ting Ni: Assistant Professor, Department of History, *Saint Mary's University of Minnesota*

Ashakant Nimbark: Ph.D., Professor and Chair, Department of Sociology, *Dowling College,* Oakdale, New York

Virginia Davis Nordin: Attorney and Associate Professor, *University of Kentucky,* Lexington

Levi Obonyo: Ph.D. Student, School of Communication and Theater, *Temple University,* Philadelphia, Pennsylvania

William A. Paquette: Professor of History, *Tidewater Community College,* Georgia

Yovanna Pineda: Assistant Professor, Department of History, *St. Michael's College,* Colchester, Vermont

Marguerite R. Plummer: Assistant Professor of History, Department of History and Social Sciences, *Louisiana State University in Shreveport*

Cynthia Pope: Assistant Professor, Department of Geography, *Central Connecticut State University, New Britain*

Zoltán Raffay: Research Fellow, Transdanubian Research Institute, Center for Regional Studies, *Hungarian Academy of Sciences,* Pécs, Hungary

Danielle Raquidel: Associate Professor of French and Spanish, *University of South Carolina,* Spartanburg, South Carolina

Monica Rector: Professor, Department of Romance Languages and Literatures, *University of North Carolina at Chapel Hill*

Raul Reis: Ph.D., Assistant Professor, Department of Journalism, *California State University Long Beach*

Terry Robertson: Ph.D., Assistant Professor, Department of Communication Studies, *University of South Dakota,* Vermillion, South Dakota

Meshack Sagini: Associate Professor, Department of Social Science, *Langston University,* Oklahoma

Charlene Santos: Graduate Student and Teaching Assistant, Department of Educational Policy Studies and Evaluation, *University of Kentucky*

D. R. SarDesai: Emeritus Professor of History, *University of California,* Los Angeles

Samuel Sarri: Ph.D., Professor, Economics, Business, Philosophy, Political Science, *University & Community College System of Nevada*

Elizabeth D. Schafer: Professional writer

Carol L. Schmid: Ph.D., Professor of Sociology, *Guilford Technical Community College,* Jamestown, North Carolina

Manoj Sharma: Associate Professor, Health Education, *University of Nebraska at Omaha* and *Walden University,* Minneapolis, Minnesota

Ronald E. Sheasby: Assistant Professor of Writing, English Department, *Loyola University,* Chicago, Illinois

Philip D. Supina: Professor and Lecturer, Legal Studies, *Merrill College University of California at Santa Cruz*

Blair Tindall: Visiting Lecturer in Journalism, Department of Communication, *Stanford University,* California

N. Prabha Unnithan: Professor, Department of Sociology, *Colorado State University,* Fort Collins, Colorado

William Wardrope: Assistant Professor of Management, *Southwest Texas State University,* San Marcos, Texas

Clay Warren: Professor of Communication, *The George Washington University,* Washington, D.C.

Rob Weir: Master's student, *University of Missouri*; copy editor, *Star-News* Wilmington, North Carolina

Duffy Austin Wilks: Associate Professor, Department of Social Science, *Western Texas College,* Snyder

Jean Boris Wynn: Ph.D., Assistant Professor of Anthropology, Division of Social Science, *Manchester Community College*

Sherry L. Wynn: Special Lecturer, Rhetoric Program, *Oakland University,* Rochester, Michigan

Linda Yoder: Coordinator of the West Virginia Council of International Programs, *West Virginia University,* Morgantown

INTRODUCTION

Welcome to the second edition of the *World Press Encyclopedia: A Survey of Press Systems Worldwide.* In these two volumes, readers will find comparative, in-depth essays on the press systems of 232 countries and/or territories. *World Press Encyclopedia (WPE)* is unique and valuable to users because, in addition to essays on each country's press system, *WPE* also contains custom-made graphs and statistical tables, as well as regional maps, useful appendices, and an extensive index.

This comprehensive, authoritative source of information allows for easy comparison between essays with a standard format or set of "rubrics" used whenever possible (see section titled **"Essay Components"**). Each essay also features basic data information—such as official country name, literacy rate, language(s), and number of daily newspapers—clearly marked with headings at the beginning of each entry. Additionally, *WPE* 's contributors include scholars, professionals, and educators from across the United States and around the world; each essay has a byline (also see the **"Contributor Notes"** section).

NEW FEATURES

Although this is the second edition, *WPE* has been completely reconceptualized and **100 percent revised** from the first edition, which was published in 1982. Differences include:

- All essays have been freshly researched and written for this edition.
- Essays now appear in alphabetical order.
- The standard format has increased consistency, which eases comparison.
- *WPE* includes "new" countries since the last edition due to the dissolution of the Soviet Union and Yugoslavia; it also includes renamed countries such as Myanmar, which was formerly known as Burma.
- Essays include information, when available, on topics such as new political philosophies and their impact upon the press and the role the Internet has played in changing the manner in which news is disseminated.
- Essays include custom-made graphs.
- The appendix tables provide regional and country statistics.
- Three appendix components have been recreated in their entirety along with capturing more pertinent data elements.
- *WPE* now includes regional maps.

VOLUME BREAKDOWN

- Volume 1: Afghanistan-Myanmar
- Volume 2: Namibia-Zimbabwe, Appendixes, Index

CONTENTS OF ESSAYS

Essays in the *WPE* were individually researched and written by more than 80 authors. Essays range in size from about 200 to around 30,000 words. The essays' standard rubrics (see section titled **"Essay Components"**) such as **"Background & General Characteristics"** and **"Press Laws"** allow for ease of comparison. Even the smaller essays include such information when applicable.

The **"Essay Components"** section lists all possible rubrics. Please note that authors were allowed to use other subheadings than those listed, but those listed give the reader an idea of what to expect under that particular heading. For example, The "Background & General Characteristics" heading should contain the nature of the audience, comments on the quality of journalism, and the largest daily newspapers by circulation. The "Press Laws" heading should contain information on constitutional provisions, laws affecting the press, and licensing of newspapers and journalists.

Important to Note

- Statistics presented in "Basic Data," graphs, and tables may differ slightly due to the large number of sources for this information. Additionally, figures presented in "Basic Data," graphs, and tables were not compiled by the authors of the essays, so the text may present somewhat different numbers at times.
- Common acronyns may not be defined in all essays. Some examples include: GDP (gross domestic product), GNP (gross national product), UNESCO (United Nations Educational, Scientific and Cultural Organization), and NGO/ONG (non-governmental organization).

Appendices

WPE contains three unique and comprehensive appendices:

- Appendix 1 contains nine tables of press-related statistics on such topics as newspaper advertising expenditures, number of television sets, and personal computer users (including those with Internet access). The tables may include regional rankings and percentages, as well as brief explanations of the data gathering methods. **Please note that not all countries appear in these tables since not all countries report the necessary data.**
- Appendix 2 includes three different sets of information: **"The World's 100 Great Dailies," "News Agencies of the World,"** and **"Press-Related Associations, Organizations, and Unions."** The "Great Dailies" includes the title and country of publication and is presented both alphabetically and by region and country. "News Agencies" lists full contact information (with E-mail and URL when available) along with languages the service is provided in. The "Press-Related Associations" provides a wealth of data such as full contact information, a general description of their activities, awards given, publications produced, and conventions/meetings held.
- Appendix 3 contains a list of all 232 countries and their corresponding regions, which in turn correspond to the maps that are also included in this section.

General Index

The **"General Index"** contains alphabetic references to items mentioned within the essays such as significant terms, trade and professional associations and organizations, names of individuals and countries, government agencies, significant court cases, and key legislation.

Inclusion Criteria

In determining which countries and/or territories should be included, the editors found it best to rely upon several means, a small portion of which were decidedly subjective. We consulted many Internet sites, as well as other Gale products and an advisory board. We included many small countries and/or territories that are, admittedly, difficult to research, hence, the shorter essays.

In addition, we tried to overlook territorial disputes and political issues when compiling the essay list. For example, Israel and West Bank/Gaza Strip have separate essays, as do Indonesia and East Timor.

We also chose to use some more common names such as Lao instead of Lao People's Democratic Republic and North Korea instead of Korea (Democratic). The official country names are given within the "Basic Data."

Finally, the authors were asked to maintain an objective point of view when compiling and writing their essays.

Acknowledgments

The editors wish to express their gratitude to the authors of the essays for their invaluable work and patience.

Following is a list of the copyright holders who have granted us permission to reproduce material in *WPE*. Every effort has been made to trace copyright, but if omissions have been made, please let us know.

Copyrighted material in *WPE* was obtained and/or reproduced from the following: From *2000 World Development Indicators*. The World Bank, 2002. Copyright 2002 by the International Bank for Reconstruction and Development. All rights reserved. Reproduced by permission.—From the International Telecommunication Union. All rights reserved. Reproduced by permission. The sole responsibility for selecting extracts for reproduction lies with the beneficiary of this authorization alone and can in no way be attributed to the ITU. The complete volume(s) of the ITU material, from which the texts reproduced are extracted, can be obtained from: International Telecommunication Union, Sales and Marketing Division, Place des Nations-CH-1211 GENEVA 20 (Switzerland). Telephone: 41 22 730 61 41 (English)/41 22 730 61 42 (French)/41 22 730 61 43 (Spanish). Fax: 41 22 730 51 94. E-mail: sales@itu.int. http://www.itu.int/publications.

All maps were created by Maryland Cartographics on behalf of Gale Group.

Comments & Suggestions

Comments and suggestions are most welcome. Readers are invited to send their thoughts to:

Editor/World Press Encyclopedia
Gale
27500 Drake Rd.
Farmington Hills, MI 48331-3535
Telephone: 248-699-GALE
Toll-free Phone: 800-347-GALE
Toll-free Fax: 800-339-3374
E-mail: BusinessProducts@gale.com
Web Site: http://www.gale.com

ESSAY COMPONENTS

BACKGROUND & GENERAL CHARACTERISTICS

General Description

The Nature of the Audience: Literacy, Affluence, Population Distribution, Language Distribution

Quality of Journalism: General Comments

Historical Traditions

Distribution by Language, Ethnic & Religious Orientation, Political Ideology, Geography

Size: Regular/tabloid; Average Number of Pages per Issue

A.M., P.M.; Sunday Newspaper; Magazine Sections

Foreign Language Press

Minority-owned Press; Other Special-Interest Press

Number of Cities with Newspapers/with Competing Newspapers

Number of Newspapers by Circulation Groups (below 10,000; 10,000 to 25,000; 25,000 to 50,000; 50,000 to 100,000; 100,000 to 500,000; 500,000 to 1 million; over 1 million)

10 Largest Newspapers by Circulation

Three Most Influential Newspapers

ECONOMIC FRAMEWORK

Overview of the Economic Climate & its Influence on Media

Newspapers in the Mass Media Milieu: Print Media versus Electronic Media

Types of Ownership: Individual, Corporate, Government, Ruling Political Party, Opposition Party

Types of Newspapers: Elite, Popular, Yellow

Concentration of Ownership: Newspaper Chains & Cross-Ownership; Decline or Growth in Competition; Monopolies; Antitrust Legislation in Force

Distribution Networks: Concentration in Distribution

Newsprint Availability: Policies Relating to Newsprint Import and Allocation; Average Cost of Newsprint per Ton

Advertisers' Influence on Editorial Policies: Ad Ratio

Influence of Special-Interest Lobbies on Editorial Policies

Industrial Relations: Strikes; Major Labor Unions; Influence of Unions on Press Freedom; Total Employment and Average Wage Scales; "Reporter Power"

Circulation Patterns; Average Price & Recent Price Hikes; Percentage of Circulation Accounted for by the Top 10

Distribution of Printing Methods (Offset etc.); Impact of New Printing & Editing Technologies

PRESS LAWS

Constitutional Provisions & Guarantees Relating to Media

Summary of Press Laws in Force

Registration & Licensing of Newspapers & Journalists

Compulsory Posting on Bonds

Press-related Laws, such as Sunshine Laws, Shield Laws, Libel Laws, Laws against Blasphemy & Obscenity, Official Secrets Acts

Laws Protecting Privacy of Non-official Citizens

Independence of the Judiciary; General Comments

CENSORSHIP

Agency Concerned with Monitoring the Press

Pre-publication Censorship Procedures; Modes of Compliance

Case Studies

Composition, Functions, and Operations of Press/Media Councils

Administrative Rules Restricting Officials from Giving Information to the Press; Freedom of Information Acts

STATE-PRESS RELATIONS

Organization & Functions of Information Ministry/Department

The Right to Criticize Government: Theory & Practice

Managed News

Editorial Influence on Government Policies: Case Studies

Suspension & Confiscation of Newspapers

State Control over the Press through Subsidies, Allocation of Newsprint, Advertising Support, Labor Union Manipulation, Import Licenses for Printing Equipment, Licensing of Journalists

ATTITUDE TOWARD FOREIGN MEDIA

Accreditation Procedures for Foreign Correspondents

Special Visas for Foreign Correspondents

Bannings & Jailings of Foreign Correspondents

Import Restrictions on Foreign Publications: Ban on Sales

Foreign Ownership of Domestic Media
Foreign Propaganda & Its Impact on Domestic Media
Domestic Contacts with International Press Organizations

News Agencies

Domestic News Agencies: Organization; Relations with the State; Number of Subscribers
Foreign News Bureaus: Number of Subscribers; Exclusive Contracts with the State
Issues Related to News Flow

Broadcast Media

General Overview
State Policies Relating to Radio & TV News

Electronic News Media

Focusing on Internet Press Sites
Issues Related to Online News Flow

Education & Training

Review of Education in Journalism: Degrees Granted
Journalistic Awards & Prizes
Major Journalistic Associations & Organizations

Summary

Conclusions
Trends & Prospects for the Media: Outlook for the Twenty-First Century

Significant Dates

Highlights of Press History during Recent Years

Bibliography

FOREWORD

INTRODUCTION

The second edition of the *World Press Encyclopedia* is a magisterial survey of the state of the press at the beginning of the twenty-first century. The two decades since the first edition was published have been turbulent and momentous in world history. It will be remembered for the collapse of the Soviet Union; the rapid spread of world communications, including the Internet and the computer; and the dominance of the United States as a superpower. Globalization is now accepted as the wave of the future, but it is marked by two contradictory trends: the marginalization of non-Western cultures on the one hand and the growth of nationalism and separatist tendencies on the other. The threat of terrorism on a global scale is a new phenomenon that bodes ill for the future. The second edition of *World Press* thus deals with a world far different from the one described in the first.

Like the world it reflects and reports on, the press has gone through several mutations. As the principal carrier of information in a troubled world, the press has entrenched itself as a powerful and pervasive institution with a host of roles and functions. For the first three centuries of its existence beginning in the seventeenth century, it was locked into its traditional role as a purveyor of information: it reported and occasionally commented on the events of the day. Beginning in the twentieth century, it expanded its functions in several directions: on the one hand it became a partisan platform for various ideologies of the day; on the other hand it assumed the mantles of an educator, watchdog, moderator of national debates, advisor, chronicler, promoter of new ideas, setter of national agendas, investigator, national bulletin board, and propaganda machine. In this transformation, it was aided by technology, which enabled it to collect, print, and broadcast news faster than ever before.

World Press Encyclopedia uses the term "press" in its broadest sense—a dispenser of information. It encompasses not only the print media (including magazines and other periodicals) but also what is known as the electronic media (including television, radio, and Internet publications). It also covers the profession of journalism, journalism education, censorship, political communications, advertising, and freedom of the press. The word "press" has been retained in the title rather than more nebulous words, such as "media" and "information," because the print media remains the mother lode of all methods of communication. Even the most cynical futurist does not foresee the complete displacement of the print media by electronic media in the near future.

REGIONAL PRESS TRENDS

World Press Encyclopedia provides a country-by-country assessment of the state of the press, but regional presses share some characteristics derived from the social, political, and economic status of the member countries.

Africa

Africa produces the fewest newspapers of any continent. Of the world's thousands of daily newspapers, fewer than 150 are published in Africa. Africa's newspapers are scattered and concentrated in a handful of coastal cities. Historically, the product of colonialism, the press has been battered and buffeted since independence by a succession of dictators in all major countries. Newspapers remain small and undercapitalized, with limited circulation and sparse advertising. Potential readership is constrained by illiteracy and poverty. Government and party-controlled newspapers dominate the field, forcing independent publications to cut back or fold. Journalists became civil servants doing the bidding of politicians. Newspapers not under direct government control are harassed in various ways, and editors are often forced out of their jobs and exiled.

In the words of a respected Kenyan editor, Hilary Ng'weno, "Nothing has really changed from the bad old days of colonialism." In addition to political barriers, the growth of the African press is hobbled by social constraints, poor literacy, linguistic fragmentation, and transportation and production difficulties.

South, Southeast, and East Asia

The Asian press has both a developed and an underdeveloped sector. Japan, Korea, and Singapore have a highly developed press, while most other countries are severely handicapped because of low literacy, dependence on foreign news agencies, and stringent government controls. In most countries, freedom of the press does not exist. There is also a tradition of self-censorship that has its historical roots in the colonial days. Governments have promoted a guidance concept used in conjunction with national development goals. The guidance principle is a subtle form of control offered to journalists by governments who want to diminish the adversarial role of the press. In deference to the administration, the press avoids investigative reporting, includes all government speeches and news releases, and ignores the opposition. Frequently, officials offer publishers unsought "advice," which must be followed without dissent.

Most Southeast Asian and many East and South Asian nations require annual licensing of newspapers, and some require prohibitively expensive security deposits. Security, public order, and libel and sedition laws are applied to both domestic and foreign journalists and publishers. Another form of control includes economic restraints through government control of newsprint and official advertisements. In Bangladesh the state rents printing presses to newspapers and controls newsprint and equipment allocations. Many other states subsidize newspapers that practice "healthy" journalism.

Another problem for the press concerns the sources of news. Although regional news agencies have been in existence for decades, they are overshadowed by the multinational giants, such as Reuters, Associated Press, and Agence France Presse. Nearly all countries have national news agencies, but their credibility is suspect because of close government ties.

Europe

The European press has the longest history among continental presses, but there are differences in national tradition, economic development, and political systems. Despite these differences, the press has followed similar evolutionary curves, although at varying rates. The political partisan press is a typically European institution and is still active in many countries. Existing alongside is a commercialized, advertiser-supported press. Commercialization accelerated after World War II. Nevertheless, newspapers have not lost their political labels and are known for their conservative or liberal sympathies. There also has been increasing concentration not only in the print media but in cross ownership of print and electronic media.

The Northern European press has differed in important respects from the press in Western Europe as well as that in Southern Europe. A large proportion of newspapers are aligned with political parties, but the press system in general is highly developed. As in Southern Europe, the distinction between popular and elite newspapers is less clear than in Western Europe. The Eastern European press is still trying to find its true mission and to rid itself of the vestiges of Communist authoritarianism. The press is conscious of its power to mediate in political and social disputes and takes an active role in social engineering. In Western Europe, as in North America, the capitalist nature of the economy influences the media in many ways. There is a heavy concentration of ownership of the traditional elite media, which is offset by the proliferation of alternate media opposed to the establishment.

Increasing competition from television and radio has forced newspapers to adopt innovative strategies to survive. "Journalism in Education" is one such program by which newspapers reach high school students and inculcate in them the habit of newspaper reading.

Latin America

The Latin American press has always been at the center of the political storms that have whirled around the continent in the nineteenth and twentieth centuries. The elite press has experienced confrontations with governments, including censorship and direct attacks on journalists. Journalists have often been politicians and vice versa. The elite press also represents almost exclusively the interests of the upper classes to which the press lords belong. Despite these problems, the role of the press in the formation of public opinion and the expression of political debate continues to be significant.

The Interamerican Press Association has been influential in maintaining freedom of the press in the region, even during dictatorships and coups. The redemocratization of the region in the 1980s has helped the press to assert itself and to open new vistas of growth.

The Latin American press can be grouped into three large categories. The first is made up of traditional newspapers that are generally owned by wealthy families and tend to reflect conservative ideologies. The second group is made of politically moderate newspapers, some of them Roman Catholic in orientation. The last is the popular press, which tends to support leftist causes.

Despite overall poverty, circulation tends to be high, relative to other developing regions. For example, Chile, with a literacy rate of 90 percent, has newspapers with a daily circulation of more than 500,000. The percentage of space devoted to advertising is also high.

Middle East

The Middle East generally refers to the crescent of countries extending from Morocco to Central Asia where Islamic culture is concentrated. Politically and economically, it excludes Israel, which is geographically a part of the Middle East. Called the Arab press (although it is a misnomer since a number of print and electronic media are in French, English, and other languages), it is one of the unsettled institutions in the region.

The influence of the "street" on the Arab media is so strong that it is difficult to describe it in conventional terms. Governments play a double role in their control of the media. On the one hand, they deny the press any semblance of freedom in reporting and use every means in their power to keep it subservient. On the other hand, they use the press as a safety valve against Islamic fundamentalism.

In comparison with the rest of the world, the percentage of Arabs who read newspapers is small, and the percentage who buy newspapers is even smaller. The higher illiteracy rates among Arabs, coupled with social and cultural traditions that discourage reading (many Arabs prefer to watch television or listen to the radio) contributes to this phenomenon. The most important disincentive is the historic distrust of the press. There is also a lack of credible writers and investigative journalists—the few who make a mark in their profession often are jailed or forced to emigrate.

North America

As in Europe, the press in North America is a major force in national life. As in other regions, there are problems, many of them dating back to the nineteenth century. The most persistent problem is the concentration of the ownership of print media and television and radio broadcasting networks in a few hands. Also, readership of newspapers has historically been lower in the United States and Canada relative to other developed countries, especially in Europe. Another problem is the overreliance on advertising revenue. Principally carriers of local advertising, newspapers as a whole comprised the largest advertising medium, followed by television and direct mail, generally garnering about two-thirds of all media advertising revenues. Whereas advertising is allotted only two-thirds of total newspaper space, it accounts for more than four-fifths of all newspaper revenues. When the economy slumps, as it does periodically in capitalist countries, the press is hit hard. Paradoxically, along with the focus on fragmented audiences, there is increasing standardization. Syndicated columns, comics, features, and news service reports provide a major portion of the homogenized editorial content. A further extension of the trend toward standardization was made possible by satellite technology with regional editions of the same newspaper sponsored by regional and national advertisers.

Fundamental social shifts are also affecting both print and electronic media. As radio and television broadcasting and, later, cable television, began to challenge newspapers as purveyors of news and advertising, the latter responded by acquiring a stake in the new media. Cooperative rather than competitive strategies were used to create a new synergy called convergence. However, even as joint ventures were adopted, newspapers continued to depend on their unique existing assets: printing and distribution facilities, intimate knowledge of local advertisers and their needs, and experience in information-gathering and processing. With stiffening competition to supply electronic information services by means of new technologies, newspapers catapulted into the information market by acquiring unrelated companies, such as telephone and computer firms, banks, brokerage firms, direct mailers, and retailers. An example of the press's entry into this market is its commitment to "front-end systems," or computerized editorial systems that permit direct links between the paper and outside electronic networks. Once information is stored in newspaper computers, it can easily be transformed into new information products for electronic distribution.

The press also has encountered increasingly sweeping and sophisticated moves by government agencies and private corporations to define and shape news. Managing the news is a new presidential function consisting mainly of spin, trial balloons, and photo ops. The independence of the press has received some setbacks in the courts and has tended as a result to shrink in certain areas. Nevertheless, the press as a watchdog and investigator has continued to play a valued role in the evolution of American democracy.

Impact of New Media Elements

Media is not merely business; it is an extension of the democratic processes in any form of representative government. The influence of the media is evident in almost all major political developments in the twentieth century. Since the 1970s scholars have grappled with the implications of the new media taking shape through advances in telecommunications and computers. In doing so they have addressed classic political questions: Who controls these media elements? Whose interests are served by changing technologies? Do they advance or slow the interests of the people?

Control is a central issue because communications technology serves the interests of those who own it. At least four competing perspectives have emerged from discussions of control. The first is a democratic marketplace view, which sees technology as ultimately controlled by marketplace needs and preferences within the context of democratic institutions. The second view is a technocratic one, characteristic of critics of the media. It argues that the communications media is controlled by a technocratic elite driven by a need to advance their own interests and who shape public preferences through marketing techniques. The third view is the pluralist view in which the media is controlled by a variety of players whose contradictory interests result in an equilibrium. The fourth view is reinforcement politics, which regards communications technologies as malleable resources controlled by a dominant coalition of interests within a society. Technologies enhance the power of already powerful groups and thereby reinforce the existing power structure.

Are the new technologies neutral or are they biased toward the status quo or are they powerful enough to shift the balance of power in a society? There are four competing perspectives that view the new media as neutral, democratic, elitist, and dual. The first views the new media as politically neutral, if not apolitical. It argues that the nature of the content, not the technology, shapes the effects of a medium. The second view regards the new media as democratic and points to its effects in the liberation of Eastern Europe from Communist ideology. According to Edwin Parker, the new media provides the public with more information, segmented and packaged according to audience, with greater variety in contents and greater feedback. They thus accelerate the erosion of hierarchies and power monopolies and bring more people into the agenda-setting process. They also break down communication barriers between cultures, classes and nations. The third view, on the other hand, holds that the media is elitist in nature and exercises bias by creating bottlenecks and by assuming a gatekeeper role in communications. The complexity of high technology further distances elites from a public that is increasingly uninvolved and uninformed, thus creating a new knowledge gap. The new media simply erects more efficient vertical communication networks between elites and masses rather than horizontal networks among the public. The fourth view is that communication technologies are inherently contradictory and can achieve seemingly opposing results. For example, new communication technologies can be intrusive and thus erode privacy, yet at the same time they may reinforce the isolation of the individual from social pressures and reinforce privacy. They contribute to a more informed public, yet they facilitate manipulation of public opinion. Differential access to electronic media translates into disparities in access to political power. More affluent members of the public have greater access to the new media, thus increasing existing inequities rather than leveling the playing field. Also, the relation between citizens and institutions is altered by the migration of information from the former to the latter.

The array of public communication facilities offered by the new media encouraged social planners in the 1960s to envision an electronic highway into every home and business to carry all kinds of information and service. The potential for integrating broadcast, cable, data, and telephone communications networks generated both utopian and dystopian versions of a "wired nation." These visions faded with the growing recognition of the limitations of interactive cable and the rise of a host of newer media. In the 1980s there emerged a new vision of a marketplace of electronic networks and services, including telephones, cable, televisions, and videocassettes. But instead of opening the door to more democratic patterns of public communications, the newer media lessened diversity, increased concentration of ownership, pushed up the cost of communications, threatened privacy, and widened the gap between the information poor and the information rich.

Globalization has made the rise of the new media into a worldwide phenomenon. In communications there are no national boundaries, and national governments have lost their ability to control the flow of information across borders. However, the new media, with its heavy reliance on technology, reinforces the dominance of Western nations. Communication networks are complex and costly and can be financed only by wealthy nations. Although consumers now have greater choice, they have no control over content and even less control over production and distribution and the technological infrastructure. International communication infrastructures represent nothing less than new trade routes over which developed nations can export communication products and services. The lack of national controls over the new media raises concerns over the maintenance of cultural traditions and values in underdeveloped countries. It also poses great danger to the concept of privacy as data files could be processed in the so-called data havens where there are no safeguards on how the data should be used.

Government-Media Relations and Freedom of the Press

At no time in history has there been complete freedom of the press nor is there any country today that enjoys complete freedom of the press. Even from the beginning of the press era in the seventeenth century, there have been controls of some sort on the press that have varied from time to time. In more democratic countries, the control is limited to laws, regulations, and procedures that safeguard "public interest." These include laws against libel, pornography, monopoly, and breach of national security. Under more authoritarian regimes, these laws extend to licensing of newspapers and journalists, newsprint quotas, censorship, defamation of government officials, and promotion of national ideals. As a result, there is constant interaction between government and the media in which the press is often on the losing side. In relation to the state, the press has adopted six postures which media scholars have described as antithetical, adversarial, symbiotic, bureaucratic, partisan, or subservient.

The antithetical press is opposed to any links with the government. It is intensely radical and outside the power structure. *The Nation* in the United States is a good example of the antithetical press. The adversarial press is not anti-government, but it challenges the political values of the establishment. It defines a relationship with the government in its own terms, and usually engages in muckraking and investigative reporting to embarrass the government. Although many journalists consider themselves as adversarial, most are often deferential to the political leadership. *Le Monde* in France is a prominent example of an adversarial daily that often functions as a national scold. In most democracies, the periodical press is more adversarial than the daily press. The symbiotic press functions as spokesperson for the government, using some government-manipulated news to fill its pages. Commercial wire services practice a form of journalism characterized as symbiotic. Especially in times of crisis and war, they hew closely to the government versions of events and rarely question their sources or their veracity. Commercial radio also appears more symbiotic, simply because they have no time for the extended analysis needed to ferret truth from the overlay of propaganda. Small-town newspapers also tend to be more symbiotic because they do not have the resources to go beyond soft news to the kind of hard news that only investigative journalism can provide. Some analysts feel that some newspapers go beyond being merely symbiotic to being safety valves for the ruling elites. The bureaucratic press is the official or state-owned press that exists in the vast majority of the nations. A good example is the British Broadcasting Corporation (BBC) , which is owned by the government even though Britain is a classic democracy. The United States has no functional equivalent to the BBC, but it has covert interests in many news organizations. In the West most of the bureaucratic press is electronic, such as Canadian Broadcasting Corporation (CBC), Radiotelevisione Italiana (RAI), and Telediffusion de France (TDF) but, in most other countries, there is state-owned print media as well. Bureaucratic press shies away from reporting on government scandals or failures. The partisan press has direct and formal ties with active political parties. In the late eighteenth century, the partisan press was the only form of press that covered politics and government. In the nineteenth century, party affiliations were included in the name of the newspaper. In Europe, parties pioneered the newspaper business in the eighteenth and nineteenth centuries. As late as the early twentieth century, Canadian journalists were seated in the parliament galleries according to party label. However, since World War II, partisan press has declined both in number and influence. The subservient press exists more often in nondemocratic countries. It functions as an arm of the government and often receives state subsidies in return for editorial favors.

Throughout press history both print and electronic media have moved toward a more open system where government influence, while still subtle, is muted. One reason may be a more educated readership, which is able to detect propaganda disguised as news. The press corps also has become more discriminating and resistant to crude pressure from official sources. The courts have been more liberal and pro-press in many of their decisions involving sedition, libel, and other laws.

News Agencies

News agencies form the first link in the chain of news. They are also the primary gatekeepers of news; all news has to pass their turnstiles to get into print or broadcasting. The fact that the big five agencies are all Western explains the dominance of the Western media in the world. News agencies themselves were historically adjuncts of colonialism, a network of communications that served as trade routes to reinforce Western commercial and economic interests. Until the end of World War II, Western news agencies formed a cartel dividing up the world into spheres of influence. Even today, the influence of the old cartel is evident in the way the news agencies function. The news flow patterns continue to reflect the hegemony of Western economies. Although, in contrast to other forms of the news media, news agencies are relatively invisible, their anonymity was challenged as pressure built up in the 1970s and 1980s in the Third World against what was perceived as a monopoly of a few agencies controlling the flow of news and photographs. It led to the movement to create a New International Information Order. The movement fizzled out in the 1990s as the economic clout of Western powers increased and that of the Third World declined.

ADVERTISING

Advertising and the media are Siamese twins; one cannot exist apart from the other without defying the laws of economics. The twentieth century marked dramatic changes in the advertising industry. Before 1890, agencies focused on selling space, analyzing media markets, and trying to convince businesses that they should advertise. By the end of the twentieth century advertising represented an increasing range of creative and business functions. Through the use of jingles, artwork, typeface, and layout, advertising became a Pavlovian psychological exercise, trying to persuade people to do what the advertisers want them to do. Trademarks and trade characters were developed to enhance corporate identities. Target audiences were identified and relentlessly studied and pursued; infomercials were developed in which a commercial message was subtly wrapped in supposedly educative material.

The press was a major beneficiary of the explosion in advertising strategies and techniques. It enabled both print and electronic media to exploit new markets at home and abroad. Television and radio had the added advantage that one need not be a literate to watch television or listen to the radio. In industrialized countries, the domestic market was saturated with advertising, in all forms of the media, promoting a lifestyle based on consumerism and conspicuous consumption. Outside the developed world, advertisers enticed the more affluent with the same message. In the process, advertising helped to create a homogenized consumer culture and thus drive globalization. The youth were particularly susceptible to the siren song of advertising. The primary focus of advertising was not merely marketing, but public consciousness.

The success of advertising was such that it was adopted by divergent fields as politics. It has become common in the United States and Western democracies for politicians and political policies to be promoted like commodities. Presidential advisors are increasingly drawn from advertising and public relations as well as polling industries.

In the twenty-first century, advertising has become a multinational industry underwritten by large transnational corporations. Using the national media as their principal forum, these advertisers use the same images with only slight variations in the different countries in which they operate. Advertising enables transnational corporations to exercise influence over the local media as their major source of revenue. Advertising agencies that expand into foreign markets may choose one of several methods of entry. One is to establish a new branch in the country; another is to set up a joint agency with a domestic agency. This is an effective approach in countries like Japan that are difficult to penetrate because of laws that discourage foreign direct investment. Yet another alternative is to join an agency network system. This is often done when a particular market is not large enough for a full-fledged office.

Like the press, advertising faces a variety of regulations whose nature and stringency vary from country to country. Although regulation of advertising is on the increase, there are cases where the prevailing trend is opposite. In the European Union, for example, there is a strong effort to harmonize laws and to drop or relax some of the more restrictive ones. Nevertheless, regulators everywhere are concerned about certain types of advertising message content. Advertising controls are generally directed toward political correctness, especially advertisements that poke fun at minority groups or women, corrupt morals, use false comparisons, encourage energy consumption, or mislead. A rising force in the regulation of advertising is the worldwide consumer movement, which seeks to defend the consumer's rights to privacy, safety, choice, and redress in case of wrongdoing. Some countries have added linguistic chauvinism to the menu. In France and many Middle European countries, use of foreign expressions is banned unless they are readily intelligible to a general audience. There is a stronger trend toward regulation of advertising in countries that are more economically developed and have more militant consumer movements.

Advertisers face regulatory issues in most countries. The first regulatory concern is misleading advertising. Omissions, ambiguous statements, self-serving comparisons, deceptive uses of typefaces, or demonstrations and partly true statements are considered misleading. The second is sexism and decency, both legally elusive and nebulous concepts, but they are sensitive issues likely to offend the very audience that advertisers are trying to reach. In many countries, the rubric "decency" would cover references to contraception, vulgar language, feminine hygiene goods, cigarettes, alcoholic beverages, pornographic materials, and violence. Sexism applies to the exploitation of women—including the overuse of young attractive women in situations not related to the use of the product or service. The third concern is the use of foreign languages, which is banned in certain countries to satisfy linguistic purists and to protect consumers. The fourth is advertising directed primarily at children.

The main arguments for regulating ads to children are: such ads create wants among children, which parents cannot or should not gratify; they teach children overly materialistic values; they encourage consumption of junk foods; they take advantage of children's credulousness and lack of experience; and they exploit children's difficulty in distinguishing between program materials and advertising messages.

If an advertisement is false, misleading, deceptive, or unfair, it can be challenged after the fact in most countries. However, many countries do not favor this approach (since the damage has already been done) and have adopted a system of pre-clearances (pre-vetting in Britain) mandating the approval of advertising materials by the authorities before they are released to the press. Most countries have pre-clearances for all broadcast materials while others have pre-clearances for specific categories, such as drugs, games, lotteries and contests, food and drink, cigarettes, alcoholic beverages, financial services, tourism, cinema, and children's products. In many countries, codes of ethics and guidelines have been developed by advertising associations and there are international codes such as that of the International Chamber of Commerce (ICC).

What kind of an influence does international advertising have on the editorial and entertainment content of the press? There are conflicting answers to this question. In the developed countries, advertisers have less influence on the press than in developing countries. The print media is not as dependent on advertising revenue as the broadcast media since newspapers and magazines derive at least a part of their revenue from subscriptions. In many developing countries and the United States, television depends solely on advertising revenue. In other countries, where television and radio are state-owned or subsidized, the revenues come from a mixture of advertising, appropriations from the general tax revenues, and contributions from private industry or the public at large. According to a UNESCO study, there is a discernible trend throughout the world toward greater commercialization of the communications media. In the print media, this is reflected in the substantial increase in commercial as opposed to editorial content. In the case of radio and television, commercial time is increasing as a percentage of total broadcast time. To counteract this trend, some countries have mandated the grouping of commercials within certain time slots, keeping the rest of the programming free of all advertising. This is a common pattern in Western Europe. The United Kingdom allows commercials only during breaks in the program. In the United States, commercials are placed within programs, but viewers with the appropriate technology can skip them.

Quality of Journalism: The Elite Newspapers

A majority of the world's newspapers reflect the type of mass market journalism formerly known as yellow journalism—characterized by low professional standards, trivial subject matter, sensationalized treatment, irresponsible propaganda, news gaps, and stereotypes. However, there is a core group of serious newspapers in a few countries that defy this trend. These are the elite (or quality) newspapers that provide rational analysis and reliable news. Their number is not large, their overall impact is not very great, and their share of the market is probably minuscule. Yet, their philosophy is important, their staffs are dedicated, and their influence is far greater than indicated by the circulation numbers. The British call these papers quality or class papers, distinguishing them from mass or popular papers. The French call them *journaux de prestige* while Germans call them *Weltblatter,* stressing their international focus.

What characterizes the elite press? These are the newspapers of record that hold a mirror up to the world and incite the reader to think and reflect. They rarely play to the passions or prejudices of the reader. An elite newspaper does not merely report events, it places them in historical context and interprets their significance. It expresses opinions even when they are unpopular. It is a leader and reformer, trying to winnow the news and discard the chaff. It aims at coherence and clarity, for credibility and understanding. Unfortunately, the elite newspaper does not have the crackle and pop that characterizes the general press. Many of them, in fact, are dull in appearance. The *Neue Zurcher Zeitung,* for example, has an antiquated page makeup: the headlines are small, the pictures are few, there are no comics, no crossword puzzles, and no women's page.

While the elite press is difficult to define, it has certain characteristics that stand out. It attempts to do what the Commission on Freedom of the Press in 1947 said the press should do for society: "to present a truthful, comprehensive and intelligent account of the day's events in a context which gives them meaning." Within this framework, there are variations. There are analytical newspapers, such as *Le Monde* and *Frankfurter Allgemeine* and newspapers of record such as *The Times* of London and *The New York Times.* There are quality newspapers such as Switzerland's *Neue Zurcher Zeitung*, Germany's *Die Welt,* and Sweden's *Dagens Nyheter*. There are prestige newspapers such as Mexico's *El Nacional* and Vatican's *Osservatore Romano.* There are conservative newspapers such as the *Chicago Tribune*, Sweden's *Svenska Dagbladet*, *The Times* of London, *The Scotsman* of Edinburgh, *Corriere della Serra* of Milan, and the *Frankfurter Allgemeine* of Frankfurt am Main. The liberal newspapers would include *The New York Times*, *The Guardian* of England, *Dagens Nyheter* of Sweden, *Post-Dispatch* of St. Louis, *Le Monde* of Paris, *Neue Zurcher Zeitung* of Zurich, and *Suddeutsche Zeitung* of Munich. Among the weeklies, the elite press would include *Die Zeit* of Hamburg, *Weltwoche* of Zurich, the *Sunday Times* of London, and the *France Observateur* of Paris.

But labels have little to do with quality. All elite newspapers manage to create a bond of confidence between the paper and its reader. It establishes a link between the events and the ideas and people behind events and uncovers patterns in seemingly unrelated happenings. The readers receive a continuing education every day rather than merely news, and there is a distinct effort to avoid prurience, voyeurism, and sensationalism. Quality newspapers also strive to achieve clarity through the economical and efficient use of language. Some of them become noted for their unique style and usage, as in the case of *Time* magazine. Good reporting, as Albert Camus said, requires conciseness of expression, a feeling for form, flexible and free-flowing style, and incisive and honest interpretation. In a sense, the elite press serves as the conscience of the nation. Key to such a role is continuity and consistency in editorial policy. Editorial policy comprises practices, rules, and principles that the paper sets as a guide and standard for itself. It determines the character of the institution. It answers two important questions: What shall we print and how shall we print it? Sometimes it is written down as a manual and sometimes it is not, but both the editors and the readers come to expect that standard maintained in the paper every day.

Some countries have a stronger elite press than others. In Great Britain, for example, the serious national dailies perform the conscience-of-the-nation role better than in other countries. In the United States, where there is no national press, the major dailies, with a few exceptions, are generally unfocused and try to be all things to all people, offering bits of entertainment, comics, sports, puzzles, fiction, columns, and a grab bag of commentary.

The elite press has four other defining qualities. First, it is internationalist and cosmopolitan. It understands the interconnectedness of global systems and extends the same serious concern to events in foreign countries as to domestic issues. Second, it has an aura of dignity and stability, both in tone and style. It has a balanced approach to issues that helps it avoid hysteria and panic during crises. Third, it is courageous. It has a reputation for speaking out on issues when it is not popular to do so and when it may lose subscribers as a result. It attempts to lead and not follow public opinion and imposes the same standards that it follows on others. Fourth, the elite press is responsible and reliable. It views its role as a sacred trust for public good.

Elite newspapers tend to attract influential and thoughtful readers by the depth and breadth of their coverage, and they also tend to be more often independent and critical of government. According to Wilbur Schramm, the great newspapers tend to focus on big news of the day, both national and international, at the expense of local news and sensational human interest items, and they treat these larger events at greater length. Surveys have established five criteria for evaluating elite newspapers: (1) independence, financial stability, integrity, social concern, and good writing and editing; (2) strong opinion and interpretative emphasis, world consciousness, and nonsensationalism in content and makeup; (3) emphasis on durable issues in politics, international relations, economics, social welfare, culture, education, and science; (4) technically-skilled editorial and production staff; and (5) a well-educated and intellectually active readership and a desire to influence leadership in politics and society.

Press Councils

The development of press councils is associated with the emergence of the social responsibility theory in the twentieth century. A socially responsible press is fair and responsive to its readers. Governmental and private commissions investigating press performance in various countries have prescribed voluntary regulation to guard against abuses not covered by press laws. At least 14 free press countries have functioning arbitration boards to resolve conflicts and abuses. Generally publishers and journalists voluntarily cooperate with these councils. They are similar to medical or bar associations that enforce professional ethics except that the press council decisions are generally non-binding. The primary objective of every press council is to enforce the right of readers to reply and other access issues. Journalists and publishers constitute the majority membership in most press councils. Lay people usually account for between 20 and 33 percent of the membership.

Among the primary tasks of press councils are the preservation of the freedom of the press and the maintenance of professional standards and rights of access. Thus, they have a dual function—self-defense and self-control. In addition, press councils engage in other activities, such as ensuring a flow of information, preventing press concentration and monopoly, promoting education and research in education, supporting technical improvements, and representing the press in national and international forums. They may also represent the press in deliberations and hearings in the legislature. By and large, all press councils limit their purview to problems affecting newspapers.

There are debates about the pros and cons of press councils. Media watchers list seven positive features. They provide a litigation-free resource for readers with a grievance, and they provide an independent forum for discussion of media responsibilities and performance. They protect the interests of the press especially in legislative forums. Acting as a watchdog, they tend to enhance the credibility of the press. Press councils promote accountability and professionalism in the industry, and they provide broad guidelines and cut down excessive competitive zeal. Further, they help to create consistency in codes of ethics across national boundaries. Among the negative features are: threatening the freedom of underground and alternative newspapers that are often more audacious in their reporting and comments; potentially turning into a machinery for self-censorship; encouraging conformity and timidity among editors; lacking due process because there is no appeal against its decisions.

Press Laws

The history and development of press laws has been shaped largely by the interplay of three competing philosophies. The authoritarian view is that the press must serve the interests of the state and keep the ruling elite in power. The libertarian view is that the press should be free of any control—governmental, religious, economic, or otherwise. The third view of social responsibility holds that the press exists to serve society and its prevailing value systems. The authoritarian view has become more or less moribund as democratic forms of government have displaced monarchic and autocratic regimes. But press laws based on this view still flourish even in democratic countries. For example, in Israel the law permits the official censor to prohibit the publication of any matter prejudicial to public order. Violation of such legal provisions constitutes a criminal offense. Furthermore, even an indication that the censor had deleted some information was prohibited.

Most common-law systems have adopted Blackstone's doctrine that legal limitations over press freedom cannot be applied before publication. In his *Commentaries*, Blackstone stated that the liberty of the press is indeed essential to the nature of a free state, and this theory is the cornerstone of the libertarian view. It asserts the individual's and, consequently, the publisher's and editor's right to think and say what he or she pleases. Despite Blackstone, governments possessed ample power through criminal law to punish objectionable expression. One was the doctrine of seditious libel, which treated criticism of the government as subversive. This principle has persisted, although the Alien and Sedition Act was overturned in 1964 by the Supreme Court of the United States. The court held that newspapers could not be held liable unless the allegedly defamatory statements were made with actual malice—that is with the knowledge that the statements were false or with reckless disregard of truth.

The libertarian view does not distinguish between freedom of the press and general freedom of expression. Consequently, journalists do not enjoy any special professional privileges because libertarians do not concede any social function to the press. Social responsibility proponents, while sharing the libertarian antipathy to government, hold that the press has a special legal status because of its social significance. At issue is the reporters' privilege, the legal recognition that a reporter is immune from the general obligation to disclose the sources of information. Journalists contend that they need to protect their sources of information in order to provide the public with true and reliable information. The Freedom of Information acts also reflect the theory of social responsibility and recognize the public's "right to know" as a fundamental right. Although the Freedom of Information acts do not grant the press a legal status, they concede that society depends on information and that journalists need some protection. The flip side of the social responsibility theory is that it imposes certain legal obligations on journalists and calls for their regulation in the same fashion as other professions, such as medicine and law.

Press laws around the world represent a curious mixture of all three theories of the press. There is lip service in all constitutions to a "free press" and to "freedom of expression," but the press everywhere is engaged in a cat and mouse game trying to use its strengths against the constant danger posed by the state. One redeeming feature is the provision in certain countries of specific constitutional guarantees of press freedom accompanied by judicial review. But many countries, especially in Europe, have press statutes that amount to a comprehensive regulation of the press. They deal with registration, the legal obligations of editors and publishers, and accountability, and they provide for severe penalties for infractions of these regulations. But although the codes are severe, the courts themselves are less so and often cut the press some slack in the actual observance of these regulations.

Radio and Television

Next to print, radio is the most universal of all media. In certain regions, such as the Middle East, it is more popular than print or television. It is ideally suited for propaganda and even evangelism, as religious broadcasters discovered as early as the 1940s. In Egypt, for example, Radio Cairo under Nasser was one of the principal inciters of anti-Western propaganda, and Radio Ghana in the 1950s often excelled in anti-colonial rhetoric that effectively stirred up mass hysteria. Even poor nations, such as Bangladesh, have international radio services more as a status symbol than as a means of communication. Most international services, outside of religious broadcasting, are financially supported, operated, or supervised by governments and remain the voice of the state. There are a few commercial stations that depend on advertising to meet its bills and that provide a varied fare of music. There are also clandestine stations affiliated to lost causes or exiled political leaders trying to dislodge their rivals from power. News and news-related programs, such as editorials, commentaries, and cultural features, take up the largest single segment of program time on government-supported services. Popular music runs a fairly close second. Most international commercial radio stations devote little or no time to news, a major exception being France's SOFIRAD (Societie Financiere de Radio Diffusion). The largest of the international radio services may broadcast in as many as forty languages routinely and may be on the air for between 1,400 and 2,000 hours a week. The most popular of the international services is the BBC, which is listened to by people all around the globe.

The spectrum space in the short wave bands is allotted by the International Telecommunications Union (ITU), but all the desirable spectrum space has long been taken by the developed nations. ITU's World Administrative Radio Conferences have tried to mediate the dispute in favor of the Third World countries, but the spectrum remains congested and reception has tended to deteriorate. Some nations have tried to jam international broadcasts from unfriendly nations calling them "air pollution." The proliferation of communications satellites has made it easier for the larger nations to relay broadcasts to their overseas relay transmitters. Because of the costs involved and the need to get satellite space, Third World nations find themselves at a greater disadvantage.

Unlike radio, there are no international television services; nevertheless, television images are transmitted within minutes by satellites and appear on screens around the world. In no other medium is the term "global village" more of a reality than in television. Because of its direct impact, both the message and the medium are important in television. Cable has expanded the range of television; it is said that more than 500 channels can be watched in an average day (if one has the time to do it).

Playing a key role in television news packages, giving coherence to its varied contents and styles of presentation, are the anchorpersons. They are the visible messengers, the towncriers of the twenty-first century who bring the news of the day to the public; their personalities often serve as filters that color the news. Their inflections, gestures, and expressions play a crucial part in how the news is received, cueing and channeling audience reactions. Many are celebrities who are courted by politicians.

National newscasts are carried by a network of stations, but there may also be local news programs assembled by individual stations. There is also a trend toward "happy talk"—on more or less the same format as talk radio or call-in radio, consisting mostly of chatter. "All news" formats are becoming popular, especially in cable, with CNN being the prime example.

News is a perishable commodity with a shelf-life of not more than 24 hours, and television news has to contend with the need to present the most important news at the shortest notice. They are also faced with other problems, especially those relating to audience ratings; if the ratings fall, they are out of business. There is also the lengthening shadow of the sponsors or advertisers who underwrite the program. Censorship is not a major problem in free societies, but there are unwritten codes of conduct relating to sex and violence that most television program directors observe scrupulously. The compression of news into short bites, the attention deficit disorder from which most television viewers suffer, and the competition from other television and radio news channels highlights the need to dramatize and personalize every event and to grip the interest of the audience. For social scientists, television remains a performance theater in which the dividing line between entertainment and reality is blurred. Television news also is highly selective because it has a short amount of time to cover the world without going into a lengthy analysis. Despite these limitations, many people in many countries derive their information about world events from television rather than from newspapers or the radio.

Conclusion

In a free society, the press finds the right environment for growth in influence and financial stability. Technology has made the collection and dissemination of news faster and more dependable. There is a large corps of trained professional journalists, commentators, and anchorpersons who combine good investigative, writing, and speaking skills with dedication to their job and a commitment to the objective presentation of facts. The press has become a vital component of the functioning of a democratic society.

According to Marshall McLuhan, the twenty-first century will be the age of the media because information and news are forms of energy that energize all activities. The *World Press Encyclopedia* looks at this phenomenon as it plays out in all the countries of the world. No encyclopedia can deal with a grander theme.

—George Thomas Kurian

AFGHANISTAN

BASIC DATA

Official Country Name:	Islamic State of Afghanistan
Region (Map name):	East & South Asia
Population:	26,813,057
Language(s):	Pashtu, Afghan Persian (Dari)
Literacy rate:	31.5%
Area:	647,500 sq km
Number of Television Stations:	10
Number of Television Sets:	100,000
Television Sets per 1,000:	3.7
Number of Radio Stations:	9
Number of Radio Receivers:	167,000
Radio Receivers per 1,000:	6.2

BACKGROUND & GENERAL CHARACTERISTICS

When the Taliban took control of the capital—Kabul—on September 26, 1996, the Islamic State of Afghanistan began a period of regulation regarded by many as the most restricted in the world. Five years later, shortly after September 11, 2001, when terrorist attacks on the World Trade Center and the Pentagon destroyed the former and severely damaged the latter, these restrictions began to ease, largely as a result of U.S. ''war'' strikes against the Afghani-based Al Qaeda (The Base) terrorist group held responsible for the attack.

Afghanistan has a population of around 25 million people composed of two major ethnic groups, Pashtun (38 percent) and Tajik (25 percent); however, additional ethnic groups include Aimaq, Balulchis, Brahui, Hazaras, Nuristanis, Turkmens, and Uzbeks. Most people are Muslim (Sunni: 84 percent, Shi'a: 15 percent). Many speak one of the official state languages (Dari: 50 percent, Pashtu: 35 percent), although there are some 30 viable dialects, and the official language of the religious leadership is Arabic. Between 1996 and 2002, religious police enforced codes of conduct that imposed comprehensive constraints on females.

A paternalistic background dominates the role communications has played in the country. Up to the time of this publication, the industry may be characterized as small, state-controlled, and subject to heavy censorship by religious fundamentalists. In 2001 newspaper circulation rates were estimated by objective data-gathering sources to be operating at the 1-percent mark. The Taliban Ministry of Information and Culture maintained that more than a dozen daily newspapers existed under their regime. These state-owned organs featured Taliban official announcements, news of military victories, and criticism of any opposition. Because there were no newsstands, the papers were distributed largely to political/religious institutions.

Low readership, in addition to low circulation, characterizes this country's journalism. The potential newspaper audience is small because Afghanistan has a literacy rate thought to be among the lowest in Asia (around 31 percent, according to UNESCO estimates), although education is officially compulsory for children between the ages of 7 and 13. Few matriculate to any form of higher education.

Restricted press life and low readership levels extend backward well beyond the Taliban. In fact, only one period may have permitted the operation of truly independent journalism—the supposed decade of democracy (1963-

73) under the rule of King Zahir Shah, Pakistan's last monarch who reigned from 1933 to 1973. With his overthrow, media restrictions increased geometrically under President Mohammad Daud (1973-78), the Communist People's Democratic Party of Afghanistan (1978-92), the provincial *Mujahidin* (fighters in a holy war) (1992-96), and the Taliban (1996-2002).

The first regularly published Afghani newspaper was the *Saraj-al-Akhbar* (''Lamp of the News'') debuting in 1911 and published in Afghani Persian (Dari), eight years before Afghanistan gained independence on August 19, 1919, from Great Britain. Founder Mahmud Tarzi was outspoken and opposed, among other things, the official position of friendship between Great Britain and Afghanistan. After King Shir Ali Khan died, the ''Lamp'' was replaced by *Aman-i-Afghan* (''Afghan Peace''). From that initial period of attempted enlightenment until the 1950s through 1970s, when professional journalists facilitated a brief period of growth, Afghani journalism remained limited and mostly a vehicle for resonance with ruling thought.

By 2001 the two most influential dailies were *Anis* (''Companion'' or ''Friendship''), founded in 1927 with a circulation estimated at 25,000 and published in Dari but including articles written in Pashtu and Uzbek, and *Hewad* (''Homeland''), founded in 1959 with a circulation estimated at 12,000 and published in Pashtu. Both are based in Kabul and controlled by the Ministry of Information and Culture. These four-page ''dailies'' came out only several times a week, however, and reached only 11 per 1,000. Nevertheless, such a distribution rate represents a marginal increase from the 1982 rate of 4 per 1,000.

Other principal dailies, estimated at no more than 14, were headquartered in Kabul and in such provincial centers as Baghlan, Faizabad, Farah, Gardiz, Herat, Jalabad, Mazar-i-Sharif, Shiberghan, and Qandahar. These provincial papers mostly relied on the Kabul dailies for news, and averaged around 1,500 in circulation.

An independent Afghani press, then, has not existed in Afghanistan since 1973. The nearest relative to such an entity would be an Afghan-owned daily that began operations in Peshawar, Pakistan, in the late 1990s. With formal news channels so restricted and unidimensional, informal news networks have flourished in the bazaars of Kabul and other cities. A mixture of fact and fantasy, this news has circulated orally and through *shahnamahs* (night letters).

ECONOMIC FRAMEWORK

Afghanistan has had a modern history of oppression, war, and poverty. A mountainous, landlocked country in southwest Asia, with dry climate and temperature extremes, its arable land is only around 12 percent. Nevertheless, almost 70 percent of its labor force is engaged in agrarian activity. In general, the population has a small per capita income (around U.S. $170) and a life expectancy that is the lowest in Asia (around 47 years-of-age).

The Hindu Kush Mountains separate the country into northeast and southwest sections, roughly speaking, a division that has impeded commercial and political relations between these areas. The Taliban, an Islamic fundamentalist militia, ruled approximately 80 percent of Afghanistan between 1996 and 2002. The Northern Alliance, their last remaining opponents with a stronghold in the northeast corner, laid claim to the remaining 20 percent.

Modern printing machines began operating in Afghanistan in 1927, although the printing standards remain behind the times. Much of the type continues to be set by hand.

Questions relevant to journalism in technologically advanced countries—competition, advertisers' influence, reporter power, and the like—simply are not relevant to Afghanistan. As a country entrenched in the beginning stages of progress, in fact, Afghanistan has substantial barriers to media development. These obstacles include inhospitable terrain, mixed ethnic groups with historic conflicts, language differences, low literacy and income levels, underdeveloped educational and other social welfare institutions, and a governmental structure dominated by religious intolerance.

PRESS LAWS

The 1964 Constitution of Afghanistan and the Press Law of July 1965 provided for freedom of the press subject to comprehensive articles of proper behavior. According to the Press Law, the press was free (i.e., independent of government ownership) but must safeguard the interests of the state and constitutional monarchy, Islam, and public order. When the government was overthrown in July of 1973, 19 newspapers were shut down. Western-style freedom of the press has systematically eroded during the regimes of dictatorship, communism, *Mujahidin* factions, and the Taliban.

CENSORSHIP

By 2002 it appeared that traditional forms of press freedom were simply nonexistent in Afghanistan. Because the ruling movement strictly interpreted Muslim Sharia law and banned representation of people and animals, for example, newspapers were picture-free—censorship in which Afghanistan stands alone in the world. Had newspapers been allowed to print photographs, women would have appeared only in full veil and men in full beard. This suppression of freedom of expression extended to a complete ban on music and films.

Self-censorship also has been a problem because of the threats received by journalists after writing articles critical of the Taliban. Afghan journalists, working both locally and in exile, have been subject to warnings as well as *fatwas* (death threats) for writing unpopular reports. These threats have sometimes materialized into murder.

ATTITUDE TOWARD FOREIGN MEDIA

The Taliban enforced heavy restrictions on foreign journalists who were provided with a list of 21 rules. The principal positive rule required journalists to give a ''faithful'' account of Afghani life. The succeeding rules represented a series of restrictions, the umbrella of which was a prohibition on journalists traveling unaccompanied by Taliban ''minders.'' These watchdogs were there to ensure that journalists abided by the limitations, which included bans on entering private houses, interviewing women, and the like.

Foreign journalists, as well as Afghani journalists, often have been harassed. A number of examples exist of reporters who have been wounded, kidnapped, or murdered—grim reminders of the dangers journalists face while trying to perform their job in an unstable country.

The only foreign broadcaster permitted entry to Afghanistan has been Al Jazeera, an independent satellite television station home-based in Qatar and seemingly owned, at least indirectly, by the Qatari government. Although the channel may not always promote ''Arab brotherhood,'' as defined by the Arab States Broadcasting Union's code of honor, it also has been willing to air anti-American views and statements by Osama bin Laden, even after the terrorist attacks on September 11, 2001. Labeled a maverick, and regarded as the most popular television channel in the Arab culture, Al Jazeera may come closest to uncensored programming among Arab media.

NEWS AGENCIES

The Bakhtar News Agency, responsible for domestic news collation and distribution to all domestic media, reports to the Ministry of Information and Culture. Leaders in both these units traditionally have been appointed based on their loyalty to the ruling government.

Two Pakistani-based news agencies have been launched by Afghani refugees—the Afghan Islamic Press and the Sahaar News Agency. They manage to produce bulletins with varying degrees of accuracy for mostly Western wire services.

Because of the dangers to journalists based in Afghanistan, foreign news bureaus have shrunk. By 2001 only three countries were represented by news agencies in Kabul: Czechoslovakia, Russia, and Yugoslavia.

BROADCAST MEDIA

Color television broadcasting began in 1978. The Taliban banned television and closed the station in 1996. Taliban religious police smashed privately owned television sets and strung up videocassettes in trees in a form of symbolic execution by hanging. Anyone found harboring a television set was subject to punishments of flogging and a six-month incarceration.

In the northeast, however, Badakhshan Television broadcast news and old movies for three hours every evening. Financed by the Northern Alliance, the station's audience was limited to around 5,000 viewers (among 100,000 residents in Faizabad without electricity) who could muster some kind of home-generation power source. Although a marginally effective news channel, it became a symbol of light in a more freely communicating society in direct opposition to the darkness imposed by the Taliban.

Radio is the broadcast medium of choice in Afghanistan, an option well suited to a low-literate society, although most people do not have a radio (radio ownership is around 74 per 1,000). The Radio Voice of Sharia (Islamic law), founded in 1927 as Radio Kabul and controlled by the Ministry of Information and Culture, was programmed by the Taliban to provide domestic service up to 10 hours daily in Dari and Pashtu; daily domestic service of 50 minutes in Nurestani, Pashai, Turkmen, and Uzbek; and 30 minutes of foreign service in English and Urdu. Broadcast topics were mainly of religious orientation, unrelieved by music.

SUMMARY

The history of mass media in Afghanistan, especially recent history, is dominated by such adjectives as restricted, censored, under-developed, and nonexistent. Its future undoubtedly relies on the establishment of peace, prosperity, and a philosophy of communication that promotes civil government. Because country development and modern communications technology are correlated, Afghans would do well to create a society that offers freedom of information and human respect, regardless of demographic label, to all.

SIGNIFICANT DATES

- 1996: Taliban capture Kabul and Jalalabad, effectively assuming control of Afghanistan. Ban television. Impose heavy restrictions on radio and print media.
- 2001: Terrorist attacks on the World Trade Center and on the Pentagon in the United States. Al Qaeda,

a terrorist organization headquartered in Afghanistan, held responsible. United States responds with air and ground strikes aimed at destroying the Taliban, who refuse to surrender Al Qaeda.

- 2002: Taliban overwhelmed. A measure of freedom returns to Afghanistan as freer press, music, and television begin a resurgence.

BIBLIOGRAPHY

Abu-Fadil, Magda. ''Maverick Arab Satellite TV: Qatar's Al-Jazeera Brings a Provocative New Brand of Journalism to the Middle East.'' *IPI Report* 5, no. 4 (1999): 8-9.

''Afghanistan.'' *The Europa World Yearbook 2001,* 365-385. London: Europa Publications, 2001.

''Afghanistan: Media Chronology Post-11 September 2001.'' *BBC Monitoring International Reports,* 16 January 2002. Available from http://www.lexis-nexis.com.

''Afghanistan.'' *The World Fact Book 2000,* 1-3. Washington, DC: Central Intelligence Agency, 2000.

''Afghanistan.'' *World Press Freedom Review 2000,* 110-111. Columbia, MO: International Press Institute, 2000.

Farivar, Masood. ''Dateline Afghanistan: Journalism under the Taliban.'' *CPJ Briefings: Press Freedom Reports from around the World,* 15 December 1999. Available from http://www.cpj.org.

Goodson, Larry. *Afghanistan's Endless War.* Seattle: University of Washington Press, 2001.

Kaplan, Robert D. *Warrior Politics: Why Leadership Demands a Pagan Ethos.* New York: Random House, 2002.

Lacayo, Richard. ''The Women of Afghanistan: A Taste of Freedom.'' *Time* 158, no. 24 (2001): 34-49.

Lent, John A. ''To and from the Grave: Press Freedom in South Asia.'' *Gazette* 33, no. 1 (1984): 17-36.

Marsden, Peter. *The Taliban: War and Religion in Afghanistan.* London and New York: Zed Books, 2002.

Rashid, Ahmed. ''Heart of Darkness.'' *Far Eastern Economic Review* 162, no. 31 (1999), 8-12.

———. ''The Last TV Station.'' *Far Eastern Economic Review* 162, no. 38 (1999), 38.

Razi, Mohammad H. ''Afghanistan.'' *Mass Media in the Middle East: A Comprehensive Handbook,* eds. Yahya R. Kamalipour and Hamid Mowlana, 1-12. Westport, CT: Greenwood Press, 1994.

The World Almanac and Book of Facts 2001. New York: World Almanac, 2001.

World Association for Christian Communication. *U.S. Pressures Al-Jazeera,* November 2001. Available from http://www.wacc.org.uk.

—Clay Warren

ALBANIA

BASIC DATA

Official Country Name:	Republic of Albania
Region (Map name):	Europe
Population:	3,510,484
Language(s):	Albanian, Greek
Literacy rate:	93.0%
Area:	28,748 sq km
GDP:	3,752 (US$ millions)
Number of Television Stations:	9
Number of Television Sets:	405,000
Television Sets per 1,000:	115.4
Number of Radio Stations:	21
Number of Radio Receivers:	810,000
Radio Receivers per 1,000:	230.7
Number of Individuals with Computers:	25,000
Computers per 1,000:	7.1
Number of Individuals with Internet Access:	3,500
Internet Access per 1,000:	1.0

BACKGROUND & GENERAL CHARACTERISTICS

Albania is a land of clans. For centuries the clans of Albania have feuded with each other, making this eastern Adriatic region susceptible to occupation by stronger empires. For two decades in the fifteenth century the clans of Albania united in an alliance against the Ottoman Turks under the leadership of Gjergj Kastrioti (1403-1468), better known as Iskander Skanderberg. The Turkish surrender to Skanderberg in 1444 brought Albania a brief period of decentralized national unity. Skanderberg's death in 1468 from wounds at the battle of Lezhe against the Ottoman Turks returned Roman Catholic Albania to the Muslim control of Constantinople. A red flag with Skanderberg's heraldic emblem remained the symbol of Albanian independence under five centuries of Ottoman occupation.

In the nineteenth century Albanian intellectuals standardized the Albanian language, a unique mixture of Latin, Greek, and Slavic dialects, creating a literary style for educational use. The Society for the Printing of Albanian Writings, founded by Sami Frasheri in 1879, sought national reconciliation from Muslim, Catholic, and Eastern Orthodox Albanians and the use of the Albanian language in the region's schools. For most of Albania's history, education in Muslim-controlled Albania was under the jurisdiction of the Ottomans and their surrogates, the Greeks, who banned Albanian language-based education and required Albanians to be educated in Turkish or Greek. Albanian exiles in Romania, Bulgaria, Egypt, Italy, and the United States kept the Albanian language alive by writing and printing textbooks and smuggling them into their homeland.

The gradual economic and political disintegration of the Ottoman Empire in the late nineteenth century and the empire's military defeats in the twentieth century against successful nationalistic waves of independence by Serbians, Romanians, Greeks, Montenegrins, and Bulgarians provided the Albanian people with the opportunity to seek their own independence. Albanian guerrilla movements within Albania worked with Albanian supporters of the Young Turk movement throughout the Ottoman Empire to destabilize it. Albanian efforts brought fleeting rewards. In 1908 the Ottoman government restored the Albanian language as the educational language for instruction and offered some local political autonomy; however, a new Turkish government in 1909 immediately reversed its position on Albania. Albanian resistance ultimately was successful when Ottoman overlords granted Albania local autonomy in 1911, extending to Albanians local control over the educational system, military recruitment, taxation, and the right to use the Latin script for the Albanian language.

A series of Balkan wars in 1912 and 1913 by Bulgaria, Serbia, Greece, and Montenegro against the Ottoman Empire offered Albania the opportunity to declare its own independence in the city of Vlores in November 1912. The London Conference of 1913 on the Balkans ultimately granted Albania full independence from the Ottoman Empire under the protection of Europe's Great Powers (Russia, Great Britain, France, Austria, and Germany). As would be true for most of the twentieth century, Albania's future was shaped by other nations, not by the Albanian people. The Great Powers acceded to the demands of Serbia and Montenegro for Albanian districts. Albanians living in Kosovo and western Macedonia were placed under the jurisdiction of Serbia, not Albania.

An independent Albania was constituted as a constitutional monarchy ruled by an imported German prince, Wilhelm zu Wied, who was unprepared for the realities of Albanian politics. Prince Wilhelm barely controlled the major cities of Durres and Vlores. He left his country after a brief six months. World War I brought deals from the Allies in exchange for support from Albania's neighbors. Italy, Montenegro, and Serbia were each promised Albanian land in return for military assistance against the German and Austrian armies. Albania's future was again determined by other nations unwilling to allow all Albanians to be part of a ''Greater Albania.''

U.S. diplomatic intervention kept Albania independent after World War I. The newly formed Kingdom of Yugoslavia (Serbs, Croats, and Slovenes) backed Albanian chieftain Ahmed Bey Zogu, believing him a pliable tool for Belgrade's interests in the acquisition of additional Albanian territory. Zogu first established his control within Albania and then turned on his Yugoslav benefactors by making himself President of Albania in 1924 and King in 1928. King Zog turned to Italy for international support against Yugoslavia. Over the next 15 years, Albania came under greater Italian control. Roman Catholic schools were established to replace Muslim ones and Italian became the language of education. Zog's regime was both repressive and censorious. In 1939 King Zog was overthrown by the Italian military. He fled into permanent exile leaving Albania under the control of Rome until Italy's defeat and surrender in 1944.

King Zog and his ministers were never accorded Allied recognition as a government-in-exile. The only major internal resistance in Albania against Italian and German troops was a communist insurgency led by Enver Hoxha. British support provided the critical leverage creating a People's Republic of Albania in 1944. During the next five years all opposition to Hoxha's communist government was eradicated. The media was seized by communist authorities in 1944 but not nationalized until 1946. All media forms were used to instill Marxist values and justify communist rule. Albanian writers and artists were commissioned to rewrite Albania's past to depict a population both backward and besieged, thankful for the advances a communist regime could offer. The press, radio, and television urged implementation of communist economic programs and supported antireligious campaigns and literacy promotion. The media was instructed to appeal to Albanian nationalism to force the public's acceptance of the communist dictatorship's agenda. All newspapers were under the control of the communist government and printed only what they were told. Albania's few radio and television stations spoke only the communist credo. All journalists, editors, film directors, and television and radio producers were either communist party members or severely subjected to the discipline and guidelines of the party. For the next four decades Albania under President and Communist Party leader Enver Hoxha brutally suppressed all dissent, denied the Albanian people human rights, and isolated Albania from all European countries with only distant China, little Albania's primary ally. The communist party published the nation's most important newspaper, *Zeri I Popullit* (*Voice of the People*).

A 1984-study commissioned by Amnesty International identified Hoxha's Albania as one of the world's most repressive regimes. Albanians were denied the freedoms of expression, religion, movement, and association in contradiction to the country's 1976 constitution, which stated the nation's political liberties. The only information available to the Albanian people came from the government-controlled media. Hoxha's death in 1985 led to minor improvements in the communist rule of Albania under Hoxha successor, Ramiz Alia. Alia loosened some of the nation's harshest restrictions on human rights and the media. Internal dissent and mounting demonstrations in Albania led Alia to sign the Conference on Security and Cooperation in Europe, which guaranteed Albanians both human and political rights as part of the Helsinki accords of 1975. After press laws were liberalized in 1990, *Zeri I Popullit* rapidly lost circulation. Opposition papers were printed; the most popular newspaper became *Rilindja Demokratike.* To regain subscribers *Zeri I Popullit* removed the hammer and sickle and the Marxist slogan from its masthead and relinquished its role as the mouthpiece of the Communist Party.

In 1990 Albania reorganized itself into a multiparty democracy. Student unrest in 1990 led to violent clashes. The political party, the Democratic Front and its daily newspaper, *Bashkimi,* covered the clashes, arrests, and police activity. This was Albania's first public criticism in the media since the 1944 communist takeover. Albania's government acted with a new sense of responsibility, and the Council of Ministers proceeded to liberalize the laws regulating the media, reduced the Communist Party's control of the press, and legalized the nation's first privately owned opposition newspaper, *Rilindja Demokratike.*

Albania adopted a new constitution in 1998 to bring the nation into full compliance with the constitutions of Europe's other nations and to facilitate Albania's need for foreign investment in the nation's financial future. Under the 1998 constitution the nation's head of state is a president elected for a five-year term by the legislature. The president, who is advised by a cabinet, appoints the prime minister. Albania has a unicameral legislature (*Kuvendi Popullor*) with 155 members serving four-year terms. Most legislators are elected by direct popular vote with a smaller number elected by proportional vote. Part Two of the constitution, The Fundamental Human Rights and Freedoms, guarantees the Albanian people human rights and freedoms that are indivisible, inalienable, and inviolable, and protected by the judicial order. Article 22 provides for freedom of expression, and freedom of the press, radio, and television. Prior censorship of a means of communication is prohibited. The operation of radio and television stations may require the granting of a government authorization. Article 23 guarantees the right to information. All Albanians have the right, in compliance with the law, to get information about the activities of the government and about the individuals exercising governmental authority.

In 1996 Albania published five national dailies with a combined circulation of 116,000. In 1995 the four largest newspapers were the Albanian language morning dailies *Zeri I Popullit,* 35,000 circulation; *Koha Jone,* 30,000 circulation; *Rilindja Demokratike,* 10,000 circulation; and the Albanian and Italian language morning daily *Gazeta Shqiptare,* 11,000 circulation. *Dy Drina* is published in northern Albania and has a circulation of 1,000. According to 1995 statistics, general-interest biweekly periodicals circulated as follows: *Alternativa,* published by the Social Democratic Party, 5,000 readers; *Bashkimi,* published by the Democratic Front, 5,000 readers; and *Republika,* published by the Republican Party, 8,000 readers. Weekly general interest periodicals are *Ax,* 6,000 readers; *Drita,* 4,000 readers; and *Zeri I Rinise,* a Youth Confederation publication, 4,000 readers. *Lajmi I Dites,* published by the ATS News Agency, has three issues per week and a circulation of 5,000. Special interest publications are the monthlies *Albanian Economic Tribune* in both Albanian and English with 5,000 readers; *Arber,* published by the Ministry of Culture with 5,000 readers, and *Bujqesia Shqiptare,* published by the Ministry of Agriculture with 3,000 readers. Weekly special interest periodicals are *Mesuesi,* published by the Ministry of Education, 3,000 circulation, and *Sindikalisti,* circulation 5,000. The University of Triana publishes the biweekly *Studenti,* with a circulation of 5,000, and the quarterly *Gruaja Dhe Koha* has 1,000 readers. The quarterly *Media Shqiptare,* founded in 1999, caters to journalists and provides news about the profession.

The Albanian print media is generally characterized as an extension of political parties. It is perceived as more opinion than factually based. Albanian newspapers have distribution problems. They are sold in the cities, which omit 60 percent of the population residing in the countryside. Newspapers lack adequate revenue to cover printing costs and salaries for a professional staff. Since 1999 newspaper circulation has dropped from 75,000 to 50,000 readers. A majority of Albanians believe that the print media are a negative national influence. Polls indicate that Albanians prefer to receive their news via electronic means.

Albania has had one government owned radio station, Radiotelevizioni Shqiptar. The nation's previously government-owned television station is also called Radiotelevizioni Shqiptar. In 1999, both stations were merged into a public entity no longer financed by the state and without direct linkage to the government. Radiotelevizioni Shqiptar (RTSH; Albanian Radio Television) is under the jurisdiction of the National Council for Radio and Television and regulated by a committee whose members are chosen by Albania's parliament.

ECONOMIC FRAMEWORK

The population of Albania is 95 percent Albanian. The remaining 5 percent of the Albanian population is Greek (3 percent) and Vlachs, Gypsies, Serbs, and Bulgarians (2 percent). Albania is overwhelmingly Muslim (70 percent). Albanian Orthodox Christians represent 20 percent of the population, and 10 percent of Albanians are Roman Catholic.

Albania is one of Europe's poorest nations. The transition from a communist, highly centralized economy to a privatized capitalistic system has had serious repercussions for Albanians. Albania suffered a severe economic depression in 1990 and 1991. The economy improved from 1993 to 1995, but political instability led to increasing inflation and large budget deficits, 12 percent of the gross national product. In 1997, the Albanian economy collapsed under pressures from a financial pyramid scheme to which a large segment of the population had contributed. Severe social unrest led to over 1,500 deaths, the destruction of property, and a falling gross national product. A strong government response curbed violent crime and revived the economy, trade, and commerce. Albanian workers overseas, primarily in Greece and Italy, represent over 20 percent of the Albanian labor force. They contribute to the nation's economic well being by sending money back to their families in Albania. In 1992, most of Albania's farmland was privatized, which increased farming incomes. International aid helped Albania pay for ethnic Albanians from war-torn Kosovo living in refugee camps in Albania. Albania's work force is divided among agriculture (55 percent), industry (24 percent), and service industry (21 percent). The nation's major industries are food processing, textiles and clothing, lumber, oil, cement, chemicals, mining, basic metals, and hydropower.

Due to international pressure, under the leadership of Ramiz Alia Albania relaxed political and human rights controls. National amnesties in 1986 and 1989 released political prisoners held for years. By 1990, Alia supported a more open press and freedom of speech. The press covered controversial topics, sometimes resorting to sensationalism to increase circulation.

Albania is poorly represented in the telecommunications field with an obsolete wire system. Telephone wires were cut in 1992 by villagers and used to build fences. There is no longer a single telephone for each Albanian village. It is estimated that there are two telephones for every 100 Albanians. The lack of a telecommunications network is being alleviated by Vodafone Albania, a subsidiary of Vodafone Group Plc. Vodafone competes with Albania Mobile Communications (AMC) for the sale of cell phones in a nation without regular telephone communications. State run Albtelecom was privatized in 2002. Albtelecom has two Internet Service Provider licenses supporting ISDN and NT connections in five major Albanian cities and plans to expand and serve the university population. The competition of all three companies will allow Albania to catch up in the telecommunications industry on a level compatible with the European Union nations.

International communication is frequently carried by microwave radio relay from Tirana to either Greece or Italy. During the communist era radio and television were exclusively used for propaganda purposes. In 1992 the government owned and operated all 17 AM radio stations and the sole FM station, which broadcast two national programs as well as regional and local programs throughout the country. Popular Albanian broadcast frequencies are AM 16 and FM 3. There are two short-wave frequencies. Albania has nine television stations. Programming is broadcast in eight languages and reaches Albanians in Africa, the Middle East, North and South America, and Europe. Until the early 2000s all radio and television stations were broadcast exclusively over government-controlled frequencies and were usually propaganda based. This has changed significantly with the restructuring of the RTSH.

PRESS LAWS & CENSORSHIP

Albania's rapid transition from an isolationist communist state to western-style democracy was fraught with difficulties. The 1999 Country Reports on Human Rights Practices reported that the nation's security forces usually respected Albania's Law on Fundamental Human Rights and Freedoms, but there were incidents in 1999 where journalists were beaten. The report noted that the media were given the freedom to express views, but the press seldom used self-restraint in what it printed. News stories were given to sensationalism and lacked professional integrity, contained unsubstantiated accusations, and sometimes included complete fabrications. In 1999 Albania's political parties, labor unions, and professional and fraternal groups and organizations published their own newspapers and magazines. In that year, there were at least 200 such publications available on a daily or weekly basis. Newspaper sales were falling because the public lacked trust in what was being reported. In 1999 new privately owned radio and television stations began to emerge to compete with the print media for circulation. At least 50 television and 30 radio stations competed with the RTSH, formerly run by the state. To control a proliferation of broadcast media stations, the government approved new licensing requirements. The National Council of Radio and Television was created to regulate the licensing of radio and television stations. The Council's membership is equally divided between the government and the opposition political parties.

The *2001 World Press Freedom Review* noted that the Albanian press showed increased maturity and professionalism in reporting the news. Professional standards for the hiring of journalists reflected a significant improvement. In 2001, the media's professionalism was increasingly evident in their reporting on the conflict in neighboring Macedonia with its large ethnic Albanian population and Albania's general elections of June 2001. A lack of financial resources forced the Albanian media to increasingly depend on foreign news sources for international coverage. Journalists' bias and opinion are now more likely to appear in newspaper editorial pages than in the newspapers front-page articles. The *World Press Freedom Review* criticized the media for a lack of critical analysis about political candidates running for public office and the failure to cover some important national events. Press coverage on the Socialist Party (the former Albanian Communist Party) was criticized in the report for being overly critical and biased. The broadcast media were noted as providing more balanced coverage. Only the public television channel TVSH was sited for biased reporting with 40 percent of the coverage focused on the Socialist Party and 11 percent of the coverage for all the other opposition parties. As a result the National Council for Radio and Television fined TVHS for bias in reporting for the Socialist Party.

In 2001, Albania's government debated a new media law, Article 19 for Freedom of the Press, to regulate the media. Opposition lawmakers feared Article 19 might compromise press freedom by making journalists responsible for what was printed regardless of who authorized the article. Article 19 also required all journalists to register with a Journalists' Registry and to be experienced before being licensed by the state, and made publishers legally liable for hiring unlicensed journalists. Article 19 required journalists to report only truthful and carefully checked news stories. False news articles would be considered a criminal offense. A national debate concluded that Article 19 was likely to be in contradiction to European Union media practices, which required the media to police and discipline itself.

NEWS AGENCIES

For the majority of its media history, Albania has had only one principal news agency, Agjensia Telegrafike Shqiptare. There are three media associations, the Journalists Union, the Professional Journalists Association, and the Writers and Artists League. E.N.T.E.R. is the first Independent Albanian News Agency. Founded in 1997 by a recognized group of well-known independent journalists, E.N.T.E.R. negotiates contracts for the sale and distribution of news with independent newspapers, private radio stations, state radio and television stations, state institutions, and international organizations. E.N.T.E.R. is divided into three departments, Interior News, Foreign, and Technical, with correspondents in Albania's 12 administrative districts. Tirfax offers information in English but not a single Albanian newspaper uses it.

BROADCAST MEDIA

The National Council for Radio-Television regulates broadcasting. The president appoints one member, and the Commission on the Media, which is made up of representatives selected equally by the government and the opposition parties, chooses six members. The National Council broadcasts a national radio program and a second radio program from 14 stations. Statistics for 1997 indicated that Albanians owned 810,000 radios and 405,000 television sets. The electronic media law of September 30, 1998 provides for the transfer of the state-owned RTSH to public ownership under the authority of the National Broadcasting Council. An amended state secrets law, passed in 1999, eliminated references to punishing media institutions and journalists for publishing classified information. Penal code punishments have not been dropped.

In 2000, many Albanian television stations operated illegally without government licenses. There were 120 applications with 20 television stations competing for two national channels. The National Council for Radio and Television granted the two national channels to TV Klan and TV Arberia. TV Shijak, one of the television losers, criticized the decision as being politically motivated. Other television stations were granted licenses for local broadcasting including TV Teuta. Most television and radio stations are joint ventures with Italian companies. Despite the criticism, Albanian media is increasing in number and reflecting the political and economic stability of the nation. RTSH tends to provide more government information as it makes the transition to a private network system. It is the only station to broadcast throughout the entire country.

Radio Koha, Radio Kontakt, Radio Stinet, Radio Top Albania, and Radio Ime are Albanian's most popular radio stations. Their programming emphasizes music, news, and call-in shows. Albanians receive FM broadcasts from the Voice of America, British Broadcasting Corporation, and Deutsche Welle on short wave.

ELECTRONIC NEWS MEDIA

Electronic media in Albania is a relatively recent addition to the media. The list of electronic media is growing at a rapid rate. AlbaNews is a mailing list dedicated to the distribution of new and information about Albania, Kosovo, the Former Yugoslav Republic of Macedonia, Montenegro, and Albanian living around the world. Major contributors to AlbaNews are Kosova Information Center, OMRI, Albanian Telegraphic Agency, Council for the Defense of Human rights and Freedoms in Kosova, and Albanian Weekly (Prishtina). Electronic Media newsgroups for Albania include soc.culture.albanian, bit.listserv.albanian, clari.news.Europe.Balkans, alt. news.macdeonia, soc.cuture.yugoslavia, and soc. culture.europe.

The Albanian press with Internet Web sites are Koha Jone, Gazeta Shqiptare, Gazeta Shekulli, Gazeta Korrieri, Sporti Shqiptar, Zeri I Popullit, Republicka, Revista Klan, and Revista Spekter. Internet sites are available for a number of Albanian print media, which includes the Albanian Daily News, AlbaNews, Albania On-Line, ARTA News Agency, Albanian Telegraphic Agency, BBC World Service Albanian, Dardania Lajme, Deutsche Weel-Shqip, Kosova Crisis Center, Council for the Defence of Human Rights and Freedoms, Kosova Press, Kosova Sot, and the Kosova Information Center. Albanian periodicals with Internet sites are Blic, Fokus, International Journal of Albanian Studies, International War and Peace Report, Klan, and Pasqyra.

Albanian radio stations with online sites are Radio 21, Radio France Internationale, Lajme ne Shqip, and Rilindja. Albanian television stations with Internet sites are Radio Television of Prishtina Satellite Program, Shekuli, TV Art, TVSH-Programi Satelitor, and the Voice of America Albanian Service.

Albaniannews.com was the nation's first electronic media to go online in 1991 as a private company. The company's Independent Albanian Economic Tribune, Ltd. was Albania's first economic online monthly. In 1995, the English-language *Albanian Daily News* was of-

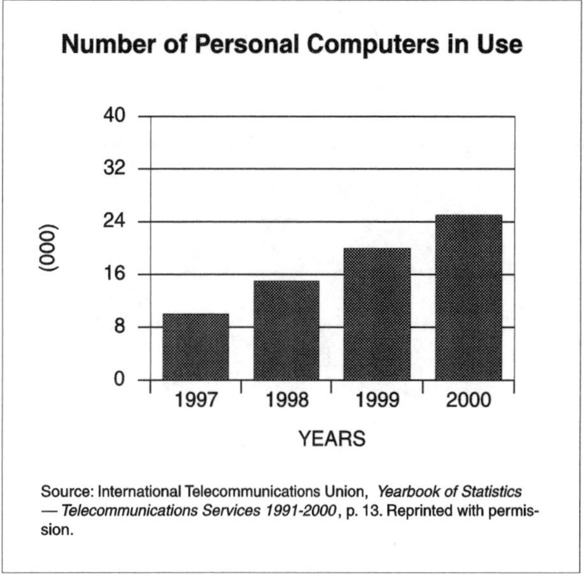

Source: International Telecommunications Union, *Yearbook of Statistics — Telecommunications Services 1991-2000*, p. 13. Reprinted with permission.

fered to foreigners on the Internet. Albaniannews.com plans to add a third Internet site to present news about Albanians residing overseas.

EDUCATION & TRAINING

The only institution of higher learning in Albania to offer degrees in media related careers is the University of Tirana. Founded in 1957, the University of Tirana is a comprehensive university with seven colleges and 14,320 students. The faculty of History and Philology, a college that also includes history, geography, Albanian Linguistics, and Albanian Literature, offers a degree in journalism. The University of Tirana's increasing cooperation with European Union institutions offers Albanian students the opportunity to transfer to universities outside Albania for programs of study in the media not offered there.

SUMMARY

Albania is a nation beset with a multitude of problems generated by centuries of isolation and control during the rule of the Ottoman sultans and the interventionism by Yugoslavia, Italy, and the Soviet Union in Albania's internal affairs. World War II and the ultimate victory of communist insurgents led to four decades of xenophobic control and the isolationism of Albania from the rest of Europe. The development of a democratic system has resurrected internal feuding among newly organized political parties that occasionally reflect Albanian clans likely to renew historic feuds. Ethnic Albanians living in the Serbian province of Kosovo and the Former Yugoslav Republic of Macedonia involve the Republic of Albania in the politics of its neighbors.

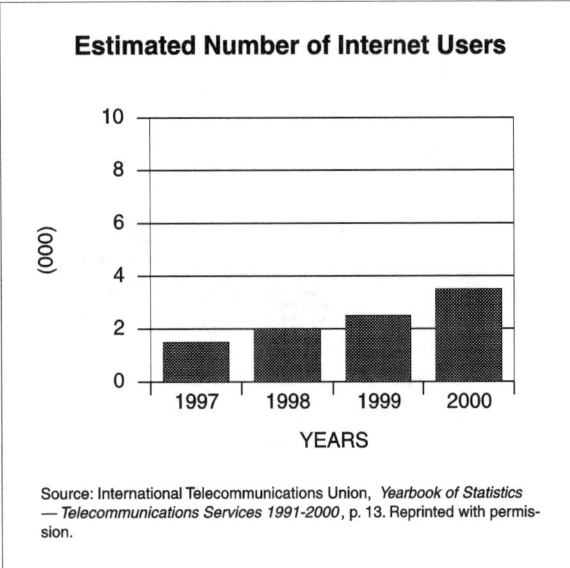

Source: International Telecommunications Union, *Yearbook of Statistics — Telecommunications Services 1991-2000*, p. 13. Reprinted with permission.

Albanian refugees from Kosovo and Macedonia living in Albania claim that the Albanian government discriminates against them in providing access to education, public-sector jobs, and representation in the government. A poor nation, Albania is the route for drug trafficking from Southwest Asia in opiates, hashish, and cannabis and cocaine from South America. There is some opium and cannabis production in Albania. Whether Albania will be able to integrate successfully into a Europe of multiparty democracies depends on Albania's position about ethnic Albanians in war torn Kosovo (a part of Serbia) and the Former Yugoslav Republic of Macedonia. Albania has limited financial resources and needs foreign investment. Political stability and respect for human rights will directly affect foreign economic investment and Albania's future. The violence that once characterized Albanian politics and the media's journalists and radio and television stations is rapidly on the decline. The print media will need to regain public confidence now enjoyed by the broadcast media. Although freedom of expression is freely exercised in Albania, freedom of movement for journalists has risks because of the large number of rifles owned by Albanians and an absence of public order outside Albanian cities. Whether Albanians living overseas will return home and help the nation rebuilt may determine the nation's future.

SIGNIFICANT DATES

- 1985: Death of Enver Hoxha, Communist leader of Albania since 1944.
- 1990: Albania begins the transition to a multiparty democracy.
- 1997: Pyramid financial investment scheme collapses causing an economic crisis.
- 1998: Approval of a new constitution.

BIBLIOGRAPHY

1999 Country Reports on Human Rights Practices, Albania. Washington, DC: United States Department of State, Bureau of Democracy, Human Rights, and Labor, 2000.

2001 World Press Freedom Review. Available from www.freemedia.at/wpfr/albania.htm.

Glenny, Misha. *The Balkans, Nationalism, War and the Great Powers, 1904-1999.* New York: Viking Press, 2000.

International Journalists' Network. Available from www.ijnet.org.

Kaplan, Robert. *Balkan Ghosts.* New York: St. Martin's Press, 1993.

Turner, Barry, ed. *Statesman's Yearbook 2002.* New York: Palgrave Press, 2001.

World Mass Media Handbook. New York: United Nations Department of Public Information, 1995.

Zickel, Raymond, and Walter R. Iwaskiw, eds. *Albania: A Country Study.* Washington, DC: United States Government Printing Office, 1994.

—William A. Paquette, Ph.D.

ALGERIA

BASIC DATA

Official Country Name:	People's Democratic Republic of Algeria
Region (Map name):	Africa
Population:	31,736,053
Language(s):	Arabic (official), French, Berber dialects
Literacy rate:	61.6%
Area:	2,381,740 sq km
GDP:	53,306 (US$ millions)
Number of Television Stations:	46
Number of Television Sets:	3,100,000
Television Sets per 1,000:	97.7
Number of Radio Stations:	34
Number of Radio Receivers:	7,100,000

Radio Receivers per 1,000:	223.7
Number of Individuals with Computers:	200,000
Computers per 1,000:	6.3
Number of Individuals with Internet Access:	50,000
Internet Access per 1,000:	1.6

BACKGROUND & GENERAL CHARACTERISTICS

The development of the Algerian press can be categorized into five periods: 1962-65, when the editors of newspapers were intellectuals of the *FLN* (National Front of Liberation) who enjoyed a certain autonomy; 1965 to 1988, a period when the intellectuals were replaced by civil servants who were docile instruments of the state bureaucracy; 1988 to 1992, when the press enjoyed greater freedom and several new papers appeared; 1992 to 2000, when journalists were restricted and threatened; and the period after 2000, when journalism had regained some of the freedom lost during the early 1990s.

Since the 1960s, when Algeria became independent from France, the press has been controlled by the ruling party, the *FLN*. Three years into the nation's independence, freedom of press became unknown to journalists and newspapers. Before the late 1980s, Algeria was home to three main government-run newspapers, *El-Moudjahid* (The Freedom Fighter) in French, *Ech-Chaab* (The People) in Arabic, and the weekly *Algérie Actulalité* in French. In the nineties, readership of these newspapers declined and *Algérie Actualité* was discontinued. Numerous privately owned newspapers have been created since.

In 1988, popular pressure brought about the explosion of the Algerian political system and the liberalization of the press. About two years later, new legislative elections were on the verge of placing the Islamists in power when the army, under the pretext of saving a young democracy, cancelled the elections and seized power. Over 100,000 Algerians were victims of the civil war that followed. Journalists and intellectuals were assassinated by armed Islamist groups and by the military in power.

According to the Algerian government, mass media should be under complete government control. Capitalist inclinations and individualism have been discouraged. Algeria has followed the populist socialist path. Capitalism is rejected, and instead, focus is placed on the public sector. Before the events of October 1988, it was impossible for journalists to investigate or publish material relating to government activities, unless the government furnished said information. Radio and television were government-run and censored, and the print media was published either by the government or the *FLN* (the party that ruled Algeria for 30 years.) The authorities also tightly controlled the circulation of foreign journals.

The military-backed regime that came to power in January 1992 curtailed the press and restricted freedom of expression and movement. In the 1990s, a number of newspapers were shut down, journalists were jailed and some disappeared, while others were openly assassinated. In some of the murder and disappearance cases, both the Islamists and the government have attracted suspicion.

In 1990, a ministerial decision guaranteed two years of salary to journalists in the public sector that created or worked for new independent or partisan newspapers. As a result, a virtual stampede of journalists and editors founded new publications. Like new political parties, new newspapers appeared. However, in 2000, it was reported that state controlled printers delayed the publication of certain newspapers for political reasons. Some newspapers accused the state of favoritism when it came to distributing government advertising.

One hundred journalists and other media workers have been murdered from May 1993 to August 1997. While Islamists were blamed for most of the killings, the Algerian government was believed to have played a role in some of the killings. The fate of many other journalists is unknown as of 2002.

Circulation In 1993, there were 117 publications: 21 dailies, 34 weeklies and 62 periodicals, 57 of which were printed in the Arabic language and 60 in the French language. In 1996, the number of publications went down to 81: 19 dailies, 44 weeklies and 10 magazines. The total number of journalists was 1,700. Most of the big political parties used to have their own newspapers; however, due to financial constraints, the majority were discontinued. Nevertheless, among the remaining newspapers, many tend to take positions with different political parties. Dailies and weeklies such as *La Tribune*, *L'Autentique*, *El Sabah* (the morning), El Djadid (the new), *El Houria* (the freedom), *Le Quotidian d'Oran* were created after 1992.

Amongst the most read French newspapers are *El Watan*, *Le Matin*, *Le Soir d'Algérie*, *Le Quotidien d'Oran*, *Liberté*, *La Tribun*, *L'Authentique*, *Horizons* and the newly created *L'Epression*. *El Watan* is known for being unbiased. *Le Matin* and *Le Soir d'Algérie* are anti-government. *Le Quotidien d'Oran* is known for the high quality of its journalists. As for the latest addition, *L'Expression*, its editorials tend to defend the government and justify its actions.

The most respected Arabic newspapers are: *El Khaber* (The News) and *El Youm* (today.) Older newspapers, such as *El Moudjahid* and *Ech Chaab*, have lost grounds to more independent publications.

The media's effort to spread information to the different socio-economic classes has, for the most part, been unsuccessful. The educated and affluent elite that controls the content and dissemination of mass media to the whole of Algerian society often fails to reach classes outside of itself. Many rural Algerians are illiterate and too poor to own a television or buy newspapers. Those who do have access may not understand the Standard Arabic and French used in all forms of the media.

The present circulation the *El-Moudjahid* is about 40,000 for the entire country while *El-Watan* prints about 100,000 daily. The annual circulation of the Algerian newspapers is estimated at 364 million. Due to the high illiteracy rate in Algeria (41 percent in 1990), especially among the older generation, readership is confined to the elite.

Most of the Algerian urban population lives in the northern 10 percent part of the country. The southern part, the Sahara, is sparsely populated. Consequently, most publishing and other media activities are concentrated in the northern part of Algeria.

ECONOMIC FRAMEWORK

The government officially announced in 1998 that a budget of 400 million Algerian dinars (about $6.5 million) had been allocated to aid the press. By 2001, 500 million Algerian dinars had been committed to aid journalists who opted to leave the public sector in favor of the private sector. This aid came in the form of two years of guaranteed salary.

From the establishment of a private press in 1990 until Dec. 31, 1995, the state subsidized the publishing costs by paying the difference between the actual cost and what the newspapers were able to pay. The state has also made available three press centers to public and private newspapers.

PRESS LAWS

The Information Act, Law No. 90-7 (dated April 3,1990) regarding information forbids newspapers to publish any stories or information about political violence and security from any source other than the government. Algerian legislation prohibits criticism of the regime system as it is considered a crime affecting the state's security.

In 1999, an attempt to pass a law to end government monopoly over advertisement failed. During the same year, the government ended its monopoly over the Internet and opened the market to private Internet Service Providers.

Algerian journalists have the right to keep their sources of information and news confidential, a right considered one of the most prominent aspects of freedom of expression. This protects the journalists' resources against retribution and guarantees the flow of information.

CENSORSHIP

Algeria imposes through legislation a clear prior censorship on the content of media. The import of foreign periodicals through Algeria should be through a prior license issued by the concerned department after consultation with a higher council. The import by foreign corporations and diplomatic missions of periodical publications meant for free distribution is possible after obtaining a license from the concerned department.

Before the 1988 riots, it was impossible for journalists to investigate or publish material relating to high-level government corruption, unless the government provided said information. The print media was published either by the government or the *FLN*.

Nevertheless, during the last few years of the second millennium and the beginning of the third millennium, the Algerian press offered a wide range of news, events, comments and stories that were previously taboo such as AIDS, prostitution and corruption.

Additionally, two democratic and independent organizations, the Association of Algerian Journalists (AJA) and the National Union of Algerian Journalists (SNJA), were formed during the state of emergency that was in place after the 1988 riots. In the late nineties, the SNJA organized large demonstrations demanding the return of suspended newspapers.

STATE-PRESS RELATIONS

The government controls the supply of newsprint and owns the printing presses and is therefore able to put economic pressure on the newspapers. The state also exercises authority over the distribution of advertising, giving preferential treatment to the newspapers whose content is in line with the views of the government. President Bouteflika has stated that the media should "ultimately be at the service of the state."

Harassment of the privately owned press, whether legal, economic or administrative, was common practice. In mid-October, 1998, the state-run printing presses decided to stop printing the two most read newspapers, the dailies *El Watan* and *Le Matin* after they were given a 48-hour ultimatum to pay their debts in full. This came despite the April agreement to pay any debts in installments until December 31, 1998. The suspension decision came after *El Watan* and *Le Matin* published a series of articles and letters directing accusations against the Minister of Justice and a close advisor of the President of the Republic. Subsequently, both officials were forced to resign. The public (and the journalists) saw the suspension of the newspapers as a punishment for exposing government officials. Four newspapers owned by a former advisor to the president were also in debt, but continued to print.

In solidarity with the two suspended newspapers, many other newspapers voluntarily stopped the printing of their publications. This incident gave more credibility to the privately-owned press; subsequently, Algerians realized the importance of independent newspapers.

During the period 1993-98, journalists and media workers were targeted by the various extremist Islamic terrorist groups. As a result, 60 journalists and 10 media workers were assassinated, while five journalists were reported missing. Both the extreme Islamic groups and the government were suspected to have participated in their disappearance.

For security reasons, about 600 journalists have been housed in hotels and other housing units in proximity of Algiers under the protection of security guards. The government assumes full responsibility of the incurred costs.

When the journalists are spared death, they are faced with imprisonment, fines or suspension of their newspapers if they do not comply with state law. As the state continues to exert leverage over private newspapers through its ownership of the country's main printing houses, it also possesses the power to summon journalists to court.

ATTITUDE TOWARD FOREIGN MEDIA

Foreign correspondents have restricted access to Algerian affairs. Foreign media have accused the Algerian government of implementing a restrictive policy toward the granting of entry visas to foreign journalists. However, government-released figures show that in 1998, 626 foreign journalists were allowed to enter the country. These foreign journalists, mostly European, have reported limited access to opposition figures and to local sources who are willing to discuss political violence and other sensitive issues.

The authorities tightly control the circulation of foreign journals. In the 1980s, the Paris-based weekly political magazine *Jeune Afrique* that dealt with African affairs (and had a large readership among the Algerian educated class) was banned. The French daily *Le Monde* and other French publications were tightly controlled and periodically seized for carrying articles the government found objectionable. However, there were always ways for Algerians to obtain such "popular" issues.

For the most part, Algerians prefer watching foreign TV channels such as the Arabic channels *MBC*, *ART*, *Al-Jazeera*, and French channels such as *TV5*, *TF1*, *France 2* and *FR3*. In a 1988 survey for the Portuguese Manata Company, Algeria had 1.5 million satellite dishes, the highest proportion of dishes to population in the world.

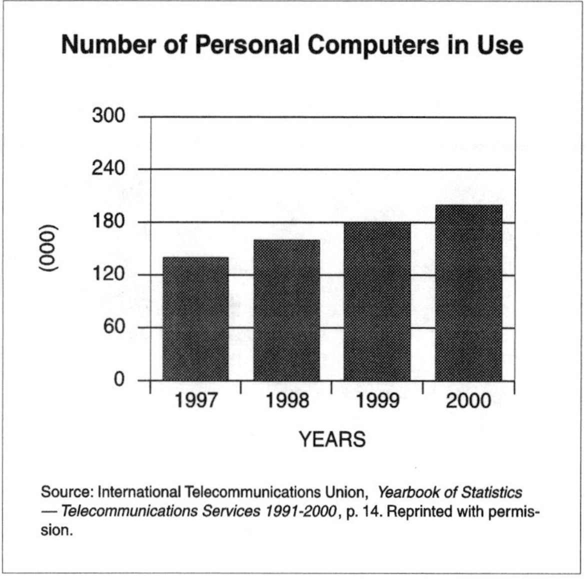

Source: International Telecommunications Union, *Yearbook of Statistics — Telecommunications Services 1991-2000*, p. 14. Reprinted with permission.

NEWS AGENCIES

Algeria has one news agency. The Algerian Press Service (APS) is located in Algiers and is run by the state. APS was founded in 1961. In 1994 it launched its first computerized editorial office and in 1998 its satellite broadcast. The agency is represented in twelve foreign capitals: Washington, Moscow, Paris, London, Brussels, Rome, Madrid, Cairo, Rabat, Tunis, Amman and Dakar.

BROADCAST MEDIA

Television and radio are public institutions run by the Algerian government. The Algerian television channel (ENTV) and the three main radio channels maintain regular news service and are the channels of the dissemination of official political discourse. The television presents news in three languages, Arabic, French and English.

The three national radio channels are: *Channel 1* (Arabic), *Channel 2* (Berber), and *Channel 3* (French and some English.) Numerous regions of the country have their own radio stations.

ELECTRONIC NEWS MEDIA

Most newspapers are available on the Internet. In Algeria, journalists at the much-censored *La Nation* were able to post an edition of the weekly at the web site of *Reporters sans Frontières*, a French freedom of expression organization, after *La Nation* closed its doors in 1996.

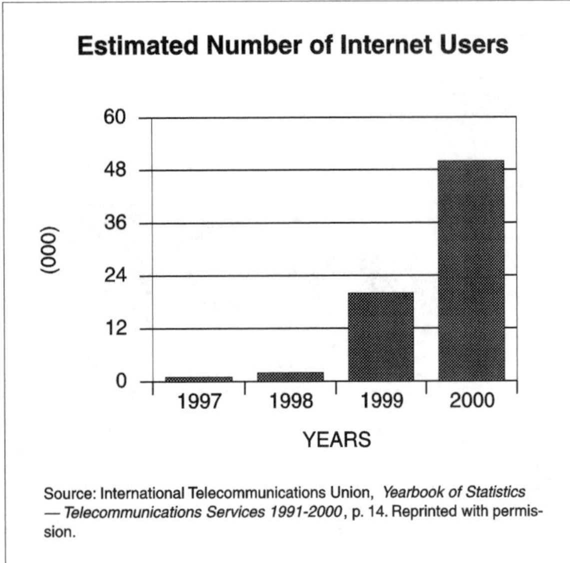

Source: International Telecommunications Union, *Yearbook of Statistics — Telecommunications Services 1991-2000*, p. 14. Reprinted with permission.

When private dailies in Algeria went on strike in October 1998 to protest pressure from state-run printing presses, they published bulletins daily on the Web to mobilize support for their cause.

Algerians can visit numerous web sites mounted by Islamist groups that are banned and have no legal publications inside Algeria, including the Salvation Islamic Front (*Front Islamique du Salut—FIS.*)

Perhaps the most defiant use of the Internet in a country without a freedom of the press is the use of the Web as a substitute for censored media. Newspapers censored in Algeria have placed banned stories online, where they circulate widely to the Algerian emigrants and foreigners.

EDUCATION & TRAINING

In addition to journalism schools, a number of training opportunities are available to practicing journalists. For instance, in 2001 the U.S. Agency for International Development funded a one-week training session in Algeria for 15 print journalists. This training focused on investigative reporting in the areas of human rights and rule of law, as part of a 15-month project implemented by the *RIGHTS Consortium* and headed by *Freedom House*.

SUMMARY

Algerian press, despite the controversies and the bad publicity it received in the nineties, is considered one of the freest in the Arab World. Since 2000, no journalist has been jailed, killed or threatened, and no newspaper has been shut down. The restrictions placed on the press protect the sovereignty of the state; therefore any defamation or personal attack against government and military officials is punishable by imprisonment or fines. The government contends that journalists must choose to use the government presses and respect its laws, or get their own presses. An argument deemed fair to some and unfair to others. While the current political climate is improving, journalists in Algeria stand to meet higher standards of practice to complete with western sources of information as most publications lack objectivity. More importantly, it must find a way to sustain independent financial support so as not to rely on the over conditional government sources needed to disseminate information.

SIGNIFICANT DATES

- 1998: National Union of Journalists is created. The state printers suspend the printing of several privately owned daily newspapers. The state requires journalists to obtain agreement of the authorities before publishing any information dealing with issues regarding security. Physical attacks on journalists that started in 1993 have receded.
- 1999: Early elections. Mr. Bouteflika is the uncontested new President of the Republic.
- 2001: New libel law that would penalize defamation against President Abdel Aziz Bouteflika or other senior government and military officials by imprisonment of up to one year and fines of 250,000 dinars (US $3,500).

BIBLIOGRAPHY

Committee to Protect Journalists. *Attacks on the Press*. 1996. Available from http://www.cpj.org/

Chagnollaud, Jean-Paul, ed. *Parole aux algériens: Violence et politique en Algérie*. (Essays by Algerian journalists, politicians and ordinary citizens). Paris: Harmattan, 1998.

Faringer, Gunilla L. *Press Freedom in Africa*. New York: Praeger, 1991.

International Press Institute. *Algeria: World Press Review*. 2001. Available from http://www.freemedia.at/

Mahrez, Khaled and Lazhari Labter. *1998 Report on the Situation of the Media and the Freedom of the Press in Algeria*, International Federation of Journalists Algiers. 1999. Available from http://ifj.org/

Rugh, William A. *The Arab Press: News Media and Political Process in the Arab World*. Syracuse University Press: Syracuse, 1987.

Smail, Said. *Mémoires torturées: un journaliste et un écrivain algérien raconte*. Paris: Harmattan, 1997

Stone, Martin. *The Agony of Algeria*. Columbia University Press: New York, NY, 1997.

Stora, Jenjamin. *Algeria: 1830-2000. A Short History.* Ithaca: Cornell University Press, 2001.

Waltz, Susan E. *Human Rights And Reform.* Berkeley: University of California Press, 1995.

Willis, Michael. *Islamist Challenge Algeria.* New York: New York University Press, 1996.

—*Karima Benremouga*

AMERICAN SAMOA

BASIC DATA

Official Country Name:	American Samoa
Region (Map name):	Oceania
Population:	65,446
Language(s):	Samoan, English
Literacy rate:	97%

American Samoa has been occupied by the United States as a territory since 1900, but it is believed to have been inhabited since 600 B.C. Today, the country's five islands and two coral atolls, which lie near Western Samoa in the Pacific Ocean, are managed by the U.S. Department of the Interior and a local, popularly elected Governor. The legislature consists of a House of Representatives and a Senate, and the country also sends an elected delegate to the U.S. House of Representatives. The population of American Samoa is estimated to be 607,000. The literacy rate is 97 percent. Most Samoans are bilingual in English and Samoan, a dialect closely related to Hawaiian and other Polynesian languages. The economy revolves around tuna fishing and tuna canning. The government is also a major employer. Efforts to diversify the economy have been hindered by the country's geographic isolation and a fierce hurricane season.

As a territory of the United States, American Samoa enjoys the press freedoms provided under the U.S. Constitution. American Samoa has two newspapers: the *Samoa News* and the *Samoan Post.* Stories in both newspapers appear in English and Samoan. The *Samoan News* is printed Monday through Saturday; its circulation is approximately 4,000 a day in addition to an online edition. The *Samoan Post* publishes Sunday, Tuesday and Thursday. Its approximate circulation is 1,500.

Three FM stations and three AM stations serve approximately 57,000 radios. One television station broadcasts over three channels to approximately 14,000 TV sets. It is owned by the Office of Public Information of the American Samoan government. Samoanet is the country's sole Internet service provider.

BIBLIOGRAPHY

''American Samoa,'' *CIA World Fact Book 2001.* Available from http://www.cia.gov.

''American Samoa,'' FCC AM Radio Query 2002. Available from http://www.fcc.gov.

''American Samoa,'' FCC FM Radio Query 2002. Available from http://www.fcc.gov.

''Samoa News,'' 2002 Home Page. Available from http://www.samoanews.com.

—*Jenny B. Davis*

ANDORRA

BASIC DATA

Official Country Name:	Principality of Andorra
Region (Map name):	Europe
Population:	66,824
Language(s):	Catalan, French, Castilian
Literacy rate:	100%

Located in the Pyrenees Mountains between Spain and France, the Principality of Andorra was the last feudal state in Europe until 1993, when it became a constitutional democracy. Its constitution transferred power from the two previously governing bodies, the French president and the Spanish bishop of Seu d'Urgel, to a popularly elected legislative body called the General Council of the Valleys. Although the President and the Bishop remain the titular heads of state, all governmental operations are now overseen by Andorran officials. Andorra's population is approximately 67,000, and the country boasts a literacy rate of 100 percent. Tourism accounts for approximately 80 percent of the economy, but international banking is also an important revenue source. Catalan is the official language, but Castilian and French are also spoken.

Andorran law fully guarantees freedom of the press. Although Andorra only encompasses 175 square miles, it supports two daily newspapers, *El Periodic d'Andorra* and *Diari d'Andorra.* Both are available online. There are also two major weekly newspapers, *Informacions* and *7 Dies.* All four publications publish in Catalan from the country's capital, Andorra La Vella.

Two radio stations, one of which is state-owned, broadcast to approximately 16,000 radios, and six television stations reach approximately 27,000 televisions. Andorra has one Internet service provider.

BIBLIOGRAPHY

''Andorra,'' *Encyclopedia Britannica 2002.* Available from http://www.britannica.com.

''Andorra,'' *CIA World Fact Book 2001.* Available from http://www.cia.gov.

''Andorra,'' *TvRadioWorld 2002.* Available from http://www.tvradioworld.com/.

Diari d'Andorra, 2002. Available from http://www.diariandorra.ad.

El Periodic d'Andorra, 2002. Available from http://www.elperiodico.com.

—Jenny B. Davis

ANGOLA

BASIC DATA

Official Country Name:	Republic of Angola
Region (Map name):	Africa
Population:	10,145,267
Language(s):	Portuguese, Bantu,Kikongo, Kimbundo, Umbundo, Chokwe, Mbunda, Oxikuanyama
Literacy rate:	56%

Angola was the location of the world's perhaps most prolonged and severe civil war in the last quarter of the twentieth century. Upon independence from Portugal in November 1975, the country was plunged into civil war with the ruling Popular Movement for the Liberation of Angola (MPLA) fighting a rebel movement, the National Union for the Total Independence of Angola (UNITA), for control of the country. Democratic elections were held in 1991, but UNITA disputed the result. Despite a peace accord in 1994, civil war raged until the death of UNITA leader Jonas Savimbi in February 2002, when prospects for peace seemed the best since Angolan independence. In the first 16 years of the civil war it was estimated that 300,000 people had been killed out of a total population of 12 million.

Angola possesses significant petroleum resources, in some years supplying 5 percent of the U.S. international supply, and is the location of significant diamond deposits, although the national economy remains one of the worst performers in the world and the living standards of the Angolan people is one of the lowest. Throughout the civil war both sides distrusted the media and neither side was prepared for media coverage of their activities, a situation that made journalism in Angola one of the most hazardous occupations in the world. The ascendancy of the MPLA as the governing party has not made the situation for journalists any more secure; the government feels even freer to stifle independent opinion and restrain any free press.

The press, television and radio were nationalized in 1976 and thus the government dominates the media. The government controls the only news agency (ANGOP), the only daily paper (*Jornal de Angola,* with a circulation estimated at 40,000 but a readership of probably more than 100,000), the national television network (Televisao Popular de Angola) and the national radio station (Radio National de Angola). The national radio broadcasts in Portuguese, English, French and Spanish as well as nine local indigenous African languages. There is an independent press, namely *Folha 8,* a Luanda-based weekly, and *Actual* and *Agora* two other independent weeklies. WT Mundovideo is a local television broadcaster in Luanda, and Radio Morena and Radio Lac Luanda are independent radio stations in Benguela and Luanda, respectively. Luanda-Antena is an independent commercial radio station. Radio Ecclesia is a Roman Catholic FM station generally agreed to be the most vociferous critic of the government and it has been the target of much state-sponsored criticism and pressure to modify coverage. It has suspended daily broadcasts on occasion as a protest against government pressure and hate campaigns. Both government and private sector advertising is discouraged in independent newspapers, and hence, financial viability of the independent media is always in question.

The constitution of the Republic of Angola specifically codifies freedom of expression and of the press, but often this is not respected. During the civil war a number of journalists were killed or imprisoned and this has continued into the twenty-first century. Journalists from the government news agency and from *Folha 8,* and *Agora,* as well as BBC, Voice of America and Portuguese television correspondents have been singled out for attack, threats and harassment. One figure stands out in this regard, Rafael Marques, a local freelance journalist and human rights activist, who repeatedly has been detained and interrogated for articles he has written and jailed for defamation of the president. As a result, the combination of government censorship and fear of government reprisals has meant most journalists practice self-censorship. A new draft media law was introduced in 2000 but was withdrawn later that year after much criticism.

There is a Committee to Protect Journalists (CPJ), an Angolan media Women's Association and a Union of Angola Journalists (UAJ), the latter formed primarily of government-employed journalists and with little credibility outside Angola. However, UAJ is leading the way in providing education and training for journalists and in providing the first school of journalism in the country's advanced education system. Foreign news agencies cover Angola from Johannesburg (Reuters and AP), while the BBC and Portuguese media have a greater presence in Angola owing to their former colonial role in the region. While their entry into the country is not restricted, some restrictions have been placed on their movement inside the country—ostensibly for their safety—and on rebroadcast of transmissions.

Angola faces an uncertain future. In practice the civil war ended with the death of Jonas Savimbi, but media freedom has not followed. A 25-year legacy of distrust and disrespect is not easily removed. At the same time, Angola remains one of the world's poorest nations with poorly developed infrastructure, including Internet communications, and a desperately poor people. The prospect of greater wealth arising from petroleum and diamonds is present, but much will have to change in the form of removal of corruption, economic mismanagement and political power arising from resource control. These are explosive issues the media must confront in order to fulfill a role in national development—and it can expect much opposition.

BIBLIOGRAPHY

''Angola.'' BBC News Country Profile. Available from-http://news.bbc.uk.

''Crackdown on Angola's Independent Media Condemned.'' Human Rights Watch, 2000. Available from http://wwwhrw.org/press/2000.

''Media Outlets in Angola.'' Available from http://www.Angola.org.

''Media Situation deteriorates in Angola'' Digital Freedom Network. Available from http://www.dfn.org/focus/angola/media-deterioration.htm.

U.S Department of State Country Reports on Human Rights Practices, 2001. Available from http://www.state.gov.

— Richard W. Benfield

ANGUILLA

BASIC DATA

Official Country Name:	Anguilla
Region (Map name):	Caribbean
Population:	11,797
Language(s):	English
Literacy rate:	95%

Anguilla is the most northerly of the British Leeward Islands and is bordered by the Caribbean Sea to the south and the Atlantic Ocean to the north. Under British rule since 1650, it spent more than 150 years as an incorporated dependency with neighboring islands called the West Indies Associated States. After a long struggle for secession, Anguilla was finally recognized as a separate British dependency in 1980. The British monarch serves as chief of state, represented in the island's government by a Governor. A Chief Minister presides over the legislative body, called the House of Assembly. English is the island's official language. The population is estimated at approximately 12,000, with a 95-percent literacy rate. Luxury tourism and offshore financial services comprise the largest sectors of the Anguillan economy, with fishing, construction and remittances from émigrés abroad providing smaller contributions.

As a British dependency, laws governing freedom of the press are the same as those in the United Kingdom, providing for an unrestricted free press. Journalists can, however, be compelled to reveal their sources or face contempt of court charges. Anguilla supports two weekly community newspapers, *The Light* and *The Anguillian.* *The Light* is published by ''What We Do in Anguilla,'' which publishes a namesake monthly visitor's magazine. *The Anguillian* launched in December 1998. Both titles publish in English from Anguilla's capital, The Valley. For more timely print news, Anguillan's read the *Daily Herald,* a St. Martin newspaper that publishes Monday through Saturday and arrives on Anguilla by late morning, and *The Chronicle,* which is published in Dominica.

Five AM and six FM radio stations, and one television station, broadcast to approximately 3,000 radios and

1,000 television sets. There are 16 Internet service providers.

BIBLIOGRAPHY

''Anguilla,'' *BBC Holiday Shopping Guide 2001.* Available from http://www.holiday.beeb.com.

''Anguilla,'' *CIA World Fact Book 2001.* Available from http://www.cia.gov.

''United Kingdom Country Report,'' *U.S. Department of State Country Reports on Human Rights Practices 2001.* Available from http://www.state.gov.

—Jenny B. Davis

ANTIGUA AND BARBUDA

BASIC DATA

Official Country Name:	Antigua and Barbuda
Region (Map name):	Caribbean
Population:	66,422
Language(s):	English
Literacy rate:	89%

The Caribbean islands of Antigua and Barbuda, located east-southeast of Puerto Rico between the Caribbean Sea and the North Atlantic Ocean, became an independent state within the British Commonwealth of Nations in 1981. The government is a constitutional monarchy. Great Britain appoints a Governor General, who in turn appoints a Prime Minister. The Prime Minister presides over a Senate and a House of Representatives. The population is estimated at 65,000 with an 89-percent literacy rate. English is the official language, but many local dialects are spoken. Tourism is by far the largest source of revenue, accounting for more than half of the gross domestic product. Remaining revenue comes from agriculture, fishing and light industry. Efforts to develop an offshore financial sector have been stymied by sanctions and money laundering scandals.

Although the constitution guarantees press freedom, the media industry is nearly entirely controlled by the Prime Minister or members of his family. When one of the country's daily newspapers, the *Daily Observer,* started a radio station that aired political messages from the opposition, the editor and publisher were arrested for operating a radio station without a license. Print media, however, is generally allowed to operate unhindered. The country's press center is Antigua, which at just over 100 square miles is nearly double the size of Barbuda and claims 98 percent of the population. Every major newspaper publishes from its capital, St. John's. There are two dailies, the *Antigua Sun* and the *Daily Observer,* both of which are available online. Weekly publications include *The Nation's Voice, The Outlet,* and *The Worker's Voice.*

There are six radio stations, four AM and two FM, serving 36,000 radios. Two television stations broadcast to 31,000 televisions. Sixteen Internet service providers provide online access.

BIBLIOGRAPHY

''Antigua and Barbuda,'' *CIA World Fact Book 2001.* Available from http://www.cia.gov.

''Antigua and Barbuda,'' *U.S. Department of State Country Reports on Human Rights Practices 2001.* Available from http://www.state.gov.

''Antigua and Barbuda,'' *The World Press Freedom Review 2001.* Available from http://www.freemedia.at.

Antigua *Daily Observer,* 2002 Home Page. Available from http://antiguaobserver.com.

Antigua Sun, 2002 Home Page. Available from http://antiguasun.caribbeanads.com.

Benn's Media, 1999, Vol. 3, 147th Edition, p. 246.

—Jenny B. Davis

ARGENTINA

BASIC DATA

Official Country Name:	Argentine Republic
Region (Map name):	South America
Population:	37,384,816
Language(s):	Spanish (official), English, Italian, Germany, French
Literacy rate:	96.2%
Area:	2,766,890 sq km
GDP:	284,960 (US$ millions)
Number of Daily Newspapers:	106
Total Circulation:	1,500,000

Circulation per 1,000:	61
Total Newspaper Ad Receipts:	1,136 (US$ millions)
As % of All Ad Expenditures:	35.00
Number of Television Stations:	42
Number of Television Sets:	7,950,000
Television Sets per 1,000:	212.7
Number of Cable Subscribers:	6,034,700
Cable Subscribers per 1,000:	163.1
Number of Radio Receivers:	24,300,000
Radio Receivers per 1,000:	650.0
Number of Individuals with Computers:	1,900,000
Computers per 1,000:	50.8
Number of Individuals with Internet Access:	2,500,000
Internet Access per 1,000:	66.9

Top Ten Daily Newspapers
(2000)

	Circulation
Clarín	514,000
La Nación	171,000
Popular	90,000
Crónica	80,000
La Voz del Interior	65,000
Ole	50,000
La Gaceta	46,000
La Capital	39,000
Los Andes	30,000
El Día	30,000

Source: World Association of Newspapers and Zenithmedia, *World Press Trends 2001*, p.38

BACKGROUND & GENERAL CHARACTERISTICS

Argentina is the second largest country in Latin America after Brazil, with a total area of 2.8 million square kilometers. It is a federal republic made up of 23 provinces and the city of Buenos Aires, home of the federal government. The total population according to the 2000 national census is 36 million, of which 13 million live in the city of Buenos Aires and surrounding suburbs. Argentines are Spanish speakers, mostly Catholic (around 87 percent of population; 35 percent practicing), have a very high literacy rate (96 percent of population), and a fairly large middle class. The country's gross domestic product (GDP) in 2001 was $281 billion and per capita GDP was $7,686. At the end of 2001, the country entered a severe economic crisis that led to a sharp depreciation of the currency (previously pegged to the dollar), a high increase in the unemployment rate to 23 percent as of July 2002, a banking crisis that included the freezing of individual accounts, and the fall of two presidents in just a few weeks.

Argentines are avid readers of newspapers, having the highest newsprint consumption in Latin America according to UNESCO. Data on newspaper circulation differs depending on the source, with the World Bank reporting 138 newspapers per 1,000 individuals in 1994, UNESCO showing 123 in 1996, and the Buenos Aires Press Workers Union (UTPBA) recording 56 newspapers for the same number of people in the year 2000. Although the national market is shared fairly even between newspapers printed in the city of Buenos Aires and those printed in the interior provinces, the national press is concentrated in the former. Those newspapers printed in the interior are primarily part of provincial circulation. Newspapers of national circulation do not tend to include matters that are mostly of provincial concern, a void filled by several local papers. The city of Buenos Aires has at least 12 major national newspapers and the provinces a few hundred local newspapers.

The 10 largest national newspapers—which may vary depending upon the source referenced—are: *Clarín* (800,000 circulation; 1.2 million on Sundays); *La Nación* (500,000 circulation; 800,000 on Sundays); *Ámbito Financiero* (300,000 circulation); *Crónica* (300,000 circulation); *Diario Popular* (300,000 circulation); *Página 12* (150,000 circulation); *La Prensa* (120,000 circulation); *El Cronista* (100,000 circulation); *Buenos Aires Herald* (100,000 circulation); and *Olé* (100,000 circulation).

The most influential national newspapers are *Clarín* and *La Nación,* both based in the city of Buenos Aires. The one with the highest circulation in the country is *Clarín,* founded by Roberto Noble in 1945. It is considered the most widely read newspaper in Spanish-speaking Latin America. It belongs to a multimedia conglomerate that owns two radio stations (*Mitre* and FM100), two television channels (cable channel *Multicanal* and open air *Canal 13*), the newspaper *Olé* (the only major daily dedicated entirely to sports news), and shares in at least three provincial papers as well as in the news agency *DYN.* It employs approximately 900 people and

Daily and Non-Daily Newspaper Titles and Circulation Figures

	1996	1997	1998	1999	2000
Number of Daily Newspapers	101	101	100	102	106
Circulation of Dailies (000)	2,350	2,335	2,160	1,944	1,500
Number of Non-Daily Newspapers	NA	NA	NA	1	3
Circulation of Non-Dailies (000)	NA	NA	NA	NA	NA

Source: World Association of Newspapers and Zenithmedia, *World Press Trends 2001*, pp. 8, 10, 17, 19. Note: NA stands for not available.

publishes supplements on culture, sports, economics and world affairs, as well as a Sunday magazine and occasional books on specific topics. On a weekday it has on average 52 pages and on weekends 71 pages. *Clarín*'s editorial tendency is considered to be moderate center-left.

The second largest paper, *La Nación* was founded in 1870 and has been one of the most influential newspapers in the country's history. It has 500 employees and has bureaus all over the country. *La Nación* owns parts of the main national company dedicated to the commercialization of newsprint and has shares in at least two provincial dailies and in the news agency *DYN.* In the last few years it has invested over $100 million in the modernization of its operating plant, including color editions and faster printing mechanisms. On weekdays it has on average 18 pages in its main section, and 8 additional pages for regular supplements. On Sundays it has 24 pages in its main section in addition to special supplements and a magazine. *La Nación* is considered to have a center-right editorial position.

The newspapers *Ámbito Financiero* and *El Cronista* are the largest ones dedicated to economic issues. They are considered the best source for daily financial activity and analysis of the local markets, including articles by well-known economists. Neither one is published on Sundays. *Ámbito Financiero* owns a smaller newspaper, *La Mañana del Sur,* that is sold in three southern provinces. It has innovated by establishing plants in the interior of the country to speed up the publishing process and improve circulation. *El Cronista* was founded in 1908 and was one of the largest and most influential newspapers in the decades between 1930 and 1950. Its editorial opposition to the last military government (1976-83) generated numerous threats to its journalists, including the kidnapping and ''disappearance'' of its director, Raúl Perrota. Since the year 2000 *El Cronista* is wholly owned by the media group *Recoletos* from Spain, which is itself owned by the Pearson Group, editor of the *Financial Times.*

The newspapers *Diario Popular* and *Crónica* are considered sensationalists and are known to compete for the same readership, which comes mostly from the popular sectors. The first one is a left-leaning paper that emphasizes crime and catastrophic news and includes supplements for the suburbs of Buenos Aires, where it is published. The second one is a nationalist paper with an anti-U.S. and anti-England perspective (particularly following the 1982 war with England), and it is published in three daily editions.

The main leftist newspaper in Argentina is *Página 12,* which began its publication in 1987 and rapidly gained a niche within the intellectual and progressive readership. *Página 12* has been consistently critical of government policy. Many well-known leftist intellectuals and journalists contribute or have worked for this newspaper. It has an innovative style, mixing humor and irony with a literary flair in covering the news. On weekdays it has an average of 36 pages. The newspaper includes weekend supplements on culture, media, economics, and foreign affairs.

The only major foreign language newspaper is the *Buenos Aires Herald,* founded in 1876 and published in that city. It is written in English with editorials in both English and Spanish. It played an opposition role to the military government that ruled Argentina between 1976 and 1983, which led to recurring threats that resulted in its editor, Graham Yoll, leaving the country in exile.

The provinces of Argentina, where more than half of the country's population lives, are home to several newspapers that provide a wealth of local news. According to the Argentine Association of Newspapers from the Interior (ADIRA), provincial newspapers, with 90 percent of the share, dominate the newspaper market outside the city of Buenos Aires and surrounding metropolitan area. The four largest provinces are those of Buenos Aires, Cordoba, Santa Fe, and Mendoza. In the province of Buenos Aires, where the large cities of La Plata and Mar del Plata are located, there are about 150 newspapers; in Cordoba, home of the second biggest city in the country, there are at least 16 newspapers, including the biggest regional newspaper in the country, *La Voz del Interior* founded in 1904. In Santa Fe there are 12 newspapers, and in Mendoza there are three newspapers of which *Los Andes,* founded in 1882, is the most important.

The smaller province of Entre Rios has a large number of newspapers, at least 22, but the most famous one is *Hora Cero.* The province of La Pampa has 3 newspapers, including one of the oldest in the country, *La Arena,* founded in 1900. Another provincial newspaper with a long history is *La Gaceta* from Tucumán, founded in 1912. The province of Santa Cruz is the home of at least 9 local newspapers; the provinces of Chubut and Tierra del Fuego have 7 newspapers each; the province of Formosa has 6; Rio Negro has 5; the provinces of Corrientes, Jujuy, Misiones, and San Juan have 4 newspapers each; Catamarca, Chaco, La Rioja, Salta, Santiago del Estero, and San Luis have 2 newspapers each; and the province of Neuquen has only one big local newspaper.

The history of the press in Argentina is deeply intertwined with the rich and convoluted history of that land. Its origins can be traced back to colonial times. The first newspaper edited in what is now Argentina was *La Gazeta,* a monthly publication of eight pages that began in the year 1764. During the first decades of the following century several publications began to propagate the ideas of the independence movement, such as the *Correo de Comercio* or *La Gazeta de Buenos Ayres.* Some others like the *Redactor del Congreso Nacional* had an important historical role in publishing the transcripts of the convention that declared independence in 1916. In the years that followed independence, the antagonist relations between the port city of Buenos Aires and the interior, which eventually evolved into a civil war, promoted the emergence of various provincial newspapers such as *La Confederación* from the province of Santa Fe. Under the control of Governor Rosas (1829-32; 1835-52) from the province of Buenos Aires, we find the first period of widespread censorship, including the closing of newspapers and the killing of several journalists critical of the government.

The period of peace and growth following the civil war begins in 1870. It is at this time that *La Nación* and *La Prensa,* contemporary newspapers, began their publication. President Bartolome Mitre founded *La Nación.* During the decade of the 1880s, coinciding with Argentina's frontier wars, many newspapers with high nationalist, militaristic, and expansionist content began to be published. In the 1920s the new press tended to be run by some of the conservative forces in control of the government. At that time newspapers like *El Cronista* and *Noticias Gráficas* began to be published. In the year 1945, when Juan Peron entered the political scene, several newspapers of more populist tendencies were initiated, including today's largest newspaper *Clarín.* President Peron (1946-52; 1952-55) exerted strong pressure against the independent media, including censorship and the closing of the opposition newspaper *La Prensa.* In 1951, during Peron's second term as president, television was first launched in the country, 21 years after the establishment of the first national radio station. After a military government that deposed Peron, a wave of repression was initiated against the prior president's supporters in the media. Under a subsequent regime, the state news agency *Telam* was founded in 1959. During the 1960s numerous leftist publications were started, including the magazine *Panorama* and the newspaper *Crítica.*

Advertising Expenditures — 1999

(US$ millions, in current prices)

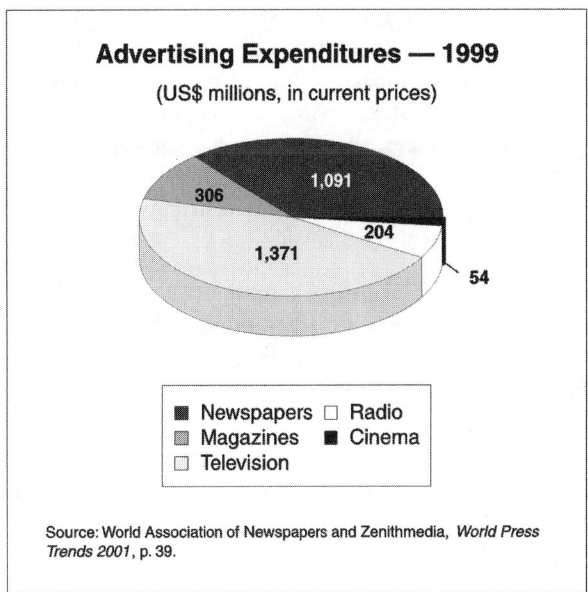

Source: World Association of Newspapers and Zenithmedia, *World Press Trends 2001*, p. 39.

ECONOMIC FRAMEWORK

As of mid-2002, after four years of recession and a drastic financial crisis, the short- and medium-term economic prospects for media corporations, as well as for most other businesses, seem bleak. Newspapers have recently hiked prices by at least 20 percent (to $1.20 pesos), pressured by a corresponding drop of about 50 percent in advertising demand. Financial difficulties have also led national newspapers to reduce their personnel by almost 20 percent and to undertake a general reduction of salaries. The situation of the two largest newspapers, *Clarín* and *La Nación,* is particularly difficult because in recent years they proceeded with a series of investments that required substantial capital, which led them to acquire large dollar debts. These liabilities in foreign currency became major a problem after the Argentine peso depreciated sharply to less than one-third of its previous value within the first six months of 2002.

In light of the serious financial situation faced by the local news media, Congress is debating a law limiting the share of foreign companies in cultural enterprises. According to the bill, foreigners will have a 20 percent limit in the share of national media companies. The purpose of the new law is to prevent foreign companies from capturing a local market, where many companies face serious cash shortages and are near bankruptcy. One big newspaper, *La Prensa,* which had a circulation short of 100,000, has recently started free distribution, hoping to increase readership and advertising revenue.

Newspapers from the interior of the country were also hit hard in recent times. Not only did the increasing costs of foreign imports and the freezing of local credit hurt them, but they also had to suffer a 100 percent increase in the price of newsprint (mostly of national origin). The organization that brings together these provincial newspapers (ADIRA) has recently called for the mobilization of journalists in defense of what they see as a threatened profession.

In the year 2000 the government of Fernando de La Rua was facing a serious budget deficit and decided to increase the value added tax applied to cable television from 10.5 percent to 21 percent, an increase that was not extended to print media. The Inter-American Press Society (SIP) recently asked the Argentine government to abolish the added value tax on newspapers given the tenuous financial situation of the press and the excessive burden of the rates in place. The same source accused the government of having the highest tax rates in the region.

According to the press organization FLAPP (*Federación Latinoamericana de Prensa en Periódicos*), advertising revenue during the year 2001 was approximately $2.8 billion. Half of that advertising money is spent on television, 37 percent is spent in newspapers, almost 5 percent in magazines, over 6 percent in radio, and the rest in newspaper supplements. Although figures have not been released yet, there is a consensus that investment in advertising dropped significantly in 2002.

Ownership of media companies is fairly concentrated. This has generated numerous complaints and threats of new regulations, but in practice Congress has been reluctant to pass new legislation. The "*Clarín Group*" is the biggest conglomerate, controlling the newspaper of the same name in addition to shares in two major provincial newspapers, the sports daily *Olé,* cable channel *Multicanal,* open air channel *Canal 13,* radio *Mitre,* radio FM100, part of the news agency *DYN,* the press *Artes Gráficas Rioplatense S.A.,* the publishing company *Aguilar,* the magazine *Elle,* the TV studio Buenos Aires Television, and other investments, such as a cellular company in the interior of the country.

The second largest media company is *La Nación S.A.,* which runs the newspaper of the same name and is partial owner of the national satellite *Paracomstat.* The two major groups are associated in several commercial ventures. In 1978 they started *Papel Prensa S.A.* with the goal of producing newsprint. The company now produces 165,000 tons of paper a year, covering a major part of the local market. Both groups are also partners with the Spanish "Correo Group" in a company called CIMECO, which owns the regional newspapers *La Voz del Interior* and *Los Andes,* each one dominant in their local markets (83 percent and 73 percent of provincial circulation respectively). *Clarín* Group and *La Nación S.A.* also have shares in the news agency *DYN.*

Argentina has three other important media groups also located in the city of Buenos Aires: *Atlántida* Press, *Crónica* Group, and *Ámbito Financiero* Group. The editorial group *Atlántida* has been an important player in the magazine business for several decades. It owns eight magazines (*El Gráfíco, Gente, Teleclic, Para Ti, Chacra, Billiken, Plena,* and *Conozca Más*), part of a TV channel *Telefé,* and radio stations Continental and FM Hit. The group *Crónica* has, in addition to the newspaper of the same name, the magazines *Flash* and *Ahora,* the TV news channel *Crónica* TV, the television studio *Estrella,* and the newspaper *El Atlántico* from the biggest coastal city, Mar del Plata. The group controlling *Ámbito Financiero* also publishes the Patagonian newspaper, *Mañana del Sur,* and owns a TV channel in the province of Rio Negro. Another major consortium led by Eduardo Eurnekian (owner of radio stations America and Aspen) had been a major player in the media business until recently, but it has recently sold off its shares in the television stations America 2 and *Cablevisión* and the newspaper *El Cronista* (to a Spanish company). A new upstart player includes the group led by journalist Daniel Hadad, who runs the financial newspaper *Buenos Aires Económico,* a radio station, and the television channel *Azul TV.*

In the interior of the country we find several smaller media groups built around local newspapers. The group El Día in the city of La Plata publishes the newspaper of the same name in addition to the national newspapers *Diario Popular* and the news agency *NA.* The group *Nueva Provincia* from the city of Bahia Blanca has the newspaper of the same name, the magazine *Nueva,* and shares in the national television channel *Telefé* and in a local FM station. The group *Supercanal* from the province of Mendoza controls the newspaper *Uno* in addition to a television channel and at least three radio stations. The group *Territorio* from the province of Misiones owns the newspaper of the same name and the cable company in the provincial capital. In the province of Salta the group *El Tribuno* has the newspaper of the same name, which is also popular in the province of Jujuy, and shares in local TV channels. The group *Rio Negro* from Rio

Negro province owns the newspaper of the same name and the provincial cable channel. The groups *Territorio, El Tribuno,* and *Rio Negro* also have shares in the news agency *DYN.*

Antitrust legislation was passed in 1997 under the name "Law to Defend Competition." It restricts and regulates monopolies or oligopolies across the country as well as determines the possible merging of different companies. The law provides monetary fines, penalties, and even jail sentences for those found breaking it. This legislation mandated the creation of a National Commission to Defend Competition, an agency independent of the executive branch. Because most of the large media conglomerates were created in the years after deregulation in 1991 and prior to this law, they cannot be forced to dismember now, but future mergers need to correspond to the regulations of the new law.

The two main workers' organizations in the press are the Buenos Aires Press Workers Union (UTPBA) and the Argentine Federation of Press Workers (FATPREN), itself a national labor organization composed of over 40 individual unions. Industrial relations have been difficult, particularly over the reform of severance packages and the deregulation of the health funds run by the unions. Since the health fund system opened up, many press workers have left the poorly performing press union fund for other competing organizations, reducing an important source of revenues and political power. Unions provide individual journalists with legal counseling in case of conflict with management or in judicial matters.

Sometimes union disputes have become violent. In May of 2000 several armed groups invaded eight distribution centers for the provincial newspaper *La Gaceta* from Tucumán, hitting employees and burning the Sunday edition of the paper. Many reports associated the incident with an internal conflict. The newspaper had been involved in a labor dispute with members representing the street newspaper vendors (*canillitas*) over the reduction of commissions given to the workers. However, there was no judicial finding on whether the incident related to such a dispute, or if it was in response to other crime-related news published in the paper.

PRESS LAWS

The constitutional reforms of 1994 incorporated several provisions upholding freedom of expression and codifying state-press relations. Article 14 of the Constitution establishes that all inhabitants of the Argentine Republic have the right to "publish their ideas in the press without prior censorship. . ." and Article 32 specifies that. . . "The federal Congress cannot not pass laws that limit freedom of the press or that establish over them a federal jurisdiction." The right to confidential press sources is specifically protected by constitutional Article 43. Article 75 section 19 of the same Constitution gives Congress the power to regulate broadcasting media.

Argentina has incorporated into the Constitution several international treaties that deal specifically with press rights. A document that has been important in cases related to freedom of the press is the American Convention on Human Rights or "Pact of San José, Costa Rica," which establishes the following rights:

Article 13. Freedom of Thought and Expression

- 1. Everyone has the right to freedom of thought and expression. This right includes freedom to seek, receive, and impart information and ideas of all kinds, regardless of frontiers, either orally, in writing, in print, in the form of art, or through any other medium of one's choice.
- 2. The exercise of the right provided for in the foregoing paragraph shall not be subject to prior censorship but shall be subject to subsequent imposition of liability, which shall be expressly established by law to the extent necessary to ensure: (a) respect for the rights or reputations of others; or (b) the protection of national security, public order, or public health or morals.
- 3. The right of expression may not be restricted by indirect methods or means, such as the abuse of government or private controls over newsprint, radio broadcasting frequencies, or equipment used in the dissemination of information, or by any other means tending to impede the communication and circulation of ideas and opinions.
- 4. Notwithstanding the provisions of paragraph 2 above, public entertainments may be subject by law to prior censorship for the sole purpose of regulating access to them for the moral protection of childhood and adolescence.
- 5. Any propaganda for war and any advocacy of national, racial, or religious hatred that constitutes incitement to lawless violence or to any other similar action against any person or group of persons on any grounds including those of race, color, religion, language, or national origin shall be considered as offenses punishable by law.

Article 14. Right of Reply

- 1. Anyone injured by inaccurate or offensive statements or ideas disseminated to the public in general by a legally regulated medium of communication has the right to reply or to make a correction using the same communications outlet, under such conditions as the law may establish.

- 2. The correction or reply shall not in any case remit other legal liabilities that may have been incurred.
- 3. For the effective protection of honor and reputation, every publisher and every newspaper, motion picture, radio, and television company, shall have a person responsible who is not protected by immunities or special privileges.

In the year 1992 the president of the country, Carlos Menem, filed a suit against journalist Horacio Vertbisky for *desacato*—in this case disrespect to the president of the country—a common restriction to press freedom across many countries in Latin America. The journalist took the case to the Inter-American Commission on Human Rights (*CIDH*), who ruled in favor of Vertbisky and demanded that the Argentine government take action. In friendly terms the Argentine government agreed to change its stance and nullified the law in the year 1993.

In addition there are provisions in the Penal Code and the Civil Code as well as Supreme Court decisions that regulate the work of journalists and freedom of the press. The Penal Code has typified the crimes of ''slander'' (*calumnias*) and ''insult'' (*injurias*). In Article 109 it states, ''Slander or false accusation of a crime that results in public action is punishable with a prison term of one to three years.'' Article 110 reads, ''Anyone that dishonors or discredits another will be given a fine of between $1,000 and $100,000 Argentine pesos or jail term of one month to one year.'' When an individual feels that he has been a victim under these rules, he can file a suit. The effect of these articles extends to those who publish or reproduce these declarations made by others and to those who are considered as authors of the original statement. Articles 114 and 115 specify that editors in news organizations that publish such statements can be forced by the plaintiffs to publish the judicial sentence or extend some retribution for the offenses. And a safety valve was introduced in Article 117, which allows offenders to avoid penalties if they publicly retract before or at the same time they respond to the legal suit.

The articles in the Penal Code related to ''slander'' and ''insult'' have generated controversy with civil libertarians because such provisions have been used in many occasions to punish news organizations. As of 2002 the federal Congress is debating a bill that would restrict the extent of these articles by excluding those individuals who have become involved in issues of public interest (i.e., government officials) and by reducing or eliminating the liabilities of news organizations that publish such statements. In a publicized case, the news magazine *Noticias* was fined $60,000 dollars for having published reports of political favoritism involving President Menem and an alleged love affair.

The Civil Code also has provisions that protect an individual's honor. If someone is found guilty of ''slander'' or ''insult,'' the court can establish an amount of money to be paid in compensation to the victim. As of the middle of 2002, there is a bill in the Senate that would modify Article 1089 of the Civil Code to limit its reach. The intended bill is similar to the project to reform the Penal Code, in that it excludes those individuals who have become involved in issues of public interest, and it eliminates the liabilities of news organizations that publish such statements.

The Supreme Court of Argentina ruled in 1996 in a legal case against journalist Joaquin Morales Sola over statements published in his book *Asalto a la Ilusión* that the person filing the suit needs to prove that the information contested is false and that the party publishing the statements knew they were untrue. This position, known as the doctrine of ''real malice,'' is similar to the arguments advanced by the Supreme Court of the United States in the case of *New York Times Co. v. Sullivan* in 1964.

A few years before this case, the Argentine court had issued another ruling with important implications for the press. This is the case known as ''Campillay,'' which started after three major newspapers published an article that attributed certain crimes to the recently detained Julio Campillay, an ex-police officer. The newspaper articles included an almost literal copy of the police reports without specifying the original source. The ruling against the newspapers established that to avoid litigation, press reports needed to specify the appropriate source, use a corrected verb tense to avoid imputing the crime to the alleged offenders, or leave the identity of those implicated in an illegal act unknown.

The press has also been affected by Supreme Court rulings and civil code regulations over the right to privacy. Article 1071 of the Civil Code protects the right to privacy, and allows judges to impose financial penalties and force public retractions to those found guilty of having violated another person's right to privacy. The most famous ruling on this matter came on December of 1984 in a case originated after the national magazine *Gente* published a front-page photo of Ricardo Balbin (ex-presidential candidate and leader of the political party UCR) dying in the intensive care unit of a hospital. The court found that because the picture had been taken without the permission of the family, and because it was not a public event, the magazine was in fault and had to pay compensation to the wife of Mr. Balbin.

Many press organizations have complained against recent Supreme Court decisions that they see as unconstitutional and contrary to international treaties, such as the ''Pact of San José, Costa Rica,'' mentioned before. In one case the highest court found journalist Bernardo Neustad guilty for comments made on his television show *Tiempo Nuevo* by one of his guests, who implicated a local judge in controversial (i.e., illegal) activities. The journalist, the television channel, and the guest who made the comments were all fined heavily. In another case the Supreme Court refused an appeal by journalist Eduardo Kimel, who in 1999 was found guilty of insulting a former judge in his book *La Masacre de San Pedro,* which narrates the killing of five priests during the military government. The journalist was given a jail sentence in addition to a fine of $20,000 dollars.

Another legal provision that affects free speech is the ''defense of crime speech'' (*apologia del delito*). It is a judicial term for a free speech violation that involves the diffusion and promotion of crime. It is usually very difficult to prove, but it has been used against politicians, former military or police personnel, and others for comments usually reproduced in the media.

The courts have had mixed responses to the use of hidden cameras, a growing modality in investigative journalism for television. Sometimes the courts have used them as key evidence, but on other occasions they have not taken such filming into consideration. Many well-known television shows like *Telenoche Investiga* use hidden cameras, which have been very useful to uncover widespread evidence of corruption in many segments of public life. At the moment the country lacks regulations regarding the use of hidden cameras.

The labor law regulating working conditions for journalists is called the *Estatuto del Periodista,* and it was originally enacted in 1945. It has provisions for working hours, vacations, severance pay, and seniority, among other issues. The number of working hours established under this statute is 6 a day, with overtime pay equal to double the regular hourly rate. Vacation time starts at 20 days a year (5 more than most other workers) and increases with seniority. In regard to severance payments, journalists enjoy a special clause that provides them with a better compensation than most other workers, originally included to protect an allegedly unstable profession.

The actual implementation of this statute, among other things, has been severely undermined by the severe economic situation of the last few years. The only part that until recently had been regularly respected was the severance pay provision. Until recently journalists in Argentina were receiving a sum equal to 10 months of work plus an extra month for each year of work, but now even that seems to be disregarded. In a case involving the lack of enforcement of this provision, a judge sided with the firing of the journalist by the press company, which paid a severance amount equal to a typical worker. Forced reductions of salaries have also been challenged legally. So far, they have not been overturned.

In regard to a journalistic code of behavior or ''Ethics Committee,'' Argentina lacks both. There is disagreement among the different actors in the press with regard to the establishment of a code of ethics for the profession. The Association of Press Entities of Argentina (*ADEPA*) has come out strongly against any such rule, which it sees as a violation of press freedom. However both major newspapers, *Clarín* and *La Nación,* have in place a code of ethics that apply to their writers and editors. Some of the main requirements imposed by it include:

- A clear differentiation between advertising sections and news sections to avoid misleading readers and suggestions of editorial endorsement.
- News articles should clearly differentiate between personal opinion and factual reporting, using editorial pages to present individual perspectives on issues.
- Journalists must avoid slander and insult, and must respect the privacy of individuals.
- Reports on crime should not assign culpability until after a judicial sentence on the case.
- Journalists are entitled to preserve the anonymity of their sources of information.
- Journalists cannot receive outside monetary compensation for publishing newspaper articles.
- According to the law, the name and photographs of minors involved in judicial proceedings cannot be published, nor can those of rape victims.
- It is forbidden to offend or insult people because of their race, religion, and color of their skin, or political ideas.

CENSORSHIP

The most dangerous time to be a journalist in Argentina was certainly under the military government that controlled the country between 1976 and 1983. According to the Buenos Aires Press Workers Union (*UTPBA*), during that period a total of 84 journalists were kidnapped and disappeared. The military rulers exercised explicit censorship in all of the media and pushed many press organizations to close. At least 10 national newspapers were shut down, and those that survived were subject to government controls. The military had a tight grip over all of the state media, including all national television channels. The media's inability to openly address the widespread human rights violations in the country and the disinformation spread during the military conflict with England in 1982 are two of the most grotesque cases of state censorship in this period.

The process of democratization initiated at the end of 1983 brought about a radical change in freedom of the press, including the dismantling of the state censorship apparatus and increasing access to government information. Currently Argentina does not have governmental institutions dedicated to censoring press material before it is published. Nevertheless political pressures, by interest groups or government officials, have allegedly surfaced on occasion, such as in the control over state advertising funds, apparently helping to soften or to avoid certain news. Publications that include pornographic material are required to have a plastic cover with a warning sign prohibiting their sale to minors below the age of 18. The Federal Broadcasting Committee (*COMFER*) supervises and controls radio and television, including language and time of broadcasting, but it does not affect printed media like newspapers and magazines.

Argentina currently lacks any specific laws over journalist access to public government information. If a public agency were to refuse information to reporters, they could initiate a legal case, which would require proof of public interest in the information requested and of the arbitrary nature of the decision made by the public official. If a judge finds merit in the petition, a judicial order can force the agency to release the information. There are no laws limiting speech by government officials. There is currently a bill being debated that would expand on the issue of state information, including the forced declassification of government information after 10 years.

In regard to data about an individual that the state may have, the constitutional reform of 1994 introduced the right of *habeas data.* According to Article 43 of the Argentine Constitution, any individual can have access to information about himself that is in public registries or databases as well as in some private databases. In case of untruthfulness or discrimination, the individual affected can demand the nullification, correction, confidentiality, or actualization of such information. In addition, the state cannot alter the secrecy of confidential sources for journalists.

In the decades that followed the return of democracy, intimidations, threats, and violence diminished but did not go away completely. In many cases the local police or corrupt public officials were the alleged agents undertaking the repression of investigative journalists. The Buenos Aires Press Workers Union (*UTPBA*) reported 1,283 cases of violent aggression toward journalists between 1989 and 2001. The years with the highest number of reported abuses were 1993, with 218 cases and one murder, and 1997, with 162 cases and also one journalist killed.

Since 1993 newspapers have called attention to the murder of three journalists: Mario Bonino, José Luis Cabezas, and Ricardo Gangeme. The first victim in the 1990s was Mario Bonino, a journalist for the newspapers *Sur* and *Diario Popular* and a member of the press office of the *UTPBA*. He was found dead in the Riachuelo River four days after disappearing on his way to a seminar in November 1993. The judicial official in charge of the investigation found that the journalist had died under suspicious circumstances. According to Amnesty International, the death of Bonino occurred in the context of an increased campaign of threats and intimidation against journalists. Soon before his death, in the name of the *UTPBA*, he had denounced the death threats received by journalists in the province of San Luis. More recently, on April 19, 2001, the television show *Puntodoc/2* presented footage where a former police officer from the province of Buenos Aires implicated other police agents in the killing of Bonino. The case remains open.

The brutal assassination of photojournalist José Luis Cabezas in January of 1997 is the most famous case of violence against the media in recent times. The 35-year-old magazine news photographer was found handcuffed and charred in a cellar near the beach resort of Pinamar. He had been shot twice in the head. A few days after his death, thousands of journalists, citizens, politicians, and members of human rights groups wore black ribbons while marching through the streets of Buenos Aires in silence as a sign of protest to the murder. As a journalist for the magazine *Noticias,* Cabezas had recently photographed reclusive Argentine businessman Alfredo Yabran, accused of having Mafia ties. Mr. Yabran committed suicide in May 1998, after a judge ordered his arrest in connection with the murder of Cabezas. In February of 2000, 8 out of 10 persons accused in this crime received sentences of life in prison. Three of those with life sentences were members of the Buenos Aires police department.

The more recent case involves the murder of Ricardo Gangeme, owner and director of the weekly *El Informador Chubutense* from the southern city of Trelew, on March 13, 1999. He received a gunshot as he arrived home. The journalist, who had previously worked as an editor at Radio Argentina and as a reporter for the Buenos Aires newspaper *Crónica,* was known for investigating corruption in government and business, and had reported threats to the police. Prior to his murder Gangeme wrote about irregularities in three legal suits involving the directors of the Trelew Electrical Cooperative. Six months after Gangeme's murder, the judicial official in charge of the investigation determined the arrest of six people allegedly involved in the killing. The arrested were associated with the administrative board running the city's electricity cooperative, which had been accused of corruption by Gangeme.

According to the Argentine Association for the Defense of Independent Journalism (*PERIODISTAS*):

> . . .1997 was the year of the greatest regression in press freedom in Argentina since the restoration of democracy

in 1983. If in previous years, repressive bills on press freedom and lawsuits against journalists presented by government officials threatened the consolidation of a right won with great difficulty, in 1997 the murder of photographer José Luis Cabezas, the proliferation of attacks, threats and insults against journalists, official treatment of the press as a political rival and the encouragement by President Carlos Menem to attack the press by saying that citizens had 'a right to give (the press) a beating': all helped put freedom of thought and expression in a serious predicament.

There are also several reports from *PERIODISTAS* and the *UTPBA* that in the last few years reporters have been physically attacked or seriously threatened by a variety of social actors such as police officers, union activists, politicians, agitators, party militants, public officials, and individuals associated with the prior military regime. In one case in the province of Santa Cruz, the radio station *FM Inolvidable* was attacked four times (including a firebomb) after reporting on the drug trafficking and car robberies in the port city of Caleta Oliva.

In addition there is the case of illegal spying on journalists by state agencies. One case that gained notoriety in recent years involved the illegal spying on reporters by the intelligence services. According to reports in *Página 12* and *Crónica,* during 1999 the Air Force's intelligence services, concerned about investigations by journalists on the privatization of the country's airports, initiated an illegal inquiry that included spying on eight journalists from major newspapers. Following a judicial investigation, five members of the military were arrested and charged with plotting the illegal search.

STATE-PRESS RELATIONS

The state had a dominant role over the media between the years of 1973 (when General Peron returned to power) and 1983 (when the military government fell, and elections were called). From 1973 to 1976 television was in the hands of the government, run during that time by the Peronist party (*Partido Justicialista*). The state took an aggressive stand to gain control of television, confiscating private channels and taking advantage of license expirations. The government also moved to organize a state media bureaucracy that had under its jurisdiction the news agency *TELAM,* National Radio and its 23 affiliates in the interior of the country, 36 other radio stations, the National Institute of Cinematography, the national television channel (*Canal 7*), and four other television channels. Poor management and large financial losses characterized these agencies throughout this period.

The military government that took power in 1976 also extended its grip over state media, seeking to perpetuate the control they had already imposed in other areas of Argentine public life. Struggles within the different branches of the armed forces led to a division of control over media outlets. In this regard, the presidency exerted control over Channel 7, the army over Channel 9, the air force had Channel 11, and Channel 13 was shared among them. An important technical development during this period came in 1978, with the hosting of the soccer World Cup. The improvements made for the event included direct satellite communication with over 400 broadcasting units within the country and the move to color television, which formally started in May of 1980. Another related event during this period was the passage of a broadcasting bill, "Law 22,285" in 1980, which opened the door for the slow introduction of a private role in television and radio. In particular, the law sought to prevent businesses involved in printed journalism from expanding into broadcasting media and also to restrict the creation of national television networks. Under this law, one channel (*Canal 9*) was privatized in October of 1982. The first private owner was Alejandro Romay and his company *TELEARTE S.A.*

The new democratic period began at the end of 1983 following the election of Raúl Alfonsin from the UCR party. During his government drastic changes occurred in the areas of freedom of the press and stopping the violent attacks of the preceding era. On the legal front the new democratic government did not alter the status quo, and no important media privatization projects were undertaken under this government.

The next president, the Peronist Carlos Menem, was elected in 1989 and again in 1995. He introduced major changes in the regulations of television and radio, privatizing several state television channels, permitting the creation of national networks and introducing greater foreign participation. While on the one hand Menem benefited private ownership of the press, on the other hand he had a very contentious relationship with journalists. Public encouragement by President Carlos Menem to attack the press by saying that citizens had 'a right to give (the press) a beating' is one example. According to the independent organization *PERIODISTAS,* by the end of 1997:

> . . .The decision of a private TV channel to pull two of its shows because of pressure from the government created a new type of threat against freedom of expression: that of media owners who have other business interests. In the case of the programs *Día D* led by journalist Jorge Lanata, and *Las patas de la mentira* produced by Miguel Rodríguez Arias, the main shareholder of the América TV channel which aired the programs is also in one of the groups bidding in the privatization of 33 domestic airports. Information on the cancellation of the journalists' contracts was communicated by people close to government before it was announced by the channel authorities.

The media companies that had been part of the state for decades were reorganized by an executive decree in January of 2001. The government created a new multimedia state company, *Sistema Nacional de Medios Públicos Sociedad del Estado,* that merged with other smaller agencies. In the process it dissolved the state companies that ran the television channel ATC, the news agency *Telam,* and the Official Radio Broadcasting Service, whose functions are now part of the new state conglomerate. In 2002 another decree placed a government official to oversee the restructuring of this state company.

Accusations of political uses of advertising money by the state have surfaced in a number of occasions in the last few years. The agencies running the advertising decisions of the state have been political appointees (i.e., "partisan allies") of the administration in place. The board running the state multimedia company has ample powers to determine the allocation of advertising for every sector of the executive branch, including state-dependent companies. There is no auditing agency or independent control mechanism over decisions made regarding state advertising. Allegations of pressures to withdraw state (federal and provincial) publicity funds have grown, including some that eventually led to the filing of legal suits. The main victims have apparently been the poorer media organizations in the interior of the country that many times are heavily dependent on these funds to make a profit. Such allegations have surfaced in the provinces of San Luis, Mendoza, Chubut, La Rioja, Santa Cruz, and Rio Negro.

The relationship between governors and the media has been controversial in many provinces. In the province of Salta, the main newspaper *El Tribuno* is owned by the governor. This has led to questions about press independence in that area of the country. In the province of Santiago del Estero a serious dispute between journalists and provincial political party "machines" has grown in the last few years. A judicial ruling from an allegedly friendly provincial judge ruled against the newspaper *El Liberal* and ordered the payment of monetary compensation to the women's branch of the local Peronist party. This is the third such judicial ruling, which carried a penalty of $600,000 from 11 different criminal counts. According to Danilo Arbilla, president of the Inter-American Press Society (SIP), "we are surprised that public agencies from Santiago del Estero and from the federal government have not acted on this matter yet, given their knowledge that this is clearly a campaign directed by the provincial administration, which uses a judicial system of little independence, to punish a news media organization for criticizing the public administration and their political activities." The controversy started after *El Liberal* from Santiago del Estero reproduced reports, published in the newspaper *La Voz del Interior* from the neighboring province of Cordoba, that were critical to the women's branch of the dominant Peronist party run by the governor's wife. Since then, political groups allegedly connected to governor Carlos Juarez have responded with distribution and working barriers against both newspapers.

The relationship between legislators and the media turned sour in the year 2000 after newspapers reported on a bribe scandal in the Argentine Senate. This halted progress on an important bill protecting press freedom, which had been demanded by journalists for some time. A judge investigating the scandal said that it appeared that government officials bribed senators of the opposition Peronist party, as well as some of its own senators, to vote for a controversial labor reform bill. These allegations rocked the De La Rua administration, which had been elected with a mandate to fight corruption a year before. One of the 11 legislators called to answer questions before a judge was Senator Augusto Alasino, who was forced to give up his job as leader of the opposition Peronist Party in the upper house. In an apparent effort to get back at the press, Alasino later introduced a bill rejecting "the unlimited use of freedom of expression." The bill never passed.

As of mid-2002 the president of the country had a radio show on the public station *Radio Nacional.* The show, called *Dialogando con el Presidente,* was broadcast twice a week for two hours.

ATTITUDE TOWARD FOREIGN MEDIA

Foreign correspondents need an accreditation provided by the Ministry of Foreign Affairs. This credential, renewable every year, is issued by the ministry after a specific request by the media company hiring the journalist. The Association of Foreign Correspondents in Argentina has a special agreement with the government, and requests for such permits can be processed at its office instead of the government's agency. To be able to work inside governmental buildings such as the National Congress or the president's office and residence, a special accreditation provided by the respective institutions is required. According to this foreign press association, in Argentina there are around 150 foreign correspondents, half of which are Argentines working for foreign media companies.

The current government of Argentina does not review or censor cables or news sent abroad by foreign journalists working in the country. The last time some type of censorship mechanism was imposed was during the last military government (1976-83), when the state checked on foreign correspondents' activities as part of their overall objective of controlling the news flow. There are no established procedures for government relations with the foreign press. The holding of a special presidential press conference for the foreign media on a monthly occasion is now a not-so-regular event.

Foreign ownership of media companies started to increase with the withdrawal of state companies and the slow deregulation of the market that began after the election of Menem to the presidency. In 1989 the government dropped the 10-year residency requirement for receiving a broadcasting license. In regard to the newspaper business, companies from Spain have made important inroads in the market. The Spanish group *Recoletos* has recently acquired 100 percent of shares in the leading financial newspaper *El Cronista* and the magazines *Apertura, Information Technology,* and *Target.* The Spanish group *Correo* is a partner with the two leading Argentine newspapers in a company called *CIMECO,* which owns the regional newspapers *La Voz del Interior* and *Los Andes,* each one dominant in their local markets (83 percent and 73 percent of provincial circulation respectively).

An Argentine investor sold the first privatized television channel, *Canal 9,* to the Australian company Prime Television for $150 million in 1997. Two years later the Spanish company Telefonica bought it for $120 million. And in 2002 it was bought by an Argentine consortium. Another foreign player in broadcasting is the Mexican group CIE Rock & Pop, which currently owns eight radio stations.

In light of the serious financial situation faced by the local news media, Congress is discussing a law limiting the share of foreign companies in cultural enterprises. According to the new project, foreigners would have a 20 percent limit in the share of national media companies. The bill passed the Senate, but it still needs the approval of the lower chamber.

News Agencies

Argentina has three major news agencies, one of which belongs to the state. A board appointed by the government, which often seems to reflect political interest more than professional aptitude, controls the state agency *Telam.* Recently the state multimedia company that runs *Telam* has entered a major restructuring, and the future of the agency is uncertain. The other two big national agencies, *DYN* and *Noticias Argentinas (NA),* are run by major newspapers. The former is partly own by the two biggest newspapers *Claín* and *La Nació,* and the latter belongs to the group that controls *Diario Popular.* They are both national agencies that supply information to national and provincial media.

Two other smaller news agencies are the *Agencia de Diarios Bonaerenses,* based in the province of Buenos Aires, and the *Agencia Informativa Católica Argentina,* which is a Catholic Church agency focusing on news related to religious and church matters. There are also news agencies run by universities, such as the University of La Plata (*AIULA*) and the University of Lomas de Zamora (*ANULZ*). These two agencies are run by journalism students and are self-financed with their revenues from selling information mainly to newspapers and local radios.

Major foreign news agencies with bureaus in Buenos Aires include: ANSA (Italy), Associated Press (United States), Bloomerang (United States), EFE (Spain), France Presse (France), Reuters (UK), United Press International (United States), and Xinhua (China). Some other foreign press news organizations in the country include: Deutsche Press (Germany), Europa Press, Bridge News (United States), BTA (Bulgaria), Milliyet (Turkey), Pravda (Slovakia), Vatican Information Service, Inter Press Service, Novosti (Russia), Agencia Latinoamericana de Informacion, Prensa Latina (Cuba), Zenit, and Duma (Bulgaria).

Broadcast Media

As of 2002 about 10 million Argentines own television sets. According to the World Bank, Argentina has the highest rates of cable television subscribers in Latin America, with 163 per 1,000 individuals in 1998. The country has 46 channels of open television: 2 belong to the state, 11 to provincial governments, 4 to national universities, and 29 are private channels. Only 7 cities have more than one local TV channel: Buenos Aires, Tucumán, Rosario, Mendoza, Cordoba, Bahia Blanca, and Mar del Plata. The city of Buenos Aires has 5 national channels of open broadcast TV. One of these, *Canal 7,* is the only state-owned channel that broadcasts all over the country. Provinces have at least 2 channels of open TV that rebroadcast programs from the national stations. In addition there are 4 national cable channels and over 100 other cable channels that rebroadcast national and foreign shows.

Argentina has approximately 260 AM radio stations and 300 FM stations. Of these, 32 are located in the city of Buenos Aires. The number of illegal radio stations has increased dramatically in the last 20 years. It is calculated that there are over 1,000 unlicensed radio stations. To counter the increasing number of clandestine radio stations, the government has recently extended a large number of licenses and has also begun a program to facilitate the legalization of existing stations. Argentina has approximately 650 radios per 1,000 individuals.

According to the main umbrella organization for private media businesses in Argentina, CEMCI (*Comision Empresaria de Medios de Comunicación Independientes*), radio and television generate employment for 35,000 people, offering one of the highest wage rates in the country.

In 1989, soon after President Menem came to power, he modified press law 22,285 first passed under the military government and began the deregulation of broadcasting media. After this four television channels that used to be state-owned were privatized. This was the first major privatization of television channels since 1982. In 1999 the government of Menem also introduced important changes to the legislation affecting broadcast media. Radio and television regulations were affected by an executive decree (1005/99), whose main provisions were: (1) to increase the number of licenses given per business nationwide from 4 to 24, and maintain the limit of 1 per district and type of service, (2) to allow the creation of national networks, (3) to permit the transfer of licenses, (4) to drop the 10-year residency requirement for receiving a license, and (5) to give television and radio stations benefits regarding their own publicity.

The subsequent government of De La Rua limited the total number of television licenses issued to 12 out of those 24. It intended to limit the possible reach of such a network to only half of the country, which has 24 provinces. In regard to radio station licenses, the government now increased the prior limits to 4 as long as it accounts for no more than 25 percent of the local offer. In order to have 2 radio stations belonging to the same group, a minimum of 8 radio stations have to be in place in that locality. In practice the transfer of licenses is complicated to track down, since limitations were dropped and in some cases licenses are requested after the transfer has been in effect.

The Federal Broadcasting Committee (*COMFER*) is the government agency in charge of regulating radio and television, including language and time of broadcasting. The *COMFER* issues licenses to broadcast within the available frequencies, regulates transfers of licenses, and determines their expiration. First established in 1972, it is the agency in charge of enforcing the broadcasting law 22,285/80, the regulating executive decree 286/81, and complementary laws across the nation. The *COMFER* has a Supervision Center in the city of Buenos Aires and 32 delegations across the country, as well as an Assessment Area. A main task is the control of broadcasting material that is considered to be harmful to children. The broadcasting law 22,285 determines the agency's reach into areas such as the content of the transmissions (section 14), the use of offensive language (section 15), audience protection (section 16), protection of minors (section 17), participation of minors (section 22), advertising (section 23), time limits for commercials (section 71), and free broadcasting (section 72). The executive decree 286/81 also regulates advertising (articles 4 and 5) and the broadcasting time for protection of minors (article 7) among other matters.

In the application of the law, the *COMFER* can issue sanctions (i.e., infraction fees) and control the revenues that would come in the application of the federal broadcasting law. In practice, if the agency finds a violation through one of its monitoring centers across the country, it needs to start a file recording the alleged infraction. If the problem refers to the content of a broadcasting show or commercial, it goes to the Assessment Area, where the file is analyzed according to regulations and if a breach is confirmed, it is forwarded to the Infractions Area of *COMFER.* If the file arose in respect to direct violations (films with inappropriate rating for the time of broadcasting, advertising on medicines, advertising overtime, transmission of gambling events, etc.), it is forwarded to a different unit (*Dirección de Fiscalización*), and if the breach is confirmed, it is also sent to the Infractions Area. This latter office is the one required to notify the individual with the license and to present the appropriate documentation of the case. The alleged offender can appeal to the Judicial Directorate of *COMFER.*

Until recently *COMFER* had been receiving close to $140 million from tax collections earmarked to them. According to regulations, 25 percent of what television provides has to be invested in cinematography, 8 percent of revenues go to support the National Institute of Theatre, and the rest goes to the National Treasury. The government financially supports national radio and public television from other tax resources.

ELECTRONIC NEWS MEDIA

According to official figures, Argentina has 7.5 million telephone lines and 4 million active cellular phones. In 1999 the number of Internet users was calculated to be 900,000, which is equivalent to 2.5 percent of the population. The proportion of Internet users in the population is similar to that found in Brazil and Mexico. According to the World Bank, Argentina has 28 Internet hosts per 10,000 individuals.

On the legal front, Internet press continues to be regulated in a similar fashion as the press in general. Regarding Internet privacy, the Argentine Federation of Press Workers (*FATPREN*) has opposed a bill being debated in Congress because of its position against a provision that would allow employers to check employees' e-mail messages.

All major media organizations have Internet Web sites. These press sites provide users with a variety of news, information, and entertainment. Several include up-to-the- moment news together with access to their editorials, archives, live radio, or television. Some of these sites include:

- Agencia Diarios y Noticias (DYN) (http://www.dyn.com.ar/)

- Ambito Financiero (http://www.1.com.ar)
- Buenos Aires Herald (http://www.buenosaires herald.com/)
- Clarín (http://www.clarin.com)
- Cuyo Noticias, from the provinces of Mendoza, San Juan, and San Luis (http://www.cuyonoticias.com.ar/)
- El Cronista (http://www.cronista.com/)
- El Día, from the city of La Plata (http://www.eldia.com.ar/)
- La Gaceta, from the province of Tucumán (http://www.gacenet.com.ar)
- La Nación (http://www.lanacion.com.ar/)
- Olé, a sports news site (http://www.ole.com.ar/)
- Página 12 (http://www.pagina12.com/)
- Parlamentario.com, a site with legislative news (http://www.parlamentario.com/)
- Periodismo.com, which includes links to over 20 radio stations (http://periodismo.com.ar/)
- La Razón (http://www.larazon.com.ar/)
- Río Negro On Line (http://www.rionegro.com.ar/)
- TELAM, the state news agency (http://www.telam.com.ar/)
- TELEFE Canal de television (http://www.telefe.com.ar/)
- TN24horas.com, from Todo Noticias cable channel (http://www.tn24horas.com/)
- La Voz del Interior from the province of Cordoba (http://www.lavozdelinterior.com.ar/)
- El Zonda, from the province of San Juan (http://www.diarioelzonda.com.ar/)

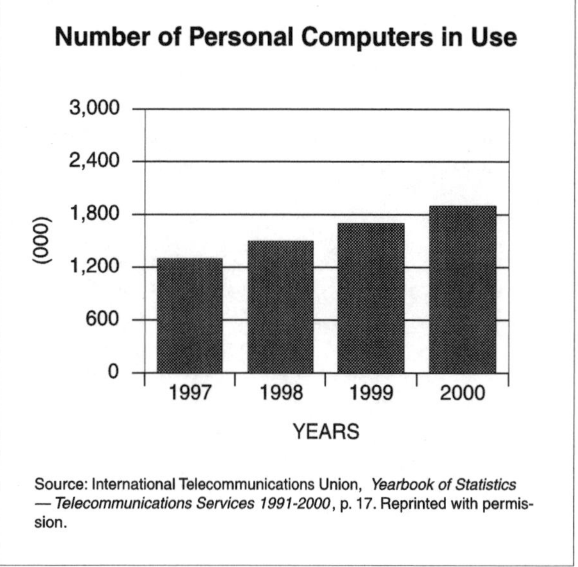

Source: International Telecommunications Union, *Yearbook of Statistics — Telecommunications Services 1991-2000*, p. 17. Reprinted with permission.

Education & Training

Educational institutions in Argentina offer undergraduate as well as graduate degrees in journalism and in communication studies. There are also several colleges that provide technical training for people interested in a career in journalism. Media companies have been recruiting students with journalism degrees, but it is not a common requirement for entering the profession. Generally speaking all educational entities provide students with training in writing for the press and speech for public broadcasting. In addition, classes also provide students with a more general education in the social sciences.

All major universities offer graduate degrees in journalism. In addition, since 1999, the two major newspapers have began to offer a one-year masters degree. *La Nación* has a program in association with the University San Andrés, and *Clarín* has a program in association with University Di Tella and Columbia University in New York. Students of these educational institutions enjoy the opportunity to intern in these very influential newspapers for six months. Most other educational institutions have also established internships with a variety of media organizations. Internship opportunities provide students with the chance to write stories for newspapers as well as to participate in live broadcasts.

Some of the universities offering degrees in journalism include: Universidad de Buenos Aires; Universidad Abierta Interamericana; Universidad Argentina de la Empresa; Universidad Argentina John F. Kennedy; Universidad Catolica Argentina; Universidad de Belgrano; Universidad de Morón; Universidad de San Andrés; Universidad Nacional de La Matanza; Universidad Nacional de La Plata; Universidad Nacional de Luján; Universidad Nacional de Quilmes; Universidad Nacional de Lomas de Zamora; Universidad Austral; Universidad Nacional de Córdoba; Universidad Nacional de Tucumún; Universidad Catolica de Salta; Universidad Nacional de Rosario; Universidad Nacional de Entre Rios; Universidad Nacional de San Luis; and Universidad del Museo Social Argentino.

In addition there is a state-sponsored Institute of Higher Education in Broadcasting (*ISER*) founded in 1951 and run by the Federal Broadcasting Committee (*COMFER*). Based in the city of Buenos Aires, the institute has three radio studios (two FM), two television studios, editing rooms, and a computer lab.

Argentina has two major awards targeted to the press and show business. The Konex foundation, a nonprofit

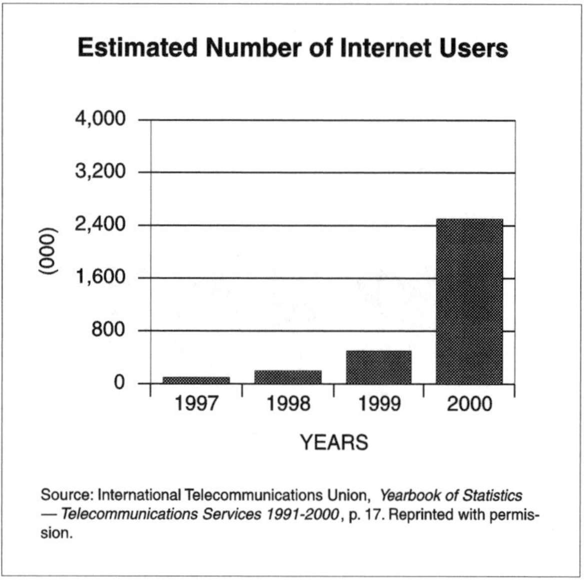

Estimated Number of Internet Users

Source: International Telecommunications Union, *Yearbook of Statistics — Telecommunications Services 1991-2000*, p. 17. Reprinted with permission.

organization dedicated to stimulate cultural, educational, philanthropic, social, and scientific activities, awards yearly prizes to journalists, the press and broadcast media. There is also a yearly event organized by the Association of Television Journalists (*Asociación Argentina de Periodismo Televisivo*), which awards the ''Martín Fierro'' prizes. The jury is composed of well-known personalities in broadcasting media, and awards are given to news programs, sports, entertainment, humor, and soap operas. The awards given by this highly watched event also include radio programs.

A smaller yearly event in recognition of the press activities involves the ''Santa Clara de Asís'' awards, given by the League of Family Mothers. They are targeted to broadcasting shows that have excelled in the defense of family values, culture, and ''healthy'' recreation. Another award to radio and television shows includes those handed out by the ''Broadcasting Group,'' which beginning in 2002 takes into consideration public votes in its selection of prizewinners.

The main umbrella organization for private media businesses in Argentina is the ''Independent Media Business Committee'' or CEMCI (*Comision Empresaria de Medios de Comunicación Independientes*). It brings together six other major organizations: the Association of Newspaper Editors from Buenos Aires, the Association of Magazine Publishers, the Association of Newspapers from the Interior, the Argentine Association of Broadcasting Stations, the Cable Television Association, and the Argentine Association of Private Radio Stations.

Some other press organizations in the country include:

- PERIODISTAS: Founded in 1995 by a group of renowned independent journalists, it is a nonprofit organization supported by membership contributions. The membership includes newspaper directors, editors in chief, writers, and broadcasting journalists. It has maintained an independent trajectory and cultivated a plurality of views that has made it the main independent organization of journalists defending freedom of the press.
- Buenos Aires Press Workers Union (UTPBA): This is a labor organization that represents journalists from the city of Buenos Aires. It performs union activities, such as collective bargaining, as well as defending the individual rights of press workers. The organization has a training and research center, a library, and runs the press workers' health fund. In the last years it has maintained a critical position against the government and defended legislative threats to the welfare of its workers.
- COMUNICADORES: This is a recently established organization of journalists active in labor and freedom of the press issues. The membership of this organization is mostly from journalists who do not occupy management, editorial, or other hierarchical positions in media organizations.
- Association of Foreign Correspondents in Argentina: The Association of Foreign Correspondents is located in the city of Buenos Aires. Its membership of 130 includes journalists from all foreign media companies working in Argentina. It provides an avenue for foreign correspondents to meet and exchange information as well as a voice in public issues related to freedom of the press. In addition it helps foreign correspondents with accreditation paperwork and sometimes offers educational courses.
- Association of Press Entities of Argentina (ADEPA): This organization brings together owners and upper management of media companies (i.e., television, radio, and newspapers). It lobbies on matters that affect the economic and legal status of media businesses as well as freedom of the press. It has recently emphasized its support for government deregulation of the media and its opposition to restrictive judicial rulings.
- Association of Photojournalists from Argentina (ARGA): The association has a membership that extends all over the country. It is concerned with legal issues affecting the profession as well as press freedom and militancy. The latter became salient after the murder of photojournalist José Luis Cabezas in 1997.

- The Argentine Federation of Press Workers (FATPREN): This is a national labor organization composed of over 40 individual unions.

SUMMARY

The press in Argentina has undergone significant changes over the last three decades. After suffering under a repressive military regime for seven years, it emerged as one of the institutional building blocks of democracy. As the country struggles with the difficult task of building a free society, journalists have consistently put themselves at risk in order to bring news to Argentine homes. As a profession, journalism has grown stronger in both political and economic influence. Many individual journalists, also the victims of a depressing economic panorama, have excelled in their professional achievements, winning international awards and helping locally to uncover government fraud, mafia activities, and human rights violations.

Media companies have also grown economically stronger under favorable legislation. The move to a more business friendly set of regulations started under President Menem. These changes allowed for a growth in private ownership of media companies never seen before. Many critics have lamented the decreasing role of state intervention and have accused big media conglomerates of monopolizing the market. Unions and the left have also protested what they see as excessive political influence of big media conglomerates. Whatever advantages these companies accumulated during the last decade, now they are forced to confront the ills of heavy liabilities.

The difficult economic situation in Argentina in mid-2002 leads most analysts to conclude that the short-term prospects for the country are bleak. This will seriously affect the press, not only as it suffers from the general malaise, but also for the consequences of possible violent social conflict on press freedom. For small media companies and provincial newspapers the panorama appears to be even worse. On the legal front, the slow erosion of norms benefiting press workers and the constant use of presidential decrees to undertake major changes in media regulation have opened the door to policy volatility in the next few years.

The rapid growth of electronic media and instant access to information also pose new challenges to old fashioned newspapers that have to adapt to a rapidly changing professional environment. The accelerated growth of Internet sites and availability of broadcasting media online will probably continue to grow in the near future, despite economic hardships.

Overall the future of the press seems complex and uncertain. Many important legal and economic issues that affect the profession are now being debated in Congress. Under the currently difficult state of affairs, the role of the Argentine press has, if anything, grown even more important.

SIGNIFICANT DATES

- January 1997: Photojournalist José Luis Cabezas is murdered, resulting in a national outcry.
- 1997: Antitrust legislation is passed, limiting the growth of media conglomerates.
- March 1999: Murder of journalist Ricardo Gangeme in the southern city of Trelew.
- September 1999: Presidential decree modifying broadcasting laws and favoring greater concentration of media ownership.
- 2000: Following press reports over illegal activities, the Argentine Senate becomes embroiled in a bribery scandal.
- January 2001: Decree reorganizing all state media companies under one central unit

BIBLIOGRAPHY

Alemán, Eduardo, Jose Guadalupe Ortega, and James Wilkie, eds. *Statistical Abstract of Latin America.* Volume 36. Los Angeles: UCLA Latin American Publications, 2002.

Amado, Ana Maria. *El ABC del Periodismo Sexista* [The ABC of Sexist Journalism]. Buenos Aires: ILET, 1996.

Avellaneda, Andres. *Censura en la Argentina* [Censorship in Argentina]. Buenos Aires: Editorial CEAL, 1986.

Blaustein, Eduardo, and Martin Zubieta. *Deciamos Ayer: La Prensa Argentina bajo el Proceso Militar* [Yesterday We Said: The Argentine Press under the Military Government]. Buenos Aires: Editorial Colihue, 1998.

Casullo, Nicolas. *Comunicación, la Democracia Difícil* [Communication, the Difficult Democracy]. Buenos Aires: ILET, 1983.

Fernandez, Juan. *Historia del Periodismo Argentino* [History of Argentine Journalism]. Buenos Aires: Prelado Editores, 1943.

Fraga, Rosendo. *Prensa y Analisis Políticos* [Press and Political Analysis]. Buenos Aires: Centro Nueva Mayoría, 1990.

Galvan, Moreno. *El Periodismo Argentino* [Argentine Journalism]. Buenos Aires: Claridad, 1943.

Halperin, Jorge. *La Entrevista Periodistica* [The Press Interview]. Buenos Aires: Editorial Planeta, 1990.

La Nacion. *Manual de Estilo y Ética periodistica* [Manual of Style and Journalism Ethics]. Buenos Aires: Editorial Espasa, 1990.

Laiño, Felix. *Secretos del Periodismo* [Journalism Secrets]. Buenos Aires: PlusUltra, 1987.

Llano, Luis. *La Aventura del Periodismo* [The Adventure of Journalism]. Buenos Aires: Editorial Peña, 1978.

Mitre, Bartolomé. *Sin Libertad de Prensa no hay Libertad* [Without Press Freedom there is no Freedom]. Buenos Aires: Fundacion Banco Boston, 1990.

Moncalvillo, Mona. *Entre lineas* [Between Lines]. Buenos Aires: Editorial Planeta, 1993.

OAS, Secretariat for Legal Affairs. ''Treaties.'' Available from http://www.oas.org.

Periodistas. ''Report on Press Freedom.'' Available from http://www.asociacionperiodistas.org.

Ramos, Julio. *El Periodismo Atrasado: La Tecnologia es Ráro los Medios de Prensa Lentos* [Backward Journalism: Technology is Fast but the Media is Slow]. Buenos Aires: Fundacion GADA, 1995.

Rivera, Jorege, and Eduardo Romano. *Claves del Periodismo Actual* [Keys to Contemporary Journalism]. Editorial Tarso, 1987.

Salomone, Franco. *Maten al Mensajero: Periodistas Asesinados en la Historia Argentina* [Kill the Messenger: Journalists Murdered in Argentine History]. Buenos Aires: Editorial Sudamericana, 1999.

Sidicaro, Ricardo. *Las Ideas del Diario La Nación* [The Ideas of the Newspaper La Nación]. Buenos Aires: Editorial Sudamericana, 1993.

Sirven, Pablo. *Quien Te Ha Visto y Quien Te Ve: Historia Informal de la Television en la Argentina* [Informal History of Television in Argentina]. Buenos Aires: Editorial la Flor, 1988.

Sortino, Carlos. *Leyes en la Prensa Argentina* [Argentine Press Laws]. La Plata: Universidad de La Plata, 1990.

———. *Dias de Radio: Historia de la Radio en la Argentina* [Radio Days: History of Radio in Argentina]. Buenos Aires: Editorial Espasa, 1995.

Ulanovsky, Carlos. *Paren las Rotativas: Historia de los Grandes Diarios, Revistas y Periodistas Argentinos* [History of the Big Newspapers, Magazines and Journalists in Argentina]. Buenos Aires: Editorial Espasa, 1990.

Ulanovsky, Carlos, Silvia Itkin, and Pablo Sirven. *Estamos en el Aire: Historia de la Television en la Argentina* [History of Television in Argentina]. Buenos Aires: Editorial Planeta, 1993.

World Bank. *World Development Indicators 2000.* Washington, D.C.: The World Bank, 2000.

—Eduardo Alemán and Martin Dinatale

ARMENIA

BASIC DATA

Official Country Name:	Republic of Armenia
Region (Map name):	Middle East
Population:	3,336,100
Language(s):	Armenian, Russian
Literacy rate:	99.0%
Area:	29,800 sq km
GDP:	1,914 (US$ millions)
Number of Television Stations:	4
Number of Television Sets:	825,000
Television Sets per 1,000:	247.3
Number of Cable Subscribers:	3,420
Cable Subscribers per 1,000:	0.9
Number of Radio Stations:	16
Number of Radio Receivers:	850,000
Radio Receivers per 1,000:	254.8
Number of Individuals with Computers:	25,000
Computers per 1,000:	7.5
Number of Individuals with Internet Access:	50,000
Internet Access per 1,000:	15.0

BACKGROUND & GENERAL CHARACTERISTICS

Within the Republic of Armenia, newspaper circulations are small and the press industry represents a tiny portion of an emerging market economy. The country's tepid investigative journalism accompanies comparable democratic development. In the late 1980s the former Soviet Republic joined others in the move to independence that resulted in the collapse of the USSR. The official proclamation came in April 1991, at which time the International Covenant of Civil and Political Rights (ICCPR) was signed and accepted as the basis for developing domestic law. The National Assembly adopted its own Law on the Press and Mass Media in October 1991, guaranteeing the right of access to information, freedom of speech, and a free and independent press. The same principles are embodied in the 1995 Constitution. However, these "guarantees" remain subject to the interpretation of a constitutionally powerful executive. New civil and criminal codes were enacted in 1999, a new broadcast media law in 2000, and a new licensing law in 2001. All three were passed in reaction to the October 27, 1999, terrorist attack on the Armenian Parliament that killed the Prime Minister, Speaker, and six others. The new laws have facilitated the power of government to encroach upon the freedom of the press. However, Armenia also became a member of the Council of Europe in 2001, which carries obligations to guard against threats of excessive state powers restricting a free and independent media.

Armenia's Department of Information registered 642 newspapers and 166 magazines in 2001, but only 150 of these were regularly active. It is safe to say that total newspaper circulation in the Republic is very limited, even though numbers are extremely unreliable. They are based on print runs rather than on actual sales, providing the opportunity to manipulate them for economic gain.

Dailies are issued five times a week, Tuesday through Saturday. Of the 47 registered dailies, the Department of Information estimates a total circulation of only 40,000 copies, or about 1 copy per 83 persons. The major papers circulate between 2,000 and 6,000 daily copies. Many papers circulate only in the several hundreds. Non-dailies may appear two or three times a week, weekly, monthly, or irregularly. Non-daily circulation numbers can run comparatively higher, such as the 30,000 copies for the crime reporting weekly *02* (Police Messenger), a publication of the Ministry of Internal Affairs.

Armenia has no newspaper chains. Private media groupings are only beginning to appear. Nonetheless, newspapers are privately owned, with the exceptions of *Hayastani Hanrapetutyun* (Republic of Armenia, in Armenian, circulation 6,500) and *Respublica Armenia* (in Russian, 3,000). Both are joint ventures between the National Assembly and the newspaper staffs, founded in 1991. Ownership of other papers is organized in corporations of both open and closed joint stock companies. The media industry is structured in a manner that separates newspaper editorial offices from the printing and distribution services. Both of the latter were state-owned monopolies until the privatization process that began in 2001. Newspapers operate with extremely limited resources, and therefore none are completely independent of patronage from political parties, economic interest groups, or wealthy individual sponsors. Private ownership of the print media suffers from a lack of self-sufficiency due to low circulation and weak advertising markets, as well as the little revenue generated by advertising.

The media industry is concentrated in the capital city of Yerevan. Some rural regions of the country see no newspapers at all, and other areas have print runs as low as 100 copies. Newspapers address a limited and elite audience: a mere 5 percent of the population takes its news from papers. Broadcast media represents the widest market share: radio at 10 percent and television commanding 85 percent. Most media organizations, and particularly newspapers, either represent a definite orientation toward some particular political party, or express views constrained by the need to retain their financial sponsors. Low circulation numbers reflect the small target audience. This allows newspapers to be sponsor-oriented, as opposed to reader-oriented. Profit expectations are low, and subsequently business investment and advertising are low as well. In 2002, after a decade of independence from Soviet rule and exposure to the process of emerging markets, the newspaper industry still did not operate as a profitable business.

Armenia is one of the most ethnically homogeneous regions of the former Soviet Union: 96 percent Armenian; 2 percent Russian; 1 percent Kurdish; and 1 percent Yerdish. In 1993, with the outbreak of conflict over the Nagorno-Karabakh Armenian enclave within Azerbaijan, most of the Azeri population, formerly 3 percent of the total, returned to Azerbaijan. The Armenian enclave community has tried to secede and attach itself to Armenia, but the international community would not accept the move. The Republic's literacy rate has been nearly 100 percent since the 1960s, a fact that makes low circulation rates most disappointing, as does the 3,000-year-old literary culture of the Armenian people.

According to tradition, the ancient country was founded around Lake Van, by a descendant of Noah known as Haik, and remained independent for centuries under Haikian Kings. The first historical mention of Armenia dates to the ninth century BC, with Assyrian inscriptions referring to Urartu, or Ararat. The high rugged mountains and deep fertile valleys lie at the convergence of the Anatolian, Iranian, and Caucasus plateaus, where the headwaters of the Tigris, Euphrates and Araxes Rivers take rise. It has been a land frequently invaded, conquered and divided among various regional powers since ancient times: Assyrians, Medians, Persians, Parthians, Macedonians, and Romans.

Armenians converted to Christianity very early, and formed the world's first Christian state in AD 301. The Armenian Apostolic Church then played a principle role in establishing and preserving the literary traditions of the language. There was a national alphabet by the fifth century. Grabar, the classical religious language, was also the written language of the Armenian cultural community, which drew its identity based on this linguistic distinctiveness and the adaptation of ancient myths to it. The early Christian state lasted until the seventh centuries. The Bagratid Golden Age ran through the ninth and tenth centuries. Beginning in the eleventh century a series of invasions, migrations and deportations led to the dispersion of Armenian communities outside the historic homeland. Nevertheless, the Kingdom of Lesser Armenia, or Cilicia, in the southeast corner of Anatolia, lasted from the twelfth to fourteenth centuries. Cilicia fell to Genghis Khan, and then was destroyed by Tamerlane. By the sixteenth century, when the Ottoman Empire ruled, most Armenians in eastern Anatolia survived as peasant farmers. Diaspora communities had resettled in Istanbul, Smyrna, and various cities along the eastern shores of the Mediterranean, becoming artisans, traders and moneylenders.

Trade and commerce led to growing Armenian communities in various regional centers from India and Persia, to the Levant, across the eastern Mediterranean basin and into Europe. The successful Armenian Diaspora drew upon commercial skills, polyglot capacities, and international contacts. Wherever they went, their clerics and intellectuals took the Armenian literary traditions with them. The fourteenth century *Dasatun* (Scriptorium), located in Aleppo, was famous for the art of calligraphy and illumination of liturgical, canonical, and other religious manuscripts. It maintained special workshops for the manufacture of parchment and paper, ink and pigments, and the binding of manuscripts. The tradition of copying Armenian liturgical books began to decline after the seventeenth century, however, with the popularization of printing.

The first Armenian-language printing establishment was founded at Venice in 1565. Papal restrictions on liturgical works led to it being moved to Istanbul in 1567. Still, more than one hundred Armenian titles were published in Europe between 1695 and 1777. The Armenian printing press in Amsterdam, founded in 1660, produced the first printing of the classical Bible in 1666, and functioned for 57 years free from Papal restrictions. The New Julfa community in Persia printed their first book, *Saghmor* (Psalms), in 1638, followed by *Harants-Vark*, (Lives of the Church Fathers) in 1646. The first Armenian newspaper was published at Madras, India, in 1794, 60 years before any would appear in the homeland. From 1794 to 1840, only 15 Armenian journals appeared throughout the world. Between 1841 and 1915, however, 675 new Armenian periodicals were published. The boom resulted from the linguistic innovation of a Benedictine order of Armenians founded by the monk, Mkhit'ar of Sebastia.

The Mekhitarist innovation fundamentally altered Armenian literary expression by producing a vernacular, Ashkharabar, which became the medium of an increasingly nationalistic movement. Cultural and political revival in the late nineteenth century generated formation of secret revolutionary societies. Newspapers assumed the role as organs of political parties.

The first journal printed in the new vernacular was *Ararat* (Morning), published in Tiflis in 1849. The political party Armenakan was founded in France in 1885 and published *Armenia* in Marseilles. In the Caucasus, *Mshak* (Cultivator) was printed between 1872 and 1920. *Zang* (The Ring) was an organ of the Hnchakists political party and published from 1910 to 1922. The Dashnak party published its journals *Ararat* from 1909 to 1912 and *Ayg* (Dawn) from 1912 to 1922.

After a history of subjugation to other powers, Armenia revived as an independent state in May 1918. It did not last long, caught between the forces of a Nationalist Turkey and a Bolshevik Russia. One million Armenians were lost to a holocaust engineered by the emerging Turkish Republic. The Red Army installed a communist-dominated government, the Transcaucasian Soviet Federated Socialist Republic, that combined Armenia with Azerbaijan and Georgia. The printed press came under strong central control from Moscow, which lasted until the Soviet Union's demise. The Russian language was also imposed.

The circulation numbers of Soviet-era print media were far larger (in the tens of thousands) than the numbers of the infant private press in the transitional environment of the early twenty-first century. However, there has been an explosion of journalistic activity. In the 1980s, *perestroika* and *glasnost* permitted the public discussion of issues as well as access to some information. A language and cultural revival inspired the awakening of national consciousness, and the creation of dozens of new journals and newspapers. Armenian replaced Russian as the primary language in schools and newspapers. The push for greater autonomy, democracy and loosening of Russian political domination began in 1987-88. Despite this encouraging environment for explosive journalistic growth, the story also includes many failed enterprises and defunct newspapers. In 1993 there were thirteen major Armenian language magazines and journals covering such topics as science and technology, politics, art, culture, and economics, one satirical journal, one journal for teenagers, and one for working women. In early 1994 the Ministry of Justice reported twenty-four magazines, nine radio stations, twenty-five press agencies, and 232 active newspapers, compared to the 150 that existed in 2002.

The vast majority of news outlets are located and based in the capital of Yerevan. The circulation of 40,000 daily newspapers is well down from the 85,000 reported in 1995. News is comprised of political reporting on government and parliament, and content extends to the arts, culture, religion, sports, and some limited foreign news. The major privately owned national dailies offer a wide variety of opinions, but newspapers in general do not encourage investigative reporting. Only one newspaper, *Delavoy Express* (Business Express), concentrates on business and economic news. The situation of careful criticism and no aggressive investigative reporting has been exacerbated by the October 1999 attack on the Armenian National Assembly, as well as by the onslaught of the war on terrorism governments internationally have confronted since September 11, 2001.

The major daily papers in the Republic, in addition to those mentioned above, include:

- *Aravot* (Morning): established in 1994 by editorial staff. (circulation 5,000-6,000)
- *AZG* (Nation): founded in 1991, centrist, coverage of Diaspora. (4,000)
- *Hayots Ashkhar*: founded in 1997 by private owner, politicized. (3,500)
- *Haykakan Zhamanak*: founded in 1997 by the Democratic Motherland Party and the Intellectual Armenia, a social-political organization. (2,500)
- *Yerkir* (Country): founded in 1991 by the Armenian Revolutionary Federation Dashnaksutyun (ARF), commonly known as Dashnak; covers religion and the activities of the party; one of the media outlets closed when ARF was suspended by presidential decree in 1994, prior to national elections the next year; resumed publication in 1998 when ARF reinstated. (2,000)

All are printed in either A2 or A3 format, range from 8-16 pages, and have an average price of 100 drams (about 20 U.S. cents).

The major non-daily publications include:

- *Ayzhn*: organ of the National Democratic Union (NDU) issued weekly. (4,000)
- *Dzain Zhoghovrdi* (Voice of the People): a weekly established in 1999 as a joint-stock company, issued and financed by the People's party. (3,000)
- *Golos Armenii* (Voice of Armenia, in Russian): covers news from Russia with an opposition, left-wing orientation. (5,230)
- *Garant*: a weekly entertainment journal. (30,000)
- *Grakan Tert* (Literary Paper): issued by the Armenian Union of Writers.
- *Hay Zinvor*: issued weekly by the Ministry of Defense. (10,000)
- *Hayk*: founded in 1989 as an organ of the Armenian Pan-national Movement (APM); features party news, entertainment, and foreign news. (3,500)
- *Iravunk* (Law): founded in 1989; published without interruption. (7,000-12,000)
- *Kumairi*: printed in Armenia's second city of Gyumri, suffers frequent interruptions, depends on local authorities for financing. (1,000)
- *Novoye Vremia* (New Time, in Russian): centrist with financial support from a private Moscow-based businessman. (3,000-5,000)
- *Nzhar*: published weekly by the Ministry of Justice.
- *Riya Taze* (New Way): a Yezidi ethnic weekly.

The primary printing method in the early twenty-first century remained offset printing. Computer-based (electronic) typesetting has become more popular as imagesetter systems have been introduced to Armenia. The state-owned publishing and printing house, Tigran Met, formerly known as Periodica, was privatized in 2001 and now functions as a commercial enterprise. There are still government-held shares, but no visible government intervention. Tigran Met remains the largest facility, although there are some 20 printing companies registered with the Ministry of Justice; most are very small.

The price of newsprint is a major portion of printing costs. Armenia has no local production and imports newsprint from Russia. Costs are double those in Russia, due to the small market size and transportation costs. Newsprint in Armenia averages $1,200 per ton. Of course, the larger the volume of the purchase, the lower the price, which benefits Tigran Met. The Armenian print media consume 51 tons of newsprint per month; down from Soviet-era figures as high as 920 tons. The average print run fell from 185,000 copies in 1988 to 5,000 in 1997.

The Soviet-era system of subscriptions for newspapers and magazines ceased to exist in 1993. The Nagorno-Karabakh conflict, and subsequent economic blockade and gasoline crisis, brought deliveries to a stop and the system of subscriptions evaporated—another factor contributing to low circulation numbers. The state-run Hayamamoul distribution company began the privatization process in 2001. Since regaining independence the distribution network has consisted of a system of some 200 kiosks scattered throughout the capital city, Yerevan, and in some of the other regions. Kiosk operators are guaranteed a minimum income (U.S. $20-30 per month) based on sales. There is a financial penalty for unsold papers, so Hayamamoul has developed a "no return" policy that establishes a set circulation amount and a guaranteed low cost on returns. The alternative "return" policy gains the paper a higher percentage of kiosk sales, but there is a high collection cost incurred on returned papers. Most papers choose the ''no return'' policy for the guaranteed revenue. Corruption has worked its way into this process, as circulation numbers are often kept artificially low while the printing house prints overruns (beyond the agreed number), sells them, and keeps the profits. The printing process also serves as a form of censorship, as print runs will be stopped if they contain controversial articles.

ECONOMIC FRAMEWORK

The bleak economic environment in the Republic of Armenia since regaining its independence is yet another factor hindering the media's reformation and depressing circulation numbers. The prevailing conditions result from a combination of tensions that include: the transition from Soviet political and economic centralization to market-based economics and democratic politics; the 1988 earthquake that killed 25,000 and left 500,000 homeless; the ethnic tensions in the Nagorno-Karabakh conflict between Armenia and Azerbaijan; and the global war on terrorism. These macro-economic social and political factors, along with the government's inability to account for and tax as much as 40 percent of economic activity, combine with the micro-economic realities of low newspaper readership and lack of a viable advertising market, to create a difficult environment for the Armenian press.

Limited resources and readership act as overwhelming constraints on the development of advertising revenues, the lifeblood for any independent media. Political sponsorship or some form of patronage of the media is an accepted substitute for business performance. Ownership often remains hidden. This lack of transparency affects the media in that professional standards tend to give way to economic survival. Often a paper's allegiances can be deciphered through the biases in the reporting.

By signing the Alma-Ata Declaration in December 1991, Armenia became a founding member of the Commonwealth of Independent States (CIS), an economic community, if not political union, of former Soviet Republics. In reaction to the Nagorno-Karabakh conflict, Turkey and Azerbaijan have imposed an economic blockade against Armenia for a decade. The longer the status of the enclave remains unresolved, the longer it continues to disrupt economic development.

Armenia has claimed 3.5 percent to 5.5 percent annual economic growth between 1993 and 2002. This is misleading, because there has been little improvement in investment, exports, or job creation. The growth numbers suggest a supportive climate for business, but they cloak a failure to create improved conditions for consumers. There is serious income inequality and widespread poverty, and levels of unemployment and emigration are rising. The government reports unemployment at 12 percent, but it is at least double the official number. Estimates are that nearly half the population lives below the poverty line, and in need of government assistance.

Newspapers also must search for funds to pay for their high printing and other production costs. Extremely limited resources mean dependence on patronage from interest groups or individuals. Editors turn to sponsors as the most common way of meeting financial need. Businessmen contribute to pro-government newspapers for political connections. Sponsors solidify government connections in seeking preferential consideration. Paternalism and clientalistic networks permeate the industry.

The National Assembly tried to encourage journalistic expansion through tax policy. The print media receives an exemption from the value-added tax (VAT), legally stipulated in a 1997 law. However, the editorial offices pay the tax indirectly in costs imposed by the printing houses, for whom the exemption does not apply.

Economic assistance from foreign aid programs and the diaspora community has been on the increase. George Soros' Open Society Institute has invested in media projects since 1996. In 1999 the United States Agency for International Development (USAID) contributed to the media law reform program. The International Research and Exchanges Board (IREX) has introduced technical assistance through its Pro-Media program. The Eurasia Foundation helped establish Gind, a private publishing house, to challenge Tigran Mets' monopoly. In May 2001 Gind discontinued Haykakan Zhamanak because of unpaid debt. Questions about political influence in the decision have been raised. The European Institute for the Media (EIM) is a non-profit association under German law working towards integrating the CIS states into a civil digital society by developing cross-border media. EIM also conducts programs to advance research, the media's relationship with democracy, the European television and film forum, and a library documentation center. The funding comes from a variety of European sources.

PRESS LAWS

Constitutional and legal protections for journalists exist in Armenia, but enforcement is ambiguous and uneven. Based on the ICCRP, the 1991 Law on the Press and Mass Media conforms to many accepted European standards. Article 24 of the Constitution, established in 1995, reiterated the protections of freedom of speech and press. Armenia's acceptance into the Council of Europe in 2001 should help provide structure and oversight in protecting freedom of speech. This legal and regulatory framework supports an independent media in principle. In practice the application of constitutional guarantees has fallen far short of expectations.

The registration of journalists and news agencies is mandated in the 1991 law. In 2001 a law on licensing was enacted that requires re-registration of all media companies. The cost has been a burden for all newspapers, which are forced to operate on narrow margins as is.

Article 2 of the press law forbids censorship. However, Article 6 imposes restrictions on types of information that can be published, e.g., appeals to war, violence, and religious hatred. The law also prohibits the publication of "false or unverifiable information," a clause often invoked by the government in its dealings with the media. There exists further invitation for abuse, manipulation, and intimidation on part of the government in any conflict with journalists over the issue of revealing sources. In court cases sources must be revealed, which encourages self-censorship. Libel is a criminal offense in Armenia. However, it is vaguely defined, and this leaves journalists facing legal suits and criminal arrest for conducting their professional responsibilities.

CENSORSHIP

There is no official censorship, but freedom of expression in the press is limited. Armenia's judiciary is hindered in protecting press freedoms by the executive's oversight capacity, and its ability to restrict the jurisdiction of the courts. Judges and prosecutors are dependent on the executive for their employment. Constitutional human rights and press freedoms are, therefore, not safeguarded. The judicial system itself continues to be in transition: in 1999 both prosecutors and defense counsels began a process of retraining and recertification as mandated by the Constitution.

Even though the opposition press criticizes government policies and leaders, journalists see the 1991 press law as inadequate for both their own personal protection and the development of their profession. Criminal defamation, as covered in Article 131 of the 1999 Criminal Code, is a strong instrument for government restriction on press freedom. Fines and compensation for damages are steep, and punishment now includes imprisonment for up to three years. As a result, journalists are tepid investigators, hoping to avoid the retribution some have experienced in recent years on the part of powerful officials and other individuals. The case of Vahram Aghajanian in Nagorno-Karabakh is a reminder that the enclaves' self-proclaimed authorities are less restrained than in the Armenian Republic itself. In June 2000 Vahang Gnukasian suffered incarceration and was beaten at the Interior Ministry, according to the Committee to Protect Journalists (CPJ).

Self-censorship is common in reporting on such issues as the conflict in Nagorno-Karabakh, national security, or corruption. In covering domestic policy and political issues, self-censorship has been reinforced by the strengthened libel laws in the criminal code. The news media is not required to reveal sources under the 1991 law, except when involved in a court case. To avoid appearing in court, sources are rarely cited, and "news" stories read more like commentaries than reporting. The need to retain or seek economic patronage is another important factor in self-censorship.

The Armenian journalistic community itself has not developed effective mechanisms to protect itself. An absence of self-regulation norms promotes a false sense of freedom, but gives room to critics who desire to shorten the media's pen. Because journalists have determined no rules themselves, such cases go to the courts.

STATE-PRESS RELATIONS

The constitutional protections and institutional legal structure defining the role between the state and a potentially free and independent press have been taking legislative form for a decade. The printing and distribution agencies, however, have until recently been state-owned. The privatization process was advanced in 2001, but problems persist and success is yet to be verified.

The pursuit of journalism as a profession has been answerable to the government's protection of state secrets and maintaining state security. There are reported transgressions against journalists and media firms by security forces as well as privately hired thugs. Both have delivered beatings and other forms of intimidation to journalists, including fires and destruction of editorial offices. These crimes are rarely solved or even thoroughly investigated, and because the judiciary is constitutionally submissive to the executive, journalistic independence has only uncertain state protection.

Nine political parties were banned prior to the 1995 Parliamentary elections, which resulted in the closure of the media organizations owned by or associated with those parties. The politics of media control was evident in the case of Dashnak's printing house, Mikael Vardanyan, a Canadian-Dashnak joint venture, which was suspended, closed, and looted. Operations remained closed for four years, until re-legalized in February 1998. Similar transgressions preceded the 1999 election.

The degree of political influence on the content of newspaper reporting has intensified since the 1999 attack on the National Assembly. The attack has brought increased tensions between the government and the press, and even among the press themselves. The Yerevan Press Club's extensive media-monitoring project has determined that an ''information war'' over differing opinions about the parliamentary attack began in early 2000. One group, supported by the political opposition, linked the terrorist activity to associates of President Robert Kocharian. The other group has accused the investigators of political involvement and bias, and views Kocharian as the only guarantor of stability and justice. The increased government monitoring of the press, and demand for the names of sources, has only served to increase self-censorship on the part of journalists.

Corruption and lack of transparency continue to characterize the environment in which the media must operate. Accepting bribes is a criminal offense, punishable by up to 8-15 years imprisonment, plus confiscation of personal property for repeated crimes. Despite these severe penalties, bribery remains widespread and the most common form of media corruption. The shadow economy and money-making potential of influence-peddling serve to advance the hidden and non-transparent exercise of power through manipulation of the press.

ATTITUDE TOWARD FOREIGN MEDIA

There are no legislative restrictions on access to international news coverage and reception of satellite television, and no censorship of imported printed materials. The free flow of information is protected under the ICCPR and membership of the Council of Europe. Foreign reporters must register with the Ministry of Justice; a presidentially appointed commission conducts licensing of foreign media companies. There is a variety of Russian broadcasts and printed news (Russian is the second language for 40 percent of the population), as well as news presented in translation from the BBC, Euronews, and CNN.

Diaspora Armenians support organizations and associations that produce newspapers and published materials both in the Republic and throughout the world-wide diaspora communities. One-sixth of the 6 million Diaspora population resides in Russia. The Soviet regime had banned diasporic activity in Armenia. There is an active relationship between Russian media and shareholders, whether Armenian or not, and the Armenian Republic. The flow of information, however, is predominantly from the homeland to the dispersed communities, rather than the reverse.

NEWS AGENCIES

The Armenpress News Agency is the state service that dates from the early Soviet era. It covers political, economic, and cultural news from the homeland and abroad in Armenian, English, and Russian (http://www.armenpress.am).

There are about twenty-five private services registered with the Ministry of Justice. They cover news both in the Republic and the Armenian Diaspora Communities. Some of the major services include the following:

- Agragil, an English-only service covering daily news from Armenia; it feeds *Azg*, *Yerkir*, *Hayastani Hanrapetutyun*, *Respublica Armenia*, and *Golos Armenii*. (http://www.aragil.am)
- The Armenian Daily News Service, a service offering news, press reviews, and articles from columnists on domestic issues, the Nagorno-Karabakh conflict, the Transcaucasus region, and the Armenian Diaspora. (http://www.armeniandaily.com)
- ARKA, a service created in 1996, specializing in financial, economic, and political information in English and Russian. (http://www.arka.am)
- Noyan Tapan, a multi-media company and information center offering an advertising service and video documentary programming. (http://noyan-tapan.am)
- SNARK, the first independent news agency in Armenia and the Caucasus when it was established in 1991. (http://www.snark.am)
- The SPYUR Information Service, founded in 1992, offering an information and inquiry service about companies and organizations in Armenia. (http://www.spyur.am)

BROADCAST MEDIA

From its inception in 1991, the law has treated the print media as separate and distinct from the broadcast media. The Law on Television and Radio Broadcasting was adopted in October, 2000, of which several aspects have caused alarm in the industry. The Armenian president is given the exclusive right to appoint all nine members to a governing body that regulates and licenses the media. Thus it is seen as a political tool of the executive. Article 9 requires that television and radio stations devote 65 percent of airtime to locally produced programs in the Armenian language. This has caused concern over the financial burden of production. The libel law's vagueness and threat to journalists applies to broadcasters as well as print media.

In 2002 the Ministry of Information reported 850,000 radios in the country and 825,000 television sets. There were 55 radio stations and 48 independent television companies. All media outlets have been required to register with the Ministry of Justice since re-independence in 1991. The government implemented a re-registration and licensing program in 1999. The same law also prohibited individuals from founding a media company. All programming is in Armenian, although foreign films are shown with Russian translation.

As of 2002 there were two state-owned TV channels. H 1, or National Television of Armenia, was a state-owned closed joint stock company. It was founded in 1954 and was able to reach the whole Republic by satellite. The broadcast day was limited to 6 hours until January, 1999, when it was extended to 15. The second channel was founded in 1978 and made available to the concentrated urban, industrialized and population of the Ararat valley. In 1995 it was named Nork, and has become known for its presentation of a liberal political orientation. Programming on Nork was abruptly stopped in early 1999. It was replaced with programming from the channel Kultura.

Shant TV was founded in April 1994 at Gyumri, the second largest city in Armenia. A new Independent Broadcast Network was founded in 2000 by a consortium of Ashtarak TV, A One Plus, Shant TV, and five other smaller companies. A new channel, Biznes TV, focused on computing, education, and televising courses during the day over the Russian ORT frequency. Biznes operated a professional studio for computer graphic production and produces all its own programming. Broadcast days varied station to station. H 1 had two segments: 9 a.m. to noon, and 5 p.m. to 1 a.m. The independent channel, A One Plus, broadcast 24 hours a day.

Executive control over the licensing process to manipulate the information flow is a blunt political tool. In January, 2001 the government stopped re-broadcasting ORT due to a financial dispute. Broadcast was subsequently resumed on a different frequency when the dispute was settled. Two independent broadcasting companies, A-One Plus and Noyan Tapan, were stripped of their licenses in April, 2002. The action was consistent with past government attempts to quiet opposition ahead of elections. These closures have left Armenia with no major independent broadcast outlets. The frequencies were awarded to other media firms without news broadcasting experience: Sharm, an entertainment company; and Shoghakat, which is associated with the Armenian Apostolic Church.

As a member state of the Council of Europe, Armenia accepted the European Convention on Transforntier Television, which entered into force in March, 2002. The parties are to ensure freedom of expression and information in accordance with Article 10 of the Convention for the Protection of Human Rights and Fundamental Freedoms, guarantee reception, and not restrict retransmission of program services.

Electronic News Media

The Internet and Information Technology (IT) have only begun to appear in the beginning of the twenty-first century. The Ministry of Justice registered 43 IT firms in 2001. However, a local business association put the estimate at 200 companies. It is believed 4,000 people were employed in this sector. As of 2002, the main challenges to growth were a shortage of skilled labor and the required educational transformation. Cost and needed technical training keep the Internet within reach of a limited few.

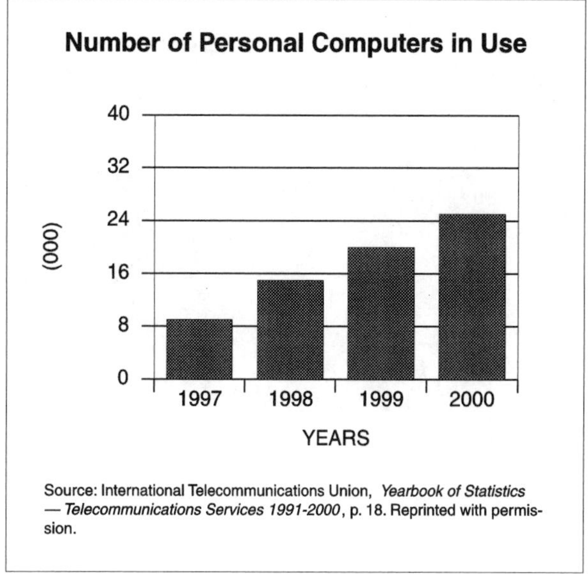

Source: International Telecommunications Union, *Yearbook of Statistics — Telecommunications Services 1991-2000*, p. 18. Reprinted with permission.

Education and Training

Armenian universities have provided undergraduate and graduate degrees in journalism since the Soviet era. The system has been characterized by the journalistic theory lingering from the former Soviet system. The transitional institutional reforms taking place in Armenia throughout the 1990s have introduced some significant changes. Curriculum changes are being made in order to improve journalistic professionalism and quality of reporting.

Private professional organizations are working to improve the quality of journalism and the environment that journalists work in. The Armenian Union of Journalists dates back to the Sovietera, and organizes courses for the journalistic community. The Yerevan Press Club (YPC) was established during a seminar organized by the European Institute for the Media in June 1995. The YPC issues a bulletin, organizes press conferences, seminars, and journalism courses. It also monitors the media and operates a press center. The Mass Media Association of Armenia was created in 1997 with the purpose of participating in the privatization process of the print production and distribution companies.

Summary

The demise of the Soviet Union left an unstable political, social, and economic environment in the Republic

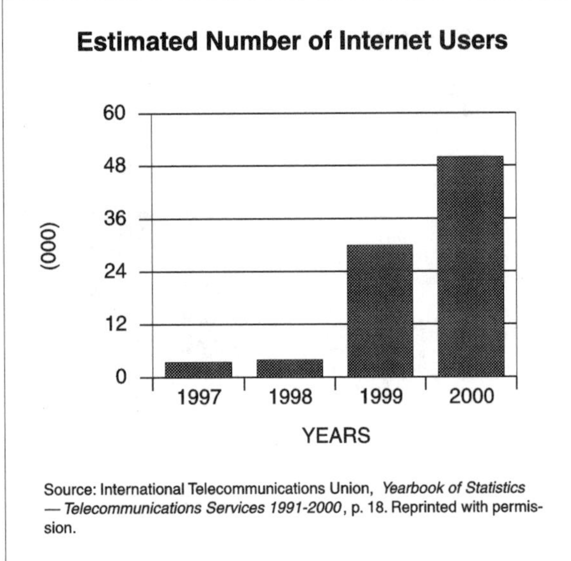

Source: International Telecommunications Union, *Yearbook of Statistics — Telecommunications Services 1991-2000*, p. 18. Reprinted with permission.

of Armenia. Political structures and economic practices that had long dominated society were undermined. The situation has remained relatively unstable, and was made worse by the 1988 earthquake and the armed conflict in Nagorno-Karabakh.

The newspaper industry was privatized in 1991, and editorial offices have helped facilitate limited public discourse. Political opposition and criticism of the government has been allowed. However, the print media does not function as an economically viable business. Advertising and circulation revenues are not sufficient to cover the costs of printing and distribution. The transition from a state-supported towards a privately-owned and market-based media has been difficult. In the 1990s there has been an increase in foreign and diaspora aid for the training of journalists. The profession is beginning to show some improvement in the quality of reporting. At the same time, government regulation and surveillance in the name of national security is on the increase. Tension results from the government's need for security and the media's need to protect sources. The legal questions facing the editorial offices only distract them from the effort to increase readership and advertising revenues, as well as begin to engage in investigative reporting. In general, news-oriented papers are not a profitable business. Entertainment orientation of the news and publications enjoy greater profitability. In this regard, Armenia is not unusual.

SIGNIFICANT DATES

- 1991: The Republic of Armenia becomes an independent state with the demise of the Soviet Union.
- 1995: The Constitution of the Republic of Armenia is ratified by referendum.
- 1996: The Law on Advertising enacted.
- 1999: The National Assembly passes new civil and criminal codes; on October 27, the National Assembly is attacked and several government officials were killed.
- 2000: The National Assembly enacts the new Law on Television and Radio Broadcasting.
- 2001: The new Law on Licensing enacted which mandates the re-registration of media outlets.
- 2002: The new Law on Printed Press is under legislative review.

BIBLIOGRAPHY

''Armenia.'' *Europa World Yearbook 2001*. Vol. 1, A-J. London: Taylor and Francis Group, 2001.

''Armenia.'' *Media Sustainability Index 2001*. Washington, D.C.: IREX, 2001.

ArmenPress. Available from www.armenpress.am/.

Azg Newspaper. Available from www.hntchak.com/newsarm.html

Bardakjian, K.B. *The Mekhitarist Contributions to Armenian Culture and Scholarship*. Cambridge: Harvard College Library, 1976.

Bedikian, A. A. *The Golden Age in the Fifth Century: an Introduction to Armenia*. New York: Literature in Perspective, 1963.

Berberin, H. *Armenians and the Iranian Constitutional Revolution of 1905-1911*. Boulder, CO: Westview Press, 2001.

The Central Intelligence Agency (CIA). *International Economic Statistics*. Washington, D.C.: GPO, 2001.

The Central Intelligence Agency (CIA). *World Factbook 2001*. Directorate of Intelligence, 2002. Available from www.cia.gov/.

Chaqueri, C. *The Armenians of Iran: The Paradoxical Role of a Minority in a Dominant Culture, Articles and Documents*. Cambridge, MA: Harvard University Press, 1998.

European Institute of the Media. *Media in the CIS*. Duesseldorf, Germany: European Institute of the Media, 1997. Available from www.internews.ras.ru/books/media/contents.html.

Hovannisian, R.G. *The Republic of Armenia*. Berkley: University of California Press, 1996.

International Monetary Fund Report on Armenia. Washington, D.C.: IMF Economic Reviews, 1993.

Media in Armenia. Soros, 1997. Available from soros.org/armenia.at/archive97/world.html.

Nercessian, R. *Armenia.* Santa Barbara, CA: ABC-Clio, 1993.

Noyan Tapan Information and Analytical Center. Available from noyan-tapan.am/.

Open Society Assistance Foundation-Armenia. Available from www.soros.org/natfound/armenia/.

Suny, R.G. *Looking Toward Ararat: Armenia in Modern History.* Bloomington: Indiana University Press, 1993.

Sussman, L.R. and K.D. Karlekar, eds. *Annual Survey of Press Freedom.* New York: Freedom House, 2000.

Toloyan, Khachig. ''Elites and Institutions in the Armenian Diaspora.'' *Diaspora.* Vol. 9, no. 1. Toronto: University of Toronto Press, 2000.

UNESCO. *Annual Statistical Yearbook.* Paris, France: Institute for Statistics, 1999.

United States Agency for International Development. *Armenia.* Washington, D.C.: GPO, 2000.

World Radio TV Handbook (WRTH) : The Directory of International Broadcasting. Vol. 56. Milton Keynes, UK: WRTH Publications Limited, 2002.

Yerevan Press Club. August 2002. Available from www.ypc.am/.

—Keith Knutson

ARUBA

BASIC DATA

Official Country Name:	Aruba
Region (Map name):	Caribbean
Population:	69,539
Language(s):	Dutch, Papiamento, English, Spanish
Literacy rate:	97%

Located off the coast of Venezuela, the Caribbean island of Aruba is an autonomous member of the Kingdom of the Netherlands. Formerly part of the Netherlands Antilles, it seceded in 1986 and began moving toward full independence—a move it chose to halt in 1990. The population is estimated at 70,000 with a 97 percent literacy rate. The official language is Dutch, but Spanish, English, Portugese and Papiamento, a derivation of Spanish, are also spoken. The government is based on Dutch traditions. The Dutch monarch selects the Governor; the Prime Minister is appointed by the Staten, who in turn are elected by a popular vote. Tourism is by far the largest source of revenue for Arubans, followed by oil and gold.

Freedom of the press, as guaranteed under Dutch law, is observed in Aruba. Aruba has five major newspapers. The *Corant* newspaper publishes in Papiamento, as do the more widely read daily newspapers, *Diario Aruba* and *Bon Dia Aruba,* which is also published online. *The News* and *Aruba Today* both appear in English—*Aruba Today* is published by the same company that produces *Bon Dia.*

There are no Dutch-language newspapers published on the island, but three titles that originate from the neighboring island of Curacao, in the Antilles, distribute in Aruba and dedicate special sections and reporters to its news and events. The most widely read of these newspapers are *Amigoe,* a daily print and online newspaper that debuted in 1884, *Algemeen Dagblad,* a daily, and *De Curacaosche Courant,* a weekly.

Four AM and six FM stations broadcast to approximately 50,000 radios. One television station reaches approximately 20,000 televisions. Aruba's only Internet service provider is Setar, the government-operated telephone company.

BIBLIOGRAPHY

Amigoe, 2002 Home Page. Available from http://www.amigoe.com.

''Aruba.'' *Aruba On-line 2001.* Available from http://www.arubatourism.com.

''Aruba.'' *CIA World Fact Book 2001.* Available from http://www.cia.gov.

''Aruba.'' *KrantNet, 2002.* Available from http://www.krantnet.f2s.com.

Bon Dia, 2002 Home Page. Available from http://www.bondia.com.

Diario Aruba, 2002 Home Page. Available from http://www.diarioaruba.com.

—Jenny B. Davis

AUSTRALIA

BASIC DATA

Official Country Name:	Australia
Region (Map name):	Oceania
Population:	19,357,594
Language(s):	English, native languages
Literacy rate:	100.0%
Area:	7,686,850, sq km
GDP:	390,113 (US$ millions)
Number of Daily Newspapers:	48
Total Circulation:	3,030,000
Circulation per 1,000:	196
Number of Nondaily Newspapers:	233
Total Circulation:	374,000
Circulation per 1,000:	24
Newspaper Consumption (minutes per day):	35
Total Newspaper Ad Receipts:	581 (Euro millions)
As % of All Ad Expenditures:	41.60
Number of Television Stations:	104
Number of Television Sets:	10,150,000
Television Sets per 1,000:	524.3
Television Consumption (minutes per day):	177
Number of Cable Subscribers:	1,305,600
Cable Subscribers per 1,000:	68.0
Number of Radio Stations:	608
Number of Radio Receivers:	25,500,000
Radio Receivers per 1,000:	1,317.3
Radio Consumption (minutes per day):	138
Number of Individuals with Computers:	8,900,000
Computers per 1,000:	459.8
Number of Individuals with Internet Access:	6,600,000
Internet Access per 1,000:	341.0
Internet Consumption (minutes per day):	6

BACKGROUND & GENERAL CHARACTERISTICS

In its infancy Australian communication was dominated by a single goal—to improve connections to the motherland, Great Britain. Even though Australia had already been joined with Britain via overseas cable in 1863, it was not until 1910 (38 years later) that it was linked via cable to the rest of its own Pacific region. The Australian federal government focused time, money, and attention on communicating with Europe rather than with the more remote regions of Australia. Press coverage and broadcast media programming reflected a Eurocentric outlook. The later twentieth century, however, saw the increased presence of aboriginal people in the media and greater coverage of the Asia-Pacific region. Long influenced by British, continental and American trends, Australia began to come into its own as a media force.

The Nature of the Audience Literacy rates in Australia are very high, with 100 percent of those over 15 able to read and write. English is the primary language, but a number of aboriginal languages are spoken as well. Caucasians make up 92 percent of Australia's population, Asians 7 percent, and aboriginal and other racial groups 1 percent.

Australia is a democratic, federal-state system that recognizes the British monarch as sovereign. The Australian judiciary system is based upon English common law. Although Australia is the world's smallest continent, it is the sixth-largest country. Its population is concentrated along the eastern and southeastern coasts.

Newspaper History The first newspaper in Australia was the *Sydney Gazette and NSW Advertiser*. A government-controlled weekly, its first issue was produced on March 5, 1803. The printer and editor was former convict George Howe. At that time and for several decades to come, the British colonial governors had absolute control not only of the penal colonies of Australia, but also its print publications. Total censorship was lifted around 1825 and a few independent newspapers began in urban areas. One of the earliest was the Sydney Morning Herald, which became the sole property of the Fairfax family during the 1850s and which remains under their control. In 1856, the company became known as John Fairfax and

Sons. After World War II, the Fairfax group moved into broadcast media by purchasing radio and television interests. A new newspaper, The Australian, began publication on July 15, 1964. In 2002 it remained the only national newspaper for general interest news.

In the mid-1980s, metropolitan daily newspapers in Australia experienced a rash of acquisitions and mergers. During this period, of the 18 urban newspapers, 12 changed ownership; three of them changed ownership twice. Also in the mid-1980s changing ownership affected all Australian commercial television broadcasters. By the end of the 1980s Rupert Murdoch's News Corp claimed 60 percent of the national television audience, while Fairfax Television Properties had only 20 percent. During this period financial transactions involving both print and television properties allowed the marketplace, rather than government strategic planning, to determine media ownership.

Top Ten Daily Newspapers
(2000)

	Circulation
Herald Sun	545,000
Daily Telegraph	412,000
Sydney Morning Herald	223,000
Courier Mail	212,000
West Australian	206,000
The Advertiser	200,000
The Age	191,000
The Australian	133,000
Australian Financial Review	93,000
The Mercury	49,000

Source: World Association of Newspapers and Zenithmedia, *World Press Trends 2001*, p. 42.

Australia's Coverage of the Pacific Region Prior to World War II there was relatively little coverage of the Pacific region by Australian newspapers or radio. Following the war, the coverage expanded dramatically, but there has been a continued trend to focus on disasters and political turmoil in the region. As Anthony Mason points out in his article "Coups and Conflict," "Essentially, the Australian media is only interested in covering the Pacific if it involves a coup, a conflict, or a natural disaster. The only positive stories are primarily related to tourism" *(57)*. Mason also describes the media outlets in Australia, New Zealand, and other industrialized nations that engaged in "Parachute Journalism." This refers to the practice of sending reporters into a media hot spot only for the time needed to cover an event. Currently some Australia media such as The Australian, The Australian Broadcast Corporation (ABC), and the Special Broadcasting Service (SBS) have full time or senior correspondents responsible for the Pacific region.

Number of Newspapers by Circulation Groups In Australia in 2000, there were a total of 48 daily newspapers consisting of 10 metropolitan, 2 national and 36 regional papers. There were 10 Sunday newspapers.

The largest newspaper in Australia is the *Herald Sun,* published in Victoria by the Herald and Weekly Times, a News Corp property. It is a tabloid with a circulation of over half a million. The second largest is the tabloid *Daily Telegraph* of New South Wales, published by Mirror Australia Telegraph Publications, also a News Corp holding. Its average circulation is 412,000. The *Sydney Morning Herald* of New South Wales, published by John Fairfax Publications, is the third largest newspaper. It is a broadsheet with a circulation of 223,000. The fourth largest is *Courier Mail* of Queensland, published by Queensland Newspapers, a News Corp property. It is a broadsheet with a circulation of 212,000. The tabloid *West Australia,* located in Western Australia, is the fifth largest newspaper. It is published by West Australian Newspapers and has a circulation of 206,000. The sixth largest is *The Advertiser,* located in South Australia, and published Advertiser Newspapers, a News Corp property. It is a tabloid and the average circulation is 200,000. The broadsheet *The Age,* of Victoria, is the seventh largest newspaper. Published by John Fairfax Publications, its circulation is 191,000. The eighth largest is *The Australian,* published by Mirror Australia Telegraph Publications, a News Corp holding. It is a broadsheet, and circulation averages 133,000. The ninth largest newspaper is the *Australian Financial Review,* published by John Fairfax Publications. It is a tabloid and average circulation is 193,000. The tabloid *The Mercury,* of Tasmania, published by Davies Bros., a News Corp property, is Australia's tenth largest newspaper. It has a circulation of 49,000.

Top Media Companies

News Corp Limited News Corp is a highly diversified global corporation that engages in the production and distribution of audiovisual products in Australia, the United States, Europe, and Asia. News Corp has interests in motion pictures, television programming, satellite and cable broadcasting systems, the publication of newspapers, magazines, and books, and the production of online programming. The major properties of News Corp in the United States are Twentieth Century Fox Movie Studios, Fox Television Network, Fox All-News Network, and various book publishers. Many American movie and television productions appear in Australian theaters or on commercial television channels as part of News Corp's global marketing strategy.

Daily and Non-Daily Newspaper Titles and Circulation Figures

	1996	1997	1998	1999	2000
Number of Daily Newspapers	49	49	48	48	48
Circulation of Dailies (000)	3,121	3,120	3,107	3,083	3,030
Number of Non-Daily Newspapers	148	235	244	229	233
Circulation of Non-Dailies (000)	NA	NA	NA	NA	NA

Source: World Association of Newspapers and Zenithmedia, *World Press Trends 2001*, pp. 8, 10, 17, 19. Note: NA stands for not available.

News Corp makes about 25 percent of its profits from global businesses, with fully 75 percent of that coming from its U.S. investments. News Corp global revenues are about $15 billion (U.S.) annually.

A major News Corp property is Fox Studio Australia. Fox Studio is a multi-use facility and movie studio. Located on a 60-acre site, it includes entertainment, shopping, and dining and sponsors a number of events. It is the only Twentieth Century Fox studio outside the United States, and has offered complete services for major international films such as *Moulin Rouge*, *Star Wars Episode 2*, *Babe 2*, and *The Matrix*.

News Corp owns several newspapers across Australia in both large and small markets. It also operates Fox Sports Australia. In addition, News Corp owns 25 percent of FOXTEL, a pay television service offering a number of movie, sports and news channels. FOXTEL began operation in 1995 and is available via cable or satellite to more than 70 percent of Australians.

Media magnate Rupert Murdoch and his family hold about 30 percent of the company's shares. He was born in 1931 in Melbourne to newspaper manager and editor Sir Keith Murdoch. Sir Keith was a working journalist in both England and Australia and ultimately managed a chain of Australian newspapers headquartered in Adelaide, Australia, which later became News Corp's world headquarters.

Sir Keith died in 1952 and the control of two of his newspapers passed to his young son, Rupert Murdoch. Rupert attended Oxford and had just finished apprenticeships in England at the *Birmingham Gazette* and Fleet Street's *Daily Express* when his father died. The two newspapers in Australia that he inherited were the *Adelaide News* and a Sunday paper, the *Weekly Times*. Rupert Murdoch quickly turned the *Adelaide News* into a financial success and in the late 1950s he expanded the company with the profits. He bought the *Perth Sunday Times*, started the successful *TV Week*, and in 1958 he entered the television business.

In the 1960s Murdoch expanded his print properties with the purchase of the Cumberland newspapers as well as the *Sydney Daily* and the *Sunday Mirror*. Over time he added more magazines, book publishers, film and record companies in Australia.

During the 1970s Murdoch began buying properties in England, most notably BSkyB satellite system. In the United States he established a major media presence with purchase of Twentieth Century Fox movie studios, Fox Television Network, and other properties. News Corporation was established as a public company in 1979. In 1985, Murdoch became a U.S. citizen in order to meet regulatory requirements for the purchase of Federal Communication Commission controlled licenses for the U.S. television industry. He expanded into Asia with Star TV, a satellite based system that broadcast across many nations, particularly India and China, acquiring 64 percent of it in 1993. In 2002 Star TV posted a profit for the first time. Rupert Murdoch's youngest son, James Murdoch, and his Chinese-born wife, Wendy Ding, run Star TV jointly. Rupert Murdoch's daughter Elisabeth served as general manager of BSkyB in the 1990s but has since left the company. She continues to be involved in mass media by running her own production company. The eldest son, Lachlan, is a senior executive at News Corp.

In addition to its broadcast media holdings, News Corp also controls Harper Collins Publisher and also owns Triangle Publications, which publishes *TV Guide* and global magazines such as *Seventeen*. Murdoch also has made major investments in the Internet and is attempting to link his diverse print media for Internet traffic and sales. News Corp has been particularly active in developing Web sites for its major properties in Australia and elsewhere. Approximately 50 percent of News Corp's revenues come from electronic media properties and the balance from print media, with the bulk of the profits for the global corporation currently coming from holdings in the United States.

John Fairfax Publications Fairfax Community Newspapers has 28 community publications located mainly in Australian urban regions. The company dates back to 1865 and publishes some of the oldest community newspapers in Australia.

APN News and Media APN is Australia's largest operator of regional newspapers, radio broadcasting and outdoor advertising, with interests in specialist publishing, pay television and the rapidly expanding digital market.

APN was listed on the Australia Stock Exchange for the first time in 1992. At this time it was a publisher of regional newspapers in Queensland and NSW.

Rural Press Limited Rural Press is a specialist agricultural and regional publisher. Its first publication was *The Land*, launched in 1911 by a group of people who felt that farmers and grazers needed a strong advocate in the face of agriculture's falling political power. *The Land* is the principal carrier of information to people whose lives and work revolve around the Australia land. The Rural Press is dedicated to enhancing the economic, political and social well being of the rural and regional communities throughout Australia.

The Rural Press also serves rural people in New Zealand and the United States. Rural Press operates three principal divisions: Agricultural Publishing, Regional Publishing, and Printing. The Agricultural Publishing Division produces a range of weekly and monthly newspapers that serve Australia and New Zealand's primary producers and agribusinesses.

West Australian Newspapers Limited West Australian Newspapers is the publisher of *The West Australian* and 19 other West Australia regional newspapers. *The West Australian* was first published in 1833. Still in existence, the newspaper sells about 210,000 copies Monday through Friday and 385,000 for the weekend edition on Saturdays, which has more than one million readers. The principal activities of the WA Newspapers consist of newspaper publishing, commercial printing and radio communications.

Trading Post Group Trading Post Group's *The Melbourne Trading Post* was founded in 1966. In 1968, both the *Sydney Metropolitan Trading Post* and the *Personal Trading Post* in Brisbane commenced publication. Today, the Trading Post Group publishes 11 Trading Post publications around Australia as well as *Autotrader* in Perth, *Buysell* in Sydney, *Collectormania* and the leading Web site tradingpost.com.au. The group is also now part of Trader.com, a global leader in classified advertising.

ECONOMIC FRAMEWORK

Overview of the Economic Climate & its Influence on Media Australia has a free-enterprise market economy. Australian media operates in a mixed ownership milieu with both public sector media outlets such as ABC, and private sector commercial properties. These two sectors are highly professional, competitive, and seek long-run strategies to remain competitive in the greater Asian pacific region. Because the media depend upon advertising revenue as a major source of income, they depend upon a healthy economy in order to prosper.

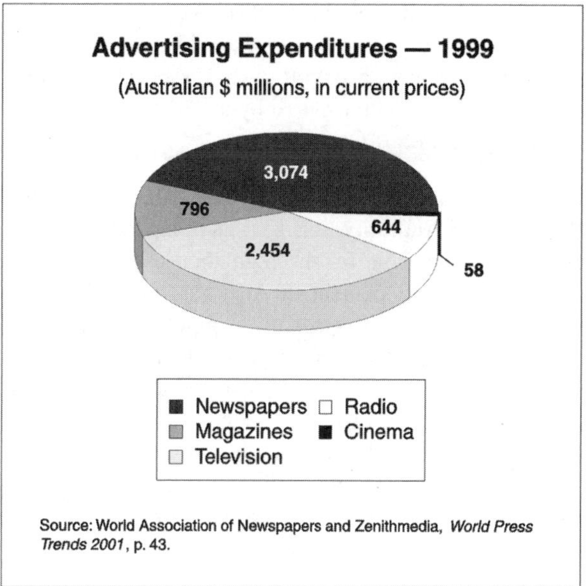

Source: World Association of Newspapers and Zenithmedia, *World Press Trends 2001*, p. 43.

Newspaper Chains & Cross Ownership Prime Minister Howard's federal government in Australia announced in 2002 a new cross media ownership bill. The bill sought to mandate that print newspapers and television stations owned by the same owner must maintain separate decision making structures, such as journalists and editors. This provided for two separate bureaus even in the same city in order to have distinct editorial staff, policy, and guidelines. Although technologies were converging, particularly with digital formats, it is interesting to note that Australia was attempting to maintain the old analog distinction between content and carrier. The chairman of the Australian Broadcasting Company, David Flint, was responsible for examining companies with multiple operations in the same city to ensure that they were complying with the recent legislation.

PRESS LAWS

As a result of the Australian media's early focus on European news and affairs, the expansion of radio, cable and other wireless technologies across Australia was not a federal priority. However, this did leave room for urban areas to continue to rely on newspapers for their national news. For international news these papers depended upon the Reuters cable feed from London and once again a Eurocentric slant was the prism through which Australians saw the world, even though geographically they were in the Pacific rim.

The 1993 Racial Vilification Legislation, which came into effect in October 1995, provides for complaints about the accuracy of the portrayal of Aboriginal people in the media. It is administered by the Human Rights and Equal Opportunities Commission.

Federal Government Activities The Australian Broadcasting Authority (ABA) is an independent federal authority responsible for the regulation of radio, television, and Internet content in Australia. One of ABA's major activities is overseeing compulsory regulatory standards in regards to commercial television with Australian content. These rules are designed to promote Australian culture, history, and ideas, and to provide employment for Australians in the audiovisual industries. They were created because of the growth and domination of American content, particularly during prime time hours. These objectives to provide an Australian identity and promote cultural diversity have sometimes been questioned by commercial television operators. Standards that took effect on March 1, 1999, call for 55 percent of all programming broadcasts on an annual basis to be Australian in creation or in content. There are also specific rules concerning children's educational programming and content. Certain provisions permit some New Zealand programming to be counted as part of the Australian quota.

The ABA's oversight for radio involves monitoring and assistance with technical planning and the assignment of the broadcast service band. The ABA commenced a study in 1992 to completely reframe radio broadcasting services across Australia. The report was completed in 2001, but with the introduction of new services, particularly digital and audio broadcasts via the Internet, much of the study had been rendered obsolete.

Created by the Australian government, the Federal Department for Indigenous Affairs protects indigenous people and their cultures. This includes not only promoting indigenous art and ceremonies, but also returning to original Aboriginal owners land that was confiscated by British and Australian authorities in past centuries.

Aboriginal Media The treatment of aboriginal people throughout Australia's history is a topic of much contention. Much of the information about the treatment and handling of Aboriginals is contained in the 1991 Royal Commission into Aboriginal Deaths in Custody. In general, the media coverage of Aboriginals and Aboriginal issues has focused on negative news. Because of the Eurocentric nature of the early history of Australia, concepts of race, class, and what constitutes appropriate behavior were imported from Europe and imposed on the Aboriginals.

The 1991 Royal Commission made four recommendations concerning the role of the media in terms of the broader Aboriginal environment in Australia. These recommendations were:

- Recommendation 205. That (a) Aboriginal media organizations should receive adequate funding where necessary in recognition of the importance of their function; (b) all media organizations should be encouraged to develop codes and policies relating to the presentation of Aboriginal issues, the establishment of monitoring bodies, and the putting into place of training and employment programs for Aboriginal employees in all classifications.
- Recommendation 206. That the media industry and media unions be requested to consider the establishment of and support for an annual award or awards for excellence in Aboriginal affairs reporting to be judged by a panel of media, union and Aboriginal representatives.
- Recommendation 207. That institutions providing journalism courses be requested to: (a) Ensure that courses contain a significant component relating to Aboriginal affairs, thereby reflecting the social context in which journalists work, and, (b) Consider in consultation with the media industry and media unions the creation of specific units of study dedicated to Aboriginal affairs and the reporting thereof.
- Recommendation 208. That in view of the fact that many Aboriginal people throughout Australia express disappointment in the portrayal of Aboriginal people by the media, the media industry and media unions should encourage formal and informal contact with Aboriginal organizations, including Aboriginal media organizations where available. The purpose of such contact should be the creation on all sides of a better understanding of issues relating to the media treatment of Aboriginal affairs (McKee 11-12).

There are some examples of positive media coverage. In 1994 ABC television produced a drama series entitled *Heartland*. It had a cast that consisted of Aboriginals as well as non-Aboriginals. It examined the reconciliation between Aboriginal and non-Aboriginal Australians and through its various episodes dealt in a sensitive way with the different approaches and hopes of both groups and their cultures. Following the Royal Commission, a Council for Aboriginal Reconciliation was established. One of its main tasks was to brief media organizations, editors, and journalists about Aboriginal history, culture, languages, people, and future goals.

In the early 2000s, the indigenous media sector in Australia was one of the fastest growing. The National Indigenous Media Association of Australia (NIMAA) promotes the fight against racism and exclusion and establishes a National Aboriginal broadcasting authority across Australia. The NIMAA reported that there were almost 100 community radio stations that carry at least some Aboriginal community programming. Some community television programming exists as well. However, Aboriginals were most often those listening to Aboriginal radio or reading Aboriginal newspapers with relatively little crossover to non-Aboriginal groups.

In 1978 the Video Education Australasian (VEA) was created. It produces and markets video with two educational institutions across Australia and the Pacific region. VEA produces a number of videos dealing with indigenous Australians. The group promotes Aboriginal bands, Aboriginal books for children, Aboriginal civil rights, Aboriginal history and other educational programs for Australians as well as the international education market. VEA currently has 58 items dealing with Aboriginal themes.

In 1987 ABC television created a division entitled Aboriginal Programs Unit, which it later renamed the Indigenous Programs Unit. It produced a number of documentaries such as *First Australians* and *Indigenous Current Affairs Magazine*. ABC's employment policy strives for Aboriginal representation in 2 percent of its labor force. Currently it exceeds this goal. As a minority group, Aboriginals for the past number of years have received significant coverage across all media, but a substantial amount of the coverage is negative, focusing on crime, unemployment, and other problems.

CENSORSHIP

Australia has a long and mixed history in terms of censorship. From the early twentieth century there was a federal government censor office, which rated a vast array of print and video materials, ranging from movies to greeting cards. In 1956 a Film Censorship Board was established to classify movies and later video. In 1988 this board was replaced by a broader Office of Film and Literature Classification (OFLC) with a full time chief censor reporting to the Attorney General's office. The censorship classification system proved controversial and calls for reform were constant. A new set of guidelines was enacted in 1999 but they turned out to be more restrictive. In 2000, after the Office banned a popular art film entitled *Romance*, there were additional criticisms of the entire censorship process. In 2002 new legislation was being debated concerning Internet censorship issues as the activities of the OFLC have continued to attract critics.

In addition to the OFLC there is a separate category and process for television. Under this structure, which is the responsibility of the Australian Broadcasting Authority, television stations report to the Minister for Communications.

Press Councils The Australia Press Council (APC) was established in 1976 as the self-regulatory body for Australian print media. It has two goals: to help preserve the freedom of the press and to encourage the free press to act ethically and responsibility. In order to accomplish these goals there is a formal complaint mechanism. Participating newspapers and magazines fund the APC, and a 21-member council that represents publishers, journalists, and public members runs it.

The APC is concerned with the need to balance individuals' rights to privacy with the media's goal of informing the public about significant issues that are in the public interest. The council is also active in promoting discussion concerning the role and necessity of press freedom as well as educational initiatives including an APC fellowship, along with a number of public forums and publications detailing current media issues.

Freedom of Information Acts The Western Australia Freedom of Information Act 1992 (F01) gives Australians the right to apply for access to government documents. There is also an Information Commission that in 1993 set up the Freedom of Information regulations.

STATE-PRESS RELATIONS

A major new Broadcasting Act was passed in 1942. The same year, the government created the Gibson Committee, which sought to make recommendations to control the growth of radio in a more orderly fashion for both the private and public sectors. The Gibson Committee made a series of recommendations, of which one was implemented in 1948, amending the 1942 Broadcasting Act to create the Australian Broadcast Control Board (ABCB). It was charged with regulating and controlling broadcasting in order to ensure that adequate radio, television and other communication services were developed to serve the public interest.

In 1953, a Royal Commission on Television was created. The Australian television industry began to dominate public discussion about the mass media as well as federal government policy from that time onward. The witnesses called to appear before the Royal Commission were split between those who advocated an almost purely commercial television network across Australia and those opposed to such a concept. The latter group promoted a single, national, publicly financed television system, like England's BBC television, with no commercials at all. The final report of the Commission contained 68 recommendations. The report led to the awarding of commercial licenses in both Sydney and Melbourne. ABC television was given public stations in both major cities about the same time. From the start, the commercial television stations were dominated by existing newspaper barons. The young Rupert Murdoch communicated with the Royal Commission, on the side of promoting the introduction of commercial television in Australia. It did not take long before there was a public concern over the number of American shows on the commercial television stations, which led to the formation of the Vincent Committee in 1993. Its report, known as the Report of the Senate Select Committee on the Encouragement of Australia Productions for Television, examined the situation. The proposals in the report were for Australian content quotas and greater concern for the cultural impact of television across Australia.

In the early 2000s the question of television licenses was a major policy issue that remained unresolved. At that time there were three major national commercial television channels—Seven, Nine, and Ten. The Australian Communications Minister, through the Australian Broadcasting Authority, mandated a moratorium on new commercial television licenses until 2007. In an era of deregulation, privatization, and liberalization, this policy came under increasing criticism, including criticism from other federal departments such as the Australian Treasury and Finance Departments, and even from the Prime Minister's Office. Given the financial windfall that commercial television operators experienced, a number of organizations were eager to submit applications for new commercial licenses. They did not want to wait until 2007 while the current three commercial television networks enjoyed limited and restricted competition.

ATTITUDE TOWARD FOREIGN MEDIA

Foreign Media Holdings in Australia CanWest Global Communications Corporation of Canada has a major investment in Australian mass media. CanWest Global is an international media company with vast holdings of print and electronic media in Canada as well as television properties in Australia, New Zealand, and Ireland. CanWest Global has a 57.5 percent equity stake in Australia's TEN Television Network. The voting share of the parent company limits CanWest Global to 15 percent of the overall voting shares. It became involved in Australia broadcasting with TEN networks in 1998.

Regulation of Foreign Ownership Under government policy, all proposals for foreign companies to establish a newspaper, or acquire an interest of 5 percent or more of a newspaper, are subject to case-by-case examination by the Federal Treasurer.

The policy sets the following foreign ownership limits: for national and metropolitan newspapers, the maximum permitted foreign interest is 25 percent, while other unrelated foreign interests can have an additional 5 percent. For provincial and suburban newspapers (which are not usually published daily) foreign interests are limited to less than 50 percent for non-portfolio shareholders. These limits may be exceeded with approval from the Federal Treasurer. When this policy was introduced, the Federal Treasurer allowed existing foreign investors to remain in place.

NEWS AGENCIES

Domestic News Agencies The **Australian Associated Press** (AAP) was formed as a cooperative in the 1930s. The cooperative model for press bureaus is similar to the one utilized by the Associated Press of the United States. AAP was designed to provide overseas news from bureaus based in London and New York. Today AAP is the largest news and information association in Australia. AAP works through a national pool of journalists that have bureaus and share their collective input. They have also opened a bureau in Jakarta, Indonesia. AAP established a communication company in 1984 and in 1991 established a telecommunications company, the third largest in Australia.

Four different media groups own AAP. They are News Corp, Fairfax Group, Western Australia Newspaper, and Newspapers & the Harris Group. AAP offers digital artwork for advertising and timely racing and financial information for the growing Internet trade. The international operations of AAP include AsiaNet, which is based in Sydney, and represents a consortium of Pacific region news agencies. Their material is rewritten to suit the Australian AAP media outlets. AAP also operates AsiaPulse, a real time commercial intelligence and news service covering the Asia region. AAP offers a NewsCentre, a print monitoring service also available to business and government clients; MediaNet, a customized media list; NewsTrack, a 24-hour real-time international; and Australian news service via the Internet for subscribers.

BROADCAST MEDIA

State Policies Relating to Broadcasting The federal government delegates many regulatory matters to Australian Broadcasting Tribunal (ABT) and thus the Minister of Communication has considerable control over awarding licenses, policy, and control of strategic planning. During the 1970s and '80s the Australian Broadcast Act of 1942 was amended many times. In 1980 there was an investigation of Australian television content resulting in Television Program Standard 14, which mandates that 50 percent of prime time programs be Australian. In the 1990s, the introduction of pay television was a major policy issue. Several commercial television stations changed hands as did several metropolitan daily newspapers.

Television North Queensland was acquired in part by Canadian company Can West. Canadian Conrad Black purchased Fairfax Broadcasting, which had suffered financial problems for much of the 1980s.

The Broadcasting Service Act of 1992 replaced the much-criticized ABT with the Australian Broadcasting Authority (ABA). Under the new regime, both privatization and liberalization became more apparent across the media sectors. The philosophical movement toward deregulation being promoted by two prominent conservative politicians, Margaret Thatcher of Great Britain and Ronald Reagan of the United States, also made its way to Australia. Although there was continuing concern about Australian cultural policy and activities, the dominance of a market driven economy relegated cultural issues to a second tier.

During the closing decades of the twentieth century, immigration patterns shifted considerably in Australia. The net inflow of Asian immigrants clearly outpaced European immigrants. As result, coverage and concern about Asian affairs began to displace European affairs in the media. Also at this time Australian Aboriginals began to promote their lifestyle, culture, and creative activities, demanding greater coverage by the mainstream media in Australia, particularly the government-run media outlets. An investigation by the federal government in the 1980s into Aboriginal affairs and tactics of previous governments led to a major policy change, particularly in terms of the proper role and promotion of Aboriginal rights. This study was a Royal Commission and set the groundwork for future pro-Aboriginal legislation across Australian society, including, of course, the media. With the introduction of satellites, broadcasting took a major shift in Australia; both radio and television stations began to broadcast across Asia as part of their activities.

The Federation of Australian Commercial Radio Broadcasting (FARB) was established in 1930 to represent the interests of commercial radio broadcasting. It began with only 33 members and currently has 241 members, which represent 98 percent of commercial radio operators in Australia. In the 1990s, there were a series of mergers and in 2002, 38 radio operators controlled 80 percent of the market. These operators formed into 12 national networks. The commercial radio industry generated close to $800 million (Australian dollars) in advertising revenue in 1999-2000.

Special Broadcasting Service (SBS) is Australia's multicultural and multilingual public broadcaster, which began as an experiment in 1975. SBS Radio provides materials in 68 languages and is designed to reach the more than 2.5 million Australians whose native language is not English. It does this by producing over 650 hours of programming each week. Its mandate is to define, foster, and celebrate Australia's cultural diversity. It does this through radio and television programming which is intended to both entertain and educate. It is to be a reflection of Australia's multicultural society (particularly Aboriginals) and to promote understanding among different groups. More than 7.5 million Australians view SBS Television weekly. The programming is either Australian-produced or international programming, which focuses on other cultures, religions or issues.

Australia Broadcasting Corporation (ABC) Radio went on the air July 1, 1932. At that time ABC consisted of twelve outlets: two in Sydney, two in Melbourne, and one each in Brisbane, Adeline, Perth, and Hobart, with relay stations in four smaller cities. As with the British BBC, the early funding for this non-commercial radio came from a license fee for each radio. During the early years, all programming was live, and the stations were on the air only in the mornings and the evenings. A substantial amount of their programming consisted of news from Britain of weather, politics, stocks, and the ever-important shipping news. In terms of Australian content, recording studios were established to provide music and support orchestras. In addition, sporting events were covered ranging from cricket to local soccer matches. By the mid-1930s educational radio lessons were broadcast across Australia and became a major feature of ABC's activities. During this time the Australian Newspaper Proprietors Association also provided domestic and foreign news for the radio newsreaders.

When Great Britain entered World War II, Australia as a colony also entered the war and strict censorship followed. ABC produced programs aimed at boosting national spirits since the Japanese were overtaking major portions of Asia. During the war years ABC established a broadcasting unit in the Middle East to report on the actions of Australian troops. Also in 1942 the Australian Broadcasting Act was passed, giving the Cabinet Minister the right to direct broadcasting in the public interest. By 1946 ABC was required to broadcast Parliament, and in 1948 the license fee approach was changed. Future funds would come from an annual appropriation from Parliament.

ABC television was created in 1953 as a single national channel but with only two stations, one in Sydney and the other in Melbourne. Other television stations were added in other cities very quickly. Commercial television stations also went on the air during this period. ABC continued to attempt to create and reflect the diversity and perspectives of Australians. ABC television commissioned and supported children's programming, music and drama.

In the early 1980s, ABC radio began Aboriginal broadcasts and these shows increased greatly over time.

An Aboriginal Broadcasting Unit was created in 1987. During the same period Parliament pressed for more Australian dramas and series in prime time to balance the growing number of American shows during evening hours. In 1983 the Australian Broadcasting Corporation Act was passed, replacing the 1942 Act. The new act created a board to ensure ABC's objectivity and independence. In 1985 a Concert Music Department was created, reflecting the continuing subsidy to several world class orchestras and making ABC one of the biggest promoters of orchestral music in the English speaking world.

In the 1990s ABC began to focus its regional coverage on the Asian region, rather than Europe and Great Britain. News and public affairs continued to be the defining characteristic of ABC's media role. It has restarted its short wave radio service to Asia and provides Radio Australia to 110 rebroadcast partners across Asia via cable, satellite and the Internet.

ABC receives funding from two sources. The bulk of its funding comes from government appropriations that are an annual budgetary allocation from the tax revenue accumulated by the Australian National Government. A second source of revenue comes from the sale of goods and services, particularly reruns of popular ABC drama and comedy shows. In 1999-2000, ABC revenues were $678 million from the federal purse and $150 million from other sources. Financial concerns related to the movement from an analog transmission environment to a digital transmission environment. From time to time the Australian Senate establishes a select committee to investigate particular aspects of either ABC management or ABC operations in order to insure that the government's policies and objectives about public interest and nation building are maintained. Some critics are concerned about political pressure and threats to the independence of the ABC, since it is responsible to the federal Department of Communications, Information Technology and the Arts (DCITA). The cabinet minister for the department is responsible to the Australian Parliament for all of ABC's activities including budgetary and policy items.

ABC is working in a changing environment. The entire role and scope of government activities is being challenged in an era of liberalization and privatization. With technologies creating new services and distributors, ABC competes with many audiovisual suppliers, including the Internet, for a limited audience. ABC's federal funding, like many public broadcasters' around the world, has decreased by almost one third since the mid-1980s.

Television History In 1953 the Television Act created a national public service, ABC-TV, and approved issuing licenses for commercial stations as well. The commercial sector via TCN-9 broadcast the first television signal in September 1956. Two months later ABC broadcast television in Sydney, and two weeks after that in Melbourne. ABC made television service available in Brisbane by 1959, and in Adelaide, Perth and Hobart in 1960.

Early Australian television broadcast a number of important shows. One of these was *Melbourne Tonight*, which debuted on May 6, 1956. The legendary Graham Kennedy hosted the program. He continued to host this extremely popular variety show until 1975, when the Australian Broadcasting Control Board banned Kennedy from broadcasting live, claiming that he had used inappropriate language on live television. The variety show, in terms of format, mimicked aspects of the U.S. television legend Johnny Carson's *Tonight Show*. Another important early television show was entitled *Four Corners*. Modeled after a highly successful BBC program called *Panorama*, it was a public affairs program; with no national newspaper at that time in Australia, it dominated public debate about major national issues. The program touched on politically sensitive issues and often criticized the government of the day.

During the earliest years of television in Australia, American series and movies dominated almost 80 percent of the schedule. British TV comprised part of the balance, particularly BBC productions. Even when Australian television produced its own materials, sets, and shows, they frequently mimicked either U.S. or British video production models.

ELECTRONIC NEWS MEDIA

In the early 2000s in Australia there were well over 250 Internet Service Providers (ISPs) and nearly 8 million Internet users: There were 12 national and 8 foreign Internet news sources, ranging from Australian news and Bloomberg to One World. The number of Internet newspaper Web sites jumped from a mere 5 in 1997 to over 150 by the year 2000. Overall, Australian sites are not very popular compared with U.S. and British sites. Two notable exceptions are John Fairfax Holdings' widely respected f2 Network. The f2 Network consists of over 30 Internet sites, which are aimed at specific databases. Services range from car and house advertisements, career and business information, to entertainment and restaurant choices. Another notable web site is ABC online, which has other niche news sites such as Asia-Pacific and Indigenous affairs. ABC online also draws information from CNN, and BBC World Service, Reuters, and Agence France-Presse.

Today all of the Australian newspaper publishers are active in developing their own online interests. The newspapers' strategies consist of building strong traffic and revenues by focusing on revenue-generating services such as classifieds, finance, auctions and directories.

Some industry spokespeople have speculated that the long term success of online classifieds will have a negative impact on traditional newspaper classified pages.

EDUCATION AND TRAINING

In Australia there are a number of Research Institutes, such as:

- University of New South Wales Communication Law Center
- Melbourne CIRCIT Research Institute
- Griffith University, Brisbane
- Institute of Cultural Policy Studies
- Sydney University of Technology
- Center for Independent Journalism
- Australia Film, TV, and Radio School (Sydney)
- Publisher of Media Information Australia
- Course Concentrations MacQuarie University and Charles Stuart University
- Queensland University, long history in a Department of Journalism
- Deakin University Journalism Program
- University of Canberra Graduate International Communication Program

Journalism as a career in Australia is attracting a large number of people. Many have university degrees, frequently in journalism or communication. However, openings in media outlets are scarce, and there is a large group of qualified individuals seeking entry-level positions. As compared to the United States, where over 80 percent of the working journalists have university degrees, primarily in journalism, fewer than a third of Australians have a baccalaureate degree. The major media outlets accept hundreds of applications, but frequently only hire the top 10 or 20. Some of those selected for the highly coveted full time training positions have degrees in Journalism or Communication, while others have degrees in other areas. In Australia there are two main newspaper groups: Rupert Murdoch's News Corp, and Fairfax. They take the bulk of the university journalism graduates. There is still a debate as to whether journalism schools are teaching the appropriate skills, or whether degrees in some other areas such as economics, political science, or Asian studies might not be more appropriate. Since many of the established editors and managers of media outlets in Australia rise up through the ranks without journalism degrees, they often prefer experience to education. In Australia as elsewhere, there is criticism that university graduates have a background that is ideologically driven and intellectually rigorous, but that the graduates lack practical training in how to write or how to use equipment.

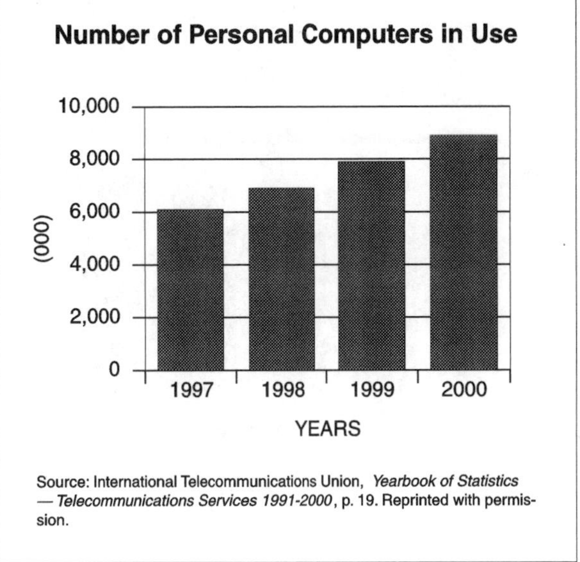

Source: International Telecommunications Union, *Yearbook of Statistics — Telecommunications Services 1991-2000*, p. 19. Reprinted with permission.

Australia's first professor of journalism was John Henningham, who retired as Professor of Journalism at the University of Queensland. His forte was providing writing skills needed for the media, rather than focusing on broader areas offered in programs with a media studies focus. Although journalism as a profession is not held in high esteem in Australia, many high school graduates are turning to university programs with a journalism orientation.

Five Major Journalism Programs

- Charles Stuart University (Bathurst, New South Wales). This program was founded in 1975 and is a mixture of theory and practice. A number of graduates have been placed in leading Australia media outlets.
- R.M.I.T University (Melbourne). Founded in 1972, this program has a strong liberal arts components and practical radio/newsroom training. The teaching staff includes a number of former Australian journalists.
- University of Queensland (Brisbane). This program was founded in 1921, making it the oldest in Australia. The program has a strong slant toward reporting and writing skills as well as a mix of professional courses dealing with law, ethics, theory, etc. It still retains the basic print orientation, with electronic media being electives.
- University of Southern Australia (Adelaide). This program, founded in 1973, has a practical focus, but also now teaches aspects of online journalism.
- University of Technology (Sydney). This program was founded in 1978. It aims to educate students

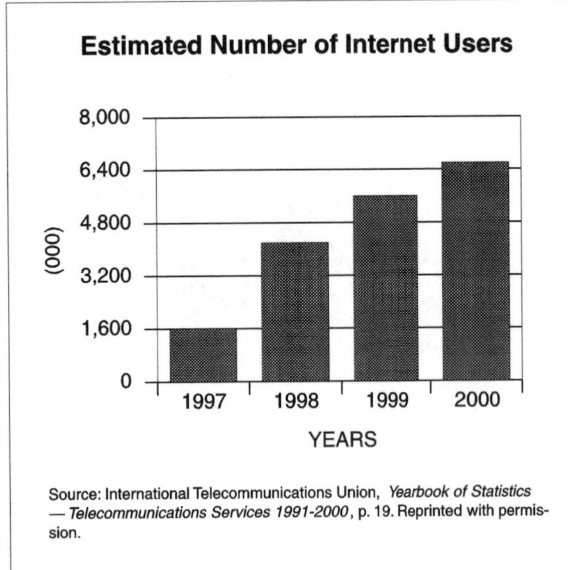

Source: International Telecommunications Union, *Yearbook of Statistics — Telecommunications Services 1991-2000*, p. 19. Reprinted with permission.

about the role media plays in a democratic society. It teaches critical thinking as well as the ethical and political aspects of the journalism discipline. A number of graduates serve as senior reporters for various Australian media outlets.

Journalism Education Association (JEA) The JEA was formed in 1975 by a small group of concerned journalism academics. The goals of the association are to raise the standard of teaching in journalism across Australia, as well as develop closer ties between mass media practitioners and the academic community. During its initial meetings, members discussed at length the transition for working journalists who, later in their careers, had become academics and were teaching journalism in Australia. As the association grew, it began to accept memberships and academic paper presentations from New Zealand and other countries in the Asian region. Their newsletter evolved into a journal known as the *Australian Journalism Review*. The association continues to grow in strength and importance particularly given the substantial number of universities that teach courses in journalism, communication, media studies, and film.

Two programs deserve particular mention. The first is the University of Wollongong. Its graduate School of Journalism offers coursework and a degree in English in Hong Kong. A Master of Journalism degree is available electronically through a variety of multimedia materials. Professors sometimes visit Hong Kong to work with students.

In 1973 the Australian government founded the Australian Film, Television, and Radio School (AFTRS), headquartered in Northwestern Sydney with branches in Melbourne and Brisbane. The school also has representatives in other cities across Australia. There are full time programs as well as part time programs and short courses. Most of the course work is at the post-Baccalaureate level. In part due to government funding, the full time program is only available to Australian citizens or legal permanent residents. A variety of courses ranging from script writing, cinematography, directing, and producing, to radio digital media, documentary and television are offered. Some course work is available online and in early 2000 AFTRS planned to introduce the Global Film School (GFS). The GFS is designed to become the premier film making school around the world by offering courses online. It is a joint partnership of UCLA, AFTRS, and the National Film and Television School (NFTS). The NFTS is a full time MA program, offering course work in ten specialized areas. This film school is British and has a long and prestigious history in the area of documentary filmmaking.

Journalistic Awards and Prizes In Australia the most prestigious awards for journalism are the annual Walkley Awards. The Walkleys were established in 1956 with five different categories. Each category has various subgroups. The three top prizes are the Gold Walkley, Most Outstanding Contribution to Journalism and Journalistic Leadership. There are several sub-categories for radio, television, print and wire services, and other media. Over the years, ABC Radio and Television have received several awards as well as have major newspapers such as *The Australian*.

SUMMARY

The Australian mass media has its origins in its strong ties to British press traditions. The early years of the press were dominated by censorship laws and controlled by British government agencies. In the twentieth century, with the arrival of greater competition, there was a lessening of government control and influence. The Australian press operates in a democratic environment. It also is served by a strong and attentive Australian Press Council.

Recently the Australian press has begun to include a larger role for Aboriginal media and issues. In addition, the Australian press is beginning to cover more of the Asia-Pacific region, leaving behind its historical preoccupation with Europe, particularly Great Britain, and the United States.

BIBLIOGRAPHY

Appleton, Gillian. *How Australia Sees Itself: The role of commercial television*. Sydney: Australia Broadcasting Tribunal, 1988.

Bell, Phillip and Roger Bell. *Implicated: The United States in Australia*. Melbourne: Oxford University Press, 1993.

Brown, Allan. *Commercial Media in Australia*. St. Lucia: University of Queensland Press, 1986.

Carmen Luke. ''Media and Cultural Studies in Australia.'' *Journal of Adolescence and Adult Literacy* 43:8 (1999): 622-626.

Craik, Jennifer, Julie James Bailey and Albert Moran. *Public Voices, Private Interests: Australia's media policy*. Sydney: Allen & Unwin, 1995.

Cunningham, Stuart. *Framing Culture: Criticism and culture in Australia*. Sydney: Allen & Unwin, 1992.

Cunningham, Stuart and Toby Miller. *Contemporary Australian Television*. Sydney: The University of New South Wales Press, 1994.

Hartley, John and Alan McKee. *The Indigenous Public Sphere*. Melbourne: Oxford University Press, 2000.

Holden, W.S. *Australia Goes to Press*. Detroit: Wayne State University Press, 1961.

Mason, Anthony. ''Coups and Conflict''. *Pacific Journalism Review*. Vol. 7, no. 1. 2001.

Mayer, H. *The Press in Australia*. Sydney: Landsdown Press, 1968.

McKee, Alan. *Australian Television: A genealogy of great moments*. Victoria: Oxford University Press, 2001.

McPhail, Thomas. *Global Communication: Theories, Stakeholders, and Trends*. Boston: Allyn & Bacon, 2002.

Osborne, Graeme, and Glen Lewis. *Communication Traditions in Twentieth century Australia*. Melbourne: Oxford University Press, 1995.

Prue, Torney-Parlicki. *Somewhere in Asia—War, Journalism and Australia's Neighbours 1941-75*. New South Wales: University Press Ltd., 2000.

Rohm, Wendy. *The Murdoch Mission*. New York: John Wiley, 2002.

Shawcross, William. *Rupert Murdoch: Ringmaster of the Information Circus*. London: Chateo and Windus, 1992.

Wilson, H, ed. *Australian Communications and the Public Sphere*. Melbourne: Macmillan, 1989.

World Press Trends. Paris: World Association of Newspapers (WAN), 2001.

—Thomas Lawrence McPhail, Ph.D.

AUSTRIA

BASIC DATA

Official Country Name:	Republic of Austria
Region (Map name):	Europe
Population:	8,150,835
Language(s):	German
Literacy rate:	98.0%
Area:	83,858 sq km
GDP:	189,029 (US$ millions)
Number of Daily Newspapers:	16
Total Circulation:	2,503,000
Circulation per 1,000:	374
Number of Nondaily Newspapers:	120
Newspaper Consumption (minutes per day):	57
As % of All Ad Expenditures:	31.10
Number of Television Stations:	45
Number of Television Sets:	4,250,000
Television Sets per 1,000:	521.4
Television Consumption (minutes per day):	221
Number of Cable Subscribers:	999,540
Cable Subscribers per 1,000:	123.4
Number of Satellite Subscribers:	1,450,000
Satellite Subscribers per 1,000:	177.9
Number of Radio Stations:	
Number of Radio Stations:	63
Number of Radio Receivers:	6,080,000
Radio Receivers per 1,000:	745.9
Radio Consumption (minutes per day):	61
Number of Individuals with Computers:	2,270,000

Computers per 1,000:	278.5
Number of Individuals with Internet Access:	2,100,000
Internet Access per 1,000:	257.6

BACKGROUND & GENERAL CHARACTERISTICS

As of the early 2000s, Austria had a population of eight million people; nearly a fifth of its residents lived in the capital, Vienna. The population was ethnically, religiously, and linguistically homogenous, 78 percent Roman Catholic and 98 percent German-speaking. The country was divided into nine provinces. In the west the Vorarlberg borders Switzerland; Tyrol borders Germany and Italy. Carinthia borders Croatia and Slovenia to the south. Styria and Burgenland are bounded by Hungary and Slovakia in the east. Lower Austria (Niederösterreich, which surrounds Vienna) borders the Czech Republic, and Upper Austria (Oberösterreich) borders Germany to the north. The Salzburg province lay between Tyrol and the other provinces, sharing a short border with the German state of Bavaria. About 300,675 aliens also resided in Austria, around 60 percent of them workers (or their descendants) from the former Yugoslavia or Turkey who came during the post World War II reconstruction era. A small Slovenian minority lived in southern Carinthia, and groups of Croatians and Hungarians lived in Burgenland.

Public education began in 1774 and became compulsory in 1869. As of 2002, the literacy rate was 98 percent. A high standard of living and a long life expectancy (eighty-one years for women, and seventy-five for men) created a strong market for print media. Three-fourths of Austrians read a daily paper, spending a half-hour to do so, and three-quarters of an hour on weekends. On average Austrians watched about two-and-one-half hours of television per day, considerably less than in the United States. Surprisingly high numbers of young Austrians read newspapers: 68.6 percent of those between the ages of 14 and 19, and 72.6 percent of young people between 20 and 24. The better educated and self employed are more likely to read newspapers (80-85 percent of them do so) than unskilled workers or those who lack secondary education, about two-thirds of whom read a daily paper. Beginning in 1995 a private association, *Zeitung in der Schule* (Newspapers in the Schools) encouraged mainstream readership by providing free subscriptions and instructional materials for school classes, serving 60,500 pupils in 2000-01.

The first printing press arrived in Vienna in 1483, spurring development of early newssheets and broadsides. *Der postalische Mercurius*, a twice-weekly paper which first appeared in 1703, soon became an official organ of government, and its descendant, the latter-day *Wiener Zeitung*, could thus claim to be the oldest daily newspaper continuing as of 2002 in existence.

The democratic revolution of 1848 sparked an explosion of newspapers; about 90 dailies soon appeared in Vienna. *Die Presse*, also later titled *Die neue freie Presse*, was founded in 1848 and survived the political repression which followed the unsuccessful revolution. Karl Marx contributed articles as the paper's London correspondent between 1861 and 1862. Censorship of the press was officially abolished in 1862, although true freedom of the press could not be warranted until nearly a century later. The paper attracted a liberal middle class audience, especially assimilated Jews who opposed the clerical, conservative press. The Zionist Theodor Herzl served as Paris correspondent and literary critic for *Die Presse* from 1891 to 1904. Suppressed by the Nazis in 1938, the paper continued as of 2002 as the oldest of the country's general-purpose quality newspapers, defining itself as conservative and politically independent.

In the second half of the nineteenth century, compulsory education, the resulting increase in literacy, coupled with industrialization, urbanization, and the rise of the social democratic movement created an increasing demand for newspapers. In 1889 the Socialist Party founded the *Arbeiter Zeitung*, whose circulation reached 100,000 in the 1920s. During the 1930s a much smaller version was printed in Czechoslovakia and smuggled into Austria. Sensational tabloids sprang up in the late 1800s, among them the *Illustrierte Kronen Zeitung*, Austria's largest daily paper as of 2002.

The Hapsburg monarchy ruled Austria from 1273 until the end of the World War I. The Austro-Hungarian Empire governed Hungary, parts of Poland, the Czech Republic, Slovakia, Romania, Italy, and much of the territory that in the early 2000s was called Slovenia, Croatia, Yugoslavia, and Bosnia-Herzegovina. Vienna, a capital city designed for an empire of 50 million, presided in 2002 over a federal republic of some eight million Austrians. The city boasted a long and prestigious tradition of theater, opera, and music. In the early 2000s, it was the nation's press capital as well, home of the largest newspapers, the national press agency, the journalists union, and press club.

Austria's modern press began to develop rapidly after World War I in the transition from the Hapsburg monarchy to a federal democracy. The lifting of a ban on street sales of newspapers in 1922 stimulated the rise of a tabloid press, and within a few years Austrian newspapers were circulating 1.5 million copies, of which 1.2 million were in Vienna. The Nazi takeover in 1938, however, suppressed political expression. Before that, *Die Presse* had been forced to cease publication because several of its editors were Jewish. The *Wiener Neueste Nachrichten* became the leading Nazi organ. Of the 22 dailies in Vienna at the time of the *Anschluss*, only four remained in operation at the end of World War II.

The victorious Allies divided Austria and its capital into four zones of occupation; the country did not regain full independence until 1955. The Allies set up newspapers in their zones of occupation, first the Soviets' *Österreichische Zeitung*, which appeared in April 1945. The American occupying powers established *Salzburger Nachrichten* and *Oberösterreichische Nachrichten* in their zone, and the French and Americans supported the *Tiroler Tageszeitung*. These three papers were soon transferred to Austrian ownership. The postwar period also saw the appearance of the *Kleine Zeitung*, re-founded in Styria and Carinthia by the Catholic Press Association. *Kurier*, launched by the Americans, was bought by an Austrian industrialist in 1954; for decades it was the country's second largest newspaper with a circulation of nearly a half million. With the exception of the Soviets' *Österreichische Zeitung*, all of these dailies continued to occupy a strong position in Austria in the early 2000s. The socialist daily *Express* was taken over by *Kronen Zeitung* in 1975, making that center-left newspaper larger than its rival, the right-wing *Kurier*. The small tabloid *Wiener Zeitung*, with a circulation around 30,000 in the 1970s, held exclusive rights to publish government notices and advertising until 1996.

Die Presse was re-founded in 1946 as a weekly paper in Vienna, and then in 1948 it resumed daily publication. The Federal Chamber of Commerce owned an 80 percent share in *Die Presse*, whose independence and journalistic freedom were nonetheless guaranteed. In 1985 it became the first European newspaper to install an electronic editing system, and in 1993 the paper introduced color photos and graphics. The Federal Chamber of Commerce withdrew from ownership in 1991, and Styria Verlag, publisher of the *Kleine Zeitung*, took over *Die Presse*. Two years later it adopted a smaller format, necessitated by print machinery, and the need to compete for kiosk display space with the smaller *Standard*, founded in 1988 as the youngest of the country's dailies continuing in existence as of 2002. In September 1996 *Die Presse* went online and rapidly gained readers, claiming 316,000 in 1997. Its liberal opposition stance meant boycotting the nationwide spelling reform in 1997 and publishing prices in Euros as well as Austrian schillings before the Euro replaced national currencies in 2002.

Political party ownership of newspapers appeared to be a safeguard against the type of censorship and propaganda which had existed under the Nazis, but the role of parties in the press declined throughout the second half of the twentieth century. The postwar period witnessed the appearance of *Neues Österreich*, published by the fledgling provisional Austrian government and its newly established political parties: the Christian Democrats, Socialists, and Communists. The conservative Austrian People's Party founded the *Kleines Volksblatt* (which ceased in 1970); the Socialists resumed publication of the *Arbeiter Zeitung*, and the Communists created the *Volksstimme*. *Neue Zeit* also began as a weekly owned by the Socialist Party in 1945 and was purchased by its employees in 1987. It had 16,000 subscribers and an estimated 80,000 readers in the late 1990s. Yet even a $2 million press subsidy from the federal government in 2000 did not suffice to prevent bankruptcy, and the paper ceased publication in 2001. The Socialists' *Arbeiter Zeitung*, begun in 1889, followed a similar path to independence as a left liberal paper in 1989 and was renamed *Neue Arbeiter Zeitung*, only to close for good two years later. The Austrian People's Party's (ÖVP) *Neue Volkszeitung* was sold to a private corporation in 1989, with the ÖVP retaining just a 10 percent share. In 1953 newspapers owned by political parties accounted for half of all circulation, while in 2002 for only 2.2 percent or 62,000 copies combined. Those papers remaining in party ownership were the two owned by the Austrian People's Party, *Neues Volksblatt* and *Salzburger Volkszeitung*, and the Socialists' *Neue Kärntner Tageszeitung*, which was managed and distributed by the largest Austrian media conglomerate, Mediaprint, from 1990 into the early 2000s.

Given its high concentration of population, Vienna is also Austria's press and media capital, with five daily general-purpose newspapers: *Neue Kronen Zeitung*, *Kurier*, *Die Presse*, *Der Standard*, *Wiener Zeitung* and the financial daily, *Wirtschaftsblatt*. *Krone*, (the newspaper's abbreviated title) published regional editions in Salzburg, Styria (Graz), Tyrol (Innsbruck), Oberösterreich (Linz), and Carinthia (Klagenfurt). *Kurier* published regional editions in Graz, Innsbruck, Linz, and Salzburg. Other cities large enough to have their own daily newspapers were (in order of size) Graz (*Kleine Zeitung*), Salzburg (*Salzburger Nachrichten*), Linz (*Oberösterreichische Nachrichten*), and Bregenz (*Vorarlberger Nachrichten* and *Neue Vorarlberger Tageszeitung*). *Salzburger Nachrichten* was the only national newspaper not headquartered in Vienna. Two federal states, Niederösterreich and Burgenland, depended on neighboring Vienna for their news and had no dailies of their own, although a short-lived daily, *Guten Tag Niederösterreich*, was launched in 1990.

By far the largest Austrian newspaper is Vienna's tabloid *Neue Kronen Zeitung*, also the most widely circulated Austrian newspaper abroad. It was published daily

Daily and Non-Daily Newspaper Titles and Circulation Figures

	1996	1997	1998	1999	2000
Number of Daily Newspapers	17	17	17	17	16
Circulation of Dailies (000)	2,382	2,500	2,669	2,896	2,503
Number of Non-Daily Newspapers	121	125	128	121	120
Circulation of Non-Dailies (000)	383	370	385	377	374

Source: World Association of Newspapers and Zenithmedia, *World Press Trends 2001*, pp. 8, 10, 17, 19.

and featured short articles that occupied less space than the numerous color photographs and cursory coverage of politics, culture, sports, and large numbers of classified ads. A photo of a naked female model always appeared on page six or seven. It sold over twice as many copies as its next closest rival, *Kleine Zeitung* (Graz). The tabloid *Kleine Zeitung* brought out more substantial news coverage, more international news of politics, economics, culture, and sports, and fewer color photos. In third place was *Kurier*. The country's most influential papers, those most widely quoted and distributed abroad, were *Die Presse*, *Der Standard*, and *Salzburger Nachrichten*. The latter was a standard sized independent paper, offering more color photos than *Die Presse* or *Der Standard* in its reports on politics, economics, and sports. Styria Media, Inc. published *Kleine Zeitung* and owned 51 percent of *Die Presse*. As of February 2001 it also owned 98 percent of Croatia's largest newspaper, *Vecernji List.*

Neue Kronen Zeitung's leadership in circulation and advertising revenues was occasionally challenged between 1985 and 2000. In April 1988 Oscar Bronner of Berlin's Springer publishing house, launched a new liberal daily, *Der Standard*, the first new daily in previous 16 years. *Der Standard* was a quality paper of standard format with a distinctive salmon-pink color, rivaling *Die Presse*. It appealed to a younger audience, claiming that 57 percent of its readers were under 40. It offered broad coverage of international news, economics, politics, culture, and a substantial editorial section on its last page. In 1992 a former owner of *Krone*, Kurt Falk, launched *Täglich Alles*, printed in four-color intaglio. *Täglich Alles* sold for three schillings at first, about a third the price of other tabloids, but it doubled in price five years later. It fought to gain readership by distributing free copies and offering games and prizes. It featured sensational headlines, a large television section, and took a strong stance opposing the European Union. A year after its start-up, it boasted 1.1 million readers, but soon it lost advertising revenue because of its sensationalism and political stance. It reached second place with 423,000 daily copies sold in 1998 but lost money and closed for good in August 2000, though it continued to appear online. In April 2001 *Neue Zeit*, with a subscription list of 26,000 and some 80,000 estimated readers, declared bankruptcy and folded. *Kleine Zeitung* gained the most in circulation with the demise of *Neue Zeit* and *Täglich Alles*.

Another new daily, *Wirtschaftsblat*, began publication in 1995 with an initial print run of 58,000, intending to compete with *Der Standard*. It was financed by an Austrian syndicate and the Swedish publishing group Bonnier and distributed by Mediaprint. It published financial and economic news Tuesdays through Saturdays and was available only by subscription.

Through the 1980s and 1990s, the media scene in Austria was characterized by shrinkage in the number of daily newspapers and increasingly overlapping ownership, with several major papers owned partially by foreign firms. In 1998 Austria had 17 dailies, or 28 titles (accounting for regional editions), with a total circulation estimated at 2.9 million. In 2002 Austria was home to 15 daily newspapers, a small number in relation to its population. Switzerland, with a slightly smaller population of 7,283,000 has 88, and Germany, whose population is 10 times the size of Austria's, has 375 daily papers. Even after Austria's entry into the European Union in 1995, foreign newspapers failed to gain a readership in Austria, despite the common language the country shares with Germany. Three-fourths of those who read a daily newspaper choose an Austrian publication.

Media development in the postwar age was characterized by a lack of political opposition, with overlapping membership in the political establishment, government, and big business. Not until the late 1970s did Austrian newspapers begin to investigate, question, and oppose government policies, such as those surrounding nuclear power and ecological issues. The Chernobyl catastrophe of 1986 and the resulting popular rejection of nuclear power in Austria resulted in increased environmental coverage and greater questioning of government decisions, a process strengthened by the formation of Austria's Green Party in the 1980s.

NEWS WEEKLIES

In the early 2000s, among Austria's 40-odd news weeklies were several regional newspapers with local news for rural areas less well served by the large national dailies. The two newspaper-format weeklies were *Niederösterreichische Nachrichten*, whose 27 local editions reach 10.7 percent of the weekly news market in Lower Austria, and *Oberösterreichische Rundschau* with 11 percent of the market in Upper Austria. Lower Austria (Niederösterreich), which surrounds Vienna, had no regional daily to compete with the larger city papers. Many other weeklies were political party organs, or published by the Catholic Church.

One special niche filled by weekly papers was to serve minority groups which spoke languages other than German. Klagenfurt in Carinthia was home to three Slovenian language weeklies, *Nedelja*, *Slovenski Vestnik*, and *Nas Tednik*. A Croatian language weekly, *Hrvatske Novine*, was published in Eisenstadt in Burgenland. These papers might receive special press subsidies or be partially supported by the Catholic Church.

Austria's weekly news magazines reflected the same pattern of consolidation under overlapping ownership as the country's dailies. *Profil* and *Trend*, founded in 1970, were the first Austrian news magazines to outsell such German publications as *Der Spiegel*. Kurt Falk, half owner of *Krone*, launched *Die ganze Woche* in 1985 and sold it in 2001 to a company owned by his sons. With a press run of 700,000 and a reach of 37 percent, it became the third largest mass-media organ in the country, after *Krone* and ORF, Austria's public radio monopoly. In the mid 1990s *Wochenpresse*, which reported weekly on economic news, ceased publication, and *Profil* moved further to the left along the political spectrum

Brothers Wolfgang and Helmut Fellner introduced *News*, then *TV-Media* and, around 1997, *Format*, which reported every Monday on news, politics, economics, and science. Three-fourths of Fellner publishing was then sold to Bertelsmann, (Germany's largest book publisher) with a 30 percent share in *News* then owned by Mediaprint (WAZ). *News* reached 19.3 percent of the market in 2000, *Format* 7.1 percent, and *Profil* another 9.4 percent. The rival weekly, *Trend*, reported on economics and sold about 64,209 copies weekly, with a market reach of 8.1 percent. In early 2001 *News* and *Trend /Profil* merged, giving Bertelsmann and WAZ control over 59 percent of the Austrian news weekly market.

ECONOMIC FRAMEWORK

Austria enjoyed economic stability and increasing prosperity after 1945. The most significant recent economic and political developments resulted from Austria's joining the European Union (1995) and adopting the EU's Euro as its official currency, in 2000 for banking and paper transactions, and for all trade and purchasing in 2002.

Top Ten Daily Newspapers
(2000)

	Circulation
Neue Kronen Zeitung	1,052,000
Kleine Zeitung	287,000
Kurier	270,000
U-Express	150,000
OÖ Nachrichten	127,000
Die Presse	123,000
Der Standard	119,000
Tiroler Tageszeitung	118,000
Salzburger Nachrichten	105,000
Vorarlberger Nachrichten	73,000

Source: World Association of Newspapers and Zenithmedia, *World Press Trends 2001*, p. 47.

The three largest newspapers, *Neue Kronen Zeitung*, *Kurier*, and *Kleine Zeitung* and *Oberösterreichische Nachrichten* were all tabloids, measuring approximately 9 by 12 inches and costing 9 or 10 schillings (US$.70 to US$.80). The quality papers read by the better educated and more affluent (*Die Presse*, *Der Standard*, and *Salzburger Nachrichten*) were about equal in size of readership and larger in format: about 12 by 18 inches. *Die Presse* cost the same price as the tabloids, while *Salzburger Nachrichten* and *Der Standard* cost about US$1.00 per issue. These three papers were distributed nationally by subscription, with a combined circulation of 321,000, or about 11.3 percent of the total national circulation of daily newspapers. *Kleine Zeitung* also touted that 93 percent of its copies were sold by subscription. The average monthly subscription in 2000 for six days of postal delivery cost around US$17.50, but the quality papers *Die Presse* and *Der Standard* cost about US$26 per month. Newspapers might be purchased as single copies at state-controlled tobacco shops or kiosks or subscribers might pick up their copies there, an arrangement that cost less than home delivery. The financial daily, *Wirtschaftsblatt*, which cost about US$1.50 per issue, was the most expensive of all.

Neue Kronen Zeitung, *Kurier*, and *Kleine Zeitung* dominated Sunday sales, since regional dailies and *Presse* and *Standard* did not publish on Sundays. The *Wiener Zeitung* did not publish Saturdays or Sundays and was available by subscription only. Many papers charged higher daily prices Wednesday through Saturday or on weekends.

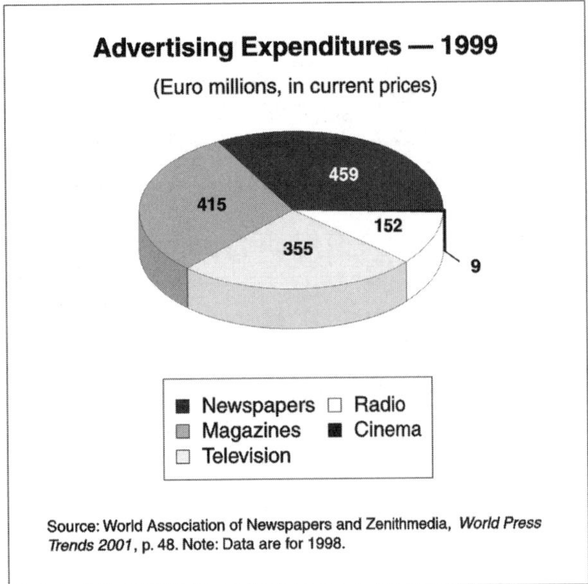

Source: World Association of Newspapers and Zenithmedia, *World Press Trends 2001*, p. 48. Note: Data are for 1998.

Austria's *Österreichische Auflagen Kontrolle* (Circulation Control, ÖAK,) was founded in 1994 to verify circulation counts for advertisers. In 2000 the ÖAK revised the way newspaper circulation was calculated and the *Neue Kronen Zeitung* and *Kurier* participated in the count for the first time. According to the revised definition, papers were evaluated by the number sold on weekdays during the third quarter of 2000. The findings indicated that *Neue Kronen Zeitung* sold the most with 874,442 copies reflecting 43.4 percent of the market.

In the mid-range of distribution was *Die Presse* (76,216 copies, 5.4 percent). The smallest distribution registered was for *Neue Vorarlberger Tageszeitung* (7,426 copies, 0.8 percent) (*VÖZ-Jahrbuch Presse 2001—Dokumentationen, Analysen, Fakten*, November 2001). Two small papers, whose circulation was estimated at 20,000-25,000, did not participate in the official circulation count: *Neue Kärntner Tageszeitung* (Klagenfurt) with a reach of 1.2 percent, and *Neues Volksblatt* (Linz).

Sources estimated that the *Neue Vorarlberger Tageszeitung* sold fewer than 10,000 copies. In the 10,000 to 25,000 circulation range there were two papers: *Salzburger Volkszeitung* and the *Wiener Zeitung*, which specialized for decades in government announcements and advertising. *Wirtschaftsblatt*, financial information from the Viennese stock exchange, was the only daily in the 25,000 to 50,000 bracket. Five newspapers sold between 50,000 and 100,000 copies: the two large format Viennese quality papers *Der Standard* and *Die Presse*, and *Tiroler Tageszeitung*, *Salzburger Nachrichten*, and *Vorarlberger Nachrichten*. Some 100 to 500 copies were sold daily by the *Oberösterreichische Nachrichten*, *Kurier*, and *Kleine Zeitung*. Only the *Neue Kronen Zeitung* sold over 500 copies per day.

The economic framework of Austrian newspaper publishing in 2002 had been shaped by a series of mergers and the advent of foreign media conglomerates during the 1980s and 1990s. Germany's *Westdeutsche allgemeine Zeitung* publishing group (WAZ) entered the Austrian market in November 1987, purchasing 45 percent of *Kronen Zeitung* and increased its share to 50 percent in 1993. With a print run of nearly 2 million per day and a 43 percent share of the market, *Krone* dominated the scene. *Westdeutsche allgemeine Zeitung* purchased 45 percent of *Krone*'s closest rival, *Kurier*, in 1988 and increased its share to 49 percent in 1993. By 1992 *Krone* and *Kurier* were also publishing regional editions for the provinces. Austrian media analysts referred to this concentration of media power in German hands as KroKuWAZ, an acronym blending *Krone*, *Kurier*, and *Westdeutsche allgemeine Zeitung*. In 1988 WAZ founded a company called Mediaprint, which managed and distributed these two major dailies, as well as the Socialists' smaller *Kärntner Tageszeitung*. The group bought a 74 percent share in the Viennese publisher *Vorwärts*, where the heavily indebted *Arbeiter Zeitung* was printed. That old Socialist daily was forced to cease in 1991. In 2002 Mediaprint employed a workforce of 3,500, and its papers reached over half of all Austrian newspaper readers.

Another major German player in the Austrian media market was Oscar Bronner, of Germany's Springer publishing group. In the 1960s he launched two weekly magazines, *Profil* and *Trend*. In 1988 he initiated the *Standard*, in which Germany's *Süddeutsche Zeitung* also owned a share. That paper originally reported on political and business news on days when the Viennese stock exchange was open, but soon it expanded to cover culture and sports as well. In 1989 the Springer Company bought a half share in the *Tiroler Tageszeitung*. Mediaprint (WAZ) launched a price war against *Tiroler Tageszeitung* in 1999, reducing subscription prices to its papers *Krone* and *Kurier* in Tyrol by nearly one half, to just $13 per month. At the same time, Mediaprint raised its prices in Vienna, Niederösterreich, and Burgenland by 7.2 percent. The *Tiroler Tageszeitung* complained to the courts, which ordered Mediaprint to cease taking advantage of its dominant market position.

These media conglomerates competed in distribution as well as advertising and subscription sales. In the mid 1990s the left-liberal *Standard* sued Mediaprint for refusing to distribute its paper, while still distributing other newspapers not owned by Mediaprint (*Wirtschaftsblatt*), but *Standard* lost the suit. In addition to the very common distribution via subscription or kiosk sales, the *Neue Kronen Zeitung* and *Kurier* sold papers by hawking them on the streets, in cafes, and in traffic during rush hours.

Daily newspapers attracted about 30 percent of all the money spent on advertising in Austria, with another

23 percent going to television and 8 percent to radio. Weeklies and other magazines accounted for an additional 23 percent of money spent on advertising. In the 1990s revenues from advertising accounted for over half the revenues of newspaper publishers, becoming more lucrative than newspaper sales. At the same time, papers needed to continue to attract a readership interested in and capable of purchasing the products advertised. Thus the better-educated, more affluent consumer was the newspaper publisher's target audience. In 2000 Austrian advertisers spent $2.24 billion, of which $1.257 billion, or 54 percent, went to print media. Fifty-two per cent of print advertising went to daily newspapers, and 48 percent to magazines.

Like newspaper sales, advertising revenues were concentrated at the top of the circulation pyramid, with Mediaprint's *Kronen Zeitung* and *Kurier* attracting about two thirds of all advertising revenues, leaving a much smaller share for lesser competitors. Regional papers struggled to support themselves through small classified ads, regional advertising, and sales. Through the 1980s newspapers lost advertising revenue to television and radio, where advertising on Sundays and holidays became legal. In 2002 the Mediaprint papers and large regional dailies *Kleine Zeitung*, *Oberösterreichische Nachrichten*, *Salzburger Nachrichten*, *Tiroler Tageszeitung*, and *Vorarlberger Nachrichten*, all turned a profit.

Until 2002, newspapers received preferential postal rates, which accounted for only 17 percent of the true cost of mailing publications; however, this cost affected more weeklies than daily newspapers, which were often bought at kiosks or tobacco shops. Regional newspapers in rural areas were most dependent on the postal delivery system. Despite objections by the Association of Austrian Newspapers, postal rates were raised in two stages, effective January 1, 2002 and January 1, 2003. When the transition was to be complete, rates for mailings up to sixty grams would have risen 282 percent over 2001, and rates for mailings heavier than 100 grams would have risen 157 percent. Saturday postage rates would have increased at an even higher rate. In 2001 the former rivals *Standard* and *Presse* began a common home delivery system to residents of Vienna, Niederösterreich, and northern Burgenland. However, home delivery by the publisher was the most expensive method of distribution.

In 1985 *Die Presse* was the first Austrian paper to use an all-electronic editing format. *Der Standard* made the leap to on-line publishing in February 1995, followed in September by *Vorarlberger Nachrichten*. That paper began four-color printing in 1994, and *Täglich Alles* began printing in four-color intaglio in 1992. In 1995 the *Tiroler Tageszeitung* opened a modern four-color printing plant as well. By 2002, four-color offset printing was the industry standard.

Mediaprint, as the country's largest newspaper publisher, also had the newest printing facilities. In 1989 it purchased 35 percent of one of Austria's largest offset printing firms, Tusch Druck. Its new printing plant in St. Addrä/ Lavanttal opened in summer 2002 and employed 180 workers. It printed a total of 300,000 copies of its two major dailies, *Krone* and *Kurier*, and the entire print run of the *Kärntner Tageszeitung*.

The two largest suppliers of newsprint were Steyrermühl (in 2002 part of UPM Kymmene), and Bruck/ Norske Skog, part of a Norwegian paper producer, the second largest in Europe. Norske Skog, located in Graz, produced 120,000 metric tons of newsprint a year, while Steyrermühl, located in the town of the same name in Upper Austria, produced 480,000 metric tons of newsprint and uncoated magazine paper. Each year a group within the Association of Austrian Newspapers would negotiate a general agreement with these two producers, and then individual publishers would negotiate the details. There was no shortage of newsprint in Austria, but price increases in the double digits appeared in 2001. About three-fourths of the paper and cardboard produced in Austria was exported.

PRESS LAWS

The Austrian constitution guarantees freedom of the press, and there is no state censorship of the media. A Media Act of 1981 guaranteed objective and impartial reporting, ensured the independence of journalists and broadcasters, and required all media to disclose their ownership. The Media Act also protected individuals from invasion of their privacy, slander, libel, and defamation of character. Anyone who believed these guarantees have been violated had recourse to the Austrian Press Council, an independent watchdog agency founded in 1961 by the Association of Austrian Newspapers and the Austrian Journalists Union. The Austrian Press Council also represented interests of the press, radio, and television in negotiations with government agencies. The Media Act was amended in 1993 to require media to present opposing viewpoints and to offer citizens the right of rebuttal.

In the early 2000s, all newspapers, regardless of size, ownership, or general financial condition, received a general press subsidy, under an arrangement which originated in the mid 1970s. Beginning in 1973, Austrian newspapers were subject to a value added tax at a reduced rate of 10 percent. After complaints by the newspaper editors and publishers association, state subsidies for newspapers and magazines were introduced in 1975 in order to ensure the survival of a broad spectrum of public opinion. While the existence of such government subsidies might reduce press criticism of the state, a governing committee of representatives of the chancellor's office, the journalists' trade union, and the Association of Austrian Newspapers ensured that such pressure did not apply. In 2001 the country spent about $64 million on general newspaper subsidies awarded to the 16 dailies then in existence. Larger newspapers received more funding, so the subsidy did not effectively promote the publication of smaller papers or a broader range of viewpoints. Effective in the early 2000s, Austria could not refuse the general press subsidy to newspapers dominated by foreign ownership because doing so is prohibited by the European Union.

A Press Promotion Law of 1985 defined recipients of a second, special press subsidy (amounting to more than the general subsidy) as ''daily newspapers of particular importance for the formation of public opinion which do not have any dominant market position.'' To qualify for special press subsidies, a paper had to reach between 1 percent and 15 percent of the population of its province, or a maximum of 5 percent nationwide. Advertising must not amount to more than 22 percent of total pages. In 1993 the press subsidy system was revised and new regulations were put into place to control future mergers in the media industry. In 2001 six papers received special subsidies totaling $80 million, excluding *Neue Zeit*, which closed, despite having received a special subsidy of $2 million the previous year. The *Standard* and *Salzburger Nachrichten* were denied subsidies for exceeding the limit on the proportion of space that could be devoted to advertising three times within the previous five years. The special subsidies awarded amounted to $2.8 for *Die Presse*, $1.5 million for the *Kärntner Tageszeitung*, around one million apiece for the Neues Volksblatt and the Neue Vorarlberger Tageszeitung, and slightly under one million for the *Wirtschaftsblatt*. Beginning in 1979 subsidies were also awarded for the education and training of journalists, to a total of nearly three-quarters of a million dollars in 1997. Since 1983 further subsidies supported the modernization or construction of new printing plants. Provinces may also subsidize newspapers, in some cases through direct investment, elsewhere through measures such as tax breaks for new printing plants.

Austria did not enact major anti-trust legislation until 1993, believing that media consolidation strengthened the country's position against outside competition. But the large role played by *Westdeutsche allgemeine Zeitung* and other foreign owners stimulated a change of philosophy. Those media conglomerates already in existence, however, such as Mediaprint, were not obliged to diversify. *Wiener Zeitung* lost its monopoly on federal government announcements and advertising in 1996 because the monopoly violated regulations of the European Union, which Austria had joined a year earlier. Formerly owned by a department of Austria's State Printers, it became independent in 1997.

In January 2001 a legal decision based on Austrian cartel law defined the media market in such a way as to find no violation in the concentration of ownership in weekly news publications. Yet discussions about the necessity of examining the joint impact of print, radio, and television and of reforming cartel law and breaking up existing conglomerates rather than merely forbidding new mergers have surfaced in the Austrian media.

The Association of Austrian Newspapers (which in 2002 maintained a Web site at www.voez.at) often lobbied the federal government on matters affecting the media. In 2001 the organization urged repeal of a law requiring that advertisements to be subject to a special tax, which could range as high as 30 percent. Austrian firms could advertise their products and services in foreign media without paying the special tax. This policy, unique to Austria, placed the country at a disadvantage in attracting advertising in the international market.

Austria also regulated the content and nature of advertising, which had to be identified as such, not masked as advice or commentary. Advertisers had to be able to prove the truth of statements made about their products. Newspapers could refuse to publish certain advertisements or newspaper inserts without stating any cause. Austrian law prohibited advertising directed at children from attempting to persuade them that the possession or enjoyment of certain products is a goal in and of itself and warned that parents should not be portrayed as negligent nor children as inferior if they do not own or buy certain products. Violence in advertising was forbidden. The dignity of women should be respected in advertising, and women should not be portrayed as incompetent in using technology or driving, for example, or shown predominantly as housewives or lower-ranking employees.

CENSORSHIP

Austria had several federal laws which guaranteed freedom of expression and prohibited censorship, particularly a 1981 federal law on the press and other journalistic media. This law required all media to disclose their ownership and stipulated that confiscation or withdrawal from publication could occur only after a court order. Broadcasting must be objective and must represent a diversity of opinion. Private citizens were protected from libel, slander, defamation, or ridicule in the media.

All major media groups subscribed to *Ehrenkodex für die österreichische Presse* (the code of ethics of the Austrian press). It stated that readers must be able to differentiate between factual reporting and editorial commentary. Journalists should not be subject to external influences, whether personal or financial. The economic interests of the publisher should not influence content to the point of falsifying or suppressing information. Racial or religious discrimination was not permissible, nor was the denigration or mockery of any religious teaching by recognized churches or religious communities. The intimate sphere of public figures had to be respected, especially where children were concerned. Protection of the individual's rights must be carefully weighed against public interest, which might mean exposure of serious crimes or risks to public security or public health. Photographs of the intimate sphere of public figures could only be published if the public interest outweighed voyeurism. Retouched photographs or photo montages should be identified as such. Travel and tourism reports should mention the social and political background of the region, for example serious human rights violations. Reporting on automobiles should contain energy consumption and environmental information. Moreover, courtroom television, live radio broadcasts, and photography of court proceedings were prohibited. Journalists who quoted pretrial court proceedings could be punished with up to six months in prison.

Violations of this code of ethics were brought before the Austrian Press Council for deliberation. It represented the press within federal government bodies, ensured press freedom, and watched over citizen complaints. While the Press Council lacked legal means to enforce its decisions, it was generally respected by over 100 print media who subscribed to its code of ethics. In 2001 the Austrian Press Council debated 35 violations of the code of ethics, many concerned with the publication of sensational or gruesome photographs. Other cases concerned failure to disclose conflicting financial interests, inappropriate portrayal of public figures, and unfair coverage of a political party. The Council's sanctions were limited to requiring offenders to publish apologies or rebuttals; it had no authority to impose legal penalties or financial settlements. Its jurisdiction was limited to the content of print media and excluded their business dealings such as attempts to recruit readers. Furthermore, it had no authority over online publications.

State-Press Relations

After World War II, Austrian media policy aimed to establish strong national media, with interlocking interests represented in newspaper publishing, the state monopoly radio system, and the Austrian Press Agency. The arrival of German groups, such as the *Westdeutsche allgemeine Zeitung*, stimulated calls for revisions of media policy, yet Austrian cartel law functioned to protect those conglomerates already in power, such as Mediaprint, and as of 2002 no breakup had occurred. Two years before Austria joined the European Union, the European Court for Human Rights condemned Austria's radio monopoly, ORF. Further impetus toward action came from the need for a legal framework governing the development and use of the Internet as a broadcast medium. While private radio and television existed in Austria in 2002, it did not yet rival the formidable public network. Overall, the thrust of media policy had been to use federal funds to subsidize newspapers, magazines, printing plants, and even the education and training of journalists, rather than to dismantle the media conglomerates and promote stronger competition to diversify Austria's print and broadcast media.

In the early 2000s, protection of the freedom of information attracted greater attention. The Austrian Press Council watched over infringements against freedom of the press or the right to know, which it saw as threatened by military and police security, particularly in the wake of terrorist attacks on the United States in September 2001.

Attitude toward Foreign Media

In the early 2000s, foreign journalists were welcome in Austria and did not need special permission to gather news in the country. Foreign news agencies such as the Associated Press, Reuters, Agence France-Presse, TASS, and the German news agency had headquarters in Vienna. Foreign newspapers were available in the major cities, and foreign radio broadcasts and television stations might be received wherever the country's terrain made reception feasible.

News Agencies

The Austrian Press Agency (APA) founded in 1946 was, as of 2002, the country's leading organization of journalists and reporters and the largest source of information about Austria. The country's national radio broadcast monopoly was its largest shareholder. It maintained correspondents in each of the provincial capitals and at European Union headquarters in Brussels. All of Austria's major newspapers and the Austrian Broadcasting Corporation (ORF) were represented in its governance structures.

As of 2002, it produced over 180,000 news reports annually, covering domestic and foreign affairs, economics, culture, science, education, and sports. It also supplied photographs and graphics for print or on-line media. Its services included data banks, content management, information technology, multi-media services, financial reports, and an original text service, which enabled public relations agencies or offices to send press releases directly into the APA system. It published a financial monitor with news of the Vienna stock exchange. In 2001 its reports were circulated to 37 news agencies, 281 daily papers, 48 weeklies, 171 radio and television broadcasters, and 100 press offices. Its headquarters in Vienna housed the International Press Center, and the agency maintained an important Web site: www.apa.at.

Vienna was also home to the Concordia Press Club, founded in 1859, a professional organization of reporters, editors, and publishers. Concordia gave prestigious annual awards each May for human rights and freedom of the press (www.concordia.at). The Austrian Journalists Club (www.oejc.or.at), Concordia, and the Austrian Press Agency were all headquartered in Vienna.

BROADCAST MEDIA

Austrian radio began in 1924 with the establishment of *Österreichische Radioverkehr AG* (RAVAG) in Vienna, a corporation whose shares (82 percent) were publicly owned and funded by users' fees. Radio advertising began in 1937, as music and art programming gave way to Nazi propaganda. At the end of World War II, the four Allied Powers established the Austrian Radio Corporation (*Österreichischer Rundfunk*, ORF) for radio broadcasts, and television broadcasts began in 1957. Broadcasting was regulated by the federal government rather than the nine provinces, and it was overseen by the *Österreichische Rundfunk Gesellschaft*, where proportional representation from several constituencies was intended to ensure fair use of the airwaves. The late 1960s saw new provisions for public citizens to broadcast counter statements if they felt they had been misrepresented on the air. Subsequent statutes also guaranteed journalistic freedom and objective reporting. In 1967 ORF became politically and economically independent. These provisions for its independence were extended in 1974 to ensure objectivity, a wider variety of opinion, and fair and balanced programming. By 1970 ORF consisted of three radio networks and two television channels. During the cold war years, Austrian news was eagerly received in Hungary, Czechoslovakia, and Yugoslavia, where many people continued to know German. Unlike the overtly political broadcasts that West Germany aimed at the German Democratic Republic during those years, ORF maintained strict neutrality in radio and television news. As of 2002 ORF maintained regional studios in all nine provinces and broadcasts on four networks, as well as to the United States, Africa, Asia, Australia, and the Near East.

Demand for opening the airwaves to private broadcasters began in the 1980s, a campaign led by the Association of Austrian Newspapers, which expected to own and control most private facilities. Media politics became a hotly debated topic in national elections, and disagreements between the Austrian Socialist Party and the Austrian People's Party over the ownership of frequencies delayed diversification for a decade. Private radio stations did not begin broadcasting until 1988, and then only in Styria and Vorarlberg. Regional and local licenses in the remaining provinces were finally granted and private broadcasting on 43 local networks began there in 1998. Antenne Radio, one of the largest private radio networks, broadcasted in Styria, Carinthia, Salzburg, and Vienna but achieved only modest success. Five years after its founding, *Antenne Steiermark* (Styria) reached just 24 percent of the regional market.

As of 2002, the result of this gradual liberalization process had not brought significant diversification; the most powerful media players remained dominant. In that year and estimated two-thirds of Austrians watched domestic television broadcasts and 80 percent listen to ORF. Private radio reached only around 15 to 25 percent of the market in its own province and attracted chiefly younger listeners, one-third of Austrians between the ages of 14 and 49. Newspaper conglomerates dominated the private airwaves as well as the country's print media. In 1998 a new Viennese radio station, *Wiener Antenne Radio* began broadcast, with *Die Presse* owning a 24 percent share, and another large share in the hands of Fellner publishing. *Krone* Media, Bertelsmann publishing, the *Tiroler Tageszeitung*, and *Vorarlberger Nachrichten* were also major players in regional markets. A ruling prohibiting newspapers from holding more than a 26 percent share in a regional radio station or more than a 10 percent share in two others, which must be in different provinces, was lifted in 2001. In that year *Neue Kronen Zeitung* established a private foundation to own a majority share in Danube Radio Vienna, broadcasting as 92.9 FM *Krone Hitradio*. Its one dozen stations reached 5.7 million people, making it a strong competitor of *Antenne Radio*.

ORF held the largest share in the Austrian Press Agency which prevented it from supplying audio news to private radio stations, thus ensuring ORF's virtual monopoly on the dissemination of news. Its first program, Ö1, broadcasts news headlines three times a day, with longer broadcasts in the evening. The remaining three ORF stations broadcasted a mix of music, talk shows, and cultural reports.

In 1988 ORF, Swiss public television, and Germany's *Zweites Deutsches Fernsehen* (its second public television channel) joined forces to offer satellite programming for the three German-speaking countries. About 41 percent of Austrian households had satellite television and received about a dozen foreign channels. The most popular were Germany's public television networks *Allgemeine Rundfunk Deutschlands* (ARD) and *Zweites Deutsches Fernsehen* (ZDF). Cable television viewers preferred SAT, Pro Sieben, and RTL. Two-thirds received CNN and about one-third received Euronews. Border areas closest to Germany, Switzerland, and Italy also received foreign radio broadcasts, although Austria's mountainous landscape made transmission difficult in some locations.

Each state studio of ORF local television broadcasted a half-hour local news program Mondays through Fridays and headlines as much as five times a day. News and politics consumed about 16-18 percent of television broadcast time, but only about 17-19 percent of television viewers watch the news.

Austria's print and broadcast media often shared journalists and collaborated in formulating media policy. In 1985, for example, ORF and VÖZ agreed to the expansion of radio and television advertising into Sundays and holidays, with the proviso that ORF renounce future broadcasts of regional advertising in local television markets. Another agreement in effect from 1987 to 1995 provided for local daily and weekly newspapers to establish private regional radio pilot programs under the aegis of ORF. This maneuver effectively excluded entities other than newspapers from access to radio.

The Association of Austrian Newspapers generally succeeded in insisting that ORF should be funded by user fees rather than advertising, which accounted for about 42 percent of its revenues in the early 2000s. ORF was also prohibited from airing advertising of a regional nature. ORF's four broadcast networks reached 75.9 percent of possible listeners in Austria (5.3 million people), and private radio served only about 22.8 percent, or 1.6 million. In April 2001 Austria established a new regulatory authority for radio, KommAustria, with jurisdiction over the distribution of private television broadcast licenses and the responsibility to watch over the increasingly interwoven telecommunications networks.

Electronic News Media

Austria was relatively late in developing widespread Internet access, in part because of high telephone rates from the provinces for long-distance calls to Internet service providers. Austria's first Internet sites were produced by universities. *Media Analyse*, an Austrian monitoring agency, found that in 1999 some 7.4 percent of Austrians had used the Internet on the day preceding their survey, just under a half million people. Computers were still not ubiquitous in Austrian schools, nor were information literacy skills part of the general curriculum. In Vienna, teletext access was also available through cable television for about 220,000 subscribers.

Through the mid 1990s all Austrian dailies established Web sites on the Internet. *Der Standard*, the first Austrian newspaper to appear online, was still ranked first as of 2002, with over 280,000 hits daily. Several regional papers followed the lead of *Vorarlberger Nachrichten*, which offered regional news via Internet beginning in September 1995. In 2002 *Der Standard* and the weekly *Falter* offered Vienna online, *Oberösterreichische Nachrichten* covered Upper Austrian regional news, and the *Kleine Zeitung* published Styria and Carinthia online. The Austrian Press Agency supported and assisted these electronic developments.

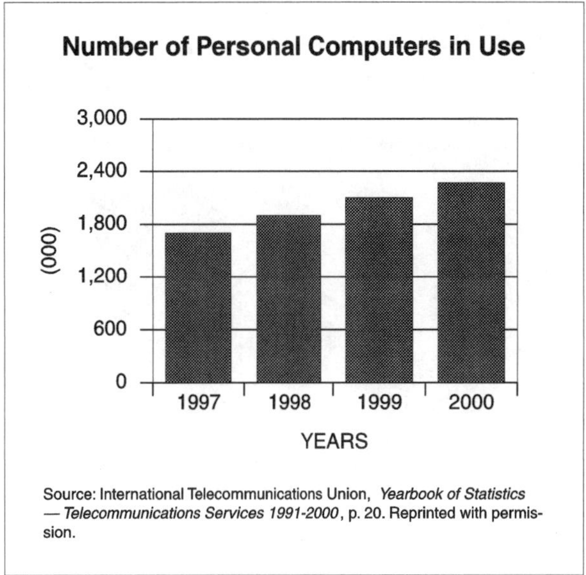

Source: International Telecommunications Union, *Yearbook of Statistics — Telecommunications Services 1991-2000*, p. 20. Reprinted with permission.

In 2001 the Association of Austrian Newspapers demanded protection of intellectual property of journalists and reports because electronic news digests supplied headline news on line without crediting the sources and thereby reduced demand for printed papers.

Education & Training

The universities of Vienna and Salzburg had departments of communication and journalism where students could earn a master's degree or a doctorate. (Austria had no real equivalent of the American baccalaureate degree). The University of Salzburg's Institute for Communication Science also prepared an annual report on the state of journalism in Austria. *Kuratorium für Journalistenausbildung* (the Board of Trustees for Journalist Training), founded in 1979, was also located in Salzburg and Vienna. Journalists might be admitted to its *Journalisten Kolleg* (educational programs) after passing an examination; no particular academic degree was required. It offered 12-week training seminars spread over a 9-month period, covering such topics as electronic media, online publishing, interview techniques, and press law.

Until 2001, journalists were represented through the Union for Art, Media, and Freelance Work, Journalists

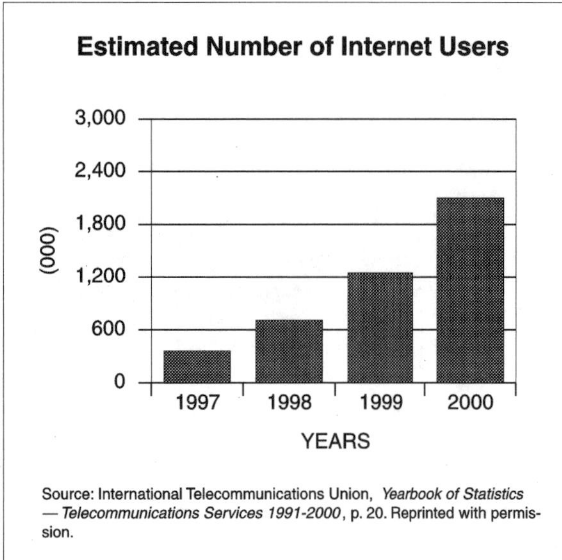

Source: International Telecommunications Union, *Yearbook of Statistics — Telecommunications Services 1991-2000*, p. 20. Reprinted with permission.

Section, headquartered in Vienna. In June 2001, some 97.2 percent of Austria's 3,651 unionized journalists voted to separate from that labor union and establish their own media union together with printers. Afterward, they were represented by the Print and Paper Union, Journalists Section. In general Austrian employers and employees viewed themselves as social partners cooperating to reach common goals without labor disputes that would disrupt production. Thus, as of the early 2000s, Austria's postwar media history was free of major strikes.

SUMMARY

Austria's remaining 15 daily newspapers might, as of 2002, face further shrinkage in coming years. Particularly the small dailies, such as *Neue Vorarlberger Tageszeitung* and the *Neue Kärntner Tageszeitung*, might be more dependent on the special press subsidy or might become vulnerable to bankruptcy as they face increasing competition for advertising revenues, rising newsprint costs, and higher postage rates which become effective in 2003. Austria's strong system of public transportation would continue to support newspaper readership; in contrast to Americans who commute to work by car, Austrians travel by train, subway, or streetcar, past kiosks where they can buy a daily paper and in vehicles where they can read instead of drive.

Print media appeared subject to change only through economic concerns; an examination of the membership of organizations such as the Association of Austrian Newspapers, the Austrian Press Agency, or the Board of Trustees for Journalists' Training revealed very few women or minorities. Journalism and its leadership appeared to be securely in the hands of the interlocking hierarchies of government, Catholicism, and the established business community.

SIGNIFICANT DATES

- 1988: WAZ acquires a 45 percent share in *Krone* and *Kurier*, founds Mediaprint to handle the joint printing, distribution, and advertising sales of its papers.
- 1987-1991: this year marks the end of political party-owned newspapers *Arbeiter Zeitung* and *Volksstimme* (KPÖ).
- 1988: *Der Standard* is launched.
- 1992: *Täglich Alles*is launched by Kurt Falk in four-color intaglio.
- 1994: *Vorarlberger Nachrichten* is first traditional Austrian newspaper to print in four colors.
- 1995: *Der Standard* is first online newspaper in the German language in the world.
- 1995: *Wirtschaftsblatt*is launched with an initial run of 58,000 copies.
- 1996: *Wiener Zeitung* loses its monopoly on the publication of government announcements and job postings.
- 2000: *Täglich Alles* ceases print publication but is still available online.
- 2001: *Neue Zeit* ceases publication.

BIBLIOGRAPHY

Austria: Facts and Figures. Vienna: Federal Press Service, 2000.

Bruckenberger, Johannes. ''Zeitungen im Zeitraffer—Chronologie des Medienjahres 2000/01.'' *VÖZ Jahrbuch Presse 2001—Dokumentationen, Analysen, Fakten.* Vienna: Verband österreischischer Zeitungen, 2001. http://www.voez.at/dynamic.

Burtscher, Klaudia. ''Between Sensationalism and Complexity: A Statistical Analysis of the Environment as a Topic in Austrian Media.'' *Innovation: The European Journal of Social Sciences,* 6 (1993): 519-532.

Düriegl, Günter and Andreas Unterberger. *Die Presse, ein Stück Österreich.* Vienna: Vienna Historical Museum, 1998.

Geretschlaeger, Erich. *Mass Media in Austria.* Vienna: Federal Press Service, 1998.

Grisold, Andrea. ''Press Concentration and Media Policy in Small Countries; Austria and Ireland Compared.'' *European Journal of Communication,* 11 (1996): 485-509.

Hummel, Roman. ''''A Summary of the Media Situation in Austria. '''' Innovation: The European Journal of Social Sciences 3 (1990): 309-331.

May, Stefan. ''Kein Mensch schaut uns an: Österreichs Medien in Deutschland.'' *Academia,* 52 (2001): 10-12.

Pfannhäuser, Harald. ''Formil macht mobil.'' *Academia,* 52 (2001): 7-9.

Pürer, Heinz. ''Österreichs Mediensystem im Wandel.'' *Presse Handbuch,* 1989: 5-15.

——— *Presse in Österreich.* (Schriftenreihe Medien & Praxis, Band 2). St. Polten: Verband Österreichischer Zeitungsherausgeber und Zeitungsverleger, 1990.

Sandford, John. The Mass Media of the German-Speaking Countries. London: Oswald Wolff, 1976.

Verband Österreichischer Zeitungsherausgeber und Zeitungsverleger. *Presse Handbuch.* Vienna: annual volumes.

—Helen H. Frink

AZERBAIJAN

BASIC DATA

Official Country Name:	Azerbaijani Republic
Region (Map name):	Middle East
Population:	7,771,092
Language(s):	Azerbaijani (Azeri) 89%, Russian 3%, Armenian 2%, other 6%
Literacy rate:	97.0%
Area:	86,600 sq km
GDP:	5,267 (US$ millions)
Number of Nondaily Newspapers:	329
Total Circulation:	122,000
Circulation per 1,000:	22
Number of Television Stations:	2
Number of Television Sets:	170,000
Television Sets per 1,000:	21.9
Number of Cable Subscribers:	2,400
Cable Subscribers per 1,000:	0.3
Number of Satellite Subscribers:	200,000
Satellite Subscribers per 1,000:	25.7
Number of Radio Stations:	28
Number of Radio Receivers:	175,000
Radio Receivers per 1,000:	22.5
Number of Individuals with Internet Access:	12,000
Internet Access per 1,000:	1.5

BACKGROUND & GENERAL CHARACTERISTICS

A member of the Commonwealth of Independent States (CIS), the Republic of Azerbaijan (*Azarbaycan Respublikasi*) gained its political independence, in 1991, in the wake of the former USSR collapse. It is a country of Turkic Muslims that remains in territorial conflict with adjacent Armenia, over the Azerbaijani Nagorno-Karabakh. This conflict has had an enormous human and economic cost of over 750,000 refugees and internally displaced persons (IDPs), representing slightly less than 10 percent the total population of 7.8 million Azerbaijanis.

Azerbaijan's average life span is short, with less than seven percent of the population above the age of 65. The mortality rate is nearly twice the birth rate (9.5 births per 1,000, and 18.5 deaths). Most of the population speaks Azeri, but minorities also speak Russian and Armenian. Ethnically almost all of the population is Azeri, and 93 percent are Muslims, although few practice. Literacy is high at about 97 percent.

Geographically situated within southwest Asia, Azerbaijan is a land of 33,400 square miles. It borders the Russia and Georgia to its north; Iran to the south; Armenia to the west; and the Caspian Sea to the east. Its capital city is Baku with a population of about 2 million people, or about 25 percent the total population. Historically, Azerbaijan was the home of the Scythian tribes, incorporated into the Roman Empire. Overrun by the Ottoman Empire in the eleventh century, it was occupied by the Russians in 1906 and 1913. In December 1922, it was officially annexed by the USSR. In 1936, it metamorphosed into a constituent part of the Soviet Union. On December 26, 1991 it spun out from the Soviet orbit and became politically independent. Fights between Muslim Azerbaijan and neighboring Christian Armenia escalated between 1992 and 1994 over the enclave of Nagorno-Karabakh, over which both proclaim sovereignty.

Mr. Haydar Aliyev, a pro-Russian former communist, was democratically elected president of Azerbaijan,

Top Ten Daily Newspapers
(1999)

	Circulation
Yeni Musavat	16,000
Bu gun	11,000
Azadliq	9,000
Xalq qezeti	7,000
Azerbaijan	7,000
525-ci qezet	7,000
Zerkalo	6,000
Respublika	5,000
Edalet	5,000
Zaman	5,000

Source: World Association of Newspapers and Zenithmedia, *World Press Trends 2001*, p. 50.

and a national constitution has ensued since 1995. The infant media reflects the nascent political entity. Newspaper circulation remains weak at 28/1,000 people (compared to 267/1,000 in Russia and 228/1,000 in the USA). In 1998, a presidential decree abolished censorship, but media and press restrictions continue.

ECONOMIC FRAMEWORK

The international statistical news and descriptive media, as well as the local sources, present Azerbaijan as empirically a uniquely oil-rich country. For, despite a decline in oil production, over the late nineties, a trend reversal has emerged, in particular at the aftermath of the Production-Sharing Arrangements (PSAs) negotiations and deals with a multitude of foreign transnational corporations (FTCs). These FTCs have committed over $60 billion to oil field exploration, development, implementation, trade, and worldwide consumption. Naturally, these major international currency funds ought to trigger industrial and economic activities, pre- and post-oil realizations. The majority of the population, 60 percent, still lives under the poverty level. The Azerbaijani media is instrumental in reporting such major economic problems. The national budget stands at about $800 million whereas public spending is at a relatively higher point of approximately one billion dollars. It is incumbent upon the Azerbaijani press and media, including the nascent Internet technology and e-journalism, to spread the word about the considerable Azerbaijani economic opportunities and challenges.

PRESS LAWS

In addition to the Articles 47 (Freedom of Thought and Speech) and 49 (Freedom of Information), many ordinances and decrees (particularly, the sweeping anti-censorship decree of 1998) promote free and open information. *Hayat, Khalg Gazeti, Bakinskii Rabochii,* the weekly English newspaper, ANS, Azertag, BBC Azerbaijan, the Media Press Agency, Internews Azerbaijan, Azerbaijan Broadcasting Agency, Azerbaijan State TV, and foreign media are all entitled to open and free news. Journalists and media companies, however, must pass the screening tests of the Information Ministry, Ministry of Culture, and other governmental authorities. This includes paying fees and posting bonds, supporting the government against terrorism and the Armenian occupation of the Karabakh enclave, avoiding obscenity and rebellious incitements against the government, protecting the constitutional rights of the Azerbaijani people, reporting fraud and crimes, and supporting the constitutional institutions.

The Mass Media, National Politics, and Elections The current Azerbaijani Constitution and a number of press laws fully support the use of mass media (print, audiovisual, videoconferencing, satellite communications, cyberspace, etc.) to spread the word on the democratic, frontier capitalism experiment in Azerbaijan. The Constitution encourages Azerbaijanis living overseas to be in touch with the home media, foreign-linked media, and even to form their own press (e.g., the *Azerbaijan International Magazine*) to spread news and information about the local politics, elections, and socio-economic development national issues.

The Mass Media, Liberal Political Democracy, Frontier Market Economy, and Socio-Economic Development Articles 15 and 16 of the Constitution express that Azerbaijan's vision is to establish a political liberal democracy in conjunction with a free market economy. The mass media are asked to play a crucial role in informing, disseminating, and reporting about these ideals, the constitutional foundations, and the means of their achievement. Even diplomatically, this new transitional capitalist power aims, via the media diffusion within and without Azerbaijan, to foster relations with the industrialized capitalist West, principally Western Europe and the USA. The press and media prides itself in informing about the cooperative efforts with the USA in fighting and jointly combating ''. . .terrorism, [instituting] the modernization of frontier troops, and [the] coordination of efforts on non-proliferation of mass destruction weapons, trade and preparation to admit Azerbaijan to the WTO, and humanitarian sphere.'' (local media, azertag.com, president.com, etc.). The media was eager to report that The Bush Administration, within the 2002 fiscal year framework and the subsequent ''Freedom Support Act'', allocated $50 million to Azerbaijan. Pentagon military assistance, privatization enhancement, agricultural assistance, and education cooperation are other media-publicized U.S. elements of economic help.

CENSORSHIP

The Constitution, the anti-censorship decree of 1998, and a variety of other government documents assert that the independence of the mass media in Azerbaijan is "an established fact." For example, in an interview of the Head of the Azerbaijani Parliamentary delegation, Mr. Ilham Aliyev, at the Council of Europe (COE/September 29, 2001), he states:

> Correspondent: How will you comment [on] (the) yesterday's statement of the Chairman of the Council of Europe Parliamentary Assembly on journalists?
>
> Ilham Aliyev: Today in Azerbaijan every condition for independent mass media is established. When I asked you how many newspapers are published in Armenia, you said about 6-7. But we have over 100 [including regional and small] daily newspapers, which mainly represent numerous circles of political establishment. Censorship has been abolished in Azerbaijan, freedom of speech is guaranteed and not under control. There are, of course, cases when the officials are subject to different critics. In some cases, even the journalists are brought to court, because they use unverified facts, often slanderous, then the court passes a decision against the newspaper. This is a democratic mechanism and there is no another. Therefore, to say that there are problems in the mass media of Azerbaijan, I think, is not right.

Effectively, since the newly introduced Constitution, the Azerbaijani mass media have proliferated and acquired a myriad of investigative, reporting, and broadcast rights. The Parliament, the Ministry of Justice, the Ministry of Information, private journalist organizations, and the foreign media provide a variety of safeguard devices against censorship, reporting official bureaucratic abuses, bribery and corruption, violation of the constitutional civil rights of the Azeri people, and the freedom and independence of journalists. Gradually, however, particularly in virtue of more training, journalistic education, openness, and objective but courteous reporting, censorship should eventually be eliminated.

The Mass Media as A Bearer of Open Media The Constitution purports an open and uncoerced media and press system in Azerbaijan. Thanks to international satellite communications, such a media policy is, to some extent, observed. The Parliament News and the Press Service of the Ministry of Justice, albeit the many faces of governmental control, use the media to promote freedom of expression, human rights, the freedom of assembly and peaceful strikes, ecological integrity, academic freedom, diversity and tolerance, etc. During a visit by the Council of Europe (COE), the Head of the Justice Ministry stated that Azerbaijan was a member of a number of international conventions against racism, religious intolerance, genocide, apartheid, and censorship (Azerbaijan media, March 28, 2002).

STATE-PRESS RELATIONS

As stated above, the 1995 Constitution guarantees many press and media rights and responsibilities. Precisely, Article 28 stresses the Right to Freedom, Article 40 emphasizes the Right to Culture (the arts, literature, humanities, communication and media, lingual and religious diversity, etc.), Article 47 focuses upon the Freedom of Speech, and Article 49 zeroes in on the Freedom of Information. There is a need for the State of Azerbaijan and related institutions, principally the Ministries of Culture, Information, Justice, Education, and Foreign Relations to facilitate the role, tasks, functions, dynamics, and objectives of the Azerbaijani media and foreign-linked media. The media are expected to keep tabs on the government as well. However, further reform is required with respect to circumventing corrupt reporting; promoting the media coverage of the whole nation; fairly representing the national identity and culture; and emancipating the media and press from the yet visible tight hold of the State. The press and media are justifiably a necessary tool to building democracy and contributing to the artistic, scientific, technologic, political, and socioeconomic development of any country, and specifically to Azerbaijan's internal and global prosperity, the intercultural and inter-civilizational harmony amongst nations, and planetary peace.

Government & Political Framework There is a strong correlation between the type of governmental structure, dynamics, and ends-in-view and the press and media system within a specific country. Generally, the more democratic and participatory a nation, the more liberal and uncoerced the press and media, and vice versa.

Although the Democratic Republic of Azerbaijan came into being, historically, on May 28, 1918, it did not regain its autonomy until August 30, 1991 from the Soviet Union. The press and media, throughout seventy-three years of Soviet political and economic satellitism, were the replicas of the central Moscow government. *Pravda* and *Moscow News*, formulated, delivered, and manipulated most of the information system in Baku and beyond.

On November 12, 1995, the country adopted a democratic constitution that went into effect two weeks later. Its main six intentions are territorial integrity, democracy, civil society, a secular state, a free market-centered economic system that shall foster higher standards of living for every Azerbaijani, and a faithful ideology in human universal values and international law. Precisely, its basic tenets are: i) universal suffrage at 18 years of age; ii) a national civil law system; iii) the change of name from Azerbaijan Soviet Socialist Republic to the Republic of Azerbaijan (Azarbaycan Respublikasi); iv) the inception and the administrative autonomous re-organization of the country into 59 rayons, 11 cities, and 1 autonomous republic; v) an open press and media system throughout the nation; vi) regular presidential elections via popular vote every five years; vii) regular elections of a Unicameral National Assembly (*Milli Mejlis*) of 125 members, for a five-year mandate, via popular vote; viii) multipartism, hence multi-media/multi-press systems; ix) promotion and advent of political pressure groups and leaders; x) presence and maintenance of open and mutually fruitful relations with all sovereign nations via membership into a variety of world entities; and xi) the fostering of a free democratic, market-like, and capitalist transitional society, based on free competition, cooperation with the CIS, religious tolerance, state secularism, and the promotion of macro-growth and economic development in Azerbaijan as well as the participation in the causes of peace and prosperity worldwide. Many challenges and threats remain, principally because of the Azerbaijani-Armenian conflict, the surrounding conflicts (the Gulf and Mideast problems, and the Pakistani-Indian crisis) and the anti-terrorism war in Afghanistan.

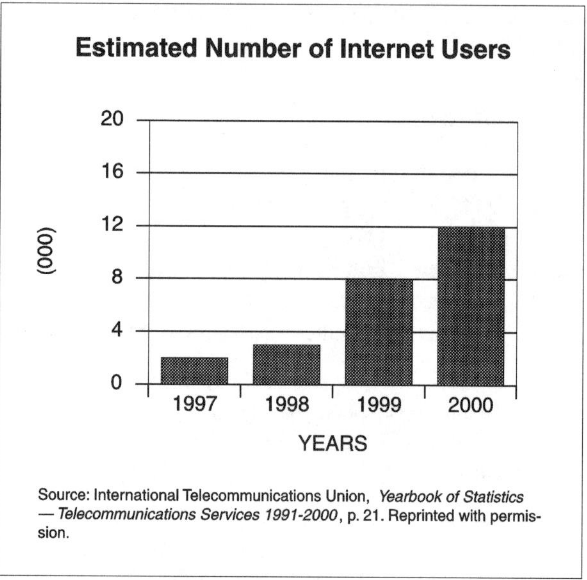

Source: International Telecommunications Union, *Yearbook of Statistics — Telecommunications Services 1991-2000*, p. 21. Reprinted with permission.

ATTITUDE TOWARD FOREIGN MEDIA

Azerbaijan has formed a variety of agreements with foreign media that are for the most part open and intended to be constructive. Azerbaijanis are eager to read, watch, and listen to the foreign media, particularly Western European and American. To those with the financial means, access is available to international broadcast via satellite, as well as publications such as the *New York Times*, *Le Monde*, and the *Wall Street Journal*. Foreign journalists can easily access Azerbaijan by acquiring a visa through the Azerbaijan embassy in their home country. If national media is suppressed in content or delivery, people will increasingly look at the foreign media and private radios, television channels, and press systems. The danger may be the loss of some of the national identity and culture.

ELECTRONIC NEWS MEDIA

As early as 1992, Azerbaijan began to be exposed on the Internet. Today, there are over 10 years of articles, reports, documentaries, journalistic pieces, and a myriad of other writing with regard to Azerbaijan on the World Wide Web. The writing relates to the Azerbaijani culture, languages, politics, economy, society, education, territorial integrity, art, dance, folklore, the relations with the CIS and UGUAM (Ukraine, Georgia, Uzbekistan, Azerbaijan, and Maldovia), international relations, technology, the environment, refugees, and especially the oil and natural gas resource-endowed Azerbaijan. Azer.com, for example, is one of the most comprehensive search engines on this country. There can be some difficulty on Azerbaijani sites due to orthographic differences between transcriptions of Azeri and Russian. An early law, passed by the Azerbaijani Parliament on December 25, 1991, envisioned such problems and therefore adopted an altered, Latinized alphabet to substitute for the Cyrillic.

Issues Related to Online News Flow Some of the frequently broadcast topics and themes include, but not limited to, the Azerbaijani culture, the arts, the territorial conflict with Armenia, the IDPs and refugees, the oil and gas economies, frontier capitalism, public policy in Azerbaijan, state secularism, technology in Azerbaijan, international and diplomatic relations, education, the media and press themselves, crimes, unemployment, corruption and bureaucratic inefficacy, censorship, tourism, business, the role of the Azerbaijani women, elections and politics, and the Constitution. One advantage of the Internet is that it has been able to make the Constitution more accessible. Articles 47 and 49, which specifically address the freedom of speech and the freedom of information, have been particularly of interest to the media. Internet publishing has been strongly influenced by Western business media.

EDUCATION & TRAINING

Higher Learning Institutes in Azerbaijan are rapidly growing and diversifying. The largest concentration of these educational and formative institutions is in the capital Baku, with 17 major schools. The Azerbaijan State Pedagogical University, Baku State University, and Khazar University are some of the main higher learning centers for training in the field of mass media and press. At Khazar University (KU), a Bachelor of Arts in Journalism is offered. It aims at acquiring strong journalistic, press and media, professional and practical skills, along with a social science and training background in ESL and ESP. Specifically, this major offers a broad education and training in the print and broadcast news professions, predicated upon the ongoing needs and changes in the Azerbaijani and world societies. It also encourages the student, or potential journalist, in learning and acquiring on-hand experience via the KU Press activities, the Khazar View Magazine, and the KU Radio and TV studios.

A miscellany of awards is conferred, from the academic training and graduation to the professional, governmental, and international echelons. The Business Journalists Association in Baku is an entity that fosters competition amid economic and business journalists, allocates monetary prizes, and facilitates trips and journeys. Within many of the major daily newspapers, and State and foreign mass media groups, bonuses and awards are afforded. In fact, the media profession is an attractive career, although compensation and wages are still comparatively low.

SUMMARY

Since gaining its independence from the USSR in 1991, Azerbaijan has worked to foster a system of free press. Under the new constitution, the rights to free speech and free press are protected, but there is still censorship both by the government and by journalists. Conflict with Armenia and the struggle to build a democratic country have slowed efforts to improve the press system. Many universities offer journalism programs, and the media is becoming a more and more popular career choice for many people, even though it is still developing.

BIBLIOGRAPHY

Azerbaijan International. Available from www.azer.com/.

The Central Intelligence Agency (CIA).*World Factbook 2001.* Directorate of Intelligence, 2002. Available from www.cia.gov/.

Economist. Available from www.economist.com/.

Ellits, M. *First English Long Travel Guide to Azerbaijan with Georgia.* Yorkshire: Trailblazer Publishing, 1999.

Embassy of the Republic of Azerbaijan. Available from www.azembassy.com/.

Goltz, T. *Azerbaijan Diary.* White Plains, NY: M.E. Sharp, 1998.

International Monetary Fund. *Finance & Development.* 2002.

Said, K. and J. Gramen. *Ali & Nino.* New York: Overlook Press, 1998.

Sarri, S. *Ethics of the International Monetary Systems.* Philadelphia: University of Pennsylvania Press, 1998.

————. *Prolegomena to Islamology.* LeGlobe, 1988.

————. *Poetic Reflections.* Rosethorn Press, 1991.

————. *Visions.* EMW Publishing, 2000.

————. *Middle Easterners & North Africans in Las Vegas (MENAs)-A Socio-Economic and Geo-Political Survey.* EMW Publishing, 2002.

————. *Applied Financial Economics.* La Jolla, CA: Copley Press, 2001.

————. *Twenty-first Century Macroeconomics.* Redding, CA: CAT Publishing, 2000.

————. *Twenty-first Century Microeconomics.* Redding, CA: CAT Publishing, 2000.

Swietochoswki T. and Collins, B. *Historical Dictionary of Azerbaijan.* Lanham, MD: Scarecrow Press, 1999.

U.S. News. Available from www.usnews.com/.

The Wall Street Journal. Available from www.wsj.com/.

The Washington Post. Available from www.washingtonpost.com/.

—Samuel Sarri

The Bahamas

Basic Data

Official Country Name:	Commonwealth of the Bahamas
Region (Map name):	North & Central America
Population:	294,982
Language(s):	English, Creole
Literacy rate:	98.2%

Seven hundred islands make up the Bahamas, located just south of Florida in the Caribbean Sea. Although the country was granted independence from Great Britain in 1973, important ties remain between the two countries. The Bahamas is still a member of the British Commonwealth, and the British monarch serves as its titular head of government. The real leader of the country, however, is the Prime Minister, who presides over a Senate, which is appointed, and a House of Assembly, which is elected. English is the official and most common language spoken, though Creole is spoken by the country's immigrant Haitian population. The estimated population is 300,000 with a 98-percent literacy rate. Tourism is the largest segment of the economy, but offshore banking also produces a significant amount of revenue.

Bahamians enjoy freedom of press and speech. There are two independent, national newspapers that publish from the capital, Nassau. The *Nassau Guardian,* which has been publishing continually since 1844, is the leading daily with an estimated circulation of 15,000 and an online presence. Close behind with an approximate circulation of 13,000 is *The Tribune,* which publishes every day but Sunday. The *Bahama Journal,* also published from Nassau, is a weekly newspaper that reaches 4,000 to 6,000 readers and is also available online.

The *Nassau Guardian* publishes local editions for Freeport (*Freeport News*), Andros Town (*Andros Chronicles*), George Town (*Exuma Sentinel*), Governor's Harbor (*Eleuthere Advocate*), and Turnbull (*Long Island Mail*). The *Abaco Journal,* established in 1987, publishes monthly from Marsh Harbour. A government publication, the *Official Gazette,* publishes weekly. Total circulation for daily newspapers in 1996 was 99 per one thousand population.

There are six radio stations, three AM and three FM, and one television station, which is owned by the government. Bahamians own approximately 215,000 radios and 67,000 television sets. There are 19 Internet service providers.

Bibliography

The *Bahama Journal,* 2002 Home Page. Available from http://www.jonescommunicationsltd.com/journal.html.

''The Bahamas,'' *CIA World Fact Book, 2001-2002.* Available from http://www.cia.gov.

The *Nassau Guardian,* 2002 Home Page. Available from http://www.thenassauguardian.com.

New York: 2000, *United Nations, Department of Economic and Social Affairs, Statistical Division, Statistical Yearbook,* 44th issue, 1997.

—Jenny B. Davis

Bahrain

Basic Data

Official Country Name:	State of Bahrain
Region (Map name):	Middle East

Population:	634,137
Language(s):	Arabic, English, Farsi, Urdu
Literacy rate:	85.2%

Bahrain (*Al Bahrayn*), its name meaning ''two seas,'' is the principle island in an archipelago of some 36 islands that make up the Kingdom of Bahrain (*Al Mamlakah al Bahrayn*— previous to February 14, 2002 the conventional form was the State of Bahrain and the local long form was *Dawlat al Bahrayn*. The local short form remains unchanged as *al Bahrayn*). The country boasts connection with the ancient civilization of Dilmun existing 5,000 some years ago when it was also considered an island paradise by the Sumerians; a kind of Valhalla or Elysian Fields where the wise and brave enjoyed eternal life. Bahrain is situated in the Persian Gulf about 28 kilometers northwest of the Qatar Peninsula and 24 kilometers east of Saudi Arabia. Bahrain became accessible by automobile as of November 1986 when it established a causeway with Saudi Arabia. A causeway with Qatar is also expected in the near future having become a possibility as of March 2001 when the International Court of Justice (ICJ), finding in favor of Bahrain, resolved a longstanding ownership dispute concerning the Hawar islands.

Febuary 14, 2002 Bahrain adopted a new constitution changing its status from emirate to monarchy. This fulfilled a portion of a referendum drafted in late December 2000 that has met with overwhelming public support. Other aspects of the referendum to be implemented by 2004 include an elected bicameral parliament and an independent judiciary. The referendum continued a trend toward increasing respect for human rights, religious tolerance, and freedom of expression in Bahrain. In May of 2000 the Emir (Sheikh Hamad Bin-Isa Al-Khalifah) appointed women and non-Muslims to the Consultative Council for the first time — a move welcomed by much of the international community — and immediately preceding the December referendum the Emir ordered the release of all political prisoners. In February 2001 the 1974 State Security Law and the 1995 State Security Court were abolished. As well, Bahrain has licensed the Bahrain Society for Human Rights, has promised NGO's increasing favor in the eyes of the government, and has granted citizenship to Shi'ite Muslims of Iranian descent who have had numerous generations living in Bahrain. This is especially important due to the ruling Al-Khalifah family, in power since 1783 upon expelling the Persians, being part of the Sunni Bani Utbah tribe while the majority of the population is Shi'ite.

Bahrain, the smallest of the Persian Gulf states, still has a commendable set of communications media that far precedes its political independence gained in 1971. The press began during the 1930s and maintained independent status until 1957 when the government curtailed all independent press functions due to their support of 1950s riots and labor group strikes. Then, the Bahrani government issued a press law in 1965 that allowed for newspaper production to begin again according to unambiguous regulations that essentially disallowed for criticism of state interests in the broadest sense. However, even under these stringencies the press began to reemerge.

In 1967, *Akhbar al Khaleej*, Bahrain's first Arabic daily opened under the possession of Abdulla Mardi. Today there are four dailies with a fifth that has offices in Manama (the capital), but originates in the United Arab Emirates (UAE). The two Arabic dailies are *Akhbar al Khaleej* or *Gulf News* (circ. 17,000) and *Al-Ayam* or *The Days* (circ. 37,000). The two English dailies are the *Bahrain Tribune* (circ. 12,500) and the *Gulf Daily News* (circ. 50,000). The fifth daily originating in the UAE is the *Khaleej Times* (circ. 72, 565). There are also about eight weeklies that circulate and tend to have more pronounced political leanings than the dailies. Among the largest weeklies are *Al-Adwhaa'* or *Lights* (circ. 7,000), *Al-Bahrain ath-Thaqafya* and *Huna al-Bahrain* published by the Ministry of Information, *Al-Mawakif* (circ. 6,000), *Oil and Gas News* (circ. 5,000), and *Sada al-Usbou'* which circulates in various Gulf states (circ. 40,000).

There are 15 periodicals that circulate currently, many of which are business and tourism related. Some of these include *Bahrain of the Month* (monthly circ. 9,948), *Discover Bahrain*, *Gulf Construction* (monthly circ. 12,485), *Gulf Panorama* (monthly circ. 15,000), *Al-Hayat at-Tijariya* or *Commerce Review* (monthly circ. 7,500), *Al-Hidayah* or *Guidance* (monthly circ. 5,000), *Al-Musafir al-Arabi* or *Arab Traveller* (bimonthly), *Shipping and Transport News International* (bimonthly circ. 5, 500), and *Travel and Tourism News Middle East* (montly circ. 6,333).

Bahrain's television and radio media are respectively run by an agency with state ties — previously state-owned, in 1993 ruled an independent corporation to be committee-run by the Emir — and a commercial agency: Bahrain Radio and Television Corporation (BRTC) and Radio Bahrain. The BRTC operates on five terrestrial TV Channels, broadcasting in Arabic and English. The main Arabic and English channel each accept advertising. BRTC's signals are strong enough to cover eastern Saudi Arabia, Qatar and the UAE. For its radio programs the BRTC utilizes two 10-kilowatt transmitters and also broadcasts in Arabic and English. Radio Bahrain broadcasts in English and Arabic 24 hours a day. Its programming includes news, music, the arts, sports, and religion.

There are two other factors which play into the traditional electronic media situation in Bahrain. First, English language TV and radio programs can be received by Bahrani's from Saudi Arabian Saudi Aramco and from the U.S. Air Force in Dharan. And, while satellite TV is officially banned, as of 1999 roughly 6 percent of the country's 230,000 homes had access. Statistically, people owning televisions in 2000 was 402 per 1,000 and owning radios was 545 per 1,000.

In 2000 there were an estimated 40,000 Bahraini internet subscribers representing nearly 6 percent of the population as compared with 2,000 in 1995. In 2000 there were approximately 138.7 personal computers per 1,000 people, while there had only been 50.3 in 1995. The government maintains an official Web site and has links leading to newspapers, periodicals, radio, and television stations also available on the internet. Routing of all traffic occurs on only seven secure servers.

Bahrain maintains positive relations with foreign agencies. Agence France-Presse (AFP), Associated Press (AP), Reuters, and Gulf News Agency all maintain offices in Manama. As well, contributing to strong ties with the foreign press and maintaining the governmental trend toward increasing press respect, the Bahrain Journalists Association was allowed and founded in 2000 and maintains a membership of 250 members.

Though the press and the country as a whole are experiencing relaxed government control there are a few issues that have caused concern as of late. First, in November 2001, Hafez El Sheikh Saleh, a journalist with the daily *Akhbar al Khaleej* was charged by the justice minister as betraying national unity and creating writings antithetical to the National Charter and the constitution. Nabil Yacub al-Hamer, the information minister, banned Saleh from traveling abroad or practicing journalism. Second, in November 2001, Bahrain prohibited the London published Arabic daily *Azzaman* from being printed in the country because it had been accused of criticizing the emir of Qatar therefore breaking the press and publications law. Third, at the end of March 2002 the Bahraini government blocked at least five Web sites said to have offensive content, lies and questionable information. Sites blocked included one run by Islamic fundamentalist Abdel Wahab Hussein, one by the Bahrain Freedom Movement — a political opposition group, and *Al-Manama*—an online newspaper. Finally, in May of 2002, Bahrain refused to let Qatari based Al-Jazeera TV cover municipal elections. Al-Hamer said Al-Jazeera was "trying to harm Bahrain" and was "infiltrated by Zionists." Reporters Without Borders (Reporters sans frontières - RSF) wrote that it was suggested that Al-Jazeera was refused due to earlier unauthorized coverage of Bahraini protests in Manama against Israeli incursions into the West Bank.

While the material presented here sounds a somber note, overall the future appears positive for Bahrain. King Al-Khalifah has worked extraordinarily hard to facilitate reform while maintaining political stability in the country. Bahraini Political trends, technological development, and public desire all suggest expanding frameworks for freedom of the press, freedom of expression, and inclusive citizenship.

BIBLIOGRAPHY

Akhbar Al-Khaleej (Gulf News). Available: http://www.akhbar-alkhaleej.com

Al-Alyam (The Days). Available: http://www.alayam.com

All the World's Newspapers. Available: www.webwombat.com.au/intercom/newsprs/index.htm

Atalpedia Online. Country Index. Available: http://www.atlapedia.com/online/country_index

Bahrain Tribune. Available: http://www.bahraintribune.com

BBC News Country Profiles. Available: http://news.bbc.co.uk/hi/english/world/middle_east/country_profiles

Boyd, Douglas. Broadcasting in the Arab World: A Survey of the Electronic Media in the Middle East, 3rd ed. Ames, IA: Iowa State University Press, 1999.

CIA. The World Factbook 2001. Available: http://www.cia.gov/cia/publications/factbook/

Clarke, Angela. Bahrain: Oil and Development, 1929-1989. London: Immel, 1998.

Dabrowska, Karen. Bahrain Briefing: The Struggle for Democracy. London: Colourmast, 1997.

Gulf Daily News. Available: http://www.gulf-daily-news.com

International Press Institute. World Press Review. Available: http://www.freemedia.at/wpfr/world.html

Kingdom of Bahrain Ministry of Information. Available: http://www.moi.gov.bh/english/index02.htm

Kurian, George, ed. World Press Encyclopedia. New York: Facts on File, Inc., 1982.

Maher, Joanne, ed. Regional Surveys of the World: The Middle East and North Africa 2002, 48th ed. London: Europa Publications, 2001.

Radio Bahrain. Available: http://tv.gna.gov.bh/radiobahrain.asx

Redmon, Clare, ed. Willings Press Guide 2002, Vol. 2. Chesham Bucks, UK: Waymaker Ltd, 2002.

Reporters Sans Frontieres. Bahrain Annual Report 2002. Available: http://www.rsf.fr

Reporters Sans Frontieres. Middle East Archives 2002. Available: http://www.rsf.fr

Russell, Malcom. The Middle East and South Asia 2001, 35th ed. Harpers Ferry, WV: United Book Press, Inc., 2001.

Sadaa Al-Esbua. Available: http://www.sadaalesbua.com

Stat-USA International Trade Library: Country Background Notes. Available: http://www.stat-usa.gov

Sumner, Jeff, ed. Gale Directory of Publications and Broadcast Media, Vol. 5 136th ed. Farmington Hills, MI: Gale Group, 2002.

The Library of Congress. Country Studies. Available: http://lcweb2.loc.gov/frd/cs/

The Middle East, 9th ed. Washington, DC: Congressional Quarterly Inc., 2000

UNESCO Institute for Statistics. Available: http://www.uis.unesco.org

Wheatcroft, Andrew. The Life and Times of Sheikh Salman bin Hamad al-Khalifa: Ruler of Bahrain 1942-61. London: Kegan Paul Intl., 1995.

World Bank. Data and Statistics. Available: http://www.worldbank.org/data/countrydata/countrydata.html

World Desk Reference. Available: http://www.travel.dk.com/wdr

Zahlan, Rosmarie Said, and Owen, Roger. The Making of the Modern Gulf States: Kuwait, Bahrain, Qatar, the UAE and Oman. Reading: Ithaca Press, 1997.

—Clint B. Thomas Baldwin

BANGLADESH

BASIC DATA

Official Country Name:	People's Republic of Bangladesh
Region (Map name):	East & South Asia
Population:	131,269,860
Language(s):	Bangla (official known as Bengali), English
Literacy rate:	56.0%
Area:	144,000 sq km
GDP:	47,106 (US$ millions)
Circulation per 1,000:	254
Number of Television Stations:	15
Number of Television Sets:	770,000
Television Sets per 1,000:	5.9
Number of Radio Stations:	26
Number of Radio Receivers:	6,150,000
Radio Receivers per 1,000:	46.9
Number of Individuals with Computers:	200,000
Computers per 1,000:	1.5
Number of Individuals with Internet Access:	100,000
Internet Access per 1,000:	0.8

BACKGROUND & GENERAL CHARACTERISTICS

Bangladesh has the dubious distinction of being the most densely populated country in the world and one of the poorest. Roughly 85 percent of its population lives in villages, where there is a frequent possibility of natural disasters such as floods, severe storms or tidal waves. Around two-thirds of the people live on agriculture and there is little industry. Illiteracy is at an unacceptable high; only 38.1 percent of the population, age 15 or older, can read and write. Of these, the ratio of males to females is 2:1. The per capita income is $380, which may not take account of lots of economic transactions in the countryside because they are barter transactions or do not enter the government statistics.

On the plus side, despite the apparent economic misery, the people always seem tremendously interested in public affairs and eager to know what appears in the press or over the radio and television, even though only a small segment can afford a television set. The people are ethnically homogeneous, 98 percent of them speaking Bengali, which is the national language, mandatory in all government offices; English is understood by the elite and serves also as an official language. Most of the press as well as radio and television broadcasting is consequently in Bengali although the small English-language press — newspapers and weeklies — has an influence far out of proportion to its circulation numbers.

The predominant religion is Islam (88.3 percent), with Hindus (10.5 percent) as the principal minority, adherents of Buddhism, Christianity and others account for 1.2 percent. Officially, the Republic of Bangladesh is a secular democracy with everyone above the age of 18, regardless of race, religion or gender having the right to vote. An amendment to the constitution adopted in 1988 established Islam as the state religion. Also in practice, Islam is supported by the government, which disallows any criticism of it in the media. However, despite the religious affinity with the Islamic world, culturally Bangladeshis feel closer to the speakers of the Bengali language in the Indian part of Bengal, sharing with them the rich cultural traditions manifested in literature, music and the arts. The press and media reflect such a love among the citizens of Bangladesh and regularly publish special articles and features on Bengali culture.

History and Recent Politics From August 1947 when the British carved out the two dominions of India and Pakistan until Dec. 16, 1971, the present area of Bangladesh comprised the Eastern wing of Pakistan, designated as East Pakistan. In the absence of genuine social, cultural and economic integration between the two wings of Pakistan, East Pakistan remained neglected and disgruntled as its cultural ethnic identity overwhelmed the common Islamic tie with West Pakistan, whose bureaucracy and military gave a disproportionately low representation to East Pakistanis, who numbered 55 percent to West Pakistan's 45 percent.

The diverse differences came to the fore in December 1970 when in the elections to Pakistan's Constituent Assembly and provincial assemblies, Sheikh Mujibur Rahman, of the Awami League (AL), campaigning on a "Six-Point Programme" which included greater autonomy for East Pakistan, won 167 out of 169 seats there. The victory gave AL an overwhelming majority in Pakistan's Constituent Assembly and made Mujibur Rahman a legitimate contender for the position of Prime Minister of Pakistan. The total reluctance of President Yahya Khan and of Zulfikar Bhutto, leader of the Pakistan People's Party (PPP), to implement the electoral results led to Mujibar Rahman's declaration of a political strike (hartal) and the AL's assumption of power in East Pakistan. In March, 1971, Yahya Khan cracked down on Dhaka, East Pakistan's capital, massacring thousands and arresting Mujibur Rahman and detaining him in West Pakistan on charges of treason. The AL was declared illegal, an action which drove its leaders into India where in April 1971, they formed the Constituent Assembly of Bangladesh in Exile. They also formed the Mukti Bahini, a force composed of Bengalis in Pakistan's army and volunteers, as "freedom fighters" setting the stage for a civil war between the two wings of Pakistan. A million East Pakistanis crossed the border into India as refugees.

Partly to resolve the problem of the refugee burden and partly to help the Mukti Bahini in its political goals, the Indian Army joined in the war against Pakistan's military forces beginning Dec. 16, 1971. Two weeks later, with the surrender of the Pakistani troops, the nation of Bangladesh was born. On Jan. 12, 1972, Mujibur Rahman, released from Pakistani jail, returned to Dhaka a hero to become the first Prime Minister of the People's Republic of Bangladesh.

The Constituent Assembly of Bangladesh, consisting of those elected in 1970, adopted a constitution effective December 1972, providing for a parliamentary democracy based on four principles: democracy, socialism, secularism and nationalism. A series of natural disasters, economic problems and domestic disorder led to the proclamation of a National Emergency in December 1974 and the adoption of the fourth amendment to the Constitution enabling Mujibur Rahman to become the President, dissolve the Parliament and replace the AL with a new party, the Bangladesh Peasants and Workers League (BAKSAL). He banned all other parties. It was the worst year for fundamental freedoms, including freedom of expression. The government imposed restrictions on the press and the media which remained in place for the large part until the mid-1990s.

The reaction to the emergency was swift. On August 15, 1975, some elements in the army assassinated Mujibur Rahman, some of his family and close supporters, and prevailed on Khondakar Mostaque Ahmed, a former minister of commerce, to become the President. He dissolved the BAKSAL, declared martial law but restored the parliament. He was soon replaced by an army general. The political position remained fluid moving from one point of instability to another until in 1978, under the revised constitution, General Ziaur Rahman (Zia) became President and leader of a new party, the Bangladesh Nationalist Party (BNP) and abolished the martial law. His assassination in 1981 led to instability again until in March, 1982, Lieutenant-General Ershad assumed authority. He established the Jatiya party (JP) and by the end of the year became President, remaining in that position until 1990, when he was deposed, subsequently tried and convicted of a number of offenses and sent to prison.

In February 1991, following elections, Begum Khaleda Zia, the widow of former president Zia, became the Prime Minister leading the majority of the BNP members in the parliament. In September, the constitution was revised. The country returned to a parliamentary system of government, ending 16 years of executive presidential rule. In early 1996, the press played a key role in persuading the BNP government, whose term of office had just ended, to hand over authority to a caretaker government in April and thereby set the stage for national elections in June. The media succeeded; the general election of June 1996 held by the caretaker government put a coalition government under the AL's Sheikh Hasina.

The victory of the press in enabling a transition of government through the mechanism of a "caretaker government'' led to the adoption of a constitutional amendment at the end of 1996. The ''Caretaker Government Amendment'' made it obligatory that, in future, all general elections in Bangladesh would be held by a neutral, non-partisan caretaker administration headed by the President. Accordingly, on July 13, 2001, Hasina stepped down as Prime Minister handing over the charge to a caretaker administration. The general elections of October 2001 held by the caretaker administration brought in a new government, this time under the BNP's Khaleda Zia as Prime Minister.

History of the Press The early history of the press in Bangladesh is inextricably linked to the Bengal presidency, which covered the present Bangladesh and the Indian states of West Bengal and parts of Orissa and Assam under the East India Company (until 1858) and thereafter under the direct British rule. Calcutta, being the capital of all the British Indian possessions, became a major center for newspapers and magazines.

Looking narrowly at the history of the press in the area covered by the present Bangladesh, one readily sees the importance of Bangladesh's capital, Dhaka (formerly Dacca) as the second major center (after Calcutta) for the concentration of newspapers and magazines. Two of the earliest magazines in Bengali — *Kabita Kushumabati* and *Dhaka Prakash*—were published around 1860 in Dhaka. Over the following two decades, Dhaka published several newspapers in Bengali: *Mahapap*, *Bangabandhu* and *Balyabibah*. Lesser centers like Banshal published *Gram Dut*, *Balaranjika*, *Hitasandhani* and *Barishal Barta*; Rajshahi published *Hindu Ranjika*. Also of note is the fact that a newspaper of great distinction on the Indian sub-continent, *Amrit Bazar Patrika*, was first published in Jessore in 1868.

With the partition of the Indian sub-continent and the emergence of Pakistan in two wings — West and East — in 1947, East Pakistan began publication of two dailies: *Purba Pakistan* and the *Paigam* and a weekly, *Zindagi*. In the following year, the daily *Azad* and the morning *News*, which were published in Calcutta since 1936 and 1942 respectively shifted to Dhaka. Two more Bengali dailies, which grew into being the most important newspapers in Bangladesh — the *Sangbad* and the *Ittefaq*— began publication in 1950 and 1955 respectively while another daily, the *Pakistan Observer* in English started in 1948.

The period around the birth of Bangladesh witnessed the birth of many new papers and magazines. Such include: *Banglar Bani* (1971), *Ganakantha* (1971), *Samaj* (1972), *Janapada* (1973), *Bangabarta* (1973) — all in Dacca; *Andolan* (1973), *People's View* (1970), *Dainik Michiil* (1972), *Dainik Swadhinata* (1972) — all in Chittagong and Daily *Janabarta*, *Dainik Prabha* and *Tribune* in Khulna.

Modern Press Statistics of number of newspapers and their circulation vary with different sources. According to the *Editor and Publisher International Year Book* 1999, there were 40 daily newspapers in Bangladesh, and the number of cities with competing newspapers is substantial. Dhaka, for example, is the home of 21 newspapers, four of which boast a circulation of more than 100,000. Five of Dhaka's newspapers are printed in English, and 16 in Bengali.

The city of Chittagong prints seven newspapers — five in Bengali and two in English — one with a circulation of more than 20,000; four with a 10,000; and two with 5,000. Khulna has six newapapers, one of which is printed in English. Four have a circulation of greater than 5,000. Jessore has three papers, all printed in Bengali; Rajshahi has two Bengali newspapers; and Dinajpur has one Bengali newspaper.

Of these, the largest two dailies in Bengali — the *Ittefaq* and *Dainik Inquilab*— are published from Dhaka with a circulation of 215,900 and 180,140 respectively in 1999.

The total circulation of the eight English language dailies was a little over 145,000; those published in Dhaka had a circulation of nearly 117,000. Although only about 10 percent of the total circulation of all newspapers, the English press is very influential because it is read by intellectuals, academics, sophisticated politicians and foreign diplomats. Many of its columnists enjoy an international reputation for their superior abilities in reporting and analysis.

The newspapers suffered a major blow when most of them came under fire under the Emergency Regulations in 1974. In 1972, the Mujibur Rahman government took over the ownership and management of four daily newspapers and one periodical: *Morning News*, *Azad*, *Observer*, *Dainik Bangla* and *Purbodesh*. The government imposed severe controls over those which survived the onslaught. By 1997, following the return of the Awami League Party to power, the controls were relaxed though four publications still remained under the government-controlled trust. These were: *Dainik Bangla*, *Bangladesh Times*, weekly *Bichitra* and fortnightly *Ananda Bichitra*. Except for these, most of the newspapers in Bangladesh at present are entirely owned privately, mostly by limited liability companies.

ECONOMIC FRAMEWORK

For years after its independence, Bangladesh needed massive economic assistance because of a series of natural disasters, governmental mismanagement and rampant corruption all of which hampered development. In the last decade or more, economic conditions have improved. The economy is market-based, but the Government owns all utilities, most transport companies, and many large manufacturing and distribution firms. A small, wealthy elite controls much of the private economy, but a middle class is emerging.

Bangladesh needs industrial development and massive foreign direct investment, which is currently very low, concentrated in the gas sector and in electrical power generation facilities. Remittances from workers overseas in Saudi Arabia, Kuwait, United Arab Emirates, Oman, Qatar, Malaysia and Singapore enable the government to bridge the gap between exports ($5.1 billion) and imports $8.01 billion), for example, in 1998. The exports are principally in garments, jute and jute goods, frozen fish and seafood, with the United States being the best destination (33 percent), Germany (10 percent) and the United Kingdom (9 percent). Imports have been largely of machinery and equipment, chemicals, iron and steel, raw cotton, food, crude oil and petroleum. The principal trading partners in imports are India (12 percent), China (9 percent), Japan (7 percent), South Korea and Hong Kong each 6 percent. Foreign aid ($1.475 billion in fiscal 1996-1997) remains an important source of the much-needed foreign exchange; the external debt was an estimated $16.5 billion in 1998.

Financial Condition of Newspapers Newspaper ownership and content are not subject to direct government restriction. However, if the Government chooses, it can influence journalists through financial means. Government-sponsored advertising and allocations of newsprint from the state-owned newsprint mills in Khulna are central to many newspapers' financial viability. At times, the government creates an ''artificial scarcity'' of newsprint and denies allocation or delays allocation of newsprint to certain newspapers, which are even mildly critical of the government. The Newsprint Control Order of 1974 entrusted the Ministry of Commerce and Foreign Trade as well as the Ministry of Information and Broadcasting with control over the production, consumption and distribution of newsprint.

Government-sponsored advertising is the largest source of revenue, taking 50 percent of the space of the newspapers. In allocating advertising through the Department of Films and Publications, the Government states that it considers circulation of newspapers, implementation of wage board recommendations, objectivity in reporting and coverage of development activities. In the past, commercial organizations often were reluctant to advertise in newspapers critical of the Government due to fear of government or bureaucratic retaliation, however, this appears no longer to be the case.

Under the State of Emergency regulations of 1974, most newspapers were closed down or regulated. At that point, the government itself took over some newspapers and prominent political weeklies. By 1997, most such restrictive regulations were removed except that four publications continue to be financed and managed by the government-appointed trust: *Dainik Bangla. Bangladesh Times*, weekly *Bichitra* and fortnightly *Ananda Bichitra.*

Among the well-funded publication groups in the private sector are the Ittefaq Group and the Inquilab Group. *The Ittefaq*, which commands the largest circulation. was founded by the late legendary Tofazzal Hossain; it is now run by his son, who claims it is non-partisan and meant for all classes. Its non-partisan claims are sometimes questioned particularly because its editor/owner has been a minister in two governments. The financial independence of the other popular daily, *Sangbad*, is also well assured partly because of the support of the industrialist, Ahmadul Kabir.

PRESS LAWS

Article 39(1) of the Constitution provides for freedom of speech, expression and the press but Article 39(2) makes the enjoyment of these rights subject to ''reasonable restrictions'' in the interests of ''the security. of the state, friendly relations with foreign states, public order, decency and morality in relation to contempt of court, defamation or incitement to an offence.''. Numerous Acts inhibit these freedoms, most notorious in this respect being the Special Powers Act (SPA) of 1974, whose rigor was marginally lessened in 1991 by allowing bail for journalists and others arrested under that Act. The SPA made it an offense, punishable by five years' imprisonment and/or fine ''to print, publish or distribute prejudicial reports.'' Journalists were required to identify all sources of information and authorities were given draconian powers to seize documents and newspapers, to ban publications and to search premises. Section 99A of the Code of Criminal Procedure made any printed matter, defamatory of the country's President or the Prime Minister, an offense punishable by imprisonment from two to seven years.

The worst years for legislation limiting the freedom of the press were 1973 to 1975, following the brief honeymoon with Prime Minister Mujibur Rahman, who had emerged as the nation's hero after the birth of Bangladesh. Besides the SPA, a State of Emergency declared in 1974 empowered the government to ban any foreign periodical. By June 1975, 20 dailies and all political weeklies were banned except those taken over by the government: *Dainik Bangla*, *Bangladesh Times*, weekly *Bichitra* and fortnightly *Ananda Bichitra.*

The Press Council Act of 1974 ostensibly entrusted the Press Council (PC) with preserving the freedom of the press. Its responsibilities included responsibility for devising a code of conduct for maintaining high professional standards. In practice, the PC would help the press to avoid a conflict with the government through self-censorship. The PC Act held the PC responsible for protecting the fundamental rights of the citizens against any ''unscrupulous or irresponsible'' newspaper or journalist. The Act did provide the right of the journalists to confidentiality of a news source. The PC has no powers to take action against the government for transgressing the freedom of the press, nor does the government consult the PC before taking action against a newspaper or a journalist.

The Government's human rights record has remained poor in many significant areas. It has continued to commit serious abuses, although it respected citizens' rights in some areas. The Police committed a number of extra-judicial killings, and some persons died in police custody under suspicious circumstances in the 1990s. Police routinely use torture, beatings and other forms of abuse while interrogating suspects. Police frequently beat demonstrators. The government rarely punishes persons responsible for torture or unlawful deaths. It continues to arrest and detain persons arbitrarily under the Special Powers Act (SPA) and Section 54 of the Code of Criminal Procedure.

A silver lining of the situation is that the higher levels of the judiciary display a significant degree of independence and often rule against the Government; however, lower judicial officers tend to toe the line of the executive, and are reluctant to challenge government decisions.

Despite such restrictions, self-censorship and governmental abuse of power, the press, numbering hundreds of daily and weekly publications, provides a lively forum for a wide range of views. The free spirit of the Bengalis prevails. While most publications support the overall policies of the government, several newspapers report critically on government policies and activities, including those of the Prime Minister.

Censorship

All publications are subject to Press and Publication Act of 1973, which requires four copies of each issue to be sent to a ''designated government agency.'' While the government categorically denies the existence of censorship, in practice, papers are ''guided'' by the advice and briefings of the Principal Information Officer of the Ministry of Information and Broadcasting as well as by the External Publicity Division of the Ministry of External Affairs. The President's Council of Advisors controls the newspaper editors informally. In general, criticism of economic policies is more likely to be tolerated than sensitive political issues.

Foreign publications are subject to review and censorship. Censorship most often is used in cases of immodest or obscene photographs, perceived misrepresentation or defamation of Islam, and objectionable comments about national leaders. In October 2001, the BNP Government banned the popular Calcutta-based, Bangla-language magazine *Desh*. The Government alleged that the magazine was offensive to the country and its citizens.

A government Film Censor Board reviews local and foreign films, and may censor or ban them on grounds of state security, law and order, religious sentiment, obscenity, foreign relations, defamation or plagiarism. In general, the Film Censor Board looks kindly at the Bangladesh-made films, occasionally suggesting some cuts. However, the Board has habitually banned the screenings of several imported English-language movies for their pornographic content. Video rental libraries provide a wide variety of films to their borrowers, and government efforts to enforce censorship on these rental films are sporadic and ineffectual. The Government does not limit citizens' access to the Internet.

State-Press Relations

Journalists and others are potentially subject to incarceration when criminal libel proceedings are filed by private parties. Members of Parliament from the ruling party have, in the past, filed separate criminal libel suits against several newspapers after articles were published that the politicians viewed as false and defamatory. The journalists in all cases received anticipatory bail from the courts, and none of the cases moved to trial. Sedition charges remained pending, and those persons accused remained on bail.

In November 2000, a new sedition charge (there was another sedition charge already pending against him) was filed against an editor, Bahaudin, for publishing a parody of the national anthem mocking the Prime Minister. When the police arrived at Bahauddin's residence to arrest him, he was not there, so they arrested his brother, Mainuddin, instead under the PSA and, therefore, not eligible for bail. Mainuddin was not charged; after 16 days he was released. Charges against editor Bahauddin remain pending in both sedition cases.

Virtually all print journalists practice self-censorship to some degree, and commonly are reluctant to criticize politically influential personalities in both the Government and the opposition; however, some journalists do make such criticism. Many journalists cite fear of possible harassment, retaliation, or physical harm as a reason to avoid sensitive stories. Violent attacks on journalists and newspapers, and efforts to intimidate them by government leaders, political party activists, and others frequently occur. Violence against journalists has increased since 2001. Political parties and persons acting on their behalf conducted attacks both on media offices; individual journalists were targeted for their unfavorable news reporting. These crimes largely remained unresolved and the perpetrators, often identified by name or party affiliation in press reports, have not been held accountable. Attacks by political activists on journalists also are common during times of political street violence, and some journalists were injured in police actions.

BROADCAST MEDIA

To start with, East Pakistan, as Bangladesh was then known, had very poor telecommunications. Between 1959 and 1963, the first 100 KW medium wave and short wave transmitters were installed in Dhaka in order to improve communication between the two wings of Pakistan separated from each other by over 1,200 miles. There were relaying stations in Chittagong, Sylhet, Rangpur, Rajshahi and Khulna.

The 1971 war for the liberation of Bangladesh destroyed most of the facilities particularly in Khulna. Immediately after liberation, the government established the Bangla Betar Radio (BBR) with eight regional stations. In June 1975, Bangladesh opened its first earth satellite radio station at Betbunia, 140 miles south-west of Dhaka with $8 million from the Canadian International Development agency.

Television began in 1964, thanks to Nippon Electric Company as part owner of the pilot TV project. By the end of the 1960s, there was a satellite station operating from Chittagong along with two relay stations in Khulna and Rajshahi. By 1970, there were 35 hours of weekly telecasts, mostly in Bengali. Following the liberation of Bangladesh, Mujibur Rahman nationalized TV Bangladesh (BTV) Corporation with the government as the controlling stockholder and Nippon Electric as a major stockholder. The BTV has expanded considerably since then with its headquarters in the Rampura sector of Dhaka.

The Betar Radio (BR) has eight radio stations in Dhaka, including one for overseas service. There are FM facilities in Dhaka, Sylhet, Chittagong, Rajshahi, Rangpur and Khulna. As for television, there were 15 broadcast stations in 1999 with an estimated 1.5 million sets in 2001. Programs are aired nationwide and to the other countries of South Asia, South and Southeast Asia, Middle East, Europe and the US. The BTV covers 95 percent of the population with relay stations in Dhaka, Rangpur, Mymensingh, Noakhali, Satkhira, Sylhet, Khulna, Natore, Rangamal, Chittagong, Cox's Bazar, Jenaidah, Thajurgaon, Brahmanpura and Patunkhali.

Together, the BR and BTV have a workforce of nearly 4,000 and are responsible to the Parliamentary Committee for their functioning. In practice, they are virtually controlled by the Ministry of Information and Broadcasting.

In the early 1990s, Cable TV was introduced. It became quickly popular and was availed of in more than one million homes with about 2,000 cable operators having an average of 200-250 subscribers, mostly in Dhaka and Chittagong. In 2002, they charge an average $3 or about 175 takas per connection. All operators need a license from the BTV, costing them an annual 25,000 Takas in the four main cities and 10,000 Takas in other urban centers.

In 1991 and 1996 elections, both the principal political parties —the AL and the BNP— called for a free, national and democratic broadcasting system under an independent authority. On Sept. 9, 1996, the AL government appointed a 16-member committee to recommend measures and authorize private TV and radio. In 1997, the committee submitted its report. The US Department of State's Report on Human Rights, 2001 observes that the Bangladesh Ministry of Information and Broadcasting thought the recommendations for privatization were "unrealistic." The first measure toward privatization was, however, taken in March 1999, authorizing privately owned Ekushey TV to go on air by the end of 1999. It has agreed to follow the existing censorship guidelines.

The government owns and controls virtually all radio and television stations with the exception of a few independent stations, such as Ekushey Television (ETV) and Radio Metrowave. The activities of the Prime Minister occupy the bulk of prime time news bulletins on both television and radio, followed by the activities of members of the Cabinet. Opposition party news gets little coverage. As a condition of operation, both private stations are required to broadcast for free some government news programs and speeches by the Prime Minister and President. In 1996, a government committee recommended measures for authorizing autonomy for radio and television broadcasts. On July 12, 2001, Parliament approved two bills granting autonomy to state-run Bangladesh Television (BTV) and Bangladesh Betar (Bangladesh Radio). Even with passage of these laws, the public still believes that there is no real autonomy for BTV and Bangladesh Radio. Government intrusion into the selection of news remains a pervasive problem. Many journalists at these stations exercise self-censorship out of regard for what they feel were the government's wishes.

SIGNIFICANT DATES

- 1996: Free and Fair elections; press plays a major role in the proposal for a pre-election care-taker government.

- 1997: The Government disbands the state-controlled trust which was in charge of publishing four important newspapers since 1974.
- 1999: Private television ownership permitted.

BIBLIOGRAPHY

Ahmed, Q.Z., *Development News in the Newspapers of Bangladesh*, (unpublished doctoral dissertation), Washington, D.C., Howard University, 1998.

Al-Mujahid, S. *Broadcasting in Asia and the Pacific: A Continental Survey of Radio and Television*, Philadelphia, Temple Univ. Press, 1978

Anam, M. *Walking the Tightrope: Press Freedom and Professional Standards in Asia*, AMIC, 1998.

Anwar, M.T., ''Bangladesh: Fewer 'Black Laws''' in *Press Systems in SAARC*. AMIC, 23-27. Singapore: 1994.

APT (Asia-Pacific Telecommunity), *The APT Yearbook 2000*. Bangkok and Surrey.

Billboard Publications. *World Radio and TV Handbook 2001*. Amsterdam: 2001.

Bhuiyan, S.I. and Gunaratne, S.A.. ''Bangladesh'' In *Gunaratne, S.A..Ed. Handbook of the Media in Asia*. Sage, 39-66. New Delhi: 2000.

Editor & Publisher. *Editor & Publisher International Yearbook 2000*. New York.

French, D. and Richards, M., Eds. *Contemporary Television: Eastern Perspectives*. Sage. New Delhi: 1996.

Gunaratne, S.A., Hasim, M.S.., and Kasenally, R. ''Small is Beautiful, Information Potential of three Indian Ocean Rim Countries'' *Media Asia*. 24, 188-205. 1997.

Lent, J.A. ''Bangladesh'' *Newspapers in Asia: Contemporary Trends and Problems*. Heinemann Asia, 428-441. Hong Kong: 1982.

''Media Monitors in Bangladesh,'' In *Venkateswaran, K.S., (Comp)., Media Monitors in Asia*. AMIC, 12-16. Singapore: 1996.

Montu, A.T., ''CATC in Bangladesh,'' *Satellite & Cable TV, 7,3*. May1999. Available from http://www.Webmaniacs.com/

Moslem, S., ''Bangladesh,'' In *Asian Communication Handbook*, A. Goonasekara and Holaday, D., Eds., 5-15. AMIC, Singapore: 1998.

Network Wizards, *Internet Host Survey*: Online.

Salam, S.A., *Mass Media in Bangladesh: Newspapers, Radio and Television*, Dhaka, South Asian News Agency, 1997.

Ullah, M., ''Bangladesh,'' In *Communication Development and Human Rights in Asia*, Hamelink, C.E. and Mehra, A., Eds., AMIC. Singapore: 1990.

UNESCO, *Statistical Yearbook*. Paris: 2000.

U.S. Department of State. *Bangladesh: Country Report on Human Rights Practices*. 2001. Available from http://www.state.gov/

World Association of Newspapers (WAN)., *World Press Trends*. World Association of Newspapers. Paris: 2000.

—Damodar Sar Desai

BARBADOS

BASIC DATA

Official Country Name:	Barbados
Region (Map name):	Caribbean
Population:	274,540
Language(s):	English
Literacy rate:	97.4%

Barbados, located northeast of Venezuela, is considered the Little England of the Caribbean. Not only were the British the original settlers — the island was uninhabited when they arrived in 1627—but the island remains an independent state within the British Commonwealth. The British monarch serves as the titular head of government and is represented by a Governor General. The Governor General appoints a Prime Minister, who presides over a bicameral Parliament that consists of a Senate, which is appointed by the Governor General, and a House of Assembly, which is popularly elected. The population of Barbados is approximately 275,000 and the literacy rate tops 97 percent. English is the official language. Sugarcane and molasses were once the most important Barbadian industries, but in the 1990's tourism took precedence as the largest contributor to the economy.

Freedom of speech and press are respected. The island's two largest newspapers, the *Barbados Advocate* and the *Daily Nation,* both publish daily in print and online. *Caribbean Week,* a business and travel guide to the region, publishes weekly print editions and posts print content and daily updates on the Web portal cweek.com. Among the island's independent weekly newspapers are the *Weekend Investigator* and *The Broad Street Journal,* a business publication in print and online that serves Barbados and the surrounding area. Other weeklies are published by the companies behind its two daily newspapers; The Advocate Co. puts out *Sunday Advocate* and Nation Publishing Co. produces *Eastern Caribbean News, Sunday Sun* and *Weekend Nation.*

There are six FM stations and two AM stations broadcasting to approximately 237,000 radios. There is one television station, which is government-owned. Nineteen Internet service providers operate in Barbados.

BIBLIOGRAPHY

''Barbados,'' *CIA World Fact Book 2001.* Available from http://www.cia.gov.

Benn's Media, 1999, Vol. 3, 147th Edition, p. 246.

The Barbados Advocate, 2002 Home Page. Available from http://www.barbadosadvocate.com.

Daily Nation, 2002 Home Page. Available from http://www.nationnews.com.

''Using this Site and Caribbean Newsstand,'' *Caribbean Week.* Available from http://www.cweek.com.

—Jenny B. Davis

BELARUS

BASIC DATA

Official Country Name:	Republic of Belarus
Region (Map name):	Europe
Population:	10,350,194
Language(s):	Byelorussian, Russian, other
Literacy rate:	98.0%
Area:	207,600 sq km
GDP:	29,950 (US$ millions)
Number of Television Stations:	47
Number of Television Sets:	2,520,000
Television Sets per 1,000:	243.5
Number of Cable Subscribers:	332,000
Cable Subscribers per 1,000:	33.2
Number of Satellite Subscribers:	60,000
Satellite Subscribers per 1,000:	5.8
Number of Radio Stations:	76
Number of Radio Receivers:	3,020,000
Radio Receivers per 1,000:	291.8
Number of Individuals with Internet Access:	180,000
Internet Access per 1,000:	17.4

BACKGROUND & GENERAL CHARACTERISTICS

The Republic of Belarus is an independent state formed after the disintegration of the Soviet Union. It is a legal heir to a former Soviet Socialist Republic of Belarus. On July 27, 1990 the Supreme Soviet (Parliament) of the Republic adopted a declaration on national sovereignty. In 1991 this document received a constitutional status. Belarus is a founding member of the Organization of the United Nations. On June 26, 1945, it signed the Statutes of the UN. It is a founder of Commonwealth of Independent States and forms a Union with Russia.

Throughout the centuries the territory of contemporary Belarus was divided among different countries: Lithuania, Prussia, Poland. Different languages and religions left their marks on culture and literature of this region. Before World War II the republic had a considerable Jewish population that was annihilated in the Holocaust.

The main distinctive feature of the Republic is that its Slavic population speaks mostly Russian and not Belo Russian. In the eighteenth century the Catholic influence from Poland, in the nineteenth century Russian Imperial policy of assimilation and non-recognition of Belo Russian as a language, the division of the country between Poland and USSR in the interwar period, all created a unique situation when the majority of press and literature published in Belarus are in Russian language.

The link to the Soviet past is perhaps more visible in Belarus than in any other of the 14 former USSR republics. Belarus keeps a Soviet-era coat of arms, flag, and the music of the national anthem. The state security service continues to be called KGBELARUS (KGB). Significantly as of 2002, the names of the main Soviet era newspapers and magazines had not been changed. Their preeminent position in the market also had been kept intact. These particular features explain in part why undemocratic and authoritarian tendencies in Belarus after 1991 had a significant impact on the media.

As of 2001, Children under the age of 15 accounted for 20 percent of the population. The adult population was 58 percent and senior citizens over 60, some 21 percent. The population is mostly urban: 70 percent live in the cities and 30 percent in the rural areas. The literacy rate is high. In 2000, some 1,547 million studied in secondary schools while 95,000 had graduated. About 281,000 students attended courses in universities and colleges. At the same time 61 million books and brochures were published. Total stock of books in public libraries amounted to 77 million copies. There are 296 telephones per 1000 people. Belo Russians accounted for 81 percent of the population; Russians, 11 percent; Poles, 4 percent; Ukrainians, 2.4 percent; and Jews, .3 percent.

The major cities are Minsk (capital), with the population of 1.7 million; Gomel, .49 million; Vitebsk, .34 million; Mogilev, .36 million. The size of national economy was in 2002 some 3 percent of neighboring Russia. The pace of post-communist reforms in this country is slow. The transition to the market economy is not as fast as in neighboring countries. As of 2000, the total percent of the population who worked in foreign owned companies was only .4; those who worked in mixed joint ventures (national and foreign capital) numbered 1.3 percent. In the government sector of the economy, workers numbered 57 percent, and in privately owned businesses, they numbered about 42.5 percent.

At the beginning of the twenty-first century, the biggest political party continued to be the Communist. The Human Rights issues were advocated by the Khartiia 97 movement. The nationalistic movements, unlike in other post-Soviet republics, constituted the opposition. Belo Russian National Front, United Civil Party, and *Narodnaia gromada* (Social Democratic Party) were allowed to operate, but their access to the media was insignificant.

The first newspaper on the territory of contemporary Belarus is believed to have been *Gazeta Grodzen'ska* (1776). It was published in Polish in a two-page format. Starting in 1838 the official newspapers were published in Russian (since it was an official language of the Russian Empire): *Vitebskie gubernskie novosti* (Vitebsk Provincial News, also Grodno, Minsk, and Mogilev). In 1862-63 K. Kalinoiskii published an underground newspaper, *Muzhytskaia prauda* (Peasant Truth) in Belo Russian language. The first authorized printing house for Belo Russian language publications was opened in 1906, *Nashe Delo* (Our Cause). After the October 1917 socialist revolution led by Lenin, several republican and provincial newspapers were established. In 1924 (district), in 1938 (regional), and in 1954 (papers at both district and region levels).

The most distinctive feature of journalism and media in general is that it is practiced in Russian. That makes sense since in a century before the 1917 Bolshevik revolution only 13 out of 249 publications were in Belo Russian language. During the years of independence the number of magazines and periodicals rose sharply from 129 in 1990 (those in Belo Russian language accounted for 36) to 354 in 2001 (those in Belo Russian accounted for 111). However, the yearly number of printing copies went down from 54.1 million (33 million in Belo Russian) to 16 million (4 million in Belo Russian). The rise in the number of newspapers displayed a different tendency, a jump from 224 titles (135 in Belo Russsian) to 610 (202 in Belo Russian). Total single circulation went from 5.7 million copies to 11.4 (Belo Russian language dropped from 2.3 million to 1.8 million). Annual circulation in million of copies went down from 985 million in 1990 to 635 million in 2000 (in Belo Russian language from 312 to 216). The country is open to Russian language publication from the Russian Federation as well.

Some Russian Federation newspapers have local editions: *Komsomol'skaia Pravda* prints 220,000 copies on Friday and 30,000 on a regular day. The most circulated Russian newspaper, *Argumenty I facty* (Arguments and Facts) has a 160,000 daily circulation in Belarus and includes a special local supplement.

Belarus by European standards is a closed society. Only 48,000 tourists visited the country in 2000, mostly from neighboring Poland (13,000). At the same time 1.2 million Belo Russians traveled abroad outside CIS and Russia.

As of January 1, 1995 in the republic there were published 525 newspapers. The national newspapers that belong to the government and are subsidized from the national budget date their existence back to Soviet times: *Zviazda* (Star), *Literatura I mastatstva* (Literature and Art), *Sovetskaia Belarus* (Soviet Belarus, in Russian, available on-line), *Chyrvonaia zmena* (Red Relief), *Respublika* (Republic), *Narodnaia gazeta* (People's Newspaper, in Russian), *Nastaunitskaia gazeta* (Teacher's Newspaper). Regional newspapers are: *Zaria* (Dawn, Brest), *Minskaia prauda* (Minsk Truth), *Magileuskaia prauda* (Mogilev Truth). The titles of most of these newspapers have not changed since the Soviet Era. This fact suggests the much larger and pervasive difficulties and challenges of transition from Communism to post-communist society in this former Soviet Republic.

In the capital six non-government newspapers of general interest are published. Only one of them, *Narodnaia Volia,* can be considered daily (five issues a week). The second place belongs to *Belorusskaia delovaia gazeta* (four times a week, available on-line). The rest are typical large format weeklies.

Theoretically diverse political parties, civil organizations and movements, artistic and professional groups, and private citizens, all have a right to publish their own printed media. More than 1,000 newspapers and magazines are registered in the country. In fact, 80 percent of them belong to private citizens or businesses. However, only few non-government papers have a circulation running in tens of thousands: *Narodnaia Volia,* 75,000; *Belorusskaia Delovaia Gazeta* and *Belorusskaia Gazeta,* 20,000. The vast majority of regional papers have a circulation from several hundred to two or three thousand copies. The circulation of government papers surpasses those of private at the ratio of ten to one. To this should be added a variety of official local newspapers and those published by the government ministries. *Vo slavu Rodiny* (For the Glory of the Motherland) is published by the Ministry of National Defense for the purpose of indoctrination work in the armed forces. The industrial factories and Soviet era *kolkhozy* and *sovkhozy* (collective and Soviet peasant farms) also publish their own tabloid size four-page newspapers called *mnogotirazhka.* Minsk Auto Factory (MAZ) has its own *Avtozavodets* paper.

All government papers are subsidized from the budget, either presidential or national, or from the special foundations held by industrial enterprises. Though the printing costs in the republic are high, the sales price is brought down by heavy subsidies. There are no problems with distribution for government paper. The local authorities mandate their subordinates and managers of the state firms and enterprises to subscribe to government papers, both national and regional. This is another Soviet-like feature of the press.

Language Issues The paradox of the current situation in Belarus is the fact that the government represented by the president, prime minister, administration of the president, security service (KGB), and to a large degree by the president-controlled Parliament forces, all try to impose the Soviet era style of government and the Russian language as its main instrument while the opposition promotes the national Belarus language and culture and is oriented to Western European values. Therefore the government makes systematic efforts to subvert the national press, especially the local one.

As of 2002, this typical situation could be illustrated by Baranovichy, a town in the Brest region near the Polish border. According to a population census, 83 percent of the people in Baranovichy consider Belarussian their mother tongue and 40 percent use it in everyday communication. However, there are only 3 independent newspapers in this town of 170,000, and all of them are published in Russian. *Belaruskaye Slova* (Belarusian Word), the first Belarusian language independent newspaper in the town, was founded in 1991 at the beginning of the national revival period. But in 1994 it was economically strangled; the fine imposed on the publication for an article published in it amounted to its several annual budgets. After that, the ex-editor of the newspaper tried to restore the newspaper, but extremely tough conditions of registration along with absurd prices for printing and distribution made it impossible.

The Largest Newspapers by Circulation As of the early 2000s, *Sovetskaia Belarus* (The Soviet Belarus) was published by the Administratsiia Prezidenta Respubliki Belarus' (the President's Office of Belarus). Founded in 1927, the daily paper, initially the mouthpiece of the local branch of Communist Party, had Format A2 and half a million copies. It was printed in Belorusskii Dom Pechati (Belo Russian House of Press), the main state owned printing facility in the Republic. *Respublika* (The Republic), with a circulation of 120,000, was published 250 days a year by the Soviet Ministrov (Council of Ministers) since 1991 in both Belo Russian and Russian. This paper was also printed in Belorusskii Dom Pechati. Begun in 1999, *Soiuz* (Union) was published by the Ispolnitel'nyi komitet I Parlamentskoe sobranie Soiuza Belarusi I Rossii (Executive Committee and Parliamentary Congress of Belarus and Russia), the main bodies of proposed union between Russia and Belarus. The publishers were *Belorusskii dom pechati* and *Rossiiskaia Gazeta* (Russian Newspaper), the official organ of the Russian Government. The stated circulation was of 900,000 copies. *Vechernii Minsk* (Evening Minsk), format A2 evening newspaper was published in the capital. It produced 100,000 copies, and half of the newspaper was advertising and the rest mainly local news. First issued in August 1917 in Russian in Minsk, *Zviazda* (Star) is published five times a week. Starting in 1925, it was partly Russian, partly Belo Russian and after 1927 it was exclusively in Belo Russian. It is the official newspaper covering the activities of the Supreme Soviet and the Cabinet of Ministers. The monthly supplement, *Chernobyl* (which began in 1993) deals with issues linked to the nuclear power station disaster in neighboring Ukraine in 1986. *Literatura I mastatstva* (Literature and Art) is a weekly dealing with literature, theatre, music, and cinema.

The Belarus Orthodox Church has the most members of any church functioning in the Republic. It is part of the Russian Orthodox Church. While responding to major decisions taken by the Moscow Patriarchate, it still has certain independence in internal affairs. This lack of completely independent national status for the Orthodox Church (unlike in the neighboring Ukraine and elsewhere) also reflects the somewhat incomplete nature of Belarus independence. A religiously connected magazine, *Minskie eparkhial'nye vedomosti* is published four times a year (in format 4A with 250 pages). The official church newspaper *Tserkovnoe slovo* is published on an irregular basis. The activities of foreign religious organizations as well as representatives of Vatican are severely curtailed and monitored. They are often called ''totalitarian sects'' and their religious work labeled as ''pernicious''.

ECONOMIC FRAMEWORK

Before the break up of the Soviet Union in December 1991 Belarus occupied 1 percent of the USSR national territory and accounted for 4 percent of its GDP. However, the very nature of command economy made the republic highly dependent for supplies on other parts of the country. After the proclamation of independence, hyperinflation ensued and production collapsed. Two-thirds of the capital left the country. Eighty percent of the enterprises were on the verge of bankruptcy. By the end of 1990s the economic collapse had stopped. As of 2002, according to the government data, 98 percent of the active adult population was employed in production industries. The same statistics source claimed gross domestic product (GDP) in the 1996-2000 period rose 36 percent; investment rose 13 percent; and industrial output increased 65 percent. Personal income rose 71 percent and commerce doubled. However, the published statistics in post-communist countries have to be viewed with some degree of healthy skepticism. The particular feature of Belarus is the slow pace of privatization and the absence of oligarchic structures (a mixture of former Communist Party, KGB, and government moguls that privatized huge parts of the national economy). The most important business activity is controlled, in fact, by the President's Administration Office. The government becomes in practice the main businessman in the Republic.

DISTRIBUTION NETWORKS

Most newspapers are published by Belorusskii Dom Pechati, the megaprinting house owned by the state and are also distributed by a government monopoly network, *Belpochta* (Belo Russian Mail). Belpochta sets different tariffs for government and non-government media. By illustration, the tariff set for the privately owned *Belorusskaia Delovaia Gazeta* for the second quarter of 2000 was five times higher than for the government paper, *Respublica*. Yet the format and size of these two newspapers is identical. Moreover, there are difficulties facing independent distributors. Pressures from the Association of Journalists forced Ministry of Business and Investment to issue a warning to stop discriminatory tariffs for non-government media. The Ministry of Communications, whose subsidiary is Belpochta, defended itself by stating that any medium is free to distribute its product in any possible way through government, cooperative, NGO organizations, or with the help of private citizens.

PRESS LAWS

The Belarus Constitution, adopted by the thirteenth session of the Supreme Soviet on March 15, 1994, states in its Article 5 that ''political parties and other social organizations have the right to use state media in the way it is established by the law.'' The same article prohibits the formation of the parties aimed at changing constitutional order; propaganda of war; and national, racial or religious hatred. Article 33 states: ''Manipulation of Media by the State, social organizations and by average citizens, as well as censorship are not allowed.'' Article 34 provides for the soliciting and dissemination of information about the government activities, ''political, economic and international life.'' In practice, however, the declaratory democratic pronouncements of the Constitution are de facto annulled by other Laws, Rules and Regulations.

The most significant political event regarding the press was the treatment of the figure of the President Aleksandr Lukashenko (Belarus 1954) who came to power in 1994 and managed to get reelected for a five-year term in 2001. The political climate imposed by Lukashenko's regime in the country is expressed by the ''above the law'' status of the president himself and to some degree it anticipated the pattern of Russian political development after the election of President Vladimir Putin in March 2000, which brought with it increased militarization, the appointment of security forces cadres to key government positions, and a curtailing of independent printed and electronic media.

According to the Constitution, the president is a head of state and de facto of the government, a ''guarantor of the Constitution, of rights and freedoms of people and citizens, he personifies the unity of the nation and guarantees the realization of the main directions of internal and foreign policy.'' The provision for the ''unity of the nation'' and the demonstrated practice of power have been one of many causes of serious human rights violations and suppression of the press in the Republic. As some human rights organizations, the Council of Europe, European Parliament, Conference for Security and Cooperation in Europe and others suggest this totalitarian concept of the ''unity of the nation'' is in practice a cover for the establishment of an authoritarian state in the heart of Europe.

Press Related Laws Government Decree no. 144, adopted on February 26, 1996, stipulated that purchase of printing equipment could be carried out only by the permission of the Government Committee on the Press (now Ministry of Information). Without this permit no media could operate in the republic. No license was needed in the case of certain government agencies' publications and official blanks, wrapping paper, stickers, and rice tags. The rest of the publications in order to be printed need a government license. The publishing license could be obtained if the particular medium has on staff ''professionals with University degrees, three years experience in the publishing business and those who have successfully passed a qualifying examination.'' Those without these requirements did not qualify.

The media were required to post the information about the publisher. The compulsory posting on bonds, however, did not exist, but the newspapers, especially the independent ones, had to be constantly ready to disclose all financial information to the government-controlled tax and revenue police. In fact the tax office in post-Soviet societies is one of the major instruments of government control over the media. The violation of copyright laws is prohibited as well the infringement of ''thematic scope'' and publishing in languages not authorized in the license.

Obligatory copies of certain publications are distributed widely, sent to the ministries, national libraries or book chambers. Poor printing quality is not allowed. The political control includes a ban on media use of information that is considered state secret ''or any other secret especially protected by the law,'' any appeal towards ''the violent change of existing government and social order, war propaganda, violence and cruelty, racial, national, religious supremacy or intolerance, pornography, as well as any publishing activity that contradicts the interests of the Republic or any other illegal activities.'' The government is entitled to suspend the license for up to 6 months and in case of a recurrent violation suspend the license altogether. (''Regulation on the Licensing and the Use of Licenses'' issued by the Committee on the Press on May 21, 1997).

Article 16 of the Press and Media Law that regulates the Belarus media stipulates the following steps to be taken leading up to the closure of the media. First, the Ministry of Information or a local attorney makes a written warning when the media violate the laws. Two or more warnings during a twelve-month period can lead to the closure of the media. In the year 2000 more than 50 warnings were issued. Most of the warnings dealt with article 5 of the Press Law that bans any ''dissemination of information made in the name of political parties, trade unions or any other social organizations that did not pass Government registration'' in the Ministry of Justice.

CENSORSHIP

Though the Constitution bans the censorship, some agencies monitor the press and therefore exercise strict censorship. This government system includes the State Committee on the Press (Republican Government) that in the late 2001 was replaced with the Ministry of Information. There are regional executive committees (regional governments) that have *Upravlenie po pechati* (Department on the Press) (for example, in Brest, Vitebsk, Mogilev, Gomel) or *Upravlenie obschestvenno politicheskoi informatsii* (Department of Social and Political information, in Grodno) or Upravlenie informatsii (Department of information, in Minsk). *Natsional'naia knizhnaia palata* (National Book Chamber) monitors all printing activities in the Republic in terms of collecting and filing all printed materials.

Cases of Actual Censorship *Government vs. Narodnaia volia* illustrates the point. On one occasion the most influential independent newspaper, *Narodnaia Volia* used the verb ''expelled'' in the context of the prominent Belo Russian writer, Vasil' Bykov, who lives in Germany. The Press Committee issued the official warning to the newspaper based on the interpretation of the word. It stated Bykov was not ''expelled,'' but rather ''for some time he had been living and working in Finland invited by the PEN-CluBelarus. Now he lives in Germany. He is not considered 'an expelled person' as claimed by *Narodnaia Volia.*'' A warning of this type can foretell closure and is usually signed by the Minister of Press (Information)Suspension. In August 2001 the authorities confiscated 10 computers belonging to the same *Narodnaia Volia*. The official reason was the fact the computers were not registered as belonging to the editorial office rather than to private citizens namely, the journalists. Therefore they could not be used on editorial premises. The editorial staff was left with only four computers.

Government vs. Lambda also illustrates how censorship works. In March 2002 the only gay publication in the country, *Forum Lambda*, was closed down. The license was removed because according to the government the magazine that had ''registered as scientific, popular, culturological edition, for more than a year had been published as an erotic one.'' In September of 2001 the magazine had received a first warning with the same text. It coincided with the official ban of a ''Gay Parade 2001'' in Minsk whose main organizer happened to be the magazine. The tax police immediately studied the publication's bookkeeping and tax receipts but did not find any irregularities.

The cases against government newspapers are hard to win. *Helsinki Human Rights Group vs. the Government* illustrates the point. After the 2001 Presidential election, a leading human rights association, The Bela Russian Helsinki Committee, demanded a ''refutation of slanderous data disseminated'' in the leading government newspaper *Sovetskaya Belorussiya*. The newspaper had claimed that the Helsinki Committee activities subverted the country's national security. The article in question was published in the newspaper's special issue, whose circulation was twice that of a regular one. Its main topic was candidate Alexander Lukashenko's election program. The special issue was produced in full color on eight pages and was distributed free of charge. The court first of all refused even to consider the sources for financing the issue. Then it declined to study the veracity of the information. For months after that news, the group tried hard to get this information publicly refuted. The human rights defenders addressed in vain the republican KGB, the Security Council (top national security body) and the Presidential Administration requesting these institutions to confirm or deny BHC's involvement in anti-state activities.

In April 2002, the Ministry of Information issued yet another official warning to *Narodnaia Volia* for "dissemination of baseless unsupported statements regarding the President of Belarus." It was a reply to an article, "Great Laundry" that claimed that the president's office had privatized the most lucrative part of national economy (arms trade) and the president wanted to launder those profits in Austria. The newspaper objected the reprimand because the news had been reprinted from the Web site of Radio Liberty.

The government tries to intimidate even the foreign journalists working and covering the country from abroad. In January 2002 the KGB of Belarus sent a letter to Russia's Secret Service FSB protesting against statements made by top Russian TV journalist Pavel Sheremet (Bela Russian by birth). KGB claimed public statements made by Sheremet damaged constitutional order in the country, were of anti-government nature, discredited Belo Russian leadership and as a result damaged relations between two countries. Russian authorities as a routine disregard these protests made by their closest political ally.

The censorship as an all-pervasive Soviet-style institution works as well at the local level, with municipal government publications, industrial enterprises and collective farms. For example, the director of the agricultural machinery plant, Gomsel'mash, issued an internal memo entitled "On the Relationship with Media," which ordered the editor of the factory's newspaper to review all types of documents (texts, speeches, articles, addresses, letters) that were being sent from the factory's official to the media. This document was announced to all 10,000 workers and they were specifically advised that any appearance in media had to be previously approved.

Judiciary and the Media The criminal code was adopted by *Palata predstavitelei* (Chamber of Representatives of the Parliament) on June 2, 1999 and approved by the Soviet Respubliki on June 24, 1999. It includes six chapters (out of nine) that potentially infringe on the freedom of press and individual liberties. "Crimes against Peace, security of humankind and military crimes," (propaganda of war), "Crimes against Social Security and Population Health," "Crimes against Social Order and Social Morals," "Crimes against Information Security," "Crimes against State (*gosudartsvo*) and order of execution of Government and management" (*vlast' i upravleniie*), and "Crimes against military service". (The remaining chapters are: "Crimes against Person" and "Crimes against ownership and way of conducting of economic activities.") It is one of the most repressive criminal codes in all of the post-Soviet world except perhaps some Central Asian countries.

Article 198 establishes that any impediment in any form of the lawful professional activities of journalists or forcing them to divulge or desist from dissemination of information (with violence or with the threat to use it) entails a fine or banning to occupy certain positions or imprisonment up to three years. Article 204 establishes a fine for the denial of an official to give to a citizen documents and materials concerning this citizen. Article 367, "Defamation regarding the President of the Republic of Belarus" (*kleveta v otnoshenii prezidenta respubliki Belarus*) applies to any public pronouncement, printed or publicly displayed work, or in the media that may draw a fine, correctional works up to two years, or imprisonment up to four years. Article 368, "Insult of the President" (*oskorblenie prezidenta*), stipulates that a public insult would draw a fine or two years imprisonment. The treatment of the President became the central worry of the Bela Russian state and its police and law enforcement organs. Defilement of State symbols (coat of arms, flag and anthem) draws up to one year imprisonment. Other crimes include: State secrets, official secrets, "illegal production, acquisition or sale of means for illegal receipt of information."

STATE-PRESS RELATIONS

Organization and Functions of Information Ministry On June 14, 1996 the government Committee on the Press was instituted. On October 26, 2001 it was dismantled and a Ministry of Information formed in its place which is headed by a minister appointed by the president and managed by a seven-person board.

At the provincial level the Directorates of Information exist. They are attached to the provincial executive committees (local governments). According to the law the main tasks of the ministry include: "government regulation of the spreading of information," carrying out of the government policy towards media, control, economic measures in media and publishing business and distribution of books, coordination of policies with other states, and finally the "formation of the media culture."

The Ministry of Information has a monopoly right to license media and all publishing and printing activities in the territory of Belarus. It takes measures to prevent ''abuse of media freedoms, free publishing and censorship'' and it is in charge of publishing of the ''socially important literature,'' textbooks, etc. It also makes decisions on forming, reorganizing and closing of media organizations. It forms correspondents bureaus abroad and takes care of the accreditations procedures for foreign correspondents (in conjunction with the External Affairs Ministry).

The Right to Criticize the Government (Theory and Practice) The Constitution proclaims the freedom of the press. In practice, criticism of the president as the supreme authority of the nation often is a prelude to a crackdown. this applies to all media both printed and electronic. The opposition claims that since the top management of the Belo Russian Television and Radio Company is named by the president it is totally subordinated to him. Political opposition therefore is denied any access to the government owned media.

The agreement reached in October 1999 about a wider access of the political opposition to the Government media and the creation of equal opportunities to all forms of media ownership went largely ignored by the authorities. A case of local newspaper *Pagonia* and its editors illustrates the point. Nikolai Markevich and Pavel Mazeika were tried on charges of slander against President Lukashenko. If convicted, they might face up to five years in jail, under Belarus criminal laws. Both international and domestic media freedom watchdogs denounced the criminal libel prosecution of journalists as a gross violation of the freedom of expression standards.

Suspension and Confiscation of Newspapers Newspaper *Noviny* published in Belo Russian has been popular in opposition circles. Reportedly the president of the country gave an order to the Security Council chief to file a case against the newspaper for an alleged ''insulted honor and dignity'' of the president and seek financial compensation. The claim was presented at the court and satisfied in the record short time. The amount of fine was so big that the newspaper was forced out of business. Half a year later it made an unsuccessful effort to come out under a different name.

In September 2000 several issues of the opposition newspaper *Rabochii* (Worker) published by the Confederation of Independent Trade Unions was confiscated. It had called citizens to boycott the October 15 parliamentary elections. Police and KGB confiscated 150,000 copies of the newspaper and arrested its editor-in-chief, the lawyer representing the newspaper and the director of the printing shop.

In the first four months of 2001 the printed media received 68 warnings from the Government Committee. The government lost only one trial brought against Brestskii kur'er. In the year 2000 only four trials were lost by the government.

State Control over the Press Control is exercised in a simple but effective way, the financial one. The government owned newspapers receive heavy subsidies from the budget. It allows them to establish a symbolic subscription price (less than one U.S. dollar for three months, that is, one cent a day). At the same time the distribution through the government-controlled post office for a privately owned newspaper costs four to five times more than for the government one. The competition becomes difficult, if not impossible.

The average monthly salary in the country is US$35. Potential readers must choose to purchase the most economic media product. This explains the skyrocketing circulation of the main government paper, *Sovetskaia Belarus* (half a million copies). The government also monopolizes all remaining infrastructure dealing with the press. The printing, mailing, and selling of the press is regulated by the state. The result of this protectionist policy is that the circulation of independent press is ten times smaller than the newspapers and magazines sponsored by the government.

The authorities in the little town of Smorgon in early 2001 explicitly prohibited local government offices and businesses from subscribing to the non-government newspaper *Novaia gazeta*. Atypically, its circulation was five times larger than the local official paper. The post office was required to submit the lists of all government subscribers to independent paper in order to punish them.

Different branches of the government try to exercise its influence over the press. Sometimes their interests are conflicting and damaging the State. Ministry of the Interior (police) was reportedly refusing to give accreditation to the official government newspaper, *Respublic*. The newspaper in the past had criticized the Minister of the Interior, and it had reported cases of corruption and organized crime within the police force.

ATTITUDE TOWARDS FOREIGN MEDIA

In general the attitude towards foreign media is governed by the atmosphere of strained relations with the European Union, the Organization for the Security and Cooperation in Europe, and the United States.

Accreditation procedures for foreign journalists Foreign journalists are required to submit an application in order to get a professional accreditation in Belarus. It includes personal information, a name of the organization which is requesting the procedure, and valid journalism credentials. Based on this submission, the External Affairs Ministry grants or denies the accreditation.

The activities of foreign journalists and those national citizens working for them are governed by the government *polozhenie* (statute), "On Stay and professional activities in the territory of Republic of Belarus of offices and correspondents of foreign media registered in the Republic of Belarus." More specifically, the rules are listed in the *Instruktsiia* (Instructions) issued by the External Affairs ministry. There are two types of accreditation: permanent (up to one year) and temporary (up to two months).

Apart from the application, a short note on the history and status of foreign media should be supplied with relevant information, as well as resume on professional activity of a correspondent. The same procedure is required for technical personnel. The Ministry resolves the case in two months period. When the permit is granted the Consular Division of the Ministry sends a written authorization form allowing the Belo Russian Consulate in a given country to issue a year-long multiple entry professional visa (*godovaia mnogokratnaia sluzhebnaia viza*). Once in the national territory, foreign journalist gets an Accreditation Card. Family members get a special card as well as professional visa. The temporary accreditation follows the same procedure. The only difference is the visa is granted in 20 working days after the application is received. The activities of foreign correspondents de jure are monitored by the Department of Relations with Media at the External Affairs ministry and de facto by the security service, KGBELARUS.

A common practice adopted by foreign media in Belarus is to hire local journalists and photo correspondents to cover events in the country. Doing so, however, creates additional pressure on the journalists who are local citizens and not covered by diplomatic immunity or other privileges accorded to the foreign nationals.

No diplomats, consular officials, representatives of foreign businesses, offices, or any organizations can be granted foreign correspondents accreditation. Certified national journalists can neither work for foreign media. Foreign journalists can form a professional journalistic association, can freely travel on the territory of the Republic except in case of "objects access to which is limited in accordance with the Republican legislation." In 1997 the visit of two Russian TV journalists to a forest near the Lithuanian border brought about their arrest and created an international scandal between Russia and Belarus. The Belarus authorities claimed the forest had military installations.

The Rules specifically stipulate that "rights and freedoms exercised by foreign correspondents should not damage interests of the Republic of Belarus, rights and legal interests of citizens." The specification of these obligations includes a requirement to check out the veracity of information, "present for publication objective information," not allow false or untrue assertions to be aired, to get permission for news on private life of the citizen from the citizen concerned, "while receiving information from citizens and officials notify them about the use of this information in audio, video, cinema and photo materials as well in the form of text." Rules also required journalists to carry a professional identification. Finally, a foreign journalist is required to "fulfill other obligations stipulated on journalists by the law and international treaties signed by the Republic of Belarus." The full responsibility falls upon the shoulders of foreign journalists in case they divulgate information considered state or "any other guarded by the law secret," or they are engaged in "the propaganda of war, social, national, religious, racial hatred, make calls to seize power, or violently change the constitutional order or infringement of the territorial integrity of the republic." If they stipulate the formation of "illegal social organizations, aid and make propaganda of their activities." Finally it is specifically prohibited to "attempt against the morality, honor and dignity of citizens and officials of the state, in particular dissemination of information viciously attempting against honor, dignity and business reputation (*chest', dostoinstvo I delovaia reputatsiia*) of the President of the Republic of Belarus." "Other illegal activities" are mentioned without specification. This language and practice follow closely the repressive legislation and practice of Soviet era.

The reprisals envisioned by the Ministry include the following steps: a) the first warning; and b) the reduction of the time of stay in the Republic for foreign nationals or the expulsion from the republic. Foreign journalists can be denied accreditation in the following cases: a) violation of rules after the first warning and the "dissemination of facts not corresponding to the reality," and b) in cases envisioned by the international agreements on civil and political rights. If the foreign media employ unauthorized personnel it can be denied accreditation for six months. A special Committee of the Ministry of External Affairs deals with the accreditation of journalists.

On May 8, 2001, this committee officially warned Iurii Svirko, a local journalist working for the foreign media, about violations in the "rules of order" governing foreign journalists' work. The warning was reportedly made on behalf of the president's Security Service. The Service among other priorities monitors media coverage of the president. The decree mandating this was adopted in 1998 but was never made public.

In September 2001, the Belo Russian consulate in Bonn, Germany, refused to grant visas to six German journalists. They were invited by the Belo Russian office of UNESCO as part of a bilateral exchange program. The refusal was motivated by the fact that the journalists did not have an accreditation with the Ministry of External Affairs (MID Belorussii). In fact the journalists on exchange trips unlike those traveling on business do not need accreditation.

In January 2002, the Ministry of Foreign Affairs expressed its concern with a comment made by Russian National TV channel NTV journalist Pavel Selin on the detainment of Mikhail Leonov, general director of the Minsk Tractor Factory (MTF). The NTV correspondent said: ''Products of the Minsk Tractor Factory are mainly exported to Russia. President Lukashenko is known to resist the mass penetration of Russian capital into the profitable branches of Belarus' industry. He is no less active in getting rid of those who are standing out for the strong economic relations with brotherly Russia.'' The head of the NTV bureau in Minsk was immediately summoned to the Ministry of Foreign Affairs. Commenting on this event the head of the ministry's information service, said: ''In our opinion, the comments made on the detainment of MTF director . . . were an insult to the Republic of Belarus and distorted the real picture and the fight against embezzlements.'' According to the journalist, the Ministry's official said that the conversation had the status of an official warning. He added that if NTV did not change its attitude to covering events in Belarus, the accreditation in the country might be cancelled.

NEWS AGENCIES

The government-owned Belo Russian Telegraph Agency (BELTA) was founded in January 1921. For 70 years it worked as a provincial subsidiary of the main Soviet News agency TASS. In 1991 after the collapse of the Soviet Union it became independent. It prepares daily 80 to 100 news items on mostly government approved information. It is mailed to and it is required publication material by the national and local newspapers, TV and radio stations. Some foreign subscribers, diplomatic missions, companies, and major Russian Internet companies are also among the subscribers. Photographs done by BELTA correspondents are sent to Poland, Germany, Rumania, and People's Republic of China. BELTA publishes a weekly information and analysis magazine *Sem' dnei* (Seven days) that has a circulation 100,000. Using its government status the news agency is actively involved in publishing business (books, posters, brochures, booklets). According to its official Web site, ''it is ready to fulfill any printing order.''

Another domestic news agency is BelaPAN. Created in 1991, it has a reputation for disseminating alternative source political, economic, and other information from Belarus. It is subject to all the restrictions imposed on media but can be considered semi-independent from the government not unlike the Interfaks agency in Russia. The company distributes its information to the subscribers and has its own correspondents in all regions of the country as well as in the neighboring states. It has an analytical service, advertisement agency, editorial office, and a sociological service, *Zerkalo* (Mirror). In 1999 it started publishing its own weekly *Otdykhai* (Have a Rest) geared at travel agencies and tourism.

BROADCAST MEDIA

Television Belo Russian Television began in 1955. Only 4,500 people had TV-sets at that point. One channel broadcasted six hours a day. The signal reached a radius of 60 kilometers. In 2000 the First national channel broadcasted 17 hours a day in all the republic's territory. The programming included strict schedules of newscast, division of programs in three blocks (morning, afternoon, night), variety of programs, and took into consideration different categories of viewers and TV ratings.

Radio Belo Russian Radio was inaugurated in November 1925. The broadcasts were aired in Belo Russian language with a signal range of 300 kilometers. At that time, broadcasts lasted only 30 minutes a day as compared to the early twenty-first century where it broadcasts 29 hours a day on two national channels. In June 1998 it started broadcasting into the neighboring areas of the Russian Federation and in Ukraine. Four hours a day it broadcasts abroad. The government radio station Stolitsa broadcasts 17 hours a day.

The same laws and regulations that govern the printed media apply to the Belarus Radio which is strictly controlled by the government in terms of the distribution of frequencies, equipment, and other facilities. It is considered a strategic media because the majority of the households has standard radio sets that are connected to so-called ''radio lines,'' a practice dating back from the early Soviet times. This is especially true in the rural areas where it is common scene for the government station to be heard non-stop from the loudspeaker located at the main square.

After Belarus' independence many FM stations sprang up. The most listened to is FM station ''Stolitsa'' (The Capital) broadcasting almost 18 hours a day. It has what is called in the former Soviet Union, a ''European'' style of broadcasting that combines popular music and information segments. But it is a government property and forms part of TV and radio media holding. Radio ''Belarus'' also broadcasts four hours a day in Belarussian, Russian, English, and German languages.

The government claims the official radio is popular, accessible, offers a great amount of information, is fast

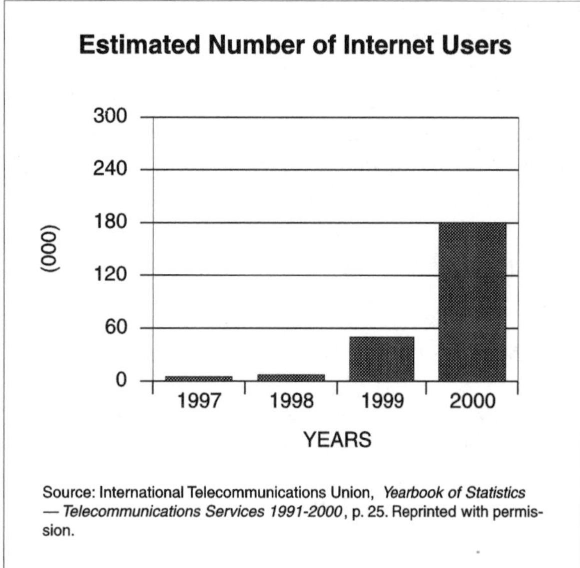

Source: International Telecommunications Union, *Yearbook of Statistics — Telecommunications Services 1991-2000*, p. 25. Reprinted with permission.

and has a high content of coverage of problematic issues. But critics argue it is a spoken version of the government's printed propaganda.

Summary—Broadcast Media The government policies regarding TV and radio broadcasts are even stricter than for printed media since no private enterprise is allowed in this type of media. Commenting during a yearly trip to the TV offices on October 12, 2001 President Lukashenko stated his criteria regarding the type of person who should lead the television company: ''It would be a person, who carries out a government policy. Television is a serious force. It will never leave from out of control of the state and will never lack its support. The new head of TV without doubt will be President's man, the same way I am your man, and all of us are people of the Government.''

ELECTRONIC NEWS MEDIA

The pioneer of the development of internet technology in Belarus—as well as in the other parts of CIS—has been the ''Open Society'' Institute, part of the George Soros Foundation. It distributed thousands of computers free of charge to civil society and non-government institutions in addition to subsidiaries of the official Academy of Sciences of Belarus. However, only in Belarus have drastic measures been taken by the security apparatus against its offices that were closed down in 1997 and its officials expelled. The mechanism used to evict ''Open Society'' represents a common pattern in dealing with independent media in both print and electronically.

There are an estimated 180,000 users of the Internet in Belarus. Almost four-fifths of them live in the capital Minsk. Users can access information on the republic from independent sources not available in printed format (the semi-clandestine National Radical Party is publishing an internet newspaper ''Molot'' otherwise it would not be able to disseminate its information). Some other media—both government and independent—are also present in electronic format. For example, republican, local, and commercial information newspapers: ''Belorusskaia delovaia gazeta,'' BELTA News Agency, ''Sovetskaia Belorussia.'' ''Vecherny Gomel'' (regional business paper), ''Press Reklama'' (newspaper with free advertising), ''Gomelskie Vedomosti,'' free-advertising newspaper ''BEKO Plus, ''''DJAM'' newspaper (advertising and information), ''Shans'' newspaper from Gomel (advertising and information), ''Smorgon News'' (the independent newspaper of Smorgon including local news, free classifields, and a photo gallery) and ''Optovick Belorussii''.

EDUCATION & TRAINING

Belorusskaia Assotsiatsiia Zhurnalistov (Belo Russian Association of Journalists), a professional group of 800 journalists, is a special interest lobby. The Association sponsors a Law Center for Media protection. The officers and experts of the Centre have acted as defense attorneys in trials against Belarusian journalists: the case of Svaboda newspaper, closed down by authorities in November 1997; the case of Pavel Sheremet and Dmitry Zavadski, Russian ORT TV network correspondents, convicted to suspended sentence in December 1997-January 1998; the cases of administrative prosecution against journalists covering peaceful mass protest actions. Russian *Tsentr ekstremal'noi zhurnalistiki* (Centre for Extreme Journalism) has its office in Belarus and monitors the violation of press freedoms.

The Journalistic education in Belarus is being carried out at the Journalism Faculty of Belarus State University in Minsk. The magazine *Kul'tura movy zhurnalista* (The Culture of Journalists' Language) has been published since 1982. The journalists formed the Union of Journalists of Belarus to represent the government-oriented media. Before its closure by the authorities and expulsion from the republic in 1997, George Soros' Open Society Institute, made a significant contribution to the civic education of journalists through generous grants and scholarships and seminars.

SUMMARY

The situation with the press and other media in Belarus represents a paradox. According to some observers the country in the heart of Europe is perhaps the only vestige left of the totalitarian culture that governed half of Europe for a significant part of the twentieth century. According to Belarus government it is an island where post-communist chaos, mafia, oligarchs, and other vice could not take hold. Living in isolation from Europe but trying to form a joint country with Russia Belarus severely curtailed personal freedoms and freedom of the press in the name of so-called national unity.

The government involvement in the media is unparallel even with former Soviet republics (Moldavia, Ukraine, or neighboring Russia). The independent media have to be printed in Lithuania or Ukraine. At the same time the country watches Russian TV and reads Russian newspapers. Russian is the de facto media language of the Republic.

As of 2002, it seemed certain that pressure for the liberalization of the country would continue. Internet technologies, TV broadcasts from other countries, and the support of democratic governments around the world and NGO for a constitutional opposition eventually may lead to the democratization of the country.

Significant Dates

- 1994: A new Constitution is adopted.
- 1994: Aleksandr Lukashenko is elected president.
- 1995: Iosif Seredich is removed by the president from the parliamentary official newspaper Narodnaia Gazeta and he starts publishing an independent Narodnaia Volia.
- 1996: A Treaty on the Formation of Commonwealth of Belarus and Russia is signed.
- 1997: A Union Treaty between Belarus and Russia is signed.
- 1997: The Council of Ministers (Government) approves a document drafted by External Affairs Ministry. It is the main code that governs foreign journalists activities in the Republic.
- 1997: Russian National TV journalists Pavel Sheremet and IuriiZavadskii are arrested in Belarus.
- 1997: President Lukashenko cancels his visit to Russia. President Boris Eltsyn demands: ''Let him free Sheremet first.''
- 1997: Sheremet and Zavadskii are freed.
- 2000: The Russian TV cameraman Zavadkii is abducted at Minsk national airport at Belarus capital. His colleague Cheremet arrives at the airport and finds Zavadskii's car at the place where the cameraman usually parked it. Dmitrii disappears without a trace. The arrest of the former Belarus Army Special Unit ''Almaz'' officer Valery Ignatovich prompts speculations about government involvement in the case.
- 2001: The authorities close down the independent newspaper Pagonia accusing it in libel against the president. It has published a limerick about Lukashenko. All equipment and all copies of the paper are confiscated. The editor replies that during the presidential campaign the newspaper has criticized all candidates.
- 2001: The Supreme Court of Belarussia in its closed session studies the case of disappearance of the cameraman Zavadskii.
- 2001: Iosif Seredich is charged with dissemination of information ''denigrating the authorities.''
- 2001: Non-government media journalists hold unauthorized protest against government closure of local opposition newspaper Pagonia. Passersby are offered toilet paper with printed message: ''Ideal Press According to the President.''
- 2000: Grodno local newspaper Pagonia is closed down indefinitely by the decision of the court. The 14 journalists protesting the closure picket and are arrested.

Bibliography

Belarus Entsyklapedychny davednik (Belarus. Encyclopedia). Minsk: Belaruskaia entsyklopedyia, 1995.

Kanstytutsyia respubliki Belarus (Constitution of Belarus Republic). Minsk: Polymia, 1994.

Knizhnoe delo. Pressa Belarusi (Book Publishing. Belarus Press). Minsk: Natsional'naia knizhnaia palata Belarusi, 1999.

Martselov, Stanislav. *Na putiakh stroitel'stva sotsializma. Pechat' Belorussii.* vol. 1926-37 gg. Minsk: Izdatel'stvo Belarus, 1972.

Pechat' Belorussii v period razvitogo sotsializma (Belarus Press in the Period of Developed Socialism). Minsk: Belarus, 1982.

Respublika Belarus' v tsifrakh. Kratkii statisticheskii sbornik (Republic of Belarus in Numbers. Short Statistical Book). Minsk: Ministertsvo statistiki I analiza Respubliki Belarus, 2001.

Ugolovnyi kodeks Respubliki Belarus (Criminal Code of Belarus). Minsk: Natsional'nyi Tsentr pravovoi informatsii Respubliki Belarus, 1999.

—Leonid Maximenkov

BELGIUM

BASIC DATA

Official Country Name:	Kingdom of Belgium
Region (Map name):	Europe
Population:	10,252,762
Language(s):	Dutch, French, German, legally bilingual (Dutch and French)
Literacy rate:	98.0%
Area:	30,510 sq km
GDP:	226,648 (US$ millions)
Number of Daily Newspapers:	28
Total Circulation:	1,568,000
Circulation per 1,000:	187
Total Newspaper Ad Receipts:	423 (Euro millions)
As % of All Ad Expenditures:	22.80
Number of Television Stations:	25
Number of Television Sets:	4,720,000
Television Sets per 1,000:	460.4
Number of Cable Subscribers:	3,840,870
Cable Subscribers per 1,000:	372.9
Number of Satellite Subscribers:	220,000
Satellite Subscribers per 1,000:	21.5
Number of Radio Stations:	87
Number of Radio Receivers:	8,075,000
Radio Receivers per 1,000:	787.6
Number of Individuals with Computers:	3,500,000
Computers per 1,000:	341.4
Number of Individuals with Internet Access:	2,326,000
Internet Access per 1,000:	226.9

BACKGROUND & GENERAL CHARACTERISTICS

Belgium's media landscape—and position in European leadership—is not described by its small land mass of over 30 thousand square kilometers. Nor do its dense population of 336 people per square kilometers and its economic viability explain its lively and diverse press. To understand its press, one must understand Belgium's historical resilience as a nation often subjected to invasion and occupation, and its status as a multilingual but linguistically segmented country.

Before housing the leadership of the European Union (EU), Belgium, which derives its name from the *Belgae* Celtic tribe, was a province of Rome. When Attila the Hun invaded what is now Germany, Germanic tribes pushed into what is now Belgium. Next the Franks took control of Belgium. Oversight of Belgium next passed to the Spanish (1519-1713) and then to the Austrians (1713-1794). After the French Revolution, Belgium was annexed by Napoleon. It was made a part of the Netherlands in 1815. In 1830, after a revolution, Belgium declared its independence and established a constitutional monarchy. The result of a coalition of the intellectual and financial elite, Catholic leadership, and the nobility, the new nation's Constitution ''may be considered a balanced compromise of the sometimes divergent interests of these social groups'' (Lamberts 314). While Belgium was occupied by the Germans during both world wars, it survived and thrived when it was liberated in 1944 by Allied forces. The early and late occupations created a nation indebted to German, French, and Dutch influences. The nation has incorporated these languages and cultural elements into different parts of its geographic and cultural landscape. Belgium's characteristic compromise may be what makes it a desirable location for EU leadership despite its lack of central proximity.

The sustained balance of three diverse regions and language communities largely explains the development and fragmented organization of the press that serves its 10 million people. The Flemish, French, and German cultural communities were granted official autonomy with a 1970 revision of the Constitution that also established three separate economic regions: Flanders, Wallonia, and Brussels. Today, after a 1993 Constitutional revision, Belgium is a federal state with three distinct regions, each with its own prime minister, council of ministers, and regional council. In the north, Flanders largely sustains a Dutch speaking community, previously referred to as Flemish, represented by a Flemish community council. In the south, Wallonia is the home of a largely French speaking community who are represented by a French community council; eastern Wallonia, however, houses a significant German speaking population who are represented by a German community council. Brussels, the capital, is a multilingual community; the French speaking people are represented by a French community council who also represent Wallonia, while the Dutch speaking members of Brussels are represented with the Dutch speakers of Flanders in a Flemish community council. While there are numerous political parties on the Belgian scene, the three major political groups—Socialists, Liberal, and Christian Social—have French- and Dutch-language parties, respectively, and are largely organized along linguistic lines. The Flemings make up 60 percent of the population (Flanders 55 percent), and the Walloons make up about 30 percent (Wallonia 35 percent). About 1 percent of the remaining Belgians are German speakers who live in Eastern Wallonia on the German border.

Literacy in Belgium is reportedly 98 percent or better. Preschool education, which begins at two and one-half years of age, is very popular and successful; more than 90 percent of Belgian youngsters attend. Education is compulsory from 6 to 18 years of age. During comprehensive education, all students specialize in technical, vocational, or college preparatory curriculum. Its oldest university, established in 1425, is the Catholic University of Louvain. In 1834 the Free Masons established the Free University of Brussels. Because of the legally bilingual nature of Belgium, both universities operate separate French and Dutch speaking campuses. A state university system was also established in Ghent and Liege in the early 1800s; other schools have followed in the 1900s. The government subsidizes 95 percent of student expenses. All these factors contribute to a highly educated and skilled workforce.

While the Belgian people are highly literate, most do not subscribe to a daily newspaper. Increasing pressure to maintain or enlarge circulation has encouraged many dailies to adopt a ''tabloid'' style to their presentation. The World Association of Newspapers (WAN) reports that many newspapers have also decreased the number of pages in their daily publications, making the texts more compact. In 1995 ''the overall circulation of the Belgian press amounted to 1,543,623, the Flemish press taking 993,229 or 64.3 per cent of sales, and the French-language press 550.394 or 35.6 per cent of sales'' (de Bens 2). Only about 36 percent of Belgians were reported to subscribe to a newspaper in 1995 (2). While circulation figures have declined in the latter part of the 1990s, tabloid strategies have reportedly been adopted by many dailies to enhance their market share. From 1996 to 2000 circulation declined 3.3 percent overall in Belgium. While WAN further reports that Belgian daily circulation increased slightly, 0.2 percent in 2000, overall newspaper sales in the European Union have fallen 2.5 percent from 1996. A May 2002 conference hosted by WAN examined strategies to revamp Web sites and enlarge circulation in uncertain times. Overall, television and Internet expansion offer preferred choices to print media, especially in light of the consolidation of papers into major publishing groups with similar content.

Top Ten Daily Newspapers
(2000)

	Circulation
Het Laatste Nieuws/De Nieuwe Gazat	286,000
Het Nieuwsblad/De Gentenaar	218,000
La Meuse/La Lanterne/Nouvelle Gazette/La Province	146,000
Le Soir	125,000
Gazet van Antwerpen	121,000
Het Volk	111,000
Het Belang van Limburg	104,000
Groupe Vers l'Avenir	101,000
De Standaard	82,000
La Dernière Heure/Les Sports	78,000

Source: World Association of Newspapers and Zenithmedia, *World Press Trends 2001*, p. 53.

Of the 41 newspapers published in Belgium, most are dailies. Belgians additionally have ready access to both EU and non-European publications. Circulation figures gathered within the 135th Edition of the *Gale Directory of Publication and Broadcast Media* (2001) indicate that 14 newspapers have a circulation of 100,000 to 500,000. About six publications have circulation figures in the range from 50,000 to 100,000, an additional six have circulation figures from 25,000 to 50,000, and five have circulation figures of 10,000 to 25,000. The rest have circulation rates of less than 10,000 copies. Of the 11 largest daily Belgian newspapers by circulation, 8 serve the Dutch speaking community; 3 are published in French. Note that these figures may vary from source to source. Of the Dutch publications, *De Standaard/Het Nieuwsblad/De Dentenaar,* established in 1914, has a circulation of 372,410; *De Gentenaar,* established in 1879, has a circulation of 372,410; *Het Laatste Nieuws,* established in 1888, has a circulation of 308,808; *De Nieuwe Gazet,* established in 1897, has a circulation of 306,240; *Gazet Van Mechelen,* established in 1896, has a circulation of 177,898; *De Nieuwe Gids,* established in 1955, has a circulation of 171,350; *Gazet Van Antwerpen,* established in 1891, has a circulation of 148,095; and *Het Volk,* established in 1891, has a circulation of 143,330. The French publications with large circulation figures are: *Le Soir,* established in 1887, which circulates 178,569 copies; *L'Avenir Du Luxembourg,* established in 1897, which circulates 139,960 copies; and *Vers L'Avenir,* established in 1918, which circulates 139,960 copies. The only German daily, *Grenz Echo,* a Catholic publication founded in 1927, has a circulation of 12,040.

The many newspapers vary not only in their language of publication but also in their coverage and target audience. *De Standaard,* one of two dailies that share the largest circulation status, is decidedly the most strident Flemish nationalist newspaper. *Het Laatste Nieuws,* which shares *De Standaard's* circulation breadth, *De Morgen, La Derniere Heure* are less nationalistic, characterized as progressive-liberal newspapers, with a ''relatively lowbrow populist tone'' (Elliott 187). *Le Soir* is a respected French daily; *La Libre Belgique* sports a ''perceived upper-class readership and a firmly 'keep-Belgium-united' stance'' (187). Business coverage comes in the form of *L'Echo,* French, and *De Financieel-Ekonomische Tidj,* Dutch. English favorites such as *The Wall Street Journal, The Financial Times, The Times* and the *Herald Tribune* are all reprinted for a Belgian audience.

ECONOMIC FRAMEWORK

Initially most newspapers were offshoots or instruments of a political party, union, or pillar, such as the Catholic Church, the liberals, and the socialists (Witte 290; Lamberts 328). While the Catholic Church and the liberals still hold a strong representation in newspapers, papers today are increasingly held by large conglomerates, thus making the papers a little more ideologically independent. Financial constraints have virtually eliminated small party representation in the press, and as such Socialist Party coverage was diminished entirely (the *Volksgazet* and *Le Peuple*) or was redirected toward a more general public (*De Morgen*), thereby obscuring party affiliation (Lamberts 291). Starting in the 1960s, newspapers have been increasingly absorbed by these large conglomerates, thereby decreasing competition. Of the cities with circulation statistics available, 29 appear to have competition, whereas 9 (roughly 25 percent) do not. Only about 10 newspapers are truly autonomous; the remaining publications vary only slightly in coverage and format from the market leaders (de Bens 1).

In Flanders three conglomerates dominate the newspaper business. Vlaamse Uitgeversmaatschappij (VUM) publishes *De Standaard, Het Nieuwsblad, De Gentenaar,* and *Het Volk.* De Persgroep owns *Het Laatste Nieuws, De Nieuwe Gazet,* and *De Morgen.* Regionale Uitgeversmaatschappij (de RUG), an alliance between N.V. De Vlijt and N.V. Concentra, publish *Gazet van Antwerpen* and *Het Belang van Limburg* (Witte 290; de Bens 1).

Until 1998 the Francophone press was dominated by three groups: 1) N. V. Rossel, who owns *Le Soir, La Meuse, La Lanterne, La Nouvelle Gazette, La Province;* 2) IPM who owns *La Libre Belgique* and *La Derniere Heure;* and 3) Mediabel, who publishes *Vers l'Avenir, Le Jour/Le Belgique, La Courrier de l'Escaut, l'Avenir de Luxembourg,* and *Le Rappel* (de Bens 1). The Francophone press is nearing duopoly status because *Vers l'Avenir* acquired 51 percent of IPM in the late 1990s (de Bens 2). As a result, readers of one publication have banded together in a readers' association to demand diversity of the press and editorial staff independence (1998 World Press Freedom Review). Finally, while the German speaking region has *Grenz Echo,* published by an independent publishing house, Rossel now owns 51 percent of *Grenz Echo* shares.

In 1995 Belgian press circulation was 1,543,623; the Flemish press accounted for 993,229 or 64.3 percent of sales, while the French-language press accounted for 550.394 or 35.6 per cent of sales (de Bens 2). Only about 36 percent of Belgians are reported to subscribe to a newspaper (2). As circulation figures have declined in the latter part of the 1990s, strategies have reportedly been adopted by many dailies to enhance their market tabloid share (de Bens; Elliott). VUM and Rossel have adapted well and are market leaders in sales and advertising revenue (de Bens 2).

While newspapers are attempting to make an economic comeback, 1999 layoffs in smaller regional papers that regrouped in Sud-Presse and layoffs in the national wire service sorely tested efforts to offer diverse press coverage. It appears that readership in Brussels and the Dutch speaking regions of Belgium is increasing, as it is decreasing in the Francophone region (1999 World Press Freedom Review). The print media is largely free of subsidies that it was granted in 1975; subsidies were found to have little effect on market trends and/or to be too small to make a difference (de Bens 4). In 1999 Flanders eliminated direct subsidies because all of its newspapers had been bought by larger media groups. While direct subsidies are decreasing, indirect assistance remains. The print media continues to operate value added tax (VAT) free today, thereby assisting the struggling newspaper and magazine market.

PRESS LAWS

Title II of the Constitution, ''Belgians and Their Rights,'' includes three articles that have bearing on the press. Article 25 specifically grants Belgians the right to a free press: ''censorship can never be established; security from authors, publishers, or printers cannot be demanded.'' It further states that when the author is a known resident of Belgium, neither the publisher, nor the printer, nor the distributor can be prosecuted'' (Adopted 1970, as revised 1993). In addition to establishing a free press, Article 25 also protects Belgian journalists and publishers from prosecution—or, so it would seem. Contemporary cases that challenge this protection include the 1990s Dutroux pedophilia case and the 2002 fining of two *De Morgen* journalists.

Article 19 [Freedom of Expression] grants Belgians, ''freedom of worship, public practice of the latter, as well as freedom to demonstrate one's opinions on all matters.'' The Constitution also includes a Freedom of Information clause; according to Article 32, ''Everyone has the right to consult any administrative document and to have a copy made, except in the cases and conditions stipulated by the laws, decrees, or ruling referred in Article 134.'' In addition to its own constitutional provisions, as a member of the EU, Belgium is party to a Green Paper that seeks to broaden access to public documents and extend freedom of information across Europe.

The Belgian media is not tightly regulated by extra-constitutional legal provisions; most of the laws and statutes guiding press actions are characterized by insiders as ambiguous. Belgium leadership is therefore often criticized by human rights groups and liberals for pursuing a largely laissez-faire media policy (de Bens 4). To fill this regulation void, the Belgian Association of Newspaper Publishers, the General Association of Professional Journalists of Belgium, and the National Federation of the Information Newsletters came together in the Belgium Press Council and drafted the Belgium Code of Journalistic Principles in 1982. This Code articulates the importance of: 1) a free press; 2) unbiased collecting and reporting of facts; 3) separation of facts reported and commentary on the facts; 4) respect for a diversity of opinions and publishing of different points of view; 5) respect for human dignity and the right to a private life make it necessary to avoid physical and/or moral intrusion; 6) restraint from glorifying violence; 7) commitment to correct previously reported false information; 8) protection of source confidentially ; 9) thwarting efforts to prevent freedom of press in the name of secrecy; 10) editorial judgment when freedom of expression appears to conflict with fundamental human rights; 11) resisting outside pressure on newspapers and journalists; and 12) presenting advertisements in such a way as not to be confused with facts (International Journalists' Network). The Code continues to be the most important regulator of press conduct in Belgium despite efforts to draft laws and statutes that guide the behavior and legal treatment of journalists.

As of result of 1990s scandals, the Minister of Justice convened a hearing for interested parties such as judges, lawyers, politicians, journalists, and academic experts, where issues such as the protection of sources for journalists, treatment of press trials, and the need for an Order of Journalists were discussed. Conflict, particularly about ethical issues, made the implementation of laws too difficult; it was decided that the journalistic codes should continue to handle ethical problems. The Belgian Press continues to be self-regulated by the Federation of Editors—a body to which all newspaper editors belong.

Starting in the late 1990s, there was much discussion of bringing press violations such as advertising, tract distribution, and racism to magistrate courts, whereas ''ordinary'' violations would still be evaluated by a jury per the Belgian Constitution (1998 World Press Freedom Review). Amendments to the ''right of reply'' also have been examined but not enacted.

While a 1998 law had mandated speech to the press from the highest public prosecutor, journalists complained that contact was difficult to establish. Minister of Justice Tony Van Parys, therefore, ordered that prosecutors needed to designate spokespeople who could provide journalists with investigation updates in 1999 (World Press Freedom Review). Such a move was welcomed by journalists and press freedom groups.

Prior to 1980 the Belgian press was subject to the following laws: 1979 Press Law, 1987 Belgian Media Law, 1987 Flemish Speaking Law for Commercial Television, and the 1980 Royal Decree on Execution of the 1979 Press Law.

CENSORSHIP

Oversight of the press comes primarily in the form of a Deontological Council of the Belgian Association of Professional Journalists and its Code of Ethics. While Belgium's Constitution encourages an independent media, journalists are increasingly being targeted for lawsuits and/or to divulge confidential sources. Since 1999 journalists and the papers that employ them have increased their insurance policies to cover penalties imposed by Belgian courts (World Press Freedom Review). While the trend is for courts to fine journalists, this trend is often offset in appeal. Cases continue to be brought before Belgian courts, however, and many press freedom groups lament the trend.

In June 2002 Douglas de Conick and Marc Vendemeir, journalists for *De Morgen,* were fined 25 euros (approximately $23 per day) for failing to reveal their sources for a May 11, 2002, story in which they reported that the Belgian State Railway had overshot its budget for a high-speed train. The case will likely join a similar 1995 case on the docket of the European Court of Human Rights, a Strasbourg court that has often affirmed the right of journalists to keep their sources confidential.

On August 9, 2000, a Belgian court granted an emergency injunction to stop *L'Investugatuer* editor Jean Nicolas from publishing a list of convicted or suspected pedophiles. The court further ordered that if Nicolas failed to comply, circulation of the list would lead to a fine of about $22,000 per copy (2000 World Press Freedom Review). The court found that publishing the list would violate the rights of the accused. Journalists and Belgian citizens, however, saw this action as another example of court indifference to victims and potential victims.

On November 16, 1999, two *Le Soir Illustr* journalists were fined 55,000 euros for implying that a police officer had failed to make a proper inquiry into allegations of sex abuse by a minor. Likewise, fines were levied on Michel Bouffioux and Marie-Jeanne Van Heeswyck, *Télé Moustique* reporters, who labeled the same police officer a ''manipulator'' in their story (World Press Freedom Review). Reviewers argue that the lower courts are increasingly siding with public officials and law enforcement officers against the press.

In 1997 the police searched the office of Hans Van Scharen, a *De Morgen* journalist, and confiscated items related to his coverage of a ''hormone mafia'' case; he was accused of improperly possessing judicial documents (1997 World Press Freedom Review).

The most controversial cases, however, concern the 1996 Marc Dutroux case and a 1997 child custody case. Dutroux, a pedophile, raped and killed young Belgian girls. The press was very active in the investigation, while the government was seen to have foiled the case. The complete transcript of the case was made available to a Web site by a journalist; the Web site was later ordered shutdown. In the custody case, the justice system and judiciary were criticized for potentially favoring a notary who was accused of molesting his two sons. In both cases, the justice system was seen at odds with efforts of the press to secure justice. The European Court of Human Rights ruled that accusations made by the journalists appeared to be justified and awarded them legal costs of 851,697 Belgian francs (about US$24,500) (1997 World Press Freedom Review).

Therefore, while censorship is officially absent, Belgian courts' rulings against journalists in libel and source confidentiality cases, particularly where government or judicial figures are criticized, appear to be growing as of the late 1990s and early twenty-first century. Human rights advocacy groups and press freedom groups continue to watch the situation closely.

State-Press Relations

As the press law and censorships sections suggest, Belgium's print press is not subject to strong state control. Its audiovisual media, however, is primarily state run, but commercial and foreign expansion efforts have met a favorable climate. Telecommunications are overseen by the Minister of Telecommunications, while the print news media is self-regulated.

All forms of the press can and do criticize the government. Until the mid-1990s, journalists faced few attempts to interfere with their reporting. Recent court cases levied by state officials may indicate a change in practice. A 1996 case particularly concerns international journalists and human rights groups. A licensed Kurdish station, MED-TV, was forced to close when the Belgian police raided its offices and confiscated its archives. The International Centre against Censorship argued that Belgium was bound by Article 19 of the International Covenant on Civil and Political Rights, which among other things guarantees freedom of expression and the right to ''seek, receive, and impart information.''

The Belgian government has also done little to limit the creation of media conglomerates. Broadcast monopolies were legally legitimate until the late 1980s. On the more positive side, increased access to prosecutorial spokespeople has liberated the flow of information from the state to the citizen on important government and criminal matters.

Attitude toward Foreign Media

As the home of EU leadership, Belgium is frequented by and home to many international journalists. If there is a complaint about coverage in Belgium, it is that regional and national coverage of Belgium itself is often diminished in favor of covering EU issues.

According to non-Belgian journalists, it is very expensive to have a full-time correspondent in Brussels because it is at the periphery of Europe. While large agencies and organizations like Reuters and the BBC have people based in Belgium, some smaller countries and networks contract with a freelance journalist who supplies coverage to more than one agency. Belgium's specific coverage in other European countries is often limited because the correspondents largely address their coverage to EU issues.

News Agencies

Belgium has its own press agency, Belga Press Agency, which covers both daily national and international news. It was originally offered as the Belgium Telegraphic Press Agency (*Agence Belga*) in 1920. According to its home page timeline, the agency distributed its first press release on January 1, 1921, to 45 newspapers, 16 banks, the government, and 9 commercial companies. In 1925 Belga created its home desk; its editorial structure was split into a French- and Dutch- speaking desk in 1970. Using the Hermes system, Belga computerized its editorials and became the country's first electronic press company in 1981. This was followed in 1984 with real-time dispatches to the government's Bistel information network. A client-specific system was developed in 1986 to provide selective information to interested markets by fax or e-mail. Most recently in

2000 Belga entered a joint venture with news *aktuell* International, a subsidiary of the German Press Agency, to distribute specialized press releases. Today Belga dispatches information on politics, cultural issues, finance, sports, and public personalities in the public venue to the traditional media—newspapers, radio, and television. It also offers a subscription service for business and government clients. Belga's press releases are distributed to an international market, too, through contracts with the world's largest foreign press agencies. Belga prides itself for autonomy, accuracy, and timeliness

Foreign press agencies offer coverage in Belgium as well. Reuters Belgium is a regional office of Reuters International that supplies news information on business and finance. The BBC offers extensive coverage of Belgium.

BROADCAST MEDIA

Like the print media, television and radio are divided primarily along linguistic lines. As a result, many Belgians know their regional news and programs yet face limited access to information and stations of other Belgian regions in favor of programming from the rest of Europe and the United States (Elliott 184). It is quite likely that someone in Wallonia has more access to English and international programs than those from the Dutch regions of Belgium itself.

A number of private radio stations were aired after 1923, including Radio Belgique, which was supported by both the royals and the Belgian business world (Lamberts 359). The National Institute for Radio (NIR), a public radio network, was funded by the Belgian Parliament in 1930. It was modeled on the British Broadcasting Corporation (BBC). Unlike the BBC, the NIR, however, was required to allocate air time for party-affiliated organizations, thereby limiting its objectivity and political investigative scope (Lamberts 359). The three main parties demanded broadcasting time; staffing was also influenced by the pillars who sought and gained an employment policy of proportional representation (Witte 291). Thus, the Belgian network, public by statute, was dominated by the country's religious and ideological pillars (Lamberts 359). This public monopoly effectively controlled the radio waves until a 1987 law that allowed for private broadcasting.

Public service programming is supported by an annual licensing fee on automobile radios. Home radios are not subject to licensing (Elliott 185). A ban on radio advertising was revoked in 1985, thus clearing the way for more commercial stations. While the political parties ensured that change was slow to take hold, the public service radio broadcaster currently struggles to survive amid competition from Internet news programming and commercially supported programming in the twenty-first century.

The main radio stations today continue to be state run. RTBF1 and VRT offer mixed programming. Radio 1 is one of the five public radio networks offered by the VRT. Radio Vlaaderen International (RVI) offers programming like ''Flanders Today'' for the Flemish speaking community as well. Radio 1's news and current affairs programs explore social issues and controversies, economic indicators, and cultural events in depth. Radio 2 is Flanders' largest radio network. It provides its listeners with local news and popular music. Radio 2 offers regional program coverage in the five Flemish provinces. Radio 3 is a high-brow station, targeted to the more liberal, intellectual listener. Radio 21 plays current releases and news to the Francophone population, whereas StuBru offers such tunes and coverage to the Dutch speaking community. The BBC World Service is offered in both English and German. There are over 79 FM, 7 AM, and 1 short-wave stations as of 1998. There are over 8.075 million radios in the country; access to radio coverage and alternative programming, however, has broadened substantially with Internet radio coverage.

Belgian television began in 1953 and has become an important information and leisure tool. Like Belgian radio, television was initially dominated by a public monopoly. By the 1980s, however, these monopolies were challenged by commercial stations that were allowed to broadcast their own programs. Since the introduction of audiovisual media, the print media has lost subscriptions, leading to the many mergers. For a time before the mergers, starting in 1975, subsidies were used to sustain the print media (Lamberts 376). These were largely found to be unsuccessful in the face of competition from radio and television.

The main government TV networks are VRT in Dutch and RTBF in French. The Belgian Dutch are also served by VTM, a private station that developed after the implementation of a 1987 decree that allowed for one private station to be created (Witte 291). The Francophone region is also served by RTL.

Ninety-four percent of Belgian households with televisions are equipped with cable, making it the most densely cabled country in the world. When cable programming first became available, it primarily distributed national programming. In fact, only foreign public service stations were allowed cable access in the Belgian market initially (de Bens 3). Today viewers can access over 30 national and foreign channels. International news programming includes CNN, BBXI, and CNBC.

The Belgian market includes pay channels like Canal Plus and satellite dishes. While there is strong support for expanded television options in Belgian policy, pay television has not become as popular in Belgium as in the United States. For example, after 10 years of operation in Flanders, one such pay venture, Filmnet, only had about 120,000 subscribers. It merged with Canal Plus, but still has not attracted a significant number of subscribers (de Bens 4). Some locations in Belgium also have statutes that limit or prohibit such access.

As of 1997 data, there were over 4.72 million televisions for Belgium's 10 million people (*CIA Factbook*). Like car radios, color televisions in Belgium must be licensed. There are additional fees for cable access (Elliott 185).

While public corporations still own and operate most radio and television systems, private ownership is growing. The public corporations that support public broadcasting receive most of their financial support from the annual licensing fees paid by owners of automobile radios and color television sets. As the economic market continues to influence the media, it is likely that commercial and alternative programming will grow to meet the needs of very specific audiences, while public sponsored media will diminish. In addition, the journalists themselves are occupying more presence in political and social debates.

ELECTRONIC NEWS MEDIA

Because Belgium is the most cabled country in the world, the Internet is easily accessible. All agencies, organizations, and government documents are accessible via the World Wide Web. Belgium has several Internet access providers. Belgacom is Belgium's telephone and Internet service provider. Belgium's country code is BE. Skynet is the nation's largest provider because it has a special relationship with Belgacom. Other providers include Aleph-1, Be On, and BIP. The list of providers and free providers is growing in the country daily.

Most large circulation national and regional print newspapers are available online. A survey of web news information sources reveals that the sites are very attractive with lots of color, photography, and links to additional information and news archives. Some publications, such as *E-Sports* (French), *MSR* (Dutch), *Politics Info* (French and Dutch), and *Vlaamse Volksbeweging* (German, French, Dutch, and Spanish) exist solely online as national publications. Belgian expatriates have several choices for news from home via the Internet, including *Expatica.com* and *xPats.com. The Belgium Post,* a foreign publication offered by World News.com, offers daily coverage of Belgium for an English speaking audience. The trend for electronic news is growing because information can be updated throughout the day, and corrections can be made more efficiently.

The European Union is actively involved in creating policies for the dissemination of information on the Internet, including an Internet Rights Observatory. In 1997 Belgian journalists won a case over reuse of their work against Central Station, who had argued that it could reprint their work without permission or compensation.

EDUCATION & TRAINING

There are a number of European news organizations and training institutions available to Belgian journalists and editors; while these associations serve greater Europe and/or the European Union, some are based in Belgium itself.

The European Newspapers' Publishers Association (ENPA), a nonprofit organization, represents some 3,000 daily, weekly, and Sunday titles from 17 European countries. More than 91 million copies are sold each day and read by over 240 million people. Based in Brussels, ENPA works toward ensuring a sympathetic European legislative and economic environment for the independent newspaper industry. Its primary goal is to fortify freedom of both the editorial and commercial press. It lobbies for the inclusion of freedom of the press in a Charter of Fundamental Rights to protect newspaper publishers in the event of cross border disputes. ENPA promotes multimedia access and diversity as foundational structures of a democratic nation. Among its other important causes, ENPA actively promotes discussion of intellectual property rights in a technology transformed world; it fiercely defends author ownership of press content against unauthorized reproduction. Finally ENPA would like the European print press to be covered by a more coherent policy like that being drafted and enacted for the Internet.

The European Journalism Centre (EJC), founded in 1992, is an independent, nonprofit multimedia training support center based in the Netherlands, whose membership and services are widely utilized by Belgian journalists, editors, and educational institutions. EJC offers guidance on how to increase European media presence and thereby gain greater and more accurate coverage of European current issues. It provides an assessment of media developments in several countries, including Belgium, and describes the changing nature of Europe's media overall. It also provides media links and tools to help journalists conduct more effective research and to share their working knowledge.

The European Journalism Training Association and its member schools organize and facilitate conferences and colloquia on academic and pragmatic journalism education. It acts as a resource and information broker for its members and provides essays on educational and social challenges facing European journalism programs. The Institut des Hautes Etudes des Communications Sociales and Katholieke Hogeschool Mechelen/Afdeling Journalistiek-De Ham are Belgium member schools.

The International Federation of Journalists (IFJ), based in Brussels, represents over 450,00 journalists in over 100 countries, including the organization's home country, Belgium. The largest of journalist organizations, the IFJ was initially established in 1926 and was launched again in both 1946 and 1952. IFJ exists to promote and defend freedom of the press, social justice, and independent trade union activities. IFJ is nonpartisan, but instead promotes a global human rights agenda. It opposes the use of media for propaganda and/or to promote hate. The IFJ is called upon to represent journalists within both the United Nations and the international trade union movement. It maintains a safety fund for humanitarian assistance for journalistic endeavors. The IFJ agenda is set by a Congress that meets every three years; its actions are carried out by the Brussels-based secretariat who works under the direction of an elected Executive Committee. In addition, since 1992 the IFJ has awarded the Lorenzo Natali Prize for Journalism, one of the world's most valuable journalistic prizes, awarded to print and/or online journalists who have demonstrated a striking insight and particular dedication to the reporting of human rights issues within the context of the development process.

The Pascal Decroos Fund promotes special journalism in the written and audiovisual press in Flanders by granting working grants to journalists who are willing to work on a special project. New and experienced journalists are encouraged to apply. Pascal Decroos (April 20, 1964 - December 2, 1997) was a prominent producer and journalist who died early in his career. He was known as a passionate journalist who promoted the cause of society's underprivileged and who brought a keen and critical eye to investigative journalism. His creed, ''do not let yourself be carried along the stream of superficial news, but submerge. Do not content yourself with drawing the obvious conclusion, but investigate and probe until you find the truth,'' motivated the development of this scholarship that allows journalists to probe a topic deeper and provide more in-depth coverage than the average news story. This working grant is supported by the Flemish community, but is available to any qualifying journalist.

There are also three important media organizations in Belgium. The Association of Belgian Journalists (AVBB) in Brussels, the Belgian Association of Publishers (BVDU), and Febelma, the association of publishers of magazines.

Belgian and European educational institutions offer undergraduate and graduate courses of study in communication and journalism—institutions like Universiteit Leiden, which offers baccalaureate degrees in journalism and news media, Universitaire Faculteiten Sint-Ignatusia (UFSIA), which offers graduate degrees, and VLEKHO and Erasmushogeshool, which both offer postacademic training for journalists. Opportunities to study journalism are enhanced by generous course offerings in the use of technology for investigative journalism and online journalism in both the college and journalism organization settings.

SUMMARY

On the one hand, Belgian press access is expanding with the daily increase of media outlets on the Internet. On the other hand, the coverage offered in mainstream newsprint is becoming more streamlined with media mergers in both the Dutch and the Francophone press. Barriers between French, Dutch, and German speakers continue to grow in this multilingual nation, as is evidenced by a separate higher education system, regional and national news coverage, and economic growth trends in their respective sectors. Press coverage within each region, however, appears to discourage interregional diversity. Smaller political and social movements find the Internet a friendly option for their ideas and publications, as they increasingly find the print media closed to them. While Belgium has sustained internal conflict throughout its history of occupation by different language speakers who ultimately shaped its regional triad, it remains to be seen if Belgium can continue to placate the various groups, as economic success moves closer to the Dutch population, who were once viewed as the inhabitants of a largely agrarian and recession-prone region. The French and German peoples are more and more overshadowed by Flemish radio, publications, and nationalism, which may lead to further conflict.

Belgium's situation as the economic and leadership center of the EU also influences the development of its press coverage. While its role as an economic leader and exporter grows, we must wait to see if its rich culture will be more visible and known to greater Europe and the rest of the world. Information about Belgium's history and culture is still not well documented in the West and English language publications. To further complicate matters, it appears that its EU membership will increasingly determine its position on such matters as freedom of information and Internet commerce.

While Belgium is not hostile to its journalists—it does not license, torture, or imprison them for their investigative work—documented cases of censorship and fines are cause for closer attention. It remains to be determined whether or not technological expansion will ultimately sustain or erode press freedom. While more voices are enabled to provide media coverage—some that have been virtually eliminated or never viable in print—the commercial and compact characteristics of most media present journalists and readers in Belgium with a contradiction. It may be that this contradiction will be sustained and absorbed, as has been the case in most of Belgium's political and social history. It may also be that the news media is changing globally to reduce the gap between entertainment, advertising, and investigative reporting. If that is the case, the news media will further become a menu of options for cultural and selective consumption, thus further reducing the importance of the news media, even as it expands.

SIGNIFICANT DATES

- May 1997: *Vers l'Avenir* obtains 51 percent of IPM to create near-duopoly situation in the Fracophone press.
- 1998: *Le Matin* is taken over by *Vers l'Avenir,* a Catholic publication, thus placing the nation's only remaining leftist paper—whose sales have not improved—at risk of ceasing publication.
- Law enacted that limits press prosecution press releases to the highest public prosecutor. Minister of Justice Tony Van Parys later orders (1999) that prosecutors must designate spokespeople to provide journalist with investigative updates after complaints that the highest public prosecutor was too unavailable for comment.
- 2000: Belga Press Agency enters a joint venture with news *aktuell* International, a subsidiary of the German Press Agency, to distribute specialized press releases.
- August 2000: A Belgian court grants an emergency injunction to stop *L'Investugatuer* editor Jean Nicolas from publishing a list of convicted or suspected pedophiles.
- June 2002: Two *De Morgen* journalists are fined for failing to reveal their sources for a May 11, 2002, story in which they reported that the Belgian State Railway had overshot its budget for a high-speed train. The case will likely join a similar 1995 case on the docket of the European Court of Human Rights, a Strasbourg court that has often affirmed the right of journalists to keep their sources confidential.

BIBLIOGRAPHY

de Bens, Els. ''The Belgian Media Landscape.'' In *European Media Landscape.* European Journalism Centre, 2000. Available from http://www.ejc.nl.

Boudart, Marina, Michel Boudart, and Rene Bryssinck, eds. *Modern Belgium.* Palo Alto, CA: Society for the Promotion of Science and Scholarship, 1990.

Central Intelligence Agency (CIA). *The World Factbook.* CIA Publications, 2000. Available from http://www.cia.gov.

Elliot, Mark. *Culture Shock: A Guide to Customs and Etiquette.* Portland, OR: Graphic Arts Center Publishing Co., 2001.

Freemedia. ''World Press Freedom Review: Belgium.'' Freemedia Home Page, 2000. Available from http://www.freemedia.at.

Lamberts, E. ''Belgium Since 1830.'' In *History of the Low Countries,* Ed. J. C. H. Bloom and E. Lamberts. Trans., James C. Kennedy, 313-386. New York: Berghahan Books, 1999.

Stallaerts, Robert. *Historical Dictionary of Belgium.* Series: European Historical Dictionaries, No. 35. Lanham, MD: The Scarecrow Press, Inc., 1999.

Witte, Els, Jan Craeybeckx, and Alain Meynen. *Political History of Belgium from 1830 Onwards.* Trans. Raf Casert. Brussels: VUB University Press, 2000.

World Association of Newspapers. ''World Press Trends: On Circulation.'' World Association of Newspapers Organization Web site, 2001. Available from http://www.wan-press.org.

—Sherry L. Wynn

BELIZE

BASIC DATA

Official Country Name:	Belize
Region (Map name):	North & Central America
Population:	249,183
Language(s):	English, Spanish, Mayan, Garifuna (Carib), Creole
Literacy rate:	70.3%

Formerly known as British Honduras, the Central American country of Belize broke from Great Britain to become an independent country in 1981. Despite its independence, the English monarch is still the chief of state, represented locally by a Governor General. A Prime Minister leads the bicameral National Assembly, which consists of an appointed Senate and an elected House of Representatives. English is the official language of Belize, but many Belizeans speak Spanish, Mayan, Creole, and Garifuna, a Caribbean dialect. The population is approximately 256,000 and the approximate literacy rate is 75 percent. The basis of the Belizean economy is agriculture, especially sugar and bananas, but tourism and construction are becoming more important every year.

The Belizean Constitution provides for general press freedom, and the media operates freely. The government has occasionally been sensitive to criticism: in 2000, the editor of the *San Pedro Sun* was publicly threatened by a government minister for criticism about the government's environmental policy.

The capital of Belize is Belmopan, but the media center of the country is Belize City. Belize has no daily newspaper; most newspapers publish weekly, and all are printed in English. Politics play a large part in the country's publications. The most widely read weekly is *Amandala,* which began in 1969 as a stenciled newsletter for the United Black Association for Development and now publishes in print and online. *The Belize Times,* published in English and Spanish and posted online, bills itself as the official newspaper of the People's United Party. *The Guardian* (known as *The People's Pulse* before 1998) is the official newspaper of a rival political group, the United Democratic Party. It also maintains an online presence. Beyond politics—and the mainland—is *The San Pedro Sun,* which publishes every Friday from San Pedro Town, located on Ambergris Caye, the largest of some 200 cayes off the coast of Belize. The content is also posted online. *The Reporter* is also a popular Belize City weekly.

There are 12 FM stations and one AM station serving approximately 133,000 radios in Belize. Two television stations broadcast to about 40,000 televisions. There are two Internet service providers.

BIBLIOGRAPHY

''Belize.'' The Central Intelligence Agency (CIA). *The World Factbook.* Available from http://www.cia.gov.

''Belize.'' *World Press Freedom Review.* International Press Institute 2001. Available from http://www.freemedia.at.

The Belize Times, 2002. Available from http://www.belizetimes.bz.

Benn's Media, 1999, Vol. 3, 147th Edition, p. 247.

The Guardian News Online, 2002. Available from http://www.udp.org.bz.

The San Pedro Sun, 2002. Available from http://www.sanpedrosun.net.

''Welcome.'' *Amandala 2002.* Available from http://www.belizemall.com.

—*Jenny B. Davis*

BENIN

BASIC DATA

Official Country Name:	Republic of Benin
Region (Map name):	Africa
Population:	6,395,919
Language(s):	French, Fon, Yoruba
Literacy rate:	37%

The tiny state of Benin in West Africa is home to about 15 dailies and more than 20 periodicals. A precise figure is difficult to gauge as newspapers are continually launched while others close down just as frequently. Circulations are small, typically less than 3,000 due largely to a low literacy rate, estimated at about 37 percent for its more than 6 million citizens, and a poor distribution service. The press is largely concentrated in Contonou, the seat of government, and Porto Novo, the official capital.

Newspapers are mostly privately owned and while many are short-lived, a few such as the dailies *La Matinal,* founded in 1997, *Le Point au Quotidien* and *Les Echoes de Jour,* are maintaining a fairly constant presence. The Catholic-oriented *La Croix du Benin,* founded in 1945 and published fortnightly, is one of only two newspapers that could be considered established. The other is the state-owned daily, *La Nacion,* which was founded in 1967. A state news agency, Agence Presse Benin (APB), was founded in 1961.

Although Benin is considered to have a free press, journalists receive poor salaries and thus are susceptible to bribery from businessmen and politicians seeking to embellish their image. The government has sought to address this problem by offering 300 million CFA francs, about U.S.$400,000, in aid to privately-owned media every year since 1997.

The increasing number of Beninese with college degrees, and the establishment of training programs for journalists as well as the government's recognition of the value of a free press—athough libel is still punishable by prison—means the press in Benin is edging toward stability and is one of the freest in Africa.

BIBLIOGRAPHY

Adjovi, Emmanuel, ''Media Status Report: Niger,'' Partners for Media in Africa, Research and Technology Exchange Group, June 2001. Available from http://www.gret.org/mediapartner/uk2/ressource/edm/pdf/benin.pdf.

''Benin.'' Central Intelligence Agency, *The World Factbook 2001.* Available from http://www.cia.gov.

''Benin.'' International Press Institute. *2001 World Press Freedom Review.* Available from http://www.freemedia.at/wpfr/benin.htm.

Benin, The Press. In *The Europa World Yearbook 2000,* 667-8. London: Europa Publications, 2001.

''Benin: Press Overview.'' International Journalists' Federation, 2001. Available from http://www.ijnet.org/Profile/Africa/Niger/media.html.

''Niger.'' Committee to Protect Journalists, Africa 2001. Available from http://www.cpj.org/attacks01/africa01/benin.html.

—Denis Fitzgerald

BERMUDA

BASIC DATA

Official Country Name:	Bermuda
Region (Map name):	North & Central America
Population:	62,997
Language(s):	English, Portuguese
Literacy rate:	98%

Bermuda, which lies east of North Carolina in the North Atlantic Ocean, was settled in 1609 when a group of English colonists shipwrecked there on the way to Virginia. Today the country is still linked with Great Britain, as a self-governing overseas territory. A referendum on independence was defeated in 1995, and the chief of state remains the British monarch, represented locally by a Governor. Presiding over a bicameral Parliament with an appointed Senate and an elected House of Assembly is the Premier, usually the majority leader of Parliament. The population of Bermuda is approximately 65,000, and the literacy rate is 98 percent. The official language of Bermuda is English, but Portugese is also spoken. Bermudians have one of the highest per-capita incomes in the world thanks to an economy based on financial services and luxury tourism.

Bermuda's newspapers are independent, but the government retains controls over broadcasting content. Tobacco ads are banned on television and radio, and there are restrictions on alcohol advertising. In 2002, the adoption of a ''minimum local content'' law for broadcasts was being debated. Bermuda's publishing hub is the capital city of Hamilton, and all major newspapers are printed in English. Bermuda's only daily newspaper is *The Royal Gazette.* Founded in 1828, the independent *Royal Gazette* publishes every day but Sunday and public holidays and claims to reach more than 90 percent of the adult market with its circulation of 16,000 and its online edition. The *Mid-Ocean News* publishes on Friday. Although it is the sister publication of *The Royal Gazette,* it maintains editorial independence. The *Bermuda Sun,* which publishes on Wednesday and Friday and maintains an online edition, has a reported circulation of 12,300 and publishes the island's official government and legal notices. Prior to March 2001, the *Sun* was known as the *Official Gazette.*

There are eight radio stations, five AM and three FM, broadcasting to 82,000 radios. Bermuda has three television stations serving approximately 66,000 televisions. There are 20 Internet service providers.

BIBLIOGRAPHY

Benn's Media, 1999, Vol. 3, 147th Edition, p. 247-248.

''Bermuda,'' The Central Intelligence Agency (CIA). *World Fact Book 2001.* Available from http://www.cia.gov.

Bermuda cable, daily and other newspapers, magazines, radio & television, Bermuda Online 2002. Available from http://www.bermuda-online.org.

Bermuda Sun, 2002 Home Page. Available from http://www.bermudasun.bm.

The Royal Gazette, 2002 Home Page. Available from http://www.theroyalgazette.com.

—Jenny B. Davis

BHUTAN

BASIC DATA

Official Country Name:	Kingdom of Bhutan
Region (Map name):	East & South Asia
Population:	2,005,222
Language(s):	Dzongkha
Literacy rate:	42.2%

Bhutan is a small country in South Asia that had a population of about 2 million in 2001. (Official statistics do not include people of Nepalese origin and thus place the count at 800,000.) Nearly 90 percent of the population lives in rural areas. The literacy rate is nearly 42 percent. The four main languages spoken in Bhutan are Dzongkha (the national language and spoken largely in Western Bhutan), English (the language of instruction), Nepalese (with its dialects spoken by close to 1 million people of Nepalese origin in Bhutan), and Sharchopkha (spoken in Eastern Bhutan). The main occupations, which employ 94 percent of the population and account for 40 percent of the Gross Domestic Product, include agriculture, animal husbandry, and forestry.

Bhutan is a monarchy, run by a king and a unicameral *Tshogdu* (National Assembly). Jigme Singye Wangchuk has been the king of Bhutan since 1972. He has paved the way for a gradual modernization of this traditional country. His slogan is that Gross National Happiness (*Gakid*) is more important than Gross National Product.

Journalism is fairly small-scale and new to the country of Bhutan. Bhutan has only one newspaper, one radio station, one television station, and one Internet provider, Druknet, which was started in 1999. The government monitors these enterprises closely, under the guise of preserving culture and tradition, and restricts freedom of speech and the press. Bhutan's only regular publication is *Kuensel*, a weekly newspaper that is published and controlled by the government. Its circulation is about 10,000, and editions are published in *Dzongkha* English, and Nepalese. An online version of the newspaper was introduced in 1999. The government ministries regularly monitor the subject content and have the constitutional right to prevent or alter publication of the content. There are no tabloids published in Bhutan, but some Indian and Nepalese tabloids are available.

In 1989, the Bhutan government banned reception of all private television and ordered dismantling of satellite dishes and antennas. It introduced a local television service through the Bhutan Broadcasting Service. In early 2002, the daily programming consisted of about four hours of programs with half of it in Dzongkha and the other half in English. The programs consisted of imported programs from other countries, such as the British Broadcasting Corporation and *Doordarshan* (India). In 1997 it was estimated that about 11,000 television sets were being used in Bhutan.

Bhutan's one radio station includes one short-wave program and one daily FM broadcast from Thimphu, the national capital. In 1997 it was estimated that there were about 37,000 radios in Bhutan.

Bhutan is a traditional country that is slowly modernizing but resists Western influences. In such milieu, the press has focused more on providing information to the people, assuming an objective reporting style, and serving as the long arm of the government.

BIBLIOGRAPHY

The Central Intelligence Agency (CIA). *The World Factbook 2001*. Directorate of Intelligence. Available from http://www.cia.gov/.

Central Statistical Organization, Planning Commission. *Bhutan at a Glance*. Thimphu, Bhutan, 1999.

Cooper, Robert. *Bhutan*. New York: Marshall Cavendish, 2001.

Dompnier, Robert. *Bhutan: Kingdom of the Dragon*. Boston, MA: Shambhala Publications, Inc., 1999.

Karan, Pradyumana P. *Bhutan: Environment, Culture, and Development Strategy*. Columbia, MO: South Asia Books, 1990.

Planning Commission. *Eighth Five Year Plan 1997-2002*. Thimphu: Royal Government of Bhutan, 1998.

Savada, Andrea M. *Bhutan Country Study*. Washington, DC: Federal Research Division, Library of Congress, 1993.

—Manoj Sharma

BOLIVIA

BASIC DATA

Official Country Name:	Republic of Bolivia
Region (Map name):	South America
Population:	8,300,463
Language(s):	Spanish (official), Quechua (official), Aymara (official)
Literacy rate:	83.1%
Area:	1,098,580 sq. km
GDP:	8,281 (US$ millions)
Number of Television Stations:	48
Number of Television Sets:	900,000
Television Sets per 1,000:	108.4
Number of Cable Subscribers:	79,680
Cable Subscribers per 1,000:	9.6

Number of Radio Stations:	321
Number of Radio Receivers:	5,250,000
Radio Receivers per 1,000:	632.5
Number of Individuals with Computers:	140,000
Computers per 1,000:	16.9
Number of Individuals with Internet Access:	120,000
Internet Access per 1,000:	14.5

BACKGROUND & GENERAL CHARACTERISTICS

The only landlocked Andean country of South America, La República de Bolivia (The Republic of Bolivia) is bordered by Brazil, Peru, Chile, Argentina, and Paraguay. The country's population is approximately 8 million, about 40 percent of which live in rural areas. Bolivia has the unique claim to having two national capitals, La Paz (the seat of government) and Sucre (the seat of the judiciary). Other major cities include Santa Cruz, Cochabamba, and El Alto. The country is 425,000 square miles, about twice the size of Texas.

The people of Bolivia suffer from various economic and social problems. Two-thirds of the population live in poverty, one of the biggest issues facing the Bolivian government. The country's literacy rate is about 83 percent, one of the lowest in South America. There are three official languages in Bolivia: Spanish, Quechua, Aymara; about half of the population speaks Spanish as their first language. There is a huge wealth gap within the population, especially between wealthy city residents and poorer urban farmers and miners. Approximately 55 percent of the people are of indigenous descent (Quechua, Aymara, or Guarani), 30 percent are *mestizo* (mixed European-indigenous heritage), and 15 percent are white. The predominant religion is Catholic (95 percent), followed by various Protestant and non-Christian religions.

Like most of its neighbors, Bolivia's journalistic tradition began as an extension of Spanish colonial culture and rule. After it gained independence from Spain in 1825, Bolivia's newspapers continued to be official state publications of the new country. One of these newspapers was *La Gaceta de Gobierno* (*The Government Gazette*), established in 1841. Various political factors created and controlled other politically oriented newspapers throughout the 1800s, a characteristic known as *caudillismo.*

Today, Bolivia boasts 18 daily newspapers, most of which are published in La Paz, where the combined daily circulation is approximately 50,000 copies. Among the most distributed newspapers are *El Diario, La Razon,* and *El Deber* (*The Daily, The Reason,* and *The Duty,* respectively). The country's overall circulation is not very high, averaging about 55 readers per 1,000 people. There are several reasons for the relatively low circulation, including distribution and infrastructure problems, a high poverty rate, and the high illiteracy rate.

The volatile political nature of Bolivia has made the journalism profession often dangerous, especially for reporters. Numerous incidents over the last few years have resulted in harm to various media professionals. In 2000 staff at *La Presencia*—a daily newspaper in La Paz—received death threats and a bomb scare after the paper investigated a major drug trafficking story in the country. A year later in 2001, reporter Juan Carlos Encinas was killed while covering a conflict between two companies fighting over a limestone cooperative. Then in 2002, journalists were placed at danger while covering protests after the government closed a coca place. Other similar events, some of which have involved the Bolivian military, have also been recorded.

Despite these dangers, the Bolivian media is responsive to its obligations to its readers. Different newspapers have participated in projects highlighting civic responsibility and freedom of information. In 1998, *El Nuevo Dia* (*The New Day*) published a two-page questionnaire, ''Discover if you are part of the problem,'' which was intended to make people think about their social responsibility to fight corruption. This undertaking was part of a larger project to promote democracy in Bolivia.

ECONOMIC FRAMEWORK

Bolivia is the poorest country in South America. Recovering from severe recession in the 1980s, it enjoyed moderate growth in the 1990s, until the economy slowed down after the Asian financial crisis in 1999. Periods of hyperinflation over the last two decades—which peaked at 24,000 percent—caused a generally unfavorable economic environment for the struggling media in the country and also created civil unrest, which exacerbated already-difficult working conditions for journalists. Foreign investment and the privatization of several key Bolivian companies resulted in investment capital for infrastructure improvements in the mid and late 1990s, but the only aspect of communication to benefit directly was the telecommunications industry (telephone and Internet). The primary business sectors in Bolivia are energy, agriculture, and minerals. Many of these resources, especially mining, have not been developed to their full potential.

The success of media in Bolivia is dependent not only on the general state of the economy itself, but also upon its relationships with political and private entities. Generally, media that are most visibly pro-government receive more business than those media who are openly critical. Media that criticize the government rely on small, often limited, private funding, a condition that promotes self-censorship. The La Paz newspaper, *El Pulso* (*The Pulse*), which is noted for its sometimes unfavorable reporting of political events, is owned mostly by journalists. Reporters may also find writing about corruption in the corporate sector difficult because of the close ties between media owners and businesses.

PRESS LAWS

Historically, Bolivia has maintained laws designed to protect the rights of individuals, companies, and the media. One of the first pieces of legislation of this type was the Print Law of 1925, which guaranteed the confidentiality and legal protection of sources. In 2000, a legislative proposal to repeal this law was introduced, but was withdrawn following a march on the national capital by Bolivian journalists, who are called *periodisticas.* Periodisticas, like all Bolivian citizens, are guaranteed freedom of speech under Article 7 of the *Constitution Politica del Estate de 1967* (Constitution of the States). Yet many legal parameters exist for journalists, such as the Electoral Code Reform Law of 2001, which gives the National Electoral Court the legal right to suspend media who do not follow carefully constructed rules for political advertising. Periodisticas can also invite sanctions from the government for reporting that is slanderous or too critical.

One of the biggest areas of Bolivian press law is related to defamation. Defamation is almost always treated as a civil violation; although, if it is directed at a public official, may carry criminal penalties. The Telecommunications Law of 1995 sets forth mandates requiring infringers to pay damages, and another law provides for 40-member juries (some members of which may actually be journalists) in each municipality to hear cases of defamation and award civil damages. A 1997 amendment to the Penal Code also strengthened copyright laws, making infringement a public crime, allowing police enforcement if necessary. Consequently, Bolivian journalists tend to exercise extreme self-regulation and caution when covering government corruption and politically sensitive topics.

According to Bolivian law, all journalists must have a university degree in journalism and register with the National Registry of Journalists in order to exercise their profession inside the country. Some exceptions can be made through official channels of the Ministry of Education for experienced journalists who lack an academic degree. People who call themselves journalists without complying with these legal requirements are sanctioned and can be criminally prosecuted. These laws are considered a violation of human rights by the Inter-American Court of Human Rights but are still in effect, although not necessarily enforced.

CENSORSHIP

The press in Bolivia plays an especially important civic role, serving as a primary means of challenging governmental corruption. Like many other South American countries, a free political process is still a relatively new concept; many countries in South America, including Bolivia, did not replace dictatorships with full-scale democracies until the middle part of the twentieth century. Thus, authoritarian traditions and attitudes are still widespread within these societies and still may impede the complete liberties of periodisticas.

There is currently concern in Bolivia that the press does not enjoy complete freedom to investigate and report on politically sensitive issues such as government and corporate corruption. Although the Bolivian constitution guarantees free speech to all citizens, under the existing Penal Code, journalists—or any citizen, for that matter—who defame or insult public officials can be jailed. Greater sentences can even be imposed if the defamed official is high-ranking, such as the president or a cabinet minister. Even implied defamation can carry consequences. For example, a special tribunal was called in La Paz in 1999 after the magazine *Informe R* published a photo of then-President Banzer with Augusto Pinochet, former authoritarian leader of Chile.

Other examples of censorship exist in recent Bolivian history. In 2000, after protests over a proposed water rate hike, the military took control of three radio stations in an effort to control coverage of the event. Also during that year, Ronald Mendéz was initially jailed on criminal defamation charges after he reported on alleged embezzlement by officials at a local water company. He was cleared before serving his sentence, however.

In 2001, senator and former government minister Walter Guiteras resigned office after being accused of intimidating media to suppress coverage of his alleged assault on his wife and for presumably bribing police officers to cover the incident. In a protest march from Cochabamba to La Paz, journalists were assaulted by police, and later that year Bolivian security forces allegedly fired at reporters in Chaparé. However, the journalists in both cases were present in conflict zones, and there was no evidence that the journalists themselves were the actual targets of police force.

STATE-PRESS RELATIONS

The relationship between the Bolivian government and the press is tense. These tensions exist for a number of reasons, including the past violence as previously described, conflicting free expression laws in the Criminal Code, the country's stressful economic conditions, and more recent legislation controlling the media's coverage of political campaigns. Moreover, the Bolivian government reserves the right to withhold information about any topic, including those issues of public interest, which further restrains the press.

ATTITUDE TOWARD FOREIGN MEDIA

All media activity in Bolivia is subject to the rules of the Ministry of Government Information. Many foreign press organizations have bureaus in Bolivia, including the U.S.-based Associated Press. Most major developments in Bolivia are covered by a host of international journalists from organizations such as CNN and the British Broadcasting Corporation. Foreign journalists must be accredited through the Ministry of Education in order to work in the country.

Bolivia cooperates with the *Comisíon Interamerica de Telecomunicaciónes* (Inter-American Telecommunication Commission), an entity of the Organization of American States, which coordinates and develops telecommunications among governments and private sectors of countries throughout the western hemisphere. The country also participates in exchanges and fellowships with media professionals from other countries, such as David Boldt, a retired journalist from the *Philadelphia Inquirer,* who trained Bolivian journalists as part of a Knight Fellowship from 2001 to 2002.

NEWS AGENCIES

Several main news agencies operate in Bolivia. The largest agency, La Agencia Boliviana de Información, is operated by the government under the Ministry of Government Information, and provides information for Virtualísimo, an online news site. La Agencia Nacional de Noticias Jatha, a widespread private news agency in existence since 1992, offers national news and business news. Other agencies include La Agencia de Noticias Fides, which is owned and operated by the Catholic Church, and Le Agence France-Presse Worldwide, a France-based agency, which maintains an office in La Paz.

BROADCAST MEDIA

Over the last decade, the broadcasting industry in Bolivia has matured, particularly in regards to the television market, which is the principal advertising media—as of 2002 there are over 900,000 television sets owned by Bolivia's 8 million people—followed by newspapers and radios, respectively. Several major television *reds* (networks) exist, including the privately owned P.A.T. network and the state-owned Empresa Nacional de Televisíon Bolivania, which broadcasts on seven stations in different parts of the country.

Altogether, Bolivia has 48 television stations, 73 FM radio stations, and 171 AM radio stations. Eight television stations are operated by various universities; one radio station is state-owned.

Like the Federal Communications Commission in the United States, the Bolivian government also has an agency that regulates electronic media. All broadcast stations, cable systems, and Internet services are subject to the control of La Superintendencia de Telecomunicaciónes (SITTEL), whose office is administered under the Ministry of Economic Development. SITTEL's vision to ensure ''more and better communications at less cost'' also involves protecting the legal rights of businesses and consumers. In Bolivia, television piracy (receiving services without paying for them) is a serious problem, with a piracy rate of about 95 percent. The Dirección General de Televisión, an office under the auspices of SITTEL enforces the general regulation of television service, which includes penalties for illegal broadcasts.

ELECTRONIC NEWS MEDIA

Despite a poor communication infrastructure and expensive telephone rates, Bolivia leads its South American neighbors in the area of online newspapers. At least 10 print newspapers in La Paz, Santa Cruz, and Cochabamba also maintain online sites. Various online services such as Bolnet, offer links to official news, education, business, and country events.

EDUCATION & TRAINING

Many of Bolivia's universities offer programs in telecommunications, journalism, and communication science. Students receive a *licenciatura,* the equivalent of a bachelor's degree, which qualifies them to register with the National Register of Journalists. Several universities operate local television stations that schedule cultural and public interest programming. One example is La Televisión Universitaria, which has been in operation at the Universidad Autonómia Juan Misael Saracho in Tarija for 25 years. Although under the auspices of the SITTEL, this station and other university-run media outlets are free to maintain their own programming without governmental influence.

Students with interests in print or electronic communication follow structured *plan de estudios* (programs of study) depending on their particular intended academic focus. Earning a licenciatura typically involves three to four years of full-time school, assuming a student takes five to six courses per semester. Some universities, such as la Universidad Católica Boliviana and la Universidad Mayor de San Andres, offer postgraduate and certificate programs in telecommunications and related areas.

Students studying journalism and broadcasting complete *cursos especialidades* (specialized courses), which are structured very similarly to academic programs found in the United States. Bolivian college students majoring in communication generally take the equivalent of general education courses, including mathematics, sociology or psychology, natural sciences, and political science, which are integrated with courses in their major field. Students receive licenciaturas with emphases in communication science, telecommunications, journalism, or other closely related fields. Specialized programs such as the Ingeneiería de Telecomunicaciónes (telecommunications engineering) at the Catholic University of Bolivia include courses in satellite and digital technology, as well as other technical aspects of mass communication.

In addition to courses in writing, editing, communication law, ethics, and technology, a Bolivian journalist's academic training may also include courses related to religion, culture, philosophy, or behavioral studies. Credit may be received for courses based on lecture hours, laboratory work, or special workshops.

SUMMARY

Because Bolivia is a country that has not yet reached its economic and social potential, its press faces various political barriers. Rigid defamation laws and potential censorship by the government hinder reporters' effectiveness in bringing information to the public. Violence due to social unrest in the country represents a danger to journalists, who may be directly or indirectly harmed by civilians or police. In short, Bolivia has not fully embraced the freedom of expression guaranteed by its constitution.

Moreover, a low literacy rate and widespread poverty restrict the extent to which the populace consumes information, especially print material. The wide reach of television compensates for this limitation, especially for advertisers in the larger metropolitan areas, whereas newspaper circulation remains relatively low.

On a more positive note, although infrastructural problems still need to be solved, Bolivia has taken great strides in introducing technology into the press industry. Despite the comparatively small size of the country, both in area and population (its neighbors, particularly Brazil, are much larger in both respects), Bolivia is a leader in electronic media in South America. Its universities keep abreast of current technological innovations and provide students with a well-rounded liberal arts education.

As Bolivia continues to solve its internal problems, it will no doubt lead the region in state-of-the-art print and broadcast journals. Its abundance of natural resources and its strong cultural history will serve to enhance its potential as an information-rich nation.

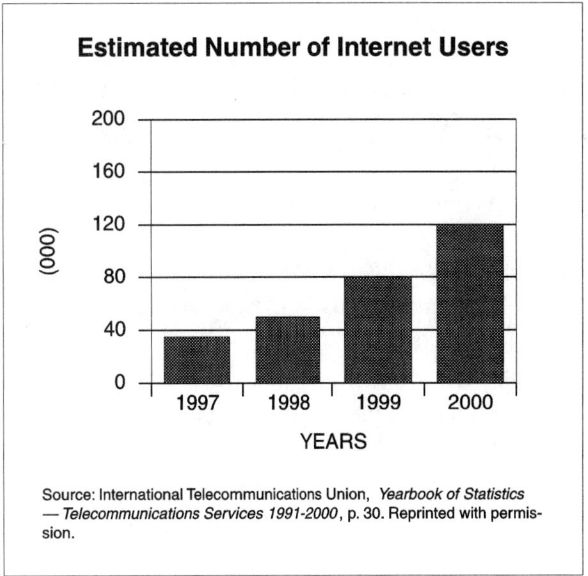

Source: International Telecommunications Union, *Yearbook of Statistics — Telecommunications Services 1991-2000*, p. 30. Reprinted with permission.

SIGNIFICANT DATES

- 1994: Constitution is revised.
- 1995: Telecommunications Act is passed, establishing current defamation laws.
- 2001: Electoral Code Reform Law is passed; reporter Juan Carlos Encinas is killed while covering a conflict between two companies fighting over a limestone cooperative.

BIBLIOGRAPHY

''AFP Worldwide.'' Agence France-Pressne, June 2002. Available from http://www.afp.com.

''Agencia Boliviana de Información.'' La Agencia Boliviana de Información, June 2002. Available from http://www.comunica.gov.bo/abi.

''Background Note: Bolivia.'' U.S. Department of State, April 2001. Available from http://www.state.gov.

''Bolivia.'' The Central Intelligence Agency (CIA) *World Factbook*, June 2002. Available from http://www.cia.gov.

''Bolivia.'' The Committee to Protect Journalism, June 2002. Available from http://www.cpj.org.

''Bolivia.'' Inter-American Press Association, March 2002. Available from http://www.sipiapa.org.

''Bolivia.'' International Intellectual Property Alliance, June 2002. Available from http://www.iipa.com.

''Bolivia Country Commercial Guide.'' U.S. Commercial Service. Available from http://www.usatrade.gov.

''Bolivia: Marketing U.S. Products and Services.'' *Tradeport,* June 2002. Available from http://www.tradeport.org.

''Bolivia: Media.'' *World Desk Reference,* June 2002. Available from http://www.travel.dk.com.

''Bolivia: Media Outlets.'' International Journalists' Network, June 2002. Available from http://www.ijnet.org.

''Bolivia Newspapers.'' Onlinenewspapers.com, June 2002. Available from http://www.onlinenewspapers.com.

''Bolivia: Press Overview.'' International Journalists' Network, June 2002. Available from http://www.ijnet.org.

''Bolivia: World Press Freedom Review.'' International Press Institute, June 2002. Available from http://www.freemedia.at/wpfr/bolivia.htm.

''Bolnet.'' Available from http://useradmin.bolnet.bo.

''Country Profile: Bolivia.'' BBC News, March 2002. Available from http://www.news.bbc.co.uk.

''Diplomado en Gestión de Información y Documentación en las Organizaciones.'' Universidad Mayor de San Andrés, June 2002. Available from http://www.umsanet.edu.bo.

''Education.'' Bolivia Web, June, 2002. Available from http://www.boliviaweb.com.

''Golden Eagle Praised by Gold Mining Coop in Bolivia's Largest Circulation Newspaper.'' SocialFunds.com, 16 April 2002. Available from http://www.socialfunds.com.

''Inter-American Telecommunication Commission.'' CITEL, June 2002. Available from http://www.citel.oas.org.

''Knight Fellows to Train Journalists in Four Continents.'' International Journalists' Network, 2001. Available from http://www.ijnet.org.

''Latin America.'' The International Media and Democracy Project, June 2002. http://www.centralstate.edu.

''Licenciatura en Ciencias de La Comunicación Social.'' Universidad Católica Boliviana-La Paz, June 2000. Available from http://www.ucb.edu.bo.

Meyer, Eric K. ''An Unexpectedly Wider Web for the World's Newspapers.'' *Newslink,* June 2002. Available from http://newslink.org.

''Misión—Visión.'' Superintendencia de Telecomunicaciones, June 2002. Available from http://www.sittel.gov.bo.

''Paseo por el Periodisma: A History of Journalism in Latin America and Spain.'' University of Connecticut Library, June 2002. Available from http://www.lib.uconn.edu/exhibits.

''Periodismo.'' Universidad Privada de Santa Cruz de la Sierra, June, 2002. http://www.upsa.edu.bo.

''Plan de Estudios,'' Universidad Católica Boliviana-Cochabamba/San Pablo, June 2002. Available from http://www.ucbcba.edu.bo.

''Plan Curricular de Ingeneiría de Telecomunicaciónes.'' Universidad Católica Boliviana-Cochabamba, June 2002. Available from http://www.ucbcba.edu.

''Press Freedom in Latin America's Andean Region.'' The International Women's Media Foundation, 2001. Available from http://www.iwmf.org.

''Press Laws Database.'' Inter-American Press Association, June 2002. Available from http://www.sipiapa.org.

''Quienés Somos,'' Bolivision, June 2002. Available from http://bolisiontv.com.

''Serivicios de Comunicación.'' Universidad Autónoma Juan Miseal Saracho, June 2002. Available from http://www.uajms.edu.bo.

''Telecomunicaciónes.'' La Universidad de Aquino Bolivia, June 2002. Available from http://www.udabol.edu.

BOSNIA-HERZEGOVINA

BASIC DATA

Official Country Name:	Republic of Bosnia and Herzegovina
Region (Map name):	Europe
Population:	3,922,205
Language(s):	Croatian, Serbian, Bosnian
Literacy rate:	NA
Area:	51,129 sq km
GDP:	4,394 (US$ millions)
Number of Television Stations:	33
Number of Radio Stations:	25
Number of Radio Receivers:	940,000
Radio Receivers per 1,000:	239.7

BACKGROUND & GENERAL CHARACTERISTICS

Until the late 1990s, most Bosnians were identified simply as Bosnians. However, since the end of the war and the division of Yugoslavia, Bosnians have become more divided along ethnic and religious lines. Most (more than 95 percent) speak the same language, Bosnian or Serbo-Croatian, and most share the same ethnic racial background. Where they are divided is in their religions. Bosnians of Catholic faith, or whose ancestors were Catholic, are identified as Bosnian Croats, and make up 17 percent of the population. Those with Eastern Orthodox backgrounds are Bosnian Serbs, and comprise 31 percent of the population. The largest group is the Muslim Slavs, descendent from Christian Bosnians who approximately 500 years ago adopted Islam, with 44 percent of the population. Although the country is increasingly secular, strong hatred remains between the three groups.

Bosnia-Herzegovina's dynamic press has been characterized by diversity and change, and has been extremely influential in the political development and public opinion of the country, although it still has not been effective in the citizenry's understanding of its rights and national identity.

The Bosnia-Herzegovina (BiH) press had during the early 1980s potential to become an independent, vibrant and a free voice of the people; however, media in general became a propaganda tool during the war which ultimately split Yugoslavia. The media became dependent, not only on political bankrolls, but upon the fast and loose reporting style of the propaganda machine. Even now, accuracy and fact checking are not widely valued, and most print and electronic media remain extremely slanted and divided politically and ethnically. Since 1995, and the signing of the Dayton Peace Accord, BiH has remained mainly peaceful, but journalists have had some difficulty adjusting to press freedoms and their new roles in post-war news gathering and delivery. Readers are as reluctant to cross over to objective media as reporters are to adopt fair reporting styles and policies necessary to establishing a democracy. The tendency on the part of readers has been to continue to purchase newspapers and magazines which are aimed primarily at their specific political party or ethnic/religious demographic.

After the war heavy nationalist attitudes took hold. Fear and ethnic and religious bigotry negatively impacted the press, even though prior to the 1990s, the press had been very diverse despite a long history of dictatorship and censorship. From 1945 to 1990, although religious freedoms were terribly impacted throughout Yugoslavia (Muslims, Christians and Jews alike were banned from public worship), cultural freedoms (an active press included) were fully supported both philosophically and financially by the government. A long economic boom in the Communist country also helped support emerging media. Unfortunately, during the time of political unrest and war, the media also became a tool for differing political parties. Parties and governments supported media that espoused their political views, and punished, in direct financial actions as well as intimidation, those who did not. Those that complied became dependent on the political funding. They also became dependent upon easy-to-get information, and never questioned its truth or validity. Even though journalists in BiH can take advantage of Freedom of Information laws, many do not because they are largely untrained in the concept and practice.

Although technically BiH has a free, or partially free, press guaranteed by its Constitution, in practice the press is still heavily controlled by the government, and by advertisers or vendors who will not support publications with editorial opinions that differ from their own ideologies. State-supported businesses are prohibited from advertising in independent, non-government newspapers and electronic media.

The BiH media landscape is highly saturated. In a country of approximately 4 million, there are 376 media groups in BiH: 138 newspapers and reviews, 168 radio stations, 59 television stations and 11 news and photo agencies. Although on the surface those figures are impressive for a country that is still relatively new to having and supporting a free press, they represent a significant decrease from the BiH press' most active and diverse period. Ironically, the war which divided Yugoslavia (into the current countries of BiH, Croatia, and Slovenia) nearly destroyed the media. Newspapers were, before the war, largely subsidized or completely supported by the government. In the age of democracy and a free press, many businesses, particularly during lean economic times, have found survival impossible. For example, in Sarajevo alone there are three daily newspapers and five newsmagazines. The over-saturation is forcing the media industry to consolidate, but the independent media in particular are ill equipped to deal with consolidation. Many of the media are over- or under-staffed, and many are managed poorly and lack proper technology. Further, limited understanding of still-developing media laws and the media's new and emerging role in a developing free society negatively impacts publishers' ability to effectively manage their businesses. The newly-created press laws made survival even more difficult as censorship, sometimes blatant and at other times subtle, has remained very much a reality.

In 1991 there were 377 newspapers and publications. The diverse media was a key player in the early stages of the socialist system's disintegration. Young journalists in the early 1990s launched opposition newspapers, and in the fall of 1990 the first multi-party elections were held in Yugoslavia. During that tumultuous time, the press was fairly free-swinging, and although it had been censored and controlled previously, during the war years, papers from a wide variety of political slants and ethnic backgrounds published and survived, or even in a few cases flourished. However, after the country's first free elections, many newspapers were punished by government officials who had faced opposition in the media. Newspapers that espoused philosophies opposite theirs, or who had dared criticize candidates and officials, were suddenly raided, and audited and fined. In other cases journalists were sued for libel, threatened, or physically assaulted. However, as professional associations develop, media professionals will benefit from more education and legal support.

The BiH media is still largely under the influence of the government, and of political parties, and most independent newspapers suffer lower circulation and fewer resources. *Dnevni Avaz* had been prior to 1999 controlled mainly by the Party of Democratic Action (*Stranka Demokratske Akcije*, SDA), but distanced itself and adopted more fair and professional reporting standards. It remains the most widely circulated daily paper in BiH. *Dani* and *Slobodna Bosna* are the most influential independent magazines in the BiH federation. The weekly newsmagazine *Reporter* is the most influential independent weekly.

Two true independents, *Oslobodjenje* and *Vecernje Novine*, combined have lower circulation with 25,000 readers than their former SDA supporter *Dnevni Avaz* with 30,000 readers.

ECONOMIC FRAMEWORK

Bosnians are still suffering the aftermath of the war. Unemployment is high—nearly 50 percent—and earnings are low. Many major cities are being rebuilt from ruins after being bombed. Prior to the war, employment was high in the mainly industrial country. Earnings were fair in the Bosnian region, though not as high as in the former Yugoslavia's northernmost area, Slovenia.

PRESS LAWS

Government officials are still in the process of developing media and press laws. Most of the media and press laws were formed in 1995 with the signing of the Dayton peace agreement. The Constitution provided for a free press and by law prohibited censorship, but did not properly protect media professionals or provide for adequate flow of information between state and press. Further, the financial structure of most media was not yet ready to sustain a free press and break free from government support and subsidy.

Following the Dayton agreement, the government failed to comply with free press provisions, and it was not until the late 1990s that the government began to view seriously the importance of a free press. The shift in attitude came only after years of pressure from European and American democratic countries.

In 1999 the Helsinki Committee for Human Rights directed the BiH government to decriminalize libel and defamation. Prior to that, libel laws were so restrictive that journalists and publishers could be sued for exorbitant amounts of money for honest criticism of the government and its leadership. Steep fines and court actions created a serious chilling effect in the media, and virtually prohibited the media from engaging in honest journalistic pursuits.

In 1999 and 2000, the process had come to a halt, and the media was largely adhering to the draconian laws imposed in pre-war Yugoslavia. The former laws restricted the information flow from the government to the media.

Even newer laws negatively impact the media. The laws were designed to protect the country's current government in light of the threat of NATO military strikes. Under the Public Information Act of 1998, the public and government officials can still sue the media for publishing material that is not patriotic, or is "against the territorial integrity, sovereignty and independence of the country." Further, rebroadcasts of foreign media and news services are strictly banned.

The law, which has been criticized as "extremely vague and selectively enforced," makes it "practically impossible to engage in any type of journalist work," according to the U.S. State Department. Further, libel laws only apply to independent newspapers, not to government-sponsored papers. Approximately 25 percent of BiH newspapers are independent and some of the state-run papers are partly privatized.

When NATO bombing began in 1999, independent media outlets were shut down completely. Journalists were not allowed to report on the military, or on casualties, and the media was generally censored during that time. When the bombing concluded, more than one third of all the radio and television stations failed to resume operations.

The laws are changing slowly. In July 1999, the United Nations called for new legislation to deal with defamation and libel. In 2000, a new Freedom of Information law was passed, guaranteeing access to official government records.

CENSORSHIP

Although technically BiH has a free, or partially free, press guaranteed by its Constitution, in practice the press is still heavily controlled by the government, and by advertisers or vendors who will not support publications with editorial opinions that differ from their own ideologies. State-supported businesses are prohibited from advertising in independent, non-government newspapers and electronic media. Further, the media professionals themselves have had some difficulty adjusting to the concept and practice of a free press, designed to educate rather than to persuade readers or create nationalist sentiment.

Under the Dayton Accords, peacekeeping forces have the authority to monitor and penalize the news media. Although used rarely, it remains as a pressure with which journalists must contend. Two agencies have been developed for regulating print and electronic media. In 2000, the Council for the Press was formed. The Communications Regulatory Agency (the CRA) had been operating for several years prior to the print counterpart's development.

The primary difference between the two is that the CRA may discipline outlets while the Council has no sanctions at its disposal, and cannot, for example, prevent a paper from printing. The CRA, however, can close outlets which are in violation of media laws.

The Council oversees voluntary compliance with laws and journalistic standards, while the CRA was given the task of cleaning up the saturated and cluttered broadcast scene. Broadcasters who continue to air inflammatory and unprofessional programming are shut down. While it seems backward that a government agency is given this power after the war (during the war the press had free reign to print or broadcast whatever it pleased, and was often encouraged to become the mouthpiece for various political parties) the goal is to establish a fair, democratic and professional press.

However, media professionals in BiH, accustomed to political divisiveness and bickering, complain the CRA is too heavily controlled by foreign entities and adheres too strictly to foreign press objectives, which are generally more similar to the western world's concept of a free and democratic society. They have therefore resisted compliance with the new standards and media laws.

Freedom of Information Act (FOIA) Legislation passed in 1998 guarantees the press access to public information, however, they must request in writing the documents they need. Although the government has only recently began complying with FOIA legislation, perhaps the even greater issue is journalists unfamiliarity with the types of information available to them, and the process for requesting such material. The shortcomings on the part of the media professionals are generally caused by lack of training and reporting in a free press society.

Attitude Toward Foreign Media

Media professionals and consumers alike are distrustful of foreign media. During the war, foreign media professionals fell for different public relations efforts, though the BiH media professionals fell just as hard.

Most notably was the news coverage generated by the American public relations firm, Ruder Finn, hired on behalf of Serbia's enemies. The firm has been accused by some of exaggerating and dramatizing circumstances and events during the war, which foreign journalists, particularly Americans, reported as fact. According to National Post reporter Isabel Vincent, one of the firm's best customers was Kosovo, which paid the firm more than $230,000 in six months.

''For that Ruder Finn focused its efforts on building international support for actions designed to prevent 'ethnic cleansing' by Serb forces in Kosovo,'' Vincent reported. Bosnian journalists and readers alike grew wary of foreign media, and Vincent quoted one Bosnian reporter as saying, ''You people in the international press really don't know what you are writing about. You buy into to the whole Ruder Finn line, and you don't really do any independent reporting. That's the reason I really don't believe in a free international press.''

Broadcast Media

The largest broadcasters in BiH are Radio Television Bosnia and Herzegovina (RTV BiH) and Radio and Television of Republika Srpska (RTRS). According to the U.S. State Department, the international community launched the Open Broadcast Network (OBN) in 1997 as a cross-entity broadcaster and source of objective news and public affairs programming. However, only a minority of viewers watches the OBN as their primary source of news. Independent outlets include TV Hayat, Studio 99, OBN Banja Luka affiliate Alternative TV, and other small stations throughout the country. Of the smaller stations, most of which were municipal stations prior to 1995, some have been partially privatized, but none have been fully privatized, and as yet the ownership status of nearly all is still unclear.

The matter of privatization will likely be sorted out in the first part of the twenty-first century. The media industry began a restructuring in July 1999, and it has yet to be fully implemented. Under the restructuring the state-run broadcast industry was to be liquidated, including the liquidation of RTV BiH, and to create a statewide public broadcasting corporation, The Public Broadcasting System of Bosnia and Herzegovina (PBS BiH). Elements of OBN will be incorporated into PBS BiH, but details have not yet been fully determined.

As part by the OBN of the restructuring new guidelines have been established and ''programming must be based on truth, must respect human dignity and different opinions and convictions, and must promote the highest standards of human rights, peace and social justice, international understanding, protection of the democratic freedoms and environment protection.''

Radio broadcasting in BiH is diverse. According to the State Department, opposition viewpoints are reflected in the news programs of independent broadcasters. Independent or opposition radio stations broadcast in BiH, and Radio Pegas report a wide variety of political opinions. Local radio stations broadcast in Croat-majority areas, but they are highly nationalistic. Local Croat authorities do not tolerate opposition viewpoints. One exception is Studio 88, in Mostar, which broadcasts reports from both sides of the ethnically divided city.

The Independent Media Commission was established in 1998 and is empowered to regulate broadcasting and other media. The IMC licenses broadcasters, determines licensing fees, establishes the spectra for stations, and monitors adherence to codes of practice. The IMC also controls punishment of broadcasters for noncompliance. Warnings, fines, suspension and termination of licenses, equipment seizures and shut-downs are among their tools for controlling the broadcast media.

Although incidents of selective enforcement have decreased since 1995, the number of fines in the year 2001 was still substantial, and the broadcast media is often left wondering exactly where their boundaries lie.

Education and Training

As yet, major associations and organizations within BiH are still not developed, although the international community has stepped forward to assist in training, developing media policy and even in financing struggling papers.

Although several international media groups are trying to establish a journalism training program in Sarajevo, very little training is available, and media professionals by and large are unaware of the country's new media laws and how they impact their rights and ability to work. The journalism outlets that currently exist have largely been tainted by years of corruption and government censorship and financial control. Many talented journalists left Bosnia-Herzegovina during that period when they were restricted and forced to become part of the propaganda machine during the war. Still others were fired by their editors or publishers, when political parties threatened or pressured them to quiet dissenting or even fair-minded journalists. There are few experienced professional mentors with an understanding of a balanced press left to train young journalists in BiH.

Summary

Although the media in Bosnia-Herzegovina remains weak and generally poor, a few examples of progress have emerged, particularly since 1998 and the adoption of a few still-developing media laws.

Still, a few factors will continue to plague the media scene for several years. First are the poor management practices in the media. During a period of consolidation of the media, few publishers are prepared. They lack business skills and financial resources to survive, and the financial infrastructure is not equipped to support them.

Another factor is the aftermath of the war, and how the country suffered as it remained in survival mode for most of the 1990s. There is a serious lack of educated and talented journalists in the country, and most young journalists learned their trade during the war years, and are not prepared to write objective news. They are still eager to be spoon-fed their information from official outlets, which are often not above spinning stories to the point of being untruthful.

Further, the country is technologically disadvantaged. Many media have not the resources to purchase and maintain advanced computer hardware and software, and few journalists are trained to use the technology available to them.

Although a variety of media are available, Bosnians have few choices in independent and fair media outlets. Broadcast media in particular are still heavily dominated by the government and its influence, and Bosnians are bombarded with slanted and narrow views in the media.

Significant Dates

- October 1999: The *Nezavisne Novine* editor-in-chief lost both legs in a car bomb. Later the following year, he was threatened numerous times by unknown people. In June, 2000, authorities arrested six people for attempted blackmail, but although they were also suspects in the acts against the editor, police were not able to charge them with the bombing.
- October 1999: *Oslobodjenje* is forced to reduce its staff from 250 to 160, in the wake of poor economic conditions. Prior to the war, the paper was the largest daily in Bosnia, selling 60,000 copies daily. In 1999, circulation dropped to about 14,000.
- April 2000: A *Dnevni Avaz* journalist is assaulted by the driver of Federation Prime Minister Edhem Bicakcic after the journalist wrote articles criticizing Bicakcic.
- June 2000: Edin Avdic, a journalist from the weekly *Slobodna Bosna*, was assaulted outside his home after receiving threats from the Chief of Cultural Affairs. The victim claimed the Chief, Muhamed Korda, demanded he stop writing articles about the cultural activities of the government, and had threatened to kill him if he would not stop.

- June 2000: Tax authorities raided, without explanation or court order, the daily *Dnevni Avaz*. Distribution of the paper was delayed and the authority billed the paper $450,000 for 1998 unpaid taxes. The raid came after the newspaper's split from partisan reporting in favor of the nationalist SDA (the Party of Democratic Action) party, and adopted a more neutral and fair reporting style. Prior to the raid, the paper had been threatened. The paper's editor in chief said the reason for the raid and the audit was a series of stories and editorials about corruption, implicating SDA leadership.
- August 2000: A journalist from the *Ljubisa Lazic* was assaulted after a series of threats and harassment by Marko Asanin, president of the regional board of the Srpsko Sarajevo Independent Party of Social Democrats. Asanin had previously attempted to exclude local media from assembly sessions.
- May 2001: Daily paper, *Oslobodjenje*, stopped publishing for the first time in nearly 60 years. The closure was due to an employee strike. The paper resumed printing one week later, and the labor dispute was resolved. Among employee complaints were late paychecks, and 20-percent pay cuts. Employees argued they had tolerated the financial instability during the war, but some five years later, were still waiting to be compensated fairly.

BIBLIOGRAPHY

Aumente, Jerome. ''Profile in Courage,'' Committee to Protect Journalists, CPJ Online. 15 December 1999. Available from http://www.cpj.org.

''Bosnia and Herzegovina Media Analysis,'' IREX-ProMedia. April 2000.

''Bosnia 2001 World Press Freedom Review,'' 2002. Available from http://www.freemedia.at/wpfr/bosnia.htm.

Gjelten, Tom. *Sarajevo Daily: A City and its Newspaper Under Seige.* New York: Harper Collins Publishers Inc., 1995.

Glenny, Marsha. *The Fall of Yugoslavia.* New York: Penguin Books, 1992.

Helsinki Committee for Human Rights, ''Bosnia and Herzegovina—Republika Srpska: Freedom of expression and access to information.'' November 1999.

Howard, Ross. ''Mediate the Conflict,'' Radio Netherlands. 22 March 2002.

Ivanova, Tanja. ''Sarajevo: Newspapers in the Wringer,'' AIM Press. 25 Oct. 2001. Available from http://www.aimpress.org.

Perenti, Michael. *To Kill a Nation.* New York: Verso, 2000.

''U.S. Department of State Report: Bosnia and Herzegovina,'' 23 Feb. 2001. Available from http://www.state.gov.

Vincent, Isabel. ''International media under attack in Serbia,'' National Post. 23 November 1998.

—Carol Marshall

BOTSWANA

BASIC DATA

Official Country Name:	Republic of Botswana
Region (Map name):	Africa
Population:	1,576,470
Language(s):	English, Setswana
Literacy rate:	69.8%

BACKGROUND AND GENERAL CHARACTERISTICS

Botswana (bot-SWA-na) is a landlocked country in southern Africa, which used to be known as Bechuanaland. It covers 224,610 square miles, making it slightly bigger than Texas. Botswana is bordered by South Africa to the south, Zimbabwe to the northeast, Zambia to the north, and Namibia to the west and north.

In the 1800s, Bechuanaland became a British protectorate, meaning that it was under the protection and control of Britain. After undergoing a series of governmental structures, including the use of white and black advisory councils, in 1965 the county attained self-government, with Sereste Khama as its first African head of government. After further successful negotiations with Britain, on September 30, 1966, the former Bechuanaland became the sovereign Republic of Botswana, with Khama as the new president. In the early 20th century, Botswana was one of the truly democratic African countries. The 1.6 million citizens of this sparsely populated semi-desert country have enjoyed democratic freedoms found in few other African countries.

Print Media In the early twenty-first century, there were four print news media outlets in Botswana. The *Botswana Daily News*, published in English and Setswana, was established in 1964. With a circulation in the 25,000 to 50,000 range, it was the country's largest newspaper in 2002. Below it, with circulations from 10,000 to 25,000, were the *Botswana Guardian*, an English weekly established in 1982; *The Botswana Gazette*, another English weekly; and *Mmegi wa Digmang* (The Reporter), also a weekly, published in English and Setswana, established in 1984. The *Daily News*, *Mmegi wa Digmang*, and the *Botswana Guardian* were Botswana's largest and most influential newspapers. The *Daily News* was state owned. The others were privately owned.

PRESS LAWS

The Botswana independence constitution of September 1966 (amended in August and September 1997) guaranteed freedom of expression to all residents. Unlike many African countries, where the ruling party bans opposition views and news from newspapers, radio and television, Botswana has allowed a diversity of views and allowed robust debate in the electronic and print media. As of 2002, journalists were not licensed or required to register. Newspapers and journalists did not have to post bonds to do their work. There was no censorship, but journalists operated according to community standards by avoiding material that would be considered obscene or offensive. Foreign media and journalists also operated freely and openly. The University of Botswana was establishing a Department of Journalism, which will provide training.

BROADCAST MEDIA

In 2002, Botswana television offered MultiChoice Botswana and Gaberone Television. The latter was owned by Gaberone Broadcasting Corp. and was a private television channel that reached about 20 percent of the population. South African television was also accessible in most of Botswana. As of the early twenty-first century, however, radio remained the most common means of mass communication in Botswana. The number of radio receivers increased from 180,000 in 1994 to 230,000 in 1996, while the number of television receivers rose from 24,000 to 29,000 during the same period. Government-owned Radio Botswana broadcast in English, the official language, and Setswana. Its work was complemented by Radio Botswana 2, an FM channel accessible only in Gaberone, the country's capital. There were also two private radio stations: GABZ-FM and VA RONA-FM.

NEWS AGENCIES

The Botswana Press Agency (BOPA) is a government-owned domestic news agency. Foreign news agencies, including the South African Press Association and Reuters, have operated freely in the country.

SUMMARY

The Botswana print media are robust, operate with little or no government restrictions and relations with the government are good. The broadcast media are government controlled, but are not abused by government officials. For the first 26 years of Botswana's independence, democracy has prevailed, and the future looks bright for the media.

BIBLIOGRAPHY

Africa. New York: Worldmark Press, Ltd., 1988.

Africa South of the Sahara. London: Europa Publications, 2002.

Ainslie, R. *The Press in Africa*. New York: Walker and Co., 1966.

Barton, F. *The Press of Africa*. New York: Africana Publishing Co., 1979.

Country Profile: Botswana. London: British Broadcasting Corporation, 2002.

International Year Book. New York: Editor and Publisher, 2002.

Liebenow, J. Gus. *African Politics*. Bloomington, IN: Indiana University Press, 1986.

Merrill, John C., ed. *Global Journalism: Survey of International Communication*. Boston: Longman, 1993.

Middleton, John, ed. *Encyclopedia of Africa: South of the Sahara*. New York: Charles Scribner's Sons, 1997.

—Tendayi S. Kumbula

BRAZIL

BASIC DATA

Official Country Name:	Federative Republic of Brazil
Region (Map name):	South America
Population:	174,468,575
Language(s):	Portuguese (official), Spanish, English, French
Literacy rate:	83.3%
Area:	8,511,965 sq km
GDP:	595,458 (US$ millions)
Number of Daily Newspapers:	465

Total Circulation:	7,883,000
Circulation per 1,000:	61
Number of Nondaily Newspapers:	2,020
Total Newspaper Ad Receipts:	1,490 (US$ millions)
As % of All Ad Expenditures:	23.90
Number of Television Stations:	138
Number of Television Sets:	36,500,000
Television Sets per 1,000:	209.2
Number of Cable Subscribers:	2,334,480
Cable Subscribers per 1,000:	13.7
Number of Satellite Subscribers:	1,195,000
Satellite Subscribers per 1,000:	6.8
Number of Radio Stations:	1822
Number of Radio Receivers:	71,000,000
Radio Receivers per 1,000:	407.0
Number of Individuals with Computers:	75,000,000
Computers per 1,000:	429.9
Number of Individuals with Internet Access:	5,000,000
Internet Access per 1,000:	28.7

BACKGROUND & GENERAL CHARACTERISTICS

Newspaper circulation and readership in Brazil have traditionally been low if compared to the rates in most developed countries: 61 daily newspapers per 1,000 people in 2002. However, the fifth most populous country in the world—170 million people in 2000—boasts a very lively and energetic press, which in the 1990s played an important part in exposing problems such as political corruption, homelessness, and environmental degradation, and thus spurring significant changes in the structure of Brazilian political and economic institutions.

Relatively low literacy rates (85 percent) and high production and distribution costs have been consistently blamed for small newspaper circulation in Brazil. An estimated 465 newspapers circulated daily in Brazil, more than in Germany, Mexico or Russia. Although there are no national newspapers in the country, the largest circulation dailies attract audiences that extend beyond their regional geographic markets. Brazil has no large newspaper chains, and most publications are still family-owned. Several of those family-owned companies, however, are in fact regional or local media conglomerates that also own television and radio stations within their metropolitan or state markets. A handful of those corporations also own and operate publishing houses, news agencies, as well as cable and satellite television companies.

When it comes to press freedom, Brazil has had a somewhat spotty historical record. Until 1808, Portuguese colonizers prohibited printing presses in the country. As a result, a strong newspaper tradition was not established in Brazil until the mid to late 1800s. From 1889 on, with the creation of the Brazilian Republic, the country's political system has alternated between authoritarian and democratic phases. Consequently, freedom of the press has been restricted and in some cases completely abolished for significant periods in Brazilian history.

Brazil occupies half of South America's landmass. The country is the fifth largest in the world, after Russia, Canada, China, and the United States, although its geographic area is larger than the 48 continental U.S. states. Brazil shares a border with every South American country, except for Ecuador and Chile. The Amazon rainforest, which occupies at least half of Brazil's landmass, is probably the country's most prominent and well-known geographic feature. The country also has wetlands, savannas, subtropical forests, mountains, and semi-arid areas. Those geographic characteristics were very important in the establishment of Brazil as a country and in the development of the Brazilian media system. Until the mid-1970s, most of the country's population was concentrated in the southern and southeastern areas of Brazil, as well as along the northeastern Atlantic coast. Consequently, newspaper circulation (as well as magazine readership and even television watching) until the 1970s used to be concentrated in these populated urban areas.

The 26 Brazilian states, some of which are larger and more populous than other Latin American countries, are commonly grouped in five different regions: North, Northeast, Center-West, Southeast and South. In terms of population and socioeconomic indicators, the North and Northeast are usually regarded as poorer and less populated than the other three regions. The Southeast alone, with just 11 percent of the country's area, had 42 percent of the Brazilian population, 62 percent of the GDP and over 70 percent of the country's industry in 1996. The

Daily and Non-Daily Newspaper Titles and Circulation Figures

	1996	1997	1998	1999	2000
Number of Daily Newspapers	380	400	372	465	465
Circulation of Dailies (000)	6,472	6,892	7,163	7,245	7,883
Number of Non-Daily Newspapers	938	892	1,251	1,780	2,020
Circulation of Non-Dailies (000)	NA	NA	NA	NA	NA

Source: World Association of Newspapers and Zenithmedia, *World Press Trends 2001*, pp. 8, 10, 17, 19. Note: NA stands for not available.

three largest Brazilian cities, São Paulo, Rio de Janeiro, and Belo Horizonte, are located in this region.

The four top circulation newspapers in the country—*Folha de São Paulo* (560,000), *O Globo* (350,000), *O Dia* (250,000), and *O Estado de São Paulo* (242,000)—are also located in the Southeast region, *Folha* and *Estado* in São Paulo and *Globo* and *Dia* in Rio.

Although it displays less impressive numbers, in terms of quality of life, socioeconomic indicators, and distribution of wealth, the South might be considered the most prosperous Brazilian region. With a heavily mechanized agriculture and most of the country's cattle, the Center-West, which has recently achieved economic importance, occupies one-fourth of the country's area, but has less than one-twelfth of its population.

Brazil is an essentially urban country. According to the official census data, the percentage of the population living in urban areas sprung from 36 percent in 1940 to 76 in 1991. That number rose again to 81 percent in 2002. The census also indicated that more than 85 million Brazilians lived in cities of 100,000 or more in the early 1990s.

In terms of ethnic and cultural characteristics, the Northern region is mostly populated by the descendants of native Indian groups. Known as *caboclos*, men and women of this sparsely populated Brazilian region (where most of the Amazon forest is located) live along the banks of the many rivers and creeks that constitute the Amazon river basin. Most of those *caboclos* rely on subsistence crops, fishing, and hunting as their main economic activity. Many of them still preserve much of the physical and cultural traits that characterized their native Brazilian ancestors. In the Northern region, the influence of Portuguese and other European immigrant groups can best be felt in larger cities, such as Belém and Manaus. Newspaper readership in the northern region is also concentrated in those two cities, as well as in a few other smaller urban areas.

In the Northeast, the *sertanejo* is the equivalent of the Northern *caboclo*. *Sertanejo* is the term usually employed to describe peasants and small farmers that populate the arid and poor inland areas of that region. The Northeastern coast received the largest numbers of African slaves brought from across the Atlantic. Today's *sertanejos* are the result of centuries of racial integration between African and local native groups. The African influence is still heavily felt in the region's largest cities, especially Salvador and Recife. Most cities and state capitals located in this area have their own daily newspapers, but readership tends to be low.

In terms of ethnic diversity, the Southeast and Center-West regions are the best examples of the ''melting pot'' of cultures and traditions described in earlier paragraphs. There is no one dominant ethnic group in those regions of the country, where the African, European and native Brazilian presences can be equally measured. However, heavy European and Asian immigrations have radically altered the ethnic make-up of the five Brazilian regions in the twentieth century. The most important ''recent'' ethnic groups are Germans, Japanese, and Italians. Their immigration to Brazil started in the late 1800s and early 1900s, and continued throughout the first half of the century. The Japanese population, concentrated in the states of São Paulo (Southeast), Paraná (South), and Pará (North), has grown to 1.2 million over the decades. German immigrants concentrated in the three Southern states, where many rural areas are still referred to as ''little Germany,'' while a very large number of Italian immigrants concentrated in São Paulo and also in the South.

Brazil's history as a nation goes back to the year 1500, when Portuguese *navegadores* (sailors) set foot on what is now the state of Bahia. Before the Portuguese, several different native populations occupied Brazil. Despite wildly divergent estimates, most historians believe the country was heavily populated along its lush 4,600 mile-long shoreline, and only sparsely occupied inland.

Years before they discovered Brazil, the Portuguese had already claimed the eastern half of South America, when they signed the Treaty of Tordesillas with Spain in 1494. The colonization of Brazil, which started 30 years after discovery, was justified by economic, political and religious reasons. Portugal needed not only the abundant raw materials (wood, sugar cane, spices) free for the taking in the new colony, but it also took upon itself the duty of converting to Christianity the native population it encountered in the new land.

Portuguese colonization was very important in determining the future of the Brazilian press system. Literacy and education were highly discouraged by the Portuguese rulers. Universities, book publishing and newspaper printing were not seen in Brazil until 1808, when the Portuguese royal family had to settle in Rio de Janeiro to escape the Napoleonic Wars in Europe.

Portugal granted Brazil independence in 1822, but unlike what happened in former American colonies such as the United States or Mexico, Brazilian ruling classes opted for a monarchic regime that lasted until 1889. During the so-called First and Second Empires (1822-1889), limited access to education, low literacy rates and widespread poverty prevented newspapers from reaching a mass audience. Newspapers were often associated with political parties and specific interest groups, such as the freemasons. Despite their limited reach, and because of their influential role in forming public opinion among the educated elite, newspapers and journalists were often in the center of the political action.

The situation was not very different throughout the *Velha República* (Old Republic), which lasted from 1889 to 1930. Newspapers and prominent editorial writers influenced decisions made by the Brazilian ruling classes—landowners, merchants, and political and military figures—but never attained the kind of mass circulation reached by the Penny Press in the United States at the same time period.

Political disenfranchisement of the masses and general dissatisfaction with economic policies led to the collapse of the Old Republic and the establishment of the Vargas Era (named after President Getulio Vargas) in 1930. Vargas ruled Brazil from 1930 to 1945, and then again from 1951 to 1954, alternating as dictator (1930-1934), congressionally elected president (1934-1937), dictator again (1937-1945), and finally popularly elected president (1951-1954). Throughout this time, Vargas had a very turbulent relationship with the press. The government created an official propaganda department; press freedom was suppressed for extended periods of time; journalists and writers were persecuted and jailed; newspapers were routinely censored.

It was not until the end of World War II in 1945 that Brazil started to enjoy a period of democracy and economic growth. From 1945 to 1964, civil liberties and press freedom were finally restored, as a new Constitution was drafted and approved by Congress. The country was industrialized, a new capital (Brasilia) was built, and a strong middle class emerged. Universities were created or expanded in every Brazilian state, and literacy and newspaper readership increased.

The democratic period ended in April 1964 with the military coup d'état that removed President Goulart. The military regime that ruled Brazil from 1964 to 1985 was particularly fierce in its limitation of press freedom. From 1968 to the mid-1970s, for example, a presidential executive order (called AI-5, short for Ato Institucional n. 5) severely restricted civil liberties in the country, and established de facto media censorship.

During the two decades of military rule, several daily newspapers refused to abide by the government's limitations, but these publications had to pay a high cost for serving as the country's moral and social conscience. In the late-1960s and early-1970s, it was not uncommon for newspapers to be censored on a daily basis. Individual journalists also suffered government persecution, and, in the case of at least one prominent journalist, paid with their own lives.

Brazilian mass media, especially newspapers and magazines, were instrumental in pressing for and overseeing the transition from military to democratic rule in the late-1970s, a process known as abertura politica. The restoration of democracy, civil liberties and the rule of law also immensely affected the press in the 1980s. In the 1990s, newspapers and journalists played a very important role in denouncing social and economic problems such as poverty, homelessness and political corruption.

In the early 1990s, newspapers and newsmagazines were the first institutions in the country to investigate allegations of corruption and abuse of power against then President Fernando Collor. The subsequent media frenzy, which has been dubbed by some as the ''Brazilian Watergate,'' eventually led to the impeachment of Collor by Congress in 1992.

Throughout the 1990s and into the twenty-first century, the Brazilian press has continued to take very seriously its role as government watchdog. According to an international media survey conducted in 1997, newspaper circulation and readership were up in Brazil, and, more importantly, newspapers ranked number one in terms of public credibility, ahead of government, congress and other institutions.

History of the Press As opposed to what happened in the Spanish and English colonies in the Americas, where printing presses were used since the 16th and 17th centuries, Brazil did not know printing until the early nineteenth century. According to historians, some basic differences in the Portuguese, Spanish and English colonization schemes account for that delay. While the Spanish colonizers had to fight to replace advanced indigenous civilizations (the Incas and the Aztecs) with their own culture, counting on colonial universities and printing presses to better prepare their local elite, the Portuguese found in Brazil indigenous groups only loosely organized and sparsely located along the country's Atlantic coast, which did not pose a threat to their colonizing efforts. Moreover, the Portuguese royalty saw books, even in the metropolis, with extreme distrust. Until the late 1700s, any material published in Portugal had to be examined by three different kinds of censors-the local Church authorities, the Inquisitors sent in by the Holy See, and the censors working for the King. As a result, printing was a very restricted activity in Portugal, and most books were religious in nature.

Throughout colonial times, books were illegally brought to Brazil by military and intellectual figures that visited or studied in Europe. Some of those illegal books were actually used as incriminating evidence against clandestine groups that fought for Brazil's independence from Portugal. Among the forbidden publications were the French and American Constitutions.

The first printing press that entered Brazil legally came with the Portuguese royal family, in 1808. One of the first official acts of the recently transplanted Portuguese rulers was to establish the Royal Press in Rio de Janeiro. From the offices of the Royal Press was printed the first Brazilian newspaper, the *Gazeta do Rio de Janeiro*, on September 10th, 1808. The *Gazeta* was first a weekly, and then a daily newspaper. The newspaper served merely as the official mouthpiece for the royal family, publishing news from Europe and official government acts.

One of the first influential Brazilian newspapers, the *Correio Brasiliense*, was published not in Rio, but in London. Its founder, Hipólito da Costa, justified his choice of printing his paper abroad by reminding local critics of the fierce Portuguese censorship, and of the risks that would threaten editors who dared to criticize the King. Although the *Correio*'s first issue was published on June 1st, 1808, three months before the *Gazeta* first appeared, the latter is still considered by most historians the first Brazilian newspaper, since the former was published abroad.

Neither the *Gazeta* nor the *Correio* were informative, news-filled periodicals. While the *Gazeta* was an official newspaper, the *Correio* was a partisan one, very much interested in educating Brazilian readers about themes such as abolitionism and political emancipation. Although it was published in London, the *Correio* was a very influential newspaper, read by the political, intellectual and commercial elite both in Brazil and Portugal.

Other newspapers that started in Brazil at the time, such as the *Idade de Ouro do Brasil*, which was published in Salvador, Bahia, and first appeared in May 1811, presented themselves as informative and impartial, but in reality were very much attuned with the national and local ruling classes. Most of these ''official'' periodicals lasted only until 1822, when Brazil became independent from Portugal.

The Brazilian independence is explained by most historians as a long economic and political process in which the Brazilian commercial upper classes saw the Portuguese royalty as an obstacle to their goal of exporting and trading freely with any country they wanted, besides Portugal. The Portuguese King and ruling classes wanted Brazil to trade exclusively with the metropolis, and this economic dispute over trade monopoly eventually culminated with the rupture between the two countries.

Historians believe that an emerging rebel or insurgent Brazilian press played an important part in convincing and uniting the local economic and political elite around the independence ideals. Newspapers promoting the independence and rupture with Portugal flourished in Brazil in 1821 and 1822. Even before 1822, local newspapers appeared in cities such as Salvador and Belém, sponsoring radical and even revolutionary ideas.

After the independence, printing presses and newspapers multiplied in several Brazilian states, from Pará, in the north, to Rio Grande do Sul, in the south. Reading, writing and printing books and newspapers were seen not only as desirable but as necessary and even patriotic activities.

During the so-called First and Second Empires (1822-1889), the Brazilian press experienced an unprecedented boom. It was during this phase that the tradition of a strong partisan press was established in Brazil. Newspapers multiplied in every major Brazilian city. In 1827, an imperial decree abolished censorship of the press. The tradition of a lively and engaged press, patronized by political groups as well as the general population, was thus born. In the state of Minas Gerais alone, about a dozen daily newspapers appeared between 1823 and 1833.

Brazilian newspapers of the period were both informative and partisan. It was not uncommon to find newspapers articles openly and strongly criticizing the imperial government, as well as local authorities and rival political groups. This period of political emancipation and economic development in Brazil cemented the public's trust in the press, as well as the habit of reading several daily newspapers. It was not uncommon for the general population in cities such as Rio de Janeiro, São Paulo and Ouro Preto to subscribe to competing dailies.

During that time, besides Portuguese-language newspapers, French and English dailies, such as the *Courrier du Brésil* and *The Rio Herald*, also circulated in Rio de Janeiro. Those newspapers circulated mainly among the English and French nationals with commercial and financial interests in Brazil, but they also influenced local politics. French immigrants played an especially relevant role in developing not only newspapers, but also printing and typography in general in Rio de Janeiro.

In the 1830s and 1840s, as the country went through a phase of political upheaval as separatist and republican movements spread throughout the provinces, to the well-established daily newspapers were added the *pasquins*, openly partisan newspapers and pamphlets, many of them without regular periodicity. Those *pasquins* were extremely popular and influential, appearing (and disappearing) during times of intense political disputes. Historians attribute the emergence and popularity of the *pasquins* to the increasing literacy rates and the need many Brazilians felt to be better informed during a period of intense political battles.

From the 1850s on, daily newspapers and *pasquins* played an important role in two crucial national issues in Brazil: the end of African slavery and the end of the monarchy. Throughout the 1850s, abolitionist and republican newspapers multiplied in Brazil, not only in cities such as Rio de Janeiro and Ouro Preto, but also in the less-developed provinces, such as Pernambuco and Bahia. It was at this time that the political cartoons and political satires, very influential journalistic features of the Brazilian press, also appeared.

Besides their heavy interest in local and national politics, the Brazilian newspapers of the time also gave a space to the arts, especially literature. In a country where book publishing is still an extremely expensive activity, newspapers specialized in publishing short stories, essays and even serialized novels written by some of the most important Brazilian writers of the time. Following a tradition prevalent in countries such as England and France, where the serialized novels of Charles Dickens and Victor Hugo first appeared on the pages on local newspapers, Brazilian dailies enlisted intellectuals such as José de Alencar and Machado de Assis, two of the most important writers of the nineteenth century, to publish new stories and novels on their pages. Actually, most writers of any renown at the time either started at or wrote exclusively for newspapers, as daily reporters and editors.

It was also during the 1850s and 1860s and some of the most important daily newspapers were first published. *Diário do Rio de Janeiro*, *Jornal do Comércio* and *Correio Mercantil*, all of them influential daily newspapers in Brazil, appeared in the 1860s. The daily *O Globo* was also revitalized, under new ownership, at that time.

The end of slavery, in 1888, and the end of the monarchy, in 1889, started a new phase for Brazilian newspapers. Readers and subscribers favored newspapers that sponsored republican ideals. In 1891, the influential *Jornal do Brasil* was first published. Many well-known journalists were called to be part of the first republican government.

At the end of the nineteenth century and beginning of the twentieth, the Brazilian press made an effort to modernize its production. Larger newspapers, such as *Jornal do Brasil*, already had photography departments, and most dailies published cartoons and drawings. The period also signals a shift in management and ownership models, and most newspapers grow from small, individually-owned enterprises to larger, family-owned corporations. At that time, most large dailies owned and operated their own industrial printing complexes.

The beginning of the twentieth century also saw one of the first efforts to consolidate and professionalize the press-many small newspapers folded or were absorbed by larger dailies. Most cities still maintained the tradition of competing daily newspapers, which prevails to this day in Brazil, but most smaller papers and *pasquins* had to give way to market pressures.

The tradition of a partisan press and the heavy involvement of newspapers and journalists in the political life persisted throughout the first half of the twentieth century. The trend towards consolidation and modernization also persisted. As Brazil moved from an agricultural, rural society to an industrial, urban one, newspapers tried to follow the lead. As urban newspapers modernized their production departments, old printing presses were being sold to smaller, rural newspapers.

By the end of World War II, every state capital and major Brazilian city had at least one daily newspaper. It was not uncommon for cities with 100,000 people or more to have two or three rival dailies. Newspapers were often still affiliated with political groups or local powerful families. As competition increased, the need for professionalization of the news business and modernization of printing also grew.

In the 1950s, most Brazilian newspapers were already following the news model introduced by their North-American counterparts, with the use of the lead and the inverted pyramid; as well as independently-verified and gathered information; the use of an ''objective'' narrative style; and the reliance on independent news sources.

Paradoxically, the 1964 military coup, discussed in more detail on a separate section, also contributed to turn Brazilian newspapers into more modern and politically independent enterprises. After political parties were extinct and the multi-party system substituted by a bipartisan, quasi-official political system, newspapers focused on the ''straightforward'' news of the day and on more efficient business practices. It was also in the 1970s that most journalism and mass communication courses started, and a new law demanded an accredited university degree for the credentialing of new journalists by the Labor Department. By the 1970s, most, if not all Brazilian newspapers were independent from political organizations, and used off-set printing techniques.

By the early 1980s, some newspapers were already introducing computers in the newsrooms and production departments, and many were experimenting with color printing. Market pressures and successive economic crises led many Brazilian newspapers to fold in the 1980s and 1990s. Some markets have consolidated into one major daily newspaper, but in the beginning of the twenty-first century, most Brazilian cities still have two or three competing dailies.

A city such as São Paulo, for example, has three major dailies, *Folha de São Paulo* (circ. 560,000), *O Estado de São Paulo* (circ. 242,000), and *Gazeta Mercantil*, and still has enough space for popular newspapers, tabloids, and niche-filling publications. The same is true for Rio de Janeiro, with *O Globo* (circ. 350,000), *O Dia* (circ. 250,000), and *Jornal do Brasil* being the most important and influential regional newspapers, and still having smaller tabloids and specialized dailies.

Besides full-color printing and digital and satellite production, most Brazilian newspapers have simultaneous Internet versions. In many cases, those electronic versions are updated throughout the day, and have as many or more readers than the traditional paper versions.

ECONOMIC FRAMEWORK

Up to the 1930s, Brazil's economy relied heavily on the production and export of primary goods (especially timber, spices, gold and precious gems, and coffee). During colonial times, Portugal strongly enforced economic policies that reduced the country to a mere exporter of raw materials. Local industry was virtually non-existent, and land ownership and commercial trade were the only means to economic prosperity.

Heavy industrialization started in the 1930s and accelerated through the 1940s and 1950s, culminating with the creation of a national steel and automotive industry in the mid-1950s. The industrial self-sufficiency policy implemented by the government in the 1950s created strong working and middle classes; increased living standards, education and literacy; substituted imported manufactured products for national ones; and established the basis for a strong, diversified economy that persists into this century.

Media analysts have observed that throughout twentieth century Brazil, real media power was wielded not by newspapers, but by radio and television. That is true, to a large extent, because of the fact that both radio and television benefited not only from the same economic growth that affected newspapers, but also from the added benefits of economic policies that expanded Brazil's telecommunications infrastructure.

Ironically, newspaper circulation and readership in Brazil have increased even during desperate economic situations, such as the hyperinflation crisis of the late 1980s. Analysts believe that happened because the Brazilian press has been particularly effective at covering economic and financial news, keeping readers abreast of all the latest economic policies and measures implemented by the government.

An interesting characteristic of the Brazilian press system is that a law enacted by the military in the mid-1960s prevents foreign ownership of Brazilian media companies. The law, which at the time forced U.S. media giant Time-Life to sell its interests in the then-emergent broadcasting company TV Globo, has made sure that only Brazilian companies and Brazilian nationals control mass media firms. However, in April 2002, legislation working its way through the Brazilian Congress was proposing to open the domestic media market to foreign investors. The bill, already approved in the Chamber of Deputies, was waiting for ratification by the Senate and then by the President to go into effect. Even before the new law was approved, many international media conglomerates, such as Time-Warner and Pearson (which publishes the Financial Times), were already announcing in April 2002 their intention to vie for a slice of the Brazilian media market.

Brazil represents the largest Latin American market for both investors and advertisers. In 1995, advertising expenditures in Brazil amounted to US$ 6.5 billion, compared to US$ 3.1 billion for Mexico and US$ 2.6 billion for Argentina, respectively the second and third largest markets. But while in Mexico newspapers accounted only for 12 percent of advertising expenditures (US$ 366 million), in Brazil newspaper advertising expenditures represented almost 28 percent of the total (US$ 1.8 billion).

PRESS LAWS

The Brazilian Congress enacted in 1967 a Press Code (*Lei de Imprensa*) that addresses and ensures freedom of the press in the country. The first article of the law states:

''It shall be free the expression of thought and opinions and the search, reception and transmission of information and ideas, by any means, and without censorship, and everyone shall be responsible, in the terms of the law, for the abuses he or she might commit.''

The subsequent paragraphs, however, build in exceptions to prohibit war propaganda, subversion of the social and political order, and the diffusion of racist messages. The second article of the Press Code specifically ensures the right to a free press:

''It shall be free the publication and circulation, within the whole national territory, of books, newspapers and other periodicals, unless these are clandestine or offend the standards of public decency.''

The exceptions built into both articles of the law were used by the military regime to justify censorship between 1968 and the mid-1970s, without having to actually revoke the then newly created code.

The 1967 Press Code's third article prohibits media ownership by foreign companies or foreign nationals. The subsequent article goes even further, stating that only Brazilian-born citizens might be responsible for managing, editing and producing news shows, including news stories, debates, opinion and commentary. The code prohibits journalists from using aliases and writing anonymous pieces, but guarantees the media's right to maintain anonymity of sources. The second part of the code prescribes the penalties (citations, fines, and sentences) for violating each article of the law.

Telecommunications Policies in Brazil A new Telecommunications Code (*Lei Geral das Telecomunicações*) was enacted in 1997 to guarantee universal access to telecommunications to all Brazilian citizens. The new code also created a national telecommunications agency (*Agência Nacional de Telecomunicações*), now responsible for granting telecommunications licenses. In Brazil, as in the United States, the government rules the airwaves, but the private sector owns them. The Ministry of Communications, which still controls the granting of broadcast licenses, as well as Embratel, were created by the military government in 1967 to foster both technological development and political control over broadcasting.

If in the 1960s and 1970s the process of government supervised licensing was used chiefly as a means of political control and censorship, in the 1980s and 1990s the distribution of new broadcasting licenses was used by Brazilian governments for bargaining power, and as a means of increasing political support. Broadcasting licenses are granted by the federal government and subject to Congressional approval. The exchange of broadcasting licenses for political support was taken to extremes by former President José Sarney, himself a media mogul in his native state of Maranhão. From 1987 to 1990 alone, the federal government distributed 850 new radio and television licenses.

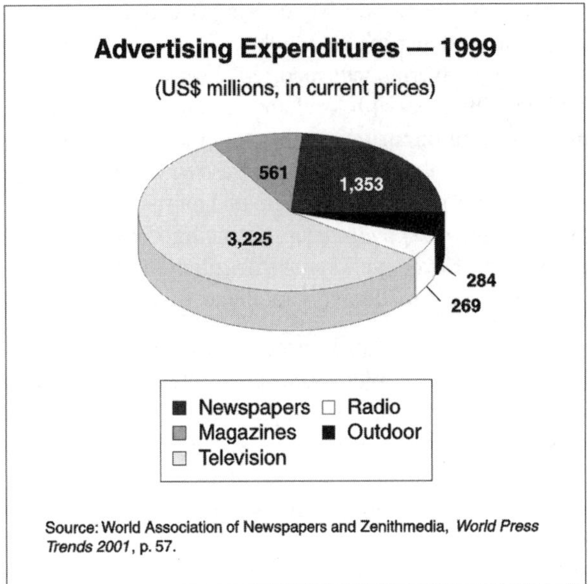

Source: World Association of Newspapers and Zenithmedia, *World Press Trends 2001*, p. 57.

A federal law prior to the military regime established the Brazilian Code of Telecommunications, in 1962. The law created the Conselho Nacional de Telecomunicações (National Council for Telecommunications; Contel), an agency that also works as a regulatory body, supervising the granting of licenses, authorizations and permits, and also the agency that applies penalties.

Analysts have noticed that the military regime had a tremendous impact on broadcasting policies in Brazil. That influence was translated both into the already mentioned technological changes, and into the establishment of direct censorship. After the coup d'état of 1964, censorship was not only openly exerted, but also unofficially authorized by the new Press Code, enacted in 1967.

When the military government stepped down and Brazil went back to civilian rule, in 1985, a democratic process engendered a new Constitution, adopted in 1988. Under the new Constitution, censorship of the media is not only condemned but also expressly prohibited.

According to the new Telecommunications Code of 1997, most of the duties and responsibilities of the old Conselho Nacional de Telecomunicações were transferred to the newly created Agência Nacional de Telecomunicações (Anatel).

CENSORSHIP

Censorship affected the Brazilian press throughout the country's history, from imperial times (nineteenth century) to the Old Republic (1889-1930), and then again during the Estado Novo (1937-1945) portion of the Vargas regime. De facto censorship was reinstated during the military regime (1964-1985), particularly during the implementation of the AI-5 (1968-mid-1970s).

During the Estado Novo, Vargas created a federal propaganda department, which was in charge of disseminating government supported news and information; building alliances with local and regional media owners; and silencing opposition voices, both through economic and political censorship. The Vargas regime was also responsible for persecuting writers and journalists who disagreed with the government, enforcing censorship and repression of even well known Brazilian literary figures, such as Jorge Amado and Graciliano Ramos.

Censorship was also enforced during the military regime. Opposition voices were persecuted, silenced, and driven underground. Several newspapers were outright closed down, and the ones that survived were quick to learn how to adapt to the realities of the new regime. Ironically, the Brazilian Press Code was enacted in 1967, during the military dictatorship. That law guaranteed freedom of the press, but it also contained built-in mechanisms to allow for persecution of dissenting voices, if those were considered subversive or threatening to national security.

A presidential executive order promulgated in December 1968 (AI-5) suppressed civil liberties, including direct elections for most executive and legislative positions, individual rights, and press freedom, and established a de facto police state in Brazil. Censorship of the mass media was openly enforced by the military between 1968 and the early 1970s. Major newspapers at the time, such as *Jornal do Brasil* and *O Estado de São Paulo* even had their own censors in the newsroom. Those federal government employees were responsible for reading major stories ahead of time, before they went to press, and recommending the appropriate changes, if necessary. Several times, important news stories were yanked from page one, and newspapers tried to alert readers by replacing them with cooking recipes, or even by printing blank columns.

Media censorship was eliminated once the democratic rule was reestablished in 1985. However, one of the first controversies faced by the newly elected civilian ruler, President José Sarney, was caused by his decision to prohibit a French movie he deemed offensive to the Catholic Church.

STATE-PRESS RELATIONS

In the 1990s, the Brazilian press stepped up its role as government watchdog. Since then, newspapers have been at the forefront of the struggle against political and economic abuse of power. Newspaper and newsmagazine circulation and readership increased partly due to the press' efficiency in investigating and publishing stories that expose social ills such as poverty and corruption. Historically, that has not necessarily been the case. The relationship between government and the press in Brazil was very strained during the 1930s, and then again during the military regime. Journalists and writers were often censored, jailed, and in some cases, killed, for pursuing stories that exposed corruption or political repression.

During the late 1930s, President Getulio Vargas used the media, particularly radio, to gain public support for his regime. During the late 1940s and 1950s, a very polarized press alternated support and criticism of the newly democratic government. In the 1950s, most newspapers in Brazil were still affiliated with political parties, openly supporting and campaigning for candidates, or, on the other hand, publishing editorials and articles criticizing political opponents.

During the military regime, the new rulers fiercely silenced the opposition, and newspapers learned to conform and adapt to the new political reality. In the 1960s, as the traditional political parties were outlawed, the old tradition of a strong partisan press also died out. Throughout the military dictatorship, newspapers, for the most part, tried to maintain their independence, but in many occasions had to tone down criticism and go along with government policies they would not have otherwise endorsed.

On a very few occasions during the military regime did newspapers openly disagree or criticize the government. One of those occasions was caused by the death of journalist Wladimir Herzog, who worked at TV Cultura de São Paulo, a state-owned educational channel. Herzog's death during questioning at a local police station in 1975 represented a major turning point not only for the relationship between the military and the press, but also for the return of democratic rule in Brazil.

Two Brazilian press institutions played a very significant role in the transition to democratic rule in the 1970s—the Brazilian Press Association (Associação Brasileira de Imprensa—ABI) and the National Federation of Journalists (Federação Nacional dos Jornalistas—FENAJ). The former congregates not only journalists, but also editors, publishers and newspaper owners, while the latter is the most important professional organization for journalists in the country.

Most of the mass media in Brazil are privately owned and there are no government subsidies for media companies, except for educational radio and TV-usually one public broadcasting company in each state owns and operates educational television and radio stations. The 1997 Telecommunications Code created a federal agency that oversees the license-granting process to telecommunications companies in the country.

ATTITUDE TOWARD FOREIGN MEDIA

All major foreign media, including newspapers, magazines, news agencies, and broadcasting companies, have offices and correspondents in Brazil. Those offices are usually either in Rio de Janeiro or São Paulo, with several of the correspondents in the national capital, Brasilia. International journalists have their own organization in the country, the Association of Foreign Correspondents in Brazil (Associação dos Correspondentes de Imprensa Estrangeira no Brasil-ACIE).

Until 2002, foreign ownership of media companies was not allowed in Brazil. In April 2002, new legislation was approved by the Chamber of Deputies to allow foreign nationals and companies to own interests in Brazilian media organizations.

Foreign mass media, especially entertainment and news television channels, are very popular in Brazil, and accessible through cable or pay TV subscription services. Foreign newspapers and magazines are available in all major Brazilian cities, at newsstands or bookstores.

The Impact of Foreign and National Media Some Brazilian analysts and scholars worry about the negative impact of foreign and national mass media in Brazil. They worry that much of what was considered the ''authentic,'' traditional Brazilian culture is being lost because of the widespread penetration of television.

Small towns in Brazil still gather around communal television sets to share the electronic ritual of watching television. Some remote villages in the Amazon jungle do not even have electricity. On the other side of the spectrum, urban areas enjoy communication technologies comparable to those in use at the world's most industrialized regions.

Recent studies that examined the impact of mass media on traditional communities of the Brazilian Amazon observed that many of the authentic, traditional cultural and social activities were being transformed as a consequence of television's pervasiveness. Remote rural villages seemed to be ready and eager to incorporate cultural and social norms that have been long associated with Brazilian urban areas.

The same studies showed, for example, that the networks' strict schedules were changing local residents' concept of time, which was moving from a more fluid, qualitative state to a more strict, quantitative one. Television was also thought to have a negative influence on the continuity of local cultural traditions, such as traditional religious practices and ceremonies; as well as on some long held economic practices, such as subsistence fishing. However, mass media was also seen as contributing to social and political participation, by elevating the educational level of local residents, and by keeping them informed of major national, regional and state political and economic developments.

NEWS AGENCIES

Brazil has several national news agencies, maintained by the major newspapers in the country, and operating under subscription agreements with affiliated news organizations throughout the country. The most important of those are Agéncia Folha, Agéncia Globo, Panorama Brasil, and Agéncia Estado. There is also a government-owned news agency, called Agéncia Brasil, and other regional news services.

Agéncia Estado, sponsored by the newspaper *O Estado de São Paulo*, bills itself as the largest news agency in Brazil. It has hundreds of subscribers throughout the country, and sends out an average of 230 news items per day, plus photos. Besides using traditional wire technology, Agéncia Estado delivers news to clients through satellite links and the Internet.

Agéncia O Globo is sponsored by the newspaper *O Globo*, from Rio de Janeiro, and is associated with the TV Globo corporation. It was created in 1974, and distributes approximately 120 news items per day.

Agéncia Folha was created and is maintained by *Folha de São Paulo*, the largest daily newspaper in Brazil. It employs approximately 500 journalists, and has offices and correspondents spread throughout the country.

All major international news agencies, such as Reuters, Associated Press, and Agence France-Press, have offices in Brazil. The Associated Press, for example, has offices in Rio de Janeiro, São Paulo and Brasilia. Other news agencies that have offices in Brazil include EFE (Spain), ANSA (Italy), Deutsche Presse-Agentur (Germany), Kyodo Tsushin (Japan), and Xinhua (China).

BROADCAST MEDIA

Broadcasting airwaves are public in Brazil, and a federal government agency grants licenses to media companies operating radio and television stations. There are five large privately owned national television networks-TV Globo, SBT, TV Record, TV Bandeirantes, and TV Manchete, as well as hundreds of local and regional television stations (256 stations in 1992) operating under an affiliation system similar to the United States'.

Broadcast TV has an immense influence on virtually all aspects of Brazilian culture and society. Television programming is often a topic of conversation at school and in the workplace, in the house and among friends. Television is an extremely important source of information for Brazilians of every socio-economic stratum. Brazilians across the board refer to reports they have seen on Jornal Nacional-TV Globo's most watched evening newscast, or to the latest plot twist in one of the soap operas.

The introduction of cable, satellite and pay TV is a relatively recent (1990s) phenomenon, but these sectors' growth has been astounding. In 1993, only 0.8 percent of Brazilian households had pay TV, in contrast to 28 percent of homes in Argentina. A year later, the number had jumped to 2.3 percent, or 700,000 subscribers. In early 1996, Brazilian homes with cable TV neared 1.5 million. That number had doubled by March of 1998.

Radio ownership in Brazil follows a format similar to that of television. However, radio networks are a phenomenon of the twenty-first century. Until the turn of the century, most radio stations were still family owned. In April 1996, there were 1,822 radio stations in Brazil, and radio was still the most pervasive mass media in the country (88 percent of households).

The growth of television viewership in Brazil is a unique and impressive phenomenon yet to be completely explored. TV sets numbered only 200 in the entire country on September 18, 1950, when commercial broadcasting started in São Paulo. By the end of 1980, only 30 years later, there were estimated 20 million TV sets in the country. By that time, Brazil alone had more TV sets than the rest of Latin America combined. Television households increased from 7 percent in 1964 to 51 percent in 1979, and then again to 75 percent in 1990, easily reaching more than 80 percent by the end of the century. More recent data estimated a total of 36.5 million TV sets in Brazil, and 209 TV sets per 1,000 people in 2002. Television broadcasts now reach all of Brazil.

The growth of viewership in Brazil both was stimulated and reflected the huge industrialization process that took place in the country from the 1940s on. In 1954, the development of an autonomous national industry was made possible by the creation of the National Steel Company and its peripheral heavy equipment manufacturers.

Brazil is today the world's eighth largest economy. Although strangled by the largest foreign debt in the world, the country's economy presents signs of vitality, with a strong currency, inflation under control, and a record trade surplus. The middle class represents one third of the country's population of 170 million, making up the second largest market for TV and consumerism in the Western hemisphere.

Brazilian media organizations were clearly aware of the country's economic potential. They took full advantage of the "expansion and integration" process that led the military dictatorship to create the Empresa Brasileira de Telecomunicaçães (Brazilian Telecommunications Enterprise, or Embratel), in 1967, and to launch a development plan that, by 1986, had virtually every Brazilian covered under a satellite blanket.

Television Pioneers The first Brazilian network, called TV Tupi, was established in São Paulo in 1950 by Diários e Emissoras Associados, a media conglomerate headed by journalist Assis Chateaubriand. A second TV Tupi station was launched in Rio de Janeiro on January 20, 1951. Diários e Emissoras Associados owned more than 30 daily newspapers, 18 TV stations and 30 radio stations. The conglomerate also had its own news agency, advertising agency, and some public relations firms. It published several magazines, including the influential *O Cruzeiro*, which was until 1967 the largest selling magazine in Latin America.

Television in Brazil was established following a trial and error pattern similar to the one experienced by American networks. Programming was adapted from other media, particularly radio and film. During the first years of Brazilian TV, there was little to no experimenting, television was a second-hand medium, absorbing formats which had their origins in radio, newsprint media, film, and theater. TV Tupi's broadcast included news, comedy and "filmed theater," or "teleplays."

Throughout the first half of the 1950s, television was a very elitist medium. Only a small percentage of the population (namely, wealthy families in Rio de Janeiro and São Paulo) had television sets. Consequently, programming was directed to that segment of the population. The situation changed in 1955, when television lost its "novelty for the wealthy" appeal and became a household item. Around that time, it became common, for example, to present newlyweds with television sets. Aware of the new trend, TV Tupi's broadcast became more sensationalist.

During most of the 1950s, TV Tupi's leadership remained unchallenged. That situation changed in the 1960s, when three competing networks—TV Excelsior, TV Record, and TV Globo—were launched. TV Record, which chose to produce well-structured journalism and music programs, had a particularly great impact on the market.

TV Excelsior was born in 1964, already in the age of soap operas, and excelled in this genre and in musicals. TV Globo came to challenge the leader, also aiming its programming at the lower economic strata. Competition among four different TV networks, combined with economic expansion, stimulated television's growth. In 1950, viewership was limited to large cities, such as São Paulo and Rio de Janeiro, due mostly to the cost of TV sets. But if sets were only 200 in 1950, in 1965 they were already 3 million, spread throughout the country.

Unlike other Latin American and European countries, where either monopolistic and/or government-owned broadcasting traditions were established, Brazil consolidated in the 1960s a major trend towards commercial television and multiple, privately-owned national networks, a format that had the American television system as its model and inspiration.

It was also in the 1960s that Brazilian television created its own specific style, best translated in the *telenovela* or simply *novela* (soap opera) genre. Interestingly enough, Colgate-Palmolive's line of cosmetics had been one of the major advertisers in 1940s Brazilian radio, when soap operas first became popular in the country. One of the reasons why Brazilian *telenovelas* were created by the networks was to provide a product in which advertisements could be placed. For ten years, Brazilian TV had struggled to find the right formats for its potential advertisers. Most shows were short in duration (15 minutes, on average), because of the conditions in which they were produced and broadcast—virtually every program aired was a live presentation. Even the early soap operas followed that format. Advertisers were reluctant to invest in a medium that failed to grip the audience's attention in a habit-forming fashion.

Throughout the 1960s, networks decided to resuscitate some of radio's most popular soap operas. Although soap operas had been a common staple of Brazilian broadcasting since the early 1950s, the Cuban drama *Direito de Nascer* (A Right to be Born), a radio favorite of the 1940s, is believed to have originated the *telenovela* audience phenomenon in Brazilian television. First aired on December 7, 1964, the soap opera experienced an overwhelming success which continued to its final daily installment, broadcast live from an over-crowded sports arena in Rio, in August of the following year.

TV Globo TV Tupi dominated Brazilian television during the 1950s and 1960s, but in the 1970s and 1980s, TV Globo became the largest television network in the country. TV Globo, also known as *Rede Globo* (Globo Network) was, well into the 1990s, the world's most consistently watched private TV network.

In 1998, TV Globo was still the fourth largest network in the world, regularly attracting 55 percent of the country's audience, and about 70 percent of the advertising revenue. However, with the growth of cable and satellite television, Globo started to experience a decline in ratings, dipping just under half of the audience for the first time in almost 30 years.

As late as April 2002, Brazil's giant media organization was still one of the top five commercial television networks in the world, commanding an estimated daily viewership of 100 million people at prime time. Advertisers responded to this large number of viewers. In 1995, US$ 3.6 billion were spent in television advertising in Brazil, with an estimated half of that total ending up in TV Globo's coffers.

The network thrived during the military regime (1964-1985), when it received special treatment and financial incentives from successive governments. The conglomerate both reflected and legitimated the authoritarian regime's ideology of "development and national security."

TV Globo initially aimed its programming at the lower economic strata of the population, competing directly with then leader TV Tupi. By the end of the 1960s, Globo had succeeded in attracting a large audience, mostly in detriment of TV Tupi's audience. The rise of Globo in the popular preference coincided with the death of media mogul Assis Chateaubriand, which detonated a process of internal disputes and bad management that ended up by destroying TV Tupi, which went bankrupt in the 1970s.

Television critics have characterized Rede Globo's role at gaining public support for the military regimes as subtler than mere propaganda. Some of them have noticed that the first military governments (1964 to 1974) pursued exclusionary policies that led them to rely on continued repression to maintain hegemony.

The following period (1975 to 1985) marked a so-called transition from military to civilian rule. Legitimacy, then, had to be obtained more through the construction of cultural and ideological hegemony than through overt repression.

TV Globo played a key role in both periods. In the first one, widely watched *telenovelas* worked to create a positive, happy and optimistic image of the country and its people, when the so-called Brazilian 'economic miracle' was emphasized to support the idea that "Esse é um país que vai pra frente" ("This is a country that moves forward," a popular government slogan of the time).

In the second period, when loss of legitimacy due to economic recession led the military regimes to propose the alternative of transition to civilian rule, Rede Globo threw all the heavy weight of its news coverage to support indirect transition (a civilian president indirectly elected by an electoral college), as opposed to a president chosen by the popular vote. The main consequence of the tactic was a complete ignorance of the unprecedented popular demonstrations demanding *diretas já* (direct elections now).

The second largest Brazilian network, Sistema Brasileiro de Televisão (SBT), was launched in August 1981. Owned by game show host Silvio Santos, SBT has nine local stations, including its national broadcasting center in São Paulo, and 76 affiliated stations throughout the country. The network's programming is a mix of game shows, sensational journalism, soap operas (in-house productions and Mexican imports) and popular comedy shows.

SBT prides itself on being Brazil's second-largest network. The network's penetration is strongest in São

Paulo. According to the Nielsen data furnished by SBT on its Internet home page, in 1997, the network had 30 percent of the advertising market share in São Paulo in 1995. *Globo* had 43 percent; Bandeirantes 11 percent; Manchete 10 percent; Record two percent and independent stations four percent.

It is worth noting that the third largest Brazilian television network, TV Record, is owned by Igreja Universal do Reino de Deus (Universal Church of the Kingdom of God, UCKG), an evangelical, revivalist Christian church that emerged in 1977, and that has now become one of the fastest-growing religious groups in the country.

In 1996, the UCKG owned TV Record and its 25 affiliates, besides 35 radio stations and two mass circulation newspapers. Its controversial leader, the self-appointed Bishop Edir Macedo, was investigated in the early 1990s for alleged links to a Colombian drug cartel, and has attracted the wrath of the all-powerful media mogul Roberto Marinho, who founded and, until the late-1990s, ran the Globo media empire. In the late 1990s, with its mix of sensationalism and crass programming, TV Record was seriously threatening the audience leadership of TV Globo in parts of the country.

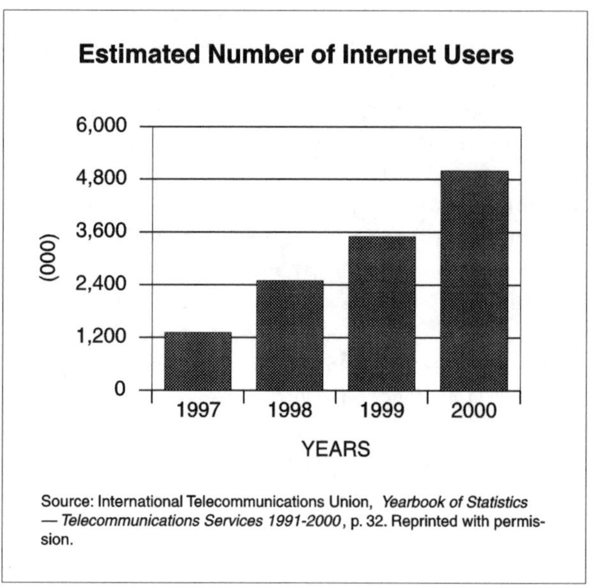

Source: International Telecommunications Union, *Yearbook of Statistics — Telecommunications Services 1991-2000*, p. 32. Reprinted with permission.

ELECTRONIC NEWS MEDIA

Brazilian media ratings firm Ibope estimated in August 2001 that 20 percent of Brazilians living in urban areas had Internet access. According to Ibope and NetRatings (the Internet arm of the Nielsen ratings corporation), those numbers had put Brazil ahead of countries such as Spain and France, in terms of Internet users.

Comparatively, only 1.9 percent of Mexico's population was connected to the Internet in June 2001, according to the Organization for Economic Development & Cooperation. Widespread adoption of computers and the Internet by Brazilian consumers led the U.S. Yankee Group to predict that 42.3 million Brazilians will be surfing the Web by 2006.

As happens in other developed or emerging countries, most Internet users report using it to search for news and information. In fact, out of the three most popular Brazilian Web portals—UOL.com.br, Globo.com.br, and iG.com.br—only the last one is not funded, sponsored or supported by a major news organization. News stories, however, play a very prominent part in the design and content of all of those sites.

Because of its cheap, global and ''boundary-less'' nature, the Internet has also become a very important (and in some cases the only) way of delivering unrestricted and uncensored news outside of particular countries and regions. Similarly, the Web has become the preferred news delivery medium for Brazilian expatriates wanting to keep up with current affairs back at home and for all other foreign users with social, economic and political interests in particular countries or regions.

EDUCATION & TRAINING

Journalism and mass media university programs became very popular in Brazil in the early 1980s. By the end of that decade, new university-trained journalists were fast replacing reporters and editors with no formal training in television and newspaper newsrooms across the country.

In the early 1990s, an overwhelming majority of practicing journalists had undergone university training in mass communications. Up to the previous decade, most journalists had been recruited out of political science, law, Portuguese, and sociology courses.

That change was partly due to the fact that in the 1980s, *sindicatos dos jornalistas* (journalists unions) pressured the federal government to recognize and accredit the profession. As a consequence, university programs strove to receive professional and government accreditation, and news organizations were pressured to hire more university-trained journalists.

A national organization called Intercom (short for Sociedade Brasileira de Estudos Interdisciplinares da Comunicação), congregates journalism educators and students in the country, promoting research and education in the field of mass communication.

SUMMARY

Despite the country's inconsistent tradition as far as press freedom, Brazilian newspapers have developed throughout the 1980s and 1990s a keen sense of independence and social responsibility. As a result of that process, and of their newfound watchdog role, circulation and readership have been up, and Brazilian newspapers enter the twenty-first century with renewed hopes and high expectations.

The Brazilian democracy and the country's economy have been stable for more than a decade, and newspapers seem to be taking full advantage of economic prosperity and institutional stability. Although readership is still low, if compared to most industrialized countries, the most popular dailies reach an ever increasing audience, with the top four papers maintaining a combined circulation of 1.4 million copies daily. Both the broadcasting industry and the Internet have experienced an astounding growth in the 1990s and early 2000s, which also bodes very well for the future of these emergent technologies in Brazil.

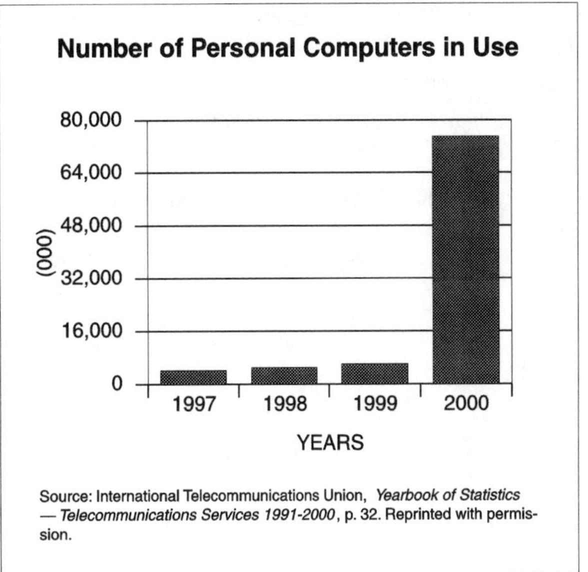

Source: International Telecommunications Union, *Yearbook of Statistics — Telecommunications Services 1991-2000*, p. 32. Reprinted with permission.

SIGNIFICANT DATES

- 1992: Newspapers play a very important role in exposing corruption and irregularities that lead to the impeachment of President Fernando Collor.
- July 1997: Brazil enacts its new Telecommunications Code, which creates a new federal agency responsible for granting telecommunications licenses.
- August 2001: An estimated 20 percent of Brazilians living in urban areas have access to news and information on the Internet.
- April 2002: A bill proposing to open Brazilian mass media to foreign ownership is approved by the Chamber of Deputies and expected to be ratified by the Senate and the President.

BIBLIOGRAPHY

Brazil: A Country Study. Washington, D.C.: Library of Congress, 1998.

''Brazil.'' *Encyclopaedia Britannica Online*. 2002. Available from www.britannica.com/.

''Brazil.'' *Encyclopedia of the Third World*. 4th ed., Vol. I. New York: Facts on File, 1992.

''Brazil.'' *The Europa World Year Book*. Vol. I. London: Europa Publications, 2001.

''Brazil.'' *The World Almanac*. New York: World Almanac Books, 2002.

Brown, Robert U. (1997). ''Latin Press Thriving.'' New York: Editor & Publisher, 1997.

Camargo, Nelly, and Pinto, V. B. N. *Communication Policies in Brazil*. Paris: The Unesco Press, 1975.

Census Data 2002. Instituto Brasileiro de Geografia e Estatistica (IBGE). Available from www.ibge.gov.br/.

Federico, M. E. B. *História da Comunicação: Rádio e TV no Brasil*. Petrópolis, Brazil: Editora Vozes, 1982.

Hoineff, Nelson. *A Nova Televisão: Desmassificação e o Impasse das Grandes Redes*. Rio de Janeiro, Brazil: Editora Dumará, 1996.

''Ibope: 20% of Metropolitan Residents Have Internet Access.'' *Business News Americas*. 2001.

''Internet Penetration Estimates Vary Widely.'' *Business News Americas*. 2001.

Kottak, C. P. ''Television's Impact on Values and Local Life in Brazil.'' *Journal of Communication*. 1991.

Lei de Imprensa (Brazilian Press Code). Enacted on 9 February 1967.

Lei Geral das Telecomunicações (Brazilian Telecommunications Code). Enacted on 16 July 1997.

Levine, Robert M. ''Elite Perceptions of the Povo.'' In Conniff, M., & McCann, F., Eds., *Modern Brazil: Elites and Masses in Historical Perspective* (pp. 209-224). Lincoln, NE: University of Nebraska Press, 1989.

Mattos, S. *The Impact of the 1964 Revolution on Brazilian Television*. San Antonio, TX: V. Klingensmith Independent Publisher, 1982.

''The Media Market.'' *Advertising Age*. Vol. 68, No. 2. 1997.

Miranda, R., & Pereira, C. A. M. *Televisão: O Nacional e o Popular na Cultura Brasileira*. São Paulo, Brazil: Editora Brasiliense, 1983.

Necchi, S. H. ''Brazil: A Mogul's Muscle.'' *Columbia Journalism Review*. Vol. 28, No. 4. 1989.

Oliveira, O. S. ''Mass Media, Culture, and Communication in Brazil: The Heritage of Dependency.'' In G. Sussman, & J. A. Lent, Eds., *Transnational Communications* (pp. 200-213). London: Sage, 1991.

Queiroz, A. *TV de Papel: A Imprensa como Instrumento de Legitimação da Televisão*. Piracicaba, Brazil: Editora Unimep, 1992.

Reis, Raul. ''The Impact of Television Viewing in the Brazilian Amazon.'' *Human Organization, Journal of the Society for Applied Anthropology*. Vol. 57, No. 3. 1998.

———. ''What Prevents Cable TV from Taking off in Brazil?.'' *Journal of Broadcasting & Electronic Media*. Vol. 43, No. 3. 1999.

Roett, Riordan. *Brazil: Politics in a Patrimonial Society*. Westport, CT: Praeger, 1992.

Schneider, R. M. *Brazil: Culture and Politics in a New Industrial Powerhouse*. Boulder, CO: Westview Press, 1996.

Serbin, Ken. ''Brazilian Church Builds an International Empire.'' *Christian Century*. Vol. 113, No. 12. 1996.

Sistema Brasileiro de Televisão (SBT). Available from www.sbt.com.br/.

Sodré, M. *O Monopólio da Fala*. Petrópolis, Brazil: Editora Vozes, 1977.

Straubhaar, Joseph D. ''Mass Communication and the Elites.'' In Conniff, M., & McCann, F., Eds., *Modern Brazil: Elites and Masses in Historical Perspective* (pp. 225-245). Lincoln, NE: University of Nebraska Press, 1989.

Thomas, G. ''Closely Watched TV.'' *Censorship Brazil*. Oxford, UK: Oxford University Press, 1979.

Tunstall, J. *The Media Are American*. New York: Columbia University Press, 1977.

Wentzel, Laurel. ''Rede Globo Dominates Brazil's TV Prime Time, Ad Revenues.'' *Advertising Age*. Vol. 69, No. 39. 1998.

''Yankee Predicts 42 million Internet Users in 2006.'' *South American Business Information* (07/11/2001).

—Raul Reis

BRUNEI DARUSSALAM

BASIC DATA

Official Country Name:	Brunei Darussalam
Region (Map name):	Southeast Asia
Population:	336,376
Language(s):	Malay, English, Chinese
Literacy rate:	88.2%

Brunei Darussalam, a tiny country situated on the northwest corner of the island of Borneo, has a media and press system that is highly censored and uniform, with little diversity or freedom.

The primary English-language daily newspaper is the *Borneo Bulletin*. The Malay-language newspaper is the *Media Permata*. The country also has one independent English-language daily, the *News Express*, and an online news service, Brunei Direct. The country has only one television station, state-controlled Television Brunei, with broadcasts in the Brunei's official language, Malay, as well as English. The country's one radio station, state-controlled Radio Television Brunei, broadcasts in Malay, English, Mandarin Chinese, and Gurkhali. Foreign broadcasts can be accessed through a cable network, lending diversity to the population's information access.

Brunei's press, although not considered free by Western standards, is what the government describes as a ''socially responsible Press,'' which balances the rights of the individual and those of society. The authoritarian government, led since 1967 by Sultan Hassanal Bolkiah, rejects a press that is too liberal and free to print caustic criticism of its political leaders. The government is considered a Malay Muslim Monarchy and has maintained its independence, first by rejecting in 1963 the option of joining the Malaysian Federation (the country remained a British dependency), then by separating from the British monarchy in 1984, thanks to its newfound wealth of oil and gas deposits.

The country's population is well educated, well read, and enjoys one of the highest standards of living in the world, with an average annual per-capita income of US $24,620. Brunei citizens pay no income taxes and enjoy free medical care and education.

Although newspapers and foreign media are censored, the government has loosened control somewhat in the early twenty-first century. However, religious leaders in Brunei have expressed their concern over less censorship because they believe the society will fall into moral decay, according the BBC News.

BIBLIOGRAPHY

''Committee to Protect Journalists Statement,'' 25 Sept. 2001. Available from http://www.brudirect.com

''Country Profile: Brunei.'' *BBC News*, 26 Feb. 2002.

''Country Reports on Human Rights Practices, Brunei.'' Bureau of Democracy, Human Rights and Labor, U.S. Department of State. 4 March 2001.

"Global Press Freedom Declines." *Freedom House,* 29 April 2000. Available from http://www.freedomhouse.org

Hesseldahl, Arik. "Tough Times in Brunei." *Forbes,* 14 Sept. 2000.

"The World's Largest Prison for Journalists—Annual Report Asia 2002." *Reporters Without Borders,* 25 April 2002. Available from http://www.rsf.fr

—Carol Marshall

BULGARIA

BASIC DATA

Official Country Name:	Republic of Bulgaria
Region (Map name):	Europe
Population:	7,707,495
Language(s):	Bulgarian, secondary languages closely correspond to ethinic breakdown
Literacy rate:	98.0%
Area:	110,910 sq km
GDP:	11,995 (US$ millions)
Number of Daily Newspapers:	43
Total Circulation:	1,400,000
Circulation per 1,000:	203
Number of Nondaily Newspapers:	114
Total Circulation:	1,750,000
Newspaper Consumption (minutes per day):	16
Total Newspaper Ad Receipts:	39 (Lev millions)
As % of All Ad Expenditures:	26.40
Magazine Consumption (minutes per day):	15
Number of Television Stations:	96
Number of Television Sets:	3,310,000
Television Sets per 1,000:	429.5
Television Consumption (minutes per day):	78
Number of Cable Subscribers:	1,066,820
Cable Subscribers per 1,000:	130.1
Number of Satellite Subscribers:	160,000
Satellite Subscribers per 1,000:	20.8
Number of Radio Stations:	119
Number of Radio Receivers:	4,510,000
Radio Receivers per 1,000:	585.1
Radio Consumption (minutes per day):	40
Number of Individuals with Computers:	361,000
Computers per 1,000:	46.8
Number of Individuals with Internet Access:	430,000
Internet Access per 1,000:	55.8
Internet Consumption (minutes per day):	58

BACKGROUND & GENERAL CHARACTERISTICS

Bulgaria is undergoing a renaissance. In 2001 the Bulgarian people elected exactly half of the members of the national Parliament from a novice political party, the National Movement for Simeon II (NMSII), formed only a few months before the election, supporting Bulgaria's former king, Simeon II. Simeon II created a coalition government with the Movement for Rights and Freedom (DPS), representing the Turkish minority to form a working parliamentary majority. His Majesty became His Excellency Prime Minister Simeon Saxe-Coburg-Gotha. In 2002, in a surprise election upset, President Petar Stoyanov, representing the Union of Democratic Forces (UDF), was defeated for reelection by former Communist and Bulgarian Socialist Party (BSP) leader, Georgi Purvanov. A president who is a former Communist and a prime minister who was once its king lead Bulgaria in 2002.

Bulgaria's history extends back to the seventh century, when the first Bulgar tribes formed a nation-state created and recognized by the Byzantine Empire in 681. In the ninth century Bulgaria's first kings or czars successfully fought the armies of the Byzantine Empire. Czar Boris I accepted Christianity, the Eastern Orthodox rite, for his people. Bulgaria's first golden age and the first Bulgarian Empire reached its peak during the reign of Czar Simeon I (893-927). The country's first period of independence ended after successive defeats to the Byzantine armies. In 1018 Bulgaria was incorporated into the Byzantine Empire.

The Bulgarian state was reestablished in 1185 under Princes Asen and Peter. A second Bulgarian Empire, created in 1202 under the leadership of Czar Ivan Asen II (1218-1241), saw Bulgarian culture again flourish. After Czar Ivan Asen's death, internal strife, invading Tartars, a militarily more powerful Byzantine Empire, and a peasant revolt fueled by the nobles' excessive taxation, ended Bulgaria's independence, and returned the nation to the rule of Christian Constantinople. A brief national resurgence under Mikhail Shishman and Ivan Aleksandur only postponed Bulgaria's ultimate absorption into the Muslim Empire of the Ottoman Turks (1385). The collapse of the Christian Byzantine Empire in 1453 brought all of Eastern Europe under direct Muslim rule. Attempts at Bulgar insurrections brought swift and brutal retaliation from the Ottoman Turks.

Under centuries of Ottoman control the flame of Bulgarian independence and culture was kept alive by Bulgarian exiles Hristofor Zhefarovich who wrote *Stematografía,* a seminal work on Bulgaria's history (1741), and Paisi of Hilendar's History of the Bulgars (1762) written in vernacular Bulgarian. Bulgarian money and men supported Serbian and Greek rebellions against Turkish rule in the early 1800s. Bulgarian independence remained an ideal in the cultural and intellectual realm outside the region but not in Bulgaria. In 1824 Dr. Petur Beron published the first educational primer in colloquial Bulgarian. Beron's primer and educational philosophy were gradually adopted in nineteenth-century Bulgaria's schools. The development of an educational system awakened Bulgars to their history and culture, and the realization of the oppressive nature of Ottoman rule. Bulgarians seeking higher education went to Russia and France. European beliefs in constitutional government and the French Revolution's ideas of liberty and equality were carried back to Bulgaria and deposited as the intellectual ''seeds of independence.''

The first Bulgarian periodical was printed in 1844. Its focus was the recapitulation of earlier journals printed outside Bulgaria in Romania and beyond Ottoman censorship. As the nineteenth century progressed, an increasing number of periodicals printed by Bulgarian émigrés and smuggled into Bulgaria fueled beliefs in independence. Soon Bulgarian cultural and charitable organizations operating from Constantinople nurtured the idea of Bulgaria's freedom when they established the *chitalishte* (reading room), which served as a center for adult education, social gatherings, lectures, performances, and debates, where Bulgarians could discuss their future. By 1871, 131 reading rooms spread the Bulgarian language and culture among the Bulgars. Dobri Chintulov wrote the first poetry in modern Bulgarian and helped begin a cultural revival among the Bulgars. Western literature, translated into the Bulgarian language, presented Bulgarians with knowledge of the political, social, and economic changes occurring in the rest of Europe.

As the Bulgarian national identity developed, so did the desire of the Bulgarian Orthodox Church to be independent of the Greek Patriarch in Constantinople. Decades of petitions and protests brought results. In 1870 the Sultan in Constantinople designated the Bulgarian Church as separate from and outside the control of the Ecumenical Patriarch in Constantinople. Bulgarian revolutionaries used the organizational structure of the Bulgarian Orthodox Church as the skeletal framework for a future state.

A series of Bulgarian uprisings in 1835, 1841, 1850, and 1851 were brutally suppressed by the Turks. The failure of the revolts led Bulgaria's independence movements to split, with each one suggesting a different approach to end Turkish domination. Eventually the gradual disintegration of the Ottoman Empire led Great Britain and France to intervene and forced the Turkish government to implement political, economic, and social reforms within the Bulgarian region.

Under the leadership of Georgi Rakovski, Bulgaria launched its first major rebellion against their Turkish overlords in 1862. Serbian betrayal dashed the dream of Bulgarian independence and led to generations of feuding between Serbians and Bulgarians. Fortunately for the Bulgarian people even Rakovski's death in 1867 did not end the Bulgarian dream of independence. The insurrections of September 1875 and April 1876 on behalf of independence were poorly organized and collapsed under the onslaught of a trained and equipped Ottoman army. However, the deaths of over 30,000 Christian Bulgarians raised European concern about the integrity of the Ottoman Empire. The possibility of Russian military intervention in the Eastern Mediterranean in support of the Bulgars forced the convening of an international conference on the Bulgarian question. Russia took the opportunity to charge the Turks with the slaughter of Christians. Turkish refusal to allow the creation of two semiautonomous Bulgarian states was the excuse Czarist Russia needed to declare war on the Ottoman Empire, with the ulterior motive being Russia's desire to gain access to and control of the Black Sea.

Russian intervention on Bulgaria's behalf and with British connivance, witnessed the rapid advance of Russian troops into Bulgaria and on to Constantinople. Through the conference of Berlin in 1876, a smaller Bulgarian state was recognized. Bulgarians in Eastern Rumelia remained under Turkish rule but with a Christian governor. The Treaty of Berlin allowed Bulgaria to adopt a constitution, elect a prince, but continue as a vassal state to the Ottoman Sultan. Europe's exclusion of Bulgarians living in Macedonia, Thrace, and Eastern Rumelia would remain a contentious issue for the next century and lead to numerous Balkan wars.

In 1879 an assembly of Bulgarians meeting in Turnovo, the medieval capital of an independent Bulgaria, wrote a constitution, elected legislators, and selected a German prince, Prince Alexander of Battenberg, to govern them. The principality of Bulgaria's politicians quickly divided into competing factions of liberals and conservatives. Each established its own party newspaper: the *Nezavisimost* for the liberals and the *Vitocha* for the conservatives. Within a few years Bulgaria had 19 weekly newspapers publishing around the country.

The brief reign of Prince Alexander of Battenberg (1879-1886) was fraught with great difficulties. A nephew of the Russian czar, Alexander II, Prince Alexander initially enjoyed Russian support for a conservative regime in Bulgaria. However, Bulgaria's conservatives did not have the people's support. The assassination of Alexander II had a tremendous impact on Bulgaria's future. The new Russian czar, Alexander III, did not like his Bulgarian cousin, Alexander of Battenberg. Although the cousins were both conservatives, the Russian czar demanded the Bulgarian Parliament institute his changes, which diluted many freedoms and liberal clauses guaranteed in the Constitution. The unpopularity of the conservatives ultimately forced Prince Alexander to restore the liberals and revoke the Russian-imposed constitutional changes. Prince Alexander's decision to block increasing Russian influence in Bulgaria by denying the permit for the construction of a railroad for Russia in Bulgaria and the increased presence of the Russian army in Bulgaria led to a serious split between the two nations. In 1885 Prince Alexander's increasing assertions of independence led to the union of Bulgaria and Eastern Rumelia against the wishes of Russia. Russia retaliated by placing army officers inside Bulgaria who led the 1886 coup, which ousted Alexander of Battenberg.

Russia then imposed a three-man regency council on Bulgaria. The regency quickly rejected Russian interference in Bulgarian affairs. An embittered Russia withdrew from Bulgaria and for a decade only hostility existed between the two nations. Under the leadership of Stefan Stambolov as prime minister, the Bulgarian legislature elected, against Russian advice, Ferdinand of Saxe-Coburg-Gotha, a German Catholic and a cousin of Queen Victoria, as Prince of Bulgaria. Although Ferdinand was Bulgaria's new ruling prince, the real power remained Stambolov, who moved quickly to limit constitutional freedoms and squelched the press with strict government censorship. Bulgaria's first national newspaper was the Stambolov creation *Svaboda* (Freedom). Later when Stambolov was out of office, the former prime minister used *Svaboda* to criticize Prince Ferdinand. The newspaper was written with a "racy sarcasm" and included articles that were withering attacks on the government and Prince Ferdinand. It was alleged that Stambolov leaked negative stories about the Bulgarian government to the foreign press. The government unsuccessfully tried to convict Stambolov for defamation of Prince Ferdinand's character in the foreign press. Bulgaria's courts rejected the government's argument. Prince Ferdinand responded by allowing government ministers to leak stories to the newspapers that compromised Stambolov's moral and political integrity.

Europe's Great Powers did not recognize Prince Ferdinand as the ruler of Bulgaria for a decade. Stambolov ruled as a virtual dictator who suppressed political parties, the press, and extreme nationalists. The prime minister remained in power because he neutralized the army leadership, shifted the national economy into profitable capitalism, and won support from the Bulgarian Orthodox Church. Stambolov acquired many enemies, and in 1894 Ferdinand had consolidated enough power and support from the various factions within his country to dismiss the prime minister. Stambolov continued to use *Svaboda* to attack the government, both the new prime minister and Prince Ferdinand. When Stambolov was assassinated in 1895, *Svaboda* accused Prince Ferdinand of engineering the former prime minister's death. The ascension of Czar Nicholas II to the throne of Russia in 1896 brought Russian recognition of Ferdinand as Prince of Bulgaria. Prince Ferdinand continued to increase his political powers over the next two decades by maintaining a semblance of parliamentary rule, supporting industrialization, and encouraging Bulgarian nationalism at the expense of the Ottoman Empire. In 1908 Ferdinand felt secure enough to break all ties to the Ottomans and declare himself King of Bulgaria. Numerous small newspapers began circulation in the cities of Sofia, Plovdiv, and Varna. The nation's new leading print media were the *Vetcherna Poschta* (Evening Courier) and *Dnevnik* (Journal). Advertising as a source of revenue increased the number of newspapers to 239 publications in 1911. Ironically *Svaboda* still published, but as the government's newspaper.

The press in Bulgaria suffered during World War I because of a shortage of newsprint and strict military censorship. The defeat of the Central Powers and the overthrow of Europe's three emperors in Russia, Germany, and Austria-Hungary, forced the politically astute King Ferdinand to abdicate in favor of his eldest son, Boris, to save the dynasty. Ferdinand opted for permanent exile from Bulgaria and a life of comfortable exile in Coburg, Germany.

The reign of Boris III (1919-1943) was beset by severe crises on all fronts. As a defeated nation, Bulgaria lost territory, was forced to pay war reparations, and suffered from parliamentary instability. Under Agrarian Party leader and prime minister, Alexander Stamboliiski, Bulgaria underwent severe economic reforms. The government took control over the grain monopoly, ended land monopolies, and redistributed land to the nation's poor, passed a progressive income tax, enacted an obligatory labor law, and made secondary education compulsory. Stamboliiski garnered many enemies from among the other political parties and Bulgarian nationalists from Macdeonia. In June 1923 he was assassinated.

The Bulgarian Communist Party, Europe's oldest, attempted to overthrow the new coalition government in 1923 and in 1925 attempted to kill the king by blowing up the Sofia cathedral with the czar in attendance. The Bulgarian press reacted to the nation's political instability, experiencing periods of some freedom to publish, followed by severe repression and censorship when the military ruled Bulgaria in the king's name. Prior to World War II, the press restrictions under the royal dictatorship of King Boris were relaxed. Each of Bulgaria's many political parties published a newspaper but did so with great care, fearing censorship or closure.

World War II brought Bulgaria into the conflict on the Axis side, as it once again sought territory from its neighbors, which Bulgars inhabited. King Boris skillfully navigated a tightrope between Hitler's increasing demands for war contributions and Boris's desire to keep his nation out of the spreading conflict. In 1943, after returning from a stormy meeting with Hitler in Germany, Boris III died under mysterious and still unresolved circumstances. The throne passed to his six-year-old son, Simeon, and power to a Regency Council of three.

The brief reign of Simeon II was affected by the approaching Soviet armies and the increasing power of the Bulgarian Communist Party. The three regents were charged with treason in 1945 and executed. Until September 1946 and the abolishment of the monarchy, Bulgaria rapidly witnessed the closure of the media, suppression of political parties and the execution of their leaders, and the conversion of a capitalistic economy to a Communist one. The 1947 People's Republic of Bulgaria Constitution, known as the Dimitrov Constitution for Prime Minister Georgi Dimitrov, guaranteed all Bulgarian citizens equality before the law, freedom of speech, press, assembly, and the inviolability of person, domicile, and correspondence. All these rights were qualified by a constitutional clause prohibiting such freedoms if they jeopardized the attainments of the Communist revolution of 1944.

During the Communist era Bulgaria was regarded as one of the most loyal of the Soviet Union's allies. Religious, press, and speech freedoms were gone. On Stalin's demand, Bulgarian Communists viewed as sympathetic to Yugoslav Communist maverick, Marshal Tito, were purged from the party. Under Stalin protégé Vulko Chervenkov (1950-1956), Bulgaria faced one of its harshest periods of repression against any who failed to follow party line. Bulgarian nationalism, culture, and the arts all suffered. All farmland was collectivized.

After the death of Stalin and a period of Soviet liberalization under Nikita Khrushchev, Bulgaria adopted some mild reforms. Newspapers and journalists were permitted more latitude in writing news articles. The Hungarian Revolution of 1956 again forced further repression within Bulgaria. Attempting to reassure the Soviet Union of Bulgaria's steadfast loyalty, Chervenkov purged the leadership of the Bulgarian Writer's Union, and all liberal journalists and editors were fired. In 1962 Soviet Premier Khrushchev selected Todor Zhivkov as Bulgaria's next prime minister, who served in that position until his overthrow 27 years later (1989). During those three decades Bulgaria had brief periods of improved press-state relations followed by longer periods of repression. Detente in the early 1970s briefly benefited the Bulgarian press. The 1978 murder of exiled Bulgarian writer Georgi Markov, believed ordered by the Bulgarian secret police, harmed the nation's international image and signaled a return to stricter press regulation. Discontent in Communist Poland (1980) could not be reported for fear of encouraging domestic dissent.

Under Communist rule Bulgaria published 13 daily newspapers, 5 in the provinces, and 8 in Sofia, the capital. The leading newspapers were still the Communist Party organs *Rabotnichesko Delo* and *Otechestven Front.* A Communist youth newspaper, *Narodna Mladezh,* was the third most influential newspaper. Thirty-three newspapers published as either weeklies or twice a week. The Bulgarian Orthodox Church printed its own newspaper but with a careful eye to government censorship. During periods of economic crises, the newspapers reduced the number of pages from 6 pages to 4 and the number of days of publication from 7 to 6 or even 5 days. Each newspaper targeted a specific audience within Communist Bulgaria. They were not subject to circulation concerns or worried about advertising revenue. Bulgaria's other major newspapers published during the Zhivkov era were *Trud,* the trade unions newspaper, agricultural dailies *Koopernativno Selo* and *Zemedelsko Zname, Vecherni Novini,* the only newspaper to give considerable space to advertising, and *Narodna Armiya,* published by the Ministry of Defense. Only 2 provincial newspapers had wide circulation, the Varna newspaper *Narodno Delo* and *Otechestven Glas,* published in Plovdiv.

During the 1980s Zhivkov temporarily eased state oppression of Roman Catholics and the Bulgarian Orthodox Church. The media was permitted to cover and publish more news events. This brief liberalization period was attributed to the influence of Zhivkov's daugher, Liudmilla, who was chairman of the Commission on Science, Culture, and Art. Her death in 1984 witnessed Bulgaria's return to greater repression of basic freedoms. In 1987 Bulgaria had 17 daily newspapers, most of them local. *Rabotnichesko delo* remained the nation's leading daily and continued as the mouthpiece for the Bulgarian Communist Party. The weakening of Communism in Eastern Europe and the Soviet Union led to the emergence of dissident Bulgarian groups protesting the lack of human rights and environmental issues. The Bulgarian government's forced assimilation of its Muslim Turkish minority, denying them their culture, religion, and language, met strong internal resistance and international criticism. Public demonstrations across Bulgaria in 1989 denouncing the Communist government led to the dismissal of Zhivkov and the holding of Bulgaria's first multiparty elections in 1990 since the 1930s. Elections led to the adoption of a new constitution.

The Constitution of Bulgaria was adopted July 12, 1991, creating Bulgaria as a republic and a parliamentary democracy. Its chief of state is a president elected by direct popular vote for five-year terms. The head of the government is the prime minister, who serves as the chairman of the Council of Ministers. The prime minister is nominated by the president and normally heads the largest voting block in the legislature. Since July 2001 Bulgaria's prime minister is its former King Simeon II, now Simeon Saxe-Coburg-Gotha. Bulgaria's legislature (*Narodno Sobranie*) is a unicameral legislature of 240 seats elected by popular vote every four years.

The Ministry of Transport and Communication, under the department of public administration, oversees Bulgarian communications. The Ministry follows public investment policy in communications, prepares projects for international treaties and agreements in communication, and organizes and guides the preparation of communication during crises, maintaining working communications nationwide for the armed forces and security forces. This Ministry designates representatives to international communications organizations, determines the communications budget, participates in the National Communications System, and controls the actions of authorized legal entities, which receive licenses, permits, and certificates from appropriate government personnel.

Article 34 guarantees the freedom and confidentiality of correspondence and all other communications as inviolable, except when the judicial authorities permit investigation to discover or prevent a crime. Article 38 states that no one shall be persecuted or restricted in his rights because of his views, nor shall be obligated or forced to provide information about his own or another person's views. Freedom of expression (Article 39) is guaranteed, entitling everyone to have an opinion and publicize it through words, written or oral, sound, or image, or in any other way. This right shall not be used to the detriment of the rights and reputation of others, or for the incitement of a forcible change of the constitutionally established order, the perpetration of a crime, or the incitement of enmity or violence against anyone. Article 40 governs the press and the media. The press and the mass information media are free and shall not be subjected to censorship. An injunction on or a confiscation of printed matter or another information medium shall be allowed only through an act of the judicial authorities in the case of an encroachment on public decency or incitement of a forcible change of the constitutionally established order, the perpetration of a crime, or the incitement of violence against anyone. An injunction suspension shall lose force if not followed by a confiscation 24 hours. Under Article 41 of the Constitution, the people of Bulgaria are entitled to seek, obtain, and disseminate information. This right shall not be exercised to the detriment of the rights and reputation of others, or to the detriment of national security, public order, public health, and morality. Citizens of Bulgaria are entitled to obtain information from state bodies and agencies on any matter of legitimate interest to them that is not a state or official secret and does not affect the rights of others.

In 1996 Bulgaria had 1,053 newspapers, 635 periodicals, and published 5,100 books. Forty-six newspapers are considered national newspapers with 1,464,000 readers (1995). The major dailies are all morning newspapers. They include: *24 Chasa, Chernomorski Far, Continent, Democraciya,* published by the Democratic Forces Union, the Socialist Party newspaper *Duma, Glass, Narodno Delo, Novini,* the business newspaper *Pari, Standart, Trud, Zemedelsko Zname,* printed by the Agrarian Union, and the Socialist Party *Zemya.* Additional daily newspapers published in Sofia are *Abv, Banker Daily, Chassa Daily, Daily Monitor, Democratsiya, Demokratsia Daily, Dneven Trud, Dnevnik Daily, Duma Daily, Ikonomiceski Zivot, Kkk, Kontinent Daily Newspaper, Mladezhko Zemedelsko, Monitor Daily, Novinar Daily, Pari Daily, Podkrepa, Politika/Bulgaria, Sofia News, Standart Daily, Troud Daily, Trud Daily, Vecerni*

Daily and Non-Daily Newspaper Titles and Circulation Figures

	1996	1997	1998	1999	2000
Number of Daily Newspapers	30	33	33	36	43
Circulation of Dailies (000)	1,328	1,267	1,112	1,350	1,400
Number of Non-Daily Newspapers	156	156	112	115	114
Circulation of Non-Dailies (000)	891	947	1,240	1,620	1,750

Source: World Association of Newspapers and Zenithmedia, *World Press Trends 2001*, pp. 8, 10, 17, 19.

Noviny, Vek 21, and *WAZ Bulgarian Newspaper.* Bulgaria's weekly newspapers are *Chassa Weekly, Kapital Weekly, Kultura Weekly, Media and Reklama Magazine, Media Sviat Magazine,* and *Sofia Echo.* Three major dailies are printed outside Sofia, *Chernomorski far* (Bourgas), *Demokraticesko zname* (Plovdiv), and *Narodno Delo Daily* (Varna).

Bulgaria's major general interest periodicals (with 1995 circulations in parentheses) are the weeklies *168 Chasa* (65,000), *Bulgarska Korona* (15,000), *Cash* (70,000), and the *Stolista* (15,000). Special interest periodicals are the business weeklies *Bulgarski Business* (25,000) and *Capital Press* (15,000). *Darzhaven Vestnik,* published by the National Assembly, has 30,000 readers. The Ministry of Culture publishes *Kultura* (8,000). *Lechitel* is a health magazine with 90,000 subscribers. A major women's magazine is *Nie Zhenite* (10,000). *Pogled,* published by the Journalists Union, has a circulation of 5,000. New periodical publications are *Paralleli Magazine,* published by the Bulgarian News Agency, *Capital Weekly, Century 21, Otechestvo, Sports Plus, Bulgarian Journalist, Debati, Geopolitical Weekly, Literaturen Forum, Radio & TV Center,* and *Reforma.*

ECONOMIC FRAMEWORK

The population of the Republic of Bulgaria is 83 percent Bulgarian, a Slavic ethnic group. The rest of Bulgaria's population is distributed among Turks (8.5 percent), Roma or Gypsy (2.6 percent), and Macedonian, Armenian, Tatar, Gagauz, and Circassian (5.9 percent). The Bulgarian Orthodox Church accounts for 83.5 percent of Bulgarian worshippers followed by Muslim (13 percent), Roman Catholic (1.5 percent), Uniate Catholic (0.2 percent), Jewish (0.8 percent), and the remaining 1 percent divided among Protestant, Gregorian-Armenian, and others.

Bulgaria is a former Communist country establishing a capitalist economy. A severe economic recession in the Balkans in 1996 and 1997 confronted Bulgaria with triple-digit inflation. The governments of Bulgaria since 1997 have stabilized the economy, promoted privatization of state-owned industries, and undertaken major administrative reorganization of the government bureaucracy. Bulgaria is aggressively seeking membership in the European Union and NATO. The labor force in Bulgaria is divided between agriculture (26 percent), industry (31 percent), and the service industry (43 percent). Bulgarian industry produces electricity, gas and water, food, beverages and tobacco, machinery and equipment, base metals, chemical products, coke, refined petroleum, and nuclear fuel. Major exports are clothing, footwear, iron and steel, machinery and equipment, and fuels. Bulgarian agriculture produces vegetables, fruits, tobacco, livestock, wine, wheat, barley, sunflowers, and sugar beets.

Bulgaria began major reforms within the government's bureaucracy, particularly its judicial system, which previously was subject to executive influence, corruption, and structural and staffing problems. A major breakthrough came in 1989 when Bulgaria's Turkish minority was emancipated and given equal rights with the rest of the Bulgarian people. A nationalistic wave threatening Bulgaria's internal peace was avoided when Bulgarian Turks were given the right to run for political office. The political party representing Bulgaria's Turks is part of a governing coalition with the National Movement for Simeon II.

By 1991 Bulgaria had eight national newspapers printing without restriction both national and international news stories. Tainted by decades of association with the Communist era, the newspaper *Rabotnichesko delo* changed its name to the *Duma,* adopted more moderate newspaper coverage, and changed the newspaper's format. The leading newspapers in 1991 were the *Duma, Demokratsiya* (an independent), *Trud* (a trade union daily), and *Zemia* (a rural daily). Popular weekly newspapers were *Pogled, Sturshel* (a publication featuring folk humor), and *168 Chasa,* which parodied the West's more sophisticated papers.

With the end of Communism the media became more critical of past regimes and demanded public inquiries. Major Bulgarian news stories were about the nation's Kozloduy Nuclear Power Plant, Chernobyl, and the 1978 murder of writer Georgi Markov. The new openness in Bulgaria extended to the government's decision to open its files to allow the media to investigate whether or not Bulgaria had a role in the 1981 attempted assassination of Pope John Paul II. The new press freedom did not eliminate government lawsuits against individual publications for alleged treasonous stories. A 1991 poll conducted by *168 Chasa* indicated that 46 percent of the Bulgarian people still believed that the government was trying to regulate and control the media. By 2001 and 2002 the respective Union of Democtratic Forces (UDF) parliamentary and presidential defeats were not based on opposition to government policies, but because privatization of state industry was moving too slowly, there was still considered widespread government corruption, and the economy had not rebounded. The Bulgarian press freely reported these stories with each major political party sponsoring a daily newspaper. The freedom to publish extended to Bulgaria's publishing houses.

Top Ten Daily Newspapers
(2000)

	Circulation
Trud	440,000
24 Hours	245,000
Sega	58,000
Nosten Trud	55,000
Standart	45,000
Monitor	35,000
Novinar	32,000
Duma	30,000
Demokratsia	28,000
Pari	14,000

Source: World Association of Newspapers and Zenithmedia, *World Press Trends 2001*, p. 59.

Bulgarian book publishers gained international attention in 2001 when Adolf Hitler's *Mein Kampf* was published, and the publication was widely advertised. Press clamor claimed that Bulgaria was anti-Semitic. The truth is closer to the Bulgarian people's desire to read publications long denied them during World War II and the Communist era. Bulgarian King Boris III died under mysterious circumstances after returning from a meeting with Hitler in 1943. Mein Kampf continues to be published in the West without incident. The vast array of book titles published each year in Bulgaria accurately represents a greater freedom to publish.

In 1996 King Simeon II returned to Bulgaria after a 50-year exile. At a Brookings Institute forum in Washington, D.C., in 2002 Prime Minister Simeon Saxe-Coburg-Gotha commented that he was surprised how little had changed in Bulgaria since his 1946 departure outside of industrialization. However, the prime minister noted that in the last five years, Bulgaria had dramatically changed. Prime Minister Saxe-Coburg-Gotha stressed that Bulgaria was always intellectually ''European'' even if separated by the wall of Communism from the rest of the continent. He preferred to have Bulgaria designated a part of southeastern Europe rather than the Balkans, because the latter term indicates a negative image of backwardness and instability, which Bulgaria is not.

Bulgaria's prime minister stressed the need for further judiciary reform. The Ministry of Justice is reviewing Bulgaria's laws and seeking authority to bring them into compliance with the Western democracies. When this is accomplished, Bulgaria's media will be legally protected to print and broadcast with less fear of legal recrimination from government officials. In 2002 Bulgaria's media are uncensored, foreign satellites broadcast programming in Bulgaria, and Western journalists have freedom of movement within the nation. More state industry needs to be privatized, which will affect employment. International bids are encouraged. The issue of pre-Communist era land ownership awaits a final resolution. The prime minister actively courts foreign investment.

The Bulgarian people have high expectations. The prime minister wants to see these expectations met, which was why he was on a tour of Europe and the United States to push for Bulgaria's membership in both the European Union and NATO. To reject Bulgarian membership in both organizations could have a devastating impact on the nation. Bulgaria needs a deadline and a commitment for dates of admittance. The prime minister stated that Bulgaria has already accomplished many changes to meet membership requirements, and even if all required changes are not complete, this should not keep Bulgaria from membership. Should membership be denied, Prime Minister Saxe-Coburg-Gotha feared that Bulgaria's relatively new democracy would be harmed, there would be tremendous public disappointment, and the nation could face a major destabilizing effect. However, Bulgaria's support for the United States against world terrorism and offers of assistance in Afghanistan reflect the new maturity of the Bulgarian nation. It is clear that Bulgaria is moving rapidly to adapt, modernize, and be a strong multiparty democracy.

PRESS LAWS & CENSORSHIP

In the decade after the fall of Communism, Bulgaria has moved more rapidly than other nations of southeastern Europe in becoming a Western style democracy. The 1991 Constitution guarantees basic press and speech freedoms. However, obstacles still confront the Bulgarian

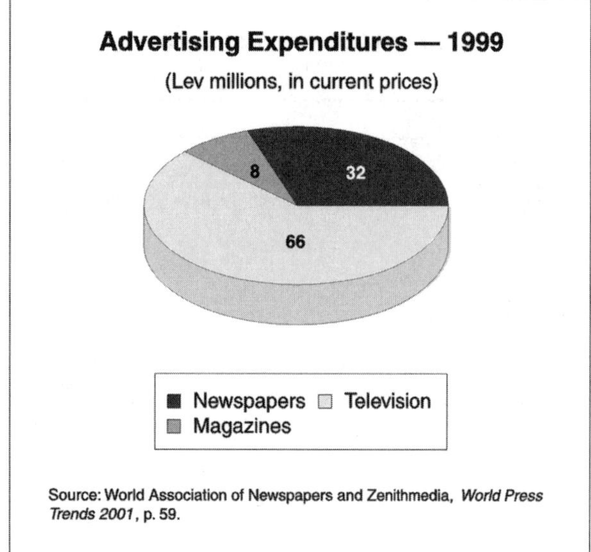

Source: World Association of Newspapers and Zenithmedia, *World Press Trends 2001*, p. 59.

government, preventing it from achieving full press freedom.

In January 2000 the Bulgarian Parliament changed the press law, which imposed prison sentences on journalists. Under the new law, public officials must bring libel charges against journalists instead of the government agency bringing legal suit. Government officials must pay their own legal bills and hire their own attorneys. The press law ended the imprisonment of journalists but increased the fines for journalists if found guilty. Bulgaria's president vetoed the measure. The president also vetoed the Electronic Media bill, approved by Parliament in October 1998, because the bill prohibited commercial advertising on television during prime time. Parliament overruled the president. The ban on commercial advertising was ended February 2000.

The Law on Radio and Television and the Law on Telecommunications both regulate Bulgaria's electronic media. The Law on Radio and Television is criticized because the oversight agency, the National Council on Radio and Television, which issues broadcast licenses and reviews possible violations of editorial policies, was not made an independent regulatory agency. The Telecommunications Law assigns broadcast frequencies and determines regulatory rules but is criticized because the complexity of the rules might deter broadcasters with limited resources from operation. A national debate continues on both laws because they fail to conform to European Union standards on the media.

In 2000 the European Union (EU) invited Bulgaria to participate in its Media II Program. The EU's strategy encourages Bulgaria to implement EU policies on economics, science, and culture. The Media II Program is designed to strengthen the audiovisual industry by providing support for the training of film industry personnel, develop audiovisual projects, and encourage transnational distribution of audiovisual projects. Bulgaria has achieved progress in the European Union's Media II Program by adopting a new broadcasting law and its ratification of the EU's Convention and Protocol on Transfrontier Television, but both measures await implementation by the government and Bulgarian media.

News Agencies

Bulgaria has three major news agencies, the Balkan Information Pool, the Bulgarian Telegraph Agency, and the Sofia Press Agency. Two recent additions are the Bulgarian News Agency and LEFF Information Agency. The Independent Journalists Union and the Journalists Union are Bulgaria's two major press associations.

Broadcast Media

Broadcasting in Bulgaria is regulated by the state-controlled Bulgarian National Radio and Bulgarian Television agency. There are four national and six regional radio programs. Bulgaria's major radio station is the government-owned Bulgarian Radio. Privately owned radio stations are *Daric,* Radio FM, and TNN. A radio service is broadcast for tourists from Varna. Bulgaria has two independent television stations, *Nova TV* (New Television) and *7 Dni* (Seven Days). The government-run Bulgarian-TV is considered the nation's leading television station. Bulgaria receives television transmissions from the French satellite channel TV5.

The National Council on Radio and Television (NCRT) regulates the broadcast industry and appoints the directors of Bulgaria's national radio and television systems. NCRT members are appointed on the recommendation of nongovernmental agencies. Parliament selects four from the list of potential appointees, and the president appoints three. The NCRT is criticized for being too influenced by government opinion in the selection of its members. On January 30, 2001, 200 Bulgarian journalists protested to the government that the NCRT was a politicized agency. The dispute stemmed from the NCRT's failure to approve radio directors in a nonpartisan manner.

Since 1991 Bulgaria has licensed 80 radio stations and 18 national and local television stations. There are over 200 local cable stations for both radio and television. Private radio stations are rated as having more professional employees, being financially solvent, and are alleged to number as many as 160 stations because all are not legally licensed. Bulgarian National Radio (BNR) is generally given high marks for its professionalism and generally rated better than Bulgaria's print media. BNR has two national stations, *Horizont* and *Christo Botev,* which provide local and regional programming, as well as foreign language broadcasts in Turkish, Greek, Serbo-Croat, French, and Italian. The BBC, *Deutsche Welle,* Radio Free Europe, and the Voice of America freely broadcast inside Bulgaria.

Private radio stations broadcasting in Bulgaria (with the broadcast site in parentheses) are Agency Balkan (Sofia), Alma Mater (Sofia), Alpha (Varna), Aura (Blagoevgrad), Berkk (Berkovitsa), Bravo FM (Varna), Classic FM (Sofia), Contact Radio (Sofia), Darik (Sofia), Express (Sofia), FM+ (Sofia), Glarus (Bourgas), Iujen Briag (Bourgas), RFI (Sofia), Tangra (Sofia), Valina (Blagoevgrad), and Vitosha (Sofia).

Television networks are fewer in number in Bulgaria because of the high start up costs and limited revenue from advertisers. The Bulgarian National Television (BNT) operates the country's two national television channels, Channel 1, which offers entertainment, westerns, and variety shows, and *Efir 2,* whose focus is the arts and documentaries. Media mogul Rupert Murdoch was granted the right to convert *Efir 2* into a private channel in 1999, leaving Bulgaria with only one government channel. A third television channel was approved for nationwide broadcasting using the frequency formally used by Russian television channel, ORT. The third station will only reach about 55 percent of Bulgarian people but is required to expand coverage gradually to the entire nation. Small television stations offer pirated programming. Cable television is limited by the inability of the people to afford the additional costs and a general lack of advertising revenue. Media frequently judged critical of the government were less likely to get needed advertising revenue during the decade of the nineties. Bulgarian public and private television stations, except for TRI V&X Ltd. in Blagoevgrad, are Sofia based and include 24 Chassa, 7 Dni, BTV, Bulgaria Cable, Bulgarian National Television, Bulgarian Television, Canal 3, MSAT TV, and Nova TV.

ELECTRONIC NEWS MEDIA

The Internet has achieved great popularity in Bulgaria with an estimated 150 Internet service providers. The Ministry of Telecommunications lost a 1999 case legally raised by the Internet Society of Bulgaria challenging the law licensing Internet service providers as a direct denial of the public's right to information.

An increasing number of Bulgarian media offer online services. State-run media with Internet services are the Bulgarian Telegraph Agency (www.bta.bg) with an English version (www.bta.bg/indexe.html), The Bulgarian National Television (www.bnt.bg), and Bulgarian National Radio (www.nationalradio.bg). Political parties with Internet service are the National Movement for Simeon II (www.novotovreme.bg) and the Union of Democratic Forces (www.eunet.bg/bgnews/democracy). Bulgarian television stations online are 7 Days Bulgarian Television Online and Bulgarian Internet Television (www.bgitv.com). Bulgarian radio stations with Internet connections are *Darrik Radio* (www.netissat.bg/), 107.9 FM (www.hit7.com), 97.6 FM (ww.radiovitosha.com), and Radio Free Europe/Radio Liberty (www.rferl.org). Important news services with Internet addresses are News Bulgaria (www.news.bg.com), Mediapool, which offers daily updates of Internet information and analysis about Bulgaria (www.mediapoolbg@mediapoolbg.com), Bulgaria OnLine (www.db.online.bg/bg/news.main), and NI (www.netinfo.bg).

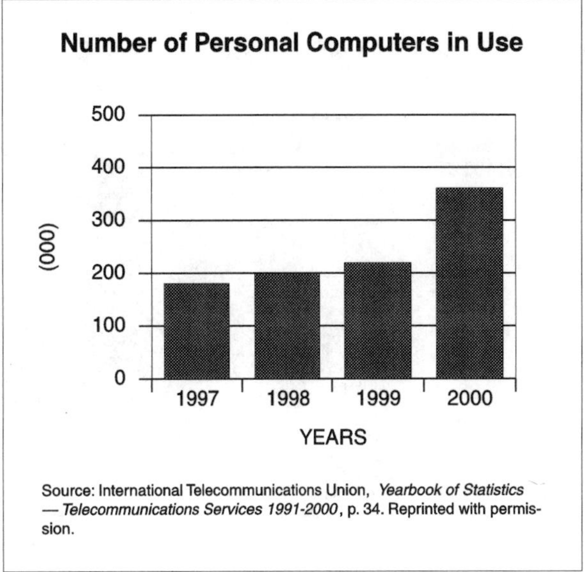

Source: International Telecommunications Union, *Yearbook of Statistics — Telecommunications Services 1991-2000*, p. 34. Reprinted with permission.

Specialized media offering Internet services are *Bulgarian Business News* (English version), *Bankers* (www.banker.bg), the English weekly *Capital* (www.capital.bg/old/weekly/index.html), and the *Daily Chronicle* (http://chronicle.capital.bg). Major economic publications online are the *Bulgarian Financial & Business News Daily,* English version (www.news.pari.bg/cgi-bin/pari-eng.home.cgi) and the *Bulgarian Economic Review,* a biweekly publication (www.pari.bg/doc/BER/berindex.htm).

Print media with online editions include Bulgaria's three largest publications, *Standart News* (www.standartnews.com), *Monitor* (www.zone168.com), and *Sega Daily* (www.segabg.com). Additional Bulgarian newspapers with Internet editions are the English language *The Sofia Independent, Duma, Trud, Sega Weekly, Novinar, Kultura, Bulgar Voice,* and *The Insider.* The *Bulgarian Press, Nedelnik Weekly, The Bulgarian-*

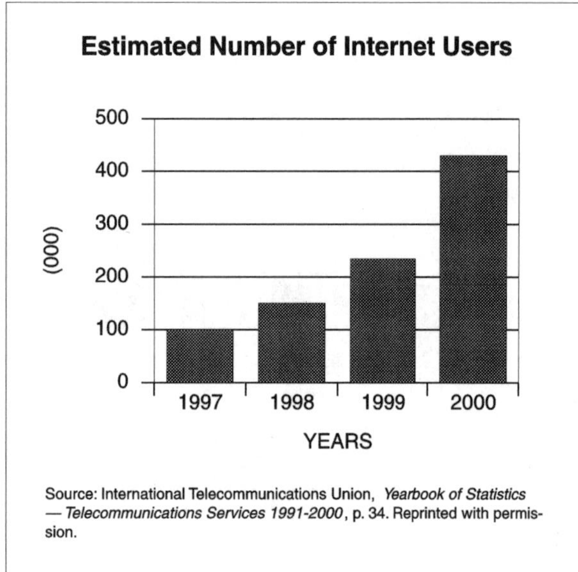

Source: International Telecommunications Union, *Yearbook of Statistics — Telecommunications Services 1991-2000*, p. 34. Reprinted with permission.

Macedonian National Education and Cultural Center, The BG-Reporter, and the *Bulgarian Room in the Balkan Info Home, The Sofia Echo, 7 Sport,* and *Mmatch* offer Internet editions. *Vox,* an online magazine for literature, was Bulgaria's first independent literary magazine. It was banned by the Communists, but emerged as an underground publication for political journalism and literature in 1989, first called *Samizdat* and later *Vox Glas.*News

EDUCATION & TRAINING

Sofia University St. Kliment Ohridski is Bulgaria's oldest university, founded in 1888 with three academic faculties: History and Philology, Physics and Mathematics, and Law. The school became a university in 1904 with the addition of degree granting programs in medicine, agriculture, forestry, theology, and economics. By 1938 Sofia University contained 9 colleges and 72 institutes and clinics. New higher education programs won government approval from 1947-52: the Higher Institute of Economics, the Medical Academy, the Veterinary-Medical Institute, the Academy of Agriculture, and the Bulgarian Academy of Science.

Sofia University is the major institution of higher learning in Bulgaria for a degree in the media, offering undergraduate and graduate programs in the Department of Journalism and Mass Communication. The department specializes in the fields of press and book publishing, communication and public relations, history and theory of journalism, and radio and television. The Department of Journalism and Mass Communication has a working relationship with several major Bulgarian newspapers, *Monitor, Capital, Kontinent, Pari Daily, Sega,* and *Standart.* Affiliation with European Union nations allows Bulgarian students in a variety of media fields to study outside Bulgaria at major universities in Western Europe and North America.

SUMMARY

Bulgaria has had few periods of complete independence. In the Middle Ages Bulgaria was twice briefly free before being absorbed by either the Byzantine or Ottoman Empires. In the nineteenth and twentieth centuries more powerful neighbors manipulated the future of the Bulgarian people, most notably the Turks and the Russians. Attempts to unite all Bulgars under one national flag failed because Bulgaria's neighbors, Greece and Yugoslavia, claimed the same lands. The desire for a Greater Bulgaria, led the nation to make the ultimately disastrous decisions to join both the Central Powers and the Axis in two world wars to achieve the union of all Bulgars.

Independent since 1879, Bulgaria was denied the right to unite all Bulgars under one national flag, and its governments were interfered with and destabilized by more powerful neighbors, particularly Russia under the czars and the Soviet Union under Communism. Throughout Bulgaria's history, human rights and press freedoms existed for only brief periods. Political instability led to political assassinations and coups. Constitutions were replaced and even though each one guaranteed press, speech, and expression rights, those rights were usually ignored, reduced, or suspended altogether. Within a decade of Communist dictator Todor Zhivkov's overthrow, Bulgaria has begun a remarkable transformation into becoming a modern democratic state. The paradox of a former king leading his nation as a prime minister out from under the shadows of decades of Communist rule has achieved great attention in Europe and the United States. Prime Minister Simeon Saxe-Coburg-Gotha is politically astute, cultured, and is completely dedicated to making Bulgaria a modern nation of the twenty-first century. The change in Bulgaria began in 1997 with the election of the Union of Democratic Forces. The momentum must be continued, and it will be if Bulgaria's progress is rewarded with membership into the European Union and NATO.

SIGNIFICANT DATES

- 1997: Union of Democratic Forces (UDF) win the presidency and control of Parliament from the Bulgarian Socialist Party, the nation's former Communist Party.
- 2001: Exiled King Simeon II wins parliamentary elections and becomes prime minister of a coalition government with the Turkish minority party
- 2002: Bulgarian Socialist Party leader and former Communist, Georgi Purvanov, is elected president.

BIBLIOGRAPHY

Assenova, Margarita. "New Freedoms, Old Problems." *The World and I,* 1 November 1999.

Constant, Stephen. *Foxy Ferdinand, Tsar of Bulgaria.* New York: Franklin Watts, 1980.

Constitution of the Republic of Bulgaria.

Curtis, Glenn E., ed. *Bulgaria, A Country Study.* Washington, DC: United States Government Printing Office, 1993.

Dimitroff, Pashanko. *King of Mercy.* London: Wexford & Barrow, 1986.

Embassy of Bulgaria. Available from http://www.bulgaria-embassy.org.

Glenny, Misha. *The Balkans, Nationalism, War and the Great Powers, 1804-1999.* New York: Viking, 1999.

Groueff, Stephane. *Crown of Thorns.* Lanham, MD: Madison Books, 1987.

International Journalists' Network. Available from http://www.ijnet.org.

Kaplan, Robert D. *Balkan Ghosts.* New York: St. Marti's Press, 1993.

Saxe-Coburg-Gotha, Prime Minister Simeon. Washington, DC: Brookings Institute, 24 April 2002.

Turner, Barry, ed. *Statesman's Yearbook 2002.* New York: Palgrave Press, 2001.

World Mass Media Handbook, 1995 Edition. New York: United Nations Department of Public Information, 1995.

Zhelev, Veselin. "Hitler's Autobiography Doing Well in Sofia." *AP Worldstream,* 11 December 2001.

—William A. Paquette

BURKINA FASO

BASIC DATA

Official Country Name:	Burkina Faso
Region (Map name):	Africa
Population:	11,946,065
Language(s):	French, native African languages
Literacy rate:	19.2%

Burkina Faso, a landlocked country in western Africa (formerly known as Upper Volta) received its independence from France in 1960. Turmoil in the 1970s and 1980s led to the name change and subsequently to the installation in 1987 of President Blaise Compaoré.

The country is prone to droughts and repeated population movements and has high poverty and low literacy levels. The official language is French, but the major languages are Moré, Dioula, and Fufuldé. Much of the population has only limited contact with the press.

Independent presses exist, but markets are nonspecific, and presses often distribute papers and leaflets that are passed from hand to hand and recopied. Media are also on-line, including TNB: *Tévision nationale du Burkina*; *Sidwaya* (Burkinabè daily newspaper); "news" pages from the Burkina government; *L'Opinion* (weekly magazine); *Afrinews Burkina*; *L'Observateur Paalga*; and *Le Journal du Jeudi* (Thursday newspaper, satirical weekly newspaper).

Under President Compaoré, press rules relaxed. However, the 1993 Information Code, says media outlets can be closed if charged with "endangering national security or distributing false news." CSI, the Supreme Council on Information, is charged with media oversight. Non-legal constraints also exist. Norbert Zongo, a journalist investigating the murder of David Ouedraogo, chauffeur of François Compaoré, brother of Blaise Compaoré, was assassinated. Four of the five presidential guards charged with chauffeur's death were later charged with Zongo's death. Reporters Sans Frontièrs, French press freedom advocates, were expelled for investigating Zongo's death. The "Norbert Zongo Festival pour la Liberté d'Expression et de Presse," partly a Zongo remembrance, was initially accepted by the government which later asked for festival cancellation.

Le Collectif, a coalition of human rights advocates and local independent journalists, was charged in December 1999 with "undermining state security" when it attempted to organize a demonstration calling for a final investigation of the murder of Zongo; charges were later dropped. Radio station Horizon FM aired a Le Collectif press release on April 14, 2000, requesting people attend a Zongo rally. Police shut the station down; it reopened late in May. Asked if the charges and closures resulted from Horizon's discussion of the president's family being involved in Zongo's assassination, Bakery Hubert Pare, CSI official said, "Democracy is fine, bur journalists have to know that the interests of the country come first. Journalism is not about insulting state officials."

International organizations see press freedoms in Burkino Faso as problematic. The 1999 listing of press freedom from Freedom House: Press Freedom Survey

1999 designated the Burkina Faso press as ''partly free.'' CAF/SCO, a Dutch foundation supporting independent media, added Burkina Faso to the list of countries in which journalists are at risk. The International Journalists' Network reported harassment of journalists. The Committee to Protect Journalists revealed restrictive methods in Burkina Faso in 2002. The World Audit awarded Burkino Faso 57 out of 100 for press freedom. (Lower numbers are preferred: for example, the US is 11/100 and United Kingdom is 16/100.) Reporters Sans Frontièrs lists Burkina Faso as not respecting freedom of the press.

BIBLIOGRAPHY

Africa Report. *The Press Is Free, but Will Burkinabè Buy It?* September-October 1991.

Burkina Faso: World Audit Democratic Profiles. 2001. Available from http:www.worldaudit.org/.

Central Intelligence Agency (CIA). *The World Factbook 2001*. 2002. Available from http://www.cia.gov.

Citizens for Public Justice. *CPJ Dangerous Assignments*. 3 April 2001. Available from http://www.cpj.org/.

Communication Assistance Foundation/Stichting Communicatie Ontwikkelingssamenwerking (CAF/SCO). 2000. Available from http://www.villamedia.nl/cafsco/us/.

Embassy of Burkina Faso. 2002. Available from http://burkinaembassy-usa.org/.

Freedom House. *Press Freedom Survey 2000*. 2000. Available from http://freedomhouse.org/.

Freedom House. *Freedom in the World: Burkina Faso*. 2001. Available http://www.freedomhouse.org/.

International Journalists' Network (IJN). *Repression of Freedom Continues This Year in Much of Africa*. 26 April 2001. Available from http://www.ijnet.org/.

International Media Issues. *French-speaking Nations Assailed on Press Restrictions*. 27 August 1999. Available from http://www.freedomforum.org/.

International Media Issues. *Watchdog Group Says Burkina Faso Journalist Likely Slain over Critical Reporting*. 6 January 1999. Available from http://www.freedomforum.org/.

L'Association de l'Institut d'Enterprise. *The Burkinabé Media Are On Line!*. 2002. Available from http://www.iie.cnam.fr/.

Tanau, Sarah. *Burkino Faso: Spotlight on Press Freedom*, ANB-BIA Supplement. 15 August 1999. Available from http://www.peacelink.it.

—Emily Dial-Driver

BURUNDI

BASIC DATA

Official Country Name:	Republic of Burundi
Region (Map name):	Africa
Population:	6,054,714
Language(s):	Kirundi, French, Swahili
Literacy rate:	35.3%

BACKGROUND & GENERAL CHARACTERISTICS

Burundi is a small parliamentary democracy in Central Africa, south of Rwanda, west of Tanzania, and east of the Democratic Republic of Congo (DRC). Lake Tanganyika forms Burundi's southwest border. The country's capital is Bujumbura. Over the past decade, Burundi's six million people have experienced some of the worst ethnic violence on the African continent. Since 1994 over 200,000 have been killed in ethnic conflict linked to the genocide that took place in neighboring Rwanda that year.

Burundi's two major ethnic groups are the Hutus (majority) and the Tutsis (minority). The imbalance of power among ethnic groups instigated through the manipulations of European imperialists in the nineteenth and early twentieth centuries underlies the violence that continues to beset the region. The major language groups in Burundi are Kirundi and French, both of them official languages, and Swahili. Most Burundians are Christian (principally, Roman Catholic) or practice indigenous religions.

In 1993 Melchior Ndadaye, a political leader of Burundi's Hutus, who previously had been excluded from power, was elected president in Burundi's first democratic elections following independence from Belgium in the early 1960s. With Burundi's newly elected parliament, the National Assembly, led by the Hutu Front for Democracy in Burundi (Frodebu) party, Ndadaye became Burundi's first Hutu head of state in a country whose politics long had been dominated by Tutsis. However, a few months after his election, Ndadaye was assassinated, sparking renewed ethnic violence in Burundi that evolved into nearly a decade of civil war. Early in 1994 Burundi's Hutu-dominated parliament elected Cyprien Ntaryamira, another Hutu, as president. Unfortunately, President Ntaryamira's tenure as Burundi's head of state was very short, as he was killed—along with Rwanda's president—in a suspicious helicopter crash in April 1994, an event that sent neighboring Rwanda into a genocidal civil war of its own.

In October 1994 another Hutu was appointed president of Burundi, Sylvestre Ntibantunganya, following talks between the key parties in parliament. Just a few months later, however, the Union for National Progress (Uprona) party, a largely Tutsi party, already was withdrawing from the government and the parliament, and further ethnic violence erupted. Pierre Buyoya, a Tutsi, seized power in July 1996 and has remained president as of 2002. Buyoya first took power in Burundi in 1987 by overthrowing another Tutsi leader, but stepped down from the presidency in 1993 when Melchior Ndadaye was elected president.

In November 2001 a new power-sharing agreement was signed by President Buyoya, 17 political parties (10 Tutsi based, seven Hutu based), and the National Assembly in order to inaugurate a transitional government. However, the principal rebel groups refused to acknowledge or abide by this accord, and the fighting between rebel groups and government forces continued.

While the death toll in Rwanda exceeded that in Burundi many times over, the loss of life and levels of brutality and human suffering over the past decade in the two countries, as well as in neighboring DRC and in nearby Uganda and the Sudan, has been enormous. Ethnic violence continued in Burundi in early August 2002, and ongoing peace efforts had not yet produced a peace accord simultaneously agreeable to Buyoya's Tutsi-led government and the two main Hutu rebel groups: the Forces for the Defense of Democracy (FDD) and the National Liberation Forces (FNL).

Although peace talks to settle the conflicts plaguing Burundi have been frequent and mediated by such notable figures as former South African President Nelson Mandela and former Tanzanian President Julius Nyerere, no firm solution to problems of power sharing, continuing ethnic violence, and refugee return had yet been found by early August 2002, when new peace talks were slated to begin in Tanzania. As of mid-2002, some 600,000 to 800,000 Hutu civilians—about 12 percent of Burundi's population—were housed in ''regroupment camps'' in Burundi. The Tutsi-led government portrayed these persons as being held in the camps for their own protection against potential further ethnic violence by Tutsis seeking vengeance for earlier massacres of Tutsis at the hands of Hutu extremists—and also to prevent any Hutu rebels likely to attack Tutsis from hiding among other Hutus. Sadly, many of the internally displaced Hutus in Burundi were starving and/or dying of disease in the camps. The Tutsis who were forced from their homes in 1993 at the start of Burundi's civil war also have suffered greatly. They, too, remain housed in camps, unable as of mid-2002 to return to their homes. They are also dangerously vulnerable to diseases and to attacks from Hutu rebels, much as the Hutus in the regroupment camps are susceptible to attacks from the Tutsi-dominated government army. Another 400,000 Burundian refugees were said to be living in neighboring countries, according to an October 2001 report by the Committee for Refugees cited by the Committee to Protect Journalists. Many Burundian refugees, including members of one of the anti-government rebel factions still fighting the Burundian government, were housed in camps in Tanzania in mid-2002.

The media are strongly influenced if not outright controlled by the government. As the BBC Monitoring service notes, ''The government runs the main radio station as well as the only newspaper that publishes regularly.'' The principal newspaper in the country is *Le Renouveau,* the government-owned paper. *L'Avenir* is another newspaper favorable to the government, as is *La Nation,* a private, pro-government paper. The Tutsi-based National Recovery Party publishes the private newspaper, *La Vérité.* The Catholic Church publishes its own newspaper, *Ndongozi.* The Hutu-backed Frodebu party published *La Lumière,* the only opposition paper in the country until it, too, ceased publication in March 2001 after its publisher, Pancrace Cimpaye, left the country to go into exile. Cimpaye had begun receiving anonymous death threats after publishing lists of government military officers—most of them, Tutsis from Bururi province—identifying their home provinces and the shares they owned in parastatal companies.

Despite the challenges posed to the private media, independent forces are skillfully addressing problems inherent in the national reconstruction of an interethnic community and fostering peace and reconciliation. Studio Ijambo, based in Bujumbura, is part of one very successful effort at creating new types of programming to counteract the kind of ''hate radio'' promulgated in the early 1990s that contributed heavily to the genocide in Rwanda that overflowed into Burundi. Working in partnership with a Tanzanian radio station, Radio Kwizera, in mid-2002, Studio Ijambo aimed to build tolerance and understanding between Tutsis and Hutus by creating news and educational programs in Kirundi and French for broadcast on state and private radio stations in Burundi, over the Internet via www.studioijambo.org, and on a community radio station in the eastern part of the Democratic Republic of Congo. Outlining the goals of this positive initiative, the directors of Studio Ijambo and Radio Kwizera noted, ''As the facilitated repatriation continues, there is a critical need for accurate, balanced and objective information on both sides of the Burundi border. The

Studio Ijambo—Radio Kwizera collaboration aims to rise to this challenge, using the power of radio to reunite Burundian refugees with their compatriots in Burundi.''

ECONOMIC FRAMEWORK

Burundi is heavily dependent on agribusiness for its economy. Much of the economy is based on coffee, and tea, sugar, cotton, and hides are the other principal exports. Per capita annual income is only about US $110—one of the lowest incomes in the world.

The private press is significantly challenged by government attempts to control information viewed as potentially able to destabilize the country or to critique government policy or actions.

PRESS LAWS

The Transitional Constitution Act does not limit press freedom. However, the government does limit freedom of speech and of the press. Additionally, according to a press law, a government censor must review newspaper articles four days before publication. ''Newspapers are sometimes forced to close, then reappear again,'' according to BBC Monitoring.

Although Burundian law does not require owners of private news agencies to complete a registration of copyright, the director of Netpress, a privately owned news agency in the country, was arrested and charged in June 1999 with neglecting to complete such a registration. The editor of Netpress was arrested and detained for one week in December 2001 by government authorities, who also stopped Netpress from issuing news briefings during that same period. Eventually the charges against the editor were dropped, but only after his family paid a fine without his knowledge or consent.

CENSORSHIP

Journalists carefully practice self-censorship, but some room for the expression of a range of political views in the media does exist. The government also actively censors the media, harassing and detaining journalists at times and searching and seizing their property, such as cameras. This pertains especially to attempts by journalists to provide balanced coverage of the ongoing civil war.

STATE-PRESS RELATIONS

Government-press relations are usually strained, if not outright conflictual, in Burundi except for media owned and operated by the government itself. The country's only newspaper able to publish without interruption is the government-owned paper, *Le Renouveau,* issued three times a week.

However, in April 2001 the government saw the benefits of having active, private radio stations when hardline Tutsi soldiers naming themselves the Patriotic Youth Front overran the government's own station, Radio Burundi. The rebels had overtaken the government radio and begun announcing that Buyoya had been overthrown. The private media essentially came to the country's assistance by enabling government officials to use private radio stations to broadcast messages designed to reassure Burundians that a coup in fact had not occurred and to coordinate troop movements to stop the attempted coup. As the Committee to Protect Journalists observes, ''The implications of the independent media's role in crushing the coup were not lost on Burundians, as President Buyoya praised private stations for offering a counterbalance to extremist opinions in the country.''

Just one month earlier, however, according to the U.S. Department of State, Burundi's Minister of Communications in March 2001 ''threatened to prosecute journalists and shut down news organizations that the Government believed were 'disseminating false information, divulging defense secrets, promoting the enemy, or promoting panic.'''

In October 2001 government gendarmes arrested and beat a journalist, Alexis Sinduhije, who worked as a reporter for Radio Publique Africaine (RPA), a new private station employing both Hutu and Tutsi staff and advocating ethnic reconciliation. Sinduhije had met with visiting foreign military officers from South Africa, brought to Burundi secretly by the Burundian government in an attempt to address internal security problems associated with the repatriation of Hutus into the country. Sinduhije was fined and released the next day.

ATTITUDE TOWARD FOREIGN MEDIA

The government tolerates broadcasting from foreign-backed and foreign media such as RPA, the BBC, the Voice of America, and Radio France Internationale. Burundians have been permitted to work as local reporters for these stations.

NEWS AGENCIES

The government-controlled news agency is Agence Burundaise de Presse (ABP). The private news agency, Netpress, which operates in French and in English, has been sorely challenged by repressive government action, as already noted above. Another privately owned news agency, Azania, operates in French. Netpress and Azania have produced almost-daily newssheet faxes, projecting the political views of mainly Tutsi-based parties. Other electronic news agencies, such as *Le Témoin,* also are active in the country.

BROADCAST MEDIA

Because of the high levels of illiteracy and poverty in Burundi, radio is the most popular forum for the exchange of public views via the media. Few private broadcasting services exist in Burundi. The government runs the principal radio station, Radio Burundi, which broadcasts in several languages: Kirundi, Swahili, French, and English. Beginning in 1996 Radio Umwizero (''Hope'') began broadcasting as a private station, funded by the European Union, with the aim of fostering peace and reconciliation in the country. That station later became Radio Bonesha, which met with difficulty in March 2001 when one of its journalists, Gabriel Nikundana, and its editor-in-chief, Abbas Mbazumutima, were arrested and fined after the station broadcast an interview with an FNL spokesman. Radio Public Africa, mentioned above, another independent station, began broadcasting in May 2001 in French, Kirundi, and Swahili.

Electronic News Media

Various Internet sites make news and perspectives on the reconciliation and peacebuilding process available to Burundians within and outside of Burundi. One example, already noted above, is Studio Ijambo, at http://www.studioijambo.org. Another is In-Burundi Diffusion and Communication, at http://www.in-burundi.net.

Summary

After nearly nine years of civil war, much of the Burundian population appears to be welcoming the return to a more stable political situation, although ongoing ethnic violence between the two main rebel, Hutu-based groups and the Tutsi-led government was still ongoing in mid-2002, even as close as a few miles from the capital, Bujumbura. While some doubted the long-term success of efforts to create a final peace accord and to keep the transitional government installed in November 2001 for the entire three-year period during which it was intended to serve, others appeared hopeful that a new climate of peacebuilding and reconciliation was possible.

The contributions of the private media have been no small part of this changing mood in the country, where any serious effort to secure lasting peace will necessarily have to involve people of all ethnic groups living in the country. By offering opportunities for Hutus and Tutsis to work together developing programming and broadcasting educational and news programs together aimed at fostering more positive outcomes for Burundi as a whole, media outlets such as Studio Ijambo and Radio Publique Africaine appeared poised in 2002 to make significant contributions to the future of the country.

The potential of Burundi's media, especially radio, either to foment war or to contribute to the establishing the conditions for peace was readily apparent to most Burundians, both within and outside the country. Along with the peace talks scheduled to take place in August 2002, the flourishing of private media oriented toward greater accuracy and more tolerance in reporting and interpreting events seemed to bode well for the prospect of transforming Burundi into a country where the political opposition could co-exist with the ruling party and all would have room for the free expression of their ideas.

Significant Dates

- July 1996: Pierre Buyoya seizes power and becomes president of Burundi.
- March 2001: La Lumière, the only political opposition newspaper in the country published on a regular basis, ceases publication when its publisher, Pancrace Cimpaye, flees the country after receiving death threats.
- March 2001: Editor-in-chief and journalist of Radio Bonesha, a private radio station, are arrested and fined after broadcasting an interview with a rebel spokesman.
- April 18, 2001: Calling themselves the ''Patriotic Youth Front,'' 30 hard-line Tutsi soldiers take over Radio Burundi, the government radio station, and announce Buyoya's overthrow, but are soon counteracted by government troops and broadcasters temporarily using private radio stations to assure Burundians that a coup in fact has not occurred and to coordinate government troops.
- November 2001: Transitional government installed, involving power-sharing among President Buyoya, 17 political parties (both Hutu and Tutsi), and members of the National Assembly (parliament), but without the support of the two main rebel groups, who continue their fight against the government.
- December 2001: Netpress, a private news agency, temporarily halts operations when its editor is arrested and fined by the government.
- August 2002: New peace talks scheduled, with rebel groups failing to fully participate.

Bibliography

Amnesty International. ''Burundi.'' *Amnesty International Report 2002.* London: Amnesty International, May 28, 2002. Available at http://web.amnesty.org/web/ar2002.nsf/afr/burundi!Open.

BBC Monitoring. ''Country profile: Burundi.'' Reading, UK: British Broadcasting Corporation, March 7, 2002. Available at http://news.bbc.co.uk/1/hi/world/africa/country_profiles/1068873.stm.

BBC News. ''Truce call ahead of Burundi talks.'' August 5, 2002. Available at http://news.bbc.co.uk/1/hi/world/africa/2173091.stm.

Bureau of Democracy, Human Rights, and Labor, U.S. Department of State. ''Burundi.'' *Country Reports on Human Rights Practices 2001.* Washington, DC: Bureau of Public Affairs, U.S. Department of State, March 4, 2002. Available at http://www.state.gov/g/drl/rls/hrrpt/2001/af/8280.htm.

Committee to Protect Journalists. ''Burundi.'' Attacks on the Press in 2001: Africa 2001. New York, NY: CPJ, 2002. Available at http://www.cpj.org/attacks01/africa01/burundi.html.

In-Burundi Diffusion & Communication. ''*Communiqué* [Press Release]: Studio Ijambo.'' June 13, 2002. Available at http://www.in-burundi.net/Contenus/Rubriques/Lejournal/06_13ijambo.htm.

newafrica.com. ''Thousands flee Burundi capital as rebels attack military positions.'' June 5, 2002. Available at http://www.newafrica.com/news/.

Reporters without Borders. ''Burundi.'' *Africa annual report 2002.* Paris, France: Reporters sans frontiers, April 20, 2002. Available at http://www.rsf.org/article.php3?id_article=1724.

—Barbara A. Lakeberg-Dridi, Ph.D.

Cambodia

Basic Data

Official Country Name:	Kingdom of Cambodia
Region (Map name):	Southeast Asia
Population:	12,212,306
Language(s):	Khmer, French, English
Literacy rate:	35%

War and political strife have stifled modern Cambodia's media. The Cambodian government controls both the print and electronic press. Officials often intimidate, fine, or imprison journalists who stray from accepted media policies, particularly concerning human rights issues. Reporting is often hazardous, especially during volatile elections. Because the Khmer Rouge purged journalists, training programs teach media skills to inexperienced reporters. The Khmer Journalists Association encourages Cambodian journalists to act professionally; however, underpaid journalists sometimes resort to extortion to supplement their incomes.

Most media is centered in Khmer. More Cambodians acquire information from radio than from any other media. There are an estimated one million radios in Cambodia. Broadcasts are accessible in all provinces, and people who do not own radios can hear broadcasts on market loudspeakers. The Khmer Rouge seized control of Phnom Penh's radio station in 1975 to broadcast propaganda. After Vietnamese forces defeated the Khmer Rouge and temporarily occupied Cambodia, radio services were gradually restored. The Kampuchean Radio and Television Commission was established in 1983. The Voice of the Kampuchean People (VOKP), later called Voice of Cambodia, was on the air by the late 1980s. Rebel Khmer Rouge forces continued to broadcast from remote locations. The Cambodia Radio Journalists' Training Project, aiming to improve Cambodia's 13 radio stations, was initiated in 1999.

There are only 100,000 televisions in Cambodia, and more urban dwellers than rural have access to television media. Skeptical Cambodians were convinced that Khmer Rouge dictator Pol Pot had died when his corpse was broadcast on television. In March 1986, Television Kampuchea (TVK) first broadcast in Phnom Penh. By the twenty-first century, six television stations broadcast various programming.

Phnom Penh is the nucleus of print journalism. The largest daily Khmer-language newspaper, *Rasmei Kampuchea*, has a circulation of 15,000. When United Nations peacekeepers encouraged democracy, more English-language newspapers began to be printed. The biweekly, independent *Phnom Penh Post* (http://www.phnompenhpost.com/) started in 1992. Newspapers *Phnom Penh Daily* (http://www.phnompenhdaily.com/), *Cambodia Daily*, *Cambodia Times* (which ceased publication in 1997), and magazines *Bayon Pearnik* and *Indradevi* feature contrasting views. Journalists have successfully countered government efforts to make Cambodia's press laws more restrictive. Several Internet sites also post Cambodian news.

Bibliography

Mehta, Harish C. *Cambodia Silenced: The Press Under Six Regimes*. Introduction and photgraphs by Tim Page. Bangkok: White Lotus Company Ltd., 1997.

Ross, Russell R., ed. *Cambodia: A Country Study*. 3rd ed. Washington, D.C.: Federal Research Division Library of Congress, 1990.

Schanberg, Sydney H. *The Death and Life of Dith Pran*. New York: Viking, 1985.

—Elizabeth D. Schafer

CAMEROON

BASIC DATA

Official Country Name:	Republic of Cameroon
Region (Map name):	Africa
Population:	15,421,937
Language(s):	African language groups, English, French
Literacy rate:	63.4%

BACKGROUND & GENERAL CHARACTERISTICS

Officially independent since January 1, 1960, the Republic of Cameroon was constituted from the merging of the former French and British Cameroons in 1961. It borders Nigeria, Equatorial Guinea, Chad, the Central African Republic, the Republic of Congo, and Gabon. With 402 km of coastline and 4,591 km of borders, Cameroon's area is about 475,440 square kilometers. Its capital is Yaounde. The climate varies from tropical to semiarid. With a 2001 estimated population of 15,803,220 growing at the rate of 2.41 percent, Cameroon had an estimated literacy rate of 63.4 percent in 1995.

The Press The national press developed considerably in the 1990s, and at the beginning of the twenty-first century there were several daily newspapers, including *Mutations* and *Ciel d'Afrique* (African Sky), born in 2000. *Africa New Destiny* is a daily international general information magazine. Published from Monday to Friday, the bilingual *Cameroon Tribune* was started in January 2000. In two years it went from 7,000 to 25,000 copies and from 25 to 32 pages.

The main weeklies are *Le Patriote* (The Patriot) and *Le Messager* (The Messenger), which started in 1979. Other weeklies include *L'analyste* (The Analyst), *Le Temps* (The Times), *Le Triomphe* (The Triumph), *Voix d'Afrique* (African Voices), *Les Nouvelles d'Afrique* (African News), the French-English Catholic publication *L'effort Camerounais*, centered in Douala, and *L'informe* (The Informer). Bi-weeklies include *L'aurore* (The Dawn) and *Dikalo*. Tri-weeklies include *La Détente* (Relaxation), *Le Jeune Detective* (The Young Detective), and *La Nouvelle Expression* (The New Expression), published since 1992. There is also the *Herald*, published in English.

There are several monthly publications such as *Mensuel Panafricain d'Analyses Politiques* (The Political Analytical Panafrican Monthly), *L'anecdote* (The Anecdote), the *Dschang News*, dedicated to the Dschang urban community, and *Mefoe Ya Nlam*, which distributes information in French to the Southern province. Other topical publications include *Patrimoine* (Patrimony), about culture and debates, and *La Plume sur le Rocher* (The Feather on the Rock), a Catholic publication.

In 2002, *Le Francophone*, a bimonthly, was started by l'Alliance Panafricaine pour Promotion de la Francophonie. (The Panafrican Alliance for French Language Promotion). Two other bimonthlies are *Le Gri-gri International* (The International Amulet), a panafrican satirical publication, and *Le Serment* (The Oath).

Outside publications that are read in Cameroon include *Le rendez-vous de l'Afrique* (African Rendez-Vous), *Toute l'actualité de l'Afrique* (Current African Events) and *Governance Alert on Cameroon Human Rights*. There is also a French quarterly *Impact Tribune*. Other important publications include *Polemedia*, *Le Journal de l'Agence Intergouvernementale de la Francophonie*, *L'écluse* (The Lock) and *L'action* (Action).

NEWS AGENCIES

Cameroonian news agencies in 2002 included the YFIA Francophone News Agency, the Agence de Presse, and the IEPF (L'Institut de l'Energie Périodique Francophone). Also active were AJIC (l'Association des Journalistes Indépendants du Cameroun), and the CJSC (Club des Journalistes Solidaires du Cameroun), founded in 2000. Every year on May third, Cameroonians celebrate World Press Freedom Day in an effort led by UNESCO to promote freedom and independence of the press.

BROADCAST MEDIA

In 1998, there were eleven AM radio stations, eight FM stations, three short wave radio stations and one television station. Four years later, under Cameroon Radio Television alone there are ten regional radio stations and one national, three FM urban commercial channels, and one television station with thirty-two diffusion centers. There are also some international stations such as Radio Africa No. 1, Afro Caribbean Music, and Radio France Internationale. In 1997, there were 2.27 million radio sets and 450,000 TV sets in Cameroon.

ELECTRONIC NEWS MEDIA

In 2000, there was only one Internet provider and 20,000 users. However, as of 2002 there were 11 cyberpapers and many magazines online. Some of these include *Le Patriote*, *Afrik'Netpress*, a bilingual daily, *La Nouvelle Expression*, for investigation and analysis, *Tam Tam*, and *The Cameroon Tribune* a French-English paper. *Sujet Tabou* (Taboo Subject), an evangelistic journal, and *L'action*, a democratic site on politics, economics and sports give topical information. The Internet is growing in popularity as a source of international media. International sites such as the BBC, L'équipe.fr, CNN, and *Le Monde* have the largest Cameroonian readership.

BIBLIOGRAPHY

The Central Intelligence Agency (CIA). *World Factbook 2001*. Directorate of Intelligence, 2002. Available from www.cia.gov/.

Cameroon Info.Net News. Available from www.cameroon-info.net/.

Ciel d'Afrique. Available from www.cieldafrique.fr.st/.

—*Danielle Raquidel*

Number of Satellite Subscribers:	968,000
Satellite Subscribers per 1,000:	30.6
Number of Radio Stations:	594
Number of Radio Receivers:	32,300,000
Radio Receivers per 1,000:	1,022.4
Number of Individuals with Computers:	12,000,000
Computers per 1,000:	379.8
Number of Individuals with Internet Access:	12,700,000
Internet Access per 1,000:	402.0

CANADA

BASIC DATA

Official Country Name:	Canada
Region (Map name):	North & Central America
Population:	31,592,805
Language(s):	English, French
Literacy rate:	97.0%
Area:	9,976,140 sq km
GDP:	687,882 (US$ millions)
Number of Daily Newspapers:	104
Total Circulation:	5,167,000
Circulation per 1,000:	206
Total Newspaper Ad Receipts:	2,995 (Canadian $ millions)
As % of All Ad Expenditures:	38.70
Number of Television Stations:	80
Number of Television Sets:	21,500,000
Television Sets per 1,000:	680.5
Number of Cable Subscribers:	7,989,520
Cable Subscribers per 1,000:	259.4

BACKGROUND & GENERAL CHARACTERISTICS

Canada is a very large country, at least in terms of landmass. It extends over nine million square kilometers. The largest single administrative entity is Nunavut, an Arctic territory that constitutes 21 percent of the nation's landmass while having its smallest population, 28,200. In contrast, Canada's largest central provinces of Ontario and Québec have a combined population of 19,281,900. These two provinces are the nation's largest media market, and constitute 26.2 percent of the country's landmass. Canada borders on three oceans: the Atlantic, the Pacific and the Arctic. Its most immediate neighbor is the United States, which it touches on two borders, one to its south and the other to the north. Nine out of 10 Canadians live within ninety miles of the United States. In terms of density, in the majority of the country there is less than one person per 49 square kilometers of land space. Sharing to a significant degree a common heritage and a common language with the United States, issues focusing on national cultural survival dominate much of the political debate in Canada. Media issues and press policies are critical players in this debate. The arguments have become more acute since Canada joined the United States in a free trade agreement in 1984 and agreed to extend the arrangement to include Mexico in 1988.

Europeans came to what is now Canada in the early 16th century as agricultural and industrial revolutions on the continent left hundreds of thousands of displaced persons searching for new lives and new endeavors. In 1534 the French master pilot Jacques Cartier left the port of Le Havre in command of two ships and 61 sailors, anxious to inquire about economic and settlement prospects in a new and unfamiliar world which had been seen some 40 years previously by explorer John Cabot. Cabot's discoveries led to the establishment of the Newfoundland and Atlantic fisheries, but anything beyond sporadic settlement had yet to take place. Cartier was determined to explore all opportunities, so he sailed beyond where the Atlantic fishery was located, having become a mainstay in the economic life of continental Europe. That year, Cartier explored the many islands, bays, and inlets which dotted the shoreline of the Gulf of St. Lawrence, but he would have to wait until his second voyage to the New World in 1535 before sailing down the river which drained into the Gulf.

Cartier hoped to find a civilization that could trade with or perhaps rival that of Europe. What he discovered instead were two very poor native settlements, one on the current site of the city of Montréal and the other at the contemporary city of Québec. He came to the conclusion that this was a land for the taking and between 1541 and 1543 worked diligently to encourage settlements in the frontier. The hostile climate and lack of interest would prove to be fatal for Cartier. It would remain for others to complete the work that Cartier had begun.

The Atlantic fishery moved closer to shore when drying part of the catch became a necessity for preservation, and contact with the native communities along the St. Lawrence shores became more frequent. The aboriginal settlements possessed furs, a commodity valued by the Europeans. Realizing the value of fur in the European market place, many fishers gave up the ocean to explore the economic potential of the vast beaver population. Canada had launched its first and most important economic enterprise, one that would last well into the early years of the 19th century. As the Canadian economic historian Harold Innis noted in his study of the fur trade, the wholesale exploitation of raw products, which began with the beaver, set Canada on an economic path which focused on the extraction of the raw materials that Innis referred to as staples. With the fur trade came an increased need for settlements and established economic ties to Europe. Trapping required alliances with the native populations who, like the French, prospered until overkill forced the trade westward to the rivers of the great plains provinces of contemporary Manitoba, Saskatchewan and Alberta, eventually reaching the North West Territories, where the cost put the price of furs beyond the reach of traditional consumers in Europe.

Despite France's loss of Canada to Britain in 1759, the presence of the French in Canada has had a lasting impact. French remains the official language in the province of Québec and enjoys significant legal and practical status in New Brunswick, Ontario, Manitoba and parts of Western Canada. It has equal status with English in all federal jurisdictions such as Parliament and the judiciary system. Québec still retains the core aspects of the Napoleonic civil code. The linguistic arrangement that was forged between the British and the French following the conquest of 1759 remains reflected in the media in contemporary times.

There is no evidence to suggest that the French colonies at Québec had any interest in journalism or the press. In fact, there is no evidence to suggest that printing existed in the colony prior to the British conquest in 1759 although there is some suggestion in historical texts that religious tracts were published for the literate minority. The majority of colonists were farmers and skilled crafts people who labored under a form of continentally inspired feudalism that faded with the British invasion. The lack of journalistic development in the French colonies put Canada nearly a century behind the soon to be independent United States in the link between the press, government, democracy and an educated citizenry.

The emergence of journalistic practice took place in the British possessions before the conquest of Québec and the successful rebellion of the thirteen colonies. The first newspaper of record was Benjamin Harris' *Publick Occurrences Both Foreign and Domestick* which appeared in Boston after Harris left a British debtors prison and immigrated to America. Harris, a well-known agitator, incurred the wrath of the colonial authorities and his newspaper did not survive beyond one issue. In 1735, a civil jury dismissed a charge of criminal libel against Peter Zenger, a German immigrant who had founded and published the *New York Weekly Journal.* Zenger was brought to court for an inflammatory article he had written about the Governor of New York. With the dismissal of the case, the concept of free speech, democracy, and a free press became incorporated in the political culture of western society. The simple equation that a democracy cannot exist or function properly without a free press was born out of the Zenger decision. The case would not mark the end of attempts by both business and industrial elite to control the distribution and content of the daily press, a problem which continues to exist on both sides of the border today.

Journalism came to what was to become Canada just a few years before Britain lost her thirteen colonies to the new republic of the United States. A Bostonian, Bartholomew Green, moved up the coast to Nova Scotia where he opened a printing concern and announced that he would soon begin publishing a newspaper. Green died before he could launch his new journal, but his work was soon assumed by an old Boston compatriot, John Bushell, who published the first edition of the *Halifax Gazette* in 1752. As Canadian historian Douglas Fetherling has noted, Canadian journalism was born with the launch of this newspaper.

Printing and newspaper publication got a boost after 1776 when Loyalist printers flooded Canada. Twenty newspapers were founded by the end of the War of 1812 with a combined circulation of 2,000 copies. Of these, five were published in what is now Québec, one in what is now Ontario and the remainder in the Atlantic provinces and other territories. Douglas Fetherling notes that these papers were primarily ''journals of ecumenical rationalism, full of scientific and literary materials picked up from foreign publications and used to fill the columns between the official proclamations and what in some cases amounted to plentiful advertising, much of it related to land sales, shipping schedules and the like.''

By 1836, mechanical printing presses were being manufactured in Upper Canada. There were now 50 newspapers operating in Ontario and Québec with Ontario leading the way with 60 percent of the journals located in that colony. Journalism was becoming seriously involved in the political life of the citizenry. The population had split between Tories, rooted mainly in the Loyalist communities who had come to Canada to preserve their monarchial connections and Reformers unwilling to separate church and state. The colony's newly founded newspapers found themselves dividing along political lines.

William Lyon Mackenzie changed the course of Canadian journalism, specifically its relationship to the ruling classes. Mackenzie was a political and economic liberal who had great difficulty abiding the colonial government, which he labeled ''The Family Compact.'' Very few of the ruling elite could claim blood ties to the British monarchy, Mackenzie claimed that they behaved as royalty, and thus the name. Mackenzie was an admirer of William Cobbett, the English journalist and reformer who published parliamentary debates. Cobbett's name regularly appeared when one spoke of the impact of the 1832 Reform bill and the Chartist movement. He was also connected to the American president Andrew Jackson, who was no lover of the currency and banking system. Cobbett published the *Colonial Advocate* for ten years between 1824-34. In 1836 Mackenzie began publishing the *Constitution* which he devoted to the coverage of serious news. He was also plotting to carry out a violent rebellion in league with French speaking rebels led by Louis-Joseph Papineau. Their joint efforts led to the outbreak of armed confrontation in December 1837. Within hours of the beginning of the uprising, the rebels were routed and Mackenzie had to flee to New York to save himself from the gallows.

The Mackenzie-Papineau rebellion was not without positive results. In May of 1838, John George Lambton, Earl of Durham, arrived in Québec City with a mission to investigate and report on the problems that led to the ill-fated rebellion. In the winter of 1839 Durham issued one of the most important documents in Canadian history, the *Report on The Affairs of British North America.* It would have a serious impact on developing Canadian press policy, in particular the relationship between a citizenry and its government and the role that journalists assume as the information intermediaries of this relationship. Although Durham commented on a number of Canadian problems, in particular the thorny relationship of the English and French speaking communities, the majority of his report was devoted to dismantling the semi-feudal rule of the Family Compact and its allies and the installation of a representative democracy.

In 1867 the British Parliament united Ontario, Québec, New Brunswick and Nova Scotia with the British North America Act. The legislation made no mention of the role of the press, and, unlike the American Constitution, it did not contain a bill of rights. Canada would not have its own constitution until 1982. Between the passage of the British North America Act and the arrival of radio in the early twentieth century, the press in Canada enjoyed one of its most productive periods.

Following Confederation, the federal government adopted a policy to extend the nation from Atlantic to Pacific. British Columbia joined the union in 1870 when the federal government promised to build a railway from Montréal to Vancouver. Eventually, the territories located between Ontario and British Columbia and owned by the Hudson's Bay Company were turned over to Canada, from which three new provinces and three new territories were carved. The 10 year old *Victoria Gazette* and the *Anglo American* and the French language *Le Courier de Nouvelle Caledonie* (Nova Scotia Courier) and the *British Colonist* existed on the west coast to serve the growing population. Newfoundland and Labrador followed in 1949.

The 1857 A. McKim Directory of Newspapers listed 291 publications available in Canada. By 1900 this number had increased to 1,226, of which 121 were daily newspapers. Along with this growth the characteristics of the press changed considerably in the second half of the nineteenth century. In many respects, newspapers abandoned the pointed and sometimes vitriolic partisanship that was symbolic of the newspapers of the first half of the century. The political position of the paper was more likely to be found on a page dedicated to editorial opinion. There was no mistaking that the Toronto *Globe* supported the Liberal Party and the *Toronto Telegram* supported the Conservative Party. The most significant change to come out of the nineteenth-century Canadian media was the evolution of the press from primarily weeklies to dailies and the entrenchment of newspapers in the rapidly developing technological and market economy.

The country also took its first steps to becoming a new, urbanized society. From 1900 until 1911, Canada was the fastest growing nation in the world. Newspaper circulation in 1900 stood at 650,000 and it doubled by 1911. The Canadian growth was only truncated by the First World War.

Once the First World War ended the country entered a crippling depression that lasted until 1921. Relative prosperity followed and new technical innovations made Canadian newspapers more efficient. The cost of wire services such as Canadian Press and the Associated Press in the United States decreased significantly when the teletype was introduced. In many ways, more efficient technologies only benefited a few relatively solvent publishers and owners. While there were 121 dailies in the country in 1900, by 1951 this had dropped to 94. In 1900, 18 Canadian urban areas published two or more dailies. By 1951, only 11 Canadian cities would have competing newspapers. Since 1960, several major Canadian newspapers have closed their doors including the *Toronto Telegram,* the *Montreal Star,* the *Ottawa Journal* and the *Winnipeg Tribune.* This decline was partially offset by a new series of tabloids published under the *Sun* masthead in Toronto, Winnipeg, Ottawa, Calgary and Edmonton. Other new ventures began in Halifax, Montréal and Québec City. In 1998, the Hollinger corporation converted its business newspaper *The Financial Post* into a daily operating under the masthead of the *National Post.* It is now a member of the Can West Global communications corporation.

In the early 1970s the use of computers in the newsroom not only sped up the production and editing process, it succeeded in destroying the power of one of the country's oldest unions, the International Typographers Union (ITU), an organization that fiercely resisted the introduction of digital technology into the newsroom. As early as 1964 the ITU struck all three Toronto dailies, *The Globe, The Star* and *The Telegram* to fight the introduction of computers in the newsroom. By 1987, the *Toronto Star* which had at one time employed more than 150 unionized typographers, had reduced the staff to 30. The arrival of digital technology has changed the concept of reporting and newspapers themselves.

Canada's federal government is a constitutionally structured bilingual parliamentary monarchy, both English and French are equals in any federal jurisdiction. Each province can decide whether to be officially bilingual or not which can result in an odd combination of polices. Québec is the only officially unilingual Canadian province with French as its official language. Although French is not among the official languages of Ontario, Prince Edward Island, Nova Scotia, Saskatchewan, Alberta and British Columbia its use is widespread. New Brunswick is the country's only official bilingual province. Ontario government documents are usually issued in both languages. The Ontario province government-owned television system offers full time English language service on TVOntario and full time French language service on TFO, *Télévision Français d'Ontario.* On the national level the government owned and operated Canadian Broadcasting Corporation—La Société Radio—Canada operates two radio and two television networks. Canada also has an official multicultural policy so that the political and judicial structures address the needs of those outside the French and English communities and the aboriginal populations.

Canada has a population of more than 31 million, 68.6 percent of which are between the ages of 15 and 64. Like many other western industrial nations, Canada faces an aging society in the coming decades of the twenty-first century. There are now 3,917,875 persons over the age of 65, constituting 12.6 percent of the population. Although it constitutes the smallest demographic range, it is not far off the 18.8 percent of the population between the ages of 0 and 14. The majority of Canadians live within a narrow corridor bordering on the United States of America.

Although Canada has a vast land area, the highest concentration of the population, or around 35 percent, lives in the central Canadian provinces of Ontario and Québec. The western provinces, especially Alberta and British Columbia, with their staple products of gas, oil, and forestry products, have proven attractive to those wishing to move. Combined, Alberta and British Columbia constitute about 12 percent of the Canadian population. The remainder live either on the prairies, in Atlantic Canada, in the Northwest Territories or in Nunavut.

The 1996 Canadian Census recorded the immigrant population in the country. There were 4,971,070 persons who reported that they had been born outside the country. Of these 1,054,930 arrived before 1961. A further 788,580 came between 1961 and 1970. The number of immigrants began to climb again in 1971. In the subsequent decade 996,160 persons arrived. This number increased to 1,092,400 in the ten years following 1981. In the final decade of the twentieth century, 1,038,990 persons immigrated to Canada.

The most significant increase in the immigrant population was comprised of those who identified Eastern Asia as their home area. Only 20,555 of these people reported coming before 1961. But in contrast, 252,340 arrived at Canadian ports between 1991 and 1996. A further 140,055 reported coming from Southern Asia and 118,265 reported that they came from Southeast Asia. The main ports of attraction were in Vancouver and other points on the Pacific coast and the central Canadian city of Toronto. African, Caribbean and Middle Eastern immigrants also significantly increased in number during the same years. Canada during the past four decades is decreasingly a white, Anglo-Saxon, and predominantly Christian state.

Despite immigration from areas of the world where English is primarily a second language, it is still claimed by 16,890,615 Canadians as their mother tongue. A further 6,636,660 Canadians reported French as their mother tongue. A total of 4,598,290 persons reported speaking a third tongue, which was not classified as official. These included persons who came from China, Italy, Germany, Poland, Spain, Portugal, India and Pakistan, the Ukraine, Saudi Arabia, Holland, the Philippines, Greece, and Vietnam. Inside Canada, both Cree and Inuktitut were recognized as third, nonofficial languages. There were 1,198,870 more who reported speaking languages other than English, French, or those listed in the nonofficial columns of the census reports.

There are a number of media outlets directed to populations whose primary language is neither English nor French. As one of Canada's oldest multilingual broadcasts, Toronto radio stations CHIN-AM and CHIN-FM have continued since the mid-1960s. Multilingual television station CFMT-TV serves not only Toronto, but also communities in southwestern Ontario through a system of satellite transmitters and cable companies, most of which are owned by Rogers Communications. Canada's large Asian population can subscribe to the cable pay service Fairchild TV in most parts of the country. Toronto's large and well established Italian community is served by the daily *Corriere Canadese.* There is an established practice that broadcasting stations operating primarily in one of the country's two official languages offer programming in a third language. Toronto's local CITY-TV still follows this practice.

The Canadian newspaper industry has found a niche in the complex, multicultural, and multilingual Canadian media market. Ranging from punchy, colorful tabloids such as the *Sun* newspaper, to the more intense and serious *National Post, Le Soleil,* and the *Globe and Mail.* Fifty-seven percent of all Canadians read a newspaper daily in 2001, according to the Canadian Newspaper Association. This represents 11.8 million readers which is an increase of 3 percent over the 11.3 million readers who had reported reading a newspaper daily in the year 2000. This reversed a downward trend of the previous two decades.

The statistics become more revealing when broken down into separate demographic categories. In the major markets of the country, there are 4.8 million adults between the ages of 18 and 49, 85 percent of which reported reading a newspaper at least once a week. Younger readers between the ages of 18 and 24 have the highest five-day readership, at 80 percent. The most difficult demographic for the Canadian newspaper industry to reach were the 25 to 34 year olds, with just half reporting reading a newspaper the previous day. Sixty-eight percent of people with an income of $100,000 CDN per year read a daily newspaper. In 2001, 71 percent of university educated persons read a newspaper at least once a week. Eight out of 10 senior managers reported reading a newspaper in the past week and 74 percent read one each day.

Top Ten Daily Newspapers
(2000)

	Circulation
The Toronto Star	496,000
The Globe & Mail	334,000
The National Post	294,000
Le Journal de Montréal	279,000
The Toronto Sun	255,000
La Presse Montréal	203,000
The Vancouver Sun	200,000
The Province, Vancouver	167,000
The Ottawa Citizen	147,000
The Gazette Montréal	146,000

Source: World Association of Newspapers and Zenithmedia, *World Press Trends 2001*, p. 64.

Of cities with a population over 150,000, the Manitoba capital of Winnipeg reported the highest weekly newspaper readership with 89.9 percent of its citizens over the age of 18 having read one in the past week. Calgary, Alberta and Windsor, Ontario were tied for second place at 89.5 percent each. The Alberta provincial capital of Edmonton was 87.7 percent. Hamilton, Ontario reported reading at 87.2 percent and Halifax, Nova Scotia was at 85.5 percent. St. Catharines, Ontario, Regina, Saskatchewan, Québec City, Québec, and Victoria, British Columbia were all over 84 percent. In larger cities, readership has remained fairly constant. In many ways, the Ontario provincial capital of Toronto reflected the trends. Of adults over the age of 18, 56 percent reported that they had read a newspaper the previous day. A further 77 percent reported reading a newspaper at least once per week and 84 percent reported having done the same by the end of the week. Figures were similar for Montréal. In the category of having read a newspaper the previous day, the figure stood at 48 percent of all adults. In the category of having read a newspaper at least once per week, the number was 68 percent and finally, those reporting having read a newspaper by the end of the week, the figure stood at 79 percent. In British Columbia's largest city, Vancouver, the numbers stood at 56 percent, 77 percent and 79 percent respectively. The national capital city of

Ottawa reported 57 percent, 79 percent and 84 percent respectively, in figures released by the Canadian Newspaper Association.

The largest owner of Canadian newspapers is Southam Publications (Can West Global) with 27; next is Osprey Media Group Inc. with 18; Sun Media (Quebecor, Inc.) owns 15 papers. Hollinger Canadian Newspaper Limited Partnership owns 10 and Power Corporation of Canada owns seven. The next largest all own five papers each: Independents, Horizon Operations BC Limited, and Torstar Corporation. Annex Publishing and Printing own two. Bell Globe Media and Black Press each own one newspaper.

Canadians claim that they have the oldest surviving newspaper in North America. The *Québec Gazette,* once the voice of the provincial capital's then extensive English speaking population, began publishing on June 21, 1764. It was eventually folded into the present-day weekly publication, the *Québec Chronicle-Telegraph.* The next oldest publication is the Southam-owned *Montréal Gazette,* which began publication on June 3, 1778. It is the longest continuing daily in the country.

Newspapers in Canada continue to hold their own in attracting advertising dollars. In 1996, they secured 32 percent of the overall market in contrast to television's 32.3 percent. In 1997, the figure increased slightly to 34.1 percent in comparison to television's 31.1 percent, but it began to decline again as the turn of the century approached, with 32.4 percent of the market in comparison to television's 31.5 percent. However, the volume of dollars attracted, expressed in millions, did continue to increase, from $1,960 (Canadian funds) in 1996 to $2,303 in 1997 and finally $2,379 in 1998.

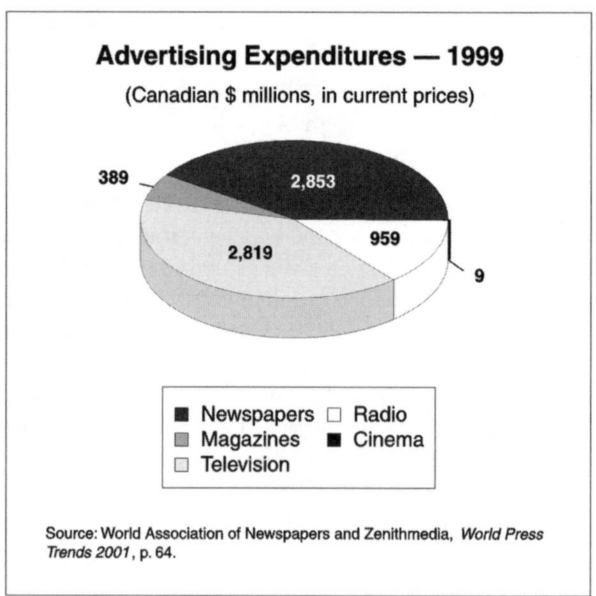

Source: World Association of Newspapers and Zenithmedia, *World Press Trends 2001*, p. 64.

ECONOMIC FRAMEWORK

In the spring of 2002, 66.6 percent of all Canadians over the age of 15 were participating in the labor market. Viewing the statistics on a province to province basis shows some disparity. Participation rates are highest at 72.2 percent in Alberta, a province wealthy from extensive gas and oil royalties. The participation rate is the lowest in Newfoundland and Labrador, where the economy for years was built on fishing in the Atlantic. It is only in recent years that economic diversification has been attempted, with oil and gas exploration on the Hibernia grounds at sea and through hydro electric development at Churchill Falls in Labrador.

Since 1997, the country's unemployment rate, seasonally adjusted, has dropped significantly. That year it stood at 9.5 percent across the nation and in 2002 it stood at 7.2 percent. Again, the statistics must be seen in their relationship to the country's provinces. The rate for Newfoundland and Labrador in the spring of 2002, stood at 16.6 percent. In contrast, the rate in Alberta was 5 percent, Manitoba 5 percent, and Saskatchewan 5.8 percent. Ontario, with the most diversified economy of Canada's provinces, had a rate of 7 percent and British Columbia 9 percent.

In March of 2002, Canada's Consumer Price Index stood at 117.7, based on the index start date of 1992 of 100. Between March 2001 and March 2002, the overall index increased only 1.8 percent. However, that figure is somewhat distorted because tobacco and alcohol products increased by 14.8 percent. Food was also higher, increasing by 3.3 percent over the same period. Only two categories showed a decline, one of which was clothing and footwear (although the decline was insignificant at 0.7 percent). The cost of energy actually declined by 3.3 percent. Shelter and recreation, education and reading all increased 1.1 percent. Household furnishings and operations increased by 2.2 percent, transportation by 0.3 percent, and health and personal care by 0.9 percent. Compared with incomes in 1992, the relative purchasing power of the dollar in March 2002 was 85 percent.

While personal disposable income in Canada increased by 3.3 percent from the fourth quarter 2000 to the fourth quarter 2001, corporate profits declined by 29.9 percent. The gross domestic product at market prices seasonally adjusted at annual rates (SAAR) declined by 0.1 percent. Business investment in machinery and equipment declined by 5.6 percent. Personal expenditure on consumer goods increased by 2.3 percent. Overall, personal savings rates declined by 0.3 percent.

All Canadian media outlets experienced growth in advertising revenue in the years between 1996 and 1998, the last year figures are available. The numbers below are expressed in millions of dollars in Canadian funds. Spending on advertising in all major media increased from $6.1 to $7.3. Newspapers increased their share from $1.9 to $2.3. Television jumped from $1.9 to $2.3. Radio thought to be on its way out as a major medium in Canada in the early 1990s actually attracted $.9, an increase from $.7 two years earlier. General magazines increased from $.31 to $.38. Trade magazines increased from $.233 to $.277. Outdoor advertising increased from $.200 to $.250.

PRESS LAWS

In 1982, the Government of Canada repatriated the British North America Act from the parliament at Westminster. Although many of the clauses of the new Canadian constitution did not vary significantly from those of its predecessor, it did include a Charter of Rights and Freedoms. Under those matters deemed to be fundamental freedoms the role of the press was defined for the first time. The four basic freedoms that emerged did not exist in the British North America Act. These were defined as: freedom of conscience and religion; freedom of thought, belief, opinion and expression, including freedom of the press and other media of communication; freedom of peaceful assembly; and freedom of association.

Freedom of expression and freedom of the press, although similar and related concepts, are not one-and-the-same in Canadian law. In fact, serious limitations exist which clearly differentiates freedom of the press in Canada from that of its southern neighbor. The Charter of Rights and Freedoms only defines those rights of the individual in his or her relationship to the state. As law scholar Robert Martin has pointed out, the law does not address freedom of expression issues that arise involving media owners and managers.

As noted earlier, Canada is a constitutional monarchy consisting of ten provinces and three territories. The federal parliament consists of a lower chamber, the House of Commons, whose members are chosen by the electorate in a cycle that must not exceed five years. The federal electoral districts called ridings are loosely defined on the basis of population. At the turn of the most recent century, five parties sat in the House. The Liberal Party had the largest number of members and thus formed the government with its leader assuming the role of Prime Minister. The largest opposition party is the Canadian Alliance. Minor parties include the New Democratic Party, the Progressive Conservatives and Le Bloc Québeçois. Although rare, there are occasions when members sit without party affiliation. The upper chamber is the Canadian Senate, which represents the interests of the provinces. Members are appointed on the recommendation of the Prime Minister with the consequence that a long sitting government may have a majority of members in both houses. Senators must retire by the age of 75. The head of state is the Governor-General who acts as the representative of the Queen in Canada. Although constitutionally endowed with extensive powers, the actual role of the Governor-General is largely ceremonial, although no piece of legislation in Canada becomes law without his/her signature.

The 10 Canadian provinces hold considerable powers such as control of health, welfare and education, which make them virtually independent states inside the confederation. Their powers are defined in Sections 92, 92A and 93 of the constitution. Federal powers, which tend to be national in scope, can be found in Section 91. Section 95 defines those areas in which both levels of government may make law, in particular in areas such as agriculture and immigration. Some of the most important clauses in the constitution are contained in Section 33 known as the "not withstanding clauses" which allow any constitutionally enabled government to override court decisions for a five year period after which the enacting government must give adequate justification for continuing to use the clauses. One such case was when Québec language laws, which gave preference to the French language, were declared unconstitutional.

Because the British North America Act was written in 1867, some technologies were not addressed, such as broadcasting. In 1929 the French-language province of Québec passed legislation to regulate broadcasting within its borders. The federal government retaliated by taking the matter to court. In 1932 the Judicial Committee of the Privy Council decided that broadcasting was a matter of national interest and therefore under the jurisdiction of the federal government. Also at this time, Canada had entered into treaties with both the United States and Mexico regarding allocation of broadcast channels. Section 132 upheld the right of Canada to make such treaties, thus confirming federal jurisdiction in this media field.

As in most modern democracies, Canada has a series of laws pertaining to defamation. Virtually all of them have something to do with press coverage of certain events. The most common set of statutes is referred to as "civil libel laws," although the definition for criminal libel still exists on the books. In some jurisdictions, the definition distinguishes between slander and libel that is written or portrayed. In other jurisdictions, the word defamation is used to define all kinds of libel. In Canada, anything presented by a media outlet is subject to potential action under the law. This includes news, classified ads, advertisements, comic strips, and even the publication of materials from outside sources.

Criminal libel is divided into three categories: seditious libel, defamatory libel, and blasphemous libel. The clauses have traditionally been used to clamp down on political speeches. The last case involving seditious libel took place in the 1940s when the Jehovah's Witnesses delivered a tract accusing the Premier of the province as being a God-hating demagogue. When the case finally arrived at the Supreme Court, the judges divided five to four in throwing out the case against the sect. As a consequence of that decision, it is now virtually impossible to get a conviction on the charge.

The definition of defamatory libel is similar to civil libel, but can result only when two persons decide to exchange inflammatory words leading to a confrontation. As Robert Martin points out, the law was first passed by the British Star Chamber in the seventeenth century to discourage debates from descending into duels. In Canada the most famous case took place in the 1930s when a man in Edmonton distributed a pamphlet with the names of nine prominent persons on one side of the sheet listed under the title "Bankers' Toadies." On the other side, he wrote the words "God Made Bankers' Toadies just as He made snakes, slugs, snails and other creepy crawly, treacherous and poisonous things. Never therefore abuse them—just exterminate them." He was arrested, tried, and convicted of defamatory libel.

Blasphemous libel has much to do with religious practice. The statute allows for serious religious debate but not for the defamation of religious belief or those who hold views that may be controversial. There has never been a case under this law in Canada, but in Britain a decision ruled that only the Christian religion need be defined under this law.

CENSORSHIP

Libel action in the minds of some observers can be used as a censoring device in the hands of those with the ways and means to hire expensive lawyers. In the mid-1980s it was rumored that two wealthy business families in Toronto had sent letters threatening legal action to authors who were writing about their respective family histories. However, this does not appear to be a large or significant problem in Canada. Surveys by the Canadian Daily Newspaper Association throughout the 1980s clearly demonstrated that few had serious concerns about large lawsuits. In Canadian law, an apology will officially end any libel action. In many cases, the defendant can ask the court to impose expensive bonds on a plaintiff that that person runs the risk of losing. Favorable court decisions result in low awards that won't cover the expenses incurred.

There are two levels at which censorship operates, in the boardrooms of media outlets and in the judicial system. The first is easy to define since it has historical precedents. The first media in Canada were established with clear, political objectives in mind, namely the support of the patron who paid the way. When newspapers evolved into independent entities supported by advertising in the late Victorian period, they gave the illusion of being politically independent. Yet many of these journals were operated by strong willed individuals who used the media to promote personal causes, some of them beyond politics. Joseph "Holy Joe" Atkinson of the *Toronto Daily Star* was an adamant temperance man who forbid liquor advertising forbidden in that newspaper. A policy that lasted for a number of decades after his death. Opposing views on the question did not appear with any regularity in Atkinson's newspaper. In another example, there was little doubt that the mission of the French language journal *Le Devoir* during the First World War was to prevent Canada from being involved in what its founder Henri Bourassa viewed as Britain's war in Europe.

In more recent times, the relationship between the press and the judiciary has become a flashpoint of controversy. Courts regularly prohibit the publication of evidence. In a notorious murder case that took place in St. Catharines, Ontario, a young couple kidnapped, tortured and murdered two young schoolgirls. The proceedings against the female defendant were closed to the media. She had arranged for a plea bargain to two counts of manslaughter in return for her testimony against her husband. The trial judge ruled that public exposure of the conditions of her plea bargain could possibly contaminate the proceedings against her husband. A series of videotapes of the kidnapped girls were also suppressed. In other cases, such as the need to protect witnesses, Canadian courts regularly forbid the publication of certain types of information.

One of the more interesting cases in Canadian history surrounds the revision of the statutes governing the behavior of juvenile defenders and the consequent introduction of the Charter of Rights and Freedoms in 1982. The Juvenile Delinquents Act states that trials of juveniles must take place without publicity. In 1981, a Supreme Court decision declared that all persons involved in any specific case against a juvenile had to remain anonymous. Trials were to be held *in camera,* defying the public nature of the judicial system. When the Charter of Rights and Freedoms became law, the *Ottawa Citizen* sent a reporter to cover a juvenile case. She was turned away. In the end, the Supreme Court upheld the right of public access to judicial proceedings but it also upheld the right of a juvenile accused of a crime to anonymity.

The most restrictive piece of legislation for the Canadian media was passed in 1914 under the title of the War Measures Act. It was to be used in only the direst of circumstances because its key initiative was to remove the law making right of Parliament and to transfer it to the federal cabinet. Citizens' participation in government was therefore suspended and censorship legalized. It was first enacted in 1914 when Canada joined Britain in the First World War. Although the war officially ended in 1918, the law remained in effect until 1920.

The government used the law to ban publications during the war years. Among these were a number of German language publications, but socialist and social democratic magazines and newspapers were also banned, as well as a few Irish nationalist publications. Any publication that questioned the direction of the war could potentially be banned. Publications advocating temperance were also banned on the premise that such journals would weaken the morale of men overseas. The Act resurfaced in 1939 when Canada went to war against Germany. As in the First World War, the provisions of the act continued on for two years after the hostilities ceased.

The most controversial application of the law came in October 1970. Québec had been the scene of disturbances over the right of the province to secede from the Canadian Confederation. The debate began in the mid-1950s and escalated in the early 1960s. Terrorists using the name FLQ (*Front de Liberation Québeçois*) placed bombs in a mailbox in the English speaking district of Westmount and threatened other English language institutions. In 1970 they kidnapped the British trade minister, James Cross, and the provincial minister of labor, Pierre LaPorte. Cross was eventually released but LaPorte was murdered by his captors, which led Prime Minister Pierre Trudeau to invoke the Act. No significant armed insurrection appeared and the Act was eventually revoked. When the City of Vancouver used the Act to clean up the downtown from various types of undesirables, the government amended the legislation to allow for regional imposition and changed its name to The Emergencies Act. However, provisions for media censorship are still in the law.

A few Canadian journalists have also run afoul of the Official Secrets Act. In 1979 a Toronto journalist, Peter Worthington, became convinced that there was an extensive Soviet spy network in Canada and that the government was ignoring it. He had come into possession of documents that supported his case and he published one of these in the *Toronto Sun.* As a result, he was charged under the Official Secrets Act. However, he was acquitted of violating the Act when the judge decided that although the material Worthington published qualified under the provisions of the law, the document was no longer secret. The prosecution in the case decided to let the matter drop.

STATE-PRESS RELATIONS

In Canada, the state and the media have never been completely separated, even during the short period between 1919 and 1932 when the emergence of radio broadcasting was primarily a private affair. The tradition of state and press integration can be traced to the evolution of a strictly partisan press in the eighteenth and nineteenth centuries. As noted earlier, even when the press freed itself from direct party control, most newspapers and many magazines remained outlets for, if not totally partisan political views, at least polarized moral issues such as temperance and women's rights. When broadcasting entered onto the scene in the 1920s, the only state involvement was the issuing of radio licenses through the Department of Marine and Fisheries. However, in 1929 the relationship was to undergo radical change.

As the twenties came to a close, Canadian political elite became increasingly concerned that the commercial messages and entertainment-driven values from American radio stations that freely drifted across the border were eroding Canadian culture. The most popular radio show in Canada was the American produced situation comedy *Amos n' Andy.* In 1929 the Liberal government of Mackenzie King commissioned three men to study and report on the state of broadcasting in the country, beginning a relationship between the state and the media that has not weakened since. The three were Sir John Aird, a banker, Charles Bowman, a journalist with the *Ottawa Citizen,* and Augustin Frigon, an engineer at L'Ecole Polytechnique in Montréal. The commissioners studied virtually every form of radio broadcasting in existence during the year of the investigation.

By the time Aird delivered his report, the Liberals were out of office and a new Conservative Prime Minister, R. B. Bennett was in control. It was up to Bennett to decide which form broadcasting would take in Canada. Like King, Bennett was deeply concerned that American influence, especially its views on liberalism and republicanism, would soon dominate Canadian thinking. But in spite of his own concerns, he did not opt for a pure system of public broadcasting. Instead, his government founded the Canadian Radio Broadcasting Commission (CRBC) with a mandate to both build and operate stations and to produce programming for its own outlets, as well as the private sector. The concept proved unworkable.

Badly injured politically by the Great Depression, Bennett was out of office in 1935 and King returned with a vision for a stronger and more Canadian oriented public broadcasting system. The King government essentially threw out Bennett's legislation and created the Canadian Broadcasting Corporation (CBC) in 1936. The CBC was to own and operate stations, produce programming for both itself and the private sector, but, above all, it was to act as a regulator for the private sector which remained subservient, but intact.

Although the CBC was designed to act as an outlet for Canadian ideas and Canadian programming, radio dials remained tuned to stations south of the border. In fact, the CBC itself carried a significant amount of U.S. programming to help pay its bills. American influence also extended to the stage, film, dance, and music worlds, as well as to publications on a myriad of themes. As the Second World War came to a close, government officials began to realize that the CBC alone could not encourage or preserve what ''produced in Canada'' culture existed. As a consequence, the government called upon Vincent Massey, brother of the actor Raymond Massey, to conduct an inquiry into the state of the arts in Canada. In 1951 the Massey commission concluded with the now familiar ''the Americans are taking us over'' theme. The commission concentrated its investigation on the state of the arts, but did note that newspapers were critical actors in the dissemination of knowledge in any given country. In reference to radio, Massey concluded that the medium had three critical functions: to inform, to educate, and to entertain.

In spite of Massey's warnings, American influence in Canada continued unabated. This was assisted in part by the 1948 arrival of television in the United States, four years prior to the opening of the first Canadian station in Montréal. Following a pattern established in radio some three decades previously, television dials in Canadian cities began to lock on to U.S. channels. It was hardly a rebellion against nationalism. In fact, when the dust began to settle over the question as to whether loyal Canadians would reject American broadcasting, the issue had really became one of variety. It remained to be seen whether or not the CBC should remain the dominant provider of broadcasting product in Canada. The answer was a firm no.

Yet another commission had been looking into the business of broadcasting in Canada. Robert Fowler delivered his report to the government on March 15, 1957. It was here that the principle of a single broadcasting system consisting of both public and private participants first saw the light of day. Although Fowler felt that private broadcasters in general had to be forced to deliver a good product or lose their respective licenses, he also conceded that the private sector, in spite of having existed in a subordinate position for twenty years, had refused to go away. To this end, Fowler added one more condition to the purpose of broadcasting, essentially creating a vehicle for advertising. His most dramatic recommendation was the removal of the regulatory powers of the CBC, which he felt should be seated in a neutral body. In 1958, the federal government acted on his proposal and created the first independent regulatory agency, the Board of Broadcast Governors. Within months, the new agency opened the way for private, independent television stations to take to the air. It was the beginning of the alternate development in Canadian television which would see the emergence of CTV (Canadian Television) as the country's first privately owned and operated system.

Broadcasting was not the only thing on the government's mind during this time period. It was also concerned about the state of magazine publishing in the country. Yet another Royal Commission was charged with investigating the situation chaired by one of the government's most solid supporters, Senator Grattan O'Leary, an Ottawa-based newspaper publisher. O'Leary targeted what he felt was unfair competition in the magazine industry, in particular two journals, *Time* and *Reader's Digest.* Both magazines were owned and operated by American interests although they published a Canadian edition. Usually these editions were only a small part of the overall magazine. As a consequence, advertising rates for Canadian businesses were far lower than those of purely domestically produced. O'Leary wanted the government to remove the tax credits that Canadian advertisers received for expenses involved in placing ads in these journals. The outcry from Washington was predictable, but in 1976 the Liberal government enacted O'Leary's recommendations and eventually extended it to advertisers who used border television. Just before the turn of the century, *Sports Illustrated* successfully fought a government regulation to extend government support for the industry although the tax legislation remains intact, exempt for the time being under the cultural provisions of NAFTA (North American Free Trade Agreement). In 1998 the government passed Bill C55, which eliminated the discrimination against U.S. magazines publishing in Canada.

Although Canada has had a magazine industry since the *Nova Scotia Magazine* and *Comprehensive Review of Literature and News* first appeared in 1789, they have never played a significant financial role in the history of Canadian media. Most attempts to establish a magazine industry in the country during the period when newspapers were enjoying significant prosperity were inconsistent to say the least. Some such as J.S. Cunnabell's *Acadian Magazine* and *Halifax Monthly Magazine* did enjoy brief prosperity. By the mid point of the nineteenth century, Toronto had become the major magazine publication center in the country, but as in previous instances, most magazines, such as *The Canadian Journal* and the *British Colonial,* did not last very long.

The French language press did enjoy more success following Confederation. A Montréal publisher, Georges Edouard Desbarats launched his *Canadian Illustrated*

News in December 1869, which he followed with a French language edition, *L'Opinion Publique* in 1870. In Toronto, a young artist with a political wit launched *Grip* magazine, a collection of cartoons and political satire which published for two decades. Both Queen's University and McGill launched successful academic journals during the second half of the nineteenth century. In 1887 *Saturday Night,* a collection of consumer news and pointed political coverage, first hit the newsstands of Toronto. The longest lasting and most stable of all Canadian periodicals, the *Busy Man's Magazine,* which eventually took the name of its founder, *Maclean's—Le Magazine Maclean,* was first published in 1896. *Maclean's* remains one of the country's largest publishers of trade periodicals in concert with its weekly newsmagazine. However, without government support, it is doubtful that Canada could support a magazine industry.

Government once more wielded its power in 1968. Dissatisfied with the performance of the Board of Broadcast Governors and recognizing that a new broadcasting environment was taking shape, the government again amended the Broadcasting Act. Faced with rising nationalism in Québec, it wanted the broadcasters to play a larger and more influential role in defining Canadian unity. One of the changes to the act was to charge the CBC primarily with this task. As well, the new act brought both cable casting and educational broadcasting under the jurisdiction of the new federal regulatory body, the Canadian Radio and Television Commission (CRTC).

One of the driving forces in the 1960s was the behavior of the private sector in the media. Like private entrepreneurs everywhere, the desire to expand and control lucrative markets became a cause in itself. Watching as one after another independent operator came under the umbrella of a major corporation, the government once again resorted to a commission of inquiry to investigate the potential problem. As always, it chose one of its own to head the investigation, Senator Keith Davey, known in Liberal Party circles as the Rainmaker. The 1970 report revealed much of what had been suspected about media economics and patterns of ownership. But the Davey inquiry did not stop at that point. It looked at the role of journalism in media, how journalists behaved, and how they were educated. Much to the chagrin of the owners, there were extensive comments on the workplace morale of many media workers.

One of the consequences of the Davey commission was the establishment of press councils across the country. Initially they emerged in Ontario, Québec and Alberta but soon thereafter spread across the country. Now they are almost an institutional way of life for most Canadian dailies and weeklies. Of these, the Ontario Press Council is the largest, with 226 members as of July 2001. The councils attempt to mediate complaints about coverage when these are received. However, should a complaint go to a formal hearing, and should the newspaper lose the case, it must publish the results in a prominent place as soon as possible after a decision has been rendered to retain its membership.

In spite of what appears on the surface to be a relatively healthy newspaper market in Canada, serious concerns have been raised, as they have been elsewhere, about the diminishing number of corporations who now own the vast majority of the largest and most influential Canadian dailies. The situation has received the attention of the Federal Government on two occasions, once in 1970 when Liberal Senator Keith Davey was charged with investigating various aspects of the media situation in the country and again in the early 1980s when Thomas Kent chaired a commission investigating concentration of ownership in Canada's newspaper industries.

In 1980 two corporate giants, Thomson of Toronto and Southam of Hamilton, decided to reduce competition in their respective markets. Thomson closed the *Ottawa Journal* and Southam closed the *Winnipeg Tribune.* It was not lost on the government that these two owners actively competed with each other in both cities and that the closures were destined to ensure that no competition existed. As a consequence, the government chartered another Royal Commission, this one under former civil servant Tom Kent, to investigate the state of affairs in the industry. Overall, the Kent Commission felt that concentration of ownership was dangerous for the Canadian democracy and should be curbed. The industry did not agree and the Kent recommendations were denounced on virtually every editorial page in the country. The government retreated and did not implement any of the recommendations. Realizing the vulnerability of their respective positions, the industry now actively embraced the work of the press councils which they argued would provide meaningful checks on their more outrageous activities.

The issue emerged once again in 2002 when the Asper family of Winnipeg, owners of Can West Global Communications, announced that they would be centralizing editorial writing three days per week at the company's head office. The company had just finished the purchase of the Southam properties previously owned by Hollinger. The journalists rebelled by removing bylines, but the company stood fast to its premise that it had a right, if not an obligation, to promote its views in its newspapers. The senior executives at Southam reminded the journalists that it was they, and not the journalists, who owned the newspapers and thus had the power to make and enforce the decisions. As with the Can West Global situation, the newspaper industry in 2002 was in what could be described as its third consolidation phase.

In keeping with tradition practiced by previous governments, when the Conservatives, under the leadership of Brian Mulroney, came to power in 1984, yet one more Royal Commission was chartered to investigate broadcasting policy in Canada. It received its charge on April 9, 1985. The commission was jointly chaired by Gerald Caplan, a former national secretary of the New Democratic Party which sat in opposition to the ruling Conservatives and by Florian Sauveageau, a communications professor at Laval University in Québec City. They were given a wide mandate to investigate and make recommendations on the future of the Canadian broadcasting system. Suspicion ran high in public broadcasting circles that the Conservatives were about to use the investigation to either downgrade or destroy the CBC.

Once again, the investigation did not downplay the much-desired Canadian nationalist ideal. In fact, it reinforced the concept, although it dismissed the belief that the CBC should take the lead in promoting national unity. Instead, it argued that the CBC should focus on developing what it termed ''a national consciousness.'' The commissioners also wanted to extend the concept of broadcasting to include other forms of media, namely provincial agencies, native groups, community groups, and those in minority languages and cultural communities. It saw these and other smaller groups as part of a larger public community. Although many of the recommendations were not formally acted on, the country now enjoys the presence of a national cable network operated by aboriginal peoples, multilingual radio and television services in most of the major cities and community programming aired through designated channels on cable television. The Broadcasting Act was finally amended, which removed the CBC from the business of promoting national unity. The Act did not, however, relieve the public broadcaster from the responsibility of generating part of its own operating revenue through the solicitation of advertising.

Attitude toward Foreign Media

As noted above, Canadian broadcasting policy has been driven since the arrival of radio by the concept that foreign intervention threatens the national identity, and that it is the responsibility of Canadian-owned and operated media to give access to Canadian creators and performers in order to offset the overwhelming influence of the American media in Canada. This is less of a problem in Québec, where the predominant language is French, though broadcasters there carry dubbed versions of the *Ally McBeal* and *West Wing* television shows. The Caplan Sauvageau Commission found that of the 52,000 yearly hours of broadcasting they investigated, only 370 were produced in Canada. Since 1986, the situation has changed significantly, with the CBC now boasting an all-Canadian prime time broadcast day. The recent inclusion of foreign specialty channels has once again brought the nationalist question to a head. Fundamentally, one thing has not changed since Caplan Sauvageau: the majority of major hits such as *The West Wing* dominate the top ten television shows in Canada on a weekly basis.

Although Canadian private broadcasters regularly espouse the virtues of a free market and a lack of regulation, they often turn to government for assistance in protecting their private spheres. Foreigners cannot own or control through proxy any Canadian broadcast media. On numerous occasions, the federal government has attempted to protect the Canadian magazine industry through tax protection or outright subsidy. Foreign booksellers are not allowed to set up competing shops in Canada. The Borders Books and Music chain was forbidden entry into the country to compete with a similar Canadian chain called Chapters. Eventually the person who attempted to bring Borders to Canada opted to begin her own chain, called Indigo. When Chapters fell on hard times, she merged the Indigo operation with Chapters. When Canadian press baron Conrad Black attempted to accept a seat in the British House of Lords, the Canadian government reminded him that he would have to relinquish his Canadian citizenship and consequently his newspaper chain. Black did for the most part cut ties to Canada, selling his principle holdings to broadcaster Can West Global.

Other than ownership requirements, the Canadian media industries are supported by government actions determined to either curb the influence of foreign media or to keep it out altogether. As noted earlier, the amendments to the Income Tax Act which removed the ability of Canadian advertisers to claim deductions for expenses made outside Canada is just one model. Another is the simultaneous substitution rule in cable that has caused friction between the Canadian and American governments since its implementation in the early 1970s. The policy was inspired to a significant degree by the first of a series of spectacular failures initiated by the CRTC, albeit unwittingly. In July 1972, it awarded a license to Global Communications for a regional television network to operate in southern Ontario. Global was to be an agency that purchased programming from independent producers in Canada, as opposed to producing the material themselves. The network came on the air in early 1974, but by the end of the spring, it was apparent that it was in serious difficulty and that its very survival was at stake. The CRTC, rather than let its prize project go down the drain, intervened.

Part of the bailout followed up on an experiment that had been tried earlier in Western Canada. It involved the removal of commercial messages from programs imported from the United States when they were being transmitted on cable. American broadcasters were not happy with this arrangement and did their best to make it difficult. Viewers soon caught on to something being wrong when they missed touchdowns on NFL games or returned to a program part way through an American commercial message. The Commission decided on the simultaneous substitution rule, aimed directly at U.S. broadcasters.

It works this way: when a Canadian broadcaster is carrying a U.S. program at the same time as the American network, Canadian cable operators can only carry the Canadian signal. As an example, when NBC broadcasts *The West Wing*, CTV broadcasts the program at the same time. Both Canadian and American audiences see the same show, but the Canadian audiences see commercial content produced and funded in Canada. And, since the U.S. signal is blocked on Canadian cable systems, any multinational advertiser must buy space on the Canadian program to reach a Canadian audience. In effect, artificially inflated ratings for these programs exist because there is no choice, and, as a consequence, advertisers pay higher prices for the advertising space. Canadian television programmers worked to ensure that any American product they purchased was shown at the same time as any one of the commercial networks in the United States.

News Agencies

Canada instituted telegraph service not long after Samuel Morse first demonstrated the viability of his invention. In the beginning, most of the telegraphs transmitted commercial messages, but to keep the operators occupied between messages, it was decided that they could use the service to send information to local newspapers. Eventually, telegraph companies bought rights of way along major railway lines. Noting the success of the business, the Canadian Pacific Railway (CPR) decided to get into the news business. In 1894 it obtained a monopoly franchise to distribute Associated Press material in Canada. When the CPR attempted to double its price in 1907, a group of newspapermen in Winnipeg decided to set up the Western Associated Press in competition with the CPR. They challenged the railway's rate structure, won the battle and, in 1910, the railway got out of the news business entirely, selling its assets to the Western Associated Press. In cooperation with regional news sharing cooperatives in Central Canada and the Maritimes, a company called Canadian Press was born.

It was not until 1916 that a group of Canadian publishers reached agreement on how to fund and operate a national service. Part of the income for the new venture came from a $50,000 annual subsidy from the federal government. On September 1, 1917, Canadian Press opened an office in Toronto under general manager Charles Knowles, with a staff of 15 (Canadian Press employed a total of 72 staff across the country). For quite some time, Canadian Press was a non-profit cooperative news gathering agency designed to service only the newspaper industry. By the mid-1930s, the newly emerging radio industry began to discover the advantage of newscasting. In 1933, Canadian Press and the CBC signed a contract that bound the agency to write and air a 1,200-word newscast nightly on the network. It was the first step into broadcast for Canadian Press.

Canadian Press (CP) showed no interest in expanding its horizons in broadcast beyond the CBC. As a result, an American organization devoted to servicing only broadcasters signed up 25 Canadian stations when Associated Press refused to serve them. The agency, Transradio, operated out of a Toronto office. Another American agency, the United Press set up a Canadian broadcast subsidiary that is called British United Press in an aim to attract clients in Canada. In retaliation, Canadian press expanded its broadcast service to three, 1,000-word reports daily. In 1939 Canadian Press signed a deal with the CBC that gave it access to all of CP's content. In 1940 Transradio withdrew from Canada, and in 1941, the CBC founded its first, in-house broadcast news operation. Other than the CBC Radio and now television service, the only remaining broadcast news service in Canada is Broadcast News, an arm of Canadian Press. Although CP has been close to demise on a number of occasions due to battles among its members, it continues as the only major domestic agency to provide national and international news to Canadian media. Reuters also operates a small Canadian bureau, as does the French language service *L'Agence France Presse,* along with small and dedicated services such as the business service Canada News Wire.

Broadcast Media

As in most industrialized nations, the broadcast media are significant players. In Canada, there is a mixed private and public system. Until 1958, as noted above, the public Canadian Broadcasting Corporation dominated the system, owning stations, producing programs, and regulating the private sector. Private stations were allowed to exist, but in areas without CBC service, they were expected to broadcast a significant proportion of CBC programming. In many cases, this led to a great amount of duplication in the marketplace. Before CHCH-TV in Hamilton, Ontario, became an independent in the early 1960s, it broadcast a full schedule of CBC programming, although it was only about 30 minutes away from the CBC production headquarters in Toronto. With the granting of licenses to private operators in 1960 and the subsequent birth of CTV, the Canadian Television Network, the pendulum swung toward the private sector. In the first years of the twenty-first century, Canada remained a nation with a mixed public and private system, although some levels of government have indicated that they wish to divest themselves of broadcasting responsibilities.

The Canadian Broadcasting Corporation operates four major television networks, two in English and two in French, in addition to a limited service covering the nation's Arctic regions. Two networks are targeted to mass audiences in both English and French Canada. Although the content is primarily produced in Canada by Canadians, these two networks differ little from any American commercial network in tone and appearance. To a significant degree, they are supported by advertising. Since the CBC receives an annual subsidy from the federal Parliament of $795 million out of a total budget of $1.32 billion, private broadcasters have often complained that the corporation is involved in unfair competition. The corporation's other two networks, News World in English and RDI in French, are cable channels. They are information channels with some similarities to CNN and they are supported by advertising to a significant degree.

Radio service in Canada reflects that of television. The CBC operates four radio networks, two in English and two in French. The primary networks are dedicated to extensive news, information, and current affairs coverage. Both stereo services are primarily in the business of programming music, with a classical music base and many live concerts. In the late twentieth and early twenty-first centuries, the CBC has abandoned a number of AM licenses to the private sector with the aim of converting most of its broadcasting service to FM. Together with the private sector, the CBC operates four specialty channels: Galaxie, a 30-channel continuous music broadcaster; ARTV, which focuses on arts; the Canadian Documentary Channel; and Country Canada. All of these are offered as subscriber operations. The CBC continues to sign affiliation agreements with private owners to broadcast CBC produced programming, especially on television. The CBC also operates Radio-Canada International, a short-wave service operated out of New Brunswick. It broadcasts in English, French, Spanish, Chinese, Arabic, Russian and Ukrainian. The service has faced closure on several occasions as CBC public funding fell.

The second most important segment of the public sector is provincial operations. There are six such operations, and one, ACCESS Alberta, is a hybrid: privately owned and operated with the bulk of its programming contracted to the provincial government. It operates both radio and television stations. The largest and most dominant of the educational networks operates in Ontario. It has both an English language service, TVOntario, and a French language service, *Télévision Français d'Ontario* (TFO). In some ways, programming resembles that of the American public television system (PBS), but there is a stronger reliance on locally produced programming. TVO and TFO are one of the largest producers of children's programming in both the English- and French-speaking worlds. For the most part, the system is funded by the government of Ontario. However, the system does have frequent membership fundraising drives. Along with TVO-TFO, educational television systems exist in Québec (*Télé-Québec*), in British Columbia (The Knowledge Network), the Maritime provinces (MITV), Alberta (ACCESS), and Saskatchewan (the Saskatchewan Community Network). As well as public television and radio, and educational channels, the Canadian legislatures operate channels to broadcast parliamentary proceedings and the Canadian version of C-Span, called C-PAC, can be found on cable systems across the country.

Much of the remainder of the radio and television system across the country can be found in corporate and private hands. The largest is BellGlobeMedia, owners of both the CTV Television Network and Canada's national newspaper the *Globe and Mail.* Until recently, the CTV network was owned by a cooperative operated by the CTV affiliates, each of whom owned the same amount of shares. As new stations began to join the system, individual share percentages dropped. As a consequence, an offer was made by Toronto's Baton Broadcasting, then owners of CFTO-TV, to purchase the majority shares. The CRTC approved the deal, and the cooperative ceased to exist. CTV is now free to make affiliation agreements with other privately held stations without surrendering share value. The other private, national network is operated by Can West Global Communications, which also is a major newspaper owner. Global began life as a regional, private network in 1972. After a bankruptcy scare, it changed hands several times until it was purchased by the Asper family of Winnipeg, the current owners.

The remainder of the Canadian media market is divided among several smaller players. The most significant player in this field is CHUM Limited of Toronto, which owns a number of radio and television stations across the country. Their most visible television presence is Much Music, the Canadian counterpart to MTV. Much Music operates three channels, one for everyday hits, one for older tunes and a new digital channel called Music Music Loud, created for heavy metal listeners. The owners of A-Channel, a western-based media family, were expanding into Ontario at the turn of the twenty-first century. They were granted a license to serve Toronto, with a new outlet planned for 2003. The emphasis of Corus Entertainment, an offshoot of the Shaw cable interests from Calgary, remains mainly in radio. Other players include Rogers Communications, the country's largest cable operator, who also owns television and radio stations as well as the Québec based Telemedia Corporation.

In Québec, the privately owned and operated counterpart to the English-language CTV is TVA, headquartered in Montréal. It has a smaller competitor, *Télévision Quatre Saisons* (Four Seasons Television), which has teetered on the brink of insolvency in the past.

At the turn of the twenty-first century, Canadian television had access to 82 specialty channels. Some, such as CBC News World and RDI, were part of the cable packages that both cable operators and satellite systems offered as part of their extended basic services. They were packaged with regular, off-air channels at a monthly fee. Others were packaged with U.S. superstations such as WGN Chicago or WSBK Boston as pay-TV channels. Recently, a new cast of digital channels became available, all of which are sold through separate subscription systems. Canadians wishing to access the most television channels can either subscribe to a cable service or opt for connection to a satellite system such as Direct TV or Star Choice.

The operating revenue for Canada's commercial television stations in 2000 was $1,887,221. Operating expenses amounted to $1,708,607, leaving an operating profit of $178,614. After corporate taxes were applied, this amount dropped to $105,225. The results do not include cable television operations, pay television, or any non-commercial endeavors.

Cable television has existed in Canada for a long time. It was begun in London, Ontario by Edward Jarmain when he decided a large receiving antenna on an elevated piece of land would vastly improve signals arrived in that city from the United States. London was geographically close to major U.S. cities, but not close enough to get reliable reception from the network stations that broadcast from those localities. In its early years, cable was promoted as a reliable way to receive interference free and reliable signals from distant stations. In Toronto in the mid-1960s, cable companies carried Buffalo's PBS station, WNED, in order to attract upper-income Ontarians to the systems. For some time, WNED could not be received off air in Toronto. Other cable companies in other communities also used similar techniques resulting in rapid cable growth. By 1975, six out of ten Canadians subscribed to a cable system. Provincial governments in Québec and the Prairies challenged federal jurisdiction over cable citing the fact that cable systems did not cross provincial boundaries and therefore should be provincially regulated. In 1977 the Supreme Court of Canada disagreed, and cable remained under federal jurisdiction.

Since the technology existed to import more and more distant channels, mainly from the United States, pressure was put on the CRTC to open more channels for this purpose. The commission was concerned that importing channels to areas where those channels were not licensed to serve would fragment the audience of Canadian-based stations and negatively impact their incomes. As a result, when cable companies asked the regulator to include some of these channels, they were often refused. For years, the Fox outlet in Buffalo, WUTV, was not allowed on Canadian cable systems in Ontario. This kind of scenario repeated itself many times across the country. Not only were cable companies subject to this kind of regulatory practice, they were also forced to set aside a channel for community programming which was intended to be advertiser free. There are now over two hundred of these operating in Canada with a variety of local programming, ranging from live sports, church services, bingo games, political talk shows, and interview programming to local documentary features. The cable industry also finances and operates the aforementioned C-PAC, the Public Affairs Access Channel.

Cable came into its own in the early 1980s when the CRTC decided to license a number of channels with the express purpose of operating as cable-only channels. Initially, these channels were offered on a subscriber basis only, but eventually, most of the original cable-only services became part of cable's basic package. Throughout the remaining years of the twentieth century, cable operators added a number of new services, including movie channels, digital channels, and home shopping channels. Analog systems in Canada now regularly feature up to 78 channels consisting of everything from locally produced community shows, regular CBC, CTV and Global service and any one of a number of channels from outside Canada. Near the end of the 1990s, Rogers Cable in Toronto introduced a high-speed Internet service through its cable system. Other major players such as Shaw, Groupe Videotron, and Cogeco have followed. To accommodate the new services and in anticipation of local and long distance telephone licenses, cable companies in Canada launched an extensive capital investment into converting their service to wide band fiber optics cable.

At the turn of the century, the cable industry was faced with choosing a massive expansion strategy or merging with companies devoted to doing so. Revenues remained high for cable operators, coming in at $2,055,956. However, expenditures outstripped revenues, with a resultant overall loss of $192,666. The largest single expenditure was on technical services at $724,893. In all, Canadian systems operated 219,000 kilometers of line in the country.

Electronic News Media

By the late 1990s, virtually every major news medium in the country operated a web site. Only the smaller ones, such as Saskatchewan Community Television, did

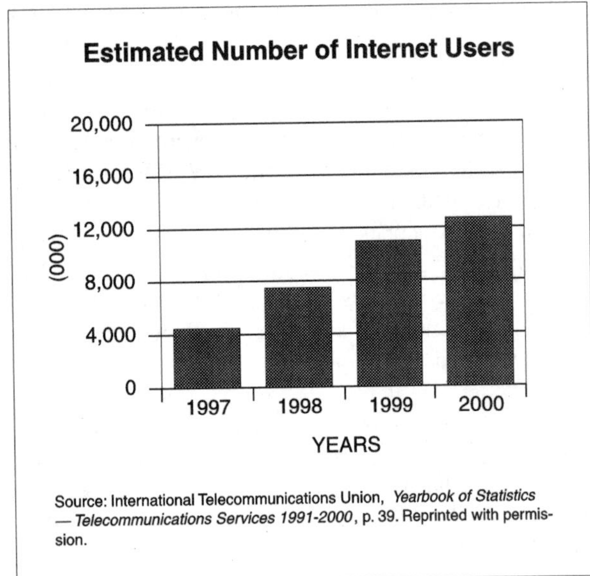

Source: International Telecommunications Union, *Yearbook of Statistics — Telecommunications Services 1991-2000*, p. 39. Reprinted with permission.

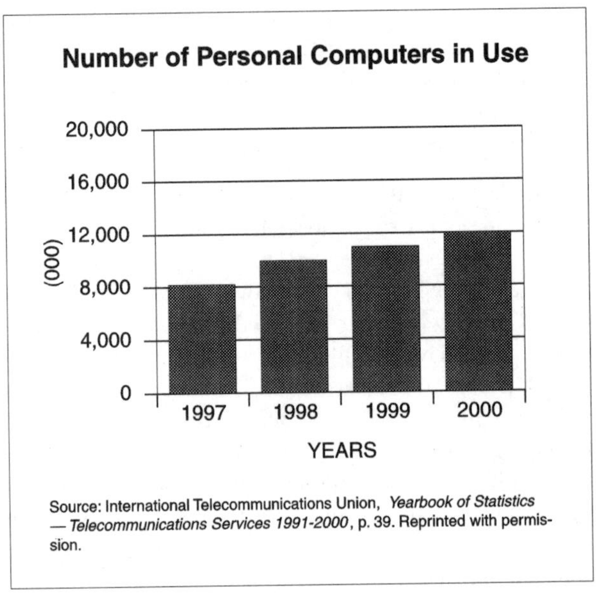

Source: International Telecommunications Union, *Yearbook of Statistics — Telecommunications Services 1991-2000*, p. 39. Reprinted with permission.

not. BellGlobeMedia designed an instant update news site and the CBC site is also operated on a frequent update system. Others change information daily and some weekly. However, very few sites were used to originate news. Most copy came either from a newspaper's city room or from radio and television newsrooms. Internet usage in Canada during the 1990s and onwards continued to grow. In 2000, 51 percent of all Canadian households measured by Statistics Canada had at least one family member who was an Internet user. That represented an increase from 42 percent in 1999. The study covered 34,000 households. The majority of users reported that home was the best place for them to access the Internet. The most significant growth was the rise of cable as a major access provider. In the year 2000, an estimated 1.6 million Canadian households were connecting to the Internet through their cable companies. This represents an increase of 155 percent over those who reported in 1999. However, 3.7 million households connected by telephone lines, representing a growth rate of 29 percent in the same period. Close to 50 percent of all users connected read the news. This falls well behind interest in general browsing, seeking information about health and travel, and the use of e-mail. However, it did exceed other Internet factors such as e-banking and e-commerce. Higher income families tended to use the Internet more often.

EDUCATION & TRAINING

Until recently, communications and media studies have been in short supply in Canadian universities. For years, Canadian post-secondary education closely followed the British model, in which the arts, sciences, humanities and social sciences formed the core of the institution and were complemented by prestige professional faculties in law, teaching, engineering, and medicine. Journalism was treated largely as a technical skill, and, as a result, the largest number of journalism programs was offered by junior colleges of applied arts and technology across the country. This practice stands in contrast to the American experience where journalistic and press training often reside side by side with academically driven communications studies programs in major universities.

In Canada, the newest member of the journalistic community came to the University of British Columbia in the late 1990s as the result of a large grant by the Sing Tao newspaper chain. The program offers a two-year Master of Arts degree to a small number of students wishing to study newspaper journalism. The University of Western Ontario has Canada's oldest journalism program, which opened in 1947. It currently operates the program under the umbrella of the Faculty of Information and Media Studies and has a significant academic program combined with professional training. Carleton University in Ottawa also opened a journalism program in 1947 only a few short days after the Western program opened. It offers a four-year Bachelor of Arts degree in journalism as well as a Masters in Journalism (M.J.). Carleton also offers extensive educational opportunities at the graduate level in mass communications studies. The University of Regina, King's College University in Halifax, the University of Québec at Montréal, Concordia University in Montréal, and Ryerson Polytechnical University in Toronto also offer undergraduate degrees in journalism. Ryerson also offers a separate degree in Radio and Television Arts as well as a two-year post-degree program for those holding a Bachelor's degree from another institution. In the late 1990s, there was massive growth in universities who began to offer interdisciplinary programs in media and communications studies. These programs are mostly oriented toward academic, not professional, study.

SUMMARY

In most respects, Canada remains a healthy media market, although concerns about concentration of ownership continue to be voiced. In spite of several government commissions that have investigated this situation, little has changed since the introduction of television in the early 1950s. Most of the nation's media, including newspapers and magazines, broadcasting stations, and Internet sites, are now owned and operated by large, profit-driven corporations. Unlike other states in the western world, in particular the United States, public broadcasting continues to exist and in most cases thrive in spite of tightening budgets and calls for privatization. With the exception of the Canadian Broadcasting Corporation's television networks, the significant majority of public broadcasters are also educational broadcasters. As a consequence, the daytime schedules of these stations are primarily focused to attract younger viewers, especially those in school. In the evening, most of these stations turn their attention to culturally enriched programming such as documentaries, other forms of current affairs programming combined with high quality dramatic series, many of which are imported either from Britain or France. Some operations, such as TVOntario, use membership lists in order to raise funds.

Although the Canadian Broadcasting Corporation calls itself a public broadcaster, in most respects it behaves more like a commercial broadcaster. With very few exceptions, notably those in news and current affairs programming, the corporation attempts to attract advertisers. Although its programming content is primarily produced in Canada and reflects Canadian issues and themes, its on-air presence has a very commercial look to it. Each spring, as the hockey playoffs begin, the CBC regularly reschedules its evening programming content to cover the competition for the Stanley Cup, even if this means shifting its popular 10 PM newscast to a different time. Non-hockey fans have long voiced their objection to the predominance of hockey games, which can occupy Canadian Broadcasting Corporation screens from late March to early June on a nightly basis. The CBC has long argued that it needs the revenue that these events generate.

American media and some broadcasting from Europe are available on Canadian cable systems and through direct home satellite services. The American networks NBC, CBS, ABC, WB and UPN are not unfamiliar to Canadians. In fact, the most viewed programs in Canada often originate from outside the country. In that respect, Canada is becoming more international in its production perspective. Due to the relative decline in value of the Canadian dollar, many American production companies find it to their advantage to shoot both television series and films in Canadian locations. The popular *X-Files* program was, for most of its life, shot in Vancouver, British Columbia. One of the country's largest production firms, Alliance-Atlantis, is involved in both film and television production and regularly sells its products to both Canadian and American television outlets.

Canadian publications are directed to audiences in Canada for the most part. With the exception of Toronto and Montréal, and to some degree Vancouver, Canadians can receive only one daily local newspaper. However both the *Globe and Mail* and the *National Post* have attempted to convince Canadian readers that they are national in scope in spite of the fact that both are published in Toronto. Due to satellite hookups and contracts with localized printing firms, both newspapers can arrive at homes and businesses across the country on a same day publication and delivery system. As with television, the country's most popular periodicals are, for the most part, imported from the United States. Canada does have a small, but volatile magazine industry. The largest and most popular publication is *Maclean's—Le Magazine Maclean* which is a weekly public affairs journal. Most other stable magazines in the country are tightly targeted journals aimed at specific, but often small constituencies such as hunters, homemakers, brides, or car aficionados.

Electronic, digitally based communications systems have been readily adapted by Canadian consumers. Cable television penetration has always been very high in Canada, due in the most part because signals from the United States could not be received with any technical stability, except in those regions where American transmitters existed in relatively close proximity to Canadians. When direct-to-home satellite service came to Canada, rural communities not wired for cable soon joined the international viewing community. Both services laid the groundwork for the rapidly growing Internet connections, as noted above. Canada is a world leader in the manufacture and use of fiber optics technology. Canada continues to wire its remaining communities at a rapid pace.

If there is any genuine fear about the future of the media in Canada, it is the potential take-over of Canadian media by American interests. Canadians have not forgotten the 1920s, when RCA's David Sarnoff declared that North America, in his mind, was one giant media market. Canada has continued to implement protective measures such as those noted above. Although NAFTA supporters continue to argue that the agreement exempts Canadian cultural industries from the free trade provisions of the treaty, NAFTA opponents continue to argue that the clauses are weak. Only time will tell who is correct.

BIBLIOGRAPHY

''57% of Canadians read a daily newspaper.'' Canadian Newspaper Association. Accessed May 2002. Available from http://www.cna-acj.ca/newspapers/facts/history.asp.

''Address Listings for Daily Newspapers.'' Canadian Newspaper Association. Accessed May 2002. Available from http://www.cna-acj.ca/newspapers/facts/history.asp.

Buckley, Peter. *The National Link.* Toronto, Ontario: The Canadian Press Association, 1997.

''Canadian Circulation Data.'' Canadian Newspaper Association. Accessed May 2002. Available from http://www.cna-acj.ca/newspapers/facts/history.asp.

''Canadian Daily Newspapers Advertising Expenditures.'' Newspaper Association of America. Accessed May 2002. Available from http://www.naa.org/info/facts00/29.html.

''Canadian Daily Newspaper Trivia.'' Canadian Newspaper Association. Accessed May 2002. Available from http://www.cna-acj.ca/newspapers/facts/history.asp.

''The Canadian Encyclopedia.'' Historica. Accessed May 2002. Available from http://www.histori.ca.

Canadian Press Association. *A History of Canadian Journalism.* Toronto, Ontario: Canadian Press Association Historical Committee, 1908.

Crack, W.A. *A History of Canadian Journalism Volume 2.* Toronto, Ontario: The Ontario Publishing Company Limited, 1959.

Creighton, Donald. *The Story of Canada.* London, U.K.: Faber and Faber, 1971.

''The Daily.'' Statistics Canada. Accessed May 2002. Available from http://www.statcan.ca.

Desbarats, Peter. *Guide to Canadian News Media.* Toronto, Ontario: Harcourt, Brace and Jovanovich, 1990.

''The Evolution of Newspapers.'' Canadian Newspaper Association. Accessed May 2002. Available from http://www.cna-acj.ca/newspapers/facts/history.asp.

Fetherling, Douglas. *The Rise of the Canadian Newspaper.* Toronto, Ontario: The Oxford University Press, 1990.

Kesterton, W. H. *A History of Journalism In Canada.* Ottawa, Ontario: The Carleton Library No. 36, 1967.

Martin, Robert. *Media Law: Essentials of Canadian Law.* Concord, Ontario: Irwin Law, 1997.

Osler, Andrew M. *News: The Evolution of Journalism In Canada.* Toronto, Ontario: Copp, Clark, Pitman, Ltd., 1993.

''Ownership of Canadian Daily Newspapers.'' Canadian Newspaper Association. Accessed May 2002. Available from http://www.cna-acj.ca/newspapers/facts/history.asp.

Raboy, Marc. *Missed Opportunities: The Story of Canada's Broadcasting Policy.* Montréal and Kingston: McGill-Queen's University Press, 1990.

Resnick, Philip. *The Masks of Proteus: Canadian Reflections On The State.* Montréal and Kingston: McGill-Queen's University Press, 1990.

Singer, Benjamin, and Craig McKie, eds. *Communications In Canadian Society Fifth Edition.* Toronto, Ontario: Thomson Educational Publishing, 2001.

Sotiron, Minko. *From Politics To Profit: The Commercialization of Canadian Daily Newspapers, 1890-1920.* Montréal and Kingston: McGill-Queen's University Press, 1997.

Taras, David, and Helen Holmes. *Seeing Ourselves: Media Power and Policy in Canada.* Toronto, Ontario: Harcourt, Brace and Jovanovich, 1992.

Television Bureau of Canada. Accessed May 2002. Available from http://www.tvb.ca.

Vipond, Mary. *Listening In: The First Decade of Canadian Broadcasting 1922-1932.* Montréal and Kingston: McGill-Queen's University Press, 1992.

—David R. Spencer

CAPE VERDE

BASIC DATA

Official Country Name:	Republic of Cape Verde
Region (Map name):	Africa
Population:	401,343
Language(s):	Portuguese, Crioulo
Literacy rate:	71.6%

Cape Verde is an archipelago of small, volcanic islands off the coast of western Africa in the North Atlantic Ocean. Colonized by the Portugese in the fifteenth century, the islands won their independence from Portugal in 1975. The population of Cape Verde is approximately 400,000, and the literacy rate is about 71 percent. Portugese is the official language, but most citizens speak Creole or Crioulo, which mixes Creole Portugese with West African words. A President acts as the chief of state, and a Prime Minister heads the government. The legislative body is the popularly elected National Assembly. Cape Verde is a largely poor country, and government launched programs in the 1990s and early twenty-first century to develop the private sector and attract foreign investment. Most of the current economy is service-related, including commerce, transportation and public services.

When the new President took office in 2001, some agencies that monitor world press freedoms reported allegations of governmental interference with the media. The new authorities shut down the country's only daily newspaper, the *Horizonte,* citing a need to develop new information policies. The country does have other publications, however. *A Semana* is a weekly newspaper. *Opiniao, Noticias,* and *Agaviva* are monthly periodicals. *Novo Jornal Cabo Verde* is a government publication that appears twice weekly, and *Terra Nova* is issued monthly by the Catholic Church. All publications are printed in Portugese.

Cape Verde has 11 FM radio stations but no AM stations. There are approximately 73,000 radios on the island. There is one television station broadcasting to approximately 2,000. Cabonet is the country's only Internet service provider.

BIBLIOGRAPHY

''Cape Verde Islands,'' Central Intelligence Agency (CIA). *World Fact Book 2001.* Available from http://www.cia.gov.

''Country Report: Cape Verde,'' *The Committee to Protect Journalists, 1998.* Available from http://www.cpj.org.

U.S. Department of State Bureau of Democracy, Human Rights and Labor. ''Cape Verde Country Report.'' *Human Rights Practices for 1998 Report.* Available from http://www.usis.usemb.se.

''Cape Verde,'' *Worldinformation.com 2002.* Available from http:www.worldinformation.com.

—*Jenny B. Davis*

CAYMAN ISLANDS

BASIC DATA

Official Country Name:	Cayman Islands
Region (Map name):	North & Central America
Population:	34,763
Language(s):	English
Literacy rate:	98%

This series of three Caribbean Islands between Cuba and Honduras was originally sighted by Christopher Columbus in 1503 during his fourth and final voyage to the New World. Ships from the Netherlands, Great Britain, Spain, and France used the islands for watering and provisioning.

The Cayman Islands enjoy the press freedoms of British citizens. The *Caymanian Compass* is the national daily newspaper. It is published Monday through Friday by the Cayman Free Press Ltd., which lists circulation at ten thousand. The *Cayman Net News* publishes a weekly tabloid-style print newspaper. Its online edition is updated regularly every Tuesday and Thursday and contains unique content.

There are five FM radio stations and one AM radio station for approximately 36,000 radios. There are about 7,000 televisions in the country and four local television stations. There are 16 Internet service providers.

The islands came under British rule when Oliver Cromwell's army captured Jamaica from the Spanish in 1655, and British continued to colonize the islands via Jamaica through the nineteenth century. When Jamaica became an independent state in 1962, however, the Cayman Islands remained a British dependency. Population is estimated at forty thousand, with a literacy rate of approximately 98 percent. English is the official language, but Jamaican Patois and dialects of Spanish are also spoken. The chief of state is the British monarch, represented locally by an appointed official called the Governor and President of the Executive Council, which is the cabinet. There is a unicameral, eighteen-seat Legislative Assembly. Caymanians enjoy a high standard of living predominantly due to tourism—especially diving—and offshore banking industries.

BIBLIOGRAPHY

Cayman Islands Web site. 2002. Available from www.caymanislands.ky.

Cayman Islands Government. 2002. Retrieved February 28, 2002, Available from www.gov.ky.

The Central Intelligence Agency (CIA).*The World Fact Book 2001*. 2001. Available from www.cia.gov.

Worldinformation.com, Country Profile. 2002. Available from www.worldinformation.com.

Cayman News Net. 2002. Available from www.caymannetnews.com.

—*Jenny B. Davis*

CENTRAL AFRICAN REPUBLIC

BASIC DATA

Official Country Name:	Central African Republic
Region (Map name):	Africa
Population:	3,512,751
Language(s):	French, Sangho, Arabic, Hunsa, Swahili
Literacy rate:	60%

BACKGROUND & GENERAL CHARACTERISTICS

The Central African Republic (*Centr'Afrique*, *Centrafrique*, or CAR) is located in the heart of Africa, south of Chad and the Sudan and north of Congo and the Democratic Republic of Congo. Its capital is Bangui. The CAR's 3.8 million people have experienced significant political instability since gaining independence from France in 1960. When French troops finally left the CAR in 1997, internal security was facilitated by the presence of UN troops, the UN Mission to the Central African Republic (MINURCA), the transformed version of a French-financed peacekeeping force composed of troops from several Francophone African states. Most of the UN peacekeeping force withdrew in March 2000.

Ange-Félix Patassé, a member of the Sara ethnic group, is the CAR's elected president, in power since 1993. He was most recently elected to office in 1999, winning out over nine other candidates in an election seen as neither free nor fair. Civil unrest has been high since independence and built to excessive proportions in 2001. On May 28, 2001, a coup attempt led by former President André Kolingba, an ethnic Yakoma, and soldiers loyal to him was halted after ten days of fighting in which over 200 people were estimated to have been killed. Government troops, assisted by foreign mercenaries, put down the rebellion. Another coup attempt took place in November 2001 when fighting re-erupted, with civilians, including women and children, reportedly killed in the crossfire.

The print media in the CAR are less popular and less influential than the broadcast media, due to the high level of illiteracy in the country and the high costs of printed newspapers, which are out of reach for the average citizen. The CAR's principal languages are French and Sangho. Newspapers and television broadcasts do not typically reach the areas outside the capital or other urban areas. Radio broadcasts are the most widely used means of spreading news.

The government produces three newspapers that represent the perspectives of the MLPC, the president's party. They are *Centrafrique Presse*, the Agence Centrafricaine de Presse (ACAP) bulletin (an irregularly published news source), and *Be African Sango* (not published in 2001 due to financial constraints). Eight to twelve independent newspapers also are published, though not all on a regular basis. *Echo de CentrAfrique* presents views aligned with the president's party but is a private daily paper. Other independent papers are *Le Citoyen*, *Le Novateur*, *L'Hirondelle*, and *Le Démocrate*.

Although both government-run and private newspapers criticized public policies and alleged corruption prior to an increase in civil unrest during 2001, the government has increasingly restricted freedom of the press and of expression since 2001. Journalists have been fined, arrested, imprisoned, tortured, and threatened with death for covering news about political violence or for publishing reports viewed as unfavorable to the government.

ECONOMIC FRAMEWORK

The Central African Republic is one of Africa's most richly endowed countries in terms of natural resources, but its economy is substantially underdeveloped. Diamonds, timber, cotton, coffee, and tobacco are the country's principal exports. Annual per capita income is only about US $290. Life expectancy is very short—just 42 years for men and 46 years for women.

PRESS LAWS

The Constitution guarantees freedom of speech and freedom of the press. However, government censorship is widely felt.

CENSORSHIP

In the months following the May 2001 attempted coup, the government tried controlling the news media and in November 2001 stopped a press conference from taking place where attorneys planned to protest the government's detention of Assingambi Zarambaud, a lawyer accused of participating in the May coup. In September 2001 police had beaten Advocate Zarambaud in the street for his article in Le Citoyen critical of the government inquiry into the arrest and mistreatment of Abdoulaye Aboukary Tembelé, a human rights defender, in February 2001. Zarambaud was held for three months without being charged.

Late in 2001 the former military chief of staff of the CAR's armed forces, General François Bozizé, who was accused of participating in the November 2001 coup, reported that the government was preventing him from making press statements to Agence France-Presse ''because apparently they [his statements] are sensational.'' Bozizé and his supporters later fled to Chad.

STATE-PRESS RELATIONS

Relations between the government and the press have been inimical since the 2001 coup attempts. Although at the start of the new millennium President Patassé was allowing the media to operate without significant government interference, he made it clear that the press would be restricted if journalists were to use it ''to incite rebellion.'' In February 2001 Abdoulaye Aboukary Tembelé, a journalist and key defender of human rights, was beaten and tortured at the National Gendarmerie headquarters after an opinion poll he produced, deemed unflattering to the president, was published in the *Journal des Droits de l'Homme*. Entitled ''Should President Patassé Resign?,'' the poll indicated that most citizens supported the idea of the president's resignation.

Later in 2001 government security forces seized printing equipment and issues from the *Groupement des Editeurs de la Presse Privé* (GEPPIC), an association of editors of the independent press, for criticizing government behavior in the May 2001 attempted coup.

Father Tonino Falagoista, the director of the Roman Catholic radio station *Radio Notre Dame*, was held by the government for two months after being arrested by the Mixed Commission, set up by the government to investigate the May coup attempt. Father Falagoista had refused to deny his authorship of a report of three mass graves of persons killed by the security forces in the unrest and for criticizing the killing of Yakomas (members of the former president's ethnic group) in the coup attempt.

Many Yakoma journalists fled abroad after May. After the coup attempts even journalists from President Patassé's Sara ethnic group were obliged to subdue their criticism of the regime. According to the Committee to Protect Journalists, ''The few who dared to speak out against the violence, such as editor Maka Gbossokotto of Le Citoyen, were quickly silenced with death threats.''

At the close of 2001 some of the journalists who had left the country during the civil unrest had returned to the CAR. By that time, state media workers, perceiving ''the smallest margin for free speech'' as being destroyed by ''political censors,'' themselves were protesting government interference in their work.

ATTITUDE TOWARD FOREIGN MEDIA

Africa Number One, a private radio station belonging to a French broadcasting network and broadcasting from Libreville, Gabon, reaches listeners in the CAR. Radio France International broadcasts in the CAR and includes local reporters among its staff.

BROADCAST MEDIA

Radio Ndeke Luka, a Bangui-based broadcasting station established by the Swiss foundation, Hirondelle, financed by foreign governments and development organizations, and sponsored by the United Nations, offers balanced news coverage and rebroadcasts programs from international sources. Radio Ndeke Luka broadcasts on both FM and short-wave frequencies.

Although private television broadcasting is legally permitted, the government has effectively controlled television broadcasts. Its High Council of Communications has exercised authority over all television programming in the country.

The government-run Radiodiffusion-Centrafricaine Television provides other radio and television stations whose programs have little to say about the political opposition. Radio Centrafrique is the main government station. Radio Notre Dame, financed by the Vatican, is a Roman Catholic station based in Bangui. Radio Nostalgia is another alternative to government radio.

Broadcasting by Radio Centrafrique was briefly halted during the May 2001 coup attempt when rebel soldiers destroyed its main transmitter. During that time the government temporarily replaced its radio broadcasts with those from an impromptu government station, Radio Paix et Liberté, set up in the president's home.

Private satellite and cable television stations are permitted to broadcast their programs into the CAR, but few people can afford satellite or cable television.

ELECTRONIC NEWS MEDIA

The government does not limit Internet access. Domestic Internet service and e-mail service are available through a private telecommunications company. A cyber café, Bangui 2000, offers citizens Internet access.

SUMMARY

Civil unrest and violence have damaged the ability of journalists and the press to operate freely and without fear of government repression in the Central African Republic. Decades of political instability and questionable democratic practice have made it imperative for alternative news sources, including those financed by outside, foreign sources and non-governmental organizations, to find their way into the CAR. Due to the high levels of illiteracy and poverty that persist in the CAR despite the country's natural richness, radio is the preferred means of news communication and the most popular medium for public expression.

BIBLIOGRAPHY

Amnesty International. ''Central African Republic.'' *Amnesty International Report 2002*. London: Amnesty International, May 28, 2002. Available from www.amnesty.org/.

BBC Monitoring. ''Country profile: Central African Republic.'' Reading, UK: British Broadcasting Corporation, 2002. Available from news.bbc.co.uk/.

Bureau of Democracy, Human Rights, and Labor, U.S. Department of State. ''Central African Republic.'' *Country Reports on Human Rights Practices 2001*. Washington, DC: Bureau of Public Affairs, U.S. Department of State, 2002. Available from www.state.gov/.

Committee to Protect Journalists. ''Central African Republic.'' *Attacks on the Press in 2001: Africa 2001*. New York, NY: CPJ, 2002. Available from www.cpj.org/.

Reporters without Borders. ''Central African Republic.'' *Africa Annual Report 2002*. Paris, France: Reporters sans frontiers, April 20, 2002. Available at www.rsf.org/.

—Barbara A. Lakeberg-Dridi

CHAD

BASIC DATA

Official Country Name:	Republic of Chad
Region (Map name):	Africa
Population:	8,424,504
Language(s):	French, Arabic, Sara, Sango
Literacy rate:	48.1%

BACKGROUND & GENERAL CHARACTERISTICS

Chad is a large, politically unstable, militarized, multiparty democracy located in central Africa, south of Libya, west of the Sudan, north of the Central African Republic and Cameroon, and east of Nigeria and Niger. Its capital is N'Djamena. Chad's 8.5 million people live in one of the poorest countries in the world, despite the fact that many lucrative natural resources, including oil, gold, and uranium, are to be found which could be developed to yield significantly greater prosperity and social benefits for Chad's population. Thirty years of civil war and internal conflict have impoverished the people of Chad and made even rudimentary economic and social development extremely difficult.

Only in the early twenty-first century was a 650-mile oil pipeline project started in Chad and neighboring Cameroon in order to bring oil up from the expectedly numerous deposits lying below the surface of these two countries. The Exxon-Shell pipeline project, officially known as the Chad-Cameroon Oil Pipeline, will take 25 to 30 years to complete and involves drilling nearly 600 oil wells. The pipeline project is likely to bring an influx of multinationals and to increase the potential for government corruption and scandals as the oil industry is developed. It also has been remarked that the increasing oil wealth should be closely watched so as to avoid government corruption, particularly since radical Islam is on the rise in Chad and could easily become a stronger political force given oil profits or corrupt officials misusing oil monies.

The World Bank in mid-2002 was deliberating adding its financial support to the oil pipeline project and was scheduled to take a vote on this in October 2002. Much concern has been expressed by environmentalists and human rights activists that the project not follow the same path as oil development in Nigeria, which has devastated the originally pristine natural environment and destroyed the health and welfare of thousands, if not millions, of indigenous peoples living in the oil industry's way. On the positive side, the World Bank appointed an International Advisory Group (IAG) to examine the implications of the Cameroon-Chad pipeline project for the region's poor and to monitor government use of oil revenues. The IAG apparently was welcomed by at least some of Chad's journalists, who believed an independent monitoring body would better protect the country from government corruption.

The main languages used in Chad are Arabic in the north and French in the south. In terms of religious affiliation and ethnicity, the northerners are mainly light-skinned Arab Muslims and the southerners dark-skinned Christians, similar to the situation in neighboring Sudan. Decades of political violence linked to religious and ethnic differences and exploited by those hungry to take or remain in power, combined with severe drought conditions, have prevented Chad, primarily a desert nation, from developing a workable infrastructure, social services, and political stability. In consequence, the expected lifespan in Chad is quite short: 45 years for men and 50 years for women.

As of 2002 the president of Chad was Idriss Déby, who took power initially in 1990, promising ''no journalist will be prosecuted and from now on newspapers are free.'' However, as Reporters without Borders pointed out in their annual report for 2002, this desirable state of affairs had not yet materialized, nearly a dozen years later. Idriss' initial rise to the presidency was backed by Libya. After eight years of enduring a difficult political situation in which the north of the country was governed by one ruler and government and the south of Chad by another regime, Chad held its first multiparty elections. Though falling considerably short of international standards for free and fair electoral practices, the 1996 election confirmed Idriss as president, as he received about two-thirds of the vote on the first ballot. Violent unrest erupted throughout the country following the contested election for several weeks, several state electoral commission members resigned from their posts to protest the apparently fraudulent election, and the opposition candidates who ran against Déby threatened lawsuits due to the high levels of fraud that marked the election.

Since the 1996 election, continued armed rebellions have plagued the country, especially in the north. Riots in southern Chad in October 1997 left 80 unarmed civilians dead, massacred by government security forces from primarily the president's own ethnic group. In March 1998, apparently 100 additional unarmed civilians were killed.

The most popular, prevalent form of media is radio, owing to the high levels of illiteracy and poverty in the country. The government, opposition parties, and other private parties such as the Catholic Church and non-governmental human rights groups all publish newspapers.

The government directly controls two newspapers, *Info Tchad* and *Victoire* and shapes the weekly paper, *Le Progres.* Numerous private newspapers publish in the capital, including *N'Djamena Hebdo,* an independent weekly, *L'Observateur,* an independent bi-monthly, and two other key independent papers, *Le Temps* and *Le Contact.*

Very little freedom of expression or of the press exists in Chad. As Amnesty International's 2002 annual report put it, ''Freedom of expression continued to be threatened and human rights defenders worked in a climate of intimidation and danger.'' Criticizing the president or other government officials, reporting on the northern rebellion, or casting government officials in an unfavorable light are sufficient causes for landing journalists and parliamentarians—and occasionally even private citizens—in jail. For example, one Member of Parliament, Yorongar Ngarleyji, was imprisoned for several months after criticizing the oil pipeline project.

ECONOMIC FRAMEWORK

Chad has only recently begun to develop its oil resources. Its main exports are much less technologically complex: cotton, livestock, and textiles. Annual per capita income is quite low—only about US$200. The population in the north of Chad consists primarily of nomadic pastoralists, herding livestock to make their living. The southerners, on the other hand, depend more heavily on settled agriculture and urban trade, since Chad's major cities, including the capital, are located in the southern half of the country.

The private press suffers to some extent from the imposition of high government licensing fees. Nonetheless, a number of private newspapers are published, and many do not hesitate to openly criticize government officials, policies, and practices.

In 1994 a fund was legally established to assist the privately owned presses. However, none has ever been granting funding from this purse. Government-run media also are subject to financial problems, since funding is less than plentiful to replace outmoded, broken equipment. Consequently, broadcasting via the Radiodiffusion nationale tchadienne (RNT), the government-owned radio station, can only be effectively accomplished in major urban areas.

PRESS LAWS

The 1996 multiparty Constitution officially guarantees freedom of speech and freedom of the press. However, in practice the government severely restricts press freedom and to a somewhat lesser degree, freedom of speech.

The government communication regulatory authority, the High Council of Communications (HCC), ruled in April 2001 that political debates during the election campaign would be banned from broadcasts on private radio stations, that no one would be permitted to comment on news bulletins, and that radio stations found to be in non-compliance with the stipulations would be banned from all broadcasting for the period of the entire election campaign. Overall, the HCC is designed to operate as an intermediary to encourage free access to the media, but it has no real enforcement power.

CENSORSHIP

As observed above, considerable censorship exists in Chad—both self-censorship practiced by editors, journalists, and broadcasters, and active censorship by the government, anxious to preserve its position and to not risk losing control again of the country in a coup or riot situation.

In 2001 Michael Didama, the acting editor of the privately owned newspaper, *Le Temps,* appeared to be hit especially hard by government censorship and repression of the media. Apparently having alleged in 2000 the involvement of the president's own nephew and other relatives of the president in various coup attempts, Didama was arrested and given a six-month suspended sentence early in 2001 for having allegedly committed the crime of defamation. Harrassment of employees at *Le Temps* also reportedly occurred, with members of the government armed forces entering the newspaper offices after an article appeared that reported the number of deaths suffered in the north of Chad in the ongoing armed rebellion.

Other journalists and members of the media likewise suffered from government mistreatment, abuse, jail sentences, and fines in 2001, particularly around the elections. Even the state-owned media were not immune from attacks by the government, which exercised censorship both officially and unofficially. The official media also tended to report much more about the government, especially in a favorable light, than about the political opposition.

STATE-PRESS RELATIONS

Particularly during the presidential and parliamentary elections of 2001, relations between the government and the press were strained. When FM Liberté, a privately owned radio station, objected to the government ruling on press limitations during the 2001 election campaign, the station was threatened in May 2001 with closure by the HCC if it continued to broadcast programs on the campaign. A compromise agreement ultimately was reached, with the station permitted to cover the campaign except for its program entitled, *''Le club de la presse.''*

ATTITUDE TOWARD FOREIGN MEDIA

During the election campaign in 2001, two election observers from the Ivory Coast and Roger-François Hubert, a reporter working for an Ivoiran daily, *Le Belier,* were expelled from Chad after government officials accused them of not having proper legal clearance.

NEWS AGENCIES

The government operates one news agency in the country.

BROADCAST MEDIA

Only one television broadcasting service exists in Chad, government-owned Teletschad. Regarding radio, the government-owned Radiodiffusion Nationale Tchadienne, based in the capital, broadcasts nationally. As already noted, FM Liberté is a private station owned by a group of human rights organizations. *La Voix du Paysan* is the Catholic Church-owned radio station.

Private satellite TV channels and cable channels, while permitted by the government, reach only a small percentage of Chad's population due to low income levels and the high costs of owning a television set and accessing special broadcasting services. One new private television station was registered in Chad in 2001. A privately owned cable television station distributes foreign broadcasting to audiences in Chad, with programming in French and in Arabic, but few can afford the cost of the cable service. A South African cable company also operates a television station in the country via subscription.

ELECTRONIC NEWS MEDIA

Just one Internet access service provider exists in Chad, and it is owned by the government telecommunications monopoly. Although the government does not restrict public access to the Internet, the relatively affordable prices offered by the government Internet monopoly and the decent quality of service function as effective deterrents to the establishment of other competitive, privately run, Internet services within the country.

EDUCATION & TRAINING

During the presidential and parliamentary election campaign season in May 2001, the state media ridiculed the independent press, claiming journalists in the private media were poorly trained and unprofessional.

SUMMARY

Because Chad has undergone so many decades of internal conflict that have not yet been resolved and do not yet appear to be coming to a close anytime soon, it is unlikely that the country will develop a free and independent media in the near future. Continued government repression is expected to limit the capacity of journalists and broadcasters to freely publish and transmit a wide range of viewpoints. However, with the impending development of the oil industry through the Chad-Cameroon Oil Pipeline project, the World Bank is likely to send international monitors to observe the development of the industry, the use of oil profits, and the involvement of Chadian government officials in the development process. This may bode well for the future of free expression and freedom of the press in the country, since it will be harder for the government both to unduly influence or to repress private parties, be they oil companies or the private press, or to mishandle oil profits if the country and its leaders are being watched more closely by responsible observers from the outside.

Nonetheless, it is difficult to imagine the free development of the oil industry without excessive government intervention, considering the scenario of Nigeria and other African states where lucrative natural resources have been discovered and developed. This is especially the case in the context of the ongoing civil violence in the north of Chad. Certainly, foreign investment is unlikely to be attracted to Chad or to thrive if the country is rampant with continuous violent ethnic and religious conflict, nor are investors likely to ignore the problems of civil unrest without attempting to instill a measure of control themselves on the situation, as has so sadly and disastrously happened in many of the oil-rich regions of Nigeria. For the benefit of human rights and the future of the Chadian people, it is imperative that journalists and the media, whether state-owned or private, be given the means to flourish as freely as possible, in order to act as watchdogs on the future development of their country and to ensure that neither government leaders nor multinationals nor the international community interfere with their own welfare in ways that go unchallenged.

SIGNIFICANT DATES

April 2001: The HCC, a regulatory commission established by the government, rules that political debates during the election campaign will be banned and no commentary on news bulletins will be permitted, and radio stations that fail to comply will be temporarily shut down.

BIBLIOGRAPHY

Amnesty International. ''Chad.'' *Amnesty International Report 2002.* London: Amnesty International, May 28, 2002. Available at http://web.amnesty.org/web/ar2002.nsf/afr/chad!Open.

BBC Monitoring. ''Country profile: Chad.'' Reading, UK: British Broadcasting Corporation, June 29, 2002. Available at http://news.bbc.co.uk/1/hi/world/africa/country_profiles/1068700.stm.

Bureau of Democracy, Human Rights, and Labor, U.S. Department of State. ''Chad.'' *Country Reports on Human Rights Practices 2001.* Washington, DC: Bureau of Public Affairs, U.S. Department of State, March 4, 2002. Available at http://www.state.gov/g/drl/rls/hrrpt/2001/af/8307.htm.

Committee to Protect Journalists. ''Chad.'' *Attacks on the Press in 2001: Africa 2001.* New York, NY: CPJ, 2002. Available at http://www.cpj.org/attacks01/africa01/chad.html.

Friends of the Earth. ''Chad-Cameroon Oil Pipeline.'' Accessed 6 August 2002 at http://www.foe.org/international/worldbank/chadcameroon.html.

Reporters without Borders. ''Chad.'' Africa annual report 2002. Paris, France: Reporters sans frontiers, April 20, 2002. Available at http://www.rsf.org/article.php3?id_article=1727.

— Barbara A. Lakeberg-Dridi, Ph.D.

CHILE

BASIC DATA

Official Country Name:	Republic of Chile
Region (Map name):	South America
Population:	15,328,467
Language(s):	Spanish
Literacy rate:	95.2%
Area:	756,950 sq km
GDP:	70,545 (US$ millions)
Number of Daily Newspapers:	53
Total Circulation:	348,000
Number of Nondaily Newspapers:	9
Total Newspaper Ad Receipts:	110,225 (Pesos millions)
As % of All Ad Expenditures:	35.00
Number of Television Stations:	63
Number of Television Sets:	3,150,000
Television Sets per 1,000:	205.5
Number of Cable Subscribers:	682,480
Cable Subscribers per 1,000:	44.9
Number of Satellite Subscribers:	100,000
Satellite Subscribers per 1,000:	6.5

Number of Radio Stations:	261
Number of Radio Receivers:	5,180,000
Radio Receivers per 1,000:	337.9
Number of Individuals with Computers:	1,260,000
Computers per 1,000:	82.2
Number of Individuals with Internet Access:	2,537,000
Internet Access per 1,000:	165.5

BACKGROUND & GENERAL CHARACTERISTICS

Before 1973, Chile was a model of political freedom among Latin American nations. The press was relatively free to publicly criticize government officials and their regimes. In 1970, Chilean citizens elected the Socialist politician Salvador Allende as national president. As of 2002, Chile remained the only country in the Americas to have democratically elected a Socialist president to power. From 1970 to 1973, the media flourished and freely reported on the political infighting, economic crises, and mass public demonstrations characteristic of President Allende's government.

However, on September 11, 1973, General Augusto Pinochet overthrew Allende's Socialist government and imposed a military regime. Pinochet ruled as president and dictator of Chile from 1973 until a freely elected president was installed in 1990. During his seventeen-year military dictatorship, Pinochet largely used the media to promote his newly imposed economic and anti-democratic policies. He also implemented state security measures that limited the civil rights of individuals as well as severely curtailed freedom of the press, expression of opinion, as well as flow and access to information.

In 1980, Pinochet wrote a new Chilean Constitution and implemented the *Ley de Seguridad Interior del Estado* (State Security Law), which was intended to control and maintain social order for the purposes of expanding the economy. He suppressed free speech and both print and broadcast media by enacting Article 6(b) in Chile's State Security Law. The Article declared it was illegal for anyone to publicly slander, libel, or offend the president of the Republic or any other high-level government, military, and police officials. The term, offense, was used to describe acts of disrespect or insult. Generally, the law gave discretionary power to supporters of the Pinochet regime to control the media and restrict free speech.

The provisions of the State Security Law also gave judges unrestricted power to place gag orders on alleged controversial issues and to ban press from court proceedings. Pinochet chose conservative pro-military individuals to support and enforce his policies. Pinochet also expanded the role of government censorship offices and widely increased the types of material that could be censored. In most cases, military members headed the censorship offices. People arrested for violating the provisions of the State Security Law were tried in a military court in which members of the military quickly reached guilty verdicts and imposed punishments. Defendants could be imprisoned for up to five years. These provisions radically curbed the print and broadcast media's freedom to report information without the threat of harassment or imprisonment.

Regulations permitting freer press and censorship laws gradually took place in the decade following the end of Pinochet's dictatorship. Although Pinochet left political office in 1990, he remained as chief commander of the armed forces until 1998 and as senator-for-life until his resignation in July 2002. The regulations in Article 6(b) and the 1980 Constitution that increased censorship and limited freedom of the press and information remained in effect until June 2001.

After 1990, the center-left parties, the Christian Democrats and Concertación Coalición (Concerted Action Coalition), had national power. The center-left presidents worked to pass freer press laws and repeal some of the repressive provisions of Pinochet's 1980 Constitution and State Security Law. The process to pass freer press and censorship laws took well over a decade. The slowness was in part due to the continued presence of Pinochet in the military as chief commander and in politics as senator and through his right-wing political party, the Independent Democratic Union. Moreover, the two right-wing parties in Congress, the National Renovation and Independent Democratic Union, supported Pinochet's policies of social order and regulating media.

In 1990, the first democratically elected president since 1970, Patricio Alywin, took office. During his presidential term, Alywin began the process of creating a freer and more democratic society, including liberalizing press laws to allow greater expression of opinion and flow of information. The ''Law on Freedoms of Opinion and Information and the Practice of Journalism'' was first proposed in 1993, though it was not passed until 2001 in part due to opposing forces in Congress.

In the late 1990s, President Eduardo Frei and his coalition, Concerted Action, led the struggle to pass more permissive censorship and opinion laws for the press and cinema. By 1997, the press operated far more freely than in 1990. However, Article 6(b) of the State Security Laws remained in effect and continued to limit journalists' rights to free speech. The regulations, for example, permitted judges to bar controversial topics and information from being freely expressed in the media. At times, judges imposed gag orders rather liberally and suppressed print and broadcast media from reporting freely.

In 2001, the "Law on Freedoms of Opinion and Information and the Practice of Journalism" passed in Congress and went into effect when President Ricardo Lagos signed it on May 18. The new press law repealed Article 6(b) and permitted the Chilean print and broadcast media to operate far more freely than it had been able to in thirty years. The law also repealed legislation that gave judges discretionary power to ban press coverage of court proceedings.

The "Law on Freedoms of Opinion and Information and the Practice of Journalism" passed in part because of events connected to Pinochet's arrest for human rights violations in London in October 1998. In Chile, these events led to the reawakening of bitter feelings over two decades of repression. In the late 1990s, Chilean citizens supported and voted through Congress provisions for free speech, freedom of expression, and access to information without persecution.

Chilean journalists were relieved with the repeal of Article 6(b). Nevertheless, some journalists believed that the press and information laws could go further to promote a truly independent press without government regulation.

Print Media Most press activity occurs in the populous central valley of Chile, particularly in Chile's largest city, the capital Santiago. In 1996, Chile had 52 newspapers and newsprint consumption was 5,326 kilograms per one thousand inhabitants. However, in 2002, the number of published dailies had decreased to approximately 40 newspapers. This decline in dailies was in part due to the Chilean recession that began in 1999. Many small-scale publishers were bankrupted as it was difficult to maintain circulation and advertising revenue during the recession.

In 2002, the dailies ranged from nationally distributed and high quality newspapers to small-town tabloids. These newspapers were distributed between four and seven times per week. Distribution ranged from as much as 300,000 copies for *El Mercurio* (in its Sunday edition) to 3,000 copies of a regional paper. Chile's capital, Santiago, has nine major newspapers with a combined daily circulation of approximately 479,000. The circulation of local dailies in the regions outside Santiago was approximately 220,000. Assuming an average readership of three persons per newspaper, total readership countrywide could be estimated at more than 2 million readers per day.

Nearly all towns with populations of 50 thousand or more had newspapers that focused on local news and events. Apart from the publications of Chile's two newspaper chains, there were approximately 25 other independent regional dailies. These had a small circulation within their towns. One of the most important regional dailies was Concepción's *El Sur*, with a circulation of approximately 30 thousand.

Other important and widely read periodicals were the nondailies that appeared two to four times per month and were published for a nation-wide readership. The biweekly newsmagazine, *Ercilla* had an approximate circulation of 12 thousand. Other nondailies with relatively large circulations were the three business-oriented monthly magazines, *America Economía*, *Capital*, and *Gestión*. The two popular magazines, *Cosas* and *Caras* were biweeklies with *Life* magazine format. They published interviews with popular stars and athletes, as well as political interviews of national and international interest. Other widely-read publications in Chile included the following weekly and monthly magazines: *El Siglo*, the Communist Party's official weekly publication; *Punto Final*, a biweekly publication of the extreme-left group *Movimiento de Izquierda Revolucionario* (Revolutionary Left Movement); *Paula*, a women's magazine; *Mensaje*, an intellectual monthly magazine published by the Jesuits; and several sports and TV/motion picture magazines. Circulation information was not available for these nondailies.

In 2001, two newspaper chains operated in Chile. Each chain was responsible for publishing the two most widely read newspapers, *El Mercurio* and *La Tercera*. The first chain, the *El Mercurio*-chain, was owned by the Edwards family since the nineteenth century. It published and was affiliated with 15 dailies circulating throughout Chile. As of the early 2000s, *El Mercurio*, was Chile's longest-running and most influential paper. The *El Mercurio*-chain also published two other widely read dailies, the mass-oriented, *Las Últimas Noticias* and *El Mercurio*'s afternoon supplement, *La Segunda*. According the official statistics by the United States Department of State, the daily *El Mercurio* attracted conservative audiences.

The second media chain was *Consorcio Periodístico de Chile* (COPESA), owned by Alvaro Saieh, Alberto Kasis, and Carlos Abumohor. COPESA published the news daily *La Tercera* for national distribution. *La Tercera* was a Santiago-based national newspaper with a 2002 daily circulation of about 210,000. As of that year, this number was the highest daily readership in Chile. *El Mercurio* competed with COPESA's *La Tercera* for newspaper readers. COPESA also published three other periodicals for national distribution: the popular magazine, *La Cuarta*; the free daily tabloid, *La Hora*; and the newsweekly, *Qué Pasa*, which offered political analyses of current events. In 2002, *Qué Pasa* had an approximate circulation of 20 thousand readers. COPESA created sites on the Internet for its publications. The publisher also had affiliations with smaller-scale print and digital publishers. One such affiliation was with the digital company that produced "RadioZero," a music Internet site for younger audiences.

The Nature of the Audience In the early 2000s, the Chilean newspaper audience was in general well educated. School attendance was obligatory for children under the age of 16. The Chilean Ministry of Education made it obligatory that all children in the school system complete the eight-level system, ideally within eight years. Most children go beyond the eight years of elementary learning to attend secondary schools and university. In 1995, of those age 15 and over, some 95.2 percent of the total population was literate. Generally, high levels of literacy indicate a high number of potential readers.

At the beginning of the twenty-first century, most publishing and other media activity were concentrated in central Chile, particularly in the capital of Santiago. Nearly 90 percent of the population was concentrated in central Chile, in the area between Coquimbo in the north and Puerto Montt in the south. Chile was not a densely populated country. Even in the central area, with the exception of the Santiago metropolitan area, the average population density did not exceed 50 inhabitants per square kilometer (130 per square mile). The average population density for the country was 17 persons per square kilometer.

In 1995, some 86 percent of the total population lived in urban centers and 41 percent of the total population lived in urban agglomerations of one million or more. For the press, it is advantageous to have markets concentrated in urban centers so as to obtain easy access to larger numbers of readers. As of July 2001, the population of Chile was estimated at 15,328,467 and population growth rate was 1.13 percent.

In the late 1980s, Chile's prosperity—due to Pinochet's aggressive free-market and trade policies—led to an increase in immigration. Migrants came from as close as neighboring Argentina and Peru and from as far away as India and South Korea to work as shopkeepers, doctors, musicians, and laborers. Many stayed on illegally after entering with tourist visas. In the 1990s, over 3 thousand Koreans legally registered as immigrants. Most set up small shops in which to sell textiles or imports from South Korea. In 1996, there were 814 legal Cubans, mostly working as musicians. The Cuban community estimated that as many as 6 thousand Cubans might be working illegally in Chile. Generally, immigrants assimilated into Chilean culture. However, there were imports of foreign dailies particularly from the United States, Asia, and European Union countries. The growing Cuban community also had small local publications that listed events and local news.

Chile's official language is Spanish. The two main ethnic groups are white and mestizo, which composed in 2002 some 95 percent of the population. Mestizo is a mix of European and Native American peoples. The Native American population composed 3 percent of the population. Some of the indigenous populations still used native languages, mainly the Araucanian language. Indian groups were largely concentrated in the Andes in northern Chile, in some valleys of south-central Chile, and along the southern coast.

In the early 2000s, the typical Chilean was not affluent. According to a report by the U.S. Central Intelligence Agency, in 1998, about 22 percent of the total Chilean population were below the poverty line. In 2000, the unemployment rate was 9 percent. The underemployment rate was estimated at nearly 20 percent. There were wide discrepancies between the poor and rich, which is a common characteristic among countries that impose fast-paced privatization and market-oriented policies. Pinochet's policies, for example, included tax relief for business and international investors, new marketing strategies, and massive trade expansion with foreign countries. His policies eliminated previous full-time jobs in state-run industries. He failed to create new jobs or train these former employees for existing higher-skilled jobs or for the new computer-technology occupations in the late 1980s. The new market system created few jobs for low skilled, state workers, which in part explains the high levels of under- and unemployment.

In 1998, the poorest 10 percent of Chilean households received only 1.2 percent of the national income, while those in the richest tenth possessed 41.3 percent of national wealth. Furthermore, in the bottom 10 percent, the proportion earning less than the minimum wage grew from 48 to 67 percent, indicating a serious deterioration of the conditions of the working poor.

In Chile, the most extensive mass medium was radio and not newspapers. For the most part, Chilean radio was a relatively inexpensive form of obtaining daily news. Nearly all homes had radios, so these constituted the prime source of current news to millions of Chileans.

Quality of Journalism: General Comments Although some newspapers and nondailies reported tabloid news, employed bold headlines, numerous photographs, and techniques of strong popular and entertainment appeal, locally produced news were generally of high quality and drew large audiences through radio and readership. Laws current in 2002 required that all journalists obtain a university education and be professionally trained at a recognized journalism school. In most cases, professional journalists had sufficient training and developed a sense of duty for providing readers with accurate and important news pieces.

Historical Traditions Chile was established and colonized by Spanish conquistadors in the 1540s. It developed as an isolated frontier with low levels of Spanish immigration and relatively large numbers of Indian groups in the northern Andes region and southern part of the country. In the early nineteenth century, Chile came into being as a nation-state when it joined in the independence wars against Spain. It declared independence from Spain on September 18, 1810.

Before 1810, all printed matter (newspapers, magazines, and books) had been published in Spain or in other European countries and brought through the ports of the Viceroyalties of Peru (ca. 1526) or Buenos Aires (1776). After the independence and civil wars in 1823, Chile began establishing its economy, politics, and press systems. Supreme Director, General Ramón Freire encouraged the flourishing tradition of free and polemical journalism. Between 1823 and 1830, over a hundred newspapers (many were short-lived) were printed. The country's first formal paper, *El Mercurio*, was founded in Valparaíso in 1827. It circulated daily beginning in 1829.

By the 1840s, Santiago was growing as a lively urban center. An important feature of urban life was the growth of the press. *El Mercurio* was by then the most prestigious paper in the country. From Valparaíso, the publishers of *El Mercurio* printed special Santiago editions and sent, via steamship, supplements of the paper along the coast and up to Panama.

The Chilean government subsidized a few papers in the mid-1800s to promote readership and spread news information. The government quickly discovered the benefit of using the press to promote policies and current leaders. By 1842, Santiago began publishing its first daily; unfortunately, it was short-lived. In 1855, *El Ferrocarríl* (The Railroad) became Santiago's most distinguished newspaper; it ran until 1911. The decade of the 1860s saw further good quality dailies like *El Independiente* (1864-91) and *La República* (1866-78). *El Independiente* represented the interests of the Conservative Party and *La República*, those of the Chilean Liberal Party.

The Spanish conquistadors introduced Roman Catholicism in the 1540s. All indigenous populations were christened en masse and called Christians when the Spaniards arrived and settled. From the colonial to twenty-first centuries, the Roman Catholic Church continued as the dominant religion in Chile. The Church began publication of its weekly magazine, *Revista Católica*, in 1843. This magazine continued its publication as of 2002. *Revista Caólica* was Chile's longest-running magazine.

By the early 1900s, the government promoted literacy and education through mass public campaigns in the cities and countryside. The results were greater literacy and schooling among the general population. Also, journalism gained new prominence as a profession. The higher literacy rates and increased number of full-time, professional journalists led to the growth of the press, in particular the provincial press flourished. Nearly every town published at least one newspaper reflecting on religious or political bias.

By the 1920s, dailies published in the urban areas diversified and expanded their topics to attract a greater number of readers. Santiago's most popular local paper was *Zig-Zag*, which was owned by the Edwards Family (*El Mercurio*-chain). There was also a rise in papers published for specific clientele, such as those that catered to socialists, anarchists, workers, or a political party.

By the mid-twentieth century, Chile was gaining reputation as a place of diverse publications. Chile had printed more than 4 million books (1,400 separate titles) and published a variety of magazines (political, humorous, sports, feminine, right-wing, left-wing, Catholic, Masonic) and newspapers (including tabloids). Chile's largest newspaper, *El Mercurio*, had a daily circulation of 75 thousand readers.

Before September 1973, Chile's press was thriving and considered an important component of its democratic society. The press was very diverse and represented all levels of the political spectrum from ultra-right to ultra-left. Broadcast media also operated relatively freely and without fear of political repression. The press was relatively independent and investigative journalists operated without excessive regulation and certainly without threat of persecution. Politics were polarized ideologically and heated debates among politicians were commonplace. The press freely reported on all ideological polarization, political debates, and scandals.

Nonetheless, on September 11, 1973, General Pinochet led a coup and established an authoritarian government wherein little or no meaningful political competition or media freedom existed. In the 1970s and 1980s, the military government heavily regulated news media through regulation and the government censorship office. Pinochet passed press laws that restricted newspapers and magazines from making political commentary that could be termed libel, slander, or offensive. It was illegal and punishable by imprisonment for reporters to publish what could be considered negative or controversial reports on the leaders of the regime.

Pinochet used both broadcast and printed media to push his economic and social order policies. For example, he used the media to downplay or justify the repression that ensued after 1973. Although Pinochet stepped down from power in 1989, the laws restricting freedom of the press were in effect until June 2001.

In 2001, President Ricardo Lagos signed into effect the new press laws permitting journalists more freedoms including the right to criticize political leaders and their policies. Since 2001, journalists and legal advocates of free speech have actively ensured that their rights to free speech and access to information are never infringed upon again.

One of the most important conditions of the new press laws of 2001 was that reporters could once again question and criticize the decisions of government authorities. For example, on June 13, 2002, President Lagos announced that only two media sources would be allowed access on his international and domestic trips. Lagos's decision immediately provoked criticism from members of the press corp. The director of the National Press Association, a union of over 80 publications, deemed the announcement "unacceptable." The director said that Lagos was inhibiting the freedom of the press and the people's access to the news. The School of Journalists also criticized Lagos' decision. Due in part to pressure from distinguished journalists, Lagos responded and explained his actions in detail. His doing so was significant because in this case the press showed that it would question and criticize unjust policies. These events also indicated that journalists could expect responses from the president without the fear or threat of persecution.

Distribution by Language, Ethnic and Religious Orientation, Political Ideology Most dailies were printed in Spanish, but there were a few foreign language dailies. In 2002, *Condor* was the German-language newspaper. A century earlier, the largest numbers of immigrants to Chile had been Germans, who colonized southern Chile. Germans had a larger impact in the colder regions of several southern Chilean cities. There were also several English-language economic and financial newspapers published in the metropolitan center of Santiago. These were *The News Review*, published twice a week, and the daily *Santiago Times*. These two publications also had Internet sites. On its Internet site, the *Santiago Times* provided free access to its daily headline only.

The majority of the population practices the Roman Catholicism. Approximately 89 percent of the population is Roman Catholic and 11 percent are Protestant. One of the longest running magazines in Chilean history, *Revista Católica*, has circulated since the nineteenth century. *Mensaje*, an intellectual monthly magazine published by the Jesuits, had a nation-wide readership. During the military dictatorship, Pinochet increased the role of the Catholic Church. He established a strong public relationship with Cardinal Francisco Javier Errazuriz, who also delivered Pinochet's resignation letter of his senator-for life post. Pinochet's public relationship with the Church was perhaps intended to divert attention from accusations of human rights violations during his dictatorship.

Since independence (except during years of military dictatorship), Chilean press reflected a strong political orientation and represented the political interests of the conservatives, liberals, ultra-rights, and ultra-lefts. In the nineteenth century, *El Independiente* represented the interests of the conservative party and *La Republica*, of the Chilean Liberal Party.

By 2002, nearly all political parties had their own Internet site. They also published pamphlets and small-scale periodicals to promote their political ideologies, strategies, and candidates. Most politically active groups regularly used the mainstream media to promote their policies and ideologies. Some of these political groups and their publications are: the Communist Party (legalized in Chile in 1990) which published *El Siglo* on a weekly basis; and the ultra-left group, *Movimiento de Izquierda Revolucionario* (Revolutionary Left Movement), which published the bi-weekly *Punto Final*. The center-left group, the Concertación (Concerted Action) a coalition of Socialists, Communists, and some factions of the Christian Democratic Party, was in power in 2002 and led by President Ricardo Lagos. Each faction within the coalition printed a weekly publication. The two right-wing/pro-military parties, Independent Democratic Union and National Renovation, also distributed propaganda.

Papers, particularly the two leading dailies *La Tercera* and *El Mercurio* were professional and well organized. These two top dailies had sections for news, commentary, editors' letters, sports, finance, business, economy, politics, as well as for cultural events and reviews. The most up-to-date news came from their Internet sites. They updated their headlines every 30 to 60 minutes during business hours.

The most prestigious daily, *El Mercurio*, has both a morning and an evening edition. Its largest sales came from the Sunday edition with a distribution in 2002 of 300,000 copies. *El Mercurio* was considered the right-wing/conservative paper for middle-aged and up audiences. *La Tercera* seemed to appeal to popular and younger audiences.

ECONOMIC FRAMEWORK

After the independence wars in the nineteenth century, Chile became one of the wealthiest and most political-

US 212 MI US 218 US 430 US 131
US 73 US 127 US 611
Chicago US 68 US 40 US 120 Harlem US 219
US 34 US 118 US 422 US 23 US 74
US 19 OH US 50 US 57 US 240 MD
US 27 US 32 US 42 US 220 US 140
US 71 US 52 Memphis US 21 US 217
US 67 US 241 US 15 US 170 US 117
AL US 78 US 72 US 12 FL US 175
US 25 US 29 US 41 US 129 US 341
US 231 Atlanta US 90 Miami

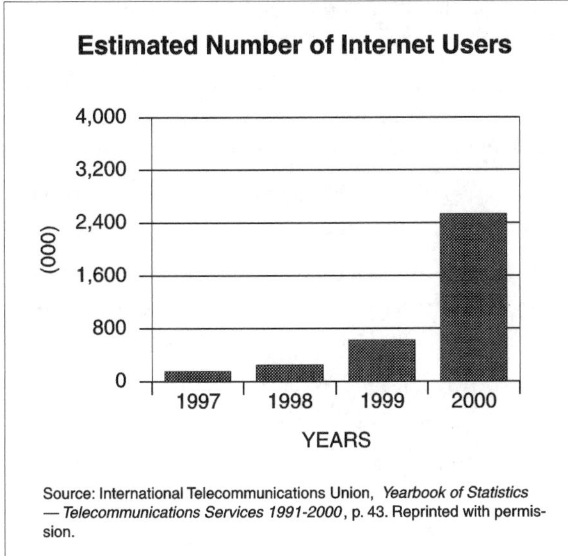

Source: International Telecommunications Union, *Yearbook of Statistics — Telecommunications Services 1991-2000*, p. 43. Reprinted with permission.

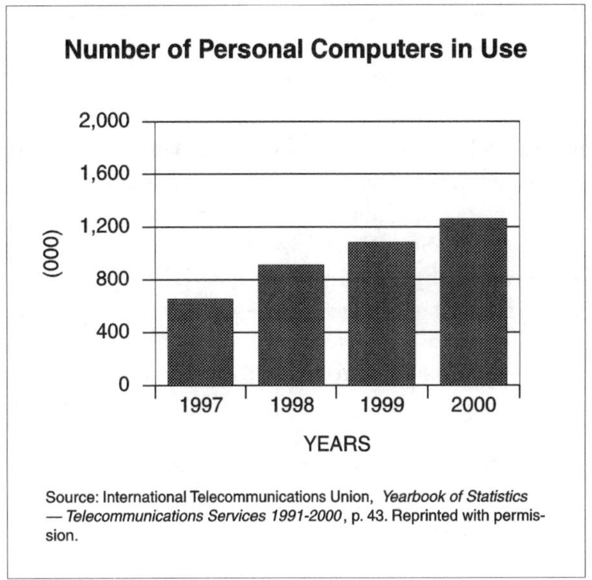

Source: International Telecommunications Union, *Yearbook of Statistics — Telecommunications Services 1991-2000*, p. 43. Reprinted with permission.

providers and an estimated 625,000 Internet users. Chile's internet code was.cl.

Some of the on-line newspapers included: *Agencia Chile Noticias*, *Condor* (German-language); *Crónica*, regional paper of Concepción; *Diarios regionales*, published by the *El Mercurio*-chain; *El Chileno* (weekly); *El Díario* (Firms, Economy, and Finance); *El Mercurio* (national circulation); *El Mercurio de Valparaíso* (Regional edition); *El Mostrador* (Santiago daily); *El Siglo Digital* (weekly in Santiago); *El Sur*, regional paper of Concepción; *Estrategía* (Business magazine); *Infoweek*, a weekly on business, Internet, and technology. Many others existed that reflected the diverse reading culture of Chile.

Other online news media included: *La Cuarta Cibernética*; *La Otra Verdad* (The Other Truth), which was written by independent citizens; *La Tercera*, the Santiago-based paper published by COPESA; *Las Últimas Noticias*, published by COPESA; *La Voz Arauco*, a local paper of Canete; *Prensa al Día*, compilation of news of the day published by Chilean newspapers; *Prensa Austral*, a local paper of Punta Arenas; *Primera Línea*, an online only newspaper; and last, the *Santiago Times*, an online daily in English-language.

Education & Training

Chile has fully accredited journalism and mass media programs. By law, any Chilean in pursuit of a career in journalism must attend an accredited and recognized journalism school to receive the full title of journalist. In 1987, students graduating from all schools of journalism in the country numbered 4,058, of which 2,690 were women.

Two of the larger and more prestigious journalism schools in Chile were the *Facultad de Comunicaciones de la Pontificia Universidad Católica de Chile* (Faculty of Communications of the Pontific Catholic University of Chile) and *Escuela de Periodismo de la Universidad de Chile* (School of Journalism of the University of Chile). Both were established in the late 1950s and early 1960s.

In 1983, the School of Journalism of the University of Chile expanded its centers and established the Center for the Study of the Press. The Center had affiliations with press firms and published the magazine, *Cuadernos de Información*. In 1987, the School of Journalism expanded its degree programs to include the credential of *Licenciado en Información Social* (equivalent to a bachelor's degree in social information) to the professional title of Journalist.

At the start of 1998, the School of Journalism of the University of Chile continued to expand and created the Faculty of Communications, which was a part of the School of Journalism. On May 1, 1998, the school was approved for acceptance in the Accrediting Council of Education and Mass Communication. This latter association unites the best institutions of journalism in North America.

Summary

From 1973 to 1989, the Chilean press was reduced to pro-regime rhetoric under Pinochet's repressive rule. After 1990 the Chilean press gradually regained its confidence and actively promoted freer press laws. In 2001, the "Law on Freedoms of Opinion and Information and the Practice of Journalism" was signed into law. Although it had some features that promoted a less-than-independent press, the law was a huge feat for a country that had been under military rule for nearly two decades. A free, responsible press is a necessity to the operation of a truly democratic society.

Moreover, Chilean journalism was improving in quality and promoted high-quality reports. Journalists were using the Chilean National Ethics Committee (self-regulating organization similar to the former national news council in the United States) to promote high caliber journalism by reporting scrupulous coverage by competing investigating journalists. Moreover, in the late 1990s, there was increased media competition. This was ideal in part because it made news organizations evaluate and criticize competitors. In the past, this competition helped to increase the diversity and quality of news reporting. Fernando Paulsen Silva, editor of *La Tercera*, noted that increasing media competition in Chile made news organizations watch and compare the quality of programming. On February 27, 2000, his newspaper complained to the Chilean National Ethics Committee. He accused one of his competitors of inventing bylines to give readers the impression that it had sent staff members around the world to cover soccer games, when in fact he said the news was being rewritten from the Internet.

Under Chilean President Lagos, the press was active in reminding the president that they refused to be relegated to an auxiliary position. More important, in Latin America generally, efforts were made by presidents to free archival police files covering up the disappearances of hundreds of victims during covert government operations against alleged dissidents. Overall, the future of the press in the Latin American region, and particularly the Chilean press, was bright and members of the press and others hoped that one day it would promote even freer laws.

Significant Dates

- 1989, 1993, 1997: The democratically elected presidents, Patricio Alywin and Eduardo Frei, sign into law amendments to Pinochet's Constitution of 1980 in order to allow more permissive press dispersal of information.
- Autumn 1998: Pinochet is arrested in London and placed under house arrest for human rights abuses. Pinochet steps down as commander of the armed forces.
- 2001: Chilean president Ricardo Lagos signs the ''Law on Freedom of Opinion and Information and the Practice of Journalism.''

Bibliography

Association of Independent Journalists (South American Cone). ''Chile.'' Available from www.asociacionperiodistas.org/ultimagresion/chile.htm.

Bethell, Leslie, ed. *Chile Since Independence.* Cambridge: Cambridge University Press, 1993.

The Central Intelligence Agency (CIA). *World Factbook 2001.* Directorate of Intelligence, 2002. Available from www.cia.gov/.

''Chile'' *World Press Freedom Review, 1997-2001.* Available from www.freemedia.at/wpfr/.

''Chile gauges impact of increased immigrant population.'' CNN Interactive, World News Storypage, October 14, 1996. Available from www.cnn.com.

''Chilean Media.'' 2002. Available from www.corporateinformation.com/clsector/Media.html.

''Chilean regime signs electoral pact with Communist Party.'' 2002. Available from www.wsws.org/.

Collier, Simon and William F. Sater. *A History of Chile, 1808-1994.* Cambridge: Cambridge University Press, 1996.

''Pinochet Quits Senate Post.'' July 2001. Available from news.bbc.co.uk/.

Spooner, Mary Helen. *Soldiers in a Narrow Land: The Pinochet Regime in Chile.* Berkeley: University of California Press, 1994.

U.S. Department of State. ''Chile—Country Commercial Guide.'' 2001.

Wilkie, James, Eduardo Alemán, and José Guadalupe Ortega, eds. *Statistical Abstract of Latin America,* vol. 36. Los Angeles: UCLA Latin American Center Publications, University of California, 2000.

—Yovanna Y. Pineda

China

Basic Data

Official Country Name:	People's Republic of China
Region (Map name):	East & South Asia
Population:	1,273,111,290
Language(s):	Standard Chinese or Mandarin, Yue, Minbei, Minnan, Xiang, Gan, Hakka dialect
Literacy rate:	81.5%
Area:	9,596,960 sq km

GDP:	1,079,948 (US$ millions)
Number of Daily Newspapers:	816
Total Circulation:	50,000,000
Circulation per 1,000:	54
Number of Nondaily Newspapers:	1,344
Total Circulation:	138,000,000
Circulation per 1,000:	148
Total Newspaper Ad Receipts:	12,776 (Yuan Renminibi millions)
As % of All Ad Expenditures:	32.50
Number of Television Stations:	3240
Number of Television Sets:	400,000,000
Television Sets per 1,000:	314.2
Number of Cable Subscribers:	77,138,750
Cable Subscribers per 1,000:	61.1
Number of Radio Stations:	673
Number of Radio Receivers:	414,000,000
Radio Receivers per 1,000:	325.2
Number of Individuals with Computers:	20,600,000
Computers per 1,000:	16.2
Number of Individuals with Internet Access:	22,500,000
Internet Access per 1,000:	17.7

Background & General Characteristics

As a monopolistic regime, the Chinese Communist Party (CCP) is committed to the Marxist-Leninist-Maoist emphasis on the central control of the press as a tool for public education, propaganda, and mass mobilization. The entire operation of China's modern media is based upon the foundation of ''mass line'' governing theory, developed by China's paramount head of state, Mao Zedong. Such a theory, upon which China's entire political structure hinges, provides for government of the masses by leaders of the Communist Party, who are not elected by the people and therefore are not responsible to the people, but to the Party. When the theory is applied to journalism, the press becomes the means for top-down communication, a tool used by the Party to ''educate'' the masses and mobilize public will towards socialist progress. Thus the mass media are not allowed to report any aspect of the internal policy-making process, especially debates within the Party. Because they report only the implementation and impact of resulting policies, there is no concept of the people's right to influence policies. In this way, the Chinese press has been described as the ''mouth and tongue'' of the Party. By the same token, the media also act as the Party's eyes and ears. Externally, where the media fail to adequately provide the public with detailed, useful information, internally, within the Party bureaucracy, the media play a crucial role of intelligence gathering and communicating sensitive information to the central leadership. Therefore, instead of serving as an objective information source, the Chinese press functions as Party-policy announcer, ideological instructor, intelligence collector, and bureaucratic supervisor.

China's modern media, which were entirely transplanted from the West, did not take off until the 1890s. Most of China's first newspapers were run by foreigners, particularly missionaries and businessmen. Progressive young Chinese students who were introduced to Western journalism while studying abroad also imported the principles of objective reporting from the West. Upon returning home, these students introduced the methods of running Western-style newspapers to China. The May Fourth Movement in 1919, the first wave of intellectual liberation, witnessed the publishing of Chinese books on reporting, as well as the emergence of the first financially and politically independent newspapers in China. However, the burgeoning Chinese media were suffocated by Nationalist censorship in the 1930s. Soon after the Kuomintang (KMT) gained control of China in 1927, it promulgated a media policy aimed at enforcing strict censorship and intimidating the press into adhering to KMT doctrine. But despite brutal enforcement measures, the KMT had no organized system to rein in press freedom, and when times were good, it was fairly tolerant toward the media. The KMT gave less weight to ideology than the CCP eventually would and therefore allowed greater journalistic freedom.

Chinese journalism under CCP leadership has gone through four phases of development. The first period started with the founding of New China in 1949 and ended in 1966, when the Cultural Revolution began. During those years, private ownership of newspapers was abolished, and the media was gradually turned into a party organ. Central manipulation of the media intensified during the utopian Great Leap Forward, wherein excessive emphasis on class position and the denunciation of objectivity produced distortions of reality. Millions of Chinese peasants starved to death partly as a result of media exaggeration of crop production.

During the second phase (1966-78), journalism in China suffered even greater damage. In the years of the Cultural Revolution, almost all newspapers ceased publication except 43 party organs. All provincial CCP newspapers attempted to emulate the ''correct'' page layout of the *People's Daily* and most copied, on a daily basis, the lead story, second story, number of columns used by each story, total number of articles, and even the size of the typeface. In secret and after the Cultural Revolution, the public characterized the news reporting during the Cultural Revolution as ''jia (false), da (exaggerated), and kong (empty).''

The third phase began in December 1978, when the Third Plenary Session of the Eleventh Central Committee of the Chinese Communist Party convened. Deng Xiaoping's open-door policy brought about nation-wide reforms that nurtured an unprecedented media boom. The top agenda of media reform included the crusade for freedom of press, the call for representing the people, the construction of journalism laws, and the emergence of independent newspapers. Cuts in state subsidies and the rise of advertising and other forms of financing pointed the way toward greater economic independence, which in turn promoted editorial autonomy.

The Tiananmen uprising in 1989 and its fallout marked the last phase. During the demonstrations, editors and journalists exerted a newly-found independence in reporting on events around them and joined in the public outcry for democracy and against official corruption, carrying banners reading ''Don't believe us—we tell lies'' while marching in demonstrations. The students' movement was suppressed by army tanks, and the political freedom of journalists also suffered a crippling setback. The central leadership accused the press of engaging in bourgeois activities such as reflecting mass opinion, maintaining surveillance on government, providing information, and covering entertainment. The once-hopeful discourse on journalism legislation and press freedom was immediately abolished. With the closing of the political door on media expansion, the post-Tiananmen era witnessed a dramatic turn towards economic incentives, allowing media commercialization to flourish while simultaneously restricting its freedom in political coverage. These developments produced ''the mix of Party logic and market logic that is the defining feature of the Chinese news media system today'' (Zhao 2).

The media expanded more rapidly after Mao's death than at any other time in Chinese history. As of October 1997, China had more than 27,000 newspapers and magazines. Chinese newspapers can be divided into several distinct categories. The first is the ''jiguan bao'' (organ papers). *People's Daily* and other provincial party newspapers are in this category. The second is the trade/professional newspapers, such as *Wenhui Ribao* (Wenhui Daily), *Renmin Tiedaobao* (People's Railroads), and *Zhongguo Shangbao* (Chinese Business). The third is metropolitan organs (Dushibao), such as *Beijing Qingnianbao* (Beijing Youth Daily), *Huaxi Dushibao* (Western China Urban Daily), and other evening newspapers. The fourth is business publications, such as *Chengdu Shangbao* (Chengdu Business Daily) and *Jingji Ribao* (Economics Daily). The fifth is service papers; *Shopping Guide* and *Better Commodity Shopping Guide* are two examples. The sixth is digest papers, such as *Wenzhaibao* (News Digest), and finally, army papers: *Jiefangjun Ribao* (People's Liberation Army Dail) belongs to this category. Besides these types of formal newspapers, there are tabloids and weekend papers. The Chinese ''jietou xiaobao'' (small papers on the streets) are the equivalent of tabloids, which are synonymous with sensationalism in China. In addition to tabloids, major newspapers seeking a share of the human-interest market also created zhoumo ban (weekend editions). In 1981, *Zhongguo Qingnianbao* (China Youth News), the official organ of the Central Committee of the Chinese Communist Youth League, published its first weekend edition in an attempt to increase readership. The paper was an instant success. By the end of 1994, one-fourth of all newspapers had weekend editions. Weekend editions sell well because they are usually more interesting than their daily editions, with more critical and analytical pieces on pressing social issues, as well as various entertainment components.

As of March 2000, China had 2,160 newspapers with a total annual circulation of 26 billion (Sun 369). However, these numbers are estimates because newspaper circulation is actually unknown in China. Except for several successful ones, most papers do not give real numbers thus discrepancies exist depending upon the source used. The numbers cited below can only be used as an indication of the general trends. Also, circulation does not necessarily reflect popularity or influence, due to mandatory subscription or larger populations in some areas. The following table lists the 10 largest newspapers with their circulations (Press Release Network, 2001).

- *Cankao Xiaoxi* (Reference News) 9,000,000
- *Sichuan Ribao* (Sichuan Dail) 8,000,000
- *Gongren Ribao* (Workers Daily) 2,500,000
- *Renmin Ribao* (People's Daily) 2,150,000
- *Xinmin Wanbao* (Xinmin Evening News) 1,800,000
- *Wenhuibao* (Wenhui Daily) 1,700,000

Daily and Non-Daily Newspaper Titles and Circulation Figures

	1996	1997	1998	1999	2000
Number of Daily Newspapers	647	697	740	816	NA
Circulation of Dailies (000)	41,757	43,948	44,348	50,000	NA
Number of Non-Daily Newspapers	1,516	1,524	1,313	1,344	NA
Circulation of Non-Dailies (000)	137,015	138,639	137,759	138,000	NA

Source: World Association of Newspapers and Zenithmedia, *World Press Trends 2001*, pp. 8, 10, 17, 19. Note: NA stands for not available.

- *Yangcheng Wanbao* (Yangcheng Evening News) 1,300,000
- *Jingji Ribao* (Economic Daily) 1,200,000
- *Jiefang Ribao* (People's Liberation Army Daily) 1,000,000
- *Nanfang Ribao* (Nanfang Daily) 1,000,000
- *Nongmin Ribao* (Farmer's Daily) 1,000,000
- *Zhongguo Qingnianbao* (China Youth Daily) 1,000,000

The most popular newspaper appears to be *Cankao Xiaoxi* (Reference News), which is a collection of foreign wire service and newspaper reports in translation with a circulation of approximately 7 to 8 million. It contains international news, including commentary from media sources in Western countries, Hong Kong, and Taiwan. It gives a glimpse into behind-the-scenes domestic policy debates and factional struggles. Initially limited to cadres at or above the jiguan ganbu (agency level), it was as of 2002 available to the Chinese public.

In terms of influence, the next most important newspaper is *People's Daily*, whose huge circulation is benefited by the mandatory subscription of all Chinese working units. *People's Daily* runs five subsidiary newspapers, including its overseas edition, which is the official organ for propagating the Party line among the Chinese-reading public overseas. The other four editions include two editions covering economic news, a satire and humor tabloid, and an international news edition. Under Deng Xiaoping's economic reforms, Party and government media organs are no longer simple mouthpieces; they have become business conglomerates.

Beijing Youth News is one of the most influential newspapers among younger Chinese audiences. It began on March 21, 1949, as an official organ of the Beijing Communist Youth League. The paper has been able to make the most of opportunities created by reform and commercialization. Since the early 1980s, it has implemented a series of successful management reforms, refused to accept any ''back door'' job placements, pioneered the system of recruiting staff through open competition, and eliminated lifetime tenure. From 1994 to 2001, it changed from a daily broadsheet with eight pages to a daily broadsheet with 46 pages, including 14 pages of business information. Its circulation reached 400,000 in 2001, and its advertising income concurrently skyrocketed to 640 million in the same year. In the 1990s, the newspaper grew from a small weekly into a conglomerate that publishes four papers and runs 12 businesses in a wide range of areas.

As of 1997 there were 143 evening newspapers in China. Three of them have circulations of over 1 million. They are the *Yangcheng Evening News*, *Yangzi Evening News*, and *Xinmin Evening News* (China National Evening Newspaper Association). Local evening papers, usually general interest dailies, are among the best sellers. They are under the direct control of the municipal Party propaganda committee and with more soft news content closer to everyday urban life are aimed at urban families.

The huge gap between Chinese urban and rural areas in terms of living standards is reflected in the access to the media and information. Although the majority of the Chinese population are peasants (79%), Chinese media basically serve urban populations since they are more educated and enjoy greater consumption power. Because of high illiteracy rates and the rapid increase of radio and television sets among Chinese peasants, rural residents increasingly use television as their source of information rather than newspapers.

As of 2000, there were 14 English newspapers in China. They are perceived as reporting on China's problems with less propaganda. *China Daily*, published by the *People's Daily*, was the first English newspaper to appear in China. It serves as the CCP's official English organ, directed particularly at foreigners in China.

Nationwide, 6 percent of Chinese belong to 56 ethnic minority groups. Just as there are no privately owned newspapers in China, there is no minority-owned newspaper. The overwhelming majority of Chinese newspapers are published in the official Chinese language,

Top Ten Daily Newspapers
(2000)

	Circulation
People's Daily	2,500,000
Xin Ming Evening News	1,800,000
Yangchen Evening News	1,300,000
Yangzi Evening News	1,100,000
Beijing Evening News	900,000
Jie Fang Daily	800,000
Economic Daily	700,000
Beijing Daily	800,000
Guangzhou Daily	700,000
Jin Wan Bao	700,000

Source: World Association of Newspapers and Zenithmedia, *World Press Trends 2001*, p. 69.

Mandarin Chinese. But some government newspapers are published in minority languages, like Mongolian, Tibetan, and Uygur. Mongolian language newspapers are published in eight provinces and autonomous regions, including Inner Mongolia, Xinjiang, Gansu, Qinghai, etc. *Tibet Daily*, *Tibet Youth Daily*, *Tibet Legal Daily*, *Tibet TV Broadcast Daily*, *Tibet Technology Daily* are published in Tibet, in addition to a Chinese version of each. Similarly, some newspapers published in Xinjiang are also published in Uygur and Kazak. There is even a Uygur version of *Reference News*.

Between 1949 and 1990, almost all Chinese newspapers were distributed through the postal system. However, this changed when *Luoyang Daily* and *Guangzhou Daily* started their own distribution company in the late 1980s, followed by a host of other newspapers. As of the beginning of the twenty-first century, 800 newspapers among more than 2,000 distribute through their own networks. Others reach consumers through a variety of channels, such as post offices (both institutional and private subscription), street retail outlets, automatic newspaper dispensers, and occasionally, copies posted on public billboards. While institutional subscriptions provide newspapers to offices, street retail outlets are the major source of newspapers to private homes. In the office, reading free newspapers is considered legitimate political education as part of the job, but newspapers sold on the streets must compete not only among themselves but also with other commodities and for the urbanite's leisure time and cash.

ECONOMIC FRAMEWORK

Because Chinese media have historically been under such strict control of the CCP, unsurprisingly, until the start of economic reform, almost every aspect of media operation was entirely subsidized by the state. Reform and opening gradually promoted financial independence so that at the end of 1992, one-third of the 1,750 registered newspapers were no longer reliant on state support. In 1994, the government began to implement plans to phase out virtually all newspaper subsidies, with the exception of a few central party organs. Several factors have made financial autonomy and commercialization an economic necessity for Chinese media. First, the opening up of China since the 1980s has created a growing demand by foreign and domestic enterprises for effective advertising channels. Second, Chinese governments at all levels have been relatively deprived since economic reform began, due to economic decentralization and the lack of effective tax laws. Finally, public demand for better media service also stimulated investment in new stations, in more newspapers, and in extended broadcasting hours.

Advertising is the most important form of commercialization in the new Chinese media. In 1992, the four major media—television, newspapers, radio, and magazines—received RMB 4 billion in advertising income, or 64 percent of the total advertising revenue of RMB 6.78 billion. At the beginning of the twenty-first century there were 33 newspapers earning more than RMB 100 million from advertisement.

Commercial sponsorship of specific media content is another form of media commercialization. There are several ways of sponsoring news and information content. In the print media, a sponsor can put its stamp on news, photos, feature articles, and opinion pieces on every page by promoting some sort of competition, usually paying the paper for organizing the contest and providing the cash awards. Sponsors can also support regular newspaper columns or create special columns on chosen subjects under their own names. In the broadcast media, a common form of commercial sponsorship is joint production of feature and information programming. In these programs, government departments or businesses provide money and material while stations produce and broadcast the program.

The new dependence on advertising and sponsorship has had a significant impact on Chinese media. Rather than focusing on political topics, many newly established newspapers and broadcast channels are almost exclusively devoted to business and entertainment. Ratings systems also help advertisers target audiences more effectively. The commercialization of media has also caused the decline of national and provincial organs and the rise of metropolitan organs since the former have more responsibility to cover government policies and political issues while the latter can devote more space to issues of interest to the urban population.

Along with more financial freedom, commercialization has also brought journalistic corruption to China. Journalists, media officials, editorial departments, and the subsidiary businesses of the media often take advantage of their connections with news organizations to pursue their own financial gains. These range from relatively harmless exchanges such as paid travel and accommodations to encourage positive reporting about the news source, to crimes such as "paid journalism," in which journalists receive bribes for publishing promotional material disguised as news or features. Since the late 1980s, systemic journalistic corruption has developed rapidly, expanding from business clients to government clients, from an individual practice to a collective custom, and from small gifts to sizeable cash sums and negotiable securities. Studies comparing Chinese media over the past one hundred years to other Asian and Western media show that the particular connection between news and business in the Chinese media is unique. Chinese journalism corruption is a structural problem, rooted in the contradictions between the Party's ideology and the commercialized environment under which the modern press operates.

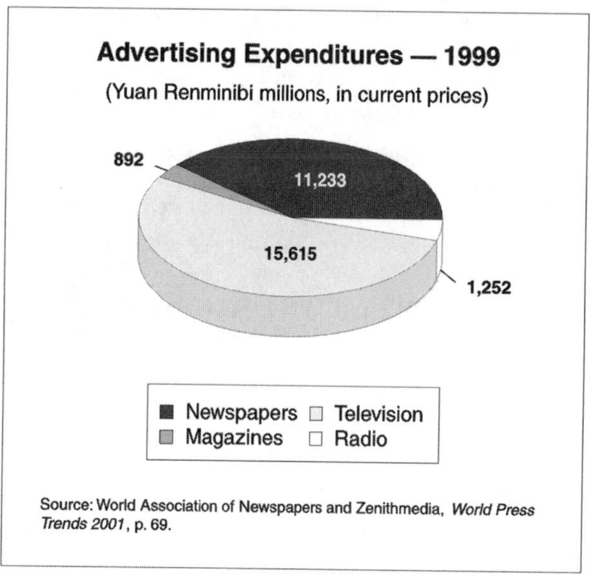

Source: World Association of Newspapers and Zenithmedia, *World Press Trends 2001*, p. 69.

PRESS LAWS

Article 35 of the Constitution of the People's Republic of China (adopted on December 4, 1982) stipulates that "citizens of the People's Republic of China enjoy freedom of speech, of the press, of assembly, of association, of procession and of demonstration." Although there has not been any law specifically ascribed as press law, many regulations and administrative orders have been issued to control publications and their distributions since 1949. In late 1994, the Propaganda Department's Six No's were circulated in top journalism and news media research institutions: no private media ownership, no shareholding of media organizations, no joint ventures with foreign companies, no discussion of the commodity nature of news, no discussion of a press law, and no openness for foreign satellite television. This kind of statement, by far the most important media policy statement made by the Party in the 1990s, illustrates the informal and reactive nature of media policy-making by the Chinese Communist Party.

The first step necessary for the Chinese government to control the media was a strict registration and licensing system. As stipulated by the 1990 Provisional Regulations on Newspaper Management, all applications for publishing newspapers must be approved by the State Press and Publications Administration (SPPA), the government's official media monitor. All newspapers must carry an official registration number. Moreover, with the exception of party organs, all must have an area of specialization and must have a "zhuguan bumen" (responsible department) that maintains leadership and control. Thus, even papers that are seemingly not related to the Party are actually controlled by ministries that are under Party control. This prevents the independent launching of a second general interest newspaper in an area to compete with the party organ. With the exception of party organs, all newspapers focus on specific subjects, like the economy, the legal system, health, education, or culture. They may also target specific audiences like intellectuals, workers, women, farmers, or youth. This focus effectively prevents newspapers from being independent civil institutions outside the Party/state apparatus.

Another powerful weapon that the CCP uses to check information flow is to classify an enormous range of information as "state secrets," including harmless information already in the public domain. The Notification on Forbidding Openly Citing Internal Publications of Xinhua News Agency (1998) states that "to maintain the secrecy of the internal publications concerns the Party's and national interests." It made it clear that news media are not allowed to cite any classified documents. This regulation has been conveniently used to imprison citizens who spread critical ideas and information outside of established channels.

Besides maintaining control of the media, the CCP authorities try to tackle the problem of journalistic corruption partly due to public pressure and partly due to concern for the party organ's reputation. A series of codes of ethics have been released since 1991. The first one was the Moral Code for Chinese Journalism Professionals, which emphasizes the principles of news objectivity and fairness. According to the code, journalists "should not publish any forms of 'paid journalism'. . . should not put news and editorial spaces up for sale, nor accept nor extort money and gifts nor obtain private gain.'' It also pronounced that ''journalism activities and business activities should be strictly separated. Reporters and editors should not engage in advertising and other business activities nor obtain private gain.'' In January of 2000, the ''Chinese Newspaper Self-Discipline Agreement'' was released, which stipulates that journalists must strictly follow all regulations and rules passed by the government and assume social responsibilities. Reporters should not ''issue false numbers, make untruthful advertisement and groundless accusation, and mix news reporting with advertising activities.'' The Advertising Law of the People's Republic of China (February 1995) is yet another kind of code of ethics, calling for media institutions and journalists to adhere to the principle of truth, abide by the law and professional ethics, maintain honesty in performing their duties, and defend the reputation and image of the Chinese media. However, these codes of ethics are not binding at all. Enforcement of regulations is weak, often belated, and full of loopholes.

Since the 1980s reformist journalists, educators, and researchers have pushed for a press law that would safeguard journalists' professionalism beyond the vague ''freedom of the press'' provision in Article 35 of the Chinese Constitution. For different reasons, functionaries concerned with the news media's potential to hamper official business and harm reputations also pushed for such a law, hoping that it might restrain the press from excess zeal. The suppression of the 1989 Student Democracy Movement, however, killed all discussions on a press law. As of 2002, there was no sign that China would pass such a law.

CENSORSHIP

Censorship defines the environment in which the Chinese press has operated since the late nineteenth century. The Communist Party, however, exerts the most rigorous and institutionalized forms of censorship in Chinese press history. Vertically, the CCP's Central Propaganda Department commands the propaganda departments of CCP committees at five government levels—central, provincial, municipal, county, and township, as well as individual enterprises and institutions. Horizontally, it controls China's print and broadcast media, journals, books, television, movies, literature, arts, and cultural establishments.

As a matter of control, newspapers have a strict editing system. The Central Committee Secretariat inspects important manuscripts at the *People's Daily* and the provincial CCP secretary or the secretary in charge of supervising propaganda work inspects provincial newspaper articles. Shendu or shending (media monitoring) is usually performed by special teams of veteran Party ideologues. For editors and journalists, the danger of post-publication retribution is omnipresent. Punishment ranges from being forced to write self-criticism to imprisonment. Although pre-publication censorship is not prevalent, the threat of post-publication sanction results in fairly vigilant self-censorship.

However, China's news apparatus exhibits far more flexibility than a strictly totalitarian model would lead one to expect. In a nation as large and complex as China, authorities cannot hope bring every aspect of the media fully under control. Communication between the Party and the masses is subject to leaks, inference, and distortion. Press censorship cannot always achieve its purpose since the Chinese have learned the art of decoding newspaper messages over the years. For example, if some senior members of the Party are missing from the participants' list on an important CCP gathering, the public learns to interpret this as a sign of a factional struggle within the higher echelons of the CCP, and those missing names indicate a purge.

The fate of the *Shijie Jingji Daobao* (World Economic Herald) provides a case study of censorship in China. The Shanghai-based *World Economic Herald* was created in June 1980 as a result of Deng Xiaoping's economic-reform policies which allowed enterprises to start newspapers to promote the exchange of business information and to provide a means of advertising. In order to obtain relative freedom and autonomy in the newspaper's organization and to escape government control, Qin Benli, the founder of the *World Economic Herald*, established a board composed of prominent scholars and officials to formulate the *Herald*'s guidelines. He not only appointed some previous ''rightists'' but also recruited a group of talented young reporters and editors. The *Herald* had no government funding and started with RMB 20,000 of prepaid advertising money, but sound management led the paper to expand rapidly.

The principle of the paper was to serve as a ''mouthpiece for the people'' to promote reform and opening. Quickly, the newspaper became a yardstick for measuring the extent of political freedom in the country. In a sense, the paper was the harbinger of the 1989 Student Democracy Movement. Fearing the paper's growing political and financial autonomy, the government wanted to oust Qin Benli and take over the paper. Such efforts were twice defected by reformists at the top of the Party's hierarchy. But on April 24, 1989 the *World Economic Herald* published an article expressing sympathy for the former General Party Secretary, liberal Hu Yaobang, criticizing those who purged him in 1987. Two days later, Qin Benli was dismissed and the paper was taken over by the Shanghai Municipal Committee. Party officials in Shanghai announced that the *World Economic Herald* had never been an official newspaper and Qin had never received formal certification regarding his appointment.

STATE-PRESS RELATIONS

Theoretically, Chinese citizens have the right to criticize the government. According to the 41st Article of the Constitution,

> ''Citizens of the People's Republic of China have the right to criticize and make suggestions regarding any state organ or functionary. Citizens have the right to make to relevant state organs complaints or charges against, or exposures of, any state organ or functionary for violation of the law or dereliction of duty, but fabrication or distortion of facts for purposes of libel or false incrimination is prohibited. The state organ concerned must deal with complaints, charges or exposures made by citizens in a responsible manner after ascertaining the facts. No one may suppress such complaints, charges and exposures or retaliate against the citizens making them. Citizens who have suffered losses as a result of infringement of their civic rights by any state organ or functionary have the right to compensation in accordance with the law.''

This right is, however, by no means guaranteed. The Fifty-first Article indicates that national, societal, and collective interests cannot be damaged due to individuals' exercise of freedom and their rights. ''Citizens of the People's Republic of China, in exercising their freedoms and rights, may not infringe upon the interests of the state, of society or of the collective, or upon the lawful freedoms and rights of other citizens.'' The CCP General Party Secretary, Jiang Zemin (1997-2002), defines the relationship between the Party's leadership of the press and the people's rights in this way: ''The news project of our country is a part of the cause of our Party. So in the press, we must adhere to the principles of keeping the Party's spirits, and maintaining a correct orientation for public opinion. It is not permitted to use so-called 'people's rights' to deny our Party's leadership over the news project.'' Thus, the Constitution leaves a significant loophole regarding citizens' right to criticize the government. Only the state can determine what national, societal, and collective interests are deemed important enough to override individual rights.

An apparatus for tightening administrative supervision of the press is the State Press and Publications Administration that was set up in January 1987. In addition to offices in charge of policies and regulations, copyrights, foreign affairs, newspaper, periodicals, books, distribution, audio-video, technology development, personnel, and planning and finance, it also governs about 20 publishing houses. It is a ministry-level agency with corresponding agencies at provincial and municipal levels. The Administration serves as the ideological police of every newspaper and magazine in China. It is also in charge of drafting and enforcing press laws, licensing publications, and monitoring texts. However, this agency is under the supervision of the Party's Propaganda Department and thus has no authority over central party newspapers, such as *People's Daily* and *Guangming Daily*.

ATTITUDE TOWARD FOREIGN MEDIA

In both Nationalist and Communist China, foreign correspondents have never been provided information adequately by official sources. Foreign journalists must develop alternative sources, such as embassy personnel, the foreign community in China, and Chinese intellectuals, artists, and dissidents. Sometimes they even make an effort to meet officials under informal, off-the-record circumstances or to befriend the children of high-level officials. Foreign journalists must take extraordinary pains to protect their Chinese sources. In general, foreign correspondents are subjected to surveillance, including the monitoring of telephones and mail. Chinese staff, such as interpreters, drivers, cooks, and maids, are also instructed on their duty to keep an eye on foreign correspondents during their work.

After the Tiananmen student movement in 1989, three sets of regulations were announced for external reporters. The first two sets were for Taiwan, Hong Kong, and Macao reporters, issued respectively on September 16, 1989, and October 27, 1989. The third set, ''Regulations Governing Foreign Reporters and Permanent Foreign News Apparatus,'' has been in effect since January 1990, and it delineates the procedure of accreditation and operation of foreign journalists in China. According to the regulations, the Information Department of the Foreign Ministry is in charge of foreign journalists. As for the accreditation process, any news organization must first register with its home government. The Chinese government then has the right to acknowledge or reject its status in China. Finally, foreign journalists must register with the Information Department in order to get ''Foreign Correspondent Cards.''

In 1991 the Chinese Foreign Ministry directed Chinese embassies abroad to impose stricter standards in screening foreign reporters' visa applications, including extensive background checks, and a review of the political content of each applicant's previous reporting. Chinese missions were held accountable for unfavorable stories by reporters that they cleared. The Chinese government also required special permission to visit areas of minorities.

Even in special economic zones, areas in which foreigners could expect a certain degree of leniency, control over communications has been tightened. In April of

1996, the government issued a 25-article regulation to centralize the distribution of business, economic, and financial news and data. It ordered foreign news providers and their subscribers to register with the state monopoly, Xinhua News Agency. Because business news items have become hot commodities, foreign news services such as Reuters and Dow Jones have developed networks worth tens of millions of dollars by selling up-to-minute stock market quotes and news to more than one thousand private and company clients in China. The regulations not only put strict curbs on foreign news services in reaping profits from this lucrative business but also allowed Xinhua to filter news that is "forbidden" or that "jeopardizes the national interest of China." The real-time information providers as well as news wire and online service providers are required to pay a certain amount of monitoring fees. Xinhua has the authority to decide how and at what price foreign-produced business news can be distributed.

According to Chinese law, no foreign capital can enter Chinese media. The only joint venture that is allowed by the Chinese government is the magazine, *Jisuanji Shijie* (Computer World), run by a Chinese and an American company. Although a Hong Kong company and a Swiss investor tried to invest in two Chinese newspapers secretly, they were soon discovered and forced to leave. Chinese sources indicated that the situation would remain the same even after China entered the World Trade Organization.

Overall, foreign reporting influence on China has been marginal. Reporters are restricted to urban areas and cannot communicate directly with peasants in the countryside or with industrial workers, partly due to language barriers and partly because of the Chinese government's restrictions. Common problems faced by foreign correspondents include isolation, being treated with distant respect, and being subjected to staged propagandistic events. Although foreign reporters of Chinese descent can be more resourceful and less recognizable in China than their non-Chinese counterparts, there is no evidence that they have been any more influential on China's development. So far, journalists, scholars, and government analysts have not penetrated central politics.

Nonetheless, external challenges to the Chinese media system have never been so strong since China started economic reforms in the 1980s. The news media of Hong Kong and Taiwan are increasingly influential with better economic integration and a common cultural background. Western media influences come in many technological forms, from short wave radio to satellite television to the Internet, and are driven by both political and commercial imperatives. More than 100 international media outlets have set up branch offices in China, including CNN, Reuters, Bloomberg, AP Dow Jones, *Newsweek*, *Fortune*, *New York Times* and many others. Therefore, morning news events in Beijing are likely to be picked up by international wire or TV networks in the afternoon and broadcast worldwide. Generally speaking, the foreign media in China go after political stories and sensitive, provocative issues such as Tibet, human rights and Taiwan's independence movement. And they tend to add a controversial touch or political twist—even in business reports.

Reprinted news dispatches of foreign journalists based in China have been widely perceived in China as more informative about internal developments than Chinese newspapers. Evidence shows that Western reporting on the Democracy Wall movement in 1978-1979 prompted Chinese authorities to halt the movement because the foreign media amplified the effect of the movement. Likewise, Western coverage of the 1983-1984 spiritual pollution campaign helped moderate the intensity of the campaign since the coverage raised foreign investors' concern over the Chinese investment environment.

In addition to international correspondents, foreign short wave radio has also become an important alternative source of news, particularly for intellectuals and university students. A 1990 survey found that 10.6 percent of the Beijing population frequently listened to nearly 20 foreign radio stations. As of 1993, some 27 outside broadcasters (including five in Taiwan) provided Chinese-language broadcasts, comprising a total of 185 channels. Influential foreign short wave stations, like the Voice of America (VOA) and the British Broadcasting Company (BBC), have played a critical role in challenging the CCP's monopoly on information, especially with their reports about events in China during political upheavals such the Tiananmen movement.

Besides journalists and radio stations, direct satellite television broadcasting is also a threat to the CCP's monopolistic control of news and ideology. In addition to CNN and the BBC, more than twenty outside television channels broadcast by satellite to China, including both commercial and government-sponsored stations in such places as Hong Kong, Australia, Japan, France, Germany, and Russia. Although the Chinese government, out of fear of ideological influence from the West, generally forbids the reception of all external television, foreign satellite television has gained considerable inroads in China because the original business in satellite dish sales to business institutions quickly expanded to individual households: by late 1993, more than 11 million Chinese households had satellite dishes. The most wide-reaching outside television threat comes from Hong Kong-based Star TV offering MTV, sports, BBC World Service news (partially translated into Mandarin), family entertainment, and a channel of broadcasts in Mandarin, all on the air 24 hours a day. Star TV was originally controlled by the Hong Kong tycoon Li Jiacheng, who has many business interests in China and close ties with China's top leadership. But in July 1993, Li suddenly sold 64 percent of Star TV to Rupert Murdoch's News Corporation. This change of ownership from a friendly Hong Kong businessman to an international media tycoon further diminished the Chinese government's possibility of cutting off unwanted news. In late 1993, Star TV programs were seen in more than 30 million Chinese households.

Moreover, access to the Internet is expanding rapidly and the Party's Propaganda Department is again falling behind government departments that have technological and commercial interests in promoting it. China's first electronic mail message was sent through an international connection to a German mail gateway in September, 1987. Among the more than 190 national and regional computer networks registered in China in 1996 are two major academic networks, the China Education and Research Network (CERNET), and the China Academic Science Network (CASNET). These two networks link hundreds of Chinese universities and research institutions to the outside world. In addition, the Ministry of Posts and Telecommunications operates Chinanet, which began to provide commercial access to the Internet in May 1995. The Ministry of Electronic Industry is also installing an Internet service. By early 1996 about 100,000 people in China had logged onto the Internet. With the growing popularity of telephones and home computers, many more institutions and urban households will soon access the Internet, and the Propaganda Department will find it hard to restrict computer and telephone use without damaging the economy.

News Agencies

Xinhua News Agency enjoys a monopolistic position as the only CCP-mandated news agency in China. The Chinese Communist Party's news agency, the Red China News Agency, was established on November 7, 1931. Six years later, it was changed to New China (Xinhua) News Agency. The agency not only sent reports to the outside world but also used army radio to collect outside news, mainly dispatches of the Nationalist government's Central News Agency. These were edited and printed in Reference News, which was distributed to Party leaders. Xinhua's tradition of providing intelligence for high-level Party leaders continued as of 2002. By the end of the 1980s, Xinhua had become the largest news organization, with three major departments: domestic with bureaus in all provinces; international with more than 100 foreign bureaus; and the General Office with both domestic and international news editing bureaus, sports news bureau, photo editing bureau, news information center and Internet center. As of 2001, it puts out almost forty dailies, weeklies, and monthlies. Its important subsidiaries include Zhongguo Zhengquan Bao (China Security), a daily that specializes in business news and the stock market, and *Xinhua Meiri Dianxun* (Xinhua Daily Telegraph), a general interest daily that carries the agency's own news dispatches.

Although Xinhua belongs directly to the highest governmental body, the State Council, its daily operations rely heavily on instructions from various levels of the Party bureaucracy, from the Politburo to the central Propaganda Department. It has the largest and most articulated internal news system of any organization in China, which can be divided into three classes: secrecy, top secrecy, and absolute secrecy. It functions on a need-to-know basis. Those highest in the hierarchy get most fully briefed, while a stream trickles out to the lower level. The system creates a news privilege pyramid. The higher the privilege, the richer the news, the more comprehensive the secrets contained, and the more authoritative the ideas.

Broadcast Media

By the end of the 1980s, Central People's Broadcasting Station (CPBS) and China Central Television (CCTV) had monopolized the broadcast media. They are under the jurisdiction of the Ministry of Radio, Film, and Television, which serves as both a news organization and a broadcasting administrative bureaucracy. CPBS's 6:30 to 7:00 morning news and CCTV's 7:00 to 7:30 evening news are transmitted nationwide everyday, making them the most important news programs in the country.

The Central People's Broadcasting Station (CPBS) has established 34 stations nationwide and provides broadcasting and music programs to 34 countries. Popular programs include ''Selections from News and Newspapers,'' ''Local People's Broadcasting Stations' Programs,'' ''Small Loudspeaker,'' ''Reading and Appreciation,'' and ''Hygiene and Health.'' Besides CPBS, every province has at least one radio station under the provincial government, with at least two different channels providing general interest, as well as original programming in specialized areas such as music and business news.

Radio Beijing is the only national station that broadcasts to the world. From 1947 to 1949 all its broadcasts were in English. Then Japanese language programming was added. At the beginning of the twenty-first century, it used 43 languages to broadcast to most countries in the world. After 1984, it opened programs to foreigners in Beijing, and twelve provinces followed suit. It provided programs to more than 20 countries (*Zhongguo xinwen chuban dadian* 619).

CCTV, the country's most powerful and influential station, went on the air in 1958. As a state-owned and party-controlled instrument of propaganda, television had limited penetration prior to the 1980s and thus figured insignificantly compared with newspapers and radios before the reform period. However, due partly to a more open political atmosphere and an emerging market economy, and partly to the Chinese Communist Party's intent to use television as an effective means for political and cultural propaganda, television programs became increasingly interesting and more relevant to Chinese daily life. This development resulted in an expansion of television stations, a growth of television-set ownership, and the emergence of an extensive cooperative relationship among stations, commercial financing institutions, and government agencies. CCTV now has 12 channels, including news, social economy and education, entertainment, film, opera, agricultural news, and western China development. CCTV has established relations with more than 120 stations within about 80 countries. As local stations strengthened their capacity for newsgathering and also for producing entertainment fare, they began to be a major program source for CCTV. In 1981, CCTV aired a total of 4,186 news stories; 44 percent of them were furnished by local stations. Of the 118 television dramas that CCTV broadcasted, 81 percent came from local stations.

With the introduction of cable in the mid-1980s, many municipalities and counties, as well as large government units and businesses with their own residential areas for employees, established local cable networks. Because cable stations charge monthly fees, they do not need government investment. As a result, they have developed at an explosive rate and have become highly decentralized. As of the first half of 1993, there were more than 2 thousand cable networks in the country reaching into 20 million households. Approximately 800 were full-scale cable stations, broadcasting videos or self-produced programming. Two hundred of these were run by large-scale state-owned business enterprises. At the end of 1995, the number of full-scale cable stations had reached 1,200, with an estimated audience of 200 million.

CCTV commenced international newscasts on April 1, 1980. The reception from foreign television news services, such as Visnews (Britain) and UPI Television News Service (The United States), broadened CCTV's world news coverage. China also joined Asiavision, a television consortium among Asian countries, and exchanged news with the African Broadcasting Union and World Television Network.

ELECTRONIC NEWS MEDIA

The Internet age undoubtedly poses major challenges to the Chinese propaganda authorities. With the advent of the Internet, an unlimited audience can access information. There is no need for licenses to launch electronic publications. The Internet has opened a system of two-way communication, which is the opposite of China's longstanding indoctrination-oriented propaganda system. The advent of chat rooms via Internet technology has provided the Chinese people with a channel for the free flow of information and opportunities for participants to speak their minds.

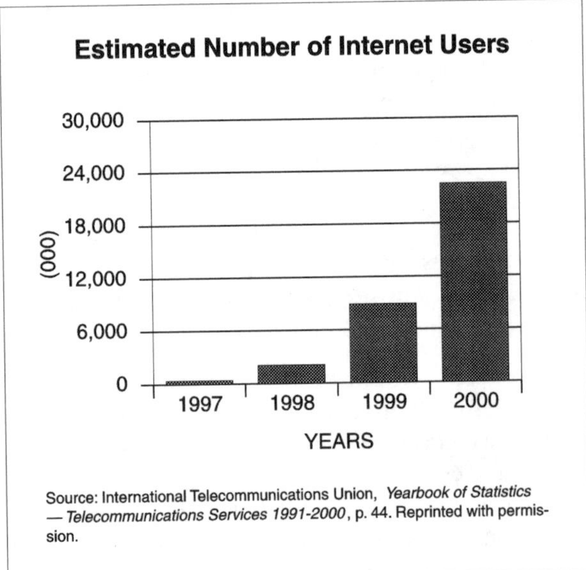

Source: International Telecommunications Union, *Yearbook of Statistics — Telecommunications Services 1991-2000*, p. 44. Reprinted with permission.

By 2000, China had 10 million Internet users. About 18 percent of households in Beijing, Shanghai, Guangzhou, and Shenzhou enjoy net access. Twenty-seven percent of China's Internet users chatted on AOL's messaging service. China now has 3,000-odd enterprises engaged in Internet-related and other value-added endeavors. As of June 2001 almost 1,000 Chinese newspapers—nearly half—were on online. Some well-known Internet press sites included People's Web, established by *People's Daily* in 1997 and one of the biggest Chinese news web. By providing easy access to a wide range of business information, photos and syndicated cartoons, chinadaily.com.cn has grown into an influential provider of information for people in and outside China. It was the only English-language newspaper Web site that made it into the country's top 10 news portal list. It was recommended by America Online as one of the global leading news websites. Another influential press site is the Qian Long Xin Wen Wang (Thousand Dragon Newsnet), which was formed by nine press institutions in Beijing on March 17, 2000. Its aim is to become the biggest newsnet for Chinese worldwide. A third popular newsnet is Saidi Wang (Saidi Net). It was started by eight information technology institutions in March of 2000. In the south, almost at the same time, Shanghai Liberation

Daily, Wenhui-Xinmin Joint Newspaper Group, Dong Fang Radio Station and Dong Fang TV Station started to discuss the formation of Shanghai Dong Fang Net. Both Thousand Dragon Newsnet and Shanghai Dong Fang Net are based on joint efforts between the printed media and the broadcast media.

The Chinese government has issued a number of rules and regulations to control the content of the Internet. Regulations issued in January 2000, for example, stated that media must obtain a qualification certificate to disseminate information online. It also ruled that Internet users charged with violating China's strict security laws could face sentences of up to life in prison. In November 2000, Beijing issued "Temporary Regulations on Internet News Business Management," which stipulated that electronic news media have the right to report news while Internet business sites can only repeat news items that are reported by the news media.

At least seven people have been arrested for Internet-related journalism in China, and more arrests are likely. Lin Hai, the first person in China sentenced in connection with the Internet, was arrested due to his supply of 30,000 e-mail addresses to an overseas electronic newsletter. Huang Qi's website "www.6-4tianwang.com" grew out of an electronic billboard for missing persons and developed into a discussion forum where people reported human rights abuses that were neglected by the official Chinese press. He was detained by the public security department in Chengdu, Sichuan in June 2000.

About twenty provinces were creating Internet "police" forces, according to Xinhua, with the task of "maintaining order" on the Internet. Meanwhile, criminal statutes were revised to allow for the prosecution of online subversion, limiting direct foreign investment in Internet companies and requiring companies to register with the information that might harm unification of the country, endanger national security, or subvert the government. Promoting "evil cults" (an obvious reference to Beijing's campaign against Falun Gong) was similarly banned, along with anything that "disturbs social order." The regulations also covered chat rooms, a popular feature of many Chinese sites, where the anonymity of cyberspace fosters discussion of democracy and the shortcomings of the ruling elite. Under the new rules, all service providers had to monitor content in the rooms and restrict controversial topics.

The explosion of electronic news media also creates copyright issues in China. In China's first Internet copyright lawsuit, a Beijing court ordered an Internet company to compensate six prominent writers for publishing their work without consent. The court ruled Century Internet Communications Technology Co. had violated copyright laws by putting the works on Beijing Online's Web site at http://www.bol.com.cn. The six writers sued the company in July 1999. They include Wang Meng, appointed culture minister in the 1980s but fired months after China's 1989 crackdown on dissent, Zhang Chengzhi, Bi Shumin, Liu Zhenyun, Zhang Jie and Zhang Kangkang. The Internet is becoming the latest battleground for press freedom in China. While the Chinese authorities intend to turn the Internet into nothing more than a vehicle for e-commerce and state-controlled information, Western enthusiasts are hopeful about the Internet as a powerful tool in political reform.

Number of Personal Computers in Use

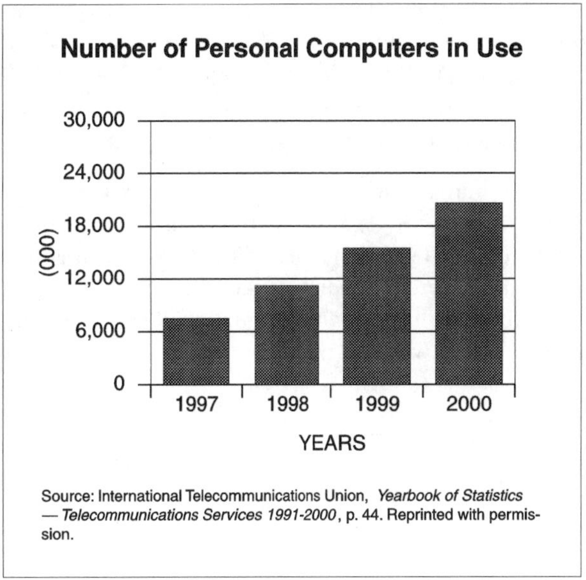

Source: International Telecommunications Union, *Yearbook of Statistics — Telecommunications Services 1991-2000*, p. 44. Reprinted with permission.

EDUCATION & TRAINING

Journalism is becoming an increasingly popular subject among Chinese youth. As of April of 2002, journalism studies were offered in 232 colleges and universities in China. The most popular subjects are TV-broadcast editing and news anchoring. The journalism departments at Beijing University, Wuhan University, and People's University are the most prominent in the country. Beijing University, which opened the first journalism course in China over 80 years ago, re-opened its School of Journalism and Communication in 2001. The new school consists of three departments and one institute. They are the Journalism Department, the Communication Department, the New-Media and Internet-Communication Department, and the Institute of Information and Communication Research. The curriculum and research fields cover journalism, communication, international communication, advertising, editing and publishing, Internet communication, and inter-cultural communication.

The Journalism Department of Wuhan University was founded in 1983. It became the College of Journalism and Communication in 1995. The college has six departments: Journalism, Broadcast Television, Advertisement, Print Communication, Packaging Design, and Internet and Communication. It also offers graduate journalism degrees.

The Journalism Department in People's University was established in 1955, and it became the School of Journalism in 1988. It is one of the two programs that offer Ph.D. degrees nationwide, and the only key subject under the State Education Commission. The department also publishes two magazines, *Journalism Studies* and *International News Media*.

In 1980 many young journalists started to take English-language journalism courses from foreigners who began teaching Western journalistic norms in several schools in Beijing and Shanghai. Chinese-language journalism departments, such as those at People's University and Sichuan University in Chengdu, also began expanding their curriculum and embracing the ideal of objectivity, using the American media as an example to be emulated.

However, compared to other subjects of study, journalism is still one of the most guarded. All journalism students are required to take political indoctrination courses on works by Marx, Lenin, and Mao on journalism, and Deng's ideas about the socialist market economy. Reporters and editors nationwide are being forced to attend refresher courses on the role of the media in China's Communist society. Also, anyone who wants to work for a government agency such as Xinhua must become a member of the Communist Party first.

There are four major journalistic organizations in China, and they are all government organizations. The All-China Journalists Association is the first professional organization for Chinese reporters. The organization has a domestic department and foreign affairs department. The former is responsible for training reporters, organizing newsgathering, and sponsoring discussions. The latter is in charge of exchanging programs with foreign journalists and holding press conferences.

China Radio and Television Society was founded in 1986. There are 36 subdivisions, seven offices and seven research committees nationwide. Its objectives are organizing members' research activities to improve the quality of broadcasting and TV programs, giving policy advice, organizing conferences, publishing society's reports, documents, and research results.China Newspaper Publishers' Association (CNPA), founded in 1988, is under the Press and Publication Administration, and affiliated with the *People's Daily*. It publishes a monthly magazine, Newspaper Management. Membership has reached more than 1,000.

Chinese Publishers Association was created in December, 1979. Besides ordinary functions assumed by other professional organizations, such as assisting government propaganda nationwide and promoting cultural exchanges with foreign counterparts, organizing academic activities is one of its major functions. It issues Taofen Prize, named after a famous Chinese journalist and writer, every two years. It also publishes *China Publication Yearbook*.

SUMMARY

China's entry into the World Trade Organization (WTO) in 2001 undoubtedly brought changes to Chinese media and publication businesses. According to the State Press and Publication Administration, within one year after joining WTO, China would probably allow foreign media to set up joint book and newspaper retail stores in five special economic zones and eight cities. Mergers would also become increasingly prevalent in China's WTO era. Media conglomerates emerged in the mid-1990s at provincial level and in major cities. These newspaper giants published books, magazines, audio-video materials and newspapers, and they run radio, TV stations, and Internet sites. As of the beginning of 2000, there were 15 media giants in China. The two reasons for the merger fever are media heads' frequent visits to their counterparts in Western countries and the desire to combat increasingly intense competition on China's media market. In January, 1996, the Press and Publication Administration approved the creation of China's first newspaper group, Guangzhou Daily Newspaper Group, the richest Chinese newspaper at the time. By 1998, it had increased to ten newspapers and one magazine with a circulation of 920,000. The advertising income reached 1.5 billion. Based on the successful operations of Guangzhou Daily Newspaper Group, Beijing approved two other newspaper conglomerates in Guangzhou in May of 1998: Nanfang Daily Newspaper Group and Yangcheng Evening Newspaper Group. *Guangming Daily* and *Economic Daily* are the first two newspapers in Beijing that formed newspaper conglomerates. Some of the newspaper groups are now trying to enter the stock market overseas to obtain more funds for expansion. It is predicted that by 2010 China will develop 20-30 more newspaper conglomerates (Sun 327).

The goals that the Press and Publication Administration set for Chinese press to achieve in the first decade of the twenty-first century are:

- double the publication volume of both newspaper and audio-video material
- build 5-10 publishing groups with an income between RMB 1 billion and 10 billion and 20-30 of about RMB 1 billion

- advertising income will make up 80% of total income of newspaper companies
- promote newspaper retail by developing newspaper dispensers

At the beginning of the twenty-first century, in order to win press reform, undertake investigative journalism, and truly function as their society's watchdogs, Chinese media still have a long way to go. Since the start of reforms, the Chinese news media have been in the paradoxical situation of at once being changed and remaining the same. Economic reforms and an open-door policy introduced market logic into the party-controlled news media system. But the discourse on media democratization that emerged was suppressed in the crackdown on the democracy movement in 1989. Ironically, this promoted media liberalization by forcing the Chinese press to turn to market forces in a vacuum of political freedom. These developments produced the mix of party logic and market logic, forging the tension, contradiction, and uncertainty that is the unique hallmark of the Chinese media system.

SIGNIFICANT DATES

- October 1997: The first English Edition Chinese newspaper, China Daily, Hong Kong Edition, is issued (Zhongguo Chuban Nianqian (China Publication Yearbook), 1999. Chinese Publication Yearbook (ed.), 1999: 41).
- June 1998: The ''three fixes'' are implemented to streamline the administrative structure of the press. The three fixes mandate: ''fix the number of employees, fix the workload and fix the post.''
- August 2000: China's first TV station, Sun TV, starts its program in Hong Kong.
- January 2001: Shanghai begins China's first digital TV program. Other cities, such as Shenzhen, Qingdao, and Hangzhou, follow suit quickly.
- December 2001: The largest Chinese media, China Broadcasting and Television Group, is created in Beijing.
- December 2001: China Human Rights Web site (http://www.humanrights-china.org/) goes online. A project of the China Society for Human Rights Studies (CSHRS), it is the official Chinese human rights Web site, with reports of current human rights conditions, government documents and White Papers, relevant laws and regulations, and links to various state organizations, NGOs, and academic institutions.
- January 2002: China's Ministry of Radio, Film and Television and American Time and Warner start broadcasting 24 hours daily CCTV English news (CCTV, Channel 9) in New York, Houston, and San Francisco. In return, China allows Time Warner's Mandarin programs (ETV) to broadcast in southeast China. This is the first foreign TV program to be shown in China.

BIBLIOGRAPHY

Berlin, Michael J. ''The Performance of the Chinese Media during the Beijing Spring.'' In *Chinese Democracy and the Crisis of 1989: Chinese and American Reflections*. Eds. Roger V. Des Forges, Luo Ning, Wu Yen-bo, 263-273. Albany, New York: State University of New York Press, 1993.

Britton, Roswell S. *The Chinese Periodical Press, 1800-1912*. New York: Paragon, 1966.

''China Release New Rules for Foreign News Agencies.'' *Wall Street Journal*, 17 April 1996, PB7(W), PB9(E), col. 1.

China Publication Yearbook. Beijing: China Publishers Association, 1999.

Des Forges, Roger V., et. al. *Chinese Democracy and the Crisis of 1989: Chinese and American Reflections*. Albany, New York: State University of New York Press, 1993.

Dobbs, Michael. ''Journalists Link Press Freedom with Aims of Student Protesters.'' *Washington Post*, 23 May 1989, p. A18, 28.

Faison, Seth. ''The Changing Role of the Chinese Media.'' In *Perspectives on the Chinese People's Movement: Spring 1989*. Ed. Tony Saich, 144-162. Armond, New York: M. E. Sharpe, 1990.

Holman, Richard L. ''Press Freedom in Hong Kong.'' *Wall Street Journal*, 6 Oct. 1993, p. A14(W), p. A12(E), col. 2.

———. ''Chinese Journalists Warned.'' *Wall Street Journal*, 5 August 1993, p. A9(W), p. A4(E), col. 4.

———. ''China Reduces Media Access.'' *Wall Street Journal*, 22 Oct. 1991, p. A16(W), p. A17(E), col. 3.

Kristof, Nicholas. ''Beijing Delays Law on Free Press.'' *New York Times*, 27 June 1989, p. A4(N), col. 1.

Lee, Chin-Chuan. *China's Media, Media's China*. Boulder, CO: Westview Press, 1994.

———. *Voices of China: The Interplay of Politics and Journalism*. New York: The Guilford Press, 1990.

Lin, Yutang. *A History of the Press and Public Opinion in China*. New York: Greenwood Press, 1968.

Liu, Liqun. ''The Image of the United States in Present-Day China.'' In *Beyond the Cold War: Soviet and American Media Images*. Eds. Everette E. Dennis, George Gerbner, and Yassen N. Zassoursky, 116-125. Newbury Park, CA: Sage Publications, Inc., 1991.

Lynch, Daniel C. *After the Propaganda State: Media, Politics, and "Thought Work."* In *Reformed China.* Stanford, CA: Stanford University Press, 1999.

MacKinnon, Stephen R. "Press Freedom and the Chinese Revolution." In *Media and Revolution.* Ed. Jeremy D. Popkin, 174-188. Lexington, KY: The University Press of Kentucky, 1995.

———. "The Role of the Chinese and U.S. Media." In *Popular Protest and Political Culture in Modern China: Learning from 1989.* Eds. Jeffrey N. Wasserstrom and Elizabeth J. Perry, 206-214. Boulder, CO: Westview Press, 1992.

MacKinnon, Stephen R., and Oris Friesen. *China Reporting: An Oral history of American Journalism in the 1930s and 1940s.* Berkeley, CA: University of California Press, 1987.

Nathan, Andrew. *Chinese Democracy.* Berkeley, CA: University of California Press, 1985.

"New Law for Journalists Proposed," *New York Times,* 9 Sept. 1980, p. 3(N), p. A6 (LC), col. 3.

Southerland, Daniel. "China Issues Code for Foreign Journalists; New Regulations Seem Designed to Tighten Government Control." *Washington Post,* 21 Jan. 1990, p. A359.

Sun, Yanjun. *Baoye Zhongguo* (Newspaper in China). Beijing: China Three Gorge Publishing House, 2002.

Ting, Lee-hsia Hsu. *Government Control of the Press in Modern China, 1900-1949: A Study of Its Theories, Operations, and Effects.* Cambridge, MA: Harvard University Press, 1974.

Tyson, Ann Scott. "China Steps Up Harassment of Correspondents," *Christian Science Monitor* 1 March 1990, 82, no. 65, p. 59.

Widor, Claude. *The Samizdat Press in China's Provinces, 1979-1981: An Annotated Guide.* Stanford, CA: Hoover Institute, Stanford University, 1987.

Wu Guoguang. "Developemnt of Chinese Mass Media and the Progress of Democratization of Chinese Society." In *Essay Collection of Symposium on Election System and Democratic Development in China, Taiwan, and Hong Kong.* Ed. Hu Chunhui, 453-491. Hong Kong: Hong Kong University, 1999.

Yang, Meirong. "A Long Way toward a Free Press: The Case of the World Economic Herald." In *Decision-Making in Deng's China: Perspectives from Insiders.* Eds. Carol Lee Hamrin and Suisheng Zhao Armond, 183-188. New York: M. E. Sharpe, 1995.

Zhao, Yuezhi. *Media, Market, and Democracy in China: Between the Party Line and the Bottom Line.* Chicago: University of Illinois Press, 1998.

"Zhongguo Xinwen Chuban Dadian." In *Encyclopedia of World Media.* Beijing: China Archive Publishing Company, 1994.

—*Ting Ni*

CHRISTMAS ISLAND

BASIC DATA

Official Country Name:	Christmas Island
Region (Map name):	Oceania
Population:	2,564
Language(s):	English, Chinese, Malay
Literacy rate:	N/A

Named for the day of its discovery in 1643, Christmas Island is the top of a 50 million-year-old extinct volcano rising out of the Indian Ocean, south of Indonesia.

Islanders enjoy freedom of speech and press. Because the population is so small, no major newspapers are printed locally. The only publication is a newspaper called *The Islander*, which appears fortnightly. The full-color, tabloid-sized publication is produced by the Shire of Christmas Island, the local government body.

There is one radio station on the island, transmitting on both AM and FM frequencies for approximately 1,000 radios. It is staffed by volunteer announcers. Islanders own approximately 600 televisions, but there are no local broadcast stations. There are two Internet service providers.

The island has never had an indigenous population, but British settlement began in the late 1800s, and it was annexed by the United Kingdom in 1888. Under British rule, the island became a major region for phosphate mining, a mineral byproduct of volcanic eruptions.

In 1958, the UK transferred sovereignty of the island to Australia. The population of Christmas Island is approximately 1,300, and inhabitants speak a mix of English, Chinese, and Malay. Christmas Island is administered by Australia under the Australian Department of the Environment, Sport, and Territories. The Christmas Island Shire Council is popularly elected to one-year terms. Although phosphate mining ceased temporarily between 1987 and 1991, the island has sustained considerable environmental damage. Today more than two-thirds of the island has been declared a national park, and local authorities are cooperating to restore the landscape and preserve the nesting sites of endangered birds. These goals also support the island's economy, as environmental-based tourism is a growing business.

BIBLIOGRAPHY

Christmas Island Web site. 2002. Available from www.christmas.net.

Central Intelligence Agency (CIA). *World Fact Book 2001.* Available from www.cia.gov.

—Jenny B. Davis

COLOMBIA

BASIC DATA

Official Country Name:	Republic of Colombia
Region (Map name):	South America
Population:	40,349,388
Language(s):	Spanish
Literacy rate:	91.3%
Area:	1,138,910 sq km
GDP:	81,283 (US$ millions)
Number of Daily Newspapers:	24
Total Circulation:	1,093,000
Circulation per 1,000:	41
Number of Nondaily Newspapers:	4
Total Circulation:	131,000
Circulation per 1,000:	5
Total Newspaper Ad Receipts:	307 (US$ millions)
As % of All Ad Expenditures:	11.30
Number of Television Stations:	60
Number of Television Sets:	4,590,000
Television Sets per 1,000:	113.8
Number of Cable Subscribers:	575,280
Cable Subscribers per 1,000:	13.6
Number of Satellite Subscribers:	79,000
Satellite Subscribers per 1,000:	2.0
Number of Radio Stations:	515
Number of Radio Receivers:	21,000,000
Radio Receivers per 1,000:	520.5
Number of Individuals with Computers:	1,500,000
Computers per 1,000:	37.2
Number of Individuals with Internet Access:	878,000
Internet Access per 1,000:	21.8

BACKGROUND & GENERAL CHARACTERISTICS

Colombia is one of the more complicated and interesting of the world's nations. Its history has a significant connection to its media and its press traditions. From its founding as a nation into the twenty-first century, it maintained a tradition of freedom of the press, and it attained an extensive and high quality press. However, violence threatens the country as a democratic entity as well as the health of its media.

Colombian History The territory that came to be called Colombia was originally populated by Chibcha Indians, who were conquered by Spanish *conquistadors* (colonialists). The Spanish used the term, Indian, which derived from *indigena* (indigenous). Although the nation was named for Columbus, the explorer never actually set foot on the land. Spain colonized the territory in the 1600s after conquering the Chibchas.

Originally part of Gran Colombia, which included what are now Panama and Venezuela, Colombia developed a constitution and government in 1811. It began its efforts towards independence from Spain in 1812. When Gran Colombia was liberated at Boyoca in 1819, under the leadership of Bolivar, it became an independent nation. Ecuador joined Gran Colombia in 1822. Panama became part of Colombia in 1821, after gaining its independence from Spain.

The Gran Colombia constitution was a model of popular democratic government. It established a two house or bicameral Congress, guaranteed the inviolability of persons, homes, and correspondence, and also guaranteed freedom of the press. By 1828, however, Bolivar, had returned from liberating other South American nations and had become a dictator and a self-proclaimed president for life. The people of Gran Colombia organized a constitutional convention in 1830, at which time Bolivar resigned. In the process, Ecuador and Venezuela seceded from Gran Colombia, and Gran Colombia collapsed. That left Colombia and Panama as the remaining entities and they essentially became Colombia.

Ethnic Groups As of 2002, about 58 percent of the people are *mestizo* (mixed Spanish and Chibcha Indian), and whites are 20 percent. The Spanish brought African slaves who were from the areas now called Angola, Nigeria, and Zaire. Mulattos (mixed black and white) are 14 percent; blacks, 4 percent; and mixed black-Amerindian 3 percent. In addition, Amerindian represent 1 percent of the population.

Population Density The 2001 estimate of the Colombian population, 40,349,388, suggested a population density of 92 persons per square mile. About three-fourths of the population was classified as urban. One-third of the Colombia people are young. The age distribution was given as follows: younger than 14 represented 31.88 percent; between 15 and 64 represented 63.37 percent; those 65 years and older constituted 4.75 percent. The overall population growth rate was 1.64 percent. The birth rate was 22.41 births per 1,000 population and the death rate was 5.69 deaths per 1,000 people. The population was decreased slightly by a few more people leaving the country than moving to it.

Literacy and Education The *Encarta Encyclopedia* estimated that 97 percent of all Colombians could read and write by 2001. In 1996 some 4.9 million pupils attended primary schools and 3.3 million secondary schools. Elementary education was free and compulsory for five years. Most schools were controlled by the Roman Catholic Church, but even governmentally-funded schools required Catholic religion educational content, an arrangement which reflects the close ties between the nation and the Church. There were some Protestant schools, primarily in Bogotá. The government paid for elementary education in communities that could not afford to do so; it also financed secondary and university-level schooling. Late 1990s data showed that 4.9 million pupils annually attended primary schools. Another 3.3 million attended secondary schools including vocational training and teacher training institutions. Of the 235 institutions of higher education some were public and others were affiliated with the Roman Catholic Church.

Religion & Language In the early 2000s some 95 percent of the people were Roman Catholics. The Concordat between Colombia and the Roman Catholic Church gave that religion a special status in the nation. The rest of the population included some Protestant groups as well as a small Jewish population, many of whom were descendents of individuals who fled Nazi Germany.

Spanish is the dominant language in Colombia. But the 1991 Constitution recognized diverse ethnic groups and made some provision for bilingual education. Dialects characterize different regions of Colombia, and Colombians take special pride in their language and some believe Colombian Spanish to be most closely related to the mother tongue Spaniards brought to Latin America.

Colombian Newspapers There are 37 Spanish language daily newspapers in Colombia, in addition to two English language dailies, *The Colombia Times* and *The Bogotá Daily*. According to *2001 International Year Book: The Encyclopedia of the Newspaper Industry* four of the Spanish language papers had circulations of fewer than 10,000; eight had circulations between 10,000 and 25,000; eight others had circulations from 25,000 to 50,000; five had circulations from 50,000 to 100,000; and three had circulations from 100,000 to 500,000.

In Colombia, there were two daily (except for Sunday) newspapers, *La Cronica* and *Diario del Quindio* The capital city of Bogotá had several newspapers: *Diario*, *El Espacio* (The Space), and *El Espectador* (The Spectator), considered one of the most influential newspapers in Colombia and Latin America. In Barranquilla, an important port city, there were two newspapers (daily except for Sunday), *El Heraldo* (The Herald) and *La Libertad* (The Liberty).

Established in 1925, *El Nuevo Siglo* was a morning Bogotá paper which also has a Sunday edition and a circulation of 68,000. Begun 1988, *La Prensa* (The Press), a morning paper without a Sunday edition, had a circulation of 38,000. Started in 1953, *La Republica* (The Republic), a morning daily newspaper without a Sunday edition, had a circulation of 55,000. Operating since 1911, *El Tiempo* (The Time), the largest in Bogotá and the nation, had a daily circulation of 265,118 and its Sunday edition, which included supplements, had a circulation of 536,377. *El Vespertino* (The Evening) was also available afternoons in Bogotá.

In Bucaramanga, *El Deber* (The Duty) is a morning daily which does not publish on Sundays. *El Frente* (Forward) is a morning daily without a Sunday edition, with a circulation of 10,000. Finally, *Vanguardia Liberal* (Liberal Vanguard) is a daily with a Sunday edition and a circulation of 48,000.

In the city of Cali, *El Caleño* is a tabloid paper in operation since 1977. Cali also had *El Crisol*, a morning daily without a Sunday edition, and *Occidente*, a morning

Daily and Non-Daily Newspaper Titles and Circulation Figures

	1996	1997	1998	1999	2000
Number of Daily Newspapers	23	25	23	24	NA
Circulation of Dailies (000)	1,089	1,152	1,072	1,093	NA
Number of Non-Daily Newspapers	5	5	3	4	NA
Circulation of Non-Dailies (000)	65	71	33	131	NA

Source: World Association of Newspapers and Zenithmedia, *World Press Trends 2001*, pp. 8, 10, 17, 19. Note: NA stands for not available.

newspaper without a Sunday edition. Cali's *La Republica* (The Republic) published both morning and Sunday editions and had a circulation of 20,000. *El Pais* (The Country) was as of 2002 Cali's largest circulation newspaper. It had both morning and Sunday editions and circulations of 60,000 on weekdays, 120,000 on Saturdays, and 108,304, for the Sunday edition with supplements.

The resort city of Cartagena had *El Periodico de Cartagena* (The Newspaper of Cartagena) and *El Universal* (The Universal) which published both daily and Sunday editions with supplements. In Cucuta, the newspapers included *Diario la Frontera* (Frontier Daily) and *La Opinion* (The Opinion). In Girardot, the newspaper was *El Diario* (The Daily). In Ibague there were two papers, *El Cronista* and *El Nuevo Dia.* The town of Manizales had *La Patria* (Homeland), a morning paper established in 1921.

The major city of Medellin, in Antioquia, had *El Colombiano* (The Colombian) which was established in 1912. This newspaper published morning and Sunday editions and had an extensive circulation of about 90,000. It was one of the three most influential in the nation, along with *El Tiempo* and *El Espectador* of Bogotá.

Many smaller towns had one or more papers. In Neiva there are two newspapers, *Diario de Huila* (Huila Daily) and *La Nacion* (The Nation). In Pasto, the two papers were *El Derecho* (The Right) a morning publication established in 1928, and *El Radio* (The Radio). In Pereira, *El Diario* (The Daily) provided a daily but no Sunday edition, and *Diario del Otun* (Otun Daily) put out an evening newspaper. *La Tarde* (The Afternoon) was an evening newspaper in Pereira. The morning paper without a Sunday edition, *El Liberal* (The Liberal), was established in 1938 in Popayan and had circulation of 6,500. The newspaper in Santa Marta was *El Informador* (The Informer). In Tunja, there were two newspapers, *Diario de Boyaca* (Boyaca Daily) and *El Oriente*, a daily. In addition to these general interest daily newspapers, there were many specialized newspapers in Colombia, some dealing with the economy and some with sports. There were also a large number of general interest and special interest magazines published in the country.

Colombian Newspapers: Characteristics and Orientations Newspapers are an important part of Colombian life. According to the *World Almanac and Book of Facts* in the early 2000s there were 55 newspapers daily per thousand persons. However, historically there was little communication among the various distinct regions of Colombia. For example, the Department of Antioquia, with its capital of Medellin, was quite distinct geographically and culturally from the capital city of Bogotá and other major cities such as Cali. News and information tended to be local. Moreover, Colombian industry was divided by region. In some sense, each major part of the nation could be seen as a separate nation. These divisions were partly caused by geography. As of 2002, roads were difficult to travel, especially through the high Andean mountains. Air travel, though widely available, was expensive. Therefore, interaction among the regions was not common, and pervasive violence, kidnappings, and robberies discouraged people from going too far from their homes.

Generally, newspapers were of high quality—well-written, well-edited, and generally independent. Colombians depended upon and tended to trust their newspapers, which were widely available and read even across regions. Many of the larger newspapers were readily available through the Internet.

It is possible to infer, from their names alone, the political persuasions of many dailies. Some had ''liberal'' in their titles, for example. Then, too, the government was an important factor in newspaper business because of its extensive advertising. However, Human Rights Watch and other sources reported that despite the intimidating violence and disorder in the nation, news media independence persisted and papers presented a wide range of political views.

In the early 2000s, Colombian newspapers were mostly owned by wealthy individuals. Human Rights Watch indicated that there was a high concentration of media ownership and, at the same time, fewer advertisers than there had been in the past. Since advertising funds are valued and government is one of the major advertis-

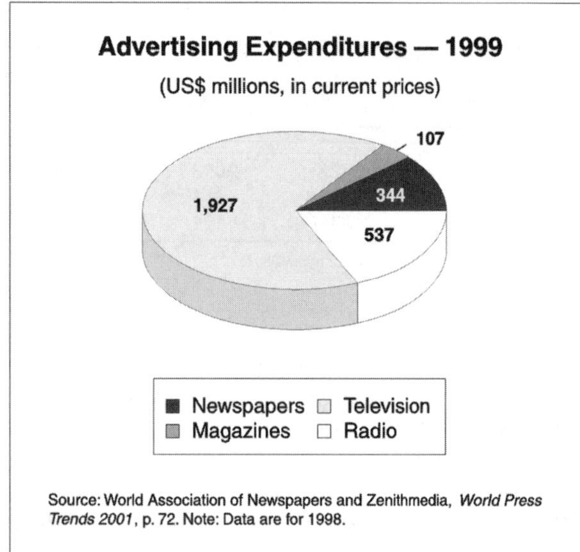

Source: World Association of Newspapers and Zenithmedia, *World Press Trends 2001*, p. 72. Note: Data are for 1998.

ers, Human Rights Watch suspected that newspapers increasingly practiced self-censorship. Elizabeth Dirnbacher, a journalist in Colombia, called the nation the most dangerous in Latin America for her profession. She stated:

> Colombia's leading television networks and newspapers are run by members of long-standing political and economic elites. The Santo Domingo group, Colombia's largest industrial conglomerate, owns the Caracol TV and radio networks as well as the *El Espectador* newspaper. The rival RCN TV and radio network is controlled by the Ardila Lulle beer empire. Other prime-time TV news shows and the weekly political magazine *Semana* are owned by family members of former presidents of the two traditional Conservative and Liberal parties that have held power for the last 150 years.

She also noted that the president elected in 1998, Andres Pastrana, was a former journalist from the Conservative Party.

Robert N. Pierce noted that there was a longstanding Colombian tradition of national leaders who mixed politics and the direction of newspapers. Two other presidents who were newspaper directors preceded Pastrana, Laureano Gómez of the no longer existing *El Siglo* and Eduardo Santos of *El Tiempo*. Clearly, newspapers though free are closely tied to the political system.

Economic Framework

Colombia's wealth comes from a number of sources. It has natural resources in petroleum, natural gas, coal, iron ore, nickel, gold, copper, emeralds, and hydropower. Agriculture is a major industry and the following statistics on its land and land use are significant in understanding its magnitude: arable land, 4 percent; permanent crops, 1 percent; permanent pastures, 39 percent; forests and woodland, 48 percent; and other, 8 percent. The nation's agricultural products include coffee, cut flowers, bananas, rice, tobacco, corn, sugarcane, cocoa beans, oilseed, vegetables, and forest products. It exports petroleum, coffee, coal, clothing, bananas, and cut flowers. In all, it exports US$14.5 billion, half of which goes to the United States, 16 percent to the other Andean nations, 14 percent to Europe, and two percent to Japan. In addition, the country imports industrial equipment, equipment for transportation, chemicals, consumer goods, paper products, and electricity. Although it imports electricity, Colombia produced as of 2002 more than 75 percent of its electricity by hydropower, a renewable and relatively inexpensive source of energy.

The economy of the country has been shrinking. In 1998, Colombia had a gross domestic product of US$102.9 billion, but in 1999 a gross domestic product of only US$88.6 billion. Of course, this gross domestic product figure does not account for sales of illegal drugs, such as cocaine, which constitute a major agricultural crop and industry in the country. According to the Central Intelligence Agency, the cultivation and manufacture of coca, opium, cocaine, and heroin are growing industries in Colombia. The potential production of heroin in 1999 was eight metric tons. As of the early 2000s Colombia supplied 90 percent of the cocaine used in the United States and was a major supplier of the substance to other nations. It supplied large quantities of the heroin brought to the United States. Clearly, the illegal narcotics business contributed to the economy in ways that were contrary to the notions of healthy growth for the nation. These illegal activities were not taxed, a minor issue compared to the fact that much of the earnings from narcotics went into building the narcotics business and into supporting the anti-government forces who threaten to destabilize the nation. These anti-government forces were also responsible for kidnapping and murdering many journalists. So the narcotics trade, in several ways, countered the economic and social growth of Colombia as a nation.

Of course, the narcotics business contributed to the Colombian official economy. For example, individuals operating narcotics productions pay farmers for the produce. They pay employees who process coca and opium into cocaine and heroin and those who traffic in the substances. Those who are paid in turn put their money into the economy by paying for their food, transportation, and shelter. In these and other ways, illegal transactions affect the legal economy. One might also argue that the drug industry also brings U.S. funds into the country: it induces U.S. concern and encourages the United States to send Colombia large sums to use in counteracting the production and distribution of drugs.

In the early 2000s, of the total legal Colombian legal economy, US$61.5 billion of the gross domestic product was composed of services and US$24.4 billion was industry. The remaining US$14.1 billion came from rich Colombian agriculture. On the Caribbean coast, there are mangroves and coconut palms. The forest areas have a variety of trees, including mahogany, cedar, pine, and balsam. Other plants yield rubber, chicle, ginger, vanilla, and many other products. Of course, Colombia is known worldwide for its coffee. The country also produces textiles.

Socioeconomic Structure In the early 2000s, the Central Intelligence Agency estimated that the lowest 10 percent of the Colombian population, by income, had about one percent of the household income and the top ten percent had about 44 percent of the income. The per capita annual income was about US$6,200 and the inflation rate was nine percent. According to the *Encarta Encyclopedia*, the upper socioeconomic class in Colombia was largely composed of white people who might trace their family histories to the Spanish colonial period. Their wealth largely came from owning land and other forms of property. Some of these individuals earned their wealth through commercial activities.

The nation had a growing middle class composed of educated, professional people who were successful in business and industry. Some middle class members were teachers, government employees, and professionals in law and medicine, for example.

The lower class lacks adequate housing, health care, and education. In the early 2000s, the Central Intelligence Agency estimated that 55 percent of the Colombian population was below the poverty level. Many lived in rural areas and were employed by wealthy landowners. Labor unions helped to improve the situation of some working poor. Some human services programs were incorporated into the structure of many businesses and industries. In some businesses, the social services programs equaled in value the workers' pay. These social services provided basic education, some counseling, and vacation resorts for workers and their families. Nonetheless, the predominance of low wage employment remained a factor in the growth of the illicit drug industry, which was itself the most important economic and social development in recent Colombian history. In the early 2000s, the total labor force, at all levels, was estimated to be about 18.3 millione. Forty-six percent of those were in service work, 30 percent in agriculture, and 24 percent in industry.

Government As of 2002, Colombia was divided into 32 departments and the one capital district, which was officially called Distrito Capital de Santa Fe de Bogotá. The nation operated under the 1991 constitution which defined three democratic governmental branches. Men and women age 18 or older were eligible to vote.

As of the early 2000s, Colombia was a republic dominated by an executive branch. The executive branch was headed by a president who was elected for a four-year term. The president governed with a cabinet, which was a coalition of representatives from the two major political parties. There was also a vice-president elected by popular vote. In the 1998 elections, runoffs were needed when no candidate initially received more than 50 percent of the vote. The president and vice-president who were elected in 1998 received just slightly more than 50 percent of the vote each in the runoff.

The *Congreso*, Colombia's bicameral legislature, consisted of the *Senado* (Senate) with 102 members elected for four year terms and the *Camara de Representantes* (House of Representatives) with 163 members also elected for four year terms. Of the two main political parties, the Liberal Party and the Conservative Party, the Liberal Party had a much larger proportion of the Congreso membership (about half) than the Conservative Party. Smaller parties were also usually represented. In 2002, the president was an independent.

Although the Colombian law is based on Spain's, the judiciary was organized similarly to the system maintained in the United States. The judicial system could, for example, exercise judicial review, not a common function of courts in the Spanish tradition.

In addition to the two traditional parties, there were the Patriotic Union (UP), a legal party formed by the Revolutionary Armed Forces of Colombia (FARC), the Colombian Communist Party (PCC), and the 19 of April Movement Party (M-19).

Besides political parties, the country contended with powerful insurgent groups that caused great difficulty for the government. The two largest were the National Liberation Army (ELN) and the Revolutionary Armed Forces of Colombia (FARC). The largest paramilitary group is United Self-Defense Groups of Colombia (AUC). As of 2002, both received part of their financing, perhaps much of it, from drug operations. They controlled lands that were used for the cultivation and manufacture of cocaine and heroin. The profits from those drugs amply financed the revolutionary groups. The government's troops constituted a third force of violence in the nation, although their task was to control or eliminate the revolutionaries.

Press Laws

Article 20 of the Colombian Constitution stipulated a series of guarantees regarding freedom of the press. It guaranteed freedom of expression as well as freedom for journalists to carry on their work. It also guaranteed the right of individuals to begin media companies and the right of journalists to keep their sources secret. The constitution promised to protect journalists. It set up a complicated body to monitor and defend press freedom with elected persons representing the media who must have experience in the media professions. The group had to be representative of the wide range of media—newspapers, radio and television, public, for profit and non-profit, regional, and national. Pierce wrote that Colombia had greater press freedom than any of its Latin neighbors. That tradition continued through decades of conflict that the nation faced and periods of insurrections which occurred toward the end of the twentieth century.

The World Bank reported that the nation's ''Colombia Portal,'' a plan for increasing information available to the public and providing for ready access to information about the nation, made a strong commitment to open information on purchasing, budgets, and planning. Part of the commitment was the establishment of Web sites for the Colombian government and all its agencies, making them available through the Internet. All government regulations since 1900 were to be accessible on the government Web site.

Human Rights Watch generally agreed that the Colombian press was free. It stated that the media are generally free of legal restrictions by the government. It noted, however, that some laws under the penal code and anti-corruption laws prohibited the publication of some kinds of information connected to criminal investigations. Pervasive interior conflict made these laws necessary.

For a time, Colombia had government requirements for professional journalists. The Law of the Journalist required new entrants into journalism to have university degrees. Continuing journalists were ''grandfathered'' into the professon. However, those laws were abolished in 1998.

CENSORSHIP

Even though as of 2002 no theoretical restrictions on press freedom or official censorship existed in Colombia, practical aspects media work led to the kinds of self-censorship that actually constituted restrictions. Dirnbacher reported that in the 1980s investigative reporting increased sharply. That was an understandable development in a nation torn by revolutionaries, guerillas, and government troops accused of human rights violations. But there was also a tendency toward other kinds of crimes in some segments of the society. She noted that *El Espectador* reported on secret financial deals involving Colombian banks. The banks withdrew their advertising from the newspaper, throwing it into financial crisis, she reported.

ATTITUDES TOWARDS FOREIGN MEDIA

In the early 2000s, illegal factions in Colombia were hostile to foreign media. However, official media outlets in the country associated heavily with international and regional organizations and sometimes provided leadership to them. For example, Colombia was a member of the InterAmerican Press Association. Moreover, U.S. media such as *Time* and *Newsweek* were popular in the nation, and many exchanges of all kinds took place between Colombia and the United States, the primary non-Latin American foreign nation with which it deals. Still, journalists were targets of hostile acts, including kidnapping and murder by rebel groups. Clearly, foreign and local journalists who become deeply involved in reporting on violent groups could be threatened by those groups.

Violence Against Journalists In the early 2000s, the major news stories about Colombia dealt with its descent into chaos and violence. Connected to issues of press freedom, much of the violence was directed against journalists. As a result of a series of violence events, the president issued presidential decree 1592 which created in 2000 the Program for the Protection of Journalists.

According to Colombia Policy Briefs, 11 journalists were killed in the midst of Colombia's armed conflicts in 2000. A total of 169 had been killed since 1977, according to the Colombian Committee for the Protection of Journalists. At least 15 journalists were kidnapped, and 13 left the country after receiving threats. Six more were killed between January 1 and July 11, 2001. Kidnapping and abductions were a widespread problem, a common tactic used by the revolutionary and anti-government guerilla groups.

Dirnbacher wrote about the murder of several journalists. A reporter for *El Espectador* was killed in 1998. He had been investigating connections between bullfighting and organized crime. A political reporter and professor in Cali was shot as he left his university in 1998. He had helped the National Police establish a FM news radio station. In that same year, a teacher and journalist who was news director of Radio Sur, a subsidiary of the National Radio Chain, was shot. He had alleged there was corruption among members of former municipal administrations.

In 1999, a journalist and satirist who served as a go-between for families of kidnap victims who were taken by left-wing groups was shot on the way to his radio station. In that year, the FARC group kidnapped seven journalists because, FARC said, they had not reported the truth about guerillas and paramilitary groups committing atrocities against farmers. Also that year a bomb exploded near the offices of the *El Tiempo* in Bogotá. A FARC member said the bomb was set because of an article in that newspaper about FARC's attacks on the oil industry.

The editor-in-chief of *El Tiempo*, Francisco Santos, had to leave Colombia in 2000 because of death threats issued against him, probably by FARC, probably a result of his leadership of an anti-kidnapping organization. Santos had been held hostage with other journalists in 1990 by Pablo Escobar, as a protest against government threats to extradite drug traffickers to the United States for prosecution.

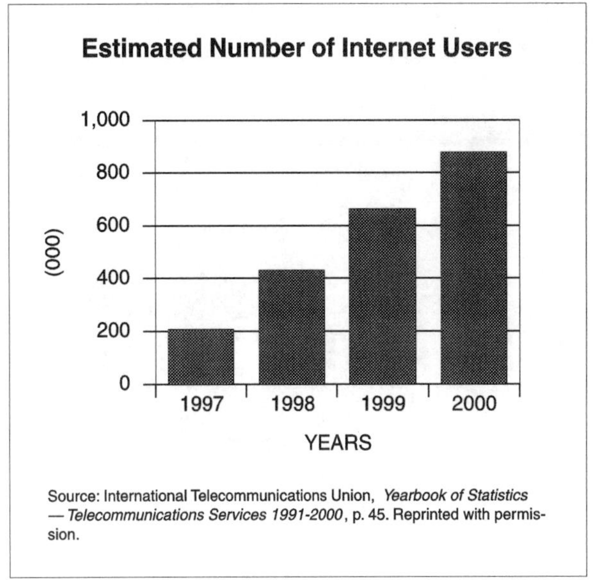

Source: International Telecommunications Union, *Yearbook of Statistics — Telecommunications Services 1991-2000*, p. 45. Reprinted with permission.

NEWS AGENCIES

As of 2002 Colombia had several news agencies, notably the CNTV, the Comision Nacional de Television, and ERBOL. The Associated Press also was active in Colombia as were other private news services, such as UPI and Reuters. Cox News Service had a long presence in Colombian journalism and in reporting about Colombia. The government also provided a news service.

BROADCAST MEDIA

In addition to newspapers, Colombia has extensive radio and television coverage. According to the Central Intelligence Agency, as of 2002, there were 21 million radios in the nation (155 radio sets per thousand people, according to the *World Almanac and Book of Facts*). There were also 454 AM radio stations and 34 FM stations. In addition, there were 27 short-wave stations and 60 television stations. *World Almanac and Book of Facts* reported that there were 188 television sets per thousand.

These media outlets were served by a variety of government and private organizations. The agency responsible for regulating AM, FM, and television frequencies and regulations is the Comision de Regulacion de Telecommunicaciones (CRT). Other government broadcasting agencies, according to TV Radio World, were Inravision and the Ministerio de Comunicaciones (Ministry of Communications). In addition, television was served by the nation's National Television Broadcasting, Regional Television Broadcasting, and Satellite/Cable Television Networks. There was also a government organization, the Instituto Nacional de Radio y Television de Colombia, that operated several radio and TV stations on behalf of the government.

There were a number of national radio networks, the best known of which was a conglomerate, *Caracol* (Snail.) It consisted of several networks including a sports operation, salsa and rock music networks, and other programming units.

The Radio Cadena Nacional (National Radio Chain, RCN), which called itself La Radio of Colombia, included a love music stereo network, a sports programming operation, a network that combined information and romantic music, another that was music and news-oriented, one that transmitted pop and rock music for young listeners, another that presented Colombian folk music, and the Rumba Digital Stereo network which focused on various dance music such as the salsa, *cumbia*, *merengue*, and *el porro.*

Generally, the broadcast media were covered by the same constitutional guarantees as the print media. However, the broadcast media could be taken over by government in emergency situations, a procedure that is similar to that followed for emergencies in the United States. The Colombian government may exercise the right to censor radio and television in times of emergency, especially those associated with violence.

ELECTRONIC NEWS MEDIA

The nation has a few Internet news providers that provide news only. However, many of the newspapers and some of the radio networks sponsor news sites that provide extensive coverage of news information from the Internet.

EDUCATION & TRAINING

As of 2002, Colombia had 20 institutions of higher education that offered study in *periodismo* (journalism). (A journalist is a *periodista.*) ''Social communication'' programs offered much more than traditional journalism in their academic programs. They may teach advertising, public relations, media management, and electronic journalism as well as print.

Journalism education programs in Colombia were organized into the Association of Faculties of Social

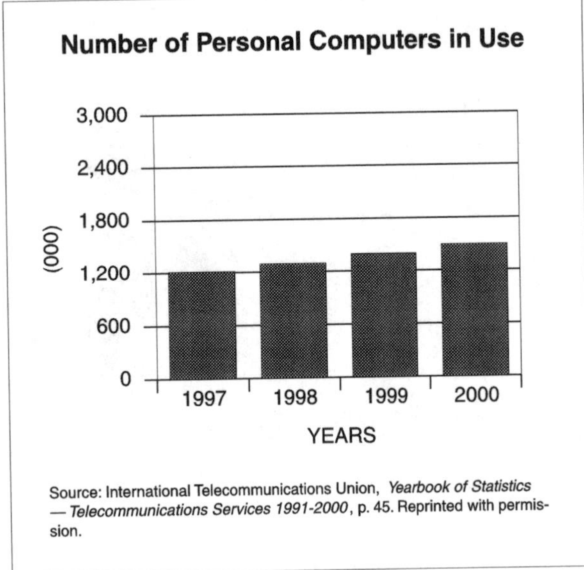

Source: International Telecommunications Union, *Yearbook of Statistics — Telecommunications Services 1991-2000*, p. 45. Reprinted with permission.

Communication (what were usually called departments or schools in the United States are referred to as *faculties* in Colombia.) The Association, in turn, belongs to the Latin American Federation of Faculties of Social Communication.

In the early 2000s, the Colombian journalism faculties presented curricula spanning 10 semesters or five years of study. Content included theoretical and practical information that might be found in U.S. schools of journalism as well as other subject matter. The programs typically included field experiences, too.

There were associations of journalists in Colombia, in addition to those involved in journalism education. There was an effort in the 1970s to organize Colombian journalists in a labor union. However, Colombia did not have a member organization of the International Federation of Journalists, the international group that oversees and coordinates such efforts.

SUMMARY

In the early 2000s Colombia was, in many ways, a nation of contrasts. That was especially true of its press and journalism. The press was essentially free from governmental interference and was also generally of high quality. That appeared to be true of both print and electronic media. It treated journalists as major figures and had presidents who came from the field of journalism. Its education of journalists was sophisticated and widespread.

However, Colombia was also a nation that was beset with internal conflicts. One of the results of those conflicts was the spread of the illegal drug trade, especially the production and distribution of cocaine. It was also a producer of heroin. Rebel groups were believed to finance themselves with proceeds from the production and distribution of drugs. The drug issue was further complicated by the economic deprivation experienced by many Colombians so many of whom lived in poverty. Growing the raw material for drugs and otherwise engaging in the drug trade was a route out of poverty for many economically disadvantaged Colombians.

The internal conflicts also involved journalists and press officials, some of whom were kidnapped or assassinated or who faced threats of such violence. Therefore, the press and journalism were difficult areas of employment in Colombia. Perhaps they were more dangerous in that nation than in any other.

Therefore, what may well be considered a high quality press industry was tempered by one of the world's most complex and unstable social environments—in which inordinate numbers of public facilities and the nation's infrastructure were subject to constant threat. In addition, numbers of people, including journalists, were kidnapped, murdered, and displaced by the activities of rebel groups. The violence facing Colombia, although warring parties and the factors in the violence might characterize the end of the twentieth century, was a part of Colombian life for a half century.

It was inadvisable to generalize about this nation of contrasts. In many ways, it was an inviting environment for press work while in others it posed dangers to those who worked in the field.

SIGNIFICANT DATES

- 1998: Andres Pastrana, former journalist and candidate of Conservative Party, is elected president of Colombia, begins negotiations with rebel groups to end violence, and establishes ''control zones,'' where rebel groups are able to control territories they had conquered.
- 1998-1999: More journalists and other media personnel kidnapped, forced into exile, or murdered, and media facilities are bombed.
- 1998: Law of the Journalist terminated.
- 2002: FARC again bombs, kidnaps, and murders Colombians. President Pastrana announces that peace with rebel groups will not be achieved during his presidency. Álvaro Uribe Ve'lez elected president as an independent.

BIBLIOGRAPHY

Allman, T. D. ''Blowback.'' *Rolling Stone,* 9 May 2002.

''Colombia.'' Central Intelligence Agency (CIA). *The World Factbook*. Available from http://www.cia.gov.

"Colombia." *Microsoft Encarta Online Deluxe Encyclopedia 2001.* (3 Apr. 2002). Available from http://encarta.msn.com.

Contreras, Joseph. "Colombia's Hard Right." *Newsweek International,* March 25, 2002. Available from www.msnbc.com/news.

Defensoria del Pueblo Colombia report. Available from http://www.colombiapolicy.org.

Dirnbacher, Elizabeth. *Journalism in Colombia.* Available from http://www.Freemedia.at/journali.htm, 2000.

Famighetti, Robert. *The 1999 World Almanac and Book of Facts.* New York: St. Martin's Press, 1999.

Ferriss, Susan. "Colombians Elect President amid Violence." *The Colombia State.* (May 27, 2002): A7.

Forero, Juan. "Colombia Voters are Angry, and Rebels May Pay Price." *The New York Times.* (May 26, 2002): 4.

Guillermoprieto, Alma. "Letter from Colombia: Waiting for War." *The New Yorker.* (May 13, 2002): 46-55.

Human Rights Watch. Available from http://www.Hrw.org/americas/colombia/.

International Year Book: The Encyclopedia of the Newspaper Industry, 2001. New York: Editor and Publisher, 2001. Available from http://www.editorandpublisher.com.

Library of Congress, Federal Research Division. *Colombia Country Studies, Area Handbook Series.*

Marquis, Christopher. "The U.S. Struggle to Battle Drugs, Just Drugs, in Colombia." *The New York Times.* (May 26, 2002): wk 7.

Pierce, Robert N. "Colombia." *World Press Encyclopedia.* New York: Facts On File.

"Two Bombs Explode in Colombian City." *The Colombia State.* (April 8, 2002): 3A.

U.S. Department of State, Bureau of Democracy, Human Rights, and Labor. *Colombia Country Reports, Human Rights Practices for 1996, January 30, 1997.*

WWW.Virtual library: Latin America Resources. Available from www.etown.edu/vl/latamer.html

TVRadioWorld. Available at http://www.tvradioworld.com

Wikipedia: The Free Encyclopedia. Available from http://www.wikipedia.com.

World Development Indicators database, July 2000. Available at www.colombiapolicy.org.

—Leon Ginsberg

THE COMOROS

BASIC DATA

Official Country Name:	Islamic Federal Republic of the Comoros
Region (Map name):	Africa
Population:	578,400
Language(s):	Arabic, French, Comoran
Literacy rate:	57.3%

The archipelago *La République Fédérale Islamique des Comores* (Federal Islamic Republic of the Comoros) is situated off the east African coast, between Mozambique and Madagascar. It is composed of three main islands (Grande Comore or Njazidja, Mohéli or Mwali, and Anjouan or Nzwani) and a number of islets. The capital, Moroni, is located on the west side of Grande Comore. The population in 2000 was about 670,000, and was 98 percent Sunni Muslim, the other 2 percent being Roman Catholic. The official languages are Arabic, and French, and Comoran, a mixture of Arabic and Swahili, is also spoken.

Comoros gained its political independence from France in 1975, save for Mayotte in the southeast, which is still French-dominated. Political instability reigns: 19 coups d'états have occurred since it became in independent nation. In 1999, the military chief Colonel Azali seized power, and within the Fomboni accord, he vowed to calm the severe political instability, and pursue socioeconomic development for this divided and profoundly impoverished nation. The human development index (HDI) in 2000 was at a very low ranking of 139. GNP per capita was at $400, life expectancy was 59 years, literacy at 55 percent, and deaths at 65 per 1,000.

As of the early twenty-first century, there were no daily newspapers in Comoros, and the press circulation was at a 1 in 1000 ratio. There were two weekly newspapers, the state-owned *Al Watany* (The National) and the independent *l'Archipel* (The Archipelago). There existed only one state-dominated radio system with a few independent services, and no television service was available, though France has promised to finance the islands' first TV station. There is no media liberalization or autonomy, notably in the wake of the bloody 1997 separatists attacks on Anjouan and the May 1998 police brutal seizure of an independent radio station that was critical of the State.

BIBLIOGRAPHY

Central Intelligence Agency (CIA). "The Comoros," *World Fact Book 2001.* Available from http://www.cia.gov.

—*Samuel Sarri*

CONGO

BASIC DATA

Official Country Name:	Democratic Republic of the Congo
Region (Map name):	Africa
Population:	51,964,999
Language(s):	French, Lingala, Kingwana, Kikongo, Tshiluba
Literacy rate:	77.3%

BACKGROUND & GENERAL CHARACTERISTICS

Brief Socio-political Background Several socio-political discussions, including ethnography, geography, and literacy are necessary for an appreciation of the press in the Republic of the Congo (the Congo). The Congo formed part of French Equatorial Africa (FEA) until its independence from France in 1960. FEA included what are now known as the Congo, Gabon, Cameroon, the Central African Republic, and Chad. Brazzaville was the capital of FEA and remains the capital of the Congo. In its long-standing history as capital first of FEA then of the independent Republic of the Congo, it has been privileged in terms of education, industry, government, and commerce. The only other major town is Pointe-Noire, almost due west of Brazzaville, on the Atlantic Ocean. It is the center of the Congo's oil exploration and export.

Ethnography and Geography The *Bakongo* ethnic group predominates. Next to the *Bakongo* are the *Bateke*, who live to the immediate north. Further north are a good number of small speech communities that are not active participants in Congolese socio-political life. The languages spoken in the Congo belong to the Bantu family. The *Bakongo* are divided into eleven sub-groups with strong attachment to their group membership and equally strong claims of speaking a dialect of *Kikongo*. The strength of these sub-group attachments has resulted in a simplified form of *Kikongo* known as *Kituba*. The *Bateke* as well as the *Bakongo* accept *Kituba* as a Congolese lingua franca to cross ethnic and linguistic boundaries. As a result the vast majority of the citizens of the Congo speak *Kituba* as well as their own languages or dialects. The Congo River separates the Republic of the Congo from the Democratic Republic of the Congo (Congo-Kinshasa; previously Zaire). *Lingala*, another Bantu language, has evolved as yet another lingua franca up and down the Congo River. It has spread both east and west and has become quite established alongside *Kituba* in the Congo. During the French colonization, French language and culture were superimposed upon all of these peoples and languages. Upon independence, the Congo emerged with five languages: *Kikongo*, *Kiteke*, *Kituba*, *Lingala*, and French. As the language of colonial power, French evolved as the language for all formal contexts, including most importantly elite education and communication. French has remained the official language in government and education at all levels. A citizen of the Congo must be quadrilingual, speaking *Kiteke*, or a dialect of *Kikongo*, *Kituba*, *Lingala*, and French, in order to negotiate successfully through Congolese life. The government attempts to the extent of its means to promote *Kituba* and to a lesser extent *Lingala*, but these efforts have not succeeded in overcoming French.

Literacy and Education The total population of the Congo is about 53 million. Literacy for those between the ages of 15 and 25 is claimed to be as high as 81 percent (as of 2000). The percentage of those over 25 years of age with no schooling at all as of 1984 was 58.8 percent. The number of students in primary schools as of 1996 was almost half a million. The number of students in secondary and vocational schools again in 1996 was almost quarter of a million. Those attending university (Université Marien Ngouabi) numbered about 14,000 in 1993. Although literacy is high, there is a sharply decreasing rate of access to education as one progresses from primary school to university education. All figures regarding education and attained rates of literacy regard learning in French. Not surprisingly, the reading public reads largely in French.

The Press Four daily newspapers are currently published within Congo: *Aujourd'hui*; *L'Eveil de Pointe-Noire*; *Journal de Brazzaville Mweti*, and *Kikongo*. Several news-related periodicals are available as well:

- Bakento ya Congo (Quarterly, Brazzaville, Kikongo, circulation 3,000)
- Bulletin Mensuel de la Chambre de Commerce de Brazzaville (Monthly)

- Bulletin de Statistique (Quarterly, Brazzaville)
- Le Choc (Weekly, Brazzaville)
- Combattant Rouge (Monthly, Brazzaville)
- Congo-Magazine (Monthly, Brazzaville, circulation 3,000)
- Effort (Monthly, Brazzaville)
- Le Flambeau (Weekly, Brazzaville)
- Le Forum (Weekly, Brazzaville)
- Le Gardien (Fortnightly, Brazzaville, circulation 2,500)
- Jeunesse et Révolution (Weekly, Brazzaville)
- Le Madukutsekele (Weekly, Brazzaville, circulation 5,000)
- La Nouvelle République (Weekly, Brazzaville)
- L'Opinion (Monthly, Brazzaville)
- Paris-Brazzaville (Weekly)
- Le Pays (Weekly, Brazzaville)
- La Rue Muert (Weekly, Brazzaville, circulation 3,000)
- La Semaine Africaine (Weekly, Brazzaville, circulation 7,500)
- Le Soleil (Weekly, Brazzaville)
- Le Stade (Weekly, Brazzaville, circulation 6,500)
- Voix de la Classe Ouvrière (six a year, Brazzaville, circulation 4,500)

The numbers given for the specialized periodicals would suggest a total readership in substantial numbers within the literate-schooled population. It is revealing that with one exception they are all published in Brazzaville and again with one exception they are all in French.

Press Laws & Censorship

The Congo has been under severe political stress in the late twentieth and early twenty-first centuries. Publications reflect the publishers' political orientation. There is recent legislation to protect the freedom of the press (which is currently listed as "not free" by Freedom House) except for libel against individuals, the president, and the judiciary and for incitement of inter-ethnic conflict. However, laws exist which state that journalists must demonstrate unwavering support of the government. Huge fines exist for any found guilty of libel, slander, and inciting ethnic violence. Almost any criticism could be construed as incitement of inter-ethnic conflict, and it is often so interpreted.

State-Press Relations

The newspapers and periodicals may not all be available at all times. Some may cease publication for a period of time or permanently. New ones may appear for indeterminate periods. Editors and editorial boards may change suddenly. This instability reflects the political and social stresses within which both the press and the political body at large exist and interact. The socio-political status of the Congo has not evolved to a point where one could consider the government, the press, the economic sector, the judiciary, the military, and so on, as distinct entities. The individual participants in these various sectors all belong to a small French educated elite. There is a great deal of mobility of participants from one sector to the other. Hence, the relationship between the state and the press is ambiguous as well as in flux. If there is a constant factor it is ethnic allegiance.

Attitude toward Foreign Media

In addition to the publications listed earlier within the Congo, Brazzaville and to some extent Pointe-Noire provide for ample access to French publications such as *Le Monde*, *Jeune Afrique*, and *Le Nouvel Observateur*. These are of special interest to the expatriate communities as well as the university educated Congolese community. Several major countries have cultural centers in Brazzaville. Their libraries make available promotionally oriented publications in their respective languages. *Newsweek*, *Time*, and *The Herald Tribune* are available through the American Cultural Center and in hotel newsstands.

The governing elite does not seem to have a policy on foreign publications. One major reason is that only the educated elite who can afford these publications would read them. Another reason is that for the most part the expatriate community reads them, and they insist on having them available. A third reason, and likely the most important one, is that criticism within the foreign media is rarely initiated internally.

Broadcast & Electronic News Media

Dissemination of news in Congolese African languages finds an outlet through radio broadcasts and television. Only 33,000 own television sets but 341,000 possess radios. French fills the greatest amount of time in either venue. Limited amounts of time are allocated to African languages. Radio Congo (transmitters in Brazzaville and Pointe Noire) broadcasts in *Lingala* and *Kikongo* as well as in French. *TéléCongo* operates on a limited daily schedule mostly in French with a restricted amount of time in *Lingala* and *Kikongo*. Whereas radios are readily available and are indeed owned by most Congolese, television sets are economically restricted to the upper middle class of society. Kinshasa, the capital of Congo-Kinshasa, is directly across the Congo River from Brazzaville. The two Congos have not been on good terms, but the populations of Brazzaville and Kinshasa have easy access to radio and television transmissions from both cities. Radio Congo's and *TéléCongo*'s choices of *Lingala* and *Kikongo* is meant to reach a large segment of the Congo-Kinshasa population which speaks these two languages. Kinshasa radio and television transmissions tend to have a larger portion of airtime given to African languages. African languages, especially *Lingala*, *Kikongo*, and *Kiswahili* from Kinshasa, find a significant outlet on both sides of the Congo River in the famous Congo-Jazz style of song and rhythm, and more recently in rap style in *Kiswahili*. These venues and styles of music could legitimately be considered to correspond to the American college town ''alternative press.''

Although several newspapers have online editions, very few are able to access them, as Congo only has one Internet Service Provider and 500 users within the country.

BIBLIOGRAPHY

Acct, Cerdotola, Equipe National du Congo. *Atlas Linguistique de L'Afrique Central, Atlas Linguistique du Congo*. Brazzaville: Centre pour l'Etude des Langues Congolaise, Université Marien Ngouabi, 1987.

Africa South of the Sahara. 30th Edition. London: Europa Publications, Taylor & Francis Group, 2001.

''Congo (Brazzaville).'' *Freedom House*. Available from http://www.freedomhouse.org.

The Central Intelligence Agency (CIA). *The World Factbook 2001*. Available from http://www.cia.gov.

UNESCO. *African Community Languages, and their Use in Literacy and Education*. Dakar, 1985.

UNESCO. *Statistical Yearbook*. Lanham, MD: Berman Press, 1999.

—Haig Der-Houssikian

COOK ISLANDS

BASIC DATA

Official Country Name:	Cook Islands
Region (Map name):	Oceania
Population:	20,407
Language(s):	English, Maori
Literacy rate:	N/A

The Cook Islands, named after the British naval captain who first sighted them in 1770, are located in the south Pacific Ocean, between Hawaii and New Zealand.

The Cook Islands enjoy freedom of the press and freedom of speech. A Cook Islands Media Council, based on the Australian and New Zealand model of press self-regulation, operated between 1995 and 1999 to respond to a perceived threat of government regulation. When the threat passed, the council disbanded. No formal council currently exists, but proposals surface periodically to revive the model.

The country supports two main English-language newspapers: the daily *Cook Islands News* and the weekly *Cook Islands Herald*. The *Cook Islands News* began in 1944 as a one-page news sheet and was developed in the late 1960s as a government-owned publication. It was privatized in 1989 and is the country's largest independent newspaper, publishing Monday through Saturday. Its estimated print run is 2,000; its online edition, which is updated every Wednesday, contains selected stories from the print edition. The *Cook Islands Herald*, which is published every Wednesday, started in 1997 as a guide to television programming but it adopted a newspaper format in 2000. Its estimated print run is 1,300, and it maintains an online edition.

There are three radio stations in the country, one AM and two FM. Radios number approximately 14,000. Two local television stations broadcast to approximately 4,000 televisions. There are three Internet service providers.

The island chain consists of seven sparsely populated coral atolls and eight volcanic islands. The country became a British protectorate in 1888, but administrative control had been transferred to New Zealand by 1900. In 1965 Cook Islanders chose self-government in association with New Zealand, meaning islanders are responsible for their internal affairs through a parliamentary democracy, and New Zealand takes care of external affairs in consultation with island government. The estimated population is 20,600, and the literacy rate is 95 percent. The country's economy is based on agriculture, but fruit processing and tourism are also important. The official language is English, but Maori and Pukapukan are also spoken.

BIBLIOGRAPHY

Australian Press Council. *Country Profile—Cook Islands*. 2002. Available from www.presscouncil.org.au.

Central Intelligence Agency (CIA). *World Fact Book 2001*. Available from www.odci.gov.

Cook Islands News. Retrieved May 31, 2002. Available from www.cinews.co.ck.

—Jenny B. Davis

COSTA RICA

BASIC DATA

Official Country Name:	Republic of Costa Rica
Region (Map name):	North & Central America
Population:	3,773,057
Language(s):	Spanish (official), English spoken around Puerto Limon
Literacy rate:	94.8%
Area:	51,100 sq km
GDP:	15,851 (US$ millions)
Number of Daily Newspapers:	6
Total Circulation:	275,000
Circulation per 1,000:	99
Number of Nondaily Newspapers:	27
Total Circulation:	149,000
Circulation per 1,000:	54
Total Newspaper Ad Receipts:	18,408 (Colones millions)
As % of All Ad Expenditures:	36.00
Number of Television Stations:	6
Number of Television Sets:	525,000
Television Sets per 1,000:	139.1
Number of Cable Subscribers:	72,580
Cable Subscribers per 1,000:	19.1
Number of Radio Stations:	112
Number of Radio Receivers:	980,000
Radio Receivers per 1,000:	259.7
Number of Individuals with Computers:	600,000
Computers per 1,000:	159.0
Number of Individuals with Internet Access:	250,000
Internet Access per 1,000:	66.3

BACKGROUND & GENERAL CHARACTERISTICS

Costa Rica is a nation of 3.7 million people that boasts a long history of democracy, no army, and relatively peaceful political development, which is in stark contrast with the war-torn legacies of most of its Central American neighbors. Long thought a stellar democracy wherein the press basked in unlimited freedom, the murder of a popular radio journalist in 2001 revealed a darker side to the country that has often been referred to as the Switzerland of Central America.

Costa Rica covers 51,000 square kilometers and is divided into seven provinces. The nation's capital, San José, is home to one-third of all Costa Ricans. The vast majority, 97 percent, of Costa Ricans are of European or *mestizo* (mixed European and Native American) descent, although a growing number of immigrants from neighboring Nicaragua are slowly beginning to transform the nation's homogenous demographics. Roman Catholicism is the dominant religion but evangelical Protestantism is growing at a rapid pace. In San José, the number of evangelicals doubled in the 1980s and it is estimated that by 2010, 20 percent of the population will be Protestant.

In July 2001 the murder of the popular radio journalist, Parmenio Medina, shocked the nation. Medina was murdered the night he was to receive an award from a Costa Rican nonprofit organization for defending freedom of expression. He was shot three times at close range and died on the way to the hospital. Medina, Colombian by birth, was well known for his 28-year-old radio program, *La Patada* (A Kick in the Pants) that often denounced official corruption. Medina's muckraking approach to journalism left him with many potential enemies. He had recently aired accusations about alleged fiscal improprieties at a local Catholic radio station, Radio María. His reporting led to the station's closure and an investigation into the actions of its former director. Some believed that Medina could have been killed for investigating money-laundering activities by a large drug-smuggling cartel. A year after his murder no one has yet been brought to trial although national TV and newspapers have reported that four members of a criminal gang are suspected of having been paid to assassinate Medina.

A survey taken by the nation's leading newspaper, La Nación a month before Medina's murder, found that 55 percent of the 97 journalists polled said they had received some kind of threat during their careers. Though some threats were physical, most journalists were threatened with defamation suits. Some journalists have said that they are reluctant to investigate important cases, such as Medina's murder, because Costa Rica has a harsh penal code that could lead to imprisonment or heavy fines.

These recent events are a strict departure from the typical belief that Costa Rica is an oasis of peace and stability in the historically war-torn and impoverished region of Central America. Latin America's longest-standing democracy, Costa Rica is more known for its eco-tourism trips, as a U.S. retirement community, and the Nobel Peace Prize-winning former president, Oscar Arias, than for political violence. The nation has had little violence despite its proximity to Guatemala, El Salvador, and Nicaragua, all countries that suffered from devastating civil wars in the 1980s. Costa Rica has one of the highest literacy rates in the region with 95 percent of the adult population considered to be literate. Indeed, Costa Rica has a historical precedent for supporting education, beginning universal free public education in 1879. It has the region's highest standard of living, and a life expectancy comparable to that of the United States. In general, an educated public with higher per capita average than the region's norm at US$3,960 has enabled the rapid development and expansion of all forms of media.

Although Columbus stopped over briefly on Costa Rica's Caribbean coast in 1502, for most of the colonial era, Costa Rica remained a forgotten backwater since it had little that the Spanish colonialists were looking for, namely, a significant labor supply and/or mineral wealth. An isolated and neglected province of the kingdom of Guatemala, Costa Rica did not have much in the way of publishing. Guatemala was the center of publishing for two hundred years having had its first press installed there in 1641.

In 1824 an elected congress chose Juan Mora Fernandez as the first chief of state. The first newspaper appeared shortly after his re-election in 1829 although a local citizen had to subsidize the purchase of an English printing press. The first regular weekly newspaper, *Noticioso Universal,* was issued on January 4, 1833. *Noticioso Universal* closed after two years because the early development of the press in Costa Rica had three strikes against it: there was not a sufficient literate and economically viable audience to sustain a local newspaper; the weekly in existence had to compete with the more established newspapers arriving from Guatemala and South America; and finally, there was little available and affordable paper on which to print the news. Between 1833 and 1860, ten different newspapers existed in Costa Rica, none of them lasting for more than two years. The government began operating its own press in 1837, primarily printing decrees, orders, and laws.

It was not until the introduction of coffee in 1808 that Costa Rica began to attract a significant population. Coffee brought wealth, a class structure, and linked the nation to the world economic system. The coffee barons, whose growing prosperity led to rivalries between the wealthiest family factions, vied with each other for political dominance. In 1849, members of the coffee industry elite conspired to overthrow the country's first president, José María Castro, who had established a newspaper and a university. The President believed that ignorance was the root of all evil and that freedom of the press was a sacred right. Unfortunately, Castro's rule was interrupted by William Walker, the U.S. citizen who believed in the manifest destiny of the United States to rule other peoples. Walker already controlled Nicaragua in 1855 and he invaded Costa Rica the following year. His unintended role in Costa Rican history was to help unite its people, who roundly ousted him the same year.

During the 1880s the national leadership was under the helm of the liberal elite who stressed the values of the enlightenment, although charismatic leaders often held sway over political ideologies and programs. The free press, however, increasingly guided public opinion, and Costa Ricans became accustomed to hearing critical discussions of ideas as well as the ideas of political candidates. Yet political rivalries often resulted in moments where the press was repressed. For example, in 1889 the new president Jose Joaquin Rodriguez, caught between the country's liberal and conservative factions, suspended civil liberties, including the closure of opposition papers. He dissolved congress in 1892 and imprisoned a number of journalists. Rafael Iglesias, Rodriguez's successor, did much to beautify the capital, but he also declared that the violently critical newspapers had turned his people against him and he clamped down on the press, even going so far as to flog some of his detractors publicly. During the first century of the country's independence, the freedom and the power of the press was seen as a double-edged sword by many of the nation's leaders. In this context, in 1902 one of the nation's longest lasting press laws was established which protected the "honor" of individuals from being attacked in the press.

The intertwined role of the media and politics is a strong theme in recent Costa Rican history. For example, a 1942 speech broadcast on radio by future president, José Figueres, against the communist-affiliated president, Rafael Calderón, proved to be pivotal to the latter's political demise. The press was generally critical of Calde-

Daily and Non-Daily Newspaper Titles and Circulation Figures

	1996	1997	1998	1999	2000
Number of Daily Newspapers	6	6	6	6	6
Circulation of Dailies (000)	NA	238	265	290	275
Number of Non-Daily Newspapers	25	25	25	27	27
Circulation of Non-Dailies (000)	NA	117	130	138	149

Source: World Association of Newspapers and Zenithmedia, *World Press Trends 2001*, pp. 8, 10, 17, 19. Note: NA stands for not available.

rón's successor, Teodoro Picado, and frequently charged his government with tyranny and oppression. The press remained free to the point that newspapers even printed personal attacks against the president with little repercussions. The publisher of the daily newspaper *Diario de Costa Rica,* Otilio Ulate, was politically prominent and served as president in the 1950s. Ever since the presidencies of Figueres and Ulate, the position has rotated between the country's two primary parties: the PLN (National Liberation Party) and the PUSC (Social Christian Unity Party).

Costa Rica has six daily newspapers nationwide. The total circulation is 88 papers per one thousand inhabitants. The largest newspaper, *La Nación,* was started in 1946 and represented the commercial interests of the business elite. *La Nación* was close to the Nicaraguan Contras and served as a voice for their cause during the U.S.-backed Contra-Sandinista war of the 1980s. *La Nación* distributed a weekly supplement called *Nicaragua Hoy,* directed from Miami, Florida, by Pedro Joaquín Chamorro, son of the murdered editor of the Nicaraguan daily, *La Prensa. La Nación* also publishes a number of magazines including *Perfil, Rumbo,* and *Ancora.* The paper had a circulation of 110,000 in 1997.

The nation's two other dailies, *La Prensa Libre* and *La República* share the conservative tendencies of *La Nación.* Both newspapers were originally seen as alternatives to the nation's premiere daily, but both have moved to the right since their founding. The morning paper, *La República* was founded in the 1950s and was sympathetic to President Figueres, and for years represented a true counterpart to the ideological stance of *La Nación.* In the mid-1990s it had a circulation of 55,000 and is known for being only slightly less conservative than *La Nación. La Prensa Libre* is an afternoon paper with a circulation of about 45,000. It was founded in the 1960s. One of the only newspapers to originate outside of San José is *El Sol de Osa,* a general interest newspaper published in Puerto Jimenez.

Some smaller papers offer a more liberal view but their influence is limited by their relatively small circulation. *Semanario Universidad,* is the official paper of the University of Costa Rica and it has gained an international reputation for its coverage of politics and the arts. It is characterized by a leftist editorial perspective. In late 1988 the newsweekly *Esta Semana* appeared. All of these publications originate in San José, Costa Rica's capital. A number of supplements are published on a weekly basis. These include Sunday's *Revista Dominical,* an events showcase with interviews of local personalities. An educational supplement *Zurqui* appears on Wednesdays and targets a younger audience; on Thursdays two other supplements appear. *En forma* (In Shape) reports on health and wellness issues; and *Tiempo libre* (Free Time) lists the calendar of social events in the capital. Other daily newspapers include *El Heraldo* and *Extra.*

The nation's primary English language newspaper, the *Tico Times,* was founded by Elisabeth Dyer in 1956. According to the paper's first editorial, it was "begun in order that young people interested in journalism could receive practical, on the job training, and in so doing to provide the English speaking public of Costa Rica with a newspaper of special interest to the American and British colonies and Costa Ricans who know, or are learning, English." For its first four years, the *Times* was a volunteer effort, produced by members of the English-speaking community, including high school students. The paper's circulation has grown to 14,500 and is printed in Costa Rica and California and distributed free. The paper remains a training ground for journalists and for those who want work experience in Latin America, and many of its former volunteers have gone on to influential media positions in the United States and Europe.

By 1980, the *Times* was respected internationally for its investigative journalism and its coverage of Central America, especially of the Nicaraguan revolution and the Iran-Contra affair. The *Times'* reporter Linda Frazier was among those killed in the May 1984 bombing of the Nicaraguan contra leader Edén Pastora's press conference on the Nicaraguan border and the paper campaigned vigorously to expose the truth behind the bombing. With civil unrest diminishing in Central America the paper's special interests have centered on tourism and environmental concerns, at times an uneasy balance, as much of the paper's advertising revenue is from real estate developers.

Costa Rica's relative prosperity in Latin America provides a large and literate audience to sustain a number of magazines, whose topics range from glossy tourism monthlies, to evangelical Christian publications, to conservation issues. Eco-tourism publications have acquired a growing number of international subscribers. *Gente 10,* a magazine that targets a gay and lesbian audience, was founded in 1995. Scholarly journals are also published, including *Káñnina* (past tense of ''to dawn'' in the indigenous Bribrí language) published by the University of Costa Rica, which showcases scholarship in fine arts, the humanities, and the social sciences.

San José has long dominated Costa Rican society and the vast majority of the nation's publications originate there. Radio, however, is more important than daily newspapers outside of the nation's capital as the primary way in which people receive information. All of the newspapers follow the tabloid-sized format.

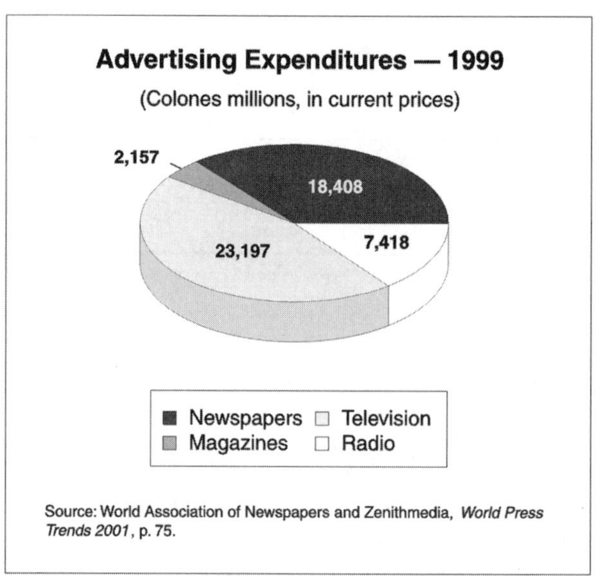

Source: World Association of Newspapers and Zenithmedia, *World Press Trends 2001*, p. 75.

ECONOMIC FRAMEWORK

Costa Rica's economy is based primarily on agriculture, light industry, and tourism. Traditionally considered to the strongest economy in Central America, Costa Rica's gross domestic product in 2001 grew only 0.3 percent and inflation stood at around 11 percent, triggered by low world coffee prices. The last 20 years have seen Costa Rica move away from its social welfare past and into the free market reforms of present-day Latin America. The nation has also faced economic crises and increasing distance between the social classes. In the mid-1980s, for example, the top 10 percent of society received 37 percent of the wealth while the bottom 10 percent had 1.5 percent. Costa Rica became the first underdeveloped country to suspend debt payments in 1981. The worst of the crisis was over by 2002, but the nation continued its ''structural adjustments.'' From 1982 to 1990 the U.S. Agency for International Development gave over 1.3 billion U.S. dollars to Costa Rica. The foreign aid and economic recovery came with the imposition of harsh austerity measures, a restructuring of financial priorities, and a revamped development model.

The last four presidents, despite coming from two different political parties, have followed the same path of economic liberalism, stressing free trade, export promotion, and less money for the public sector. Hurricanes have also damaged the economy in recent years beginning with César in July 1996 that caused several dozen deaths and cut off much of southern Costa Rica from the rest of the country. The Inter-American Highway was closed for about two months and the overall damage was estimated at about US$100 million. In November of 1998 Hurricane Mitch caused substantial damage to Costa Rica, although not as much as in the northern-most Central American countries, Nicaragua and Honduras. That same year, the Social Christian Unity Party's Miguel Angel Rodríguez won the presidency. A conservative businessman who made the economy his priority, he went on to privatize state companies and encourage foreign investments in an effort to create jobs. By the time of the February 2002 elections, Costa Ricans were displeased with the lack of government transparency and the questionable deals between political figures. These misgivings resulted in a ''no win'' election, and voters returned in April 2002, choosing Abel Pacheco, also of the PUSC.

The majority of the media in Costa Rica is privately owned and there are a few media conglomerates that own the majority of the media in the entire nation. *La Nación* stockholders also hold interests in the daily paper, *La República,* as well as the popular radio stations, Radio Monumental and Radio Mil. The owners of the major media tend toward conservative politics and their power as media owners allows the news to lean to the conservative side of issues.

In the 1980s there was a good deal of concern that the ownership of the media in Costa Rica might have a tendency to deliver politically-biased news accounts. The discussion was brought to the forefront as the nearby war between the U.S.-backed Contras and the Marxist-inspired Sandinistas escalated in Nicaragua. Four of the five privately owned major TV stations broadcast a barrage of sensationalized news reports warning of the *sandino-comunista* threat. Analysis of news coverage in the 1980s found that national stations rarely ever interviewed Nicaraguan officials yet they gave considerable coverage to the Reagan administration's viewpoint. Former Nicaraguan contra leader Edgar Chamorro also testified in the World Court that CIA money was used to bribe journalists and broadcasters in both Costa Rica and Honduras.

Many journalists in Costa Rica argue that the media owners and the media in general are considerably to the right of the general population, but that alternative media has not been able to develop because of the conglomerate nature of the media. One journalist who tried to start up an alternative newspaper, commented that his efforts were hampered since media and business owners were "one and the same."

PRESS LAWS

While the constitution provides for freedom of speech and the press, and the government largely respects these rights, a number of outmoded press laws have caused controversy as well as internal and international pressure for reform. In 1999, President Miguel Angel Rodríguez presented a bill to congress that attempted to make improvements in press legislation. Specifically, it proposed the abolishment of Article 7 of the old Press Law from 1902 which makes publishers liable for offences by third persons in their news outlets. It would also increase to 15 days the time allowed to respond to a lawsuit and include a provision that exempts from responsibility those who have only provided the material means for publication or sale of slanderous, libelous or defamatory reports. The proposed changes also pushed for removing the burden of proof from the journalists to demonstrate that their published information is true.

In 2001 the murder of Parmenio Medina re-focused attention on the need to revamp the nation's antiquated press laws. But this was not the only event to spur legislative change since a few months before his murder, the Inter-American Press Association (IAPA) analyzed the Costa Rican constitution in light of the Chapultepec Declaration of 1994 (also known as the Declaration of Free Speech for the Western Hemisphere) and found that four of the ten points recommended for guaranteeing freedom of the press were absent in Costa Rica. In effect, IAPA found that there was insufficient legal support for journalists to protect their sources, harsh repercussions for journalists who criticized public officials, restrictions on the free flow of information and censorship.

The most controversial aspect of Costa Rican legislation has been the long-standing *desacato* or "insult" law which protects public figures from critical journalists. The Legislative Assembly voted on March 26, 2002 to eliminate Article 309 of the Criminal Code which made it a crime to "insult" the dignity of the president and other public officials. This aligns the code with the "actual malice" standard, first articulated by the U.S. Supreme Court in 1964. This standard requires plaintiffs to prove not only that published information about them is false, but also that the journalists knew or should have known it was false at the time of publication. Until the change in this law, journalists faced potential jail sentences of anywhere from a month to two years in prison, or as much as three years in prison if the offended party is a higher-ranking official such as the President.

The legislation also contains a neutral reporting standard, which says that journalists cannot be sued for accurately reproducing information from an explicitly mentioned source. For years, the international and local press communities and the Inter-American Commission on Human Rights had urged elimination of "insult" laws. The elimination of the law suggests greater press freedom will follow since journalists are no longer threatened with jail time for reporting on political or powerful personages in a less than flattering manner.

The World Free Press Committee (WFPC) is still pushing for the following changes in the Costa Rican legal code:

- Article 149, which establishes the "evidence of truth" (*prueba de la verdad*) as a necessary standard for journalists to prove. The WFPC recommends that the article should be revised to bring it into conformity with press freedom principles.
- Article 151, which as it currently stands establishes some "exclusions" of responsibilities to people who have been accused. Reform would increase the number of such exclusions.
- Article 152, which as it stands is most restrictive, penalizes the "reproduction of offenses." The WFPC suggest introducing instead the principle of "faithful reproduction," which is recognized by the Inter-American Commission on Human Rights.

Although the *desacato* law had been invoked infrequently, journalists say its existence had a chilling effect on news reporting. In 2001 another San José criminal court ordered Rogelio Benavides, editor of *La Nación's* TV supplement *Teleguía,* to pay a fine equivalent to 20 days' wages or face a jail sentence. Enrique González Jiménez, a beauty pageant promoter, sued Benavides based on a review of the pageant that appeared in a 1999 issue of *Teleguía* (TV Guide). While article 151 of the Penal Code holds that press reviews cannot be characterized as "offenses against honor" the court nonetheless convicted Benavides of libel and ordered that its ruling be published in *Teleguía.*

While welcoming repeal of the *desacato* law, many Costa Rican journalists say it is a minor obstacle to press freedom in Costa Rica. There is concern that repeal will lead lawmakers to claim that enough was done toward reform, and that officials will fail to act on the nation's far more troublesome and complex libel, slander, and defamation laws. Unlike those in most other democracies, Costa Rica's defamation laws are criminal, rather than civil statutes. This means that journalists can receive prison sentences and heavy monetary fines for convictions.

While not common, these statutes have been employed far more often than journalists would like. Up until the repeal of the *desacato* law, news media in Costa Rica had more than a dozen criminal defamation actions pending, with penalties totaling thousands of dollars. In June 2001, for example, the Costa Rican Supreme Court upheld a libel verdict against three journalists from *La Nación.* The case stemmed from a 1997 article reporting that a former justice minister had been accused of appropriating state-owned weapons and an official car for his personal use. The politician was awarded damages of US$34,000. The decision also required that *La Nación* publish the first seven pages of the decision in their entirety. One of the arguments used to justify such a large fine was that the articles were available on the Internet, and therefore reached a larger audience for a longer period of time. The court also ordered *La Nación* to remove all links from its web site that could lead the reader to the contested articles. The judges ruled that the journalist had shown malicious intent by continuing to investigate the case despite testimony from two former Costa Rican presidents who vouched for the politician's integrity.

Other problematic legislation includes the ''right of response'' law passed by congress in 1996. This law provides persons criticized in the media with an opportunity to reply with equal attention and at equal length. While the print and electronic media continued to criticize public figures, the law has proven difficult for media managers to administer. On occasion, some media outlets delayed printing responses because submissions were not clearly identified as replies to previously published items.

Costa Rica's government has also tried to foster political tolerance and dialogue through laws like the one that requires broadcasters to accept political ads during campaign periods. During the highly charged political climate of the 1980s, Costa Rica managed to maintain its democratic political tradition during the presidential campaign. With a battle raging in bordering Nicaragua, Costa Rica's right-wing candidate Rafael Angel Calderón Fournier, a godson of former Nicaraguan dictator Anastasio Somoza García, was shown talking one-on-one with Ronald Reagan, Margaret Thatcher, and Pope John Paul II in televised advertisements. His opponent, Oscar Arias Sánchez, brought in liberal American consultants, who used polling to identify what was worrying the large bloc of undecided voters and refocus the campaign appropriately. By promising jobs, housing, and peace, Arias was able to overcome Calderón's wide lead in early polls to win the presidency in February. The fact that Arias was allowed to advertise on television indicates that the Costa Rican media carry a wider range of views than those of less democratic countries. There have been times, however, when there have been unconfirmed allegations that the government withheld advertising from some publications in order to influence or limit reporting.

Censorship

While little outright censorship exists, reports that journalists and editors are forced to monitor what they write and publish have been increasingly frequent. Editors say they censor themselves and their reporters routinely, for fear of incurring penalties that could mean imprisonment, loss of their jobs, or corporate bankruptcy. A survey done by *La Nación* which asked journalists a number of questions about their profession showed that many of them practiced some sort of self-censorship. Limiting access to information can be seen as a subtle form of information control and a number of journalists complained that public officials were not forthcoming in this regard. For example, a majority of the journalists interviewed said that while they had direct access to public officials, there were many ways in which these sources avoided their attempts to interview them. Often, it was difficult for journalists to make it through the ''screen'' of intermediaries (press secretaries, secretaries, assistants, and others). If an interview was obtained journalists complained that public officials pled ignorance or claimed confidentiality agreements prohibited an answer.

State-Press Relations

As mentioned before, many of the laws governing the press in Costa Rica have been designed to protect the honor of public officials, complicating the relationship between the state and the press. The ability of the press to be critical of the state without repercussions is not secure. The strict libel laws, for example, resulted in the firing of two reporters who investigated fraudulent business deals related to PLN President-elect José María Figueres in 1993: one reporter from Channel 7 was reportedly dismissed from her job because of pressure from the PLN after she reported on private sector corruption; a reporter from *La República* said that he had left his editorial position because of alleged pressure from officials close to the President-elect. The reporter had been working on several articles that linked Figueres to alleged fraudulent mining deals.

In 1995 the *Tico Times* reported that the popular television program, ''Diagnóstico'' had been cancelled by the government-run National Radio and Television System (SINART). Critics of the decision to cancel the program, which aired weekly on Channel 13 and had been running for 10 years, alleged that it was one of the few shows where guests felt free to discuss a number of important issues in Costa Rica. The show's host, a politician named Alvaro Montero, referred to it as the most liberal program in the country and said that he had to struggle for years to keep it on the air. According to the *Tico Times,* the administration of President Rafael Angel Calderón Jr. first tried to shut down the program by terminating an airing in mid show. The Figueres administration SINART officials reportedly tried to end the program by cutting off its funding. Montero financed the show out of his own pocket for two years. The government claimed the show was cancelled out of a conflict of interest given that Montero was a potential candidate for president in the 2002 elections.

ATTITUDE TOWARD FOREIGN MEDIA

The nation's democratic political structure, tourism industry, and large retirement community from the United States make it very receptive to foreign media. The international station, Radio For Peace International (RFPI), has studios and transmitters located in El Rodeo, Costa Rica, and with the revocation of the *colegio law* in 1995, there are no longer any restrictions on foreign journalists working in Costa Rica. The end of civil wars in Central America has also made the entire region safer for foreign journalists reporting there.

Until 1994 there were legal limits to the ownership of national media by foreigners. After the government revoked this law, it opened up the way for the Hollinger group, headquartered in Canada, to buy the newspaper *La República.* Foreign ownership, however, is subject to a number of bureaucratic constraints.

With the advent of cable, satellite dishes, and the Internet, foreign media entered Costa Rican society with substantial force over the last two decades of the twentieth century. Foreign-funded periodicals have left their imprint on Costa Rican media. Primarily sponsored by aide organizations, such publications have made an important contribution to the dissemination of information. The merging of local and foreign media is representative of many joint ventures here. For example, in 1994 an international council began funding a far-reaching demographic analysis of Costa Rican society and the resulting publication appears annually as *Estado de la Nación* (State of the Nation) and appears on the Internet. Costa Ricans watch Venezuelan and Mexican soap operas, soccer matches, and dubbed U.S. programs on commercial channels. Despite a law limiting imported programs to 75 percent of broadcast schedules, about 90 percent are imports. In addition, U.S. programs dominate the cable channel offerings in parts of the capital, San José.

NEWS AGENCIES

There are a number of news services that operate in Costa Rica. These include *Agence France Presse, Telenoticias,* Rainforest Alliance, *Diario La Nación,* and the *Tico Times.* The Internet also provides rapid information access to news desks.

BROADCAST MEDIA

Radio is extremely popular in Costa Rica and is especially important for those Ticos who live outside of the capital city. In 2002 about 130 radio stations existed. Daily radio programming included talk shows and soap operas, political and social commentary, educational and religious programming, and sports coverage. Until Medina's murder, *La Patada* was one of the most popular radio programs in Costa Rica. It generally provided a light-hearted perspective on the news mixed with humor and political criticism. Another show, *La Opinion*, offers serious news commentary and is broadcast on Radio Reloj.

Evangelical Christian stations have blossomed since the 1980s. American missionaries were the first to broadcast the Protestant message by radio and television. The radio station *Faro del Caribe,* for example, has been broadcasting since the 1940s and includes programs targeted for the instruction and entertainment of children, mothers, and young people through Bible study, radio theater, advice, and music. Radio programming has also fulfilled other goals. In 1993 the government established the Costa Rican Institute of Radio Education in an effort to provide access to education to residents in rural areas. Programs such as "The Teacher in Your House" are broadcast from 12 noncommercial stations and complement correspondence courses in public schools. Lessons in English are also immensely popular.

Of the many radio stations in Costa Rica, Radio Reloj has the most listeners and it is also fairly conservative in nature. The news station Radio Monumental is also quite conservative and reflects the right-leaning opinions of its owners. Many radio stations carry Voice of America (VOA) and other U.S. Information Service programs including Radio Costa Rica which devotes about half its broadcast time to VOA programming. VOA's "Buenos Dias, America" feeds to 28 radio stations in Costa Rica. The most liberal station currently broadcasting is Radio America Latina which has proved responsive to the concerns of the popular movement.

Costa Rican television transmission began in the 1950s and today there are a dozen commercial stations and one government-run station. The most viewed stations are Channel 4 Multimedia, Channels 6 and 9 Repretel, Channel 7 Teletica, and Channel 2 Univisión. The Picado family owns the cable network, Cable Tica, and Channel 7. Angel Gonzalez, who is based in Florida, partially backs Channels 4 and 9. The other channels are privately owned with the exception of the national television network which is publicly owned and SINART (Channel 13), a government-controlled cultural channel.

Over 90 percent of Costa Rican households have at least one television set. Cablecolor, the local cable service, broadcasts the U.S. government's daily program as well as CNN's 24-hour news service. Channel 7 leads the others in terms of viewers, and is trying to assert full control of the medium through the professionalization of its "Telenoticias" news program. Channel 7, formerly owned by ABC, is of the same ideological stripe as the major print media. Channel 4 has gained in popularity over the last few years, perhaps due to offering a left-leaning political perspective, and hence, a contrast to the majority of Costa Rican media. A public station founded by the PLN during a previous period in power, Channel 13 offers a more liberal take on current events and offers a wide array of cultural programming. Costa Rican television also broadcasts programs from the rest of Latin America.

There has been little interference with the operation of television stations, with some exceptions. A Costa Rican court decision made in 2001 required a privately owned station to invite all 13 presidential candidates to appear, rather than just the frontrunners. The Inter-American Press Association called the court order a "flagrant interference in the news media's editorial and journalistic independence." The order was issued by a majority of justices of the Costa Rica Supreme Electoral Tribunal, upholding a request for injunction filed by three minority political party candidates to the Costa Rican presidency who had not been invited to take part in a debate scheduled to be aired by the privately-owned Channel 7 TV. The station only invited the four leading candidates, who between them were estimated to account for 95 percent of the public vote.

ELECTRONIC NEWS MEDIA

By 2000 about 150,000 people in Costa Rica, or 3.9 percent of the population, were Internet users, accessing it through either one legal or two illegal Internet service providers. Most of the important newspapers also have an online presence, as do many of the national magazines.

La Nación publishes an online summary of news events in English and has news archived since 1995. AM Costa Rica is a website updated Monday through Friday targeting the English-speaking retired community in

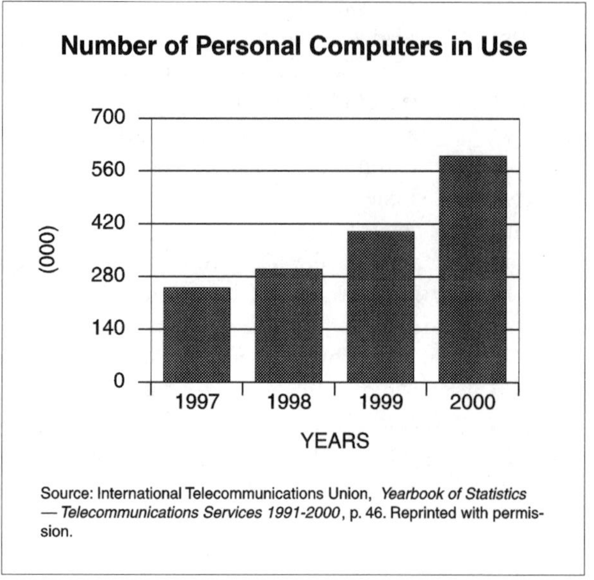

Source: International Telecommunications Union, *Yearbook of Statistics — Telecommunications Services 1991-2000*, p. 46. Reprinted with permission.

Costa Rica. It is published by Consultantes Río Colorado, S.A., a Costa Rican corporation.

The following newspapers and magazines have websites:

- *La Nación:* www.lanacion.co.cr
- *La República:* www.larepublica.co.cr
- *Tico Times:* http://www.ticotimes.co.cr
- *AM Costa Rica:* http://www.amcostarica.com
- *Diario Extra:* http://www.diarioextra.com
- *El Heraldo:* http://www.elheraldo.net
- *La Prensa Libre:* http://www.laprensalibre.co.cr

These radio stations are broadcast over the Internet:

- Radio Columbia (primarily sports coverage): http://www.columbia.co.cr
- Radio Monumental: http://www.monumental.co.cr
- Radio Reloj: http://www.rpreloj.co.cr

EDUCATION & TRAINING

To professionalize its media Costa Rica passed a law in 1969 that required national news reporters to graduate from the University of Costa Rica's journalism school (*colegio de periodismo*). The so-called *colegio* law has been controversial almost from the outset since it acts, at times, as a restrictive licensing measure. Furthermore, during the first few years after the law's inception, the University of Costa Rica did not have a journalism program in operation making the law impossible to uphold. As a result, journalists were allowed to be members of the *colegio* if they had at least five years of consecutive journalistic experience or ten years intermittent experience.

The *colegio* system has been controversial throughout Latin America since it has been interpreted as a professional licensing board that can curtail the freedom of individual journalists to exercise their profession. In 2001 *La Nación* published an article detailing the history of the *colegio* and its many failures to support journalists over the last 25 years. Most of the charges included instances of aggression against the press when the *colegio* failed to back individual journalists, radio and television stations, and newspapers, motivated by the licensing board members' conservative political alliances with the national government.

In 1994 the *colegio* began lobbying for passage of a constitutional amendment to permanently ensure its ability to define who exercises journalism in the country. The amendment would have protected the *colegio* from international criticism such as that issued by the inter-American Human Rights Court which ruled the licensing practice a violation of press freedom. *Colegio* leadership argues that the body serves to create professional standards, minimize cultural imperials and protect journalists' rights. The *colegio* has a code of ethics with 17 articles that was approved by the organization's general assembly in October 1991.

The *Tico Times* successfully took a case to the Inter-American Court of Human Rights over a Costa Rican law requiring the licensing of journalists. The *Times* claimed harassment by the *colegio* for over 20 years even though the *colegio* admitted it was unable to supply enough qualified journalists. In 1995, the Costa Rican Supreme Court addressed the problems inherent to the *colegio* system and declared the licensing of journalists unconstitutional. This was seen as a major victory for advancing legislative support of freedom of expression in the country.

Journalism degrees are awarded by the University of Costa Rica and the Latin University of Costa Rica. In addition a number of organizations sponsor seminars and conferences related to the practice of journalism. Costa Rica is one of the most popular spots for international journalistic conferences dealing with Latin America. The International Center for Journalists sponsored seminars on the media and freedom of expression in the Americas in Costa Rica. The Costa Rican *colegio* also organized conferences and workshops on social communication, human rights and the media, taking place frequently in San José. The city often hosts special courses to train media specialists in radio and television. A radio station from the Netherlands, Radio Hilversum, held a series of such workshops in San José open to all Latin American and Caribbean journalists. The World Bank Institute's Governance and Finance Unit and Radio Nederland Training Center, located in Costa Rica, also organized a course in investigative journalism conducted over the Internet.

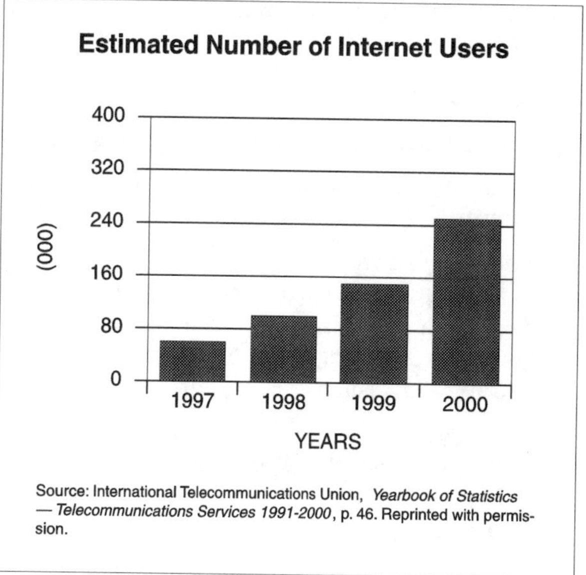

Source: International Telecommunications Union, *Yearbook of Statistics — Telecommunications Services 1991-2000*, p. 46. Reprinted with permission.

SUMMARY

The Costa Rican mass communications industry can support both pessimistic and optimistic predictions. For the pessimist, it is easy to point out that a popular muckraking journalist was killed in cold-blood and that his attackers have yet to be officially identified or tried. Costa Rica's press freedom and development is also limited by the concentration of the media in the hands of a powerful few, and an increase in U.S. influence in the country, both economically and also culturally. For the optimist, the openness with which *La Nación* conducts and publishes interviews with journalists about their profession suggests that there is indeed a greater level of freedom of expression than one would imagine given the survey's critical findings. Also, during most of the 1990s, the media in Costa Rica was becoming more aggressive in its interrogation of government officials suspected of incompetence, corruption, and influence peddling. In addition, the repeal of the *colegio* law in 1995 and the recent repeal of the "insult" law also suggests that the protection of the rights of journalists to practice their profession without the fear of being fined, imprisoned, or expelled is being institutionalized.

Historically, the nation's emphasis on both education and freedom of the press have resulted in a great resistance to any attempt to restrict these rights and even greater resilience to bounce back quickly from those moments when such rights have been constrained. Medina's murder has resulted in greater discussion about freedom of the press and changes to provide the legislative teeth to ensure those freedoms. The nation's literacy rate, the public's increasing access to the Internet, and the rich opportunities for journalists and other media professionals to receive on-going training, suggests that the press in Costa Rica will endure.

Significant Dates

- 1995: Costa Rican Supreme Court issues a decision saying that the licensing of journalists was unconstitutional.
- 1996: Legislative Assembly passes ''right of response'' law which provides persons criticized in the media with an opportunity to reply with equal attention and at equal length. The law has proven difficult to enforce and administer.
- 1999: President Miguel Angel Rodríguez proposed a bill to the Costa Rican legislature, the Law to Protect Press Freedom, intended to make important improvements in press legislation.
- 2001: Popular radio journalist Parmenio Medina was murdered in what is assumed to have been retaliation for Medina's investigative journalism. No one had been arrested for his murder as of 2002. The tragedy sent shockwaves through the nation and spurred on legislative attempts to update outmoded legislation.

Bibliography

Alemán, Eduardo, Ortega, José Guadalupe, and Wilkie, James W., eds. *Statistical Abstract of Latin America.* Los Angeles: UCLA Latin American Center Publications, 2001.

Attacks on the Press: A Worldwide Survey. New York: Committee to Protect Journalists, 1994.

Baldivia, Hernán, ed. *La formación de los periodistas en América Latina: México, Chile, Costa Rica.* México D.F.: CEESTEM, 1981.

Biesanz, Mavis Hiltunen, Biesanz, Richard and Biesanz, Karen Zubris. *The Ticos: Culture and Social Change in Costa Rica.* Boulder and London: Lynne Rienner Publishers, 1999.

Borders Without Frontiers, Costa Rica Annual Report 2002.

Helmuth, Chalene. *Culture and Customs of Costa Rica.* Westport, CT and London: Greenwood Press, 2000.

IPI Report, The International Journalism Magazine (November/December 1995).

Lara, Silvia, with Barry, Tom, and Simonson, Peter. *Inside Costa Rica: The Essential Guide to its Politics, Economy, Society, and Environment.* Albuquerque, New Mexico: Resource Center Press, 1995.

Marshall, Oliver. *The English-Language Press in Latin America.* London: Institute of Latin American Studies, University of London, 1997.

Martínez, Reynaldo. ''Sociedad Interamericana de Prensa (SIP) considera que en nuestro país se violentan cuatro principios que garantizan este derecho.'' *La República,* July 2, 2001.

Skidmore, Thomas E. and Smith, Peter H. *Modern Latin America.* New York and Oxford: Oxford University Press, 1997.

Solano Carboni, Montserrat. ''The Silence: A Year Later the Murder of a Popular Costa Rican Journalist Remains Unsolved.'' New York: Committee to Protect Journalists, July 2, 2002.

Uribe, Hernán O. *Ética Periodística en América Latina: Deontología y estatuto professional.* México D.F.: Universidad Naciónal Autónoma de México, 1984.

Vega Jiménez, Patricia. *De la Imprenta al Periodico: Los inicios de la comunicación impresa en Costa Rica 1821-1850.* San José, Costa Rica: Editorial Porvenir, 1995.

World Press Freedom Review, 2000.

—*Kristen McCleary*

Côte d'Ivoire

Basic Data

Official Country Name:	Republic of Côte d'Ivoire
Region (Map name):	Africa
Population:	16,393,221
Language(s):	French (official), 60 native dialects with Dioula the most widley spoken
Literacy rate:	48.5%
Area:	322,460 sq km
GDP:	9,370 (US$ millions)
Number of Television Stations:	14
Number of Television Sets:	900,000
Television Sets per 1,000:	54.9
Number of Radio Stations:	13
Number of Radio Receivers:	2,260,000
Radio Receivers per 1,000:	137.9
Number of Individuals with Computers:	90,000

Computers per 1,000:	5.5
Number of Individuals with Internet Access:	40,000
Internet Access per 1,000:	2.4

Background & General Characteristics

Located in Western Africa, Côte d'Ivoire Republic (La République de Côte d'Ivoire, French) borders the North Atlantic Ocean, Liberia, Guinea, Mali, Burkina Faso, Ghana, and the Gulf of Guinea. It is a little larger than the state of New Mexico. Its climate is tropical along the coasts, but semi-arid in the far north. It possesses some significant natural resources, including bauxite, cocoa, copper, petroleum, natural gas, diamond, manganese, iron ore, and hydropower. Since gaining its political independence from France, on August 7, 1960 it has acquired a steady, but insufficient, flow of foreign direct and indirect investment funds particularly from the ex-French metropolis. Its export-led strategies, primarily dependent on the cocoa production, have triggered consistent economic growth but not necessarily harmonious socio-economic development outcomes. The severe decline in cocoa prices in 1999 and 2000, coupled with the first military coup d'état since 1960 and the exclusion from the October 2000 national elections of opposition leader Alassane Outtarra produced violence and political turmoil. After this election, Mr. Laurent Gbagbo replaced Mr. Robert Guei, ending 10 months of military dictatorial control.

The population of Côte d'Ivoire in the early 21st century was approximately 16.5 million, but AIDS has ravaged the nation, killing 72,000 Ivorians in 1999 alone. The average life expectancy in the early 21st century was only 45 years. The country has absorbed many refugees from neighboring countries, particularly Liberia. Ethnically, Akans represented Ivorians at 42 percent, Gurs or Voltaiques at 18 percent, Mandes (North and South) at 26.5 percent, and Krous at 11 percent. Religiously, 34 percent of the Ivorians were Christians, 27 percent Muslim, and 15 percent Animist. The official language is French but some 60 dialects are spoken, predominantly Dioula, and the literacy rate has remained above the world average, at about 50 percent.

The Press The mass media and press system in Côte d'Ivoire has remained fundamentally French, as in numerous ex-colonies of Western European powers. In the early 21st century, there was a very low daily newspaper circulation of 16 per 1,000 people compared to 228 per 1000 in the USA, 237 per 1000 in France, or 14 per 1000 in Liberia. This was despite the existence of 12 major daily newspapers, including *Fraternié-Matin* and *Ivoire-Soir* (government-owned), *La Nouvelle République*, *Le Jour*, *AFP-Côte d'Ivoire*, *AllAfrica*, *IRIN*, and *Abidjan Net*. Other statistics recorded one television set per 17 people, one radio set per seven people, and one telephone per 123 people.

Economic Framework

The Ivorian real (adjusted for inflation) GDP amounted in 2000 to slightly over $26 billion. The real GDP per capita, in addition, was a low $1600. The GDP was 32 percent based on agriculture, 18 percent on industry, and 50 percent on services. The labor force remained mostly absorbed by agriculture at the beginning of the 21st century, as Côte d'Ivoire has continued to be a major world producer and exporter of beans, cocoa, coffee, and palm oil. The Ivorian economy is at the mercy of world commodity price variations, climate, and internal and external politics. Public revenues in 2000 were $1.5 billion while public expenditures were some $2.1 billion. Official unemployment was at a high 13 percent. Exports amounted to about $4 billion and imports added up to $2.5 billion. Again, cocoa represented the lion's share of the exported goods at about 35% while consumer goods, capital products, transport material, and fuel were the main imports.

Press Laws & Censorship

At the wake of major protests by students and workers in February 1990, against President Félix Houphouët-Boigny, the first ever-democratic multiparty elections were held in October 1990. Although Mr. Boigny retained his office, the Ivorian National Assembly introduced gradual media and press legislation to promote freedom of the press, freedom of information, and non-censorship, at least in principle. Factually, censorship still reigns as Côte d'Ivoire remains unsure due to political instability, the plummeting of world prices, AIDS, and an enormous influx of refugees from neighboring countries. Laws and ordinances have been introduced to fight the spread of AIDS, poverty, the uneven regional development, child labor exploitation and slavery, and discrimination. The major Ivorian press and the Internet are paramount to the goals of the new government. Telco, a quasi-monopoly partially owned by the state, is legally encouraged to engage broadcast media, press, other mass media, and journalists and news operators to embark on the Internet to promote social and economic justice.

Broadcast & Electronic News Media

In 2002 one main state-owned television service and one state-owned radio system existed, as well as four in-

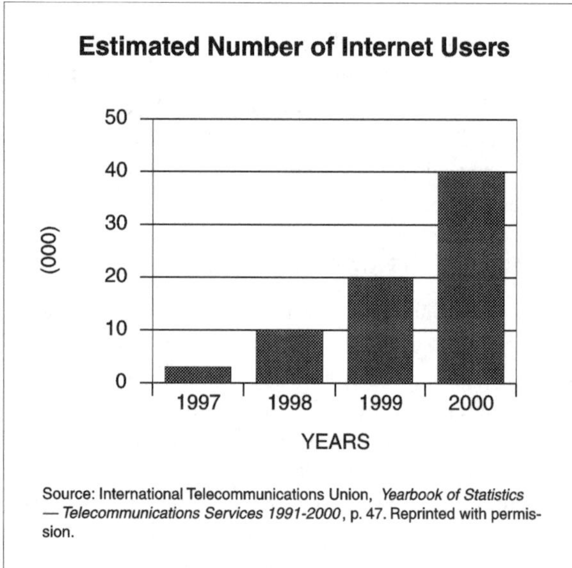

Source: International Telecommunications Union, *Yearbook of Statistics — Telecommunications Services 1991-2000*, p. 47. Reprinted with permission.

dependent services. The electronic media was extremely weak, though the political, administrative, financial, and academic structures were beginning to acquire and use cyberspace and information technology, particularly in the capital, Abidjan. Some major web sites include those of the Ivorian President, the Ministry of Culture, the National Office of Tourism, the Front Populaire Ivoirian, Agence France Presse, and several major newspapers.

ATTITUDE TOWARDS FOREIGN MEDIA

The Ivorian people have generally been open to foreign media, usually French. The successive governments, since the 1960 post-colonial régimes of Boigny, Bedié, Guei, and Gbagbo have varied in their perceptions, authorizations, and usage of the foreign press and media. In the years 2000 and 2001, Côte d'Ivoire saw its worst political nightmares, as opposition leader Alassane Ouattara was illegally excluded from the October 2000 elections. In fact, following the Supreme Court decision to exclude Ouattara, the streets of Abidjan were the scene of unprecedented violence. Relations with the foreign media, therefore, were tense and exclusionary. The UN, the EEC, and the OAU refused to assist with the parliamentary and presidential elections. Other protests, governmental and media, ensued from France, South Africa, Senegal, Morocco, and many others. Gradually, however, since Mr. Gbagbo took over in October 2000, replacing the military junta and dictatorship of 10 months, the country has begun to return to democratic internal press and media usage, and external media and press cooperation.

EDUCATION & TRAINING

Many journalists in Côte d'Ivoire are educated and trained in France, principally in colleges, universities, and journalism schools in Paris, Lyon, and Bordeaux. A few are trained in Western and North-African countries, such as at L'Université de Dakar in Senegal and l'Université Mohammed V in Rabat, Morocco. Abidjan is becoming a major educational and training center for journalists, news anchors, and photojournalists.

BIBLIOGRAPHY

afrol.com. Available from www.afrol.com/Countries/CIV/news_civ.html.

"Cote d'Ivoire," *CIA World Fact Book 2001*. Available from http://www.cia.gov.

Sarri, Samuel. *Ethics of the International Monetary Systems*. UPA: New York, 1998.

The World Almanac and Book of Facts, 1995 through 2001. K-III Reference Co.: New Jersey.

—Samuel Sarri

CROATIA

BASIC DATA

Official Country Name:	Republic of Croatia
Region (Map name):	Europe
Population:	4,334,142
Language(s):	Croatian, other (including Italian, Hungarian, Czech, Slovak and German)
Literacy rate:	97.0%
Area:	56,542 sq km
GDP:	19,031 (US$ millions)
Number of Daily Newspapers:	12
Total Circulation:	595,000
Circulation per 1,000:	154
Number of Nondaily Newspapers:	245
Total Circulation:	653,000
Circulation per 1,000:	169
As % of All Ad Expenditures:	14.00

Number of Television Stations:	36
Number of Television Sets:	1,220,000
Television Sets per 1,000:	281.5
Number of Cable Subscribers:	167,200
Cable Subscribers per 1,000:	38.0
Number of Radio Stations:	119
Number of Radio Receivers:	1,510,000
Radio Receivers per 1,000:	348.4
Number of Individuals with Computers:	361,000
Computers per 1,000:	83.3
Number of Individuals with Internet Access:	250,000
Internet Access per 1,000:	57.7

Top Ten Daily Newspapers
(2000)

	Circulation
Vecernji List	252,000
Jutarnji List	150,000
Republika	120,000
Slobodna Dalmacija	55,000
Novi List	48,000
Sportske Novosti	40,000
Vjesnik	22,000
Glas istre	21,000
Glas Slavonije	11,000
Zadarski List	5,000

Source: World Association of Newspapers and Zenithmedia, *World Press Trends 2001*, p. 78.

BACKGROUND & GENERAL CHARACTERISTICS

At the beginning of the twenty-first century, the state and future of the Croatia's media can be viewed in the context of two defining events. The first was the end, in the early 1990s, of the socialist period of government that lasted 45 years following the end of World War II. The second event was the effect of the ethnic conflict in the Balkans from 1992 to 1996, followed by the peacetime influence of the government of President Franjo Trudjman from 1996 to 1999, which ended with his death on December 10, 1999. Consequently, Croatia's media have been moving out from under the heavy control and influence of the government toward independence and autonomy. It is this movement that characterizes Croatian media today and guides its evolution in the twenty-first century.

The media in Croatia are delivering news and commentary to a highly educated, literate population that values news and debate in the early 2000s. Notwithstanding a population that has a low per capita income by European standards of US$4,000 per annum in 2001, there are numerous media and a wide range of political positions among them. A distinct concentration of media is in the capital, Zagreb, in large part due to the concentration of population in the city and in the surrounding region. According to the 2001 census, the population of the city of Zagreb was 770,058; however, coupled with a population of 304,186 in the surrounding county, the Zagreb metropolitan area contains 1,174,244 persons, which is over 25 percent of the nation's population of over 4.3 million. Moreover, the country is not geographically large, so print media and national electronic media have little difficulty in providing national coverage. Within that national coverage, the presence of significant minorities—particularly Slovenes and Italians in the northwest, Hungarians in the Northeast, Serbs in the East, and Bosnians in the Southeast and Southwest—have spawned opportunities for the creation of some publications in these regions in languages other than Croatian.

The quality of journalism would generally be scored a 7 out of 10. Much of the poor journalism can be attributed to journalists who historically worked under the former socialist system and who are often not trained as journalists and have acquired and maintained their positions through political patronage and their willingness to deliver a loyal party line. Many of these journalists have shown an inability to adapt to a more critical, wide-ranging, issue-oriented role after the end of the socialist government, and as such, the quality of journalism suffers. In contrast, journalists who were not trained under the socialist system and were at the forefront of the criticism of the government during the Balkan conflict have created a class of critical writers and observers that provide perceptive commentary on the situation in the region. With the increasingly open media, this type of journalist is in the ascendancy.

Most newspapers are in a tabloid format with over 50, and sometimes up to 70, pages in length. The exception is the newspaper *Vjesnik,* which is regular size. National, regional, and international news dominate the first one third of the newspapers, features and television programming the middle third, with the final third devoted to weather, sports and cultural topics. Newspapers retailed for less than US$1 in 2002. Sunday newspapers

Daily and Non-Daily Newspaper Titles and Circulation Figures

	1996	1997	1998	1999	2000
Number of Daily Newspapers	10	11	10	11	12
Circulation of Dailies (000)	522	502	510	536	595
Number of Non-Daily Newspapers	194	220	224	237	245
Circulation of Non-Dailies (000)	531	576	568	624	653

Source: World Association of Newspapers and Zenithmedia, *World Press Trends 2001*, pp. 8, 10, 17, 19.

have significantly more content, but not to the extent of newspapers in other European cities or the United States. Weekly magazines fulfill a major role in the Croatian media, for they represent the most vociferous and sensational outlets for news and commentary on social, political, and economic issues. During the Trudjman regime these weekly periodicals were the major organs for dissent and the major outlets for investigative journalism, a role they continue to play today. There is no dedicated Croatian English-language magazine or newspaper, but same-day international editions of English-language newspapers and magazines are readily available, and hence the need or market is not apparent. Minority media in Croatia include newspapers dedicated to religion, particularly the Catholic Church (*Glas Koncila*), and other ethnic language newspapers such as Serbian language newspapers. These weekly newspapers have fewer pages (usually 32) and, in the case of the Catholic newspaper, are devoted to more ecclesiastical matters than the political and cultural focus of mainstream newspapers.

Other cities in Croatia do not have significant competing newspapers; rather, national papers tend to have regional specialization. For example, the national newspaper *Slobodna Dalmacija* exhibits a regional coverage bias in favor of the Dalmatian coastal region containing the second- and third-largest cites of Split (population 300,000) and Rijeka (population 225,000). Official circulation figures of newspapers are unobtainable and vary widely depending on the source, but it is believed that the most important newspapers by unofficial circulation figures are: *Vecernji List* (120,000), *Jutarnji List* (90,000), *Slobodna Dalmacija* (30,000), *Novi List* (15,000-20,000), and *Glas Slavonije* (a regional Slovenian newspaper; 10,000) and *Vjesnik* (8,000).

Although *Vecernji List* and *Jutarnji List* are the highest circulation news-related publications, numerous popular publications also exist, including *Gloria,* a weekly magazine specializing in fashion, yellow journalism, and personalities, with a circulation of 90,000; *Globus,* a weekly similar to *Gloria* with a circulation of 70,000; and *Teen* and *OK,* teenager magazines with 55,000 and 50,000 readers, respectively. Additionally, the fashion weekly *Mila,* the political weeklies *National* and *Arena,* and the fashion monthly *Cosmo* also outsell one of the largest newspapers, *Slobodna Dalmacija.* Three other publications are noteworthy: *Autoklub,* a monthly motoring magazine, has 30,000 readers; *Playboy* magazine, with 22,000 subscribers, outsells the fourth and fifth best-selling newspapers; and the weekly *Feral Tribune,* with 20,000 copies in circulation, is noteworthy as it was the most vocal critic of the Trudjman regime in the 1990s. Although the *Feral Tribune* fell on hard times in large part as a result of ongoing legal judgments passed down on the basis of lawsuits filed during the Trudjman era, it remains one of the most outspoken publications in Croatia.

ECONOMIC FRAMEWORK

The economic climate of Croatia is a direct result of the repercussions of the Balkan war and the rule of President Franjo Trudjman, which lasted until 1999. The ravages of war have meant that recovery has been slow, a pace that many independent media have blamed on continuing government corruption and mismanagement. A change of government following the death of Trudjman has resulted in little improvement. In contrast, the neighboring country of Slovenia, although less affected by the Balkan war, has made significant economic progress. Progress in Slovenia is such that it has become a viable candidate for European Union membership, a status many in Croatia would like to achieve. The result of this economic climate has been a more vigilant press, intent on exposing corruption and mismanagement and generally critical of the nation's economic progress. This role has been confined to the printed media because the national television and radio networks are still government controlled and hence muted in their criticism. Much internal and external media criticism has been directed at government control of the television network, which serves as the primary source of information for an estimated 70 to 90 percent of Croatians; over 50 percent obtain their news from television's early evening news program.

In contrast to the television network, all newspapers are owned either by individuals or large corporate bodies.

Indeed, the acquisition of most Croatian newspapers by two corporate giants, Europa Press Holdings, a German conglomerate, and Styria, an Austrian based media conglomerate, has lead to fears that Croatian media has gone from being de facto government controlled to corporate controlled. The Croatian government is expected to address such potential monopolistic issues in the future. The newspapers that exist can be characterized as a mixture of popular and yellow journalism. This reflects not only the need to impart the news but also to build circulation, which provides the justification for inclusion of yellow journalism. The only exception to this group is *Vjenik,* which is much more elitist. As the former organ of the ruling party, it has fallen to fifth in popularity but its articles are longer and more in depth, and it is generally agreed that the quality of the journalism and its increasing distance from one-party affiliation will make it increasingly more popular and accepted, leading to a rise in circulation.

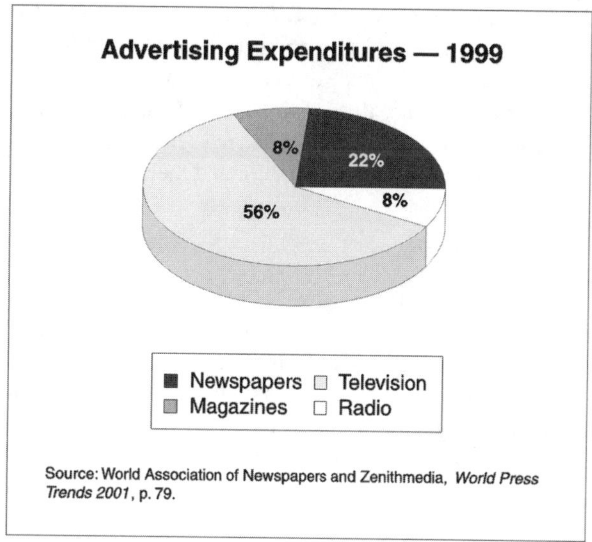

Source: World Association of Newspapers and Zenithmedia, *World Press Trends 2001*, p. 79.

A major issue in Croatia is the print media's near monopolistic distribution network, owned by the Tisar company, which controls distribution, including most of the kiosks where print media are sold. Tisar's uncertain financial situation was of major concern beginning in 2000. In the early 2000s the company was acquired by Europa Holdings, resulting in renewed concern over too much vertical integration within the media.

Unlike many other countries, newsprint is readily available to all who wish to publish, and there are a large number of private printing houses with modern offset printing presses. Hence, control of print production is not an issue. Moreover, there have been no strikes or work stoppages in either the journalistic community or the printing community that have affected media production. Wages in the media are on a par with the national average; however, a difference does exist between employees of the state-controlled television network and the print media. Notwithstanding a large bureaucracy and a situation of over-staffing, television network salaries are always forthcoming and relatively inflation proof. In contrast, in the print media circulation wars are ongoing and staffing is a critical cost area; thus, journalists are often paid only a small retainer and receive a bonus or commission based on the story they obtain or, more problematic, on the degree of sensational impact the story has on the publication's audience or overall circulation. Sales and circulation as a source of revenue is particularly important because advertising in Croatian national newspapers is very limited (usually less than 20 percent of the newspaper and often less than 10 percent), and most advertising dollars are generated by multi-national companies or commercial endeavors placing classified ads. This lack of local advertising revenue can be attributed almost solely to the lack of marketing funds for most Croatian companies. Journalists in Croatia belong to a union but as yet have neither a collective bargaining system nor a contract. Each journalist negotiates his or her own contract.

PRESS LAWS

The constitution of the Croatian Republic guarantees freedom of the press and freedom of speech. Specific laws governing the press uphold these rights but identify such subjects as pornography, official state secrets, and obscenity as areas where censorship is imposed. However, as subsequently noted, the constitutional right and ostensibly liberal publishing laws has not stopped extensive litigation, particularly slander suits, by politicians. For example, a cartoon depicting a person urinating was the basis for a lawsuit citing the cartoon as pornographic material. The existence of more restrictive press laws and their use to restrain journalists was certainly more prevalent under the reign of President Trudjman. For example, a law under the Trudjman regime made it a penal offense to criticize the president and five other members of the executive branch of government. This law has now been repealed, but the sentiment that it expressed is still prevalent under the existing government. As much of the judiciary is appointed by the government, it is generally agreed that the courts are more sympathetic to the plaintiff (in cases of newspapers being sued for libel). In general, the Croatian courts are more likely to consider libelous reporting as serious offenses, suits that in the European and American press would probably be considered trivial or without foundation and thrown out of court. In two of the decisions handed down in 2002, the daughter of a prominent politician was awarded 100,000 kunas (US$12,000.00) for suffering "mental anguish" after a journalist negatively criticized her sculpture, and the *Feral Tribune* was fined 50,000 deutschmarks for causing ''moral pain'' to a plaintiff in a 1994-1995 lawsuit. As a counter balance to the press laws, the Croatian Association of Journalists maintains a 10-member council that monitors journalists and may pass nonbonding judgments on their ethical behavior and their newspapers.

CENSORSHIP

There is no official government body that monitors the press and no official censorship. However, considering that there were some 10,000 cases pending against journalists before the courts in 2002, the court system serves as the major source for policing the media. If a journalist loses a case, imposed fines can be high (and journalists' private bank accounts have been raided to pay these fines). Because of their meager salaries, journalists have a large incentive to avoid the courts and thus self-censor. In addition, the fact that many official agencies are still government-owned and yet to be privatized has meant that journalists guard their official sources closely. The prevailing policy might be described as ''not biting the hand that feeds you.''

There are, nonetheless, a significant number of examples, both during the Trudjman era and after, in which the power of the press to influence public opinion and indeed to cause general outcry against perceived wrongs has been such that dramatic change has occurred. For example, the resignation of the former mayor of Zagreb was a direct result of the media's exposure of the fact that he left the scene of a car accident while intoxicated.

STATE-PRESS RELATIONS

The most significant feature of state and press relations is the paradigm change from pre-1990 when, under the socialist regime, the media was purely a tool to disseminate state and party information, to the post-2000 era when journalists are free to write what they wish. For the political elite this change is difficult to accept. As a result it is generally the political elite that become offended when even mildly criticized by European standards, and it is primarily they who have launched the large number of lawsuits alleging slander, defamation of character, and the like before courts in the early 2000s. The effect has been that the newspapers have been forced into lengthy, time-consuming and costly court battles to defend freedom of the press whereas the government has seen this as an effective way to stymie the press. Given the precarious financial state of some publications, it may ultimately have the effect of removing some small independent media voices. Acting as a counterforce to this government legal pressure are organizations such as the Organization on Security and Cooperation in Europe (OSCE) and International Research and Educational Exchange (IREX), whose responsibilities include the monitoring of government interference in the media and recommending legislative change to create greater freedom in the media.

ATTITUDE TOWARD FOREIGN MEDIA

The Croatian government is generally tolerant of foreign media. There are no special requirements for foreign journalists in Croatia, and certainly there have been no restrictions placed on journalists or foreign correspondents. This was not entirely true under Trudjman, who often railed against the foreign press, but since his death this kind of diatribe has ceased. It must be noted that the ever-widening connection to cable systems and satellite transmissions has made foreign reporting even more available, and CNN is now considered the de facto voice of the U.S. government voice in Croatia. Under the IREX program of USAID (U.S. Agency for International Development), widespread dissemination of cable systems has been provided, and the office closely monitors the various government policy and legislative measures that affect the provision and functioning of an independent media. It may serve as a measure of the dramatic change that has occurred in the media since the death of Trudjman to observe that U.S. assistance in the provision of an independent media has changed in the new millennium from a focus on training journalists in investigative reporting, media law, and avoidance of libel to one of business practices and financial management. In addition to the United States, the European Union's Council of Europe has sent a number of delegations to Zagreb to recommend changes to laws governing the media and in particular those laws that relate to changing the state-owned television and radio network into an independent public broadcasting system.

NEWS AGENCIES

There is one domestic news agency, the Croatian News Agency (HINA), that acts as the official government voice. It is generally considered reliable and all print and electronic media and correspondents both in Croatia and overseas use its releases. The usual companies represent foreign news agencies: Associated Press, Reuters, and Agence France-Presse. APAD, the Russian news agency, like a number of other agencies, covers Croatia from Belgrade. The government does not receive foreign news agency wires and hence news outside Croatia usually emanates from International News services.

BROADCAST MEDIA

As was previously noted, the state controls national television and radio. Three channels are broadcasted: one devoted to sports, the second to entertainment, and the third to news. An independent board supposedly guides the national network, but in fact programming directors and producers have significant autonomy and produce programming that is very pro-government in orientation. However, some liberalization has occurred during the early 2000s. For example, those critical of the government and who would not appear on television may now be seen and heard.

ELECTRONIC NEWS MEDIA

Like in many other nations, the Internet is only now becoming widely accessible owing to the falling cost and availability of computers and the ability of the telecommunications network to handle Internet traffic. Anecdotal reports suggest that approximately 10 percent of the population have personal computers, but there are 290,000 Internet users, mostly available at Croatians' employment sites; thus, there is increasing access to online news flow. During the Trudjman era, the Internet was a major medium for dissent and protest over curbs on the media, but the gradual liberalization of the media since 1999 has meant that the Internet is no longer primarily a protest vehicle.

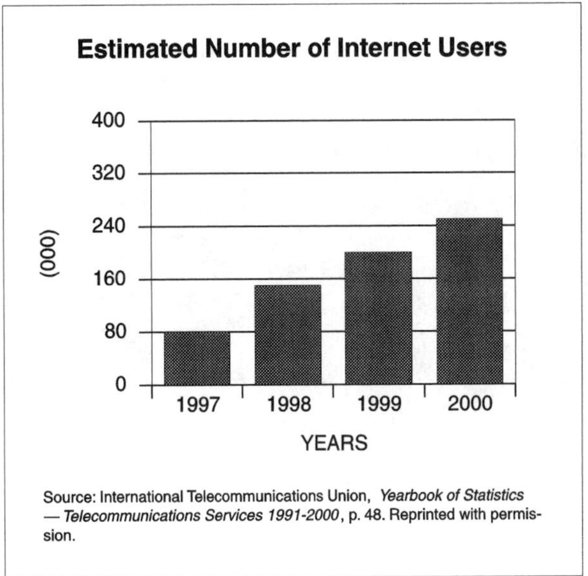

Source: International Telecommunications Union, *Yearbook of Statistics — Telecommunications Services 1991-2000*, p. 48. Reprinted with permission.

EDUCATION AND TRAINING

The only school of journalism in the country is at the University of Zagreb. The school graduates approximately 100 journalists each year, and there appears to be a strong market for graduates as most find employment in the numerous newspapers, magazines and electronic media. More prevalent is the situation where university graduates seeking employment are hired by someone they know in the media. The Croatian Association of Journalists upholds the status and stature of journalism in Croatia. It acts as an oversight body, a refuge against threats from outside, and as a representative body for journalists. The association has a yearly awards program that recognizes and promotes excellence in journalism.

In recognition of the difficulties Croatian print media had establishing independence during the Trudjman era, *The Feral Tribune* received a number of international awards from international press institutes for their pursuit of press freedom.

SUMMARY

In the last 10 years of the twentieth century the media in Croatia was placed in an invidious position. From 1992 to 1996 a "homeland defense war" was conducted against its neighbors Serbia and Bosnia-Herzegovina. The media was, of necessity, required to state its allegiances, and these positions were essentially set for the decade. It created a situation where growth of the fourth estate was stunted by the necessity to remain nationalistic and in some cases jingoistic in order to retain an audience and appease the government. Today there are still remnants of this overt nationalism. According to a survey by the Zagreb Civic Human Rights Commission, in 10 issues of *Slobodna Dalmacija* in 2001, hate speech appeared 75 times, was judged to incite violence, attacked individuals and institutions it judged enemies of the state, and was overly nationalistic and extreme in its orientation. Presenting a voice of opposition is still clearly difficult and fraught with danger. However, the opposition media did discover a role as unofficial opposition during the Balkan crisis, and upon the death of Trudjman the emergence of an independent free press was much easier to attain. In the early 2000s, that process is in place.

The prognosis for the development of an independent, vibrant media in Croatia appears promising. Like many European countries outside the European Union, the prospects for Croatia obtaining membership in the Union is highly dependent on the state of the government's relations with the media. In this regard, the pressure being exerted on the government by the European Union, and the positive reaction by the present government, in contrast to the Trudjman era, would appear to bode well for the media. The presence of the large number of outstanding litigation cases before the courts is not only a serious constraint to the development of the present media but also to the development of an independent media in the future, not only because of the legal issues involved but also because the motivation for such lawsuits is based on a fear or distrust of the media by the political elite. The value of and need for an independent media has yet to be realized by the powerful elite in Croatia. Journalists perceive that after the problems of the Trudjman era things are getting better, although many believe not enough has changed. They point out that eco-

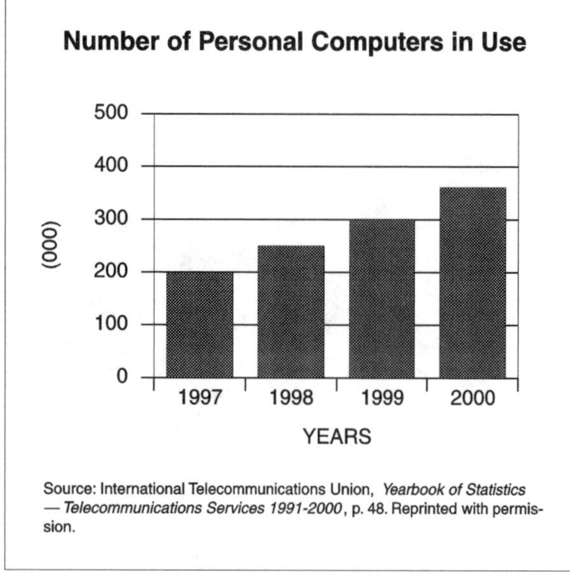

Source: International Telecommunications Union, *Yearbook of Statistics — Telecommunications Services 1991-2000*, p. 48. Reprinted with permission.

nomic independence is not the same as journalistic independence nor does economic openness guarantee press freedom. In essence they believe that they ''won the war but are still fighting the battles.'' The future will thus come down to whether the media recognize the role they have to play in public opinion formation, whether the government can learn to live with an independent media, realizing that the media will not go away, and whether the media can settle into a role of comment, reaction, and rethink instead of adversary, opposition, and foe.

SIGNIFICANT DATES

- 1992-1996: Balkan Conflict. President Trudjman attempts to control the media in efforts to bring about strong nationalism. Independent News media strongly criticizes the conduct of the war.
- 1999: President Franjo Trudjman dies.

BIBLIOGRAPHY

Croatia 2001 World Press Freedom Review. Available from http://freemedia.at/wpfr/croatia.htm.

''The Media in the Republic of Croatia: Facts and Information.'' Zagreb: State Publishing House, 1998.

''Report on Public Affairs and Media.'' Organization for the Security and Cooperation in Europe. Available from http://www.osce.org.

''Country Reports on Human Rights Practices 2001.'' U.S Department of State. Available from http://www.state.gov.

—Richard W. Benfield

CUBA

BASIC DATA

Official Country Name:	Republic of Cuba
Region (Map name):	North & Central America
Population:	11,184,023
Language(s):	Spanish
Literacy rate:	95.7%
Area:	110,860 sq km
Number of Television Stations:	58
Number of Television Sets:	2,640,000
Television Sets per 1,000:	236.1
Number of Radio Stations:	225
Number of Radio Receivers:	3,900,000
Radio Receivers per 1,000:	348.7
Number of Individuals with Computers:	120,000
Computers per 1,000:	10.7
Number of Individuals with Internet Access:	60,000
Internet Access per 1,000:	5.4

BACKGROUND & GENERAL CHARACTERISTICS

General Description The press situation in Cuba ranks as one of the most complicated in the world due to the political and physical distribution of the Cuban people. Since the victory of the Castro-led forces in 1959, a significant Cuban exile community has flourished in the United States, especially in South Florida. This offshore Cuban community has generated a significant volume of information during its decades of exile. Part of their output has been in English, designed for the audience in the United States, while the remainder has been in Spanish, aimed at consumption by the population of Cuba. Similarly, the press offerings on the island, including both the government-sponsored media and those of the opposition, have been divided between those aimed at domestic and international audiences.

The press situation in Cuba is one of the most restrictive in Latin America. Over the more than four decades since the accession of the Castro government, neither freedom of expression nor freedom of the press have existed on the island. The Castro regime maintains a monopoly on information throughout the nation, confiscating the property of independent media and maintaining a policy of constant repression.

The Nature of the Audience: Literacy, Affluence, Population Distribution, Language Distribution In 2001, the U.S. government estimated the population of Cuba at just over 11 million. Of these, 21 percent were aged 0-14, 69 percent were aged 15-64, and 10 percent were over age 65. The population was estimated to be growing at a rate of .37 percent annually. The ethnic mix of the nation includes 37 percent persons of European descent, 11 percent persons of African descent, and 51 percent people of mixed races. Despite its history of slavery, the significance of race is less of an issue in Cuban society than it is in the United States. Eighty-five percent of Cubans were nominally Roman Catholic prior to Castro coming into power. The remaining religiously identified Cubans included Protestants, Jehovah's Witnesses, Jews, and Santeria.

The government's figure for overall literacy is 95.7 percent of all persons aged 15 and older, although this figure is based on the unique Cuban definition of literacy. In 1961, the Castro-led government initiated a Literacy Campaign that claimed remarkable results, dropping the nation's illiteracy rate from nearly 40 percent to below 4 percent in a single year. In the years since the revolution, Cuban officials have consistently placed the nation's illiteracy rate at figures of three or four percent, a rate better than that in Switzerland. However, the Cuban definition does not conform to world standards for measuring literacy. In the Cuban model, the literacy rate describes the proportion of those persons between the ages of 14 and 44, whom the government believes capable of learning how to read, who could read and write according to a standardized Cuban test. In the early 1980s, when the Mariel boatlift refugees came into the United States, many of them were tested for literacy in Spanish by local school districts for the purpose of placement in the second language programs of American public schools. The results of these tests placed their literacy rate at more plausible levels of between 70 and 80 percent. These and other objective measures of Cuban literacy demonstrate that the efforts of the Cuban government to improve literacy have been effective, although not nearly as effective as Cuban propaganda and UNESCO sources would suggest.

Quality of Journalism: General Comments The state-employed journalists of Cuba are very literally the voice of the Cuban government. Because of the severe restrictions in content as well as in style that are placed upon these writers and editors, the work is described as "a very somber and unimaginative journalism" by Dr. José Alberto Hernández. Hernández, president of CubaNet, a nonprofit, nonpartisan organization based in the United States that works to foster press freedom in Cuba, points out that upon separation from the government-controlled media, an independent journalist, while achieving some freedom of expression, loses access to both ends of the journalistic process. Sources that were once openly available become utterly unapproachable to the independent. Likewise, publication proves elusive to the independent journalist. Therefore the choice for the Cuban journalist is between a dull and highly controlled career within the state-sponsored media or a precarious and difficult one outside of that media.

The most noticeable trait in journalism concerning Cuba is the omnipresent bias. On one side the bias is the pro-government slant found in the government-controlled press organs that flourish on the island and in the scattered press organs around the world that sympathize strongly enough with the Castro regime to overlook its cavalier treatment of press freedom. These press outlets serve effectively as apologists for all Cuban government activities and sounding boards for Cuban-based criticism of the West, especially the United States. However, the bias on the other side of the divide is equally severe. Given the difficulty of serving as an independent journalist inside Cuba, only those with powerful and typically anti-Castro agendas tend to endure the hardships associated with this career. Similarly, a huge amount of writing originating outside of Cuba flows from the exile community in South Florida, from the Radio Martí airwaves and from other anti-Castro activists.

Those who would serve as impartial observers face difficulties from both directions. The Cuban government, while extremely accommodating to those members of the foreign press who they perceive as representing the "reality of Cuba," provide virtually no real access to journalists whom they do not feel they can utilize. Political and bureaucratic opposition to objective coverage of Cuba for American journalists can make the endeavor seem not worth the effort.

Historical Traditions Cuban journalism traces its history to an early beginning during the Spanish colonial rule, with the first Cuban press put into operation by 1723. The history of the nation's press can be divided into five periods. The first period, the Colonial, reaches from the earliest days until 1868. The second period, the time of the Independence Revolution, spans the period from 1868 to 1902. A third period, the Republican period, runs from 1902 until the overthrow of the dictator Machado in 1930. The third period, the Batista era, lasts from

1930 until 1959. The final and current epoch of the Castro era runs from the triumph of the communist revolution in 1959 up to the present.

In comparison with Spanish colonies in other parts of the world, Cuba developed a printing press at a rather late date. However, compared to the rest of the Caribbean and Central America, the Cuban press came early. The nation's first newspaper, *Gazeta de la Habana,* began publication in 1782, followed in 1790 by the colony's first magazine, *Papel Periódico de la Habana.* These early publications and those that came into being over the following century operated under Spanish press laws that had been in place in Spanish America since the late sixteenth century. During the early years of the nineteenth century, Spanish regulations on the press became relaxed, partly due to the decreasing power of Madrid on its distant colonies and partly in response to the political currents flowing from the French Revolution.

The second phase of the Cuban press began in 1869 with the first war of independence, when the colonial government issued a press freedom decree with the aim of gaining favor from the reformist circles. In the months following this decree, a series of reform-minded periodicals began publication, of which the most important was *El Cubano Libre,* appearing on the war's first day. Other new periodicals included *Estrella Solitaria, El Mambi* and *El Boletín de la Guerra.*

In 1895, at the outset of the second war of independence, the most important newspaper of the reform party was *Patria,* which had been founded in 1892. Providing the spark that began *Patria* was José Martí, who had earlier written for a wide variety of newspapers and magazines, including *La Nación* of Buenos Aires and the *New York Sun.* Journalism provided Martí with his most direct, immediate, and constant form of expression. Martí, who served as the inspiration and organizer of the War of Independence in Cuba, saw newspaper essays as a key force in the development of modernism and the inspiration of his fellow revolutionaries as they struggled to free themselves from Spanish rule.

With the establishment of the Republic of Cuba on May 20, 1902, the history of the Cuban press entered its third period, which lasted until 1930 when the dictator Gerardo Machado was overthrown. During this period Cuban journalism enjoyed a time of prosperity in which at least a dozen dailies flourished in Havana. In the opinion of Jorge Martí, this large number arose due to the ease with which one could start a newspaper or magazine, the willingness of political parties to serve as sponsors, and an overall strong economy. Faced with increasing political opposition and an often-hostile press, in 1928 Machado attempted to co-opt the press by providing significant government subsidies to periodicals in exchange for support. This move prefigured the difficult times to follow.

Machado's fall began in 1930, brought about by earlier economic difficulties and aggravated by the 1933 political instability. With this, the golden days of Cuban journalism faded, brought to an end by the combination of labor unrest from within and the increased government attempts at control from without. The declining state of the Cuban press might have been much worse had it not been for the improvements brought by twentieth-century technological advances. The arrival of steam-powered printing presses and the increased commercial sophistication of the publishers served to expand the journalist's audience and prestige across the country. During this period, a succession of authoritarian regimes which culminated in that of Batista in 1952, exerted increasing control over the nation's press.

In 1959, with the victory of the Castro-led communists, the history of the Cuban press entered its current phase. This phase might be described as simply a continuation of the movement toward government domination and control of the press that began in 1930. The four decades following the Cuban revolution have been marked by very tight government authority over all press outlets. Although opposition has worked throughout this period to counter the government's propagandistic journalism program, only in the 1990s with the emergence of the Internet as a new medium has independent journalism began to pose a significant challenge to the government control of information.

Although often castigated by the Castro regime, the American press played a vital role in the establishment of an independent Cuba by leading the charge toward America's entry into a war with Spain. At the forefront of this effort stood two giants of American journalism, publishers William Randolph Hearst and Joseph Pulitzer. Both men saw in the conflict with Spain a rare opportunity for increased circulation of their newspapers. Correctly perceiving in the spirit of the day an increased patriotic sense, the two publishers directed their newspapers to publish sensational anti-Spanish stories. These stories were often illustrated graphically by some of the most gifted artists of the day, including Frederic Remington, and written by top quality writers such as Stephen Crane. Working in competition with each other, Hearst and Pulitzer ironically worked together in creating a war frenzy among the American people as they reported the alleged brutality of the Spanish toward the Cuban rebels. At the same time, the violent acts committed by the Cuban rebels were rarely mentioned in the papers' coverage. When the USS Maine exploded in Havana Harbor, the pro-war coverage instigated by Hearst and Pulitzer had sufficiently built national war sentiment that President McKinley felt it a political necessity to bow to pressure and enter into a war with Spain.

While the press under the Castro-led government from 1959 to the present has received significant criticism from world press organizations and advocates of a free and open press, it should not be forgotten that a history of free expression is not found in years before 1959. Where the Castro regime has used direct state control of media outlets since the 1960s, the previous governments exercised control of a privately owned media through frequent closures of newspapers and censorship. The nation's 1940 Constitution reacted against the censorship that had plagued the Cuban press since 1925, providing strong protections for the press and free expression. Despite these provisions, ensuing rulers returned to the censorship practices of their predecessors, effectively ignoring the law. Fulgencio Batista, who came to power in a coup on March 10, 1952 established very strong censorship during his nine years of leadership. Censorship under Batista was explained as a response to the threats posed by the rebel movement that would eventually unseat him. The Union of Cuban Journalists (UPEC), in discussing the issue of press freedom, asserted that ''press freedom only existed in the colonial and republican life of Cuba for the powerful ones and rulers.''

During the difficult economic times of the 1990s, significant problems afflicted the Cuban press as a result of the ongoing financial distress of the nation. Budgetary shortages brought about drastic consequences, including a 40 percent reduction in hours of radio and television programming and an 80 percent reduction in the budget of the print media.

Foreign Language Press Although many of the national press services in print, broadcast, and digital media are published with English-language counterparts aimed primarily at international consumption, no significant non-Spanish press exists on the island.

Leading Newspapers Three national periodicals circulate in Cuba. The newspaper with the largest circulation is *Granma,* which since its founding in 1965 has served as the official news organ of the Communist Party. The other two national publications are *Juventud Rebelde* and *Trabajadores.* Regional newspapers are published in each of the fourteen provinces of the island. Also, the nation boasts various cultural, scientific, technical, social science, and tourism magazines, which appear at various intervals.

The most important newspaper in Cuba is *Granma.* In 1998, *Editors and Publishers International Yearbook* placed the circulation of the daily at 675,000, which ranked it as the 88th most widely circulated newspaper in the world. The international reach of *Granma* expanded significantly with the advent of the Internet. The website *Digital Granma Internacional* brings much of the print edition's content to the web, presenting it in Spanish, English, French, Portuguese, and German. In all of its incarnations, the propaganda role of *Granma* is impossible to avoid. Typical front-page headlines include roughly equal numbers of stories vindicating and celebrating government policies and position along with frequent stories censuring the political leadership of the United States for perceived abuses. In both its print edition and Internet counterpart, this daily newspaper contains national and international news, cultural reporting, letters, sports, and special thematic features.

Juventud Rebelde, the nation's newspaper with the second highest circulation is, as all professionally produced publications on the island, controlled and created by the government. Under the editorial leadership of Rogelio Polanco Fuentes, the newspaper has maintained a focus on news about and for Cuban youth culture. In pursuing this aim, *Juventud* covers many of the same stories as the more adult-oriented *Granma.* Comparisons between the coverage of stories in these two leading newspapers show that the *Juventud* articles tend to be briefer, composed of shorter sentences, and drafted with a less challenging vocabulary. The daily runs a regular feature entitled ''Curiosidades,'' in which brief, peculiar news stories of the sort that the U.S.'s National Public Radio *Morning Edition* runs at half past the hour are related. *Juventud,* like its adult-oriented counterpart *Granma,* also covers cultural and sporting events but from a more youth-focused angle. The focus on popular music, nearly nonexistent in *Granma,* is a prominent example of this contrast. However, rather than pandering to a youth culture, *Juventud* actively works to indoctrinate the young people of Cuba into a belief system that serves the state's interests. The newspaper runs regular articles celebrating the heroes of the revolution and frames pieces in such a way as to encourage its young readers to identify with these heroes.

A prime example of the journalism of identification practiced by *Juventud Rebelde* can be seen in the ongoing coverage throughout late 2001 and 2002 of the incarceration within the United States of the so-called ''Cuban Five.'' Rene Gonzalez Sehwerert, Ramón Labanino Salazar, Fernando Gonzalez Llort, Antonio Guerrero Rodriguez, and Gerardo Hernandez Nordelo, were arrested in the United States on charges of espionage against South Florida military bases. The Cuban government and the five men themselves have claimed since their arrest in September 1998 and throughout their trial and imprisonment that they were merely attempting to monitor the activities of right-wing anti-Cuban groups in Florida. The five were convicted in June 2001. Since that time, the Cuban press has provided daily focus on these men, branding them the ''five innocents'' and portraying them, after September 11, 2001, as fighters against terrorism.

The differing coverage of this issue between *Granma* and *Juventud Rebelde* is illustrative of the audience differences between the two dailies. In *Granma*, the focus of the stories regarding these five prisoners has been in placing them into a larger context of both history and world politics. The five are compared favorably with Cuban heroes of old and their actions are portrayed within the context of a longer struggle against the imperialist forces of the United States. In *Juventud Rebelde*, the political and historical context is less important. Instead, readers are urged to identify with these young men. In fact, the young age of the prisoners is a regular focus in *Juventud*, despite the fact that, in their mid- to late thirties, most of these men are considerably older than the readership of this newspaper. *Juventud* also places much more emphasis on the families of the prisoners.

The third national publication in Cuba is *Trabajadores* (Workers), which is much more political and polemical than either *Granma* or *Juventud Rebelde*. As the official organ of the government-controlled national trade union, *Trabajadores* also is the most noticeably and consistently Marxist in orientation of the three.

ECONOMIC FRAMEWORK

All of the official media outlets on the island of Cuba are controlled by and almost exclusively funded by the government. The nominal subscription fees charged to Cuban nationals for the three major print media fail to cover the marginal production costs of the publication. Since the advertising carried within the newspapers is essentially all purchased by the state, the subsidies provided to cover the shortfall in the publications' budgets take the form of inter-agency transfer payments. Subscription rates for a weekly edition of *Granma Internacional* cost US$50 per year, again an amount insufficient to cover the cost of production. Broadcast media are similarly supported by government funds. The amount of the subsidies paid to the various press organs is not public knowledge.

The government controls some 70 percent of all farmland on the island as well as 90 percent of production industries. Although the government brings in considerable revenue from exports, especially sugar, Cuba's economy has been in deep difficulty since the early 1990s. Credits and subsidies from the Soviet Union totaled an estimated US$38 billion between the years 1961 and 1984. As much as US$4 billion was transferred from the Soviet coffers to those of Cuba during the late 1980s. The collapse of the Soviet bloc, which deprived Cuba of both its leading aid donor and trade partner, severely damaged the nation's economy. During the early 1990s the annual gross national product was about US$1,370 per capita. The annual government budget included approximately US$14.5 billion in expenditures, offset by only US$12.5 billion in revenues.

A journalist can earn a respectable income by Cuban standards; however, the salaries paid to all Cuban workers are problematic. Wages have not risen markedly over the 40 years since the revolution. In addition, wages paid in Cuban pesos are of questionable value as shortages of goods in the nation's stores leaves consumers with no use for their earnings. Since the peso is not a widely recognized currency, even those workers with access to external markets find themselves unable to participate.

The economic structure of the non-governmental press is even more difficult. Since the independent journalists working on the island are not able to sell their work in any form that could provide sufficient income for personal support, most of the independent journalists work out of a sense of devotion to their profession rather than for hope of material gain. Those independents who do sell their work to paying markets abroad run the risk of imprisonment.

The anti-Castro press/propaganda structure centered in South Florida, while carrying advertisements, is largely a political construct. Advertisers support these media not because of the benefit that the advertisement promises to their businesses but because of their devotion to the anti-Castro cause.

PRESS LAWS

Constitutional Provisions & Guarantees Relating to Media Article 53 of the 1976 Cuban constitution recognizes freedom of both expression and the press, but subordinates and limits those freedoms to the ''ends of the socialist society.'' Constitutional Article 62 limits press freedoms further, and Article 5 grants to the Communist Party on behalf of the society and the state the duty to organize and control all of the resources for communication in order to realize the benefit of state.

Summary of Press Laws in Force There is no formal press law in Cuba, and aside from the vague statements in the constitution, press freedom is not guaranteed legally. The Communist Party, according to a resolution approved by the first party congress in 1975, regulates the role and function of the press. In 1997, the state passed Resolution Number 44/97, which regulated the activities of the foreign press. In the stipulations of this resolution there was established a Center of International Press to provide oversight to foreign journalists. This resolution, composed of three chapters and 26 articles, established that no foreign press agency could contract directly with a Cuban journalist to serve as a correspondent without the permission of the state. Law 80, approved in December 1997 under the title of the ''Law of Reaffirmation of National Dignity and Sovereignty,'' stipulates in Article 8 that no journalist may in any way, directly or indirectly, collaborate with the journalists of the enemy. The 1999 Law 88, called the ''Law of Protection of National Independence and the Economy of Cuba'' provides more specific limits to the rights of free expression and the press with the nation in the law's Article 7. Part of this act provides a prison term of up to 15 years to anyone that directly or indirectly provides information to the United States, its dependents or agents, in order to facilitate the objectives of the U.S. Helms-Burton Act. The law also prescribes an eight-year prison term to those who reproduce or distribute material deemed to be subversive propaganda from the U.S. government. Specifically, the law forbids collaboration ''in any way with foreign radio or television stations, newspapers, magazines or other mass media with the purpose of . . . destabilizing the country and destroying the socialist state.'' Other provisions of the law create further penalties for press activities considered detrimental to the state or the communist party or beneficial to the nation's enemies.

At the passage of Law 88, the communist youth daily *Juventud Rebelde* ran stories that demonstrated the government's propaganda position. ''Independent journalists are mercenaries: The [U.S.] Empire pays, organizes, teaches, trains, arms and camouflages them and orders them to shoot at their own people,'' they wrote. Castro, in public speeches, denounced the independent journalists, branding them as counterrevolutionaries. The government has long claimed that the independent journalists receive considerable funding from anti-Castro forces, especially those in the large Cuban exile community in Miami. Naturally, the independent journalists deny such charges.

CENSORSHIP

In Cuba, no law exists that either establishes or prohibits censorship. The role of censor is carried out by the Department of Revolutionary Orientation, which answers to the Ideology Secretary of the Political Bureau of the Communist Party. This department was created in the mid-1960s, first bearing the name of Commission of Revolutionary Orientation, and was charged with creating propaganda and propagating the government ideology. The department is also responsible for the design and creation of all official political communications.

Independent Press The most pressing issue related to censorship in any study of the Cuban press is the treatment by the authorities of those who attempt to create an independent press. In the late twentieth century, as the number of these independent reporters mushroomed, the reaction of the government was forceful. The policy of official repression, which had been allowed to relax in previous years, returned powerfully in the 1990s. The government's actions included imprisonment, physical violence, and house arrest.

Only those journalists that are members of the state-controlled UPEC are allowed accreditation to practice their trade in Cuba. UPEC does not function in the manner of a press organization in a free country but instead serves as an extension of the government, assisting in their control and prior approval of the information allowed in the press. A 1997 Communist Party publication stated overtly that UPEC serves as an ideological organ of the party and that they are charged with spreading the thoughts of the revolution. Not all journalists belong to UPEC, however. In reality various independent organizations exist, though banned by the government. These groups are typically formed by dissident and opposition journalists, indisposed to undergo the control of the government. In many cases the government has removed accreditation from journalists involved with these unofficial groups.

STATE-PRESS RELATIONS

The Committee to Protect Journalists (CPJ) has, since the early 1990s, included Fidel Castro on its annual ''Ten Worst Enemies of the Press'' list, a distinction that he shares with such regulars as Ayatollah Ali Khamenei of Iran, President Jiang Zemin of China and Prime Minister Mahathir Mohamad of Malaysia. In 2002, the CPJ named Cuba as one of the 10 worst places in the world to be a journalist, noting that ''The Cuban government is determined to crush independent journalism on the island but has not yet succeeded. . . .'' Journalists are constantly followed, harassed, intimidated, and sometimes jailed.

In early 2002, the CPJ noted with approval the recent release from prison of two journalists, but lamented the continued detention of Bernardo Arévalo Padrón, jailed since 1997. Arévalo is serving a six-year sentence imposed for ''disrespecting'' President Fidel Castro. The exact nature of Arévalo's offense was to refer to Castro as a ''liar'' when the president failed to enact democratic reforms that he had promised. Previously, the journalist had garnered ill will from the government when he made public the members of the Communist Central Committee who appropriated cattle for their own use at a time of food shortage. As of August 2002, he held the distinction as the lone journalist in the Americas behind bars for his work.

While some independent journalists find outlets in America and Europe in both Spanish and English language venues, others attempt to publish as best they can in Cuba itself. One such independent publisher, Adolfo Fernandez, creates his own quarterly newsletter with a production run of roughly 1,000 on a photocopier. He then passes these newsletters out to friends and acquaintances. Fernandez admits to withholding some criticism in his stories, preferring to moderate his tone and avoid government clampdowns. Fernandez also gets his message off of the island through radio communications and occasional offshore publication. He has taken on the role of a watchdog over the two most important government publications, *Granma* and *Juventud Rebelde*. Fernandez is typical of the independent journalists, many of whom formerly worked within the government information apparatus and who found the censorship and propaganda that rule those outlets unbearable.

The police in Cuba perpetuate violence and harassment against the independent press operatives. Their actions include constant surveillance, late-night visits, and the confiscation of the tools of their trade. Another favorite method of the revolutionary government is to make an accusation of injury or slander against the independent journalists, as in the case of Bernardo Arévalo Padrón.

The Right to Criticize Government: Theory & Practice Reporters who work outside the state-sanctioned press system are forced to meet informally, often in the homes of individuals, to discuss ideas and utilize fax and telephone services to convey uncensored articles to editors of Spanish-language newspapers, radio and Internet news services located across Europe and the United States.

These journalists complain of abuse and persecution at the hands of the authorities. In some cases the telephone company cuts off service to homes from which these independent journalists work, and the police routinely maintain surveillance on these buildings and the reporters. Journalists report that relatives have been deprived of jobs in state-run businesses and that they are followed by the agents of the Committees for the Defense of the Revolution. Another frequent complaint is that the police routinely place these reporters under house arrest in response to events featuring the political opposition. Another tactic involves rounding up opposition reporters and driving them into remote parts of the country in order to keep them out of circulation temporarily. According to the French group *Reporters sans Frontières,* in 2001 a total of 19 of these harassed Cuban journalists chose to continue their work from exile rather than submitting to the continued persecution.

Although harassment of both low and high intensity has greeted opposition journalists throughout the years of the Castro regime, the government has not succeeded in stemming the flow of reporting from risk-taking reporters working throughout the island. Instead, the latter half of the 1990s saw an explosion in this activity. As recently as 1995, these journalists amounted to some twenty individuals working for five separate organizations. Estimates in 2002 placed the number of unofficial news agencies currently operating from within the island's shores at around twenty, representing a staff of some 100 journalists.

While some of this increase in numbers of opposition reporters might be attributed to the end of the Cold War and an increasing sense that the Castro government is nearing its twilight, it must not be ignored that the government itself, notwithstanding its continued harassment, has become more open to the idea of an independent press system. In May 2001, a group of 40 journalists banded together to effect the formation of the first independent association for journalists recognized under the Castro government. They were spearheaded by Raul Rivero, the former Moscow correspondent for *Prensa Latina*, the Cuban government's official news agency.

In 2001, three journalists were released from prison. Jesús Joel Díaz Hernández, the executive director of *Cooperativa Avileña de Periodistas Independientes,* obtained his release after serving two years of a four year sentence for ''dangerousness.'' No explanation accompanied his release, except the warning that he could be jailed again if he returned to work as an independent journalist. Díaz Hernández, arrested on January 18, 1999, in the central province of Ciego de Avila, was sentenced the next day to a four-year prison term. The charge against Hernández was that he had six times been warned about ''dangerousness.'' The second released journalist, Manuel Antonio González Castellanos, who served as correspondent for the independent news agency Cuba Press, obtained his release in February 2001. His October 1998 arrest had been based upon charges of insulting Castro while being detained by state security agents. The final freed reporter was José Orlando González Bridón, who had been imprisoned since December 2000 serving a two-year term for ''false information'' and ''enemy propaganda.''

González Bridón, the head of the small opposition group the Cuban Democratic Workers' Confederation, was the first opposition journalist to receive a prison sentence arising from an Internet publication. Writing since the fall of 1999 for the Miami-based Cuba Free Press, Bridón's arrest followed an August 5, 2000 article that alleged police negligence in the death of an activist killed by her ex-husband. The trial, held in a single day and not open to the public, ended with a guilty verdict and a two-year sentence, although the prosecution had only requested a one-year sentence.

Throughout the year 2001, state security agents continually harassed independent journalists and their families. In January, Antonio Femenías and Roberto Valdivia, both of whom worked for the independent news organization Patria, were detained and interrogated for three hours by state security agents after they met with two

Czech nationals. The Czech representatives, accused of holding ''subversive talks'' and conveying ''resources'' to dissidents, were detained for nearly a month, a move that worsened already strained relations between Cuba and the Czech Republic.

One of Cuba's most widely known dissident journalists, Raúl Rivero, has for many years served as the unofficial leader of the nation's independent press movement. Throughout that time, Rivero has faced constant harassment from the Castro government and its security agency. Born in 1945, Rivero graduated from Havana University's School of Journalism in the early 1960s as one of the first in a group of journalists to be trained after the 1959 revolution. In 1966 he co-founded the satirical magazine *Caián Barbudo* and from 1973 until 1976 he served as the Moscow correspondent for the government news agency, *Prensa Latina.* In 1976, Rivero returned to Cuba to assume leadership of the *Prensa Latina* science and culture desk, a post that he held until his break with the agency in 1988. In 1989, Rivero resigned from the government's National Union of Cuban Writers and sealed his status as an opposition leader in 1991 when he became one of ten journalists, and the only one to remain in Cuba, who signed the *Carta de los Intelectuales* (Intellectuals' Letter), which called for the government to free all prisoners of conscience. The same year, Rivero declared official journalism to be a ''fiction about a country that does not exist.''

Since 1995 Rivero has headed CubaPress, one of the nation's leading independent news agencies. Viewed as a dissident for his independent work, Rivero, like all independent journalists, is prohibited from publishing on the island. His only outlets for publication are on the Internet and abroad, although in publishing internationally he runs the risk of a jail term for disseminating ''enemy propaganda.'' He has been notified that while he is free to leave Cuba, his re-entry to the country will be denied. Rivero's celebrated February 1999 article, ''Journalism Belongs to Us All,'' reflected on the efforts of Cuban journalists attempting to freely report the news from that nation. In this article he proclaims that no law can make him feel like a criminal for reporting the truth about his homeland. ''I am merely a man who writes,'' he asserts. ''One who writes in the country where I was born.''

ATTITUDE TOWARD FOREIGN MEDIA

The relationship between the Castro government and the foreign press has long been troubled as the government attempts to provide some access to foreign news organizations in order to serve their own ends while also attempting to effect control of the material flowing out of the country. A constant refrain in the speeches of the president is the unfair and negative tone so often evident in foreign accounts of Cuba. British journalist Pascal Fletcher, Reuter's news agency correspondent assigned to Cuba, has received especially severe attacks in the government-controlled press. In January 2001, *Granma* described Fletcher as being ''full of venom against the Cuban revolution,'' while a television program aired three days later complained of the journalist's ''provocative, tendentious and perfidious attitude.''

President Castro, in a televised speech broadcast on January 17 and 18, 2001, complained of the foreign press and described their stance as ''completely unobjective.'' While not mentioning any media or journalists in particular, he struck out at journalists ''who dedicate themselves to defaming the revolution'' or who ''transmit not only lies, but gross insults against the revolution and against myself in particular.'' In the speech, Castro threatened to cancel the operating permits of foreign media, noting that it would be effective to remove permission to report from Cuba from an agency instead of simply deporting a single reporter.

Foreign journalists also suffer from the repressive actions of the Cuban government. In August 2000, three Swedish reporters were detained, ostensibly for immigration violations, after having conducted interviews with various independent journalists.

Foreign Propaganda & its Impact on Domestic Media

The most significant foreign broadcast presence in Cuba comes through the expense and effort of the United States government and their Radio Martí and TV Martí programs. In 1985, Ronald Reagan signed the Radio Broadcasting to Cuba Act, which established a nine-member advisory board to oversee the expansion of Voice of America services to include specifically Cuban broadcasts. The administrators of this service describe themselves as follows: ''The Office of Cuba Broadcasting (OCB) was established in 1990 to oversee all programming broadcast to Cuba on the Voice of America's Radio and TV Martí. In keeping with the principles of the Voice of America Charter, both stations broadcast accurate and objective news and information on issues of interest to the people of Cuba.''

Radio Martí initiated programming from studios in Washington, D.C. in May 1985. Their programming runs seven days a week and twenty-four hours a day over AM and short-wave frequencies. The broadcast schedule includes news, news analysis, and music programming. Roughly half of the Radio Martí broadcast day is composed of news-related programs. Besides traditional news coverage, the broadcasts include live interviews and discussions with experts and correspondents around the world. The station also carries live coverage of congressional hearings of import to Cuba as well as speeches by

Latin American leaders. The fiscal year 1998 budget for Radio Martí was US$13.9 million. According to the OCB, Cuban arrivals in the United States indicate that Radio Martí is the most popular of Cuban radio stations, although the Cuban government goes to great expense and effort to jam the broadcasts. In 2002, in response to increasingly effective Cuban efforts to jam the Radio Martí signals, the broadcaster requested that the government of Belize allow them to use the transmitters located in that country, which were already used to broadcast Voice of America programming throughout Central America, for Cuban transmissions. The government of Belize declined this request, attempting to avoid involvement in worsening U.S.-Cuban relations. Radio Martí transmits over the air and also provides a streaming audio version of both their live programming and periodic news reports over the Internet.

Television Martí joined its radio counterpart on March 27, 1990. The programming for TV Martí originates from studios in Miami and is then transmitted to the Florida Keys via satellite. The antenna and transmitter for the station are mounted onto a balloon that is tethered 10,000 feet above Cudjoe Key, Florida. Cuban government jamming of the TV Martí signal has proven far more successful than the radio-jamming efforts, partly due to the highly directional broadcast signal used to target the broadcast into the Havana area. Because of this jamming, the signal is randomly moved to regions east and west of the capital in order to reach Cuban televisions without jamming.

News Agencies

The main internal Cuban news agency is AIN, *Agencia Cubana de Noticias* (Cuban News Agency). Founded in May 1974, AIN operates from Havana under the direction of Esteban Ramírez Alonso. As a key organ in the promulgation of government information, AIN predictably carries key stories that support government policies and reinforce the regime's interpretation of world affairs. For example, in the aftermath of the terrorist attacks of September 11, 2001, AIN condemned the actions of Al Qaeda but spent considerably more time castigating the United States for its responses in Afghanistan and elsewhere. However, not all AIN coverage can be dismissed as propaganda. Presented in both English and Spanish, the news stories on any given day include speeches and comments by Castro and coverage of world events from a pro-government point of view, as well as less politically charged stories regarding scientific advances, cultural events, and other ordinary stories.

The Cuban government also supports and controls *Prensa Latina* (Latin Press), which they refer to as a Latin American Press Information Agency. While attempting to appear in the guise of an Associated Press-style news agency, the propaganda function of this service is apparent to any attentive observer. Describing themselves as the "Premier News Agency in the Republic of Cuba," *Prensa Latina* provides a daily news service including synthesis of materials regarding Cuba; a daily section containing the principal Cuban news stories; a Cuban economic bulletin (in Spanish and English); and a summary of vital Cuban economic, commercial, and financial news. They also publish a daily English-language "Cuba News in Brief," and the English-language "Cuba Direct," which provide translations of articles regarding Cuban news, politics, sports, culture, and art. Other occasional features include tourism news, medical news, women's issues, and coverage of Cuban and Caribbean science and medicine.

While a number of news organizations from the United States, including CNN, the Associated Press, the *Chicago Tribune* and the *Dallas Morning News* maintain permanent bureaus in Havana, foreign reporters visiting the nation are frequently harassed, threatened or even expelled.

Broadcast Media

The government maintains 5 national and 65 regional radio broadcast stations along with the international service of *Radio Habana Cuba*. Along with the radio services, the government supports 2 national and 11 regional television stations. The most important of these is *Cubavisión*, which is tightly controlled by the government. In September 2001, the government announced the establishment of a third television channel dedicated to educational and cultural programming at a cost of $3.7 million. In 1998, the nation supported 225 radio broadcast stations, 169 AM, 55 FM, and 1 short-wave. Four Internet Service Providers were in operation in 2001, although access to Internet services remained closely restricted.

A 1997 estimate set the number of radio receivers in the nation at 3.9 million, or roughly one for every three persons. The number of television sets stood at 2.6 million, or one for every four persons.

The most significant domestic television news provider in Cuba is *Cubavisión Internacional.* Like virtually all of the media outlets on the island, *Cubavisión Internacional* is controlled completely by the government.

A recent addition to the services offered by *Cubavisión* is a streaming Internet feed, *TV en Vivo,* through which the current programming on the network is available internationally. Again, in view of the tiny proportion of Cubans who possess any Internet service whatsoever (roughly half of one percent in 2000), this service must be considered as an offering for those in other parts of the world and not for the inhabitants of the island. In 2002, the broadcast day on *Televisión Cubana* ran from 6:30 a.m. until 6:00 p.m. A 90-minute, light news program began the day. A one-hour news show and several brief news updates provided the main news coverage. Typical news coverage included political and economic coverage, stories on science, culture, society, and sports. The network also broadcast more developed special reports, some of which were considered to be propaganda pieces.

Despite the government control of the television news, the voice projected is not a completely monolithic one. One popular segment of the news is *Preguntas y Respuestas* (Questions and Answers) in which listeners are allowed to pose a question for the reporters to answer. The network's web site provides a feedback option as well, allowing a newsgroup-style threaded discussion of selected topics. Both of these features, while allowing a certain amount of openness, either demonstrate a lack of true dissent or are censored before they appear publicly.

CHtv represents itself as the channel of the capital, focusing its news broadcasts on the local news of Havana. CHtv has been serving Havana since 1991, and presents a two-hour-per day news program six days a week.

The other television outlet in Cuba is *Telecristal*, broadcasting from Holguín. The first broadcast from *Telecristal* was transmitted in December 1976. Along with running news broadcasts from the central government, *Telecristal*'s reporters provide periodic regional news and generally benign editorial comments.

Electronic News Media

Only 60,000 Cubans had access to the Internet in 2000, a figure that represented one-half of one percent of the population. At the center of the Cuban Internet presence is CubaWeb (www.cubaweb.cu), a large directory of government and government-controlled web sites. The main CubaWeb site appears in both Spanish and English versions and many of the subsidiary sites are available in languages beyond Spanish, suggesting that the target audience for the site is not on the island where Spanish is the primary language. Aside from links to news stories, CubaWeb provides links to media organizations, political and government entities, technology providers, cultural and arts organizations, non-governmental organizations, tourism bureaus, business groups, and health care providers.

While access to email and the Internet is not permitted to the independent press, the Cuban government maintains more than 300 websites dedicated to the press and official institutions. The government's monopolistic control of the Internet has become extreme. For more than a year, journalist and writer Amir Valle edited an online periodical about Cuban literature titled "Letras de Cuba." Although Valle was not collaborating with foreign journalists and had demonstrated no political dissent, his site was suddenly suspended because, according to the authorities, no independent publications were allowed.

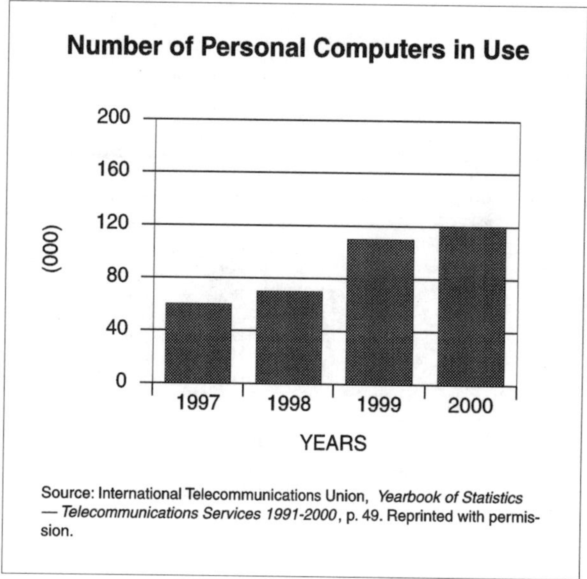

Source: International Telecommunications Union, *Yearbook of Statistics — Telecommunications Services 1991-2000*, p. 49. Reprinted with permission.

Although the severely curtailed press freedom for non-government-affiliated media makes the printing of independent newspapers virtually impossible, the Internet has allowed an expanded voice for the independent press voices of the nation. The most prominent web-based newspaper in operation currently is *La Nueva Cuba*, which has been in operation since 1997. Under the guidance of Director General Alex Picarq, *La Nueva Cuba* provides coverage of international and national news, culture and economic events, sports, and editorials. The editorial slant of the publication, both on its opinion page and in its reporting, is decidedly anti-Castro, the content proving to be as far toward propaganda for the opposition as is the content of *Granma* for the government. While the web site lists addresses for correspondents in New York, Madrid, and Rome, no addresses are found referring to Havana or elsewhere on the island. In fact, on close examination, *La Nueva Cuba* proves far more oriented to the expatriate population of South Florida than to the inhabitants of the island. The advertisements on the site, mostly for businesses from the United States, suggest a mainland audience. Given the fact that a very small percentage of Cubans enjoy access to the Internet and that those who do are overwhelmingly affiliated with the government, the penetration of the content of this site to the population may be slight.

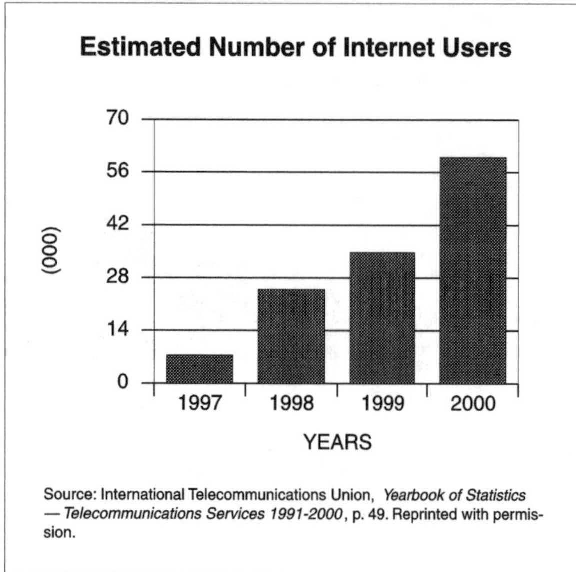

Source: International Telecommunications Union, *Yearbook of Statistics — Telecommunications Services 1991-2000*, p. 49. Reprinted with permission.

EDUCATION & TRAINING

Review of Education in Journalism: Degrees Granted The leading journalism school in Cuba is the University of Havana. The typical journalism student there will earn a bachelor's degree in communication specializing in journalism. The bachelor's degree is a five-year course of study that includes a wide range of courses drawn from the sciences, social sciences, and humanities as well as more traditionally journalistic studies. The degree also requires six semesters of English. Students may elect courses in new media, photojournalism, and other specialties in addition to their required studies. After completion of a bachelor's degree, the journalism student may proceed to a master of science degree in communications, a program that begins in January of each year and generally requires two and a half years of study. Two of the three specializations offered for the master of science degree are related to journalism. Students may specialize in journalism, public relations, or communications science.

Similar undergraduate degrees are offered at most of the regional universities throughout the island. Graduate studies in journalism are available at the University of Holguín and the University of the Orient in Santiago.

In 1996, the Jose Martí International Institute of Journalism, founded in 1983 by the UPEC, resumed operations after a brief hiatus. Officially this interruption of services came as the result of "an obligatory recess brought on by the current economic difficulty in Cuba." The institute fashions itself as an "Institute of the South" and attempts to foster the continued education of Cuban journalists as well as allowing them to interact with their peers in other countries. The institute offers a variety of workshops, seminars, training programs, and other courses of a postgraduate as well as adult education nature. They also fund a selection of research projects concerning social communication on the national and international levels.

Journalistic Awards & Prizes The highest award in journalism given in Cuba is the "José Martí National Award of Journalism." Established in 1987 by the UPEC, the Martí Award is granted in honor of a lifetime body of work. The first award was made in 1991. In 1999, in honor of the seventh UPEC Congress, 15 journalists were given the award.

In 1989, the UPEC established an award recognizing exceptional work over a year of journalism. This award is named in honor of Juan Gualberto Gómez, an exceptional nineteenth-century Cuban journalist. Each year, Gómez awards are granted in four categories: print journalism, radio, television, and graphic design.

A third award, the Félix Elmuza Distinction, is also granted to journalists, both domestic and foreign, who have earned renown through one or more of several avenues. Among the merits warranting the Elmuza Distinction are a career of 15 or more years of meritorious service, exceptional contributions to journalism, promotion of journalistic collegiality, foreign journalistic work that "reflects the reality of Cuba," or establishment of goodwill between the press and government or society.

Major Journalistic Associations & Organizations The Unión de Periodistas de Cuba (Union of Cuban Journalists) serves as the journalists' professional organization for anyone who wishes to work in the recognized media in Cuba. Formed on July 15, 1963 from several pre-revolution organizations, UPEC is ostensibly a non-governmental organization, although membership in this union is required for professional employment in the government-controlled media and the organization's direction is in line with government policies.

In their own documents, the UPEC states its primary obligations as the assistance of journalists in the "legal and ethical exercise of the profession," in achieving the proper access to sources, and in the general support of reporting. The organization also describes itself as being charged with "contributing to the formation of journalists in the best traditions in Cuban political thought, and in the high patriotic, ethical and democratic principles that inspire the Cuban society." The reader can see how such objectives can be read to support the government.

The UPEC code of ethics contains many statements that would seem familiar to journalists in other parts of the world. Reporters are charged with the protection of sources and with the obligation to go to multiple sources in order to ensure an accurate report. Reporters are also said to have a right to access all information of public utility. What constitutes useful information, however, is not defined. Most problematic among the ethics code provisions is Article 12, which states that ''The journalist has the duty of following the editorial line and informative politics of the press organ in which he works.'' Since all of the press organs represented have their editorial lines prescribed by the government, this article essentially dictates that all reporters must follow the government line. The ethics code provides disciplinary sanctions for violations ranging from private admonishment to expulsion from the organization and, hence, the profession.

SUMMARY

Conclusions Cuban media speaks in several voices, yet this polyphony is different than in most countries. Rather than supporting an array of media outlets that span a spectrum of viewpoints, Cuba possesses a large, relatively well-funded, and monolithic state-controlled media engine paired with a small and struggling independent press. Added to these two voices are the propaganda efforts of expatriate Cubans publishing from abroad and targeting both Cuban and international audiences. Finally, the government adds an international voice as it directs a great deal of its news output toward an international audience. This cluster of voices makes a full understanding of the Cuban media more complex than it might seem on the surface.

Trends & Prospects for the Media: Outlook for the Twenty-first Century The 1990s were a difficult period for Cuba. After the collapse of the Soviet Union, Cuba lost the considerable subsidies that flowed into the nation each year. The ensuing economic hardships are only lessening 10 years after they began. Just as the first 30 years of the Cuban revolution's history cannot be separated from the Superpower relations of the Cold War, the history of the 1990s and any future events cannot be separated from Cuban relations with the United States. The continuation of the American economic boycott effectively caps the potential for Cuba's economic prosperity. Without economic dealings with the United States, it is hard to imagine the future holding a great deal of promise for Cuban journalists. Recent years have seen budgetary cutbacks expressed in reduced sizes of newspapers and a reduction in the broadcast hours of radio and television. Continued economic privation would promise more of this sort of contraction.

Just as important over the last decade has been the development of the Internet and its consequent opening of potential modes of publication for dissident journalists. As personal publishing power expands through the spread of the Internet and other media, one can expect an increase in the number and effectiveness of independent journalists in Cuba. How the government will react to such an increase, however, is not at all certain. In recent years, the Castro government has shown no interest in relaxing their stranglehold on information. While it is conceivable that the government will relax their restrictions in the face of public pressure, it is just as likely that they will redouble their efforts toward maintaining control and increase the level of harassment directed at the independent press.

Perhaps the single most important issue for the future of the Cuban media is found in Fidel Castro. After more than four decades in control of the nation, it is difficult to envision a Cuba without Castro. In the spring of 2002, former U.S. President Jimmy Carter visited Cuba and encouraged a relaxation of tensions and the policies of both nations. The Bush administration has demonstrated no interest in pursuing such a relaxation, leaving Castro isolated but in firm control.

SIGNIFICANT DATES

- 1990: Economic subsidies from the Soviet Union valued at US$4 to US$6 billion annually are ended, plunging Cuba into a lengthy recession.
- 1997: The government sentences Bernardo Arévalo Padrón, founder of the independent news agency *Linea Sur Press,* to a sentence of six years for insulting President Fidel Castro and Vice President Carols Lage.
- 1997: Resolution 44/97 is passed, establishing the Center for International Press, a government-controlled group tasked with providing oversight and direction to foreign journalists.
- 1997: Law 80, the ''Law of Reaffirmation of National Dignity and Sovereignty,'' is passed, making journalistic collaboration with ''the enemy'' a criminal offense.
- 1999: Law 88, the ''Law of Protection of National Independence and the Economy of Cuba,'' creates a wide range of penalties for journalistic activities deemed to be contrary to the benefit of the state.
- 1999: Six-year-old Elian Gonzalez is rescued after his mother's death as they, along with others, attempt to raft to the United States. A heated legal and journalistic battle rages for months before the boy is returned to his father in Cuba in April 2000.
- 2000: Three Swedish journalists are detained briefly after interviewing independent journalists.
- 2000: 3,000 Cubans seek to escape Cuba on homemade rafts and boats. The United States Coast Guard intercepts roughly 35 percent of these.

BIBLIOGRAPHY

Anuario Estadístico de Cuba. Havana, published annually.

CubaWeb: Cuban Directory. Available from http://www.cubaweb.cu.

Elliston, Jon. *Psywar on Cuba: The Declassified History of U.S. Anti-Castro Propaganda.* Melbourne: Ocean Press, 1999.

Franklin, Jane. *Cuba and the United States: A Chronological History.* Melbourne: Ocean Press, 1997.

Latin American Network Information Center (LANIC). Available from http://info.lanic.utexas.edu/.

Lent, John A. ''Cuban Mass Media After 25 Years of Revolution''. *Journalism Quarterly.* Columbia, SC: AEJMC, 1999.

Perez-Stable. *The Cuban Revolution: Origins, Course, and Legacy.* New York: Oxford University Press, 1993.

Salwen, Michael B. *Radio and Television in Cuba: The Pre-Castro Era.* Ames, IA: Iowa State University Press, 1994.

—Mark Browning

CYPRUS

BASIC DATA

Official Country Name:	Republic of Cyprus
Region (Map name):	Middle East
Population:	762,887
Language(s):	Greek, Turkish, English
Literacy rate:	94.0%
Area:	9,240 sq km
Number of Daily Newspapers:	8
Total Circulation:	46,000
Circulation per 1,000:	94
Number of Nondaily Newspapers:	10
Total Circulation:	43,000
Circulation per 1,000:	88
Total Newspaper Ad Receipts:	7.6 (Cypriot Pound millions)
As % of All Ad Expenditures:	9.40
Number of Television Stations:	8
Number of Television Sets:	300,300
Television Sets per 1,000:	393.6
Number of Radio Stations:	90
Number of Radio Receivers:	366,450
Radio Receivers per 1,000:	480.3
Number of Individuals with Computers:	150,000
Computers per 1,000:	196.6
Number of Individuals with Internet Access:	120,000
Internet Access per 1,000:	157.3

BACKGROUND & GENERAL CHARACTERISTICS

The dual media systems on the island of Cyprus, situated south of Turkey, reflect the contentious ethnic divisions between its Greek and Turk constituencies. The press situation is active and politically driven, in a nation with a high rate of literacy. Political divisiveness fosters an immediate, practical interest in competing ideologies and in organs reflecting those views. Much press activity is colored by the political agendas of the sponsors. By mid-2002, no political settlement to effect national unity had been reached.

The independent Republic of Cyprus (*Dimokratia Kyprou*—Greek; *Kibris Cumhuriyeti*—Turkish) was established in 1960 and joined the Commonwealth in 1961. Effective partition came in 1974, when a Greek-led initiative triggered intervention by Turkey. By 1983, the independent Turkish Republic of Northern Cyprus (Kuzey Kibris Tÿrk Cumhuriyeti, TRNC) was established. Though formal recognition has come only from Turkey, the United Nations and the United States have acknowledged official spokesmen of the Turkish Cypriots.

Since 1974, the Greek majority has controlled the southern sector, with more than half the land mass, and over three-quarters of the population, and a preponderance of the wealth. Some 200,000 Greek Cypriots found refuge in the south after 1974, evacuating their former homes in the north. The Turkish minority commands the rest of the island. The centrally located capital, Nicosia (renamed Lefkosia by Greeks in 1995), sits astride the east-west dividing line, and in 1996 had a population of some 211,000 Greeks and 40,000 Turks in its two respective sectors.

Greek-dominated cities in southern Cyprus include Limassol (population in 2000: 162,000), Larnaca (73,000), and Paphos (39,000). The major urban center in the northern sector, aside from the Turkish part of Nicosia, is Gazi Magusa (Famagusta), population 27,742. For the year 2000, UN population estimates were 793,000 for the Republic of Cyprus and 177,120 for the TRNC. In the late 1990s, nearly seventy percent of Cypriots were urban. Greek and Turkish are official languages in the south, while Turkish predominates in the north. English is widely spoken everywhere. Compulsory education and suffrage are the pattern in Cyprus. The proliferation of politically focused print media in both sectors reflects this, as does an adult literacy rate of about ninety-five percent (in 2000).

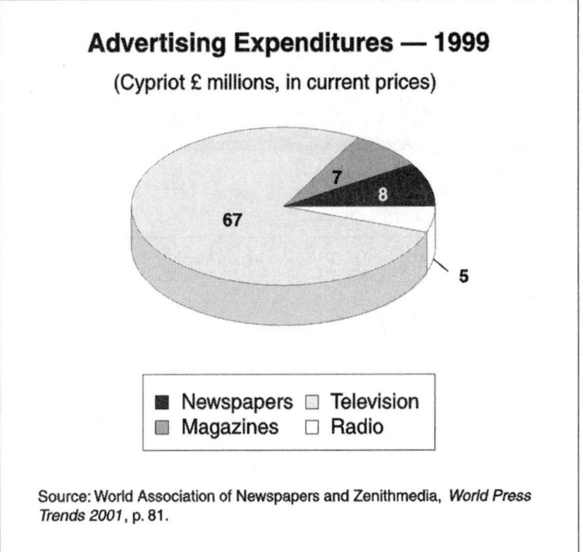

Source: World Association of Newspapers and Zenithmedia, *World Press Trends 2001*, p. 81.

Greek Sector Press and News Agencies Figures for 1994 show eight daily newspapers published in Nicosia in Greek (English translations of titles and circulation figures listed as daily averages are to be found in parentheses): *Phileleftheros* (Liberal; 21,886), an independent paper; *Apogevmatini* (Afternoon; 7,291), independent; *Simerini* (Today; 7,290), right-wing; *Haravghi* (Dawn; 6,927), the organ of the (Communist) Progressive Party of the Working People (AKEL); *Alitha* (Truth; 4897), right-wing; *Agon* (Struggle; 4,069), right-wing; *Eleftherotypia* (Free Press), moderate; and *Machi* (Battle), right-wing. In 1996, nine daily newspapers had a total circulation of 84,000, and 31 other papers had a combined circulation of 185,000, indicating a very high readership rate per capita. News agencies with offices in Nicosia include numerous foreign bureaus and the Greek-sector Cyprus News Agency (Kypriakon Praktoreion Eidiseon—KPE).

Turkish Sector Press and News Agencies The 1985 constitution of the TRNC guaranteed freedom of the press, with exceptions intended to guard public order, national security, public morals, and the workings of the courts. As of the early 1990s, the following daily Turkish newspapers were published in Nicosia: *Kalkin Sesi* (Voice of the People); *Birlik* (Unity), a right-wing publication of the National Unity Party (UBP); *Avrupa* (Europe), an independent organ; *Yeni Demokrat* (New Democrat), an organ of the Democratic Party (DP), with a conciliatory stance; *Yeni Dÿzen* (New Order), an organ of the Republican Turkish Party (CTP), which is Marxist; *Ortam* (Situation), an organ of the Communal Liberation (Socialist Salvation) Party (TKP), a leftist group; and *Yeni Çag* (New Era), an organ of the New Cyprus Party (YKP). *Kibris* (Cyprus, previously the weekly *Special News Bulletin*) had by the 1990s become the official monthly publication, circulating 4,500 copies in early 1998. Additionally, a number of mainland Turkish papers have circulated in the northern sector, principally *Sabah* (Morning), *Milliyet* (Nationality); *Hÿrriyet* (Liberty) and *Yeni Yÿzyil* (New Century). The news agencies in the Turkish sector are Turkish News Cyprus (Tÿrk Ajansi Kibris—TAK) and the Northern Cyprus News Agency (Kuzey Kibris Haber Ajansi).

BROADCAST MEDIA

Greek Sector Broadcast Media Before the 1974 division, the quasi-governmental Cyprus Broadcasting Corporation (Radiofonikon Idryma Kyprou—RIK) and the state-owned Radyo Bayrak and Radyo Bayrak Televizyon controlled national broadcasting. A law of June 1990 allowed commercial radio and TV to operate. In 1995, there were four TV stations (with 225 low-power repeaters). Into the late 1990s and the new millennium, RIK provided radio service in the Greek sector, with three additional island-wide stations and twenty-four other local stations. Broadcasts are mainly in Greek but also in Turkish, English, and Armenian. RIK has also provided television service from a transmitting station at Mount Olympus. In the late 1990s, the Greek channel ET-1 was being rebroadcast on Cyprus, with the BBC East Mediterranean Relay and the British Forces Broadcasting Service, Cyprus, also providing radio service. In 1998, Greek Cypriots had one short-wave, seven AM, and 60 FM radio stations. In 1997, they owned about 310,000 radios and 248,000 television sets. Broadcasts in one sector are usually accessible in the other.

Turkish Sector Broadcast Media Legislation passed in June 1990 permits the operation of commercial radio and TV stations. In the 1990s, Radyo Bayrak (RB) and Radyo Bayrak Televizyon (RBT) provided radio and TV service to the Turkish sector, where residents owned

Daily and Non-Daily Newspaper Titles and Circulation Figures

	1996	1997	1998	1999	2000
Number of Daily Newspapers	8	8	8	8	8
Circulation of Dailies (000)	68	53	53	45	46
Number of Non-Daily Newspapers	6	7	7	10	10
Circulation of Non-Dailies (000)	78	33	34	43	43

Source: World Association of Newspapers and Zenithmedia, *World Press Trends 2001*, pp. 8, 10, 17, 19.

about 268,000 radios and 82,000 TV sets in 1994. Two independent radio stations, First FM and Kibris FM, were broadcasting, as were two private television channels, one private pay-per-view TV channel, two foreign broadcasting stations, and numerous local radio stations. In 1995, four TV stations (with five repeaters) operated. In 1998, one short-wave, three AM, and eleven FM radio stations were on the air in the Turkish sector.

ELECTRONIC NEWS MEDIA

Figures for the year 2000 showed six Internet providers and about 80,000 Internet users on the island. In August 2002, the Cyprus News Agency maintained a web page that was available in Greek at www.cna.org.cy, and program summaries in English of some broadcasts of the Cyprus Broadcasting Corporation were available on the Internet at www.countrywatch.com/cw_wire.asp. Additionally, The Cyprus Weekly, The Cyprus Mail, and The Cyprus Communications Centre (a daily Internet newspaper in Turkish) all had web sites. Live radio broadcasts from Cyprus were available (for a fee) at www.vtuner.com, and a complete listing of Greek radio stations was available at www.media.net.gr.

SIGNIFICANT DATES

- 1985: Constitutional freedom of the press (with specified restrictions) is guaranteed in the Turkish sector.
- 1990: A law allows commericial radio and TV in the Greek sector.

BIBLIOGRAPHY

Banks, Arthur S. and Thomas C. Mueller, eds. *Political Handbook of the World.* Birminghamton, NY: CSA Publications, 1999.

The Central Intelligence Agency (CIA). *CIA World Factbook 2000.* Directorate of Intelligence, 9 May 2002. Available from http://www.cia.gov/.

Turner, Barry, ed. *The Statesman's Yearbook: The Politics, Cultures, and Economies of the World.* 136th edition. New York: St. Martin's Press, 1999.

World Almanac and Book of Facts. New York: World Almanac Books, 2002.

—Roy Neil Graves

THE CZECH REPUBLIC

BASIC DATA

Official Country Name:	Czech Republic
Region (Map name):	Europe
Population:	10,264,212
Language(s):	Czech
Literacy rate:	99.9%
Area:	78,866 sq km
GDP:	50,777 (US$ millions)
Number of Daily Newspapers:	75
Total Circulation:	1,704,000
Circulation per 1,000:	199
Number of Nondaily Newspapers:	62
Total Circulation:	765,000
Circulation per 1,000:	89
Total Newspaper Ad Receipts:	5,086 (Koruna millions)
As % of All Ad Expenditures:	19.30
Number of Television Stations:	150
Number of Television Sets:	3,405,834
Television Sets per 1,000:	331.8
Television Consumption (minutes per day):	194

Number of Cable Subscribers:	959,960
Cable Subscribers per 1,000:	93.2
Number of Satellite Subscribers:	570,000
Satellite Subscribers per 1,000:	55.5
Number of Radio Stations:	352
Number of Radio Receivers:	3,159,134
Radio Receivers per 1,000:	307.8
Radio Consumption (minutes per day):	178
Number of Individuals with Computers:	1,250,000
Computers per 1,000:	121.8
Number of Individuals with Internet Access:	1,000,000
Internet Access per 1,000:	97.4
Internet Consumption (minutes per day):	40

BACKGROUND & GENERAL CHARACTERISTICS

Since the dissolution of the Soviet Bloc in 1989, the Czech Republic has become a crossroad for new ideas and lively journalism. Newspapers which are both regional and national appear in a number of languages including Czech, English, German, and Russian.

Enterprising young journalists flocked to the Czech Republic to seek their fortunes in a new Eastern Europe. Likewise, western investors moved swiftly into an open arena of opportunities. Except for those papers once associated with the Communist Party or those with a deliberate left bias, most Czech newspapers are owned by non-Czech western conglomerates or cartels from Germany, Switzerland, or the Netherlands.

On January 1, 1993, a new political entity in Central Europe appeared from the shattered remains of the Soviet Bloc of the Cold War: the Czech Republic. The capital was the historic city of Prague, once a capital of the Holy Roman Empire during the Middle Ages, the site of the Hussite Rebellion in 1415, and the beginning of the Thirty Years War in 1618. When Czechoslovakia finally emerged as one of the few authentic democracies in East Central Europe during the interval between the world wars of the twentieth century, the nationalist yearnings of the Czech people had finally found expression, largely through the help of the expatriate Czech-Slovak communities in the United States and their influence on President Woodrow Wilson. However, the agitation of the powerful German minority living in the Sudetenland bordering Germany caused these lands to be carved away as a consequence of Hitler's Munich Accord in 1938. In the winter of 1939, Hitler's armies occupied the remaining parts of the country, allowing Slovakia to exist as protectorate and placing Bohemia and Moravia under German rule.

The outbreak of World War II was only months away. Czechoslovakia reappeared as a European country in 1945, and by 1948 it had become part of the Soviet Bloc for the remaining decades of the Cold War. In 1968 reformers under the leadership of Alexander Dubceck attempted to create a peaceful reformation of the communist system from within, known as the ''Prague Spring,'' only to be defeated by the invasion of a Soviet army. After the fall of Communism in 1989, the Czech Republic continued to exist as Czechoslovakia within the borders originally defined by the end of World War I, the disappearance of the Hapsburg Empire, and its reconstitution after World War II. The collapse of Communism and the emergence of a democratic Czechoslovakia under the leadership of such individuals as the author and later president Václav Havel was called the ''Velvet Revolution'' because of the absence of violence. Such seminal events in Czech history have acquired signature labels, another example being the democratic and revolutionary ''Prague Spring'' of 1968 that was crushed under Soviet military force. The union of Czechs and Slovaks, which had been taken for granted in the West, had never been a comfortable alliance. Unexpectedly, nationalists of both groups, in keeping with similar trends sweeping across Eastern and Central Europe, suddenly won the day, and Czechoslovakia became the separate Czech and Slovak Republics. In Czech parlance, this is called the ''Velvet Divorce'' that created two distinct republics with separate languages, traditions, and not very well concealed mutual animosity.

At the new millennium, the Czech Republic is a land-locked, heavily forested country that encompasses the historical and medieval kingdoms of Bohemia and Moravia, which were once central to the Holy Roman Empire, with an estimated population of over 10 million inhabitants. At 81 percent, the Czechs are the dominant ethnic and linguistic group, followed by the Moravians at thirteen percent. The remaining ethnic and linguistic groups include Poles, Germans, Hungarians, Slovaks, Silesians, Roma (Gypsies), and even Vietnamese, as well as other expatriate foreigners such as Americans.

Newspapers Newspapers in the Czech Republic are divided into two categories: national and regional. Most of

Daily and Non-Daily Newspaper Titles and Circulation Figures

	1996	1997	1998	1999	2000
Number of Daily Newspapers	22	21	18	18	75
Circulation of Dailies (000)	2,224	2,082	1,802	1,764	1,704
Number of Non-Daily Newspapers	78	77	75	71	62
Circulation of Non-Dailies (000)	821	812	804	801	765

Source: World Association of Newspapers and Zenithmedia, *World Press Trends 2001*, pp. 8, 10, 17, 19.

the national press is centered in Prague, capital of the Republic. The Prague location also allows for the existence of an international press that includes Internet sites, which are an innovation in Czech journalism.

Among national papers, as reported by the *Prague Post*, the *Mladá-fronta Dnes* (Today), a daily founded in 1945 with a circulation of over 400,000 and owned by the German RBVG, once had the largest circulation as a national paper, and includes a TV magazine. The tabloid *Blesk* follows behind. The third paper is *Právo* with a Saturday magazine supplement *Magazin Právo*, a communist past under the title *Rudé Právo*, and a circulation of around 300,000. The fourth paper, *ZN Zemské* (Earth News), a family daily with agricultural news of regional focus, a Thursday supplement called *Hobby*, a Saturday TV magazine, and a print run of about 160,000. It is owned by MRV Bohemia (Germany). The fifth newspaper is *Hospodárské Noviny* (Business News), specialized paper focusing on economic and political news with a daily insert pertaining to the stock market, *Burzovni Novini*, and a daily print run of about 110,000.

The sixth of the national newspapers is *Lidové Noviny* (Peoples' News), which targets a highly educated readership with intellectual commentary and analysis, a print run near 105,000 copies, and a German owner, RBVGmbH. The seventh newspaper is *Slovo* (World), a politically independent daily with a Saturday magazine, *Slovodené Slovo* and a print run of about 100,000. The only national sports daily, *Sport*, published by the national sports organization, prints about 90,000 copies, and has a Friday color supplement, *Volno Sport*. Two unranked dailies are *Halo Novini*, an opposition left-wing paper published by Futura, a.s. and *Denik Spigl* (Daily Mirror), a tabloid in competition with *Blesk* for sensational stories. Finally, the *Metro*, which is named after the Prague subway system, is a nationally oriented paper given away free in the subway.

Regional newspapers are divided according to the following geographical labels: Jihocesky kraj (Southern Bohemia), Jihomoravsky kraj (Southern Moravia), Praha Prague, Severocesky kraj (Northern Bohemia), Severomoravsky kraj (Northern Moravia), Stredocesky kraj (Central Bohemia), and Vychodesky kraj (Eastern Bohemia).

With the exception of Prague, there are at least 38 local and regional news papers in these categories, some with the name of the city or region of location in their titles, some with more of a local focus, others offering a broad menu of news ranging from national to international to local topics, and most with some sort of supplement bonus magazines for the readership. This is where the foreign conglomerates have had the most influence. With the exception of papers in the Prague region, all are printed in the Czech language.

Examples of some of these news papers are as follows:

- The *Plzensky Denik* (Daily Pilsen), owned by the Passauer group, covers Western-Northern Bohemia with ten regional daily editions with a print run of over 80,000 copies, and depending on the paper, a menu of supplements on Thursday, Friday, or Saturday and advertisers on Tuesday and Wednesday.
- The *Hradecke Novini* (Hranice News), again part of the Passau chain, covers Eastern Bohemia with four regional dailies covering both national and international news and offering its readership a Saturday supplement.
- The Moravian *Den* (Day), in which MRV Koblenz has 99 percent ownership, has a press run of over 60,000 copies, and provides world and local news as well as a Friday magazine. The city of Prague has its own local newspaper, *Vecernik Praha* (Evening Prague), again owned by the Passauer group, and offering its readership Prague news and a regular Friday color supplement and a printing run in the neighborhood of 80,000 copies.

International Press The cosmopolitan character of the city of Prague with its million-plus inhabitants has been a magnet for foreign journalists and newspapers, founding weeklies or even monthly newspapers to begin their own enterprises in a sort of capitalist free-for-all, in which competition for advertising on the open market and a paying readership were located not only within the Czech Republic but also internationally. The most salient of these is the English-language *Prague Post*, founded in 1992 and practicing Western-style investigative journalism, which has sometimes annoyed Czech government officials as well as indigenous Czech journalists and newspapers. One of the oft-spoken criticisms of the *Post* is that Czech newspapers blur the difference between news and opinion, that unsophisticated readers in the general Czech public have difficulty discerning between news and advertisement, and that there is often unsubstantiated reporting. A critical journalist must be analytical.

Other English language papers in Prague include the weekly *Prague Business Journal*, which focuses on business and economic topics, and the monthly *Prague Tribune*, which is a bilingual Czech-English publication. In terms of layout and design, some 60 percent of the articles are in Czech. At Prague's Charles University, the weekly English-language *Carolina* has appeared as a student publication. German interests have their own weekly German-language *Prager Zeitung* (Prague Newspaper). The single Russian-language newspaper is the weekly *Czekhiya Sevodnya*.

Magazines are also representative of the print media in the Czech Republic. They are heavily reliant on advertising as a primary source of revenue in addition to newsstand sales and subscriptions, and as such, are in a very competitive market. In 1998, the Czech Republic had more than 2,100 magazines, but a year later, only about 1,200 had survived. Some of those, including the news magazine *Tyden* (Time), were operating at a deficit, even though *Tyden* was owned by the Ringier-Springer Conglomerate, as was its TV magazine, *Tydenik Televize*.

Three popular magazines were founded during the ''Prague Spring'' of 1968, and have survived the vicissitudes of history. The first is *Vlasta*, a women's magazine owned by VNV, Holland. The second is *Story*, a lifestyle weekly owned by the same company. The third magazine is also a Holland product, *Tydenik Kvety*, a lifestyle weekly.

Each magazine has an average circulation of well over 200,000 copies. Other titles targeting specific readerships and niches in the market place are products of the post-Communist era, and include *Ekomom* (1991), *EURO* (1998), *Tydenik Respekt* (Times-Respect) (1990), *Tydenik Rozhlas* (Radio Times), *Prekvapeni*, a women's publication, and finally *Tydenik Televize* (TV-Times), owned by Ringier-Springer.

In a saturated media-magazine market, Czech publications also compete with Czech versions of popular western publications such as *Esquire*, *Rolling Stone*, and *Cosmopolitan*. The Czech edition of *Reader's Digest* with a monthly average of 200,000 copies is one of the nation's favorite general magazines.

Top Ten Daily Newspapers
(2000)

	Circulation
Mlada fronta DNES	338,000
Blesk	329,000
Pravo	220,000
ZN Zemske noviny	105,000
Lidove noviny	91,000
Hospodarske noviny	77,000
Sport	61,000
Zapadoceske Deniky Bohemia	60,000
Severoceske deniky Bohemia	56,000
Vychodoceske deniky Bohemia	52,000

Source: World Association of Newspapers and Zenithmedia, *World Press Trends 2001*, p. 83.

ECONOMIC FRAMEWORK

As of 2002, the Czech Republic was a member of NATO (North Atlantic Treaty Organization) but not the EU (European Union). In line after Poland and Hungary, the Czech Republic is scheduled to enter the EU where its economy can partake of the opportunities available to Western Europe. In preparation for that event, the economy continued to restructure in banking, energy, among others. Of the post-Communist states, the Czech Republic was the most stable and prosperous. In 2000 and 2001 the steady growth of the economy reduced the rate of unemployment to 8.7 percent, and held inflation to a moderate 3.8 percent.

After the fall of communism, the Czech Republic returned to the mixed capitalist-social welfare society characteristic of Western Europe. Private property is recognized in the constitution. The Czech Republic inherited the industrial base of old Czechoslovakia, which included such firms as Skoda, once known for armaments and now a producer of consumer goods such as automobiles.

In comparison to Western Europe and the EU, per capita income is low, thus providing incentive for ambitious and educated young people to move westward in search of work and at the same time, depriving the Czech Republic of its intellectual capital. The Czech beer industry is considered to be a producer of high quality products and helps to spur the economy. Since the fall of Communism, the Czech Republic has seen an increase in the tourism industry as well.

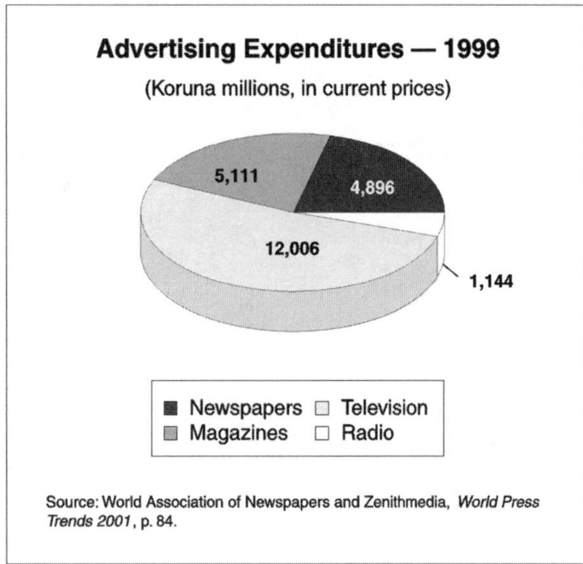

Source: World Association of Newspapers and Zenithmedia, *World Press Trends 2001*, p. 84.

PRESS LAWS

The Czech Republic's formal statement of rights and freedoms can be found in the *Charter of Fundamental Rights and Freedoms* that was issued at the rebirth of a democratic Czechoslovakia in 1990. In Division Two of the *Charter Article Seventeen*, the freedoms of speech and of the press are defined, but not without the ambiguity rooted in the totalitarian Communist past. Paragraph One guarantees the freedom of expression and the right to information. Paragraph Two guarantees the right of every person to express freely his or her opinion by word, writing, in the press, in pictures or in any other form, as well as to seek freely, receive and disseminate ideas and information irrespective of the frontiers of the State. Paragraph Three prohibits censorship. However, Paragraph Four introduces an element of contradiction and ambiguity to the interpretation of the preceding three paragraphs. One may also draw the same conclusion regarding Paragraph Five which permits organs of the State and of local self government to provide information on their activities in an appropriate manner.

CENSORSHIP

Ironically, the first mini-constitutional crisis reflecting these constitutional ambiguities and contradictions involved the banning of Adolf Hitlers's *Mein Kampf*, which had been published by a small press specializing in historical documents. Czech editions of the book had been published in 1936 and 1993, but this edition without commentary was banned in 2000. In a report by Jan Tracy in the *Prague Post* of June 14-20, 2000, the Czech criminal code articles of 260 and 261 were identified as the basis of the censorship: The publishing of the book gave support or enlisted support for a movement, the aim of which was to abolish citizens' rights and freedoms, and was punishable by fines and up to five and eight years in prison. The Czech Republic had joined its neighbors, Germany, Austria, and Hungary, in its prohibition of a book that was freely available in Britain and the United States. By the winter of 2001, the *Prague Post* reported that a superior court invalidated the conviction of the publisher, Michael Zitko, on procedural grounds. Zitko summarized his situation and the potential situation of future publishers with the comment that in a world of absolutes, there was freedom of speech and its principal enemy, censorship. In the world that was the Czech Republic there was everything in between. The *Prague Post* had condemned the censorship action with the observation that despite noble intentions, no good could come from censorship. A half century after the war, fear of the past of nazism and communism were still operative in Central Europe. The constitution expressed the idealism of a newly minted democratic political order, yet the burden of history was evident. The disorder of the 1990s in the Balkans as well as the appearance of Georg Haider on the political scene in Austria gave the government incentive to pursue right-wing groups.

In a *Post* editorial, James Pitkin observed that expediency prevailed in a country not yet ready to grasp democracy's inner spirit, criticizing the underlying assumption of the Czech courts that freedom of speech would be fine if the people could be trusted. Freedom of speech was not a perk that came with an open society, rather that open societies grew out of a deep commitment to such ideals. To compromise was corrosive and pointless.

STATE-PRESS RELATIONS

Once the Communist legal system was overthrown, there was an effort to expunge its legal legacy, and both the Czech and Slovak Republics have gravitated back to the civil laws of the old Austro-Hungarian Empire in keeping with the requirements of the Organization on Security and Cooperation in Europe. The Czech Republic is a parliamentary democracy with a bicameral parliament consisting of an 81-seat Senate elected by popular vote for six-year terms, one-third elected every two years, and Chamber of Deputies (*Polslanecke Snemovna*) of 200 members elected to a four-year term by popular vote. The executive branch consists of a President or chief of State (Václav Havel since 1993), a head of government known as the Prime Minister with deputy Prime Ministers from the legislative majority, as well as a Cabinet appointed by the President on the recommendation of the Prime Minister. The Judicial Branch of government consists of a Supreme Court and a Constitutional Court with a chairman and deputy chairman appointed for 10-year terms.

The fall of communism provided the press in Czechoslovakia and later the Czech Republic with the opportunity to relearn the realities of a market economy, the requirements of capitalism and its function within the ideals of a new democracy. The disintegration of the old order was rapid and unexpected, leaving the Czech press paralyzed. In a communist society, the press was an arm of the state's propaganda apparatus, both in terms of personnel and finances. It was isolated from the democratic presses of the west in many respects, and was unschooled in the rough and tumble of a capitalistic journalism. For reform-minded journalists, the ''Velvet Revolution'' led by the Civic Forum offered golden opportunities; for those rooted in the old communist system, the future was less rosy. However, journalism was also difficult for western-style reporters, as was noted by Martin Huckerby, who wrote that in a country where the citizen was a supplicant, where basic statistics were often lacking, and where existing information was guarded with tenacity, such reporters were often unwelcome.

ATTITUDE TOWARD FOREIGN MEDIA

Reflecting the principle of physics that nature abhors a vacuum, western media conglomerates and cartels were swift to move into the new Czech Republic, in particular from Germany, Switzerland, and the Netherlands. After all, 43 percent of the Czech Republic's foreign trade was and has been with Germany.

These cartels include *Rheinisch-Bergische* VG mbH, *Passauer Neue Presse*, and Springer Verlag, all from Germany, Ringier of Switzerland, and VNV of the Netherlands. Large newspapers on the political left are independent of the western conglomerates because of their core hostility to capitalism. These include *Právo* (Rights), a daily with a circulation of about a quarter of a million and once the house organ of the Communist Party, now the Labor Party, and *Halo Noviny*, an opposition left-wing daily owned by Futura, a.s.

Ringier-Springer owns the second-largest daily *Blesk* (Flash), a sensationalist tabloid in the image of Springer's German language *Bild Zeitung* with an emphasis on banner headlines, pictures, and scandal. With a circulation of nearly 300,000 as of January 2000, the paper has continued to grow in influence. *Blesk* offers a supplement, and in a bid to attain a little more respectability, proposed a Sunday newspaper, *Nedeni Novini*, to appeal to urban intellectuals. The potential of *Blesk* to antagonize the status quo can be found in a lawsuit that President Václav Havel was moved to file against the newspaper in 1998. As of April 2001, *Blesk* had surpassed *Mladá fronta Dnes*, the oldest of the current newspapers in terms of total circulation.

Given the thorny relationship with its German neighbor, the Czech parliament has tried to limit the presence of German conglomerates, particularly the *Passauer Neue Presse* (PNP)and *Rheinisch-Bergische VG* (RBVG), to a market share of 40 percent with what is a very ineffective law, because the cartels had already carved out their market niches in the Czech newspaper world by buying most of the regional daily newspapers. Government bureaucracy has often been reluctant to recognize the investigative nature of western-style journalism, although theoretically the constitution guarantees freedom of the press.

NEWS AGENCIES

The single Czech news agency centered in Prague is CTK or Ceska Tiskova Kancelar, which functions in both English and Czech. Its subsidiary CT Teletext is a pre-cyber-era format of delivery within the boundaries of the Czech Republic. While Prague is as technologically advanced as Western Europe, the same cannot be said for outlying regions.

BROADCAST MEDIA

Broadcast media is divided into radio and television. According to the Central Intelligence Agency's *World Factbook 2001*, the Czech republic had 31 AM stations, 304 FM stations, and 17 short-wave stations as of the year 2000. Only the Czech Parliament's Television and Radio Broadcast Conical can authorize additional frequencies. Of particular significance is the fact that Radio Free Europe/Radio Liberty was moved from Munich to Prague in 1995. RFE/RL broadcasts in English, Russian, Byeloruss, Ukrainian, Armenian, Azerbaijani, and more. Its Czech subsidiary Radio Slobodna Europa broadcasts in Croatian, Serbian, Albanian, and Bosnian. The Czech-owned state radio, Radio Praha, broadcasts in Czech, English, German, French, and Spanish. CRo 1-Radiozurnál broadcasts in Czech from Prague. The venerable BBC can be heard from England, as well as German and Austrian broadcasters to the west, Deutsche Welle and Österreichische Rundfunk. The stations follow the news, music, features, and sports formats of most western European countries.

The Czech Republic had 150 television broadcast stations and 1,434 repeaters as of 2000. Transmission signals from neighboring Germany and Austria also have an audience in the Republic. Approximately half of the TV market share is dominated by the giant TV Nova and is followed by TV Prima, which commands approximately seventeen percent of the viewership. Czech TV1 and Czech TV2 are state-owned enterprises and have about a third share of the total market. Cable and Satellite TV, which can access international stations such as CNN and the BBC as well as commercial satellite broadcasts, is just a little over five percent of the market. Most Czech

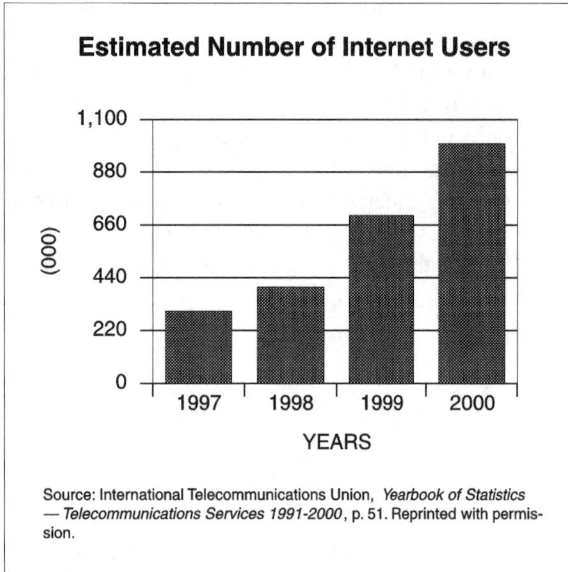

Source: International Telecommunications Union, *Yearbook of Statistics — Telecommunications Services 1991-2000*, p. 51. Reprinted with permission.

viewers receive broadcast signals over the air using antennae, and the mountainous landscape in parts of the country can hinder reception. Cable TV is widely available in spa and resort towns such as Carl Vary, which service an international tourist clientele. As in the print media, Western conglomerate owners such as Rupert Murdock have been active and swift in moving into the Czech media market, given the fact that there is a need for an orderly media policy from the government.

In 2001, this confusion was illustrated by the struggles of a new news-oriented TV station, TV3, to find its market niche. Limited by such problems as regional licensing, it reached only 25 percent of the nation's viewers. Like the newspaper industry, television is also dependent upon advertising revenues, and is, in fact, in competition with the print media. There was reluctance to grant more broadcasting frequencies because the national question of analog versus digital television had not been settled, even though there was the expectation that digital would replace analog within the coming decade.

ELECTRONIC NEWS MEDIA

The development of the Internet into a major source of news has had just as revolutionary an impact as elsewhere in the world. Internet sites originate in Prague, and include *Ahasewbnovy Noviny*, *Cesky Novinu* (Czech News), www.ceskenoviny.cz/ (the cyber arm of CTK), *Cesky Vyber Lupa* (Magnifying Glass), *Neviditelny Pes* (Invisible Dog), and *Sportonoviny* (Sporting News), all of which are in Czech.

An Internet weekly, *Dnes* (Day), is published in both Czech and German. *The Prague Business Journal* features business, politics, and national news.

An English Web site located in Prague is the *Prague Daily Report*. *Lidové Noviny* maintains an Internet alternative to its paper edition at www.lidovenoviny.cz. Other print newspapers with websites include *The Prague Post*, www.praguepost.cz; *Právo*, www.pravo.cz; *Carolina*, www.cuni.cz/cucc/carolina/carolina.html; and *Hospodarske Novini*, www.ihned.cz. *Svobodne Slovo* (Words of Liberty) has the Internet address of www.slovo.cz. The Czech Republic's Ministry of the Interior sponsors a weekly site, *Verejná správa* (Public News), www.mvcr.cz/vespra.

This arena of news activity is very likely to continue and to expand as the Internet becomes an ever-greater source of news and information.

EDUCATION & TRAINING

In some respects, the press in the Czech Republic has exhibited many of the same characteristics of the media in the United States, a rough and tumble capitalistic market place where understanding of the market place supersedes the Communist-era formal academic qualifications. Czech universities such as the flagship Charles University in Prague offer Media Studies with a curriculum quite similar to their western counterparts. Individual companies and organizations are free to set their own qualification standards. There are industry expectations regarding the level and depth of general and when necessary specialized knowledge.

SUMMARY

The Czech Republic stands at the beginning of a new democratic age with the hope and expectations of a prosperity concurrent with Western Europe that is recognized through admission to the EU (European Union) and all of the accompanying economic and cultural benefits. As such, the media in the Czech Republic is at the center of the action. In some respects, this economic globalism works against the ethnocentrism that is a curse of all past members of the Austro-Hungarian Empire. The unsettled claims of the Sudeten Germans as well as the social conflicts centering on the Roma provide the Czech media with opportunities to exercise the principles of a hard-won democracy as well as to educate the Czech public in them.

BIBLIOGRAPHY

''Breaking into the Newspaper Business'', *The Prague Post.* 3-9 October 2001. Available from http://www.praguepost.com.cz.

Central Intelligence Agency (CIA). *The World Factbook 2001.* 2002. Available from http://www.odci.gov.

Charter of Fundamental Rights and Freedoms. Available from http://www.psp.cz.

Cornej, Peter. *Fundamentals of Czech History*. Prague: Prah Publisher-Martin Nopenka, nd.

Czech Info Center News. Available from http://www.muselik.com/czech/new.html.

Czech Republic Newspapers. Available from http://www.eojeda.com/Inter/Diarios/Europa/Czech%20 Republic.html.

Czech Today. Available from http://www.europeaninternet.com/czech.

''English-Language Publication Changes for Czechs'', *The Prague Post*. Available from http://www.praguepost.com.cz.

Independent Media Center Prague. Available from http://www.prague.indymedia.org.

The Internet Public Library (IPL) Reading Room Newspapers. *Czech Republic*. Available from http://www.ipl.org.

Kidon Media-Link. *Newspapers and other Media Sources from the Czech Republic*. Available from http://www.kidon.com.

''Largest National and Regional Daily Newspapers'', *The Prague Post*. 13-19 January 1999. Available from http://www.praguepost.com.cz.

''Media Über Alles'', *The Prague Post*. 5-11 December 2001. Available from http://www.praguepost.com.cz.

''Media Wars'', *The Prague Post*. 11-17 April 2000. Available from http://www.praguepost.com.cz.

''Print publication, daily and weekly,'' *The Prague Post*. 12-18 January 2000. Available from http://www.praguepost.com.cz.

''Stable Media Market Looks to Sunday for Action,'' *The Prague Post*. 12-18 January 2000. Available from http://www.praguepost.com.cz.

Strohlein, Andrew. ''The Czech Republic: 1992 to 1999,'' *Central European Review*, 13 September 1999. Available from http://www.ce-review.org.

—Beverly J. Inman

Democratic Congo

Basic Data

Official Country Name:	Democratic Republic of the Congo
Region (Map name):	Africa
Population:	53,624,718
Language(s):	French, Lingala, Kingwana, Kikongo, Tshiluba
Literacy rate:	77.3%

Background & General Characteristics

A nominal republic with a history of autocratic leadership, the Democratic Congo has kept its media under iron-fisted government control. In the cities, jailing of non-conformist journalists continued into 2002. An interview conducted that year with a provincial radio executive and reported through French media shows tyranny by government bureaucrats operating in the provinces. Both ongoing patterns have violated free expression and worked against the expansion of TV and radio stations that other constituencies in the Democratic Congo have been trying to achieve.

Situated in west-central Africa, the Democratic Republic of the Congo (*Républic Démocratique du Congo* or DRC, also known as Congo-Kinshasa, formerly Zaire and the Belgian Congo) is the second largest of the sub-Saharan states, with an area that includes the bulk of the Congo River basin. The country is not to be confused with the Republic of the Congo (Congo Republic, Congo-Brazzaville).

Democratic Congo had an estimated population in July 2001 of 53,624,718, up from some 30,000,000 in the 1984 census. Ethnographically the country is a mosaic of several hundred groups, with various Bantu tribes comprising the largest segment.

Having a population density of sixty-one persons per square mile, Democratic Congo is thirty percent urban, with population centers in the capital, Kinshasa (est. 5,064,000), and in the cities of Lubumbashi (967,000), Mbuji-Mayi, Kananga, and Kisangani. The Congolese are about fifty percent Roman Catholic and twenty percent Protestant, the rest being Muslim or following indigenous practices.

French, the official language, dominates the media. Local languages include Kikongo, Kiswahili, Lingala, and Tshiluba. About seventy-seven percent of Congolese adults can read in at least one language. Education is compulsory through age twelve. Suffrage is universal and compulsory.

Following the withdrawal of United Nations peacekeeping forces in 1964, Maj. Gen. Joseph Désiré Mobutu took over as self-proclaimed president of the ''Second Republic''. The 1967 constitution provided for a strong presidential presence, with amendments and revisions in the 1970s further linking governmental and party institutions. Constitutional and military struggles in the 1990s ended with the ousting and exile of Mobutu and the installation of President Laurent-Désiré Kabila. In mid-2002, a 1998 draft of a new constitution had yet to be ratified.

Government corruption and economic decline characterized the 1980s and 1990s. Inflation in the mid-1990s peaked in the thousand-percent range. Adding to the mix of problems have been the influx of refugees after 1994 from ethnic bloodshed in neighboring Rwanda and the presence (in 1999) of more than a million adults with HIV/AIDS.

After Mobutu's removal from office, exile, and death in 1997, Gen. Kabila, the leader of the rebel forces, ruled by decree, alienating the United Nations as well as national allies. The rebels agreed to a cease-fire on August 31, 1999. Kabila was assassinated early in 2001, and his son, Joseph Kabila, succeeded him.

Newspapers Mobutu's regime repressed journalists and restricted the number of legal newspapers. The pattern continued under the two Kabilas. Robert Menard, the general secretary of the Paris-based watchdog group Reporters without Borders, said in February 2002 that the situation for journalists was still deteriorating in the Democratic Congo.

A number of independent newspapers generally critical of the Mobutu government began publication about 1990. Early in 1991 two directors of *Elima*, an evening daily, were detained by the government after publishing pieces alleging official corruption. A bomb destroyed the newspaper offices later that year, and the government shut down the paper late in 1993.

Such instances have persisted. National agents arrested journalist Guy Kasongo Kilembwe in February 2001 for caricaturing Joseph Kabila and his ministers. In December, police also arrested Freddy Embumba, who worked for the Kinshasa daily *L'Avenir*, and seized two editors of the paper *Pot-Pourri*, which had published an article satirizing Kabila II. In February 2002 the status of the three latest detainees was unknown. Reporters without Borders reported that officials arrested twenty-six Congolese journalists during 2001. The ongoing press situation continues to be unstable in this climate.

Earlier, in 1995, Democratic Congo had had nine daily newspapers with a combined circulation of 120,000, about three copies per 1,000 people. Daily French-language newspapers published in major cities during the 1990s included *Salongo* (in Kinshasa, circulation 10,000), *Mjumbe* (in Lubumbashi), and *Boyoma* (in Kisangani). *Le Passeport Africain*, a weekly, resumed publication in mid-1994 after a hiatus.

BROADCAST MEDIA

Government-controlled radio and television stations (with color by SECAM) have been in charge of broadcasting. In 1999, the country had one short-wave, three AM, and twelve FM radio stations. The national radio station *La Voix du Congo* and one educational station were also in operation. Television Congolaise has been the government-run commercial channel. In 1998, the populace owned about a half-million radios (79 for every 1,000 people) and more than that number of TV sets. Figures for 1999 show twenty television stations operating in the country.

In 2002, a complaint emerged through French media from Freddy Molong, chair of the association of community radio stations in the DRC, about the government's heavy taxation and routine ''administrative harassment'' of community radio stations, especially in Katanga and Kasai provinces. Local bureaucrats, Molong said, were demanding ten percent of the stations' gross income and even a ten percent tax on every obituary announcement, along with a back payment of $10,000 for the year 2001, even though most of these radio stations were less than two years old and were non-profit, operated by volunteers on shoestring budgets.

NEWS AGENCIES

Congolese Press Agency (CPA) is the main press agency. *Agence France-Presse*, Xinhua, and Reuters have bureaus in Kinshasa.

ELECTRONIC NEWS MEDIA

Statistics for January 1998 show about one hundred Internet users, and those for 1999, about fifteen hundred. Two Internet service providers operated in 2000.

SIGNIFICANT DATES

- 1990: Papers critical of the Mobutu government emerge.
- 2001: Officials arrest a number of journalists for criticism of the Kabila regime.
- 2002: Bureaucrats pursue petty harassment of struggling community radio stations. Reporters without Borders finds press situation deteriorating.

BIBLIOGRAPHY

Banks, Arthur S., and Thomas C. Muller, ed. *Political Handbook of the World, 1999.* Binghamton, NY: CSA Publications, 1999.

The Central Intelligence Agency (CIA). *The World Factbook 2000.* Directorate of Intelligence, 8 May 2002. Available from http://www.cia.gov/.

''DRC: Community Radio Stations Complain of Heavy Taxation.'' Radio France Internationale. An interview with Freddy Molongo by Kamanda wa Kamanda. Trans. from French by FBIS. *CountryWatch: Congo (DRC).* CountryWire Search Engine, 8 May 2002. Available from http://search.countrywatch.com.

''RSF Condemns Arrest of Journalists in Kinshasa.'' Panafrican News Agency, 1 February 2002. *Country-Watch: Congo (DRC).* CountryWire Search Engine, 8 May 2002. Available from http://search.countrywatch.com.

Turner, Barry, ed. *The Statesman's Yearbook: The Politics, Cultures, and Economies of the World, 2000.* 136th ed. New York: St. Martin's Press, 1999.

World Almanac and Book of Facts, 2002. New York: World Almanac Books, 2002.

—Roy Neil Graves

DENMARK

BASIC DATA

Official Country Name:	Kingdom of Denmark
Region (Map name):	Europe
Population:	5,352,815
Language(s):	Danish, Faroese, Greenlandic (an Inuit dialect), German (small minority)
Literacy rate:	100.0%
Area:	43,094 sq km
GDP:	162,343 (US$ millions)
Number of Daily Newspapers:	31
Total Circulation:	1,481,000
Circulation per 1,000:	347
Total Circulation:	66,000
Circulation per 1,000:	16
Newspaper Consumption (minutes per day):	27
Total Newspaper Ad Receipts:	5,475 (Krone millions)
As % of All Ad Expenditures:	50.80
Magazine Consumption (minutes per day):	7
Number of Television Stations:	25
Number of Television Sets:	3,121,000
Television Sets per 1,000:	583.1
Television Consumption (minutes per day):	174
Number of Cable Subscribers:	1,403,440
Cable Subscribers per 1,000:	264.8
Number of Satellite Subscribers:	800,000
Satellite Subscribers per 1,000:	149.5
Number of Radio Stations:	357
Number of Radio Receivers:	6,020,000
Radio Receivers per 1,000:	1,124.6
Radio Consumption (minutes per day):	128
Number of Individuals with Computers:	2,300,000
Computers per 1,000:	429.7
Number of Individuals with Internet Access:	1,950,000
Internet Access per 1,000:	364.3
Internet Consumption (minutes per day):	10

BACKGROUND & GENERAL CHARACTERISTICS

The Kingdom of Denmark comprises the North Sea archipelago and islands of continental Denmark, the Faroe Islands, and Greenland. Continental Denmark has coastlines totaling 7,400 kilometers (4,600 miles) and a land border with Germany of only 67.7 kilometers (42 miles). The population of continental Denmark was estimated at 5.14 million in 1989, and projections anticipate little growth in the future. The Danes are descendants of the Norsemen (Vikings) who were dominant in Scandinavia and England during the eleventh century. The Danes are closely linked with the Swedes and Norwegians in cultural heritage and language—a derivative of East Scandinavian German. The Germans in South Jutland constitute the only non-Danish citizen minority and they comprise about 1 percent of the population. In the 1990s, an influx of Arabic Muslim workers created a new minority for which accommodations of housing, amenities, and education are made by the Danish welfare state.

The 18 Faroe Islands, with a landmass of about 1,399 square kilometers, lie to the northwest of Denmark in the Atlantic Ocean between the Shetland Islands and Iceland. During World War II, Great Britain occupied and protected the Faroes from German invasion from 1940-45. The Faroes have been governed by Denmark since the fourteenth century, but a high degree of home rule was attained in 1948 and affirmed in the revised Danish Constitution of 1953. The 45,661 inhabitants (July 2001 estimate) are primarily descendants of Viking settlers who arrived in the ninth century. The Faroese language derives from Old Norse and Danish, and is similar to Icelandic and Norwegian.

Greenland (Danish: Gronland, Greenlandic: Kalaalli Nunaat), situated in the North Atlantic, was claimed in its entirety by Denmark in May 1921. Denmark colonized Greenland in the eighteenth century at the same time it established trading companies in the West Indies. Greenland's capital, Nuuk (formerly Godthab), is the oldest Danish settlement on the island (1721). In 1917, the United States purchased the Danish West Indies islands of St. Thomas, St. Croix, and St. John (now the U.S. Virgin Islands) and, at the same time, relinquished all U.S. claims to the Peary Land, the north Greenland area explored by Robert Edwin Peary. Norway's claims to land on the eastern coast settled by Norwegian fishermen were declared invalid in 1933 by the Permanent Court of International Justice at The Hague.

Greenland, the largest island in the world, encompasses 2.18 million square kilometers (840,000 square miles) of land and ice. Except for about 410,450 square kilometers (18,430 square miles), a polar ice sheet, glaciers and smaller ice caps cover the island. Sometimes the ice sheet reaches a depth of 4,300 meters (14,000 feet). Less than 342,000 square kilometers (132,000 square miles) are suitable for habitation. More than 90 percent of Greenland's population lives along the southern and western coasts of the island.

Greenland's population of 56,376 (2002 estimate) are Inuit (Eskimo) or Greenland-born Caucasians, and the balance are mainly Danish. The primary language is Greenlandic, a mixture of Inuit and Danish, but Danish also is an official language. The Danish Constitution of 1953 integrated Greenland into Denmark, and gave Greenland the right to elect two representatives to the Danish parliament. In a January 1979 referendum Greenlanders voted for home rule and formed their own seven-member executive body, the *Landsstyre*, and a 31-member parliament, the *Landting*.

From 1660 to 1849, Denmark was an absolute monarchy. Absolutism ended on June 5, 1849, when King Frederik VII signed a constitution that made Denmark a constitutional monarchy with a bicameral parliament modeled on that of England. However, continual conflict between the Crown and the powerful *Landting* (Upper House) on the one hand, and the more liberal *Folketing* (Lower House) on the other, led to constitutional changes in 1866, 1901, and 1953. The reforms resulted in a constitutional monarchy, unicameral legislature (*Folketing*) and a government organized by ministries that administer the present welfare state.

Newspapers came into existence in Denmark during the years of the absolute monarchy (1660-1849). Four newspapers founded in the eighteenth century still dominate the market. The oldest daily paper is the *Berlingske Tidende* in Copenhagen, founded by the Berling family in 1749, 35 years before *The Times* in London. The *Berlingske Tidende* adopted a moderate conservative viewpoint that appealed to the great landowners that made up the *Landting* and to business interests in the capital. Hence, from the beginning it has specialized in foreign and financial news as well as political debate, but also covered literature and the arts.

Three papers founded in the eighteenth century are the *Stiftstidende* dailies published in Aalborg (1767), Odense (1772), and Aarhus (1794). All three are independent, but the *Fyens Stiftstidende* in Odense expressed conservative views, while the other two took a liberal stance. Initially, each of these influential dailies published morning and evening editions. Political and social developments occurring simultaneously with industrialization during the latter half of the nineteenth century led to the establishment of a four-party political system and a parallel four-paper system.

Two major political parties that emerged from the bicameral legislature of 1849 were the *Venstre* (Liberal Party) and *Det Konservative Folkeparti* (The Conservative People's Party). A constitutional revision in 1866 led to the rise of two more political parties, the radical Social-Liberal Party (*Det Radikale Venstre*), representing small landholders and some of the intelligentsia who broke away from the Venstre in 1905; and the Social Democratic Party (*Socialdemokratiet*) that played a major role in the Danish labor movement. Each of the four political parties established a nationwide network of opinion-shaping newspapers that espoused the ideas of the party and resulted in a four-paper system.

The *Venstre* (Liberal Party), representing agricultural interests, and *Det Konservative Folkeparti* (Conservative Party) representing primarily the middle class, formed networks of about 60 newspapers each. The *Berlingske Tidende* and its sister paper in Copenhagen, the *Nationaltidende,* voiced conservative views in two editions daily. Both papers devoted sections to business interests such as shipping and agriculture, law and politics, and issued a special weekly sheet devoted to women's interests. A chief regional daily with conservative views was the *Jyllandsposten* (founded in 1871), a morning paper published in Aarhus. The *Jyllandsposten* rapidly gained a reputation for quality coverage of foreign and national business and commerce.

The Social-Liberal network grew to approximately two dozen papers, the most influential of which was *Politiken* (1884) in Copenhagen. *Politiken* became the most cosmopolitan paper in all of Scandinavia. It introduced the English system of small pages, prominent headlines, and heavy use of illustrations. Many important persons in the political and social movements of Denmark contributed columns and articles to this newspaper. Danish literature and art were well represented in its pages. *Politikin*'s owners also issued a successful evening paper, the *Extrabladet* (1904), which promoted social-liberal views.

The first Social-Democratic Party daily, the *Social-Demokraten* (later changed to *Aktuelt*), appeared in Copenhagen in 1872. By 1900, there were 20 more Social-Democratic papers in circulation in the provinces. The Social-Democrats agitated for revision of the constitution and were instrumental in gaining recognition of the principle of parliamentary government in the constitutional revision of 1901. This ended many years of deadlock between the *Folketing* on one side, and the Crown and *Landsting* on the other. The Social-Democratic papers also played a vital role in obtaining the vote for peasants, workers, and women, and became the voice of the labor unions in Denmark.

Ironically, the government reforms of 1901 that were urged by the press, lessened to some extent the power of the press to shape opinions, as the reorganization of the government spread responsibilities among ministries and their accompanying bureaucracies.

When Henrik Cavling took over *Politiken* in 1905, he initiated changes in the newspaper world that would shift priority from politics to news and a broad range of social and cultural topics. The new trends in journalism set by *Politiken* led to steady increases in media consumption, and by 1913 there were 143 independent dailies in 30 Danish towns, reaching almost 100 percent of the Danish populace. However, the need for more reporters to serve the growing numbers of newspapers increased the costs, as did technological advances in the form of telephones, telegraph, typesetting machines and rotary presses. Between 1925 and 1938, competition for readers and advertising revenues to meet rising costs led to mergers and closures that reduced the number of daily newspapers to 60.

The surviving dailies faced competition from 15 illustrated weekly magazines with a combined circulation of 2.2 million, and 330 local district papers and advertising weeklies distributed free of charge to 1.3 million households. City newspapers increasingly focused on news and matters of general interest as well as editorial comment. Provincial dailies cultivated local material, but included hard news, background, and a range of topical interests. District weeklies reached 80-90 percent of the adult population of Denmark. Newspapers owned more than half the district weeklies, accounting for 60 percent of the total circulation.

Papers with similar content have been published, but with less than daily frequency, in Greenland (i.e., *Atuagagdliutut/Gronlandposten*). Political viewpoints are more pronounced in the Faroe Islands by the moderate *Dimmalaetting,* the independent *Dagbladid,* and the state paper, the Social-Democratic *Socialurin.*

Weekly magazines fell into two primary categories: family and women's magazines. Typically, content was and is dominated by fashion, home and life styles, and serialized fiction. Popular early weeklies were the *Familie Journal* and *Hjemmet.* Illustrated weeklies like *Ilustreret Tidende* focused on news from the entertainment world. In appearance, they resembled the *Illustrated London Times.*

The magazine press includes highly specialized journals that focus on topics of interest to particular readers. Some are periodicals and bulletins published by trade unions and social organizations for their membership. Others are professional journals and technical publications. Two early monthlies, *Tilshueren* and *Gads danske Magasin,* were scholarly journals, while the popular *Klods-Hans* was a sort of Danish *Punch.*

World War II and the occupation of Denmark by the Germans from 1940-45 interrupted the publication of many papers, and after the war, much of the production equipment was worn out or had been destroyed. Only a few new post-World War II papers were established. These included the bipartisan *Kristeligt Dagblad,* the financial daily *Bersen,* the Communist organ *Land og Folk,* and *Information,* the latter two originally publications of the Resistance.

The Constitution of 1953 created a unicameral parliament (the *Folketing*) and organized the Danish government into multiple ministries, headed by a prime minister. This led to the formation of more political parties representing special interest groups, so that the four-party system no longer applied. In the 1960s, under pressure of competition from radio and television, changes in reader interests, and increasing costs of technology, newspapers suffered a further decline. The number of Danish households receiving at least one daily paper dropped from 100 percent to 75 percent. Newspaper closures in 1958-71 coincided with the end of the four-party system and brought an end to the four-paper system at the same time.

In 1988 there were 46 general-interest dailies with a total circulation of approximately 1.85 million. Those figures have remained fairly constant. With the decrease in numbers, the national newspapers like *Berlingske Tidende* and *Politiken* in Copenhagen, and *Jyllands-Posten* in Aarhus, increased their market share, while Copenhagen's midday tabloids, *B.T.* and *Ekstrabladet,* and evening papers *Information* and *Berlingstke Aftenavis,* lost almost 40 percent of their circulation. Larger regional newspapers merged with or took over the market share of smaller ones and increased circulation proportionately. Dominant regional papers remaining are *Fyens Stiftstidende* in Odense, *Nordjyske Stiftstidinde* in Aalborg, the *Aarhus Stiftstidende* in Aarhus, and the *Jydske Vestkysten* in Esbjerg.

Top Ten Daily Newspapers
(2000)

	Circulation
Jyllands-Posten	180,000
Berlingske Tidende	156,000
Politiken	143,000
Ekstra Bladet	135,000
B.T.	123,000
Jydske Vestkysten	91,000
Nordjyske Stiftstidende	82,000
Arhus Stiftstidende	71,000
Fyens Stiftstidende	66,000
Dagbladet/F.A.A.	56,000

Source: World Association of Newspapers and Zenithmedia, *World Press Trends 2001*, p. 88.

In addition to keen competition for advertising revenue and modernization of technology, a major factor in the increased popularity of large national newspapers is the content emphasis on foreign and national news, business, and cultural coverage. Each of Copenhagen's two large morning dailies has five or six foreign correspondents plus ''stringers'' in various areas, though much of their foreign news comes through Ritzau's Bureau and Reuters news services. To compete with the appeal of radio and television to the general populace, the newspapers have targeted their content to well-educated people who prefer the in-depth news coverage provided by newspapers to the sound bites on radio and television.

In appearance, all the general-interest dailies have virtually the same format. Typically, the *Berlingske Tidende* has a seven-column page (56 x 40 cm), with weekday editions of about 40 pages and Sunday editions of up to 84 pages. The largest regional and provincial dailies run about 20 pages on weekdays, and smaller papers 12-14 pages. On average, one-third of space is devoted to advertising, but it can run as high as two-thirds in some issues. The major city dailies published in Denmark in 2000 and their circulation estimates are shown below.

According to Danish Circulation Control, five of the major dailies published in Denmark in 2000 and their circulation estimates are: *Berlingske-Tidende,* published in Copenhagen, founded 1749, weekday circulation of 156,000; *Politiken,* published in Copenhagen, founded 1884, circulation of 143,000; *Edstrabladet,* published in Copenhagen, founded 1904, circulation of 135,000; *B.T.,* published in Copenhagen, founded 1916, circulation of 123,000; *Jyllands-Posten,* published in Aarhus, founded 1871, circulation of 180,000.

The large daily newspapers, national and regional, are quality publications, with a high content of foreign and national news, business and commerce. The smaller provincials are less formal in tone and feature more local news and culture. Large headlines, pictures and illustrations enliven the appearance, but generally, Danish newspapers avoid lurid sensationalism.

Even celebrity-oriented illustrated magazines set limits on what is appropriate to publish. According to the 1997 *World Press Freedom Review,* one Danish magazine editor announced on the day following the death of Britain's Princess Diana in Paris that he would no longer use photographs taken by the intrusive paparazzi. The *Review* also reported that in August 1997, the Danish Press Council condemned *Se og Hoer* (See and Hear) for publishing a French paparazzo's photographs of Danish Crown Prince Frederik and a woman companion bathing in the grounds of a French chateau.

ECONOMIC FRAMEWORK

Denmark lies directly in the path of European trade flowing in all directions via the North Sea, the Baltic Sea, and the Skagerrak. A merchant fleet of more than 1,500 ships engage in overseas trade. Inland vessels and ferries connect with a network of roads, bridges, and railroads that transport goods and people to Central Europe, Norway, Sweden, and Finland. Exports include agricultural products, pharmaceuticals, motor ships, dairy equipment, cement machinery and electronic equipment. Denmark imports coal and oil from Germany, Great Britain, and the United States, and industrial raw materials from various countries.

Copenhagen (Kobenhavn), Denmark's capital and largest city, has one of the busiest airports (Kastrup) of Northern Europe. It is the terminal port for the great arc over the North Atlantic from the United States and Canada, as well as the corresponding arc across the North Pole to Japan and East Asia. Scandinavian Airlines System (SAS) operates worldwide. Likewise, Copenhagen's Free Port serves 5,000-6,000 ships annually as they exchange cargoes without the expense and formalities of clearing customs. Aarhus, Odense, and Aalborg also are centers of trade and commerce.

The fishing industry, individual and cooperative, is a major factor in the Danish economy. Denmark's 12,000 fishermen bring in cod, herring, eels, lobster and shrimp from the North Sea and numerous species of freshwater fish from the coastal waters and the fjords that penetrate deep into the interior. About half the catch is sold at auction. The skippers of fishing vessels are often the owners, but customarily, the crews share in the expense and profits.

Denmark's agricultural industry is dominated by cooperatives. About 70 percent of mainland Denmark's

Daily and Non-Daily Newspaper Titles and Circulation Figures

	1996	1997	1998	1999	2000
Number of Daily Newspapers	38	38	37	34	31
Circulation of Dailies (000)	1,631	1,617	1,583	1,528	1,481
Number of Non-Daily Newspapers	1	1	1	1	1
Circulation of Non-Dailies (000)	53	60	60	63	66

Source: World Association of Newspapers and Zenithmedia, *World Press Trends 2001*, pp. 8, 10, 17, 19.

land area (43,094 square kilometers, 16,639 square miles) is devoted to agriculture. Approximately 179,000 medium-sized farms of 10-30 hectares (25-75 acres) account for one-half the cultivated area. About 27,000 "smallholdings" (farms of 5-10 hectares) were carved out of former large estates, but some wealthy landowners' manor houses with surrounding buildings can still be seen on the landscape.

Fifty percent of the land produces crops of cereal grains, mainly barley, but also oats, rye and wheat. The feed crops complement the grasslands in serving the important cattle and dairy industries, which provide 90 percent of all farm income. Danish animal husbandry and farming are productive due to applied scientific research in the selection of grains, soil treatment, automated milking machines and mechanized farm equipment.

Since the mid-1900s, industrial development has displaced agriculture as the most important segment of the economy. Urban industries employ about 40 percent of the labor force and contribute 40 percent of the gross national product (GNP). A third of Denmark's industrial workers are employed in manufacturing. One important export is cement, including products and expertise, as Danish engineers build cement plants at home and abroad. Denmark's largest corporation, the East Asiatic Company, Inc. (founded in 1897), has 100 branch offices and 35,000 employees worldwide. It maintains a fleet of 30 ships, and owns mines, rice mills, and rubber plantations. In Australia, the company is engaged in industry and timber. In Canada, it owns forests and operates sawmills and paper factories. In Brazil, it is in the coffee trade; in Africa, timber and auto imports.

Fishing and shipbuilding are paramount in the Faroe Islands. The rocky coasts of the Faroes provide nesting grounds for seabirds but very little arable land for agriculture. Dwarf shrubs and grassy heath are suitable for grazing sheep, so principal exports include mutton and wool, along with frozen and salted fish, and fish products such as liver oil. The Faroe Islands Dairy Centre supplies all 45,000 inhabitants in the islands with fresh milk and dairy products. The Centre serves as a cooperative, giving production and marketing assistance to producers in order to advance the quality and efficiency of Faroese agriculture. Nearby oil production in the North Sea offers hope that oil deposits will be found in the Faroes, allowing more diversification in the economy and lessening dependence upon the annual subsidy from Denmark. During World War II, the Faroe Islands were occupied and protected from German invasion by the British Navy. The Faroese import-export partners are Denmark, Norway, the United Kingdom, France, Germany, Sweden, Iceland, and the United States.

Greenland, with its state-of-the-art communications and meteorological stations, is important to all nations traversing the airways and seas of the North Atlantic. When Germany occupied Denmark during World War II and threatened Greenland, the Danish minister in Washington negotiated an agreement with the United States to assume protective custody over Greenland for the duration of the war. The United States invoked the Monroe Doctrine and constructed landing fields, seaplane facilities, and installations necessary to protect Greenland and the American hemisphere. In 1947 Denmark requested an end to the 1941 wartime agreement. In April 1951 a new pact was negotiated, giving Denmark control of the U.S. naval station on Greenland, providing for joint defense areas, and authorizing members of the North Atlantic Treaty Organization (NATO) to use all naval, air, and military bases on the island. The agreement further authorized the United States to build and maintain a strategic air base at Thule in northern Greenland, about 1,500 kilometers from the North Pole.

Greenland's main industry is fishing (salmon, cod, halibut and shrimp) and dozens of fish processing plants dot the southern and western coasts. Disko Bay boasts some of the world's largest shrimp beds. In the north and east, seals, foxes and polar bears are hunted for their fur. Seabirds are hunted for meat, eggs and down. Also, the southern area provides limited areas for sheep and cattle breeding. Greenland's major exports are fish and fur. Principal trading partners are Canada, Australia, the United States, Denmark and the United Kingdom.

In 1952 the Danish government and private interests in Denmark, Sweden and Canada formed a company to exploit deposits of iron, lead, zinc, tungsten and cryolite (a mineral used in the production of aluminum) in eastern Greenland. By 1990, mining had exhausted the reserves. Deposits of coal, copper, molybdenum and uranium have been located, but not fully exploited. Thule Air Base supports a community of military and civilian personnel from the United States and Denmark.

Denmark was the first industrialized country to establish a Ministry of the Environment. But despite its advanced stage of environmental planning and worldwide activism, all of Denmark's environmental problems have not been solved. Though 98 percent of sewage is treated and sulfur dioxide emissions reduced, agricultural runoff has caused harmful algae growth in the North Sea that increasingly threatens drinking water supplies. By 1997, 32.2 percent of the country had been placed in protected areas. Denmark is still working to clean up three thousand hazardous waste sites identified in the 1980s. In 1988, in response to ecological disasters that destroyed the lobster colonies in the strait between Denmark and Sweden, the *Folketing* passed more rigorous measures to protect the environment.

Denmark includes Greenland and the Faroes in regional and international environmental agreements pertaining to air pollution and the ozone layer, ship pollution and marine life, climactic changes, endangered species and habitats. In 1985 the *Folketing* passed legislation against the future construction of nuclear power plants in Denmark and agreed to help establish a Nordic nuclear-free zone.

Denmark joined the North Atlantic Treaty Organization in 1949, the European Free Trade Association (1959), and the European Economic Community, now known as the European Union (1972). In 1992 Danish voters rejected the Maastricht Treaty, which provided for increased integration of currency and politics with the European Union, creating considerable political controversy within the government. Denmark remains a member of the EU, and elects 16 members of the European parliament. Greenland joined the EU with Denmark in 1972, but withdrew in 1985 due to a dispute over fishing quotas. The Faroe Islands are not part of the EU.

PRESS LAWS

Freedom of the press is guaranteed under Denmark's Constitution of 1849, and this right is respected in practice. The chief limitation of fair comment in speech and writing has been to protect the privacy and reputation of the individual. Most press libel cases since World War II have hinged on this issue. Libel cases have rarely resulted in sentences of imprisonment, but in those few cases where it has, terms in prison have never exceeded three months. Under press law, legal responsibility for a signed article rests with the author, but for the unsigned article and other materials, legal responsibility rests with the editor. The trend in interpreting press law is toward increased freedom for journalists to protect sources. A special national agency operates as a ''corrections board'' to hear complaints about a newspaper's refusal or failure to print a correction of any factual material that has been incorrectly or wrongfully printed, and a fine may be imposed if the board holds the paper liable.

A new legal provision, resulting from the Danish experience under the Nazis, declares that no citizen may be deprived of liberty because of political or religious convictions or descent. The official state-supported church is Evangelical Lutheran, to which 91 percent of the Danes belong. Citizens do have the right to form other congregations for the worship of God. Citizens cannot be required to pay taxes to support a denomination to which they do not belong, but neither are they permitted to form a religious group and engage in practices that are ''at variance with good morals or public order.'' This affects the press indirectly, in that aberrant religious practices may become the subject of reporting and editorial comment.

The 1997 *World Press Freedom Review* reported that for the first time in Denmark's history, a prison sentence was handed down for threats made against a journalist. The case grew out of a three-year war between the Hells Angels and Bandidos biker gangs that left 12 people dead and more than 70 wounded. The gangs threatened journalists who covered the trials. One Bandido was jailed for two months for threatening Per Rasmussun, a freelance photographer filming outside the court building where a Bandido member was on trial. Two other Bandidos were tried for making repeated visits to the home of photographer Flemming Keith Karlsen and threatening him with death. Conviction of the Bandidos was seen as a major victory for the press.

CENSORSHIP

For more than 200 years under the absolute monarchy, Denmark's newspapers were subject to censorship. Since the adoption of the Constitution of 1849, which guaranteed freedom of the press, the Danish government has exercised no control over the press. Nor has it attempted to control the flow of news and information from government administrative agencies to the press.

The only exception is the censorship exercised by the Germans who occupied Denmark during World War II. A 1939 non-aggression pact with Germany allowed the Danes a measure of control over their legal and domestic affairs until 1943. But in 1943-1945, rigid censorship was imposed, and all publications were compelled to print only the news and articles approved by the Nazis.

STATE-PRESS RELATIONS

Denmark's newspapers consistently have opposed direct financial aid from the government, but as an increasing number of newspapers failed, government expanded its indirect subsidies to the press. Subsidies take the form of relief from value-added taxes, reduced rates for telephone and postal charges, and government payments for agency advertisements and printing the results of the national lottery. Low-interest loans also are available from the government-created Financial Institution of the Daily Press to which the government makes annual contributions.

The Joint Council of Danish Newspapers (*Danske Dagblades Faellesrepraesentation*) is made up of representatives of political associations, editors and publishers. Founded in 1936, this organization speaks to the authorities and the general public on behalf of the newspapers. The council has developed a code of ethics and a directive treatise on Good Press Habits in Reporting Criminal Cases. The Danish Press Council (*Pressenaevnet*) was established in 1965 for the purpose of passing judgment on interpretations and alleged violations of the code.

Most newspapers are members of the Danish Newspaper Publishers Union. The union handles common economic issues with the exception of wage agreements with typographical workers, which are handled by a special employers' union. On occasion, the government may be called upon to mediate a labor dispute such as the 1977 strike that shut down *Berlinske Tidende* and two other newspapers for six months.

The government has exerted greater control of radio and television media. From 1925 to 1964, the state maintained a monopoly over radio broadcasts, and from 1962 to 1998, a state monopoly of television.

Radio Denmark (Danmarks Radio or DR), an independent public monopoly, has sole rights to present radio and television broadcasts under the Broadcasting Act (*Radioloven*) of June 11, 1959. Until May 1987 a governing Radio Council (*Radioradet*) operated under the Ministry of Cultural Affairs. The council was charged with responsibility to establish general principles that govern the content and quality of programs. In May 1987 the *Folketing* passed legislation that replaced the Radio Council with an 11-member governing board. The Minister of Communications names the chair; the political parties in the *Folketing* select nine members; and DR personnel choose one. The board appoints the director-general of DR, and has overall responsibility for DR's operations.

A Program Committee advises the board. It is composed of 21 members, one-third chosen by listeners' and viewers' associations, two-thirds chosen by organizations representing business, labor, education, religion, art, sports, and consumers. The Program Committee authorizes program plans, suggests additional broadcast series, discusses political items and events, elections, and parliamentary transmissions that impact upon broadcast content and schedules. Complaints about DR are heard by a three-member independent agency.

DR operates two public television stations. Both are subject to public service obligations with regard to news and educational programming. Since 1988, local commercial television stations have been permitted to broadcast advertising. Since 1997, television stations are allowed to form networks. The government appoints a five-member board to manage the commercial station, TV2. Advertising commercials may be run only at the beginning and end of a program. No advertising is permitted for medicines, beer, wine, spirits or tobacco. No ads may be run for special interest organizations, political parties, or religious groups. DR is required to meet public service requirements, but commercial stations like TV2 are not.

In 1983 the *Folketing* enacted a temporary law, made permanent in 1987, allowing the operation of local and private radio and television stations. Stations must acquire a permit to operate from a board appointed by the municipal government. Stations cannot be operated or controlled by commercial interests or newspapers, but they may make agreements with newspapers to supply news programming. They are allowed to sell time to political parties and religious entities.

NEWS AGENCIES

Ritzau's Bureau, founded in 1866, is the primary supplier of national and international news to Danish media. Since 1947 Ritzau's Bureau has been owned cooperatively by the Danish press. The Bureau disseminates more than 10,000 words of foreign copy per day, of which 50-55 percent comes from Reuters, 25-30 percent from AFP, and 6-7 percent each from DPA and the Swedish TT. Ritzau's Bureau handles all distribution of Danish news abroad. Content of the foreign-bound material is about 86 percent news and 11 percent information.

There is an International Press Center in Copenhagen, where the Foreign Ministry's Press and Information Department provides services to the Foreign Press and the foreign correspondents of Danish media. The Association of Danish Newspapers, Danish District Weeklies, and Danish Specialist Press, all headquartered in Copenhagen, serve their respective newspapers and other publications. Most Copenhagen papers import newsprint and equipment through a cooperative purchasing agency, and share distribution costs through their own agency, the A/S Bladkompagniet.

BROADCAST MEDIA

Amateur radio broadcasts began in Denmark about 1920, and by 1923 three Copenhagen newspapers were broadcasting news via radio. In 1925 Statsradiofonien, a state radio monopoly was established that lasted until 1964. During the 1930s, radio became an important news media, reaching 75 percent of all Danish households. In 1959, competing radio newscasts were replaced by a single radio news service (Pressens Radioavis, renamed Danmarks Radio or DR), with major newspapers editing the news. Additional radio channels were added in 1963-1964 when the state monopoly was broken.

DR operates four channels: Programme 1 (P1) broadcasts information and cultural programs; Programme 2 (P2musik) airs mainly classical music; Programme 3 (P3) is a music and news channel aimed at younger listeners; and Programme 4 (P4) broadcasts regional news and entertainment. In 1983, local radio stations appeared, initially financed by voluntary contributions from various organizations, but since 1988 also by advertising. Radio 2, a national commercial station, has been on the air since 1997.

DR began television news transmissions in 1953. Though the state television monopoly was not broken until 1988, the rapid growth of satellite and cable television channels posed serious competition for newspapers, tabloids and weekly entertainment magazines. In 1996 DR added a second television channel.

On October 1, 1988, TV2 began transmissions and in October 2000, TV2 added a second channel. The first commercial station in Denmark was TV3, owned by the international media group SBS, which began broadcasting from London via satellite on January 1, 1988. Since April 1997, TvDanmark has broadcast in eight regions, with programming primarily focused on entertainment and regional news. Since 2000, TvDanmark has operated two channels.

The four public service stations are partly or fully financed by license fees.

In 1999, DR channels 1 and 2 garnered 31 percent of the viewing audience, while TV2's share was 36 percent. TV3 gained 11 percent, and TvDanmark 8 percent. All other channels shared 14 percent of the market. The market report estimates that the average Danish viewer watches television for 2 hours and 38 minutes per day.

Radio Denmark has radio and television studios at Copenhagen, Aarhus, Abenra, Aalborg, and Odense. In 1986 there were 49 radio transmitters serving 2.05 million receivers and 32 television transmitters with 1.95 million receivers. Though TV2 generates advertising revenues, radio and television are financed primarily from license fees required of all radio and television set owners. Usually, the television license also covers radio use, but if the household has no television, it must have a license for radio receivers only. Radio licenses cost about one-fourth the fee for television licenses. A reduced fee applies for senior citizens and disabled pensioners.

Radio Greenland (Kalaalit Nunaata Radio or KNR) is an independent public entity administered by a seven-man board appointed by the Greenland government. A management committee operates KNR-Radio and KNR-TV, broadcasting daily radio and television programs throughout Greenland. KNR-TV annually broadcasts about 300 hours in Greenlandic and 2,000 hours in Danish. It also transmits television news from DR daily. KNR-Radio broadcasts 2,500 hours in Greenlandic, 900 in Danish, and 2,200 hours of music each year. KNR has news departments in Nuuk, North and South Greenland and Copenhagen, and delivers news to Greenlanders in both Greenlandic and Danish languages. Local radio and television productions are culturally oriented, and financed partly by advertising revenue. KNR has its own production studios in Nuuk, the capital, where it employs about 120 people.

Faroese Radio is not under the jurisdiction of DR, but like Greenland, cooperates with it. Faroe Islanders are served by the state radio Utvaap Foroya, and Ras 2 radio station. Sjonvarp Faroya (SvF), the Faroes' national television company, is the only television station broadcasting in Faroese. The station transmits 40 hours a week, covering news, documentaries, entertainment, culture, sports and drama. The station employs 35 people plus 15-20 freelance workers and specialists. The station reaches about 13,000 households throughout the islands. Surveys confirm that SvF commands 70-80 percent of viewers, especially for local news and productions.

The Voice of Denmark shortwave radio service transmits daily 45-minute programs in Danish and 30-minute programs in Spanish and English. Transmissions are beamed to South America, North America, the Far East, Southern Asia, Africa and Greenland. Programs are generally free of political propaganda; they focus on news, commentaries, and interviews related to events in Denmark. The primary purpose of the foreign broadcasts is to promote a broader awareness of Denmark and its culture. A related publication, *The Voice of Denmark,* is published four times a year, and provides information about the shortwave broadcasts in Danish, English and Spanish.The expansion of broadcast media has placed increasing pressure on the print media, particularly tabloids and weekly entertainment magazines.

ELECTRONIC MEDIA

Most major radio and television channels in Denmark have established Internet services to provide news updates, essays, film and other services, in Denmark, Greenland and the Faroes. Thirty-one Denmark newspapers provide online services. Media outlets with the resources to provide Internet services have a strong advantage in the advertising market. In the 1970s and 1980s, electronic media, radio and television took over much of the advertising market that had been dominated by the print media in the 1960s.

EDUCATION AND TRAINING

Denmark has a nine-year compulsory education system beginning at age seven.The education obligation may be fulfilled in the free municipal Folkeskole or private school, or by home schooling. In 1993 the Danish Parliament adopted a new Folkeskole Act, which led to numerous reforms aimed at achieving a balance between subject-specific and general education during the nine years of compulsory education. After completing the required education, the student make proceed to upper secondary education at either of two levels: general education qualifying for access to higher education, or vocational or technical education qualifying for access to the labor market.

All higher education is free to students, and all institutions are funded by the state, though they are self-governing and independent as to program offerings and budget decisions. The student may select the short-cycle non-university program of one to three years to study technical programs, market economics, or train as a computer specialist. These programs are primarily offered at business and technical colleges. The medium-cycle university programs of three to fours years comprise the bachelor's degree programs of universities and other higher education institutions in the university sector. The institutions collectively offer a diverse range of professional training choices in education, liberal arts, science, and medicine, in which a student may prepare for a profession or move toward a university master's degree program. The long-cycle higher education program of five to six years is research-based and offered by institutions in the university sector.

All institutions of higher education in Denmark are free to admit as many qualified applicants as they have space and qualified faculty to teach. There are no entrance examinations for students, but they must be recommended by the secondary school they attended. Each institution establishes its own criteria of selection if it cannot admit all applicants. State funding grants to the institutions are based on the specific programs offered and the number of active students per year.

The government operates a school for journalists in Aarhus, which graduates about 200 students each year. The program consists of 18 months of study, 18 months of practical experience, and a final year of study. In addition, there are vocational colleges and institutions for training production technicians in print media, radio and television, and electronic media.

SUMMARY

The Danish press has made steady progress in quality and diversification for more than a hundred years, although faced by wars, political upheavals and financial reverses. The dominant positions of several large daily newspapers founded in the eighteenth century speaks to their survival capabilities and to the Danish people's attachment to their newspapers. Without doubt, the newspapers shall maintain their constitutional freedoms, despite the indirect government subsidies they accept to lower costs.

The shift to radio and television for mass media consumption is global, and newspapers have taken the competition in stride, adjusting their services to include use of the mass media outlets of radio, television and the Internet.

It remains to be seen whether the government will relinquish its remaining controls over radio and television and allow unfettered competition. The rapid growth from two to eight television stations after the state monopoly was broken may have evoked a slowdown in the government's relaxation of restrictions in order to avoid the financial instability that often comes with rapid expansion. Economic contractions in the private sector may have severe impact on the advertising revenue of the media. Government subsidies and capital outlay for communications facilities are dependent upon projected revenues from license fees and taxes—major factors in decisions to limit or encourage growth.

The Danish press has diversified in the face of competition, and thereby increased the depth and quality of programming in newspapers, radio and television. One concern is maintaining credibility in the national media as coverage increasingly reflects the violence and immorality existing in the global society.

Another factor that may influence the future of the media is whether the Faroese and the Greenlanders will be content with home rule status or will seek complete independence from Denmark.

The Danish press—print, broadcast, and electronic—seems well able to adapt to circumstances. Constitutional freedom of the press is exercised by the print media, while radio and television are partly funded and controlled by the state. Media consumption increases along with the varieties of media. Even as the electronic media inspires more consumption of programs with international orientation, there is a corresponding rise in interest in media focused on local communities and national identity.

The Internet is both a challenge and an opportunity for the print and broadcast media to expand their reach and influence to audiences beyond Denmark, and to promote awareness of Danish culture and society at home and abroad. From its past performance and history, Denmark's press seems well able to meet the challenge and take advantage of the opportunities.

SIGNIFICANT DATES

- 1997: Commercial Radio 2 began broadcasting nationally. Television stations received permission to form networks and expand.
- 1999: Two Danmarks Radio (state) television channels, DR1 and DR2, lost market dominance to commercial station TV2.
- 2000: Commercial television station TV2 began broadcasting on two channels, and TvDanmark implemented broadcasts on two channels.
- 2001: Internet site designers in Denmark increased by 85 percent in one year.
- 2002: Thirty-one Danish newspapers and two in the Faroe Islands provide services via electronic media.

BIBLIOGRAPHY

''Danish History.'' *Usenet newsgroup soc.culture.nordic.* Available from http://lysator.liu.se/nordic/scn/faq33.html.

Danish Ministry of Education (Undervisnings Ministeriet). ''Principles and Issues in Education.'' Available from http://www.uvm.dk/publications/.htm.

''Denmark.'' *Microsoft Encarta Online Encyclopedia 2001.* Available from http://encarta.msn.com.

''Denmark.'' In *1999 World Press Freedom Review.* Available from http://www.freemedia.at/wpfr/denmark.htm.

''Faroe Islands.'' Central Intelligence Agency (CIA). In *The World Factbook.* Available from http://www.odci.gov/cia/publications/factbook/geos/fo.html.

''Greenland.'' *Microsoft Encarta Online Deluxe.* Available from http://encarta.msn.com.

Harvey, William J., and Christian Reppien. *Denmark and the Danes: A Survey of Danish Life, Institutions and Culture.* Port Washington, NY: Kennikat Press, 1915, 1970.

Kurian, George Thomas. *Facts on File: National Profiles, Scandinavia.* New York and Oxford: R.R. Donnelley & Sons, 1990.

Logan, F. Donald. *The Vikings in History.* Totowa, NJ: Barnes & Noble Books, 1983.

———. *Denmark: A Troubled Welfare State.* Boulder, San Francisco and Oxford: Westview Press, 1991.

Miller, Kenneth E. *Friends and Rivals: Coalition Politics in Denmark, 1901-1995.* Lanham, MD and London: University Press of America, Inc., 1996.

Rying, Bent, Editor-in-Chief. *Denmark: An Official Handbook.* Copenhagen: Krak, for Press and Information Department, Denmark Ministry of Foreign Affairs, 1970.

—Marguerite R. Plummer, Ph.D.

DJIBOUTI

BASIC DATA

Official Country Name:	Republic of Djibouti
Region (Map name):	Africa
Population:	460,700
Language(s):	French, Arabic, Somali, Afar
Literacy rate:	46.2%

Despite an urbanized context that might be expected to foster a thriving press, media activity is in fact not extensive in the tiny Republic of Djibouti—*Républic de Djibouti* (French), Jumhuriyah Djibouti (Arabic)—formerly French Somaliland. Constraining influences are a low literacy rate, little available advanced education, high unemployment, and the ongoing historical patterns of a socially and politically closed society.

The country has a strategic location near oil reserves on the shipping lane linking the Gulf of Aden with the Red Sea. Independence came in 1977, and a 1992 constitution provided for limited multiparty elections. A late-1994 peace accord ended a three-year uprising by Afar rebels.

The country, with barren terrain covering about 9,000 square miles, is over eighty percent urban, with most people living in the capital, Djibouti, a commercially active center serviced by several international airlines. French aid bolsters the economy, and unemployment is high.

The estimated population in the year 2000 was 460,700. Adult literacy in 1995 was 46.2 percent, with the literacy rate for men about twice as high as that for women. Students at institutions of higher education numbered 130.

French and Arabic are the official languages. The use of Somali and Afar as native tongues reflects the ethnic backgrounds of the populace, which is ninety-four percent Muslim.

Newspapers include *La Nation de Djibouti*, a pro-government weekly, and *Carrefour Africain*, a Roman Catholic publication issued twice a month. Circulation numbers are low.

The local news agency is *Agence Djiboutienne de Press* (ADP). *Agence France-Presse* also has an office in Djibouti.

The state-run *Radiodiffusion-Télévision de Djibouti* broadcasts in French, Somali, Afar, and Arabic. In 1998, citizens owned about 53,000 radios and 29,000 television sets; the one television transmitter in Djibouti was at that time on the air for thirty-five hours a week.

By 1995, about 1000 personal computers were in use, and figures for the year 2000 showed about 1000 Internet users.

BIBLIOGRAPHY

Banks, Arthur S., and Thomas C. Muller, ed. *Political Handbook of the World, 1999.* Binghamton, NY: CSA Publications, 1999.

Turner, Barry, ed. *The Statesman's Yearbook: The Politics, Cultures, and Economies of the World, 2000.* 136th ed. New York: St. Martin's Press, 1999.

World Almanac and Book of Facts, 2002. New York: World Almanac Books, 2002.

—Roy Neil Graves

DOMINICA

BASIC DATA

Official Country Name:	Commonwealth of Dominica
Region (Map name):	Caribbean
Population:	71,540
Language(s):	English, French patois
Literacy rate:	94%

In the fourteenth century, Carib settlers called the island "Waitikubuli," which means "tall is her body." But the name that has stood the test of time is Dominica, granted by Christopher Columbus in 1493 to commemorate the Sunday on which he first sighted its shores.

Dominican media enjoys full freedom of speech. There is no daily newspaper, but the island does support five weeklies, all published in English. *The Chronicle* publishes on Friday and enjoys a circulation of approximately 3,000. Independent Publishing produces *The Independent*, which rivals *The Chronicle* in circulation numbers, and *The Mirror*, which is billed as a weekend newspaper and appears every Friday. Other weeklies are the *Sun*, which appears on Monday, and *The Tropical Star*, published on Wednesday. *The Dominica Official Gazette* is the island's government-sponsored newspaper. It published weekly from Roseau, the island's capital. The island also has an online news resource, *www.news-dominica.com*, which posts news and information from local newspapers, including *The Chronicle* and *The Independent*, every Friday.

Lying between the North Atlantic Ocean and the Caribbean Sea, it was the last of the Caribbean islands to be colonized by Europeans. In 1763, Great Britain took possession of the island from France, declaring it a colony in 1805. Dominica became independent in 1978, operating as a parliamentary democracy.

The country's head of state is a President, who is elected by its legislature, the thirty-seat House of Assembly. The President then appoints a Prime Minister to head the government. The population is approximately seventy-one thousand, and 94 percent of the population is literate. English is the official language, but French patois is also spoken. The cornerstone of Dominica's economy is agriculture, especially bananas, and profitability often hinges on the weather. After devastating storms in 1994 and 1995, the government has pledged to diversify the economy by encouraging soap production, adventure tourism, and offshore financial services.

There are thirteen radio stations on the island, 10 FM and three AM, and approximately 46,000 radios. There are approximately 6,000 televisions but no local broadcasting station. There are 16 Internet service providers

BIBLIOGRAPHY

Benn's Media, Vol. 3, Ed. 147. 1999

Central Intelligence Agency (CIA). *The World Fact Book 2001*. 2001. Available from http://www.odci.gov/cia.

Country Profile: Domica BBC News. 2002. Available from http://news.bbc.co.uk.

News Dominica. 2002. Available from http://www.news-dominica.com.

—Jenny B. Davis

DOMINICAN REPUBLIC

BASIC DATA

Official Country Name:	Dominican Republic
Region (Map name):	North & Central America
Population:	8,581,477
Language(s):	Spanish
Literacy rate:	82.1%
Area:	48,730 sq km
GDP:	19,669 (US$ millions)
Number of Television Stations:	25
Number of Television Sets:	770,000
Television Sets per 1,000:	89.7
Number of Radio Stations:	180
Number of Radio Receivers:	1,440,000
Radio Receivers per 1,000:	167.8

BACKGROUND & GENERAL CHARACTERISTICS

The Dominican Republic, a former Spanish colony, occupies the eastern two-thirds of the Caribbean island of Hispaniola, which is located west of Puerto Rico and southeast of Cuba in the Greater Antilles. The Dominican Republic has an area of 48,730 sq. km (18,704 sq mi), and its population was estimated at 8.6 million by the World Bank in 2001. The island is the second largest of the Caribbean island chain strung from Cuba in the northwest to Trinidad in the south. Its only border is with the Republic of Haiti.

Although they share a common border, the two countries occupying Hispaniola are culturally and linguistically distinct. The Dominican Republic is Hispanic, Spanish-speaking, predominantly mulatto or white, while Haiti is French and African culturally, racially black, with an official language of Haitian Creole (Kreyol). The Dominican population is a racial ''melting pot'' in which the mulatto (Caucasian and black mixture) has become the dominant element numerically (73 percent). Caucasians represent 16 percent of the population and blacks 11 percent. Also adding to the ethnic composition has been the influx of diverse immigrant populations of Chinese, Japanese, and Middle Eastern nationals as well as immigrants from neighboring Caribbean countries such as Haiti and Cuba. Traditionally, race and class tend to be closely related with whites forming the elite. More recently, social trends follow Brazil's model of phenotypic upward mobility. Changing rapidly from the dominantly rural mode of the past, the population is now 61.8 percent urban with a population density of 161.7 people per sq km (rural density 293.0), a fertility rate of 2.9 live births per woman and an annual growth rate of 1.8 percent. Well over 1 million Dominicans live as immigrants in the United States, making them the second largest group of incoming migrants into the American economy and remittances from Dominicans living abroad are a substantial addition (10 percent) to the capita gross domestic product.

Since the restoration of macroeconomic stability in the early 1990s, the Dominican Republic (DR) has been the fastest growing economy in Latin America. This Spanish-speaking and strongly Roman Catholic nation has emerged from the financial crisis of the late 1980s with an unprecedented growth, which has averaged eight percent per year from 1996 to 1999 and which is having a positive impact in the quality of life of the average Dominican. Recent government estimates indicate that between 1992 and 1998 more than fifteen percent of the country's poor emerged out of poverty. This finding is consistent with improvements in other indicators of welfare such as life expectancy, access to water and sanitation, and average educational attainment of the labor force. Since the year 2000, however, this promising rate of growth has leveled off to the now current GNP growth of 4.3 percent, according to Banco Central 2001-2002 figures, a trend that leaves fewer funds available for government investment in social welfare programs.

With a 2000 income per capita of US$2,080 but a highly skewed distribution of income, two million of some 8.6 million Dominicans live in poverty. The Dominican poor share most of the characteristics of the poor across the world: large families, little or no education, and limited access to water and sanitation services. Poverty tends to be especially severe in rural areas (35 percent of the total population), where misdirected agriculture practices and insufficient public investments, particularly in education, limit opportunities. Illiteracy runs at about 16 percent and the average level of educational attainment is 4.9 years of schooling. Those able to achieve higher levels of education (5.7 percent) tend to migrate out of the rural areas leaving behind the most disadvantaged, creating in the process entrenched pockets of poverty. Nowhere is that more true than in the areas bordering Haiti, where extreme poverty is prevalent. The poor are also vulnerable to catastrophic losses as the country is routinely subjected to hurricanes. Publicly provided safety nets are practically non-existent, while the private safety nets, mainly in the form of remittances from the very large number of Dominicans living in the United States, benefit primarily the middle and higher income groups.

Considerable controversy surrounds the question of Haitians present within the Dominican Republic. Prejudice against Haitians runs through society, disadvantaging many Haitians and Dominicans of Haitian ancestry. The government has not acknowledged the existence of this discrimination nor made any efforts to combat it. Existing mostly as illegal immigrants, Haitians constitute an important economic factor as they fill the need for low-paid, unskilled labor in construction and agriculture, working with salaries as low as 8 dollars per day. Estimates range as to their numbers, but official reports are unreliable, as their presence remains undocumented. Lack of personal documentation hinders the ability of children of Haitian descent to attend school where there is one available. Despite their large numbers, as of yet there are no Haitian publications within the Dominican Republic or any appreciable publications in Kreyol, the official language of *Haití*, a fact that is not surprising given the low literacy attainment of the average Haitian. National newspapers, on the other hand, tend to reflect popular Dominican opinion concerning their presence. However, recently some radio stations have began to include broadcasts in Kreyol.

The newspaper with the largest circulation in the Dominican Republic is the *Listín Diario* with a daily circulation of 166,000, a Saturday edition with a circulation of 180,000, and a Sunday edition with a circulation of 150,000, numbers that nearly double those of any major competitor. Formerly in private hands, it is now run by Editora Listín Diario, which is owned by the BanInter Group. Other newspapers, in order of circulation, are the *Hoy* with a daily, Saturday, and Sunday circulation of 82,000; *El Nacional* with a daily, Saturday, and Sunday circulation of 42,000; and the *Última Hora* (statistics NA), all of which are published out of the capital of Santo Domingo. Other national papers are *El Caribe*, circulation 40,000, whose former editor, Germán Ornes, won special recognition from the International Press Institute in 2000 as one of 50 ''Heroes of Journalism of the last 50 years'', and *El Nuevo Diario,* circulation 20,000. The largest circulation of regional interest is *La Información* of Santiago, circulation 22,000, and one English language paper, *The Santo Domingo News*.

Most Dominican magazines that focus on the news are generally weekly productions. The most important ones are *Ahora* and *Rumbo*. Of lesser importance is the yellow press weekly *Sucesos* which specializes in graphic depictions of violent events. Religious groups also issue some publications such as *El Semenario Camino* and *Despertar!*.

The history of television in the DR has gone through various stages since its initiation with La Voz del Yuna in 1942. Today Radio Televisión Dominicana is government owned. The TV channels most watched, however, are Color Visión (Canal 9), Circuito Independencia, and Canal 6 (the only station with national availability). In total, there are seven land-based television stations to which must be added 30 cable operators whose coverage augments the average number of stations to that of 40. As concerns radio coverage, there are more than 180 stations with at least 56 FM stations throughout the country, two of which are nationally owned. These broadcast not only national news and events, but also radio educational programs such as primary grade courses directed to students living in remote areas. 1997 figures place television ownership at 770,000 units and radio ownership at 1,440,000 units.

Current Press Situation Dominican journalists reported very few restrictions on press freedom in 1999, a situation that had changed by 2001. Two major developments raised concern among the local press. In September, the electoral board passed a resolution imposing restrictions on campaign advertising for the May 2000 presidential elections. The resolution requires news organizations to accept price controls for advertising and denied them the right to reject advertisements at their own discretion. Some local journalists viewed this law favorably because it also prevents newspapers from charging different advertising fees to different candidates. Another resolution, passed in July by the National Commission on Public Performances, required newscasters and other journalists to secure credentials from the Commission before appearing on radio or television. By the end of the year, this new regulation had been used to prevent 24 journalists from going on the air. Local press groups have condemned the resolution as unconstitutional.

In the Dominican Republic, defamation is a crime punishable by jail terms of up to six months. In 1997, the penal code was amended to ban publishing montages of an individual's image(s) or quoted speech without the individual's consent, unless the product is clearly identifiable as a montage. This ''crime'' carries a prison sentence of up to two years.

The Dominican press has been accused of not providing impartial coverage of presidential elections of May 16. The government party, the *Partido de la Liberación Dominicana* (PLD), lost control in a three party split between their candidate *Danilo Medina* (PLD) and *Hipólito Mejía of the Partido Revolucionario Democrático (PRD)* and the late ex-president Joaquín Balaguer of the *Partido Reformista Social Cristiano* (PRSC). Mejía obtained a little less than 50 percent of the votes, the quantity necessary to avoid a second round of voting, but he was declared the winner by the Electoral Council, the Junta Central Electoral after the other contenders bowed down claiming that a second round of voting would lead to political and economic instability.

Press coverage of the elections came into question when newspapers partial to the PLD began to portray Mejía as violent and unstable. Other newspapers also began to publish very inaccurate results from opinion surveys, which led many to question whether these surveys had been manipulated to favor the official party.

ECONOMIC FRAMEWORK

The Dominican economy has undergone profound changes in the last two decades. Until the mid-1970s, traditional export products, mainly from agriculture, represented 60 percent of the total value of the country's exports. Over the last two decades the service sector has led the economy, particularly economic and financial services related to tourism and industrial free trade zones, which by 1995 accounted for more than 70 percent of exports. The shift came with major dislocations and economic and social imbalances. Annual per capita expenditures on education during 1987-1990, adjusted for inflation, were 40 percent of what they had been in 1980. In 1992 the gross domestic product (GDP) began to recover, and by 1996 it was maintaining an average annual growth rate of more than five percent and negative inflation. In 1999, the country was singled out as the best economic performer in Latin America after having sustained a growth rate of more than six percent for several consecutive years.

The government maintains a high tariff on imported reading materials. The high cost of these and local materials and the isolation of many areas from television coverage increase the importance of newspapers as a universal source of popular reading material and information. While the government does not subsidize the press, competition between rival publishing concerns has led to the publishing of free newspapers. The *Última Hora,* previously the leading circulating afternoon paper, is now given away free. Also *El Expreso* and *Diario Libre* are published for free distribution. The former is published by Editora Listín Diario, while the latter is published by The Hoy group. These newspapers, people speculate, are distributed freely to both increase future circulation, and to compete with *El Caribe,* which came out under the ownership of Banco Popular at RD$ 5.00, instead of RD$ 10.00 for the other newspapers. Newpaper prices are now universal for the major papers, however, now that *El Caribe* has raised its rates back to RD$10.00 with Saturday and Sunday editions costing RD$15.00. The current cost of periodic quality paper now runs at US$ 700 a ton. Transmission of pictures and the elaboration of graphics are now run off digital systems that streamline all publishing processes. Distribution of newspapers, which is completely owner controlled, has also become streamlined so that all newspapers are on sale by 8 a.m. daily despite distances of 350 km from the central publishing area of Santo Domingo, with distribution agents present at all distribution points.

PRESS LAWS

The Constitution of 1994 in Art. 8, Section 6 states that:

> All persons have the right, without being subject to censure, to express freely their thoughts in either written words or any other medium of expression, either graphic or oral. When such expressed thought be an attack against the dignity or morality of other persons, public peace, or against community standards, those sanctions as dictated by law may be applied. All subversive propaganda is prohibited, either by anonymous agents or by any other means of expression that has as its object the provocation of disobedience of law, yet without impinging by this the right to analyze or give critique of those same legal precepts.

Defamation is a criminal offence under which the press may be punished both as a crime against the press code and also under the common civic code. The difference lies in the procedure as it is handled in court. When defamation is committed as a published entity, it is subject to the guidelines established in the press code. When the defamation or slander is committed outside of the published medium (as crimes of expression), then its persecution is through common law with a penalty of up to three years with *prisión preventiva* while crimes as adjudicated within the press code carry penalties of up to 2 months in prison with no *prisión preventiva.* The law of Expression and Diffusion of Thought establishes a civil and penal responsibility in the minds of the proprietor and director of newspapers, even when they have delegated to others all or part of their executive functions.

The press code speaks of the responsibility of proprietors as indicated in Article 48: ''The owners of newspapers and other news publications are responsible for the impecunious condemnation pronounced by third parties against those persons described in conformity with Art. 1382, 1382, 1384 of the Civil Code.'' Paragraph d) of Law 1951 from the year 1949 mandates that all directors of newspapers and radio broadcasters be Dominican, of legal age, residents within the country, and in full possession of their civil liberties.

In June of 2000, former president Leonel Fernández appointed a commission to review the legislation regulating the press. The commission was to take its guidelines from the ten fundamental principles as outlined in the Declaration of Chapultepec. Fernández created a special decree to form the commission, commenting that, ''A study of the norms that govern the freedom of expression and the diffusion of opinion must be made so that mechanisms can be created that would guarantee public liberties which would eliminate legislation gaps, insufficiencies, and errors.'' The special commission was to revise and modernize Law 6132, the 1962 Law of Expression and Dissemination of Thought, within a period of 45 days so that a draft would be ready to present to Congress for discussion. Continuing work on this legislation has progressed despite the change of government from Fernandez to Mejía in August 2000. In September, President Mejía submitted a bill to revise as Law 6132. Drafted by local press organizations, newspaper executives, and media law specialists, it widens access to information and provides for civil penalties in cases of defamation committed through the press. Some local journalists criticized the proposal, arguing that there has been insufficient debate on the bill, and little disclosure of its content. The bill was still pending at year's end.

Censorship

In terms of civil liberties that influence the expression of opinion and the dispersion of news, the Dominican Republic presents a mixed picture of unbalanced censorship. World Bank reports suggest that the country presents negative indicators for voice and participation in public affairs compared to the Caribbean nations of Jamaica and Belize, but compares favorably with Cuba, neighboring Haiti, and the rest of the developing world in general. It also scored negatively in government effectiveness and level of graft. Conversely, positive growth was indicated in the areas of rule of law, absence of political instability and violence, and economic growth. USAID reports of comparative exercise of political rights varies from a 1985 high of ''free'' (one on a scale of seven) to a 1994 low of partly to not free (four) to the current score of two for relatively free.

The communication media is regulated to a considerable degree by the government and is considered only partially free, especially as this control is based on financial considerations: the press depends heavily on both the publicity that the government generates and the rates that they impose. The frequency of elections adds to the amount of influence political factions have in the reporting of the news. During the last ten years, daily newspaper ownership has shifted from being privately owned to being owned by banks and large corporations. The BanInter group now owns the *Listín Diario*, once a family-run enterprise. Banco Popular, the country's largest private bank, has purchased *El Caribe* and Editora Corripio, the publishing subsidiary of a large Dominican corporation, now owns the second largest morning daily *the Hoy*. Even *La Informacion*, the Santiago local newspaper, is owned by local economic groups, which, it would appear, have strategic interests as to how the news is told.

State-Press Relations

Strong economic growth and poverty reduction has taken place in the midst of positive changes in governance. After a deep political crisis in 1994, democratic institutions have emerged strengthened, and both the legislative and judicial systems now enjoy unprecedented levels of independence. Civil society and the organized business community are also playing an increasing role in influencing policy making through their growing demands for accountability of state actions. In this climate of limited literacy yet enhanced democratic participation, the newspaper plays a critical role in the formation of public opinion and democratic action.

A nadir reached in 1994 in press/state relations was the heavily commentated disappearance of university professor and political columnist Narciso González who had been openly critical of the then incumbent president, Joaquín Balaguer. Subsequent investigations seem to point to his death at the hands of the Dominican military at the direction of Balaguer adherents.

On a brighter note, the murderers of another presumed victim of Balaguer's military was sentenced to thirty years in jail for the assassination in 1975 of the executive director of *Ahora*, Orlando Martínez. While the Sociedad Interamericana de Prensa applauded the judicial action, they also lamented the lack of accused before the bench, commenting that the twenty-five year lapse between crime and punishment had allowed many of the perpetrators to die of natural causes. In a landmark August 4 decision, Judge Katia Miguelina Jiménez delivered stiff prison sentences to three defendants who had been found guilty in the 1975 murder of Orlando Martínez Howley, the director of the magazine *Ahora* and a columnist for the Santo Domingo daily *El Nacional*. Retired Air Force general Joaquín Pou Castro and two accomplices were sentenced to the maximum penalty of 30 years in prison, along with a 5 million peso (US$300,000) fine. On December 21, the defendants appealed the decision to a higher court. The journalist's family and friends had ignored death threats and pursued the case for years, arguing that Martínez's murder resulted from the fact that his reporting had angered then-president Balaguer and other senior officials. In 1997, President Leonel Fernández ordered the case moved to trial. Balaguer, who was 93 years old when he died in 2002, was subpoenaed but declined to testify on health grounds, although he was healthy enough to run for president again in 2000. The

August judgment was seen as a major victory for the journalist's family and others who demanded justice for press freedom and other human rights violations committed under Balaguer, president of the Dominican Republic for 22 of the last 40 years.

Dominican president Hipólito Mejía has received mixed reviews for his policy toward the press since he took office in August 2000. Although Dominican journalists are generally free to express their views, and the government does not officially restrict the press, journalists have complained of government attempts to influence coverage. President Mejía, with his blunt and sometimes confrontational style, has used insulting language when referring to journalists and editors who criticize his administration. In late June, the Santo Domingo daily *El Caribe* reported that Mejía's government had diverted funds from public works programs to buy buses for a public transportation plan. Mejía said of the story, "That is a lie. That's only in the mind of Bernardo Vega [*El Caribe's* editor], one of those idiots who writes things that are not true," according to the daily *Listín Diario*.

In an August 17 interview with the Santo Domingo daily *Última Hora*, José Tejada Gómez, then-president of the journalists' association Colegio Dominicano de Periodistas (CDP), noted that Mejía's insults were common, and that his first year in office was marked by "constant conflicts" with journalists. According to the CDP, signs of government intolerance toward the press abound. In late June, Darío Medrano and Ramón Carmona, reporter and cameraman, respectively, for U.S.-based Univisión TV network and the Santo Domingo TV channel Color Visión-Canal 9, were threatened, allegedly by government officials, for their coverage of nationwide street protests against a government-imposed economic adjustment package. Gen. Luis Rodríguez Florimón, of the National Police, meanwhile, warned in early August that he would monitor radio and TV programs and threatened to jail anybody who criticized or offended the president. The general did not carry out his threats, but his words were typical of the government's hard-line reactions to criticism. Dominican journalists have also complained about low salaries and job instability, which makes them vulnerable to bribery and other economic pressures.

Another case of the press in confrontation with civil authorities came in the investigation of alleged corruption and abuse of public trust by the department of Bienes Nacionales. In May of 2001, reporters from major news services were barred from the courtroom despite affirming their constitutional right to be there. This action by judge Adrilya Vales Dalmasí was later criticized by both the president of the Supreme Court, Jorge Subero Isa, and the Attorney General, Virgilio Bello Rosa.

In another case in July of 2001, a daily program of political commentary, "Los Hechos y la Historia" directed by ex-government representative and political party advocate Rafael Flores Estrella and lawyer Tomás Castro and produced by the radio/television chain Teleradio América was shut down. According to the station executives where the program is produced, they had received "pressure" from a high-ranking government official to close down the program on the grounds that Flores Estrella and Castro had used slanderous language meant to reflect negatively against the honor of the president. The association of journalists, the Colegio de Periodistas, requested that the station release the name of the "high government official" referred to in the incident, but that request has not yet been complied with.

That same month, cameraman Cristino Rodríguez from the program "Detrás de la Noticia" of the city of Santiago was hurt by gunfire. The director of that same program, journalist Esteban Rosario had suffered a beating earlier in the year. The police state that an investigation is underway which points to a government party member as responsible for the shooting of cameraman Rodríguez. Coincidentally, the day following the shooting Rosario was arrested under orders from a Santiago judge wherein he is accused with the rape of a minor. After arraignment and subsequent to two days of questioning, Rosario was freed under bail.

Attitude toward Foreign Media

Under Dominican law, foreign ownership of national companies or corporations is restricted to 49 percent, a law that in truth does not actually discourage foreign influence in Dominican affairs as many Dominicans eager for financing will accept a nominal role as major shareholder. As indicated by the switch in ownership of many news networks, foreign investment in Dominican journalism has increased substantially since 1990. Entry of foreign news is unrestricted both through international cable news services and the distribution of foreign news publications such as the *Wall Street Journal* and Spanish language editions of *Newsweek* magazine.

Dominican journalists have been very active in Sociedad Interamericana de Prensa which seeks to seeks to protect free press thoughout Latin America and ten news organizations are active members. In 2002, the Dominican Republic hosted their semi-annual meeting at Casa De Campo.

News Agencies

All of the newspapers mentioned are subscribers to the major international news services available such as AP, UPI, EFE, and Reuters. Others have created contracts with major news sources. *Hoy*, for example, subscribes to biweekly editions of *Fortune Americas*. International editions in Spanish of the *New York Times*, the *Miami Herald*, and the *Wall Street Journal* arrive electronically and are published by local printers daily.

The Dominican Republic also provides its own 24-hour CNN style news service through the recently organized radio-TV-Internet network entitled Cadena de Noticias CDN that is owned by Banco Popular.

BROADCAST MEDIA

The Telecommunications Law of 1966, Law 1951 of 1949, Regulation 824 of 1949, and other complementary regulations establish certain norms for television and radio broadcasting. Prohibited activities include the broadcasting of events or taped materials that would offend public moral traditions or good taste, or damage international relationships. There is also a proscription against the airing of movies that contain high erotic content, scenes or dialog that would pervert morality, and in a general sense, all material that in its detail or plot demonstrate pernicious experiences that would be inappropriate for children. Despite regulation, however, the TV media is in practical terms barely if ever regulated as to content or scheduling.

ELECTRONIC NEWS MEDIA

The Dominican Republic rates 55th worldwide as advanced in technological advancement showing a score of 0.244 as compared to Finland, the most advanced with an indicator of 0.744 and the United States at 0.733. As of the year 2000, 1.7 hosts per 1000 had Internet access, 90 percent of which were located in the capital city of Santo Domingo. With more than 709,000 telephone main lines in use, Internet use should increase substantially within the immediate future as the infrastructure for more advanced telecommunications is being expanded from the relatively efficient system based on an island-wide microwave radio relay network, one coaxial submarine cable and a satellite earth station - 1 Intelsat (Atlantic Ocean).

In the Dominican Republic, as is true in the rest of the world, Internet access is not subject to any regulation, and as such, there is no control or pressure in respect to its use. As concerns the news media, the arrival of Internet access has allowed the local journalist a wider access to international opinions and styles that in themselves have created changes of both style and substance in the way that the news is reported.

Newspapers that maintain electronic circulation on the Internet are *DEDOM* (Diario Electrónico Dominicano), *Diario Resumen* (a summary of many newspapers and sources), *Dominican Republic One* (DR), the *Hoy*, the *Listín Diario*, *El Nacional*, and the *Última Hora*.

EDUCATION & TRAINING

Even though the Colegio Dominicano de Periodistas was created by law, this has never had an obligatory character to its function. Indeed, the Supreme Court of Justice ruled in 1989 that ruling 148 in 1983 that created the institution null and void. Nonetheless, the Colegio has a disciplinary tribunal and a functioning code of ethics. The Instituto Dominicano de las Telecomunicaciones (INDOTEL) regulates the use electronic media and the interrelationship of its users, assigning television and radio frequencies and monitors its lawful use. It is currently attempting to elaborate regulations for the use of the Internet.

Most major universities such as Universidad Autónoma de Santo Domingo, the oldest university in America, Pontífica Universidad Católica Madrey Maestra, UNIBE, and UTESA maintain departments dedicated to the study of Communications. The Department of Communication Sciences at the Universidad Católica de Santo Domingo is the most renowned in the country. In actuality, the study of telecommunications gains more popularity than the more traditional studies of journalism, despite the still limited number of job positions available for this field.

Academic publishing is generally limited to publishing houses sponsored by the different universities such as the Universidad Autónomo de Santo Domingo (UASD) and the Pontífica Universidad Católica Madre y Maestra (PUCAMAIMA). National and local papers, however, welcome the input of scholarly articles, particularly in the areas of social welfare, cultural, and literary criticism. The *Listín Diario*, *El Nacional*, and *El Caribe* maintain special weekly cultural segments that focus on such issues.

SUMMARY

Beyond those stated events wherein the state has directly or indirectly blocked unrestricted reporting, there have been other events that have taken place in the last eight years which many see as just as threatening events. During this period, newspaper ownership has shifted from privately owned to be owned by banks and large corporations. The newspaper with the largest circulation, the *Listín Diario*, is now owned by the BanInter group, *El Caribe* has been purchased by Banco Popular, and the *Hoy*, the second largest morning newspaper, is now owned by Editora Corripio, a subsidiary of a large Dominican corporation. Even *La Informacion*, the Santiago local newspaper, is owned by local economic groups. Symptomatic of this trend is the introduction of the publication of "free" newspapers, an event that may greatly change the way the press is received by Dominicans. Such developments are already viewed as circulation wars among rival economic entities and most major newspapers are popularly believed to reflect media manipulation in rivaling bids for power and influence among the competing commercial alliances.

Given this transparent rivalry for media control as a means to influence the politics and economy, the future of Dominican media is not easily predicted. In a state of steady flux both in terms of financing sources and readership, even well established news sources must struggle to maintain their audience. With the rapidly expanding use of Internet, however, Dominicans may become increasingly sophisticated in the use of media sources and eventually make their own choices as to the quality and influence of news coverage.

SIGNIFICANT DATES

- 1994 - Balaguer is re-elected, but agrees to serve only a two-year term after being accused of fraud. This disputed election of Balaguer results in change of the electoral process. Presidential elections start a 4-year sequence beginning in 1996, while congressional and local elections start a 4-year sequence beginning in 1998. Journalist Narciso González disappears, and a New Constitution with media laws is approved.
- 1996: Leonel Fernández Reyna of the leftist Dominican Liberation Party (PLD) is elected president. Election of Pres. Leonel Fernández is considered by many to be the first free election in recent history.
- 1997: Forty-eight hour general strike in protest against frequent power cuts, the cost of living and deteriorating public services.
- 1998: Hurricane George causes widespread devastation.
- 2000: PRD returned to power with Hipólito Mejiá as president.
- 2001: Convictions served on defendents in the 1974 murder of newspaper editor and journalist Orlando Martínez.

BIBLIOGRAPHY

Banco Central, Departamento de Cuentas Nacionales y Estadísticas Económicas, Available from http://www.bancentral.gov.do.

CIA. *World Factbook: Dominican Republic* Available from http://www.cia.gov/cia/publications/factbook/geos/dr.html.

Committee to Protect Journalists. The Dominican Republic 2000: Country Report Available from http://www.cpj.org/attacks00/americas00/Dominican.html Wednesday, 7 March 2001.

———. The Dominican Republic 1999: Country Report. Available from http://www.cpj.org/attacks99/americas99/Dominican.html.

Dollar, David. ''Governance and Social Justice in Caribbean States.'' Development Research Group, the World Bank.

Flores, Ramon. Ciencia, tecnologia, globalizacion y educacion. Presentado al Simposio Educativo Internacional, Magisterio 2000.

Filmer, Deon, Lant Pritchett, and Yee-Peng-Tes. ''Educational Attainment Profile of the Poor. DHS Evidence from Around the Globe.'' Mimeo, Washington, DC: The World Bank, 1998.

France Telecom. ''Dominicana.'' Available from http://www.dominicana.com/radio/tv.htm.

Fullan, Michael. ''Managing Change.'' (Restructuring Brief). A publication of the North Coast Professional Development Consortium, 1993.

Inter-American Development Bank (IDB). Statistics on Dominican Republic. Available from http://www.iadb.org/int/sta/english/laignet/domsocall.htm.

ICFJ-International Journalists' Network. ''Dominican Republic'' Available from http://IJNet.org/Profile/LatinAmerica/Dominican Republic/media.html.

Inter-American Development Bank. *Economic and Social Progress in Latin America. 1996 Report. Making Social Services Work.* Washington, DC: IDB, 1996.

International Press Institute. ''Boston-Presentation of 50 World Press Freedom Heroes''. Available from http://www.freemedia.at/Boston%20Congress%20Report/boston42.html.

Listín Diario. Available from http://www.Listín.com.do/antes/040402/cuerpos/republica/rep18.htm.

Oficina Nacional de Estadistica. Estadísticas seleccionadas de la República Dominicana. Santo Domingo: Oficina Nacional de Estadística, 1999.

Revista Foro Comercio e Inversión Caribe-Estados Unidos. 1999. Edición única.

Sala de Prensa ''Academia: Rep. Dominicana''. Available from www.saladeprensa.org/academia.htm.

Shaffer, Janes, n.d. *Institutions, Behavior, and Economic Performance: Comments and Institutional Analysis* Available from http://msu.edu/user/scmid/shaffer.htm.

Sociedad Interamericana de Prensa. ''Leyes de radio y television y contenido de la información.'' Available from http://www.sipiapa.org/espanol/projects/laws-dom3.cfm.

———. ''Colegiación y exigencia de título universitario: Rep. Dominicana.'' Available from http://www.sipiapa.org/espanol/projects/laws-dom6.cfm.

———. ''Informe de Medio Ano de 20 Guatemala'' Available from http://www.sipiapa.org/espanol/publications/mid3-republica dominicana200.

UNESCO. 1999. Available from http://www.unesco.org.

UNDP. ''Today's technological transformations-Creating the network age.'' Available from http://www.undp.org/hdr2001/chaptertwo.pdf.

United States Agency for International Development (USAID). 2000. Competitiveness Program of the Dominican Republic Paper, unpublished.

The World Bank. Available from http://www.worldbank.org.

World Economic Forum (1999) Global Competitiveness Report. Available from http://www.wcforum.org.

—Virginia Davis Nordin and Charlene E. Santos

East Timor

Basic Data

Official Country Name:	East Timor
Region (Map name):	East & South Asia
Population:	827,727
Language(s):	English, Indonesian, Portuguese, Tetum
Literacy rate:	55%

East Timor—or Timor Loro Sa'e—became a nation on May 20, 2002, as the world watched. The celebration of independence ended four centuries of Portuguese colonial rule, 24 years of Indonesian occupation, and more than two years of interim rule by the United Nations. East Timor shares with Indonesia about half of a 300-mile long island in the group known as the Lesser Sundas.

After the East Timorese people voted for independence from Indonesia in 1999, rampaging militias destroyed much of the island's infrastructure, including the printing presses and computers that served the former province's few newspapers and magazines. The *Voice of East Timor,* its leading newspaper, was silenced.

As a first step in rebuilding the media, Queensland Newspapers of Australia sent equipment and expertise. After a marathon equipment set-up, the *Timor Post* (in Indonesian) published its first, four-page tabloid edition on March 2, 2000. Besides the *Timor Post,* other newspapers are *Suara Timor Lorosae* (in Indonesian), *Lalenok* (in Tetum) and *Timor Today.* Archived copies of *Timor Post* and *Lalenok* can be seen at http://www.easttimorpress.qut.edu.au.

The lone television station is TV-TL, and two radio stations are Radio UNTAET and Radio Falintil. The Internet domain is.tl.

The official languages of Timor Loro Sa'e are Portuguese and Tetum. In practicality, Indonesian and English are the two languages in broad use.

Much of East Timor's independence struggle took place on the Internet, with the help of satellite phones, and in view of the world community. It can be said to have achieved its independence in cyberspace in 1997, when its domain name was registered and administered from Ireland.

Bibliography

Hill, David T. ''East Timor and the Internet: Global Political Leverage in/on Indonesia.'' In *Indonesia,* 73 (April 2002) 25-52.

Tanter, Richard, Mark Selden, and Stephen R. Shalom. ''East Timor Faces the Future.'' In *Bitter Flowers, Sweet Flowers: East Timor, Indonesia, and the World Community,* Lanham, Maryland: Rowman and Littlefield Publishers, 2001, 243-72.

—Dr. Linda Yoder

Ecuador

Basic Data

Official Country Name:	Republic of Ecuador
Region (Map name):	South America
Population:	13,183,978
Language(s):	Spanish (official), Amerindian languages (especially Quechua)
Literacy rate:	90.1%

Area:	283,560 sq km
GDP:	13,607 (US$ millions)
Number of Television Sets:	1,550,000
Television Sets per 1,000:	117.6
Number of Cable Subscribers:	323,820
Cable Subscribers per 1,000:	25.7
Number of Satellite Subscribers:	9,000
Satellite Subscribers per 1,000:	0.7
Number of Radio Stations:	448
Number of Radio Receivers:	4,150,000
Radio Receivers per 1,000:	314.8
Number of Individuals with Computers:	275,000
Computers per 1,000:	20.9
Number of Individuals with Internet Access:	180,000
Internet Access per 1,000:	13.7

BACKGROUND & GENERAL CHARACTERISTICS

Named for its proximity to the Equator, *La República de Ecuador* (The Republic of Ecuador) is located in the northwest part of South America, bordering Colombia, Peru, and the Pacific Ocean. Originally part of the federation known as *La República de Gran Colombia* which gained independence from Spain in 1822, Ecuador became a separate country in 1830. Part of its land was lost in disputes with Peru in the early part of the twentieth century. Today Ecuador is about the size of Colorado and is the smallest country in South America.

The people of Ecuador have a diverse ethnic heritage. About one-fourth of the population is indigenous to the area, about half is mestizo (mixture of Indian and European), and the remaining one-fourth is comprised of other ethnicities, including African and Caucasian. Ecuador has a total population exceeding 13 million people; approximately 1.5 million live in the capital city of Quito. The official language of Ecuador is Spanish, although the Quichua language (an Amerindian dialect) is spoken by many people. About 95 percent of the country's citizens are Roman Catholic.

Approximately 55 percent of Ecuador's population lives in urban areas. Estimates suggest that as many as 70 percent of the people in the country live below the poverty level; in 2001 the unemployment rate was 13 percent. The largest part of the national workforce is represented by agricultural jobs in seafood, fruit, coffee, and various other crops. The literacy rate is around 90 percent, and as many as two-thirds of children drop out of school by the sixth grade, even though education is compulsory until age 14. However, government programs designed to improve early childhood education are believed to have increased enrollment in primary schools steadily over the last 20 years.

Daily newspaper circulation in Ecuador is 70 per 1,000 people; daily readership is estimated to be between 5 and 10 percent of the total population. This relatively low figure is due mostly to poverty. There are 29 daily newspapers, most of which are located in the two largest metropolitan areas: the country's capital, Quito, where *El Comercial* and *Hoy* are published, and the nation's largest city, Guayaquil, the home of *El Universo* and *El Expresso. El Universo* alone has a daily readership of over half a million people.

The press in Ecuador has always been greatly influenced by religion and politics. Under the rule of conservative Gabriel Garcia Moreno (1860-1895), standards of expression were governed by the clergy of the Catholic Church, which had the power to censor the public's reading material. When the revolution led by Eloy Alfaro in 1895 overthrew Moreno's reign, the Radical Liberal rule broke official ties with the church, secularized education, and reformed conditions related to free speech and press.

Journalism is often a dangerous profession in Ecuador, as violence toward the press there has escalated over the past few years. In 2000 TV news director Rafael Cuesta Caputti was wounded by a mail bomb, one of several that were mailed to various journalists following the quick overthrow of President Jamil Mahuad. Also in that year, journalist David Montalvo was attacked while covering an influx of Colombian refugees and Ecuadorians at the border, and there were attacks on buildings housing newspapers and the news offices of Reuters and CNN.

Other acts of violence against media agents have been staged by individuals and groups in reaction to coverage of political events in the country. In 1998, 22 journalists at the *Hoy* were assaulted by demonstrators reacting to a printed scandal regarding misappropriation of aid for *El Niño* victims. There are other examples of journalists who have been threatened, attacked, injured, or even killed while covering politically and socially sensitive stories.

Journalists in Ecuador face a number of other obstacles as well, such as government limited access to public information, conflicts of interest among media owners, and heavy workloads. Most journalists make relatively low salaries, often requiring them to take second jobs to support themselves and their families. Added to the sometimes volatile political and legal environments that reporters must confront, producing high quality articles on Ecuador is not an easy job.

ECONOMIC FRAMEWORK

Like many other South American countries, Ecuador has experienced often harsh economic conditions over the last two decades. Although the performance of country's fruit and seafood industries have been generally good, the nation succumbed to a number of problems in the 1990s that caused its economy to falter almost to the point of bankruptcy in 1999. In the years prior to that, damages caused by *El Niño,* the collapse of the banking industry, the Asian financial crisis, and a slump in the petroleum industry all contributed to stifling inflation, high unemployment, and dramatic currency devaluation. These events, as well as other economic factors, affected journalism in Ecuador in a number of ways.

For example, the banking crisis in 1999 led to media criticism of the president's handling of economic policy, causing increased tension between the government and the press. President Noboa was critical of the media's coverage and exhorted them to observe more objectivity in their reporting. In that same year, Congress had also established a 10 percent tax on newspaper and magazine distribution, an act that was met with outrage by the journalism community. Because of this reaction, and in an effort to help boost the country's economic crisis, the government repealed this tax later in the year.

During 2001 President Noboa made a number of economic reforms, including the privatization of several government industries, which created political and civic opposition and added to the potential dangers to journalists reporting related events. (Noboa, formerly the vice president, had moved into the executive position after a military coup removed his predecessor, Mahuad, two days earlier). Also during that year, protests over fuel prices by Indians contributed to the dangers faced by reporters. The administration later cut those prices, reducing much of the tension. However, because of the resulting social unrest, the government declared a national state of emergency and assumed the power to censure the media; it later prevailed upon media not to sensationalize events and to avoid creating public panic.

PRESS LAWS

Ecuador has many laws that govern the practice of journalism. The Constitution of 1998 guarantees freedom of expression to all citizens, including members of the press. Moreover, The Law of Practice of Professional Journalism, passed in 1975, grants journalists access to official information and other data in the interest of the public, and to receive assistance from state or private agencies in obtaining this information. The Law also protects journalists from revealing sources, unless cases of national security are involved.

All journalists must hold a communication degree from a university and register with the *Federación Nacional de Periodistas* (National Federation of Journalists), although this law is not always enforced. Journalists having extensive experience but no degree may be given a *certificado de profesionalización* (professional certification) by the Ministry of Education, allowing them the same full status as degreed journalists. The Inter-American Court of Human Rights has declared these licensing requirements to be unconstitutional, but as of June 2002, they are still in effect.

Slander and defamation laws in Ecuador are very strict. These laws carry criminal penalties of up to two years as well as fines, and many press agents have been punished for infractions. One of the provisions of the current Constitution holds that all citizens have the right to a good name, a good reputation, and personal and family privacy; this right places journalists in jeopardy when they report findings that can compromise any of these attributes. The law also provides the means by which offended parties can require retractions for publicized untrue statements.

Media law in Ecuador is civic oriented. For example, the National Council of Radio Broadcasting and Television regulates artistic, cultural, and moral standards, including control of content before 9:00 p.m. A strict Code of Ethics is maintained by the Ecuadorian Association of Radio and Television and the Association of Television Channels of Ecuador, which enforce the government's mandate in Article 81 of the Constitution requiring media to promote educational, cultural, and ethical values. Any publications that promote ''violence, racism, sexism, religious or political intolerance, or that offends human dignity'' are forbidden, according to The Code of Penal Procedure of 1983, which prohibits the distribution of writing that is ''immoral'' or which deal with ''obscene or dishonorable subjects,'' or when such writing may instigate criminal activity.

Most recently, The Children's and Teenagers' Code is before the Congress, a bill that would ensure educational, informational, and socially responsible programming for the country's young people. In addition, it would establish the requirement to accommodate children with communication disabilities and to include programming in indigenous languages in areas where those languages are predominant. Article 200 of the Code of Minors forbids media to publish any information that harms the privacy or good reputation of children.

Various other state laws provide that the government can require all radio and television stations to broadcast official programs, news, and announcements. There are also laws that restrict the amount of space newspapers can use for political advertising per day (Electoral Law of 1987) and laws that require newspapers to reveal the amount of money spent on political advertising. Failure to comply with these laws can result in closure of a news organization. There are also many laws to protect copyright, to guard against threats to the government, and to limit the distribution of information that compromises national security. *La Superintendencia de Telecomunicaciónes* (Superintendent of Telecommunications) oversees regulations pertaining to broadcast media.

CENSORSHIP

Although the Constitution of Ecuador guarantees media agents freedom of press, there is considerable self-censorship among journalists who write about sensitive political, social, or military issues, and for good reason: any published material that is deemed immoral, obscene, or otherwise in conflict with cultural values or "human decency" may subject a journalist to various sanctions—one of several ways the government regulates the content of news and programming.

Several instances of censorship occurred during the last decade, such as the case of Navy Captain Rogelio Viteri, who was arrested after publicly discussing details of an alleged overcharge of insurance on aircraft. In 2001 the news programs of four radio stations were suspended in Orellana Province following an Indian uprising that caused the government to declare a national state of emergency, during which the Noboa administration asked journalists to keep "balance" in the news and to avoid sensationalism. And in 2001 Malena Cardona Batallas was sentenced to a 30-day prison term and fined for slandering a government official whom she questioned about fraud allegations. Other such cases of censorship can be found in recent Ecuadorian history.

Although the Constitution requires that the state release information to the public, this law is often ignored. In cases involving the protection of national security, the government may classify certain information and, with the threat of criminal penalties, restrict journalists from releasing it. According to Article 35 of the Law of Professional Practice of Journalism, journalists who commit "offenses against the security of the state" can be prosecuted under the National Security Law and the Penal Code.

STATE-PRESS RELATIONS

Even though cases like the ones stated above exist, in most other matters the press in Ecuador enjoys limited interference from government. To a great extent, professional journalism organizations self-regulate the conduct of the press. The National Federation of Journalists' Code of Ethics (1978) provides penalties, including temporary license suspension, for ethics violations. The National Council of Radio Broadcasting and Television is charged with the responsibility of regulating broadcast programming that upholds moral and cultural standards, and can issue sanctions against stations that transmit programs contrary to these standards.

One area in which government does assert itself into the press is political advertising. The Electoral Supreme Court has the ability to sanction any news organization that fails to disclose the amount of money politicians have spent on advertising; other government bodies also limit the amount of space a newspaper can devote to political advertising per day.

ATTITUDE TOWARD FOREIGN MEDIA

Many foreign press agencies maintain offices in Ecuador, including CNN, Reuters, Associated Press, *Agence France-Presse,* and the Italy-based *Agenzia Nazionale Stampa Associata.* These organizations enjoy the same basic freedoms as Ecuador-based news groups, although foreign reporters may be required to register at the National Secretariat of Public Information in order to practice in the country. If they hold journalism or related degrees from universities in their home countries, they are fully entitled to be professionally active in Ecuador.

There are government policies, however, that limit the extent to which non-nationals participate in the ownership and administration of Ecuadorian media. Foreign investors can own only up to 25 percent of the country's broadcasting stations and companies. Managerial staff must be Ecuadorian citizens, and high-ranking media personnel must be born in Ecuador, according to the 1975 La Ley de Radiofusión y Televisión (the Law of Radio Broadcasting and Television.).

NEWS AGENCIES

Several news agencies are based in Ecuador, including *Diario El Mercurio, Diario El Telegrafo,* and the *Interpress Service.*

BROADCAST MEDIA

Radio and television permeate Ecuadorian society, especially in the larger metropolitan areas of Quito and Guayaquil. The country has approximately 324 AM and 49 FM radio stations that broadcast to 4.15 million radios, and some 300 television stations that carry signals to 1.5 million televisions in the country. All stations are privately owned except for one government-controlled station.

Seven networks operate in Ecuador, including five national channels—*Ecuavisa, Gamavision, Teleamazonas, TC-Telecentro,* and *Telesistema.* The U.S.-based Univision, a Spanish language network, is also available on major cable systems in the country.

The broadcast industry in Ecuador is regulated by the *Superintendencia de Telecomunicaciónes* (Superintendent of Telecommunications), an office comparable to the Federal Communications Commission in the United States.

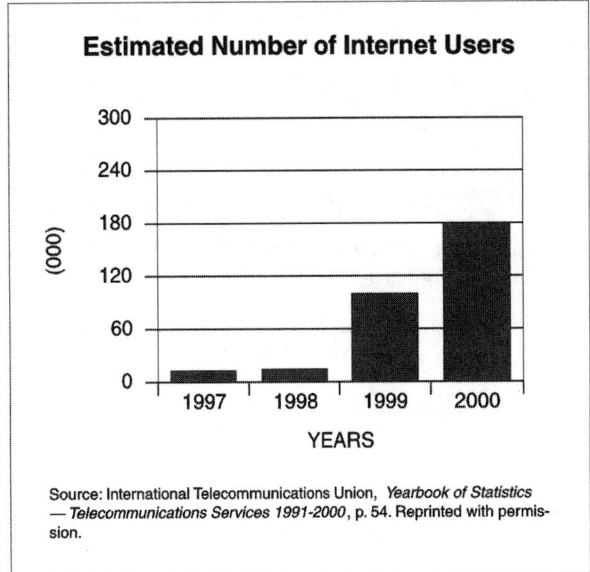

Source: International Telecommunications Union, *Yearbook of Statistics — Telecommunications Services 1991-2000*, p. 54. Reprinted with permission.

Electronic News Media

Most of Ecuador's major newspapers maintain Web sites. There are also numerous other Ecuadorian-based online sources of journalism, including *Vistazo.com* (with links to Reuters and Newsweek), *EcuaNet,* and *Quito News,* the latter of which is in English. These sites contain sections on local and international news, business, sports, culture, and other topics.

Education & Training

Several universities in Ecuador offer degrees in mass communication, including the largest programs at Pontifica Universidad Católica, Univerisdad Andina Simon Bolivar, Universidad San Francisco de Quito, and Universidad Nacional de Loja. Many programs are often called Comunicación Sociales, which is a degree that combines journalism classes with course work in public relations, web programming, culture and linguistics, and the social sciences.

Besides training in conventional university settings, other opportunities exist for the professional development of journalists in Ecuador. One workshop, sponsored by the Cox Center for International Mass Communication Training and Research Center and held in Quito in 2001, provided a forum for journalists and scientists to discuss ways to disseminate information about the ecology. Another example of educational resources is the Quito-based *El Centro Internacional de Estudios Superiores de Comunicación para America Latina* (The International Center for Advanced Study in Communication in Latin America), a nonprofit, autonomous organization that conducts research and provides training for communication professionals from all over the region.

These, and many other opportunities, speak of Ecuador's commitment to the internationalization of media and to the cultural diversity of the people whom that media serves.

Summary

Ecuador is a nation of people whose passion for civic issues provides journalists with great potential—and great risk—for doing their jobs. Battling against often formidable economic and political barriers, the men and women in Ecuador use their material and technical resources to report news that is accurate and in the public interest. The country also appears to recognize the importance of free and uncensored media, although its commitment to enforcing free journalistic practice is not always as obvious. As Ecuador continues to be a news-conscious partner with its neighbors in the region and in the world, its prominence as a leader in journalism will be realized.

Significant Dates

- 1998: Current Constitution enacted. Also, twenty-two journalists at the *Hoy* were assaulted by demonstrators.
- 1999: Economic crisis hits Ecuador, causing tensions that lead to attacks on journalists.
- 2001: Navy Captain Rogelio Viteri was arrested after publicly discussing details of an alleged overcharge of insurance on aircraft. Malena Cardona Batallas was sentenced to a 30-day prison term and fined for slandering a government official. Four radio stations were temporarily suspended in Orellana following their coverage of an Indian uprising in that province.

Bibliography

''Background Note: Ecuador.'' U. S. Department of State, April 2001. Available from http://www.state.gov.

''A Complete History of Ecuador.'' *Ecuaworld* June 2002. Available from http://www.ecuaworld.com.

''Culture Reporter.'' Update on Ecuador, June 2002. Available from http://oncampus.rishmond.edu.

"Ecuador: Annual Report 2002." *Reports Without Borders,* June 2002. Available from http://www.rsf.fr.

"Ecuador: Committee to Protect Journalists." 2001, 2000, 1999. Available from http://www.cpj.org.

"Ecuador." *Human Rights Report.* U. S. Department of State, 1999. Available from http://www.state.gov.

"Ecuador." *Infoplease.com* June 2002. Available from http://www.infoplease.com.

"Ecuador." Inter American Press Association, 2001. Available from http://216.147.196.167.

"Ecuador: Media Outlets." International Journalists' Network, June 2002. Available from http://www.ijnet.org.

"Ecuador: Media." *World Desk Reference,* June 2002. Available from http://www.travel.dk.com.

"Ecuador: Press Law Database." Inter American Press Association, 2001. Available from http://216.147.196.167.

"Ecuador: 2001 World Press Freedom Review." Freemedia, June 2002. Available from http://www.freemedia.at.

"Ecuador." *World Factbook,* June 2002. Available from http://odci.gov.

"Ecuador's Journalism Under the Microscope." ICFJ, January 2002. Available from http://www.icfj.org.

Ecuanet. June 2002. Available from http://www4.ecua.net.

El Universo. July 2002. Available from http://www.eluniverso.com.

"International Circulation & Publishing Network." Worldpaper Circulation, June 2002. Available from http://www.worldpaper.com.

"Latin America." AFP (Agence France-Presse) Worldwide, June 2002. Available from http://www.afp.com.

"Misión, Visión, y Objectivos." La Superintendencia de Telecomunicaciónes, June 2000. Available from http://www.supertel.gov.ec.

"Press Freedom in Latin America: A Survey." World Press Institute, June 2002. Available from http://www.macalester.edu.

"Press Freedom in Latin America's Andean Region." International Women's Media Foundation, June 2002. Available from http://www.iwmf.org.

Quito News. June 2002. Available from http://www.quitonews.com.

"Scientists and Journalists Join Workshop in Quito." Available from http://www.grady.uga.edu.

Vistazo.com. June 2002. Available from http://www.vistazo.com.

—William Wardrope

EGYPT

BASIC DATA

Official Country Name:	Arab Republic of Egypt
Region (Map name):	Africa
Population:	69,536,644
Language(s):	Arabic (official), English and French
Literacy rate:	51.4%
Area:	1,001,450 sq km
GDP:	98,725 (US$ millions)
Number of Television Stations:	98
Number of Television Sets:	7,700,000
Television Sets per 1,000:	110.7
Number of Cable Subscribers:	3,180,800
Cable Subscribers per 1,000:	49.7
Number of Radio Stations:	59
Number of Radio Receivers:	20,500,000
Radio Receivers per 1,000:	294.8
Number of Individuals with Computers:	1,400,000
Computers per 1,000:	20.1
Number of Individuals with Internet Access:	450,000
Internet Access per 1,000:	6.5

BACKGROUND & GENERAL CHARACTERISTICS

Egypt is one of the most pivotal of the nations of the western nations called the Middle East, which is actually an incorrect term, but is more popularly recognized by journalists and the media. It is pivotal because it is in the heart of a realm that extends over 6,000 miles longitudinally and 4,000 miles in latitude. The placement of Egypt in this realm is even more important because it is the most stable country in this region—economically, socially, culturally, and as a tourist destination.

The population of nearly 70 million Egyptians is 94 percent Muslim with the primary ethnic group being Eastern Hamitic stock (Egyptians, Bedouins, and Berbers). Only half of Egypt's citizens are literate with less than 40 percent of that number being women.

Egypt is home to the Nile River. It is by the northern end of the Red Sea, the eastern end of the Mediterranean Sea, and located in the northeastern corner of Africa across from Turkey to the north and Saudi Arabia to the east, adjacent to Israel, Islamic Sudan and militant Libya. Egypt's geographic location could condemn it, but it does not. Egypt has played host to a variety of frequent conferences, meetings and discussions that are held in Cairo, Egypt's capitol, to discuss what needs to be done to create peace in Southwest Asia, a more appropriate title for "the Middle East." However, Egypt still controls the stability in the region and therefore commands a good deal of media attention.

In the fifth century BCE (BC), the Greek scholar Herodotus described Egypt as the "gift of the Nile," but Egypt was also a product of natural protection in the ancient world. The Egyptian civilization was indeed the gift of the Nile, but the Nile itself produced a gift each year when it flooded; it deposited good, fertile soil that could grow crops that Egypt could trade. The Nile was navigable, and therefore the Nile River has been a source of life for Egypt to this day. However, control of the water is a topic that can be found in the state-controlled press of Egypt and throughout the world.

Egypt's medial landscape is defined with a simple question: for or against. Over the past few years, the system has increasingly been challenged by a growing generation of independent publications. Loyal to the idea of investigative journalism and providing information not framed by specific party lines, there are currently over 200 independent media sources in Egypt today; most of them are published off shore and brought back into the Egyptian state. Most of Egypt's media is government owned through the State Information Service of Egypt. Printed media can be divided into four categories: state owned, party owned, domestic licensed independent, and foreign licensed independent. Therefore, printed media is generally overseen by the state in Egypt and is considered not to be free; again, the State Information Service would see a great deal of what is in print in Egypt.

News Media Overall there are 18 primary newspapers and periodicals within Egypt. Some of these include:

- *Akhbar al-Adab.*
- *Akher Sa'a.*
- *Al-Ahali.*
- *Al-Ahram al-Arabit*
- *Al-Ahram Hebdo*
- *Al-Gumhuriya*
- *Al-Shaab*

The Egyptian government owns a controlling stock in three major daily Egyptian newspapers: *Al-Ahram, Al Akhbar,* and *Al-Gumhuriya.* The editors of these dailies are appointed by the president, and as appointees, they enjoy little censorship by the government. But because they are appointed and working in a state-owned newspaper, it is understood that their loyalties remain with the state. They are also given substantial leeway, given they avoid certain "taboos"—meaning government criticism is avoided since it selects and compensates them. The largest of these newspapers is the *Al-Ahram*, and it is the largest Arabic newspaper in the world; the Al Ahram Regional Press Institute has now been established, which helps Egyptian and Arabic journalists learn more current trends in journalism as well as graphic arts and legal issues associated with this practice, according to the International Journalists' Network.

Party-owned media, until recently the only true competitor for state-owned media, was the Party Press whose leaders also enjoyed limited censorship. Fourteen of Egypt's political parties have the right to publish their own newspapers, receiving a small subsidy from the government and sometimes receiving foreign interest as well. However, if they are receiving small subsidies and they enjoy very little censorship, again state domination has made its presence well known. Most party newspapers are weekly, although the main opposition, parties *Al-Wafd* and *Al-Ahrar*, maintain dailies. *Al-Shaab*, an Islamic-oriented Socialist labor party, maintains a semi-weekly publication.

Domestic-licensed independents are very rarely licensed in Egypt; hence, there are very few newspapers which fit into this category. Part of that rarity is due to the fact that it is extremely expensive and one must be cleared by all main security and intelligence agencies in order to receive a state licensure. Here again the State Information Service has control. Most of these publications are rare and done off shore, so domestic independents are few and far between. With education being questionable at best in Egypt, what specific audiences those publications would reach remains uncertain.

Offshore independents often circumvent certain constitutional rules, such as the restriction of the establishment of newspapers to legal entities, corporate bodies or political parties; many Egyptian-owned publications register in other nearby countries. Over 200 titles register abroad, mostly in Cyprus, and bring their publications back into Egyptian borders. Many owners seek licensure to print within the country, but it is too expensive and too

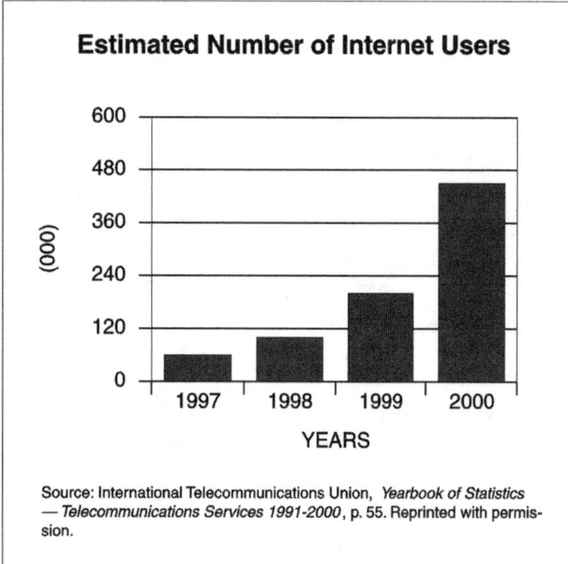

Source: International Telecommunications Union, *Yearbook of Statistics — Telecommunications Services 1991-2000*, p. 55. Reprinted with permission.

much trouble, as indicated previously. Offshore publication prevents state intervention, but this does not mean these publications are not screened. In fact, these publications are screened very carefully to maintain the stability of the region.

Nearly all magazines and newspapers are printed by one of seven government-owned printing houses. It is believed the government uses its control of the region's publishing to limit the output, access, and influence of opposition groups observable by the International Journalists' Network. They seem to be very clear in establishing an overview of the Egyptian press. If one looks at the overall picture, the Egyptian press is very state-controlled. The retention of three laws makes it increasingly easier for the government to find fault with the offshore publications. The press law, the publications law, and the penal code govern press issues and stipulate fines or imprisonment for criticizing the president, members of the government, or any foreign head of state. If the government finds something ambiguous, or if it does not screen through security properly, these media laws make it difficult for anything to bypass government screening.

Broadcast & Electronic News Media

Egyptians own over 20 million radios and nearly 8 million televisions. There are 98 television stations and 42 AM and 14 FM radio stations. The Egyptian Radio and Television Union (ERTU) works in affiliation with the Ministry of Information to operate all eight government-owned TV stations in Egypt, as well as two satellite stations and 19 local and regional stations. Egypt launched NileSat, the Arab world's first broadcast satellite, to carry Egyptian TV and radio from North Africa to the Persian Gulf.

NileSat is helping stimulate change in the area. Women are interested in seeing how other women are dressed on TV. Muslim women—who were traditionally ''covered up'' with their clothing—are now moving toward a modern, ''western''—namely American—style of dress. The media has influenced the women's movement, but the Egyptian government, oddly enough, is not censoring them on this issue.

In November 2001 a second privately-owned satellite network was also launched called DreamTV.

Egypt has made relatively good progress in making Internet access available to its people, particularly in comparison to other African countries. There are 50 Internet service providers for about 300,000 users who are able to view many of the country's newspapers online.

Bibliography

The Central Intelligence Agency (CIA). *World Factbook 2001*. Directorate of Intelligence, 2002. Available from http://www.cia.gov.

Committee to Protect Journalists. *Middle East and North Africa Country Report: Egypt*. 2001. Available from http://www.cpj.org/attacks01/mideast01/Egypt.html.

De Blij, H.J., and Peter O. Muller. *Geography: Realms, Regions and Concepts*. New York: John Wiley and Sons, 2002.

''Egypt.'' BBC News. Available from http://news.bbc.co.uk.

IJNet: International Journalists' Network. Available from http://www.ijnet.org/Profle/Africa/Egypt/media.html.

''The Press in Egypt.'' Available from http://www.sis.gov.eg/pressrev/html/pressinfo.htm.

—Pamela M. Gross

El Salvador

Basic Data

Official Country Name:	Republic of El Salvador
Region (Map name):	North & Central America
Population:	6,237,622
Language(s):	Spanish, Nahua (among some Amerindians)

Literacy rate:	71.5%
Area:	21,040 sq km
GDP:	13,211 (US$ millions)
Number of Television Stations:	5
Number of Television Sets:	600,000
Television Sets per 1,000:	96.2
Number of Satellite Subscribers:	35,000
Satellite Subscribers per 1,000:	5.6
Number of Radio Stations:	91
Number of Radio Receivers:	2,750,000
Radio Receivers per 1,000:	440.9
Number of Individuals with Computers:	120,000
Computers per 1,000:	19.2
Number of Individuals with Internet Access:	50,000
Internet Access per 1,000:	8.0

BACKGROUND & GENERAL CHARACTERISTICS

El Salvador had an estimated population as of 2002 of over 6 million, a higher population density than India, and a gross national product (GNP) of US$938 per capita. The country experienced a terrible civil war during the 1980s and the early 1990s; endured death squads that killed human rights advocates; felt population pressures; and survived earthquakes, hurricane Mitch, and the denigration of the natural environment. El Salvador has several political parties: the old moderate, center-left Christian Democratic Party (PDC); the right wing Nationalist Republican Alliance (ARENA); and the old guerilla, now leftist Farabundo Marti para la Liberación Nacional (FMLN). Through 1988, the PDC kept the presidency but the ARENA subsequently held on despite strong competition from FMLM. The Inter-American Development Bank spent millions of dollars in projects relating to health issues from the earthquakes, supported social peace, citizen security, and peaceful coexistence of political parties in El Salvador, and attempted to get at the root of these problems in dealing with massive poverty, homelessness, vagrant youths, and serious health issues. President Francisco Flores, unable to stop the terrorist kidnappings even in the midst of the national emergency of the earthquakes, was successful in gaining more freedom to criticize the government and sought both emergency and long-term planning initiatives in an attempt to establish social and economic stability.

El Diario de Hoy and *La Prensa Gráfica* were the leading daily newspapers of El Salvador. In the late 1990s their publishers allowed unheard of freedom of speech to the El Salvadorean reporters whose investigative journalism both stretched the traditional freedom of reporting and sold newspapers. Conservative media owners lamented the fading of the absolute dominance of the right-wing ARENA which won almost all elections from the end of the 1992 civil war until the beginning of the millennium and held on to the presidency in the last election only through a coincidence of events and candidates.

ECONOMIC FRAMEWORK

The working conditions of reporters improved in the late 1990s, although salaries continued to be so low that journalists were vulnerable to bribery. Even among information workers, new technologies were not always available. However, on February 18, 1998, the Inter-American Development Bank approved a US$73.2 million loan to El Salvador for expanding video libraries, interactive radio, learning resource centers for new technologies, school equipment, and computers through the ministry of education. However, even in 2002 El Salvador was a land of extremes. A suite in the Hotel Presidente, headquarters for the 1994 presidential elections, cost US$500, while a civil servant made US$4 a day and had no protection from being thrown out of his job in the next election. Luxury juxtaposed uncollected garbage, and black water filled the streets of the towns of El Salvador. According to the *CIA World Factbook*, there were 380,000 telephone lines (1998); 40,163 cellular phones (1970); 61 AM and 30 FM Radio stations (1998); 1 Intelsat (Atlantic Ocean) satellite (1997); 2.75 million radios (1997); 600,000 televisions (1990); 5 television stations (2000); 4 Internet service providers (2000); and 40,000 Internet users (2000).

PRESS LAWS

Article 243 of the Constitution prohibited the national police from allowing detained people to talk to journalists because ''it affects their good names and violates their right to due process.'' Article 272 of the El Salvadoran law stated that ''In general, penal proceedings will be public. However, the judge may order a partial or total press blackout when he deems, for valid reasons, that it is in the interest of good morals, public interest or national security, or is authorized in some specific rule.'' This blackout may be partial or complete. Article 273 stated that ''Hearings will be public, but the court may, on its own authority, order or at the request of one of the parties that said hearings be closed when required for reasons of good morals, public interest, national security or it is authorized by some specific rule.''

In September, 1996, the ARENA party pushed through a controversial bill which was the New Telecommunications Law of El Salvador. Unfortunately, although the legislature had a law that built the legal framework for democratic freedom of speech and of the press in telecommunications, major sections were excluded from the bill which actually was passed. Even the newspaper, *Diario de Hoy*, an old mouthpiece for the conservative party, admitted that the new law hurt progress towards freedom of expression and suggested that this would make the radio the only place where journalists might be free to tell the truth. This form of the telecommunications law was presented to the legislature by the Commission for Economy and Agriculture. Through a simple majority, largely of ARENA deputies, the law passed, although the representatives of the opposition parties protested and left the Assembly. The great losers were the Association of Participating Radios and Programs of El Salvador (ARPAS) and the Union of Technical Workers of Telecommunications Business of El Salvador (ATTES). These organizations had written proposals in hopes that they might be incorporated into the law and then lobbied for those proposals and their basic regulations and guarantees that the public, as well as the private, sector would be represented. ARPAS had consulted the Federal Communications Commission of the United States in making their suggestions, but nothing of their proposal was included. ARENA's law only needed the signature of then president Dr. Armando Calderon Sol, himself of the ARENA party.

In July 2000, *El Diario de Hoy* and *La Prensa Gráfica* detailed a government scandal in which government legislators were spending excessively on food, travel, and entertainment. In reaction to the news stories, the executive committee of the Legislative Assembly for a time restricted public access to any information concerning its administration and budgetary records. Since there was no member of the FMLN on the executive committee, the press coverage of the scandal could suggest that the young investigative reporters on these two periodicals were no longer afraid to report such news and the publishers were willing to sell newspapers on the basis of such reports and to back their investigative reporters.

While legislation brought forth by the Association de Periodistas de El Salvador to protect press sources languished in committee, never passing in the legislative assembly, at least the Asociacion de Periodistas de El Salvador continued to thrive. *Contraportada,* unable to secure any significant funding, all but ceased to exist. El Salvadorans had limited public access to their own government documents. Article one of the General Law of the Creation of SIGET (Superintendencia General de Electricidad y Telecommunicaciones), gave it total autonomy on all administrative and financial aspects. Article 2 required that SIGET be located in San Salvador with offices established in other locations in the country. Article 3 had it relating to other government organizations through the Ministry of Economics. Section 5 dealt with registering telecommunications stations, a big issue in El Salvador.

CENSORSHIP

For many years, journalists were controlled either by the dictates of conservative publishers or by fear of the retribution of El Salvadoran security forces. In August 1988, *Harper's* editor Francisco Goldman published a review of the Central American press that was quoted by Noam Chomsky in "Necessary Illusions": "You have to be rich to own a newspaper, and on the right politically to survive the experience. Papers in El Salvador don't have to be censored: poverty and deadly fear do the job." Fortunately, this sad state of affairs was no longer absolutely true in the early 2000s. While once the military and government were above printed criticism unless they had fallen into government disfavor and might be sacrificed to the press in the name of spin, in the 2000s investigative journalism did occasionally peek out from among the many pages devoted to reporting sports scores, advertising smart clothes, parading new brides, and making social announcements.

The 1962 El Salvadoran Constitution, Article 6, granted freedom of speech, expression, and information that would not "subvert the public order, nor injure the morals, honor, or private life of others." For the last 20 years of the twentieth century, there was a mockery of these guarantees. However, after 1982, with the installation of a democratic system of elected officials and, at last, a decline in kidnappings and violent political retaliation and politically motivated killings, fear of reporting the news in either the press or in the broadcast media began to lessen. The 1983 Constitution confirmed the rights written down in the 1962 version. Nonetheless, conservative repression, as well as the violence of the opposing left-wing terrorists groups against the press in the early 1980s, made for a kind of self-censorship. Broadcasting licenses were and continued to be sought and renewed on a regular basis. This requirement, so harmless elsewhere, functioned as a kind of censorship for radio and TV stations as there was no guarantee of the renewal of licenses. Most of the owners of the larger broadcasting stations, periodicals, and magazines were conservative so the owners of these information sources became *de facto* censors and tended to move their periodicals into a conservative camp. Fear of the ubiquitous violence in El Salvador during the 1980s and 1990s, however, caused both extreme right and left wing groups to censor themselves. Despite the need to gain broadcast licenses, owners of broadcast media tolerated greater freedom of speech than did the newspapers, where the editorial policies reflected the opinions of the editors and publishers and therefore often deviated from the realities of the events discussed.

Political parties, businesses, unions, individuals, and even government agencies, might express their opinions through the *campos pagados* (paid political advertisements) accepted by most newspapers as advertisements. Campos pagados had been one of the few means of access to the printed word available to once revolutionary leftist groups such as the FMLN-FDR, but, of course, any organization or individual had to pay the cost for this access to the public. With the victory of FMLN in the March 12, 2000 elections, censorship decreased in some ways. However, in a famous example of censorship, Juan Jose Dalton, the son of revolutionary writer Roque Dalton, lost his place on the editorial board of *El Diario de Hoy* and resigned from the paper during the election campaign after he published a piece that sharply rebuked ARENA, the fading but still strong, right-wing National Republican Alliance.

State-Press Relations

While once the state controlled the press but not the radio, as of 2002 there was a more militantly adversarial relationship between state and press and perhaps a less adversarial relationship between the two in broadcast journalism. There was a time in the 1980s when a broadcast journalist without a license would have been considered a rebel and simply shot in some parts of the country and one could largely assume that daily newspapers sought government funding and defended government decisions while radio was the medium of the people. That, to a certain extent, changed. As of 2002 even reporters on *La Prenza* and *El Mondo* occasionally stood up to government privilege and survived the experience. However, El Salvador's journalists continued to suffer from restricted access to public records and resources. These restrictions limited their ability to legally contend for this information. The penal code allowed police officers to deny the press information about who had been arrested or even to prevent reporters' access to courtroom trials. Article 339 of the El Salvadorian penal code allowed imprisoning journalists for up to three years for falsely accusing someone of a crime: ''An individual who offends the honor or dignity, by deed or word, of a public official in the performance of his duties, or threatened such an official verbally or in writing, shall be punished with a prison term of six months to three years. The punishment may be increased by one third of the maximum sentence should the offended party be the President or Vice President of the Republic, a Deputy of the Legislative Assembly, a Minister or Deputy Minister, a judge of the Supreme Court or Court of Appeals, a trial judge, or a justice of the peace.''

Unfortunately, this law was not just a threat in El Salvador. Former vice president of El Salvador, Francisco Merino of the PCN (Parotid de Conciliacion Nacional), invoked this law when he brought legal action against five journalists for insulting him even though he had been arrested for shooting a police officer. Four reporters from *La Prensa Gráfica*, Mauricio Bolanos, Alfredo Herandez, Gregoria Moran and Jose Zometa, and *El Mondo*'s Camilia Calles were all threatened with the same sort of legal action as they pursued their investigative reporting of Merino's alleged illegal transfers of property as it was being investigated and brought before Judge Ana Marina Guzman.

In perhaps a breakthrough change of editorial policy, on September 1996 *El Diario de Hoy*, traditionally the conservative supporting newspaper of the ARENA party, criticized the new Telecommunications Law passed in El Salvador against the wishes of almost every other party in El Salvador.

Attitude Toward Foreign Media

For years, rebel forces included propaganda teams and actively enlisted often poorly trained journalists, media specialists, radio operators, and technicians. Particularly in rebel territory a person caught with radio equipment would be shot. Kidnapping was rampant during the civil war and not unknown even as of 2002 as a form of income. Foreign journalists were as likely as not to be rebels who had little formal training in radio broadcasting but gained fame through the bravery of their forbidden, unlicensed broadcasting.

Journalism continued to be a dangerous occupation in El Salvador, particularly if the journalist worked for a moderate newspaper or a television or radio station. According to a July 2000 Reuters press release from London, Jorge Zedán, 60-year-old co-owner of the television station Canal 12, and one of the directors of Saltel, the telecommunications firm, was kidnapped, held for five days, and released only after a ransom was paid. The police reportedly attacked Edwin Gongora and Miguel Gonzalez, also of Canal 12, and Ernesto Rivas of *El Diario de Hoy*, beat them up, and destroyed their equipment in order to stop them from interviewing Roberto Mathies Hill, who was detained and accused of fraud. The only death associated with journalism of late was the 1997 unsolved murder of Maria Lorena Saravia, a newsreader for Radio Corporacion Salvadorena. This single death was a far cry from the murders of over 25 journalists who were killed during the civil war. One could only hope that the relative safety of journalists at the turn of the millennium would be maintained. To put things in perspective, since 1992 and the end of the civil war, there was a post-war crime wave in which murderers generally got away with murder. Of 6,792 homicides since the war ended, only 415 suspects were arrested, and *La Prenza Gráfica* reported on April 21, 1999 in ''Justicia de El Salvador reprobada'' that the Salvadoran Foundation for Economic and Social Development (FUSADES) claimed that suspects were arrested in only 6 to 8 percent of murder cases (Popkin).

News Agencies

El Diario de Hoy, the conservative full-service newspaper, also had a daily Internet presence and had worked hard in the late 1990s to rid itself of its reputation as a conservative mouthpiece of the government. In reaction to its reputation for being willing to present false news, the paper attempted to change the impression it has given the people of El Salvador. On June 3, 2002, for example, the Internet daily edition of this newspaper ran the picture of a Morazean farm worker on the cover as if to suggest that its old adversarial relationship with the leftist territories had disappeared. *El Diario de Hoy* had sections on sports, business, international and national news, and even a section called ''Do You Want to Invest in El Salvador?''

Diario El Mundo offered a daily Internet news service at El Mundo.com.SV with an amazing ''ultima hora'' service designed to compete with the swiftness of radio news, in that national and international news appeared there in less than two hours.

CoLatino or *El Diario CoLatino* claimed to be a completely independent newspaper that had news which was real, truthful or ''actualidad,'' but one had to get through the first page of sports before reaching news articles. *CoLatino*'s claim that the news was real suggested that El Salvadorans had been the victims of so much misinformation in newspapers that they continued not to trust the medium as they did radio.

La Prensa Gráfica, the premier moderate newspaper, had an extensive Web site which made news available daily on the Web as well as to those who subscribed for or bought the paper. Its subhead was ''Noticias de Verdad'' which, of course, implied that it was different from other newspapers in that its news was true. Its Web site was divided into national, international, department, economic news, features, and sports. *El Heraldo de Occidente* and *El Heraldo de Oriente*, news from the west and east, kept those interested in local events abreast of the news and made *La Prensa Gráfica* appear open and fair-minded about local issues. Margaret Popkin noted that a major factor ''that contributed to creating a climate of reform was an editorial change at *La Prensa Gráfica* . . . This traditionally conservative daily took up an editorial line that favored the peace process and judicial reform effort . . . the need for fundamental reforms and . . . protecting individual rights'' (221). The policy change was attributed to David Escobar Galinda, university president, utopian, and deservedly famous poet.

Also worth mentioning were the following sources of news: *El Noticero*, from Chanel 6; *Guanaquiemos* an electronic magazine, published in Miami, Florida by Mrs. Cecelia Medina Figueroa; *Central American News*, Salvadoran section; *El Faro*, a news service which offered up-to-date web reports on news, sports, letters to the editor, and music and which archived old articles; *Diario Oficial*, the official dissemination organ for legislative decrees. They were made available by the El Salvadorean government and published in this journal.

Broadcast Media

Radio In the capitol of El Salvador, 70 radio stations compete for advertisers. Since El Salvador is small and uses repeater stations, virtually all 103 commercial radio stations can be heard in every part of the country. There is only one government-owned broadcast station. Because broadcast media does not suffer from the handicaps of illiteracy or costly access to the public, radio is the most widely used political medium in El Salvador. The ratio of radios to television sets certainly changed in the late twentieth century. In 1985 there were an estimated 2 million radio receivers and only 350,000 TVs in the whole nation. Radio Cabal broadcasted programs of news, debate, political interest, information, and radio dramas aimed at the poor of San Salvador, but since it was linked with left-wing politics, even though it was not associated with any political party, the station had difficulty getting advertisers. Obviously, targeting the poor parts of the population limited its utility to advertisers. Radio Cabal had depended on donations from international sources, including Denmark to cover broadcasting expenses. Mellemfolkeligt Samvirke (MS), the Danish Association for International Cooperation, and Danida, the Danish International Development Agency supporting communication for development, backed the radio station both financially and with volunteers since the station's establishment in 1993.

Two of FMLN's groups, Ejército Revolucionario del Pueblo (ERP) and Fuerzas Populares de Liberacion (FPL), operated so-called clandestine stations named Radio Venceremos and Radio Farabundo Marti, respectively. (*CIA Book of Facts*, Mass Media). Of course both the openly operated station and the once secret station served as sources of information for and propaganda from the FMLN. Most of the smaller stations focused programming on music rather than politics and news, but after the mid 1980s, the news programming of smaller radio stations presented a range of political points of view including rebel material, music which had potentially leftist themes, and propaganda and news reporting. The very active amateur radio association of El Salvador is Club de Radio Aficionados del El Salvador. The radio broadcasting organization of Asocacion Salvadorena de Empresarios de Radiodifusion (ASDER) is the largest in the country. VOXFM, PulsarFM, La Femenina, LAMIL80, Radio Renacer, Radio Nacional, LaQue Buena all have Web presences that allowed them to reach El Salvadorans in the United States.

The position of radio in 2002 was partly caused by the end of the civil war, but events surrounding the legitimacy of radio stations attested to the fact that all civil strife did not cease in 1992. Many years of civil war were succeeded by the 1992 peace agreement between the left-wing guerilla FMLN and the military-supported rule, and in 1994 the peace agreement led to a truly democratic general election with, for the first time, a broad spectrum of parties participating in the election. In a dramatic contrast to the election, on December 4, 1995, the Salvadoran National Civic Police (PNC) closed 10 radio stations and confiscated their broadcasting equipment. These stations were all members of the Association of Participatory Radio Stations and Programs (ARPAS) and the World Association of Community Radio Broadcasters (AMARC). Juan Jose Domenech, president of ANTEL, the state agency with the responsibility of regulating broadcasting and telecommunications, gave the orders to close the following stations: Segundo Montes (Meanguera, Department of Morazan), Izcanal (Nueva Grenada, Usulatan), Ulua (Cacaopera, Morazan); Cooperativa (Santa Elena, Usulatan); Victoria (Villa Victoria, Cabanüas); Suchitlan (Suchitoto, Cuscatlan), Excel (Zaragoza, La Libertad), Teo-Radio (Teotepeque, La Libertad), and Nejapa (Nejapa, San Salvador). Radio Sumpul might have been closed but in Guarjila, department of Chalatenango, citizens supposedly successfully defended the station from police action. The *zona oriental*, Morazon, the home of Radio Venceremos, continued to be a stronghold of extreme political activity. Some of the radio stations there still announced revolutionary causes, espoused what would be considered extreme priorities of redistribution of land, and remained faithful to the old cold war adversarial stance.

Television As of 2002, there are 8 television channels, 8 commercial stations, and 2 government-owned stations that presented educational programming during limited broadcasting hours. Perhaps more than any other medium, television had increased freedom of speech and access to information, as well as the opinions of a diversity of political organizations. TV news crews covered events, attended press conferences, interviewed, investigated, and reported elections results. When the military, police, and security forces were accused of human rights abuses, TV crews covered these stories and interviewed those accused.

Although, like Salvadorean radio, Salvadorean television stations could transmit over the entire small country, the higher cost of the hardware minimized the influence of the medium until late 1990s. Telecommunications services were provided by the public administration of ANTEL, the Administracion Nacional de Telecomunicaciones (National Telecommunications Administration), Teledos, canal 2; canal 6, canal 12, canal 19; canal 21 and canal 23. TV 12 called itself Canal Salvadoreno and its record for investigative reporting made it popular among those who fear continued misinformation from Flores's ARENA party government. Teledos claimed to have the latest news. El Salvador had television stations on the Web, satellite television, and an international cable television network. Television broadcasting services were found at Cablecolor and Calbvisa.

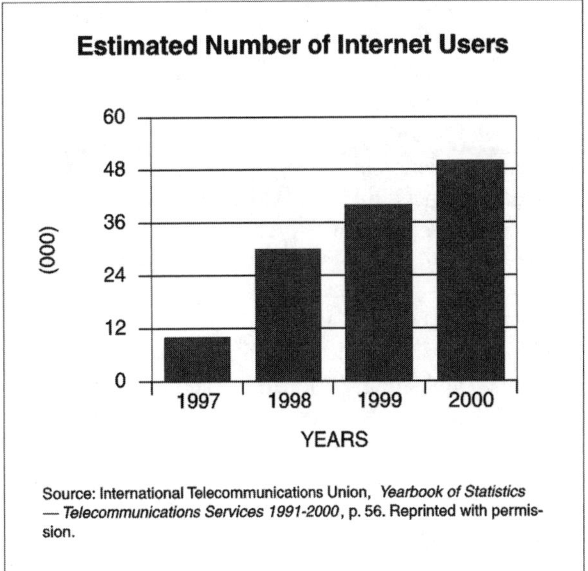

Source: International Telecommunications Union, *Yearbook of Statistics — Telecommunications Services 1991-2000*, p. 56. Reprinted with permission.

Associations important in this field are as follows. ANTEL was the state agency responsible for regulating broadcasting and telecommunications. Juan Jose Domenech was president of ANTEL and controlled the licensing system. Superintendencia de Electricidad y Telecommunicaciones (SIGET), supervised and controlled telecommunications media in El Salvador. And AMARC which covers community broadcasters.

Electronic News Media

As of 2002, providers of Internet services in El Salvador with their own Web pages were as follows: Americatel, www.americaltel.com.siv; CyTec, www. cytec.com.sv; EBNet www.gbm,net; IFX, www.ifxnet works.com; Integra, www.integra.com.sv; Intercom, www.intercom,com; Internet Gratis, www.internet gratis.com.siv; Netcom, www.salnet,net; Saltel; www. saltel.com; Telecam, www.telecam,net; Telecom, www. navegante.com.sav; Telefonica, www.telefonica.

com; Telemovil, www.telemovil.com; Tutopia, www.tutopia.com. Providers of Internet sources without Web sites or who may be working on their Internet presence at publication time are: AmNet; EJJE; El Salvador on Line; and Newcom. Companies like Genesis Technologies are certified to install and support Internet lines and construct Intranets in El Salvador. Internet de Telemovil and many other companies are involved in webhosting. Cybergate and Intersal SA de CV also were Web providers.

Consejo Nacional de Ciencia y Tecnologia (CONACYT) was publishing Rusta El Salvador Ciencia y Tecnologia for two years about the turn of the century, and the contents of this publication were available on the Web. From 1997 to 1999 Conacyt published Boletenes del CI. Those editions were still available as of 2002 on the Web as archived material.

Proceso, a weekly news bulletin from El Salvador, was published by Center for Information, Documentation (CIDAI) and Research Support of the Central American University (UCA) of El Salvador where it could be read on the university Web page, scripted into Spanish but partially or extensively obtained in English on PeaceNet. CIDAI was an impressive news service that covered political events and archived all its editions so that every issue was readily available. There were many articles relating to El Salvadoran immigrants in the United States and one of the group that might benefit from this Internet weekly news service that is uninterrupted by either advertising, sports or fashions. As of 2002, Proceso had written an editorial suggesting a reason why President Bush admired President Flores: President Flores was docile to the military objectives of the United States and had defended the war on terrorism and the installation of an American monitoring base on Salvadoran ground. The political events were presented in depth with serious academic and intellectual content often not found in other news coverage, and the editor seemed to support absolute freedom of speech.

Internet en El Salvador (SVNet) was a limited search engine set up by an act of the constitution of El Salvador on September 2, 1994, and run by a Secretariat associated with CONACYT. Phase I connected CONACYT, ANTEL, VES, Don Barco, and UCA. Phase II claimed to be adding VES San Miguel and Santa Ana, the National Library, EUSADES, and Polytechnic University. Telecam operated telecommunication services supervised by SIGET. Moreover, Telecom ran the telephone system and one of its subsidiaries, Publicar, S.A. published the yellow pages and distributed them door to door. Finally, computer magazines, *El Salvador USA. El Salvador Magazine. com* and *Revista Probidad* claimed to be nonpartisan, anti-corruption, and pro-democracy.

EDUCATION & TRAINING

There is little doubt but that El Salvador has had an increasingly professional group of print and broadcast journalists. However, under investment in education, a damaged infrastructure, relatively weak professional institutions, a legal system historically unfriendly to investigative journalism, very low salaries in the profession, and a degraded physical environment all slowed reconstruction and the stabilization of El Salvador's many communications channels and periodicals. In some ways El Salvador's universities were overwhelmed by the nation's large number of people under the age of 20. The universities did not have a sufficiently organized professional curriculum that included journalism, radio and television, and computer science. However, the technological universities, such as Universidad Politecnica de El Salvador (VPES) and the Universidad Tecnologica de El Salvador, were making rapid advances in the area of telecommunications. The University of El Salvador offered both a master's and a 5-year *Licenciatura* in Journalism with an extremely well organized plan of study through the faculty of Science and Humanities. Extensive and professional course work in newspaper writing, radio and TV was available. The University of El Salvador had a department of *periodismo* (journalism) and was dedicated to creating professionals in the area of communication.

SUMMARY

As of 2002, the media professionals in El Salvador, of necessity, had a kind of largely unspoken wait-and-see policy regarding political reform and freedom of speech. The FMLN evolved from being a guerilla army into an important political party, winning on March 12, 2000, a plurality in the legislative assembly as well as re-electing the FMLN candidate for mayor of San Salvador. Ironically, Cuba's insistence on leftist unity and that of Socialist European sponsors such as the West Germans, lessened the numbers of the dead, yet the fact remained that over 50,000 people died between the Duarte death squads and the leftist juggling for power. In the early 2000s, understandably, the desire for order and stability was great. Although the traditional El Salvadorean media were not as closely censored and restricted as Nicaraguan media, neither did they illustrate the diversity, plurality, and freedoms of the press of Costa Rica. Enjoying moderate freedom of speech and exhibiting great differences in political points of view, the press of El Salvador was self-censored. Publishers feared *la violencia* of those who would disagree with their interpretation of the news, whether opponents were right or left-wing organizations or political parties and groups. The largely conservative, business-oriented owners of the press caused a less conservative broadcast network to be the place that many El

Salvadorians found news. Literacy was as much a factor in the popularity of broadcast news as the more liberal reporting provided by broadcasters. Even though approximately 70 percent of the adult population was reported to be literate, in the capital the press's influence was still limited by considerable illiteracy and poverty.

Economic censorship was real in the often undercapitalized organizations that published newspapers and ran broadcast stations. An example of the kind of economic censorship that occurs is as follows. In June 2000, after a phone-tapping accusation by Jorge Zedán, coowner of TV DOCE, he was kidnapped but then released. *El Diario de Hoy* published a story accusing the state telephone company of tapping a huge number of phone lines, including the phone of Lafitte Fernandez, managing editor of that newspaper and by publishing the story accused a major advertiser and revenue source, France Telecom, of criminal activity. France Telecom immediately canceled its advertising in *El Diario de Hoy*. In 2002, it was too soon to suggest that all was well between the media and the government in El Salvador.

Time will tell if the government really does encourage telecommunications and sophisticated broadcast networks in and around Morazon, the old rebel capitol, and how the government uses this new technology. Nonetheless, despite significant destruction from guerrilla sabotage in the 1980s, earthquakes, and terrible economic problems, El Salvador experienced significant growth in the 1960s, 1970s, and 1990s. Powerful forces helped El Salvador restore order. The media's unrelenting pursuit of the truth, *actualidad*, gave one cause for hope for greater freedom of the press, clearer legal relationships between government and the press, and a more stable financial future for the media of El Salvador.

Significant Dates

- 1995: Confiscating their equipment, national police close 10 community radio stations that never received broadcast licenses from ANTEL but were members of the AMARC and had been operating since at least 1990.
- 1996: ARENA is able to get their Telecommunications Law passed in the Salvadorean legislature despite bills introduced by other parties and offers by telecommunication networks that are more forward-looking than ARENA's. Even *El Diario de Hoy*, usually supportive of ARENA, concedes that this bill damages freedom of expression.
- 1997: Maria Lorena Saravia, a news reader from Radio Corporation Salvadorena who also works for YSKL and canal 21 television, is murdered. The crime remains unsolved.
- 1999: Francisco ''Paco'' Flores of the Arena party begins his five-year term as president of El Salvador. The FMLN's candidate, with 29 percent of the vote, fails to disassociate himself from the violence of the civil war. Flores has spent those years teaching philosophy and managing an irrigation project with his wife, a schoolteacher. Flores, a former president of El Salvador's unicameral National Assembly, runs as a new kind of leader of ARENA, the traditionally conservative party. Flores was educated at Amherst, MA, and studies at Harvard in Cambridge, MA, and at Oxford University in England.

Bibliography

Arreaza-Camero, Emperatriz Communicacion. *Derechos Humanos y Democracia: El Rol de Radio Venceremos en el Proceso de Democeatizacion en El Salvador (1981-1994).* Available from http://lanic.utexas.edu/project/lasa95/arreaza l.html.

Belt, Juan. A.B. and Anabella Larde de Palomo. ''El Salvador: Transition Towards Peace and Participatory Development.'' Paris: unpublished paper presented at OECD workshop 21 November 1994.

Chomsky, Noam. ''Necessary Illusions: Sad Tales of La Libertad de Prensa.'' *Harper's*, (August 1988). Available from http://zena.secureforum/znet/chomsky/ni/ni/c10-s25html.

The Central Intelligence Agency (CIA). *World Factbook 2001.* Available from http://www.cia.gov.

''El Salvador, Rural Development Strategy.'' Washington, DC: The World Bank.

Galeas, Marvin. ''La prensa como contrapoder.'' *Tendencias,* no. 40. San Salvador: COOPEX.S.A., May 1995.

Gonzalez-Vega, Claudio. ''BASIS—Central American Reconnaissance Mission Report 19-24.'' Prepared for the Consortium for Applied Research on Market Access (CARMA), May 1997.

Haggarty, Richard A., ed. *El Salvador: A Country Study.* Washington D.C.: Federal Research Division, Library of Congress, 1990.

Morales, Maria. *Radio Venceremos: un medio de comunicacion alternativo en Latino America.* Mexico: U.N. A. M. (Tesis mimeografiada), 1992.

Popkin, Margaret. *Peace Without Justice: Obstacles to Building the Rule of Law in El Salvador.* University Park, PA: Pennsylvania State University, 2000.

—Merrilee Cunningham

EQUATORIAL GUINEA

BASIC DATA

Official Country Name:	Republic of Equatorial Guinea
Region (Map name):	Africa
Population:	474,214
Language(s):	Spanish, French, Pidgin English, Fang, Bubi, Ibo
Literacy rate:	78.5%

BACKGROUND & GENERAL CHARACTERISTICS

In Equatorial Guinea, a limited number of mostly government-controlled media outlets operate in Spanish, French, and local dialects from bases in the island capital, Malabo (Bioko), and the mainland city of Bata (Rio Muni).

Formerly Spanish Guinea, the Republic of Equatorial Guinea (República de Guinea Ecuatorial) is a small coastal country that gained its independence and current name in 1968. Its 1991 constitution was amended in 1995. Mismanagement and questionable elections in the 1990s are parts of a history of national instability.

On World Press Day 2002, the Paris-based group Reporters without Borders listed Minister Teodoro Obiang Nguema among thirty ''predators'' worldwide whose actions threatened the principle of a free press.

The population, under a half million, is heavily Roman Catholic and forty-seven percent urban; however, Malabo and Bata had fewer than 30,000 residents each in 1995, following the country's financial collapse and the resulting exodus of many Europeans.

Principal languages are Spanish and French—both official—and native dialects including Fang. Pidgin English operates in commerce. In the mid-1990s, the country had the second highest male literacy rate in Africa, following Zimbabwe.

In 1997, after a rift with Madrid, the government ordered state-run media to use French exclusively.

Media Activity Newspapers that have been published irregularly and in small press runs (of perhaps one or two thousand copies) at Malabo are *Ebano* and *Unidad de la Guinea Ecuatorial,* both in Spanish. In Bata, *Poto Poto* has appeared in Spanish and Fang. The first government-recognized private newspaper, the weekly *El Sol,* was started in 1994. Spain's *Agencia EFE,* operating at Malabo, is the only news agency.

Radio Nacional de Guinea Ecuatorial (RNGE) supervises broadcasts in Spanish and local languages over two radio stations at Malabo and one at Bata. *Televisión Nacional* transmits over a single, government-controlled channel at Malabo. In the 1990s a commercial radio network was operating, and cultural broadcasts were produced with Spanish collaboration. In 1995 citizens owned about 170,000 radios and 4,800 television sets.

Statistics for 2000 show one Internet service provider and about five hundred subscribers.

SIGNIFICANT DATES

- 1994: First government-recognized private newspaper appears.
- 1997: Government orders state-run media to use French exclusively.
- 2002: Reporters without Borders calls Guinean minister a ''predator'' on the press.

BIBLIOGRAPHY

Banks, Arthur S., and Thomas C. Muller, ed. *Political Handbook of the World, 1999.* Binghamton, NY: CSA Publications, 1999.

The Central Intelligence Agency (CIA). *The World Factbook 2000.* Directorate of Intelligence, 7 May 2002. Available from http://www.cia.gov/.

Turner, Barry, Ed. *The Statesman's Yearbook: The Politics, Cultures, and Economies of the World, 2000.* New York: St. Martin's Press, 1999.

World Almanac and Book of Facts, 2002. New York: World Almanac Books, 2002.

—Roy Neil Graves

ERITREA

BASIC DATA

Official Country Name:	Eritrea
Region (Map name):	Africa
Population:	4,298,269
Language(s):	Afar, Amharic, Arabic, English, Tigre and Kunama, Tigrinya other Cushitic languages

Literacy rate:	25.0%
Area:	121,320 sq km
GDP:	608 (US$ millions)
Number of Television Stations:	1
Number of Television Sets:	1,000
Television Sets per 1,000:	0.2
Number of Satellite Subscribers:	2,063
Satellite Subscribers per 1,000:	0.5
Number of Radio Stations:	5
Number of Radio Receivers:	345,000
Radio Receivers per 1,000:	80.3
Number of Individuals with Computers:	6,160
Computers per 1,000:	1.4
Number of Individuals with Internet Access:	500
Internet Access per 1,000:	1.2

BACKGROUND & GENERAL CHARACTERISTICS

Eritrea is Africa's latest nation to gain its independence from Ethiopia's 40 years of occupation. After a long, drawn-out military conflict between the two states, Eritreans won their independence on May 24, 1993. Four days later, Eritrea became a member of the United Nations.

Eritrea, at 121,000 square kilometers, is a torch-shaped wedge of the physical landscape whose size equals that of Britain. The country lies along the Red Sea coast in northern Africa and borders Sudan in the north and west, Djibouti in the southeast, and Ethiopia in the south. Its coastline is 750 miles long and is intersected with the seaports of Massawa and Assab. The northern half of the country is a highland plateau on which Asmara, the capital city, is located. The country has 10 provinces (Akele, Asmara, Barka, Denkel, Gash-Senhit, Guzai, Hamasien, Sahel, Semhar, and Seraye) (Hunter 1997). The lowlands lie to the west and east while the south is predominantly characterized by aridity (Gottesman, 2001).

Demography Eritrea's population is 4.3 million and comprises nine ethno-linguistic groups, namely Amharic, Tigra, Kunama, Hidarb, Saho, Rosdia, Blen, Arabic and Afar. The three major languages are English, Tigrinya, and Arabic. While all the languages are used in elementary school, English forms the medium of communication in post elementary and post secondary institutions. Religiously, the country is divided into half Muslim and half Christian. About 20 percent of the people live in urban areas, and 80 percent live in the rural countryside. About 15 percent are herders and farmers and less than 5 percent practice pastoralism. About 45 percent of the total population is under 15 years, 54 percent is between 15 and 64 years (life expectancy is 56 years), and a tiny fraction is comprised of senior citizens.

The literacy rate suffers at 25 percent. A quarter of a million children are enrolled in elementary school, 90,000 attend high schools, and more than 3,000 attend post secondary institutions. Of all of these, female enrollment is 48 percent, 17 percent, and 0.3 percent as compared to males respectively. The patriarchal, traditional and religious practices tend to discriminate against women. Female discrimination is more highly pronounced in higher education, the professions, and government. Press activism intended to educate the country to bridge the gap between the sexes may be regarded with distaste.

The Press Previously, Eritrea published both private-owned and government-sponsored newspapers. However, in September 2001 the government authorities ordered all eight newspapers in the private press closed. This included *Admas*, *Keste Debena*, *Mana*, *Meqaleh*, *Setit*, *Tiganay*, *Wintan*, and *Zemen* leaving *Hadas Eritrea* as the sole daily (run by the government).

STATE-PRESS RELATIONS

Historical Background Eritrea became independent from Ethiopian annexation rule in 1993. In 1994, Eritrea established a more concrete stand in international relations by being accepted as a member of the UN and OAU organizations. The first four years were a form of transitional or preparatory statehood. In May 1997, a new constitution was adopted but has never been ratified. The transitional government had a 4-year term and consisted of the presidency and the 130 member unicameral legislature. There is no judiciary branch. This national assembly consists of members of the only approved political party, the People's Front for Democracy and Justice (PFDJ). Formerly, the PFDJ was the nationalist movement that fought Ethiopia for Eritrean independence, as the Eritrean People's Liberation Front (EPLF). A marginalized opposition is centered around the Eritrean National Pact Alliance. In 1994, the PFDJ formed the Central Committee and 60 other Parliamentarians who included 11 women. The Central Committee elected the President whose constitutional responsibility is to appoint the State Council (cabinet). The transitional government had 14 cabinet ministers and 10 provincial governors. The President chairs both the State Council and the National Assembly.

In the modern world, Eritrea's historical profile, demography, political economy, constitutional and legal framework, and international relations have a profound impact in its perceptual and interpretive role of the press in an emerging democracy. These six forces form a complex interplay of factors upon which the role of Eritrean private and independent media reverberates. For instance, based on the principles of the transitional government, Eritrean government was supposed to hold general elections in September 2001. That did not happen. In a country that is perceived to be a weak but emerging democracy, the nullification of the election timetable by the government is something that makes many people skeptical, both at home and abroad. For marginalized opposition groups, an issue like this one tends to reunite, reenergize, and radicalize the opposition's challenge against the government. In the eyes of donor communities, especially the United States, whose foreign assistance to the country enables it to sustain 70 percent of its population, retaliatory diplomatic pressure on an authoritarian and ''infant democratic'' political system tends to overwhelm the influence of the powers that be. These corrupt powers are farther challenged by the work the print media, broadcast media, and electronic media display in public about them. This dissemination results in national and international awareness of the regime's political behavior in terms of its state-press relations.

Press Laws & Censorship Further evidence seems to suggest that President Isayas and his single political party (PFDJ) ''have unlawfully disallowed opposition parties from partaking in Eritrean politics. They also continue to eliminate challengers, muzzle discontent, imprison critics, persecute opponents, layoff civil servants and systematically exclude conscientious citizens in order to carryout the leadership's brutal and undemocratic activities'' (http://www.eritreal.org/). Although the Eritrean National Assembly established a commission in January 2000 for the purpose of ratifying the role and responsibility of an independent press, this constitutional and political procedure has not helped.

On February 28, 2002, ten journalists were arrested and detained indefinitely. Two unconstitutional explanations were given to justify the detention. First, since the work of some of the arrested and detained journalists is financed by foreign governments including the United States, and since the U.S. Secretary of State's office has communicated with these journalists about internal socio-economic and political conditions, there are rumors of governmental fears of exposure. Media coverage and powerful communication technology in the arena of political corruption and diplomatic pressure tend to expose sensitive bureaucratic issues which may serve to discredit democratic political rationality in Eritrea (Robinson, 2000). Second, some of those who were arrested, as the government claimed, failed to complete their mandatory military service. Journalistic detainees are members of the private press whose freedom to write, publish, educate, and communicate is in the national constitution. Irrespective of their constitutional privileges and immunities, the Eritrean Press Corps was ''silenced.'' Meanwhile, the pressmen had been on a two-month hunger strike that incapacitated one of them, a statement that was made public on April 10, 2002.

Since the laws holding the pressmen in prison are supposed to be interpreted in the context of legal jurisprudence, their interpretation remains to be challenged since the nation lacks a judicial system and since that lack is partially rooted in its ethnic and political controversies whose dynamics dictate and reinforce it.

Eritrean laws say that a detained suspect has the right to be free on bail, pending investigation, unless the suspect is a flight risk, a threat to his community or will tamper with evidence. Accordingly, the Eritrean public forum and the organization of the African commission on Human and Peoples' Rights urged the Eritrean government to consider enforcing the right to the bail of the detainees under a scheme where the movements and activities of the suspects on bail are legitimately limited in place and time, with full supervision that ensures that these suspects do not violate the terms of their bail. Freeing the journalists on bail will be necessary if the Eritrean government requires more time to complete its case against them. Such violation is inconsistent with the freedom of the press in its emblematic significance that challenges print, broadcast and electronic journalism.

BROADCAST & ELECTRONIC NEWS MEDIA

Eritrea claims only one television station and three radio stations, all of which are government-controlled as private ownership is prohibited. As of a 1997 estimate, only 345,000 Eritrean households had radios and a scant 1,000 possessed televisions.

Furthermore, in the year 2000, Eritrea had the distinction of being the last country in Africa to provide Internet access to its people. With only four Internet Service Providers and a mere 500 users in 1999 (who pay relatively high usage fees) electronic media is clearly in its infancy without much foreseeable growth.

SUMMARY

In Africa, the role, constraint, and concern of the press, as the continent struggles with democratization and other development issues, is no exception to the challenges of the Eritrean private press. The press' role in and contribution to democratic political governance and bureaucratic accountability is viewed with skepticism and distaste for its controversial stance and imperialistic overtones.

By using psychological and diverse ways of understanding and influencing the public, the press can effectively play its role as an investigator, reporter, and agenda-setter. This role is that of being a carrier because the press tends to creatively formulate and articulate agenda for public policy debates. The courage, skill, and dynamism with which the press carries out its responsibility in the Third World, in the midst of surmounting obstacles, could be different from that of its counterpart in well-established and constitutionally more tolerant democracies. Therefore, Western-oriented, ideologically intoxicated, and democratically minded private press may find it difficult if not impossible to professionally survive in Africa and particularly in Eritrea. To function well in such an environment, the press may need to learn how to adapt itself to new and challenging situations in order to capitalize on existing opportunities.

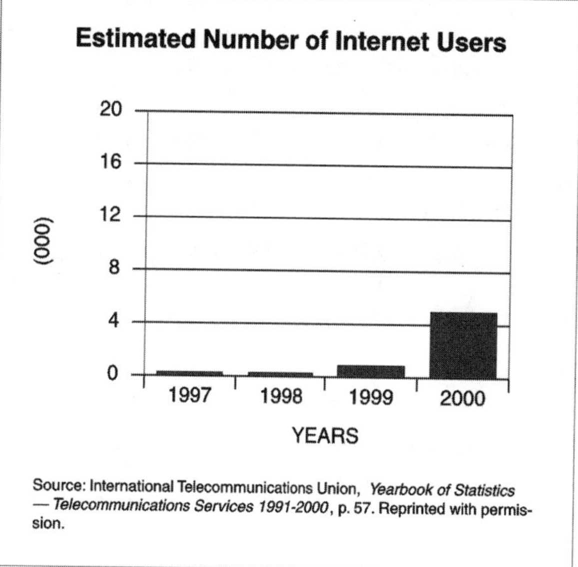

Source: International Telecommunications Union, *Yearbook of Statistics — Telecommunications Services 1991-2000*, p. 57. Reprinted with permission.

BIBLIOGRAPHY

Absuutari, Pertti. ed. *Rethinking the Media Audience: The New Agenda*. London: Sage, 1999.

AllAfrica.com. ''National Assembly Endorses Press Clampdown, Sticks to One-Party System.'' AllAfrica Global Media, August 2002. Available at http://www.allafrica.com.

——— ''Government Admits to CPJ that it is Holding Journalists in Secret Detention.'' AllAfrica Global Media, August 2002. Available at http://www.allafrica.com.

Amnesty International. ''Eritrea: Growing Repression of Government Critics.'' *Amnesty International Report 2002*. London: Amnesty International, August 2002. Available at http://web.amnesty.org.

Awde, Nicholas and Hill, Fred James, eds. *Nations of the World: A Political, Economic and Business Handbook*. Millerton, NY: Grey House Publishing, 2002.

Barnett, Clive. ''The Limits of Media Democratization in South Africa: Politics, Privatization and Regulation.'' *Media Culture and Society*, 21, 5, 649-672, 1999.

Burstien, Paul. ''Bringing the Public Back'' In: *Should Sociologists Consider the Impact of Public Opinion on Public Policy*. Social Forces, 77, 1, 27-62, 1998.

Central Intelligence Agency (CIA). ''Eritrea.'' *The World Factbook*. Directorate of Intelligence, August 2002. Available from http://www.cia.gov.

Committee to Protect Journalists. ''Eritrea: Nine journalists arrested; two others flee as crackdown continues.'' *CPJ: 2001 News Alert*. New York, NY: CPJ, 2002. Available at http://www.cpj.org.

Dayan, Daniel. ''The Peculiar Public of Television.'' *Media Culture and Society*, 23, 6, 743-765, 2001.

Diamond, Larry. *Developing Democracy: Toward Consolidation*. Baltimore, MD: Johns Hopkins University Press, 1999.

Decalo, Samuel. *The Stale Ministry: Civilian Rule in Africa, 1960-1990*. Gainsville, FL: Academic Press, 1998.

Freedom House. ''Eritrea.'' *Freedom in the World*. Freedom House, Inc., August 2002. Available at http://www.freedomhouse.org.

Gaubatz, Kurt Taylor. *Elections and War: The Electoral Incentive in the Democratic Politics of War and Peace*. Stanford, CA: Stanford University Press, 1999.

Gottesman, Leslie, D. ''Eritrea.'' *World Education Encyclopedia: A Survey of Educational Systems Worldwide*. 1, 410-419, Farmington Hills, MI: Gale Group, 2001.

Gunther, Richard and Mughan, Anthony. eds. *Democracy and the Media: A Comparative Perspective*. Cambridge, UK: Cambridge University Press, 2000.

Human Rights Watch. ''Eritrea.'' *Human Rights Watch World Report 2002*. New York: Human Rights Watch, August 2002. Available at http://www.hrw.org.

Hunter, Julian. ed. *The Stateman's Yearbook: A statistical, Political and Economic Account of the States of the World*. New York: St. Martin's Press, 1996-1997.

Linz, Juan, J. and Stepan, Alfred. *Problems of Democratic Transition and Consolidation: Southern Europe, South America, and Post-Communist Europe*. Baltimore, MD: Johns Hopkins University Press, 1996.

Mickiewicz, Ellen. ed. *Changing Channels: Television and the Struggle for Power in Russia*. Durham, NC: Duke University Press, 1999.

Milton, Andrew, K. *The Rational Politician: Exploiting the Media in New Democracies*. Aldershot, UK: Ashgate, 2000.

Mughan, Anthony. *Media and the Presidentialization of Parliamentary Elections*. New York: Palgrave, 2000.

Munck, Gerardo, L. ''The Regime Question: Theory Building in Democracy Studies.'' *World Politics: A Quarterly Journal of International Relations*, 54, 1, 119-149, 2001.

Norris, Pippa. ed. *Women, Media, and Politics*. New York: Oxford University Press, 1997.

Patterson, Thomas, E. *We the People: A Concise Introduction to American Politics*. Boston: McGraw, 2002.

Robinson, Piers. ''World Politics and Media Power: of Research Design.'' *Media Culture and Society*, 22, 2, 227-232, 2000.

Tettey, Wisdon, J. ''The Media and Democratization in Africa: Contributions, Constraints and Concerns of the Private Press.'' *Media Culture and Society*, 23, 1, 5-31, 2001.

Volkomer, Water E. *American Government*. Upper Saddle River, NJ: Prentice Hall, 2001.

— Meshack M. Sagini

ESTONIA

BASIC DATA

Official Country Name:	Republic of Estonia
Region (Map name):	Europe
Population:	1,423,316
Language(s):	Estonian (official), Russian, Ukrainian, English, Finnish, other
Literacy rate:	100.0%
Area:	45,226 sq km
GDP:	4,969 (US$ millions)
Number of Daily Newspapers:	13
Total Circulation:	262,000
Circulation per 1,000:	237
Number of Nondaily Newspapers:	49
Total Circulation:	333,000
Circulation per 1,000:	302
As % of All Ad Expenditures:	46.40
Number of Television Stations:	31
Number of Television Sets:	605,000
Television Sets per 1,000:	425.1
Number of Cable Subscribers:	126,420
Cable Subscribers per 1,000:	90.3
Number of Satellite Subscribers:	65,000
Satellite Subscribers per 1,000:	45.7
Number of Radio Stations:	86
Number of Radio Receivers:	1,010,000
Radio Receivers per 1,000:	709.6
Number of Individuals with Computers:	220,000
Computers per 1,000:	154.6
Number of Individuals with Internet Access:	391,600
Internet Access per 1,000:	275.1

BACKGROUND & GENERAL CHARACTERISTICS

Historical Traditions The pre-history of Estonia can be dated to 8000 BC when the oldest traces of human inhabitants were found, but the ethnic origins of the first settlers are unknown. By the third millennium BC, the settlers were Finno-Ugrians who migrated from the east, and Baltic tribes who came from the south. In the 13th century the Estonians were conquered by stronger medieval powers that were primarily German but also included the Danes, Swedes, and Russians. It was at this time that they were introduced to Christianity and the influence of western Catholicism. The composition of the indigenous peoples were basically *maarahvas* (country folk) while the nobility, clergy, merchants, and traders were predominantly Baltic Germans who were referred to by the local people as *saks,* a short form for Germans. The only way in which the local Estonian could hope to achieve a higher social status was to adopt the German language and customs and in effect, relinquish his Estonian identity.

The German Reformation movement reached Estonia in 1523 and created competition between the Lutheran and Catholic faiths. This precipitated the emergence of propagandist literature and led to the first Estonian book being published in 1525, which was destroyed because it was considered heretical. A more acceptable book, a catechism, was published in 1535, and in 1686 an Estonian edition of the New Testament was published. Education was always a key element in the national development of Estonia and peasants taught their children to read at home. As early as 1686, the first alphabet book in Estonian appeared. A complete translation of the Bible was published in 1739. Between 1802 and 1856, local people achieved emancipation and were given limited property rights. This freedom led to the development of an Estonian newspaper that was established in 1806. Between 1857 and 1861 *Kalevipoeg,* the national Estonian epic, was published. At that same time a new newspaper, the *Perno Postimees* (Parnu Mailman), was the first publication to refer to *essti rahvas* (Estonian people) instead of *maarahvas* (country folk) and became very popular among the Estonians. This stimulated the creation of additional publications and other newspapers followed such as *Sakala,* which was edited by Carl Robert Jakobson.

During the 19th century, the Estonian nationalist identity became stronger and by the 20th century Estonians sought independence. They achieved independence in 1918 after the First World War, known to Estonians as the War of Liberation. In 1939 Estonia was once again faced with the intrusion of a foreign power when Soviet military bases were introduced and by August 6, 1940, Estonia was annexed into the Soviet Union and forced to accept Soviet domination and influence for the next 50 years. During its occupation of Estonia, the Soviets destroyed approximately 10 to 12 million books and virtually decimated Estonian literature.

Mikhail Gorbachev, President of the USSR during the 1980s, allowed greater freedom within the various republics, a policy known as "glasnost." The Estonians took advantage of this and in 1987 launched the Popular Front, an Estonian nationalist movement. On August 20, 1991, Estonia declared itself independent from the Soviet Union and a new constitution was adopted on June 28, 1992. The final removal of Russian troops and tanks occurred in August 1994 thus terminating 50 years of Russian military presence in Estonia.

During the Soviet occupation of Estonia, journalism confronted varying degrees of censorship and the major change to occur in the Estonian media, post independence in the 1990s, was the removal of censorship. However, the evolution of this new press began as far back as 1986 when glasnost was first introduced. The Soviets began to loosen their rigid controls on the media. Periodicals began to change their style, format, and even the content of the news. Publications began emphasize the nation of Estonia and eliminate the word "Soviet." By 1989 the independent press had grown to more than 1,000 publications. These ranged from the weekly *Eesti Eks* press, a joint Estonian-Finnish collaboration, to smaller specialized journals that were short-lived.

Despite the growth and freedom afforded the press, there still existed serious problems. Similar to the other Baltic nations, the lack of a strong infrastructure resulted in several new dilemmas. The problems confronting the Estonian media included substance, structure, and regulation. The lack of quality control manifested itself in poor journalism. The analyses were simplistic, fact and opinion were not delineated, and chronology took precedence over significance of the stories. More important news was often lost in the calendar of events. More seriously, the failures of the editorial process resulted in deliberate misrepresentations that were used to gain political points. The former *Edasi,* once regarded as Estonia's best newspaper, was acquiring a reputation of deliberately twisting information and printing libelous and even plagiarized articles.

Privatization of the Estonian press proceeded slowly and in 1993 the number of publications stabilized. A major change to occur within Estonian publishing was the increasing number of foreign-language periodicals, the majority of which were in English or Swedish. In 1999 there were 105 officially registered newspapers, including 17 daily papers published in Estonia. Seventy-three of the total number and 13 of the dailies were published in the Estonian language. By the end of 1994 Estonia was considered to have the most balanced reporting of government news among the Baltic States because journalists were freer to write about political and personal issues of senior functionaries.

The media in Estonia continued to improve as indicated by a survey conducted by Freedom House that measured trends and press freedoms. Estonia improved from a rating of "partly free" in 1992 to "free" each year between 1993 and 2001.

In 1995 the major development of the Estonian press was the merger of the three largest newspapers. In 2002

Daily and Non-Daily Newspaper Titles and Circulation Figures

	1996	1997	1998	1999	2000
Number of Daily Newspapers	15	17	16	17	13
Circulation of Dailies (000)	255	260	254	273	262
Number of Non-Daily Newspapers	59	56	60	50	49
Circulation of Non-Dailies (000)	531	468	472	419	333

Source: World Association of Newspapers and Zenithmedia, *World Press Trends 2001*, pp. 8, 10, 17, 19.

the top three newspapers include: *SL Ohtuleht* (Evening Gazette), founded in 2000 with the merger of *Ohtuleht* and *Sonumileht* newspapers, a daily paper published in Estonian with a circulation of 67,200; *Postimees* (Postman), founded in 1857 and published daily in Estonian with a circulation of 60,200; and *Eesti Ekspress* (Estonian Express), founded in 1989, a weekly paper published in Estonian. The next biggest papers in terms of circulation are: *Maaleht* (Country News) founded in 1987, which deals with various aspects of country life, has a circulation of 46,000, and is published in Estonian; *Den za Dujan* (Day After Day), a weekly paper founded in 1991 and published in Russian; and *Meie Meel* (Our Mind), founded in 1991, a weekly youth paper published in Estonian.

The Nature of the Audience: Literacy, Affluence, Population Distribution, Language Distribution In 2000, the population of Estonia was estimated at over 1.4 million and consisted of 65.3 percent Estonian, 28.1 percent Russian, 2.5 percent Ukrainian, and the remaining 4.1 percent other nationalities. The native Estonian is found mainly in the rural areas, whereas the non-Estonians are found in the northeastern industrial towns. Citizenship may be obtained if one is born in Estonia or at least one parent is Estonian. Naturalization requires three years of residency in the country and competency in the language. Based on the definition of literacy to mean the ability to read after the age of 15, Estonia has a 100% literacy rate.

Economic Framework

The Estonian economy grew rapidly between the two World Wars. During that time it was principally an agricultural society with some developed industry. After World War II the economy became mainly urbanized and industrialized and enjoyed one of the highest standards of living in the Soviet bloc. By the late 1980s, the serious economic and political crises that were plaguing the Soviet Union allowed Estonia to seek sovereignty from the communist rule and work towards a free and independent nation. After independence in June 1991, the Estonian government passed an ownership act that began a privatization program that transferred almost 500 state-owned companies into the private sector. In 1992 the economy began to revive after monetary reforms were instituted and the Estonian kroon was reintroduced. In late 1995 all the Estonian railways, energy, oil shale, telekon, and ports were privatized and in gas, tobacco, and air followed in 1996. These economic reforms made Estonia one of the strongest post-communist economies of the former Soviet republics. These market reforms were also the leading factors in the much needed change in the mass media sector.

In 1998, as a ripple effect of the Russian financial crisis, Estonia experienced its first economic downturn since independence. By 2000, however, the country quickly rebounded by scaling back its budget and transferring trade from the Russian markets to the European market.

Press Laws

The Estonian Constitution provides for personal freedoms, privacy, and the right to information. According to Chapter II Fundamental Rights, Liberties, and Duties, Article 44 [Right to Information]:

- Everyone shall have the right to receive information circulated for general use.

Chapter II Article 45 [Freedom of Speech]

- Everyone shall have the right to freely circulate ideas, opinions, persuasions, and other information by word, print, picture and other means. This right may be restricted by law for the purpose of protecting public order or morals, or the rights and liberties, health, honor and reputation of others. The law may likewise restrict this right for state and local government officials, for the purpose of protecting state or business secrets or confidential communication, which due to their service the officials have access to, as well as protecting the family life and privacy of other persons, and in the interests of justice.
- There shall be no censorship.

On May 19, 1994, the Law on Radio and Television Broadcasting gave the radio and television stations the right to make free decisions about their content and broadcasts and restrictions were punishable by law.

CENSORSHIP

Newspapers and periodicals have always played an important role in the life of Estonians and have survived attempts to eliminate their language, culture, and freedom of thought. The Estonian press emerged somewhat scarred after the fifty years of Soviet occupation and censorship but has worked to rectify the problems. The Constitution guarantees no censorship, but a court decision in 1997 convicted and fined a journalist on charges of offensive remarks against a politician. This decision was questioned and criticized and many felt that it was a move against freedom of speech and came very close to censorship.

In 2002 Estonia faced new complaints from the Russian-speaking population, a large group that constitutes 28.1 percent of the population. These Russian Estonians state that there is limited programming in Russian, forcing them to receive their news from Russian broadcasts. In addition, they have complained that they also face harassment from the tax authorities and other regulators because of their background.

Another ban occurred when the parliament voted in favor of banning tobacco advertising on television and radio in 1997.

STATE-PRESS RELATIONS

The government monopoly on printing and distribution was abolished after independence was achieved in 1991 and since that time Estonia has enjoyed an independent press that is free from government interference. The major piece of legislation with which journalists are the most concerned, is the criminalization of libel. The legislature assigned the burden of proof to the media.

NEWS AGENCIES

There are two news agencies in Estonia, the BNS (Baltic News Service) and ETA Interactive. The BNS is the largest and has its headquarters in Tallinn, Estonia with regional offices in Lithuania and Latvia. There are also three press organizations: the Estonian Journalists' Union; the Estonian Newspaper Association; and the Estonian Press Council.

BROADCAST MEDIA

In 2000 Estonia had thirty radio broadcasters operating and five cable channels. The major commercial stations are: *Eesti Raadio* (Estonian Radio); *Kristlik Pereraadio* (Christian Family Radio); *Raadio Elmar; Raadio Kuku; Raadio Sky Pluss; Raadio Uuno; Raadio V6;* and Star FM.

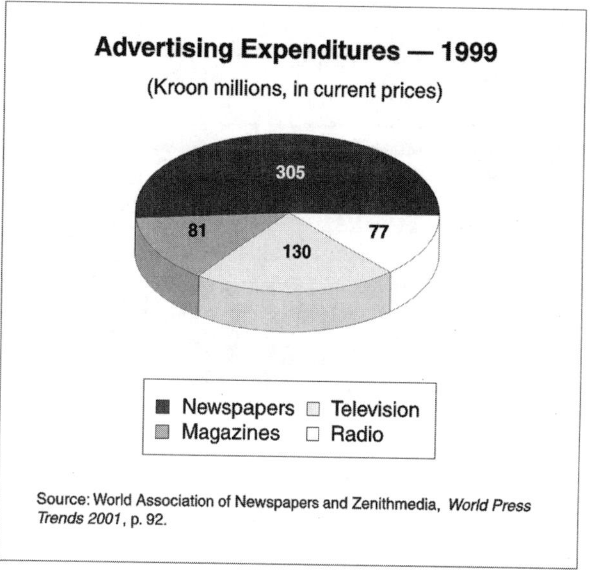

Source: World Association of Newspapers and Zenithmedia, *World Press Trends 2001*, p. 92.

There are four commercial television stations in Estonia. The state-run ETV, despite receiving government funding, faced serious financial problems at the end of the 20th century that resulted in funding decreases, employee lay-offs, and programming reductions.

ELECTRONIC NEWS MEDIA

In 2000 there were 28 Internet Service Providers (ISPs) in Estonia and all major television and radio stations and newspapers had their own web sites. According to RIPE Network Coordination Center (a regional Internet registry for Europe), Estonia is one of the most Internet-connected countries in Eastern Europe. Estonia-Wide Web (*Eesti WWW-Wäark)* provides a broad range of topics that are available online.

There are approximately 309,000 Internet users, 62 percent of which are male. About 89 percent of the total Internet users are between the ages of 15 and 39, with an average age of 29. The major reasons given for not using the Internet include cost and fear of computer use. However, the Soros Foundation's Open Estonia Foundation has supported many projects, including providing Internet-related services at medical, educational, and cultural institutions, to improve access to the Internet throughout the entire country.

EDUCATION & TRAINING

In 1995 the Estonian Association of Newspapers and the Estonian Association of Broadcasters established the Estonia Media College Foundation which was a move to-

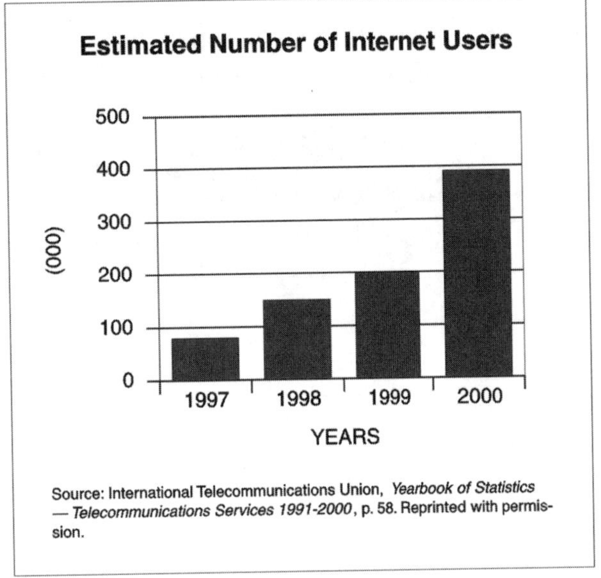

Source: International Telecommunications Union, *Yearbook of Statistics — Telecommunications Services 1991-2000*, p. 58. Reprinted with permission.

wards the establishment of the Estonian Media College. The Baltic Media Center (BMC) sponsored a course, "Cross-Border Minorities Reporting," that was attended by Estonian journalists along with participants for the other Baltic States, Russia and Poland. The course trained participants in the skills necessary to launch their own Internet-based radio station. These trends demonstrate the positive direction in which Estonia is moving in order to improve the quality of its media.

SUMMARY

The Estonian media survived censorship and subjugation by foreign powers and at the beginning of the 21st century the largest problem for the industry is economic. Since the establishment of an independent Estonia, the country has developed a growing media sector characterized by a surprisingly large number of print and broadcast outlets for the country's small population. There are a wide variety of newspapers that are privately owned and published in Estonian and Russian, private and national television channels, a state-owned public service channel, and an abundance of radio stations. The national state-owned television channel has enjoyed the highest ratings despite the competition from the independent stations. However, because of the large amount of print publications, there is fierce competition for the limited advertising and subscription revenues. Therefore, the media continues to be burdened with financial difficulties and distribution delays because debt and printing costs still plague the press.

In addition to these financial woes, sensationalism in reporting reflects the lack of law regulating media content. There is also the problem and bias against the Russian-speaking population. Despite these concerns, Estonia does enjoy an independent press. With the exception of a few legislative shortcomings, particularly regarding the criminalizing of libel, the press is generally free of government influence or control. Though the government owns the newspaper printing plant, it does not interfere with its commercial management. Overall the greatest hazard facing the press is financial loss due to limited advertising revenue.

SIGNIFICANT DATES

- 1997: Enno Tammer was named Estonian Journalist of the Year. He later became the first journalist to be honored and then convicted and fined for professional misconduct in the same year.
- 1998: A new Broadcasting Bill was introduced to the legislature that stipulates that at least 51 percent of television programs must be produced in the EU by the year 2003.
- 1999: In January, the Estonian broadcast media signed an agreement that would ban journalists from hosting programs for six weeks leading up to an election if they were also running for a parliamentary seat.
- 2000: The Internet TV portal TV.ee was started on December 4. In addition, Starman AS, a Tallinn-based cable television company bought a 60 percent stake in Comtrade and entered the Internet market.
- 2001: Vitali Haitov, who owned the two largest Russian language newspapers in Estonia, was killed near his home in Tallinn, in March.

BIBLIOGRAPHY

The Central Intelligence Agency (CIA). *The World Factbook 2001 - Estonia.* Directorate of Intelligence, 1 January 2001. Available from http://www.cia.gov/.

"Estonia." *I.P.R. Report: Monthly Bulletin of the International Press.* (December-January 1996): 35-36.

"Estonia." *I.P.R. Report: Monthly bulletin of the International Press* 43 (December 1994): 25.

"Estonia." *Nations in Transit.* 2001 Available from http://www.freedomhouse.org/.

"Estonia - Constitution." ICL. Available from http://www.uni-wuerzburg.de/law/.

The Europa World Year Book 2001, 42nd edition, vol. 1. Europa Publications 2001, 1484-1502.

Girnius, Saulus. "The Economies of the Baltic States in 1993." *RFE/RL Research Report,* 3, no. 20 (20 May 1994): 1-14.

Hickey, Neil. "A Young Press Corps." *Columbia Journalism Review* 38 (May 1999): 18.

Hietaniemi, Tapani. ''Dates from the history of Estonia.'' *Arts & Humanities IBS.* Available from http://www.ibs.ee/ibs/history.

Jarvis, Howard. ''Estonia.'' *World Press Review.* 1997-2001. Available from http://freemedia.at/wpfr/.

Kand, Villu. ''Estonia: A Year of Challenges.'' *RFE/RL Research Report* 3, no. 7 (7 January 1994): 92-95.

Kionka, Riina. ''Estonia: A Break with the Past.'' *RFE/RL Research Report* (3 January 1992)): 65-67.

Kionka, Riina. ''Estonia.'' *RFE/RL Research Report* Vol. 1, No. 39 (2 October 1992): 62-69.

Lieven, Anatol. *The Baltic Revolution: Estonia, Latvia, Lithuania and the Path to Independence.* New Haven, CT: Yale University Press, 1999.

RFE/RL Research Institute Staff. ''The Media in the Countries of the Former Soviet Union.'' *RFE/RL Research Report* 2, no. 27 (2 July 1993): 1-15.

Rose, Richard, and Maley, William. ''Conflict or Compromise in the Baltic States?'' *RFE/RL Research Report* 3, no. 28 (15 July 1994): 26-35.

—Jean Boris Wynn

ETHIOPIA

BASIC DATA

Official Country Name:	Ethiopia
Region (Map name):	Africa
Population:	65,891,874
Language(s):	Amharic, Tigrinya, Oromigna, Guaragigna, Somali, Arbic, other local languages, English
Literacy rate:	35.5%
Area:	1,127,127 sq km
GDP:	6,391 (US$ millions)
Number of Nondaily Newspapers:	149
Number of Television Sets:	320,000
Television Sets per 1,000:	4.9
Number of Satellite Subscribers:	2,000
Number of Radio Stations:	7
Number of Radio Receivers:	11,750,000
Radio Receivers per 1,000:	178.3
Number of Individuals with Computers:	60,000
Computers per 1,000:	0.9
Number of Individuals with Internet Access:	10,000
Internet Access per 1,000:	0.2

BACKGROUND & GENERAL CHARACTERISTICS

The Ethiopian context

Political context Virtually all observers of Ethiopian history and politics agree that current political events cannot be isolated from past history. The multiplicity of the Ethiopian people, and its links to ancient history and culture are reflected in traditions still very much alive today. However, Ethiopia today is said to be a ''new'' Ethiopia in the making. After decades of resistance and war against different totalitarian regimes within, a new model of state governance is being implemented. According to the authorities an ethnic federal state, with ethnically defined regions and democratic standards, has been introduced in the country. During the 1990s, many observers viewed Ethiopia's experiment in government as a bold attempt at African nation building, while others worried about what will become of the traditional ''Ethiopian entity'' after ethnic division. To attempt to describe the ongoing political changes in Ethiopia in an introductory paragraph would be overly ambitious. However, a key concern of this study is to relate the professionalism of Ethiopia's news media to human rights and democracy in the nation—to participation and pluralism.

The redefinition of the Ethiopian state on a new basis is underway, but the very foundation of that project remains controversial. In conducting our research, we have received the general impression that history is being repeated in Ethiopia. One could still say that a top-down authority is imposed on the people, this time draped in the ideological rhetoric of democracy, and again with external support, now from the West.

After decades of failed political experiments, several key issues in Ethiopian politics remain to be solved. In many situations it would be gravely misleading to analyze African democracy in terms of Western concepts. Ethiopia might and should develop democratic institutions well suited for its own society, and such institutions may differ from Western models. However, there are also certain principles fundamental to democratic modes of governance which are universal. These include open and equal opportunity for all to participate in politics, and freedom of speech and organization. Independent of local history and cultural context, these standards must be respected in a democratic society. Professionalism in a country's media allows for a constructive use of the freedom of speech, one that offers truthful, useful criticism of a country's institutions.

Ethiopia has chosen to enact a specific press bill, rather than to rely on the common law approach used in the United States and other Western democracies. These provisions would seem to create a liberal press environment. However, the absence of a free media tradition in Ethiopia has resulted in lack of adequate provisions for developing independent, professional journalism. Also lacking is a professional board or other mechanism to determine whether press content fits the press bill's criteria for press responsibility and for the taking of lawful measures. Thus most press offenses are considered by authorities as criminal, and not civic in nature.

To develop media as a viable source of information is to enable and support democracy in Ethiopia by strengthening human rights and democratic institutions. The promotion of human rights depends, among other factors, on the active involvement of the media. On the other hand, the effective operation of the media depends on a government that respects human rights and the freedom "to seek, receive, and impart information and ideas through media and regardless of frontiers" (The Press Freedom Bill). The freedom of expression may be ushered in and cultivated through professional, independent journalism.

Polarization Public debate in Ethiopia seems polarized to a first time visitor. Events and statements are easily interpreted to fit into the patterns of old conflict, and few people seem willing to engage in constructive dialogue with their adversaries. One also notices deep mistrust regarding an opponent's motives. Ethiopians who reflect on their own traditions often say "we sit on our own chairs and do not meet in the middle."

Regarding the media, this means that the independent press easily interprets all the stories in the government papers as propaganda, while the government media looks at the independent press with great skepticism, to the point of calling it an enemy of the people.

One of the causes for this polarization is the absence of a tradition of dialogue among adversaries. Some Western nations have long venerated the idea of discussion between competing parties, while physical force or other forms of intimidation have been practiced and encouraged in Ethiopia. The country's democratic movement during the 1990s has so far been neither strong enough, nor has it lasted long enough to alleviate some peoples' fears that it will backfire.

Another reason for polarization is ethnic practices. The country contains more than 80 smaller or larger ethnic groups with different languages that have played an important role in defining ethnicity in Ethiopia. The former regime called itself Marxist, but the fact that certain ethnic groups dominated it was to many Ethiopians far more important. And today the same people are far more preoccupied with the fact that the present government has its power base related to ethnicity, than that it calls itself democratic. It is our impression that the Ethiopians have developed a sophisticated ability to interpret anything that emerges from the government quarters. Their basic assumption is that what they hear is not true.

On the other hand, the polarization of the Ethiopian debate results in an added sense of personal engagement on the part of journalists, which is of vital importance to the Ethiopian press. Because of the tense ethnic situation as well as the government's softness on the enforcement of human rights, journalists take personal risks in pursuing certain stories. These risks add a dimension of reality to the debate and inspire journalists to a true devotion to their jobs. The challenge to the press is to communicate this engagement and devotion through stories and articles of high journalistic quality.

When political distrust and allegations are part of an ongoing process, one should be wary of taking any absolute stand for either side. Ethiopian political positions have become so entrenched, so defensive, that political arguments have to a large degree lost their value. Since the adversary is suspected of hidden motives, every group believes it is the only truly democratic one. Groups practice a total and unyielding criticism of each other, a moral exclusiveness, which does not allow them to expect anything but disruption and destruction from the other groups. Consequently political positions become self assertive and absolute: every new revelation of the adversary, every new suspicion instantly adds credibility to one's own position.

To get the political process on track towards an incorporating, broad based, participatory democracy, a constructive dialogue between the different actors must be established. The Ethiopian political environment seems to lack tradition for agreeing to disagree. Disagreement seems often to result in enmity and polarization. An important step towards broad and mutual participation in the country's decisions will thus be to nurture a less-biased, truth-searching media, one capable of bringing about dialogue between the different actors in the Ethiopian community. This dialogue should not seek consensus for its own sake, but in order to avoid polarization, which blocks communication and cements enmity.

Historic Development of the Media in Ethiopia Dictators have been common throughout Ethiopian history. Whatever press existed during the reign of Emperor Haile Selassie I (1930-74) and the following dictatorship behaved, with a few exceptions, like willing mouthpieces for the rulers. Only during the 1990s have signs of a free and independent press emerged. During that decade a plethora of new magazines and papers appeared on Ethiopian stands.

In a country with more than 80 languages, it is difficult to establish national newspapers and nationwide radio/TV programming. Traditionally a rather high percent of the urban population understand Amharic, and most newspapers, radio and TV programs are available in that language. Only a few programs in radio and television are produced in other major languages, such as Tigrinya and Oromiffa.

Even though many newspapers are published in Ethiopia, journalism as many Western nations practice (or at least believe in practicing) it—as an independent, critical, theoretically objective enterprise—has never really developed, and only sporadically have high-profile Ethiopians objected to the country's lack of an independent "fourth estate." Western journalists learn early on that reporting must be separated from commentary, but Ethiopian journalists routinely conflate the two, to name just one example.

Until the passage of the Press Freedom Bill in 1992, the printed press was limited. The first newspaper in Ethiopia and a few other publications emerged under Emperor Haile Selassie I. However, modern mass media was introduced in Ethiopia a century ago, during the reign of Menelik II (who ruled from 1889-1913). The first medium to be introduced was a weekly newspaper (*La Semaine d'Ethiopie,* 1890), published in French by a Franciscan missionary living in Harar. In 1905 the name of the publication changed to *Le Semeur d'Ethiopie.* The first Amharic newspaper was issued in 1895—a four page weekly newspaper named *Aemero.* The first issues were hand written. Between 1912 and 1915 weekly newspapers like *Melekete Selam, Yetor Wore* ("War News"), and many others emerged.

For the most part, these print media were controlled by the country's government, subject to official censorship and string-pulling. In 1965 Berhanena Selam Printing Press, a modern, almost monopoly instituition run by the government, was established. The Printing Press played a role in the publication of two national weekly newspapers, *Addis Zemen* (New Era), in Amharic (1941) and its English counterpart the *Ethiopian Herald,* in 1943. These two served as the main official press organs of the state and as the main source of information for literate people.

A military group called the Derg wrested power from Selassie in September 1974 and arrested him, citing his incompetence in domestic affairs (particularly in dealing with an early-1970s famine that ravaged parts of the country). Derg member Major Mengistu Haile Mariam established his own leadership within that organization in February 1977 via a shootout between his followers and those of his main rival, Tafari Banti, who died in the fighting; following this, Mengistu declared himself chairman and began his military rule over the country by 1977. During the 17 years of Mengistu's rule, the government- and party-owned publications *Meskerem* ("September"), *Serto Ader* ("Worker"), and the pre-*Derg Yezareyitu Ethiopia* ("Ethiopia Today") were published in addition to the previously mentioned *Addis Zemen* and the *Ethiopian Herald.*

In October 1992, as previously mentioned, came the proclamation of the Press Freedom Bill by the Ethiopian Transitional Government. The document states in Paragraph 3 that "1. Freedom of the press is recognized and respected in Ethiopia. 2. Censorship of the press and any restriction of a similar nature are hereby prohibited." Part Three further guaranteed the right of access to information: "Any press and its agents shall, without prejudice to rights conformed by other laws, have the right to seek, obtain and report news and information from any government source of news and information."

After the proclamation of the Press Freedom Bill, new, independent newspapers and magazines developed, especially in Addis Ababa. These offer the minority points of view often left out of government-owned publications, but suffer from inadequate fact-checking and occasional censorship, as well as the government's refusal to allow representatives from non-official papers at its press conferences.

News agencies, often government-owned, were also introduced to the country during the previous century, including the Ethiopian News Agency (ENA), begun in 1942 as "Agenze Direczion" and renamed in 1968. Walta Information Service, a more recently established news agency, is associated with EPRDF, the party in power, and is housed in the same complex as Radio Fana.

Brief Presentation of the Present Media The Ethiopian publishing industry mushroomed after the Press Bill of 1992. Figures differ, but according to the Government, 385 publications were registered between October 1992 and July 1997, of which 265 were newspapers and 120 magazines. At any one time, there are probably about 20 different newspapers for sale in Addis Ababa. More than half of the total number of papers were closed down during the same five-year period, often because of limited resources. The ''independent papers'' are owned by private share companies (business.communities, political parties or just individual business entrepreneurs). Because of a very limited middle-class, the income on advertising is also very limited. The government papers are subsidized by government funds, and partly financed by advertisements and subscribers.

Access to publications outside the capital is limited. Given Ethiopia's low literacy rate, and the relative high cost of newspapers, regular readership may be as low as one percent of the population. The Addis Ababa public consumes most of the country's newspapers (which, in total, number no more than 500,000 out of a population of 60 million, or less than one in a thousand).

As for the demand side, illiteracy, weak economy and the near non-existence of infrastructure prevent newspapers from reaching a mass readership, especially in rural areas, where newspapers (as previously noted) cannot even be distributed. In this kind of situation, it is self-evident that radio and TV are important media. Radio is important because it is inexpensive and available for group listening. TV is important for the same reasons, and both broadcast mediums are especially useful because they don't require literacy. TV sets are scarce in the rural cities and almost absent in the villages and in the remote parts of the country. Radio sets are better distributed, but are still a luxury commodity for large segments of the Ethiopian population. Even batteries for the radio sets are far too expensive in areas defined as non-monetary communities.

Broadcast media may be able to fill in some of the educational gaps created by illiteracy and language difference.

PRESS LAWS

Following the proclamation of the Press Bill, many private and party newspapers began to appear. In addition the Ethiopian Press agency now publishes four newspapers, one each in Amharic, English, Oromiffa and Arabic—respectively, *Addis Zemen* and *Ethiopian Herald,* both dailies, and *Berissa* and *Al-alem,* both weeklies. *Addis Zemen* has a circulation of 19,000, the *Ethiopian Herald* 10,000, *Berissa* 3,000 and *Al-alem* 2,500. The Press Agency lacks both the manpower and the transportation capacities to effectively deliver these papers to Addis, the regions and areas outside Ethiopia; for this and other reasons, the papers face major distribution problems.

CENSORSHIP

Ethiopia's Constitution grants basic civil liberties to its citizens, including freedom of speech and freedom of the press. However, the legislation governing the press is viewed by many as a hindrance to the development of a free press in Ethiopia.

Historically, the Ethiopian government will tolerate freedom of speech to a certain point. But opposition newspapers regularly report dramatic instances of censorship: stories of journalists harassed and imprisoned for reporting truth, etc. The appearance of such stories may, in some cases, have more to do with anti-government hostility on the part of opposition newspapers than with fact—much of these papers' content is based on rumors. A critical use of sources is a rare virtue in Ethiopian journalism of any kind, even though this is basic for developing a trustworthy journalism, and even promoters of human rights in Ethiopia are of the opinion that some journalists are asking for trouble. Journalists have a tendency to distrust open sources, and are more willing to trust what is whispered in the coffee houses. However, these points granted, one must still admit that government oppression of journalists is a reality in Ethiopia as it is throughout the world in fact, Ethiopia once imprisoned more journalists than almost any other country. Privately operating journalists are also hampered by the fact that they are cut off from part of the governmental flow of information. Direct censorship against independent newspapers is rare, but the government, on the other hand, claims that the independent press is irresponsible and untrustworthy. This is the official reason why journalists from the independent press are denied access to the government press conferences. Thus the situation is aggravated by both sides in the conflict.

The recently proclaimed Bill of Broadcasting makes independent FM radio stations legally possible in the country. Such stations could make an important contribution to Ethiopian freedom of speech, but certain civic groups expressed skepticism upon hearing the proclamation draft, citing limitations in the new law. As drafted, the bill does not allow religious organizations and political parties to run their own radio stations. Such prohibitions are regarded by some as a breach of freedom of expression.

The Ethiopian Human Rights Council (EHRC) has issued a report on journalists, documenting the arrests and imprisonment of journalists from the independent press. Lately the pressure against journalists seems to have eased a little. There are now fewer arrests, even if journalists still are brought before the courts every now and then. The new tolerance is probably connected to the country's conflict with Eritrea, a conflict on which the government press and the independent press, in general, have had similar views. The question is, will this alliance remain when the conflict is over?

STATE-PRESS RELATIONS

It is fair to say that while the makeup of Ethiopia's government has frequently changed during the twentieth century, the printing press's function, as well as that of radio, television, and news agencies, has remained the same: to serve the government in power. Media have consistently and primarily promoted government policy and activities. Consequently, Ethiopia has little or no indigenous tradition of thinking about the press as a free commercial enterprise, or as a watchdog or critic of the government. Because of the continued government control of the broadcast media, the non-government media have been limited to print, but the 1999 proclamation of a new Bill of Broadcasting in the House of Representatives may challenge this government stranglehold.

The largest newspapers and the only Ethiopian broadcasting corporation are owned by the government. If one looks at the circulation of the newspapers, the government papers hold the largest share. Non-government papers are hampered by the government's refusal to allow them to send reporters to its press conferences, as well as by an overly suspicious attitude toward the government that sometimes leads to an equally uncritical acceptance of sources critical toward it.

To illustrate how strong the tradition of control is, Government radio rarely airs a live interview. Any live interview is considered an advance for free speech.

NEWS AGENCIES

There are disturbingly close relations between the official Ethiopia Journalist Association and the government. This is emphasized by the fact that the head of the association also heads up Ethiopian Broadcasting and the country's official news bureau.

There is also an independent journalist association, the Ethiopian Free Press Journalist Association (EFJA). This association is not a legal body in Ethiopia.

Apart from these, there are no press institutions/associations in Ethiopia. This lack provides yet another illustration of the two main problems in Ethiopian journalism: its low level of development, and its dominance by the government. At the same time the Ethiopian people show a growing awareness of the importance of the media. Lobbying has increased, and various groups have introduced initiatives to improve Ethiopian media. On September 24th - 25th, 1999, the International Press Institute organized a seminar under the theme ''Ethiopian Media in Development.'' ''Independent'' and ''government'' journalists gathered under one roof for discussions about the state of their joint enterprise. For one and a half days ethical and other problems afflicting the Ethiopian media were raised and solutions suggested. The seminar was sponsored by the Austrian, British and Norwegian embassies in Addis Ababa.

BROADCAST MEDIA

Radio The government views radio as the most important mass medium in a large country like Ethiopia. The leadership in the country's only official school of journalism consider radio and TV to be important assets in promoting democracy in the rural and remote areas of the country. Radio's strategic importance is also, some suspect, the reason behind the government's reluctance to allow private radio stations.

Broadcasting, primarily the radio, reaches a much larger part of the population than does print, though Ethiopian radio is limited. Radio Voice of the Gospel, owned by the Lutheran World Federation, operated prior to the overthrow of the Emperor in 1974. Their facilities were seized under the Derg, and today there are only two radio broadcasters in Addis Ababa: Radio Ethiopia and Radio Fana. The latter is associated with EPRDF, but is not directly government owned. There is only one regional radio station in Bahir Dahr, which is associated with the regional government. The other radio station is TPLF radio in Mekele, broadcasting only in Tigrigna.

There are some regional broadcasting initiatives surfacing, of which Bahir Dahr probably is the most developed. The regional radio in Bahir Dahr, a major town in the Amhara region, is run by the Department of Culture, Tourism and Information. This region is said to have 15 million inhabitants. The regional broadcast is transmitted one hour per day, seven days a week. In addition, the studios also produce material for national television and publish a weekly newspaper and a quarterly magazine. According to this regional broadcast center, the station covers 90 percent of the region. Nobody knows the actual number of listeners. The first audience research will be conducted next year.

As previously noted, the vast majority of newspaper readers live in Ethiopia's capital, and Addis Ababa uses much of the country's other media as well. The numbers are less certain for radio than for print media, but it is believed that a similarly large difference exists between the number of urban radio listeners and rural ones, though this difference is less pronounced than the difference in the corresponding numbers for print media. Radio Ethiopia claims to have reached 50 percent of the landmass and 75 percent of the population with a good signal, making it the most influential news source in the country. However, frequency coverage does not reflect the station's actual availability to listeners, due to a lack of radio receivers. Ordinary audience research is not conducted in Ethiopia. It is too costly and too complicated. But in connection with the field work for this article, a limited audience research was conducted in Addis Ababa (count 1,200), Ambo (count 200), Awassa (count 301), Debre

Zeit (count 200) and Nazareth (count 299). The data has to be further analyzed, but it reveals the great potential radio broadcasting holds for Ethiopia.

With these facts in mind, the recent proclamation of a Broadcasting Bill by the Ethiopian House of Representatives seems an interesting and perhaps hopeful sign. Part Three of this Proclamation sets out a legal basis on which private commercial radio and television can be licensed. The Bill of Broadcasting may bring the introduction of FM radio closer to reality. This will be an enormous challenge for the media development in Ethiopia.

Television Those few Ethiopians who can watch TV, most of whom live in Addis Ababa, have only one channel's worth of state-controlled programming to watch during their evenings and weekends; during the day only the Educational Mass Media Agency broadcasts.

EDUCATION & TRAINING

The mushrooming of ''independent'' papers and the lack of professionalism in the field make it important that basic journalistic education in Ethiopia be improved, both in the long and short terms. Ethiopian media professionals at this point lack some of the basic skills necessary for the press to play a significant role in any democratization process in Ethiopia. From a quick survey of the Ethiopian press, one may safely conclude that the country badly needs education in journalism.

Few Ethiopian journalists have professional education in the field. Only a couple of people in all of Ethiopia hold advanced degrees in journalism. Many reporters operate as spokespeople for particular political views, rather than as journalists. Self-censorship is also a big problem, because some journalists would rather maintain peace between themselves and the state and thus avoid reporting any facts that may force ugly confrontations. Among the independent papers, which are under less pressure to show deference to government accounts of events, an equally unprofessional skepticism about the government pervades political reporting.

The Mass Media Training Institute (MMTI) in Addis Ababa is the only officially funded institution providing journalism education in Ethiopia. MMTI started in 1996 and runs a two-year program for approximately 100 students. Eighty percent of the students enter the school on recommendation from the government. In principle, the rest of the places are open for all. In year 2000, applicants contested these 20 openings. Most of the teachers have journalistic experience, but not all have a formal education in journalism.

Addis Ababa University also offered minor-level courses in journalism. However, plans are underway to establish a School of Journalism at Addis Ababa University. There are also independent institutions in Addis Ababa offering shorter courses in journalism, and a private college (Unity College) is giving courses in journalism.

SUMMARY

Ethiopia is emerging nearly finished with its first full decade of democracy. Freedom for journalists has not been the normal practice, but signs are hopeful. Recent legislation paves the way for democratic reforms, though these are sure to take on an African frame.

BIBLIOGRAPHY

Aadland, Öyvind. ''Ethiopia Research Report.'' Gimlekolen Mediasenter, 2001.

Azzeze, Keffeyalew, General Manager of Ethiopian Press Agency, Ethiopian Television, Radio Ethiopia and Ethiopian Herald and Chairman of the Ethiopian Journalist Association interview by Öyvind Aadland. Addis Ababa, June 16, 1999.

Bisarit Gashawtena, Vice Minister of Information and Culture, interview by Öyvind Aadland. Addis Ababa: Friday, June 18, 1999.

Bishaw, Dr. Mekonnen, Secretary General Ethiopian Human Rights Council (EHRC), interview by Öyvind Aadland. Addis Ababa, June 16, 1999.

Chemu, Ato Woldemichael, Minister of Information and Culture interview by Öyvind Aadland. Addis Ababa, June 11, 1999.

Debelko, Ato Tzehaye, Head of MMTI interview by Öyvind Aadland. Addis Ababa, June 16, 1999.

Galla, Shibberu, Director of EECMY, Communication Services, interview by Öyvind Aadland.

Hiwot, Alemayhu Gebre, Bureau Head Culture, Tourism and Information Bureau, interview by Öyvind Aadland. Bahir Dahr, June 14, 1999.

Negga, Berhanu, General Manager, EMAISC, President of Ethiopian Economic Association and Professor in Economics at Addis Ababa University, interview by Öyvind Aadland. Addis Ababa: June 10, 1999.

—Öyvind Aadland and Mark Fackler

Falkland Islands

Basic Data

Official Country Name:	Falkland Islands (Malvinas)
Region (Map name):	South America
Population:	2,826
Language(s):	English
Literacy rate:	N/A

Although the Falkland Islands lies east of southern Argentina in the South Atlantic Ocean, it has been claimed by the French, the British, and the Spanish.

Press freedoms in the Falkland Islands equal those of Great Britain. There is no daily newspaper but the country boasts two weeklies, *The Penguin News* and the *Teaberry Express. The Penguin News* is published every Friday by Mercopress, and the *Teaberry Express* is published by Falkland Islands News Network. The staunchly pro-British *Falkland Islands Newsletter* is published in London by the non-profit Falkland Island Association and appears quarterly. The Web portal Falkland Island News Network, *www.sartma.com,* provides online access to a number of publications, including the *Teaberry Express*.

There are seven FM radio stations and one AM radio station for approximately 1,000 radios. There are two local television stations, both of which are run by the British Forces Broadcasting Service. There are approximately 1,000 televisions on the island. There are two Internet service providers.

The English made the first sighting, in 1592, and the first landing, in 1690, but the French established the first colony in 1764. This colony was turned over to the Spanish two years later, and the collection of islands has been subject to sporadic territorial dispute ever since, first between Britain and Spain, then between Britain and Argentina. Tensions flared most recently in 1982 when Argentina invaded the Islands. The British beat them back and Queen Elizabeth II remains the chief of state. The head of the government is the Governor, who is appointed by the monarch to preside over a unicameral Legislative Council. The estimated population of the Falklands, which includes the two main islands of East and West Falkland and about 200 smaller islands, is nearly 3,000. English is the official language. Sheep farming and wool exports are the traditional staples of the economy, but in the late 1980s, the government began to ramp up the sale of fishing licenses to subsidize social services.

Central Intelligence Agency (CIA). ''Falkland Islands.'' *World Factbook 2001*. Available from www.cia.gov.

Falkland Islands News Network home page. 2002. Available from www.sartma.com.

Falkland Islands Tourist Board. 2002. Available from www.tourism.org.fk.

—Jenny B. Davis

Faroe Islands

Basic Data

Official Country Name:	Faroe Islands
Region (Map name):	Europe
Population:	45,296

Language(s):	Faroese, Danish
Literacy rate:	similar to Denmark proper

The Faroe Islands were settled by Vikings in the ninth century and have been connected to Denmark for more than 700 years. Located between the Norwegian Sea and the North Atlantic Ocean, the country includes 17 inhabited islands, one uninhabited island and several uninhabited islets. The country was granted self-government within the Kingdom of Denmark in 1948. Its chief of state is the Danish monarch, represented in local government by a High Commissioner. The head of government is a Prime Minister, who is elected by the majority party in the popularly elected, 32-seat Faroese Parliament. The population of the Faroe Islands is approximately 45,000 thousand. Danish is the official language, but most citizens speak Faroese, a Nordic language related to West Norwegian and Icelandic. The economy is almost totally dependent on fishing, but the recent discovery of oil may allow the country an opportunity for future diversification.

As Danish subjects, the Faroese people enjoy freedom of the press and of speech. *Dimmalaetting* is the largest of the Faroe Islands' two major newspapers, and it is generally the only profitable publication in the country. Founded in 1878, the independent publication is written partly in Danish and partly in Faroese. It appears Monday through Friday in print and online; in 2000, its approximate circulation was 10,000. *Sosialurin,* the country's second-largest newspaper, publishes in Faroese. Also politically independent, it publishes daily Tuesday through Saturday in print and online. In 2000, its estimated circulation was 7,300. The Faroe Islands has four other newspapers, with circulations in 2000 below 4,000. All four are affiliated with political parties, and all rely on the government subsidies and private contributions. *Oyggjatidindi* is published twice weekly, *Dagbladid* is published three times a week, *Norolysio* appears once a week, and *FF/FA-bladid* is published fortnightly.

The Faroe Islands supports 13 FM radio stations for approximately 26,000 radios and three television stations broadcasting to about 15,000 televisions. Neither radio nor television broadcasting runs 24 hours. There are two Internet service providers.

BIBLIOGRAPHY

Central Intelligence Agency (CIA). ''Faroe Islands,'' *World Fact Book (2001).* Available from http://www.cia.gov.

Dimmalaetting, (2002) Home Page. Available from http://www.dimma.fo.

'' The Faroese Media,'' *Royal Danish Embassy (2002).* Available from http://www.denmarkemb.org.

Socialurin, (2002) Home Page. Available from http://www.sosialurin.fo/.

Statistical Yearbook of the Faroe Islands - 2001, p. 323.

—Jenny B. Davis

FIJI

BASIC DATA

Official Country Name:	Republic of Fiji
Region (Map name):	Oceania
Population:	832,494
Language(s):	English, Fijian, Hindustani
Literacy rate:	91.6%

Fiji is located in the South Pacific Ocean between Hawaii and New Zealand. Despite the periodic threats to Fiji's democratic status, the press enjoys one of the most liberal and robust environments in the South Pacific. Successive governments have tried to use legislation to control the media, but these efforts have met with strong resistance from an organized Fiji media community.

Fiji has three daily newspapers, all published in English. The *Fiji Times*, owned by News Limited, is the oldest and biggest. Its content appears online through the *fijivillage.com* Web portal. The *Daily Post* is partially owned by the government; its content also appears on the *fijilive.com* Web portal. The *Fiji Sun* is the smallest and newest. Its news is posted online through a dedicated Web site.

There are also a variety of weekly newspapers. *Nai Lalakai* has been published by the Fiji Times Group since 1962. The same company has published the Hindi newspaper *Shati Dut* since 1935. *Na Tui*, founded in 1988, appears weekly, and *Sartag*, a Hindi weekly, also has published since 1988. The weekly *Fiji Republic Gazette* highlights local business issues.

There are 53 radio stations, 13 AM and 40 FM, broadcasting to a 500,000 radios. One television station broadcasts to more than 20,000 televisions. There are two Internet service providers.

Though Fiji was known to the European world as early as the seventeenth century, it was not until 1874 that it was pronounced a British colony, well after it had established itself as an important trade outpost. Fiji became an independent nation in 1970, with a president serving as chief of state and a Prime Minister heading the government.

The legislative branch is a bicameral, 32-seat senate and a 71-seat house of representatives. The government has, however, has been interrupted by several attempted coups stemming from the ethnic segregation of Indian and Melanesian populations. The most recent unrest was in May 2000, when terrorists stormed the Parliament and held the Prime Minister and his government hostage for 56 days. The population is just under 850,000, with a 91 percent literacy rate. Fiji's instability has harmed its economy, turning away tourists and foreign investors in its primary cash crop, sugar.

Australian Press Council. *Country Report, Fiji.* 2002. Available from www.presscouncil.org.au.

Central Intelligence Agency (CIA). ''Fiji.'' *World Factbook 2001.* Available from www.cia.gov.

Fijilive.com. 2001. Available from www.fijilive.com.

Fiji Sun. 2002. Available from www.sun.com.fj.

Fiji Village.com. Available from www.fijivillage.com/news.

—*Jenny B. Davis*

FINLAND

BASIC DATA

Official Country Name:	Finland
Region (Map name):	Europe
Population:	5,175,783
Language(s):	Finnish (official), Swedish (official), small Lapp and Russian speaking minorities
Literacy rate:	100.0%
Area:	337,030 sq km
GDP:	121,466 (US$ millions)
Number of Daily Newspapers:	55
Total Circulation:	2,304,000
Circulation per 1,000:	545
Total Circulation:	924,000
Circulation per 1,000:	219
Newspaper Consumption (minutes per day):	38
Total Newspaper Ad Receipts:	618 (Euro millions)
As % of All Ad Expenditures:	56.70
Magazine Consumption (minutes per day):	42
Number of Television Stations:	130
Number of Television Sets:	3,200,000
Television Sets per 1,000:	618.2
Television Consumption (minutes per day):	142
Number of Cable Subscribers:	954,200
Cable Subscribers per 1,000:	183.5
Number of Satellite Subscribers:	343,000
Satellite Subscribers per 1,000:	66.3
Number of Radio Stations:	189
Number of Radio Receivers:	7,700,000
Radio Receivers per 1,000:	1,487.7
Radio Consumption (minutes per day):	142
Number of Individuals with Computers:	2,050,000
Computers per 1,000:	396.1
Number of Individuals with Internet Access:	1,927,000
Internet Access per 1,000:	372.3
Internet Consumption (minutes per day):	14

BACKGROUND & GENERAL CHARACTERISTICS

Finland has a literate and well-informed society. Ninety percent of citizens over the age of 15 spend about 40 minutes reading a daily newspaper; and on average read 10 magazines per year. The Finnish national library system, with nearly 1,000 libraries, has the most books per capita compared to other European countries. Not surprisingly, more books are borrowed per capita from their national library system than from other European systems.

Finland's population, estimated at 5,195,000 in 2001, was 48.8 percent male and 51.2 percent female in 2000. Twenty-five percent were under the age of 15, 26 percent were 20 to 39, 34 percent were 40 to 64, and 15 percent were over age 65. The country's 130,160 square miles of land is divided into 20 provinces. Twenty-five percent of the population lived in the country's largest province, Uusimaa. Finland's largest cities were Helsinki (559,718), Espoo (216,836), Tampere (197,774), Vantaa (179,856), Turku (173,686), and Oulu (123,274).

Located in northern Europe, Finland is surrounded by Norway to the north, Russia to the east, the Gulf of Finland to the south, and the Gulf of Bothnia and Sweden to the west. Prior to the twentieth century its nearly 700-year association with Sweden influenced much of Finland's culture and history and its subsequent association with Russia.

The dominant language spoken in Finland was Swedish until the 1840s. In 1835 publication of the *Kalevala,* a collection of Finnish myths and legends, set in motion Finnish nationalism, which helped to restore the Finnish language to prominence. By 1900 nearly 87 percent of Finns spoke Finnish, and only 13 percent spoke Swedish. One hundred years later, 92 percent were speaking Finnish, and 5.6 percent were speaking Swedish. Both languages are officially recognized by the constitution. Ethnically the language spoken reflects the distribution of the two groups. Swedish speaking persons generally lived along the south and west coasts of Finland and in the self-governing province of Aland.

Czar Alexander I of Russia conquered Finland in 1809. For the next century Finland was an autonomous duchy of Russia. After the 1917 Russian Bolshevik Revolution, Finland declared its independence. In the decade following, most newspapers were tied to political parties. By 2000, however, most were independent of political influence.

Finnish foreign policy, deeply influenced by its history of foreign dominance, is officially neutral and has helped the country to establish and maintain friendly relationships with other countries, most notably Russia. This neutrality has three basic frameworks: a special relationship with Russia; close collaboration with the other Nordic countries (Sweden, Norway, Denmark, and Iceland); and an active membership in the United Nations and the European Union.

Finland joined the United Nations in 1955, and joined the European Union in 1995. In 1999 Finland was the first Nordic country to begin using the Union's euro currency. Prior to converting to the euro, Finland's official currency was the markka (Finmark-FMK [FIM]), which was divided into one hundred pennia.

Finns adopted a new constitution that went into effect on March 1, 2000. According to the Constitution, sovereign power belongs to the citizens who are represented by 200 members of Parliament. Finland's main political parties are the Social Democratic, Finnish Centre, and the National Coalition. The minimum age to vote and to hold public office is 18.

Finns directly elect their president, while members of the Parliament elect the prime minister. The president appoints ministers who head up each of the country's 13 ministries administering governmental policies. The responsibilities of each ministry is written in the laws, however, any matters not falling within the scope of a particular ministry are handled by the prime minister's office.

With just over 2,800 newspapers published in the country in 2001, Finland ranked 18th in the world for newspaper publications and 3rd in the world, behind Japan and Norway, for newspaper circulation per 1,000 persons. Seventy-five percent of Finland's daily newspapers are delivered to subscribers each morning; the remainder is delivered by postal service. Finnish magazines also have a high subscription rate with 80 percent having regular subscribers.

Newspapers fall into four main types: national, provincial, local, and specialist. In 2000, 212 newspapers were published at least once per week, with 29 being published on a daily basis. The 55 dailies (newspapers published four or more times a week) accounted for 48 percent of the 3.8 million newspapers circulating in the year 2002. Evening newspapers published 6 days per week accounted for 20 percent of the newspaper market share. Twice weeklies accounted for 9 percent of the market share, and once weeklies accounted for 8 percent.

Of the 186 newspapers for which the Finnish Audit Bureau of Circulations reported data for 2001, 128 (69 percent) had circulations below 10,000; 19 (10 percent) had circulations from 10,000 to 25,000; 14 (7.5 percent) had circulations from 25,000 to 50,000; 11 (6 percent) had circulations from 50,000 to 100,000; 12 (6.5 percent) had circulations from 100,000 to 500,000; and 2 (1 percent) had circulations over 500,000. None had circulations over 650,000.

The top 10 daily newspapers in 2001 (which may vary depending upon the source referenced), all of which were politically independent publications, were the *Helsingin Sanomat* (436,000); the *Ilta-Sanomat* (214,372); the *Aamulehti* (133,779); the *Turun Sanomat* (115,000); the *Kaleva* (84,106); the *Keskisuomalainen* (77,475); the *Savon Sanomat* (67,185); the *Eetla-Suomen Sanomat* (62,659); the *Satakunnan Kansa* (56,781); and the *Ilkka* (55,395). Other high circulation newspapers included the

Daily and Non-Daily Newspaper Titles and Circulation Figures

	1996	1997	1998	1999	2000
Number of Daily Newspapers	56	56	56	56	55
Circulation of Dailies (000)	2,335	2,324	2,343	2,320	2,304
Number of Non-Daily Newspapers	162	158	155	151	149
Circulation of Non-Dailies (000)	1,006	1,000	965	942	924

Source: World Association of Newspapers and Zenithmedia, *World Press Trends 2001*, pp. 8, 10, 17, 19.

Kauppalehti (85,147), a politically independent newspaper with an economic focus published three time a week, and a once weekly Christian newspaper called the *Kotimaa* (54,539). *Taloussanomat* (31,192), a recent entry to the newspaper market focusing on economic and business affairs, entered the market in 1997. *Taloussanomat* is published in Helsinki.

In 2002, 11 Finnish newspapers with a total circulation of 150,000 were published in Swedish. *Hufvudstadsbladet,* a politically independent daily newspaper published in Helsinki, was the largest Swedish language newspaper, with a circulation of 53,815 during the week and a Sunday circulation of 56,259. Finland's second largest Swedish language newspaper, the *Vasabladet,* was published six times a week in Vaasa with a circulation of 26,481.

After newspapers, magazines represent the second largest mass media sector in Finland. In 1999 magazine publishers with the highest circulation rates were *Yhtyneet Kuvalehdet Oy;* Helsinki Media Company *Oy; A-Lehdet Oy;* and *Oy Valitut Palat*—Reader's Digest Ab.

Young Finns (aged 12 to 20) are also dedicated newspaper readers. According to the 2001 Finnish Newspaper Association's national youth media usage survey, 44 percent of Finland's young people were reading a daily newspaper, with 91 percent reading a newspaper at least once a week. Twelve to twenty-year-old readers spent an average of 15 minutes a day reading newspapers. Those reading newspapers once per week were usually spending 19 minutes on Saturdays and Sundays reading them.

Newspapers have been published in Finland since 1771, when the first newspaper entitled *Tidningar utgifne av et Sallskap I Abo* (News Published by a Society in Turku) began circulating. Most print media produced for Finnish consumption is created by domestic enterprises. In 2002, 100 percent of Finnish newspapers, 98 percent of magazines and periodicals, and 84 percent of literature were domestically produced. In contrast, domestic television producers generated between 30 to 54 percent of Finland's national television programs.

The types of magazines read fell into the following categories: customer magazines (32.9 percent); family and general magazines (12.94 percent); women's general magazines (9.5 percent); women's special interest (6.0 percent); hobby magazines (6.0 percent); economy, technics, and trade (5.4 percent); living, building, gardening (4.3 percent); professional magazines (4.0 percent); comics (3.6 percent); motorsport, technics (3.4 percent); datatechnics, communication (2.0 percent); science and culture (2.0 percent); agricultural, forest economy, housekeeping, gardening (1.7 percent); young people's and children's magazines (1.6 percent); religion (1.7 percent); crosswords (0.9 percent); industry and building (0.1 percent).

The most popular magazine in each category was: *Lusto* (agriculture, forest, economy, housekeeping, gardening); *Aku Ankka* (comics); *Elakevaen Ristkot* (crosswords); *Yhteishyva* (customer magazines); *MikroBitti* (datatechnics, communication); *Taloustaito Yritys* (economy, technics, and trade); *ET-lehti* (family and general magazines); *Kolramme* (hobby magazines); *Avotakka* (living, building, gardening); *Teknilkan Maalima* (motorsport, technics); *Tehy* (professional magazines); *Kirkko ja Kaupunki* (religion); *Tiede* (science and culture); *Sotaveteraani-Krigsveteranen* (social affairs and health service); *Kotivinkki* (women's general magazines); *Hyva Terveys* (women's special interest magazines); *Suosikki* (young people's and children's magazines).

Economic Framework

In the 1990s the European economy went through a recession that affected Finland more deeply than other countries. After 1994, however, Finland's economy, led by its telecommunications industry, recovered faster than most European countries with an average 4.8 percent gross domestic product (GDP) rate of growth. Although recovery was apparent after 1994, Finnish unemployment remains higher than the European Union (EU) average in 2002 at 9.1 percent.

Manufacturing, with 497,000 employees (21 percent), employed the largest share of Finland's labor force

Top Daily Newspapers
(2000)

	Circulation
Helsingin Sanomat	447,000
Ilta-Sanomat	215,000
Aamulehti	134,000
Iltalehti	127,000
Turun Sanomat	114,000
Kauppalehti	85,000
Kaleva	83,000
Keskisuomalainen	77,000
Savon Sanomat	67,000

Source: World Association of Newspapers and Zenithmedia, *World Press Trends 2001*, p. 95. Note: Although only nine titles are listed in this table, the table does cover the largest dailies sold in Finland.

in 2001. In 1998, 49,000 Finns were employed in the mass communications sector. Fourteen thousand (28.5 percent) were employed in publishing; 16,000 (32.7 percent) were employed in printing; 8,000 (16.3 percent) were employed in advertising, news agencies, and data banks; 7,000 (14.3 percent) were employed in radio and television; 2,000 (4.1 percent) were employed in film, video, and phonograph; and 1,000 (2 percent) were employed in the manufacture of entertainment electronics.

Finland exports more books, pamphlets, newspapers, and periodicals than it imports. In 1997, 1,470,000 tons of newsprint were produced; 39,000 tons were imported; 1,211,000 exported and 298,000 consumed. Consumption per 1,000 inhabitants at 57,963 kilograms, was Europe's highest in 1997.

Finland's high rate of newspaper and magazine readership explains the preponderance of advertising dollars spent in print versus television and radio. In 2001, 58 percent of advertising dollars was spent on newspaper ads, and 17 percent was spent on magazine ads. In contrast, only 21 percent of advertising dollars was spent on television advertising, with only 3 percent spent on radio ads.

In 2000, newspaper publishing income was primarily from advertisements (61.8 percent of revenues) followed by subscriptions (32.5 percent) and sales of single copies (5.8 percent). Costs of newspaper production were fairly evenly distributed between technical production (27 percent), editing (26 percent), administration and marketing (26 percent), and distribution (21 percent).

Although individual newspaper market shares for the 10 largest daily newspapers fluctuated from 1995 to 2001, overall circulation remained relatively stable during the same period, averaging 1.4 million. For example, the largest daily newspaper, *The Helsingin Sanomat* lost 7.2 percent of its readers. On the other hand, the nation's the *Itlalehti* increased its readership by 32.2 percent.

World Bank's analysis of who controls the media, as measured by the extent to which the state owned its country's media enterprises, indicated Finland's government does not control Finland's media. All of Finland's newspapers are privately owned, reflecting a broad range of political views. In addition, the government, through its ownership of the Finnish Broadcasting Company (*Yleisradio Oy* [YLE]) controls only 48 percent of the television market which does not exceed World Bank's standard for a monopoly, which is 75 percent of the market.

Since the 1980s Finland's largest newspaper companies changed from single product lines to multiple product lines including nearly all mass media products. By the late 1990s, provincial Finnish newspapers began exchanging editorial materials, producing common weekend supplements, and sharing printing capacities to reduce production costs.

Newspaper ownership was consolidating by 1999 with mergers and acquisitions resulting in increasing numbers of newspaper chains. By 1999, 26 newspaper chains were publishing 82 percent of Finland's daily newspapers. The four largest newspaper chains, *Sanoma-WSOY* Corporation, Alma Media Group, Turn *Sanomat* Group, and the *Iikka* Group controlled more than one-half of daily newspaper sales.

In 2000 *Sanoma-WSOY* was the second largest media company in the Nordic region (Denmark, Finland, Luxemburg, The Netherlands, Norway, and Sweden). *Sanoma-WSOY* resulted from the 1998 merger of Finland's leading book publishers,Werner *Soderstrom Oy* (WSOY) and the *Sanoma* Corporation,and Helsinki Media.

Finland's largest multimedia house, *Sanoma-WSOY,* publishes the country's two largest newspapers, the *Helsingin Sanomat* (455,000) and the afternoon newspaper *Ilta-Sanomat* (219,000). *Sanoma-WSOY* also publishes four smaller daily and seven nondaily newspapers. *Helsingin Sanomat* and *Ilta-Sanomat* accounted for 30 percent of the daily circulation.

Foreign ownership of Finnish mass media companies increased in the last decade. Swedish *Marieberg* of the Bonnier Group is the single largest owner of Alma Media, Finland's second largest multimedia house. Alma Media publishes six newspapers, four of which are dailies.

PRESS LAWS

Citizens are guaranteed free speech, the right of assembly, and the right to publish uncensored texts or pictures. The Consumer Protection Act and the Act on Unfair Business Practice regulate mass media advertising. The consumer ombudsman and the marketing court control mass media advertising. Mass media advertisements cannot make unsubstantiated claims, nor can they be offensive to minority groups. The use of children in advertising is restricted, and the advertising of tobacco products is completely prohibited.

Finland acted early in its constitutional development to ensure the rights of the press by implementing the Act on the Freedom of the Press (Article Ten of the Constitution Act) in 1919. The Act guaranteed, ''. . .the right of printing and publishing writing and pictorial presentations without prior interference by anyone.'' Section Twelve of the Finnish Constitution guarantees freedom of expression, which ensures the ''. . .right to express, disseminate and receive information, opinions and other communications without prior prevention by anyone.''

The 1919 Press Law established popular control of Finland's media by giving anyone who claimed that material printed about her or him was incorrect or offensive the right to demand correction. If the publication was found to be in error, it was obligated to grant the injured party an equal amount of type-space to be printed within two days after receiving the injured party's statement. Subsequently, in 1968, organizations of publishers and journalists established the voluntary, self-regulating Council for Mass Media (CMM).

The Council's primary purpose is to interpret ''good professional practice and defend the freedom of speech and publication.'' CMM does not have legal authority; members voluntarily commit themselves to following ethical principles of the journalism profession. CMM has a president and nine members consisting of six media representatives (four editors and two journalists) and three members of the public. The Council president and its three public members are elected by member organizations, but they could not be members of any mass media organization.

Any private citizen or public official believing there is a breach of ethical principles in any form of mass media (newspaper, magazine, radio, or television) can lodge a complaint with the CMM. If the CMM finds through its investigation of the facts that ethics have been breached, it issues a notice that requires the party violating the principles to publish CMM's notice of findings. Complaints to the CMM are usually investigated in about three months at no charge to the person lodging the complaint.

CMM decisions are based on published guidelines that were accepted by the Union of Journalists in Finland in 1992. CMM investigated 120 public complaints in 1998. Historically CMM found in favor of the complaining party about 25 percent of the time.

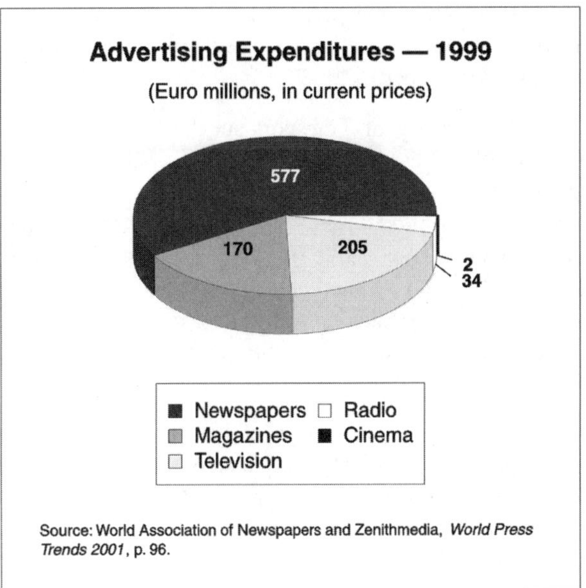

Source: World Association of Newspapers and Zenithmedia, *World Press Trends 2001*, p. 96.

In 1951 Finland adopted an Act on the Publicity of Official Documents, and in 1999 adopted the Openness of Government Activities Act. Accordingly, documents and recordings of government are considered public, unless their publication is specifically restricted by an act.

In 1966 Finnish legislation protected the confidentiality of sources by allowing journalists to refuse to reveal the identity of sources, unless it would solve a serious crime calling for a sentence of six or more years. In 1971 protection of the confidentiality of sources was extended to television journalists.

CENSORSHIP

According to Freedom House's annual ratings of press freedom, Finland's media enjoyed relative freedom throughout the late twentieth century. While there are restrictions on mass media advertising, there is no ''official'' censorship in Finland.

STATE-PRESS RELATIONS

Each of Finland's 13 governmental ministries has its own department responsible for disseminating public information and issuing press releases pertaining to its functions. Finland's government considers the media to be a ''cultural industry.'' Media-related cultural industries are mass media (radio, television, and newspapers), cinema and video, publishing (books and periodicals), and sound recording.

Governmental policies related to radio, television, and newspapers are the responsibility of the Finnish Ministry of Transport and Communications. The Ministry of Education is responsible for cinema, video, and book publishing. The Finnish Audit Bureau of Circulations is responsible for recording the circulation levels of each Finnish newspaper.

The Ministry of Transport and Communications is responsible for assuring that ''the public and the business community have safe and inexpensive transportation and communication services.'' The department's Mass Media Unit is responsible for administration of the mass media in Finland by handling television and radio broadcasting, mass media legislation, newspaper subsidies, postal services, and the economy and research of mass media.

According to the Ministry of Transport and Communications, governmental newspaper subsidies are paid to newspaper publishers to ''guarantee freedom of speech and to conserve a diverse press.'' Subsidies to newspapers declined during the 1990s. In the early 1990s the Finnish government paid nearly 500 million FIM. By 2000 the amount of subsidies declined to 75 million FIM. Indirect support for the print press was discontinued by 1996. The two forms of newspaper subsidies remaining in effect in 2002 were ''selective'' subsidies intended to lower newspaper transport and delivery costs (30 million FIM) and ''party'' subsidies granted to political parties for their publications (45 million FIM). The amount of subsidies to political parties is divided among the parties depending upon their relative representation in Finland's Parliament.

ATTITUDE TOWARD FOREIGN MEDIA

The Ministry of Foreign Affairs is responsible for providing information pertaining to Finland's government and its operations. Within the Ministry of Foreign Affairs, the Press and Culture Department handles communications with foreign media. The Ministry also makes arrangements for state and ministerial visits, and coordinates the press and cultural activities of the approximately 25 officials of Finland's Foreign Service. The Ministry of Foreign Affairs' Web site, which holds complete English translations, is the responsibility of the Ministry's Press and Culture Department.

Within the Ministry of Foreign Affairs Press and Culture Department there are four units with specific media responsibilities. The Media Unit is responsible for the International Press Center for foreign journalists and arrangements for visiting dignitaries. The Information Unit is in charge of the Ministry's external information such as press releases and media inquiries. The Cultural Unit is in charge of Finnish cultural activities and international cultural cooperation, such as cultural agreements and documents, and organizing journalists' visits related to cultural affairs. The Publications Unit handles external publications, the Press and Culture Department's library, and the maintenance of ''Virtual Finland,'' the Foreign Ministry's Web site, the journal *Kauppapolitiikka,* and the annual Press Directory.

Citizens of Nordic countries do not need a work or residence permit to work or live in Finland. Citizens of European Union countries do not need to obtain a visa to enter or work in Finland but must obtain a residence permit issued by local police departments. Foreign citizens who are not members of either the Nordic or European Union countries must obtain residence and work permits in order to stay in the country longer than three months. Valid passports and a statement from the Finnish Department of Labor (which a Finnish employer must obtain for the foreign citizen) are required to secure Finnish residency and work permits. Foreigners who become eligible to live in Finland are subject to Finnish laws as well as Finnish protections. Foreign residents can choose where to live and can freely leave the country.

NEWS AGENCIES

The 2002 Press Directory, published by the Finnish Ministry for Foreign Affairs, listed four news agencies. Two of the agencies, *Keskustan Sanomakeskus* and *Up-Uutispalevlu* are located in Helsinki. Startel News Agency, located in Sanomat, is an independent news agency. Svensk Press Janst, located in Helsinki is an independent Swedish language news agency.

In addition to the news agencies listed in the directory, Finland's Ministry of Foreign Affairs offers news analysis, parliamentary speeches, and articles about Finland from the foreign press. The service, Newsroom Finland, is available at the Ministry's Web site. The American Embassy also offers press and cultural affairs services at its Helsinki offices at the American Resource Center (e-mail: arc@usembassy.fi.)

Press Associations and Information Bureaus in the directory included the Association of European Journalists; the Association of Finnish Economic Correspondents; the Association of Finnish Foreign News Journalists; the Council for Mass Media; the Finnish Association of Magazine Editors-in-Chief; the Finnish Newspapers Association; the Finnish Periodical Publishers' Association; the Guild of Finnish Editors; the International Press Institute; the Association of Finnish Third World Development Journalists; the Political Journalists Association; *Taloudellinen Tiedotustoimisto* (Finnfacts); Union of Journalists in Finland; and the Western Foreign Press Club.

The Union of Journalists in Finland has about 10,000 members, 50 percent of whom are women. In addition, the Women Journalists in Finland, founded in 1946, is one of Finland's oldest journalist associations. The

Women Journalists association's goals are to improve the professional skills of its members and to improve the position of female journalists in newsrooms and editorial offices. They annually select a ''Torchbearer of the Year'' who, through her activities, brings consciousness and debate on a current issue or problem to the public's attention.

The 2002 Press Directory listed 19 foreign news agencies and over 120 foreign correspondents. Associated Press and Reuters, along with the other foreign news agencies, had offices in Helsinki.

BROADCAST MEDIA

Commercial and public television services entered the landscape in 1957. Four domestic national television channels and six national radio networks operate in Finland. The country's first private local radio stations were established in 1985. The state-owned Finnish Broadcasting Company (YLE) broadcasts at the national level with three channels in Finnish and one in Swedish. The Companies Act and the Bookkeeping Act legislation govern YLE.

YLE's operations are based on a license issued by the Finnish Council of State (1994 Broadcasting Act). Under the legislation of the 1994 Broadcasting Act, YLE operates or supervises all television and radio broadcasting. YLE is prohibited from advertising or carrying sponsored programs on its radio and television channels; and is required to offer services in Swedish, Sami, and other minority languages. Fifty-seven percent of all television programs were domestically produced in 2001. About one-half of the foreign-produced television programs were from other European countries and about 30 percent from the United States. Foreign television programming is shown with subtitles.

YLE's largest revenues are from license fees, providing service to television companies such as YLE, MTV3, and Channel Four. The Finnish television broadcasting companies cooperatively agree to classify programs unsuitable to children under age 16. Programs considered unsuitable are broadcast after 9:00 P.M. In January 1999 YLE transferred ownership of its broadcasting distribution network to its subsidiary Digita Ltd. In November 1999 Sonera, Finland's largest telecommunications company, bought a large share in Digita Ltd.

Cable television expanded rapidly during the 1980s, and by 1995 over one-third of Finnish households had cable television. The government issues cable licenses. Cable networks are required to carry a certain proportion of domestic productions. The state also imposes advertising quotas, stating that commercials may not occupy more than 11 percent of the programming time.

The largest telecommunication company, Sonera, announced its intent to merge with another Finnish telecommunication company, Telia, in March 2002. The merger will make them the leading telecommunications group in the Nordic and Baltic regions.

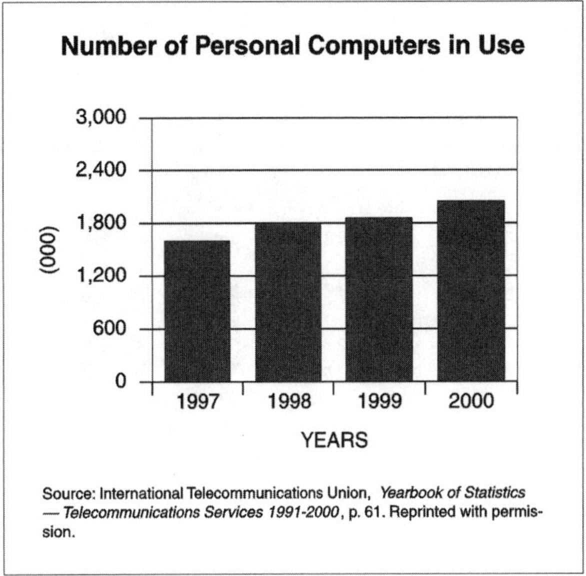

Source: International Telecommunications Union, *Yearbook of Statistics — Telecommunications Services 1991-2000*, p. 61. Reprinted with permission.

ELECTRONIC NEWS MEDIA

Finland's information technology knowledge has increased along with the industry itself. 60 percent of all Finns are able to use a computer. In 1999, 38 percent of the population had access to the internet, ranking second to the United States in per capita Internet connections. By 2000, nearly 90 percent of Finnish organizations employing more than 10 persons indicated they used the Internet. Further, 80 percent indicated they had their own home page.

In 2001 Finland's electronic news media was penetrating the print media's traditional market, with a 1 percent share of total national advertising expenditure going to Internet advertising. Nearly 200 Finnish journalistic publications were available on the Web, and all major media companies had their own Web sites, providing news and information in Finnish, Swedish, and English.

FinnFacts (*Taloudellinen Tiedotustoimisto*), a media service acting as a liaison between foreign media and Finnish industry, provides Internet accessible information about Finnish society. FinnFacts publishes business and industry information through its network of domestic and international contacts. It also arranges visits for members of the foreign media wanting to learn about the country's industries and innovations.

EDUCATION & TRAINING

Finnish commitment to reading reflects on the national commitment to education and literacy. Article

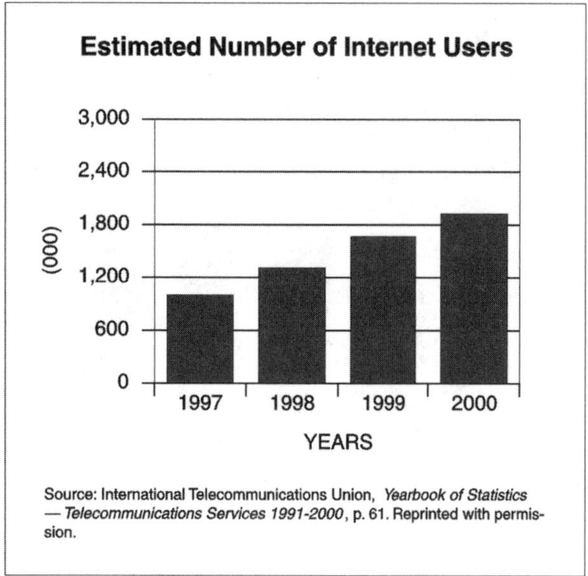

Source: International Telecommunications Union, *Yearbook of Statistics — Telecommunications Services 1991-2000*, p. 61. Reprinted with permission.

Twenty of the Finnish Constitution guarantees provision of free education through the university level. The Finnish education system is divided into four categories: comprehensive, general secondary, vocational secondary, and higher education.

In 2001 there were 10 multidisciplinary universities (*yliopisto*). In addition, there were 6 single discipline universities, 3 art academies, and over 20 polytechnic schools (*ammattikorkeakoulut*). The categories of higher education degrees offered by Finland's universities are the Bachelors, the Masters, and two graduate degrees, the licentiate and the doctorate.

Finland was the first of its Nordic cousins to offer a degree program in journalism in 1925; The University of Helsinki followed in 1965 and Jyvaskyla in 1985. In 1960 The University of Tampere became the leading Finnish university for journalism studies. Between 1960 and 1990 the University graduated 400 professional journalists (with B.A. degrees) and 900 masters degree students majoring or minoring in the field. Since 1993 Tampere's program averages 35 to 40 M.A. graduates. Annual new enrollment in journalism programs averages 80 at Tampere, 20 at Helsinki, and 20 at Jyvaskyla.

Journalism-related degree programs are available at the University of Helsinki, the University of Tampere, the University of Jyvaskyla, and the University of Arts and Design Helsinki. The University of Helsinki's Department of Communication, founded in 1978, accepts 35 students each year. Its journalism program includes courses in general communication theory, study of mass communication, organizational and interpersonal communication, communication policies and technologies, and the media. The University of Tampere's Journalism and Mass Communication program includes courses in theories of communication, media economy and policy, media analysis and criticism, media research issues, Finnish media and communication systems, and current issues in communication and information sciences in Finland. The University of Jyvaskyla's Department of Communications offers courses in journalism, speech, organizational communication, and public relations. The University of Art and Design Helsinki offers degree programs in Film and TV studies, and in Journalism Photography.

Most degree programs require 140 to 160 credits consisting of basic studies, professional studies, elective studies, job training, and a written thesis. Finland's degree students learn the fundamentals of the field in which they major, its importance in the work world, in Finnish society, and internationally. Students are also required to take language studies in both their native language and at least two more foreign languages.

Enrollment at Finland's universities in 2001 was 162,800. Eighty-five percent of Finnish university students were undergraduates. About 21,000 (15 percent) were postgraduate students. Entry was highly competitive with only 43 percent (28,400) of the 65,400 applicants being accepted. In the ''open university'' system 83,200 students were enrolled, and another 106,700 Finns participated in continuing education.

In addition to the professionally recognized journalism degree programs, the Union of Journalists, as well as media employers, offer journalism-related courses through the university centers. For example, Helsingin Sanomat, Finland's multimedia giant, offers in-house education programs in journalism, and the Finnish Broadcasting Company (YLE) has its own Radio and Television Institute for its staff. Media courses are also available at the civic colleges.

Journalism and media related centers providing research, training, and publicity related to journalism operate at the University of Tampere at the Journalism Research Centre. A regional center, The Nordic Centre for Media and Communication Research, whose focus includes Denmark, Finland, Iceland, Norway, and Sweden, headquarters in Sweden with a branch at the University of Tampere.

Non-Finnish students can obtain residency permits in order to study in the country, provided they demonstrate they have enough funds to support themselves. During the period in which they are studying at Finnish universities, foreign students are able to work without a permit. The Centre for International Mobility (CIMO), a unit of the Finnish Ministry of Education located in Helsinki, promotes international student exchange programs.

SUMMARY

Finland's overall daily newspaper circulation remains relatively stable at about 1.4 million each year, indicating market saturation has occurred. Finnish newspaper publishers have responded to the market saturation by merging companies and by reducing publication costs. Mass media consolidation leading to the creation of multimedia enterprises picked up steam in the late 1990s with more newspapers operating as chains and increased sharing of editorials, weekend supplements, and printing capacities among the provincial newspapers.

Advertisers wishing to reach consumers are likely to continue having success with newspapers, since 9 out of 10 Finnish adults read a daily newspaper. However, it is likely that in a society as well-educated as Finland that the ease of Internet access and its continually fresh content will eventually cut into not only the traditional newspaper subscriber market but also the traditional advertising market.

Since Finland liberalized foreign investment restrictions in 1993 and joined the European Union in 1995, internationalization of Finnish mass media companies has increased. Initially the increase resulted in more Finnish media companies buying companies outside the country. However, because of their closeness to and expertise in the Baltic States and the independent states of the former Soviet Union, Finns are hoping to attract more foreign investors by serving as a gateway to those countries. Finland's promotion of foreign investments will undoubtedly result in continued consolidation of its own mass media ownership under the control of fewer and fewer multimedia giants—especially those wishing to tap into the potential markets of the former Soviet Union.

SIGNIFICANT DATES

- 1999: Finland is first Nordic country to adopt the euro (European Union currency).
- 1999: Finland's state-owned television broadcaster, The Finnish Broadcasting Company (YLE), transferred ownership of its distribution network to its subsidiary Digita Ltd. Later in the year, Sonera purchased a large share of Digita.
- March 2000: Finns adopt a new constitution.
- 2002: Sonera and Telia announced their intent to merge, which would make them the leading telecommunications group in the Nordic and Baltic regions.

BIBLIOGRAPHY

Central Intelligence Agency (CIA). *The World Factbook 2002.* Available from www.cia.gov.

Finland Ministry for Foreign Affairs, Department for Press and Culture. *Finland Press Directory: 2002.* Helsinki: Edita Publishing, 2002.

Finland Ministry of Education. ''Education, Training and Research in the Information Society: A National Strategy, 2000-2004.'' Helsinki: 1999.

Finland Ministry of Finance, Statistics Finland. ''Mass communication as employer 1980-1998).'' Updated 25 September 2001.

———.''Mass media turnover 1980-2000.'' 17 June 2002.

———.''Population by age and sex 1950-2000.'' 17 June 2002.

———.''Share of domestic production in different sectors of mass communication.'' 17 June 2002.

Finnish Audit Bureau of Circulations. ''Circulations of Periodicals 2001.'' 18 June 2002.

———. ''Newspapers 1990-2001.'' 28 May 2002.

Finnish Newspapers Association. ''Facts about the Finnish Press.'' 2001.

Nordicom. ''Media Trends 2001 in Denmark, Finland, Ireland, Norway, Sweden: Statistics and Analysis.'' Sweden: 2002.

Solsten, Eric, and Meditz, Sandra W., eds. *Finland: A Country Study.* Washington, D.C.: Federal Research Division, U.S. Library of Congress, 1990.

Stockmann, Doris, Niklas Bengtsson, and Yrjo Repo. ''The Book Trade in Finland.'' 1999.

Sussman, Leonard R., and Karen Deutsch Karlekar, eds. ''The Annual Survey of Press Freedom 2002.'' New York: Freedom House, 2002.

Union of Journalists in Finland. ''Guidelines For Good Journalistic Practice.'' Adopted by the Union of Journalists in Finland in November 1991, entered into force on January 1, 1992.

U.S. Census Bureau. International Database. Washington, D.C., 2000.

U.S. Department of State. ''Background Note: Finland.'' Bureau of European and Eurasian Affairs: Washington, D.C., June 1999.

———. ''FY 2001 Country Commercial Guide.'' U.S. Embassy Helsinki: Bureau of Economic and Business, July 2000.

U.S. Department of State, Bureau of Economic and Business Affairs. ''2001 Country Reports on Economic Policy and Trade Practices.'' Washington, D.C., February 2002.

—Sandra J. Callaghan

FRANCE

BASIC DATA

Official Country Name:	French Republic
Region (Map name):	Europe
Population:	59,551,227
Language(s):	French, rapidly declining regional dialects and languages
Literacy rate:	99.0%
Area:	547,030 sq km
GDP:	1,294,246 (US$ millions)
Number of Daily Newspapers:	86
Total Circulation:	8,799,000
Circulation per 1,000:	190
Newspaper Consumption (minutes per day):	30
Total Newspaper Ad Receipts:	1,784 (Euro millions)
As % of All Ad Expenditures:	17.70
Number of Television Stations:	584
Number of Television Sets:	24,800,000
Television Sets per 1,000:	416.4
Television Consumption (minutes per day):	193
Number of Cable Subscribers:	2,662,280
Cable Subscribers per 1,000:	45.2
Number of Satellite Subscribers:	4,300,000
Satellite Subscribers per 1,000:	72.2
Number of Radio Receivers:	55,300,000
Radio Receivers per 1,000:	928.6
Radio Consumption (minutes per day):	191
Number of Individuals with Computers:	17,920,000
Computers per 1,000:	300.9
Number of Individuals with Internet Access:	8,500,000
Internet Access per 1,000:	142.7

BACKGROUND & GENERAL CHARACTERISTICS

General Description National daily press is no longer the prime information source for French people. It accounts for two percent of the titles and 14 percent of the circulation. Magazines account for 40 percent of the titles and 38 percent of the circulation. Technical or professional press leads the number of titles, 44 percent, but only accounts for five percent of the readership. The true leader in readership is the regional daily and weekly press, with 43 percent, although they only have 14 percent of the publications. French people overwhelmingly rely on magazines and on their local daily newspaper for news. In 2000, more French people read the sports daily *L'Equipe* and consulted TV guides than read the prestigious *Le Monde*. The technical and professional information press, while extremely diversified, has a very small audience. The number of new publications reflects this trend: in 1998, 427 new titles were created, among which 250 magazines and 140 technical and professional information press titles. The regional press is the most prominent media, ahead of television.

The national press remains an important segment of the industry even though it is heavily centered in Paris. The daily opinion press has practically disappeared, with main newspapers adopting a more neutral tone and limiting political commentaries to editorial articles and op-ed pages. The remaining opinion newspapers are *La Lettre de la Nation* (RPR), *L'Humanité*, which today remains the voice of the communist party, the ultra-rightist *Présent*, and the Catholic *La Croix*. The daily information press's most important titles are *Le Monde*, *Le Figaro* and *Libération*. Their influence is felt on domestic public opinion and in the other media. The most prominent popular daily newspaper is *Le Parisien-Aujourd'hui*, one of the few to have adopted a regional press strategy. *France-Soir*, another popular newspaper, lost two-thirds of its readership between 1985 and 1997, plummeting to 173,000, and survived only by adopting a tabloid format in 1998. Theme daily newspapers, by contrast, have an increasing success: the financial and economic newspapers *Les Echos*, and *La Tribune*, with the sports newspaper *L'Equipe* being the first daily newspaper. In 1993, the street press appeared; *Macadam-Journal*, *La Rue*, *Sans-Abri*, and *L'Itinérant*, weekly or monthly publications of the homeless and the unemployed, promoted their copies at train stations and in the metro. Today, their circulation is declining.

The Nature of the Audience In 2000, 18.3 percent of French people above age 15 read a national daily newspaper every day, against 38.4 percent for the regional or departmental daily press and 11 percent for the regional daily press and 95.9 percent for the magazine press. Overall approximately half the French population over 15 years of age read a regional newspaper regularly, with readership distributed equally between men and women. While the regional press reaches only 17 percent of the public in the greater Paris area, it reaches over 50 percent of the public in the provinces.

One third of all readers of the national daily press are found in the Paris region. They belong to the educated upper middle classes; 61 percent of them are actively employed men; one third of the readers are under 35 and two-thirds under 50 years of age. Readers spend an average of 31 minutes reading the newspaper, and 70 percent read the newspapers before 2 p.m.

Readers of the daily regional or departmental press are evenly distributed between men and women, with approximately 25 percent under 35, 41 percent between the ages of 35 and 59, and 33 percent over 60. Fifty-one percent were actively employed (27 percent in rural towns, 30 percent in large cities). Parisians represent 7.4 percent of this readership. Readers spend an average 24 minutes reading the regional newspapers.

The readers of the weekly regional press are the most faithful and exclusive of all readers. Thirty percent of readers are under 35, while 60 percent are under 50, and 58 percent are actively employed. Readership is distributed evenly between men and women. Readers belong to all socio-professional categories, with employees, workers, and farmers being the main groups.

Press readers have progressively gotten older, forcing the press to adopt new strategies to attract young readers, such as putting newspapers in the schools, improving the distribution system, and creating magazines especially for young readers. The magazine press in general is faring extremely well. French people read an average 7.5 magazines, mostly in their homes. Some 92 percent of young people read magazines, half of them regularly. Increases in television viewing time and universal radio listening have also cut into the press readership. Finally, the internet press has gotten a share of the market. The average press budget per household is US$132.

Top Ten Daily Newspapers
(2000)

	Circulation
Ouest France	785,000
Le Parisien/Aujourd'hui	486,000
Le Monde	393,000
L'Equipe	398,000
Le Figaro	361,000
Sud Ouest	345,000
La Voix du Nord	322,000
Le Progrès	277,000
Le Dauphiné Libéré	265,000
NRCO	255,000

Source: World Association of Newspapers and Zenithmedia, *World Press Trends 2001*, p. 99.

Quality of Journalism: General Comments The French press has long had a tradition of defending its freedoms and establishing high standards for reporting the news, political news in particular. Using it to promote democracy and educate the readers, it regularly engages in debates about what constitutes proper journalistic practice and ethics. The quality of journalism in general is very high, and the opinion press very diversified.

There is a wide range of expression, from popular newspapers to intellectually challenging ones. In the 1970s the higher quality journals gained at the expense of the popular press owing to the increased urbanization and higher educational levels of the population. *Le Monde*, *La Croix*, and *Le Figaro* all grew while popular newspapers such as *France-Soir*, *L'Aurore* and *Le Parisien Libéré* lost readers.

Historical Traditions The first French newspaper was born in 1631 as Théophraste Renaudot's *La Gazette*. The press grew slowly until the French Revolution which saw the birth of the opinion press along with information newspapers such as *Le Moniteur Universel* and the *Journal des Débats*. French public opinion was born, and, with the coming of the Industrial Revolution, the press gained a unique status of sole purveyor of information to the people. With freedom of expression guaranteed by Article 11 of the Declaration of the Rights of Man and Citizen, the press became synonymous with the pursuit of democracy, and journalists enjoyed unprecedented freedoms in the absence of police interference and professional standards to restrain the editors.

Beginning in 1815, numerous changes took place. The introduction of the telegraph in 1845 and of the telephone in 1876, together with an increase in the nation's literacy, created a fertile environment and a growing demand for news. Charles Havas created the first news agency in 1832. The development of the rotary press and the use of wood-pulp paper, the new railroad networks, and diminished production costs, made mass production possible, and enhanced distribution. The nineteenth century was the golden age of press democratization. The first low-priced newspaper targeting a general audience was Emile de Girardin's *La Presse*, created in 1836. In 1863, *Le Petit Journal* refined this formula by inventing the popular press, characterized by simple writing with an informal, familiar tone. It found immediate success. Within five years it had reached a circulation of 300,000, thus becoming a European model.

During the nineteenth century, governmental policies alternated between liberalism and authoritarianism. The press continued to play a major political role, contributing to the revolutions of 1830 and 1848, weakening Napoleon III's rule after 1860 and influencing electoral outcome during the first years of the Third Republic. The Law of 29 July, 1881 ushered in a golden age of the press, which lasted until 1914. It firmly established the principle of a free press by suppressing paperwork (authorization to publish, down payment, "timbre," or a special tax) and limiting the definition of press law violations. Subsequently the number of newspapers increased. In 1914, Paris published 80 titles, and the regional and local press flourished, toppling 100,000 in circulation in large cities. Four titles monopolized the daily newspaper market: *Le Petit Journal*, with a circulation of 1 million in 1890, *Le Petit Parisien*, founded in 1876, which had a 1.5 million circulation in 1914, *Le Matin*, and *Le Journal*, hovering around 1 million circulation in 1914. These newspapers favored information over opinion, thus giving the appearance of neutrality; they also tapped the rich vein of popular literature, publishing it in installments. News reporting, a new technique, was an added ingredient of the newspapers' success. Overall, newspapers still relied very little on publicity. In 1914 France was the first consumer of news with 244 readers per 1,000 population, the highest readership it would reach during the twentieth century.

During the war, the French press became more uniform. The war years were marked by rising production costs, inflation, the cost of now commonplace photographic reproductions, increases in the price of paper, and rising social costs. After 1933, the slump in sales made newspapers rely increasingly on publicity revenues. The press became more concentrated as larger amounts of capital were needed to operate newspapers that became real enterprises. *Le Petit Parisien* created its own society, while the remaining four major newspapers associated around Havas and Hachette monopolized the daily newspaper market. Crises rocked and divided the press, from the Dreyfus Affair in 1894-1897, to anti-Semitism before World War I, and financial scandals in the 1930s. Some newspapers implicated in anti-patriotic acts during the war lost much of their credibility, especially *Le Petit Journal*. The dependence of the press on businessmen and politicians' self-serving purposes further discredited the press.

Between the two World Wars the highly politicized weekly press was born, such as the rightist *Candide* and the leftist *Le Canard Enchaîné*, the regional daily press developed, especially in the southwest regions, and the magazine press appeared with general information titles such as Jean Prouvost's *Match* and leisure and culture magazines. The first radio program was broadcast in 1921 and several local radio stations were created thereafter, with the state exercising tight control over them after 1933. The importance of news reporting on the radio increased after the riots of February 6, 1934. During the Front Populaire, the radio began to become a political forum for parties and politicians.

On the eve of World War II, censorship began to be actively enforced and in 1940 the government increased its control of the press by creating the first Ministry of Information. On June 14, 1940 all newspapers were shut down by the Nazis. As clandestine media developed, the press and radio were divided between collaborators and resistors. The French began to rely increasingly on the radio as their main source of uncensored information. At the Liberation of France in 1944, the temporary government issued three ordinances to protect the press from the intervention of political power, but also from financial pressures and commercial dependencies. The new press was highly politicized and ideological, and the surge of freedom seemed to bode well for its future, as seen in the creation of a host of new publications, including *Le Monde* in December 1944. However, press restructuring and increased publicity revenues could not prevent circulation from falling back to 1914 levels by 1952. In 1958 the Fifth Republic solidified the press's dependence toward the executive, while radio and television began to compete for the news market. In 1947, three national daily newspapers were party organs: the MRP's *L'Aube*, the Socialist Party's *Le Populaire* and the Communist Party's *L'Humanité*. By 1974 only *L'Humanité* remained.

After World War II, the press began to receive governmental subsidies. By 1972 these subsidies represented one-eighth of the total turnover of press enterprises. A decree of 1973 fixed the conditions under which the subsidies could be granted to newspapers with a circulation under 200,000, limiting their revenues from publicity to 30 percent. The sixties and seventies were marked by an increase in regional press concentration. Emilien Amaury regionalized the daily *Le Parisien Libéré*, while Robert Hersant created one of the first French press groups that began with his *Auto-Journal* in 1950, continued through a series of regional newspaper acquisitions, and culminated with the control of *Le Figaro* in 1975, which prompted the resignation of editor Jean d'Ormesson and best-known columnist, Raymond Aron.

Daily and Non-Daily Newspaper Titles and Circulation Figures

	1996	1997	1998	1999	2000
Number of Daily Newspapers	86	85	86	81	NA
Circulation of Dailies (000)	8,656	8,952	8,799	NA	NA
Number of Non-Daily Newspapers	230	232	232	NA	NA
Circulation of Non-Dailies (000)	NA	NA	NA	NA	NA

Source: World Association of Newspapers and Zenithmedia, *World Press Trends 2001*, pp. 8, 10, 17, 19. Note: NA stands for not available.

Regionalization also characterized television, with a regional station opening in 1973 in addition to the other two state-controlled television stations. Weekly magazines such as *L'Observateur* and *L'Express*, and *Paris-Match*, founded in 1949 by Robert Prouvost, were founded with great success. Two national daily newspapers emerged in leading position at this time, *Le Monde* and *Le Figaro*. The regional press began to modernize in the early 1970s with offset, digital, and facsimile techniques. Those costly moves caused a concentration and regrouping of the titles whose number dropped from 153 to 58 between 1945 and 1994, erasing ideological and cultural differences. A few large groups dominated. Hersant controlled 30 percent of the market with *Le Dauphiné Libéré*, *Paris-Normandie*, *Le Progrès de Lyon*, *Les Dernières Nouvelles d'Alsace*, *Nord-Matin*, *Nord-Éclair*, *Le Havre-Libre*, and *Midi-Libre* among others. Hachette-Filipacchi Presse controls the south with *Le Provençal*, *Le Méridional*, *La République*, while smaller groups are centered around a newspaper. Some such examples are *Ouest-France*, *Sud-Ouest*, *La Dépêche du Midi*, and *La Voix du Nord*. *Ouest-France* is a leader with a circulation of over 800,000, 17 editions, and sells in Brittany, Normandy, and the Loire departments.

In the 1980s the press had reached a fragile equilibrium between pluralism and market constraints. Concentration continued while the Socialist government strengthened the pluralism of the press, deemed essential to the democratic debate in its law of 23 October 1984. A new set of laws of 1 August and 27 November 1986 prevented monopolies by establishing a 30 percent circulation limit to national and regional daily newspapers controlled by a single press group. As a result, groups such as Hersant began to invest abroad, notably in the former Eastern European countries, after the end of the Cold War in 1989. Economic realities also brought about restructuring of the printing and distribution networks. Between 1985 and 1990, however, profits were assured only by the growth of publicity revenues, while the national daily press experienced major difficulties.

The recession of 1989-93 brought more changes. The information revolution also prompted a radical reevaluation of the way news was written and distributed. Once rare and expensive, the news became overabundant, which dealt a severe blow to the French press, although it is a development common in other countries. Competition came not only from the Internet, but from radio and TV, which multiplied their news delivery, and also from an unexpected source, books that started dealing with current events, a field heretofore monopolized by newspapers. Due to France's experience with Minitel in the 1980s, a digital distribution system controlled by the Ministry of Posts and Telecommunication, France hesitated to embark upon yet another modernization. But the public was beginning to ask for free news. Some newspapers responded with an upscale presentation and simplified analyses, while others, like *Le Monde*, opted to serve the more educated, more sophisticated public of the modern, "complex" societies that required a new kind of information. The restructuring of the 1990s benefited the three main newspapers, *Le Monde*, *Libération*, and *Le Parisien-Aujourd'hui*, whose circulation stabilized in 2000. Press groups restructured as well. Hachette, which diversified into publishing, distributing, and radio broadcasting, Amaury, which diversified into the sports press and women's magazines, Prouvost which diversified around women's magazines and the very successful *Télé 7 jours*, and Del Duca, specialized in *La Presse du Coeur*, a popular press, and *Télé Magazine*.

ECONOMIC FRAMEWORK

Print Media versus Electronic Media In the 1980s, France was the first country to put a newspaper online by using a revolutionary system called Minitel. The publicity-free, pay-per-usage time service's profitability, added to the large investments made in Minitel explain why France was slower than other European countries to adopt the Internet in the 1990s. In 1996, France had seven online daily newspapers out of the total 84 and 19 online magazines out of all 294 online. In October 1997 *Les Echos* became the first newspaper to offer an online version with part free news and part pay-per-article. With the new millennium, however, things began to change quickly. The increase in internet use can be measured by the

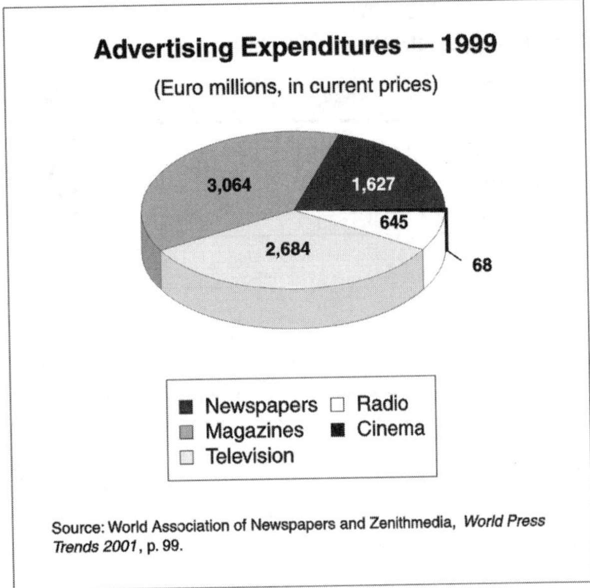

Source: World Association of Newspapers and Zenithmedia, *World Press Trends 2001*, p. 99.

number of visits to the site of *Le Monde*. In 2001 it had approximately a half million visits. In April, 2002, it had close to eight million visits, followed by *Les Echos* with 2.38 million visits, while the *Groupe Nouvel Observateur* had over one million visits, and *L'Express* and *Le Monde Diplomatique* around half a million visits. France reached the minimum profitability level of 10 percent of households having access to internet.

The best known and largest newspapers were not the first ones to go online. Their reluctance opened the door for smaller, more technologically oriented newspapers to make a name for themselves. Regional and small newspapers that embraced the new technology quickly made a name for themselves. For newspapers specialized in economic and financial news, such as *Les Echos*, the Internet was a natural medium. In 2002, a substantial proportion of newspapers had developed internet sites, especially regional newspapers.

Many titles have more than one site, showing that general and political news have lost the prominent place they once occupied. The *Groupe Nouvel Observateur*, in addition to its initial magazine site, has 14 specialized sites, including car, health, stock market, women, culture, real estate, economic and financial. *Les Echos* has seven sites, including employment, sports, and news. Online editions require substantial makeovers since site attractiveness is a must, especially in the advertisers' opinion. At first the internet press was totally dependent on publicity revenues, which it had no difficulty attracting. The new partnerships between technology and editorial policies, however, gave newspapers new revenues by developing commercial services such as e-commerce, e-bank, e-tickets, e-travel, and pay per view services. Archival services and royalties represented additional sources of revenue, and so will the use of "cookies" which was being considered in 2002. The new sites are interactive, allowing the online press to receive feedback and to monitor its audience (the first statistics were created in 1998). Employment, real estate sites, classifieds and personalized pages are among the other services offered.

Types of Partnerships/Ownership The traditional economic structure of newspapers, with limited capital and a delicate balancing act between publicity revenues, state subsidies, and sales revenues, has all but disappeared. The new technology requires the support of financial-technological support groups, thus turning the press into veritable enterprises. The new press magnates are the technological magnates, the announcers and the sponsors.

In the 1990s, the news media became a fast expanding economic sector attracting not only domestic, but European industrial and banking giants. *Libération*, a mouthpiece of the left founded in 1973 under the aegis of Jean-Paul Sartre, was taken over in early 1996 by the industrial group Chargeurs. In October 1995, the Havas publicity group together with Alcatel bought several important newspapers including *L'Express*, *Le Point*, and *Courrier International*. One of the few newspapers which remains internally controlled by its stockholders is *Le Monde*.

The editorial independence of the media appeared threatened, which caused a significant drop in circulation sales between 1995 and 1996, indicating the public's lack of confidence in the media, especially when the Tapie, Botton, and Dumas scandals revealed the extent to which investigative journalism had been choked. The press, which historically was built in opposition to political power, now seemed closely associated to it, even to the point of losing self-criticism. This new version of the power triangle between the media, big business, and politics, was somewhat addressed by an understanding between editorial offices and publicity leading to their "sacred union," and by repeated governmental measures stressing the role of the press as guarantor of democracy and pluralism.

Concentration of Ownership The late 1990s saw the formation of large press groups controlling both technology and editorial content, with the major French investor being the Vivendi group. The main press groups are: Bayard Presse, Excelsior Publications, Groupe Moniteur, Groupe Quotidien Santé, Havas, Milan Presse and Prisma Presse.

Bayard France, the first Catholic press group, regroups the press, book publishing, and multimedia. Created in 1813 with the magazine *Le Pèlerin*, it added *La Croix* in 1883, which was still in print in 2002. It publishes more than 100 magazines in the world, of which 39 are produced in France and 50 abroad. It is the leader of the educational youth press, religious press, and mature adults press. It is the fifth French group by diffusion, with 7.6 million buyers and 30 million readers worldwide. It features seven internet sites.

Prisma Presse features five weeklies, nine monthlies, and one biannual publication. *Prisma TV* deals with televised news. The group distributes 277 million copies a year and owns 18 percent of the French market. Created in 1978 within the group Gruner and Jahr, it publishes popular magazines such as *Femme*, *Capital*, *Cuisine Actuelle*, and the *National Geographic* which it co-owns since 1999 with RBA Editions.

Distribution and Printing The main press distributor remains the Nouvelles Messageries de la Presse Parisienne. In 2001 they owned more than 80 percent of the sales market with two other distributors the MLP and Transports Presse. Created in 1947 from a partnership between the Hachette bookstore and Parisian press publishers, they guarantee and promote the diffusion of the written press in France and abroad. In 1986 the NMPP began an intensive campaign of modernization that was sped by the 1989 economic crisis. After 1991 they assisted publishers in order to maximize circulation; they also created new sales locations, especially in the Paris region, and automated distributors. More modernization and geographic rationalization followed in the 1990s. In the 1990s NMPP continued to centralize and relocate in order to reduce cost and to improve service. They reduced personnel by one-third, and introduced online links with editors and press merchants.

In 2001 they represented 697 publishers and distributed 3,500 titles (dailies, magazines, and multimedia products), including 26 national daily newspapers, and over 900 foreign newspapers and magazines, for a transactions figure of 5,176 billion Euros distributed (of which 2,791 billion Euros sold), 2,658 million copies, 560,000 tons of titles. Unsold copies, averaging 46 percent, are recycled. The NMPP exported to 113 foreign destinations, 2,727 titles for an amount of sales of 286 million Euros, or 10 percent of its total sales. It employed 2,089 people. The NMPP is owned for 51 percent by five press coops and for 49 percent by Matra-Hachette which operates the firm. NMPP tariffs favor the daily press.

These issues plague NMPP: the decreasing number of newsstands in Paris and a low portion of the magazine and weekly press market. Despite restructuring, NMPP was still having financial difficulties in 2000 and for state subsidies of 250 million francs. The state was also called in to mediate a dispute in 2000 when NMPP tried to give favorable tariffs to periodicals.

Messageries Lyonnaises de Presse (MLP) regroups 200 clients and distributes 650 titles in France. In the 1990s, MLP grew considerably, cornering the magazine and weekly publications' market. In 1998 their turnover was 2.7 billion francs. Previously, in 1996, the MLP held 9 percent of the paper distributed in France which provided lesser operating costs and expanded into the Paris market.

There are 31,504 press merchants, of which includes 1,210 ''Maisons de la Presse'' stores (a combination newsstand, bookstore, and stationery store), 753 kiosks, of which 315 are in Paris, and 2,784 sites in shopping malls. The press kiosks in Paris diminished in numbers from 370 to 310 between 1999 and 2002. In 1988 there was one sales location for 2,100 Parisians, a ratio twice that in other parts of France. Editors asked the Paris mayoral office to help, since newsstands sales represent more than one-third of all sales of daily newspapers in Paris, and a press subsidies of 750,000 Euros was granted. In an effort to stem this decline, newsstands operators were given greater input about the number of copies they were assigned and press merchants signed an agreement with the Union Nationale des Diffuseurs de Presse (UNDP) in 2001 granting them a 15 percent fee. Today the situation appears to have stabilized.

Advertisers' Influence on Editorial Policies & Ad Ratio In 2000, publicity revenues for the press were 28 billion francs, a 10.2 percent increase over the 1999 revenues, roughly half the publicity revenue of all media combined. The press thus remains the main media support for publicity investments. In 2000, it attracted almost 42 percent of the media market, far ahead of television (30 percent) and radio (7 percent). The publicity revenues come from commercial publicity for 80 percent and from classified for 20 percent. The main buyers of publicity were the magazine press (40 percent), followed by the daily regional press (24 percent), the specialized technical and professional press (18 percent), the daily national press (16 percent), and in last place the weekly regional press (2 percent). 40 percent of the purchases of internet publicity space were destined to editorial sites (written press, TV and radio).

Despite the predominance of print advertising, however, over the past 20 years, the printed press lost 13 percent of the publicity market, much of it to television. In 1980 the press received 60 percent of all publicity revenue and television 20 percent, but in 2000 it received only 47.3 percent of it (including classified), whereas television received 33.5 percent. The prolonged economic crisis and the competition from television, plus the fact that alcohol and tobacco ads were curtailed, contributed to this decrease. In 2000, the turnover's ratio between sales and publicity revenues was approximately 60 and 40 percent, respectively.

By contrast, publicity on the web has increased dramatically. To finance the Internet press, several commercial methods were used: publicity, classifieds, auction sites, e-commerce, and cookies. 95 percent of e-sites were financed in 1999 by publicity, with the pay-per-view option remaining small. At first, e-publicity revenues remained small at 113 million francs in 1997, compared to 400 million francs of publicity revenue for *Le Monde* in 1998. *Les Echos*'s e-publicity revenues of 1.2 million francs in 1997 more than doubled in 1998, reaching in excess of 3 million francs, and outpaced pay per view revenues, while its printed version saw a total publicity revenue of 300 million francs. However, in 1998, the price of online publicity surpassed the printed press's publicity price, prompting many newspapers to offer an online version in order to protect their revenues, especially with regard to publicity. The price of publicity is governed by a December 1, 1986 decree which established flat publicity rates that were eliminated for newspapers with a large circulation by a *Circulaire* of October 28, 1993.

While many announcers buy space online directly, newspapers increasingly buy publicity from a middleman or specialized purchasing group. France plays a leadership role and serves as "interactive task force." Announcers who want to advertise internationally prefer to deal with French groups, whose leader is Carat with 20 percent of the investment for printed media in 1998. Carat France was the first online firm to adopt the multimedia. In 1994 it created Carat Multimédia under the sponsorship of Aegis. Besides Carat Multimédia, Ogilvy Interactive and The Network, which claims to be the first buyer on the internet market in France, Médiapolis, Optimum Media and CIA Medianetwork are the main buyers of internet space. European and international giants have an edge, however, some examples being RealMedia, Doubleclick, Interdeco (of the group Hachette Filipacchi), Accesite (dedicated to Francophone markets), or InterAd (specialized in European markets). Many purchasing groups are tied to a main client, such as France Télécom, which brought Médiapolis between 3 and 4 million francs in 1998.

France is also involved in the U.S.-based, publisher-controlled Internet Advertising Bureau, which was founded in 1996 and serves the main U.S. and foreign newspapers. France led in the creation of IAB Europe which is based in Paris, and of IAB France which in 1998 served *Libération*, *Les Echos*, and all 40 publications of the groups Hachette Filipacchi and Hersant. Several regional newspapers are also represented in IAB through their online publicity companies Realmedia and Accesite.

Another issue unfolding is whether to couple paper and web advertising. The Internet press has been banned from advertising on television since March, 1992, but the debate is ongoing, especially since CSA's decision in February 2000 to allow Internet sites, including the press sites, to advertise on television. Although the Conseil d'Etat in July 2000 reversed this decision, the debate continued, with the Syndicat de la Presse Magazine et d'Information (SPMI) favoring access to televised publicity in view of the competition from the new media.

The world of advertisers is complex and totally internationalized. One of the main advertising representatives is S'regie, an international media sales group. Headquartered in Paris and Brussels, it represents the press, TV, online, outdoor, and radio. In 2002 the publicity group Publicis bought the US Bcom3 and entered in a world exclusive agreement with the Japanese group Dentsu. The first action made Publicis the fourth publicity group worldwide, while the second action gave its clients a privileged access to the Asian market.

Special Interests and Lobbies With lobbies not much a part of the French tradition, there are few press lobbies, and they are all recent. A users' association, IRIS (Imaginons un Réseau Internet Solidaire), was created in 1997. Older, established consumer organizations such as the French Consumer Association or the National Union of Family Associations have opened departments dealing with Internet issues. In June 2001 a new group was created called Enfance et Média (CIEM) to prevent violence on television. It would produce a report in March 2002 to the Minister of Family, Childhood, and Handicapped Persons.

In France, one may consider professional associations and trade unions as lobbyists. Some of them represent their profession in governmental agencies and paragovernmental and inter-professional organizations, such as FNPF.

Journalist: An Expanding Profession The statute of journalists is defined by the collective labor contract for journalists, which was passed as Loi Guernut-Brachard in 1935. The statute was revised in 1956 under the leadership of Marcel Roëls, and then in 1968, 1974, and 1987. Since 1944 French laws have guaranteed the independence of journalists. The Articles L 761-1 to 16 of the Labor Code which were passed in January, 1973 define four kinds of journalists: (1) professional journalists who "have for their main, regular, and salaried occupation and income, the exercise of their profession in one or more daily or periodical publication or in one or more press agencies.'' This includes correspondents who work in France or abroad in the same conditions are professional journalists; (2) ''assimilated'' journalists who work in related occupations or direct editorial collaborators such as redactors-translators, stenographer-translators, redactors-copy editors, reporters-graphic artists, and reporters-photographers; (3) *pigistes*; and (4) temporary journalists or substitutes. A salary grid reveals a maze of job titles that indicates a great deal of nuances and complexities as well, listing as many as three ''categories'' differentiating the level of pay and responsibility. *Pigistes* occupy a position unique in the world of journalism, in between free lancers and tenured journalists. They are considered professional journalists since the 1974 Loi Cressard. Finally there are collaborators, namely well-known academics or specialists collaborating occasionally with an opinion piece, for which they are paid in royalties. Publicity agents and occasional collaborators are not considered journalists.

The number of card-holding journalists more than quintupled between 1950 and 2000. On the other hand, the number of new journalists showed a decline in the 1990s, with a significant drop to 1700 in 1993, during the crisis of the press. Overall, the number of journalists increased in the 1990s, from 26,614 in 1990 to 30,150 in 1998. In 1990, 9.3 percent of those were new journalists, while in 1998 this figure dropped to 6.9 percent. The profession has become less secure and increasingly competitive, with journalists leaving the profession at a high rate after a few years when their career does not take off as hoped, and employers prolonging the ''trial'' period. Also, journalism has become increasingly a second profession and students have been getting higher professional education degrees in order to be more competitive. In 1998, 90.6 percent of all journalists were considered to be employed in basic positions, with less than 10 percent in leadership positions. The number of *pigistes* among the new journalists increased between 1990 and 1998 in several media: the ''suppliers'' (photo and press and multimedia agencies), the regional television stations, and the general and specialized press. In all, one in five journalist works as a *pigiste*. There is a large proportion of *pigistes* among reporter photographers.

Overall, the average journalist today is older. Only 25 percent of journalists in 1998 were 25 and younger. The median age of journalists is 31 for men and 30 for women, with 21 percent of the new journalists being over 36 and 13.2 percent over 40, and into their second career. Men are slightly more numerous, with 51.9 percent, against 48.1 percent of women, yet they hold managerial and leadership positions in significantly larger numbers than women.

For journalists, the job market is diversified, highly competitive, and there is no sure career path owing to the changing nature of the profession. The three major sources of jobs are the specialized press for the public, the specialized technical and professional press, the daily regional press, which totaled 55.6 percent of the job market in 1998. Interestingly, the national daily press represented only 5.3 percent of the job market, in decline from 6.1 percent in 1990. Local radio stations, press agencies, and regional television stations were the next big employers, with 6 percent, 3.8 percent, and 3.6 percent respectively.

Two-thirds of all new card-holding journalists are employed in the Ile-de-France region, a number that remained steady in the 1990s, although it dropped a few percentage points to 63.7 percent in 1998. Besides Paris, three main regions attracted roughly five percent of new journalists each in 1998: Rhône-Provence, Provence-Alpes-Côte d'Azur, and Bretagne. The press offers 72.6 percent of the jobs, while radios and television stations hover around 10 percent of the market. Female journalists are more numerous in the specialized, public and specialized press, while men dominate the regional daily press, local and national radios, and local and national television stations. Women are more frequently administrative assistants, while men occupy two-thirds of the reporter-photographer jobs and almost all the jobs as photojournalists.

Employment and Wage Scales The average monthly salary of a journalist was FF 10,740 in 1998, with almost half of the journalists earning between FF 7,000 and 10,000. Salaries have not kept up with Cost of Living Allowances (COLA), thus lowering of the economic position of journalists. The majority of *pigistes* are paid below FF 7,000 a month. The lowest salaries are paid by local media, radio stations, and the suppliers (agencies). The generalist media has a large percent of regular low paid journalists and only 25 percent of its regular journalists earning salaries superior to FF 15,000.

At the level of a national daily, the pay scale varies from 1,562 Euros for an intern to 4,728 Euros for an editor-in-chief. A reporter could expect 2,612 Euros, and a photojournalist the same.

All journalists benefit from the protections granted by the Convention Collective, or Labor Contract, which includes social benefits such as paid vacation, thirteenth paid month, firing notice, indemnity of firing, unemployment benefits, medical, insurance and invalidity benefits, and pensions; as well as legal recourse in case of conflict with an employer. They also benefit from the 10 percent to 20 percent tax relief granted all taxpayers, as well as from tax deductions for professional expenses which could total up to 7,650 Euros in 2002. The state also reimburses 50 percent of the trade union membership fee.

Article L761 stipulates the conditions in which journalists receive severance pay, established an arbitration commission, and state that all work requested or accepted by a newspaper or periodical enterprise should be paid whether it is published or not. It contains provisions protecting the reproduction of articles and journalistic work. An employer-employee board established by this decree is in charge of establishing a list of newspaper or periodical enterprises who hire professional journalists, of establishing salary grids, and arbitrating disputes.

Major Labor Unions The first journalists' unions appeared in 1918 with the ''Journalist's Charter.'' Today there is a host of professional labor unions, which adapt to the many changes experienced by the profession. Among noted developments, journalists in 1991 joined the SCAM or Société Civile des Artistes Multimédia, thus joining forces with illustrators, audiovisual, radio and literature authors. Also, the European Federation of Journalists was created in France in 1952 as a branch of the International Journalists' Federation and represents more than 420,000 journalists (salaried and free-lance journalists) in more than 200 countries. It has consultant's status within the United Nations, UNESCO and WAN.

Industrial Relations: Copyright Laws and the Status of Journalists Copyright issues are complex issues that are the object of intense lobbying from journalists' associations. At issue since the 1885 Bern Convention that gave journalists ownership of their work is whether a newspaper is an collection of individual articles, or a collective work. In contrast with other European countries, France recognizes the moral right of journalists to own their work. The information revolution, by increasing both the reproduction of works and the danger of plagiarism, reopened a debate that is far from being concluded. A new issue is whether journalists or computer specialists retain editorial control of newspaper's Internet version. When *Le Monde* almost published an obituary of Communist Party Secretary George Marchais six months before his death, the world of journalism was alarmed.

Several newspapers have signed agreements with journalists' unions in anticipation of electronic developments, such as *Les Dernières Nouvelles d'Alsace* in 1995, after negotiations with the National Conciliation Commission of the Presse Quotidienne Régionale and a lawsuit, and *Le Monde* in 1997, for a two-year period. The DNA compromise gave collective property of the articles to the newspaper and paid journalists for internet and television use of their materials. Journalists retained their moral and financial rights, yet the newspaper could bear a heavy financial burden. *Le Monde* agreement recognized journalists as authors who were compensated for ceding their copyright. *Les Echos* favored a model in which the printed and electronic versions were treated as one, with journalists retaining rights for the reproduction of their articles under another form, such as a thematic dossier, or their reproduction by an external group that might censor or cut their prose and getting 5 percent and 25 percent of the proceeds, respectively. Journalists and publishers remained sharply opposed; the Havas-Vivendi directors, for example wanted journalists to renounce their copyrights. In June 1998 the Conseil d'Etat suggested to treat journalists' copyright as patents, but the problem of the extent of the newspaper's vs. the journalists' rights remains to be resolved.

In 1998, journalists organized a debate on the subject. The development of the free press in Italy and France not only created new competition but operated outside of the legal provisions of the National Labor Contract, thus prompting Italian and French journalists to create a joint coordination committee with the participation of both countries' main syndicates. USJ-CFDT also asked for a general debate about the treatment of information.

Syndicates also examined the statute of reporter-photographer whose situation is doubly precarious, owing to their status of photographers and *pigistes*. In January, 2002, with the prospect of new provisions about copyright by the Conseil Supérieur de la Propriété Littéraire et Artistique (CSPLA), the USJ-CFDT and SNJ-CGT joined forces with SCAM despite ideological differences in order to organize the defense of copyright. Editors and journalists are at odds on the subject, with lawsuits such as that of the audiovisual group Plurimedia. It appears that the CSPLA is lobbied by publishers to erode copyright. Since the tribunals have generally upheld journalists' rights, the publishers concentrate on changing the law while authors organize to devise collective contracts among multimedia, such as the ''Excelsior'' contract.

Cost, independence, and quality are three major issues, as is the statute of journalists. The creation of a new breed of ''cyberjournalists'' not covered by the legal statutes of the profession, the concentration of information, the marketing and budget pressures tending to reduce the quality of journalism, and threats to the freedom of information in the form of exclusive coverage or the control of visual information, have already raised the job insecurities. After the adoption of the 35-hour workweek, journalists pushed for a reduction to 32 hours. Citing a rising unemployment, the loss of job security, and the increasingly demanding nature of the workload, the USJ-CFDT, following the CFDT, asked for the creation of new jobs parallel to the reduction in the number of work hours.

Circulation Patterns The average price of a daily newspaper is higher than in Great Britain or Germany despite state subsidies: *Le Monde* sells for $1.25 FF while *The Times* sells for $0.30 FF. Once set at the same value as a domestic letter stamp, the price of a newspaper increased eightfold between 1970 and 1980 while the cost of living increased only four-fold. This is in part due to high distribution costs that represent 40 percent of the average sales price of the newspaper, the second highest distribution cost in Europe. Without state postal discounts and tax breaks, the price of newspapers would be even higher. Several provisions govern price and competition, especially the December 1, 1986 decrees. There is a 2.1 percent VAT on all printed media that does not apply to the internet version of newspapers and publications. In fact, European community law does not recognize electronic support as ''written press'' and electronic newspapers are thus considered data transmission, yet another non-negligible advantage.

In 1996, France exported 2,000 titles to 107 foreign countries, bringing in a turnover of $45 million FF. Approximately two thirds of sales occurred by subscription, with only one third in newsstands or libraries. The top five daily newspapers by circulation in 2000, according to *World Press Trends 2001*, were *Ouest France* with 785,000, *Le Parisien* combined with *Aujourd'hui* at 486,000, *Le Monde* selling 393,000, *L'Equipe* providing 398,000, and *Le Figaro* releasing 361,000.

PRESS LAWS

Constitutional Provisions and Guarantees Relating to the Media: Freedom of the Press Freedom of the press is one of the basic freedoms in France. It was written in the 1789 Declaration of the Rights of Man and the Citizen which established freedom of expression ''except in abusing this freedom in cases set forth by the law.'' France, which was thus one of the first countries in the world to guarantee freedom of expression, has made several exceptions to this guarantee, both in judicial decisions and legal decisions found in the Penal Code, the Code of Penal Procedure, the Code of Military Justice, the Law of 29 July, 1881, and circulars, notes, and decisions by France's supreme judicial authorities.

Summary of Press Laws in Force Press laws in force deal with the countless aspects of the media industry. There are laws for each aspect of the profession: publishers, journalists, distributors, and vendors. There are laws of the press and laws for the audiovisual industries, and now cyber laws. The main laws relating to the written press itself deal with the freedom of the press and editorial freedom, criminal offenses, collective labor contracts, copyright laws, and registration of newspapers and journalists. In addition to the laws there are scores of legislative acts providing for state regulation of the media. Those are subject to constant reorganization. In addition to national laws, France is subject to European Union laws and court decisions that have come into effect in the 1990s. The Law on the Information Society, for example, which was introduced in Parliament in June 2001, would be unthinkable outside of European Community law, especially in the areas of e-commerce, electronic signatures, and cyber criminality.

Registration and Licensing of Newspapers and Journalists Periodical publications with public circulation are subjected to strict laws. A newspaper must register with the Attorney General its intention to publish and its title, frequency of publication, name and address of the director of publication. To protect the publication's title, it must be registered with the INPI, or Institut National de la Propriété Intellectuelle. If the publication is destined for the youth, an additional declaration must be registered with the appropriate oversight committee at the Ministry of Justice. The basic Law of 29 July 1881 has been modified by the laws of 21 June 1943 and 31 December 1945, the law of 10 August 1981, a decree of 3 December 1981, a law of 27 August 1998 and a directive of 22 December 1998.

Journalists must obtain the Carte d'Identité des Journalistes Professionnels (CIJP), which is granted by a commission that was created by the Law of 29 March 1935. In 2000, the Commission delivered 32,738 such cards. Article L761-2 of the law indicates that the professional journalist is a person who ''has as his/her main, regular, and salaried occupation the exercise of his profession in one or more daily or periodical publications or in one or more press agencies, and who derives his/her main income from this work.'' Excluded from this definition are the publicity agents, although occasionally journalists may be paid for publicity work. An edict issued by the Minister of Information in October 1964 declares public relations officers and press attaches to be non-journalists. In May 1986, a statute by the State Council also excluded public servants from this definition.

In order to qualify one must have exercised or plan to exercise the profession of journalist for three consecutive months and derive more than 50 percent of one's income from it. Candidates to the CIJP must also specify which activity and which type of company they will work. The Law of 1935 created the Commission in Paris; in 1948 provisions were made to add regional correspondents.

Sunshine Laws, Shield Laws, Libel Laws, Laws against Blasphemy and Obscenity, Official Secrets Acts The basic text defining press crimes is the Press

Law of 29 July 1881. Limitations on freedom of speech include defamation, insults, offense and outrage, which are fairly broadly constructed. The Law of 1881 provided the possibility of criminal and civil action against journalists. Until the Law of June 15, 2000 the presumption of innocence and the victims' rights was reversed and the burden of proof was shifted from the accuser to the accused. The 1-year prison sentence for libel has now been abolished.

Specific cases of label are strictly regulated. The Law of 1881 punishes offenses toward public authorities, official bodies, and protected persons. This includes foreign heads of state as well as government officials and government bodies. The punishments were lessened by the law of June 15, 2000, and the right to free expression protects journalists in most cases. However, for publishing the picture of a handcuffed person without the person's approval, journalists can be fined 100,000 francs. Two laws of July 1972 and June 1990 forbid libel against persons and groups ''based on their origin, ethnic identity, race, or religion.'' The 1990 law forbids revisionism, i.e. denial of the Holocaust. In those two instances libel constitutes a press misdemeanor.

Litigation is secret as of Article 11 of the Criminal Procedure Code of 1957 which limits journalists' freedom of access to information. Revised by several circulars, most notably in 1985 and 1995, and by the Law of June 15, 2000, the law provides for exceptions, however. Public prosecutors may publish information, appeals and search notices necessary for the progress of legal proceedings, helping the accused's cause, or putting an end to the spreading of rumors and false truths. They may also correct erroneous and incomplete information about victims or make public certain elements of litigation in order to prevent false information from being published. Recently, journalists convicted before the French law have begun to take their case before the European Court of Human Rights to which France is subjected as a signatory of the European Convention of Human Rights. The ECHR does not support the secrecy of litigation. Overall, violations of Article 11 are fairly common, with journalists acting as the gadfly of a judicial system plagued by lengthy procedural delays, and with the European Community providing new guidelines. Few violations are ever punished.

The right of journalists to protect their sources has been recognized by French law since 1993, unless they abuse that right. Article 109 of the Criminal Code protects investigative reporters' journalistic sources. With recent terrorist threats, the issue of revealing information sources came anew. The Ministry of Justice in March, 2002 did not change those provisions in the wake of the new Law on Domestic Security that dealt with the war on terrorism. The official position is however that the criminal responsibility of journalists could be involved if not divulging their information sources endangered that source's life or security.

Finally a June 1998 law punishes pornography on telecommunication supports. This law is meant to protect children who are under age and is particularly severe for perpetrators of child pornography who establish contacts with their victims via a telecommunication means (Minitel or the Internet).

Cyber Communication and Copyright Online communication is protected by the September, 30 1986 law about freedom of communication. Electronic documents must be legally registered as of a law of June 1992, and illegal sites are subject to sanctions. Much French legislation in this domain is already harmonized with European legislation. The French government in the 1990s was an active participant in promoting international policies, especially in terms of uniform pricing, protection of intellectual property and authors' rights. The European Council in 1994 initiated the European Directive which created an internal market to regulate competition, protected intellectual property rights, the right to freedom of expression, and the right of general interest, and encouraged investments in creative and innovative projects. France adopted the European Directive on July 2, 1998; it protects original database content and support. A new copyright law is expected following France's adoption of the European Parliament and Council's May 2001 Resolution on Copyright.

France in November 2001 signed the International Convention on cyber criminality, which punishes copyright infractions. Cyber crimes benefit as of November 2000 of a decision of the Cour de Cassation providing for immediate litigation rather than the three-months delay granted to the printed press. Internet providers are not responsible for crimes committed by internet services except if they fail to prevent access to that service if the justice system notified them of the crime.

CENSORSHIP

Agency Concerned with Monitoring the Press Journalists and editors practice self-censorship by tradition, and because of the deterrent value of state subsidies and laws limiting the freedom of the press. Just as indirect government influence is a tradition, journalists walk a fine line when they write articles for *Le Canard Enchaîné* or skits for the television program *Les Guignols de l'Info*. In both instances they use the many registers of political caricature deftly so as to escape the accusation of libel, while providing needed distance toward reality as well as reaction against ''dominant conformism.'' A good indicator of the nature of censorship is the fact that the government has not been, nor does it plan to get involved in two major aspects of journalism: training/education and the discussion of journalistic ethics. French journalists have long been self-policing in the area of professional ethics. The professional code of journalists defines their role and responsibilities in a democratic society.

Case Studies Recent case studies show an uneven degree of tolerance for the press's behavior. In 2000, the Commission des Opérations de Bourse, which has investigative powers, conducted an investigation at the headquarters of *Le Figaro* while investigating a financial and economic scandal relating to the Carrefour-Promodes store. The journalists protested that this was a house search. In 2000 AFP was reprimanded by the government after selling prison pictures of Sid Ahmed Rezala to a newspaper. At issue was the fact that AFP had treated the picture as merchandise, not information. Publications by religious sects were not deemed subversive to the public order, and the government ruled in 2001 that transportation societies could not refuse to carry those publications to the press distributors.

The relationship between the press, power, and the judicial system in France is in a state of suspended animation. Political power can be heavy at times, such as in the presidential appointments of AFP directors. The 1975 appointment of Roger Bouzinac as AFP director provoked the resignation of Hubert Beuve-Méry who was AFP's chief administrator. Yet this practice continued in the 1980s and 1990s, signaling a political desire to control the main provider of information in France.

Relations between the press and the government became particularly tense under the second term of François Mitterrand, showing the degree of restraint of the press. After the suicide of prime minister Pierre Bérégovoy in 1993, the press asked itself whether journalists' revelations of apparently questionable financial dealings had not been responsible for his death. After President Mitterrand's death, the public learned that the press had known about his secret illness, cancer, long before disclosing it to the public, in a procedure reminiscent of the press's behavior during the last three years of President Pompidou's life, twenty years earlier. In 1997, the death of Princess Diana opened a debate about professional ethics, showing that some paparazzi's appetite for sensationalism may have contributed to the car accident that claimed her life and that of her companion Dodi Fayed.

The eruption of several political scandals in the 1990s (the Bernard Tapie, Alain Carignon, and Pierre Botton scandals) created a renewed demand for professional ethics. In May 1994, journalists formed an association to strengthen the professional ethics and denounce in particular the practice of the false ''Une'' (based on publicity rather than real news). Jean-Louis Prévost, CEO of the *Voix du Nord*, asked for a strengthening of investigative reporting and a better oversight of regional governmental accounting offices and tribunals. The public called for truth in information and voted with their purse: *Ouest-France*, *Le Télégramme de Brest*, and *Le Parisien* which improved their opinion and editorial policies, saw their circulation increase.

Composition of Press/Media Councils There are numerous governmental boards regulating the media in addition to the professional *paritaire* (employer-employee) boards which are under governmental oversight. There is no strong parliamentary oversight of the media. Governmental boards exist mostly to plan, give direction, and assist. This indicates a degree of cooperation between the public and private sectors that is a long tradition in France known as *étatisme* or *dirigisme*. The most important board is perhaps the *Commission Paritaire des Publications et Agences de Presse* whose statute was revised according to a decree of November 20, 1997 and whose function is to grant a registration number to publications and granting fiscal and postal tax exemptions. Next to it is the Commission de la Carte d'Identité des Journalistes Professionels (CCIJP) which grants the press card and the coveted journalist's status. Other boards such as the Conseil Supérieur de l'Audiovisuel or the Centre Français d'Exploitation du Droit de Copie deal with specific issues. The transportation and distribution enterprises are controlled and regulated by the Conseil Supérieur des Messageries de la Presse. Affiliated with the IFJ, the Union Syndicale des Journalistes CFDT has representatives in the main governmental and professional commissions dealing with journalism, journalistic training, ethical questions, granting of the press card, editorialists' rights, collective bargaining and arbitration commissions.

State Leadership in Promoting the Information Society The French government has taken an active role in promoting the information society and changing the educational, administrative, and communication cultures simultaneously within its own institutions and without. A flurry of decrees has been passed in the last few years, especially since the European Directive of July 2, 1998, that established the framework for the Information Society. The French government has actively defined and regulated the new technologies' uses, literary and artistic property (copyright), legal protection of databases, and e-commerce. While France provided active input on pricing, intellectual property and authors' rights, its legislation is inseparable from European Union legislation on those matters. Both the European Union and France are currently developing a plan for the new Information Society. Anticipating the European Directive in January 1998 an Interministerial Committee for the Information Society (CISI) was created to devise a governmental program to support and give direction to the development of the Information Society.

The Prime Minister's office is most important in shaping the Information Society. Several organizations dependent on his office coordinate this initiative which develops in consultation with European legislation. In November 2000 the Direction du Développement des Medias replaced an earlier committee charged with defining governmental politics toward the media and the services of the information society in order to assist the Prime Minister with drafting his decrees. The Foreign Affairs Ministry plays an important role as well as the Ministry of Education. While the former sees the development of new technologies of information and communications, or NTIC, as an opportunity to develop French presence abroad and to promote the use of French language, the latter's CLEMI or Centre de Liaison Enseignement et Moyens d'Information educates the public about the media, mostly internet. Once again, the media are seen as inseparable from education and democracy.

STATE-PRESS RELATIONS

Relations of the Press to Political Power While there is no Information Ministry in France, the relationship between political power and the media is complicated and symbiotic. In postwar France, the intervention of the state in the life of the media was qualified of "chronic illness." For one thing, there is an active revolving door policy. French politicians in the past often used the press as a political trampoline. The practice continued under the Fifth Republic. The National Assembly in 1997 counted some twenty deputies who had been journalists, nine of whom belonged to the Hersant Group which was built with the tacit approval of the authorities. This phenomenon was repeated in towns such as Saint-Etienne, Lyon, Vienne, and Dijon which had elected journalists in their midst. In 1997, the Director of France 3, the national television station, was former prefect Xavier Gouyou-Beauchamps, who was chief of the presidential press service between 1974 and 1976. In Dijon and Marseille, former rightist politicians were heading the regional television stations.

Other signs of this symbiotic relationship were a strong national monopoly at the expense of the freedom of television and radio coverage and regional coverage. This stemmed from General de Gaulle's desire to curb the regional notables' power, however, his policy failed. The only exception was Radio France, which introduced both pluralism and true local news. The 1982 law decentralizing the media further entrenched the power of notables, who now had no need to be accountable to anyone. While regional reporters have some autonomy, local reporters are often chosen by the local officials, especially the mayor's office. Local journalists are very dependent on local power and reluctant to engage in polemics, and thus less critical of the mayoral office in particular.

State Subsidies In 2001 direct subsidies totaled approximately 260 million francs, a 2 percent decrease over 2000 subsidies. The many forms and levels of subsidies form a complicated structure almost incomprehensible to the uninitiated eye, but they can be separated into direct and indirect subsidies. Among the main direct subsidies are subsidies for the national and regional dailies with low publicity revenues, transportation subsidies, subsidies for facsimile transmissions, subsidies for the expansion of the French press abroad, and subsidies for the multimedia. Since the Liberation, the government has subsidized the daily press, whether it is national or regional, departmental or local. In order to qualify a newspaper must limit its publicity revenues to 30 percent of its turnover. These provisions are updated regularly, two major updates taking place in 1986 for the national press, and in 1989 for the regional, departmental, and local press. New revisions in October 2000 benefited *L'Humanité* which had been penalized. The fund to promote the French press abroad was updated in February 1991 while on November 6, 1998 the fund for the transportation of the press was updated.

Among the indirect subsidies are subsidies for social expenses, professional membership fees, subsidies for postal transportation, preferential VAT treatment, cancellation of the professional and social contribution taxes, and a host of other measures. Those subsidies are voted yearly, with eligibility and other provisions being regularly revised. Thus reduced postal rates were last revised as per a decree of January 17, 1997.

The Finance Law of 1998 not only redirected those subsidies but created a modernization fund for the daily political and general press. In 1998-99, the amount of subsidies increased significantly, as seen in a Multimedia Development Fund offering of up to 305,000 Euros in 1999 to specific projects (or 30 percent of expenses), with a total allocation fund of 2.3 million Euros in 1999. As of 1999, approximately thirty newspapers had availed themselves of the fund, including *Le Figaro*, *FranceSoir*, *Le Nouvel Observateur*, *Phosphore*, *Le Télégramme de Brest*, and *La Charente Libre*. Other media sectors encouraged to go on line and use multimedia supports open to the public included the Institut National de l'Audiovisuel which stored television and radio programs; and radio and television programs, including RFO (Radio France Outremer) and the ensemble of the Radio-France stations broadcast online since 1999.

In the late 1990s, the French government created many subsidies for the new technologies. By a decree of February 5, 1999 the government further amended the provisions of the Ordinance of November 2, 1945 regarding the modernization of the press. Subsidies and loans were granted by an employer-employee Orientation Committee up to 40 percent of the expenses and 50 percent for collective projects, dealing with productivity increase, reduction of production costs, improvement and diversification of the reactionary format through the use of modern technologies (for acquiring, storing, and diffusing information), and reaching new categories of readers. A Control Commission was charged with overseeing the projects' execution. The RIAM (Réseau pour la Recherche et l'Innovation en Audiovisuel et Multimédia), launched in 2001, which coordinates the planning or research, or the Fonds Presse et Multimédia, created by the DDM in 1997 which purports to help increase public access to newspapers, magazines and journals on digital supports in both their on- and off-line formats.

Press distributors receive a graduated fee for their services as per a decree of February 9, 1988. In the late 1990s, given the increase in distribution costs, they were pressured to diminish their fees. The government, however, in 2000 refused to change a provision limiting a decrease of the fees to one percent for dailies and two percent for all other periodicals. In 2001, the fee was increased from 9.5 percent to 19.5 percent depending on the work conditions, in order to encourage the 15,000 of them. Provisions were also made to allow them to limit the bulk sent to them if supplies exceeded sales, and to help them computerize their sales transactions in order to better manage their business. Provisions were also made to continue the low rates of health insurance coverage of press distributors and local correspondents who have enjoyed them since 1993.

The AFP received in 2001 a 100 million FF governmental loan to help diversify its activities, services, and products. Stating that the clients are becoming more diversified, international and professional, and that their products will include photos, infography, and databases, the AFT foresaw a 2001 budget of 1.621 billion FF, with state subscriptions increasing by two percent for a total of 619 million FF. AFP is in full expansion, foreseeing a growth rate of seven percent between 2001 and 2004.

The government also took measures to help recycle old papers, of which the printed press makes a considerable amount, 2.65 million tons produced in 2000. An estimated 40 percent of that amount could be recycled, according to a study conducted in 2001.

ATTITUDE TOWARD FOREIGN MEDIA

Accreditation Procedures for Foreign Correspondents Foreign correspondents from countries outside the European Union whose stay in France exceeds three months must obtain residency permits from the French government and complete accreditation procedures with the Ministry of Foreign Affairs. If they cover presidential press conferences, they must join the presidential press association. The Foreign Affairs Ministry has created a site called CAPE or Centre d'Accueil de la Presse Etrangère to assist foreign journalists with short term missions, inform foreign correspondents and media of all conferences or programs by domestic or foreign personalities, and facilitate meetings of representatives of the foreign media.

There is no screening of cables or censorship of foreign media. Import of periodicals must get approval from the Ministry of Commerce. All major international press organizations are represented in France who voted against restrictions on newsgathering in support of the UNESCO Declaration of 1979. Distribution of foreign propaganda is strictly forbidden.

France is known for its support of human rights and freedoms. It extends this support to foreign journalists in any part of the world. Thus in the 1990s, the French press denounced the loss of freedom of the press in Islamic countries, in particular the Maghreb (Tunisia, in 1997), the expulsion of press correspondents, the closing of opposition newspapers, and noted the ouster in 1996 of the Tunisian Newspaper Directors' Association from WAN.

Foreign Newspapers in France There are a great number of foreign news publications in France, starting with the press services of foreign countries, of institutions such as the United Nations and the European Community, World Bank, and IMF. There are 45 offices representing German newspapers, radio and television stations, including a Paris representative of financial and economic newspapers such as the *Financial Times*-German edition, or *Tomorrow Business*, and a correspondent of RTL-TV-Deutschland. England has 17 foreign correspondents in France. Belgium has 10 correspondents, Spain 22, including a CNN representative, Italy 23, Poland 9, Russia 11, Switzerland 19, China 11, Japan 17, Vietnam 3, and the United States 32. All African countries together have 6 foreign correspondents, mostly from French-speaking countries (Ivory Coast, Gabon, Madagascar, Cameroon, and South Africa), and the main American TV stations such as CNN and CBS are broadcast in France.

France imports significant amounts of foreign newspapers. In 1995, the amount of press imports almost equaled the amount of press exports, in million dollars, 550 against 446. The issue foreign media access may soon be a moot point. Most Internet sites already give access to selected foreign media, while some sites such as

Courier International offer a world guide of the online press.

There are 33 international press and media professional organizations in France. Some are completely international, such as the World Association of Newspapers (WAN) while others are a partnership between France and another country (Russia, Japan, Poland). Some represent a region (Asia, Europe, Africa) while others are thematic (education television stations, environment), or regroup media genres (independent and local radio and television stations, audio-visual and telecommunications media), or professional categories (editors-in-chief, journalists). Some are sponsored by France, such as the Centre d'Accueil de la Presse Etrangère sponsored by Radio France, the CRPLF or Communauté des Radios Publiques de Langue Française, or Reporters Sans Frontières.

The *International Herald Tribune* is probably the most distinguished foreign newspaper in France. It is produced in Paris and printed in 24 press centers across the globe, mostly in Europe and Asia, by a total staff of 368, of which 56 are journalists. Since its beginning in 1887 as the *New York Herald Tribune,* it has engineered a series of journalistic and technological "firsts," none as spectacular as its successful transition from a traditional newspaper to a cross-media brand since 1978. These strategies paid off as IHT increased its circulation by 35% between 1996 and 2001, during which its sold 263,000 copies for a readership of more than 580,000 worldwide. The secret to its success lies in its ability to deliver world news in a concise format (24 pages), its commitment to excellence, and its independence. Owned jointly by the *Washington Post* and the *New York Times* since 1991, it was the first newspaper in the world to be transmitted electronically from Paris to Hong Kong in 1980, thus becoming available simultaneously to readers across the globe. It has also set up joint ventures with leading newspapers in Israel, Greece, Italy, South Korea, Japan, Lebanon, and Spain and publishes (in English) local inserts that contain domestic news. Calling itself the world's daily newspaper, it is perceived as the most credible publication by its upscale, mobile, international readership.

Small foreign newspapers are produced in France, such as *Ouzhou Ribao*, a Chinese language newspaper owned by the Taiwanese press group Lianhebao-United Daily News, which contains general information for Asia about Europe.

Foreign Ownership of Domestic Media Foreign ownership of domestic media or foreign partnerships in domestic media is a reality within the framework of the European Union. An example of foreign ownership of domestic media is *Les Echos*, owned by the British group Pearson. Olivier Fleurot, who directed the Les Echos group from 1995 to 1999, was named in 1999 general director of the *Financial Times*, which he planned to turn into the premier world financial and economic newspaper. The Italian press group Poligrafici Editoriale owns *France-Soir*. The Sygma photo agency founded in 1973 by Hubert Henrotte was bought in June 1999 by Corbis, which is owned by Bill Gates.

With the internationalization of the media in the Information Society, joint partnerships and transnational groups are bound to increase, thus blurring the distinction between foreign ownership and domestic media. The European Community has already made European television a reality with its European Convention on Transfrontier Television, which France accepted in 2002. The Arte television station is enjoying a great success in its two sponsoring countries, France and Germany, and is fast gaining a European audience. Internet groups are the most transnational thus far.

The Francophone Press and French Media Abroad
The French-speaking press has known a considerable increase in the 1990s, in great part around the Mediterranean rim. French-speaking media are diffused on all continents: in Belgium, Luxembourg, Switzerland, Canada, Quebec, Haiti, and Louisiana as well as in Lebanon, Algeria, Benin, Ivory Coast, Morocco, Niger, Senegal, Togo, Tunisia, and several other African countries.

RFO (Radio France Outremer) and the ensemble of the Radio-France stations broadcast online since 1999. Radio France International had broadcasts in French, English, Portuguese, Spanish, and Chinese every 30 minutes in addition to daily and weekly press reviews in French, English, Spanish, and German. TV5, an international television station, broadcasts on all continents; its online version features useful and local information. The television organization TVFI was charged with promoting French television programs abroad and was charged by the Foreign Affairs Ministry to offer online program offers, a repertory of French production associations, and in general to promote French programs. To further Francophone programs, the Ministry of Foreign Affairs offered a Fonds Sud Télévision to help public and private television stations in "priority solidarity zones" including sub-Saharan Africa in 2002.

All the initiatives taken by CISI have tended to develop online initiatives while putting information and communication technologies at the service of the promotion of the French language. Again, education, culture, and media are inseparable in this perspective. In addition, the educational Réseau Théophraste encourages and finances projects that develop both the media and francophonie.

NEWS AGENCIES

The Agence France Presse remains one of the main French news agencies. Founded in 1835 by Charles-Louis Havas, it was the first world news agency. In 1852, a publicity branch was created. In 1940, the publicity and information branches separated and the Office Français d'Information was born. In 1944, journalists who had participated in the Resistance rebaptized the agency AFP and gave it a new statute. In 2000 a bill was introduced in the Senate to modify this statute, but it did not pass. From the mid-1980s to the mid-1990s, important changes took place: creation in 1984 of an audio service, creation in 1985 of regional production and diffusion centers in Hong Kong, Nicosia and Washington, and creation of the international photo service, enlargement of the Nicosia regional center in 1987, where the Cairo desk was transferred, launch of an English financial news service, AFX, in 1991.

New technologies were not forgotten. In 1986, AFP started beaming news via satellites, in 1988 it created its computer graphics system, and by 1993 it was completely digitized. It opened its web page in 1995, followed by the first internet newspaper in French in 1996 and a script of televised news to the Bloomberg company. In the late 1990s, more international initiatives followed with the opening of a Spanish language desk in Montevideo in 1997 and the launching of English, Spanish, and Portuguese internet newspapers in 1999. In 2000, it launched an interactive newspaper (text and photos) on a TV frequency, expanding this service to a multimedia newspaper in Chinese with the CNA Agency of Taiwan. In 2001 it launched a video production service for the web and launched an Italian version, RITA. In 2002, its sports pictures were available to Japanese mobile phone users.

It has currently offices in 165 countries, 2000 staff members belonging to 81 nationalities, of whom 1200 are journalists and 200 photographers, while 900 live abroad. In addition AFP has 2000 free-lancers on five continents. Its main offices are organized in five regional zones: North America (Washington, D.C., 9 desks), Latin America (Montevideo, 22 desks), Asia-Pacific (Hong Kong, 25 desks), Europe-Africa (Paris, 36 desks in Europe, 16 desks in Africa), and Middle East (Nicosia, 9 desks). Its subsidiaries include financial, companies, and stock exchange news services, and German language news and sports services.

It sends 2 million words a day in six languages (French, English, Spanish, German, Arabic, and Portuguese) every day of the year, 24 hours a day, and 70,000 photos a year. Its clients include 650 newspapers, 400 radio and television stations, 1,500 administrations and companies, and 100 national press agencies. It touches directly or indirectly 3 billion people and informs 10,000 media.

Threatened by a deficit in 2001, the AFP saw the resignation of its CEO Eric Giuily after the government refused to support its five-year plan of massive and rapid investment in modernizing the agency. The 1957 statute of the agency, which mandates a balanced budget and forbids loans and capital increases, prohibits the AFP from borrowing money if it wants to grow. The 1957 statute has come under scrutiny, trying to balance financial growth with the protection of independence and objectivity. The AFP indeed lost its traditional market in the 1990s when the written press declined; while gaining new clients, especially on the international market, it did not make enough profits to finance such modernization into the digital age. The AFP proposed industrial partnerships in order to gain the capital and technology necessary to produce sound and animated pictures. Despite difficulties, the AFP has moved into the multimedia age beginning in 1997, with a rapid intensification in 1999-2000. It also diversified its services by adding financial news and sport news for its Asian market, and plans future diversification.

Smaller press agencies coexist with AFP. The Agence de Presse Editoriale is located in Marseille and specializes in the South of France. In general there has been a development of the French press in the Mediterranean, including in foreign countries such as Morocco and Lebanon. One of the reasons for this interest lies in that La Cote Bleue is devoted to stock market news. Several specialized agencies were created after 1945: Agra Presse (1949), Agence Presse Service, Société Générale de Presse, Agence Libération founded in 1971 by Jean-Paul Sartre and Maurice Clavel, Agence Générale d'Informations which in 1980 succeeded to the Agence Aigles which was founded in 1968.The newest one seems to be the Agence Centrale de Presse-Communication, which was founded in 1990.

Photographic agencies include the Agence Générale d'Images, Gamma, Magnum Photo, Sipa Press, Sygma, AFP Photo, all founded after World War II. Keystone—L'Illustration is one of the oldest one, founded in 1923.

Major Journalistic Associations and Organizations France, with her tradition of lively trade unionism, has several associations that represent the press and the journalists. In all there are 25 press syndicates in France, some more specialized than others, such as the SRGP or Syndicat des Radios Généralistes Privées, the Association des Radios Juives, the FFRC or Fédération Française des Radios Chrétiennes, or the Syndicat de la Presse Judiciaire de Province. Some syndicates such as the FPPR regroup several smaller syndicates. The FNPS is an umbrella organization for seven smaller specialized syndicates.

The most important is the FNPF or Fédération Nationale de la Presse Française, which regroups six press syndicates, the FNPS, or Fédération Nationale de la Presse d'Information Spécialisée, the FPPR, or Fédération de la Presse Périodique Régionale, the SPP or Syndicat de la Presse Parisienne, the SPPMO, or Syndicat Professional de la Presse Magazine et d'Opinion, the SPQD, of Syndicat de la Presse Quotidienne Départementale, and the SPQR, or Syndicat de la Presse Quotidienne Régionale, which represent the press with the largest circulation. The FNPF insures the study of problems related to the profession, the coordination of programs of action devoted to the study of specific problems or the defense of specific interests. It also represents collective interests of the profession in lawsuits and participates in the resolution of individual or collective work conflicts, including conciliation and arbitration. Finally, the FNPF represents the profession to the government, and para-governmental and inter-professional organizations. Examples of such cooperation include the CFC, or Centre Français d'Exploitation du Droit de Copie, the CCIJP which grants the professional journalist card, the Conseil d'Etat which rules on professional matters and governmental services dealing with information and communication technology, the FFAP or Fédération Française des Agences de Presse, and the SNE or Syndicat National de l'Edition. There is an association of press distributors called the UNDP (Union Nationale des Diffuseurs de Presse). The e-press has an association to promote the sale of e-press, Viapresse.

The same diversity is reflected in the journalists' syndicates which number over 40, some with broad missions such as the SNJ or Syndicat National des Journalistes, or the SGDL or Société des Gens de Lettres, while others are specialized either by political, religious, or professional category. The SNJ was created during World War I, in March, 1918 as an independent syndicate wanting to create for journalists a moral role equivalent to that of the Conseil de l'Ordre for lawyers. Its Charter was revised until it was finalized in 1938. Between 1920 and 1935, the SNJ fought for the recognition of the statute of journalists, which resulted in the Guernut-Brachard Law of March, 1935, followed by the creation of the Commission de la carte, the first salary grids, the first labor collective contract in 1937. The strikes of 1947 saw the syndicate fragment into smaller, political factions, while in 1948 the SNJ remained independent. Refusing to take sides during the Cold War, the SNJ remained isolated from the international federations of journalists, yet it continued to play a prominent role within the UNSJ or Union Nationale des Syndicats de Journalistes Français. In 1981 it regrouped ten autonomous organizations from different professional sectors within the ''Groupe des dix.'' Its generalism sets it apart from other syndicates regrouped around the two main labor syndicates, the CGT and CFTC.

The Union Syndicale des Journalistes CFDT, which was created in 1992, gives journalists a common structure. It claims dedication to the proper professional training of journalists. A more recent group is the Association des Journalistes Professionnels des Technologies de l'Information (AJPTI) regrouping internet, multimedia, and computer journalists. Internet services providers and users also have their associations, such as the aptly named Association of Internet Service Providers AFA, the Grouping of on-line service editors (GESTE), created in 1987, and the On-line Trade and Services Associations, created in 1980. Many associations have joined their European counterpart. AFA is a member of EuroISPA, the European Federation of Internet Access and Service Providers.

Another important category of association is those dedicated to the study and information about the media. Some such as Diffusion Contrôle and CESP (Centre d'Etude des Supports de Publicité) keep track of circulation, distribution, and numbers of publication of all ''publicity supports.'' They are often called to arbiter and testify when references are needed or in case of conflict. The Argus de la Presse which numbers over 11,000 clients, and has been in existence for 120 years, specializes in information databases and synthesis, analyzing trends, products, and competition in the written press, the multimedia, the web, and creates databases about journalists. The measurement of multimedia audience has become a flourishing industry. There are 21 such associations, including IFOP, SOFRES and IPSOS, ''general opinion analysis'' firms which have departments dedicated to the study of the media. The Institut National de l'Audiovisuel or INA, occupies a special place. For over 20 years it has archived French television programs, calling itself ''the memory of the future.'' It has opened research facilities to the public and offers multimedia support such as Vidéoscribe, a system making possible the analysis of programs frame by frame.

Among the professional organizations one must mention the advertisement societies that deal with all aspects of advertisement, from announcer's syndicates to museums to verifying publicity. They are: The Association des Agences Conseils en communication (AACC), the Bureau de Vérification de la Publicité, the Musée de la Publicité, Presspace, Union des Annonceurs, and Syndicat National de la Publicité Télévisée. Also, distributors' organizations abound, from Francepresse to the ''Messageries'' in both Paris and Lyon, and the Union National des Diffuseurs de Presse (UNDP). The cable and satellite operators have also formed associations. In all there are 13 of them, including the distributors of ''satellite bouquets'' regrouping several programs, and offering interactive programs. Four of those are cable operators associations, operate mostly for specific localities and public service.

With 375 million people in the 15 European member countries of the EU, and the prospect of six new countries and 60 million more people, understanding European news is paramount. The European Federation of Journalists, a branch of the IFJ created in 1974, is currently working on several issues, of copyright, sources' disclosure, editorial democracy and independence, media convergence, and access to information. All these tend to support journalists' rights, freedom of access to information, and editorial independence, in an effort to promote democracy. The EFJ, also created in 2000 an expert group on collective bargaining to draft a model contract on working conditions. *Europ Magazine* is the electronic publication of the EFJ, and gives news about Europe, and provides links to all activities and publications of European journalists. EFJ trains world journalists to European affairs and institutions. EFJ also calls for professional regulation, rather than European Community law, of the issue of cyberjournalists' handling of financial information.

Reporters sans Frontières supports journalistic freedoms worldwide, informs on the condition of imprisoned journalists, denounces abuses against the press, informs on new law initiatives, and features links to new publications the profession and the news, and supports professional charters. Thus it promoted a Charter on the security of journalists in battle zones or conflict areas. It tracks the fate of French journalists detained, harassed, or imprisoned abroad and publishes a yearly report on the liberty of the press worldwide. In 1992 RSF organized the first International Day of the Freedom of the Press. Held on May 3rd, it has been recognized in 1994 by the United Nations as an official day. RSF also does not believes in restricting freedom of expression on the internet, a libertarian position that it uses to fight censorship worldwide.

BROADCAST MEDIA

In 1997 French people spent only 30 minutes reading the newspaper, against 3 hours 20 minutes watching TV. The French press lost readers during the 1990s mostly to television reruns.

State Policies Relating to Radio and TV News Until 1982, radio and television stations were under a state monopoly. Radio and television remained under state control with the RTF, or Radio et Télévision Française office, which was reorganized in 1959 and in 1964 became ORTF. In 1965, the popular suffrage election of the president of the republic opened television to presidential candidates for debates. In 1974 ORTF was replaced by seven national societies: four program societies, TF1, Antenne 2, FR3, and Radio France; one production society the SFP (Societé Française de Production) and one technical and distribution society TDF (Télédiffusion de France), with the seventh being the archives and research institute INA. This restructuring caused clashes between syndicates and management in the fall of 1974.

In July 1982, state monopolies of radio and television ended, giving birth to eighteen private radio stations. The Loi Fillioux of 29 July, 1982 guaranteed the independence of the communication media from political power, and placed all television and radio networks with the exception of the Franco-German channel Arte, under the authority of an independent regulatory agency renamed Conseil Supérieur de l'Audiovisuel (CSA) after 1989. In 1989 the Loi Tasca encouraged the development of public television stations.

Current State of Radio and Television Stations Some 250 French and foreign channels are accessible by cable and satellite. Among those, Eurosport, MCM for music programs, and LCI (La Chaine Info), the first continuous news network which was started in June 1994. It broadcasts a news program every 30 minutes along with debates, interviews, or continuous coverage when needed. Digital TV started in 1996 and reached one million subscribers within two years. A new tendency is to regroup several networks into a ''bouquet'' of programs. Canal Satellite, owned by Canal Plus, offers 750,000 viewers a 9-network deal, starting in 1998. Other such networks include TPS (created around TF1, France Télévision M6 and the CLT), AB Sat, and others that offer pay-per-view programs.

There are 16 national radio stations, 2 national radio stations aimed at international broadcasts, 25 local radio stations, and five car/traffic/circulation radio stations. In addition, there are 18 theme radios, mostly with ethnic, religious or cultural specializations. Nine television and radio stations also broadcast on the internet.

Radio France in April-June, 2002 controlled 27.6 percent of the market with 505 thousand program hours, including 250 thousand hours of original programs and 250 thousand hours of network broadcasting, with only 5 thousand hours of rebroadcast. It employed 4,020 personnel of whom 595 were journalists and 1,500 *pigistes*. It featured 7 stations: France Inter, France Info, France Culture, France Musiques, France BLEU, Le Mouv' and FIP and had a budget of 486 million Euros. Radio France broadcast 24 hours a day every day, and had 139 studios, 61 in the ORTF location in Paris, 73 in local radio stations, and 5 at FIP. In addition to these activities, Radio

France was devoted to help orchestras and choirs such as the Orchestre National de France, l'Orchestre Philharmonique, and the Maitrise de Radio France.

This growth was achieved mostly between 1982 and 1992. By 1992, there were more than 30 television channels. The public stations remain favorites for the 8 p.m. news broadcasts on TF1 and France 2, which have been called ''national rendez-vous.'' A certain number of specialized channels offer pay-per-view programs in sports, music, concerts, or film. There are approximately 20 cable channels and seven Hertz-diffused channels. Four of these are public stations financed by a tax of $122 FF in 1998, by state subsidies, and by publicity (France 2, France 3, Arte, and La Cinquième). Three stations are private. TF1 and M6 are financed by private stockholders and publicity; Canal Plus is a pay-per-view channel that has advertisement revenues. In 1992, France 2 and France 3 were grouped as France Télévision, in order to insure their coherence and ability to compliment each other. France 2 has more of a national, general profile. It informs, entertains, and educates, and has 25 percent of the market. France 3 has a national and regional vocation, broadcasting regional and local news several times a day. France 3 has close to 20 percent of the market.

Arte was created following the Franco-German Treaty of 1990. It broadcasts cultural programs, debates, and reporting between 7 pm and 3 am. The Belgian Radio-Télévision has joined it, and it has a public of 27 million regular viewers in Europe. La Cinquième was created in December 1994. It is the first educational channel devoted to knowledge, formation, and employment. It shares its channel with Arts and broadcasts between 6 a.m. and 7 p.m.

TF1 was privatized in 1987 and enjoys 35 percent of the market. Its reputation, history and expertise, combined with its long-standing monopoly, its popular tone, made it the first French television station. It broadcasts games, sport, varieties, and popular films. It controls 55 percent of the television publicity receipts and is controlled by the BTP Bouygues group, in association with Bolloré. M6, owned jointly by the Compagnie Luxembourgeoise de télédiffusion and the Lyonnaise des Eaux-Dumez, broadcasts fiction and music. Half of its public are less than 35 years of age.

Created in 1984, the pay-per-view Canal Plus is the oldest of the private chains. It is pay-per-view with an encryption. It has been the biggest success of the television industry with a budget of $2.25 billion FF in 1997 and a tendency to export its formula to Spain, Belgium, and Poland. It banks on films and sport, and a famous series ''Les guignols de l'info,'' a parody of sports, political, and artistic leaders by puppets. Canal Plus is controlled today by Vivendi which uses it for the audio-visual activities, Havas for its editing, multimedia and publicity activities, and Cegetel for the telecommunication industries. In general, French television stations are very supportive of the movie industry by pre-buying and co-producing movies. In 1996, Canal Plus pre-bought $100.6 million FF worth of films and co-produced 22 movies. TF1 and France 2 did the same.

Reform of the Audiovisual System The Loi Trautmann was passed in 2000 by the National Assembly. In the works for 2 years, this law aimed at strengthening the pluralism of cultural and social identities, public service, and the INA. It opposed privatization, increased subsidies, and curbed publicity on television, which had increased from 2 minutes a day in 1968 to12 minutes per hour in 1998. By creating a group of public television and radio stations with independent regulatory mechanisms, the government recognized the need to maximize their industrial potential. The law contained guarantees of pluralism of creation as well and reinforced the role of CSA against a greater concentration of multinational communication groups. Existing television stations were given two years to adopt a digital production system. The new public television holding France Télévision (France 2, France 3, La Cinquième), got 9 channels. Each private TV station got 5 channels. New groups, such as Pathé and Lagardère, were created, as well as associative non-profit televisions. By the time that the law is fully implemented, there should be in all approximately 50 channels, 10 for France Television, 15 for TF1 Canal+ and M6, and ten for the new televisions.

ELECTRONIC NEWS MEDIA

Development of Internet France, which had seemed frozen in the monopolistic digital technology known as Minitel, quickly overcame a technology gap at the end of the 1990s. In December 2001, 30 percent of French households were connected to the internet, below the 38 percent European average, yet showing a 3-4 percent monthly growth since March, 2001, i.e. the fastest growth rate in Europe. In April, 2001, 32 percent of Frenchmen declared logging on regularly, i.e. close to 16 million internet users. Of those, 40 percent access it at work, and 14 percent enjoy a fast connection. 44 percent log on every day, 38 percent two or three times a week, and 17 percent once a week. The search engines accounted in March, 2002 for 27.5 percent of all internet hits, with Google garnering over 45 percent of the search engine hits. 25 percent of French people reported using the Internet regularly in April, 2002. Approximately one third of internet users age 11 and older use the internet to download files.

Among the important issues are the relationships between e-version and print departments. As of 2002 the former were separate but not autonomous from the latter, although web newspapers editors are already thinking about gaining their autonomy. Radio and television had a difficult time finding the right medium and format, thus they were slower to adopt the Internet.

The nature of e-media's support and content leads each medium to attempt to be all media, such as Web-TV, and each medium wants to say it all, leading to the repetition of content among the mediums. Furthermore, this desire has also provoked radical changes in the appearance of online newspapers and TV screens which now begin to resemble each other with "boxes" and scrolled news briefs at the bottom. By updating information regularly, both television and e-newspapers are in danger of losing depth of coverage and analysis.

Newspapers that exist strictly online are growing. A number of sites such as *AdmiNet* offer electronic press clippings and feature sophisticated search engines. The oldest online newspaper is perhaps *Fil Info* which was created in 1982 as an independent information newspaper. *ActualInfo*, *ZDNet France*, *Le Journal du Net*, or *Virtual Baguette*, are e-newspapers too. Other sites, which are halfway news services and halfway encyclopedias, are organized thematically, such as the *Encyclopédie Quid.* Having forged partnerships with AFP, foreign internet access providers and publishers, it has developed local branches. It offers a membership package, feature articles from AFP with links to related topics, and a series of news arranged topically. "Last minute" developments, polls, a guide of web news sites, and an almanac-type link complete this newspaper of the twenty-first century, conceived to entertain readers who spend less and less time reading the news. *Actu-media* offers news about the media and society, sports and the arts. *Imaginet*, created in 1995, merged in 1998 with the pan-European access group COLT-Telecom which is devoted to business. *L'Argus de la Presse* is a paid service sending French and foreign press, radio, television, and web excerpts to clients, as well as serving as a database about journalists and information. Finally, a guide to the best sites of the online press, *Presse On Line*, features a search engine of 819 newspapers and over 3,000 links to the French-language press worldwide. It is organized topically, from general to local and regional newspapers, sciences, sport, ads, education, leisure, and more. *La Presse Locale sur Internet*, *PresseRadioTv.com*, and *Annuaire Fraggo!.com* are search engines to various online newspaper, radio, and television stations. *Annuaire Fraggo.com* gives links to 2,480 sites and 173 web categories. Some of those sites publish in several languages, while others give a repertory of all French-language resources. All have an international dimension, in particular *Courrier International* which features a link to *Kiosque en Ligne*, a world guide of online press.

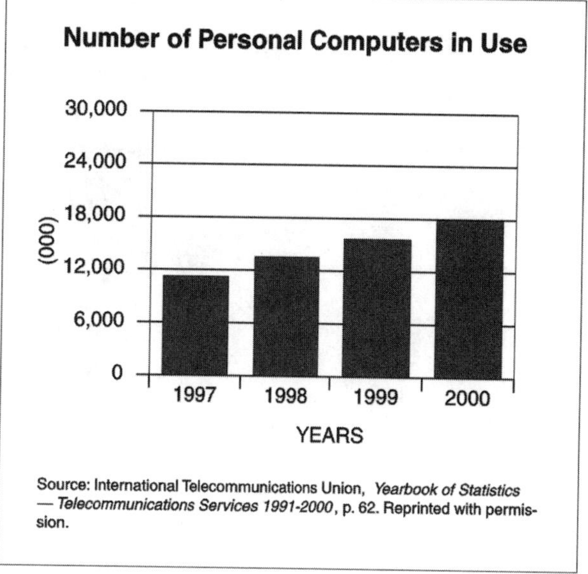

Source: International Telecommunications Union, *Yearbook of Statistics — Telecommunications Services 1991-2000*, p. 62. Reprinted with permission.

With the new interactive possibilities offered by Internet, studies about the role of publicity, the type of audience, and statistics of all kinds have become essential to the survival of the electronic news media. Sites devoted to those studies have increased exponentially. Another fast developing trend is the personalized site, made possible by the ability of online publishers to track the tastes and occupations of their audience. Of course, all online newspapers are interactive and offer chat rooms, which gives them feedback about their product and the readers' tastes. Many invite readers to submit articles for publication. Many newspapers are hiring a mediator or ethics and professional watchdog who also arbitrates in case of a disagreement between readers and editors.

Online competition comes not only from France but from French-speaking countries as well. The Swiss magazine *Webdo* was launched in September 1995, from the weekly *L'Hebdo*. It quickly developed into an interactive, original site that borrowed little from the printed version. Now among the top five percent of the world internet sites and the recipient of several prizes, it is recognized as one of the best francophone e-media sites.

Radio and TV Online The main radio and television stations now have online sites. Radio Télévision Française RFO (Radio France Outremer) and the ensemble of the Radio-France stations broadcast online since 1999. France Télévision regroups 8 public channels' internet sites, while Arte, La Cinquième, France 2 and France 3 all have online editions. Other television channels include Canal J, M6, and LCI. Online radios include BFM, Fun Radio, NRJ, RTL, Europe 1, Europe 2.

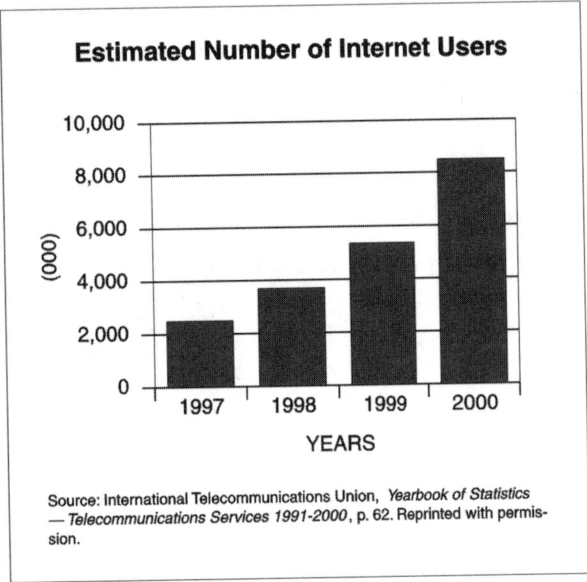

Source: International Telecommunications Union, *Yearbook of Statistics — Telecommunications Services 1991-2000*, p. 62. Reprinted with permission.

EDUCATION & TRAINING

The professional training of journalists is improving, but today still more than two thirds of all journalists have no professional degrees. In 1998, the proportion of journalists having completed formal professional schooling at a school of journalism remained at a low 22.9 percent, with roughly one third of them from non-accredited schools. Another 25 percent of journalists declared having had one or more short-term training experience in either journalism or information-communication, which deals more with the technical training aspects, half of them in settings specialized in journalistic teaching.

Of the journalists having received a formal education, in 1998 one-third received training at university schools of journalism, while 18.3 percent had a diploma in literature or foreign languages, 16.1 percent in the humanities and social sciences, 14.1 percent in law and political science, 10.4 percent in economics and business, and 13.2 percent in science, technology, or health science.

Women journalists have more years of formal training than men, averaging over 3 years of post-secondary studies consistently throughout the 1990s vs. between 2 and 2.5 years of post-secondary studies for men, reflecting a general trend in France.

An incentive for students to complete professional training is a recent provision in the national labor contract, which reduces the number of years of apprenticeship for journalism graduates to one year. Another result of this increased competition is an increase the quality of the news, together with a decrease in job security.

Review of Education in Journalism: Degrees Granted Most schools and programs of journalism are post World War II creations, except for the École Supérieure de Journalisme de Lille, a private institution attached to the Catholic University of Lille, which was created in 1924 as the first European school of its kind. In 1945, the Agence France Presse acting as a national journalism school for young journalists and the 1946 Centre de Formation des Journalistes remained the main training organizations until student demand for the democratization of education in the 1960s led to the creation of several programs, especially in the IUTs or Instituts Universitaires de Technologie. Most programs offer a 1-3 year program depending on specialization, and admission to some is granted upon successful completion of an entrance examination, such as for the CFPJ. The IUTs offer a two-year program, which is reduced to one year if the student has other university diplomas, and programs of study can also be completed as continuing education. Several schools are accredited by a *commission paritaire* composed of an equal number of representatives of employers and employees. Journalism professors are often trained journalists taking a leave from their professional obligations.

Schools of journalism are constantly redefining their curriculum, keeping up with the changing nature of the profession. The Institut Pratique de Journalisme, for example, which opened in 1978, created a department of permanent continuous training in 1981. It was recognized by the collective labor convention of journalists in 1991, joined the European Association of Journalistic Training, and became accredited in 1993. Furthermore, it has developed international educational partnerships with the Théophraste network of Francophone centers of journalistic training in 1997, and a legal education partnership with the IEP of Rennes' law and management program in 1999. Its graduates are employed by the press, radio, television, press agencies, online services, and in businesses. Most recently, with the adoption of the 35-hour work week, and budgetary crunches, it became more difficult for journalists to take time off for seminars, and IPJ started to program the dates and content of its seminars after consultation with press managers, rather than to making its schedules flexible.

The major journalism schools are the Centre de Formation des Journalistes (Paris); École de Journalisme de Toulouse; École Supérieure de Journalisme (Paris); École Supérieure de Journalisme de Lille; Institut Pratique de Journalisme (Paris); Nouvelles-L'École du Journalisme (Nice); Sciences Po-Institut d'Etudes Politiques de Paris; Institut Français de Presse (Paris); Centre de Liaison de l'Enseignement et des Moyens d'Information; Centre de Formation et de Perfectionnement des Journalistes; and Mediafor.

Several universities have schools of journalism (CELSA - Paris IV, Centre Universitaire d'Enseignement du Journalisme - Strasbourg III, Université de la Méditerranée U-II in Marseille, Paris II - Panthéon Assas, IUT of Tours and Bordeaux). In general, practical training and experience are seen as a necessary ingredient of formal training. CELSA, for example, offers continuous learning seminars along with its regular programs. To enroll in a MA program, the prospective student must have a BA, 26 years of age minimum, and 3 years professional experience. To enroll in a doctoral program, the prospective candidate must have a MA, 26 years of age minimum, and three years professional experience. The programs at CELSA range from communication to media and multimedia technology, marketing, human resources management, and institutional communication.

France, its syndicates, and the European Union recognize that continuous learning is an important part of a journalist's training. INA or Institut National de l'Audiovisuel organizes seminars on top of its regular instruction. The Centre de Formation et de Perfectionnement des Journalistes or CFPJ, labeling itself the premier center for training and perfecting journalists and press managers, holds summer workshops in addition to its regular programs, to which it admits approximately 100 students a year. Several professional associations labeled that organize summer university programs, festivals, and congresses and conferences. These sort of open forums promote discussion and exchange of ideas in a format favored by French tradition. It is important to note also that all continuous learning seminars stress professional issues and ethics as an integral part of journalistic training, and that they emphasize the theory (or philosophy) of the profession as well as its technical aspects.

Online journalists receive a formation that is part technology, part journalism. Not only French schools of journalism, but the European Community and the International Federation of Journalists have taken initiatives to address both aspects of the training. In 1992, IFJ, European Broadcasting Union, and WAN started the Medium Term Training Program aimed at training media professionals (journalists, editors, managers of press and radio-television enterprises). For the past ten years, seminars and workshops have discussed issues such as access to information, the defense of journalists' freedoms, libel, defamation, the right of respect for privacy, as well as the functioning of the media. IFJ submitted in May, 2002 a Digit Press Net Expertise to the European Commission to create a virtual campus for journalists in the framework of the Leonardo da Vinci program. All those programs are meant to increase access and pluralism in the information society.

Journalistic Awards and Prizes The Société Civile des Auteurs Multimédia or SCAM awards an impressive number of prizes for all media: photography, television and radio programs, new technologies, institutional or enterprises' work, and literary prizes. Of the journalistic prizes, the most prestigious is the Prix Albert Londres. Created in 1933 by the prematurely deceased journalist's daughter, the prize rewards the best press reporter. A second prize was created in 1985 for best audio-visual reporter.

Reflecting the internationalization of the media are two relatively recent prizes. The Prix Franco-Allemand du Journalisme rewards the best production in three categories (television, radio, written press) dealing with a topic that favors rapprochement and understanding between the two countries. Similarly, the Prix Robert Guillain awarded by the France-Japan Press Association, the Japanese Embassy in France, and other associations and businesses, rewards the best article or reporting by young journalists or journalism students about Japan. Created in 1996 and named after a long-time distinguished reporter to Japan, Robert Guillain, it carries a travel award to Japan as well as a monetary reward of 1,530 Euros. Its first recipient was *Les Echos* editor-in-chief Charles de Laubier.

Festivals also award prizes, such as the Festival International du Scoop et du Journalisme d'Angers. Others are awarded by businesses or foundations, such as Prix Crédit Lyonnais, Prix de la Fondation Mumm, Prix Georges Bendrihem. Schools of journalism also award prizes to their students, such as the Jeune Reporter Prize awarded by the INA.

Other prizes stressing an international aspect of the profession are the Prix Raymond-Charette which is awarded by the Conseil de la Langue Française to a press journalist for his/her best contribution to the French language in Quebec, while the RFI/RSF competition called "Premio RFI-Reporteros sin Fronteras" rewards the best journalistic talent in a Spanish-speaking country in order to promote their talent internationally. RSF organized in 1992 the "Reporters Sans Frontières—Fondation de France" prize rewarding a journalist who best defended freedom of information. The prize carries a monetary reward of 7,600 Euros and has been awarded every year to a foreign journalist.

SUMMARY

During the last twenty years, the French press was challenged in many ways, first through the generally depressed economic climate, then, in the 1990s, by the information revolution. A pioneer of digital communication in the 1980s with Minitel, France saw the privileged position occupied by the printed press evaporate as it struggled to make room for the new technologies. In this fast changing situation, few established national newspapers retained a position of privilege, some surviving only at the cost of major restructuring. Journalists struggled with an increasingly competitive market and a redefinition of their competencies, roles, and status. Uniformity threatened news content. Technology threatened to take over. Major ethical questions about the quality of the press and its role as guardian of democracy and pluralism emerged amidst political and financial scandals which prompted an ongoing and public philosophical debate about professional conduct and the defense of democracy, pluralism, and freedom of the press. Also, a major challenge to the French regulatory and subsidy model arose with European legislation. Despite those challenges the profession of journalist remained in constant expansion.

SIGNIFICANT DATES

- 1996: WAN Treaty on Copyright
- 1997: Creation of internet users' group IRIS (Imaginons un Réseau Internet Solidaire). *Le Monde* signs an agreement with journalists' unions about copyright. New tax dispositions grant the press bulk mailing rates. Revision of 1996 decree granting subsidies to several publications with low publicity and ad revenues. European Union begins to study dispositions of the Information Society. Directive of the European Parliament and of the Council regulating the creation of a single internal postal market for the EU.
- 1998: Creation of the first statistics about the media. Lowering of telecommunications rates in Europe. Finance Law creates a modernization fund for the daily political and general press. Prime Minister creates CISI (Comité d'Information sur la Société d'Information). Incorporation into French law of European Parliament 1996 Directive regarding the legal protection of databases. Decree modifying the 1986 decree granting subsidies to national daily newspapers with low publicity and advertisement revenues. Decree granting subsidies for fax transmission of daily newspapers. Decree granting subsidies for transportation of the press.
- 1999: Prisma Presse buys *National Geographic*
- 2000: Loi Trautmann reforming the audiovisual sector. Law strengthening the protection of presumption of innocence and victims' rights. Decree relative to the direction of the development of the media in the information society.
- 2001: France signs the International Convention on Cybercriminality. Granting of a subsidy of 100 million francs to AFP. Creation of *bouquets de programmes* on television. RFO and Radio France begin online broadcasts. Directive 2001/29/CE of the European Parliament and Council on harmonization of copyrights and related rights in the information society. Creation of lobby Enfance et Média (CIEM) to curb pornography and violence on television.
- 2002: Free distribution of the newspaper *Métro* in Paris. The journalists' union USJ-CFDT, following the CFDT lead, asks for the 32-hour week

BIBLIOGRAPHY

Bahu-Leyser, Danielle, Faure, Pascal, eds. *Médias, e-médias.* Paris: La Documentation française, 2001.

Bertolus, Jean-Jérôme. *Les Média-maîtres: qui contrôle l'information?* Paris: Seuil, 2000.

Carcenac, Thierry. *Pour une administration électronique citoyenne. Contribution aux débats Rapport au Premier ministre.* Collection des rapports officiels. Paris: La Documentation française, 2001.

Cazenave, Elizabeth, Ulmann-Mauriat, Caroline. *Presse, radio et télévision en France de 1631 à nos jours.* Paris, Hachette, 1994.

Censer, Jack Richard. *Prelude to Power. The Parisian Radical Press, 1789-1791.* Baltimore and London: The Johns Hopkins University Press,1976.

Chapel, Marina. ''30 juin 2000. Une grosse 'TAP' [Tiré à part] dans les services.'' Available from www.tv-radio.com/mediaradiotv/pages/chapel300600.html.

Charon, Jean-Marie, Furet, Claude. *Un secret si bien violé: la loi, le juge et le journaliste.* Seuil, 2000.

———. *La Presse en France de 1945 à nos jours.* 1991.

Dagnaud, Monique. *L'Etat et les médias: fin de partie.* Paris: Editions Odile Jacob, 2000.

De Broissia, Louis. ''Rapport sur le Projet de loi de finances pour 2001, adopté par l'Assemblée Nationale.'' Tome XI. Presse écrite. Available from senat.fr/rap/a00-093-11/a00-093-11.html.

De Laubier, Charles. *La Presse sur internet.* Paris, Presses Universitaires de France, Collection Que Sais-je? 2000.

———. *La Presse online en Europe.* Rapport. Novembre 1998. Available from www.scd.univ-tours.fr/Epress/sommaire.html.

Descamps, Philippe. ''Une presse docile dans une France fédérale. Misère du journalisme de province.'' In *Le Monde Diplomatique*, November 1996. Available from www.monde-diplomatique.fr/1996/11/DESCAMPS/7444.html.

Devenir journalistes. Sociologie de l'entrée sur le marché du travail. Premier ministre. Direction du développement des médias. Département des statistiques, des études et de la documentation sur les médias. Centre de recherche administrative et politique (UMR 6051 CNRS. Université de Rennes. Paris: La Documentation française, 2001.

Devillard, A., Valérie et al. *Les Journalistes français à l'aube de l'an 2000: Profils et parcours*. Paris: Editions Panthéon Assas, 2001.

Direction du développement des médias, CRAP. *Devenir journaliste*. Paris: La Documentation Française, 2001.

"Discours de Catherine Trautmann, Ministre de la Culture et del a Communication sur le projet de loi de réforme de l'audiovisuel à l'Assemblée Nationale, 18 mai 1999." Available from www.culture.fr.

European Unions. Texts of resolutions, policies, and parliamentary discussions. Available from www.europa.eu.int.

Feyel, Gilles. *La Presse en France des origines à 1944. Histoire politique et matérielle*. 2000.

———. *La Distribution et la diffusion de la presse du XVIIe siècle au IIIe millénaire*. Paris: Editions Panthéon-Assas. 2002.

Halimi, Serge. "Une presse libre." In *Le Monde Diplomatique*, September 1995. Available from www.monde-diplomatique.fr/1995/09/HALIMI/1798.html.

Ibrahimi, Hamed. "Le Maghreb confronté à l'Islam. Une presse asphyxiée, des journalistes harcelés." In *Le Monde Diplomatique*, February 1997. Available from www.monde-diplomatique.fr/1997/02/IBRAHIMI/7753.html.

Médiasig 2002. Les 7000 noms de la presse et de la communication. Premier ministre, Service d'information du Gouvernement. Paris: La Documentation Française, 2002.

Popkin, Jeremy. Revolutionary News: The Press in France, 1789-1799. Durham, NC: Duke University Press, 1990.

"Portrait de la presse magazine 2001." In *Problèmes économiques* No. 2723.

Rapport de la Cour de cassation 2001. Les libertés. Paris: La Documentation Française, 2002.

Ramonet, Ignacio. "Dessiller les yeux." In *Le Monde Diplomatique*, November 1995. Available from www.monde-diplomatique.fr/1995/11/RAMONET/1998.html.

———. "Médias en danger." In *Le Monde Diplomatique*, February 1996. Available from www.monde-diplomatique.fr/1996/02/RAMONET/2375.html.

Roustel, Damien. "Anatomie d'une désinformation. Comment Roubaix est devenue une 'ville à majoritémusulmane'." In *Le Monde Diplomatique*, June 1997. Available from www.monde-diplomatique.fr/1997/06/ROUSTEL/8738.html.

Tableaux statistiques de la presse. Données détaillées 1999. Rétrospective 1985-1999. Premier ministre. Direction du développement des médias. Département des statistigues, des études et de la documentation sur les médias. Paris: La Documentation Française, 2001.

Union Syndicale des journalistes—CFDT. Statistics and General Information. Available from www.usj.cfdt.fr.

World Press Trends 2002. World Association of Newspapers.

—Alice-Catherine Carls

FRENCH GUIANA

BASIC DATA

Official Country Name:	Department of Guiana
Region (Map name):	South America
Population:	172,605
Language(s):	French
Literacy rate:	83%

French Guiana, which sits between Brazil and Suriname on the northeastern coast of South America, has a colorful history. It boasts the speech and press freedoms of France and supports two major newspapers, *France-Guyane* (appears daily) and *La Presse de Guyane* (publishes four times per week). Both titles are French-language and are printed in the capital city of Cayenne. Neither maintains a presence on the Internet.

There are 16 radio stations operating in French Guiana (two AM and 14 FM) and three television stations, serving 104,000 radios and 30,000 televisions. There are two Internet service providers.

Originally inhabited by Carib and Arawak Indians, control of the country has shifted between France, Britain, the Netherlands, Brazil, and Portugal until it was finally confirmed as French in 1817.

Soon after, France established a notoriously brutal penal colony on Devil's Island, which lies in shark-infested waters about nine miles from shore. The prison operated until the 1950s. In 1946, French Guiana was officially declared an oversees department of France.

Accordingly, the chief of state is the French president, who operates through a prefect appointed by officials in Paris. Local administration is handled through a 19-member general council and a 31-member regional council. The population of French Guiana is approximately 175,000, and the literacy rate is 83 percent. The official language is French but Creole is widely spoken.

The economy is closely linked with France through subsidies and imports and most of the country is an undeveloped, tropical rain forest. In 1964, France established the Kourou Space Center that contributes significantly to the gross domestic product. Fishing and forestry also play important roles in the economy.

Benn's Media. Vol. 3, 147th Edition, p. 297.1999.

Central Intelligence Agency (CIA). *World Factbook 2001*. 2001. Available from www.cia.gov.

Worldinformation.com. 2002. Available from www.worldinformation.com.

—Jenny B. Davis

FRENCH POLYNESIA

BASIC DATA

Official Country Name:	French Polynesia
Region (Map name):	Oceania
Population:	249,110
Language(s):	French, Tahitian
Literacy rate:	98%

French Polynesia, a collection of volcanic islands and atolls in the eastern South Pacific, is perhaps best known for its largest island, Tahiti.

There are two daily newspapers in French Polynesia, both publishing in French and originating in Tahiti. Neither publishes on Sunday. La Děpêche is the largest and more renowned of the two; its circulation is approximately 14,000 and it maintains a website. Founded in 1961, *Les Nouvelles de Tahiti* was the island's first daily newspaper; it has a circulation of 6,700 and provides news content to the Web portal *tahiti1.com*.

The islands also support two major weekly publications. The *Tahiti Sun Press* is published in English and geared toward English-speaking tourists. It is distributed free of charge in local hotels. *TahitiRama*, which appears online and every Thursday in print, focuses on art and fashion and is a spin-off of a popular television show.

French Polynesia has three television stations broadcasting to approximately 30,000 televisions. There are 14 FM radio stations, two AM radio stations, and more than 100,000 radios. There are two Internet service providers.

The country encompasses five major island groups: the Society Islands (which include Tahiti and Bora Bora), the Tuamotus, the Marquesas, the Austral Islands, and the Gambier Islands. Today the country is a French overseas territory; French rule began in Tahiti in 1824 and spread to the other islands in the area during the latter part of the nineteenth century.

The official head of state is the French president, represented locally by a high commissioner of the republic. The local government is headed by a president of territorial government, and the unicameral, 41-seat territorial assembly also is presided over by a President. The approximate population of French Polynesia is 250,000, with the majority of the population located on Tahiti. The official language is French, although Tahitian is spoken throughout the islands. Not surprisingly, tourism makes up the largest part of the economy, making up about 25 percent of the gross national product. The black pearl industry is also an important economic sector.

Central Intelligence Agency (CIA). ''French Polynesia.'' *World Factbook 2001*. 2001. Available from www.cia.gov.

Tahiti Friendship Society. *Tahitinet.com*. 2002. Available from www.tahitinet.com.

Worldinformation.com. 2002. Available from www.worldinformation.com.

—Jenny B. Davis

GABON

BASIC DATA

Official Country Name:	Gabonese Republic
Region (Map name):	Africa
Population:	1,208,436
Language(s):	French, Fang, Myene, Bateke, Bapounou/ Eschira, Bandjabi
Literacy rate:	63.2%

BACKGROUND & GENERAL CHARACTERISTICS

Gabon is a unitary republic on the west coast of Africa, south of Cameroon and Equatorial Guinea and west of Congo-Brazzaville. Its capital is Libreville. Gabon's 1.23 million people have had the same president for 35 years: President Omar Albert-Bernard Bongo, born in 1935. Only two presidents have ruled Gabon since the country's independence from France in 1960. Bongo previously had served in Gabon's Foreign Ministry when independence was attained; prior to that, he had served two years in the French air force. Bongo was chief of staff and defense minister under Gabon's first head of state, President Leon Mba, becoming vice president in 1966. One year after Mba's death, Bongo assumed the presidency, the position he has held ever since.

Gabon is composed of more than 40 ethnic groups but has not experienced the same degree of ethnic conflict as other African states. This has been due primarily to the relative prosperity brought on by the tapping of Gabon's rich oil reserves and to the continuous presence of French troops in Gabon for nearly four decades since their reinstatement of President Mba in 1964 after he was deposed in coup. Regarding religion, the majority of Gabon's citizenry is Christian. President Bongo himself converted to Islam and took the name ''Omar'' in 1973.

Although President Bongo had made Gabon a single-party state in 1968, public protests against President Bongo in 1990 due to declining oil prices led to a new Constitution in 1991 that created a multi-party system. Nonetheless, limited space exists for full and free discussion and criticism of the president or his family by the press, as the Communications Code specifies criminal and civil penalties for what is judged to be libelous expression. While the National Communications Council (CNC) set up under the Ministry of Communications supposedly was established to ensure press freedom and high-quality journalism, the CNC actually works against journalists and freedom of expression. Through the CNC, the government is empowered to transform civil libel lawsuits into criminal suits and can initiate criminal libel suits against those issuing supposedly libelous statements against elected officials.

For the most part, the government of Gabon controls the media, though arguably somewhat less stringently than in a number of other African states. Starting in 1998 the government began to limit freedom of expression in the private media more rigorously. According to the Committee to Protect Journalists' annual report for 2001, ''Since 1998, the CNC has been using licensing regulations to trim the number of private radio stations. There are still a few apolitical private and community radio stations in Gabon, and opposition newspapers appear regularly. But local journalists say self-censorship is more pervasive than ever.''

Newspapers are almost entirely politicized. The one daily paper that exists in the country and is distributed on a national basis is government affiliated. Private weekly, bi-weekly, and monthly papers number about ten to twelve. Opposition parties produce most of the country's newspapers.

The government-affiliated newspaper is *L'Union*, which publishes daily. One of the main opposition political weekly newspapers is *Le Bucheron*, while *La Relance* is an independent weekly paper, unattached to any political party. *Le Reveil* also publishes weekly. *La Voix du Peuple*, another independent paper, publishes bi-monthly.

ECONOMIC FRAMEWORK

Gabon is heavily dependent on oil to fuel its economy. Eighty percent of the country's exports are derived from Gabon's oil. In addition to crude oil, the principal exports are timber, manganese, and uranium. Annual per capita income is about US$3,180.

Gabon's connection with oil has meant that the political atmosphere and degree of tolerance for open criticism of government leaders and policies fluctuates with the economy. When oil prices are down, as they were in the late 1980s, government acceptance of political protest has been much more limited; with rising oil prices, government permissiveness of dissent also appears to rise.

The private press often has difficulty meeting the financial requirements of the government in terms of licensing costs and the penalties that sometimes are imposed for violations of what the government considers reasonable press laws that by international standards are quite restrictive. Consequently, the number of private newspapers in print at any particular time varies.

On a questionably positive note, President Bongo made 250 million CFA francs (about US$345,000) available to the private press in January 2001 to encourage their development, but not all papers were funded, much to their chagrin. The president also stated that the private press would receive double this amount each year on a regular basis. Apparently, the president distributed the funds in such a way as to reward those papers that cast the president and the ruling Democratic Party in a favorable light. As the Committee to Protect Journalists put it, "With confounding ease, President Omar Bongo maintained his smooth-talking, iron-fisted rule by suppressing critical media voices via the Penal Code and by simply purchasing good press."

Venal rewards for journalistic coverage are rampant throughout much of Africa, making the smaller presses beholden to whoever provides them with financial support. This is no less true in Gabon, "where public expressions of unconditional support for President Bongo are often rewarded with cash-filled envelopes," according to the Committee to Protect Journalists in 2001.

PRESS LAWS

The Constitution officially guarantees freedom of speech and freedom of the press. However, the Communications Code authorizes state prosecution of journalists deemed to have breached the limits of press freedom. Journalists can be charged with both civil and criminal libel. Efforts to tighten the Code even further were made in June 2001, when the National Assembly and Senate gave their stamp of approval to a CNC proposal that publications found guilty of libel and other criminal acts be suspended for one to three months on first offense and three to six months on repeat offenses. The CNC proposal also expanded the scope of libelous conduct in order to protect the "dignity of the person" and made possible the jailing of editors and authors of articles judged to be libelous for two to six months, as well as the imposition of fines ranging from $700 to $7,000 on such guilty parties. At the close of 2001, however, President Bongo had not yet signed the new Code into law.

CENSORSHIP

Most newspapers do criticize the president, and all papers (including *L'Union*, affiliated with the government) criticize government and party leaders, risking the imposition of penalties specified in the Communications Code. Individual citizens and members of the National Assembly are accorded somewhat greater latitude to debate presidential policies and activities and to criticize ministers and other government officials, though not always without risk.

The government has censored even the pro-government paper, *L'Union*. Germain Ngoyo Moussavou, the managing editor of *L'Union*, was dismissed from his job by presidential decree in November 2001 after scathingly criticizing Antoine Mboumbou Miyakou, Gabon's Minister of the Interior, for mishandling preparations for the December legislative elections.

Over the course of several years, the government so frequently censored one satirical weekly newspaper, *La Griffe*, that by mid-2001 the paper had relocated to France. This followed the transformation of the original paper into *Le Gri-Gri*, first issued as a supplement to *La Griffe* and later as a paper in its own right. Both *La Griffe* and *Le Gri-Gri* were suspended on February 15, 2001. This marked the third suspension of *La Griffe* in less than three years. In fact, one of the paper's editors, Dorothee Ngouoni, had already left Gabon in July 1999 after being convicted of defamation.

Moreover, the CNC, the same government organ that suspended *La Griffe* and *Le Gri-Gri*, temporarily banned Michel Ongoundou Loundah, the editor-in-chief of *La Griffe*, and Raphaël Ntoutoume Ngoghe, the paper's publisher, from practicing journalism in Gabon.

Subsequently, *Le Gri-Gri* relocated to France, where it was renamed *Le Gri-Gri International* and began covering news from all of Africa, though still concentrating on politics in Gabon.

In mid-October 2001 government pressure also was applied to Mr. Barre, the manager of Sogapress, the local distributing company for *Le Gri-Gri International*. Barre was summoned before Gabon's national chief of police, Jean-Claude Labouda, who apparently acted under instructions from the Ministry of the Interior in ordering Barre to halt the paper's distribution in Gabon. Without a warrant, agents from the Ministry's investigation department on October 12 had seized the final copies of *Le Gri-Gri International* available on newsstands in Gabon, three days prior to Barre's being ordered to stop its distribution.

State-Press Relations

While ostensibly supporting the private media through state financial subsidies that began in January 2001, the government also actively censures and controls the private press. Even staff members from *L'Union* reportedly have felt themselves obliged to object to government efforts to stifle press freedom.

Interestingly, the president, his wife, and the president's sister-in-law all took *La Griffe* to court in 2001, claiming each of them was defamed in several articles published in that paper. And in 2001 Prime Minister Jean François Ntoutoume Emane chastised *Le Gri-Gri International* and similar news outlets for showing an ''appalling disrespectful attitude'' by debating questions concerning the likelihood of political change in the country.

Attitude toward Foreign Media

The BBC chose not to operate in Gabon for financial reasons. Other foreign media, including the Voice of America, Radio France International, and other international radio stations, have operated in the country without government interference, for the most part. As the U.S. Department of State noted, in 2001, ''Foreign newspapers and magazines were available widely.''

However, on December 23, 2001 Antoine Lawson, a local reporter for the British news agency, Reuters, lost his camera to police, who confiscated it and destroyed the film. Lawson had been photographing police evacuating a bar that day, when the second round of legislative elections was held and all sales outlets for alcohol were to have been closed.

If a newspaper originates in Gabon but is published abroad, government intolerance of political criticism may resemble that meted out toward the private press in Gabon, *Le Gri-Gri International* being one such example.

Broadcast Media

Few private broadcasting services exist in Gabon. As BBC Monitoring wrote, ''In October 1999 communications officials suspended four private radio and television stations after accusing them of illegal broadcasting.''

The government-owned, national broadcasting service, Radiodiffusion-Television Gabonaise (RTVG), is based in Libreville and operates two radio channels, both affiliated with the ruling Democratic Party: RTG1 (also known as RTG Chaine 1), broadcasting in French, and RTG2 (or RTG Chaine 2), ''a network of provincial stations broadcasting in French and vernacular languages,'' according to BBC Monitoring. ''Africa No1,'' a radio station based in Gabon and supported by French interests, broadcasts across Africa on both short-wave and FM frequencies.

Besides its radio channels, RTVG has two television channels, again representing Democratic Party views; one broadcasts in French to 80 percent of Gabon's territory, the other, RTG2, broadcasts only in the capital. A private satellite TV channel, TV SAT, also broadcasts from Libreville.

Electronic News Media

Internet access and use are unrestricted by the government in Gabon. Three Internet service providers were operating in the country at the end of 2001, only one of them owned by the state. Internet cafés are available in urban areas to allow Internet access at fairly reasonable prices.

L'Union Edition Web was the first weekly newspaper made available via the Internet in Gabon.

Summary

Although Gabon has developed its economic wealth to a greater extent than many of the surrounding countries in Africa, government restriction of the media has grown over time. Few journalists and editors can escape the wrath of government officials intent on prosecuting them for libel, as the Communications Code has made it possible to charge members of the media with both criminal and civil libel and to punish the guilty with jail sentences, fines, suspension of licenses, or bans on practicing journalism. Even when the private press has gone outside the country to publish critiques of government leaders, as with *Le Gri-Gri International*, journalists cannot be assured that their publications will safely make it onto the newsstands in Gabon and reach their intended audience. Journalists consequently must practice careful self-censorship or risk government repression. Winning 80 percent of the seats in the National Assembly in the December 2001 legislative elections, with 82 percent of Libreville's eligible voters choosing to remain home (as well as 56 percent of the voting public elsewhere in the country), the ruling Democratic Party has shifted Gabon increasingly toward becoming a one-party state.

In a more positive direction, however, international media have been permitted to operate in Gabon with relatively little government interference. The use of the Internet likewise has been unrestricted, and growing numbers of Gabonese are likely to resort to this form of communication if the government continues to heavy-handedly regulate public expression through the print media and broadcasting networks.

Globalization, too, appears to be making a helpful difference for Gabon's media professionals and may help shape an eventual increase in freedom of expression in Gabon. In November 2001 the Association of Free and Independent Publishers in Gabon became a member of the World Association of Newspapers. This relationship will likely offer the Gabon Association's members a certain measure of solidaristic support and some protection against government intrusion and repression as they ply their trade, at least somewhere down the line.

SIGNIFICANT DATES

- 1998: Government of Gabon increasingly attempts to use licensing withdrawals as a means of restricting the number of private radio stations operating in the country.
- July 1999: Dorothee Ngouoni, one of *La Griffe*'s editors, leaves Gabon after being judged guilty of defamation.
- October 1999: Communications officials suspend four private radio and television stations for illegal broadcasting.
- January 2001: President Bongo makes government financial support available to the private press, promising to renew such support annually, but not all newspapers receive funding.
- February 2001: *La Griffe* and *Le Gri-Gri* are suspended, a status in which they remain for the rest of the year; key staff are banned from practicing journalism.
- June 2001: The National Assembly and Senate approve a proposal to make the Communications Code more stringent.
- October 2001: *Le Gri-Gri International* is prevented from being distributed in Gabon and government officials illegally confiscate copies of the paper from newsstands.
- November 2001: Germain Ngoyo Moussavou, managing editor of the pro-government paper, *L'Union*, is dismissed from his job by presidential decree for defaming the Minister of the Interior.
- December 2001: Legislative elections are held, with a record 82 percent of eligible voters in Libreville failing to vote and 56 percent of the electorate elsewhere in Gabon choosing to do the same; the ruling Democratic Party wins 80 percent of the votes cast.

BIBLIOGRAPHY

BBC Monitoring. ''Country profile: Gabon.'' Reading, UK: British Broadcasting Corporation, June 29, 2002. Available at http://news.bbc.co.uk/1/hi/world/africa/country_profiles/1023203.stm.

Bureau of Democracy, Human Rights, and Labor, U.S. Department of State. ''Gabon.'' *Country Reports on Human Rights Practices 2001*. Washington, DC: Bureau of Public Affairs, U.S. Department of State, March 4, 2002. Available at http://www.state.gov/g/drl/rls/hrrpt/2001/af/8374.htm.

Committee to Protect Journalists. ''Gabon.'' *Attacks on the Press in 2001: Africa 2001*. New York, NY: CPJ, 2002. Available at http://www.cpj.org/attacks01/africa01/gabon.html.

Reporters without Borders. ''Gabon.'' *Africa annual report 2002*. Paris, France: Reporters sans Frontières, April 30, 2002. Available at http://www.rsf.org/article.php3?id_article=1837.

—Barbara A. Lakeberg-Dridi

THE GAMBIA

BASIC DATA

Official Country Name:	Republic of the Gambia
Region (Map name):	Africa
Population:	1,367,124
Language(s):	English, Mandinka, Wolof, Fula
Literacy rate:	38.6%

BACKGROUND & GENERAL CHARACTERISTICS

The Gambia is a very small, multi-party democracy in West Africa. The geographic territory of the Gambia, a narrow finger of land surrounded by Senegal, follows the Gambia River in an eastward direction from the Atlantic coast. The capital is Banjul. The Gambia's population of only 1.4 million, comprising a number of ethnic groups, practices Islam and Christianity. English and indigenous languages are used throughout the country.

Since independence several decades ago, the Gambia has enjoyed relatively long periods of political stability, broken by occasional coups and political violence. The current president, Yahya Jammeh, formerly served with Gambian peacekeepers in Liberia and took power from the Gambia's first elected president, Dawda Jawara, in a military coup in 1994. Two years later, President Jammeh was confirmed as president in an unfair election. He was reelected president in October 2001, this time in an election viewed as free and fair by international observers. However, after the election, allegations were made that thousands of Senegalese from Casamance, Senegal and living in the Gambia had fraudulently been registered and allowed to vote for Jammeh. The accusing journalist, Alhagie Mbye, was arrested, detained, and reportedly beaten and tortured by President Jammeh's security forces for reporting on the fraudulent voting.

President Jammeh is extremely sensitive to criticism and the possibility of renewed civil unrest in the country. Angered by his perception that the staff of Radio Gambia were siding with the political opposition and reporting unfavorably on him, the president in July 2001 threatened that anyone "bent on disturbing the peace and stability of the nation will be buried six feet deep." A large public and media outcry ensued against the president's intimidating behavior toward television and radio journalists.

Gambian government laws and practice considerably restrict freedom of expression and the media. The U.S. Department of State summarized the situation in the Gambia in 2001 as follows: "The Government significantly limited freedom of speech and of the press, and security forces arrested and detained persons who publicly criticized the Government or who expressed views in disagreement with the Government. Journalists practice self-censorship." In general, the state-owned broadcasting media are skewed in favor of the government and afford little coverage to opposition politicians, including Members of Parliament. However, during the presidential election campaign of 2001, opposition candidates were given relatively fair access to and coverage by state radio and television, at least more so than previously. This was due in part to the fact that journalists in the Gambian Press Union adopted a Code of Conduct aimed at ensuring more balanced reporting as well as to President Jammeh's July 2001 lifting of a ban on the opposition party he had ousted in 1994.

The Daily Observer is the largest-selling, independent daily newspaper in the country. Other independent and privately owned papers include *The Independent*, *The Point*, *Foroyaa*, *The Gambia News*, and *Report Weekly Magazine*.

ECONOMIC FRAMEWORK

The Gambian economy is based almost entirely on the production of peanuts. Other significant exports are fish, cotton lint, and palm kernels. Annual per capita income is only about US$330. Although the country has the Gambia River's ample water supply, much of the soil is unsuitable for farming, and only one-sixth of the land can be farmed. Peanuts are the only crop that can be easily grown. The Gambia also lacks valuable natural resources like the minerals and timber found in abundance in countries nearby.

The private press sometimes has difficulty supporting itself financially due to the excessive fees and taxes levied by the government to stifle the political opposition and silence criticism of government officials, policies, and actions. Nonetheless, several independent and private newspapers do exist, some of which are supported financially by adherents of various political parties.

PRESS LAWS

The Constitution guarantees freedom of speech and of the press. However, the government substantially interferes with the media, censoring journalists, withdrawing licenses of radio stations it wishes to censure, and exacting other penalties and sanctions on those whom government officials believe criticize or are a threat to the ruling APRC party or the president.

Amnesty International noted that in 2001, "restrictive legislation severely limiting freedom of expression remained in force." For example, Decrees 70 and 71 obstructed the free reporting of news by imposing a requirement that all newspapers either post a bond equivalent to US$6,500 or stop publishing. The bond funds were intended to cover future possible government judgments to be imposed against the papers for blasphemy, sedition, or other libelous acts.

Since at least 1999, the government has attempted to establish a National Media Commission that essentially will control free expression and interfere greatly with the practice of journalism. Although strong protests by Gambian journalists and media associations stopped the National Media Commission Bill of 1999 from passage, a yet-more-stringent bill was introduced to the Gambian parliament in March 2002.

On May 2, 2002 (ironically, the eve of World Press Freedom Day) the Gambian parliament passed the National Media Commission Bill of 2002. Amended two months later at the president's request to include a requirement that the commission's chair be a high court judge appointed by the state's chief justice, this bill awaited President Jammeh's signature in early August 2002, when the present article went to press. International media organizations and human rights associations were urging President Jammeh not to sign into law this bill, which would place even greater restrictions on journalists, requiring them to register with an obviously politicized government regulatory commission. The commission also would be empowered to impose substantial fines, jail journalists, close down newspapers, oblige journalists to reveal their sources, and take other harsh steps to control free expression. The Gambian Press Union and numerous international media associations such as the New York-based Committee to Protect Journalists, the World Editors Forum, and the World Association of Newspapers all protested this bill, pointing out that it contradicts both the Gambian Constitution and international human rights standards, including those set forth over fifty years ago by the United Nations in the Universal Declaration of Human Rights.

CENSORSHIP

As noted above, the president is especially sensitive to criticism and seeks to tighten control on the media when the international spotlight is shifted off the Gambia, as in the periods just before and just after the presidential election campaign. The president and his government show little tolerance for those who do not provide favorable coverage of government activities or policies or for those who report on the activities of opposition parties and their key leaders, particularly opposition figures known for their scathing critiques of the ruling party and president.

Interestingly, in 1999 the most popular independent daily, *The Daily Observer*, was purchased by a supporter of the ruling Alliance for Patriotic Reorientation and Construction (APRC) party. Since that time, journalists at the paper have been harassed and controlled in what they are permitted to report. This led to the June 2001 resignation of at least eight of the paper's journalists, including editor-in-chief Paschal Eze. Their managing director, Bubacar Baldeh, an APRC party propagandist, had tried preventing publication of stories related to Lamin Waa Juwara, a staunch critic of President Jammeh and controversial propagandist for the UDP, one of the Gambia's opposition parties.

One independent radio station in particular, the popular Citizen FM, has experienced especially strong government efforts to silence its programming and harass those associated with its broadcasts. For several years, the radio station has had its license suspended repeatedly by state authorities for breaching the limits of government tolerance. Moreover, in October 2001, the station's owner himself, Babucar Gaye, fell into the government's ill favor. Gaye was arrested and taken to the National Intelligence Agency (NIA), a stalwart enforcer of government restrictions on free speech and press freedom, where he was ordered to pay allegedly unpaid taxes before his station could broadcast again. Although Gaye complied and paid his supposedly overdue taxes, despite denying that he had broken any Gambian law in broadcasting the October presidential election results, at the end of 2001 Citizen FM still was not allowed to broadcast.

Also in October 2001, George Christensen, the owner of Radio 1 FM, a private radio station broadcasting in the Gambia, was arrested by the NIA and questioned for several hours about his station's finances, then released without charge. The international media protested government treatment of the two radio station owners, Gaye and Christensen.

Even one of the key staff members of the Gambia's state-run radio, Radio Gambia, was blacklisted by the government. Peter Gomez, a key producer of the station's programming, lost his job in January 2001 after refusing to broadcast a government-mandated "correction" of a news story Gomez insisted was true: namely, that President Jammeh had announced his intention to promote Shari'a (strict Islamic law) in the Gambia, an announcement made by the president when he met with a group of Muslim elders on a Muslim feast day. The Press Institute and the Gambian Press Union stood by Gomez, believing he had reported what the president in fact had said.

The government likewise interrogated three journalists from various media outlets in June 2001 for reporting on problems with accommodations and food at the 5th National Youth Conference and Festival. One of the journalists, Momodou Thomas, was held incommunicado for about eight hours by the NIA before being released.

On a more serious topic, campaigners against female genital mutilation, which is still widely practiced in the Gambia and has not yet been specifically outlawed, have been denied access to state-owned media to publicize their cause and educate the public about this widespread health hazard and abuse of women's human rights.

With deliberate attempts by the Gambian government to regulate the media and curtail press freedom, journalists typically practice self-censorship, an increasingly necessary practice for Gambian journalists wishing to avoid fines, imprisonment, or sudden dismissal from their jobs.

STATE-PRESS RELATIONS

The U.S. Department of State noted that in 2001, "Freedom of expression remained under threat as journalists from the privately owned independent media were arrested, beaten and harassed.'' Some journalists accused of publishing inaccurate or insensitive reports about the government have been arrested and detained. The State Department backed up its claim by stating that Kassa Jatta, an activist with the opposition UDP, was arrested in April 2001 after publishing an article in which he criticized the foreign policy of President Jammeh.

A court reporter, Omah Bah, who works for *The Independent*, was beaten in July 2001 by government soldiers for attempting to cover the military trial of a lieutenant in Banjul. This occurred despite the fact that Bah had been given official permission to report on the trial.

Besides government soldiers, the NIA also works as the government's strong-arm, attacking and arresting journalists deemed to be acting against the best interests of the ruling party and the president. Alhagie Mbye, another reporter with *The Independent*, was twice detained in 2001 by the NIA—once in August for three days after publishing a story about reports of coup attempts and again in November for eight or nine days. His second detention, during which he reportedly was beaten and tortured, followed a report he had sent to the British-based news magazine, *West Africa*, alleging that vote fraud had occurred by the thousands in the October presidential election. In both cases, Mbye was held incommunicado. Another journalist, Alagi Yoro Jallow, the managing editor of *The Independent*, was questioned by NIA agents for publishing an editorial in early December in which he criticized the attack on Mbye and likened the NIA to the Gestapo, Nazi Germany's secret police.

Attitude toward Foreign Media

For the most part, foreign newspapers, magazines, radio programs, and television broadcasts are permitted and distributed in the Gambia. According to the U.S. Department of State, in 2001, ''Local stations sometimes rebroadcast the British Broadcasting Corporation, Radio France Internationale, and other foreign news reports, and all were available via short-wave radio. Senegalese television and radio are available in many parts of the country.''

However, specific instances have occurred of problems faced by journalists working for foreign media. In May 2001, for instance, police held and beat a reporter for *The Daily Observer*—Alieu Badara Mansaray from Sierra Leone. Mansaray apparently had witnessed an act of bribery involving another police officer and a woman. Besides being beaten and bruised, Mansaray lost his watch, necklace, and mobile phone, all of them destroyed by the police. Released some hours later, he was never charged. Only one of the police was dismissed; the other two officers met with no punitive action.

In October 2001, Muhammed Lamin Sillah, who heads the Gambian chapter of Amnesty International and serves as coordinator for the Coalition of Human Rights Defenders, was arrested by the NIA after being interviewed for the BBC's ''Focus on Africa'' program. Having told the BBC that he believed the human rights situation in the Gambia called for improvement, Sillah was held incommunicado for four days in detention, the released on bail for US$18,000 after his case went to the High Court. The NIA accused Sillah of trying to overthrow the government and of inciting confusion and genocide, all of which Sillah denied.

Furthermore, in late July 2002, a journalist working in the Gambia for the Pan African News Agency (PANA) was arrested for supposedly running a newspaper without proper government permission. Guy-Patrick Massoloka, the journalist in question from Congo (Brazzaville), was arrested by the NIA and taken into custody. The incident provoked an international outcry from media associations and other journalists protesting government abuse and led to Massoloka's expulsion from the Gambia in early August. Massoloka was told by Immigration Department officials that he could return to the Gambia after renewing his expired visa abroad. While held by the NIA, Massoloka apparently was questioned about the likes of a French newspaper called ''*Echo du Baobab*.''

Broadcast Media

In 2001 only one private radio station regularly created its own news programming in the Gambia. Otherwise, private radio simulcasts news and programming produced by the one state-owned radio station, Radio Gambia, or broadcasts international news from such media outlets as the British Broadcasting Corporation and Radio France Internationale. Public affairs programs are occasionally developed by at least two independent radio stations.

The government runs the only television service that broadcasts nationally. Its programs cover about 60 percent of the Gambia's territory and reach those living in the eastern part of the country.

Those who can afford satellite systems are able to receive additional independent television programming such as that provided by the Premium TV Network, an external, privately owned station that transmits by Arabsat to Banjul.

Electronic News Media

Internet access is readily available and unrestricted by the government in the Gambia. Both Internet cafés and private Internet accounts make accessing the Internet affordable for many.

SUMMARY

The level of government censorship has been increasing steadily in the Gambia, despite positive measures by journalists themselves to promote balanced, fair reporting. Although the most recent presidential election was considered reasonably fair and a significant proportion of the votes cast went to opposition candidates, the legal restrictions on press freedom are increasing and the president and his National Intelligence Agency seem more determined than ever to control public expression deemed hazardous to their own political health. With the advent of international media associations on the Gambian scene, however, and the vocally courageous Gambian Press Union, it appears unlikely that the president and his ruling party will continue to expand their powers indefinitely. Surely, the time will come when both the domestic press and the international community of journalists gather sufficient strength to challenge President Jammeh's maneuvers and demand respect for the basic rights of journalists, with positive effect.

SIGNIFICANT DATES

- 1999: The most popular independent daily newspaper, *The Daily Observer*, is purchased by a major supporter of the ruling party, the APRC.
- 1999: The first National Media Commission Bill, which would severely impair press freedom, is proposed, but Gambian journalists gather enough strength to defeat its passage.
- January 2001: Peter Gomez, a key producer of the government-sponsored radio station, Radio Gambia, is dismissed after refusing to broadcast a government-dictated ''clarification'' of an earlier broadcast claiming that President Yahya Jammeh had declared his support for extending Shari'a law in the Gambia.
- July 2001: President Jammeh threatens to put ''6 feet deep'' those ''bent on disturbing the peace and stability of the nation''—a pointed remark aimed at Radio Gambia's reporting of his speeches, which he claimed were misrepresented.
- October 2001: President Jammeh is reelected to office in an election basically considered free and fair, although thousands of Senegalese are later alleged to have been allowed to register and vote for the incumbent.
- November 2001: Alhagie Mbye, a reporter for *The Independent* newspaper and the British news magazine, *West Africa*, is arrested and held for more than a week by the National Intelligence Agency, during which time he is beaten and tortured for having reported the occurrence of vote fraud in connection with the October presidential election.
- May 2002: National Media Commission Bill of 2002 is passed by the Gambian parliament, much to the dissatisfaction of supporters of press freedom; as of early August 2002, the president, faced with strong domestic and international protest from media professionals and rights associations, has not yet signed the bill into law.

BIBLIOGRAPHY

Amnesty International. ''Gambia.'' *Amnesty International Report 2002*. London: Amnesty International, May 28, 2002. Available at http://web.amnesty.org/web/ar2002.nsf/afr/gambia!Open.

BBC Monitoring. ''Country profile: The Gambia.'' Reading, UK: British Broadcasting Corporation, June 29, 2002. Available at http://news.bbc.co.uk/1/hi/world/africa/country_profiles/1032156.stm.

Bojang, Sheriff Jnr. ''Foreign Journalist Ordered to Leave.'' *The Independent*, Banjul, the Gambia, August 5, 2002. Available at http://allafrica.com/stories/printable/200208050344.html.

Bureau of Democracy, Human Rights, and Labor, U.S. Department of State. ''The Gambia.'' *Country Reports on Human Rights Practices 2001*. Washington, DC: Bureau of Public Affairs, U.S. Department of State, March 4, 2002. Available at http://www.state.gov/g/drl/rls/hrrpt/2001/af/8377.htm.

Committee to Protect Journalists. ''The Gambia.'' *Attacks on the Press in 2001: Africa 2001*. New York, NY: CPJ, 2002. Available at http://www.cpj.org/attacks01/africa01/gambia.html.

Committee to Protect Journalists. ''The Gambia: New press law would force journalists to reveal sources.'' CPJ 2002 news alert, May 6, 2002. Available at http://www.cpj.org/news/2002/Gambia06may02na.html.

Independent, The. ''International Outcry Over Media Commission Bill, Described As Second Highly Restrictive Legislation in Africa.'' *The Independent*, Banjul, the Gambia, May 10, 2002. Available at http://allafrica.com/stories/printable/200205100043.html.

Independent, The. ''NIA Swoop Down On Foreign Journalist.'' *The Independent*, Banjul, the Gambia, July 23, 2002. Available at http://allafrica.com/stories/printable/200207230472.html.

Reporters without Borders. ''The Gambia.'' Africa annual report 2002. Paris, France: Reporters sans fronti¤res, April 30, 2002. Available at http://www.rsf.org/article.php3?id_article=1840.

UN Integrated Regional Information Networks (IRIN). ''Parliament Passes Harsh Media Bill.'' July 25, 2002.

Available at http://allafrica.com/stories/printable/200207250223.html.

—Barbara A. Lakeberg-Dridi

GAZA STRIP AND WEST BANK

BASIC DATA

Official Country Name:	Gaza Strip and West Bank
Region (Map name):	Middle East
Population:	1,132,063(GS); 2,020,298(WB)
Language(s):	Arabic, Hebrew, English
Literacy rate:	N/A

Gaza Strip and the West Bank or the Palestinian Autonomous Areas are beleaguered portions of land filled with a people who have been fighting for autonomy against seemingly insurmountable odds.

Prior to the September 1993 Oslo Accords, the Palestine Authority (PA) had no broadcasting stations. They relied on the goodwill of other countries for broadcast time. After Oslo the Palestine Broadcasting Corporation (PBC) was established in outlying apartment building in Ramallah and oversees both radio and television.

Oslo accorded the PA one medium-wave and 10 FM radio frequencies. *Sawt Filastin* (The Voice of Palestine or VOP) is its flagship program. Pirate broadcasting is widespread with a 1998 estimate of 10 stations operating; the same number as officially licensed frequencies. Despite the allotted official frequencies PA media have suffered hits from Israeli military and a 2000 estimate suggests that the PBC is operating one AM station on 675 kHz with no FM or short-wave frequencies in operation.

Initial television service begin in 1995. In 1999 PBC was able to reach all areas using 11 low-power transmitters. Palestine TV is operated from both Gaza and Ramallah and there is also a Palestine Satellite Channel. Both are run by the PBC. PBC uses commercial sponsorship and receives funding from the PA to help it toward solvency. Its programming consists primarily of local interest issues. There are also at least nine other private television stations.

Newspapers include: *Akhbar an-Naqab*, *Al-Quds* (*Jerusalem*), *Al-Ayaam al-Arabi*, *Al-Haria* (*Liberation*), *Filastin ath-Thawra* (*Palestine Revolution*); and weeklies *Al-Hadaf*, *Al-Hayat al-Jadidah*, *Al-Istiqlal*, *Al-Ayyam*, and *Al-Watan Ar-Risala* (*Letter*). There are also three periodicals: weekly *Filastin* (*Palestine*) and *Palestine Report*, and the monthly *Shu'un Filastiniya* (*Palestine Affairs*). Supporting these endeavors the Palestinian Journalists' Union and the Palestine News Agency, Wikalat Anbaa' Filastiniya (WAFA), that offers news in Hebrew, French, and English.

As of 1999, 23,520 people were connected to the Internet with eight Internet service providers in operation.

The Palestine Security Services and the PA have been involved in numerous arbitrary jailings, beatings, and detainment of journalists, censorship and other limitations of freedom of the press.

BIBLIOGRAPHY

All the World's Newspapers. Available from www.webwombat.com.au.

British Broadcast Company. *News Country Profiles*. Available from http://news.bbc.co.uk.

Boyd, Douglas. *Broadcasting in the Arab World: A Survey of the Electronic Media in the Middle East*, 3rd ed. Iowa State University Press. Ames, IA: 1999.

Central Intelligence Agency. *The World Factbook 2001*. (2002) Available from http://www.cia.gov.

International Press Institute. *World Press Review*. Available from http://www.freemedia.at.

Maher, Joanne, ed. *Regional Surveys of the World: The Middle East and North Africa 2002*, 48th ed. Europa Publications. London: 2001.

The Middle East, 9th ed. Congressional Quarterly Inc. Washington, DC: 2000.

Palestine Report. Available: http://www.jmcc.org.

Reporters Sans Frontieres. *Palestine Annual Report 2002*. Available from http://www.rsf.fr.

Reporters Sans Frontieres. *Middle East Archives 2002*. Available from http://www.rsf.fr.

Russell, Malcom. *The Middle East and South Asia 2001*, 35th ed. United Book Press, Inc. Harpers Ferry, WV: 2001.

UNESCO Institute for Statistics. Available from http://www.uis.unesco.org.

Voice of Palestine. Available from http://www.bailasan.com.

World Bank. *Data and Statistics,*. Available from http://www.worldbank.org.

—Clint B. Thomas Baldwin

GEORGIA

BASIC DATA

Official Country Name:	Republic of Georgia
Region (Map name):	East & South Asia
Population:	4,989,285
Language(s):	Georgian (official), Russian, Armenian, Azeri, other
Literacy rate:	99.0%
Area:	69,700 sq km
GDP:	3,029 (US$ millions)
Number of Television Stations:	12
Number of Television Sets:	2,570,000
Television Sets per 1,000:	515.1
Number of Cable Subscribers:	13,500
Cable Subscribers per 1,000:	2.7
Number of Radio Stations:	23
Number of Radio Receivers:	3,020,000
Radio Receivers per 1,000:	605.3
Number of Individuals with Internet Access:	23,000
Internet Access per 1,000:	4.6

BACKGROUND & GENERAL CHARACTERISTICS

Georgia is situated at a crossroads between Europe and Asia. The country borders on Turkey, Russia, Armenia and Azerbaijan. It covers 26,911 square miles (about the size of Ireland) and has a population of nearly 5.5 million. The country includes two autonomous republics—Abkhazia and Ajara, as well as the autonomous region of south Ossetia. Abkhazia and the Tskhinvali region (South Ossetia) do not recognize Georgia's jurisdiction, even though no international organization recognizes the territories' independence.

Georgian history dates back more than 2,500 years, and Georgian is one of the oldest living languages in the world with its own internationally recognized alphabet, one of only thirteen recognized alphabets in the world. Although Russian is still universally spoken (except in the case of the very young), street names and most of the local press is in Georgian. Tbilisi, located in a picturesque valley divided by the Mtkvari River, is more than 1,500 years old. Much of Georgia's territory has been besieged by its Persian, Turkish and Russian neighbors along with Arabs and Mongols over the course of the seventh to the eighteenth centuries. After 11 centuries of mixed fortunes of various Georgian kingdoms, including a golden age from the eleventh to twelfth centuries, Georgia turned to Russia for protection. Russia annexed Georgia in 1801, but the first Republic of Georgia was established on May 26, 1918 after the collapse of Tsarist Russia. By March 1921, the Red army had reoccupied the country and Georgia became part of the Soviet Union. On April 9, 1991, the Supreme Council of the Republic of Georgia declared independence from the USSR.

Historically Georgia has always been a multinational country, serving as the crossroads of major trade links. Competition for such a strategic geopolitical location has been consistent. There are representatives of about 100 nationalities in Georgia. Armenians with a population of 437,211—8 percent of Georgian population—is one of the largest ethnic minorities in Georgia. Turkish-speaking Azerians, 307,556—6 percent of Georgian population—inhabit the regions of Rustavi and Azerbaijan are Shiite Moslems. Russians 341,172—6 percent of Georgian population—have no region of concentration. Today many Russians are migrating back to Moscow and the central regions of Russia. Ossetians—156,055 (3 percent), have settled in the Ossetian Autonomy Region, Gori, Khashuri, and Borjomi regions. According to the Georgian Constitution, Georgian and Abkhazians consist of North-Caucasian people related to the Adigean tribes and number 95,853—2 percent of the Georgian population. They are groups including Greeks—100,324, 2 percent; Jews, 24,795; and Kurds. At present, there are large numbers of Georgian refugees from Abkhazia living in Tbilisi with government support. These 230,000 internally displaced persons present an enormous strain on the economy. Peace in the separatist areas of Abkhazia and south Ossetia, overseen by Russian peacekeepers and international organizations, continues to be fragile, and will probably require years of economic development and negotiation.

Although Georgia has a long and close relationship with Russia, it is reaching out to its other neighbors and looking to the West in search of alternatives and opportunities. It signed a partnership and cooperation agreement with the European Union (EU), participates in the Partnership for Peace, and encourages foreign investment. France, Germany, and the U.K. all have embassies in Tbilisi, and Germany is a significant donor. There are large numbers of United States citizens and organizations contributing tens of millions of dollars per year.

History of the Press An excellent history of the press in Georgia was published in 1997 by the Caucasian Institute for Peace, Democracy and Development (CIPDD) with the support of the United Nations Development Program (UNDP). The first Georgian newspaper, *Sakartvelos Gazeti*, was published in 1819. By 1897 the average daily circulation of Georgian publications reached 3,000, the same figure as that estimated today although the population and literacy rates have both increased substantially. In soviet days, publications were run by the Communist Party and were produced on typewriters and photocopiers. In 1981, 141 newspapers were published: 12 national, 7 regional, 9 town, 66 district and 47 village, for a total circulation of 4.04 million copies.

It should be noted that during Communist rule the highest circulation was the *Comunisti* newspaper, at 700,000 copies a day. *Soplis Tshkovreba (Rural Life)* followed with 240,000, then Tbilisi at 145,000, *Zaria Vostoka (The Dawn of the Orient)* at 140,000, the Armenian language *Sovetakan Vrastan (Soviet Georgia)* at 33,000, and the *Azerbaijani Sovetan Gurjistani (Soviet Georgia)* at 35,000. The *Lelo* sports newspaper had a circulation of 120,000 while *Akhalgazrda Comunisti (Young Communists)* published 240,000 copies three days a week.

The first offset newspaper was *Tavisupleba (Liberty)*, published illegally in 1989 by the National Independence Party. The second issue was seized in the printing house by the KGB. When President Gamsakhurdia was replaced by Eduard Schvernadze in 1992, press restrictions eased although active suppression of the Gamsakhurdia press did not cease until 1994. Following soviet and European models, most early post-perestroika newspapers were organs of political parties. The first non-party paper, *7 Dghe (7 Days)* was founded in 1990, sponsored by the Journalists' Association. Only now is an independent comprehensive press beginning to emerge. Of the thirty-six registered party publications, only ten still publish.

The Press As in many changing societies, definite numerical information is difficult to come by in Georgia, in large part because all of society and the press in particular is in a state of flux.

The Georgian press is probably the most free press of all the nations of the former Soviet Union. The Georgian Parliament has enacted the strongest Freedom of Information Law in the former Soviet states which is stronger even than the U.S. Freedom of Information Act. Further, Georgian journalists have learned what the law means and how to go into court to use this law. By mid 2002 three court cases under this provision of the Administrative Code have been taken to court and three decisions have been obtained in journalists' favor. Further, the government of Georgia, although exerting pressure from time to time, is relatively tolerant of a free press. For example, Rustavi 2, the independent television station which is trying to build a quality media organization, has regularly run a nightly cartoon lampooning President Schvernadze, apparently with impunity.

Government pressure tends to come through selective enforcement of complex and ever changing administrative and tax code provisions. Otherwise, the complex regulatory provisions are seldom enforced.

Infrastructure of the Media Although a subscription system does function, it plays only a small role. Distribution of periodicals is only in Tbilisi and Kutaisi. The biggest heirs of the former *Soyuzpechat* are *Matsne* and *Sakpresa*, the former serving Tbilisi and the latter supplying the regions. Their service is so ineffective, however, that independent publications do not use either of them. *Soyuzpechat* was transformed into a joint stock company in 1993, but newspapers were discouraged from buying shared by the Ministry of Communication. This led *Alia*, *Rezonansi*, *Akhali Tacoba* and *7 Dghe* to found the Association of Free Press in 1995, which fostered professional solidarity and created a network of newsstands to bypass the distribution bottleneck. The new but already popular *Dilis Gazeta (Morning Paper)* established its own system of regional distribution using automobiles, which allows it to make speedy deliveries across the country. For instance, a car which heads for Batumi at 5 a.m. reaches the destination by 1 p.m. As a result, *Dilis Gazeta* is the only Tbilisi paper read in Batumi on the same day.

TV and radio stations use their own reporters to cover local stories and news agencies to cover stories affecting larger areas. There is little information appearing about the provinces.

The size of a newspaper's staff generally ranges from twenty-five to thirty, including technical personnel. The professional level of journalists is not satisfactory.

Many papers have their own computers at their disposal, but usually they do not have enough, and the ones they have are not the most up-to-date models. Machines fit for computer graphics are in especially short supply. Furthermore, most newspaper journalists themselves do not have access to computers, and thus are not experienced in their use.

ECONOMIC FRAMEWORK

Georgia's economic recovery has been hampered by the separatist disputes in Abkhazia and South Ossetia, a persistently weak economic infrastructure, and resistance to reform on the part of some corrupt and reactionary factions. However, the government has qualified for economic structural adjustment facility credit status, introducing a stable national currency (the lari), preparing for the second stage of accession to the World Trade Organization (the first stage has already been met), signing agreements that allow for development of a pipeline to transport Caspian oil across Georgia to the Black Sea, and passing laws on commercial banking, land, and tax reform. However, Georgia has been unable to meet International Monetary Fund (IMF) conditions recently and the new laws have yet to be implemented.

Inflation, however, ran to 300 percent in 1997, a phenomenon that steadily decreased to the 25 percent inflation rate in 1999. Tax revenues have risen somewhat, and recent tax reform encouraged by the IMF, should lead to further increases. However, Georgia needs to implement its tax legislation and take concrete steps to meet IMF programs. Although total revenue increased from 1996 to 1997, these increases were lower than expected. International financial institutions continue to play a critical role in Georgia's budgetary calculations. Multilateral and bilateral grants and loans totaled 116.4 million lari in 1997 and are expected to total 182.8 million lari in 1998 (lari were about two to the dollar).

The government says there has been some progress on structural reform. All prices and most trade have been liberalized, legal-framework reform is on schedule, and massive government downsizing is underway. More than 10,500 small enterprises have been privatized, and privatization of medium and large firms has been slow.

Georgia's transportation and communication infrastructure remains in very poor condition. Parliament has set an agenda to start the privatization of the telecommunications industry, although there is still resistance to the plan. Georgia's electrical energy sector continues to have great difficulties.

Described by the international financial press as the most corrupt country in a corrupt region, Georgia needs a stable and uncorrupt legal and financial system if it is to achieve economic progress. The IMF estimates that 70 percent of the Georgian economy is in the "shadow" or extralegal economy.

Press Economics A major problem for the Georgian press is that hardly any Georgians understand the business side of the newspaper business and few Georgian businesses can see the need to advertise especially in the countryside where businessmen tend to feel that everyone already knows what they do, and that advertising may just attract the unwelcome attentions of the tax authorities. The lack of financial stability leads sometimes to sloppy sensationalism in reporting in an attempt to expand circulation. It has also lead to hidden financial support by influential members of society such as government officials, members of prominent families and provincial government officials. These sponsorships are fairly obvious to the sophisticated reader as the sponsors' requirements are that the publication being supported defend the sponsor and attack his/her enemies; so, the positions taken by the paper make the sponsorship apparent.

At present, the Georgian press is in flux with news organizations forming and reforming for political, philosophical, financial and policy reasons. Thus, an excellent circulation survey done in 2001 is no longer valid in 2002 because many of the publications surveyed in 2001 no longer exist in 2002.

The quality of news reporting is poor, both because most newspapers pay so poorly that journalists must have additional jobs to survive financially, and because so few journalists have any professional training or experience. The excellent Journalism School sponsored by the International Center for Journalism out of Washington, D.C., is helping to change this situation. An attempt to establish a high quality newspaper called "*24 Hours*" is being undertaken by the television station *Rustavi 2,* and this effort includes the payment of higher salaries to the journalists involved.

PRESS LAWS

The Georgian Constitution and the 1991 Press Law guarantee freedom of speech and the press. At present, the Law on Press and Other Media, adopted in August of 1991 and based on the analogous Soviet law, is still in effect. The Law is acknowledged by journalists to be exemplary, but there exists no official independent watchdog body authorized to monitor its implementation and review, alleged violations and charges of non-compliance. Most journalists consider the duality of some articles of the law its main shortcoming. The Law states "the press and other mass media in the Republic of Georgia are Free". The principal of freedom of the mass media is similarly written into the Georgian Constitution adopted in August, 1995. This states, specifically, that "the mass media are free; censorship is impermissible" (Article 24.2) and that "the state or separate individuals do not have the right to monopolize the mass media or the means of disseminating information" (Article 24.3). Citizens of the Republic of Georgia have the right to express, distribute, and defend their opinions via any media, and to receive information on questions of social and state life. Censorship of the press and other media is not permitted.

Restrictions on the free flow of information via the media are enumerated in Article 4 of the law, which stipulated that "The mass media are forbidden to disclose state secrets; to call for the overthrow or change of the existing state and social system; to propagate war, cruelty, racial, national or religious intolerance; to publish information that could contribute to the committing of crimes; to interfere with the private lives of citizens or to infringe on their honor and dignity." Article 21 of the law established the rights of journalists to gather information. At the same time, the law made clear the subordination to, and responsibilities of, the state controlled media vis-a-vis the government. Article 18 stipulates that government controlled media outlets are obliged to do so only in "exceptional circumstances," such as the outbreak of war or natural disasters.

Despite the introduction of amendments and additions, the Law on Press is almost never applied in law enforcement practice. In Georgia, the Law on State Secrets, which determines the types of information that are not freely accessible due to the necessity of protecting the state security, is in force. The Law on State Secrets, adopted by parliament in September 1996, demands that the Council on National Security develop criteria of secret information to be approved by the president.

The Law on Press and Other Mass Media states that, "activities of a mass media outlet may be banned or suspended if it repeatedly violates the law thus contributing to crime, endangering national security, territorial integrity, or public order."

Censorship

During the early rule of ultra-nationalist Zvia Gamsakhurdia, political debate flourished in the pages of the Georgian press. However, as of early 1991, media freedom was systematically eroded. In October 1991, a group of TV journalists was dismissed and the majority of the personnel went on strike. Between December 1991 and January 1992, armed supporters of the regime detained several TV journalists and kept them in the basement of the presidential residence. They were freed after Gamsakhurdia's flight.

The situation altered after Eduard Shevardnadze's return to Georgia, although not immediately. While representatives of moderate opposition parties had greater access to the governmental media, certain high-ranking officials were irritated by the pro-Zviadist, as they stated it, orientation of several outlets. Independent journalists were subjected to systematic harassment and opposition newspapers were closed on the flimsiest of pretexts. However, in the case of, for instance, *Iberia-Spectri*, Eduard Shevardnadze intervened personally and ensured that publication of the paper was allowed. In 1994, a gradual relaxation of political control of the press got underway and in November 1995, several journalists confirmed that the media enjoyed greater freedom than one year earlier.

In 1996, the Independent Federation of Georgian Journalists recorded no obvious violations of the freedom of the speech. In one case, an article contradicted the criminal code. The newspaper *Noy* was closed down following the publication of anti-Semitic material. The editor (responsible for the piece) was charged with "inducing hostilities between nations" by the Office for Public Prosecution. The rather monopolistic position of the Information and Publishing Corporation Sakinform has also raised some concern, in particular regarding the provision of information. According to one observer, the "tame media always appear to be the first to receive information."

The law and the Constitution cannot always safeguard the protection of media outlets, as is illustrated by the Rustavi 2 case.

The agency Gamma Plus registered with the Ministry of Justice in 1994. The regulations of the agency envisaged the right for broadcasting and on these grounds a license allowing exploitation of the 11m-television channel was given by the Ministry of Communications. The TV channel adopted the name Rustavi 2 and soon became very popular both in Rustavi (located about 21.75 miles from Tbilisi) and in the capital. However, only several months after it went on the air, Rustavi 2 transmission was stopped. The Rustavi municipality applied to the Ministry of Communications, demanding to deprive Rustavi 2 of its right for broadcasting and to transfer its channels to an independent telecompany, Kldekari, that was set up by the municipality itself. The Ministry of Communications annulled its decision and blamed the Ministry of Justice for leading them astray. The latter also altered their position and the broadcasting of Rustavi 2 resumed. However, in July 1996 the Ministry of Communication reconsidered its verdict and once again deprived Rustavi 2 of its license on the same grounds ("invalid"). A rival company was granted permission to broadcast on the available frequency. This time, the management of Rustavi 2 decided to launch a court appeal and ultimately prevailed.

In 1992, the country's new administrative code was approved. A significant portion of the code deals with the regulation of access to information.

Religious Censorship The Georgian Orthodox Church is especially aggressive in hindering the spread of information regarding religious problems, corruption in its staff, or violations of the constitutional principle of separation of church from the school system. The church also does not want other sects or religions to receive any type of publicity. The media acquiesces in this matter, and covering of other churches is nonexistent or superficial. For example, in 1993 when an article was published on the growth of fundamentalism, the secretary of the Patriarch threatened the authors and editorial board of the paper with excommunication, along with a pair of TV announcers who had mentioned the article in their newscasts.

In 1997, an aggressive campaign against a history of religion textbook authored by Nugzar Papuashvili was carried out. Orthodox fundamentalists staged a public burning of that and other books they considered offensive. Representatives of the church said the reporting on the book burning fanned anticlerical hysteria.

State-Press Relations

The Ministry of Justice registers media outlets, while the Ministry of Communications grants (or revokes) licenses for broadcasters, manages the state printing house, the distribution of newspapers and the "subsidies" to state-owned media. The Ministry for Press and Information is, besides providing official information, responsible for the accreditation of journalists. The ministers are appointed by the president and the parliament or its president do not, *de jure*, have direct influence. The only exception is the appointment of the chairpersons of the State TV and Radio Corporation and the official Information and Publishing Corporation Sakinform, who should be approved by parliament. In addition, the parliamentary subcommittee on mass media drafts laws that concern mass media and reviews laws drafted by other bodies in view of their correlation with the current legislation on mass media.

The 1991 press law requires that journalists "respect the dignity and honor" of the president and that they do not undermine the state. The law provides penalties for publications that convey "false information" or "malevolently use the freedom of the press." There are state-owned as well as private television and radio stations. Many independent newspapers reflect different political views and suffer from varying degrees of harassment. State-owned newspapers follow the government line. While media became more independent of government control, they are not editorially independent of financial supporters.

Currently, there is a pervasive tendency toward self-censorship by Georgian editors. Journalists in state-run media fear offending government officials, while their independent counterparts worry about insulting other influential structures in society. This tendency is generally more visible among older journalists and is a residue of the Soviet era.

In June 2000, Georgian authorities tried to force "rebel" broadcast journalist Akaki Gogichaisvili out of the country, Gogichaisvili, anchor of the popular Rustavi-2 television show, "60 Minutes," had been under constant attacks from the prosecutor's office. Vasil Silagadze, a reporter for the *Eco Digest* daily newspaper in Georgia, was attacked in July 2000 by local police officers after publishing an article detailing police corruption. His attackers slashed fingers on his right hand so he "wouldn't be able to write for a while," and threatened further *retAliation* if he continued his investigations.

More recently, the murder of popular television anchor Giori Sanaia has triggered charges that he was assassinated in *retAliation* for his pursuit of government corruption on the Rustavi 2-channel talk show. The 26-year-old anchorman of Georgia's "Night Courier" program was shot dead in his apartment with a single bullet to the back on July 26, 2001. The assassination precipitated national mourning. Facing public suspicion about the role of the security ministries, the government swiftly invited the U.S. Federal Bureau of Investigation to give forensic assistance to the investigation. The police quickly arrested a man previously detained on a fraud charge, yet at this writing prosecutors had not presented sufficient evidence to indict him for Sanaia's murder. Some commentators linked Sanaia's shooting, which appeared to be expertly planned and executed, to purported knowledge or video material he had obtained, allegedly demonstrating links between law enforcement officials with criminals in Georgia's Pankisi Gorge who engaged in kidnappings and the narcotics trade.

Attitude toward Foreign Media

The U.S. Department describes Georgia's foreign relations as "excellent" and makes no remarks concerning danger to foreign journalists in Georgia while detailing its need to create opportunities for development through international and non-governmental organization (NGO) contacts. No incidents concerning the mistreatment of foreign correspondents have been noted.

Georgian media have few if any foreign correspondents and rely on contacts with news organizations in Azerbaijan, Arania and Russia. Many papers subscribe to news agencies, but basic sources are internet and foreign broadcasts.

Broadcast Media

Television The first unsuccessful attempt at independent television came when a group of staff left the State Radio-TV Company in 1990 to start their own venture. After several months of pressure from the authorities, the private TV station Mermisi (Future) was closed. The next major event was the establishment of (state-owned) Channel 2 in 1992.

Ibervisia, which joined the scene in 1992, also played an important but short-lived role in the development of independent television. Ibervisia was a joint venture of the former Komsomol leaders and the so-called Borotebi (Evils), a branch of the paramilitary Mkhedrioni organization. The controversial images of the partners paralyzed the work of the channel, which was finally closed after the weakening of the Mkhedrioni's political influence.

According to CIDD altogether 40 TV stations, including municipal channels, broadcast in Georgia today. The professional skill of their staff, together with the quality of programs, is low. Such types of stations were founded mostly by self-taught enthusiasts, who even constructed the transmission devices themselves. A primitive montage set made out of two VHS recorders is regarded as a great achievement, almost a luxury.

The Georgian television network (TNG) started its work in 1996, bringing together 15 stations not owned by the state that covered 15 cities and towns. Eighty percent of the TNG members' broadcast time consists of licensed video productions. The purchase of these programs is the main goal of the network.

In May 1996, the independent television stations started broadcasting a joint weekly program, exchanging materials with the US Internews Network. The ''Kvira'' (Week) program still presents the sole attempt at reviewing the events of the whole country.

Broadcast media continues to be the main source of information for the vast majority of Georgia's population. Television sets number around 2,570,000, while there are approximately 3 million radio receivers in the country. Over the past two years, however, there has been growing competition from independent TV companies, forcing state TV to make its programming more objective and balanced, yet it remains far from editorially independent.

The government's monopoly on television news was broken when Rustavi-2, a member of the independent television network TNG, emerged in 1998 as an important alternative to state television, after successfully resisting two years of government attempts to shut it down. It is now considered the only station other than the state-run channel with a national audience. In addition to Rustavi-2, there are seven independent television stations in Tbilisi. An international NGO that works with the press estimated that there are more than forty-five regional television stations, seventeen of which offer daily news. While these stations are ostensibly independent, a lack of advertising revenue often forces them to depend on local government officials for support. Some regions, such as Samtskhe-Javakheti and Kutaisi, have relatively independent media. Rustavi-2 has a network of fifteen stations, five of which broadcast Rustavi-2's evening news program daily. Independent newspapers and television stations continue to be harassed by state tax authorities. Stations desiring benefits and better working relations with authorities, practice self-censorship.

Since Rustavi-2, the first powerful independent TV station, survived government attempts to close it down in 1997, viewers in Tbilisi have enjoyed a much greater choice of available programming. Rustavi-2 currently attracts higher ratings than official TV and, according to 2001 data, carries about 55 to 65 percent of the national advertising market. Seven other independent TV stations compete for the TV market in the capital, but unless they receive support from powerful business or political interests, they suffer from severe financial problems. Iberia TV, supported by the Batumi-based Omega, cigarette distribution network, and Skartvelos Khma are seen to represent the views of Asian Abash, an Ajarian regional leader. Stations outside of Tbilisi struggle to maintain their independence as they continue to suffer financially. In January 2000, a 10-member United Television Network (UTN) was created to pool-advertising revenues from small regional stations.

Channel 25 is the only independent television station broadcasting in Ajara, and has been operating since 1998. On February 14, 2000, it broadcast its first uncensored news coverage. On February 19, three of the four owners of the station alleged that they were coerced by Ajaran regional government officials and Mikhail Gagoshidze, chairman of Ajaran Television and Radio, to cede 75 percent of the company's shares to Gagoshidze. The owners stated that in return they were forced to take $50,000 (100,000 laris) in cash. The same day, Batumi mayor Aslan Smirba physically assaulted Avtandil Gvas Alia, the station's commercial director. Smirba claimed that he had a right to own the station, as he had helped the company get permission to broadcast. The owners brought suit against Gagoshidze, but lost their case in Ajara regional court.

Another formidable obstacle for the Georgian media industry is the registration and licensing requirements detailed in Article 7 of the Media Law. Article 10 of that law authorizes the state of deny registration to a media outlet whose goals are considered contradictory to Georgian law.

The lack of legal definition regarding the activity of media and journalists is leading to an increase in the use of force. Georgia has many cases of violence against media professionals. One example is the case of the beating of a correspondent for the newspaper *Eco Digest*, Vasily Silagadze. On July 25, an unknown group of people approached him on the street, identified themselves as policemen, took the journalist to a park and beat him up, advising that he ''write less about the police.'' The jour-

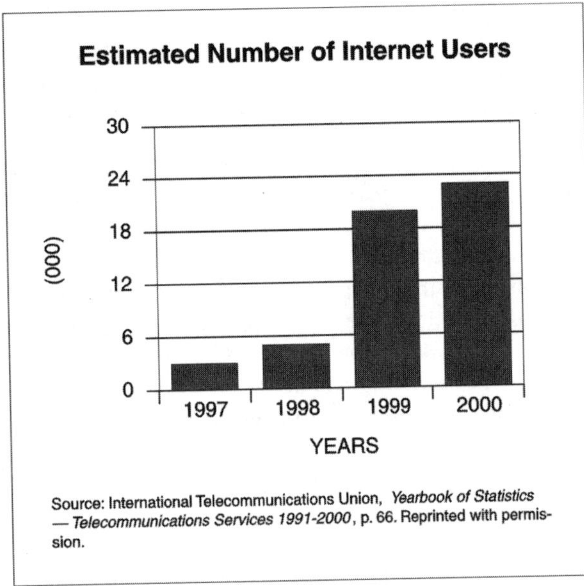

Source: International Telecommunications Union, *Yearbook of Statistics — Telecommunications Services 1991-2000*, p. 66. Reprinted with permission.

nalist also said that after his critical articles about high-ranking officials in the Ministry of the Interior, he received telephone threats. On July 28, the Tbilisi Prosecutor's Office brought criminal charges in the case of the beating. However, on September 7, Vasily Silagadze was again beaten by unknown individuals. According to Silagadze, the people who beat him were, again, police. Membership in the Council of Europe, which Georgia attained in April 1998, required Georgia to adhere to the principles of the European Convention of Human Rights, including Article 10, which guaranteed freedom of expression and information. In reality, however, certain aspects of the media landscape limit the freedom of Georgian journalism.

Radio Radio listenership varies. The Soviets did not use radio widely and a consistent listenership was not established, but many Georgians had formed the habit of listening to the Voice of America and Radio Liberty and these habits persist despite the technical difficulties in the mountainous regions. Reports differ as to whether Georgians, especially in Tbilisi, rely more on the press or TV for daily news. The Rustavi 2 nightly news program appears to reach many people.

A number of independent radio stations broadcast on AM and FM frequencies, but most of their programming consists of music. State radio continues to dominate the regions outside Tbilisi. Radio Fortuna, a privately owned, 24-hour FM station that covers the entire area of Georgia, has the largest audience with more than 620,000 listeners while the combined audience of the two Georgia state radio stations number at 580,000.

In Tbilisi the FM waves are used by one state-owned radio station and six private ones. Most stations play music and are paying less and less attention to the news. Some stations rebroadcast news in Georgian from Voice of America and Radio Liberty. One of the stations, Audientsia, broadcasts in Russian. Private FM stations operate in Kutaisi, Zugdidi, Samtredia and Batumi (although the latter actually appears to be owned by the local ruling party). Most of the FM broadcasters provide only superficial news coverage, as they find other ways to compete for the attention of teenagers, the basic listeners of private radio stations.

Electronic News Media

Only a small fraction of the Georgian population has access to the Internet. Experts estimate that the country has between 10,000 and 12,000 Internet users in a population of 5.4 million. Although this represents a significantly low percentage of the people, there has been an increase of 3,000 users since 1999.

Competition among Internet service providers is extremely high, with Sanet, ICN, and the new Georgian Online, owned by Rustavi-2, dominating the market. Some Georgian newspapers and news agencies have also launched on-line editions. Among the more popular: *The Georgian Times*; *Svobodnaya Gruziya (Liberated Georgia),* Agency Starke Information; Prime-News; The 1st channel of Georgian TV; and Virtual Georgia.

Education & Training

Academic freedom is respected in Georgia and outside support has contributed to limited improvements in Georgian media. The largest western foundations, such as United States Information Agency (now a part of the State Department), Eurasia Foundation, and TACIS have been working in the country to improve the quality of journalism. They organize various workshops, training course seminars and conferences for local media professionals. An excellent American run master's degree program in journalism, for example, has recently been initiated under the auspices of the International Center for Journalism. The Caucasus Institute of Journalism and Media Management in cooperation with the U.S. Department of State and various NGOs is dedicated to the improvement of international journalism. Other institutions that have journalism programs include the Tbilisi Institute for Asia and Africa.

Summary

While the government or local authorities continue to use administrative levers to curb freedom of the press, the trend in the past years has been towards greater freedom for the independent media, and freedom of information. The successful use of the courts by journalists to obtain information is especially heartening. Economic and organizational problems are profound as is the need for better trained professionals. So many factors and issues are in flux that a clear picture has not yet emerged.

BIBLIOGRAPHY

Assoc. of Georgian Independent TV and Radio Companies (Open Society-Georgia). ''Georgia Media Guide 2000-2001,'' Tbilisi 2001. www.mediaguide.ge.

BBC News. ''Country Profiles: Georgia'' news.bbc.co.uk

European Institute for the Media. ''Media in the CIS: Georgia'' by Yasha Lange. www.internews.ru

Freedom House. ''Survey of Press Freedom 1999'' www.rferl.org

———. ''Georgia.'' Nations in Transit 2001. www.freedomhouse.org

''Internews Guide to Georgian Non-Governmental Broadcasters,'' Tbilisi 2002 (USAID, Eurasia Foundation).

International Journalists' Network (IJET). ''Murder of Popular TV Anchor Exacerbates Political Tensions in Georgia,'' August 2, 2001. www.ijnet.org

———. ICGF, GIPA Launch New Western-Style Journalism Programs in Tbilisi. www.ijnet.org

''Media Marketing Study,'' ICFS/Pro Media II, October, 2001, Tbilisi.

Parliament of Georgia. Committee for Human Rights and Ethnic Minorities of the Parliament of Georgia. Hremcmt@parliament.ge

Press Freedom Overview. www.freemedia.at

''Report of the Public Defender of Georgia On the Situation of Protection of Human Rights and Freedoms inGeorgia,'' Tbilisi, 2001.

Telemedia. ''Georgia Media and Market Overview.'' www.telemedia.kiev.ua

United Nations Development Program (UNDP). ''Today's Technological Transformations—Creating the Network Age.'' www.undp.org

———. Bokeria G., Targamadze, G. and Ramshivili, L. ''Georgian Media in the 90's: A Step to Liberty,'' Tbilisi, 1997.

United Nations Educational, Scientific and Cultural Organization (UNESCO). 1999. UNESCO Data Base. www.unesco.org

United Nations Online Network in Public Administration and Finance (UNPAN). ''Country Profiles in Europe.'' www.unpad.org

U.S. Department of State. ''Background Notes: Georgia.'' www.state.gov

U.S. Department of State. ''1999 Country Reports on Human Rights Practices.'' www.state.gov rights/

World Bank. ''Country Profiles,'' www.worldbank.org/

—Virginia Davis Nordin

GERMANY

BASIC DATA

Official Country Name:	Federal Republic of Germany
Region (Map name):	Europe
Population:	83,029,536
Language(s):	German
Literacy rate:	99.0%
Area:	357,021 sq km
GDP:	1,872,992 (US$ millions)
Number of Daily Newspapers:	382
Total Circulation:	23,946,000
Circulation per 1,000:	375
Number of Nondaily Newspapers:	25
Total Circulation:	2,021,000
Circulation per 1,000:	32
Newspaper Consumption (minutes per day):	30
Total Newspaper Ad Receipts:	8,449 (Euro millions)
As % of All Ad Expenditures:	43.50
Magazine Consumption (minutes per day):	10
Number of Television Stations:	373
Number of Television Sets:	51,400,000
Television Sets per 1,000:	619.1
Television Consumption (minutes per day):	185
Number of Cable Subscribers:	20,286,960
Cable Subscribers per 1,000:	246.8

Number of Satellite Subscribers:	12,900,000
Satellite Subscribers per 1,000:	155.4
Number of Radio Stations:	822
Number of Radio Receivers:	77,800,000
Radio Receivers per 1,000:	937.0
Radio Consumption (minutes per day):	206
Number of Individuals with Computers:	27,640,000
Computers per 1,000:	332.9
Number of Individuals with Internet Access:	24,000,000
Internet Access per 1,000:	289.1
Internet Consumption (minutes per day):	13

BACKGROUND & GENERAL CHARACTERISTICS

For most of the twentieth century, Germany was in the forefront of media development and is almost certainly to exert a powerful role in the development of world media into the twenty-first century. This importance is all the more impressive when one considers that in 1945, following the defeat of Germany in World War II, the media were non-existent and had subsequently to be revived during a period of austerity and hardship. During the sixty years from the end of World War II until the beginning of the twenty-first century, the German media developed extensively; in fact, the world's second or third largest media conglomerate, the Bertelsmann Group, is German-based, and one of the German media barons of the late twentieth century, Axel Springer, rivaled in fame, power, and influence the media barons of the nineteenth and early twentieth centuries.

The evolution of the media in Germany in the post war years was heavily conditioned by the political evolution of the country. After World War II Germany was divided into the German Democratic Republic (East Germany), part of the so-called Eastern Bloc, and the Federal Republic of Germany (West Germany), with its political power in Bonn and as part of the western alliance. On October 3, 1990, the two Germanys were reunited under the constitution of the United German Peoples, and on March 15, 1991 the four post-war powers overseeing Germany relinquished all occupation rights. The effect on the population was to unite the 16 million East Germans with the 64 million West Germans.

The West German media virtually extinguished the existing East German media. For example, the most widely circulated newspaper controlled by the East German regime, the *Neues Deutschland* went from a circulation of over 1 million to under 100,000 in less than one year. The incentive for West German media to capture this market was certainly present, for in a country of 16 million persons over 10 million read one or more of three-dozen newspapers on the market, notwithstanding strict government censorship at the time. Similarly television and radio programming was highly controlled in East Germany, and upon reunification East German television shrank, in large part because it was possible for East Germans to receive television signals from the west during the socialist era and upon reunification they continued to view programming to which they had already been exposed and which they apparently desired. In the early 2000s, newspapers and television programs produced in the former West Germany dominate the media landscape of Germany.

General Description The target for the German media is a highly literate, affluent population that takes its media seriously. Literacy is estimated at 99 percent and, with a gross domestic product (GDP) per capita of US$23,400 (2000 est.), Germany is one of the wealthiest countries in the world. The population in Germany is highly urbanized with 87 percent of the people residing in cities and 13 percent living in rural areas. However, the spatial distribution and control of the media are based not on location of urban areas but rather on the location of the media and its public within the sixteen *Länder* (States) that make up the German Federation. It is the *Länder* that in many cases govern the media, particularly the electronic media, and it is within these regional areas that the print media deliver local and regional news. Since over 90 percent of the population is ethnic German speaking the German language, German-language newspapers predominate. However, other groups live in Germany, Turkish and Balkan people, for example.

The remarkable economic growth of the German economy in the late 1950s and early 1960s necessitated the importation of labor, and Turkish workers were actively recruited as *gastarbeiter* (guest workers) to work in German industry. As of 2002 there are some 2.4 million ethnic Turkish residents in Germany (3.1 percent of the population) who are generally concentrated in the cities of Berlin and Nurnberg. To meet their media needs, three Turkish newspapers are printed in Germany and seven Turkish TV programs are obtainable by satellite with one additional television program carried by cable. Of the Turkish language newspapers, the most widely read is *Güncel*. In addition, Turkish newspapers printed in Turkey are available. After the Balkan war between

Daily and Non-Daily Newspaper Titles and Circulation Figures

	1996	1997	1998	1999	2000
Number of Daily Newspapers	408	403	391	387	382
Circulation of Dailies (000)	25,456	25,260	25,016	24,565	23,946
Number of Non-Daily Newspapers	27	26	27	24	25
Circulation of Non-Dailies (000)	2,123	2,205	2,152	2,028	2,021

Source: World Association of Newspapers and Zenithmedia, *World Press Trends 2001*, pp. 8, 10, 17, 19.

1992 and 1996, almost one million refugees from the fighting re-located in Germany, by far the biggest recipient of Balkan refugees. Finally, the provision in the German constitution that recognizes ethnic Germans as those individuals who have families who had homes in Germany at any time has facilitated the emigration of many ethnic Germans from as far away as Russia and Central Asia. Many of these people are descendents of individuals who immigrated to Russia during the time of the reign of the German-born Russian queen, Catherine the Great, as long ago as the mid-eighteenth century. In 1997, some 11,000 ethnic Germans came to Germany from the former USSR. Many media professionals identified the growing need for publications and programming in the language of these recent immigrants which at the present is met by three newspapers, *Kontakt*, *Vostochniji Ekspresse*, and *Russkaja Germanija*, and *Deutsch Welle*, the multi-language German national radio network. However, many observers believe there is a market for additional ethnic media.

In general the quality of German journalism is high. Journalistic traditions in Germany may be traced as far back as the Weimar Republic (1919-1933) during which time reporting was considered less important than the work of high-minded, highly articulate, and erudite editors and copywriters. Thus journalism was not at this time a dynamic profession. This trend continued during Adolf Hitler's National Socialist period when, as a result of the Editors Law of 1933 drawn up by Nazi propaganda chief, Josef Goebbels, all press was placed under the control of the National Socialist government. Since then the press in Germany has been independent, vocal, and respected, and much of its excellence stems from this respect for excellent, learned writing. Another part of German journalistic tradition derive from the immediate post-war period when the occupying forces, particularly the United States and Great Britain, sent a large number of reporters as press officers to Germany to guide journalism and in particular teach ways to gather news objectively.

Politically it may be said that the German media cover a narrower part of the political spectrum than media in other western countries. This is generally explained by the desire of the German press to avoid political extremes, both the right characteristic of the Nazi regime and the left-wing positions characteristic of socialism or communism.

In 1999 there were 135 ''independent publishing units'' or businesses publishing a total of 355 newspapers that had a total circulation of 31.1 million. However, the penetration of daily newspapers in the marketplace is 78.3 percent, a slight fall from a high of over 79 percent; indeed, the number of newspapers on the market also fell in the last decade of the twentieth century. Notwithstanding these declines in readership, with a population of over 82 million persons, Germany has a readership that is among the largest in the world.

Of the 31.1 million newspaper subscribers, 17.1 million read local or regional newspapers. The only newspapers that can claim to be national in reach are *Bild*, *Süddeutsche Zeitung*, *Frankfurter Allegemeine Zeitung*, *Die Welt*, *Frankfurter Rundschau* and *Tageszeitung*. These papers generally retail for around €1.20 and are published as morning editions.

The most popular newspaper in Germany is *Bild Zeitung,* or *Die Bild,* with a circulation of 4,390,000. This size makes it the fifth most popular newspaper in the world. It is a tabloid newspaper of twelve to sixteen pages published Monday through Saturday with big letters, simple messages, often featuring female nudity on the cover or inside the front page and is the most sensational of the German newspapers. (A typical headline might read: ''Child with three arms born in a German city.'') As such *Die Bild* is the best example of yellow journalism among German newspapers. Many Germans indicate they buy it for speed of reading, television listings, and a reasonable sports section. It costs €.45 (approximately US$0.45) on the street. *Bild Zeitung* publishes regional editions and is generally right of center in its political orientation. In contrast, *Frankfurter Allegemeine Zeitung* has significantly fewer readers (approximately 400,000) but is widely known and respected both in Germany and internationally where it can be found in 198 countries. Read by the German business and political elite, it is considered one of the top newspapers in the world. National

Top Ten Daily Newspapers
(2000)

	Circulation
Bild	4,390,000
Zeitungsgruppe WAZ	1,112,000
Zeitungsgruppe Thüringen	476,000
Süddeutsche Zeitung	434,000
Freie Presse	421,000
Rheinische Post	420,000
Zeitungsgruppe Köln	417,000
Frankkfurter Allgemeine Zeitung	408,000
Sächsische Zeitung	353,000
Mitteldeutsche Zeitung	345,000

Source: World Association of Newspapers and Zenithmedia, *World Press Trends 2001*, p. 103.

newspapers generally run fifty pages and costs €1.20 per issue, but most readers in Germany have yearly subscriptions for their newspapers. Most newspapers appear as morning editions, but there are evening editions of some publications, for example, *Frankfurter Rundschau-Abend* (''evening,'' 192,000).

The lengths of German newspapers vary throughout the week as various days have different topical supplements. For instance, the *Süddeutsche Zeitung* has no supplement on Monday, specializes in travel and science on Tuesday, *Immobilienteil* (real estate) both rental and sales on Wednesday, and cultural events (theater, cinema, sporting events) on Thursday. On Friday it includes a lifestyle magazine *Süddeutsche magazin* of about twenty-six pages. Saturday's newspaper contains all the information needed for the weekend and significantly one of the biggest *Stellenmarkt* in Germany, which lists jobs in Munich, Bavaria, the rest of Germany, within Europe, and beyond. On any one day the ratio of editorial to advertisements in *Süddeutsche Zeitung* is approximately 70 percent editorial to 30 percent advertisements. In the case of *Süddeutsche Zeitung* revenues are highly dependent on subscriptions, advertisements, and in particular the widely read Saturday employment section.

Weekly newspapers sell about 2.3 million on Thursday but target primarily weekend readership. The most popular and influential is *Die Zeit* (525,500 and costing €2.80), followed by *Die Woche*. In these newspapers breaking or current news is less important than news analysis and background information. As such, it is not unusual to find a newspaper over 100 pages in length in which a full page of broadsheet size may be devoted to one topic. Also important on Sunday is the publication of Sunday editions of the dailies *Bild am Sonntag* (3,139,900 and costing €1.20) and *Welt am Sonntag* (656,000 and costing €2.10). These two are the most popular Sunday newspapers and contain more pages than their weekday counterparts (twenty pages more in the case of *Bild am Sonntag* and forty more in *Welt am Sonntag*) and more human-interest stories as opposed to their daily news publications.

Germany also has two business daily newspapers, *Financial Times Deutschland* and *Handelsblatt*, the latter the more popular of the two. Of more limited weekly circulation are the two major religious publications, *Deutsche Allegemeine Sonntagsblatt* edited by the Protestant Church, with a circulation of 50,000 and the *Rheineischer Merkur* (111,000 circulation). For both of these, as Germany becomes more secular readership is declining.

A third major component of the print media in Germany is the weekly magazine. There are some 780 general interest magazines and 3,400 specialized magazines published in Germany. The former has a total circulation of 126.98 million copies and the latter 17.7 million. The oldest (first published in 1946) and most popular is *Der Spiegel* with 1.4 million circulation. It runs about 178 pages and in 2002 cost €2.80. Generally considered liberal in its political orientation, it has a reputation for excellent investigative journalism and critical analysis of political life and politicians that often makes its findings highly controversial. Distributed to over 165 countries worldwide and with 15 percent of its sales outside Germany, it is truly an international publication and often considered to be the printed voice of Germany overseas. For many years the weekly magazine enjoyed a virtual monopoly on this part of the media spectrum, but in 1993 significant competition to *Der Spiegel* emerged with the publication of the magazine *Focus*. The format for *Focus* is modeled on the successful *Time* and *Newsweek* in the United States; it has less length to the articles, more color, and a lower price than *Der Spiegel*. This formula was immediately successful as subscriptions rose to almost 750,000 while circulation of *Der Spiegel* fell. Other magazines worthy of note are *ADAC-Motorwelt*, the German auto club magazine, with a circulation of 13 million making it the largest in Germany; *Der Stern*, another leading general interest magazine that enjoys a reputation for its liberal orientation and investigative efforts but whose circulation is steadily declining; *Aussenpolitik*, a leading magazine dealing with German foreign affairs and available in English; *German Life*, a magazine on German culture designed for Americans; *Aufbau*, a German-Jewish newspaper in German; and finally *Bunte*, a typical glossy, German, and international human-interest magazine with over 120 pages which has a somewhat dubious claim to fame with its history of fabricated stories and features of prurient interest.

Finally, as in many other European countries, Germany has seen the introduction and rise in importance of free newspapers that are placed in high pedestrian traffic areas and support themselves entirely by the sale of advertisements. Local publishing houses see these publications as a threat to their operations, and legal injunctions to limit or stop their production have occurred.

As Germany enters the twenty-first century the three most influential newspapers are *Frankfurter Allegemeine Zeitung* for its international reputation, *Die Zeit* for the depth of its news analysis, and *Süddeutsche Zeitung* for its national importance, particularly in its coverage of the all-important Bavarian political scene. It should be noted that to this list *Der Spiegel* should always be appended for its journalistic excellence and international reputation and coverage while in the future the *Berliner Zeitung* and/or *Berliner Morgenpost* will be part of such a list, not for any particular strength but for their preeminence as two of the best regional newspapers and for the rising importance of Berlin as the new or reemerging German political center.

German newspapers are generally considered more regional than urban in coverage, though to affect economies of scale and to conserve financial resources the local independent presses work closely with one another and the national media and much of the contents are produced by centralized offices rather than the *Heimatpresse* (local press). The importance and size of German regional newspapers is noteworthy. *Westdeutsche Allgemeine Zeitung*, printed in the Ruhr city of Essen, has a circulation of 1,313,400, which ranks its circulation as thirty-first in the world, while the small town of Koblenz on the Rhine with 110,000 inhabitants produces a newspaper, the *Koblenz Rhein-Zeitung* with a circulation of 250,000. Kidon Media Services in an inventory of news sources has classified German media by *Länder*. It indicates the importance of *Bayern* (Bavaria) and the Cologne, Dusseldorf, and Frankfurt conurbations as the centers of the German publishing industry and the relative unimportance of the former East German *Länder* as media centers.

Finally, although German newspapers claim to be independent and apolitical, each is generally perceived to have some political bias. However, direct ownership of newspapers by political parties as was a feature of the Weimar Republic (1919-1933) or direct control as was a feature of the National Socialist era (1933-1945) no longer exist. That said, then, it is still the case that *Vorwarts* is the official newspaper of the Social Democratic Party, and *Bayernkurier* is the mouthpiece of the Christian Social Union in Bavaria. *Rheinischer Merkusr* is often linked to the Christian Democratic Union and as noted the *Neues Deutschland* is the organ of the East German Communist party (Party of Democratic Socialism). *Bild Zeitung* and *Die Welt* are generally conservative in their viewpoints and the *Frankfurter Allegemeine Zeitung* is generally right of center, a political stance in the Frankfurt region that is counterbalanced by *Frankfurter Rundschau* which is quite liberal in its orientation. In the 1980s and 1990s, Germany saw the rise of the Green Party whose main platform is environmental policies and connected issues. Many suggest that *Frankfurter Rundschau* is its most obvious ally in the media. *Tageszeitung* and *Junge Welte* are considered the most left wing of the national dailies with the exception of a number of Marxist (*Der Funke*) and communist (*Unsere Zeit*) publications. *Tageszeitung* is an interesting study for, unlike most of the newspapers that are owned by conglomerates, it is published on a cooperative base and has several thousand owners. In the first years of the twenty-first century, it was having the most difficulty in sustaining circulation amid a sea of newspapers.

Numerous surveys indicate that the majority of Germans (51 percent) get their news from television, 22 percent from newspapers and magazines, and only 6 percent from radio (the other source, 16 percent, is from friends). Given these statistics, then, it is not surprising that despite the large number of newspapers and their popularity with Germans as a source of information, there are some disturbing trends. The number of independent newspapers has been steadily declining since the 1950s and coverage of dailies has been falling. More alarming, readership of newspapers among individuals fourteen to nineteen years of age dropped from almost 70 percent to 58 percent between 1987 and 1997. Of particular interest has been the dramatic drop in readership of newspapers in the former East Germany from 10 million in 1990 to fewer than 5 million in 1996. Sales of newspapers at newsstands have fallen and hence the increased importance of the subscription base. Finally, advertising revenues at 65 percent are the primary source of revenue (distribution and sales make up 35 percent), but the increasing competition for advertising revenues from commercial television stations is cause for concern.

ECONOMIC FRAMEWORK

From the rubble of a nation it was in 1945 following World War II, Germany has risen to become the world's third most technologically powerful economy after the United States and Japan. With a GDP of $1.936 trillion (2000 est.) as measured by purchasing power parity and a growth rate of 3 percent in 2000, Germany is one of the world's economic powerhouses. In the sixty years that it took for Germany to gain this degree of economic power, printing and publishing were major contributors with 68.4 percent of the workforce engaged in the service sector in 1999 and printing and publishing contributing 2.41 percent of gross total manufacturing output in the mid-1990s. Furthermore with the growth of German publishing in the former Eastern Bloc and other European Union

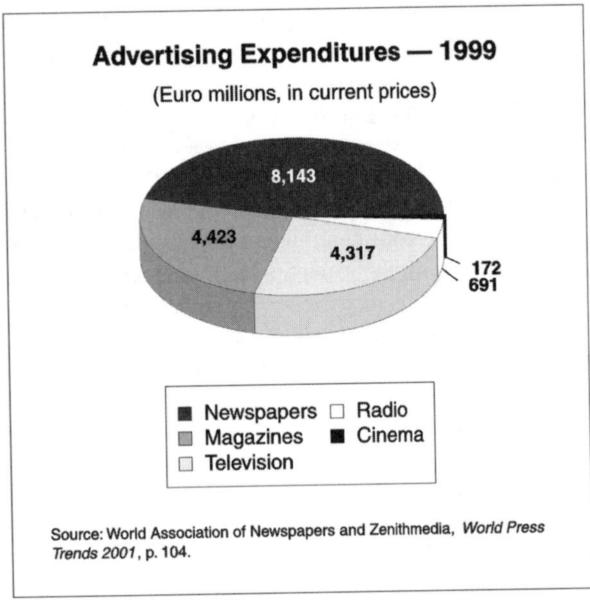

Source: World Association of Newspapers and Zenithmedia, *World Press Trends 2001*, p. 104.

countries, Germany controls an estimated 30 percent of Europe's media market. Many economic commentators noted, however, a dramatic slowing in the 1990s in the pace of the German economic surge. This is partly attributable to the debt of some US$70 billion required to effect reunification and to serious structural deficiencies in the German social system that surfaced because of an aging workforce, greater benefit payouts than income, and the cost of social benefits in hiring new workers. The result has been unprecedented unemployment and a weaker euro than desirable. Structural rigidities may in the future hamper German economic and therefore media growth.

Concentration of Ownership and Monopoly Media development during the 60 years following World War II was closely tied to the relationship between the government and the private sector and in particular the rise of large media conglomerates that as of 2002 dominate both the German media and to some extent the national political agenda. In contrast to the electronic media, the print media is privately owned and operated. The rise of the private, independent German media conglomerate is best exemplified by the rise to dominance of the Axel Springer Group, Germany's major newspaper and magazine publisher with interests also in books, film, and Internet development.

Axel Springer was born into a publishing family in Hamburg, but his empire can be traced to 1946 when the British military government in Hamburg permitted him to open a newspaper. He went on to launch a number of other newspapers in Germany most notably *Hamburger Abendblatt* in 1948 and *Der Bild* in 1956 and to acquire existing newspapers such as *Die Welt* in 1953 and *Berliner Morgenpost* in 1959. By 1968 it was estimated by the German government that Axel Springer published 40 percent of German newspapers, 80 percent of all German Regional newspapers, 90 percent of all Sunday papers, 50 percent of weekly periodicals, and 20 percent of all magazines. This market share represented two-thirds of all papers sold in German cities. Axel Springer died in 1985 but the pattern of acquisitions did not cease with his death. The 1990s were marked by expansion into Central and Southern Europe as the European Union expanded and as the former Eastern Bloc privatized former state media concerns. By 2000 the Axel Springer Group had annual sales of over DM5 billion and around 14,000 employees.

During Axel Springer's rise to prominence a parallel German conglomerate, the Bertelsmann Group, was working in other areas of the media and enjoying similar growth. A publishing house that got its start printing Bibles in the nineteenth century, Bertelsmann has wider interests than Springer, particularly in books, electronic media, and music recording. It is the world's second or third largest media conglomerate as measured by revenues with over US$16 billion (76 percent outside Germany) and 76,000 employees. In Germany its most notable publications are the most popular women's magazine, *Brigitte* and the weekly *Der Stern*, and it has a 25 percent stake in *Der Spiegel*. As a result of its lack of emphasis on newspapers, in 1999 Bertelsmann trailed Axel Springer in print circulation. Axel Springer Group enjoyed 23.7 percent of the circulation market share while Bertelsmann's Gruner and Jahr division enjoyed 3.4 percent. (With regards to the other three large media groups, Westdeutsche Allgemeine Zeitung Group has 5.9 percent market share; the Stuttgarter Zeitung Group, 5 percent; and the DuMont Schauberg Group in Cologne, which is responsible for the *Frankfurter Allgemeine Zeitung*, controls 4 percent.)

In total the ten largest publishers of dailies account for 54.8 percent of the market, and the four largest publishers of magazines enjoy 63 percent market share. This situation has given rise to an ongoing debate in Germany over the perceived monopolies of the large publishing houses and the possible need to reduce them. Most Germans are not concerned so much with the issue of monopoly as with the degree of perceived influence that such publishing houses have on political opinion and decision-making.

Control of the electronic media is different. Dominated by public broadcasting stations until the 1980s, it was traditionally independent and non-commercial but financed by license fees and subsidies and controlled by the *Länder*. These stations were and continued in the early 2000s to be answerable to public sector supervisory councils that influence programming and content. This situation changed dramatically in the 1980s with the advent of cable and satellite systems through which private interests could enter the TV market. Private stations are identifiable by the broadcast of numerous commercial messages by which they finance their operation. In addition the existing *Länder* legislation, particularly that delineating the supervisory roles of the council was anachronistic for the technology and content, and dramatic changes were required to address this new part of public broadcasting, particularly since by the turn of the century its market share was larger than that of the public broadcasting stations and increasing yearly. The power of television and its importance in the German media mix are such that political parties have become increasingly involved in policy decisions on such items as accountability, rating share, and most recently anti-monopoly concerns. Generally the relationship with German political parties has been that the conservative CDU favors privatization and more commercialization while the SPD favors the public service broadcasters.

Trade Unions The trade union movement is strong and influential in Germany, particularly in the media world. In the early 2000s the union movement is undergoing some reorganization, in large part as a reaction to the government's efforts to reduce the range of benefits and perquisites that union members enjoy. Politicians and economists are driven by the fact that in comparison to other countries, Germany is seen as having excessively generous worker benefits that some believe make it uncompetitive. Unions have a rather long history of strikes in the production departments of newspapers but rarely in the editorial offices. The most protracted and serious of these, insomuch as it was over structural change, came in the 1970s and concerned the implementation of new techniques of production.

Newspapers began using personal computers to file stories and thus German newsrooms changed. Plus, new printing presses streamlined the production process and thereby displaced workers. In the early 2000s Germany is at the forefront of new printing and editing technologies. Strikes in the German press seem to occur every two or four years, which is correlated to the prevailing contractual length. The dispute issue is usually connected to wages, and a newspaper may be on strike for some two to three weeks during which time the delivery of the daily newspaper is suspended.

Employment & Wage Scales Employment in the media in Germany is generally considered to be not lucrative. Wages for a beginning journalist in a small local or regional newspaper (50,000 circulation) is under US$50,000 per annum gross with a significant proportion of that going to taxes, health care, unemployment, and pension contribution. Salary in this case may consist of a base salary with incentives for the number of articles written by the journalist that the newspaper prints. In the larger cities and at a more prestigious media outlet, salaries may rise to around US$100,000. However, the high cost of living in Germany necessitates a modest middle-class lifestyle. Executives, TV anchors, and personalities can of course command far greater salaries and benefits. The German media use freelancers.

The fact that federal and state governments employ much of the electronic media is cause for political concern because of the excessive bureaucracy. In order to reduce this number, freelancers are hired because stations do not have to pay them benefits. Freelancers are not on a fixed salary and are free to negotiate their own remuneration and indeed they may work for a number of outlets. As a result freelancer incomes tend to be significantly higher than salaried employees at radio and television stations. Such freelancers also exist in the print media, the most famous example being the *paparazzi* (photojournalists) who sell salacious material to purveyors of yellow journalism. In 1995, some 40,000 persons were employed in television broadcasting and 11,400 in newspapers (the latter figure is from 1990 on the eve of reunification at a time when East German media were grossly over-staffed), but these figures do not take into account the large number of persons employed as freelancers or working in the large multi-national media conglomerates and the distribution network.

Distribution Most print media companies have their own distribution company, but there are also private distribution houses, which distribute a number of smaller newspapers, magazines, leaflets, and brochures. There is rarely a shortage of newsprint in Germany and prices paid reflect international rates.

PRESS LAWS

Freedom of the press in Germany emanates directly from the German *Grundgesetz* (''Basic Law,'' or constitution), which states under Article 5 (Freedom of Expression):

- 1. Everyone has the right freely to express and to disseminate his opinion by speech, writing and pictures and freely to inform himself from generally accessible sources. Freedom of the press and freedom of reporting by radio and motion pictures are guaranteed. There shall be no censorship.
- 2. These rights are limited by the provisions of the general laws, the provisions of law for the protection of youth and by the right to inviolability of personal honor.

- 3. Art and science, research and teaching are free. Freedom of teaching does not absolve from loyalty to the constitution.

While the freedom of the press and all that usually is associated with press freedom (confidentiality of sources and notes, refusal to identify sources, free access to sources) might thus be seen to be as inviolable, there are provisions for recourse in the event of perceived press violation of ethics. In particular, the Press Council is a major counter measure to full press autonomy, and legal recourse is often used. This may involve the agreement to stop printing factual errors, the agreement to print an apology or retraction, and even civil proceedings to obtain monetary damages in the most serious cases. Perhaps the most whimsical example of this was the cease and desist order directed to those in the press that falsely claimed Chancellor Gerhard Schroeder used hair coloring to remove gray from his hair.

The constitution removes the right to publish ''writings which incite to racial hatred or which depict cruel and inhuman acts.'' In the penal code relating to offences against the state, it prohibits ''betraying the country and endangering external security by betraying state secrets.'' Germany possesses the full range of libel, blasphemy, and obscenity laws. Interestingly, however, Germany is the only country in Europe that does not have a Freedom of Information Act. The argument against passage for such a law is that it is implicit within the Basic Law and that moreover it is a *Länder* responsibility. In this regard only four *Länder* have adopted Freedom of Information legislation (Brandenburg, Berlin, Schleswig-Holstein, and Nordrhein-Westphalia). Other *Länder* have proposed Freedom of Information legislation, but Bavaria, Hesse, Saxony, and Baden-Württemburg have voted down Freedom of Information legislation.

As the Federal Republic of Germany is a federal state, press law is largely a *Länder* responsibility, the Constitution setting the framework for the individual *Länder* legislation. Most *Länder* press laws were passed between 1964 and 1966 and upon the reunification in 1990 the existing models were used in the new *Länder*. The most important provisions the press laws enunciate are: the public duty of the press; the right of the press to information; the duty of the press to be thorough; identification of author or imprint; the duty of the editor; the clear distinction between advertisement and editorial; and the right of reply, regardless of veracity. All of these obligations are set out by each *Länder* in the form of a code of conduct called a *Presskodex*.

Perhaps the most controversial part of the code of conduct comes in the area of protecting the privacy of non-official citizens. The codex states under Article 8:

> The press shall respect the private life and intimate sphere of persons. If, however, the private behavior touches upon public interest, then it may be reported upon. Care must be taken to ensure that the personal rights of uninvolved persons are not violated.

The problem arises in the definition of ''intimate sphere'' and ''public interest,'' and, in the case of the German media, the yellow nature of much of the journalism. The desire for salacious material on public figures, such as politicians, athletes, movie stars, and other performing artists, often finds the German media on the edge of what is permissible and what is excessive. One notorious case of invasion of privacy is the so-called ''Caroline Case.'' In March 1992 the magazine *Bunte* published an article that purported to be an interview with Princess Caroline of Monaco, a reclusive and press-shy individual. Unfortunately the interview was entirely fabricated. The result was an DM180,000 compensation settlement.

Commonly German newspapers will publish the facts as the newspaper sees them but will not reveal the name of the central figure in those cases where scandal and sensationalism are presumed present. Rather they will print a fictitious name or only the given name and not the family name, for example a column may read: ''Richard B. was charged.'' This practice is obligatory in court cases to protect the accused. In the case of politicians, coverage is extensive but rarely involves family and indeed extra-marital relationships are also deemed private matters.

One common feature of German newspapers is the *gegendarstellung* (opposing interpretation). It is a consequence of the right to reply provision in the codex and is an expression from a complainant who believes he or she has been misrepresented. It involves the printing verbatim of the facts as the complainant interprets them. Remarkably, the compainant's response does not have to be true. It only needs to state a contrary view of the facts as the complainant sees them. In many *Länder*, the newspaper is permitted to state it is obliged to print the piece (usually by the courts) and does not necessarily agree with the sentiments expressed in it.

In the Federal Republic of Germany there is no registration of journalists though Article 9 of the codex attempts to describe a ''responsible journalist.'' Generally, journalists in Germany have some form of higher education, though particularly in the case of photojournalists newspapers and magazines will pay significant sums of money for freelance material, particularly if it is salacious, unique, or constitutes a ''scoop.'' There are no licensing requirements to be met before newspapers can publish, no bonds required, and the independence of the judiciary is not questioned.

CENSORSHIP

In Germany there is no official censorship, but as a result of the Fascist period of government and the desire to expiate the past, Nazi propaganda and other hate speech are illegal. As a result, the Freedom House Survey of Press Freedom of 1999 gave Germany one of the highest ratings for freedom of the press. In 1997 in response to concerns over child pornography and the Internet, a bill to regulate standards for child protection on the Internet was passed. It defines which online activities should be subject to licensing and other regulatory requirements. As a result of a rise in crime and the terrorist attacks of September 11, 2001, a constitutional amendment was introduced to restore broad police surveillance powers. Journalists among other professionals, however, would be exempt from bugging.

As was noted above, while there is no agency concerned with monitoring the press, Germany has an active Press Council that oversees the functions and operation of the print media. In view of its importance and influence it is worth examining in some detail its make up and mandate.

Self-monitoring Systems The German *Deutscher Presserat* (Press Council) owes its origins to the need following World War II for a body that was independent of the government to monitor the media and provide recourse for media disagreements. Formed on November 20, 1956, the German Press Council is modeled after the British Press Council. Statutes adopted on February 25, 1985 and updated in 1994 govern its structures and duties. According to Article Nine, the Press Council has the following duties: to determine irregularities in the press and to work toward clearing them up; to stand for unhindered access to the source of news; to give recommendations and guidelines for journalistic work; to stand against developments which could endanger free information and free opinions among the public, and to investigate and decide upon complaints about individual newspapers, magazines, or press services.

The Press Council consists of a consortium of twenty representatives from journalist and publisher associations. The members' assembly addresses legal, personnel, and financial matters of the body but are not involved in matters of competition and pricing. A ten-member complaints commission is an important policing unit. It should be noted that this body is entirely self-monitoring with no external authority, such as an ombudsman, involved in the decision-making process of the council. It is estimated that the council receives on average 300 and 400 complaints per year. In practice most complaints against the press are dealt with quickly and effectively, often by use of the printed apology, notes of censure, or public reprimand. Examples of the latter include reprimands for the naming of suicide victims, publication of photos of corpses, and non-authentic photographs of stories being covered. Some observers believe that the receipt of such a reprimand by a newspaper or magazine is generally seen as a black mark and is to be avoided if at all possible, while others point to the content and practices of those yellow publications and suggest that the influence of the Press Council is limited. To assist in their advisory role the Press Council provides a series of guidelines for editors and journalists to which they are advised to adhere.

The most relevant oversight body monitoring the broadcast media is the *Rundfunkrat* (Independent Broadcasting Council). This body, set up under the *Länder*, regulates the public service broadcasters. As a result of a constitutional court ruling, the *Rundfunkrat* is required to be made up of "socially relevant groups." It is composed of members of a wide range of public interest groups such as political parties, business, and labor organizations, churches, farmers, sports, women's groups, and cultural organizations. As such, it is supposed to be free of political control and influence, but in fact, party interests can become significant determinants of policy. Complaints against the broadcast media can be brought before these councils for resolution.

Satellite and Cable Issues The advent of satellite and cable systems as a means of communication necessitated new media laws to be drafted by the *Länder* to regulate media outside the existing public broadcasting regulations. Of primary necessity was the need to establish a mechanism for allocating licenses and determining what programs were to be fed into the cable systems. For this purpose, new *Länder* bodies, the *Landesmedienanstalten*, were created. These bodies closely resembled the existing supervisory bodies for the public network. By 1991, these bodies were present in the former East Germany, and in the early 2000s they govern the cable and satellite industry. As a result of criticism brought against commercial television that their offerings were particularly harmful to children, some commercial broadcasters employ a commissioner for youth protection, the *Jugendschutzbeauftragter*, that reports to the company. There are also planned informal advisory councils to advise commercial television stations on content and acceptability.

In the realm of advertising the *Deutscher Werberat* (German Advertising Council) has members from the media and advertising agencies who receive complaints and publish their decisions in a handbook. The lack of consumer representation on the twelve-person council has been cited as a major drawback to its effectiveness.

STATE-PRESS RELATIONS

Generally, the press does not abuse the German constitution which gives in practice perhaps the most wide-ranging press freedoms in the West. When the German media cover the political scene, the treatment is generally less emotional and less sensationalized than that in many other countries. Media observers attribute this objectivity to a strong organizational control in the German corporate press organization, in which reporters' opinions and criticisms are subsumed in those of the editor and lead writers. Thus rarely will one find political opinion within a story, but rather a concentration on news and business. Indeed, at election times newspapers rarely endorse one political party or candidate.

Political scandals and their effect on public life and democracy are another area of concern. The combination of the constitution, the press laws, and the Press Council codex have the effect of making the German press much more discreet and confidential than its counterparts in many western countries. However, this may be changing as several surveys indicate a decline in public attitudes towards politicians connected to scandals. Moreover it is apparent that editorial comment on such scandals strongly influences government responses given the emphasis the German public places on receipt of its news from all media sources.

ATTITUDE TOWARD FOREIGN MEDIA

The German press is an open system and as such, foreign media are accepted and contribute to a wide range of views. Indeed the evolution of the German media has been one not of protection from foreign media but rather integration to every possible extent with foreign media in order to effect growth and variety. Thus, cable systems first started with a Luxembourg-based station (RTL) and continued with such broadcasters as ARTE (a Franco-German cultural channel that is a consortium of ARD, ZDF, and the French channel La Sept), while satellite television is closely integrated with Austrian, French, Swiss, and U.S. national television stations. Deutsche Welle, as the international voice of Germany, has been particularly active in broadcasting German television programs to thirty-one countries worldwide from Berlin. Deutsche Welle Radio transmits by satellite around the globe to twenty-nine nations while Deutsche Welle World provides a multimedia service on the Internet. In the print media foreign magazines like *Paris Match*, *Elle*, *Vogue* and *W* are eagerly bought in Germany and other western newspapers are freely available. Moreover, most European media have significant representation in Germany in the form of German correspondents along with news bureaus like Reuters, Bloomberg's, AP and Agent Presse France. The German domestic news agency is the Deutsche Presse Agentur (DPA) based in Hamburg.

BROADCAST MEDIA

The German electronic media is a little like that of the BBC, but the influence and role of the sixteen *Länder* make it somewhat different. At the basis of the German electronic media is the provision in the federal constitution that the *Länder* administers radio and television. This was enacted in 1949 to ensure against no repetition of the type of state control exercised by the National Socialists during the time of the Third Reich. In 1954 the first public sector broadcasting corporation, *Arbeitgemeinschaft der Rundfunkanstalten* (ARD), was formed as a consortium of *Länder* and in the early 2000s employs 23,000 people with an annual budget of US$6 billion. The second public broadcaster, *Zweites Deutsches Fernsehen* (ZDF), was formed in 1961 and is a separate corporation with an agreement with all *Länder* to produce national programming. These public service broadcasters are marked by the production of regional news, cultural coverage, and educational programming, such as documentaries and current affairs programs. Advertising is limited to thirty minutes per day and no advertising is allowed after 8:00 p.m. or on Sundays.

This monopoly was eliminated in 1981 when *Länder* recognized their right to grant broadcasting licenses to private companies, which was passed into law in 1987. Concomitant with this legislation was the provision throughout (West) Germany of a national cable network provided by the *Deutsch Telekom* (federal post office) which today owns all the cable systems and which claims to be the world's largest cable network provider. The recent ruling by the European Union that telephone and cable systems should be ''unbundled'' or under separate ownership has led to a sell off of some of Deutsch Telekom's cable assets. By the end of the millennium, of the 33 million households that had television (owning 54 million TV sets), 70 percent had access to cable, though of the 6.6 million households in the former East Germany that had television only 12 percent had access to cable. All German television owners are required to pay a license fee with a supplementary fee required for cable subscribers.

The entrance of private companies into the TV market raised new fears of monopolies and excessive control by media conglomerates. In 2002 German commercial television is controlled by two media groups, first the Bertelsmann conglomerate that broadcasts in conjunction with a Luxembourg-based corporation and the Kirch conglomerate (headed by another German media mogul, Leo Kirch). Kirch obtained his power by buying the rights to broadcast a wide range of international programs (which are usually dubbed into German) and sporting events and which, owing to the number of rights that he holds or are under his control, is now seen as a de facto monopoly on commercial programming.

It is generally agreed that the programming on cable is much more commercial and somewhat more down market (there is a range of reality television shows, game shows, human problem confrontational shows similar to the Jerry Springer show in the United States, talk shows, and a number of pornography channels). Much of the programming on cable has been copied from the United States where similar shows have proven to be audience draws and which apparently draw German viewers. This trend in television has affected the programming on the two public service channels, ARD and ZDF. In an attempt to meet the challenge from the commercial stations, the government has decentralized control of the programming, reduced state subsidies leading program directors to turn toward more commercial type programming. For example, one of the most popular TV programs on ARD is ''Tatort,'' a crime-based soap opera in which viewers follow the work of a detective and his helpers as they expose and combat serious incidences of crime. Its success is such that it is syndicated throughout Europe. In contrast, the reduction in state subsidies and the emphasis on commercial success have meant that the German public television history of serious documentaries has lessened, for funding for such programs is now increasingly difficult to obtain. Notwithstanding the lessening importance of the German Public Broadcasting system, ARD and ZDF still command significant audience shares during their peak viewing hours (which in the case of ARD is at 8:00 p.m. and ZDF 7:30-8:00) on weeknights when the national news (*Tagesthenmen* and *Tageschau*) is broadcast, as well as on Saturday nights when the most popular TV show in Germany, *Wettendas* is shown on ZDF. This is a celebrity talk show with a game show component and a very popular host, Thomas Gottschalk. According to a 1990 survey, 49 percent of West Germans and 70 percent of East Germans watch the evening news at least five times per week.

In 1985 with the broadcast of SAT-1, satellite television became part of the media mix in Germany. While Kirch owned a large part of all SAT channels, other new entrants to the satellite market quickly emerged. Two new all-news channels appeared in 1993, one owned by Time Warner/CNN and the other, VOX, by Bertelsmann. By 1996 Kirch had introduced digital satellite TV and at the turn of the century claimed 2 million subscribers paying DM55 for service including the necessary decoder.

German radio is losing importance in the twenty-first century. As noted, only 6 percent of the public get their news from the 77.8 million radios in Germany. There were fifty-one AM stations, 767 FM stations, and four short-wave stations in Germany in 2000, with commercial radio dominating the airwaves. A city the size of Hamburg might boast over ten commercial radio stations providing programming for the full spectrum of market interests. Two German radio corporations, Deutschlandfunk (DLF) and Deutsche Welle (DW), intend to provide foreign countries with information and as such they are controlled by federal legislation. DW was founded in 1953 and has a worldwide presence, broadcasting twenty-four hours a day in 29 languages to 210 million people.

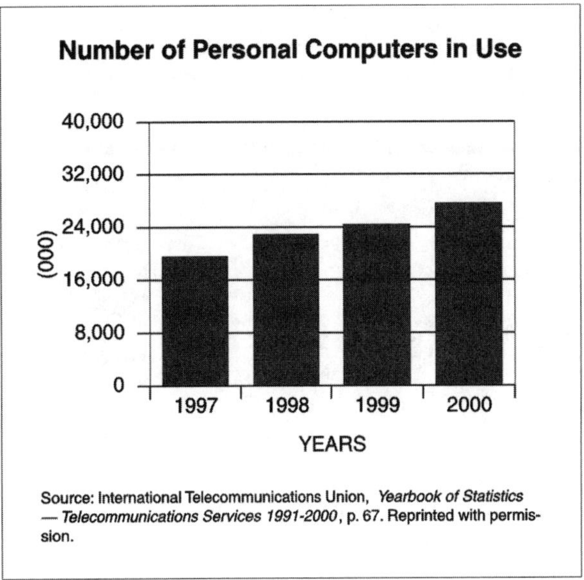

Source: International Telecommunications Union, *Yearbook of Statistics — Telecommunications Services 1991-2000*, p. 67. Reprinted with permission.

Electronic News Media

An estimated 24 million Germans have access to the Internet with 625 Internet providers in the country while at the beginning of 2000, some 176 German newspapers offered online news. As for the rest of the western world, it is difficult to assess the impact of its availability in Germany. What generally is known is that 73 percent of users are under forty years of age, of higher median income and education level, and usually male; most read online news from their residence and generally read their local newspaper. Only 29 percent read their news daily as opposed to 56 percent who read their print newspaper, and they read for a shorter time and a more limited range of topics in the newspaper. For the newspaper the issues are still ones of familiarity (it was estimated in 1989 that the median age of reporters in German newsrooms was 50 years) for an aging workforce, financial considerations, and lack of knowledge on how to market their product. In the early 2000s use of the print layout seems to be the normal method. However most German sites keep the news current and relevant.

Education & Training

Media education in Germany constitutes a large portion of the German higher educational system. The central registry of degree programs for Germany indicates that there are only twenty degree programs in Germany that award a degree in journalism, but in the more general

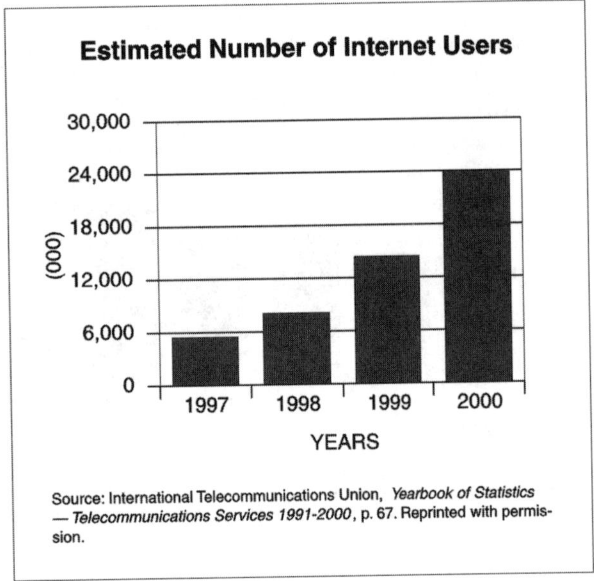

Source: International Telecommunications Union, *Yearbook of Statistics — Telecommunications Services 1991-2000*, p. 67. Reprinted with permission.

areas of media studies and publishing, 184 institutions of higher education offer some form of program. A student can obtain either a diploma, equivalent to an undergraduate degree, a *Magister* or master's degree equivalency, or a doctorate or Ph.D.

This trend toward media studies grew particularly in the 1980s and 1990s. The burgeoning interest resulted in a large number of graduates with very few positions available in any one year. For example, a small regional newspaper or radio station may hire only one or two new people every year and even the larger national newspapers hire infrequently, making the job market very competitive. This situation is exacerbated by the fact that many of the publishing houses or larger newspapers have *Volontariat* (apprenticeship) programs. While this system is not as prevalent in the early 2000s as in the twentieth century, it is still a significant option. Many media observers note that to obtain a position in the German media today a doctorate is almost becoming a necessity.

The most prestigious institutions for training journalists are the Munich Journalism School and the Hamburg Journalism School. Entrance is highly competitive for both programs, with fewer than one hundred students graduating from each institution annually. These schools owe their reputations in large part to loose affiliation with *Süddeutsche Zeitung* in Munich and the Axel Springer organization in Hamburg. It should also be noted that German media have been at the forefront of training media in such areas as investigative journalism, media management, and business planning in the newly emerging states of Central Europe, Russia, and Central Asia.

There are two major professional organizations representing journalists. One is *Deutscher Journalisten Verband* (German Journalists Association, DJV) that calls itself a trade union. It is not, however, affiliated with trade union organizations but rather acts as a professional lobby group. The second organization is the *Deutsche Journalisten Union* (German Journalists Union, DUJ), a member of the German Trade Federation. Both organizations provide ongoing training for their members, as does the European Journalism Center, an independent nonprofit training institution. As media boundaries and borders in Europe become more permeable, the goals of the EJC become more relevant. EJC goals are: to further the European dimensions in media outlets; to enhance the quality of journalistic coverage; to analyze and describe the European media landscape, and to provide strategic support for European media.

In view of the fact that the German Press Council is made up of both journalist representatives and publishers representatives, *Bundesverband Deutscher Zeitungsverlager* (BDZV), should be noted as the representative of the owners and publishers, while the *Verband Deutscher Zeitschriftenverlager* (VDZ) represents the magazine publishers. Similarly, while not members of the Press Council, but important as the industry voice in the regulation of the broadcast media, the *Verband Privater Rundfunk und Telekommunikation* (VPRT) operates as the voice of commercial radio and television.

Awards The overall excellence of the German media has garnered a large number of journalistic awards and prizes. For example, in 2001, two of the three ''World's Best-Designed Newspapers'' were, for circulation of 175,000 or more, *Die Zeit*; and for circulation in the 50,000 to 174,999 range, *Die Woche*.

In 2002 nominated as part of the sixteen finalists in the ''World's Best-Designed Newspaper'' in the 175,000 circulation and above category were *Die Welt* and the *Berliner Zeitung*. They were competing in the final with such newspapers as *The New York Times*, the *Detroit Free Press*, and the *St. Louis Post-Dispatch* from the United States; from Canada *The Globe and Mail*; and from England, *The Guardian*, *The Independent*, and *The Observer*. The winners in the category of 175,000 circulation and above were *The Hartford (Conn.) Courant*, the *National Post*, Ontario, Canada; and *Die Welt*, from Berlin, Germany. In the same competition *Die Woche* won the best newspaper award for the category of 50,000 to 174,999 circulation while *Die Zeit* won awards for ''other news'' and *Die Weltspiegel* won for its Science and Technology pages. With thirteen awards Germany received the largest number of awards of any nation.

SUMMARY

Perhaps the one factor that arises from an examination of German media is the importance it plays in German intellectual life and debate. Indeed, German media is one of the most powerful opinion makers in European, or indeed world, media for it is a highly analytical and critical tool that leads to articulation of important subjects. At the beginning of the twenty-first century, Germans debate about their past, especially under Hitler, and also turn a critical eye to politicians in their midst. The early 2000s witness a mood of disillusionment with the electorate, particularly the disgrace of former Chancellor Helmut Kohl who allegedly received large amounts of campaign contributions from industry sources. Critical analysis is the hallmark of the modern German press. Particularly at the national level, the outlook for the media in the twenty-first century is inextricably bound up with the existence of the public broadcasting networks, both radio and television. The most fundamental question is whether there is a role for state subsidized electronic media in Germany at all or whether full privatization is necessary or desirable. One problem with public broadcasting systems is the amount of investment needed for both new technologies and programming, a cost that is usually not borne by license fees or state budgets that are increasingly looking to be reduced rather than increased. In order to raise this kind of money, public broadcasting stations need to become more commercial or more revenue oriented and in order to do that, they must emulate the existing commercial operations. In the early 2000s, advertising provides roughly one-third of television revenues and one-fourth of radio revenues. If public broadcasting stations are to become more financially viable, this proportion must surely increase. They must now find a new niche in an increasingly commercial media.

At the international or global level, much like in the rest of the western world, the mission of the German media is to embrace the phenomenon of globalization. The late 1990s saw the growth of large media conglomerates, of which Germany had a significant number. These conglomerates embarked upon a strategy of vertical and horizontal integration marked by convergence of telecommunication and information technology and in particular the integration of print media, broadcast media, and the Internet. By the year 2002 as the stock market was reflecting increasing difficulty and excessive cost in achieving that convergence, the wisdom of such convergence was being reexamined. With the importance of large media conglomerates to Germany, any strategic miscalculation could have a significant impact on German economy as a whole. Thus, the outlook for the twenty-first century must be one of guarded optimism, fuelled by the incredible success story of the past sixty years but possibly tempered by the structural difficulties and rigidities that once made the economic miracle happen.

SIGNIFICANT DATES

The most significant highlights of press history during the past ten years have been the requirements within the media to integrate the former East Germany into the federal system of media operation.

- October 3, 1990: The two Germanys are reunited under the Constitution of the United German Peoples.
- 1990: The German constitution or ''Basic Law'' (*Grundgesetz*) is amended by the Unification Treaty to include the former East German *Länder* on August 31 and by Federal Statute on September 23.
- 1990: National framework of regulations between *Länder* (*Medienstaatsvertrag*) is extended to new *Länder* which join the federal republic under reunification. This action is completed in 1991.
- 1994: On February 23, the Public Principals of the German Press Council are updated.
- 1996: Digital television arrives in Germany.

BIBLIOGRAPHY

Eggleston, Roland. ''Germany: Complex Press Regulations Attempt to Divide Public, Private Spheres,'' *Radio Free Europe and Free Liberty* (May 1998). Available at http://www.rferl.org/nca/features/1998/05/f.ru.980527114711.html.

Embassy of the Federal Republic of Germany. ''Germany Info.'' Available at http://www.germany-info.org.

Esser, Frank. ''Editorial structures and Work Principals in British and German Newsrooms,'' *European Journal of Communication*, vol. 13, issue 3 (September 1998): 375.

———. ''Tabloidization of News: A Comparative Analysis of Anglo-American and German Press Journalism,'' *European Journal of Communication*, vol. 14, issue 3 (September 1999): 291.

The European Journalism Center. ''European Media Landscape.'' Available at http://www.ejc.nl.

German Culture. ''Newspapers in Germany'' and ''Radio and Television in Germany.'' Available at http://www.germanculture.com.

''Grundgesetz : Basic Law (German Constitution).'' Available at http://www.library.byu.edu.

Ketupa Net Profiles. ''Axel Springer—Profile'' and ''Bertelsmann—Profile.'' Available at http://www.ketupa.net.

Kidon Media Center. ''Newspapers and Other Media Sources from Germany.'' Available at http://www.kidon.com.

Neuberger, C., J. Tonnemacher, M. Biebl, and A. Duck. ''Online: The Future of Newspapers? Germany's Dailies on the World Wide Web.'' Available at http://www.ascusc.org/jcmc/vol4/issue1/neuberger.html.

—Richard W. Benfield

GHANA

BASIC DATA

Official Country Name:	Republic of Ghana
Region (Map name):	Africa
Population:	19,894,014
Language(s):	English (official), African languages
Literacy rate:	64.5%
Area:	238,540 sq km
GDP:	5,190 (US$ millions)
Number of Television Stations:	11
Number of Television Sets:	1,730,000
Television Sets per 1,000:	87.0
Number of Radio Stations:	21
Number of Radio Receivers:	4,400,000
Radio Receivers per 1,000:	221.2
Number of Individuals with Computers:	60,000
Computers per 1,000:	3.0
Number of Individuals with Internet Access:	30,000
Internet Access per 1,000:	1.5

BACKGROUND & GENERAL CHARACTERISTICS

Ghana has a vibrant press that plays a key role in political discourse, national identity, and popular culture. Emerging in the nineteenth century, the news media have given voice to popular campaigns for independence, national unity, development, and democracy throughout the twentieth century, establishing a distinguished history of political activism for Ghanaian journalism.

The first newspaper, *The Gold Coast Gazette and Commercial Intelligencer,* was published from 1822-25 by Sir Charles MacCarthy, governor of the British Gold Coast settlements. As a semi-official organ of the colonial government, the central goal of this Cape Coast newspaper was to provide information to European merchants and civil servants in the colony. Recognizing the growing number of mission-educated Africans in the Gold Coast, the paper also aimed at promoting literacy, encouraging rural development, and quelling the political aspirations of this class of native elites by securing their loyalty and conformity with the colonial system.

The appropriation of print media by local African elites began in mid-century with the publication of *The Accra Herald* by Charles Bannerman, son of a British lieutenant governor and a princess from the Asante royal family. Handwritten like MacCarthy's former colonial paper, *The Accra Herald* was circulated to some 300 subscribers, two-thirds of them African. Enduring for 16 years, the success of Bannerman's paper stimulated a proliferation of African-owned newspapers in the late nineteenth century, among them *Gold Coast Times, Western Echo, Gold Coast Assize, Gold Coast News, Gold Coast Aborigines, Gold Coast Chronicle, Gold Coast People, Gold Coast Independent,* and *Gold Coast Express.*

Historians of the Gold Coast press tend to explain the indigenous enthusiasm for newspapers in terms of an overall strategy by native elites to gain political power. The early Gold Coast weeklies were critical of the colonial government, denouncing specific officials and opposing policies. While the editorial positions of these papers expressed an adversarial stance, the erudite English and ostentatious vocabulary so common to journalism in this period indicates a more complex and attenuated political desire to establish an exclusive class identity as African elites while striking up a gentlemanly conversation with British officials over conditions in the colony. With occasional exceptions, the British adopted a comparatively tolerant approach to the local press in the Gold Coast, as in other non-settler colonies, colonial territories that had no substantial population of European settlers. Discussing British policy in non-settler colonies, author Gunilla Faringer points out in *Press Freedom in Africa* that ''the colonizers were more concerned with establishing trade bases and making a profit than with exercising political domination.''

Frustrated in their attempts at exercising political power within the colonial order, indigenous elites became increasingly opposed to colonial authority in the early twentieth century. The gentlemanly dialogue of nineteenth century newspapers transformed into full-blown anticolonial protest in the newspapers of the

1930s. Newspapers demanded that citizens be given political rights, improved living standards, and self-government. As the political agenda of Gold Coast journalism radicalized, newspapers began reaching out beyond the circle of elites, appealing to rural leaders and the urban poor with a more accessible language and fiery oppositional outcry. In 1948, political activist Kwame Nkrumah started *The Accra Evening News,* a publication stating the views of the Convention People's Party (CPP). Largely written by party officials, this inflammatory newspaper incessantly repeated the popular demand for ''Self-government Now!'' while launching angry attacks against the colonial government.

In contrast, the London Daily Mirror Group, headed by British newspaper magnate Cecil King, established *The Daily Graphic* in 1950. The *Graphic* sought to maintain a policy of political neutrality, emphasizing objective reporting by local African reporters. With its Western origin, The *Graphic* sought to position itself as the most professional newspaper in the Gold Coast at the time.

Lead by the anticolonial press and Nkrumah's CPP, Ghana achieved independence in 1957, becoming the first colony in Sub-Saharan Africa to gain independence from the British and win political autonomy. As the leader of independent Ghana, Nkrumah became president in 1960 when a new constitution established the nation as a republic. At independence, four newspapers were circulating in Ghana; within a few years Nkrumah had come to dominate them all. Crafting an African form of socialism, Nkrumah saw media as an instrument of state authority, using newspapers as propaganda tools to build national unity and popular support for the ambitious development projects of the new government. Influenced by Lenin, Nkrumah orchestrated a state information apparatus through a hierarchical network of institutions, including the Ministry of Information, Ghana News Agency, Ghana Broadcasting Corporation, and his own press, Guinea Press, Ltd., that published two daily newspapers, one free weekly, and several specialized publications. One of these, Nkrumah's own *Evening News,* became a ''kind of *Pravda* of the CPP,'' dominated by party news and adulations of Nkrumah.

Rejecting the commercialism of the private press as politically irresponsible, Nkrumah harassed the remaining private papers and eventually purchased *The Daily Graphic* in 1963, incorporating the paper into his state apparatus. The Kumasi-based *Ashanti Pioneer,* founded in 1939 by John and Nancy Tsiboe, remained defiant in the 1950s and early 1960s, animated by regional opposition to Nkrumah. After repeatedly subjecting the paper to censorship, eventually Nkrumah shut down the paper in 1962. The editor of the *Pioneer* was detained for seven months and the city editor spent four and half years in detention in Fort Ussher Prison for criticism against the government.

In 1966, Nkrumah was overthrown by a military coup lead by the National Liberation Council (NLC). In contrast to state domination under Nkrumah, the NLC took a more libertarian approach to the news media: releasing independent journalists from prison, closing down the more blatant instruments of state propaganda, and lifting forms of censorship and bans on foreign journalists. However, most media were then owned by the state and therefore obliged to change their editorial positions overnight, extolling the virtues of Nkrumah and African socialism one day, then lambasting the violence and corruption of his regime the next. While the president of the NLC publicly encouraged ''constructive'' criticism and the free flow of information, the main newspapers continued to experience indirect forms of state patronage and influence.

Ghana has been ruled by a series of military regimes and democratic republics since the late 1960s. In the midst of this political oscillation, the media have been subject to alternating policies of libertarian tolerance and revolutionary control. In 1981, Flight Lieutenant Jerry John Rawlings seized power from the democratically elected government of Hilla Limann. Following in the footsteps of Nkrumah, Rawlings summoned the media to actively promote revolutionary ideals of the ruling party PNDC (later NDC) while whipping up popular enthusiasm for the participatory projects of the state. The editorial staff of the state media were reshuffled or dismissed and the editorial policies of the state media were strategically shaped to suit the interests of the new regime. Throughout the 1980s, the state media apparatus applied a variety of techniques of official and unofficial censorship, including repressive laws, public intimidation and harassment, bans on oppositional publications, and arrest and detention of dissident journalists. In order to avoid state harassment, many newspapers avoided politics altogether and focused on sports reporting instead.

In 1992, Ghana returned to democratic rule with the ratification of a new constitution. Rawlings was twice elected President, first in 1992 and then again in 1996. In the democratic dispensation, Rawlings lifted the newspaper licensing law, allowing for the reemergence of the private press in the early 1990s. Newspapers such as *The Independent,* the *Ghanaian Chronicle, The Free Press,* and *The Statesman* gave voice to the angry opposition silenced in years of repression, prompting Rawlings to repeatedly denounce the private media as politically irresponsible and selfishly motivated by profit. Throughout the 1990s, the two state dailies, *Ghanaian Times* and *Daily Graphic,* continued to represent the interests of the ruling-party NDC government. In the 1996 presidential campaign, the premier state paper, the *Daily Graphic,* regularly featured a front page story celebrating the populist agenda of the state, accompanied by a large color photograph depicting the stately figure of Rawlings wielding a pickaxe or driving a bulldozer to launch a development project. These flattering portrayals were often countered in the private press by accusations of drug abuse and violent authoritarianism, featuring older photographs of a militant young Rawlings dressed in fatigues and mirrored sunglasses.

After nineteen years of Rawlings and the NDC, Ghanaians elected John Agyekum Kufour of the New Patriotic Party (NPP) as their new president in December 2000. While urging the media to be responsible, President Kufour has advocated free expression, political pluralism, and an independent media as important elements of liberal democracy—a dramatic shift from Rawlings' furious condemnations of the private press. However, President Kufour's liberal policies were challenged by a national state of emergency in April 2002 involving the assassination of the Dagomba traditional ruler and twenty-eight others in the northern city of Yendi. The Minister of Information, Jake Kufour, who is also the President's brother, has come under criticism in the midst of the crisis for requesting that journalists clear their stories on the Yendi tragedy with the Ministry in the interests of ''caution, circumspection, and wisdom.''

Currently about 40 newspapers are published in Ghana. The state funds two daily newspapers and two weekly entertainment papers. *Daily Graphic* and its entertainment weekly, *The Mirror,* are produced in Accra by the state-funded Graphic Corporation. *Ghanaian Times* and its affiliate, *Weekly Spectator,* are produced by the state-funded Times Corporation, also in Accra. *Daily Graphic* boasts a circulation of 200,000 while *Ghanaian Times* reports 150,000. *Graphic* and *Times* operate offices in all 10 regional capitals and both are distributed throughout the 10 regions via train, bus, and courier, though travel delays result in lag times of up to a week in more remote areas. In the 1970s, the government used the air force and Ghana Airways flights to minimize delays in delivery to the regions. *Daily Graphic* is the most common newspaper encountered outside Accra.

Around 16 independent newspapers provide national political coverage. The four most influential independent newspapers are *The Ghanaian Chronicle, The Independent, The Free Press,* and *Public Agenda.* In 1996, Maja-Pierce quoted the circulation figures for *Chronicle* at 40,000, *Independent* at 35,000, and *Free Press* at 70,000; though the editors for these newspapers more recently report higher numbers. With few exceptions, private newspapers are produced in Accra and circulation is concentrated there as well; though the major independents can regularly be found in Cape Coast, Kumasi, and Tamale. The commonality of English, higher literacy rates, and urban wealth all contribute to a reliable audience for independent papers in the capital. From the standpoint of production, journalists writing political stories in Accra regularly produce new stories of national relevance, while stories from the regions are more occasional and generally less sensational. However, a few independent papers regularly include coverage of regional news, following the example of the state press by maintaining offices and correspondents in the regions. The *Ghanaian Chronicle* has regional offices in Cape Coast, Kumasi, Takoradi, Koforidua, and Ho. *The Independent* maintains a regional office in Kumasi.

Despite the limitations, a few private newspapers are published outside the capital. These exceptions include *Ashanti Pioneer* in Kumasi and *The New Ghanaian* in Tamale.

To capitalize on circulation, the major private papers tend to come out on different days of the week, i.e., *Chronicle* on Monday, *Statesman* on Tuesday, *The Independent* on Wednesday, etc. In addition to circulation, another reason stems from the production process: since many of the private political papers use the same printer, the major print jobs must be staggered throughout the week. While competing against one another journalists in the private press nonetheless express a sense of solidarity against the state press. Strung together throughout the week, the private newspapers together comprise a daily independent paper, they often say, within political and economic conditions that have prevented the maintenance of such a paper.

With the privatization of the economy and opening up to global markets, growing interest in economic matters has prompted the emergence of a number of weekly and fortnightly papers devoted to business and finance. Five newspapers specialize in this area: *The Business Chronicle, Business and Financial Concord, Business and Financial Times, Business Eye,* and *Financial Guardian.*

English is the language of state in Ghana and all newspapers are published in English. This has not always been the case. During the colonial period, missionaries published materials in local languages and a few indigenous entrepreneurs published newspapers in the Akan languages of southern Ghana. After independence, local-language newspapers were produced in literacy campaigns by the Bureau of Ghana Languages, or else by churches for evangelical purposes. These papers have had limited circulation and livelihood. While newspapers have neglected local languages, many FM radio stations have introduced very popular local-language programs in Accra and in the regions. Particularly popular are the call-in programs, where disc jockeys and callers alternate between local languages and English in discussions of local, national, and global events.

ECONOMIC FRAMEWORK

By far the most prosperous news organization in Ghana is Graphic Corporation, followed by Times Corporation; both are funded by the state. With a roomful of computers, several company vans, access to world news services, more sophisticated color printing, available newsprint, and a large, well-paid staff, Graphic Corporation is able to produce a newspaper that resembles the Western prototype. Since *Daily Graphic* and *Ghanaian Times* consistently support the agenda of the state, the professional quality of the state media serves an ideological purpose, symbolizing the stability, reliability, and accumulation of the state.

The major private papers represent distinct ideological perspectives and social groups but all face similar adverse conditions, including high printing costs, lack of equipment, exclusion from state functions, hostile or fearful sources, and difficult access to timely world news. In the early 1990s economic conditions were so harsh that private newspapers could only afford to publish weekly, though many now appear biweekly and *Ghanaian Chronicle* comes out three or four times a week. Unable to break the daily news, the weekly private papers turned to political commentary and investigative stories in order to compete with the state dailies. In addition to state competition, the systematic exclusion of private journalists from state sources and assignments, combined with lack of access to wire services, has forced private journalists to design an alternative set of journalistic techniques, incorporating anonymous sources and popular rumor, resulting in a unified challenge to the conservative messages in the state media.

A copy of the premiere state paper, *Daily Graphic,* sells for 1,500 cedis or about 20 cents U.S., while most of the private papers, such as *Ghanaian Chronicle* and *The Independent,* are priced at 1,000 cedis, roughly 13 cents U.S. Although this may seem quite reasonable by American standards, minimum wage in Ghana is 5,500 cedis a day so most urban working people and rural farmers cannot afford to buy newspapers on a regular basis. The purchasing audience for the press is the white-collar working class, a growing stratum of society since the early nineties. However, in recent years the economy has slipped into a precarious condition and often newspapers are considered discretionary expenditures by this class. Most government offices, diplomatic missions, and expatriate businesses subscribe to one or both state dailies.

Nevertheless, newspapers are a ubiquitous feature of everyday life in urban Ghana. At neighborhood markets and most major intersections, crowds gather every morning and afternoon to check out the lead stories of all the current newspapers that hang across the frames of the wooden kiosks. Top stories from the major newspapers are reported and analyzed on the morning shows of many television and radio stations. People who buy newspapers often read the stories to an audience on the bus or taxi, in the office or market. Once read, a paper is never thrown away but passed around for others to read, reaching as many as 10 readers who could relay the news to a network of hundreds. Newspapers are saved and resold for use as packaging for local street foods such as fried yam or roasted maize.

In Ghana, newsprint is purchased through a central government agency, with allocations made according to circulation. Editors of private newspapers have complained that the state media receive a preferential share of available newsprint when supplies are scarce. Since 1993 the price of newsprint has increased over 300 percent, making it extremely difficult for private papers to turn a profit and stay in business. As a result, the state-funded press endures comfortably, a few private papers with established readership struggle to stay in print, while the vast majority of private papers come and go.

The government supplies a substantial amount of advertising to the state press, providing revenue beyond official state provisions. Moreover, in an uncertain political environment, many local businesses are still somewhat wary of public association with the opposition, therefore avoiding the private press and cautiously placing their ads in the state press. Foreign businesses patronize the state press almost exclusively. Advertising in the state press is not merely political, but pragmatic as well, as the state papers are daily and printed on more advanced equipment, giving a more professional appearance. As editor-publisher Kabral Blay-Amihere notes, most private papers "rely on very primitive printing facilities and therefore appear irregularly and are not well-packaged."

Although the competition for readership is intense, the sense of solidarity among journalists is remarkably strong. Ghanaian journalists are not unionized, but the Ghana Journalists Association (GJA), founded in 1949, brings all media practitioners in Ghana together for programs, lectures, and workshops designed to promote press freedom and professionalism. On the decline in the 1980s, the GJA was revitalized under the charismatic leadership of Kabral Blay-Amihere in the 1990s. Among many accomplishments, Blay-Amihere organized funding from the European Community in 1993 to house the GJA in a refurbished Ghana International Press Centre located near Kwame Nkrumah Circle. After two terms as president of GJA, Blay-Amihere was elected president of the West African Journalists Association and Mrs. Giftie

Afenyi-Dadzie became the next GJA president, exemplifying the vigorous contribution of women to Ghanaian journalism. Among the most popular GJA events are the annual State of the Media conference and the Awards Dinner-Dance. A very prominent professional organization in Ghana, the work of the GJA is supported by the Friedrich Ebert Foundation, the British Council, Westminster Foundation, United States Information Agency, the German Embassy, UNESCO, M-NET, Ashanti Goldfields Company, UNILEVER, and the Ministry of Information of Ghana. Active both regionally and globally, the GJA is a member of the West African Journalists Association (WAJA), the Union of African Journalists, the Commonwealth Journalists Association, the International Organization of Journalists, and the International Federation of Journalists (IFJ).

In the first few months of his administration, President Kufour donated a building to the GJA to be renovated as a new International Press Centre. In March 2002 GJA President Affenyi-Dadzie launched a fundraising effort to raise the 5 billion cedis ($600,000 U.S.) necessary to complete the project. The government has pledged 10 million cedis. The new venue would become the most advanced press center in the West African sub-region.

PRESS LAWS

Chapter 12 of the 1992 Constitution guarantees the freedom and independence of the media. Article 2 explicitly prohibits censorship, while Article 3 preempts any licensing requirements for mass media. Editors and publishers are shielded from government control, interference, or harassment. When the content of mass media stigmatizes any particular individual or group, the media are obliged to publish any rejoinder from the stigmatized party.

Journalists welcomed the liberal provisions of the constitution, hailing the 1990s as a new era of free expression in Ghana. Many private newspapers that had been prohibited by Rawlings' own 1989 newspaper licensing law suddenly reappeared, full of antigovernment criticism and eager to exercise the new freedoms. Despite the letter of the law, the Rawlings government continued to pressure the state press and intimidate the private press, resorting to more indirect techniques of control. State journalists whose opinions or news stories diverged from the ruling party line were chastised, demoted, or sent away on ''punitive transfer'' to remote offices in the regions, often to places where they did not speak the local language. As the private press investigated corruption among Rawlings' own cabinet, many state officials retaliated with civil and criminal libel suits against private journalists. Since journalists are prohibited from reporting on a story once it has gone to court, such libel cases had the effect of stalling the investigation while channeling the controversy out of the public eye and into the court system where state officials might expect a more sympathetic audience.

The deployment of the legal system against the press dates back to the colonial period. Many specific laws used to silence and intimidate the press in recent years bear very close resemblance to those crafted by the British to squelch anticolonial criticism among indigenous elites in the nineteenth and early twentieth centuries. Beginning in 1893 the British passed a series of Newspaper Registration Ordinances to keep track of all editors and publishers and prohibit any offensive publications. In the 1930s, the British responded to the rising tide of nationalist agitation by instituting the Criminal Code (Amendment) Ordinance, defining broad categories of sedition, including racial or class antagonism. The British were quick to bring cases of libel or sedition against journalists who criticized colonial officials or policies in print.

Signaling his commitment to free expression and independent media, President Kufour repealed the seditious criminal libel law in 2001. While commending the media for their important role in the democratic process, Kufour has nonetheless emphasized that journalists must write responsibly and ''pursue objectives that can spearhead the development of the country.'' Denouncing the pressures of commercialism, Kufour has warned the press against falsely damaging the reputations of public figures. He has called on Ghana Journalists Association to ''check any excesses'' in the press. While President Kufour is widely recognized as a friend of the media, such rhetoric is strikingly reminiscent of so many early warnings of previous Ghanaian leaders who subsequently turned to the legal system to intimidate and silence the press.

CENSORSHIP

In 1979, the government established an independent Press Commission to insulate both state and private media from state control while serving as a buffer between the state and the state media, in particular. With the suspension of the Constitution in the 1981 military coup, the state again asserted control over the state media and harassed the private press to near extinction. In 1992 democratization reintroduced the Press Commission, renamed the National Media Commission (NMC) in the new Constitution. The NMC is charged with promoting freedom and independence of media, ensuring the maintenance of professional standards, protecting the state media from government control, appointing members to the Boards of Directors, or governing bodies of the state media, and regulating the registration of newspapers.

The Commission is comprised of fifteen members, including representatives of the following: the Ghana Bar

Association, private press publishers, the Ghana Association of Writers and Ghana Library Association, the Christian Group (including the National Catholic Secretariat, the Christian Council, and the Ghana Pentecostal Council), the Federation of Muslim Councils and Ahmadiyya Mission, journalism and communications training institutions, the Ghana Advertising Association and the Institute of Public Relations, and the Ghana National Association of Teachers. In addition, two representatives are nominated by the Ghana Journalists Association, another two are appointed by the President, and three are nominated by Parliament. Following the elections of December 2000, parliament and the new president made their nominations to the NMC and the new members were subsequently sworn into office in May 2001.

Fulfilling their directive to uphold media standards, the National Media Commission issued a statement in April 2002 taking public exception to "obscene and explicit pornographic pictures" recently published in the *Weekend News and Fun Time* magazine. The Commission advised newspaper editors and publishers to be guided by public morality, decency, and professional ethics.

State-Press Relations

Since the establishment of the state media, state journalists have enjoyed a privileged relationship to government sources, information, documents, and resources. This privilege is both formal and informal. The government requests the presence of state journalists at daily "invited assignments" to state events and press conferences. At these events, state journalists are provided with official commentary as well as the printed speeches, facilitating the quick newswriting necessary for daily newspapers. The organizations of the state media post permanent correspondents to cover the president at the Castle Osu, the seat of the Ghanaian executive. Many state officials will only talk to state journalists, never private ones. Through daily involvement with government officials, state journalists develop very cordial and cooperative relationships with them. As journalists rely on these state sources for their daily supply of news stories, state journalists are quite concerned to protect these mutually rewarding relationships and hardly ever publish critical or oppositional stories about the government.

Journalists with the private press were systematically excluded from state sources and information throughout the 1980s and early 1990s. Following the lead of Rawlings, who vehemently denounced the private press at any public opportunity, state officials in the Rawlings administration were quite hostile to private journalists, denying documents and refusing interviews. Lacking official sources, private journalists were forced to rely on anonymous tips and rumors for information about the state. Frequently, ordinary people were afraid to be quoted in the oppositional private press as well. Private journalists invented alternative forms of journalistic writing and newsgathering to accommodate these restraints, often mixing anonymous and rumored information with reports in the state media to generate alternative accounts of state activities.

Until very recently, private journalists were not welcome at the Castle. Not only were they not invited to cover state events, they would be turned away if they showed up to cover the story. Under President Kufour, things have changed dramatically. Private news organizations have been invited to post permanent representatives to the Castle and Kufour invites both state and private journalists to accompany him on official visits both nationally and internationally.

Attitude Towards Foreign Media

Ghana maintains a liberal approach to foreign media and correspondents. Resident in the capital are representatives of *Agence France Presse,* Associated Press (AP), British Broadcasting Corporation (BBC), Bridge News, Cable News Network (CNN), *Canale France Internationalle* (CFI), Panafrican News Agency (PANA), Reuters, Union of Radio and Television Network of Africa (URTNA), and Voice of America (VOA). Most of these are local Ghanaians with distinguished reputations in Ghanaian journalism and strong global connections. In general they carry out their work without government interference or harassment. Outgoing information is not censored.

Incoming information is also free-flowing, though somewhat limited to elite audiences due to cost. Foreign publications such as *Time* and *Newsweek* are sold at the larger news kiosks. Foreign newspapers such as *The New York Times* and *The Washington Post* can be purchased in major hotels. BBC News is broadcast on GTV and local radio stations. CNN is available to cable subscribers.

New Agencies

Lamenting the distorted images of Africa in the international media, Nkrumah set up the Ghana News Agency in 1957 to provide more balanced representation of local, national, and continental news. Reuters initially provided guidance and technical assistance but the Agency was fully Africanized in 1961. GNA was the first wire service to be established in Africa south of the Sahara and long considered the most efficient news agency in the region. As part of the information apparatus, GNA was central to Nkrumah's effort to monopolize the production and distribution of news at home while monitoring the flow of information and images from Ghana to the outside world.

GNA was originally situated within the Information Services Department but in 1960 became a statutory corporation with a board of directors chosen by the head of state. Since 1992 the National Media Commission selects the members of the board in order to prevent state control of the Agency.

GNA maintains offices throughout the regions and districts of Ghana, channeling news stories to the head office located in the Ministries neighborhood of Accra. The Agency used to have international bureaus in major cities in 10 countries, including Lagos, London, Moscow, Nairobi, and New York; however, funding cuts have forced all but the London office to close. Over 140 organizations and diplomatic missions subscribe to the news service, which provides home news, foreign news, African news, features, and advertising. GNA has news exchange agreements with Reuters, *Agence France-Presse,* TASS, PANA, Zinhua (Chinese News Agency) and DPA (German News Agency).

Broadcast Media

Radio was introduced into the Gold Coast in 1935 when the colonial governor set up a small wired relay station, ZOY, to transmit BBC programs to some three hundred colonial residents and privileged native elites. Service was subsequently extended to Kumasi, Sekondi, Koforidua, and Cape Coast. British radio not only provided information and entertainment but also a means of countering the anticolonial campaigns of the nationalist press. In 1954, Gold Coast Broadcasting System was established, later becoming Ghana Broadcast Corporation (GBC) after independence in 1957.

GBC provides two domestic radio services, Radio 1 and Radio 2, broadcasting from Accra. Radio 1 is devoted to local-language programs, broadcasting in Akan, Ga, Ewe, Nzema, Dagbani, Hausa, and English. Radio 2 transmits in English. Both stations operate for 15 and one-fifth hours on weekdays and 17 and a half hours on weekends. The wireless Radio 3 has been discontinued due to scarce resources. In 1986, GBC began broadcasting in VHF-FM in the Accra-Tema metropolitan area, assisted by the German government. Expanding FM service, GBC opened new FM stations in the regions and districts of Ghana in the late 1980s and early 1990s. Radio GAR operates in Accra, Garden City Radio in Kumasi, Twin City FM in Sekondi-Takoradi, and Volta Star Radio in Ho. There are around 2.5 million wireless sets in Ghana, in addition to over 64,000 wired loudspeaker boxes.

Though many thought the 1992 Constitution provided for liberalization of the airwaves, the Rawlings government refused to grant licenses or allocate frequencies to private radio stations until the mid-nineties, maintaining a monopoly on radio with the state-owned GBC. In 1994 opposition politician Charles Wereko-Brobby protested this policy with a series of pirate broadcasts, the infamous *Radio Eye.* Though the government pressed for criminal prosecution of Wereko-Brobby and confiscated his equipment, his provocative action ultimately pressured the government to allow private FM stations. In 1995, the government began allocating licenses and frequencies through the Frequency Registration and Control Board. The first FM license was granted to *Radio Univers,* the small college station produced at the University of Ghana at Legon. Radio licenses are awarded for seven years, for an initial fee of $5,500. In addition, an annual broadcast fee is collected and distributed to the Copyright Society of Ghana to remunerate artists and musicians. Twelve FM stations currently operate in Ghana, all in Accra or Kumasi. Although most stations focus on musical entertainment, many have news programs and talk shows for discussion of current events in English and Twi. The most popular FM radio stations in Accra are Joy FM, Groove, Vibe, Gold, and Radio Univers.

In 1961 Ghana launched the External Service of Radio Ghana to beam information, propaganda, and messages of support to peoples struggling for freedom and self-determination in all parts of Africa. Programs are broadcast in Arabic, English, French, Hausa, Portuguese, and Swahili. The system now relies on four 100-kilowatt transmitters located in Tema as well as two high-powered transmitters, 250 kilowatts each, in Ejura in the Ashanti Region. Beyond Africa, the service reaches North America, Europe, Japan, and Australia. After Rawlings' coup, the External Service was discontinued due to "technical and financial difficulties" and then reinitiated in 1987.

Television was established in Ghana in 1965 by the Nkrumah government in collaboration with Sanyo of Japan. Sanyo wished to promote television in Ghana to support its own television assembly plant in Tema, just outside Accra. Despite Sanyo's commercial impetus, Nkrumah stressed that television should educate citizens for national development rather than merely entertain or generate profit. Radio and television broadcasting were centralized in a single unit, Ghana Broadcasting Corporation, housed in a sprawling compound in Accra. Targeted by coup leaders, GBC has frequently been seized for the public announcement of regime changes in so many "dawn broadcasts." Because of this, the GBC compound is surrounded by high walls and barbed wire and guests are obliged to remain in the small reception building outside the compound.

Currently, GBC-TV, or simply GTV, broadcasts from its central studios in Accra to transmitters at Ajankote near Accra, Kissi in the Central Region, Jamasi in the Ashanti Region, and a relay station in Tamale in the

Northern Region. In 1986, another transmitter was added in Bolgatanga in the Upper East Region and since then others have been added in Sunyani in the Brong Ahafo Region, Han in Upper West Region, Amajofe and Akatsi, both in the Volta Region. Transposers or boosters operate at Ho, Akosombo, Prestea, Sunyani, Oda, Tarkwa, Dunkwa, and Mpraeso. The Ghana television transmission standard is PAL B-5 with five low power relays. Through these transmitters, 95 percent of Ghana has access to GTV broadcasts. On weekdays, television programming begins at 5:55 AM and concludes at 11 PM. In addition, GTV provides a two-hour education program for schools on weekday mornings. On weekends and public holidays, GTV broadcasts from 6:50 AM to 11:50 PM.

After the privatization of the airwaves, the government gave approval to the allocation of frequencies to private television stations as well. Two private channels, TV3 and Metro TV, went on the air in 1997. In the Greater Accra Region, Multichoice Satellite System offers subscribers access to BBC World Service Television, CNN, Supersports, and M-Net, a South African commercial network offering mostly western movies, music videos, and television serials.

Education & Training

Three programs provide journalism training in Ghana. The majority of journalists in Ghana are trained at the Ghana Institute of Journalism (GIJ) in Accra. GIJ was founded in 1958, offering two-year diploma programs in both Journalism and Public Relations/ Advertising. GIJ also provides a number of short-term courses in advertising, public relations, writing skills, and photojournalism. GIJ has a library with 40,000 volumes for student research and a printing press for instructional purposes. While their first year emphasizes lectures and course work, GIJ students spend their second year on ''practical attachments'' to various media organizations in Accra, learning the application of journalism techniques on the job while making valuable connections for future employment.

Established in the Pan-African context of the Nkrumah period, GIJ still emphasizes that students should be trained to become ''truly African in their professional outlook.'' GIJ has trained journalists from Nigeria, Liberia, Sierra Leone, Cameroon, Burkina Faso, Swaziland, Namibia, and South Africa.

The second training institution, the School of Communication Studies, was founded in 1974 at the University of Ghana at Legon. The School offers a postgraduate training and a master's-level degree in journalism and mass communications. The School of Communications Studies publishes the quarterly journal, *Media Monitor,* dedicated to the discussion of media issues and promoting high professional standards.

In November 2001 the African Institute of Journalism and Communications (AIJC) announced a Distance Learning Scheme, providing diploma and certificate courses online in journalism, public relations, and marketing. Students throughout Ghana can enroll and access the courses via the Internet, according to Kojo Yankah, President of the Institute. For local students, the AIJC maintains an online center in Asylum Down, Accra.

In addition to formal training, journalists participate in frequent seminars on professional, political, and social issues. The German foundation, Friedrich-Ebert Stiftung (FES) is especially committed to educating Ghanaian media to contribute to democracy and development. Working closely with the Ghana Journalists Association and other local media organizations, FES has supported conferences, workshops, seminars, and publications on such topics as electoral coverage, private broadcasting, rural reporting, women in media, environmental reporting, professional ethics, and the state of the media in Ghana.

Summary

Ghana has a vigorous press with a distinguished political history. Journalism plays a crucial role in contemporary processes of democracy in Ghana, providing a common sphere of dialogue among diverse political and economic interests as well as the voices of popular culture. Journalists have enjoyed more freedom, cooperation, and respect in their dealings with the state with President Kufour in office. While seriously concerned about the economic viability of the private press, Ghanaian journalists are nonetheless optimistic that the political liberalism of the current administration is laying a foundation for the maintenance of press freedom and professionalism in the future.

Significant Dates

- 1995: Private newspapers *The Independent, Ghanaian Chronicle,* and *The Free Press* break a series of provocative front-page investigative stories alleging corruption among several government ministers. The Rawlings government directs the Commission for Human Rights and Administrative Justice (CHRAJ) to look into the allegations. Government allots licenses and frequencies to the first private FM radio stations in Ghana. Among the first on the air are *Radio Univers* and Joy FM.
- 1996: In October, CHRAJ reports the interim findings of its eleven-month investigation into press accusations of corruption. The commission censures three government ministers for financial impropriety and/or negligence and further recommends that two pay refunds to the state. President Rawlings issues

a White Paper rejecting much of the substance of these findings and refusing its recommendations for reprimand and repayment. Presidential and parliamentary elections held in December, with President Rawlings re-elected to a second term. Media analysts and political observers note that the state media, though insulated from state control, provides more coverage and advertising to the ruling party NDC throughout the campaign. Opposition candidates receive favorable coverage from private papers such as *Free Press* and *Ghanaian Chronicle.*

- 1997: The first private television stations, TV 3 and Metro TV, begin operations in Accra.
- 1999: In April, journalists for the state media report the death of the traditional ruler of Asante, Otumfuo Opoku Ware II before the death has been traditionally announced by the elders of Asante, the Asanteman Council. The news is picked up and carried in several newspapers. Outraged at this transgression of ''tradition,'' the Asanteman Council summons all journalists in Kumasi to the Palace, grilling them for the source of the leak and chastising them for publicizing the death without the permission of the Council. Ghana Journalists Association issues an appeal to journalists to ''respect time-honored institutions and practices.'' In June private newspaper editors Harruna Attah of *The Statesman* and Kweku Baako of *The Guide* found guilty of contempt of court, each fined the equivalent of five thousand US dollars and thrown in prison for thirty days for continuing to publish details on a story involving First Lady Nana Konadu Rawlings after she had launched a libel case against the papers. Journalists with the GJA form ''The Friends of Free Expression'' and march to the Supreme Court in protest.
- 2000: Presidential and parliamentary elections held in December. In a run-off election, NPP candidate, John Agyekum Kufour of the New Patriotic Party, defeats former Vice-President John Atta Mills. Observers note more balanced coverage of ruling party and opposition candidates in the state media throughout the campaign. Many private newspapers rejoice at Kufour's victory.
- 2001: Shortly after taking office, President J.A. Kufour signals his commitment to free expression and independent media by repealing the seditious criminal libel law. The repeal is ratified in parliament with bipartisan support. Unlike his predecessor, President Kufour welcomes both state and private media to the Castle Osu, inviting the private press to send permanent representatives on assignment to the Castle. During the Rawlings period, Castle correspondents came exclusively from the state press. Demonstrating extraordinary support for independent journalism, Kufour donates a building to the Ghana Journalists Association. Parliament and President Kufour make their nominations to the National Media Commission and new members are sworn into office.
- 2002: Ghana hosts the Annual General Meeting of the International Freedom of Expression Exchange (IFEX) in Accra.

BIBLIOGRAPHY

''Activities 1995: Friedrich Ebert Stiftung, Ghana Office.'' Accra, 1995.

Afele, Mwausi. ''Reporting of King's Death Touches Off Controversy.'' Panafrican News Agency, March 6, 1999.

Ainslie, Rosalynde. *The Press in Africa.* New York, 1966.

Ansu-Kyeremeh, Kwasi. *Perspectives on Indigenous Communication in Africa, Volume I: Theory and Applications.* Accra, 1998.

Ansu-Kyeremeh, Kwasi and Kwame Karikari, eds. *Media Ghana: Ghanaian Media Overview, Practitioners and Institutions.* Accra, 1998.

Apter, David. *Ghana in Transition.* New York, 1968.

Asante, Clement E. *The Press in Ghana: Problems and Prospects.* Lanham, Maryland, 1996.

Austin, Dennis. *Politics in Ghana: 1946-1960.* London, 1964.

Barton, Frank. *The Press of Africa: Persecution and Perseverence.* New York, 1979.

Blay-Amihere, Kabral. *Tears for a Continent: An American Diary.* Accra, 1994.

Blay-Amihere, Kabral and Niyi Alabi, eds. *State of the Media in West Africa, 1995-1996.* Accra, 1996.

''Broadcast Right Tears Accra Apart.'' *Daily Trust* (Abuja), January 21, 2002.

''The Censorship of the Press—An Advice.'' *Ghanaian Chronicle,* April 5, 2002.

''Communications.'' *Accra Mail,* July 25, 2001.

''Country to Host Major Media Event.'' Africa News Service, June 21, 2001.

''Daavi Ama Joins Media Commission.'' *Accra Mail,* May 28, 2001.

''Elections Dominate Ghanaian Press.'' Panafrican News Agency, December 29, 2000.

Essel, Isaac. ''We Are Not Gagging the Press—Jake.'' *Accra Mail,* April 3, 2002.

Faibille, Egbert. ''GBC Threatened with Closure in Kumasi.'' *The Independent* (Accra), March 2, 1999.

Faringer, Gunilla. *Press Freedom in Africa.* New York, 1991.

''Fears for Future of Private Press.'' *IPI Report,* Vol. 43, No. 9, Sept. 1994, p. 13.

''GJA Appeals to IGP.'' *Accra Mail,* March 25, 2002.

''The GJA Billion Building Project.'' *Accra Mail,* March 11, 2002.

''Ghana.rdquo; *IPI Report,* Nov.-Dec. 1995, p. 45.

''Ghana.'' *IPI Report,* Vol. 43, No. 12, Dec. 1994, p.30.

''Ghana Institute of Journalism: Informational Brochure.'' Accra, 1995.

''Ghana Journalists Association Thinks Big, Vendors Cry Foul.'' *Accra Mail,* March 11, 2002.

''Ghanaian Diplomat, Journalist Discuss Media in Recent Elections.'' *Accra Mail,* March 14, 2001.

Graham, Yao. ''Facing Up Against Lawsuits.'' *Media Monitor,* July-September 1996.

Hachten, William A. *Muffled Drums: The News Media in Africa.* Ames, Iowa, 1971.

Hasty, Jennifer. *Big Language and Brown Envelopes: The Press and Political Culture in Ghana.* Ph.D. Dissertation, Duke University, 1999.

''Hope for Media in the New Democracy.'' *IPI Report,* Vol. 42, No. 8, Aug. 1993, p. 7.

''Independent Radio on the Rise in Ghana.'' *Billboard,* Vol. 109, No. 2, 1997, p. 45.

''Institute of Journalism and Communications To Do Distance Learning.'' *Accra Mail,* November 6, 2001.

''Institute of Journalism Starts Degree Programme Next Week.'' *Ghanaian Chronicle,* October 18, 2001.

''Jake's Fears, the Media's Suspicions.'' *Ghanaian Chronicle,* April 3, 2002.

Jones-Quartey, *K.A.B. History, Politics, and Early Press in Ghana: The Fictions and the Facts.* Accra, 1975.

Kimble, David. *A Political History of Ghana: The Rise of Gold Coast Nationalism, 1850-1928.* Oxford, 1963.

Kitchen, Helen. *The Press in Africa.* Washington, D.C., 1956.

Koomson, A. Bonnah. *Handbook of Electoral Coverage in Ghana.* Accra, 1995.

———. *Journalism and Ethics.* Accra, 1997.

''Kufour in Full Control.'' *Ghanaian Chronicle,* April 19, 2001.

''Kufour Meets the Press.'' *Expo Times* (Freetown), May 4, 2001.

Lartey, Druscilla. ''Media Commission Sets Up 12-Man Standard Committee.'' *Ghanaian Chronicle,* March 7, 2002.

Maja-Pierce, Adewale, ed. *Directory of African Media.* International Federation of Journalists, 1996.

———. *The Press in West Africa.* Index on Censorship, 1990.

Mensa-Bonsu, *H.J.A.N. The Law and the Journalist.* Accra, 1997.

Nugent, Paul. *Big Men, Small Boys, and Politics in Ghana: Power, Ideology, and the Burden of History, 1982-1994.* Accra, 1996.

''Press Freedom in Ghana: Mixed Signals?'' *Africa Today,* Vol. 35, No. 3/4, Feb-Apr. 1988, p. 85.

''Private Press Shaken to the Core.'' *IPI Report,* Vol. 41, No. 5, May 1992, p. 13.

''Proliferation of Obscene and Explicit Pornographic Newspapers.'' *Accra Mail,* April 7, 2002.

Sharfstein, Daniel J. ''Radio Free Ghana.'' *Africa Report,* Vol. 40, No. 3., 1995, p. 46.

Shillington, Kevin. *Ghana and the Rawlings Factor.* London, 1992.

Siddiq, Sani. ''Dramatic Finale on Libel Case.'' *Ghanaian Chronicle,* February 21, 2001.

—Jennifer Hasty

GIBRALTAR

BASIC DATA

Official Country Name:	Gibraltar
Region (Map name):	Europe
Population:	29,481
Language(s):	English, Spanish, Italian, Portuguese, Russian
Literacy rate:	80%

Located at the tip of the Iberian Peninsula, the limestone rock outcropping that is Gibraltar stretches nearly to Africa and serves as a gateway to the Mediterranean. Gibraltar's media community enjoys a high degree of freedom and independence.

The city's most important newspaper is the *Gibraltar Chronicle*, which publishes daily Monday through Saturday in print and online. Established in 1801, the independent publication is one of the oldest daily newspapers in the world in continuous production. Its approximate circulation is 4,500. The weekly newspaper *Panorama* has appeared Mondays since 1975, but it also runs a daily online edition which was founded in 1997. Both print and Web editions cover local and international news. *Vox,* founded in 1955, is a weekly bilingual newspaper appearing every Friday in both Spanish and English.

There are five radio stations, one AM and four FM, serving 37,000 radios. One television station broadcasts to 10,000 televisions. There are two Internet service providers.

Gibraltar belonged to Spain until 1713, when it was ceded to Britain in the Treaty of Utrect. It has remained a sore spot ever since. In 1967, Gibraltarians chose to remain a British dependency, and Spain closed its border with the country between 1967 and 1985.

However, in 2000 Britain and Spain finally reached an agreement over the area's administrative status. Gibraltar's head of state is the British monarch, who is represented locally by a London-appointed governor and commander in chief. Heading the government and the unicameral, 18-member House of Assembly is a chief minister. The Governor does not actively participate in the government but does approve all legislation.

The population of Gibraltar is approximately 30,000, and the literacy rate is 80 percent. English is the official language, but Spanish is also widely spoken. Because of its location, Gibraltar is an international conference center and boasts an extensive shipping trade. Accordingly, it garners significant income from offshore banking, tourism, and shipping service fees. British military presence also contributes to the economy, although its percentage of the gross national product is declining.

Central Intelligence Agency (CIA). *World Fact Book 2001*. 2001. Available from www.cia.gov.

Gibraltar Chronicle home page. 2002. Available from www.chronicle.gi.

Government of Gibraltar Information Services. 2001. Available from www.gibraltar.gov.gi.

Panorama home page. 2002. Available from www.panorama.gi.

Worldinformation.com. 2002. Available from www.worldinformation.com.

—Jenny B. Davis

GREECE

BASIC DATA

Official Country Name:	Hellenic Republic
Region (Map name):	Europe
Population:	10,623,835
Language(s):	Greek (official), English, French
Literacy rate:	95.0%
Area:	131,940 sq km
GDP:	112,646 (US$ millions)
Number of Daily Newspapers:	32
Total Circulation:	681,000
Circulation per 1,000:	78
Number of Nondaily Newspapers:	14
Total Circulation:	441,000
Circulation per 1,000:	50
Total Newspaper Ad Receipts:	277 (Euro millions)
As % of All Ad Expenditures:	17.10
Number of Television Stations:	36
Number of Television Sets:	2,540,000
Television Sets per 1,000:	239.1
Number of Satellite Subscribers:	190,000
Satellite Subscribers per 1,000:	17.9
Number of Radio Stations:	118
Number of Radio Receivers:	5,020,000
Radio Receivers per 1,000:	472.5
Number of Individuals with Computers:	750,000
Computers per 1,000:	70.6
Number of Individuals with Internet Access:	1,000,000
Internet Access per 1,000:	94.1

BACKGROUND & GENERAL CHARACTERISTICS

The Hellenic Republic of Greece has a very active and vocal press greater in the number of newspapers, magazines, radio stations, and television channels than the population of less than 11 million warrants. The high number of publications is a Greek expression of freedom of the press to compensate for decades of suppression by military governments or foreign interventionists in modern Greek history, when the nation alternated between being a kingdom or a republic.

Ancient Greece represents the birthplace of democracy in the history of western civilization. Ancient Greek democracy was not extended to all city-state residents, and the Greek peninsula was a collection of city-states in competition with each other. Conflict among the Greeks led to their conquest by Philip of Macedon and the Greek incorporation into the successive empires of Alexander the Great, Rome, Byzantium, and the Ottomans. Modern Greece did not emerge until 1821, when the wars of Greek independence were waged against the Turkish rulers of the Ottoman Empire. Europe's major powers initially did not want an independent Greece, fearing a disintegrating Ottoman state would leave the eastern Mediterranean open to either Egyptian or Russian expansionism. Expatriate newspapers published in Greek in Vienna kept the Greek language and culture alive and encouraged rebellion. European public opinion, influenced by British poet Lord Byron and the romanticism of the principles of democracy in Ancient Greece, sided with the Greeks, and Great Britain was forced to accept the role of protector of the Greek people. Frequent disagreements among Greek political factions and the failure to create a unified state led Europe's three major powers, Great Britain, France, and Russia, to impose a monarchy upon the Greeks, with a foreign prince as king and neutral arbitrator to bring about national consensus. Foreign interventionism, military takeovers, and feuding Greek politicians have clouded Greek politics for almost two hundred years and forced the Greek media to struggle underground, face outright suppression of its publications, or suffer regulation by the central government censor in Athens.

The reign of King Otto, a Bavarian prince selected for the Greek people by European powers in 1832, witnessed considerable centralization of authority in the capital of Athens. The Kingdom of Greece isolated and ignored Greece's indigenous political traditions, created new hierarchies of power staffed by Germans loyal to King Otto, and failed to revive agriculture and the economy. The Greek people did not always fight back with print media. They gravitated toward oral debates, republicanism, and armed insurrection. What print media existed within Greece was considered either biased or anti-royalist. King Otto's first period of governance ended with a military coup in 1844, an internal Greek interventionist theme that would regularly be a part of Greek politics until 1975. Greece's second attempt at democracy relied more upon political patronage rather than one man, one vote democracy. Bribery, corruption, and appeals to Greek nationalism to achieve a "Greater Greece" by freeing Greeks still under Ottoman rule led to British and French intervention in Greek politics once again, and a refusal by the major powers to allow the further breakup of the Ottoman Empire. Greek nationalism was thwarted, but the desire to bring all Greeks under one national flag would add a new theme to Greek politics and newspapers. The military intervened again in 1862; King Otto returned permanently to Germany.

A new monarchy was created in 1864, once again by Europe's major powers, who extended an invitation to Danish prince William to come to Athens and become *King of the Hellenes* (king of the Greek people). Prince William adopted the reigning name of George I, and a new constitution was written with power invested in the Greek people, a single-legislative chamber, and a monarch with specific but substantial powers. Political personalities and political clubs came to characterize Greece in the late nineteenth century. Greeks regularly expressed their views in oral debates and in print—their positions frequently in opposition to government policies. Both political clubs and artisan guilds brought out the voters and imposed their views upon the nation. From 1865 to 1875, Greece witnessed a succession of seven general elections and 18 different administrations. Greek politician Kharilaos Trikoupis wrote a newspaper article about the political gridlock within Greece's national governments and criticized the king for supporting governments representing minority political groups rather than the larger parties, which dominated the Greek Parliament. Trikoupis was arrested for treason for his comments, but he was later released and went on to serve as Greece's prime minister. The political pressure applied to the monarchy by the print media led to political reform. After 1874 Greek prime ministers were usually selected from the strongest party represented in Parliament.

The reign of King George I ended by assassination in 1913 by a deranged Greek in the newly freed Greek district of Salonika. Greek media kept the public emotionally charged over the issues of a "Greater Greece," the acquisition of the island of Crete, and economic collapse. The Greek media traditionally served as spokesmen for Greek politicians and political parties, and were usually divided between the supporters of the monarchy and media supporters advocating a republic. World War I and King Constantine's attempt to keep Greece neutral led to political rivalry between the palace and Eleutherios

Venizelos, one of Greece's most influential politicians of the twentieth century. The dispute over national policy led Venizelos to claim that King Constantine was pro-German and disrespected the wishes of the Greek people to join the Allies against the Central Powers. The strategic importance of Greece in the Allied fight against the Central Powers nations of the Ottoman Empire and Bulgaria led to French interventionism in Greek politics and the disposition and exile of the king in 1917. The Venizelos press implied that King Constantine denied Greece the opportunity to expand its boundaries as a member of the Allies in the war against Germany. The monarchy remained under a figurehead king, Alexander I, a son of King Constantine. Royalists and republicans expressed their opposition to each other and polarized the Greek state. An unsuccessful attempt on the life of Venizelos and the unexpected death of the young King Alexander led to the restoration of King Constantine. The Greek nation remained evenly split between republicans and royalists. The side in power suppressed the voice of the other side. King Constantine was exiled a second time in 1922 after disastrous defeats by the Greek army at the hands of the Turks that the Venizelos press blamed on the Greek king and princes who commanded the nation's armed forces. King George II lasted less than a year on the throne and was exiled in 1923. Venizelos returned from exile to govern the Greek republic. He remained in power until the worldwide economic depression reached Greece. Venizelos' failure to revive the Greek economy led to his overthrow by the military in 1935.

The monarchy was restored in the person of King George II. The instability of Greek politics forced King George to turn to the military to govern what seemed an ungovernable state. General Ioannis Metaxas restored public order, but the cost was high. Greece became a one-party state, repressed human rights, suppressed the media, and contributed to further divisions within the Greek body politic. The secret police brutally suppressed all dissent. Political dissent led to arrest, prison, or exile. Torture was regularly used to extract confessions. The regular conflict between royalists and republicans, and the brutality of the Metaxas dictatorship led to opposition support forming around a Greek Communist Party engineered from Moscow. Germany and Italy invaded in 1941. The end of World War II and the retreat of German armies left Greece in a state of civil war between the Communists and elements of the royalist government-in-exile in London. Both Great Britain and the United States, fearful of a Communist Greece strategically located in the eastern Mediterranean threatening the Suez Canal, supported the restoration of the monarchy to counter Moscow's influence.

The defeat of the Communists in the Greek Civil War did not lead to a national healing. Royalist and republican rivalries resurfaced in the Greek press and within Greek political parties. The reign of Paul I (1947-1964) witnessed an attempt to bring economic stability to Greece with the imposition of prime ministers and political parties that were pro-Western and more rightist in political affiliation. Greek newspapers urged greater freedom of expression, which the military and the central government in Athens were not always willing to tolerate. Greece's only radio and television stations were government owned and expressed the opinions of the party in power.

Greece's last king, Constantine II, began his reign in 1964 with the nation expecting Greece to become a true constitutional monarchy, with the king and the military outside of politics. Political rivalries between Greek politicians and personalities, Konstantinos Karamanlis of the National Radical Union Party and Georgios Papandreou of the Center Union Party, during the decades of the fifties and sixties further destabilized Greek politics, placed the neutrality of the monarchy at risk, and generated fear within the Greek military that leftists allied to the Soviet Union would make Greece a Communist ally. In 1967 Greece's limited democracy was overthrown in a military coup. The regime ruled by propaganda and terror. Political parties were dissolved, the media was suppressed, closed down, or censored, and human rights were curtailed. King Constantine II attempted a countercoup to restore democracy but failed and fled into permanent exile. The monarchy remained in name until it was abolished by the military in 1973. The military regime used public interest in television for its own political and ideological interests. The views expressed in the media were ''government-controlled overt propaganda.'' During seven years of military rule, television stressed consumerism over politics. The military junta's 1974 attempt to annex the eastern Mediterranean island of Cyprus with its large Turkish Muslim population led to a war with Turkey and the collapse of the military regime. The monarchy was rejected by a national referendum in 1974, and Greece officially became a republic.

The creation of the Hellenic Republic and the adoption of a new Constitution in 1975, amended in 1986, did not immediately remove antiquated press laws dating back to the Metaxas era of the 1930s. The Constitution of 1975 created Greece as a parliamentary democracy with a president as head of state and a prime minister exercising executive authority. The prime minister is the leader of the largest party in the Greek Parliament. A cabinet is appointed with the approval of the Greek president on the recommendation of the prime minister. The president of the Hellenic Republic is voted into office by Parliament for a five-year term. The Greek Parliament (*Vouli ton Ellinon*) is a one-chamber legislative body with 300 members. The judges for the Supreme Judicial Court and

Daily and Non-Daily Newspaper Titles and Circulation Figures

	1996	1997	1998	1999	2000
Number of Daily Newspapers	22	23	28	29	32
Circulation of Dailies (000)	758	719	672	676	681
Number of Non-Daily Newspapers	13	13	18	17	14
Circulation of Non-Dailies (000)	405	422	464	NA	441

Source: World Association of Newspapers and Zenithmedia, *World Press Trends 2001*, pp. 8, 10, 17, 19. Note: NA stands for not available.

the Special Supreme Tribunal are appointed for life by the president after consultation with a judicial council.

The return of democracy brought a proliferation of Greek newspapers. The largest circulation dailies are in the capital of Athens. *Ta Nea* is Athens' largest daily newspaper with 168,800 readers (all circulations as of 1995) followed by *Eleftheros Typos* with 130,000 readers. Other leading Athenian daily papers include *Eleftherotypia* 114,000 readers, *Ethnos*, 66,100 readers, *Apoyevmatini* with 61,500 readers, and *Adesmeftos Typos*, 60,000 readers. Additional Athenian daily newspapers include *Athens News* (4,500), *Avghi* (2,500), *Avriani* (15,700), *Eleftheri Ora* (2,300), *Eleftheros* (9,800), *Estia* (3,900), *Express* (25,000), *Imerisia* (10,000), *Kerdos* (23,000), and *Nafteboriki* (35,000), financial dailies, and *Kathimerini* (35,500), *Niki* (11,800), and *Rizospastis* (16,400). The two largest newspapers in Thessaloniki are the dailies *Makedonia*, 17,000 readers, and *Thessaloniki*, 14,000 readers. New entries into the journalism field include *O Pothos*, a gay newspaper, and *Patras Today*, a daily electronic newspaper and magazine in Patras. Circulation among daily newspapers has steadily declined. Sunday newspapers have increased circulation from 857,000 papers in 1993 to 920,000 in 1998. However, 30 percent of all printed newspapers in Greece remain unsold. To compensate for lost revenues, newspapers court advertising. Automobiles, banks and other financial institutions, computers and cellular phones, and the public sector are the four primary types of advertising found in the print media. Advertising for cigarettes, educational institutions, and travel are alternative sources for print revenue.

Greek newspapers are less political then they once were. However, some of the major dailies were still clearly identified in 1991 as supporters of a particular political party or ideology. The *Akropolis*, circulation 50,800, is an independent center-right publication. *Eleftheros Typos*, circulation 135,500, is a more conservative right-wing independently owned publication. *Avgi*, with 55,000 readers, is regarded as the official mouthpiece of the Greek Left Party, and the 40,000 circulation *Rizopastis* is the print voice for the Communist Party of Greece. *Avriani*, 51,000 readers, is a center-left publication, as are the independent *Eleftherotypia* with 108,000 subscribers and *Ta Nea*, circulation 133,000. The independent *Ethnos* with circulation of 150,000 is regarded as a more left-wing paper than is *Avriani*, *Ta Nea*, or *Eleftherotypia*. A still influential politically oriented newspaper in spite of a circulation decline is the center-right publication *Kathimerini*.

A wide variety of periodicals are published in Athens. General interest magazines are *Economicos*, *Ependytis*, *Epohi*, *Exormissi*, *Experiment*, *Paron*, *Pontiki*, *Prin*, *Status*, and *To Vima*. Special interest periodicals include the women's magazine *Agonas Tis Gynaekas*, the English language *Athenian*, the political publication *Anti*, maritime periodical *Efoplistis*, economics magazine *Epiloghi*, and the business journal *Kefalaio*. The magazines *Balkan News*, *Christianiki*, *Greek News*, *Nea Ecologia*, and *Politika Themata* are all Athens-based publications. *Papaki* is a relatively new magazine created by journalism students of the Department of Communication and Media at the University of Athens.

Two percent of Greek newspapers and magazines are exported to Cyprus, the United States, Germany, and Great Britain. German and British print publications are the largest in number imported into Greece. Demand in Greece for foreign publications corresponds to the number of tourists in Greece on holiday. There are 600 newsagents and 500 subagencies in the Greek provinces for the distribution of printed media. Within Greece there are 12,000 places where the print media is sold. The number of agents, agencies, and distribution centers exceeds the demand and the general population's needs in comparison to the other nations in the European Union.

Greek radio stations ERA-1 and ERA-2 are the official government radio broadcasting stations. Athena 98.4 is a municipal radio station broadcast from Athens. There are 1200 privately owned radio stations in Greece. Top commercial radio stations, all Athens-based, are Antenna 97.1, Aristerea 90.2, Flash 96.1, Radio Athena 99.1, and Sky 100.4. Privately owned Greek radio stations include 100 FM Melodia, a Greek station based in Athens, 101.9 FM-Studio 19, 102.4 FM, 88.8 FM-STAR FM Corfu,

Top Ten Daily Newspapers
(2000)

	Circulation
Ta Nea	86,000
Eleftherotypia	80,000
Ethnos	58,000
Sportime	46,000
Eleftheros Typos	43,000
Kathimerini	42,000
To Fos Ton Spor	34,000
Espresso	32,000
To Vima	31,000
Apogevmatini	27,000

Source: World Association of Newspapers and Zenithmedia, *World Press Trends 2001*, p. 107.

which offers the top 10, dance, and the top 30 in Greek music, 9.59 FM-Fly, 9.61-Flash, a station broadcasting news and talk shows, 94.5 FM Radio Thessaloniki, and Radio ONE FM. The Greek government operates three television stations, ET-1, ET-2, and ET-3. The most popular commercial television stations, all broadcast from Athens, are Antenna-TV, Aristera TV, Kanali 5, Mega Channel, and SKY TV.

ECONOMIC FRAMEWORK

Greece is a mixed capitalist economy with the public sector accounting for almost half of the gross national product (GNP). Tourism is a key industry. Foreign exchange earnings bring needed revenue. Greek membership in the European Union has benefited Greece. The economy continues to improve as economic reforms take root. National deficits have been reduced, monetary policies tightened, and inflation rates are falling. High unemployment is still a problem, and many unprofitable state enterprises await privatization. The Greek labor force is divided among industry (21 percent), agriculture (20 percent), and services (59 percent). The nation's primary industries, in addition to tourism, are food and tobacco processing, textiles, chemicals, metal products, mining, and petroleum. Historically an unstable Greek economy was the result of political unrest among the nation's political parties, rivalry between royalists and republicans, foreign interventions, wars, and military coups. In the late twentieth century, Greek political life began to mature, become less volatile, and be stabilized by membership within the European Union.

Throughout most of modern Greek history, each political party has had its own newspaper with the party leader serving as editor. Only recently have political party newspapers separated themselves from the party. During the dictatorship of the ''colonels'' from 1967 to 1974, many newspapers were closed, censorship prevailed, and surveillance of reporters and editors was widespread. After 1974 the media in Greece has been transformed. Advertising plays a decisive role in media revenues and a partisan press has declined, while market-oriented newspapers dominate. Entrepreneurs and ship owners are the new media barons with a few publishers dominating all media. Newspapers are currently less an extension of political parties than a business enterprise. Greece's most profitable printing and publishing empires, based on sales and profits, are the Lambrakis Press, Tegopoulos Publications, Pigasos Printing and Publishing, Press Foundation, Limberis Publications, Apogevmatini Publications, and Kathimerini Publications.

Since deregulation of the media in the 1980s, Greece has grown in television and radio stations. Each station offers more advertising, imports programming from other countries, and broadcasts more political debates. With admission into the European Union, the Greek media is required to conform to the regulations established by the *Directive Television Without Frontiers*. The Greek media is debating policy issues about the amount of broadcast time allocated to advertising, program quotas, protecting minors, and the private ownership of multiple forms of the media by one person or organization.

The largest daily newspapers based on circulation remain the 17 newspapers published in Athens. There are 280 local, regional, national, daily, and Sunday newspapers published in Greece. The Sunday press is exclusively published in Athens. However, readership continues to decline. To increase readership, the Greek press has resorted to redesigning the newspapers' names and layout, publishing new papers, and offering giveaways such as free trips, houses, and consumer goods. Greece publishes more than 500 popular and special interest magazines. Most magazines are published monthly. Thirty are consumer magazines. The highest circulation magazines are television based and affiliated with game shows. An increase in specialized magazines is designed to attract younger readers in fields such as music, computers, sports, business, finance, car and motorcycles, technology, history, home furnishings, and interior design. And, yet, celebrity gossip and television magazines still have the highest circulations.

PRESS LAWS & CENSORSHIP

The Greek press is regarded as highly politicized and to gain readership is given to sensational news stories. Even though the restoration of Greek rights was guaranteed by the Constitution of 1975, the Greek government has been slow to give up monopolistic control over some media forms. The Constitution of 1975 specifically prohibits censorship in any form, and any government practice hindering freedom of the press is strictly forbidden. However, press restrictions in some form dating back to the Metaxas era of the 1930s remained in effect until August 1994.

The media played an important role in 1989 in the collapse of Prime Minister Andreas Papandreou's government, when the press revealed that media liberalization allowed Papandreou to use the power of the prime minister's office and political patronage to affect what was printed. Greek governments now have an official government spokesman to respond to the media's criticisms, a position similar to that of the presidential spokesmen in the United States. The prime minister's cabinet has a Minister of Press and the Mass Media. This office played a crucial role in both bringing the 2004 Olympic games to Greece and is coordinating the international communications that will be required for the games. There are no restrictions placed on foreign journalists or foreign media operating in Greece.

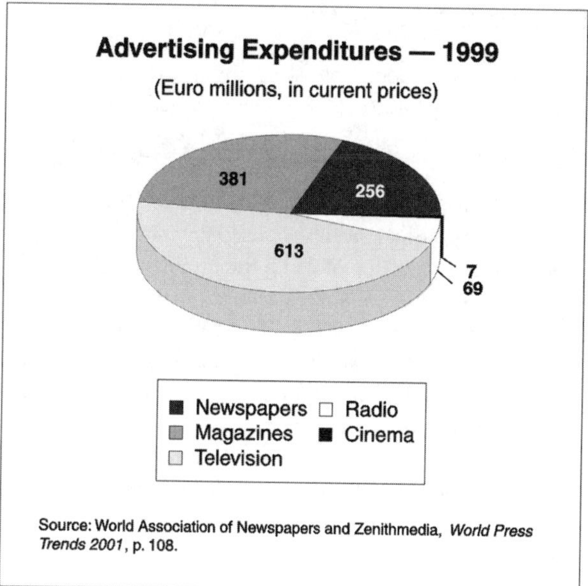

Source: World Association of Newspapers and Zenithmedia, *World Press Trends 2001*, p. 108.

In 1987 the state monopoly of radio and television ended, but until 1989 government radio and television stations continued to serve as powerful propaganda tools for the political party in power. A lawsuit brought by Athens mayor Militiadis Evert challenged the use of government stations to support candidates and was accepted for hearing by the Greek courts. In April 1989 it was ruled that the state monopoly of broadcasting violated the European Council standards. The Greek Parliament legalized the private ownership of radio and television stations in October 1989. Like the press, privatization of broadcasting led to a proliferation of new radio and television stations. The media is now a frequent critic of the Greek government's forcing the state to improve its image. Although the state-sponsored Elliniki Radiofonia Tileorasi (ERT) is still the dominant force in radio and television broadcasting, an independent committee was created in 1989 to administer ERT, improve its programming, and to weaken cabinet control of ERT.

Since the deregulation of television, most Greek households watch private television. Variety shows dominate private television broadcasting. Private television stations repeat successful formats such as soap operas. If a show lacks sufficient popularity after two years, it is cancelled. With more television channels, more Greeks are watching television. The most watched television shows are news programs, films, and series. The greatest criticism of private television broadcasting is that the shows broadcast are characterized as ''glorified tabloid newspapers.''

With deregulation the popularity of the state television channels has drastically declined, and each government channel has accumulated a substantial debt. To attract more viewers, government television (ERT 1, ERT 2, and ERT 3) is providing more entertainment features, cultural programming, environmental series, and animal interest programming. Greek series starring major Greek actors are now broadcast on government channels. ERT 3's focus is on regional programming and culture. By investing in digital television, ERT plans to regain a larger share of the viewing audience.

The National Broadcasting Council (NBC), created in 1989, oversees radio and television broadcasting and remains the buffer between the government and the broadcasters. NBC oversees advertising practices, journalistic ethics, and programming. NBC has levied fines against stations for showing ''reality'' shows and for inaccuracies in news programming. Some stations were fined for failure to pay copyright fees associated with the right to broadcast a series. The National Broadcasting Council is turning its attention to radio and television stations still failing to obtain a broadcast license.

NEWS AGENCIES

Five news agencies serve Greece: Athens News Agency (ANA), Macedonian News Agency, Athens Photo News, LocalNet News Agency, and ONA, Omogeneia News Agency. Media associations in Greece include Journalists Union of Athens Daily Newspapers (ESHEA), Foreign Press Association (FPA), Panhellenic Federation of Editor Unions (POSEY), Journalists' Union of Macedonia and Thrace Daily Newspapers, Balkan Press Center, and the Union of Editors of Periodical Press. Greece has two news ''infobanks'', InNews and the National Communications Network.

BROADCAST MEDIA

Greek radio began broadcasting in the 1930s during the Metaxas dictatorship. Television broadcasting began during the ''colonels'' dictatorship in the 1960s. Both radio and television were extensions of the state and served as propaganda instruments for the military. After 1974 Greek political parties accused the party holding the prime minister's office of using the broadcast stations for their own benefit. A state monopoly of the broadcast media continued after 1974. The Constitution of 1975 gave radio and television to the state to directly control. The state controlled the limited air frequencies and radio and television stations providing only government views and policies. Change came when the other major political party won control of Parliament. The cabinet minister in charge of the media was the nation's chief censor. Deregulation of Greek media came from outside the country when Greece applied for membership in the European Union.

In 1986 the newly elected mayors of Athens, Piraeus, and Thessaloniki were members of the opposition party. Each mayor launched new radio and television stations. Each was taken to court and won. Law 1730, approved in 1987, stated that local radio stations could belong to municipalities or local authorities or companies in which the shareholders were Greek citizens. In 1988 the mayor of Thessaloniki transmitted television programming from foreign satellite channels on UHF frequencies. The mayors of Piraeus and Athens followed suit. During the trial the Greek government realized that media reform was needed. In June 1989 a parliamentary committee was established to determine whether or not television stations in Greece should be private. Large Greek investors wanted the privatization of the broadcast media. Law 1860, approved in 1989, permitted the operation of non-state television channels and created the National Broadcast Council (NBC) to supervise the industry. Mega Channel, owned by the Teletypos publishing group, and Antenna TV, owned by a Greek ship owner, were quickly set up. Both television stations are the nation's most popular. Because there is so much unregulated broadcasting in Greece, the Greek government in July 1993 announced rules for broadcast media licensing. A change of Greek governments in October 1993 gave television licenses to Sky TV and 902 TV, whose license requests were previously denied.

The government Ministry for Press and the Media was not created until July 1994. Law 2328, approved in 1995, regulates the electronic market and determines the legal status of private television and radio stations. Only the Communist Party objected to the 1995 law. The Ministry of Press and the Media determines prerequisites for the granting and renewal of licenses to private television stations, determines programs appropriate for children, and the proper use of the Greek language in broadcasting. Licenses for radio stations must also meet the Ministry's criteria, which determines advertising parameters, and regulates the framework for private media research companies. Although the government has more strictly forced the broadcast media to obtain licenses, many are still in violation. In 1997 and 1998, 19 local stations (6 in Athens and 13 in Thessaloniki) were shut down for nonpayment of copyright fees. Over 1,200 radio stations broadcast throughout Greece. Each of Greece's 52 administrative regions has 2 or 3 local commercial stations. Many are unlicensed. The Greek government permits 3 types of radio stations to broadcast: state-owned, municipal, and private. Most Greek radio stations offer news and current events, music, Greek music, easy listening music, sports, rock music, and nostalgia music. Only one station plays classical music. News and easy listening music stations have the largest listening audiences.

With the deregulation of television, Greece went from 3 state television stations to 140 national and local stations. Mega Channel and Antenna TV control the largest share of the audience market with over 60 percent of the viewers and 65 percent of the advertising revenues. State television has a viewing audience of 8 percent and advertising revenue earned of 7 percent. Both Mega Channel and Antenna TV's popularity is based on sitcoms, satire shows, game shows, soap operas, movies, and made-for-television movies. Fewer educational and documentary programs are aired. FilmNet, the first pay-television channel, began broadcasting in 1994, showing major movies and sporting events. Super Sport and Kids TV are two additional pay-television channels that are widely popular in Greece. Cable television is currently under development. The government television channels and Antenna TV use satellites to show Greek programs to Greeks residing elsewhere. CNN, Euronews, MTV, and TV 5 are stations broadcast via satellite into Greece.

The Ministry of Press and Mass Media along with the Ministry of Transport and Communications have jointly adopted policies for digital television. Both ministries agreed that no monopoly would be permitted. A national digital platform will be a joint venture with all interested Greek parties, with the state controlling no more than 50 percent of the shareholding. It is the government's intention that the digital platform covers 100 percent of Greek territory, offers programs for Greeks living overseas, and develops domestic digital technology and industry.

ELECTRONIC NEWS MEDIA

Electronic publications are a part of the Greek media. *Diaspora WWW Project* is a bimonthly electronic publication that provides information on Hellenism. It began publication in October 1994. *Matsakoni,To* is a Greek nonprofit magazine about social movements for human rights and social liberation, and is against alienation and the hunt for profit. *Monopoli* magazine is an electronic publication about music concerts, cinema, restaurants, exhibitions, and other cultural activities. *Strategy* magazine centers on the Greek military and the defense industry. *Hellenic Resources Network (HR-Net)* is a project facilitating communication between Greeks and the exchange of news and information pertaining to Greece and neighboring countries. *I-Boom* finds anything Greek or Greek related on the web. *Greece-News Collection* provides news related to Greece. *Ariadne Hellenic News Base* offers news from well-known Greek radio stations and news agencies in both Greek and English. *Michailidis Publications* is a business and trade publication for wholesalers and retailers of consumer goods. *SV2AEL-Sava Pavlidis* is an electronic publication of photographs, awards information, and the history of Thessaloniki. Recent additions to Greek Internet Media are *Reporters Corner on-line Magazine, Eco2Day: Economy News*, *NetNews*, *NetDaily*, *I-note*, *Metapolis*, and *The Media Zone*.

The Greek Media offers Internet portals, which provide information online. These resources include HRI: Hellenic Directories & Portals, in.gr, Flash.gr, e-one, iboom Network (in Greek), iboom Network (in English), Pan.gr, Pathfinder, e-go, and Thea.gr. Online media directories are HRI: Newspapers and Magazines, Greek Media Index, The Reporter's Corner, The Greek Electronic Media Finder, Media Listings, Local Press, APN-report, Thea: Media Directory, Phantis: News and Media Directory, Eidiseis.net (multilingual), Rhodos Net: Media Index, and Mdataplus: Greek and World Press.

There has been a recent proliferation of online Greek newspapers and magazines. Online Greek newspapers include *Kathimerini* and *Kathimerini-H.-Tribune* in English, *Ta Nea*, *To Vima*, *Athens News*, in English, *Eleftherotypia*, *Avgi*, *Rizopastis*, *Agelioforos*, *Adesmeftos Typos*, publisher K. Mitsis and *Adesmeftos Typos*, publisher D. Rizos, *Apogevmatini*, *Ethnos*, *Express*, *Imerisia*, *Naftermporiki*, *Prin*, and *Athener Zeitung*, in German. Many of these online newspapers are an electronic extension of long established newspapers already in print form. The intent is to expand readership by offering an online version. Greek online magazines, some associated with a publishing group, are *HRI: Journals on Hellenic Issues* (English), *Thesis: Daily On-Line Journal of MFA* (English), *Defensor-Pacis* (English), *Lambrakis Press*, *New Europe* (English), *Oikonomikos Taxidromos*, *Evropaiki Ekfrasi* (Greek and English), *Anti* (Greek and English), *Nemecis*, *Metro*, *Defence and Diplomacy*, *Pegasus Publishers*, *Compupress Publishers* (Greek and English), and *Stratigiki Publishers*.

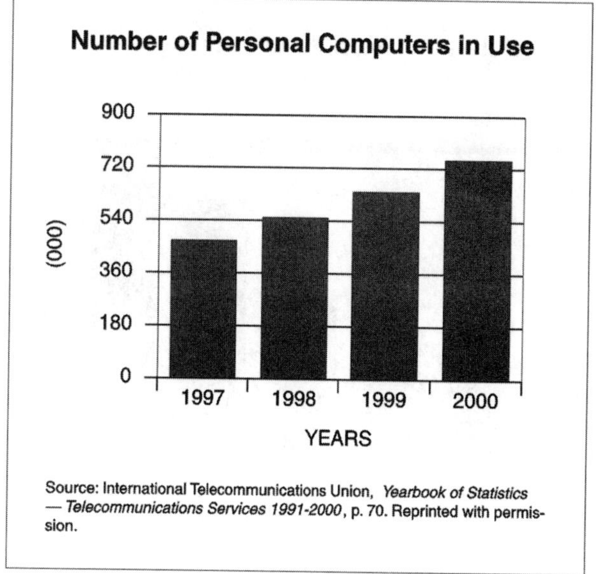

Source: International Telecommunications Union, *Yearbook of Statistics — Telecommunications Services 1991-2000*, p. 70. Reprinted with permission.

EDUCATION & TRAINING

Greeks seeking a career in the media and communication attend either the University of Athens, Panteion University in Athens, or Thessaloniki University in Thessaloniki. The Department of Communication and Mass Media at the National and Capodistrian University of Athens was founded in 1990 and offers a Bachelor, a Masters, and a Doctoral Degree in Communication and the Media. Athens' Panteion University has a relatively new program in Communication and Mass Media that offers a bachelor's degree. The Aristotle University of Thessaloniki was established in 1991 and offers a bachelor's degree in the Media in the School of Journalism and Mass Communication. Thessaloniki cooperates with a large number of European Union universities through the Socrates/Erasmus programs, enabling Greek students to attend universities in other European Union countries. Both Panteion University and the Aristotle University of Thessaloniki offer radio webcasting, and each university has its own radio station and electronic media lab.

SUMMARY

The Greek media has undergone a rapid transformation within a quarter-century. A proliferation of privately owned media exists in all forms. The media in Greece is characterized by an industry that has modern technological equipment in use, high quality printed matter, major publishing houses, a low penetration of imported printed matter in the local market, and an improved financial picture for most media owners. The Greek media is plagued

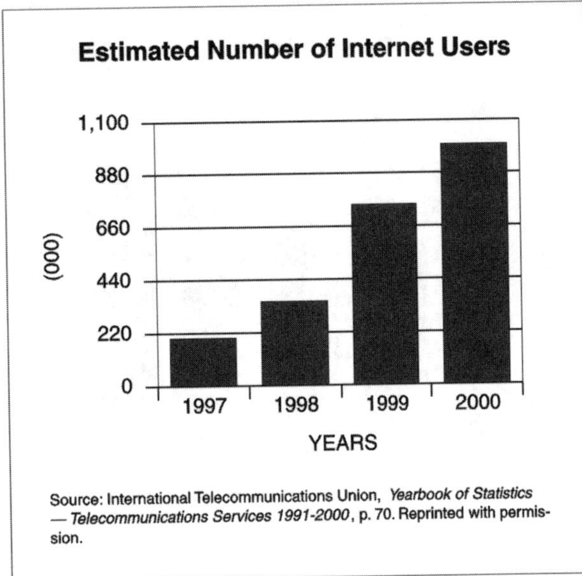

Source: International Telecommunications Union, *Yearbook of Statistics — Telecommunications Services 1991-2000*, p. 70. Reprinted with permission.

with reader disinterest resulting in lower circulation for most printed matter. There is a high dependency among the printed media on imported and expensive paper and ink. Newspapers continue to experience a high percentage of unsold newspapers, which increases production costs. The print media is too dependent on advertising revenues to balance costs; there is inadequate display and promotion, a high labor cost, and an insufficient utilization of production equipment. Since 1990 advertising expenditures represent a significant decline for newspapers and magazines. Advertising expenditures for radio fluctuates, while television advertising has steadily increased.

Greek newspapers comprise political, financial, foreign language, satirical, and sports editions. Newspapers on politics represent the largest share of the print media, but their sales continue to decline, followed by newspapers on sports. Only foreign language publications among Greek newspapers witnessed an increase in circulation. Since 1992 specialized magazines are almost 63 percent of the sales. General interest and children's magazines continue to decline in popularity. Professional journals in science, literature, and politics are seeking an audience, but their subscription numbers remain small. In an attempt to increase sales, newspapers are printing supplements in their Sunday editions that are strikingly like magazines.

Radio stations, state or municipally owned, continue to decline in popularity among Greeks. Most radio stations are privately owned with some failing to file for a license to broadcast. Deregulation undermined the government monopoly once existing over radio stations. Audiences continue to view private television networks over state television stations. Advertising revenues influence what is broadcast on private television channels. The quality of television programming continues to emerge as a national problem, with viewers complaining about too much time spent on advertising instead of programming. Rebates to attract viewers are coming under closer government scrutiny with some rebates being withdrawn because of the expense incurred.

The future direction of the Greek media will be affected by the policies adopted on proper licensing of broadcast media, cable television, and digital programming. The integrity and independence of the Greek media is directly affected by Greece's membership within the European Union. Within 25 years Greece has emerged from a political system, which institutionalized censorship and suppression, to become a democracy, which deregulated the media and is experiencing many of the same issues confronting the media as its national counterparts in Western Europe and the United States.

SIGNIFICANT DATES

- 1994: Creation of the Ministry for Press and the Media.
- 2004: Press coverage of the Olympic Games.

BIBLIOGRAPHY

Cosmetatos, S. P. P. *The Tragedy of Greece*. New York: Brentano Books, 1928.

Curtis, Glenn, ed. *Greece: A Country Study*. Washington, DC: Government Printing Office, 1995.

Hourmouzios, Stelio. *No Ordinary Crown*. London: Weidenfeld and Nicolson, 1972.

Kaloudis, George Stergiou. *Modern Greek Democracy*. New York: University Press of America, 2000.

Kousoulas, D. George. *Greece: Uncertain Democracy*. Washington, DC: Public Affairs Press, 1973.

''Local Newspapers, Magazines' Battle to Attract Readers.'' *Hermes* February 1999: 4-14.

''Mapping the Media Revolution.'' *Hermes* October 1996: 8-17.

Nash, Michael. ''The Greek Monarchy in Retrospect.'' *Contemporary Review* September 1994: 112-121.

Papadopoulos, M. George. *Two Speeches*. Athens: 1967.

Papandreou, Andreas. *Democracy at Gunpoint: The Greek Front*. Garden City, NY: Doubleday & Company, Inc., 1979.

Papandreou, Margaret. *Nightmare in Athens*. Englewood Cliffs, NJ: Prentice-Hall, 1970.

Papathanasopoulos, S. ''Mass Media in Greece.'' In-*About Greece*. Athens: Ministry of Press and Mass Media, 2001.

Tantzos, G. Nicholas. *Konstantine*. New York: Atlantic International Publications, 1990.

Turner, Barry, ed. *Statesman's Yearbook 2002*. New York: Palgrave Press, 2001.

Vaitiotis, P. J. *Greece: A Political Essay*. Washington, DC: Center for Strategic and International Studies, 1974.

Woodhouse, C. M. *Modern Greece, A Short History*. London: Faber and Faber, 1968.

———. *The Rise and Fall of the Greek Colonels*. New York: Franklin Watts, 1985.

World Mass Media Handbook, 1995 Edition. New York: United Nations Department of Public Information, 1995.

—*William A. Paquette*

GREENLAND

BASIC DATA

Official Country Name:	Greenland
Region (Map name):	North & Central America
Population:	56,309
Language(s):	Greenlandic, Danish, English
Literacy rate:	similar to Denmark proper

Greenland is the world's largest island, but more than 80 percent of its area is covered with ice, not surprising for a region located between the North Atlantic Ocean and the Arctic Ocean.

As a division of Denmark, Greenland's print media enjoys broad freedoms but independent radio stations are subject to tighter regulations. There are no daily newspapers in Greenland, but the country does support two national weekly publications. *Grølandsposten/ Atuagagdliutit* was founded in 1861 and publishes on Tuesday and Thursday. *Sermitsiak*, founded in 1958, appears every Friday in print and online. Both are printed from Nuuk, the capital, and are written in Greenlandic and Danish.

There are five AM and 12 FM radio stations serving 30,000 radios. One publicly owned television station broadcasts to 30,000 televisions. There is one Internet service provider.

Greenland came under Danish rule in the fourteenth century, and it remains a part of Denmark today as a self-governing overseas administrative division. Greenland's chief of state is the Danish monarch, represented locally by a High Commissioner. The government is headed by a Prime Minister who is elected by a unicameral, 31-seat Parliament, or Landstinget.

The population of Greenland is approximately 56,000. Most inhabitants live in settlements along the coast. The official languages are Dutch and Greenlandic, a type of Inupik East-Eskimo language. The literacy rate is 98 percent. Fish exports drive the economy, but seal and whale hunting is also important. Tourism plays a minor role, limited mostly by climate and location.

Central Intelligence Agency (CIA). ''Greenland.'' *World Fact Book 2001*. 2001. Available from www.cia.gov.

Freedom House. 2002. Available from http://www.freedomhouse.org

Worldinformation.com. 2002. Available from http://www.worldinformation.com.

Sermitsiak. 2002. Available from http://www.sermitsiaq.gl.

—*Jenny B. Davis*

GRENADA

BASIC DATA

Official Country Name:	Grenada
Region (Map name):	Caribbean
Population:	89,018
Language(s):	English, French patois
Literacy rate:	98%

The island of Grenada, located between the Caribbean Sea and the Atlantic Ocean, is one of the smallest independent countries in the western hemisphere. Yet it is the world's second-largest producer of nutmeg and was able to garner military support from the United States when a Marxist faction overthrew the government in 1983. The offensive was successful, and free elections were held again the following year. The population of Grenada is nearly 90,000, and the literacy rate is 98 percent. The official language is English, but many speak French Patois.

Grenada is a constitutional monarchy headed by the British monarch, who is represented locally by a Governor General. Heading the government is a Prime Minister, who is chosen by the Governor General. The bicameral parliament consists of a 13-member Senate and a 15-member House of Representatives. Grenada is popularly called the ''Spice Island'' for its most important export. In addition to its substantial nutmeg production, islanders also export mace, cinnamon, ginger and cloves. Tourism also accounts for a significant sector of the economy, followed by tourism-fueled construction.

Freedom of press is guaranteed by law in Grenada, and the country supports three weekly newspapers: *Grenada Today, The Informer,* and *The Grenadian Voice.* Each of these newspapers appears in English and publishes on Friday. *Grenada Today* contributes its content to the Web portal belgrafix.com.

Grenada hosts three radio stations, one FM and two AM, which serve approximately 57,000 radios. Two television stations broadcast to approximately 33,000 televisions. There are 14 Internet service providers.

BIBLIOGRAPHY

''Belgrafix.com (2002),'' Home Page. Available from http://www.belgrafix.com/.

''Benn's Media 1999,'' Vol. 3, 147th Edition, p. 251.

''Country Profile: Grenada,'' *BBC News (2002).* Available from http://news.bbc.com.

''Grenada,'' *CIA World Fact Book (2001).* Available from http://www.cia.gov.

—Jenny B. Davis

GUADELOUPE

BASIC DATA

Official Country Name:	Department of Guadeloupe
Region (Map name):	Caribbean
Population:	426,493
Language(s):	French, Creole patois
Literacy rate:	90%

Guadeloupe, in the lesser Antilles, is an archipelago of nine inhabited islands in the Caribbean Sea. In 1493, Christopher Columbus became its first European visitor, and the French settled the islands in 1635. The country remains an oversees department of France; the French President is Guadeloupe's head of state, represented locally by a Paris-appointed Prefect. The country is headed by the President of the General Council and the President of the Regional Council. Both positions are elected by the membership of their respective councils. The official language is French, but many speak Creole Patois. The population of the islands is approximately 400,000, and the literacy rate is 90 percent. Guadeloupe's economy revolves around tourism, but agriculture and light industry such as sugar and rum production also play important roles. France also provides subsidies and imports much of Guadeloupe's locally consumed food. Sugar cane was once the most important crop, but it is being edged out in importance by bananas, eggplant, and flowers.

As a department of France, Guadeloupe enjoys the European country's press and speech freedoms. Guadeloupe's primary newspaper is its daily, the *France-Antilles. Le Progrés Social* is a popular weekly. There are two newspapers sponsored by the Communist Party, *L'Etincelle,* a weekly, and *Combat Ouvrier,* a bimonthly. Only *Combat Ouvrier* is available online.

There are 17 FM radio stations and one AM station serving 113,000 radios. Five television stations broadcast to 118,000 televisions. There are three Internet service providers.

BIBLIOGRAPHY

''1999 Country Reports on Human Rights Practices: France,'' *U.S. Department of State (n.d.).* Available from http://www.state.gov.

''Benn's Media 1999,'' Vol. 3, 147th Edition, p. 251.

Combat Ouvrier, (2002) Home Page. Available from http://perso.wanadoo.fr/combatouvrier/.

''Country Profile: Guadeloupe,'' *Worldinformation.com (2002).* Available from http://www.worldinformation.com.

''Guadeloupe,'' *CIA World Fact Book (2001).* Available from http://www.cia.gov.

—Jenny B. Davis

GUAM

BASIC DATA

Official Country Name:	Guam

Region (Map name):	Oceania
Population:	154,623
Language(s):	English, Chamorro, Japanese
Literacy rate:	99%

Guam, the largest and southernmost island in the Mariana Islands archipelago, is considered the gateway to Micronesia and the hub of the Pacific. The Spanish seized control of the island in 1521, but the United States won control in 1898 following the Spanish-American war. Japan occupied Guam briefly during World War II. Today Guam is an unincorporated territory of the United States and hosts one of the most strategically important U.S. military bases in the Pacific. The population is approximately 157,000, and the literacy rate is 99 percent. English is the official language, but Chamorro, the language of the island's indigenous population, is widely spoken, as is Japanese. The U.S. President serves as the chief of state, and a Governor heads the local government. There is a unicameral, 15-seat legislature, and Guam elects one delegate to the U.S. House of Representatives. The economy is largely dependent on the U.S. military, but fish and handicraft exports also play a role. The tourism industry is growing, and the island is an especially popular destination for Japanese tourists.

Guam enjoys the press and speech freedoms of the U.S. Constitution. The country's major English-language daily is the *Pacific Daily News.* It began as the *Navy News* in 1947, when it was published by the U.S. Navy. Today it is owned by Gannett, boasts a circulation of more than 20,000, and is available online. The Sunday edition is called the *Pacific Sunday News.* There are several weeklies, many of which target the island's Asian population and Asian tourists. *Guam Chinese News* is a biweekly community newspaper printed in Chinese. Its circulation is 3,500. *Guam Shinbun,* a Japanese-language weekly, appears every Friday, boasts a circulation of 20,000, and is available online. Korean language weeklies include *Korean Community News,* which has a circulation of 2,000, and the *Korean News,* which has a slightly lower circulation. *Guam Shoppers' Guide* is an English-language community newspaper that appears every Friday and has a circulation of 20,000. *Micro Call* is a weekly published by the Communication Department of the University of Guam. Serving the American military community are the weeklies *Pacific Crossroads* (Navy) and *Tropic Topics* (Air Force). The *Pacific Voice,* also a weekly, caters to the Catholic community.

Operating on the island are four AM radio stations, seven FM radio stations, five television stations, and 20 Internet service providers. There are approximately 221,000 radios and 106,000 televisions.

BIBLIOGRAPHY

"CocoNET Wireless," *The University of Queensland, Australia. (1995).* Available from http://www.uq.edu.au/coconet/gm.html.

"Country Profile," *Worldinformation.com (2002).* Available from http://www.worldinformation.com.

"Guam," *CIA World Fact Book (2001).* Available from http://www.cia.gov.

Guam Shinbun (2001). Home Page. Available from http://www.guam-shinbun.com/.

"On the Map," *Pacific Daily News (2002).* Available from http://www.guampdn.com.

—Jenny B. Davis

GUATEMALA

BASIC DATA

Official Country Name:	Republic of Guatemala
Region (Map name):	North & Central America
Population:	12,974,361
Language(s):	Spanish, Amerindian languages
Literacy rate:	63.6%
Area:	108,890 sq km
GDP:	18,988 (US$ millions)
Number of Television Stations:	26
Number of Television Sets:	1,323,000
Television Sets per 1,000:	102.0
Number of Radio Stations:	632
Number of Radio Receivers:	835,000
Radio Receivers per 1,000:	64.4
Number of Individuals with Computers:	130,000
Computers per 1,000:	10.0
Number of Individuals with Internet Access:	80,000
Internet Access per 1,000:	6.2

BACKGROUND & GENERAL CHARACTERISTICS

In 2002, Guatemala boasted around 13 million people, more than half of whom are full-blooded Mayan Indians, many of whom could not speak Spanish, the official tongue. Two other groups included the *ladinos* (of European and Indian blood), and those of unmixed European origin, the latter controlling most of the country. Roughly two-thirds of the country is literate, with 60 percent speaking Spanish, and the remaining 40 percent one of the Amerind tongues, principally Kíché, Kaqchikel, Q'eqchi and Mam. Its religions included Roman Catholic, Protestant and traditional Mayan. Just to the south of Mexico, Guatemala occupies an area of 108,890 square kilometers (41,801 square miles).

The country is divided into a fertile coastal plain and the *altiplano* or highlands, where reside the majority of non-Spanish speaking Mayans. In 1996, a 36-year civil war between the Mayas and the government ended. In 2002, relationships between that government and its people, including the press, were still being adjusted.

Guatemala has four major daily Spanish language newspapers: *Prensa Libre, El Periódico, Siglo XXI,*—all morning publications—and *La Hora,* an afternoon paper. Also publishing are one minor daily tabloid, the somewhat sensational *Nuestro Diario,* as well as two weekly periodicals, *Critica* and *Crónica.* All except *Critica* and *Crónica* are independent. The major independent newspapers regularly criticize the government and military as well as other powerful segments of Guatemalan society. They have published reports on alleged government corruption and/or drug trafficking, using sources such as human rights groups, clandestine intelligence, or left-leaning organizations like the news agency CERIGUA, which had to operate in Mexico for most of the guerrilla war, or the Centro para la Defensa de la Libertad de Expresión (Center for the Defense of Freedom of Speech). Both *Critica* and *Crónica* had been equally independent, but the latter was the target of an advertising boycott in 1998 and was forced to sell to a conservative owner. In 2002, *Crónica* reflected the new owner's right-wing philosophy, while *Critica* continued to be critical of the government.

Additionally, there was the English-language daily *The Guatemalan Post,* as well as the oldest surviving newspaper in Central America, the *Diario de Centro America.* However, in the first decade of the twenty-first century, *Diario de Centro America* was a semi-official paper that reported legal news only, and has lacked the readership of many other papers.

The relationship between press and state in the first decade of the twenty-first century came about as a result of a history in which journalists usually wrote what the party wanted. Journalists' independence was, in 2002, less than a decade old.

Historical Background The first "journalists" in what is now known as Guatemala were Mayan dispatch runners, but the glory days of the Maya were long past when the Conquistadores arrived in the early sixteenth century. For reasons which have never been entirely clear, Mayan cities and temples were unoccupied, crumbling into decay and covered with jungle vegetation at Pedro de Alvarado's arrival.

In the post-conquest period, almost all Central America was controlled from Guatemala. In 1729, *Gazeta de Goatemala* became Guatemala's first newspaper, and only the second in the New World. It was little more than a propaganda sheet, allowed to express only opinions pleasing to governors, clergy, and crown. The press confined itself to official or Catholic pronouncements, local items, and information about Spain, with the journal's license dependent upon cooperation with the authorities. This began a history of cooperation between press and state in Guatemala, examples of which remain in recent times.

Guatemala City became the capital in 1776, and the nation gained independence from Spain on September 15, 1821. The early nation was an essentially feudal society, one in which the press continued primarily to serve the state, which was in effect a succession of large landowners, known as *caudillos,* or "old families."

In 1880 *Diario de Centro America* was founded, it is the oldest surviving newspaper in Central America. June 1922 saw the birth of *El Imparcial,* different from other papers in that it took an independent stance for many years, eventually drifting to the right until finally becoming a pro-government and anti-Communist organ as the Cold War heated up.

In the 1940s, events took a turn which had a decided impact upon the development of Guatemalan journalism. Revolution, political turmoil and mounting discontent in 1944 ushered in the era of Juan José Arévalo, a liberal president, and a freely elected government. Several newspapers from both sides of the political fence came into being, two of which still exist today, *La Hora,* which came into being in 1944, and *Prensa Libre* (1951). Something close to true freedom of the press prevailed and earned applause from many places. In the 1950 elections, Jacob Arbenz Guzmán won election as the country's president.

In 1953-54 the U.S. Central Intelligence Agency helped train and back an invasion of Guatemala launched from Honduras by a mercenary army. Although Guatemalans did not take up arms, the government lost the backing of the military and this led to Arbenz's relinquishing his office, which was seized by Castillo Armas. Guatemala gained a reputation as one of the world's worst human rights violators, and freedom of the press became non-existent.

The struggle became a 36-year-long civil war, and people who worked for newspapers were often caught in the crossfire—in some cases, quite literally—between government right-wing army troops and Mayan and/or communist guerrillas. Right-wing death squads killed or threatened to kill journalists; left-wing terror groups did the same. As an example of the entire war's effect upon the civilian population, consider the brief presidency of Jose Efraín Ríos Montt, whose counter-insurgency campaign resulted in about 200,000 deaths of mostly unarmed indigenous civilians. The military carried out many of these missions, according to the Historical Clarification Commission (CED), which estimated that government forces were responsible for 93 percent of the violations. The Archbishop's Office for Human Rights said that the military was responsible for around 80 percent of violations.

''During the long period of armed confrontation, even thinking critically was a dangerous act in Guatemala, and to write about political and social realities, events or ideas meant running the risk of threats, torture, disappearance and death,'' said the Historical Clarification Committee. *La Nación* reporter Irma Flaquer Azurdia and her son died during an ambush in 1980. Right-wing squads also have been blamed for the 1985 disappearance of U.S. journalists Griffith Davis and Nicholas Chapman Blake; in 1993, the founder and editor of *El Gráfico,* Jorge Carpio Nicolle, was ambushed and murdered by more than 30 hooded men. The Committee to Protect Journalists (CPJ) has said that more than 29 journalists were killed for doing their jobs during the conflict. In 1995, the Inter-American Press Association reported that evidence from the crime scene of the Jorge Carpio Nicolle assassination had disappeared, further hampering the investigation. In another instance, *Siglio XXI* columnist Hugo Arce's criticism of the president allegedly caused Arce to be arrested and charged with possession of dynamite and drugs. In 1993, Robert Brown summed up the position of the press with these words: ''Death threats, physical attacks with armed thugs, the burning of newspapers . . . are done with total impunity.''

The lines between journalism and politics in Guatemala often were blurred. For example, the assassinated Jorge Carpio Nicolle was not only a newspaper publisher but a candidate for several important political offices, and the same was true of his brother, Roberto. The Carpio and Marroquín families owned four of the eight dailies in 1982; Clemente Marroquín not only founded *La Hora* and was arguably the best-known journalist in the country, but also was vice president from 1966 to 1970. The founder of *La Nación,* Roberto Giron Lemus, was a presidential press secretary; General Manager Mario Ribas Montes of *El Imparcial,* who was assassinated in 1980, had been ambassador to Honduras.

During the guerilla war, several attempts to publish a paper with an anti-government point of view were made, perhaps the most typical of which was *Nuevo Diario* in the late 1970s. Not overtly seditious, it quietly attempted to investigate the government. The Secret Anti-Communist Army allegedly made death threats against Editor Mario Solorzano, causing him to flee the country. Allegations also were made that staff members were threatened, and reporters mugged or kidnapped; advertisers refused to contribute, and the newspaper collapsed in 1980.

Journalists were poorly paid. In 1975, monthly pay was supposed to range from U.S. $152 for a photographer to $253 for a reporter/editor, but very few journalists received that much. Most working reporters came from the lower middle class, with little or no training—journalism being considered a low-prestige occupation—were willing to accept the low pay in exchange for a chance to get to know the right people in politics and business and perhaps get a better job. Such reporters were not likely to be critical, and indeed, rarely were. In addition, allegations of money offered under the table for favorable reporting were often present, a form of bribery known as *fafa.* What it amounted to was that the press had a decidedly conservative bias and a strong desire to not rock the government boat.

With no redress seen for the conditions that had confined a majority of the indigenous population to the highlands attempting to live off plots of land so small they could not feed even the people who farmed them, guerrilla military activity began and reached its peak in 1980-81. The guerilla army numbered 6,000 to 8,000 armed irregulars and between 250,000 and 500,000 supporters throughout the country. In 1982, the insurgents came together to form the Unidad Revolucionaria Nacional Guatemalteca (URNG), thus creating a viable military and political entity which concerned the government's generals. Members of the ruling class coupled fear of a successful Castro-like revolution with the irregularities that characterized elections and began to question the generals' governing ability. Although the military continued to refuse to negotiate with the rebels, outside pressures came to bear in the form of peace treaties being negotiated in El Salvador and Nicaragua, as well as the ending of the Cold War.

In 1987, peace-seeking Guatemalans formed the National Reconciliation Commission (CNR) chaired by

Msgr. Rodolfo Quezada Toruño of the Catholic Church Bishops' Conference. NCR began a "Dialogo Nacional" calling for a political settlement of the civil war. Although the military and other members of the ruling class ignored them, the CNR met with the URNG in Oslo and Madrid. After an agreement in principle was reached, the guerillas agreed not to disrupt the 1990 elections, which saw Jorge Serrano elected president.

Serrano began to negotiate directly with the URNG, involving the rebels in the political process for the first time.

Serrano's record was spotty; he had some success in reducing the influence of the military and persuaded military officials to talk to the rebels directly, but in 1993 he illegally dissolved Guatemala's Supreme Court and Congress, as well as restricted civil rights and freedoms in a self-initiated coup or *autogolpe.* Faced with united opposition he fled the state, and Guatemala's Congress elected Human Rights Ombudsman Ramiro De León Carpio to complete the presidential term. Under the new president, peace negotiations intensified and a number of pacts with the rebels—for resettlement of refugees, indigenous rights, and historical clarification—were signed.

In 1995 center-right National Advancement Party (PAN) candidate Alvaro Arzú was elected to the presidency. In December 1996 Arzú signed a peace treaty with the guerrillas, ending the 36-year civil war. Along with peace came changes to the press.

Economic Framework

In 2000, agriculture accounted for 25 percent of the gross national product and employed more than half the labor force, a staggering 60 percent of whom were below the poverty line. About 2 percent of the population owned around 70 percent of Guatemala's land, with the remainder mostly not arable. Almost one-third of the population is illiterate, but that figure is much higher among the impoverished who, by and large, are Mayan. Although the four major daily newspapers are privately owned and independent, their audiences primarily consist of the relatively well off.

Although the signing of the peace accords had the further effect of diminishing violence against journalists, there are other pressures on the press. Marylene Smeets of the Committee to Protect Journalists (CPJ) said that, "Guatemalan journalists have compared this to a spigot. If they print good news, money flows in. If they print bad news, the money dries up." She also pointed out that "problems with advertisers also arise without government instigation. To write that a particular brand of automobile is the one most frequently stolen is to lose that brand's advertising."

Reporters are not without fault. *Fafa* continued to exist, albeit somewhat less frequently.

Press Laws

In 2000, the U.S. Department of State reported that the Guatemala Constitution provided for freedom of speech, including the press. By 2002, the letter of the law remained unchanged, and the government claimed to be working to improve its implementation of the law.

In addition to the Peace Accords of 1996 settling the civil war, the Accords pledged to enact reforms to the Radio Communication Law to make radio frequencies available for the indigenous Mayan communities, a matter of importance since most of that population could not speak Spanish. However, the government instead passed a law creating a public auction for radio frequencies and the resultant high cost proved an "effective barrier to rural indigenous access to radio frequencies," according to the U.S. Department of State. As of 2000, there were no radio stations solely for Mayans, although occasional broadcasts, speeches, and Spanish-language instruction was broadcast in the various indigenous tongues.

Censorship

In 2000, the U.S. Department of State found that the Guatemalan government usually respected the rights granted the press in its constitution, adding, however, that journalists had been threatened and intimidated, and finding at least two examples of "government-connected censorship." The government developed public information programs that radio and television stations had to broadcast. The government owned seven nationwide television channels; in 2002, one was being used by a Protestant group and the other by the military, with plans pending to sell the military channel to the Catholic Church. President Alfonso Antonio Portillo said the sale would provide competition for the four major stations that were monopolized by one man, Angel González of Mexico, a close friend and financial supporter of the president.

State-Press Relations

In May 2002, CPJ's Smeets reported that the press was showing signs of independence. CPJ said that "the virtual halt of violence against journalists suggests how dramatically conditions have improved for the Guatemalan press." However, that observation proved somewhat sanguine.

On June 5, 1997, a few months after the signing of the peace treaty, Jorge Luis Marroquín Sagastume, founder of the monthly *Sol Chortí,* which was investigating alleged corruption in the mayor's office of the town of Jocotaan, was murdered by two killers who, when apprehended, said they had been hired by the mayor. In November 1997, the head of the weekend section of *Prensa Libre* was stabbed by an unknown assailant, dying three hours later in the hospital.

The CPJ said that in 1997 the press had become more pluralistic and professional, but was "still hindered in its work by a climate of violence and growing tensions with the government of President Alvaro Arzú Irigoyen." It added that at least one other journalist had been killed in that year, "but against a backdrop of growing crime it was impossible to determine if the killings were motivated by their reporting."

Despite the apparent risks, journalists have reported aggressively on once-taboo subjects such as alleged government corruption, the drug trade, and possible human rights abuses by the military. Indigenous issues also have received increasing attention, not only from regional newspapers, but from Guatemala City dailies like *Siglo Vientiuno.*

President Arzú surprised everyone when he said publications were exaggerating violence in order to sell newspapers. Smeets described a publicly-funded television news show, *Avances,* supposedly in existence to inform the public about the government, but actually being used to promote the party in power.

Writing in 1998, Smeets saw violence diminishing against journalists, but felt that Arzú presented a new threat to freedom of the press. Although journalists tried to report objectively on a rising crime wave, the president felt that such reporting discouraged tourists. He continued to criticize newspapers for exaggeration and negativity, using his influence to try to deprive them of needed advertising revenue. For example, owners of the independent weekly *Crónica* felt forced to sell the magazine when all official agencies were forbidden to advertise in it. The new owners appointed right-wing and presidential friend Mario Davis García as editor, after which most of the publication's reporters promptly quit in protest.

Some Guatemalans said the well-known radio program *Guatemala Flash* changed hands from an owner who criticized the government freely to a pro-government investor because of similar pressure. Journalists were denied access to official information, on the grounds that it was privileged. It was alleged that the presidential spokesman, Ricardo de la Torre, regularly met with officials and urged them to ignore publications that were critical or negative, especially of the government. Eduardo Villatoro, ex-president of the Guatemala Journalists Association and a columnist for *Prensa Libre,* said that the "government does not realize that political space and freedom of expression are not gracious concessions of the government, but hard fought gains."

Although the CPJ found the same pressures on a free press in Guatemala in 1998, it also saw reason for encouragement. Of the three reported cases of press harassment, only one could be documented and the police officer involved was fired. Although under some financial pressure, *El Periódico* continued to improve its investigative reporting while maintaining its independence. (The newspaper had been purchased in 1997 by the same publisher who owned the independent *Prensa Libre.*) Despite government interference, the Guatemalan press as a whole became increasingly independent and professional in 1998. The CPJ said that the Asociación de Periodistas de Guatemala (APG) joined the International Freedom of Expression Exchange Clearing House.

Arzú's hostility toward the press abated in 1999 but not for ideological reasons—it was an election year. The results ended his four-year term. Arzú may have lowered his criticism but he continued to work against journalism in other ways. For instance, a radio program devoted to discrediting print journalists and opposition members was found to be run by a special advisor to the ex-president.

It had only been three years since the cessation of the guerrilla war, yet reporters often tiptoed gingerly around sensitive areas, such as any alleged links between the drug trade and the generals. Journalists were still threatened, though not as often. In May 1998 *El Periódico* revealed that two of its reporters were trailed by members of the presidential security detail. In the past, it was likely the paper would not have reported on a matter like this, so many felt progress had been made. In addition, the two brothers accused of murdering *Sol Chortí* founder and director Jorge Luis Marroquín were tried, found guilty, and sentenced to 30 years in prison.

In April 1998, a radio program called *Hoy por Hoy* (Day by Day) broadcast a series of indictments aimed at print journalists; in particular, *Prensa Libre* owner Dina García and editor Dina Fernández were singled out as incompetent reporters and immoral women, although they were neither. The staff of *El Periódico* suspected Arzú, and an investigation found a link. On June 17, headlines trumpeted: "Who's Behind *Hoy por Hoy*?" The answer: Mariano Rayo, special adviser to the Arzú. Called before a congressional hearing, Rayo offered to resign, but Arzú refused to hear of it. Eventually, Rayo was elected a deputy to the Legislative Assembly. Fernández summed up the affair: "In any other country this would have destroyed [him]. . . Here they reward him . . ."

Attempts to improve the quality of journalism were made in 1999. Media organizations tried to end *fafa,* although they were not completely successful. The APG began a dialogue about the need for a professional code of ethics.

Under the presidency of Alfonso Portillo Cabrera, and despite frequent but somewhat diminished intimidation and threats, the press continued to pursue risky activities such as investigating the military, politicians and the Guatemalan equivalent of the CIA. Former President Ríos Montt re-surfaced as president of congress and ally of the incoming president, and a target of a journalistic investigation into a conspiracy to reduce taxes on alcohol. *Prensa Libre* broke the story; editor and columnist Dina Fernández said, ''Unlike in the past, we did our job and didn't remain silent.''

On May 15, 2000, *El Periódico* accused the Estado Mayor Presidencial, or Presidential High Command, of running a clandestine intelligence agency, the director of which was an ex-military official. The previous day, a reporter for that paper had been followed by an unmarked car with concealed license plates; several other journalists on the case were either followed or received intimidating phone calls. Eight days after the story broke, *Siglo Veintinuno* said a journalist from *Nuestro Diario* was threatened during a phone call, a staffer for the radio show *Guatemala Flash* was faxed a death threat, and two reporters from *Siglo Vientiuno* itself were threatened. CERIGUA, the left-leaning news agency that had recently arrived from Mexico, also reported being threatened more than once over this case. On May 19, the CPJ sent a letter to Attorney General Adolfo González Rodas, detailing and protesting the intimidation, and calling for him to ''take adequate measures to ensure that journalists working in Guatemala are able to work safely, without threats or intimidation.''

In July, ''An Open Letter from the pro-Army Patriots to the People of Guatemala'' was paid for and appeared in *Siglo Vientiuno.* In it, *El Periódico* publisher José Rubén Zamoro was identified as one of those ''seeking to destroy the army,'' and it added that from ''now on [our intention] must be made firm and clear [it is]. . .to defend the institutionality of the army and our sovereignty.''

All of the journalists threatened in 2000 were not harmed, but some were. *Prensa Libre* photographer Roberto Martínez was shot and killed by private security guards while covering a demonstration against an increase in bus fares. The guards opened fire on the demonstrators, hitting Martínez despite his clearly being a journalist and his camera being visible. Two bystanders also were killed, and Julio Cruz, a reporter from *Siglo Vientiuno,* as well as Christian Alejandro García, a cameraman from the television news show *Notisiete* were hospitalized. Other journalists surrounded and detained the two security guards until police arrived and arrested them. The two were awaiting trial as the year ended. Centro para la Defensa de la Libertad de Expresión, or CEDEX, a newly created organization, issued a communiqué condemning the killing.

In 2001, freedom of the press somewhat deteriorated in Guatemala, as did the political stability of President Portillo's nation. In February, the staffers of *El Periódico* were threatened by a mob whose members claimed to be protesting that newspaper's investigation of corruption on the part of governmental minister Luis Rabbé. The CPJ's protest letter to Portillo said the mob tried ''to force the daily's doors open and threw burning copies of the newspaper into the building,'' additionally burning an effigy of publisher José Rubén Zamora. The police took 40 minutes to arrive and arrested nobody when they did. Portillo denounced the attack but did nothing to prevent further protests. The following month, four reporters from the paper were attacked and threatened after investigating a bank under state control. Crédito Hipotecario Nacional was revealed by Silvia Gereda and Luis Escobar to have loaned huge amounts of money to friends of the bank's stockholders and the president, José Armando Llort, who responded by taking out newspaper ads threatening libel suits against the journalists. In March, an anonymous man told Gereda that she and her friends were being filmed, and that the bank president wanted them killed. Later she was followed by an unmarked car and threatened several times. A colleague had a gun pointed to his head and was told if the investigation continued, all would die. Portillo, in the face of mounting national and international pressure, is believed to have personally asked the bank president to resign.

In April, the president of congress, Ríos Montt, whose presidency and anti-insurgency policies had resulted in the deaths of more than 200,000 mostly innocent Guatemalans, complained that the earlier investigation into the taxation of alcohol was part of a hidden agenda to discredit him and guarantee his ''political lynching.'' Seven months later, according to CPJ, the investigation ''was shelved after a highly controversial court ruling.''

In June, the Centro para la Defensa de la Libertitad de Expresión, a Guatemalan freedom of the press group, had its inaugural seminar. In November, ironically voting on Guatemalan Journalists Day, the congress required all college graduates, including journalism students, to register with *colegios* or trade associations. Portillo was asked to veto the new law by many press freedom organizations—including some international organizations and the APG—and said he would do so if he felt the bill could damage journalists.

A penalty for the murder of a journalist was carried out in February 2001 when the security guard who killed Roberto Martínez was sentenced to 15 years in the penitentiary and his company ordered to pay damages equivalent to U.S. $20,000 to his family.

As 2002 enfolded, at least one more case of journalistic intimidation had already taken place. On April 10 in downtown Guatemala City, David Herrera, a freelance reporter working for Enlaces, a group of journalists, was kidnapped and threatened with death. Herrera, working on a story recounting alleged government-sanctioned killing, was manhandled by four unknown men brandishing handguns. The men apparently wanted to know where Herrera had the notes he and a colleague had collected concerning the case. The men had searched Herrera's truck, but apparently did not find what they were looking for. The men told Herrera they were going to kill him, and when one cocked a gun, Herrera jumped from the moving vehicle and fled back to his office. Herrera required medical attention for shock. CPJ sent a letter of protest to Portillo, but three months later he had not yet answered.

Despite the arrival of peace in Guatemala, violence against journalists lingered, but at a significantly reduced pace when compared to earlier years. Although the government still did not seem willing to allow a totally free press to exist, the press itself showed great improvement in directly confronting the government, something it would not have dreamed of just a decade earlier.

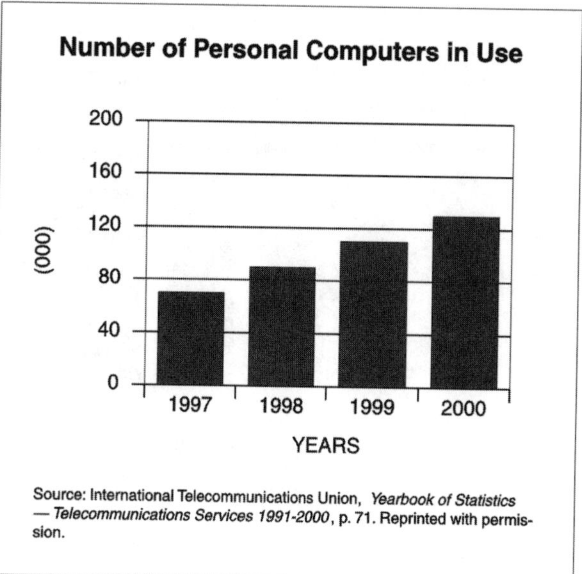

Source: International Telecommunications Union, *Yearbook of Statistics — Telecommunications Services 1991-2000*, p. 71. Reprinted with permission.

ATTITUDE TOWARD FOREIGN MEDIA

In a nation where right-wing death squads were blamed for the 1985 disappearance of U.S. journalists Griffith Davis and Nicholas Chapman Blake, conditions towards foreign journalists in post-Peace Accords Guatemala were greatly improved. Since 1996, there have been no instances of hostility reported towards reporters from other nations. The Inter-American Press was allowed to hold its "Unpublished Crimes against Journalists" conference in Guatemala City in 1997, which focused attention on cases such as the 1980 murders of journalists Irma Flaquer and Jorge Carpio Nicolle.

NEWS AGENCIES

In 2002, foreign news agencies included Reuters and the Associated Press, as well as agencies from Spain, Germany, France, Mexico, the United States and Canada. Domestic agencies included ACAN-EFE, Agencia Cimak.

The news agency CERIGUA, which had had to operate in Mexico for most of the guerrilla war due to its left-leaning philosophy, opened an office in Guatemala's capital in 1994. It provides news from a leftist perspective, and in 2002, was continuing to function as independently as possible, including reporting on attempted intimidation. During 2000, CERIGUA helped reveal the existence of a clandestine governmental intelligence agency, despite numerous anonymous threats being made to it by fax and telephone.

BROADCAST MEDIA

In 2000, there are 26 stations, with all content emanating from one of four major outlets: Canal 3, Canal 7 / Televisiete, Canal 11, and Canal 13. All are located in Guatemala City, from where all media—print and electronic— originates. The government also owns other channels, two of which were allowed to be used by an Evangelical Protestant group (Canal 21) and the military (Canal 5). In June 2002 plans were being made to allocate a channel to the Roman Catholic Church.

Radio broadcasters numbered 632 stations. The content of both radio and television was determined by the government.

Although print journalists continued to grow into their roles as investigative reporters during the postwar period, those working in radio and television were, for the most part, stagnant. Part of the problem was money; small cooperative radio stations could not afford to bid on frequencies offered at public auction. In a land where radio is the dominant medium, larger stations had more money to bid than did Mayan groups, which demanded improved media access but did not get it despite the 1996 peace accords call for specific indigenous language radio frequencies.

Violence was not limited to members of the print press. On June 16, 1997, a news reader at Radio Campesina in Tiquisate, Herández Pérez, was shot and killed while leaving the station. Also killed was a station messenger, Haroldo Escobar Noriega. In 2000, Christian Alejandro Garcia, a cameraman from the television news show *Notisiete,* was shot by security guards while covering a demonstration against higher bus fares and had to be hospitalized. In the same year, a staffer for radio show *Guatemala Flash* was faxed a death threat over that station's investigation of the government's unofficial intelligence agency. Finally, less than two years later, the

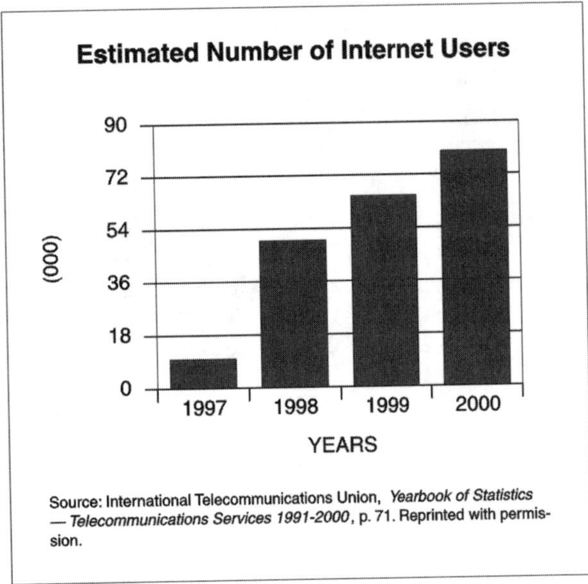

Source: International Telecommunications Union, *Yearbook of Statistics — Telecommunications Services 1991-2000*, p. 71. Reprinted with permission.

murder of another journalist took place when Linea Directa radio call-in talk-show host Jorge Mynor Alegría Armendáriz was killed just outside his home near the Caribbean coast. Some of Linea Directa's favorite topics had been government corruption and mismanagement; a colleague said that Alegría had been threatened and offered bribes. Another journalist from the same station, Enrique Aceituno, resigned in the face of threats stemming from his discussions of similar problems. The Ombudsman's Office for Human Rights decided the assassination was politically motivated, but a local prosecutor was less certain.

Governmental pressure of a subtler sort also could be seen at times. Some Guatemalans said that *Guatemala Flash* changed hands from an owner who criticized the government freely to a pro-government investor because of government pressure aimed at advertisers. A publicly-funded television news show, *Avances,* was supposed to inform the public about the government but spent most of its time criticizing the print press. The radio program *Hoy por Hoy* broadcast indictments aimed at *Prensa Libre* owner Dina García and editor Dina Fernández. President Arzú was found to be behind the false allegations.

Charges were made that it is impossible for an independent radio and television media to emerge in Guatemala because so many stations were owned by so few of the people. It has been pointed out that a Mexican national, Angel González, owns all four of the private Guatemalan television stations as of June 2002, despite laws against both monopolies and foreign ownership. Many felt that Portillo, despite his protests to the contrary, was behind González's closing of an occasionally controversial news show known as *T-Mas de Noche.* Portillo denied any involvement and invited the Inter-American Commission on Human Rights to investigate, which it did. The result was that the investigator urged the government to look into González's holdings, as well as recommending the suspension of the public auction of broadcast radio frequencies in order to make at least some of them available to the indigenous population in appropriate languages. Shortly thereafter the auctions were suspended. But in mid-2002, there were no indigenous broadcast channels for either radio or television. However, occasional broadcasts and speeches were given in Mayan tongues.

ELECTRONIC NEWS MEDIA

In the year 2000, there were five Internet service providers. The number of Internet users is rapidly increasing, especially among journalists who use it for both information and training purposes. The Internet functions government interference. Smeets said the Internet opened the eyes of Guatemalan journalists and exposed them to a more professional, better-finished, more ingenious and creative press.

In 2002, four major dailies are available on-line: *Prensa Libre* at www.prensalibre.com.gt; *Siglo XXI* at www.sigloxxi.com; *La Hora* at www.lahora.com.gt, and *El Periódico* at www.elperiodico.com. Four television stations also are online: Canal 3 at www.canal3.com.gt; Canal 7 / Televisiete at www.canal7.com.gt; Canal 11 at www.canal11.com.gt, and Canal 13 at www.canal13.com.gt. Also online is the radio group Emisoras Unidas at www.emisorasunidas.com.

EDUCATION AND TRAINING

In 1998, the Asociación de Periodistas de Guatemala began work with San Carlos University to develop journalism workshops. By mid-2002, there were individual journalism classes at that university, but no degree program. The Internet supplied some journalistic training. Regarding journalism training in Guatemala, Smeets said Guatemalan journalists need better education opportunities to learn the skills necessary to analyze current events, and that better reporting will raise reader expectations, which "opens more space for independent journalism."

SUMMARY

Before the Peace Accords, journalists were murdered, threatened, kidnapped, and were actually in the pay of the ruling classes, as were their newspapers. The print media, in particular, had become both more pluralistic and professional, as the CPJ observed in 1997. The same organization in 1998 referred to "the virtual halt of violence against journalists this year," so the profession has become safer. Although violence has escalated in recent years, it is still nowhere near what it had been. The government does try to influence newspapers, for instance, by encouraging the withholding of advertising revenue.

In the case of television and radio, there is less reason for optimism. The government's virtual monopoly over television, coupled with its control over radio channels, is a threat to freedom of the press, especially in a nation where nearly one-third of the population is illiterate. Control of these media outlets has dire consequences for the Mayan-speaking majority of Guatemalan Indians, whose primary access to the news is radio and television. In the first two years of the twenty-first century, there is neither a television nor radio station for these people, although there is an occasional radio program or speech in an indigenous language.

By the halfway point of 2002, it is not yet clear if either President Portillo or any members of the power structure he represents, including the generals, has intentions of democratization. Guatemala was brought to the Peace Accords by a combination of external pressure and the internal recognition that the war was basically unwinnable. Portillo and his backers may have intended to implement the Peace Accords and were perhaps slowly, but inevitably, progressing towards this goal. Or they may have regarded the peace process as an extension of the civil war, one in which they worked their hardest to keep the status quo while giving the illusion that they intended to become more democratic. Ultimate freedom of the Guatemalan press is dependent upon the freedom of the Guatemalan state.

One thing, however, seems evident: The full participation of the highland-dwelling indigenous people of Guatemala will be necessary before there is any sort of democracy or true freedom of the press. There is a synergistic relationship between a free press and a free and literate people; when people cannot read or at least hear and see for themselves what their government is doing, that synergy cannot exist. In Guatemala, it has never had a chance to develop.

Too many Guatemalans remain incapable of taking part in a democracy; they cannot understand the Spanish of the press, or they cannot read at all. Until they can fully participate, their nation's press continues to exist only for its literate and Spanish speaking members.

BIBLIOGRAPHY

Brown, Robert U. ''Curtailing Press Freedom.'' In *The Fourth Estate,* 128, April 8, 1995, pp. 31-3.

Bureau of Western Hemisphere Affairs. ''Background Note: Guatemala.'' Available from http://www.state.gov./r/pa/ei/bgn/2045.htm.

Central Intelligence Agency (CIA). In *The World Factbook 2002.* Available from http://www.cia.gov./cia/.

Cleary, Edward L. ''Examining Guatemalan Processes of Violence and Peace.'' In *Latin American Research Review.* January 2002, 37, no. 1, 230-246.

''Country Reports: Guatemala.'' The Committee to Protect Journalists (CPJ). 1996, 1997, 1998, 1999, 2000, and 2001. Available from http://www.cpj.org.

Ebel, Roland H. *Misunderstood Caudillo: Miguel Ydigoras Fuentes and the Failure of Democracy in Guatemala.* New York: University Press of America, 1998.

Embassy of Guatemala to the United States. Available from http://www.guatemala-embassy.org.

Jonas, Susanne. *Of Doves and Centaurs: Guatemala's Peace Process.* Santa Cruz, Ca.: Westview, A Member of the Perseus Books Group: 2000.

Lawyers Committee for Human Rights. *Abandoning the Victims: The UN Advisory Services Program in Guatemala.* New York: The Lawyers Committee for Human Rights, 1990.

Lovell, George W. *A Beauty that Hurts: Life and Death in Guatemala.* Austin, Tx.: U of Texas, 2000.

McCleary, Rachel M. *Dictating Democracy: Guatemala and the End of Violent Revolution.* Gainesville, Fl.: U P of Florida, 1999.

Nelson, Diane M. *A Finger in the Wound: Body Politics in Quincentennial Guatemala.* Los Angeles: U of California P, 1999.

Nichols, John Spencer. ''Guatemala.'' In *The World Press Encyclopedia,* George Thomas Kurian, ed. New York: Facts on File, Inc., 1982, 409-420.

Simon, Jean-Marie. *Guatemala: Eternal Spring—Eternal Tyranny.* New York: W.W. Norton Co., 1987.

Smeets, Marylene. ''Speaking Out: Postwar Journalism in Guatemala and El Salvador.'' Available from http://www.cpj.org/attacks99/americas99/americasSP.html.

''Station May Go Catholic.'' In *Chicago Sun-Times,* June 14, 2002, p. 43.

Trudeau, Robert H. ''Understanding Transitions to Democracy: Recent Work on Guatemala.'' In *Latin American Research Review,* 1993, 28, no. 1, 235-49.

Von Hagen, Victor W. *World of the Maya.* New York, New York: The New American Library, 1960.

U.S. Department of State. ''Guatemala: Country Reports on Human Rights Practices 2000.'' Available from http://www.state.gov./g/drl/rls/hrrpt/2000/wha/775pf.htm.

Zur, Judith N. *Violent Memories: Mayan War Widows in Guatemala.* Boulder, Co.: Westview Press, a member of HarperCollins Publishers, 1998.

—Ronald E. Sheasby, Ph. D.

GUERNSEY

BASIC DATA

Official Country Name:	Guernsey
Region (Map name):	Europe
Population:	64,080
Language(s):	English, French, Norman-French
Literacy rate:	N/A

Guernsey and its seven dependent islands are part of the Channel Islands, which sit northwest of France in the English Channel. The islands are the last remnants of the medieval Dukedom of Normandy and the only British soil occupied by Germany in World War II. Today Guernsey is a British Crown Dependency. The British monarch heads the state, and the head of government is a Lieutenant Governor, who is appointed by the monarch. The legislative branch is a unicameral Assembly of States. The population of Guernsey is nearly 65,000. The official language is English, but French is also widely spoken, and a Norman-French dialect is often used in rural districts. Financial services account for more than half of Guernsey's economy—light taxes and death duties make it a popular tax haven. Tourism, manufacturing, tomatoes and cut flowers also contribute to the GNP.

Citizens of Guernsey enjoy the press and speech freedoms of England. The daily newspaper of Guernsey is *The Guernsey Press.* In 1999, it changed its format from broadsheet to tabloid and shortened its name. It publishes Monday through Saturday, and its circulation is 16,000. Editorial content appears online through the thisisguernsey.com Web portal. The newspaper's parent company also publishes the island's weekly, *The Globe.* This community-oriented, tabloid newspaper appears every Wednesday and has an approximate circulation of 18,000.

Guernsey has one FM radio station, one AM radio station, and one television station. There are two Internet service providers.

BIBLIOGRAPHY

''Benn's Media 1999,'' Vol. 1, 147th Edition, p. 253.

Guernsey.net (2002), Home Page. Available from http://www.guernsey.net.

''Guernsey,'' *CIA World Fact Book (2001).* Available from http://www.cia.gov.

The Guernsey Press, (2002) Home Page. Available from http://www.guernsey-press.com.

Thisisguernsey.com, (n.d.) Home Page. Available from http://www.thisisguernsey.com/.

''What is localdial,'' *Localdial.com,* (2002). Available from http://www.localdial.com/aboutus.html.

—Jenny B. Davis

GUINEA

BASIC DATA

Official Country Name:	Republic of Guinea
Region (Map name):	Africa
Population:	7,466,200
Language(s):	French
Literacy rate:	35.9%

BACKGROUND & GENERAL CHARACTERISTICS

The government essentially runs the news media in the Republic of Guinea (Républic de Guinée), a coastal West African country where the United Nations projects a 2002 population of 7,860,000, including refugees who fled in 2001 from Liberia and Sierra Leone.

Patterns of language and literacy, population distribution, and historical modes of government have all combined against the presence of a strong press. The predominantly Muslim population, about twenty-nine percent urban, inhabits a diverse terrain. A history of colonialism followed by Marxism underlies the weak but improving economy, which is heavily agricultural. The official language is French, but natives also use tribal languages including Malinké (Mandingo). Only some thirty-six percent of Guineans are literate. Conakry, Guinea's coastal capital and communications center, has a population approaching 2,000,000.

Though the Constitution of 1991 is in force, government censorship applies, and critics charge that presidential and parliamentary elections in the 1990s were not open.

Media Activity The daily newspaper, *Fonike*, which had a circulation in the twenty thousands in the late 1990s, is state-owned. *Horoya* (Liberty) is published in French and the local languages. *Journal Officiel de Guinée* is a fortnightly government organ. A federation of Guinean workers has published *Le Travailleur de Guinée,* a monthly. *L'Indépendant* is an independent weekly.

The official news agency since 1986 has been the *Agence Guinéenne de Presse* (AGP), an offshoot of the UNESCO-supported West African News Agencies Development (WANAD) project. *Xinhua*, APN, and TASS have representations in Conakry.

The state-controlled *Radiodiffusion Télévision Guinéenne* broadcasts over eight radio stations in French, English, Portuguese, Arabic, and native dialects; in 1998 citizens owned about 390,000 radios. Interactive instruction by radio has been tried in Guinean classrooms.

State television broadcasts, which started in 1977, were reaching about 87,000 TV sets in the late 1990s. Six TV stations operated in 1997. The *Société des Télécommunications de Guinée* is forty percent state-owned.

Computer use is growing. In 1995, Guineans owned an estimated one hundred personal computers, but by the year 2000, Internet users numbered about five thousand. In mid-2002 the university at Kankan, isolated in the interior, was getting its own campus computer system and high-speed Internet connection.

SIGNIFICANT DATES

- 1977: State-sponsored television broadcasts begin.
- 2002: A college in the interior is wired for the Internet.

BIBLIOGRAPHY

The Central Intelligence Agency (CIA). *World Factbook 2002*. Directorate of Intelligence, 7 May 2002. Available from http://www.cia.gov/.

Banks, Arthur S. and Thomas C. Muller, eds. *Political Handbook of the World, 1999*. Binghamton, NY: CSA Publications, 1999.

Turner, Barry, ed. *The Statesman's Yearbook: The Politics, Cultures, and Economies of the World, 2000*. 136th ed. New York: St. Martin's Press, 1999.

USAID, 7 May 2002. Available from http://www.usaid.gov/.

World Almanac and Book of Facts, 2002. New York: World Almanac Books, 2002.

—*Roy Neil Graves*

GUINEA-BISSAU

BASIC DATA

Official Country Name:	Republic of Guinea-Bissau
Region (Map name):	Africa
Population:	1,285,715
Language(s):	Portuguese, Crioulo
Literacy rate:	53.9%

BACKGROUND & GENERAL CHARACTERISTICS

Guinea-Bissau is a small West African country situated on the Atlantic coast, directly south of Senegal and northwest of Guinea (Guinea-Conakry). Colonized by the Portuguese during the European colonial era, Guinea-Bissau became independent in 1974 after a long and violent war led by the leftist African Party for the Independence of Guinea and Cape Verde (PAIGC), with Luis Cabral at its helm. Its capital city is Bissau.

Guinea-Bissau has a population of approximately 1.3 million. The major language groups in the country are Portuguese, Crioulo, and a number of African languages. The population practices Islam, Christianity, and indigenous religions. Because illiteracy is very high—about 50 percent—news broadcasts by radio are the most practical and popular means of communicating current events and perspectives on domestic and international situations.

Kumba Yala, Guinea-Bissau's current president, won free elections held in January 2000. Yala's rise to power followed four years of civil war from 1994 to 1998 that ended with foreign mediation and two years of policing by West African peacekeepers. The country continues to struggle with internal conflicts and has a fractious relationship with the Gambia, leading to rumors from time to time that armed conflict is about to erupt between the two countries. In part, this explains the government's special sensitivity to security concerns but by no means excuses the harsh treatment meted out to members of the media.

President Yala, formerly a teacher, has supported the following goals for Guinea-Bissau: fostering national reconciliation after the civil war, balancing the national budget, making the economy more productive with an emphasis on agriculture, diminishing public spending, and canceling special benefits for government ministers.

However, he has been accused of being temperamental and authoritarian in his manner of leadership. This led to the resignation of some of his governing coalition partners in mid-2001 and made President Yala's party, the Social Renewal Party, a minority party. After this occurred, the president reportedly became more aggressive and confrontational with other members of the government and officials in the other two branches of government, the legislature and judiciary.

As the Committee to Protect Journalists (CPJ) noted in its *Africa 2001* report, ''At the end of the summer [2001], the Supreme Court declared unconstitutional the president's decision to expel members of the Ahmadiyya Islamic sect, whom he had accused of causing instability. Over the next two months, Yala went on a rampage.'' CPJ reported that four Supreme Court judges lost their positions after the president charged them with corruption. President Yala also threatened to replace most of Guinea-Bissau's public servants with persons from his own political party, and he ''threatened to shoot any politician who tried to use the army against him,'' in CPJ's words.

As Reporters without Borders noted in its annual report for 2001, ''Guinea-Bissau has still not recovered from the multiple coups d'etat and armed conflict in the past few years.'' During 2001, government limitations of press freedom increased, a pattern that was repeated if not exacerbated in 2002. In its annual report for 2001, Amnesty International reported, ''Journalists were harassed and briefly detained for publishing articles critical of the government or organizing radio debates deemed sensitive by the authorities.''

No Pintcha is the government-affiliated newspaper. A few private newspapers exist, though some have repeatedly met with government attempts to silence them. The *Diário de Bissau*, one of the leading private newspapers until late 2001, generally published several times a week, though certain stories and some of its leading staff members came under repeated government attack. In October 2001 the paper was closed down by Attorney General Caetano N'Tchama, who alleged it was not properly licensed. The same fate befell the private weekly, *Gazeta de Noticias*, allegedly for the same reason. Both papers also were accused of having caused severe damage to Guinea-Bissau's independence. Other private weeklies include *Correio de Bissau*, *Banobero*, and *Fraskera*, the latter of these a new paper added at the close of 2001.

Economic Framework

Guinea-Bissau has a very troubled economy, despite the fact that before its civil war, the country was viewed as a possible model for African development. Huge foreign debt saddles the economy of Guinea-Bissau, and the country depends heavily on international donor assistance to survive. Government corruption appears to have contributed to the sorry state of Guinea-Bissau's economy. As CPJ remarked, ''widespread allegations of corruption and mismanagement'' plagued the government in 2001.

The economy of Guinea-Bissau is basically agricultural, the principal exports being cashew nuts, shrimp, peanuts, palm kernels, and cut timber. Annual per capita income is only about US $180. By 2002 health standards were very low and average life expectancy was only 43 years for men and 48 years for women—abysmally low by international standards.

The private press often is strapped for funds because of the poor national economy and the fact that a lack of advertising in the private press often puts many independent newspapers on the edge of financial sustainability and the brink of closure. The state media does not fare much better. As Reporters without Borders observed, ''Employees of the RTGB, the national broadcasting company, went on several strikes during the year to demand better working conditions and payment of their salaries. Some RTGB journalists and technicians have not been paid for nearly two years.'' State media professionals allegedly practice self-censorship even more stringently than private journalists, in order to protect themselves from government sanctions.

The fact that all newspapers in Guinea-Bissau—public and private together—must be printed in the government printing house adds to the tenuousness of publication schedules. The printing house fees are high, and printing supplies frequently are unavailable to publish papers in sufficient quantities. No other domestic printing company is available to the country's media.

Press Laws

The Constitution guarantees freedom of speech and of the press. However, the government of Guinea-Bissau—arguably overreacting to concerns about potential, new insurrections in the country and rumors of rebel incursions supported from nearby Gambia—has acted repressively toward journalists and the private press. In March 2001 about 30 journalists signed a petition in which they protested ''censorship and detention without trial of journalists practicing their profession in Guinea-Bissau.''

The new Attorney General appointed in September 2001, Caetano N'Tchama, served as prime minister of Guinea-Bissau until President Yala dismissed him from his head-of-government position in March 2002. He had been particularly harsh toward the media. The same month he was appointed Attorney General, N'Tchama entered the private radio station, Radio Pidjiquiti, and demanded that tapes from an earlier broadcast be turned over to him. When the broadcasters refused, N'Tchama sent armed men the next day to intimidate station staff even further. He continued to demand the tapes from a program where journalists from the private newspaper, *Diário de Bissau*, had suggested N'Tchama was dismissed from his post as prime minister due to incompetence.

CENSORSHIP

In March 2001 Assistant State Prosecutor Genésio de Carvalho made an outright recommendation to Guinea-Bissau's media professionals that they practice "self-censorship." Journalists, publishers, and editors in both the private and the public media must pay attention to whether their reports and broadcasts are likely to come under criticism by the government in order to avoid government harassment, intimidation and threats, personal detention, and media closures.

Two of the latest examples of the government's ongoing efforts to silence media critiques were the respective arrests on July 17 and 20, 2002 of João de Barros, publisher and editor of a private weekly news magazine, *Correio de Bissau*, and Nilson Mendonca, reporter for the RDN. De Barros had appeared on a talk show of the independent radio station, Radio Bombolom, and had claimed that rather than being true, recent rumors of plots against the president were aimed at directing attention away from government corruption; he also discounted rumors that Gambian officials were supporting rebel activity in Guinea-Bissau. After being detained for two days, de Barros was released on the condition that he report to the authorities on a frequent, regular basis. Mendonca appeared to have been arrested for stating that the president should apologize to Gambian officials after accusing them of supporting rebels in Guinea-Bissau. Questioned about his sources, Mendonca was released after 24 hours' detention.

The World Association of Newspapers and the World Editors' Forum (the latter a subgroup of the larger association, WAN), both based in Paris, sent a letter to President Yala and denounced the arrests, reminding the president that the United Nations Universal Declaration of Human Rights guarantees freedom of expression and calling on the government of Guinea-Bissau to stop harassing journalists.

Continual efforts by President Yala to stop criticism of himself and his government by the private media and to exercise control over the types of news reported have led to repeat arrests for João de Barros, the publisher and editor of *Diário de Bissau*, and the closure of that paper in October 2001. De Barros restarted a private weekly of his that had been closed down five years earlier, *Correio de Bissau*, in December 2001; de Barros and that paper have been no less successful in escaping the wrath of government censors in 2002. Athizar Mendes, another journalist with the *Diário de Bissau*, also met with government reprisal for the stories he has covered. One of his stories, published in June 2001, alleged the president's involvement with an array of top civil servants in misappropriating large sums of money from the public treasury. Mendes and de Barros have been arrested repeatedly for their work.

In January 2001 Bacar Tcherno Dole, a state radio journalist and reporter for *No Pintcha*, the government newspaper, was arrested and mistreated for having mistakenly reported a violent incursion into the country's Sao Domingo region by rebels from Casamance in neighboring Senegal. The U.S. Department of State stated that the journalist was "abused physically and intimidated by the military and police during his detention," based on an Amnesty International report.

STATE-PRESS RELATIONS

State-press relations are none too positive in Guinea-Bissau in the aftermath of the civil war of the mid-1990s. Government censorship of the media abounds, and state as well as private journalists, publishers, editors, and broadcasters must watch their words or risk government abuse.

ATTITUDE TOWARD FOREIGN MEDIA

Upon occasion, government mishandling of the press does not stop with the domestic media. In March 2001 Adolfo Palma, a correspondent for LUSA, the Portuguese news agency, was charged with defamation after reporting on the arrest in February of persons in Guinea-Bissau. Government officials accused him of misrepresenting the truth.

Radio Mavegro, a private commercial station, includes programming from the British Broadcasting Corporation's World Service in its broadcasts.

BROADCAST MEDIA

The only television station in the country is Radio Televisao de Guinea-Bissau (RTGB). However, in 1997 the Portuguese government established a television broadcasting station, RTP Africa, comprised of a network of local stations in all the states that were formerly Portuguese colonies. The local managers are from the countries where the stations are situated, but the financing and studio equipment come from the Portuguese government.

The national radio broadcasting station in Guinea-Bissau is Radio Nacional. Private radio stations are few in number but include Radio Mavegro, a commercial station that also broadcasts some programs produced by the British Broadcasting Company's World Service, Radio Bombolom FM, and Radio Pidjiquiti. In October 2001 Attorney General N'Tchama accused the latter two private and very popular radio stations of irregularly handling "their administrative and legal situation" and threatened to close them down. However, the two stations were allowed to continue to operate—because of their usefulness to the government in broadcasting news and also because of their great popularity, according to some local journalists.

Local community radio stations previously supported by non-governmental associations did not resume broadcasting in 2001. The government does not restrict access to the Internet, which is available in Guinea-Bissau.

SUMMARY

Despite the fact that the country of Guinea-Bissau had a very promising past in terms of its economic and social development, the country today is rife with problems—economic, social, and political. In consequence, members of the media frequently are threatened and harassed by government officials who appear to seek scapegoats to blame for the problems they have not yet solved and to which they have contributed. Both state and private media professionals face problems in being irregularly or poorly paid, the state printing house frequently lacks necessary supplies that prevent the public and private press from publishing regularly, and government intimidation of journalists occurs fairly regularly. Some journalists and editors are arrested repeatedly, targeted by the government for critiquing government behavior and for supposedly adding to real or perceived national security risks.

With the greater involvement of international media associations and human rights organizations in monitoring the status of journalism and the treatment of fellow journalists, publishers, and editors, some hope exists that the media in Guinea-Bissau will see better times in the not-too-distant future. With improved access to the Internet—rapidly growing throughout Africa—government officials may find it increasingly hard to harass those who practice the delicate art of informing their fellow citizens and the world at large of the ongoing problems and challenges in their societies. Certainly the people of Guinea-Bissau will benefit from a more watchful eye by the international community of the welfare not only of media members but also of the general population. By continuing to exert influence on the shaping of public opinion regarding government policies and private practices, members of the press—both domestic and international—hopefully in the longer run will contribute to the general improvement of society and politics in Guinea-Bissau.

The crucial role of the international and domestic press in monitoring civil rights abuses, including those exacted upon media professionals as they carry out their daily work, cannot be overstressed. This is especially apparent in Guinea-Bissau, a country on the path toward national reconciliation but facing many hard challenges of leadership along the way.

SIGNIFICANT DATES

- 1994-1998—Civil war.
- 1997: Portuguese government establishes a television broadcasting station, RTP Africa, consisting of local stations from Portugal's former colonies, managed by local media staff.
- 1998-2000: International peacekeeping force composed of West Africans monitors the country.
- 2000: Kumba Yala wins free presidential election.
- March 2001: 30 journalists sign a petition protesting censorship
- October 2001: *Diário de Bissau* and *Gazeta de Noticias*, two leading private newspapers, are closed down by Attorney General Caetano N'Tchama, who also threatens to close two private radio stations.
- July 2002: João de Barros, publisher and editor of a private weekly news magazine, *Correio de Bissau*, and Nilson Mendonca, reporter for the RDN, are arrested and detained after criticizing President Yala's accusatory comments regarding Gambian government officials.

BIBLIOGRAPHY

Amnesty International. "Guinea-Bissau." *Amnesty International Report 2002*. London: Amnesty International, May 28, 2002. Available at http://web.amnesty.org.

BBC Monitoring. "Country profile: Guinea-Bissau." Reading, UK: British Broadcasting Corporation, July 5, 2002. Available at http://news.bbc.co.uk.

Bureau of Democracy, Human Rights, and Labor, U.S. Department of State. "Guinea-Bissau." *Country Reports on Human Rights Practices 2001*. Washington, DC: Bureau of Public Affairs, U.S. Department of State, March 4, 2002. Available at http://www.state.gov.

Committee to Protect Journalists. "Guinea-Bissau." *Attacks on the Press in 2001: Africa 2001*. New York, NY: CPJ, 2002. Available at http://www.cpj.org.

Reporters without Borders. "Guinea-Bissau." *Africa annual report 2002*. Paris, France: Reporters sans frontières, April 30, 2002. Available at http://www.rsf.org.

World Association of Newspapers. ''WAN, WEF Protest Against Arrest of Journalists in Bissau.'' Paris, July 3, 2002. Available at http://allafrica.com.

— Barbara A. Lakeberg-Dridi, Ph.D.

GUYANA

BASIC DATA

Official Country Name:	Republic of Guyana
Region (Map name):	South America
Population:	697,181
Language(s):	English, Amerindian dialects, Creole, Hindi, Urdu
Literacy rate:	98.1%
Area:	214,970 sq km
Number of Television Stations:	3
Number of Television Sets:	46,000
Television Sets per 1,000:	66.0
Number of Satellite Subscribers:	789
Satellite Subscribers per 1,000:	1.1
Number of Radio Stations:	7
Number of Radio Receivers:	420,000
Radio Receivers per 1,000:	602.4
Number of Individuals with Computers:	22,000
Computers per 1,000:	31.6
Number of Individuals with Internet Access:	4,000
Internet Access per 1,000:	5.7

BACKGROUND— GENERAL CHARACTERISTICS

Guyana (full name, Co-operative Republic of Guyana) is a tropical country lying on the northern coast of South America. The sparse population of the country's savannahs and highland regions consists mostly of Amerindians, Guyana's indigenous people. The capital, and the country's main harbor, is Georgetown, whose population is around 185,000. Guyana is comprised of six ethnic groups, which reflect the fact that modern Guyana began as a nation of plantations run by Dutch, French and British settlers who imported slave labor. Around 40 percent of the population is African; East Indians comprise 51 percent, and the remainder are Chinese, Portuguese, European, and Amerindian. The official language of Guyana is English, but other languages are spoken, including several Amerindian dialects, Creole, Hindi, Urdu and Creolese, which is a mixture of English and Creole. Guyana is a secular state, but everyone is guaranteed religious freedom under the Constitution. About 57 percent of Guyanese are Christian; Hindus comprise 33 percent; and 9 percent are Muslim.

The country's varied terrain, extensive savannahs, mountainous regions, and dense forests have made communication difficult and have divided the country's newspaper publication into two distinct groups: newspapers published in remote regions for local consumption, and those published in Georgetown. The largest savannah occupies about 6,000 square miles in the southwestern part of the country and is divided by the Kanuku mountain range.

The country's major newspapers are published in Georgetown and must be shipped to interior regions either by air or boat because of the country's terrain. Only unpaved roads and trails link the savannahs and interior towns. The main paved roads are located in the coastal area and extend through the towns and villages near the coast. Consequently, rivers are an important means of transportation to the country's remote areas. Air communication is the main link to the interior of Guyana, which is served by about 94 airstrips, most of which receive only light aircraft.

Regional newspapers traditionally have been small, both in readership and in the kind of news printed. By contrast, newspapers published in the capital have had a much broader scope and larger circulation. Journalists would also be affected by the country's geography. The better trained, more experienced, and better educated journalists would gravitate to the capital, where the readership was larger and press facilities were more advanced than in the smaller cities and remote villages.

Guyana's first known newspaper, the *Royal Essequibo and Demerary Gazette,* was published in 1796 by the government, but it was small and filled almost entirely with advertisements. In the nineteenth century a series of private newspapers, such as the *Creole,* frequently sprang up all over Guyana, but they usually lasted only days or months, and sometimes mere hours. They had little or no financial support and their publishers, who doubled as reporters, lacked formal training or professional experience. One of these early efforts, the *Working Man,* may have been typical of these amateur newspapers. It championed the cause of the poor and working class in opposition to powerful forces in the colony. Predictably, *Working Man* failed to attract advertisements from influential businesses and, like other small newspapers, succumbed before the year was out. By the 1940s, newspaper publication was centered in the capital. Three dailies were being published: *Daily Argosy, Guiana Graphic,* and *Daily Chronicle,* all privately owned and all serving a population of about 75,000.

Although newspapers have been part of Guyana's history for 200 years, literacy among the non-European population did not begin until 1876, when universal primary education was introduced; the establishment of secondary schools early in the twentieth century helped spread literacy. Today, the government reports an overall literacy rate of 98 percent, but research indicates that the average literacy rate is actually much lower if measured in terms of the basic ability to sign one's name. Other studies show that the overall functional literacy rate is a little more than 50 percent.

Historical Background Guyana was first populated by the indigenous peoples of the region, the Amerindians, comprised of nine aboriginal tribes. European settlement began in 1615 with the Dutch West India Company, which established plantations on the coast and brought West African slaves to work the newly established cotton and sugar plantations. The French and English soon laid claim to various parts of the region, bringing in their own slaves to work their plantations. From 1781 onwards, the British became the dominant power, ultimately uniting various colonies into British Guiana. When slavery was abolished in 1834, laborers were brought from India to work the plantations in place of the former slaves who left. Immigrants also came from Europe and China.

British Guiana gained independence in 1966, giving birth to the new country of Guyana, which adopted its own constitution in 1980 and a new economic philosophy, co-operative socialism. Many industries were nationalized, and many educated Guyanese emigrated in response to these changes and to the economic slump that hindered the country's growth into the 1990s. In recent years Guyana was attempting new economic initiatives to try to reverse the lingering effects of the recession of the 1970s and 1980s, and though it was making encouraging progress on many fronts, more than half the population lives in poverty. In an effort to relinquish control of industry, the ruling party is privatizing many businesses, and has liberalized its stance toward the media by funding professional courses in journalism at the University of Guyana.

The Guyanese press was established in 1793, and politics have sometimes played a part in which publications survived and which did not, and in how the survivors fared. During World War II, the government established the *Bulletin,* a free publication that promulgated news of the government's war efforts. Later, the *Bulletin* was expanded into a full-fledged newspaper with a circulation of around 52,000, the country's largest at the time, to deliver the state's propaganda across Guyana. The *Bulletin*'s function as a dispenser of information, not a gatherer of news, has remained the government's version of media participation ever since. Over the years, and despite the country's small population, a plethora of periodical publications have come and gone. Each group serves specific areas of the country or special groups. For example, among the journals *Polyglot: Journal of the Humanities* publishes academic research for and by linguists. Newsletters and magazines offer an economical and expedient way to disseminate information for a wide variety of groups, such as accountants, the police, the University of Guyana History Society, Georgetown Sewerage and Water Commissioners, the Adult Education Association of Guyana, various alumni associations, religious groups, political parties, and many other groups. *Visions and Voices,* the newsletter of the National Democratic Movement, focuses mainly on Georgetown's social problems. Other newsletters deal with sports, HIV/AIDs, and current topics of interest to readers. *GY Magazine* aims to offer Guyanese women "a magazine of quality" with articles on glamour, health and fitness, romance, sex, and literature. The humanities are further represented by *The Guyana Christmas Annual,* a magazine of poetry, fiction and non-fiction, and photography. *Sports Digest,* a quarterly sports magazine, covers local sports from around Guyana. *Emancipation,* a magazine started in 1993, deals with the history and culture of the African-Guyanese and contains features on villages, personalities and literature. The *Guyana Review* has established itself as Guyana's preeminent national news magazine. A monthly publication, it offers a wide range of economic, environmental, political and cultural news.

Guyana's newspapers are relatively few in comparison to the country's other print media, but the combined circulation of all newspapers in the country is a little more than 407,850. Newspapers with the largest readership are the *Guyana Chronicle,* a government-owned daily published in Georgetown, and *New Nation,* the voice of the People's New Congress, one of the two major political parties, with a circulation of about 26,000. *Dayclean,* published for the Working People's Alliance, was founded in 1979 and has a circulation of 5,000; its aim is to defend "the poor and the powerless" against abuses of power by the ruling party. The *Mirror,* owned by the ruling People's Progress Party, was begun in 1962 and grew to 16 pages by 1992. It is published twice a week in Georgetown and has developed a readership of about 25,000. *Stabroek News* is a liberal independent newspaper that started out as a weekly and increased to six times a week by 1991. *The Catholic Standard,* published by the Roman Catholic Church since 1905, has a readership of 10,000.

Several special-interest newspapers also are available. *True News,* published weekly in Georgetown, is aimed at a readership that likes sensational social, legal and medical stories. *Flame,* published in Georgetown by the National Media & Publishing Company Ltd., is a mid-week newspaper that offers "fascinating stories from Guyana, the Caribbean and the rest of the world" for an adult, mass readership. *Civil Society,* also a Georgetown weekly newspaper, offers cultural, political and social information in a manner intended to be thought-provoking. Guyana even has a weekly tabloid, *Spice,* which publishes sensational stories with racy photographs of young women.

Guyana's diverse geography has resulted in widespread racial separation, the Indians staying mainly in the rural areas and the Africans moving to the cities. Consequently, Indians on the plantation have long dominated the sugar and rice industry, and Africans now dominate the civil service and urban industries. But in the last 30 years, integration has increased as large numbers of Indians have settled in the cities, bringing new stresses as they mix with other races. The ethnic troubles of the 1960s divided the Guyanese people and have led to street violence, particularly around election times, and have raised fears of social disintegration. Turbulent politics and ethnic strife continue, and protests following the 1997 and 2001 elections increased political instability and often have threatened to bring the country's economic recovery to a halt. Through much of Guyana's history, the Anglican and Roman Catholic churches have helped maintain the social and political stability. The Roman Catholic Church and its newspaper, the *Catholic Standard,* opposed the ideology of the People's Progressive Party in the 1950s and became closely associated with conservative forces. In the late 1960s, the *Catholic Standard* became more critical of the government and, as a consequence, the government forced a number of foreign Roman Catholic priests to leave the country. By the mid-1970s, the Anglicans and other Protestant denominations had joined to oppose government abuses.

Economic Framework

Guyana's economy is dependent on a narrow range of products for its exports, employment and gross domestic product. Although Guyana is richly endowed with natural resources, it is one of the poorest countries in the hemisphere. Political antagonism and ethnic strife continue to hamper economic recovery and social reconstruction; consequently, the national spirit suffers as well. Nevertheless, some believe the biggest problem is the lack of experienced, educated people who can run the civil service, manage the country's institutions, and perform important administrative functions. A stable infrastructure and efficient bureaucracy would allow reform measures to progress and would provide the continuity the country needs in its struggle to remain viable.

Censorship

The 1980 constitution guarantees freedom of the press, but the government owns the nation's largest publication and exercises indirect control over other newspapers by controlling the importation of newsprint.

Guyana's present constitution provides for freedom of speech and of the press in the following words: "Every person in Guyana is entitled to the basic right to a happy, creative and productive life, free from hunger, disease, ignorance and want. That right includes. . .freedom of conscience, of expression and of assembly and association. . . ." The government claims that it respects these rights. Indeed, Guyanese citizens openly criticize the government and its policies, but a rancorous relationship between the press and the government has existed since the country won independence from Great Britain in 1966. Journalists have been physically attacked during public protests.

The printed press has flourished despite opposition by the government, which also has been accused of trying to control the electronic media. The independent *Stabroek News* publishes daily, and a wide range of religious groups, political parties, and journalists publish a variety of privately owned weekly newspapers. The government has its own daily newspaper, the *Guyana Chronicle,* which covers a broad spectrum of political and nongovernmental issues. The country has three radio stations, all owned by the government. A government television station plus 17 independent stations are in operation. The Ministry of Information censors the Internet and restricts public access to a variety of sites.

From 1966 onward, the government, through the newly established Guyana News Agency, has sought to control the flow of information from within and outside the country. One of the agency's assignments was to gather "information about developments in Guyana—particularly in areas outside the city—and disseminating same to the Guyana in the form of news and feature articles, etc., via the print and broadcast media." Administrations before and after the 1980 Constitution have employed a variety of other techniques to stifle opposition. In the 1960s, the government purchased the independent *Guyana Graphic,*— whose editors had criticized the government—fired the paper's editors and created its own *Daily Chronicle* and *Citizen* newspapers.

The government also brought frequent charges of libel against editors who criticized the government. The opposition *Stabroek News* survived despite these conditions and has become widely regarded as the only reliable and nonpartisan source of news in Guyana. The *Mirror,* established in 1962, also remains free of state control. Although the government has declared publicly that it allows freedom of the press, the *Mirror* details several ways the government can and does interfere with the newspaper's freedom: the government has increased the cost of bonds, which are required to publish a newspaper, pamphlet, or leaflet; the government also controls the import of printing equipment, paper, and other supplies necessary for publishing a newspaper. It also uses ''archaic libel laws'' to pressure advertisers not to advertise in certain newspapers and has forced the closure of at least one newspaper, the *Liberator.* At about the same time the *Stabroek News* expanded operations in 1991, the *Mirror* was allowed to import new presses and increase its size from four to 16 pages per issue.

The days when the media were almost completely dominated by the ruling party seem to be numbered. The government's influence over the press has lessened, and increased criticism has flourished, but whenever a party is in power, it wishes to maintain its position by controlling the media. The state has retained control over the country's radio stations and is in no hurry to relinquish whatever control it still has over other media. Political rivalry is said to be the main reason for state control of the media; no ruling party wants to silence the media—the task would be doomed to failure and would expose the government to harsh criticism from within and from foreign sources. The government simply wishes to control the kind of information that is broadcast, and to that end, it needs the media.

Ironically, the media has come under criticism in recent years, and has been accused of being dominated by ''vested interests'' that interfere with the government's efforts to improve economic and social conditions, and to privatize the media and industry. Some claim the loud and persistent questioning of government policy and other media practices distort issues, and that by reporting on the country's crime, violence, and deteriorated social conditions, the media obscures the positive gains the government has made. Many voices in the country are calling for more balanced, fair news coverage.

STATE-PRESS RELATIONS

Stabroek News regularly publishes editorials that openly criticize the ruling party and question the state of the country, and the practices of the ruling class. Although its editor has formally complained that government advertisements, a form of press subsidy, are allocated unfairly, the newspaper remains an important voice in Guyana's political and public affairs. Both of the major parties have committed themselves to the divestment of the state media. When the People's Progressive Party returned to power in 1992, it pledged that there would be ''no government or state monopoly,'' and it guaranteed ''private ownership in keeping with a pluralistic democracy and freedom of the media.'' It claimed it would also encourage ''different shades of opinion'' in the media.

Guyana's president recently joined 26 other heads of state to sign the Declaration of Chapultepec, which is based on the essential precept that no law or act of government may limit freedom of expression or of the press, whatever the medium of communication. The signing of the declaration by Guyana's president demonstrated to the international community that Guyana is not interested in returning to the ruthless denial of press freedom under the authoritarian regime that prevailed before 1992. The declaration, in part, embraces the following principles: freedom of expression and of the press is an inalienable right; every person has the right to seek and receive information, express opinions and disseminate them freely; no journalist may be forced to reveal his or her sources of information; the media and journalists should neither be discriminated against nor favored because of what they write or say; tariff and exchange policies, licenses for the importation of paper or news-gathering equipment, assigning of radio and television frequencies and the granting or withdrawal of government advertising may not be used to reward or punish the media or individual journalists; membership of journalists in guilds, their affiliation to professional and trade associations and the affiliation of the media with business groups must be strictly voluntary; and the credibility of the press is linked to its commitment to truth, to the pursuit of accuracy, fairness and objectivity and to the clear distinction between news and advertising.

The Declaration further states that ''the attainment of these goals and the respect for ethical and professional values may not be imposed. These are the exclusive responsibility of journalists and the media. In a free society, it is public opinion that rewards or punishes; no news medium or journalists may be punished for publishing the truth or criticizing or denouncing the government.'' A careful reading of these guidelines not only reveals the government's ostensible desire to improve its relations with the country's press community but also gives, by implication, a clear picture of the abuses that have persisted since the country began.

ATTITUDE TOWARD FOREIGN MEDIA

In 1980, the government established the Guyana News Agency in order to control what kind of information from foreign sources was allowed into the country. The agency was assigned the task of "channeling overseas news to the local media, government leaders and other decision-makers, and other relevant publics, in Guyana and, through its missions overseas, to the relevant publics outside Guyana." The agency was also to provide "an editing service, eventually, for overseas materials, to give them a Third World orientation and make them more meaningful to the Guyanese readership." Some observers saw the agency's mandate as a thinly veiled attempt by the government to control information flowing into and from Guyana. The government, however, could not stop criticism from the foreign press and from those journalists ousted by the ruling party. This source of information and opinion continued to be an important counterbalance to the state's attempts to stifle media criticism within the country.

In general, as a member of the Caribbean community, Guyana cannot escape scrutiny by its neighbors. Its concerns are the concerns of the whole community. Information, ideas, and issues are given voice by The Guyana Caribbean Politics and Culture Web site, which bills itself as "a unique forum for conversation on Caribbean society. . . a Center for Popular Education whose main aim is to provide information and discussion as a means of empowering Caribbean people of all classes and station in life." To that end, it devotes a special section to "Opinions Views and Commentary on Guyana," where up-to-date information about Guyana and other members of the Caribbean community may be exchanged.

BROADCAST MEDIA

Guyana's communication system includes a government-dominated television and radio network. The country's two radio stations are owned by the government, which also operates one television channel. Two private television stations relay satellite services from the United States. A large number of private television channels are available that freely criticize the government. As of 1997, the Guyanese owned 46,000 television sets.

ELECTRONIC NEWS MEDIA

By the year 2000, about 4,000 Guyanese used the Internet. Several of Guyana's publications also may be found on the Internet. *Stabroek News* is perhaps the most dependable source of unbiased online news coming out of Guyana. *Guyana Chronicle* is an online version of Guyana's largest newspaper. It follows the line of the ruling party of the day and is therefore considered unreliable as objective reporting. *Guyana Review* is a monthly, topical online magazine that offers respected articles on current events along with photographs. The magazine's regular features include a "Georgetown journal," consisting of news about the capital, national and business reports, sports information, a crime watch, interviews and obituaries.

Number of Personal Computers in Use

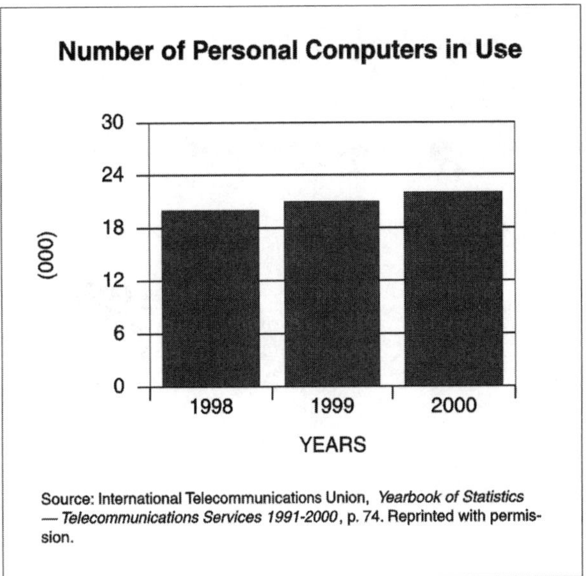

Source: International Telecommunications Union, *Yearbook of Statistics — Telecommunications Services 1991-2000*, p. 74. Reprinted with permission.

EDUCATION & TRAINING

Guyana's journalists have lacked professional training and formal education from the country's birth. Those who worked in the profession needed only a secondary education and many early reporters lacked even that much education. Wages were low and conditions were difficult. Those who wished to become established in newspaper publishing worked their way up from menial jobs to political reporting and then, if they were bright enough and committed, to an office job. Their salary would remain low, hardly enough to pay for basic necessities; they had no union, no pension, and no regular hours. They could be fined for inaccuracies in their stories, which had to be hurriedly written, and they could be dismissed without notice for insubordination or unpunctuality. To put journalists on a better footing, the government in 1975 funded a program at the University of Guyana, with the objectives "to provide development workers and planners, extension personnel, information and media practitioners. . .with a broad education aimed at improving their ability to understand and interpret social issues and the value of human communication in the development process; and, to give participants special-

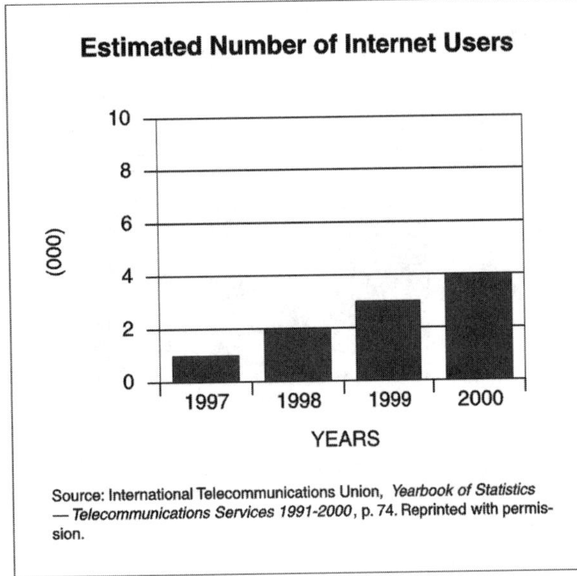

Source: International Telecommunications Union, *Yearbook of Statistics — Telecommunications Services 1991-2000*, p. 74. Reprinted with permission.

ized training the techniques of interpersonal communication and the media. . . .'' Unfortunately, this high-minded effort was subverted by the fact that entrants into the program were nominated by government agencies and approved by the government's Ministry of Information. Candidates from media that were critical of the government were effectively excluded. The program also was hampered by inadequate facilities, funding, equipment and staff. In the first four years, only 32 out of an initial 50 entrants returned to the profession. Still, the program has survived. In 1980 it was lengthened to two years and, in 1997, a four-year degree was offered.

SUMMARY

To broaden its readership, Guyana's press must rely on the government's efforts to improve the country's deteriorated educational system so more people will be better educated than they are and the dropout rate reduced. As a consequence of the decline of educational standards in recent decades, many adults are unable to read or write, and the finger of blame is pointed at Guyana's educational system, which is one of the worst in the Caribbean community. The Ministry of Education has created a ''strategic development plan'' to address this problem; meanwhile, the press suffers because many adults are illiterate. Many Guyanese feel that the country's future, not just the future of its newspapers, depends on better educating more people. To raise the quality of its profession, Guyana's press corps needs to be better trained. The University of Guyana is improving its programs in journalism, but for years the university lacked equipment, qualified staff, and other resources to offer adequate training, and progress has been slow. Without such professional training, journalists are not well respected. After a history of disorganization and poor schooling, the press corps suffers from a lack of professional solidarity and goals, professional ethics, adequate training and education, self-confidence, and self-respect. A strong union is needed to bring to all members of the country's media a sense of being among professionals whose social consciousness and training are equal to the task of gathering, analyzing, interpreting, and disseminating information for public consumption in a country still struggling to enter the new millennium.

At the same time, the government has made commendable strides toward relinquishing its control of the country's media, but the move toward total freedom of expression has not been completed.

SIGNIFICANT DATES

- 1980: in an effort to control information, the government created the Guyana News Agency, whose mandate was to ''oversee news to the local media,'' to disseminate information about Guyana to the Guyanese, and to edit ''overseas materials.''
- 2000: The Guyana Press Association, dormant since 1995, was resurrected. It offers a means by which Guyana's press corps can, as an organized and self-governing body, address their own problems and set professional standards regarding ethics, education, and social responsibility.

BIBLIOGRAPHY

Granger, David A. ''Guyana's State Media: the Quest for Control.'' *Stabroek News,* June 18, 2000.

———. ''Guyana's Press Corps and Its Problems.'' *Sunday Stabroek,* December 3, 2000.

Jagan, Cheddi. *The West on Trial: My Fight for Guyana's Freedom.* St. John's, Antigua: Hansib, 1997.

Jagan, Cheddi, and Moses Nagamootoo. *The State of the Free Press in Guyana.* Georgetown, Guyana: New Guyana Co., Ltd., for the People's Progressive Party, 1980.

Lee, Paul Siu-nam. *Development Journalism, Economic Growth and Authoritarianism/Totalitarianism.* Presented at the 38th Annual Conference of the International Communications Association at New Orleans, Louisiana, USA, 1988.

Morrison, Andrew. *Justice: The Struggle for Democracy in Guyana 1952-1992.* Published by Fr. Andrew Morrison, SJ. Printed and Bound in Guyana by Red Thread Women's Press, 1998.

Nagamootoo, Moses. *Paramountcy over the Guyana Media: A Case for Reform.* Georgetown, Guyana: The Union of Guyana Journalists, 1992.

Ratliff, William E. ''Guyana.'' In *Communism in Central America and the Caribbean,* ed. Robert Wesson, 143-58. Stanford, Calif.: Hoover Institution Press, 1983.

Sidel, M. Kent. *The Legal Foundations of Mass Media Regulation in Guyana: A Commonwealth Caribbean Case Study.* Presented to the International Communication Division of the Association for Education in Journalism and Mass Communication Annual Convention in Montreal, Canada, August, 1992.

Spinner, Jr. Thomas, J. *A Political and Social History of Guyana, 1945-1983.* Boulder: Westview Press, 1984.

White, Dorcas. *The Press and the Law in the Caribbean.* Bridgetown, Barbados: Cedar Press, 1977.

—Bernard E. Morris

Haiti

Basic Data

Official Country Name:	Republic of Haiti
Region (Map name):	North & Central America
Population:	6,964,549
Language(s):	French, Creole
Literacy rate:	45.0%
Area:	27,750 sq km
GDP:	4,050 (US$ millions)
Number of Television Stations:	2
Number of Television Sets:	38,000
Television Sets per 1,000:	5.5
Number of Radio Stations:	67
Number of Radio Receivers:	415,000
Radio Receivers per 1,000:	59.6

Background & General Characteristics

Haiti is part of an island located in the Caribbean; it occupies the western one-third of the island of Hispaniola, between the Caribbean Sea and the North Atlantic Ocean, west of the Dominican Republic. The country gained its independence from France in January 1804. Haiti's Constitution was approved in March 1987 then suspended in June 1988; Haiti returned to constitutional rule in October 1994.

As of 2002, the president was elected by popular vote to five-year terms. The prime minister was appointed by the president, and then that appointment was ratified by the Congress. The Senate had 27 seats, with members serving six-year terms. One-third was elected every two years. The Chamber of Deputies had 83 seats, and members were popularly elected to serve four-year terms.

The total population in Haiti in 2002 was estimated at nearly 7 million, with a 1.7 percent growth rate. While the birth rate is at 31.4 per 1,000 people, the infant mortality rate is a staggering 93.3 per 1,000, nearly 10 percent. More than 55 percent of the country's population is between the ages of 15 and 64; another 40.31 percent are 14 years old or younger. Blacks make up 95 percent of the population, with the other 5 percent mulatto and white. The vast majority of Haitians (80 percent) are Roman Catholic. French and Creole are the official languages.

While the Haitian Constitution actually provides for freedom of the press, putting the theoretic rights into practice was not necessarily a safe thing for journalists to do, especially in the early 2000s. The country supported several newspapers. *Haiti Progress*, the largest Haitian weekly publication, was published in French, English, and Creole every Wednesday.

As of 2002, the *Haitian Times* was the only full-color weekly newspaper distributed in the Haitian community and in Haiti. The *Times* was the only Haitian-American newspaper with full-time professional journalists. It covered Haitian and Haitian-American news; arts and leisure; entertainment, reviews, profiles and social events. Regarding sports, it covered Haitian and American soccer, basketball, and tennis. Its columns cover news from Boston, New York, and Miami, in addition to Haiti. The *Times* had a pool of award-winning writers and photographers both in the United States and in Haiti, and they were known for their authority on Haitian and Haitian-American issues.

Journalists in Haiti have long been subject to attacks, particularly by mobs on one side or another of a particular issue. In what Amnesty International called "one of the most high-profile acts of violence in recent Haitian history," prominent radio journalist and long-time democracy and human rights activist Jean Dominique was shot to death by an unknown assailant outside the courtyard of his radio station, Radio Haiti Inter. A station guard, Jean Claude Louissaint, was also killed in the attack, which occurred April 3, 2000.

Jean Dominique's death was a serious blow to Haiti, according to Amnesty International, largely because he had been such an outspoken advocate for change throughout the turbulent previous four decades in the country's history. His radio broadcasts were the first to be done in Creole rather than French, and they created an unprecedented forum for critical thought. The key was that it did so not only for the country's "educated elite," but also for Haiti's poor population, which was considerable at the beginning of the twenty-first century.

Dominique had survived imprisonment under dictator Francois "Papa Doc" Duvalier, who came to power in 1957. He was forced into exile during the reign of Jean Claude "Baby Doc" Duvalier, who succeeded his father in 1971, and again after Haiti's military coup in 1991. Subsequently, a United Nations peacekeeping force helped restore democratic rule to Haiti and restored President Jean-Betrand Aristide to office. But even after that return to constitutional order in 1994, Jean Dominique was not satisfied, pointing out anti-democratic tendencies within diverse sections of the Haitian political and societal scenes. Haitians were stunned, according to Amnesty International, by the fact such a pillar of democracy could be gunned down by an unidentified killer, after surviving so many conflicts where his adversaries were known.

Acts of violence, particularly killings, where journalists are involved regardless of their political views have a far-reaching effect on society. As noted by the Organization of American States Rapporteur for Freedom of Expression, the American Convention of Human Rights—which counts Haiti among its members—requires states to investigate effectively the murder of journalists and punish the perpetrators of such acts.

The Inter-American Commission on Human Rights (IACHR) said the lack of "an effective and thorough investigation into any criminal sanctions against the primary parties involved—and their accessories—is particularly serious because of its impact on society." When such crimes go unpunished, not only are all other journalists practicing their craft in the country intimidated, but also it has a detrimental effect on all citizens, who become afraid to report mistreatment, abuse or any other kinds of unlawful acts.

The case of the murder of Jean Dominique led to widespread questioning of the human rights situation in Haiti, even seven years after the restoration of the democratic government in Haiti. Even more significant, according to Amnesty International, was the fashion in which the investigation hit roadblocks and obstacles that illustrated the lack of human rights in Haiti. The obstacles have included lack of independence of the police force and the justice system; the failure of those institutions to confront ruling-party activists responsible for threats and much of the political violence; and acts of violence committed under the auspices of elected officials.

Even more troubling, it would seem from a journalistic standpoint, were the climbing number of attacks on journalists in the two years following the death of Jean Dominique. These started almost immediately and changed, perhaps forever, the climate in which journalists try to do their jobs in Haiti. For example, the same night Jean Dominique was killed, radio station Radio Unite, based in St. Michel de l'Attalaye, was sacked and part of its equipment stolen shortly after reporting Dominique's death. The station had reportedly received threats earlier.

Jean Dominique was buried April 8, 2000. After the funeral, pro-Famni Lavalas (FL) groups set fire to the office of *Konfederasyon Inite Demokratik* (Democratic Unity Conference), which served as headquarters to the opposition coalition. They also threatened to burn down private radio station Radio Vision 2000, which is critical of the Aristide government. Furthermore, on May 3, 2000, in Place in the Department of the South, community station *Radio Via Pelican Sid* (Voice of the Peasant Farmers of the South) was sacked. The station had reportedly already received threats. Journalist Adulate Guedeouengue, who was abducted, beaten and robbed in May 2001, was reportedly looking into Dominique's murder at the time of his attack and had been told by his kidnappers to stop investigating.

The Guedeouengue case was a perfect example of how much pressure the media faced in the aftermath of the murder of one of its biggest Haitian stars. Other Radio Haiti Inter journalists reported threats, harassment, and intimidation, including those done by people who were believed to be police. On December 15, 2000, a 34-year-old sports reporter for Port-au-Prince Radio Plus, Gerard Denoze, was shot and killed by a pair of unidentified assailants while stepping out of a car in Carrefour. The *Association Haitienne de la Presse Sportive* (Haitian Sports Press Association) said he had been receiving death threats for some time.

On December 27, 2000, the Port-au-Prince private radio station Radio Caraibes FM suspended its broadcast temporarily because it received threatening letters and telephone calls. It also reportedly received direct threats to individual journalists within its organization. The threats were allegedly made by members of popular organizations close to FL.

In January 2001, Paul Raymond, leader of Ti Kominite Legliz, a popular organization close to the FL, publicly threatened some 80 journalists, clerics, and politicians if they did not support the party. Moreover, the director of information for the Port-au-Prince-based radio station Signal FM reportedly received death threats over three days in June 2001 for questioning the behavior of some of FL's influential senators.

Later that month, on June 20, a Radio Haiti Inter broadcaster said he was followed, forced out of his automobile and threatened by two armed men. The men claimed they were police, and that they recognized the car as having belonged to Jean Dominique, the murdered director of Radio Haiti Inter. The Haitian National Police denied any of its officers had been involved, but acknowledged the men may have been ex-police. The radio station lodged an official complaint but, of course, never heard back.

On July 28, 2001, Radio Rotation FM reporters Reynald Liberus and Claude Francois did interviews with some of the alleged perpetrators of a series of attacks on police stations around Port-au-Prince. According to sources, they were allegedly arrested without warrants and mistreated by police, who were reportedly trying to get tapes of the interviews.

Jean Ronald Dupont, a journalist for Radio Maxima FM, sustained wounds to the head October 2, 2001, while covering a demonstration in Cap Hatien, the country's second largest city. The wounds were reportedly suffered when police fired at shoulder level in an attempt to disperse crowds. That same day, another radio reporter, Radio Metropole correspondent Jean-Marie Mayard, was assaulted in St. Marc, department of the Artibonite, by members of a popular organization. The attackers broke Mayard's tape recorder and threatened to kill him if he did not stop broadcasting reports critical of the Lavalas Family political party.

To close out what was a tough month for journalists, Radio Haiti Inter journalist Jean Robert Delcine was assaulted and threatened by police October 12, 2001, because he had been investigating the alleged killing of a 16-year-old by police in Port-au-Prince. Police allegedly killed the boy when they could not find his brother, who they suspected of gang activity. Radio Haiti Inter lodged a complaint against the police inspector who had mistreated their reporter, but the inspector refused to respond to the summons.

A month later, on November 27, 2001, Radio Kiskeya journalist Evrard Saint-Armand was reportedly arrested after trying to report on an incident in which a young boy was killed in suspicious circumstances in Port-au-Prince. He was taken to the local police station, where police officers reportedly beat him and broke his tape recorder to prevent broadcast of any of the interviews he had conducted.

In the most gruesome attack of the year 2001, Radio Echo 2000 news director Brignol Lindor was hacked to death by a mob including members of a pro-FL organization in Petit Goave. Several days before, according to reports, the assistant mayor for FL had called for ''zero tolerance'' against Lindor, whom the assistant mayor accused of supporting a rival party. Several of the killers admitted to the attack, and arrest warrants were issued. However, no arrests were affected for more than two months. But even after the arrest of FL-elected official Sedner Sainvilus, a member of the Communal Section Administration, Lindor's family continued to protest the failure to arrest anyone else.

Threatening leaflets were then distributed in mid-February around Petit Goave, warning the family and other journalists to stop drawing attention to the case or risk facing the same fate as Lindor. Between October 2001 and Lindor's death in December, the Federation of Haitian Journalist Associations documented 30 cases of threats or aggression against reporters by supporters of President Aristide. At Lindor's funeral, 24-year-old journalist Francois Johnson told Michelle Faul of the Associated Press he was reconsidering his life's work. ''The whole profession is traumatized by Lindor's brutal death,'' he said at the time. ''We are afraid of what is in store for us.''

When the national palace was attacked by unknown assailants in December 2001, a rush of targeted reprisal attacks took place against opposition headquarters, radio stations, journalists, and leading opposition figures. Reporters and journalists were victims of harassment and attacks, during which the Haitian police were either not present or did not respond. The Association of Haitian Journalists reported that nearly a dozen journalists left Haiti out of fear of persecution following the attack on the palace.

After the coup attempt, Aristide supporters rampaged through Port-au-Prince and Cap Haitien, the country's second largest city. Private radio stations were targeted, while other journalists were threatened and, in some cases, forced to join the mobs in singing, ''Vive Aristide!'' according to a report by OneWorld US. At the time, Garry Pierre-Pierre of the New York-based National Coalition for Haitian Rights as well as the publisher of the *Haiti Times*, called the events a ''major setback to the democratic process in Haiti.'' Mary Lene Smeets, the Latin America director of the Committee to Protect Journalists, said the climate of violence against the press was a tremendous cause for concern. She blamed Aristide for fanning the flames through his statements.

In the early 2000s, some felt that the media is as fragmented as anything else in Haiti, where military coups, government corruption, and political diversion were frequently the norm. In a forum on ethnic media in New York, the Freedom Forum Media Studies Center held a panel discussion on ''Haiti's Media: Covering News at Home and Abroad.'' The discussion centered on media issues related to Haiti, perhaps the Western Hemisphere's poorest country. Participants in the forum disagreed about the problems in the Haitian media. Some observers felt there was no such thing as neutral, fair journalism, even among mainstream media such as the Associated Press and the *New York Times*. Others felt that the bulk of Haitian media focuses on political coverage (whether fair or not) and not enough time and energy is spent covering essential issues such as ecology, justice, crime and drugs.

Radio Soleil, begun in 1991, broadcasted from Brooklyn, New York as a subcarrier radio station. In the early 2000s it claimed more than 100,000 subscribers and claimed a listening audience of more than 600,000 Haitians spread across New York, New Jersey, and Connecticut. The station broadcasted 24 hours a day, 7 days a week in three languages. Although its owner, Ricot Dupuy, agreed not enough time was spent on central issues like the ecology and crime, he pointed out that he did not have the manpower. ''We do not have the means to do in-depth coverage,'' he said. ''Everyone in Haiti is a politician. Everything boils down to politics.''

Economic Framework

In 1998, it was estimated that more than 80 percent of the Haitian population lived below the poverty line. That fact, combined with the fact that between 50 and 80 percent of the country's population is illiterate, meant most Haitians got their news from broadcast media and not the print press.

Nearly 70 percent of Haitians depend on agriculture, consisting mostly of small-scale subsistence farming and employing roughly two-thirds of the active workforce. After elections in May 2000 that were widely suspected of irregularities, the international community, including the United States and Europe, suspended almost all aid to Haiti. The result was a destabilization of the currency in Haiti and, combined with fuel price increases, a stark rise in prices in general. By January 2001, however, prices had appeared to level off.

Estimates in 1999 regarding the Gross Domestic Product of Haiti divided sources of revenue three ways: agriculture, 32 percent; industry, 20 percent; and services, 48 percent. The inflation rate, according to 2000 estimates, was 16 percent, and in 1995 the labor force was 3.6 million.

Press Laws

The Haitian Constitution, enacted in 1987 and updated in January 2002, guaranteed all Haitians the right to express their opinions freely on all matters and by any means they chooses (Article 28). It also stated that journalists may freely exercise their profession within the framework of the law, and such exercise may not be subject to any authorization or censorship, except in the case of war.

Journalists may not be compelled to reveal their sources; however, it was their duty to verify the authenticity and accuracy of information. It was also their obligation to respect the ethics of their profession. Article 28-3 of the Haitian Constitution stipulated that all offenses involving the press and abuses of the right of expression should come under the code of criminal law.

Censorship

According to the Haitian Constitution, journalists do not need to reveal their sources, although they are required to verify the authenticity and accuracy of the information they acquire. Part of the obligation includes respecting the ethics of their profession.

As of 2002, more than 200 independent radio stations existed in the country, providing the full spectrum of political views. Unfortunately, self-censorship was fairly pervasive as journalists tried to avoid offending financial sponsors or influential politicians.

State-Press Relations

Two French language daily newspapers frequently criticized the government, but with a 20 percent literacy rate, the majority of the Haitian population did not read these criticisms. Uncensored satellite television was available, but lack of funds prevented it from reaching many people.

Official harassment often happened in the early 2000s in the form of physical abuse by mobs of people. For instance, four journalists were beaten by police at an anti-crime rally in May 2000. A radio director was arrested and charged with defamation and incitement to riot a month earlier.

Regarding state and press relationships, at the beginning of the twenty-first century they are strained and oppositional in purpose. To illustrate, the key suspect in the April 2000 shooting death of Haiti's most influential journalist, Radio Haiti Inter director Jean Dominique, was Lavalas Family Party Senator Danny Toussaint. Try as he may, President Jean-Bertrand Aristide was not impressing free press watchdogs with his efforts to make press freedom a reality in his country. Indeed, Reporters Without Borders in May 2002 put Aristide's name, for the first time, on an annual worldwide list of ''predators against press freedom.'' The Reporters Without Borders list put Aristide in some distinct company: Cuba's Fidel Castro, Iraq's Saddam Hussein and Russia's Vladimir Putin, among more than 30 others.

The Paris-based organization criticized Aristide, saying he obstructed the investigation into Dominique's murder. While the investigation centered on prominent figures within Aristide's ruling Lavalas Family political party, the investigating judge, Claudy Gassant, complained of government interference and intimidation. Gassant's mandate to investigate the case ended in January, and Aristide waited three months to renew it, and did so under pressure on the second anniversary of Dominique's murder in April 2002.

The investigation into Dominique's murder provided a chance for the country to change its image. According to Amnesty International, there was ''unprecedented civil mobilization to call for justice for the popular and respected murdered journalist.'' It cut, Amnesty International stated, across the political spectrum and included human rights organizations, journalists, churches, members of the labor movement and grassroots groups. Amnesty International kept a close eye on the investigation. But Haiti's legal system protected the findings in any investigation. Still Amnesty International pointed out the country had an obligation under both international and domestic law to make sure ''full, transparent and impartial'' justice was served.

Much of the attitude toward a free press in Haiti can probably be traced to all of the political turmoil in the country. Under dictatorships since 1949, including a period from 1957 through 1986, when Haiti was ruled first by Francois Duvalier, who ruled with brutal efficiency through his secret police, the *Tontons Macoutes*. In the early 1980s, Haiti became one of the world's first countries to face an AIDS epidemic, and the disease wrought havoc on the nation's tourist industry, which collapsed, causing rising and rampant unemployment. Eventually, unrest festered in the economic crisis.

In the early 2000s Haiti's government remained ineffectual, and the country was a major point for drugs. The country also suffered from an approximately 50 percent unemployment rate, and refugees left eagerly for the United States. Aristide won re-election in 2000, and his government quelled an attempted coup in December 2001, in another event that showed the dangers of being a journalist in Haiti. After the attempt was put down, journalists were forced to seek refuge following a series of attacks by supporters of Aristide. According to the Associated Press, at least one radio station stopped broadcasting in the immediate aftermath of the attempt. Five gunmen were killed, and perhaps as many as 18 others escaped as police retook the palace. Aristide militants attacked reporters outside the National Palace the day of the assault, December 17, 2001. One radio reporter had a pistol placed against his head; others were forced by attackers to praise the president. According to Reporters Without Borders, at least a dozen reporters were assaulted outside the palace, all while police simply stood by and watched. Though no serious injuries were suffered, the reporters were forced by the mobs to leave under threat. Police did nothing, and no arrests were made. At the time, Reporters Without Borders Secretary-General Robert Menard said: ''The systematic character of the assaults shows the protesters have received instructions to attack the press.''

Aristide himself condemned the attacks on journalists, but given the treatment of reporters in the country, he did not appear to be taken seriously. At one point, he urged his supporters to respect the rights of the press. But later in the same day, Radio Ti-Moun, an educational station run by Aristide's private Foundation for Democracy, charted that the press had ''prepared the people psychologically'' for the coup. According to the Associated Press report, at least 10 people were killed in the attack on the palace and the accompanying violence. Opposition forces claimed the coup attempt was staged, and one radio reporter said he received threats after he asked a question reflecting skepticism about the coup's authenticity. Several radio stations stopped broadcasting temporarily after the attack, while others played only music. That indicated the climate in which Haitian journalists had to work.

News Agencies

As of 2002, *L'Agence Haitienne de Presse* (AHP) was Haiti's only local news agency. Founded in 1989, AHP was created to distribute news and information on Haiti and to build stronger ties with both the diaspora and the rest of the world. AHP published daily news releases in both French and English. The AHP also published an annual synopsis of the year's events. It also prepares reports on subjects of common interest, such as elections, the democratic process, and the press. All of Haiti's radio and television stations, foreign and local press, diplomatic missions and international organizations use AHP's services. AHP, according to its own Web site, has grown to a staff of 12 in its main Port-au-Prince office, with another 10 correspondents positioned around the country and one each in the Dominican Republic, Canada and the United States, where there are large Haitian populations.

BROADCAST MEDIA

In 1997, Haiti had 67 radio stations, 41 AM stations, and 26 FM stations, which reached an estimated 415,000 radios. Two television stations, plus one cable television service, reached approximately 38,000 televisions.

ELECTRONIC NEWS MEDIA

As of the early 2000s, Haiti had about 9 telephones per 1,000 citizens. Comparatively, there were 630 telephones per 1,000 users in the United States. Haiti's largest Internet provider, Alpha Communications Network, claimed a 90-percent market share of Internet users. ACN was shut down in September 1999 by the government's telecommunications regulator, the National Communications (Conatel). The shutdown paralyzed the communications ability of Haiti, stopping an estimated 80 percent of Haitian commerce and leaving government offices, embassies, and nearly everyone without Internet access.

Conatel claimed that ACN had sliced into the international business of Haiti's state-run monopoly, Teleco, by selling international phone lines and cards, causing the shutdown of ACN. The charge was later dropped, and the popular ACN was allowed to resume. ACN's popularity is understandable when one considers the average Haitian's annual salary was only US$250 a month, and that, at US$.70 a minute, Teleco's online charge would cost more than an average Haitian's annual income.

SUMMARY

At the beginning of the twenty-first century, journalists in Haiti had good reason to fear for their lives. Although President Aristide said he would do everything in his power to make sure rights were given to the press and the Constitution would be upheld, he had not been willing or able to follow through on that promise. Like Haitians of all ages and walks of life, journalists have at one time or another fled the country. When one of the country's biggest names in journalism can be shot dead in front of his own radio station, and when the government in the best case scenario is slow to investigate and in the worst case scenario actually obstructs the investigation and allows the killer or killers to go free, it does not take much to reach the conclusion that a free press in Haiti was still a long way away.

SIGNIFICANT DATES

- 1957: Francois ''Papa Doc'' Duvalier becomes Haiti's dictator.
- 1971: ''Papa Doc'' is succeeded by his son, Jean-Claude ''Baby Doc'' Duvalier.
- 1986: Facing an economic crisis brought on by the collapse of the tourist industry in Haiti caused by a burgeoning AIDS crisis, Jean-Claude ''Baby Doc'' Duvalier flees the country.
- 1991: Jean-Bertrand Aristide, a Roman Catholic priest, becomes the first elected chief executive. He is deposed in a military coup a few months later.
- 1994: A United Nations Peacekeeping force restores the Aristide government.
- 1996: Rene Preval succeeds Aristide.
- 2000: Aristide is re-elected in elections that were boycotted by the opposition and questioned around the world for their propriety.
- 2000: Jean Dominique, director of Haiti Radio Inter, is gunned down with a guard in front of the station by unknown gunmen. Radio stations and other journalists are pressured to limit their coverage of the attack.
- 2001: Reporter Brignol Lindor is hacked to death by a mob said to include members of a pro-Lavalas Family party group. When friends and family openly protest the lack of progress in the case, leaflets warning them they could suffer a similar fate are passed out in Lindor's hometown of Petit Goave.

BIBLIOGRAPHY

Demko, Kerstin. *Haitian Media Fragmentation Reflects Haiti's reality.* Available from http://www.freedomforum.org.

Faul, Michele. ''Journalists in Haiti fear for their lives.'' Associated Press, 22 Dec. 2001.

Freedom House Press Reports 2000. Available from http://www.freedomhouse.org.

Haiti History, 2002. Available from www.infoplease.com.

Human Rights Watch World Report, 2002. Available from http://www.hrw.org.

''Internet Access in Haiti.'' Digital Freedom Network, 2000. Available from http://dfn.org.

Lobe, Jim. ''Haiti's independent journalists face uncertain future.'' OneWorld US, 7 Jan. 2001.

United States State Department Report, 2001. Available from www.state.gov.

World Bank Group Reports. Available from http://www.worldbank.com.

—Brad Kadrich

HONDURAS

BASIC DATA

Official Country Name:	Republic of Honduras
Region (Map name):	North & Central America
Population:	6,406,052
Language(s):	Spanish, Amerindian dialects
Literacy rate:	72.7%
Area:	112,090 sq km
GDP:	5,932 (US$ millions)
Number of Television Stations:	11
Number of Television Sets:	570,000
Television Sets per 1,000:	89.0
Number of Cable Subscribers:	49,280
Cable Subscribers per 1,000:	7.7
Number of Radio Stations:	306
Number of Radio Receivers:	2,450,000
Radio Receivers per 1,000:	382.5
Number of Individuals with Computers:	70,000
Computers per 1,000:	10.9
Number of Individuals with Internet Access:	40,000
Internet Access per 1,000:	6.2

BACKGROUND & GENERAL CHARACTERISTICS

Originally part of Spain's empire in the New World, the Republic of Honduras was freed from Spain in 1821. After briefly being annexed to Mexico, in 1823 Honduras gained its independence and joined the newly formed United Provinces of Central America. After the collapse of the United Provinces in 1838, Honduras continued its foreign policy to unite Central America until after World War I.

U.S. companies controlled Honduras's agriculture-based economy during the twentieth century after U.S. businesses established large banana plantations along the north coast. Not long after World War II, provincial military leaders gained control of the Nationalists and the Liberals, the two main Honduran political parties. Two authoritarian administrations and a strike by banana workers paved the way in the mid-1950s for a palace coup by military reformists.

In 1957, constituent assembly elections took place and a president was elected. The assembly also transformed itself into a national legislature. From 1957-63 the Liberal Party ruled Honduras. Then in October 1963 conservative military officers deposed the president in a bloody coup. For a brief time in the early 1970s a civilian president was in charge until his administration was the victim of a coup in 1972. For the next 11 years, military men ruled Honduras. In April 1980 a constituent assembly was elected and general elections took place in November 1981. A new constitution was approved in 1982 and a Liberal Party president took office after the free elections.

In January 2002, President Ricardo Maduro of the National Party took office, becoming Honduras's sixth democratically elected president since 1981. He inherits a nation where it was estimated at the turn of the twentieth century that 85 percent of the 6.4 million Hondurans live below the poverty line, and the average annual income is U.S. $850.

Honduras's capital is Tegucigalpa. The national language is Spanish, although English is often spoken in the Bay Islands. The approximate 112,000 square kilometers of land varies from primarily mountains in the interior to narrow plains along its 820 kilometers of coastline, including the almost inhabitable eastern Mosquito Coast along the Caribbean Sea. Honduras's neighbors are Nicaragua, El Salvador and Guatemala, with a long stretch of coastline facing the Caribbean Sea and a small stretch on the opposite side of the country along the North Pacific Ocean.

In 1998 Honduras was devastated by Hurricane Mitch, which killed around 5,000 Hondurans and destroyed about 70 percent of the nation's crops. The hurricane set back the nation's development by several decades.

Not all of Honduras's problems can be blamed on the weather. Poor housing, youth gangs, crime, malnutrition, allegations of police wrongdoing, and the murder of indigenous rights groups allegedly by right-wing paramilitary groups, plague the nation.

Honduras has suffered almost 300 internal conflicts—rebellions, civil wars and changes of administrations—since gaining its independence. More than half of those conflicts have occurred in the twentieth century.

With this type of history, it is no wonder that the strict defamation laws shackle Honduran press. At times the press in Honduras is its own enemy, as journalists have been known to practice self-censorship to avoid offending the interests of media owners, and accept bribes from officials in return for favorable coverage.

Nature of the Audience More than 54 percent of Honduras's population is between the ages of 15 and 64 years, while another 42.22 percent is 14 years old or younger. In 2001, population growth was estimated at 2.34 percent annually, with a life expectancy of 69.35 years (67.51 years for men, 71.28 years for women). However, these estimates must take into consideration the country's high incidence of HIV/AIDS. From 1990 to 1996 Honduras reported 5,902 AIDS cases and another 3,132 people with HIV (the virus that causes AIDS), according to the Health Ministry.

Of the Honduran population, 72.6 percent of the men and 72.7 percent of women are literate, which is defined as those aged 15 and over who can read and write. Around 90 percent of the population is *mestizo* (mixed Amerindian and European), about 7 percent is of Amerindian descent, 2 percent is black and 1 percent is white. The overwhelming majority of Hondurans (97 percent) are Catholic, with the remainder primarily Protestant.

General Media Characteristics Honduras supports six major newspapers, with most based in Tegucigalpa. There are five national dailies, three of which—*El Periodico, La Tribuna* and *El Heraldo*—are headquartered in Tegucigalpa, as is the weekly English-language newspaper *Honduras This Week.* The other two dailies, *El Tiempo* and *La Prensa,* are based in San Pedro Sula. The government publishes its decrees in the weekly *La Gaceta.*

Political figures are a prominent part of the Honduran press. Former President Rafael Leonardo Callejas is the principal stockholder in *El Periodico*, and the paper is known for its conservative views.

Another influential political figure, Jaime Rosenthal, owns *El Tiempo.* Rosenthal, a Liberal Party leader who finished second in the Liberal Party of Honduras primary for the 1993 national election, leads the more liberal paper, which is known to criticize the police and military. As a result, the editor, Manuel Gamero, has at times been jailed.

La Tribuna and *La Prensa* are considered by most press observers to be more centrist than the others, although some would say *La Prensa* is a little more to the right of center. *La Tribuna* is owned by yet another political figure, Carlos Flores Facusse, who in 1989 made an unsuccessful bid for the presidency before being elected to that post in the November 1997 election. *La Tribuna* has close ties to the Liberal Party and to Tegucigalpa's industrial sector.

La Prensa has ties to San Pedro Sula businesses, as well as other publishing interests. Publisher and editor Jorge Canahuati Larach is a member of the family that also publishes *El Heraldo.* That paper is more conservative than *La Prensa,* and has been more favorable in its coverage of the military than other dailies. *El Heraldo* often reflects the positions of the National Party.

Daily newspapers reach about 159,000 readers, but Honduras also has smaller publications. The most significant of those—the monthly *Boletin Inforativo*—is published by the Honduran Documentation Center (Centro de Documentacion de Honduras, or CEDOH), run by the respected political analyst Victor Meza.

CEDOH and the Sociology Department at the National Autonomous University of Honduras (Universidad Nacional Autonoma de Honduras, or UNAH) publish *Puntos de Vista,* a magazine centering on social and political analysis. In addition, *Honduras This Week* covers national news and events in Central America.

Honduras's major newspapers are all members of the Inter American Press Association (IAPA), which was set up in 1942 to defend and promote the right of people of the Americas to be fully and freely informed through an independent press, according to information obtained from the IAPA. In March 2001, the IAPA announced its support for and adherence to the Declaration of Principles on Freedom of Expression during a ceremony in Washington, D.C., chaired jointly by Cesar Gaviria, secretary general of the Organization of American States, and IAPA President Danilo Arbilla.

The declaration was drafted by the Organization of American States's (OAS) Inter American Commission on Human Rights. Gaviria called it a "significant contribution to the establishment of a legal framework to protect the right to freedom of expression." He also said it would "surely be the subject of interest and study by OAS member countries." The document includes 13 principles of freedom of expression and is based on the Declaration of Chapultepec, sponsored by the IAPA and drafted in 1994. Honduras signed that declaration in July 1994, under then-President Carols Roberto Reina.

The Declaration of Principles on Freedom of Expression was adopted at the 108th regular session of the Inter American Commission on Human Rights in October 2000, and submitted for the approval of OAS member countries during a general assembly in Quebec, Canada, in April 2001.

Several periodicals are published in Honduras, as are a number of trade papers. One popular periodical is *Co-*

conut Telegraph, which features stories on vacations and travel.

Private interests own around 80 percent of newspapers. All Honduran television stations are privately owned. The government owns the radio station Radio Honduras. There is no national news agency.

ECONOMIC FRAMEWORK

In 2000, Honduras was generally seen as one of the poorest nations in the Western Hemisphere. It is basing much of its hopes for the future on expanded trade privileges under the Enhanced Caribbean Basin Initiative and on debt relief under the Heavily Indebted Poor Countries initiative.

Honduras has come back from much of the economic problems caused by Hurricane Mitch, and the gross domestic product in 2001 rose an estimated 5 percent. The labor force in 1997 was estimated at around 2.3 million. Of that labor force, about 50 percent were employed in services, agriculture employed 29 percent and industry around 21 percent, according to 1998 figures. However, in 2000 it was estimated that Honduras had an unemployment rate of 28 percent.

The Honduran economy is rebounding, and in 2001 it grew 2.5 percent, according to the United Nations Economic Commission for Latin America and the Caribbean. Inflation was at 9 percent in 2001, slightly lower than the previous year.

PRESS LAWS

The 1982 Honduras Constitution guarantees freedom of the press. However, with the news media concentrated in the hands of a small number of powerful businessmen, as well as local businessmen or their close family members, press laws are not always respected.

The Law of Free Expression of Thought came into effect Aug. 26, 1958, when it was published in La Gaceta, the official bulletin, according to the Inter American Press Association. Article 1 of that law states: ''No person may be harassed or persecuted for their opinions. The private actions that do not alter public order or that do not cause any damage to third parties are outside the action of the Law.'' According to the first part of Article 2: ''The freedoms of speech and of information are inviolate. This includes the right to not be harassed for one's opinions, to investigate and receive information, and to disseminate it via any means of expression.''

However, according to Article 6: ''It is forbidden to circulate publications that preach or disseminate doctrines that undermine the foundation of the State or of the family, and those publications that provoke, incite to or encourage the commission of crimes against persons or property.'' Clearly this leaves room for interpretation regarding what or what does not undermine the state or the family.

Honduran journalists also must adhere to the Organic Law of the College of Journalists of Honduras, an obligation that went into effect on Dec. 6, 1972. That law is, in effect, a mandatory licensing law for journalists and the OAS's Inter American Court of Human Rights has found that mandatory licensing laws such as this violate the American Convention on Human Rights. According to the OAS's Special Rapporteur for Freedom of Expression, the College of Journalists has become an ''organization that restricts freedom of expression and limits the free practice of journalism.''

The law requires that all Honduran journalists have a valid degree in journalism, be registered in the College of Journalists, and that editors, managing editors, editors-in-chief and news editors be Honduran by birth. If a journalist is caught practicing the profession without being a member, he is fined, as is the person or company that contracts the offender's services. The College of Journalists also is responsible for sponsoring courses to upgrade the profession.

The College of Journalists is charged with overseeing the regulation of professional journalism, and according to Article 2e, ''To cooperate with the State in the fulfillment of its public functions.''

Foreign journalists must abide by a strict set of laws in order to practice their profession in Honduras. Article 18 of the Organic Law mandates that foreign journalists must comply with immigration, labor laws and treaties of Honduras; have their degree revalidated at the National University of Honduras, and register with the College of Journalists.

Honduran journalists must also worry about criminal defamation laws. Article 345 of the penal code mandates jail sentences of two to four years for anyone who ''threatens, libels, slanders, insults or in any other way attacks the character of a public official in the exercise of his or her function, by act, word or in writing.'' Under Article 323, anyone who ''offends the President of the Republic'' may be sentenced to up to 12 years in prison.

Defamation is a criminal offense, and those found guilty may receive up to a year in prison, although no prosecutions were reported in 1999. Although defamation laws have been reformed, lawsuits remain a risk. Many officials still use any available legal means to stifle criticism in the press. Some government and corporate sponsors have been known to retaliate against the press by discriminately doling out advertising dollars, according to information provided by the Committee to Protect

Journalists (CPJ). In a nation trying to rebound economically, this is a particularly devastating and effective tactic.

In 2001, a government-proposed bill that would have tackled organized crime was presented to parliament. The bill (Article 7) stated "professional confidentiality cannot be cited as a reason not to cooperate" with government officials, according to Reporters Without Borders. The bill would have made it easier to tap telephones and intercept postal or electronic mail. In addition, a new penal code (Article 372) would mandate between four and seven years in prison for revealing a state secret. Although neither bill was approved by the end of the year, the fact they were put forward by the government clearly sends a message to the press.

CENSORSHIP

In theory, the rights of the press generally are respected. In practice, they sometimes appear to be breached. The media is subject to corruption and politicization, and there have been instances of self-censorship, allegations of intimidation by military authorities, and payoffs to journalists, according to a 1992 U.S. Department of State human rights report.

In a press scandal that became public in January 1993, a Honduran newspaper published information contained in documents belonging to the National Elections Tribunal (Tribunal Nacional de Elecciones) showing payments to 13 journalists. Many observers believed at the time that more than half of journalists received payoffs for stories, some from government institutions including municipalities, the National Congress, various ministries and the military.

Another problem has been self-censorship in reporting sensitive subjects, particularly issues concerning the military and national security, according to the U.S. State Department report. Intimidation, threats, blacklisting and violence also occurred at various times in the 1980s and early 1990s.

Some analysts say that despite instances of military intimidation of the press in early 1993, print and broadcast media played an important role in creating an environment conducive to the public's questioning and criticism of authorities. Honduran sociologist Leticia Salomon said that in early 1993 the media, including newspaper caricatures, played "an instrumental role in mitigating the fear of criticizing the military." He believes this diminishment of fear was an important step in the building of a democratic culture in Honduras.

Little investigative journalism is done in Honduras, and when it does occur the focus primarily is on non-controversial subjects, according to the U.S. State Department. If a journalist does try to do an in-depth report, the reporter is faced with external pressure to halt the investigation, restrictive deadlines, and often a lack of access to government documents or independent sources.

STATE-PRESS RELATIONS

As the twentieth century came to a close and the twenty-first century opened, freedom of the press in Honduras remained a difficult goal. Restrictive government policies were targeted toward silencing the independent media and corruption among journalists.

Independent journalists often faced government pressure, according to a 1999 CPJ report. Phones were often tapped, the "established" press often ridiculed them, and fear was ever present. One San Pedro Sula television journalist, Rossana Guevara, told police she had been harassed after looking into cases of government corruption. And in July 1999, someone tried to kidnap another television journalist, Renato Alvarez of Telenisa Canal 63, after he reported details of a possible coup.

In 2001, Reporters Without Borders characterized Honduras's media situation as "tense." A half dozen journalists in total were dismissed from the newspaper El Heraldo and the television station Canal 63, with all six claiming the government pressured their employers. Allegations of intervention were also leveled against former President Flores.

The Journalists Institute suspended dozens of its members in 2001. It also criticized two outspoken journalists who voiced objections against the institute's decisions and corruption among their colleagues.

The Honduran government installed in January 2002 may not try to control the press as much as past administrations have, according to the Inter American Press Association. However, threats and legal matters remain in the way of a totally free press.

The deputy of Democratic Unification, the left-wing party, has asked the National Congress to regulate press freedom, including controlling journalists and media outlets. His request was based on a recently published case in which the U.S. Embassy suspended the visas of three prominent Honduran businessmen.

The independent press also faced pressure from the government of former President Flores. The press gave prominent coverage to the more powerful politicians during the November 2001 presidential elections. Small political parties received little or no coverage and had little or no access to the media. Meanwhile, the National Party and the ruling Liberal Party flooded radio and television stations with advertisements. National Party candidate Ricardo Maduro won the race, defeating Liberal Party candidate Rafael Pineda Ponce, to become president.

It can frequently be difficult to distinguish the media from the politicians in Honduras. Former President Flores owns *La Tribuna.* In addition to *El Tiempo,* Rosenthal owns a television station, Canal 11. Other politicians are reported to own radio and television stations, according to CPJ.

The government in 2001 reportedly influenced the decision of *El Heraldo,* traditionally known for its anti-government stances, to fire opinion editor Manuel Torres and a reporter, Roger Argueta, according to CPJ. A month earlier the paper lost editor Thelma Mejia when she resigned, also reportedly under government pressure. All three had criticized the government while working at the paper. After they left, the newspaper's coverage of the Flores administration became decidedly less critical.

In September 2001, former President Flores pledged to ensure no limits are placed on press freedom after a meeting with an Inter American Press Association delegation, a meeting during which the issue of legislation to force journalists to disclose their sources of information was raised. Flores assured the delegation he would act to remove any provision that would curtail freedom of the press. In doing so, Flores cited his own newspaper background, from being editor of the daily *La Tribuna* to actually owning the paper. At the end of the year, the legislation—still with the provision—had not been acted upon.

The military allegedly has been involved in intimidating members of the press. In January 1993, an *El Tiempo* reporter, Eduardo Coto, witnessed the murder of a San Pedro Sula businessman. When *El Tiempo*'s business manager gave refuge to Coto, a bomb exploded at his home. Coto had alleged that the businessman was killed by members of Battalion 3-16, a military unit suspected in the disappearances of several people in the 1980s. Coto is said to have received death threats from members of the military. He fled to Spain, where he was given asylum.

Under the Maduro administration, many observers hope that the press will be freer than it has under previous governments. Whether that turns out to be the case or not will be determined in the coming years.

Broadcast Media

Radio Honduras is owned by the government, but the state does not own a television station. Honduras has around 290 commercial radio stations broadcasting on about 240 AM stations and 50 FM stations. Hondurans own about 2.45 million radios, according to 1997 U.S. government figures.

Honduras has nine television channels, with an additional 12 cable television stations broadcasting to approximately 570,000 televisions. Television stations primarily operate from either Tegucigalpa or San Pedro Sula. Emisoras Unidas controls three television channels, and it owns Radio HRN, a major stations. Around 87 percent of homes in Tegucigalpa have televisions, while about 90 percent have radios.

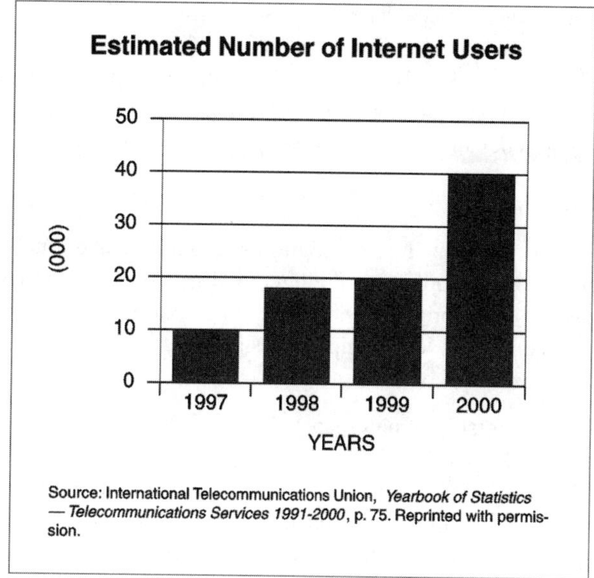

Source: International Telecommunications Union, *Yearbook of Statistics — Telecommunications Services 1991-2000*, p. 75. Reprinted with permission.

Electronic News Media

As of 2000, Honduras had eight Internet service providers, according to U.S. government figures. Honduras also reported around 40,000 Internet users. About 12 television stations air programs on the Internet, as do around 25 AM and FM radio stations, as well as several newspapers and other publications.

Education & Training

The Inter American Press Association established a scholarship fund in 1954 for young journalists and journalism school graduates. The scholarship allows U.S. and Canadian scholars to spend one academic year studying and reporting in Latin America and the Caribbean. In return, Latin American and Caribbean students spend an academic year at a recognized U.S. or Canadian journalism school. Member publications and private foundations help support the fund, and no government funding is accepted.

The primary institution of higher education in Honduras is the National Autonomous University of Honduras (UNAH), which was founded in 1847. It has around 30,000 students, with branches in San Pedro Sula and La Ceiba.

Three private universities are located in Honduras, although most observers believe UNAH remains the top educational choice. The tiny Jose Cecilio del Valle University is located in Tegucigalpa, as is Central American Technological University. The third private university is the University of San Pedro Sula. Annual enrollment in higher education in Honduras is around 39,400 students.

SUMMARY

Although its history might not appear to leave much hope for a completely unfettered and free press, Honduras has made progress. Some see greater hope for a freer press under the leadership of President Maduro, although that has yet to be proven.

Ownership of newspapers by politicians and government officials does not do much to help freedom of the press, and the kinds of harassment reported by those who criticize the government further erodes the possibility of a free press in Honduras. In addition, restrictive laws such as those requiring journalists to belong to the College of Journalists-in effect, a licensing law-further inhibits a free press. The government's pressure on the press also shackles journalists. The press in Honduras will not be free until these pressures on the media are removed.

SIGNIFICANT DATES

- 1982: The Honduran Constitution guarantees freedom of the press.
- 1998: Hurricane Mitch devastates the country.
- September 2001: Honduran President Carlos Flores pledges to ensure no limits are placed on press freedom in his country.

BIBLIOGRAPHY

Central Intelligence Agency (CIA). *The World Fact Book 2001.* Available from http://www.cia.gov.

''Country Profile: Honduras.'' BBC News, July 20, 2002. Available from http://news.bbc.co.uk.

''Country Profile: Honduras.'' Available from http://www.worldinformation.com.

''Freedom of the Press Report 2002.'' *Country Reports.* The Committee to Protect Journalists. Available from http://222.cpj.org.

''Honduras.'' *Country Reports.* The Committee to Protect Journalists. Available from http://www.cpj.org/index.html.

''Honduras.'' *Press Laws Database.* Inter American Press Association. Available from http://216.147.196.167/projects/laws-hon.cfm.

''Honduras: Constitutional Background.'' Library of Congress Country Study, 1992. Available from http://www.lcweb2.loc.gov.

''Honduras: Economic and Political Overview.'' In *Latin Business Chronicle.* Available from http://www.latinbusinesschronicle.com/countries/honduras/.

''IAPA in Honduras defends professional secrecy, rejects licensing of journalists.'' Inter American Press Association, September 7, 2001.

Reporters without Borders. ''Honduras: Annual Report 2002.'' Available from http://www.rsf.fr.

U.S. State Department. ''Honduras.'' In *Consular Reports.* Available from http://www.state.gov.

World Press Freedom Review. International Press Institute. Available from http://www.freemedia.at.

—Brad Kadrich

HONG KONG

BASIC DATA

Official Country Name:	Hong Kong
Region (Map name):	East & South Asia
Population:	7,210,505
Language(s):	Chinese (Cantonese), English
Literacy rate:	92.2%
Area:	1,092 sq km
GDP:	162,642 (US$ millions)
Number of Daily Newspapers:	48
Total Circulation:	1,528,000
Circulation per 1,000:	12
Total Newspaper Ad Receipts:	10,203 (Hong Kong $ millions)
As % of All Ad Expenditures:	37.30
Number of Television Stations:	4
Number of Television Sets:	1,840,000
Television Sets per 1,000:	255.2
Number of Cable Subscribers:	534,480
Cable Subscribers per 1,000:	78.6

Number of Satellite Subscribers:	182,000
Satellite Subscribers per 1,000:	25.2
Number of Radio Stations:	20
Number of Radio Receivers:	4,450,000
Radio Receivers per 1,000:	617.2
Number of Individuals with Computers:	2,360,000
Computers per 1,000:	327.3
Number of Individuals with Internet Access:	2,601,000
Internet Access per 1,000:	360.7

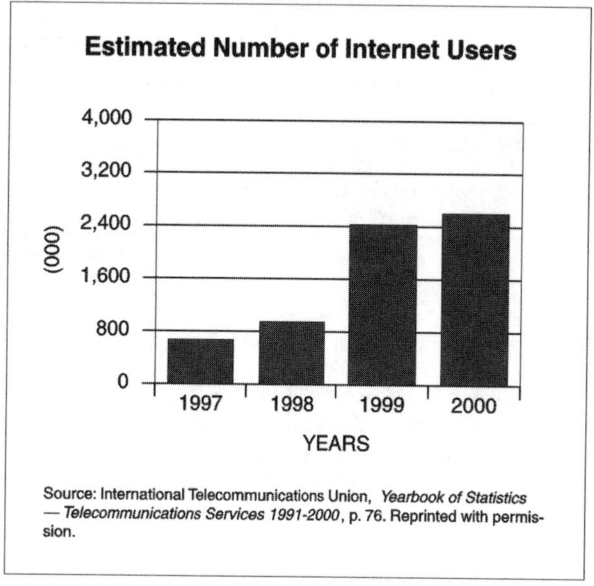

Source: International Telecommunications Union, *Yearbook of Statistics — Telecommunications Services 1991-2000*, p. 76. Reprinted with permission.

BACKGROUND & GENERAL CHARACTERISTICS

Hong Kong is a Special Administrative Region (SAR) of the People's Republic of China with a high degree of autonomy in all matters except defense and foreign affairs. On July 1, 1997, China resumed sovereignty over Hong Kong, ending more than 150 years of British colonial control. In 1984, Great Britain and China signed the Sino-British Joint Declaration, which, combined with Chinese laws enacted in 1990, provided a high degree of economic autonomy for the SAR for 50 years beyond 1997.

Hong Kong is located on the southeast coast of China. It consists of 236 islands and islets and a portion of the Chinese mainland, with a total area of approximately 1,046 square kilometers. Hong Kong Island is one of the leading trading centers in the world and constitutes the SAR's principal business and commercial center. Shipping and trade are major aspects of its economy. Tourism is one of Hong Kong's most important service activities and is the third largest source of foreign exchange earnings.

Hong Kong residents have a vast appetite for news. Their press, radio and television industries enjoy freedom from pre-censorship and minimal regulation. The Hong Kong government treats the press as a private enterprise. It has no specific regulatory body to control the media and implements no other form of direct control over the press. In this respect, Hong Kong continues to follow the colonial press regulation, which is still under debate and comes up for discussion from time to time.

Cultures of the East and the West meet in Hong Kong. Although 95 percent of the population is of Chinese descent its composition also includes those who arrived from countries like Indonesia, the Philippines, Thailand and Malaysia. Immigrants from Japan, India, Canada, Australia, the United Kingdom, the United States and other countries comprise the remainder. Hong Kong's many newspapers serve the various close-knit communities in the region. The Internet is no threat to Hong Kong newspapers, whose continued and even increasing popularity confounds claims that the press is a dying medium in the electronic age. Indeed, many newspapers now attract print readers through their online sites.

Nature of the Audience Hong Kong has an affluent population. Although Hong Kong is the most expensive city in the world, its prosperous economy is reflected in the lifestyle of its people, who have the highest standard of living in all of Asia. *Asiaweek* ranked Hong Kong as Asia's seventh best city in the world on a "quality of life" index.

There are about 7.2 million people in Hong Kong. About 1.3 million live on Hong Kong Island, around 2 million in mainland Kowloon, and the remainder in the New Territories and Outlying Islands. Almost 96 percent of the population is ethnic Chinese and 4 percent are other ethnic minorities, including a wide range of nationalities. Hong Kong is one of the most densely populated areas of the world, with an overall density of some 6,300 people per square kilometer. A British colony for 156 years, Hong Kong became a Special Administrative Region of the People's Republic of China on July 1, 1997.

There are several languages spoken in Hong Kong. The most common languages used in Hong Kong now are Cantonese and English, but as a result of the transfer of

Daily and Non-Daily Newspaper Titles and Circulation Figures

	1996	1997	1998	1999	2000
Number of Daily Newspapers	56	51	43	48	NA
Circulation of Dailies (000)	1,631	1,617	1,583	1,528	1,481
Number of Non-Daily Newspapers	NA	NA	NA	NA	NA
Circulation of Non-Dailies (000)	53	60	60	63	66

Source: World Association of Newspapers and Zenithmedia, *World Press Trends 2001*, pp. 8, 10, 17, 19. Note: NA stands for not available.

sovereignty in 1997, Mandarin is expected to become much more popular. According to the law under which the Hong Kong SAR was structured, Mandarin and English remain the official languages. Other dialects spoken include:

Hakka language; Minnan dialect, also known as Southern Min, Fukienese, Taiwanese, Amoy, Chaozhou/Tiechew, Shantow/Shahtaw; and Fuzhou dialect, also known as Northern Min or Northern Fukienese.

In addition, the characters in which Chinese is written in Hong Kong differ from those used in mainland China. Despite linguistic difficulties, literacy in Hong Kong is high: in 1998, 92.2 percent of people over the age of 15 in Hong Kong were literate.

Freedom of expression and a liberal attitude towards the press have helped to attract a concentration of prestigious international publications to Hong Kong. International publishers operating in Hong Kong manage the production, marketing and distribution of books for the Hong Kong market and export to related companies worldwide. Hong Kong printing exports amounted to over US $1 billion in 2001.

About 120 major international publishers of newspapers, magazines and books have their offices and Asian headquarters in Hong Kong, which is also the base for a number of regional publications. For example, *Asiaweek*, the *Far Eastern Economic Review*, the *Asian Wall Street Journal*, the *Financial Times*, *The Economist* and the *International Herald Tribune* are printed in Hong Kong.

International book publishers in Hong Kong include Oxford, Longman, Readers' Digest and Macmillan. In recent years, more foreign titles have been translated into Chinese, including management, personal finance and self-improvement books as well as cartoons and popular novels, especially those that have been adapted for movies or television.

Media Circulation There are a total of 54 newspapers in Hong Kong. Of these, 32 have a circulation of 2,951,000 (1993). According to the Hong Kong Government Information Center, there are 697 registered periodicals and 54 newspapers in Hong Kong. Of the 54 newspapers, 34 are in Chinese and 11 in English. UNESCO (1999) data shows that in 1996 Hong Kong published 52 dailies with a circulation of 5 million—a penetration of 78.6 copies per 100 people.

Of other non-newspaper periodicals, 347 are in Chinese, 155 in English, 115 bilingual and 17 in other languages. These magazines cover a wide variety of subjects from public affairs and politics to technical matters and entertainment.

Major newspapers circulated in Hong Kong include the following:

- *Hong Kong Standard Front Page*
- *Hong Kong Standard China Section*
- *South China Morning Post (SCMP) Internet Edition*
- *South China Morning Post China Section*
- *China Business Round Up*
- *Ming Pao Daily News*
- *Hong Kong 97 Website*
- *Sing Pao Daily News*
- *Ta Kung Pao*
- *Hong Kong iMail*
- *Apple Daily Online Newspaper*
- *Hong Kong Commercial Daily*
- *Wen Wei Po Daily*
- *Sing Tao Electronic Daily*

Of some 40 daily newspapers in Hong Kong, five are in English, including the *South China Morning Post* (circulation 101,000) and the *Hong Kong Standard* (circulation 60,000). The daily newspapers have a combined readership of over 400,000. Approximately 80 percent of the readers are Chinese. Hong Kong has the highest news readership in Asia after Japan.

Hong Kong newspapers are divided into sections—e.g., editorials, politics, education, transportation and real estate. Some newspapers cover mainly general news, both local and overseas; others cover solely entertainment, especially television and cinema news. Chinese and English newspapers belong to the Newspapers Society of Hong Kong, which was formed in 1954 and acts in the interest of the ownership, management and readership of the newspapers. Specialized periodicals, the other main sector of the press, cover a wide variety of subjects from public affairs and politics to technical matters and entertainment.

Press History Hong Kong's press history has deep roots and a close connection with Chinese politics. The British colonies of Shanghai and Hong Kong were the birthplaces of the modern Chinese press. In the 1850s, Christian missionaries first published a Chinese edition of the English language newspaper. A Chinese-owned newspaper press followed in the 1870s. At the turn of the century, both Manchurian loyalists and revolutionaries published their propaganda in Hong Kong; they aimed to reach the Chinese intellectuals on the mainland, not just to provide news but to promote enlightenment and advocate reform or revolution. There was no explicit censorship, and citizens were allowed to criticize the contending Chinese regimes, although negative discussion of the British colonial government was discouraged. After the 1967 communal riots, the colonial government felt a strong need to close the communication gap with the people. It upgraded the Government Information Services (GIS) to play the double role of news producer and news distributor to the press, both controlling and facilitating press access to government information.

When China and Britain held negotiations in the early 1980s over the future of the colony, a majority of the Hong Kong press sided editorially with the British position and cast serious doubt about the ''one country, two systems'' policy proposed by the Chinese regime. From 1984 to 1997, the press had to cope with the dualistic power structure of the colonial regime and the Chinese authorities. Throughout the 1990s, the Hong Kong press largely supported Britain's last effort to undertake democratic electoral reforms. Under the basic press law, China must allow Hong Kong to continue its present way of life, including press freedom, for at least 50 years.

In 1997, 30 Chinese dailies, 10 English language dailies, one bilingual daily and four dailies in other languages had registered with the Hong Kong government. Excluding those publications covering only entertainment or horseracing, as well as news agency bulletins registered as newspapers, Hong Kong published 15 large circulation dailies in 1999. Some dailies have distribution networks and print editions overseas, particularly in the United States, Canada, the United Kingdom and Australia. Some regional publications, such as the *Asian Wall Street Journal*, *Asiaweek*, the *Far Eastern Economic Review* and the *International Herald Tribune*, have chosen Hong Kong as their base or printing location. Many international news agencies, newspapers, and overseas broadcasting corporations have established regional headquarters in Hong Kong because of its advanced telecommunications infrastructure and the availability of the latest technology, as well as its strategically important location in Asia.

In the past, Hong Kong was known for a large number of small, diverse, family-owned newspapers. However, the new publishing economies, as symbolized by the Apple Daily, has made it difficult for smaller newspapers to survive. Newspaper publishing has become the prerogative of those individuals or corporations with substantial economic means.

Hong Kong is a regional publishing center, backed by a highly developed printing industry. Advertising sales are a major source of revenue for the printed media.

ECONOMIC FRAMEWORK

Hong Kong is the world's tenth-largest trading entity and the ninth-largest banking entity, and is one of the world's most open and dynamic economies. Its unique social system, its reputation for hard work and its strategic location combine to produce a bustling free market economy, though one highly dependent on international trade.

Hong Kong has very few natural resources and must import virtually all its raw materials; thus, it is extremely vulnerable to external influences by its trading partners. Recently, Hong Kong has achieved rapid economic growth. Traditionally, manufacturing industries, shipping, banking and tourism have been the major foreign currency earners. Textiles, clothing, toys, electronics and plastic industries employ a large percentage of the work force and contribute significantly to the GDP, accounting for some 70 percent of total domestic exports. As a gateway to China—and now as China's window to the outside world—Hong Kong is developing into a service-oriented financial center. Its active banking sector and the stock market provide the financial and administrative support for investment ventures in China.

Government policy encourages free enterprise and foreign investment. No distinction is made between local and foreign investment, and both are welcomed. Hong Kong's main trading partners are the USA, the UK, Germany, China and Japan, and the primary products are fish, fruit and vegetables. Major industries in Hong Kong include aircraft engineering, clothing, clocks and watches, electronic goods, fishing, finance and banking, iron and steel rolling, plastic products, ship repair, textiles, and toys.

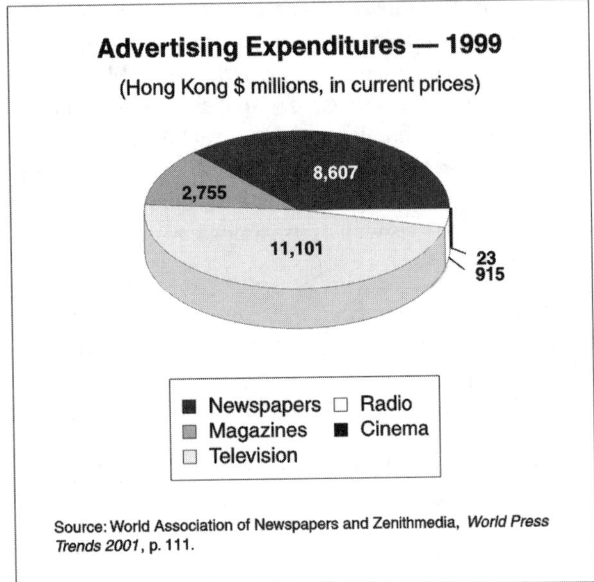

Source: World Association of Newspapers and Zenithmedia, *World Press Trends 2001*, p. 111.

Hong Kong's press is an amalgamation of privately owned and party-financed newspapers. Most newspapers in Hong Kong are owned by private investors whose main goal is profit. Contrary to widely held predictions, Hong Kong has continued to enjoy a high degree of press freedom as China seems to have kept its promise of not interfering with the SAR's internal matters.

Surveys indicate that journalists as well as citizens have perceived steady erosion in media credibility in the 1990s. In fact, many outlets like the prestigious *South China Morning Post* and *Ming Pao Daily News* have lost significant ground. Press freedom is likely to erode seriously without conscious measures to safeguard press integrity.

In 1999, the newspapers' share of display advertising revenue was 36 percent. Only television had a higher share, with 45 percent.

Press Laws

Hong Kong's press freedom is said to be the highest in Asia, except for Japan. Newspapers have enjoyed a high degree of freedom perhaps because of the British tradition. Although the colonial government had a number of laws in hand to control the press, it seldom used them.

The basic law provides for freedom of speech of the press and of publication and there was no apparent change after the Chinese takeover in the tradition of respect for these freedoms by the government. In the early 2000s, there were some instances of intolerance on the part of Chinese authorities regarding press freedom. It is perhaps ironic that in the year 2001, the Hong Kong media was affected less by political events and more by an economic slump. This has forced the closure of one publication and the slimming down of several others. Such moves have an inevitable impact on media diversity.

Censorship

There is a widespread impression among both journalists and the public that it is prudent for the press to engage in a degree of self-censorship. The pressures on journalists to self-censor usually are subtle and indirect. There is a perception of rising censorship in Hong Kong because it is a major business center where economic and political information is sensitive. Self-censorship is more pronounced on issues considered sensitive to the Chinese leadership. These include coverage of Chinese dissidents and Tibetan and Xinjiang separatists, as well as the inner workings of the Communist Party. These issues are reported upon, but reporters tend to play it safe. There are no reports of direct orders to refrain from covering a certain issue, despite a shared perception of a need for special care towards topics of particular sensitivity to China or to Hong Kong's powerful business interests.

There is no censorship of imported videos at all; the government takes the view that these are for private viewing only and not for public consumption. There are no changes to this policy planned.

News Agencies

The domestic news agency in Hong Kong is the Hong Kong China News Agency (HKCNA). HKCNA was established on November 13, 1956, in Hong Kong and offers news releases to Chinese-language newspapers in Hong Kong, Macao and foreign countries and articles for newspaper supplements. HKCNA is a regional agency that offers about 30 dispatches for over 80 clients every day covering news in the Mainland, Hong Kong, Macao, Taiwan, and Chinese communities abroad. HKCNA is a branch office of the China News Service and carries the news of both agencies.

Broadcast Media

Virtually all Hong Kong households, about 2 million, have access to television. Altogether, the TV industry provides more than 38 channels. The television stations in Hong Kong operate four channels: all commercial, two Chinese and two English. Hong Kong is also the home of major regional broadcasters, including Satellite Television Asian Region Ltd. (STAR TV), Chinese Television Network (CTN) and Chinese Entertainment Television (CETV).

Television Broadcasting International (TVBI) markets about 1,000 hours of its 2-3,000 hours of productions in 25 countries serving overseas Chinese communities. Asia Television (ATV) markets 520 hours of drama, showing 10 hours per week on air.

Radio and Television Hong Kong (RTHK), a quasi-public broadcaster, supplements commercial television. It is a government broadcasting authority, which places its programs on the other four channels. News is broadcast through Radio-Television Hong Kong and can be heard in English and Cantonese. Cantonese radio and TV programs are broadcast from Hong Kong. Recently, there have been some TV programs in Mandarin.

EDUCATION & TRAINING

The Chinese University of Hong Kong has accredited journalism and mass media programs, which are supplemented with a required period of practical training in the field. Hong Kong has many schools and colleges providing courses in mass media and journalism, which offer excellent career opportunities. Journalism and media programs aim at training students' analytical ability, independent thinking, and proficiency in language and literacy in various forms of media. The university academic program stresses both theoretical and professional training. There are five professional tracks: journalism, broadcasting, advertising and public relations, multimedia and telecommunications, and communications studies. The program's rigorous training also equips students with high adaptability and professional competence.

SUMMARY

The Hong Kong press has remained healthy and diverse despite facing competition. Because of its diversity, the press maintains high quality and high credibility and hence appears to have a bright future.

Freedom House has ranked Hong Kong as partly free regarding governance, political rights and civil liberties. Hong Kong remains a capitalist society with the government firmly wedded to a laissez-faire policy on commercial activities. After the 1997 transfer to China, the press has continued to be more vocal than most people had envisaged. However, it remains to be seen whether this trend will continue indefinitely. A threat to press freedom in recent years has been the many libel suits filed against media organizations and critics. This in effect may dampen the critical exchange of ideas and public monitoring of the press. Broadcasting regulations at the highest level rest with the Chief Executives and the advisory bodies. Under the name of market-driven journalism, yellow journalism has become the order of the day for the popular press and for some so-called ''info-attainment'' TV programs.

The decline in media ethics is evident in the growing number of complaints that people have lodged with the government monitoring body. The recent economic downturn and the fierce market competition have been another major issue in Hong Kong. As a matter of survival, many newspapers have lowered their editorial standard to attract the largest possible number of readers by offering sensational content. Intense market competition may also lead to folding of newspapers that will further narrow the spectrum of opinion.

Another danger to the Hong Kong media comes from the profession itself. The Hong Kong Press Council, which was set up by the Newspaper Society in July 2000 to consider complaints from the public about media invasion of individual privacy, announced in October that it wished to turn itself into a statutory body for protection from non-member newsgroups.

In terms of media freedom, there have been few noticeable differences since the British colonial rule in 1997. By and large, the media is free and adequately fulfils its role as a public watchdog. However, several political and corporate forces are critical of the independent media and see it as a threat or an inconvenience. Through varied means, many are intent on curtailing the activities of the press. Beating back their advances will take a vigilant and concerted effort.

BIBLIOGRAPHY

Atlapedia Online. Latimer Clark Corporation Pty. Ltd., 2001. Available from www.atlapedia.com.

Bale, Cliff. *World Press Freedom Review, 2001*. Available from www.freemedia.at/wpfr/hongkong.htm.

Goff, Peter. *World Press Freedom Review, 2000*. Available from www.freemedia.at/wpfr/hongkong.htm.

Gunaratne, Shelton A., ed. *Handbook of the Media in Asia*. New Delhi: Sage, 1982.

U.S. Department of State: Bureau of East Asian and Pacific Affairs. ''Background Note: Hong Kong.'' Available from www.state.gov/r/pa/ei/bgn/2747.htm.

—Ashakant Nimbark and Binod Agrawal

HUNGARY

BASIC DATA

Official Country Name:	Republic of Hungary
Region (Map name):	Europe
Population:	10,106,017

Language(s):	Hungarian
Literacy rate:	99.0%
Area:	93,030 sq km
GDP:	45,633 (US$ millions)
Number of Daily Newspapers:	40
Total Circulation:	1,625,000
Circulation per 1,000:	194
Total Newspaper Ad Receipts:	33,781 (Forint millions)
As % of All Ad Expenditures:	14.30
Number of Television Stations:	35
Number of Television Sets:	4,420,000
Television Sets per 1,000:	437.4
Number of Cable Subscribers:	1,576,000
Cable Subscribers per 1,000:	157.6
Number of Satellite Subscribers:	1,753,000
Satellite Subscribers per 1,000:	173.5
Number of Radio Stations:	77
Number of Radio Receivers:	7,010,000
Radio Receivers per 1,000:	693.6
Number of Individuals with Computers:	870,000
Computers per 1,000:	86.1
Number of Individuals with Internet Access:	1,480,000
Internet Access per 1,000:	146.4

BACKGROUND & GENERAL CHARACTERISTICS

Perhaps the one person that is associated worldwide with excellence in the media, innovation in communications, independent liberalism in journalism and education for the media is Joseph Pulitzer, a man of Hungarian descent. At 17, Pulitzer left Hungary for America where, in a series of newspaper ownerships, he pioneered the use of illustrations and photographs, news stunts and crusades against corruption. As a result of competition with the Hearst Group of newspapers characterized by vicious and lengthy circulation wars, Pulitzer's newspapers became renowned for sensationalism, yellow journalism and banner headlines. His name was later remembered for the foundation of the Columbia Graduate School of Journalism in New York, and endowment of the series of prizes for excellence in journalism, the Pulitzer Prizes.

Thus it is somewhat ironic that nearly 100 years after his death in 1911, the country of his birth is attempting to establish an independent media by means of sensationalism, the rooting out of corruption and mismanagement, and with a political orientation of independent liberalism that was the hallmark of Pulitzer's newspapers in his formative years as a journalist in America.

The need for an independent media results from the period following World War II, during which Hungary was part of the Eastern Bloc and therefore dominated by the Soviet Union. At that time, all media was strictly controlled as an instrument of the Communist Party. In 1989 Hungary became the first country of the Eastern Bloc to move away from the Soviet Union and its attempt to establish an independent media dates from then. The years since independence generally have been successful economically, but the transformation of the media from a state-controlled propaganda machine to an independent and self-policing vehicle of public discourse has been a hard-fought battle. At the turn of the twenty-first century the Freedom House, an independent, non-partisan organization that assess media freedom, awarded Hungary a rating of 27 out of 100, indicating almost complete freedom of the press.

The Nature of the Audience The population of Hungary is around 10 million, of which 1.8 million (18 percent) live in the capital Budapest. Other major cities are Debrecen (204,000), Miskolc (172,000), Szeged (158,000), Pécs (157,000) and Györ (124,000). Almost two-thirds of the population is urbanized and the remaining one-third has ready access to all media.

Hungary has a highly literate audience. Literacy is estimated at almost 100 percent for men and women, and the level of education is high. Thus it is no surprise that newspapers have a circulation of 194 per 1,000 people, though this is down from the early 1990s when reportedly a phenomenal 400 per 1,000 of the population read newspapers.

The Hungarian language is classified as Finno-Ugrian and is part of the Altaic group of languages. Apart from linguistic relatives in Estonia and Finland, the Hungarian language is unique in Europe, and 95 percent of ethnic Hungarians speak a language very different from other European languages. There exists a possibility the media could marginalize other ethnic groups, but the Hungarian government has made significant commitments both in the constitution and the media to recognize and cater to these groups. The most numerous of the ethnic minorities are the Roma—often called Gypsies—the exact numbers of which are unknown but may be as high as 9 percent of Hungary's population. Germans, Slovaks, Croats, Romanians, Bulgarians, Greeks, Polish, Serbian, Ruthenes and Ukrainians comprise the balance of the population. Of the 13 recognized ethnic minorities in Hungary, it is the status and accommodation of the Roma that is the most serious case for concern and which has received the most attention in the context of minority rights.

Notwithstanding the highly literate nature of the Hungarian population, the fact that the economy is in the process of recovering from the problems inherited from the socialist economic system means the affluence of the average Hungarian remains relatively low in contrast to that of its neighbors to the west. The purchasing power standard in Hungary, estimated by the European Union at 11,700 Euros, is 52 percent of the European Union average. This figure conceals significant hardships that exist in the population, not the least among the unemployed, senior citizens, and the Roma population in general. This climate of hardship and perceived injustice has created a vocal and predominantly liberal journalistic orientation.

Hungary has little in the way of historic traditions of a free media because it was effectively under the influence of the Soviet Bloc since 1945. Any history of media independence present in pre-World War II was lost in the following 45 years of Communist rule. During the Soviet period Hungary's oldest newspaper, *Magyar Nemzet*, was the principal organ of the party but was in serious decline near the turn of the twenty-first century. With mounting debts and a circulation of only 40,000 it merged with a right-wing daily, *Napi Magyarorszag*, and in recent years is Hungary's second most popular newspaper. It generally is considered the most right-wing of newspapers, and hence was the most sympathetic to the predominantly conservative governments of post-independence Hungary amid a sea of left-leaning print publications. Foremost among the liberal press are newspapers of the German-owned Axel Springer group, which have a leading position in the Hungarian newspaper market, particularly in the county newspapers outside Budapest.

Most Hungarian journalists cite a great journalistic tradition in their nation, largely a result of the early foundations of journalism during the Austro-Hungarian Empire. In the socialist years since 1945 little movement away from the party line occurred in Hungarian journalism. The only exception was during the time of the Hungarian revolution in November 1956 when many journalists and newspaper editorials supported the head of the independence movement, Imre Nagy. Following the Russian invasion to quell the revolution, a number of journalists were executed and others sentenced to long prison terms. Western observers have given Hungarian journalists a mark of 4 on a scale of 10 for quality of journalism, citing too much commentary, little quality investigative reporting and a tendency to present the newspaper's avowed political leanings with little or no attempt at balance in editorial viewpoint.

The Importance of Newspapers There are more than 40 daily newspapers in Hungary, and more than 1,600 print publications. The most popular newspaper up to 2000 was *Népszabadság* with a daily circulation of 210,000. It was surpassed in the beginning of the millennium by a new Swedish-owned, freely distributed tabloid, *Metro*, which by 2002 had a circulation of 235,000. Newspapers are in a constant circulation war, competing in a declining readership market amid an excess of publications and are increasingly turning to yellow journalism in attempts to gain market share.

Népszabadság Rt. (People's Liberty Co.) was founded in 1990 with 340 million Hungarian forints (HUF) in capital assets. Today it is a powerful business owned by the Swiss-based Ringier Corporation, with some 8 billion HUF annual revenues and it is active in other media fields. Its paper, the *Népszabadság* (Peoples Liberty) is by far the largest newspaper in circulation in Hungary. Its long-time slogan was "Hungary's Most Popular Daily Newspaper." The paper is of standard size (63 by 47 cm) and is published six times a week (Monday to Saturday). The number of pages varies during the week—Wednesday averages the most (40)—as does the ratio of advertisements—Friday averages the highest percentage (29) of advertisements. It has only a morning edition, similar to all Hungarian newspapers, with the exception of *Déli Hírek* (News at Noon), a regional newspaper circulated in the Northeast region of Miskolc and the surrounding county of Borsod-Abaúj-Zemplén. *Déli íírek* is on newsstands by noon or the early afternoon, and also has a single edition per day.

The *Népszabadság* has both permanent features and special supplements over the week. Its standard coverage consists of foreign politics with commentary, home affairs, mirror to the world, mirror to Hungary, culture, forum, market and economy, real estate market, news of the world, sport (in every day's edition), info world, green page, youth/school, the economy and technical/computer electronics. Each weekday there are special sections concentrating on popular subjects. Monday's edition has a regular supplement called "Daily Inves-

Daily and Non-Daily Newspaper Titles and Circulation Figures

	1996	1997	1998	1999	2000
Number of Daily Newspapers	38	43	40	39	40
Circulation of Dailies (000)	1,646	1,742	1,700	1,659	1,625
Number of Non-Daily Newspapers	NA	NA	1	NA	NA
Circulation of Non-Dailies (000)	NA	NA	NA	NA	NA

Source: World Association of Newspapers and Zenithmedia, *World Press Trends 2001*, pp. 8, 10, 17, 19. Note: NA stands for not available.

tor,'' Tuesday has a supplement on labor and job issues, Wednesday's special edition is dedicated to cars and motorcycles, Thursday it produces a supplement called ''At Home'' (concentrating on domestic Hungarian issues), Friday has a real estate supplement, and Saturday has ''Magazine'' and ''Weekend'' sections. The newspaper generally is considered to have a left-wing attitude, so it was quite critical towards the Hungarian government from the middle of 1998 to the middle of May 2002.

In contrast, the second largest newspaper, *Magyar Nemzet* (Hungarian Nation) has a definite right-wing bias. It is owned by Nemzet Lap és Könyvkiadó (Nemzet Newspaper and Book Publishing Co.) which consists of a number of private shareholders. It calls itself the ''bourgeois paper'' and acted as a de facto forum. Some would say it also acted as a mouthpiece for the government up to 2002, with an orientation favoring the conservative government in power. Magyar Nemzet has a circulation of about 110,000, is published six times a week from Monday to Saturday, and has permanent columns dedicated to home affairs, foreign affairs/diplomacy, the economy, culture, letters from the readers, a large sports section, and a weekend magazine on Saturday. It usually has two to three pages of advertisements and around 20 to 24 total pages. It is a full-size newspaper.

Magyar Hírlap (Hungarian News), also owned by the Ringier Group, has a circulation of around 38,000, regular (large) size pages and 24 pages on weekdays, but the Saturday edition has 28. Its motto is ''The news is intangible, the opinion is free,'' thus claiming that it is the most objective of all Hungarian newspapers. Its regular columns are the topic of the day, foreign affairs, home affairs centered on Budapest, culture, letters from the readers, world news, the domestic economy, the world economy, E-world, food market, science, sports and a weekend magazine called ''As You Like It'' in the Saturday edition.

Népszava (People's Word) a left-wing broadsheet owned and influenced by trade union interests, has about the same circulation as *Magyar Hírlap*. Its regular columns include home affairs, foreign affairs, background, opinion, world, culture, television programming, letters from readers, sports and world news.

There are two economic papers published five times a week on weekdays. In the mid-1990s they were one paper, then they split into *Napi Gazdaság* (Daily Economy) and *Világgazdaság* (World Economy). They are much more expensive than the dailies, especially *Világgazdaság*, which costs 190 HUF, and *Napi Gazdaság*'s cost of 178 HUF. In comparison *Népszabadság* sells for 85 HUF, *Magyar Nemzet* 98 HUF, *Magyar Hírlap* 99 HUF and *Népszava* 89 HUF.

In Budapest there is an English-language weekly, the *Budapest Sun*, which primarily covers topics of concern to the business community. Other European-language newspapers are readily available and often with same-day coverage as the rest of Europe. North American newspapers (*USA Today, New York Times*) usually are editions from two to three days earlier. There is no restriction on their import.

A major feature of Hungarian newspaper readership is the numbers, circulation and impact of 18 regional newspapers outside Budapest. Hungarian county newspapers and magazines are noteworthy for their dominance by the Axel Springer German newspaper conglomerate. Axel Springer is the publisher of nine county papers, or almost half of all the county papers, as there are 19 counties in Hungary. Pest County, where Budapest is located, has no newspaper of its own but owing to the dominance of Budapest in Hungarian affairs, the national dailies devote much of their news coverage to what is happening in the capital. Only three counties—Borsod-Abaúj-Zemplén, Heves and Fejér—have more than one paper. Total circulation of the nine county papers is about 250,000 with an average circulation around 37,500, thus giving them as important an impact, if not more, than the so-called national dailies. Axel Springer's county newspapers are the following: *Békés Megyei Hírlap* (Békés County News, circulation of 33,200); *Új Dunántúli Napló* (New Transdanubian Diary, 55,000); *Jászkun Krónika/Új Néplap* (Jászkun Chronicle/New People's Paper, 16,000); *Heves Megyei Hírlap* (Heves County News, 21,000); *Nógrád Megyei Hírlap* (Nógrád

County News, 17,000); *Somogyi Hírlap* (Somogy News, 25,365); *Petőfi Népe* (Petőfi's People, 50,485); *Tolnai Népújság* (Tolna People's Paper, 23,650) and *24 Óra* (Twenty-four Hours, 25,365).

The remaining county newspapers are owned either by another German-based group, Westdeutsche Allgemeine Zeitungsgruppe (WAZ), an Austrian-based conglomerate, Inform Stúdió Ltd. or the British-based Daily Mail group.

The second largest conglomerate, Pannon Lapok Társasága (Society of Pannon Papers), a division of Westdeutsche Allgemeine Zeitungsgruppe (WAZ), is one of the largest European regional media concerns, consisting of more than 160 companies and an annual turnover in excess of 4 billion Deutsche Marks in 2001. It has papers in Germany, Austria, Hungary and Bulgaria. In Hungary it has four county papers with a total circulation of around 250,000. These papers have a radio and television program color attachment called RTV-Tipp. The newspapers are: *Zala Megyei Hírlap* (Zala County News, with a circulation of about 65,000); *Napló* (Diary, 56,400); *Vas Népe* (Vas People, 64,200) and *Fejér Megyei Hírlap/Dunaújvárosi Hírlap* (Fejér County News/Dunaújváros News, 53,500 and 9,800, respectively).

The third county newspaper group in Hungary is Funk Verlag—Inform Stúdió. The publisher has Austrian majority ownership (Inform Stúdió Ltd.) but with its Hungarian center in Miskolc. It publishes three county newspapers with a total circulation exceeding 136,000. Its papers are: *Hajdú-Bihari Napló* (Hajdú-Bihar Diary, 50,400), *Észak-Magyarország* (North Hungary, 37,350), and *Kelet-Magyarország* (East Hungary, 48,750).

Finally the Rothermere family, based in Britain and publishers of the *Daily Mail* in the UK, publishes two county papers in Hungary with a total circulation of more than 150,000. The *Kisalföld* (Small Hungarian Plain) is the leading county paper in Hungary, with regional editions distributed across county borders. Its other paper is *Délmagyarország/Délvilág* (South Hungary/Southern Part).

Additionally, there are three minor county/urban county seat dailies. They are: *Békés Megyei Nap* (Békés County Daily, 10,680), *Komárom-Esztergom Megyei* (Komárom-Esztergom County News, 15,000) and the only afternoon-edition newspaper, *Déli Hírek* (News at Noon, 18,000).

In the magazine market, a company called AS-Budapest publishes most of the major magazines such as the popular women's magazines *Kiskegyed* (My Fine Lady), *Csók és Könny* (Kisses and Tears), *Kiskegyed konyhája* (Kitchen of the Kiskegyed), *Gyöngy* (Pearl), *TVR-hét* (Weekly Television and Radio Programs), *Lakáskultúra* (Homes Culture), and *Party*. AS-Budapest also publishes a Sunday paper called *Vasárnap Reggel* (Sunday Morning).

In twenty-first century Hungary there are few logistical problems with producing such a large output of print media. Most presses are modern offset presses, usually manufactured and imported from within Europe. Newsprint is readily available in adequate quantities. In a country that had a socialist history of trade union membership, there have been no strikes or work stoppages that have significantly affected newspaper production. The average print journalist's salary in Hungary in 2002 was around HUF 170,000 a month. Junior staff earn around HUF 120-150,000, more experiencedjournalists (staff members) around HUF 200-250,000, editors between HUF 250-400,000, senior editors up to 500,000, and editor-in-chiefs' salaries may go up to 1 million HUF. Television journalists are said to earn considerably more. Internet journalists earn less than the average, around 20-40 percent less than their newspaper colleagues.

Freelance journalists do not exist in Hungary in the Western sense of the term. That is, newspapers do not, or cannot, afford to pay a separate story the sum it would be worth and that helps explain why there is so little independent investigative journalism. There are journalists who do not have a single workplace and sell pieces to different publications, but their articles are public relations pieces. It is suspected that *Playboy* and similar magazines pay the largest sums for a piece, around HUF 10,000 (U.S. $39.50) per *flekk*, a Hungarian journalistic term for the length of the text, around 1,500 characters with spaces.

There also exists a strange phenomenon in Hungary because according to tax authorities, there are only a couple of journalists in the whole nation! This means that few of them are registered as being employed as a journalist in their medium, and even those who are official journalists receive only the minimum wage of HUF 50,000 per month. The remainder of their salary is paid according to an agreement with the small companies of the journalists. This way the employer can avoid paying Social Security and other taxes.

In a country the size of Hungary, the depth and extent of newspaper coverage can be viewed as remarkable. The Observer Budapest Media Watch Co. regularly examines 162 newspapers and periodicals in Hungary, although most have circulations of about 5,000 to 10,000 subscribers. The generally adverse economic climate is the major factor in the low percentage of advertising, with the result that subscriptions, circulation, market area and discretionary retail sales become major influences on newspaper viability. On the other hand, advertisers have very little influence on editorial policies. As the economy strengthens and full European Union integration brings more foreign investment, the importance of advertising to the newspaper industry can be expected to increase.

As a result of the almost homogeneous Hungarian population, most publications are printed in Hungarian. Major minority newspapers in Hungary and their ethnic audience are: *Amaro Drom* (Roma), *Ararát* (Hungarian and Armenian), *Barátság—Prietenie* (Hungarian and Romanian), *Foaia Romaneasca* (Romanian), *Haemus* (Bolgár), *Hromada* (Hungarian and Ukrainian), *Hrvatski Glasnik* (Croatian), *Közös Út—Kethano Drom* (Hungarian and Roma), *Lungo Drom* (Roma), *Ludové Noviny* (Slovakian), *Neue Zeitung* (German), *Porabje* (Slovenain) and *Srpske Narodne Novine* (Serbian).

The news media in Hungary is generally seen as having a left-wing bias, an accusation that the ruling political parties in the 1990s disliked and have attempted to counterbalance by political appointments in oversight bodies. This accusation is most prevalent in Budapest which, by nature of its population and political importance, is most affected by the political climate in Hungary. In smaller cities and towns, local news is just as important and the circumstances of individuals become more important than the political agenda. In some newspapers there have been instances of anti-Semitism that have found voice in the media, but the government moved quickly to silence such right-wing extremists.

Economic Framework

In the 10 years since the fall of the Soviet Union, the economy of Hungary has been one of the most successful in making the transition to a privatized, market economy. As Hungary entered the new millennium, inflation was at a manageable 9 percent, growth was at a robust 3.5-4 percent and productivity was among the highest of all Eastern European nations. Based on this successful economic transformation, Hungary was one of the first former communist nations to gain candidate status for entry into the European Union. Economically, the European Union has stressed that the Hungarian government needs to further reduce inflation, cut the budget deficit and reform the tax code.

The European Union also attaches considerable importance to the status of the press, with particular emphasis on freedom and independence. In addition, the European Union has used the question of the status of the Roma as a barometer upon which to judge Hungary's suitability to join the Union. In this regard the media has served in part as a barometer with which to judge Hungary's movement toward recognition and accommodation of its ethnic minorities, particularly the Roma. Some sections of the press have acted as watchdogs toward government mismanagement and discrimination, and acted to publicize and criticize racist acts directed against the Roma.

More than 80 percent of the print media and more than 70 percent of the broadcast media (in total, 30 radio stations and 29 television stations) are in private hands. The process started almost immediately after independence with the purchase of the existing media. Since independence there has been a veritable explosion of independent newspapers and magazines. Recently the print media has become highly competitive and of high quality. There is no direct control of the electronic media by the government, although there have been accusations that the government seeks to influence the media in its structuring and appointments to the Boards of Trustees.

Press Laws

The Constitution of the Hungarian Republic, written in 1949 but greatly amended upon independence in 1989, guarantees freedom of speech and freedom of the press under Act XX, Article 61, which states (paraphrased):

- Part One: In the Republic of Hungary everybody has the right to freely express their opinion and have access to and disseminate data concerning the public.
- Part Two: The Republic of Hungary acknowledges and protects the freedom of the press.
- Part Three: The amendment of the Act on the publication of data of public concern and on the freedom of the press requires a two-thirds majority of Parliament.
- Part Four: A two-thirds majority is needed for the appointment of the leaders of public radio, television and news agencies, the licensing of commercial radio and television stations and the passing of any act on the prevention of media monopolies.

These freedoms are generally respected. The most important subsequent legal qualifications were in 1994 when the Constitutional Court ruled that Article 232 of the criminal code was unconstitutional, thus removing the crime of libel from the criminal code and affirming the right of citizens/journalists to criticize public officials. In effect it meant that journalist harassment by means of libel lawsuits was no longer possible. This provision was never completely accepted by the government, and a 2000 law would permit journalists to be tried in criminal court if the journalist in question was continually charged with libel. This law has aroused much protest internally and by external media watchdogs. In 1996 a second landmark law affecting the media was passed. It was aimed specifically at the creation of commercial broadcast media and making the state public broadcasting system a separate public broadcasting service at more distance from the government. To date, the former has generally been successful while the latter has been only partially realized and is the cause of much discontent.

Finally, in 2000 the Constitutional Court removed another section of the criminal code forbidding ''deliberately spreading panic'' that in the past had been used against journalists.

It is worth noting that the Media Act (Act No. 1 of 1996 on Radio and Television services and passed by an 89 percent parliamentary majority in 1996) is one of the most problematic acts in Hungary. Reformation of this act has been on the political agenda many times since its passage with limited success. For example, Hungary is the only associate country of the European Union that has not closed negotiations with the European Union on the so-called ''audiovisual chapter.'' As a consequence, the Hungarian film industry lost access to large amounts of European Union subsidy money, as it was not eligible for support. Both the former government and the former opposition (who in 2002 reversed their positions in government) blame it on the other side. The former government (now opposition) says that the then opposition (now government) consistently voted against amendments to the media law making it impossible to close the negotiations. The opposition said that it had no real influence on the amendment as the members of the Board of Trustees consisted only of the leading government party, and that is why it voted against the amendments.

In 2002 the Board of Trustees was constituted with members from both sides. Thus the prognosis is more positive for the Media Act to be amended and harmonized with European Union requirements. The issue was raised in parliament again in the summer of 2002 for the fourth time in as many years. Principal changes will be the re-regulation of broadcasting and urban county seat requirements, the introduction of the concept of ''European program,'' the preference for programs made in Europe, stricter measures protecting youth (less violence on the screen) and the amendment of advertising rules.

There are laws codifying the privacy of individuals and these are generally respected. In Hungary the judiciary is independent under the constitution and a National Judicial Council nominates judicial appointments—other than the Supreme Court or the Constitutional court whose members are elected by parliament—at the local and county level. The Constitutional Court decides on all matters of legal interpretation and has been required to make decisions a number of times on matters affecting the media. All decisions emanating from this court have been seen as impartial and fair.

Advertising Expenditures — 1999

(Forint millions, in current prices)

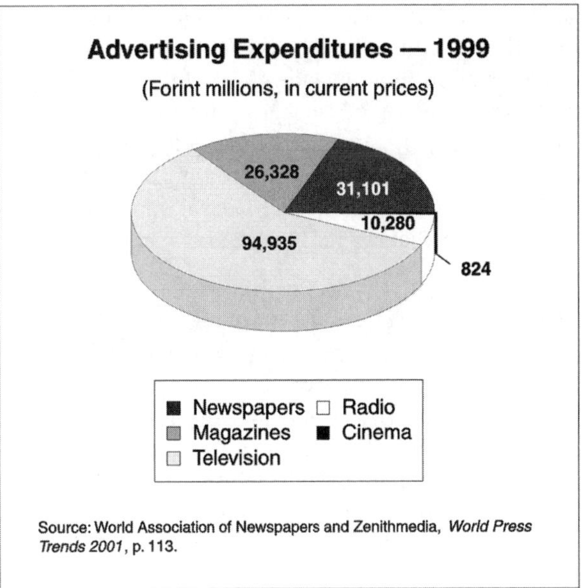

Source: World Association of Newspapers and Zenithmedia, *World Press Trends 2001*, p. 113.

CENSORSHIP

There is no government body that monitors the press, either via pre-publication censorship or modes of compliance. However in view of the general adversarial relationship between the media and the government, the International Journalists Network (IJNET) claims that information from government officials is not readily forthcoming. This is despite an existing Freedom of Information Act that provides for press access to government activities. As a result, the IJNET suggests that the media has had ''modest success'' in uncovering alleged government wrongdoing, malfeasance or illicit activities. In 1998 the government passed a law limiting information that could be revealed about official meetings, banning recordings or transcripts, and limiting information to the proposed agenda and meeting attendees.

Overall the subject of censorship is a delicate issue. For example, although there is no ''official'' censorship in Hungary, many impartial observers have noted the blatant manner in which administrations since independence (ruling from 1998 to 2002) have tried to influence the media. The most egregious example seems to have occurred during the general elections in Hungary in May 2002. The fourth general election since independence in 1989, this generally was agreed to be the most virulent campaign ever waged, with accusations of lying and hatred from both sides. In particular, public opinion polls were published in the government newspapers predicting a clear government majority and saying that FIDESZ (Fiatal Demokraták Szövetsége or Federation of Young Democrats), the incumbent party, would win again. But exactly the opposite happened. After the first round of elections, the MSZP (Magyar Szocialista Párt or Hungarian Socialist Party) had a slight advantage of only 1 percent. However, its ally, the Alliance of Free Democrats had a better position than the MIÉP (Magyar Igazság és Élet Pártja or Party of Hungarian Justice and Life), the only potential partner of the government. MIÉP is considered as an extremist right-wing party and it they had made a coalition with FIDESZ, Hungary probably would have reduced chances for European Union accession.

Between the two election rounds, then Prime Minister Viktor Orbán delivered a 40-minute speech filled with hatred, scaremongering and raising populist topics such as fear of the Communists returning, possible loss of homes and children, and religion being threatened and in danger of abolition. State television broadcast the speech in its entirety, and then rebroadcast it free of charge, not as a political advertisement (in which case it would have cost FIDESZ a fortune) but as a program of public interest.

Two days before the second round of the elections, a program defaming the MSZP candidate for prime minister was broadcast at peak evening viewing time, and on every program between the elections one could see only Orbán opening factories, talking to the people, shaking hands, crowds supporting him and so on, whereas there was hardly any news about the opposition parties campaign.

Despite this, Orbán and his FIDESZ party did not come out on top, and in 2002 Hungary elected a new government. One of the first priorities of the new government was to restructure the Board of Trustees, which governs the broadcast media. The recent board has representatives from both the government and the opposition. It is too early to judge the relationship between the new government and the media, but there is hope that it will try to exert less influence than the former government. It might also be assumed that given the left-wing bias in much of the Hungarian media, apart from *Magyar Nemzet* and a few periodicals, the media will be probably be more tolerant of the mistakes and faults of the new government.

Attitude toward Foreign Media

The Hungarian government has sometimes had a rocky relationship with the foreign media. While there are no restrictions on foreign journalists, no accreditation required and no violence against foreign media, the government is suspicious of the role foreign media plays, probably because of a perceived influence of foreign media on the process of European Union accession. In particular, the government in the past has accused foreign media of ''spreading lies about Hungary abroad,'' and in 2000 then Prime Minister Viktor Orbán took the unusual step of naming three foreign newspapers that he claimed were trying to discredit Hungary: the *New York Times, Die Zeit* and *Le Monde*, all amongst the most reputable newspapers in the world. Having said that, some commentators noted that the three are liberal in their orientation and hence their pronouncements were bound to rankle the conservative governments of that time.

As much of an irritant as foreign media are in Hungary, the oversight provided by other media watchers has proven to be effective—and mostly critical. The British Helsinki Human Rights Group, the Our Society Enlightenment Centre and domestic organizations such as the Openness Club have kept a constant commentary on press issues and freedoms in Hungary and are generally effective.

News Agencies

The official Hungarian news agency is MTI Co. (Magyar Távirati Iroda or Hungarian Telegraph Office). Founded in March 1881, then the news, reports and photographs of the MTI Co. since then have been the backbone of information released in the Hungarian press. The company has a staff of 400, including 19 county reporters and 14 reporters abroad, plus a number of photo reporters and journalists on 24-hour shifts, processing more than 10,000 pages of printed information daily. The fact that MTI produces some 700 news items per day shows how prolific it is in a country of only 10 million. As a result, there is extensive coverage of most issues in Hungary and those who use it generally see MTI Co. as fair and balanced. Almost all foreign news agencies are represented in Hungary, including Associated Press, Reuters, Interfax, Bloomberg and Dow Jones, as well as a number of European and Austrian newspapers that have offices in Budapest. The UK's *Guardian* and the *Independent* newspaper groups also have offices in Hungary.

In order to represent the Roma population more extensively and perhaps fairly, the Roma have their own news agency, the Roma Press center. In addition, Roma media television (Patrin TV News Magazine) and radio (''Roma 30 minutes'') as well as Roma Print Media (Lungo Drom, Amaro Drom, Rom Som) have offices in the larger communities outside Budapest that distribute Roma news.

Broadcast Media

Television broadcasts are in Hungarian. However, there is minority language print media, and state-run radio broadcasts two-hour programs daily in Romany, Slovak, Romanian, German, Croatian and Serbian. State-run television also carries a 30-minute program for every major minority group. This programming is written and produced by the minority groups. Moreover, those minority groups without daily programming have weekly or monthly programs in their language. These programs may be repeated during off-hours on weekends. In February 2001 the radio station Radio C, took to the national airwaves with a seven-year license to broadcast in Romany for the Roma population.

The broadcast media has been the one area of concern in the transition to a free press. In 1989 the government controlled all electronic media, but plans for dismantling this system were put in place early in the life of an independent Hungary. Early difficulties in the privatization and regulatory agencies were solved by the media law of 1996 that was one of the most influential instruments of change for media in the former Soviet Bloc. At the turn of the twenty-first century only three electronic media outlets were government owned: Radio Hungary, Hungarian Television and Duna TV. Moreover, it was estimated that state television was watched by less than 10 percent of the viewing audience in the year 2000.

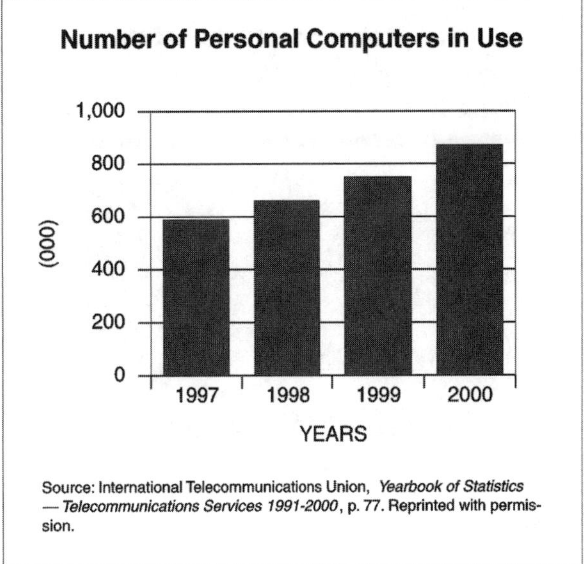

Source: International Telecommunications Union, *Yearbook of Statistics — Telecommunications Services 1991-2000*, p. 77. Reprinted with permission.

Notwithstanding this low market share, Hungarian television has been the focus of much of the discussion over the provision of a free press and the removal of government control and influence. Specifically, the state broadcast media have laid off a large number of journalists and administrative personnel, citing massive financial losses. This is almost certainly true but the government has been accused of selective layoffs, in particular firing journalists unsympathetic to the government. Moreover the Board of Trustees that governs executive positions, and ultimately programming, was weighted towards persons favoring the coalition government. Indeed, the board was incomplete with opposition seats remaining unfilled while they apparently fought amongst themselves for representation.

This infighting caused diplomats overseeing Hungary's accession into the European Union to strongly urge that this element of media affairs be resolved as it would hurt accession chances, a reprimand that is unusual and therefore indicative of a serious problem. Recently, Parliament and the Constitutional Court were embroiled in this dispute.

An example of the kind of interference in program content that has characterized Hungarian television and that has irked many Hungarians is a situation where one of Hungary's leading commercial televisions, RTL Klub, had a very popular weekly program called "Heti Hetes" (Weekly Seven), a talk show in which renowned Hungarian guest personalities (actors, writers, comedians) commented on the news of the week. It was among the two or three most popular and most watched shows on commercial television. Originally it was broadcast live, then after a few months it was filmed in a studio on Thursday night and broadcast Saturday night, starting quite late (about 10 p.m.). The program had a strong anti-government attitude but made fun of any politician, irrespective of his or her party. It was soon revealed in other media by the personalities that the best jokes were omitted from the program, notwithstanding their protests. A few weeks before the 2002 national elections, the RTL Klub announced it would cease broadcasting Heti Hetes for a few weeks until the election was over. There was a public uproar over this decision, and while the station announced that it would broadcast during the election, there was no Heti Hetes on the two Saturday nights before the elections.

Another example of government influence on the media was the case of the Hungarian writer, Péter Kende. He wrote a book called *A Viktor* about the former prime minister in which he exposed several negative characteristics of the former official. There was no formal government protest against the book nor was the writer sued, but the tax authority invaded his office the day after the book's release (the Hungarian tax authority has a history of use by the government to investigate and punish citizens) and a popular television program broadcast on state television in which Kende had an interest was taken off the air. Additionally, in many bookstores a few people were discovered wanting to buy all the books available, probably in an attempt to eliminate them from the market.

The potential for government interference in information dissemination is further exacerbated because Radio Hungary is the only radio station to cover the entire country and hence provides the opportunity for government to reach areas that television, through its limited appeal, does not. Radio Hungary also has come under much criticism as a government mouthpiece. In contrast, commercial radio stations have a limited local reach and provide little news.

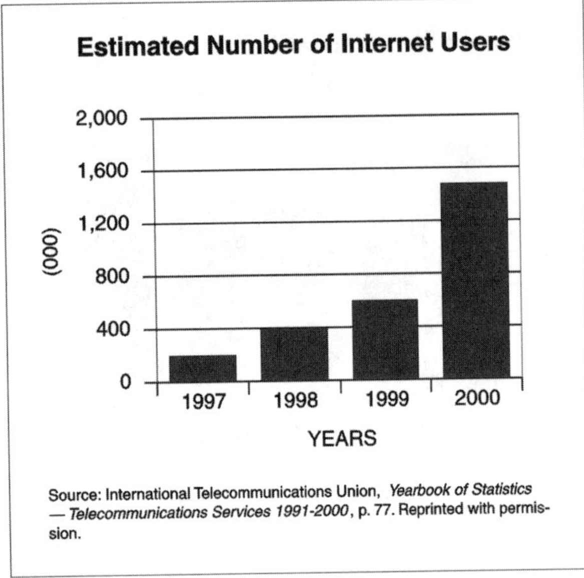

Source: International Telecommunications Union, *Yearbook of Statistics — Telecommunications Services 1991-2000*, p. 77. Reprinted with permission.

Notwithstanding these problems with a state media that controls only 10 percent of the total viewing market, private electronic media flourish to the extent that Western private consortia have opened up television channels in Hungary. However, in 2000 during a sale of local radio stations to further privatize the media, buyers with ties to Hungary's right were favored by the licensing body over bidders such as the BBC, Radio France and Germany's Deutsche Welle—an occurence leading some to comment that Hungary was not as committed to a free international press as it has claimed.

Electronic News Media

There are a large number of electronic news media sites that may be accessed by the 20 percent of Hungarian households connected to the Internet. Of significance, eMarketer believes that academic users make up more than half of the estimated Internet users, suggesting that among educated Hungarians, Internet news access may be an important trend. This is reinforced when one considers that the average Hungarian Internet user is usually between 20 and 25 years of age. Moreover, for those without Internet access, the market economy has created a large number of Internet cafes that provide access to the Internet for those who are not online at home. The major areas without Internet access are more rural, and often are areas of greater poverty. News flow is both voluminous and freely available both domestically and from international sources.

Hungary's online magazines total around 440, with some of the more popular subjects being technical and natural sciences, culture and arts, local and municipal issues, politics and public life, portals, and health and lifestyle. Overall, there is a wide variety of online magazines covering many areas of interest.

Education & Training

Since 1989 there has been dramatic growth in both the number of journalists graduating from higher education establishments and a large number of private institutions led by well-known journalists (for instance: Komlósi Stúdió) or founded by papers (*Népszabadság Stúdió*) that teach journalists. The problem is that most instructors teaching journalism in the institutions were trained during the socialist period and hence have little appreciation of the need and application of a free press and all that it entails. Thus graduating students are technically good, but lack an ability to discriminate in selection of media content or provide balance in their coverage. Moreover, they feel obliged to insert their own commentary (by liberal use of adjectives and long-winded impressions) while burying the facts.

The most prestigious journalist schools are in the communications departments in Budapest's Eötvös Lorand University and Szeged University (the latter also has a presence in Budapest). Smaller universities in the countryside have similar departments. In reality, working journalists indicate journalism schools have only one function and that is to assist students with the opportunity to practice journalism in a working editorial office for some months, and if they are good, they may have a job opportunity. Moreover, they add that with the knowledge of two Western languages a graduate of any discipline has a good chance to become a journalist regardless of writing ability.

Once employed, journalists have the benefit of ongoing training through a number of bilateral programs that bring in teachers from the BBC, major U.S. newspapers and the German media. The Independent Journalism Center in Budapest has been at the forefront of this training program, funded in the early days by the U.S. financier George Soros, who put significant financial resources into media development in his native Hungary.

Summary

The transformation of Hungary's media from a state-controlled, politically dominated institution in past years to a twenty-first-century competitive, uncensored market with the majority of print and electronic media in private hands—all in the space of 10 years—is a remarkable transformation. Moreover, the quality of journalism and programming is high. The only apparent impediment to a nearly flawless media role is the lingering tendency of government to see the press as an adversary, and thus try to mute its criticism. This situation is most apparent in the electronic media, and particularly in the regulation of state television companies. The regulating board has remained heavily politicized but the demand for change is strong, as shown in March 2001 when around 6,000 demonstrators marched in Budapest to demand an independent advisory board. The change of government in 2002 created the climate for such a change, and change must occur in order to facilitate Hungary's accession into the European Union.

SIGNIFICANT DATES

- 1989: Amendment to the Constitution of the Hungarian Republic, written in 1949, guarantees freedom of speech and freedom of the press under Act XX, Article 61.
- 1994: The Constitutional Court rules that Article 232 of the criminal code was unconstitutional, thus removing the crime of libel from the criminal code and affirming the right of citizens and journalists to criticize public officials.
- 1996: Passage of The Media Act (Act No. 1 of 1996 on Radio and Television services).
- March 2001: Around 6,000 demonstrators march in Budapest to demand an independent advisory board for state electronic broadcasting.

BIBLIOGRAPHY

Bajomi-Lázár, Péter. *Media Policy Proposals for Hungary*. The Center for Policy Studies, Open Society Institute. Available from http://www.osi.hu/ipf/pubs.html.

Country Ratings. Freedom House Media, 1999. Available from http://freedomhouse.org/pfs99/reports.html.

"Europa-Enlargement relations with Hungary." The European Commission. Available from http://europa.eu.int/comm/enlargement/hungary/index.htm.

"Hungary 2001: The Hungarian Media Today." British Helsinki Human Rights Group. Available from http://www.bhhrg.org.

"Hungary." In *World Press Freedom Review 2001*. Available from http://freemedia.at/wpfr/hungary.htm.

"Hungary." *U.S. Department of State Country Reports on Human Rights Practices*. U.S. Department of State, 2001. Available from http://www.state.gov.

"Hungary Press Overview." International Journalists Network. Available from http://www.ijnet.org/profile/CEENIS/Hungary/media.html.

—Richard W. Benfield and Dr. Zoltán Raffay

Iceland

Basic Data

Official Country Name:	Republic of Iceland
Region (Map name):	Europe
Population:	276,365
Language(s):	Icelandic
Literacy rate:	99.9%

Newspapers have been published in Iceland since 1848, when the weekly *Thjooolfur* brought domestic and foreign news to readers in Reykjavik. From that modest beginning, Iceland has grown to become one of the most voracious newspaper consuming nations in the world. Dozens of newspapers, most of them small weeklies, are published in Iceland, a remarkable occurrence given the fact that Iceland's population is only 280,000 and lives on the perimeter of an island the size of Kentucky.

The most prominent general interest daily newspapers in Iceland are *Morgunblaèiè* (Morning News) and its afternoon rival *DV*. *Morgunblaèiè*, a conservative morning paper with a circulation of 50,000 and an average size of 36 pages, is both the oldest and the largest. *DV*, the second largest newspaper in Iceland, is a liberal tabloid with a circulation of 21,000 and an average size of 20 pages.

The first successful attempt to publish a daily newspaper in Iceland was in 1910 when *Vísir* was founded. Three years later *Morgunblaèiè* was begun. Unlike most Icelandic periodicals of the day, these newspapers emphasized impartiality, seeing their primary function as publishing news rather than polemics. But the development of the powerful four-party system enveloped all newspapers, including *Vísir* and *Morgunblaèiè*, from the 1920s until the 1970s. Not until instability among the political parties combined with privatization in the late 1960s and early 1970s were daily newspapers freed from party control and encouraged to become independent and professional.

The value of professionalism for Icelandic journalists can be traced to the founding of the Union of Icelandic Journalists (BÍ) in 1942. Because it was born during the heyday of the party press, BÍ's early emphasis was on status, privilege, and collective bargaining rather than professionalism. But as the party system declined, BÍ began to devote time to seminars and conferences on the improvement of journalistic practices. The changeover to a more professional standard of journalism is evident in the ''Rules of Ethics in Journalism,'' a code enforced by BÍ since 1988. It is also evident in the education in journalism and mass communication offered by the University of Iceland.

Radio and television are major sources of news in Iceland. The state-owned Icelandic National Broadcasting Service (RUV) began radio broadcasts in 1930. According to the Broadcasting Act, the RUV is obligated to promote Icelandic language and culture and to honor democratic rules, human rights, and freedom of expression. RUV's Channel 1 broadcasts classical music and documentaries; Channel 2 broadcasts pop music and current affairs. RUV's short-wave station keeps Icelandic sailors current on happenings at home.

Since 1966 RUV has also operated a television station. Its broadcast day begins and ends with news. RUV participates in satellite program exchanges with the Eurovision network and with Nordvision, a union of public television broadcasters. News and information comprise a significant portion of RUV's programming.

Since 1985 the government of Iceland has licensed private broadcasting to complement RUV's public offerings. The result has been an expansion of broadcasting alternatives, much of which is owned by the company Finn Midill.

The highly literate Icelanders also support a large and diverse magazine and book publishing industry. Icelandic periodicals number in the hundreds, and some 1,600 book titles are published every year in Iceland. Among the largest magazine and book publishers are the privately owned Edda and Frodi and the state-run National Centre for Educational Materials. Internet publishing proliferates as well, serving an Icelandic population, 80 percent of whom either have access to or own a computer connected to the Internet.

Many Icelanders worry that the growing influence of English may diminish the preponderance of Icelandic. They cite the fact that two-thirds of television programs broadcast in Iceland are imported, mostly from the United States, and the sale of books written in English is growing. However, most Icelandic newspapers and magazines, as well as their Web sites, are written in Icelandic.

Bibliography

Jeppessen, Karl, and Dennis Moss. "Educational Television in Iceland: The Availability and Utilization of Video Resources in Schools." *Journal of Educational Television.* 16:1 (1990).

Vilhjálmsson, Páll. "Press History in Iceland: A Study of the Development of Independent Journalism in the Icelandic Daily Press." M.A. thesis. University of Minnesota, 1993.

—John P. Ferré

India

Basic Data

Official Country Name:	Republic of India
Region (Map name):	East & South Asia
Population:	1,029,991,145
Language(s):	English, Bengali, Teluga, Marathi
Literacy rate:	52.0%
Area:	3,287,590 sq km
GDP:	456,990 (US$ millions)
Number of Daily Newspapers:	398
Total Circulation:	30,772,000
Circulation per 1,000:	50
Number of Nondaily Newspapers:	98
Total Circulation:	7,774,000
Circulation per 1,000:	13
Total Newspaper Ad Receipts:	35,624 (Rupees millions)
As % of All Ad Expenditures:	50.40
Number of Television Stations:	562
Number of Television Sets:	63,000,000
Television Sets per 1,000:	61.2
Number of Cable Subscribers:	39,112,150
Cable Subscribers per 1,000:	38.5
Number of Radio Stations:	312
Number of Radio Receivers:	116,000,000
Radio Receivers per 1,000:	112.6
Number of Individuals with Computers:	4,600,000
Computers per 1,000:	4.5
Number of Individuals with Internet Access:	5,000,000
Internet Access per 1,000:	4.9

Background & General Characteristics

India is the world's largest democracy. Its mass media culture, a system that has evolved over centuries, is comprised of a complex framework. Modernization has transformed this into a communications network that sustains the pulse of a democracy of about 1.1 billion people. India's newspaper evolution is nearly unmatched in world press history. India's newspaper industry and its Westernization—or *mondialisation* as French would call it—go hand in hand. India's press is a metaphor for its advancement in the globalized world.

The printing press preceded the advent of printed news in India by about 100 years. It was in 1674 that the first printing apparatus was established in Bombay followed by Madras in 1772. India's first newspaper, *Calcutta General Advertise*, also known as the *Hicky's*

Bengal Gazette was established in January 1780, and the first Hindi daily, *Samachar Sudha Varshan*, began in 1854. The evolution of the Indian media since has been fraught with developmental difficulties; illiteracy, colonial constraints and repression, poverty, and apathy thwart interest in news and media. Within this framework, it is instructive to examine India's press in two broad analytical sections: pre-colonial times and the colonial, independent press (which may, again be classified into two: preceding and following the Emergency rule imposed by Indira Gandhi's government in 1975). The post-Emergency phase, which continues at the present, may be the third independent phase of India's newspaper revolution (Jeffrey).

The Nature of the Audience While a majority of the poor working people in rural and urban areas still remain oppressed and even illiterate, a significant proportion of people—roughly about 52 percent of the population over 15 years of age were recorded as being able to read and write. That breaks down to 65.5 percent of males and an estimate of 37.7 percent of females. After the liberalization of the economy, the growth of industry, and a rise in literacy, the post-Emergency boom rekindled the world's largest middle class in news, politics, and consumerism. Since private enterprise began to sustain and pay off, mass communications picked up as a growth industry.

In 1976, the Registrar of Newspapers for India had recorded 875 papers; in 1995 there were 4,453. Robin Jeffrey comments:

> ''Newspapers did not expand simply because the technology was available to make Indian scripts live as they had not been able to live before. Nor did newspaper grow simply because more people knew how to read and write. They grew because entrepreneurs detected a growing hunger for information among ever-widening sections of India's people, who were potential consumers as well as newspaper readers. A race began to reach this audience advertising avenues were the prizes and these would come largely to newspapers that could convince advertisers that they had more readers than their rivals. Readers, meanwhile, were saying implicitly: 'We will read newspapers that tell us about ourselves and reflect our concerns.'' (48)

Common contenders for readership and advertising are: the *National Herald,* the *Hindustan Times, Time, Illustrated Weekly, e Pioneer,* and *Filmfare.*

Historical Traditions ''Newspaper history in India is inextricably tangled with political history,'' wrote A. E. Charlton (Wolseley 3). James Augustus Hicky was the founder of India's first newspaper, the *Calcutta General Advertiser* also known as *Hicky's Bengal Gazette*, in 1780. Soon other newspapers came into existence in Calcutta and Madras: the *Calcutta Gazette*, the *Bengal Journal,* the *Oriental Magazine*, the *Madras Courier* and the *Indian Gazette*. While the *India Gazette* enjoyed governmental patronage including free postal circulation and advertisements, *Hicky's Bengal Gazette* earned the rulers' wrath due to its criticism of the government. In November 1780 its circulation was halted by government decree. Hicky protested against this arbitrary harassment without avail, and was imprisoned. The *Bengal Gazette* and the *India Gazette* were followed by the *Calcutta Gazette* which subsequently became the government's ''medium for making its general orders'' (Sankhdher 24-32).

The Bombay Herald, *The Statesmen* in Calcutta and the *Madras Mail* and *The Hindu*, along with many other rivals in Madras represented the metropolitan voice of India and its people. While *Statesman* voiced the English rulers' voice, *The Hindu* became the beacon of patriotism in the South. *The Hindu* was founded in Madras as a counter to the *Madras Mail.*

Patriotic movements grew in proportion with the colonial ruthlessness, and a vehicle of information dissemination became a tool for freedom struggle. In the struggle for freedom, journalists in the twentieth century performed a dual role as professionals and nationalists. Indeed many national leaders, from Gandhi to Vajpayee, were journalists as well. Calcutta, Madras, Bombay and Delhi were four main centers of urban renaissance which nourished news in India. It was only during and after the seventies, especially after Indira Gandhi's defeat in 1977, that regional language newspapers became prevalent.

There were nationalist echoes from other linguistic regional provinces. Bengal, Gujarat, Tamil, Karalla, Punjab and Uttar Pradesh produced dailies in regional languages. Hindi and Urdu were largely instrumental in voicing the viewpoints and aspirations of both Hindus and Muslims of the Northern provinces. As communalism and religious intolerance increased before and after partition, Urdu remained primarily the language of Muslims, as Pakistan chose this language as its lingua franca. After partition, the cause of Urdu and its newspapers, suffered a setback as Hindu reactionaries began to recognize the association of Urdu with Islam and Pakistan.

Diversity and the Language Press Naresh Khanna summarizes the trends in circulatory growth and decline varied in regional language papers during 1998-2000: In the three-year period from 1998-2000, circulation of dailies in the country increased marginally from 58.37 to 59.13 million copies. This represents a growth of 1.3 percent on the basis of data published by the Registrar of Newspapers for India in its annual reports. In this time, two distinct groups of newspapers emerge — the first including five languages that have collectively grown in

Top Ten Daily Newspapers
(2000)

	Circulation
Times of India	1,687,000
Malayala Manorama	1,162,000
Aj	982,000
Gujarat Samachar	956,000
Eenadu	776,000
Mathrubhumi	773,000
Bhaskar	768,000
Punjab Kesari	754,000
Jagran	751,000
The Hindu	720,000

Source: World Association of Newspapers and Zenithmedia, *World Press Trends 2001*, p. 117.

circulation by a healthy 5.65 percent and representing a combined circulation of 43.35 million copies. Amongst these newspapers, those in Malayalam and Bengali grew fastest at 12.9 percent and 12.8 percent respectively, while Hindi dailies grew by 5 percent and English dailies by 4.7 percent over the three-year period. Although Marathi newspapers increased circulation by 2.75 percent over the three years it would seem that they are in danger of falling out of this group and perhaps entering the phase of stagnation and circulation decline (Khanna 2002).

The second group of stagnating and declining circulations includes newspapers in seven languages with a combined circulation of 14.8 million copies in 2000. These dailies lost almost 1.8 million copies (10.62 percent) of their combined circulation in the last three years. Daily newspaper circulation plummeted most dramatically in Telugu, which fell from 2.28 million to 1.68 million copies, a fall of more than 26 percent. Urdu newspaper circulation fell by more than 12 percent and Tamil dailies' circulation declined by 10.8 percent with circulation of Gujarati dailies falling by 10.5 percent. Over the same period circulations of Oriya dailies declined by 2.8 percent and that of Punjabi dailies by 3.2 percent. Although over the three years Kannada newspapers show an insignificant fall in circulation they seem to have entered a period of stagnation and decline of their own. It would seem that in spite of new editions being added by Hindi, English, Malayalam and Bengali dailies, the print media is losing its dominance of advertising market share to television, radio and outdoor media (Khanna 2002).

ECONOMIC FRAMEWORK

India's language newspapers enjoy a relatively new entrepreneurial prowess. A mutually convenient relationship between the owners and capitalists keeps a financial balance between local/regional and national spheres in both private and public sectors. "Like coral in a reef, newspapers grew and died in a process inseparable from the creation of a 'public sphere' in the classical liberal sense. Individual proprietors sometimes brought to their newspapers a crusader's zeal for a particular cause or a diehard's loathing for a rival" (Jeffrey 105). The Second Press Commission in 1982 tried to liberate the press from the monopoly houses. In 1995 the Audit Bureau of Circulations had 165 newspapers as members, with a combined circulation of about 16 million copies a day. The top ten newspapers control roughly 50 percent of daily circulations in all languages. Bennett Coleman and the Indian Express own roughly 20 percent of daily circulations (Jeffrey 108).

While capitalists sustained national newspapers, the big houses, Dalmias, Jains, Goenka et al., monopolized and corrupted free journalism. The family and caste controlled small newspapers regionally maintain their freedom from big monopolies, thriving on their loyal supporters in north and south India. Diversity of ownership is reflective of cultural variation in India's multilingual landscape. Twenty-one newspapers control two-thirds of all circulations.

PRESS LAWS

Much of India's legal framework is built upon its colonial legacy. Legal statutes and regulations have been undergoing certain changes as India's democracy grows. India's freedom came at a high cost. The country was divided. India's border conflicts with two hostile neighbors, which forced at least three large scale wars, eclipsed other political issues. The democratic process, corrupted by criminals, unscrupulous bureaucrats and politicians, created a social climate that widened social and economic inequality.

Freedom of speech and expression is a constitutionally guaranteed fundamental right of the Indian people. Article 19 (1; a) ensures the implicit freedom but Article 19 (2) qualifies this in explicit terms. The Parliamentary Proceedings (protection of Publication) Act of 1977 and the Prevention of Publication of Objectionable Matter (Repeal Act) of 1977 further reinforce and restrict these freedoms. While constitutional guarantees ensure freedom of the press and expression, press and media are obligated by a self-regulatory system of ethics that protect individuals and organizations from libelous behavior. "Freedom of the press is an institutional freedom," wrote Sachin Sen (19). The Press Council Bill of 1956, introduced in the Indian parliament, stipulated the establishment of the Press Council of India representing working journalists, the newspaper management, literary bodies and the Parliament. The Indian Press commission

Daily and Non-Daily Newspaper Titles and Circulation Figures

	1996	1997	1998	1999	2000
Number of Daily Newspapers	399	404	402	392	398
Circulation of Dailies (000)	23,899	24,917	26,538	10,587	30,772
Number of Non-Daily Newspapers	107	113	109	102	98
Circulation of Non-Dailies (000)	8,984	8,305	8,396	7,594	7,774

Source: World Association of Newspapers and Zenithmedia, *World Press Trends 2001*, pp. 8, 10, 17, 19.

accepted the following postulate: "Democratic society lives and grows by accepting ideas, by experimenting with them, and where necessary, rejecting them. . .The Press is a responsible part of a democratic society" (quoted by Sen 42).

While The Central Press Accreditation Committee seeks to ensure quality and self-renewal, The Press Council of India was established in 1966 to uphold editorial autonomy. Restrictions on free speech were imposed after Indira Gandhi's infamous Emergency rule. The Press Council of India was abolished after editor George Verghese's criticisms of the Indira government. The Ministry of Information and Broadcasting carefully regulates the press and its liberties. The Maintenance of Internal Security Act (MISA) was enforced to intimidate reputedly autonomous newspapers in the seventies. The Press Council, resurrected in 1979, has no legal standing to impose penalties. The Indian press, generally believed as "managed," is a self-restrained institution generally reluctant to take on the governmental policies. All India Radio (AIR) and its management exemplify this "managed" system.

The Registrar of Newspapers The Registrar of Indian newspapers, among these official and professional agencies, regulates and records the status of newspapers. Electronic news, Web sites, magazines and house publications, and a number of professional organizations (like Editors Guild of India, Indian Language Newspapers' Association, and All India Newspapers Editors' Conference etc.) enrich the self-renewal process of the news enterprise. Educational and training programs are gaining importance as professionalization of specialized fields is a prioritized activity under the privatization process.

The Office of the Registrar The Office of the Registrar of Newspapers for India, popularly known as RNI came into being on July 1, 1956, on the recommendation of the First Press Commission in 1953 and by amending the Press and Registration of Books Act (PRB Act) 1867. The functions of RNI involve both statutory and non-statutory functions.

Statutory Functions The RNI compiles and maintains a register of newspapers containing particulars about all the newspapers published in the country; it issues certificates of registration to the newspapers published under valid declaration. It scrutinizes and analyzes annual statements sent by the publishers of newspapers every year under Section 19-D of the Press and Registration of Books Act containing information on circulation, ownership, etc. The RNI informs the District Magistrates about availability of titles to intending publishers for filing declaration and ensures that newspapers are published in accordance with the provisions of the Press and Registration of Books Acts. It verifies under Section 19-F of the PRB Act of circulation claims, furnished by the publishers in their Annual Statements and Preparation and submission to the Government on or before September 30 each year, a report containing all available information and statistics about the press in India with particular reference to the emerging trends in circulation and in the direction of common ownership units.

Non-Statutory Functions Non-statutory functions of the RNI include the formulation of a Newsprint Allocation Policy—guidelines and the ability to issue Eligibility Certificates to the newspapers to enable them to import newsprint and to procure indigenous newsprint. The RNI assesses and certifies the essential needs and requirements of newspaper establishments to import printing and composing machinery and allied materials.

From April 1998 to February 1999, RNI scrutinized 18,459 applications for availability of titles, of which 7,738 titles were found available for verification, while in the remaining applications, titles were not found available. During the same period, 2,693 newspapers/periodicals were issued Certificates of Registration (2,145 fresh CRs and 548 revised CRs) and circulation claims of 1536 newspapers/periodicals were assessed.

Newsprint Until 1994-95, newsprint allocation was regulated by the Newsprint Control Order (1962) and the Newsprint Import Policy announced by the government every year. Newspapers were issued Entitlement Certificates for importation and purchase from the scheduled in-

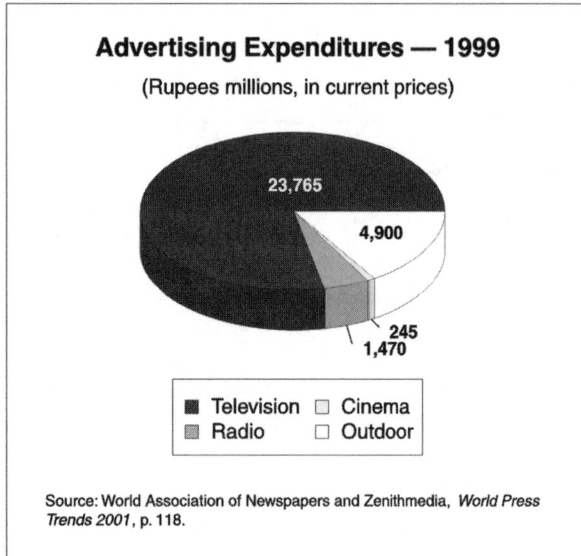

Source: World Association of Newspapers and Zenithmedia, *World Press Trends 2001*, p. 118.

digenous newsprint mills. However, Newsprint Policy is modified every year depending upon the import policy of the government. Newsprint has been placed under 'Open General License' with effect from May 1, 1995, and all types of newsprint became importable by all persons without any restriction. Under the latest newsprint policy/ guidelines for the import of newsprint issued by the Ministry of Information and Broadcasting, authentication of certificate of registration is done by the Registrar of Newspapers for India for import of newsprint, on submission of a formal application and necessary documentary evidence.

De-Blocking of Titles For the first time in the history of RNI, a massive work of de-blocking 200,000 titles was undertaken. As per the decision, all such titles of newspapers were certified till December 31, 1995, and those publications which had not registered with RNI have been de-blocked.

The work of entering registered titles has been completed and the lists have been dispatched to state governments. Nearly 150,000 of unused titles have become available for allocation to other newspapers from January 1, 1999.

Printing Machinery The RNI is the sponsoring authority for the import of printing machinery and allied materials at the concessional rate of custom duty available to the newspapers. During April 1998-February 1999, applications of four newspaper establishments were recommended for import of printing machinery and allied equipment.

Censorship

Even though India is committed to the freedom of the press, censorship is not unknown to the media. With increased privatization and entrepreneurial advancements, colonial and bureaucratic censorship no longer exists. However, the nexus of criminal politics and unethical monopolies continue to threaten the freedom of press.

Nehru famously said: "I would rather have a completely free press with all the dangers involved in the wrong use of that freedom than a suppressed or regulated press" (quoted by Kamath 272). After 1977 people's interest and involvement in regional and national affairs increased dramatically. This development helped promote the dualism of India's patriotic passions marked by linguistic chauvinism and national unity.

State-Press Relations

Public Grievances A Public Grievances Cell is functioning in the Main Secretariat of the Ministry headed by the Joint Secretary (Policy). In order to tone up the Grievance Redressal System of the Ministry, its time limits have been fixed for completion of various activities coming under the purview of the grievance redressal mechanism. Grievance Officers have been appointed in all the subordinate organizations of the Ministry who have been made responsible for timely redress of grievances. Keeping in view the need for effective monitoring of the progress in the grievance redressal, the Ministry has developed a computerized Grievance Monitoring System. The grievances received in the Ministry are sent to the concerned Grievance Officer in the attached subordinate offices of the Ministry. Periodical review meetings are held in the Ministry to ensure that the grievances are processed within a stipulated time limit.

Attitude Toward Foreign Media

India is a founding member of the United Nations Educational, Scientific, and Cultural Organization (UNESCO). UNESCO's main goal is to promote international cooperation in the field of education, science and technology, social sciences, culture and mass communication. In order to promote the communication capabilities of developing countries. The 21st Session of the General Conference of UNESCO in 1981 approved the establishment of an International Program for the Development of Communication (IPDC). India played a significant role in its inception and has been a member of the Inter-governmental Council (IGC) and also of the IPDC Bureau. India has played a leading role in its activities over the years. Being one of the founding members of IPDC, this Ministry has been a representative at the meetings of the General Conference of UNESCO and Bureau Session of IPDC.

India participated in the First South Asian Association for Regional Cooperarion (SAARC) Information Ministers Meeting held in Dhaka (Bangladesh) in 1998. The Meeting discussed the need for greater cooperation among media personnel, cooperation among news agencies, improving the programs under SAARC Audio Visual Exchange, and taking steps to project SAARC outside the region.

More indications of India's support of international cooperation is its participaton in the meeting of Asia-Pacific Regional Experts on the Legal Framework for Cyberspace from 8 to 10 September 1998 and the Third Regulatory Round Table for the Asia and the Pacific at Seoul from 14 to 16 September 1998 for finalizing the report on Trans-border Satellite Broadcasting.

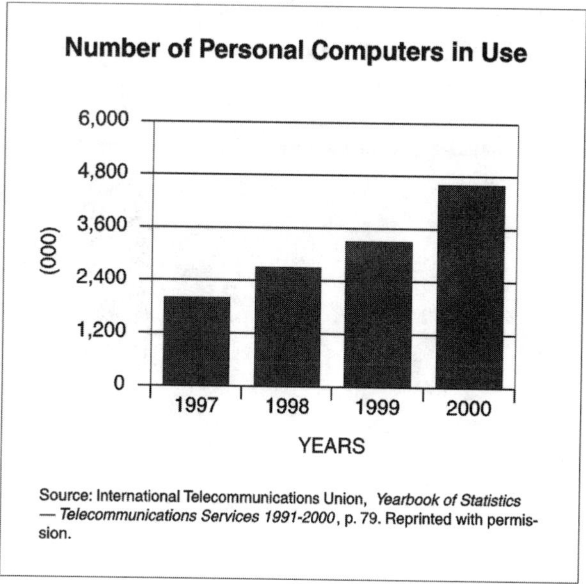

Source: International Telecommunications Union, *Yearbook of Statistics — Telecommunications Services 1991-2000*, p. 79. Reprinted with permission.

News Agencies

News agencies provide regularity and authenticity to news. K.C. Roy is credited with establishing the first Indian news agency, which became The Associated Press of India (API). However, it soon became a British-controlled agency unwilling to report about the national freedom movement. The Free Press of India News Agency came into existence under the management of S. Sadanad who had served Reuters. The United Press of India, The Orient Press, The Globe News Agency, The NAFEN News Agency, The United News of India and a number of syndicates later came to serve the news business.

The Non-aligned News Agencies Pool (NANAP), formally constituted in 1976 for the purpose of correcting imbalances in the global flow of information, is an arrangement for exchange of news and information among the national news agencies of non-aligned countries, including Asia, Africa, Europe and Latin America. Its affairs are managed by a coordinating committee elected for a term of three years. India is at present a member of the coordinating committee. The cost of running the pool is met by the participating members. The Press Trust (PTI) continued to operate the India News Pool Desk (INDP) of the NANAP on behalf of the government of India. India continued to contribute substantially to the daily news file of the Pool Network. The reception of news into the Pool Desk during the year 1998-99 has been in the range of 20,000 words per day. INDP's own contribution to the Pool partners during the year has averaged 7,000 words per day.

The organization and structure of Indian news agencies has been undergoing a controversial transformation for quite sometime. This represents a mutual mistrust between privately owned news agencies and governmental structures. Their autonomy, believed to be crucial for objectivity and fairness, is based on their role as cooperatives and non-profit groups. News agencies in general are discouraged from taking any governmental favors. There is nothing in the Indian constitution, however, that can prevent government to nationalize its news agencies. There are four dominant news agencies in India: The Press Trust of India (PTI); the United News of India (UNI); the Hindustan Samachar (HS); and Samachar Bhatia (SB).

Broadcast Media

The Ministry of Information & Broadcasting, through the mass communication media of radio, television, films, the press, publications, advertising and traditional modes of dance and drama, plays a significant part in helping the people to have access to information. It fosters the dissemination of knowledge and entertainment in all sectors of society, striking a careful balance between public interest and commercial needs in its delivery of services. The Ministry of Information & Broadcasting is the highest body for formulation and administration of the rules, regulations and laws relating to information, broadcasting, the press and films. The ministry is responsible for international cooperation in the field of mass media, films and broadcasting, and interacts with its foreign counterparts on behalf of Government of India. The mandate of the Ministry of Information & Broadcasting is to provide:

- News Services through All India Radio (AIR) and Doordarshan (DD) for the people
- Development of broadcasting and television
- Import and export of films
- Development and promotion of film industry
- Organization of film festivals and cultural exchanges

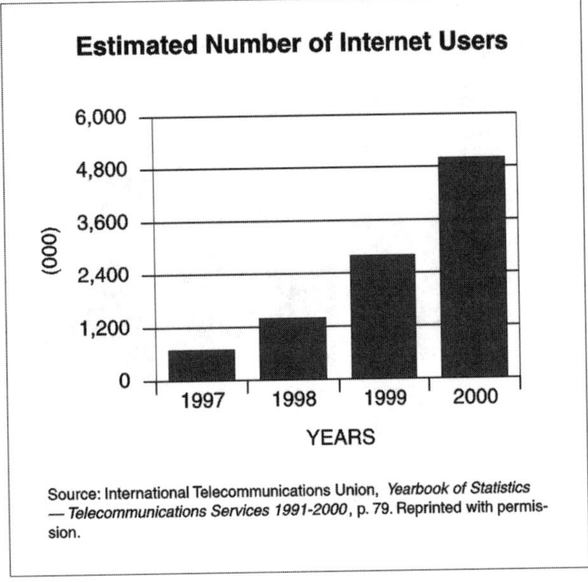

Source: International Telecommunications Union, *Yearbook of Statistics — Telecommunications Services 1991-2000*, p. 79. Reprinted with permission.

- Advertisement and visual publicity on behalf of the Government of India
- Handling of press relations to present the policies of Government of India and to seek feedback on government policies
- Administration of the Press and Registration of Books Act of 1867 in respect of newspapers
- Dissemination of information about India within and outside the country through publications on matters of national importance
- Research, reference, and training to assist the media units of the Ministry to meet their responsibilities
- Use of interpersonal communication and traditional folk art forms for information/ publicity campaigns on public interest issues
- International co-operation in the field of information and mass media

The main Secretariat of the Ministry is divided into three wings: the information wing, the broadcasting wing, and the film wing. The media units engaged in press and publicity activities include:

- Press: 1) Press Information Bureau; 2) Photo Division; 3) Research Reference & Training Division; 4) Publications Division
- Publicity: 5) Directorate of Advertising and Visual Publicity; 6) Directorate of Field Publicity; 7) Song and Drama Division
- Regulation of the Press: 8) Registrar of Newspapers for India; 9) Press Council of India
- Training: 10) Indian Institute of Mass Communication (Government of India, 2002)

ELECTRONIC NEWS MEDIA

Most Indian newspapers, magazines, and media outlets are easily accessible through the Internet. Internet Public Library (IPL) is a concise Internet source for information on Indian newspapers. The Onlinenewspapers.com Web site lists about 120 online newspapers for India with access to each of those papers for reading.

The official Web site for the Library of Congress in New Delhi is also accessible on the Internet, where e-mail contact information is provided. This directory is published biennially. The directory includes newspapers published in India, the name and language of the newspapers, circulation, frequency of publication, and names and addresses for the publishers of each paper. Paper status is also included.

Internet Public Library's list of India's contemporary newspapers exists to enable instant access to existing information resources. Among them in 2002 were 62 Indian newspapers that were available online.

EDUCATION & TRAINING

The first diploma in Journalism was offered at Aligarh Muslim University in 1938 by the late Sir shah Muhammad Sulaiman, a Judge in India (Wolseley 224). Later on, after partition, universities in Punjab, Madras, Delhi, Calcutta, Mysore, Nagpur, and Osmania offered courses at undergraduate levels. Professional education in India is largely a need-based enterprise. Journalists and other mass communicators can perform without specialized training and skills, and can succeed without advanced degrees.

SUMMARY

The media in India represents a confluence of paradoxes: tradition and modernity; anarchy and order; diversity and unity; conflict and cooperation; news and views; feudalism and democracy; the free market and monopoly.

Economic realities and relationships between press, television and those who own these engines of control and change will eventually determine the future of India's communication culture. India's complex cultural mosaic, especially linguistic and communal, strengthens its diversity. The media and press continue to play a dominant role in deconstructing the diversity discourse that sometimes flares up in explosive situations.

Capitalism, the press, and public hunger for news promote a culture of media that is fast replacing the legacy of a feudal/colonial system. While corporatization and state regulations can muffle free expression, the force of public interest and the market economy strive for greater freedom and openness. Both politics and capitalism thrive on the liberties of a democratic system that continues to evolve into a functional hybrid of chaos and order.

SIGNIFICANT DATES

- 1990: Nikhil Wagle publishes a Mumbai evening tabloid *Hamara Mahanagar*, 'Our great city' (January)
- 1991: *Mahanagar* is vandalized by a Shiva Sena gang
- 1995: The politician-proprietor of a Telgu daily embroiled in controversy was murdered, allegedly by the People's War Group (December)
- 1997: *Dainik Bhaskar*, the Bhopal-based Hindi daily opened a Jaipur edition, self-acclaimed its status as ''India's Fastest Growing Newspaper''

BIBLIOGRAPHY

Bhaskar, B.R.P. ''Understanding the Language Press.'' *Frontline,* 2 March 2001.

Bhattacharjee, Arun. *The Indian Press: Profession to Industry*. Delhi: Vikas Publications, 1972.

Government of India. *Ministry of Information and Broadcasting: Annual Report 2000-2001.* Available from http://www.mib.nic.in.

Hamill, Pete. *News Is a Verb*. New York: The Ballantine Publishing Group, 1998.

Jeffrey, Robin. *India's Newspaper Revolution*. New York: St. Martin's Press, 2000.

Joseph, Ammu, and Kalpana Sharma. *Whose News? The Media and Women's Issues*. New Delhi: Sage Publications, 1994.

Kamath, M.V. *Professional Journalism*. New Delhi: Vikas Publishing House, 1980.

Khanna, Naresh. ''Newspaper circulations in India 1998-2000.'' New Delhi, April 2002.

Mohan, B. *Democracies of Unfreedom: The United States of America and India*. Westport, CT: Praeger, 1996.

Murthy, N. Krishna. *Indian Journalism*. Mysore: Prasaranga, University of Mysore, 1966.

India: A *Wounded Civilization*. London: Penguin Books, 1987.

Naipaul, V.S. *India: A Million Mutinies Now*. London: Minerva, 1990.

Natrajan, S. *A History of Press in India*. New York: Asia Publishing House, 1962.

Nehru, Jawaharlal. *The Discovery of India*. New Delhi: Oxford University Press, 1982.

Parthasarthy, Rangaswami. *Memoirs of a News Editor: Thirty Years With The Hindu*. Calcutta: Naya Prokash, 1980.

Rau, M. Chalapathi. *Journalism and Politics*. New Delhi: Vikas Publishing House, 1984.

Sankhdher, B.M. *Press, Politics, and Public Opinion in India: Dynamics of Modernization and Social Transformation*. New Delhi: Deep & Deep Publication, 1984.

Segel, Ronald. *The Crisis of India*. Harmondsworth: Penguin, 1965.

Wolseley, Roland E. Ed. *Journalism in Modern India*. Bombay: Asia Publishing House, 1953.

—Brij Mohan

INDONESIA

BASIC DATA

Official Country Name:	Republic of Indonesia
Region (Map name):	Southeast Asia
Population:	228,437,870
Language(s):	Bahasa Indonesia, English, Dutch
Literacy rate:	83.8%
Area:	1,919,440 sq km
GDP:	153,255 (US$ millions)
Number of Daily Newspapers:	172
Total Circulation:	4,782,000
Circulation per 1,000:	36
Number of Nondaily Newspapers:	425
Total Circulation:	7,758,000
Circulation per 1,000:	59
Total Newspaper Ad Receipts:	2,100,000 (Rupiah millions)
As % of All Ad Expenditures:	25.00
Number of Television Stations:	41
Number of Television Sets:	13,750,000
Television Sets per 1,000:	60.2
Number of Cable Subscribers:	42,080
Cable Subscribers per 1,000:	0.2

Number of Satellite Subscribers:	3,900,000
Satellite Subscribers per 1,000:	17.1
Number of Radio Stations:	803
Number of Radio Receivers:	31,500,000
Radio Receivers per 1,000:	137.9
Number of Individuals with Computers:	2,100,000
Computers per 1,000:	9.2
Number of Individuals with Internet Access:	2,000,000
Internet Access per 1,000:	8.8

BACKGROUND & GENERAL CHARACTERISTICS

As of the early 2000s, the Republic of Indonesia (RI) was a fascinating site at which to study the current status of the press in a diverse, dynamic, rapidly urbanizing, and populous nation: the interplay of press and political forces, the changing economy, and, at the beginning of the twenty-first century, a vast change in the role of, expectations for, and situation of the press.

Thirty years ago Indonesia had to import its newsprint; heavily taxed, it was a drain on scarce foreign currency, driving up the price of newspapers. As of 2002 some of the world's leading pulp and paper companies exported paper from Indonesia. Until the beginning of what is known as the *reformasi* (reformation) era, beginning with the resignation of President Suharto in 1998, the strong arm of the government was seen to be the greatest restriction on the press. In 2002, however, the perceived threat was from a different source. In 2001 and 2002, violence toward and intimidation of the press were being carried out by thugs and mobs in reaction to what was being published.

Local newspapers, both urban and small city presses, had long been an accessible forum for young writers, including university students, who published their own short stories and feature articles which had been researched from the foreign press. Unlike most western newspapers, Indonesian newspapers regularly published short fiction. Moreover, although Indonesian culture was frequently characterized as a predominately oral culture, more attuned to the sounds of *wayang* (puppet theatre), a *becak* (pedicab) driver in Yogyakarta was as likely to be seen sitting in his vehicle reading the local newspaper as using it for an impromptu umbrella. He might have, in fact, gone with a half-dozen of his fellow drivers to regularly take a newspaper. Newspapers had been and remained an important part of daily life for many; the printed word was infused with mystique and authority.

In one of Indonesia's great novels, a journalist is featured as the leading character. *This Earth of Mankind*, by Pramoedya Ananta Toer, is based, along with three other novels in the series, on the life of a pioneer Indonesian journalist, Tirto Adi Suryo. Tirto Adi Suryo, a major figure of Indonesian national awakening, helped to determine the language framework of the new nation. Pramoedya first told the story to his fellow prisoners during his many years of detention, then he wrote it down in secret.

The Land and People In the early 2000s, Indonesia was the fourth largest nation in the world with a population of more than 225 million. Strung along the equator, the country is a collection of islands and peoples. Abundant in natural resources and diverse in its people, Indonesia is vast. It is longer than the United States from Maine to California is wide (5,120 kilometers from east to west). Predominately Muslim as of the early 2000s, it had been influenced by Indian, Arabic, Malay, Chinese, Melanesian, and European cultures. Indonesia was divided into seven regions: Java, Sumatra, Kalimantan, Sulawest, Maluku, West Papua, and Nusa Tenggara.

The most heavily populated island is Java, although it is far from the largest. Javanese people make up 45 percent of the country's population. Other major groups are Sundanese (mostly inhabiting West Java), 14 percent; Madurese, 7.5 percent; and Malays, 7.5 percent. A comprehensive family planning program had been in place since the early 1970s, resulting in a reduction in population growth rate from 2.3 percent in 1972 to 1.56 percent in 2000.

More than 17,000 islands make up the nation; in 2002 some 6,000 were inhabited. The large islands have interiors with high, rugged mountains and about one hundred active volcanoes. The volcanic action has contributed to a rich agricultural soil on many islands. The climate is hot, except where tempered by high altitudes, and the main variable is rainfall: there is a dry season and a rainy season.

Both Asian and European traders were attracted to the spices available on these rich islands. In 1619 the Dutch conquered a city on the northwest Java coast, burned it, and built a new city they named Batavia. It was centuries, however, before the Dutch were able to claim most of the islands, which ultimately resulted in one of the world's richest colonial possessions of all time.

The average annual income is US$570, with enormous and growing disparity between the highs and the lows. Life expectancy at birth is 64 years for females, 60 years for males. Universal suffrage is granted to those over the age of 17, and married persons regardless of age are allowed to vote.

A significant trend in the past 30 years has been urbanization. Between 1970 and 1990 the percentage of the population living in urban areas rose from 17 percent to 31 percent. A high degree of social stratification existed, yet classes were hard to clearly divide. Some argued that the Indonesian middle class was defined in 2002 mainly by patterns of consumption.

Freedom of religion was guaranteed by the Constitution to five recognized religions. They are Islam (87 percent of the population), Protestantism (6 percent), Catholicism (3 percent), Buddhism (2 percent), and Hinduism (1 percent).

Literacy & Education The official language is Bahasa Indonesia, and it is taught in all elementary schools. Most people speak at least one other regional language. In the early 2000s, adult literacy was figured at an average of 85 percent, with a higher rate for males (about 89 percent) than for females (about 78 percent). The rates for both had been increasing steadily over the previous generation. Nine years of school were compulsory, with enrollment estimated at 92 percent of eligible primary school-age children. Some 44 percent of secondary school-age children attend junior high school. About 6 percent of the population aged 19-24 was engaged in higher education.

An ever-rising rate in the consumption of print media had been fostered by the increased literacy rates, by the expansion of the middle class with the financial ability to buy newspapers and magazines, and by a growing felt importance of print media in everyday life. In the early 2000s the median age of Indonesia was quite young. The age structure of readership for print media showed that 65 percent were age 34 or younger; 35 percent were over the age of 35.

Before independence in 1945, Malay had long been used as a *lingua franca*, particularly along the coasts of Java and Sumatra. Dutch was the language of people with a formal, Western-style education, but during the colonial era there were very few of these. An important language step was taken on October 28, 1928, a day that is still celebrated as ''Pledge of Youth Day.'' At the second Indonesian Youth congress meeting in Jakarta, despite their dependence on Dutch, the language of power, and Javanese, the language of the majority, the youth pledged themselves to the language to be known as Indonesian. The *Sumpah Pemuda* (Pledge of Youth), as it is known, called for them to commit themselves to one nation, one motherland, and one language.

When the Japanese invaded the islands in 1942 and forced out the Dutch, they prohibited the use of Dutch language, which caused the educated of the populace to have to resort to Malay, later to be named Bahasa Indonesia. For this reason, among other reasons, Bahasa Indonesia was well positioned to become the national language in 1945. In 1973 the spelling of Bahasa Indonesia, which is written with the Latin alphabet, was regularized or simplified and made more similar to the spelling of Malaysian.

Local languages remain important; there are 583 still spoken. Languages with one million or more speakers are (in order of their approximate numbers): Javanese, Sundanese, Malay, Madurese, Minangkabau, Balinese, Buginese, Achenese, Toba Batak, Makassarese, Banjarese, Sasak, Lampung, Dairi Batak, and Rejang. English is the most widely spoken foreign language, and it is taught in all elementary schools.

Pancasila, the National Founding Philosophy *Pancasila* (five principles) is important to an understanding of social and political thinking in Indonesia. Sukarno, the founding president of the republic, articulated five principles on June 1, 1945, which were then written into the Constitution as the principles of the new country. His statement, although simple in form, reflected a sophisticated understanding of the complexity of the ideological needs of the new nation. *Pancasila* (five principles) reflected a culturally neutral identity, compatible with democratic, Marxist, or Muslim points of view, and it did not allow for the formation of an Islamic state.

The five principles are: belief in one supreme God, humanitarianism, nationalism expressed in unity, consultative democracy, and social justice. Sukarno presented these ideas in terms of an ideal village in which society is egalitarian, the economy is built on mutual assistance, and decision-making is by consensus.

Historical Background of the Press The Dutch established the first newspapers in the late eighteenth century. Most publications were little concerned with local events, but published news they received from Europe. In 1816, the year the Dutch took over once again after a brief interregnum by the British, the first local general interest paper was founded, *Bataviasche Courant*. The name was changed to *Javasche Courant* not long afterwards, and this newspaper was published continually until the Japanese occupation in 1942.

By the middle of the nineteenth century, about 30 Dutch newspapers were being published in islands, mostly in Jakarta, but also *De Locomotief* in Semarang, *Mataram* in Jogjakarta, and *De Preanger Bode* in Bandung.

The first Indonesian periodicals appeared in the mid-1800s. A magazine in Javanese, *Bromartani*, began publication in 1855. A newspaper in Malay called *Soerat*

Kabar Bahasa Melajoe began publication in Surabaya in 1856. Both were financed by the Dutch.

The first completely Indonesian newspaper, *Medan Prijaji* (Officialdom), began publication in 1907. Other newspapers of the early part of the century were *Darmo-Kondo* (Surakarta, Java), *Sinar Hindia* (Semarang, Java), *Oetoesan Hindia* (Surabaya, Java), *Oetoesan Borneo* (Pontianak, Kalimantan), *Benih Mardika* (Medan, Sumatra), and *Tjaja-Soematra* (Padang, Sumatra). Circulations were small, as might be expected where as few as five percent of the population was literate in Indonesian, and there was little advertising. However, these early newspapers became instruments of communication among the early nationalist movement and fired the flames created by the Budi Utomo movement founded in 1908. *Budi Utomo* (High Endeavor) at first promoted Javanese cultural values and pushed for access to Western-style education. As time went on, it became more political, promoting a nationalist spirit.

Around the same time, a flourishing publishing business grew up in the Chinese-Indonesian community. Some of the best known of these newspapers were *Sin Po* (Jakarta, 1910), which had a circulation at one time of 10,000; *Ik Po* (Surakarta, 1904); and *Tjhoen Tjhiou* (Surabaya, 1914). Another Surabaya-based newspaper, *Sin Tit Po*, was considered a leader in the nationalist movement. Most of these papers were published in Batavian Malay, a Malay language influenced by the Hokkien dialect of Chinese. *Ik Po*, however, used Chinese characters.

When the Japanese invaded the islands in 1942, all Dutch and most Indonesian newspapers were banned. The military government established several newspapers, including *Djawa Shinbun* in Jakarta and *Sinar Matahari* in Jogjakarta. An underground press sprang up, *Merah Putih* (The Red and White) in Surakarta being one of the most notable publications.

The story of the rise in national consciousness is inseparable from the history of the press. Journalists and nationalists were in close association; often they were one and the same. In the early 2000s a mythology lingered that identified journalists with the struggle, as actors in the *pers perjuangan* (the press of the struggle). This myth was in direct confrontation with a new reality: young journalists who were first generation of the urban petty bourgeoisie who had prospered in the New Order identified with the burgeoning consumerist environment of urban Indonesia, not with the idea of resistance.

Major Figures in Journalism Major figures in Indonesian journalism include Goenawan Mohamad, founder of *Tempo* magazine, prolific writer, and director of the Institute for Studies on the Free Flow of Information. Also, Mochtar Lubis (b. 1922), known widely for his searingly realistic novels, founded the newspaper *Indonesia Raya* (1949-74), which was closed down by the government. He was a prominent part of the liberal opposition to both Sukarno's Guided Democracy and Suharto's New Order and was jailed by both governments.

Recent Developments in the Press ''A bolder spirit took hold in Indonesia in 1994,'' wrote A. Lin Neumann (11), a spirit influenced partly by an international resistance movement. This movement had been sweeping much of Asia, in the Philippines first, followed by South Korea and Taiwan, and Thailand when it rejected a military government in 1992 and experienced a flowering of the press. It was perhaps inevitable that Indonesia would take part.

An important aspect of the diverse contemporary periodical publishing scene is the variety of viewpoints. Islamic publishing alone represented a wide spectrum of viewpoints. *Media Dakwah* (Media of the Proclamation of Faith), for example, made clear its campaign for an Islamic state and Middle Eastern political ideals, while the Jakarta newspaper *Republika* was brashly cosmopolitan. The title, ''Islamic Communication,'' an academic field taught in certain private Islamic universities, bore witness to the high importance placed in Islamic circles for communicating their ideas.

After reform, one Indonesian journalist categorized the press in three ways: ''establishment'' newspapers such *Kompas* and *Republika*, more ''aggressive'' newspapers such as *Rakyat Merdeka* and *Jawa Pos*, and ''extreme'' Islamic papers such as *Sabili.* It may be that the balance among these was shifting. The press in earlier years tended to exhibit many of the social norms of the polite Javanese—circumspection, self-restraint, and the practice of saying the truth gently. Readers were accustomed to reading between the lines. Aggressive journalism could, by these standards, seem insensitive and crude, but the press seemed to be going more and more in this direction.

Some analysts saw a major transition in the media that was less obvious than the freedom from governmental restrictions, but possibly more worrisome. Print journalism from its early days held to the image of a truth-seeking, idealistic force. This image was also carried in the public mind, so that even though Indonesia was rightly characterized as an oral culture, the printed word tended to be endowed with prestige and authority. The late 1990s were years of rapid industrialization of print media. Particularly in the case of electronic media, a large influx of foreign investment was changing the media picture rapidly.

News Media During the Suharto years, it took political connection, patience, and significant amounts of money

Daily and Non-Daily Newspaper Titles and Circulation Figures

	1996	1997	1998	1999	2000
Number of Daily Newspapers	77	74	79	172	NA
Circulation of Dailies (000)	4,733	4,717	5,017	4,782	NA
Number of Non-Daily Newspapers	90	90	88	425	NA
Circulation of Non-Dailies (000)	3,895	4,644	5,074	7,758	NA

Source: World Association of Newspapers and Zenithmedia, *World Press Trends 2001*, pp. 8, 10, 17, 19. Note: NA stands for not available.

under the table to get permission to publish a newspaper or newsmagazine. The years between his resignation in 1998 and the early 2000s were characterized by Indonesian people variously as *otonomi*, *demokrasi*, or *reformasi* (autonomy, democracy, or reformation), an explosion in news media occurred.

Approximately 1,000 newspapers had registered and begun publishing around the turn of the millennium. Some of these publications withered within a matter of months, as resources dried up and the market did not support them. But without a doubt, a flourishing and varied publishing industry was putting the daily results of its work out on city streets.

Major newspapers included *Kompas* in Jakarta, established in 1965 and published by Kompas Media PT. Jakob Oetoma, who served on the Press Council of the country, was both publisher and editor of this paper. *Kompas* was part of a significant publishing conglomerate under Catholic leadership, with extensive book (the *Gramedia* division) and magazine publishing, as well as six newspapers. This fact might seem remarkable in a majority-Muslim nation. Not all Indonesians viewed this fact with pride, but many saw it as evidence of their country's famed religious tolerance.

Jawa Pos, founded in 1949 in Surabaya, is widely distributed in the eastern part of the nation. The Jawa Pos group (PT Jawa Pos), headed by Dahlan Iskan, a former reporter, was known for its dynamic business policy of either buying out small regional newspapers or starting new ones. The *Jawa Pos* and others in the group made a point of attentive reporting on regional affairs, unlike many of Jakarta standard papers. It was also known for its policy of supporting paid staff journalists in news bureaus around the world, whose reporting helped bring world events to *Jawa Pos* readers and those of other newspapers in the group. Many of the newspapers in the group were recognizable for the word *Pos* or the word *Radar* in their names, such as *Kupang Pos* or *Radar Tangerang*.

Pos Kota was a popular, low-priced, Jakarta newspaper with a circulation of more than half a million. Established in 1970, it was published by P. T. Metro Pos. It was widely read by blue-collar workers in the urban area and enjoyed for its simple language and direct human interest. This was the sort of paper that *ojek* drivers (who form a collective to carry passengers on their motorbikes) tended to go as a group to buy and read together.

Republika was founded in 1991 in Jakarta as a Muslim daily, to be the official organ of the Association of Indonesian Islamic Intellectuals. From its beginning, it claimed to make the effort to serve the interests of the entire Islamic community. This fact put it at odds with more conservative Islamic organizations. In the mid-1990s, *Republika* was the object of a number of demonstrations organized by *Dewan Dakwah Islamiyah Indonesia* (Indonesia Council for Islamic Proclamation) for showing what they called a "cosmopolitan" attitude, publishing stories on art and film that were considered "very unIslamic."

One of the oldest newspapers of the country was still published regularly in Yogyakarta, Central Java. *Kedaulatan Rakyat* (Sovereignty of the People) was established in 1945 by P. T. Badan Penerbit Kedaulatan Rakyat. In the early 2000s, it had a circulation of 72,000. Another of Indonesia's oldest newspapers was *Pikiran Rakyat*, which had its beginning in Bandung in the 1920s in a different form. Published in 2002 by P. T. Granesia, it had a circulation of more than 150,000. During his student days in Bandung, Sukarno was one of its contributors. *Suara Pembaruan*, published in Jakarta with a circulation of 250,000, was considered a serious newspaper. It was started in 1987 by Indonesian Protestants after the government put their *Sinar Harapan* out of business. *Angkatan Bersenjata* (Armed Forces) was the newspaper published since 1965 in Jakarta for the armed forces. In 2002 its circulation was 52,000.

Of the three English-language newspapers published in Jakarta, the *Indonesian Observer* was the oldest (1955) and continued to be widely respected. With a circulation of 25,000, it was smaller than the subsequent newspapers *Indonesia Times* (1974) and *Jakarta Post* (1983). *Jakarta Post* moved quickly into other major cities, aggressively soliciting subscriptions. *Indonesia Times* claimed a circu-

Top Ten Daily Newspapers
(2000)

	Circulation
Pos Kota	600,000
Kompas	507,000
Jawa Pos	434,000
Suara Merdeka	261,000
Pikiran Rakyat	186,000
Media Indonesia	170,000
Republika	160,000
Waspada	99,000
Bisnis Indonesia	89,000
Analisa	85,000

Source: World Association of Newspapers and Zenithmedia, *World Press Trends 2001*, p. 120.

lation of 35,000 and *Jakarta Post* of 50,000. *Jakarta Post* was widely relied upon by the international community.

Much of the Indonesian news media, both in Indonesian and in English, could be accessed on the Web from a single site known as *Jendela Indonesia* (Window on Indonesia), created at the Illinois Institute of Technology (http://www.iit.edu/üindonesia/jendela/). In 2002, some 33 newspapers, 32 magazines, 18 journals and 4 TV station transcripts could be read in this way.

Press Coverage of East Timor Coverage of the events surrounding the vote of East Timor for independence in 1999 proved to be a test of the press's own newfound independence. The tragic aftermath of the vote shattered international goodwill that had developed following the moves toward democracy building in Indonesia. The military chose to back the bands of armed pro-Indonesia militia groups in their reaction to the vote. In a short time, the entire infrastructure of the province, including the press infrastructure, was destroyed, and two journalists were killed, one Indonesian and one Dutch. Many Indonesian journalists suffered beatings and threats, along with foreign journalists.

The military ordered Indonesian journalists to evacuate the area ''for their own protection.'' When the Australian-led peacekeeping force was sent to East Timor several weeks later, journalists began to return. World press was focused on the assault on East Timor, but the anger of the Indonesian press focused mainly on Australian ''interference.'' Editorials called for a jihad against westerners and blamed the U. N. and Western press for the independence vote. A study by the Institute for the Free Flow of Information (ISAI) later concluded that the Indonesian press had relied heavily on the Indonesian government analysis of events. As tempers calmed and the U. N. presence began to return some normalcy to East Timor, the Indonesian press began to take a more balanced view, documenting and publishing the results of government investigations into military actions in the new nation.

ECONOMIC FRAMEWORK

The economy of Indonesia was transformed from virtually no industry in 1965 to a producer of steel, aluminum, and cement by the late 1970s. During the last fifteen or so years of the century, consumer goods and paper products were produced in massive amounts to meet a growing demand from the middle class. By the mid-1990s, Indonesia ranked thirteenth among the world's economies, just behind Canada.

Before the construction of newsprint mills in the 1980s and 1990s, newspaper production was severely handicapped by the government's desire to limit the outgo of foreign exchange for the purchase of newsprint. A limited amount was imported free of import taxes and allotted to various newspapers, determined by *Serikat Penerbit Suratkabar* (Newspaper Publishers' Association, SPS). Newsprint in excess of the allotment had to be purchased on the open market with a 20 percent import tax. Furthermore, in 1978 a devaluation of the rupiah severely affected struggling publishers. It increased the cost of newsprint by 50 percent and drove newspaper prices up, causing declines in circulation. Advertising rates were also raised. As a result, many weaker publishers went under, while the larger papers became stronger.

With the barriers to publishing newspapers and magazines falling in the late 1990s, with the requirement of obtaining a license done away with, publishing began to be seen as a wide-open economic opportunity. At one point in 2001, some 1,100 publications were registered. However, the number in actual circulation afterward declined precipitously as market forces took their toll. Tabloids first began appearing in 1998, and constituted about one quarter of the number of newspapers published in 2002.

One of the most dynamic industries in the country through the 1990s was pulp and paper. The lifeblood of this industry was the country's enormous tracts of tropical rain forests, which at that time occupied about 70 percent of the landmass. By 1999, there were 81 paper mills in Indonesia producing 2.1 million tons of cultural and newsprint paper. In that year 530,000 tons of newsprint were produced, about two-fifths for domestic consumption and three-fifths for export. Almost all of the equipment for pulp and paper factories had to be imported. Domestic paper consumption (of all kinds) was 16.5 kilograms per capita in 2000.

The largest pulp and paper manufacturer in Indonesia was the Sinar Mas Group, known as Asia Pulp &

Paper Company for all of its international operations. Most paper mills were located on the vast, rugged, and forested island of Sumatra. Indonesia was expected to continue to play a continually greater role in the paper supply of Asia, because most countries of Asia, except for Indonesia, had depleted their forests.

Vertical integration was becoming an economic force with media corporations such as *Jawa Pos* owning paper mills. Distribution costs of newspapers averaged about 40 percent of cover prices. Newsprint in 1999 cost an average of Rupiah 29,000 a ton (US$36.25). Cover prices of newspapers range from US$.19 to $.20 for top end serious newspapers to US$.11 for a newspaper such as *Pos Kota*. Many readers bought their newspapers on the street, and on weekday mornings newsboys lined major intersections where traffic lights stopped the commuter traffic.

Newspaper reading patterns are dependent upon disposable income. When times are difficult, such as when the rupiah was devalued in 1978, newspaper buying tends to go down. However, during the monetary crisis of 1998, circulation actually rose because of the overwhelming interest in the political crisis. A single newspaper purchased from a street vender cost as much as a simple meal of *nasi campur* (rice and side dishes) purchased from another vendor. An annual subscription to a mainline newspaper such as *Kompas* cost about US$60 a year. When a family could buy a modest television set for US$55, the choice would most likely be the television.

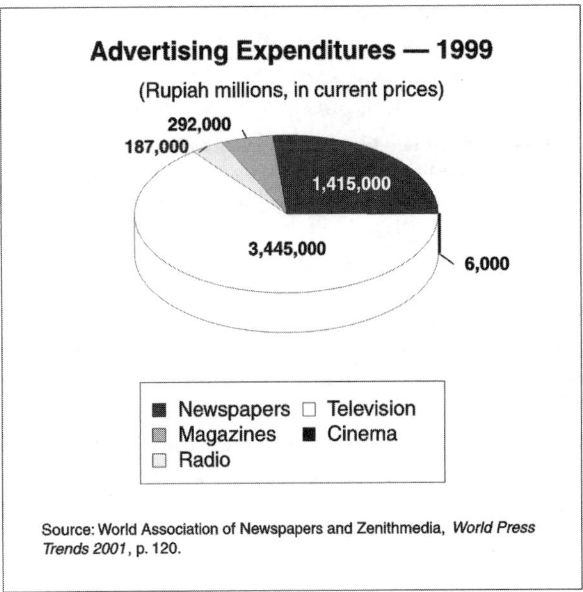

Source: World Association of Newspapers and Zenithmedia, *World Press Trends 2001*, p. 120.

PRESS LAWS

The duty of the press is "strengthening national unity and cohesion," as stated by Press Law 21 of 1982. Moreover, the Minister of Information at that time promised that a publishing license would be revoked only "when the press is not in line with the philosophy of the nation and the state." With unity as the paramount value, newspapers in general took a cautious, self-censoring stand. When some stepped out of line, they were closed down. *Sinar Harapan*, a Protestant daily with a large circulation in Jakarta, was closed in 1986 for economic reporting that was less than optimistic. (Its editorial columns had been discussing the issue of presidential term limitations as well.) *Prioritas* was closed down the following year.

With the political changes in the late 1990s, laws relating to the media also began changing in rapid succession. In September 1999, just as he was leaving office, Habibie signed Press Law 40, a law that reversed more than a generation of repressive legislation. It eliminated press licensing, removed the ability of the government to ban publications, and guaranteed freedom of the press. It called for penalties on those who would restrict press freedom and for self-regulation through an independent press council. Indonesians look back on this point as the time of *kuda lepas kandang* (the horses let loose from their pen).

A short time later, almost as soon as he took office, incoming president Abdurrahman Wahid got rid of the *Kementrian Penerangan*, the Ministry of Information, which had been used so long as a tool of propaganda and coercion under the Suharto government. It was later replaced by an agency known as *Lembaga Informasi Nasional* (LIN). However, the role of LIN was quite different. It was designed to improve the quality of public access to information and to coordinate public information in such areas as health, public services, and regulation. Although "public empowerment" was stated as one of its goals, its structure was generally a top-down system.

A decree in 2001 by President Megawati Sukarnoputri reestablished a Ministry of Information but subsumed it under the Ministry of State instead of making it a cabinet level post as it had been in for many years. There was concern by the industry that this step might be laying the foundation for a return to the policies of earlier years, but most observers remained optimistic about the situation.

As dramatic as the changes were, the Press Law of 1999 applied only to print media. There remained statutes in the Criminal Code that could be used against journalists for actions such as "leaking state secrets," "insulting the President and the Vice President," and "insulting a dead person." Nor is there any constitutional guarantee for a free press; the existing press laws could easily be changed in years to come.

The Indonesian Broadcasting Act of 1996 made official what was in fact occurring. According to existing law, *Televisi Republik Indonesia* (TVRI) was the only recognized television broadcaster; however, several private corporations had already set up operations. The new law authorized these corporations to broadcast their own news programs, in effect breaking the state monopoly on news.

In July of 2002, a comprehensive broadcasting bill, two years in the making, was being hotly discussed. A proposal to limit media-cross ownership, proposed to prevent a monopoly on opinion by major media groups, was contested by media representatives. Press Society representatives argued that the measure would serve as a barrier for new television stations which might contest the current hold on broadcasting airways (at least four of nine existing private TV stations are partly owned by family members of former president Suharto).

CENSORSHIP

Censorship was a part of the media scene in Sukarno's Guided Democracy era and Suharto's New Order. From 1974 to 1977, domestic newspapers were required to obtain, in addition to the publishing license from the Ministry of Information, a permit from *Kopkamtib*, the internal security organization. *Kopkamtib*, then was the primary agency that monitored the press. Rather than outright censorship, the agency was more likely to hold briefings telling editors what kind of news should be printed.

Censorship often took the form of pre-censorship or self-censorship. For example, in 1980 a group of prominent retired military officials and members of parliament put together what was called the Petition of 50, criticizing President Suharto for his failure to adhere to *Pancasila*, the state philosophy that is the guiding light of Indonesian thought. Editors were ordered not to allow reporting on the petition.

Periodicals were not the only publications censored during the New Order. Prominent literary figures such as dramatist W. S. Rendra and novelist Pramoedya Ananta Toer had their works banned from print. Many important foreign scholarly books deemed critical of the administration were also banned. But with all book bannings, the ubiquitous photocopy machine continued to produce books for those who wanted them, and banned books could be found around university campuses.

The Ministry of Information in 2002 included a Film Censorship board, consisting of representatives of various fields, such as foreign relations, cinematography, and culture. The board considered the educational, informational, and entertainment value of films in deciding whether they would be shown.

STATE-PRESS RELATIONS

The Press under Guided Democracy and the New Order During the years following independence, the press blossomed in freedom. Some English-language papers were introduced, many more papers in Indonesian began, and the Chinese press prospered. In 1956, Sukarno introduced the concept of Guided Democracy, abandoning the parliamentary form of government in favor of reaching a consensus among the power groups—the right-wing military groups, the powerful *Partai Komunis Indonesia* (Communist Party, PKI), and himself. Then, Sukarno instituted stringent policies regarding the press, requiring them to become active supporters of government policies. Within a few years, the number of papers and their circulation had dropped by about half.

By the early 1960s, the PKI was the largest Communist Party outside China and the USSR Tension between the army and the PKI grew and culminated on September 30, 1965, with the kidnap and murder of six generals in what appeared to be a takeover. The response was swift in the weeks and months that followed. Rightist gangs killed tens of thousands of alleged communists, especially in rural areas. Estimates of the number of deaths were placed at 500,000 and even upward. For more than a generation, an accusation of being ''involved'' could cost a person a job. Even in 2002, commentators on Indonesia both within and without would say that Indonesia had not yet come to terms with the events of 1965-66, historically, morally, or politically.

During the Suharto years (1966-98), it was a widely accepted, but also convenient, belief that a free, Western-style press was not compatible with Indonesian society and mores. Controls on the media employed many strategies: coercion, threats, or even straightforward briefings from military or governmental officials warning editors to stay away from certain happenings in the interest of national stability.

In 1980, the national government, in an attempt to bolster literacy and civic understanding, began a program called *Koran Masuk Desa*, (Newspapers for the Village). It provided a subsidy for four-page regional weekly papers, usually in Bahasa Indonesia, but sometimes in a local language. The program was augmented later with *TV Masuk Desa*, a program to supply free television sets to villages.

One New Order media closing of 1990 probably contributed indirectly to the push for greater press freedom. The upstart Jakarta tabloid *Monitor*, with a circulation of 700,000, took a poll of its readership concerning their most admired figure. The results were published, showing the Prophet Mohammad trailing Suharto, Sukarno, and Saddam Hussein. An enraged mob of Muslim youth stormed the newspaper offices, and in response the Information Minister put the tabloid out of business and charged the editor, Arswendo Atmowiloto, with blasphemy. Atmowiloto was given the maximum prison sentence, five years.

Many saw the newspaper closing and the prosecution as a response to religious pressure inappropriate in a pluralistic society. Abdurrahman Wahid, founding head of the Democracy Forum, was quoted as saying ''without [the *Monitor* case], maybe it would have taken another couple of years,'' meaning the general push toward press freedom.

After the downfall of Suharto, despite the slowness of reform on many fronts, press freedom was a part of the agenda of both Habibie and Wahid. Just before leaving office in September 1999 Habibie signed a liberal press law that did away with earlier repressive legislation and provided protection for the print media.

Pressures on the Media Some pressures on the media were long-standing. A custom known as ''envelope journalism'' persisted, where a payment was made for a favorable story or for withholding information. Other pressures resulted from the changed circumstances of the press. Organizations such as the Alliance of Independent Journalists (AJI) reported almost an epidemic of violence and threats against publishers and journalists by mobs and thugs. The alliance questioned the resolve and the ability of the government to deal with it. Much of this violence took place in rural and outlying areas. As a result, publishers and reporters inevitably became cautious. Self-censorship by a news agency in a far-flung post meant that the newspaper-reading public in the centers of power would not be aware of critical information, and the interests of the nation would not be served. Furthermore, important local stories did not get covered for fear of the hostility of certain groups.

Press Organizations and Code of Ethics As the number of newspapers and magazines burgeoned in the free atmosphere of the reformation period, so had the number of press organizations, with 36 on the record as of 2002. The longest-standing press organization was *Persatuan Wartawan Indonesia* (PWI).

In reaction to the banning of a number of weeklies in 1994, the Alliance of Independent Journalists (AJI) was formed with the backing of the editors of some of them, such as Eros Djarot of *DeTik* and Goenawan Mohamad of *Tempo*. The following year, Ahmad Taufik (the founding chairman) and Iko Maryadi, editor of *Suara Independent* were arrested on charges of insulting Suharto in print and were imprisoned for two years. Many AJI members were fired because their employers feared being shut down.

Representatives of 26 press organizations came together in Bandung in 1999 to draw up an agreed-upon code of ethics. The code of ethics stated:

- Indonesian journalists respect the right of the people to receive true information.
- Indonesian journalists follow ethical procedures for getting and releasing information, including identifying the source of the information.
- Indonesian journalists respect the fundamental presumption of innocence and do not mix fact with opinion, but always weigh and investigate the truth of the information. They do not commit plagiarism.
- Indonesian journalists do not spread information which is untrue, slanderous, sadistic, or pornographic and do not identify victims of sexual assault by name.
- Indonesian journalists do not take bribes and do not take unfair advantage of their position.
- Indonesian journalists have the Right of Refusal; they respect background information and information that is off the record according to mutual agreement.
- Indonesian journalists immediately retract or correct any wrong in the news and honor the Right to Respond.

The Presidential Decree of 2000 created a nine-member *Dewan Pers* (Press Council), with representatives from news reporters, media executives, television, radio, and one person representing the public.

ATTITUDE TOWARD FOREIGN MEDIA

During the 31 years of Suharto's government, foreign press was subject to some interference. Foreign magazines and newspapers entering the country were first given a once-over by censors. Offending articles or photographs were often blacked out. Journalists considered to be overly critical of the Indonesian government were simply denied visas. Security and immigration officials maintained a secret black list. Materials printed in Chinese characters were banned outright after the new government of 1966 was established, a ban that continued until Suharto stepped down.

In the early 2000s foreign journalists were still required to obtain a special visa to work in the country. Some reporters ignored the requirement, and some were detained and deported for that violation. In 2001 the Foreign Affairs Department banned foreign journalists from entering the trouble spots of Aceh, Maluku, and West Papua. Both Aceh and West Papua had strong separatist movements, and Maluku was the scene of repeated violence between groups with differing beliefs. Journalists found this out in January when they applied for work visas. Specifically hand-written into the permit were the words: "not valid for visits to Aceh, Maluku, and West Papua."

Indonesian nationalists working for foreign publications or agencies had to receive accreditation. They were also required to be members of the Indonesian Journalists' Association.

NEWS AGENCIES

The major and long-standing news agency was *Antara* (among or between). Founded as a private agency in 1937, it became the official agency in 1945. President Sukarno had Antara merged with other news agencies in 1963 to form the *Lembaga Kantor Berita Nasional* (National News Agency Institute, LKBN), but it continued to be referred to as Antara. Antara was closed for a time during the "attempted coup" of 1965, weeded of its left-dominated factors, and reorganized. A more recent independent agency was *Kantorberita Nasional Indonesia* (Indonesian National News Bureau, KNI).

BROADCAST MEDIA

Radio Radio is arguably the most important medium in Indonesia. Its tones are heard in the market, the village, the rice paddy, and the mini-bus. The national radio station, *Radio Republik Indonesia* (RRI) was founded in August 1945 almost as soon as independence was granted. During World War II, the Japanese occupational forces used radio as a major propaganda tool, and figures such as Sukarno and Mohammad Hatta who were to become prominent in nation-building received wide coverage, becoming household names among villagers.

One of RRI's first tasks was to encourage the Indonesian people in their struggle, as Dutch troops invaded the newly proclaimed republic. This struggle for freedom lasted for four years.

In the early 2000s, RRI was headquartered in Jakarta, with major relay stations in Medan (Sumatra), Yogykarta (Java), Banjarmasin (Kalimantan), Makassar (Sulawesi), and Jayapura (West Papua). In 2002, RRI had 53 stations staffed by approximately 8,500. RRI's overseas program, Voice of Indonesia, broadcast in ten languages: Indonesian, Arabic, Malaysian, Mandarin, Thai, Japanese, Spanish, German, English, and French. Private radio companies were in operation since 1966. They were advised to include informative, educational, and cultural programs in their broadcasts. However, they were no longer required to carry news programs produced by RRI.

Under Suharto, radio stations were required to carry the news broadcasts from the state. They were banned from doing independent reporting. The association of radio station owners was headed by Suharto's daughter, and licenses were given out to party faithfuls. Within two years after the collapse of the Suharto government in 1998, the number of independent radio stations grew by more than 30 percent, from about 750 to more than 1000 stations. Many broadcast journalists and station managers had to learn on the job. In-depth radio journalism programs or investigative reports on radio were still scarcely to be found in Indonesia. To bolster the overall quality of news and information programming, Internews (the international organization sponsored by the United States to assist fledgling broadcasters) produced three weekly radio programs and distributed them through a network of partner stations. As of June, 2000, RRI has been changed in status by presidential decree from a government-owned radio to a public broadcasting corporation (BUNM).

Television Indonesian television history illustrated a medium finding its own way, going from one state-produced official channel to a multiplicity of commercial channels. It included periods of time when advertising was banned as contrary to traditional values. *Televisi Republik Indonesia* (TVRI) began operations in 1964 and remained a major player despite the growing importance of commercial television. Since it enjoyed a long-standing monopoly with a mission of promoting the official viewpoint, it long remained in a state of stagnation. The Indonesian government early on recognized the importance of television as a policy instrument and a tool to promote national unity in these far-flung islands. This insight drove the program to provide free television sets to villages. To be able to reach the entire country, in 1974 Indonesia launched its communications satellite, *Palapa* (Sanskrit for unity).

TVRI was always hampered by a small budget, and the budget situation became even tighter in 1981, when the administration banned advertising from television. This was in reaction to the effect that advertising—western, urban, and consumer-oriented—was having on village life.

Indonesia's first commercial television station, *Rajawali Citra Televisi Indonesia* (RCTI), began operation in March, 1988, broadcasting first in Jakarta but later throughout the country. Of course, advertising was the very backbone of its existence. Corporate investments in the country and a huge consumer market with increasing amounts of money to spend put the greater part of their advertising budgets into television. Since the only legal source of news was still TVRI, RCTI and other private broadcasters created what they called "information programs" until the Broadcast law of 1996 legitimated their news programs. RCTI carried several daily programs,

Morning Nuances, News at Noon, Throughout Indonesia, and *Evening Bulletin.* These news programs, which had to complete for advertisers, carried higher entertainment values than TVRI.

Surya Citra Television (SCTV) opened a few years later, also based in Jakarta. Its news programs focused on national news, with international news accounting for about 10 percent. In August 1990, a third private station was licensed with the proviso that it focus on education. This station was *Televisi Pendidikan Indonesia* (TPI). It cooperated with TVRI extensively, with some of its advertising revenues going to TVRI. A fourth commercial station was licensed in 1993, *Andalas Televisi* (Anteve, ANTV). It attempted to profile itself in the areas of news, sports and music, and it reached a smaller audience than the others. *Indosiar* was the newcomer in 1995 and had to struggle for a viewer share. Owing to the fierce competition among these stations, there was quite a bit of similarity among them.

All five of Indonesia's private, Jakarta-based television stations—SCTV, RCTI, Indosiar, Anteve and TPI—had ties to the Suharto family. Despite the family ties, the new openness created bolder programming, even before Suharto stepped down. After that, stations offered investigative reporting and political talk shows that would have been unheard of in the New Order.

An all-news TV channel, Metro TV, began in Jakarta in November, 2000. Besides programming in Indonesian, it carried programs in Mandarin, reflecting the easing of restrictions on Chinese language and cultural media.

ELECTRONIC NEWS MEDIA

Before 1994, Internet access was limited to a very few universities, research institutions, and government offices. In late 1994, the first commercial Internet Service Provider (ISP), Indonet, was established, and by 1997 some 41 ISPs had been licensed, although all were not in service. The fast growth of ISPs was in fact largely due to government policies encouraging such growth.

The electronic news media were still in first flower when the opportunity came to test the genre in a specific way. In 1994, *Tempo*, a well-known newsmagazine, had its license to publish abruptly revoked by the government. *Tempo* had reported on a controversy concerning the purchase of used East German warships. No opportunity was given the magazine to defend itself. The news came as a shock, and although *Tempo* did win an appeal, the final ruling gave the magazine no hope of publishing again.

A little more than a year later, *Tempo* opened its electronic publication, *TEMPO Interaktif.* There was no official reaction from the government, except that the Minister of Information, when asked about it in an interview, replied that individuals and organizations in Indonesia were free to set up a Web site to promote their own activities. Since the law did not require licensing of Internet news sites, what he said was quite true.

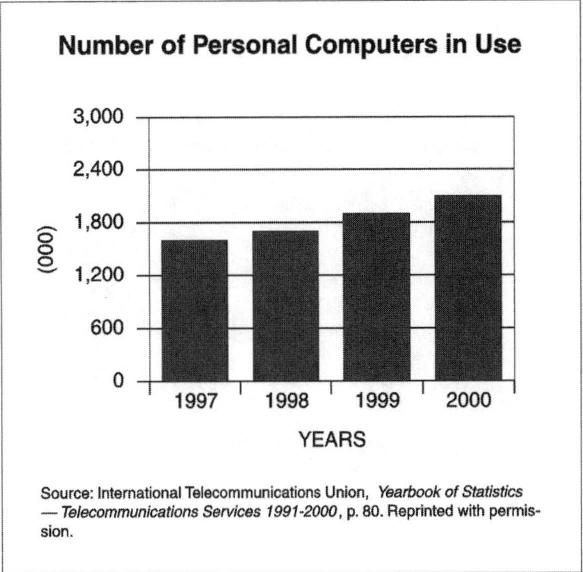

Source: International Telecommunications Union, *Yearbook of Statistics — Telecommunications Services 1991-2000*, p. 80. Reprinted with permission.

TEMPO Interaktif quickly became a popular site, becoming Indonesia's most-accessed Web publication. Enterprising students downloaded the magazine, copied it, and sold it in book form. And since a license was not needed for book publishing, *Tempo* responded by issuing the publication in book form every three months, a move welcomed by readers without Internet access.

No comprehensive survey exists to give a profile of the users of electronic news media. However, a survey carried out by *TEMPO Interaktif* identified the readership as overwhelmingly male and middle class, with the average age of readers at 27 years. The greatest number of them reported that they accessed the site from the office computer of a business. *Tempo* as a weekly newsmagazine reopened in October 1998, after the licensing requirement was eliminated.

Popular Web sites for news, some of them offering many services such as e-mail and shopping, were Astaga.com and Detik.com. Established July 1, 1998, Detik.com pioneered Indonesia's first ''real time'' electronic journalism, reporting news almost hourly. A year and a half later, thanks to foreign capital and savvy accumulation of advertising revenue, it began offering many services such as directories, chat rooms, and e-mail. At the same time, other foreign investors set up similar portals. When Astaga.com was launched, a large number of its considerable staff came from prestigious media companies, where they had made far less money. The impact

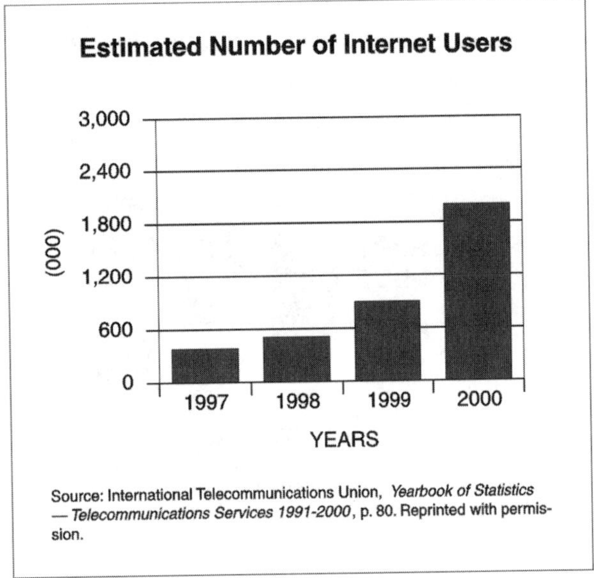

Source: International Telecommunications Union, *Yearbook of Statistics — Telecommunications Services 1991-2000*, p. 80. Reprinted with permission.

of large amounts of foreign capital remained a force to be watched.

EDUCATION AND TRAINING

Despite the importance of the media to social and political life in Indonesia, educational opportunities did not keep pace. No university listed anything like a school of journalism. Journalism education usually was offered in *fakultas* (schools) of social science and political studies. Journalism courses tended to focus on communications theory rather than on professional, practical training. But many journalists came through the ranks of a humanities education, particularly language and literature, and an unusually large number came from schools of agriculture.

Universities with respected departments in mass communication included Gadja Mada University in Yogyakarta, Hasanuddin University in Makassar, Diponogoro University in Semarang, and Pandjadjaran University in Bandung. Subsequently, some universities established schools of communication or communication science and offered degrees in *komunikasi massa* (mass communication) or *publisistik* (public relations). Of the state universities, only Padjadjaran University had a school of communication science, headed by Dr. Soleh Soemirat. The flagship state university, University of Indonesia in Jakarta, offered a graduate program in communications.

Two private universities offered a specialized school. Ibn Khaldun University in Jakarta had a School of Communication, headed by Hamid Suchas, and Islam Nusantara University in Bandung, had a School of Communication Science, headed by H. S. Insar.

Perhaps more important than universities in the training of journalists were specialized institutes. The process for introducing new curriculum at the university level was slow and cumbersome, but institutes could more quickly respond to need and serve people who were not of the usual university age.

Such an institute is The Institute for Studies in the *Institut Studi Arus Informasi* (Free Flow of Information, ISAI), founded in 1994 as a combination think tank and journalism training center. With Goenawan Mohamad as the pivotal figure, ISAI's offices in Jakarta became a gathering place for students and writers of all kinds. Meanwhile, the organization actively campaigned abroad to raise awareness of the situation of the press in Indonesia.

Other important training opportunities for journalists were the *Dewan Pers Indonesia* (Indonesian Press Council), established in 1999, and the Dr. Soetomo Press Institute (LPDS). The director of LPDS, Atmakusumah Astraatmadja, received the Ramon Magsaysay Award for journalism in 2000. Many of the leaders of the press organizations in the early 2000s were trained at LPDS. The institute also served as a think tank concerning issues of legal reform and professional ethics.

Internews, the U.S. government agency that worked throughout the world to provide assistance to journalists, provided training to more than 400 Indonesians working in broadcast media. Internews aimed to strengthen the role of the independent broadcast media by providing technical assistance; management, marketing, and advertising training; training in reporting on conflict; innovative programming and legal reform advocacy to its partner stations.

SUMMARY

The strides made by the press after 1998 were tremendous, and there was a *zeitgeist* of energy and high expectations. The proliferation of the media at all levels—from a young man rigging up the wiring from a rooftop to operate his own radio station without registration to a sophisticated urban news show such as Metro TV—were exciting developments.

Dangers to the press and thus to the citizenry included the age-old practice of envelope journalism, threats and intimidation by disgruntled groups, misuse of corporate power, and a return to the pressures on the media by the government in the absence of constitutional guarantees.

Greater media penetration would encourage greater governmental responsiveness. Better journalist training would produce a more professional and, it was hoped, a more conscientious press. Public support for a free press and for freedom-of-information laws would be necessary.

Institutions that complement a responsible media system include political parties that call for accountability on the part of public servants, effective judicial systems, and self-regulatory press councils. If the media see it as their responsibility to keep the poor and marginalized people informed, to supplement school education, and to serve the interests of all peoples, they will make a vast contribution to the future of the Republic of Indonesia.

BIBLIOGRAPHY

Anderson, Benedict R. O'G, ed. ''Cartoons and Monuments: The Evolution of Political Communication under the New Order.'' *Language and Power: Exploring Political Cultures in Indonesia.* Ithaca, NY: Cornell University Press, 1990.

Astraatmadja, Atmakusumah. ''The Media During and After 'Reformasi'.'' *Indonesia, Now and Beyond: The Indonesian Yearbook 2001.* Jakarta: Andrew Tanh Communication, 2001.

Cribb, Robert. *Historical Dictionary of Indonesia.* Metuchen, NJ: The Scarecrow Press, Inc., 1992.

Hefner, Robert. ''Print Islam: Mass Media and Ideological Rivalries among Indonesian Muslims.'' *Indonesia,* 64 (October 1997): 77-104.

Herbert, Patricia, and Anthony Milner. *South-East Asia: Languages and Literatures.* Honolulu: University of Hawaii Press, 1989.

Heryanto, Ariel, and others. ''The Industrialization of the Media in Democratizing Indonesia.'' *Contemporary Southeast Asia,* 23, No. 2 (August 2002): 327-55.

Mamora, Charlo, ''Realities and Impact of the Economic Crisis.'' *Indonesia, Now and Beyond: The Indonesian Yearbook 2001.* Jakarta: Andrew Tanh Communication, 2001.

Neumann, A. Lin. *Press, Power and Politics: Indonesia 2000.* Arlington, VA: The Freedom Forum, 2000.

Ridwan, Saiful B. ''From *TEMPO* to *TEMPO Interactif*: An Indonesian Media Scene Case Study,'' 1997. Available from http://ausweb.scu.edu.au/proceedings/ridwan/paper.html.

Sen, Krishna, and David Hill. *Media, Culture and Politics in Indonesia.* Melbourne: Oxford University Press, 2000.

Solahudin, ed. *Pro Gus Dur Runs Amok.* Jakarta: AJI (Aliansa Jurnalis) Indonesia, 2001.

Toer, Pramoedya Ananta. *This Earth of Mankind.* Trans. Max Lane. New York: William Morrow and Company, Inc., 1990.

—Linda Yoder

IRAN

BASIC DATA

Official Country Name:	Islamic Republic of Iran
Region (Map name):	Middle East
Population:	66,128,965
Language(s):	Persian, Turkic, Kurdish, Luri, Balochi, Arabic, Turkish, other
Literacy rate:	82.0%
Area:	1,648,000 sq km
GDP:	104,904 (US$ millions)
Number of Television Stations:	28
Number of Television Sets:	4,610,000
Television Sets per 1,000:	69.7
Number of Radio Stations:	82
Number of Radio Receivers:	17,000,000
Radio Receivers per 1,000:	257.1
Number of Individuals with Computers:	4,000,000
Computers per 1,000:	60.5
Number of Individuals with Internet Access:	250,000
Internet Access per 1,000:	3.8

BACKGROUND & GENERAL CHARACTERISTICS

Islam has been the official religion of Iran since the Islamic Revolution of 1979. The media is accountable to Islamic Law and heavily censored by the ruling religious clerics. Conservative Iranians believe that Islam should be the rule of law in all of Iran: men and women cannot associate in public; the press cannot criticize government leaders who are also religious leaders; and other religious tenants must be upheld in social, cultural, and political arenas. There are many conservative publications in Iran such as *Tehran Times*, *Joumhouryieh*, and *Resalaat.* However, according to the ''2001 World Press Freedom Review,'' a conservative editorial stance does not mean freedom from censorship and other forms of government control.

Reformists hold Islam in high esteem and want religion to maintain a prominent role in Iran. Reformists also desire freedom of association, freedom of the press, and a more open society: they believe a free press means a free people. Many reformist publications exist in 2002—for example, *Iran Daily*, *Hayat-e-No*, and *Iran News*—but all are frequent targets of censorship, confiscation, suspension, fining, and banning.

Journalism in Iran was a dangerous profession in the twentieth and early twenty-first centuries, particularly if an individual worked for a reformist publication or adhered to a journalistic ethic of truth regardless of personal fate, which could mean threats, arrest, imprisonment with or without formal charges, accusation of espionage, isolation, or even torture, lashes, banning, murder, and execution.

Religion is of paramount importance to most Iranians. They may not want the ruling clerics to have control of every aspect of Iranian life, but the majority of citizens want Islam to play a strong role in the country. Secularism is not supported, and the Shah is used as an example of the failure of removing religion from the official operation of the state. According to the U.S. Department of State, Shi'a Muslims are 89 percent of the Iranian population; Sunni Muslims are 10 percent; and the remaining 1 percent is Zoroastrian, Jewish, Christian, and Baha'i.

Iran has an ethnically diverse population: Persian (51 percent), Azeri (24 percent), Gilaki and Mazandarani (8 percent), Kurd (7 percent), Arab (3 percent), Lur (2 percent), Baloch (2 percent), Turkmen (2 percent), and other (1 percent). This ethnic diversity results in tremendous language diversity: Persian and Persian dialects (58 percent), Turkic and Turkic dialects (26 percent), Kurdish (9 percent), Luri (2 percent), Balochi (1 percent), Arabic (1 percent), Turkish (1 percent) and other (2 percent).

In this nation of 66 million, 1996 data from the *CIA World Factbook* estimated that 53 percent of Iranians live below the poverty line; nevertheless, some 82 percent of the population is able to read and write by 15, which is also the age of universal suffrage. The population has more than doubled from 1979, when the Islamic Revolution deposed the Shah, to 2002, with the majority (over 60 percent) of Iranians under 30 years of age.

Economic Framework

In November 2001 Iran had the second largest population in the Middle East as well as the second largest economy, OPEC production, and natural gas reserves; however, economic problems persisted. High unemployment and isolation from the global community were causing problems and leading to backlash against clerical leaders who were beginning to realize that religion needs to find a more balanced place in society, so an entire generation, which desires religion and reform, is not lost.

Press Laws

Theoretically Iran offers constitutional protection for the press, but the lengthy Press Law outlining the purpose, licensing, and duties of the press shows the true limits placed on journalists. The Press Law details a long list of don'ts for journalists, preventing free publishing under threat of punishment, which is also detailed in the Law.

Iran's Press Law established the Committee for Suspension of the Press within the Ministry of Islamic Culture and Guidance. In 2002 the Committee, dominated by reformists, monitors the press and brings charges. Any charges brought on a newspaper or journalist are heard by the conservative-dominated Press Court (Public Court 1410, Tehran); the Revolutionary Court is even known to intercede and hear cases, though press issues are not technically in the Revolutionary Court's jurisdiction. All Press Court hearings and trials are to be open to the public, but this is not what happens in reality. Juries are mostly conservative and often ignored, dismissed early, or consulted after decisions are issued. From April 2000 to mid-2002, the judges in the Press Court have been pressing charges against individuals and publications, and circumventing the Committee.

Censorship

Press censorship is most common in the capital, Tehran. Censorship certainly occurs in the city, but it is self-censorship that is the largest concern in the provinces. Provincial journalists are cautious, lack funds, and have no modern printing operations. These small provincial papers have limited circulations; thus, the power of these papers as a source of news for the population is limited. Provincial Iranians have come to rely on international broadcast media—BBC, Voice of America, and Radio Free Europe—for information.

Between 1997 and 2001, Khatami's first term, "serial newspapers" and "serial plaintiffs" became common. A newspaper is labeled a "serial newspaper" when publication of a paper is closed down, and publishers reopen with the same staff and editorial stand but under a new masthead. Examples of such serials that include three or more publications are common. "Serial plaintiffs" are those journalists who are continually charged with defying the law and offending Islam in some way.

Many reformist voices are being actively silenced in the late twentieth and early twenty-first centuries. According to the Committee to Protect Journalists (CPJ) reports, the reformist point of view can still be heard in *Iran*, *Kar-o Kargan*, *Aftab-e-Yazd*, *Norooz*, *Tosseh*, *Hayat-e No*, and *Hambasteghi*. However, the CPJ also states that many of these newspapers have mellowed in tone. They still argue for reform, but they no longer write about government officials or issues that could be perceived as national security: censorship happens in-house.

STATE-PRESS RELATIONS

Mohammed Khatami, a moderate midlevel Shi'a cleric, was reelected president in May 2001. Khatami is a reformist and seeks to offer Iranians more freedom in their daily lives: freedom of association, the press, expression, and so on. However, Supreme leader Ayatollah Ali Khamenei, a conservative committed to maintaining Islamic traditions and a more closed society, has the authority and opportunity to thwart Khatami's reform efforts, which include a freer press in Iran.

In 2002 the Islamic clerics ruling Iran held power over the media. Part democracy, part theocracy, Iran's Constitution establishes three branches of government, including an elected president and Parliament, and also offers the Supreme Leader, Khamenei, the ability to approve presidential and parliamentary candidates, and make judicial appoints. As a result Khamenei has loaded the courts with conservatives who support his positions.

According to the "World Press Freedom Review," on March 8, 2000, the conservative weekly *Harim* was banned and accused of mocking and criticizing President Khatami. Khatami, who has no control of the judiciary, pleaded over state radio on March 11 for an open jury trial for the publisher. He stated that if the press is not allowed to operate in Iran, "then people will turn to sources we have no control over."

In June 2002 the CPJ claimed that at least 52 newspapers and magazines have been closed between 1997 and 2001, despite President Khatami's reformist position on the press. These closings include student-run publications as well as licensed commercial publications. CPJ's "Iran Press Freedom Fact Sheet" confirms the following suspensions: 4 in 1998; 5 in 1999; 43 in 2000 (16 between April 23 and 24); and 16 as of September 2001.

ATTITUDE TOWARD FOREIGN MEDIA

Conservative Iranians are worried that foreign media will destroy the Islamic morals of the population, but reformist Iranians believe the foreign media, free in their home nations, are a vital part of developing democratic social structures.

Foreign correspondents face many of the same problems with censorship, banning, and harassment that Iranian journalists endure. Many foreign journalists have been imprisoned and held incommunicado. The 1997-98 case of an Iranian journalist who resides in Germany, Farah Sarkuhi, illustrates the treatment of all journalists in Iran. Sarkuhi was arrested for "anti-state propaganda," sub-

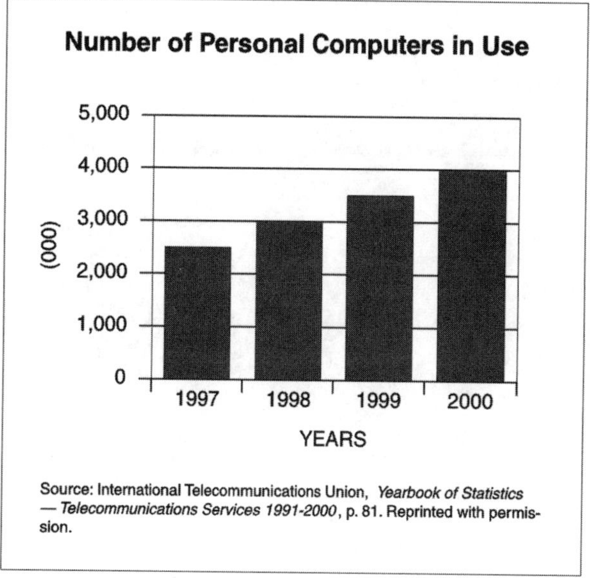

Source: International Telecommunications Union, *Yearbook of Statistics — Telecommunications Services 1991-2000*, p. 81. Reprinted with permission.

jected to a closed trial, jailed for a year, charged with espionage, cleared, released, abducted by the state, tortured, released, and finally allowed papers to return to his family in Europe.

NEWS AGENCIES

The Islamic Republic News Agency (IRNA), Iran's official news agency, will soon become an independent agency and no longer be state funded. The diverging ideas of the conservative authorities and the IRNA are illustrated in the May 10, 1998, court appearance of IRNA director general, Fereydoun Verdinejad.

Urban newspapers are not well circulated outside the cities, so the provincial readers cannot rely on an Iranian source for information on the county; this has led to a reliance on foreign broadcasts from the BBC, Voice of America, and other Western broadcast sources.

BROADCAST MEDIA

According to the Central Intelligence Agency (CIA), Iran had 72 AM, 5 FM, and 5 short-wave radio stations in 1998. Seventeen million radios were claimed to be in the country as of 1997 estimates, which meant one radio for every 3.8 people. Radio saturation is quite high, as many citizens get their news from this source.

Television's role as a disseminator of news is growing, too. Iran had 28 television broadcast stations, 450 low-power repeaters, and 4.61 million televisions, and there was 1 television for every 14.3 individuals in 1997.

The state controls most radio and television news outlets, and it is often these pro-government voices that disseminate the official hard-line rhetoric.

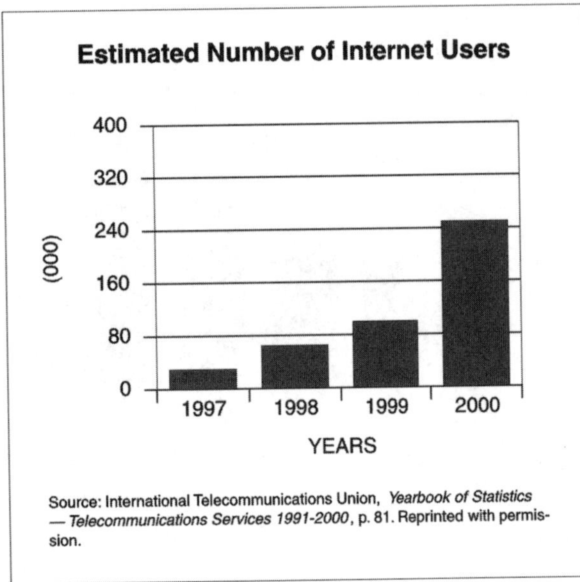

Source: International Telecommunications Union, *Yearbook of Statistics — Telecommunications Services 1991-2000*, p. 81. Reprinted with permission.

Electronic News Media

Many newspapers and news sources are available from Iran, and Iranians have tremendous access to information. The Internet is often the only source of information about the country, because newspapers are heavily censored, and the state-run broadcast media is not known for full disclosure. Traditional Islamic clerics are concerned about the Internet and its ability to alter the moral focus of young people and turn them away from Islam.

The Iranian Student News Agency (ISNA) and the Islamic Republic of Iran Broadcasting (IRIB), which owns several newspapers as well as broadcast media, both had extensive sites on the Internet in June 2002.

Education & Training

The Islamic Republic News Agency (IRNA) School of Media Studies provides long- and short-term training for journalists. The university system also offers media and journalism studies.

According to an extensive research study by Dr. Mehdi Mohsenian-Rad and Ali Entezari Rasaneh published in the summer of 1994 in *A Research Quarterly of Mass Media Studies*, 68 percent of journalists have university educations, but only a small percentage (4.6 percent) have training in communications. Between 1966 and 1994, 900 journalism degrees were awarded in Iran; 93 percent of these graduates do not work in the press. The authors and other experts speculate that the reason for this lack of journalists with journalism degrees, and the small number of those with university journalism training working for the press, is connected to the curriculum presented in the academy. Western media is studied more than Iranian media, and texts are most often translations of Western materials that do not understand the Iranian Islamic culture. In addition, most Iranian journalism curricula focus on newsgathering and interview, and pay little heed to essay writing, editorial work, and analysis.

Summary

The print media feels growing pressure from the use of broadcast and electronic media, especially among the young, those under 30 who represent over 60 percent of the population in 2001. This pressure will continue unless the conservatives are able to limit foreign broadcasting and Internet access in Iran: an unlikely possibility. However, the conflict between reformists seeking more press freedom and the hard-line conservatives is yet to be won by either side, even though the conservative clerics do hold more power and authority in 2002.

Significant Dates

- 1997: Editor dead of multiple stab wounds; Khatami elected in landslide; Sarkuhi arrested, held for closed trial, imprisoned, accused of espionage, tortured, isolated, and abducted.
- 1998: 226 new publications are licensed, bringing the total number of publications to 1,138; circulation increases from 1.5 million in 1997 to 2.9 million.
- July 1999: Student uprising protesting conservative cleric policies and supporting President Khatami's moderate reform.
- April 2000: Ayatollah Ali Khamenei gives speech accusing several papers of "undermining Islamic and revolutionary principles" ("CPJ chronicles"); at least 43 newspapers and magazines shut down.
- March 2001: President Khatami speaks on state-sponsored radio calling for a freer press.

Bibliography

Amnesty International. "Annual Report 2000: Iran," 4 June 2002. Available from http://www.web.amnesty.org.

Central Intelligence Agency (CIA). "Iran." *CIA Factbook*, 4 June 2002. Available from http://www.cia.gov.

"CPJ chronicles crackdown on Iran's news media," 16 Nov 2001. Available from http://www.freedomforum.org.

Friedman, Thomas L. "Tom's Journal." Public Broadcasting Service, 22 June 2002. Available from http://www.pbs.org.

"Iran: 2001 World Press Freedom Review," 29 May 2002. Available from http://www.freemedia.at.

"Iran's media cuts government links." *Asia Times*, 17 July 2001. Available from http://www.atimes.com.

Mohsenian-Rad, Dr. Mehdi, and Ali Entezari. "Problems of Journalism Education in Iran." *Rasaneh: A Research Quarterly of Mass Media Studies*, Summer 1994: 75. Available from http://www.netiran.com.

"Press Law," 22 June 2002. Available from http://www.netiran.com.

Sabra, Hani. "Iran Press Freedom Fact Sheet." Committee to Protect Journalists, 22 June 2002. Available from http://cpj.org.

United States Committee for Refugees. "Country Report: Iran." Worldwide Refugee Information, 6 June 2002. Available from http://www.refugees.org.

World Bank. "Country Overview: Iran," 6 June 2002. Available from http://lnweb18.worldbank.org.

—Suzanne Drapeau Morley

IRAQ

BASIC DATA

Official Country Name:	Republic of Iraq
Region (Map name):	Middle East
Population:	23,331,985
Language(s):	Arabic, Kurdish, Assyrian, Armenian
Literacy rate:	58.0%
Area:	437,072 sq km
Number of Television Stations:	13
Number of Television Sets:	1,750,000
Television Sets per 1,000:	75.0
Number of Radio Stations:	74
Number of Radio Receivers:	4,850,000
Radio Receivers per 1,000:	207.9

BACKGROUND & GENERAL CHARACTERISTICS

The Republic of Iraq is home to the Hanging Gardens of Babylon, one of the seven ancient wonders of the world. Turkey borders Iraq to the north, Iran to the east, Kuwait and the Persian Gulf to the southeast, Saudi Arabia to the south and southwest, Jordan to the west and Syria to the northwest.

In 2001 it was estimated Iraq had a population of 23.33 million. Seventy-seven percent of Iraqis are Arab, 19 percent are Kurds, and the remaining 4 percent are other ethnic groups. Iraq's Kurdish population lives in the northeastern highlands.

Iraq's official religion is Islam. A little more than 50 percent of the population is Shiite Muslims but the Sunni Muslims, who make up a little more than 40 percent of the population, tend to dominate Iraq's governmental bureaucracy. Minority religions include Christianity and Judaism. More than 80 percent of the population speaks the country's official language, Arabic. English, Kurdish, Turkish and Assyrian are among the minority languages spoken in Iraq.

Almost 42 percent of Iraq's population was below the age of 14 in 2001; 55.3 percent were 15 to 64 years of age; 3 percent were over the age of 65. Iraq's literacy gender gap is significant. Only 46 percent of Iraqi adult females are literate, while 66 percent of its adult male population is literate. Iraq's female illiteracy rate is the third highest in the world.

Iraqi society is primarily urban, with more than 70 percent of Iraqis living in urban areas. In 2001 the country's major cities were Baghdad (with a population of about 4.87 million), Mosul (1.1 million) and Irbil, (1.04 million). Baghdad is the country's capital.

Iraq was admitted to the League of Nations (the predecessor of the United Nations) after becoming a sovereign state in 1932. Iraq is a single political party republic and is governed by the Revolutionary Command Council. Saddam Hussein is president of the country, leader of the Ba'ath political party, prime minister and president of the Revolutionary Command Council, the country's highest governmental authority.

Iraq's daily newspapers are *Al-Baath Alryadi, Babil, Al-Iraq, Al-Jumhuriya, Al-Qadissiya,* and *Al-Thawra.* Newspaper circulation was 20 per 1,000 persons in 1996. Individual newspaper circulation rates were not available.

ECONOMIC FRAMEWORK

In modern times Iraq has been known for its repeated violations of basic human rights, particularly of its minority populations as well as those who express any sort of political opposition to its government. Before and after being admitted to the League of Nations, Iraq disputed the international boundaries set for it by League members. Consequently Iraq entered into numerous border conflicts with Iran. The most recent Iraq-Iran war ended in 1988. In 1990 Iraq invaded Kuwait, another area over which it claimed ancient political rights. Iraqi military forces were expelled from Kuwait by U.S.-led international forces in the 1991 military operation called Desert Storm. Immediately after the Desert Storm cease-fire, Iraq launched a military offensive against the Kurdish population residing in the Iraqi northern highlands.

As part of the ceasefire conditions Iraq was to provide proof of the destruction of its biological, ballistic and nuclear weapons and development facilities. Iraq refused to allow UN weapons inspectors into the country and continued its abuse of Kurdish and other minority groups. As a result, the United Nations imposed import/export sanctions on Iraq in 1990.

The UN sanctions prohibit exports from Iraq and imports to Iraq with the exception of medicine and other essential civilian needs not covered by the import ban. Under the UN's 1996 ''food for oil'' program, Iraq is permitted to sell set amounts of oil to fund the purchase of food, medicines and other humanitarian goods, and equipment to repair the civilian infrastructure. Since 1998 Iraq has been allowed to purchase equipment and spare parts for the rehabilitation of its oil industry.

Due to Iraq's refusal to allow UN weapons inspectors into the country and its continued abuse of Kurdish and other minority groups, UN sanctions have continued. The UN Commission of Human Rights 2000 report indicated that women, children and men continued to be arrested and detained on suspicion of political or religious activities or because they were related to members of the opposition.

According to the British Broadcasting Company (BBC), the Iraqi government and the Ba'ath Party control or own all print media in Iraq. The party and the government also control the broadcast media. Iraq's publishing and broadcast media consist of six daily newspapers, one television service, one radio service and one satellite. All are state controlled.

Uday Hussein, son of the Iraqi president, heads an extensive media empire that supposedly includes more than a dozen weekly and daily newspapers as well as the most popular of the country's three television channels. Uday Hussein also heads the national press union.

Opposition presses such as *Al-Thawra* and *Al-Jumhuriya* operate in the northern Kurdish enclaves and on the Internet. The U.S. government has operated Radio Free Iraq since 1998.

Press Laws

Criticism of Iraq's government is prohibited and a death penalty is imposed upon anyone, including journalists, criticizing Iraq's Revolutionary Command Council or the Ba'ath party.

Censorship

The Iraqi government censors all news.

State-Press Relations

The Committee to Project Journalists and the BBC independently report that Iraq's press is entirely controlled by the Iraqi state. According to BBC News, the media does not report views opposed to the Iraqi government.

Reporters Without Borders reported that Iraqi security police arrested the editor-in-chief of an Iraqi daily newspaper in 1999 after he attempted to flee the country. The editor tried to flee Iraq because Uday Hussein had reportedly threatened him when he refused the position of manager of an Iraqi magazine. In 2001 the International Press Institute reported that about 50 Iraqi journalists fled the country due to governmental press controls.

Attitude Toward Foreign Media

Foreign media, if allowed into Iraq, is closely inspected and subject to expulsion.

News Agencies

The Iraqi News Agency (INA), located in Baghdad, is controlled by the Iraqi government and is Iraq's only news agency. The INA reduced its number of foreign offices from 48 to 15 in the period following the 1990 UN sanctions.

Broadcast Media

According to the U.S. Central Intelligence Agency, 13 television stations operated in Iraq in 1997. There were 75 televisions per 1,000 Iraqis in 1997, and 208 radios per thousand. Broadcast media, particularly radio, is the most widely used media in Iraq. According to the BBC, numerous alternative radio services are aimed at Iraq, including the U.S. government-backed Radio Free Iraq.

Electronic Media

In 2000 one Internet service provider (ISP) operated in Iraq. However, the government totally controlled access to the Internet. Numerous newspapers, such as *Alef-Ba, Alwan, Al-Islam, Al-Iktisadi, Al-Ittehad, Al-Mawied, Nabdh Ashabab, Al-Raae, Al-Rafedain, Saut Alta-meem,* and *Al-Talabah,* have Arabic language Web sites.

The *Iraq Daily* and the Iraqi News Agency (INA) operate Web sites with English translations. The web address for INA is www.uruklink.net/iraqnews/.

EDUCATION AND TRAINING

Iraq's major universities are the University of Baghdad (36,000 students), the University of Mosul (20,000), the University of Basrah (18,000) and the University of Salahuddin (10,000). These Iraqi universities offer bachelor's, master's and Ph.D. degrees. Iraq's major universities offer their courses in Arabic and in English. The University of Salahuddin, located in the northern Kurdish area, offers its courses in Arabic, English and Kurdish.

In 2001 the University of Baghdad was the only university listing journalism as a course of study.

SUMMARY

Freedom of the press does not exist in Iraq. All mass media elements are either owned and or controlled by the Iraqi government. Iraq's broadcast media provides the greatest market penetration since newspaper circulation was estimated at 20 per 1,000 Iraqis in 1996. The low literacy rate of Iraq's population may explain some of the country's low newspaper circulation rate.

SIGNIFICANT DATES

- 1990: The UN imposes import/export sanctions on Iraq.
- 1996: The UN's "Food for Oil" program allows Iraq to sell oil to fund food, medicine and other humanitarian goods purchases and to purchase equipment to repair the civilian infrastructure.
- 1998: Radio Free Iraq (operated by the United States) begins operation.

BIBLIOGRAPHY

"Countries Ranked by Population." U.S. Census, International Data Base. Washington, DC, 2000.

"Focus International: Human Rights in Iraq Deteriorate." Foreign & Commonwealth Office. London, England, November 2000.

"Focus International: Iraq: Sanctions and the 'Oil for Food' Agreement." Foreign & Commonwealth Office. London, England, 1991.

"Focus International: The Work of the United Nations Special Commission in Iraq." Foreign & Commonwealth Office. London, England, October 1998.

"Iraq Annual Report 2002," Reporters Without Borders. Washington, DC, 2002.

"Literacy and Non Formal Education Sector Estimates and Projections of Adult Illiteracy for Population Aged 15 years Old and Above by Country." UNESCO Institute for Statistics, January 2002.

Metz, Helen Chapin, editor. "Iraq: A Country Study," Federal Research Division, U.S. Library of Congress. Washington, DC, 1988.

"World Press Freedom Review," International Press Institute. Vienna, Austria, 2002.

"Saddam Hussein's Iraq." U.S. Department of State. Washington, DC, September 1999.

U.S. Central Intelligence Agency (CIA). *The World Factbook 2002.* Washington, DC, 2002.

—Sandra J. Callaghan

IRELAND

BASIC DATA

Official Country Name:	Ireland
Region (Map name):	Europe
Population:	3,840,838
Language(s):	English, Irish (Gaelic)
Literacy rate:	98.0%
Area:	70,280 sq km
GDP:	93,865 (US$ millions)
Number of Daily Newspapers:	6
Total Circulation:	567,000
Circulation per 1,000:	191
Number of Nondaily Newspapers:	61
Total Circulation:	1,372,000
Circulation per 1,000:	462
Newspaper Consumption (minutes per day):	40
Total Newspaper Ad Receipts:	307 (Euro millions)
As % of All Ad Expenditures:	46.80
Number of Television Stations:	4
Number of Television Sets:	1,820,000
Television Sets per 1,000:	473.9
Television Consumption (minutes per day):	199
Number of Cable Subscribers:	672,220
Cable Subscribers per 1,000:	176.9

Number of Satellite Subscribers:	130,000
Satellite Subscribers per 1,000:	33.8
Number of Radio Stations:	115
Number of Radio Receivers:	2,550,000
Radio Receivers per 1,000:	663.9
Radio Consumption (minutes per day):	305
Number of Individuals with Computers:	1,360,000
Computers per 1,000:	354.1
Number of Individuals with Internet Access:	784,000
Internet Access per 1,000:	204.1
Internet Consumption (minutes per day):	23

BACKGROUND & GENERAL CHARACTERISTICS

The Republic of Ireland, which occupies 5/6 of the island of Ireland, is roughly equal to the state of South Carolina in terms of size and population. Half the population is urban, with a third living in metropolitan Dublin. Ireland is 92 percent Roman Catholic and has a 98 percent literacy rate. Despite centuries of English rule that sought to obliterate Ireland's Celtic language, one-fifth of the population can speak Gaelic today. Full political independence from Great Britain came in 1948 when the Republic of Ireland was established, but the United Kingdom maintains a strong economic presence in Ireland.

The printing press came to Ireland in 1550. Early news sheets appeared a century later. The *Irish Intelligencer* began publication in 1662 as the first commercial newspaper, and the country's first penny newspaper, the *Irish Times,* began in 1859. The *Limerick Chronicle,* which was founded in 1766, is the second-oldest English-language newspaper still in existence (the oldest is the *Belfast Newsletter*).

Irish newspapers are typically divided into two categories: the national press, most of which is based in Dublin, and the regional press, which is dispersed throughout the country. The national press consists of four dailies, two evening newspapers, and five Sunday newspapers. There are approximately 60 regional newspapers, most of which are published on a weekly basis. Competition among newspapers in Dublin is spirited, but few other cities in Ireland have competing local newspapers.

Roughly 460,000 national newspapers are sold in the Republic each day. The sales leader is the *Irish Independent*, a broadsheet especially popular among rural, conservative readers. The second best seller is the *Irish Times*, which is regularly read by highly educated urban professionals and managers. The *Irish Times* is probably Ireland's most influential paper. The third most popular national daily in Ireland is the tabloid *The Star*, an Irish edition of the *British Daily Star*. The *Irish Examiner* sells the least nationally, but it is the sales leader in Munster, Ireland's southwest quarter. Published in the city of Cork, the *Irish Examiner* is the only national daily issued outside of Dublin.

Some 130,000 evening newspapers are sold every day in Ireland. The leader is the *Evening Herald*, a tabloid popular in Dublin and along the east coast. The other evening paper is the *Evening Echo*, a tabloid published in Cork, and like its morning sister paper the *Irish Examiner*, popular in Munster.

Five Sunday newspapers are published in Ireland, with a total circulation of 800,000. The *Sunday Independent*, like the daily *Irish Independent*, has the largest circulation. *Sunday World*, a tabloid, comes in a close second. The other broadsheet, the *Sunday Tribune*, has a circulation of less than a third of *Sunday Independent's*. The fourth most popular Sunday paper is the *Sunday Business Post*, read by highly educated professionals and managers. The lowest circulating Sunday paper is the tabloid *Ireland on Sunday*, which is popular among young adult urban males. The other weekly national newspaper in Ireland is the tabloid *Irish Farmer's Journal*, which serves Ireland's agricultural sector.

Newspaper penetration in Ireland is about the same as that of the United States: 59 percent of adults read a daily paper. The newspapers that are most-often read are Irish. Of the 59 percent of adults who read daily newspapers, 50 percent read an Irish title only, 5 percent read both Irish and UK dailies, and 4 percent read UK titles only. Newspaper reading patterns change on Sunday, when 76 percent of adults read a paper. Of this 76 percent, 51 percent read an Irish title only, 16 percent read both Irish and UK Sundays, and 9 percent read UK titles only. The total readership of UK Sunday newspapers is 25 percent, compared with 9 percent who read UK daily papers.

Regional newspapers have a small readership, but one that is loyal, a fact that has turned regional papers into attractive properties for larger companies to buy. Examiner Publications, for example, has bought nine regional papers: *Carlow Nationalist, Down Democrat, Kildare Nationalist, The Kingdom, Laois Nationalist, Newry Democrat, Sligo Weekender, Waterford News & Star*, and *Western People*. Other major buyers of regional

Daily and Non-Daily Newspaper Titles and Circulation Figures

	1996	1997	1998	1999	2000
Number of Daily Newspapers	6	6	6	6	6
Circulation of Dailies (000)	544	552	557	567	NA
Number of Non-Daily Newspapers	61	61	61	61	61
Circulation of Non-Dailies (000)	NA	NA	NA	NA	NA

Source: World Association of Newspapers and Zenithmedia, *World Press Trends 2001*, pp. 8, 10, 17, 19. Note: NA stands for not available.

newspapers include Independent News & Media and Scottish Radio Holdings.

Unlike their national counterparts, regional newspapers carry little national news and have traditionally been reluctant to advocate political positions. This pattern did not hold during the 2002 abortion referendum, however. The *Longford Leader* was reserved, complaining that various organizations had pressured ''people to vote, on what is essentially a moral issue, in accordance with what they tell us instead of in accordance with our own consciences.'' The *Limerick Leader*, by contrast, urged its readers to vote for the referendum: ''Essentially the current proposal protects the baby and the mother. Defeat would open up the possibility of increased dangers to both.''

There are 30 magazine publishers in Ireland publishing 156 consumer magazines and 7 trade magazines. Only five percent of magazines are sold through subscription in Ireland; most are sold at the retail counter. One-fourth of magazine revenues come from advertising; the remaining three-fourths comes from sales. By far the most popular magazine in Ireland is the weekly radio and television guide, *RTÉ Guide*, which far outsells the most popular titles for women (*VIP* and *VIP Style*), general interest (*Buy & Sell* and *Magill*), and sports (*Breaking Ball* and *Gaelic Sport*).

Like Ireland's newspapers, Ireland's indigenous magazine publishers face strong competition from UK titles. According to the Periodical Publishers Association of Ireland, four out of every ten magazines bought in Ireland are imported. Magazines suffered a financial blow in 2000 when the government banned tobacco advertising, which had been the second-largest source of magazine advertising revenue. Magazines receive a very small share of Ireland's advertising expenditure: in 2000, magazines received only 2 percent; newspapers received 55 percent; and radio and television received 33 percent.

A recent survey of 46 Irish book publishers found a vital book publishing industry. Seventy percent of book publishing in Ireland is for primary, secondary, and post-secondary education. Most of the remaining 30 percent is non-fiction, but the market for Irish fiction and children's books is active. Irish book publishers sell most of their books domestically (89 percent), although export sales (11 percent) are notable. More than 800 new titles are published each year, and Irish publishers keep about 7,400 titles in print.

ECONOMIC FRAMEWORK

During the 1990s, Ireland earned the nickname ''Celtic tiger'' because of its robust economic growth. No longer an agricultural economy in the bottom quarter of the European Union, Ireland rose to the top quarter through industry, which accounts for 38 percent of its GDP, 80 percent of its exports, and 28 percent of its labor force. Ireland became a country with significant immigration. The economic boom, which included a 50 percent jump in disposable income, also led to increased spending in the media as well as increased numbers of media operators in Ireland. The underside of these achievements is child poverty, real estate inflation, and traffic congestion.

By far, the largest Irish media company is Independent News and Media PLC, which sells 80 percent of the Irish newspapers sold in Ireland. Independent News publishes the *Irish Independent*, the national daily with the highest circulation in Ireland, the two leading national Sunday newspapers, the national *Evening Herald*, 11 regional newspapers, and the Irish edition of the *British Daily Star*. Yet these properties, along with a yellow page directory, contribute only 28 percent of the revenues of Independent News; most of the rest comes from its international media properties. Despite the dominance of Independent News in Ireland, the Irish Competition Authority has concluded that the Irish newspaper industry remains editorially diverse.

The mind behind Independent News is Tony O'Reilly, whose 30 percent stake in the company is worth $430 million. O'Reilly founded Independent News in 1973 with a $2.4 million investment in the Irish Independent. Now the company includes the largest chains in South Africa and New Zealand, regional papers in Aus-

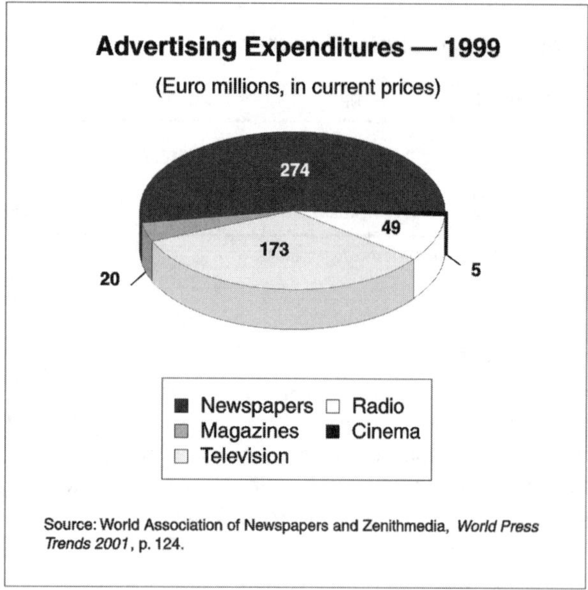

Source: World Association of Newspapers and Zenithmedia, *World Press Trends 2001*, p. 124.

tralia, and London's Independent. O'Reilly, who is the richest living Irishman with a personal fortune of $1.3 billion, has been a rugby star, CEO of the H. J. Heinz Company, and chairman of Waterford Wedgwood. He earned a Ph.D. in agricultural marketing from the University of Bradford, England, and was knighted in 2001. "I am a maximalist," O'Reilly says. "I want more of everything."

There is some media cross-ownership in Ireland. A few local newspapers own shares in local commercial radio stations. Independent News has a 50 percent financial interest in Chorus, the second largest cable operator in Ireland. Scottish Radio Holdings owns the national commercial radio service Today FM as well as six regional newspapers. O'Reilly is the Chairman not only of Independent News, but also of the Valentia consortium, which owns Eircom, operator of one of the largest online services in Ireland, eircom.net.

Most Irish journalists, both in print and in broadcast, belong to the National Union of Journalists, which serves as both a trade union and a professional organization. The NUJ is the world's largest union of journalists, with over 25,000 members in England, Scotland, Wales, and Ireland. Recently, the NUJ fought a newspaper publishers' proposal to give copyright of staff-generated material to media companies to stop them from being able to syndicate material without paying royalties to journalists.

Ireland's largest publishers are represented by National Newspapers of Ireland (NNI). Originally formed to promote newspaper advertising, it has expanded to lobby the government on major concerns of the newspaper industry.

Press Laws

Although the Irish Constitution does not mention privacy per se, the Supreme Court has said, "The right to privacy is one of the fundamental personal rights of the citizen which flow from the Christian and democratic nature of the State." Legislative measures to protect privacy include the Data Protection Act of 1988, which regulates the collection, use, storage, and disclosure of personal information that is processed electronically. Individuals have a right to read and correct information that is held about them. Wiretapping and electronic surveillance are regulated under the Interception of Postal Packets and Telecommunications Messages (Regulation) Act, which was passed after the Supreme Court ruled in 1987 that the unwarranted wiretaps of two reporters violated the constitution.

Because there is no press council or ombudsman for the press in Ireland, the main way to deal with complaints about the Irish media is to go to court. Irish libel laws leave the media vulnerable to defamation lawsuits, which are common. Libel suits are hard to defend against, so the press often settles out of court rather than go through the expense of a trial and then pay the increasingly large judgments that juries award to plaintiffs. Defamation suits cost Ireland's newspapers and broadcasters tens of millions of Euros every year. As a result, lawyers are kept on staff to advise on everything from story ideas to book manuscripts. "When in doubt, leave it out," has become editorial wisdom. The media keeps one eye on the courtroom and the other on distributors and stores, some of which have refused to carry publications for fear that they too could be sued for libel.

Defamation has not chilled the Irish press entirely, but it has made investigative journalism difficult. Veronica Guerin's exposés about the Irish drug underworld in *The Sunday Independent* are a case in point. Naming persons as drug dealers is a sure-fire way to elicit a libel suit in Ireland, unless, that is, the criminals explicitly comment on allegations made against them. So despite being threatened, beaten, and even shot, Guerin persisted in confronting drug dealers to get them to say something that she could report in the newspaper. Mostly Guerin used nicknames to identify the criminals, making sure not to use details that would make them readily identifiable. This strategy averred libel suits, because in order to sue, the criminals would have to prove that they were the persons who were nicknamed. In 1995, Guerin received the 1995 International Press Freedom Award from the Committee to Protect Journalists. The following year she was shot to death.

According to Irish law, defamation is the publication of a false statement about a person that lowers the individual in the estimation of right-thinking members of society. The Defamation Act of 1961 does not require the plaintiff to prove that the reporter was negligent or that the reporter failed to exercise reasonable care. The plaintiff does not even have to give evidence that he or she was harmed personally or professionally: the law assumes that false reports are harmful. The plaintiff merely has to show that the offensive words referred to him or her and were published by the defendant. It is up to the defendant to prove that the report is true.

The truth of media reports can be hard to prove. In 2002, John Waters, a columnist for the *Irish Times*, sued The Sunday Times of London for an article written by gossip columnist Terry Keane. The article was about a talk that Waters had given before a performance of the Greek tragedy *Medea*. Keane called Waters' talk ''a gender-based assault,'' and added that she felt sorry for Waters' daughter: ''When she becomes a teenager and, I hope, believes in love, should she suffer from mood swings or any affliction of womanhood, she will be truly goosed. And better not ask Dad for tea or sympathy. . . or help.'' Waters said that the article tarnished his reputation as a father, and the jury agreed, awarding him 84,000 euro in damages plus court costs.

As this case shows, even journalists are not reluctant to sue for libel in Ireland. But other groups sue more frequently. Business people and professionals, particularly lawyers, file libel suits most often; they are followed by politicians. Indeed, Irish libel laws favor public officials and civil servants, who can sue for defamation at government expense. If they lose, they owe the government nothing, but if they win, they get to keep the award.

Two strategies are under consideration to reform libel law in Ireland. The first is legislative. National Newspapers of Ireland (NNI) advocates changes in libel law in exchange for formal self-regulation. According to NNI, the Irish public would be better served by having the courts be the forum of last, rather than first, resort in defamation cases. NNI would like to see a strong code of ethics that would be enforced by the ombudsmen of individual media if possible and by a country-wide press council if necessary. But this system can be established only with libel reform, because as the law stands now, a newspaper that publishes an apology is in essence documenting evidence of its own legal liability.

The second strategy to reform libel law in Ireland is judicial. Civil libertarians want an Irish media organization to challenge a libel judgment all the way to the European Court of Human Rights in Strasbourg, a court to which Ireland owes allegiance by treaty. If the Irish government loses its case in the Strasbourg court, it is obliged to change its laws to conform to the ruling. Many civil libertarians pin their hope for significant libel reform upon the Strasbourg court because it has ruled that excessive levels of defamation awards impinge free expression.

Despite these strategies for libel reform, the Defamation Act of 1961 still stands because politicians tend to view the media with skepticism and have grave doubts about the sincerity and efficacy of media self-regulation. The Irish public, meanwhile, tends to believe that the media want libel reform more for reasons of self interest than for public service. Change, therefore, is slow. Political scientist Michael Foley fears that ''the Irish media will remain a sort of lottery in which many of the players win. Freedom of the press will continue to be the big loser.''

CENSORSHIP

The Irish Constitution simultaneously advocates freedom of expression and, by forbidding expression that is socially undesirable, permits censorship: ''The education of public opinion being, however, a matter of such grave import to the common good, the State shall endeavour to ensure that organs of public opinion, such as the radio, the press, the cinema, while preserving their rightful liberty of expression, including criticism of Government policy, shall not be used to undermine public order or morality or the authority of the State.'' The Constitution also says, ''The publication or utterance of blasphemous, seditious, or indecent matter is an offence which shall be punishable in accordance with law.'' Accordingly, the government has enacted and rigorously enforced several censorship laws including Censorship of Film Acts, Censorship of Publications Acts, Offenses Against the State Acts, and the Official Secrets Act.

The history of censorship in Ireland is also a history of diminishing suppression. A case in point is the 1997 Freedom of Information Act, which changed the longstanding Official Secrets Act, under which all government documents were secret unless specified otherwise. Now most government documents, except for those pertaining to Irish law enforcement and other subjects of sensitive national interest, are made available upon request. The number of requests for information under the Freedom of Information Act has increased steadily since the law was passed.

The Censorship of Publications Acts of 1929, 1946, and 1967 have governed the censorship of publications. The Acts set up a Censorship and Publications Board, which replaced a group called the Committee of Enquiry on Evil Literature, to examine books and periodicals about which any person has filed a complaint. The Board may prohibit the sale and distribution in Ireland of any publications that it judges to be indecent, defined as ''suggestive of, or inciting to sexual immorality or unnatural vice or likely in any other similar way to corrupt or deprave,'' or that advocate ''the unnatural prevention of conception or the procurement of abortion,'' or that provide titillating details of judicial proceedings, especially divorce. A prohibition order lasts up to twelve years, but decisions made by the Board are subject to judicial review.

The first decades under censorship laws were a time of strong enforcement, thanks in large measure to the Catholic Truth Society, which was relentless in its petitions to the Censorship Board. Before the 1980s, hundreds of books and movies were banned every year in Ireland, titles including such notable works as Hemingway's *A Farewell To Arms*, Huxley's *Brave New World*, Mead's *Coming Of Age In Samoa*, and Steinbeck's *The Grapes Of Wrath*. *Playboy* magazine was not legally available in Ireland until 1995. The English writer Robert Graves described Ireland as having ''the fiercest literary censorship this side of the Iron Curtain,'' and the Irish writer Frank O'Connor referred to the ''great Gaelic heritage of intolerance.''

Although the flood of censorship has slowed to a trickle, recent cases serve as a reminder that censorship efforts still exist in Ireland today. A Dublin Public Library patron complained to the Censorship Board that *Every Woman's Life Guide* and *Our Bodies, Ourselves* contained references to abortion. The library removed the books because, according to a Dublin Public Library spokesperson, ''We're not employed to put ourselves at legal risk.'' In 1994, the Oliver Stone film *Natural Born Killers* was banned. In 1999, the Censorship Board banned for six months the publication of *In Dublin*, a twice-monthly events guide, because the magazine published advertisements for massage parlors. The High Court chastised the board for excessiveness and lifted the ban on condition that the offending advertisements would appear no longer.

The potential for censorship in Ireland is real, but circumscribed. Not only have recent government censors shown restraint in inverse proportion to the power they have on paper, but most of the censorship that they have exercised is over blatant pornography. Furthermore, Ireland is awash with foreign media, so parochial censorship is likely to be countered readily by information from the UK, Western Europe, and the United States.

STATE-PRESS RELATIONS

Like other western European countries, Ireland has an established free press tradition. The Irish Constitution guarantees ''liberty of expression, including criticism of Government policy'' but makes it unlawful to undermine ''the authority of the State.'' Although not absolute, press freedom is fundamental to Irish society.

The extent to which the Irish media exercise their right to criticize government policy is a matter of perspective. Many politicians and government officials believe that the press is critical to the point of being downright carnivorous. Garrett Fitzgerald, former prime minister of Ireland, agreed with Edward Pearce of *New Statesman & Society* who said that the media ''devour our politicians, briefly exalting them before commencing a sort of car-crushing process.'' However, others disagree, complaining that the press acquiesces to the wishes of the government. ''The relationship between the media, especially the broadcast media, and the political establishment is the aorta in the heart of any functioning democracy. Unfortunately, in Ireland this relationship has become so profoundly skewed that it threatens the health of the body politic,'' Liam Fay complained in the *London Sunday Times*. While RTÉ [Radio Telefís Éireann] will never become ''the proverbial dog to the politicians' lamppost,'' said Fay, ''the station has a responsibility to do more than simply provide a leafy green backdrop against which our leaders and would-be leaders can display their policies in full bloom. Yet this is precisely what much of RTÉ's political coverage now amounts to.''

Revelations in the 1980s that the government had tapped the phones of three journalists for long periods of time helped to spur further adversity between news reporters and the government. Because the government had tapped the phones of Geraldine Kennedy of the *Sunday Tribune* and Bruce Arnold of the *Irish Independent* without proper authorization in an attempt to track down cabinet leaks, the High Court awarded £20,000 each to Kennedy and Arnold and an additional £10,000 to Arnold's wife. Vincent Brown of *Magill* magazine, whose phone was tapped when his research had put him in touch with members of the IRA, settled out of court in 1995 for £95,000.

The government office established to deal with the media is Government Information Services (GIS), made up of the Government Press Secretary, the Deputy Government Press Secretary, and four government press officers. Charged with providing ''a free flow of government-related information,'' GIS issues press releases and statements, arranges access to officials, and coordinates public information campaigns.

ATTITUDE TOWARD FOREIGN MEDIA

The government of Ireland has a cooperative relationship with foreign media. The Department of Foreign Affairs keeps domestic and international media up to date on developments in Irish foreign policy by publishing a range of information on paper and electronically, providing press briefings, and arranging meetings between foreign correspondents and the agencies about which they want to report.

Opposition to foreign media in Ireland thus comes not from the government but rather from Irish publishers, who complain of unfair competition from British media companies. One complaint involves below-cost selling. Irish publishers protest that their British competitors sell newspapers in Ireland at a cover price with which Irish newspaper companies cannot compete. Irish publishers also complain that the 12.5 percent valued added tax (VAT) on newspaper sales in Ireland causes an unfair burden. Huge British companies, which have no VAT tax at home, are able to absorb the Irish tax more easily than Irish publishers, who lack the cushion British publishers enjoy. Irish publishers claim that below-cost selling and the VAT tax have helped ensure that a significant portion of daily and Sunday newspapers sold in Ireland are British.

Besides competing with imported media, Irish companies are increasingly finding themselves competing with foreign-owned companies at home. Scottish Radio Holdings owns Today FM, the national newspaper *Ireland on Sunday*, and five regional papers. CanWest Global Communications has a 45 percent stake in TV3, as does Granada, the largest commercial television company in the UK. And Trinity Mirror, the biggest newspaper publisher in the UK and the second largest in Europe, owns *Irish Daily Mirror*, *The Sunday Business Post*, *Donegal Democrat*, and *Donegal Peoples Press*. Until recently, foreign ownership of Irish media has been limited. But the Irish media market is attractive and there is no legislation that prevents foreign ownership of Irish media, so the sale of Irish media properties to foreign (primarily British) companies is expected to continue.

NEWS AGENCIES

Because Ireland is a small country, there are no domestic Irish news agencies. Irish media use international news agencies and their own reporters for news gathering. Although some of the major international agencies have a bureau in Dublin—representatives include Dow Jones Newswires, ITAR-TASS, Reuters, and BBC—many do not, choosing instead to rely upon their London correspondents to report on Ireland as stories arise.

BROADCAST MEDIA

Since the 1920s, broadcasting in Ireland has been dominated by RTÉ, a public service agency that is funded by license fees and the sale of advertising time. RTÉ runs four radio and three television channels. Radio 1 is RTÉ's flagship radio station. Begun in 1926, it broadcasts a mixture of news, information, music, and drama. RTÉ's popular music station 2 FM is known for its support of new and emerging Irish artists and musicians. Lyric FM is RTÉ's 24-hour classical music and arts station. The fourth RTÉ station is Radió na Gaeltachta, which was established in 1972 to provide full service broadcasting in Irish. RTÉ also operates RTÉ 1, a television station that emphasizes news and current affairs programming; Network 2, a sports and entertainment channel; and TG4, which televises Irish-language programs. RTÉ is currently in the process of launching four new digital television channels: a 24-hour news and sports channel, an education channel, a youth channel, and a legislative channel.

The funding for RTÉ has been a source of contention among Ireland's commercial broadcasters, who complain that license fees contribute to unfair competition. RTÉ receives license fees to support public service broadcasting even though RTÉ's schedule is by no means exclusively noncommercial. Commercial broadcasters, by contrast, are required to program news and current affairs, but without any support from license fees. Meanwhile, because the government is loath to increase license fees, RTÉ is finding it must rely more upon advertising even as increasing competition among broadcasters is making advertising revenue more difficult to obtain.

Besides RTÉ's public stations, there are many independent radio and television stations in Ireland. There are 43 licensed independent radio stations in Ireland. In addition to the independent national station, Today FM, there are 23 local commercial stations, 16 non-commercial community stations, and four hospital or college stations. Although many of the independent stations broadcast a rather stock set of music, advertising, disk jockey chatter, and current affairs programs, some serve their communities with unique discussion programs.

Pirate radio stations have existed in Ireland as long as Ireland has had radio. Today about 50 pirate stations operate throughout Ireland. The Irish government tolerates these stations as long as they do not interfere with the signals of licensed broadcasters.

The only independent indigenous television station in Ireland is TV3. Although licensed to broadcast in 1988, TV3 did not begin broadcasting until 1998. It took ten years to find financial backing, 90 percent of which finally came from the television giants Granada (UK) and CanWest Global Communications (Canada). TV3 produces few programs in house; most TV3 programs are sitcoms and soap operas imported from the United States, UK, and Australia.

More than half of Irish households subscribe to cable TV. (Cable penetration in Dublin is an astounding 83 percent.) Those who subscribe to cable receive the three Irish television channels, four UK channels, and a dozen satellite stations. Two companies, NTL and Chorus, control most cable TV in Ireland. The US-owned NTL is the largest. Chorus Communication is owned by a partnership of Independent News and Media, the Irish conglomerate, and Liberty Media International, which is owned by AT&T.

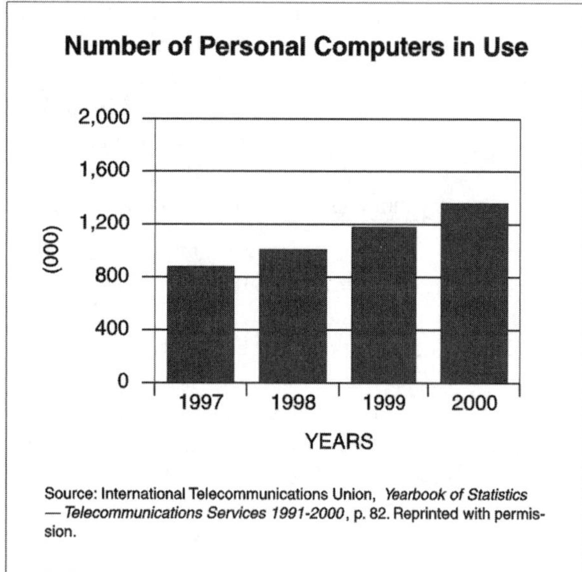

Source: International Telecommunications Union, *Yearbook of Statistics — Telecommunications Services 1991-2000*, p. 82. Reprinted with permission.

The only provider of digital satellite in Ireland is Sky Digital, operated by British Sky Broadcasting (BSkyB). Twenty percent of households in Ireland subscribe to Sky Digital. Sky offers more than 100 broadcast television channels plus audio music and pay-per-view channels. Beginning with two matches between middleweight boxers Steve Collins and Chris Eubank in 1995, and quickly followed by golf tournaments and even an Ireland-USA rugby game, Sky has bought exclusive rights to Irish sports events for broadcast on a pay-per-view basis. Sky's purchases have had the effect of making certain events exclusive that had customarily been broadcast freely. Irish viewers can no longer expect to see every domestic sports event without paying extra.

All information transmitted electronically, from broadcast to cable to satellite and Internet, is under the authority of the Broadcasting Commission of Ireland (BCI), as set forth in the Broadcasting Act of 2001. BCI is responsible for the licensing and oversight of broadcasting as well as for writing and enforcing a code of broadcasting standards.

Electronic News Media

Ireland today is a center for the production and use of computers in Europe. One-third of all PCs sold in Europe are made in Ireland, and many software companies have plants there. Indigenous companies include the Internet security firm Baltimore Technologies and the software integration company Iona Technologies.

The longest running Internet news service in the world is The Irish Emigrant, which Liam Ferrie began as an electronic newsletter in 1987 to keep his overseas colleagues at Digital Equipment Corporation informed of news from Ireland. Today, The Irish Emigrant reaches readers in over 130 countries. A hard copy version has appeared on green newsprint in Boston and New York since 1995. The Irish Internet Association gave Ferrie its first Net Visionary Award in 1999.

Virtually all broadcasters and newspapers in Ireland have a web page. The Irish Times launched its website in 1994 and transformed it into the portal site, Ireland.com, four years later. This website attracts 1.7 million visits from 630,000 unique users each month, a rate in Ireland second only to the site of the discount airline Ryanair. Following the trend among content-driven web sites throughout the world, Ireland.com began to charge for access to certain sections of the site in 2002. Ireland's Internet penetration rate was 33 percent in 2002; the penetration rate in Dublin was 53 percent.

Education & Training

Journalism education is becoming increasingly common in Ireland. At least three institutions of higher education offer degrees in journalism. Dublin City University's School of Communications offers several undergraduate and graduate degrees including specialties in journalism, multimedia, and political communication. Dublin Institute of Technology offers a B.A. degree in Journalism Studies and a Language, designed to educate journalists for international assignments or for dual-language careers at home. Griffith College Dublin offers a B.A. degree in Journalism & Media Communications as well as a one-year program to prepare students for a career in radio broadcasting. Irish students who need financial assistance in order to study journalism can apply for the Tom McPhail Journalism Bursary, a scholarship administered by the National Union of Journalists in honor of the Irish Press and Granada Television news editor who cofounded the short-lived Ireland International News Agency.

Summary

Given its relatively small population of 3.8 million, the Republic of Ireland has a rich media environment. It is served by 12 national newspapers—four dailies, two evenings, five Sundays, and one weekly—and by more than 60 regional newspapers. There are more than 150 indigenous consumer magazines and nearly 50 indigenous book publishers. Ireland has four national television stations, five national radio stations, and dozens of regional radio stations. There is a growing Irish presence on the Internet as well as an increasing Internet penetration rate in Ireland. There are also a plethora of imported books, magazines, and newspapers, as well as radio and television channels available through cable and satellite. Ireland's media environment is both populous and diverse, essential qualities for any healthy democracy.

Politically, the media in Ireland is as free from government interference as it has ever been. Before the 1990s, the Censorship Board banned hundreds of books and movies every year, a pattern that inhibited creativity at home and attempts at importing from abroad. Today the Censorship Board screens for pornography, but little more. Literature and film are free to circulate.

The government has also granted the media far wider access to its records. Until recently government records in Ireland were presumed to be private and unavailable to the public. But with the Freedom of Information Act of 1997, the press—or any Irish citizen—can now make formal requests to see government records, and with very few exceptions, those requests will be granted. The Freedom of Information Act has had the effect of encouraging more investigative reporting.

Libel, however, continues to be a problem for the press in Ireland. Libel suits are relatively easy to win in Ireland because the plaintiff has only to prove publication of defamatory statements, not their falsity, which in Ireland is the defendant's task. Furthermore, the more public the figure in Ireland, the greater the award for defamation that juries are likely to give. Such conditions make investigative reporting risky and, with the cost for lawyers on retainer, expensive. Nevertheless, the national Irish media continue to criticize government officials and discuss important social, political, economic, and religious issues. The chilling effect seems more potential than real at this point.

The media in Ireland are also facing economic challenges. One is globalization. Irish media confront stiff competition from magazines, books, and newspapers, as well as radio and television programs, that pour into Ireland from transnational UK companies with such economies of scale that they can undersell indigenous Irish products. Increasingly, media companies from the UK are buying Irish media, and large Irish companies are doing the same, so that there are fewer and fewer owners of the media. This increasing concentration is likely to diminish diversity in media content.

The public service tradition in Irish broadcasting is experiencing similar difficulties. RTÉ relies upon license fees supplemented with advertising revenue to fund its programming, which ranges from news and current affairs to entertainment and cultural programming both in English and in Gaelic. At the same time, RTÉ is facing increasing competition from commercial broadcasters that offer popular, lighter fare. Under these circumstances, RTÉ audiences will decline, making it both more difficult to generate advertising revenue and to justify increased license fees. Although RTÉ operates under a mandate to offer programs that serve viewers rather than merely satisfy them, the pressure on RTÉ is to compete with its commercial counterparts by shifting from a model of public service to a marketplace model.

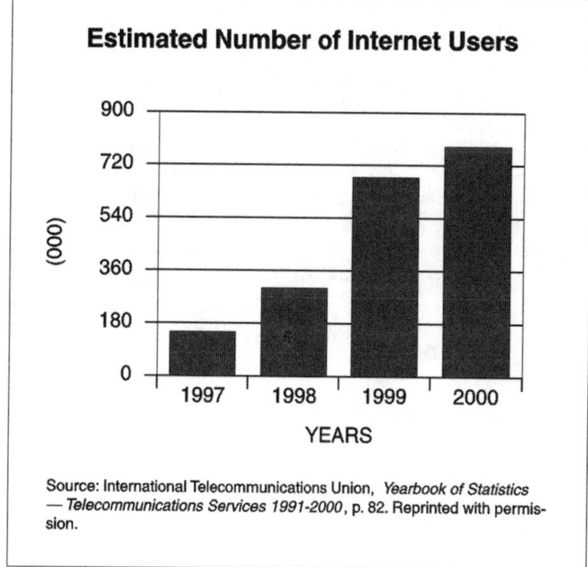

Source: International Telecommunications Union, *Yearbook of Statistics — Telecommunications Services 1991-2000*, p. 82. Reprinted with permission.

The trends toward concentration and commercialization of the media in Ireland are indeed powerful, but their effects are likely to be mitigated, at least in part, by other forces. One of these forces is technology. The Internet, with its small but growing presence in Ireland, offers the very real opportunity to contribute ideas to the public sphere that have little apparent commercial appeal. Businesses and established publishers and broadcasters dominate the Internet, but not exclusively, so the Internet will continue to be available as an avenue for dissent and other alternative expression. Furthermore, as long as the desire to preserve, promote, and explore Irish culture and language is strong, unique, and compelling, Irish communications will continue to circulate, sometimes commercially and sometimes as the result of government planning and investment.

SIGNIFICANT DATES

- 1997: Freedom of Information Act passed.
- 1998: TV3, Ireland's first commercial television station, began broadcasting.
- 2001: Broadcasting Act passed.

BIBLIOGRAPHY

Farrell, Brian. *Communications and Community in Ireland.* Dublin: Mercier, 1984.

Horgan, John. *Irish Media: A Critical History Since 1922.* London: Routledge, 2001.

Kelly, Mary J. and Barbara O'Connor, eds. *Media Audiences in Ireland: Power and Cultural Identity.* Dublin: University College Dublin Press, 1997.

Kiberd, Damien, ed. *Media in Ireland: The Search for Ethical Journalism.* Dublin: Four Courts, 1999.

———. *Media in Ireland: The Search for Diversity.* Dublin: Four Courts, 1997.

Oram, Hugh. *The Newspaper Book: A History of Newspapers in Ireland, 1649-1983.* Dublin: MO Books, 1983.

Woodman, Kieran. *Media Control in Ireland, 1923-1983.* Carbondale: Southern Illinois University Press, 1985.

—John P. Ferré

ISLE OF MAN

BASIC DATA

Official Country Name:	Isle of Man
Region (Map name):	Europe
Population:	73,117
Language(s):	English, Manx Gaelic
Literacy rate:	N/A

The Isle of Man lies between Great Britain and Ireland in the Irish Sea. Once part of the Norwegian Kingdom of the Hebrides, it came under British control in 1765. The Isle of Man has one dependent islet, the Calf of Man, which is a bird sanctuary. The Isle of Man chief of state is the British monarch, represented locally by an appointed Lieutenant Governor. The government is headed by the Chief Minister, who is elected by the members of the bicameral Tynwald, which consists of an 11-member Legislative Council and a 24-seat House of Keys. The population is approximately 73,000, and the official language is English. Many speak a dialect called Manx Celtic, and there are extensive efforts to keep this language alive. Offshore banking, manufacturing and tourism make up the largest sectors of the economy.

Citizens of the island enjoy the press and speech freedoms of England. The Isle of Man Newspapers Ltd. publishes the country's three newspapers, all of which appear weekly in English. Content from the publications appears on the Isle of Man Online Web portal, also owned by the newspaper company. The *Isle of Man Courier* is a tabloid-format newspaper that prints on Thursday. Its circulation is approximately 35,000, and it is available free of charge. The *Isle of Man Examiner* is a broadsheet that prints on Tuesday. Its circulation is approximately 15,000. The *Manx Independent,* published on Friday, is a tabloid-format newspaper with an approximate circulation of 13,000.

There are two radio stations, one AM and one FM. There are approximately 27,500 televisions, but no television station. IofM.net is the sole Internet service provider.

BIBLIOGRAPHY

The Central Intelligence Agency (CIA). *The World Factbook.* Directorate of Intelligence, 2001. Available from http://www.cia.gov/.

The Isle of Man Courier, The ADWEB UK Regional Newspaper Database Service (2001). Available from http://www.adweb.co.uk.

The Isle of Man Examiner, The ADWEB UK Regional Newspaper Database Service (2001). Available from http://www.adweb.co.uk.

The Manx Independent, The ADWEB UK Regional Newspaper Database Service (2001). Available from http://www.adweb.co.uk.

—Jenny B. Davis

ISRAEL

BASIC DATA

Official Country Name:	State of Israel
Region (Map name):	Middle East
Population:	5,938,093
Language(s):	Hebrew, Arabic, English
Literacy rate:	95.0%
Area:	20,770 sq km
GDP:	110,386 (US$ millions)
Number of Television Stations:	17
Number of Television Sets:	1,690,000
Television Sets per 1,000:	284.6
Number of Cable Subscribers:	1,147,000
Cable Subscribers per 1,000:	185.0
Number of Satellite Subscribers:	1,160,000

Satellite Subscribers per 1,000:	195.3
Number of Radio Stations:	40
Number of Radio Receivers:	3,070,000
Radio Receivers per 1,000:	517.0
Number of Individuals with Computers:	1,590,000
Computers per 1,000:	267.8
Number of Individuals with Internet Access:	1,270,000
Internet Access per 1,000:	213.9

BACKGROUND & GENERAL CHARACTERISTICS

Since the very inception of the state of Israel on May 14, 1948, as the culmination of the Zionist movement, there has been virtually no respite from one kind of violence or another between Israelis and neighboring Arab states. Though the state of Israel's creation was mandated by the United Nations, Arab states rejected the arrangement. Wars in 1948, 1967, and 1973 ensued between the newly founded state and its neighbors with Israel winning each time. While Egypt has signed a peace treaty with Israel and other Arab states have recognized its existence as a state, there continues to be no overall peaceful resolution to the differing perspectives. Israel has been embroiled in dispute over the West Bank and the Gaza Strip with the former Palestine Liberation Organization (PLO)—now known as the Palestine Authority (PA)—as they have been given semi-autonomous governance in those areas. Within this milieu, access to information and use of technology plays a vital role in the ongoing maintenance of the state.

Country Geography Israel is located on the eastern shore of the Mediterranean Sea. It is bordered by Lebanon in the north, Syria in the northeast, Jordan directly east and southeast, Egypt to the southwest, and the Red Sea directly south. Its geographical location has placed it in an area where it could not help but make news and it has been performing to capacity ever since opening day in 1948. In fact, as noted by Rami Tal, relative to its size as a nation-state Israel is the largest source of news in the world.

State of the Press The history of the press begins all the way back in 1863 during the period of the Ottoman Empire, almost a century before the state of Israel existed. *Ha-Levanon* (founded by Yoel Moshe Salomon, later a founder of the town of Petah Tikva, and Michael Cohen) and *Havazzelet* (started six months after *Ha-Levanon* and founded by Rabbi Israel Bak as a voice for the Hassidic movement) were the first Hebrew newspapers—weeklies—established in Israel. Unfortunately, each weekly had a habit of informing the authorities about alleged illegal activities by the other and so the Ottomans shut down both of the papers within a year. *Havazzelet*, however, reopened in 1870 edited by Bak's son-in-law, Israel-Dov Frumkin, and ran for forty more years through 1911; outlasting many other weeklies attempting to start up and subsequently failing. *Havazzelet* was an extremely important early activist paper calling for numerous reforms and actions on behalf of the Jews residing in Palestine during that era. For his activism, Frumkin was issued a herem—excommuniction from the orthodox community—but he continued in his cause. Among his admonitions in *Havazzelet* were calls for assistance to Russian immigrants fleeing the pogroms of the 1880s, for an ending of the Old Yishuv (Jewish community in Palestine) dependence on philanthropic donations from abroad, and for aid for the Yemenite immigrants who were being exploited by Jewish farmers in the region.

Havazzelet offered one other important contribution to the Jewish people in Palestine. In 1882, Eliezer Ben-Yehuda joined the staff of the paper to which he had contributed to as a student in Paris. Ben-Yehuda eventually took over a weekly in 1885, called *Hatzvi* (Deer), which became *Hashkafa* (Outlook) in 1901 when the Ottomans gave him a license to publish his own paper, through which he greatly aided the new yishuv and the Zionist cause. However, his most important contribution through *Hatzvi* was aiding the revival of spoken Hebrew by disseminating new vocabulary through print. His work became so important to the reemergence of spoken Hebrew that he has been labeled the "reviver of the Hebrew language."

The ending of World War I saw considerable change in the press in Palestine. Dailies began to make their appearance, but were sporadic for quite some time. In 1910, Ben-Yehuda founded the first daily paper in Palestine, *Ha'or* (The Light), edited by his son, Itamar Ben Avi, who returned from working as a journalist in France in order to take up the post. However, only *Herut* (Freedom), which was initially published as a weekly in 1909 and had become a daily in 1912, continued to appear regularly. However, by 1917, during the administration of Palestine by the British as a League of Nations mandate, people who had been exiled by the Turks returned and the situation for the press began to improve. Dailies and weeklies began to take on more of their modern differentiations. Afternoon dailies began to appear alongside the morning dailies. And already during this period the publishing exodus from Jerusalem to Tel-Aviv was beginning.

By 1925, the political press ran by particular parties, was seeing its beginning with the publication of *Davar* (Event or Word). The General Federation of Labor (Histadrut) founded *Davar* and appointed one of its leaders, Berl Katznelson, editor. Due to the work of Katznelson the paper was a large success—its Friday literary supplement attracting some of the preeminent poets and writers of the time. Almost all of the papers of the time adhered to the ''mouthpiece of a political party'' model. Only *Hadashot Ha'aretz* (News of the Land), subsequently shortened to *Ha'aretz* (The Land), which was founded in 1919 in Jerusalem and moved to Tel Aviv in 1923, followed a different path (and later also *Yediot Aharonot*, but it was not founded until 1939). *Ha'aretz* attempted to be a serious publication advocating a liberal-democratic perspective. Dr. Moshe Glickson was the editor-in-chief during this period until 1937. In 1937, a German-Jewish multimillionaire, Shlomo-Zalman Schocken, a zealous patron of high culture, purchased *Ha'aretz*. Schocken appointed his son, Gershom (Gustav), editor and this remained the case for the following decades. *Ha'aretz* is still being published as one of the most respected and influential dailies in Israel and may be accessed on the Internet.

A final historical reflection concerns the inauguration of the rivalry between *Yediot Aharonot* (The Latest News) and *Ma'ariv* (Evening Paper) which remains one of the main rivalries of Israeli press in our day. *Yediot Aharonot* produced the most popular editor and journalist of the time, Azriel Carlebach. In early 1948, about three months before Israel was established as a nation-state, Carlebach staged a ''putsch.'' He left *Yediot Aharonot* with dozens of reporters, editors, administrative personnel and staff of the printing press to begin *Ma'ariv*. *Ma'ariv* was being funded by Oved Ben-Ami (a banker and investor from Netanya). Carlebach thought that *Yediot Aharonot* would collapse, eliminating competition, but he miscalculated. The owner (Yehuda Mozes) of *Yediot Aharonot* and his son (Noah Mozes) managed to keep the daily afloat. Thus, with both dailies continuing to operate, there remains huge animosity between them. Somewhat justifiably, *Yediot Aharonot* seems to be winning the rivalry with weekday circulations at 300,000 compared to weekday circulations of 160,000 for *Ma'ariv*. *Yediot Aharonot* became the clear forerunner by circulation in the 1970s, not only above *Ma'ariv* but also any other daily in the country. It remains undisputedly in the lead as concerns circulation. However, the unexpected death of Yehuda Mozes in a car accident in 1986 has caused internal instability in the paper due to contentions for control among family shareholders. Yet, Aharon Mozes, grandson of the founder and son of Noah Mozes retained control in 2002. *Yediot Aharonot* maintains a strong editorship tradition by maintaining Moshe Vardi, who studied international relations in London. He is the son of the late Herzl Rosenbloom who was the paper's editor from 1948 to 1986.

Israel far outshines other countries by the manner in which each and every event is reported, analyzed, and reanalyzed. Thus, with Israelis' constant concern to stay in the know for the sake of safety, some of the most intensive event coverage in the world, and a population ranking a 95 percent average literacy rate, there are many of people ready to read, listen, and watch. Israel, despite recent and ongoing increases in radio and television allegiance, still maintains one of the world's highest newspaper readership rates among adult populations.

All newspapers in Israel are privately owned and managed with Tel Aviv being the main publishing nexus. This makes sense when one considers that for all practical purposes it is also the functioning capital. Jerusalem is the actual capital, but most of the embassies are located in the port city of Tel Aviv. Not only is Tel Aviv the main publication center, but all papers are produced in the larger cities. This phenomena has arisen largely owing to various economic reasons including urbanization, employer and employee living concerns, reader base per capita, and relative ease of delivery due to the small size of Israel. Actually, the population is heavily concentrated along the coastal region, with roughly two-thirds inhabiting the area between Nahariyya in the north and Ashqelon in the south. The largest circulation newspapers can drop-ship their newsprint by air to Haifa from Tel-Aviv within one hour of press time. This potential for fast and thorough circulation of papers has led to all newspapers considering themselves national rather than local papers. Weekday circulation figures of many papers receive a considerable boost on the weekends. Friday editions are typically twice the size of the weekday editions due to added supplements and prove to be popular fare as they are issued on Sabbath eve; no papers are issued on Saturday.

Newspapers, especially the morning dailies, have strong religious and/or political ties. Despite high circulation figures and advertising revenue, as in the past, most papers still end up depending on political parties, religious organizations, and/or public monies to fund their business. This has a deleterious effect on freedom of the press as there are often expectations tied with the transferring of funds. Such limitations on the press have been soundly criticized time and again, but unfortunately the papers have a fine line to walk between losing necessary operating funding and being willing to acquiesce in certain areas.

Besides the dailies, there are approximately 400 other newspapers and magazines being published. Of the four hundred, about fifty are weekly and about one hundred and fifty are fortnightly publications. Eleven languages are utilized in the publishing of these materials; two hundred and fifty of them are published in Hebrew.

Dailies Israel has around twenty-two privately owned dailies. The most influential and respected daily is *Ha'aretz* (The Land) for both its news coverage and its commentary. It attempts to maintain a non-sensational approach and Israeli decision-makers keenly scrutinize the op-ed page. Due to the way it presents its material it is able to fit twice the amount of material on each page compared to *Yediot Aharonot* and *Ma'ariv* and is the most widely read morning paper with a typical circulation of 65,000 on weekdays and 75,000 on weekends. However, its readership is dwarfed by the popular afternoon press of *Ma'ariv* (Evening Prayer)—which produces a circulation of 160,000 on weekdays and 270,000 on weekends—and Yedioth Aharonoth (The Latest News)—with a weekday circulation of 300,000 and a weekend circulation of 600,000. The weekend circulation figures of dailies are especially staggering considering that no newspapers appear on Saturday.

The most influential English language daily newspaper is *The Jerusalem Post*. It provides detailed and reliable news coverage. It publishes nationally with weekday circulation figures at 30,000 and weekend numbers at 50,000. It also publishes a weekly English international edition with circulation numbers at 70,000 and a French international edition with circulation figures at 7,500. Though its circulation numbers are low, it is disproportionately influential due the fact that it is read by the diplomatic community and all the foreign journalists in Israel.

The overall weekday daily newspaper circulation figures lie in the range of 500,000-600,000. This averages out to around 21 papers per one hundred people, but most Israeli citizens end up reading more than one daily. Newspapers are produced in a variety of languages with the majority of dailies being in Hebrew. Other languages include: Arabic, English, French, Polish, Yiddish, Amharic, Farsi, Ladino, Romanian, Hungarian, Russian, and German.

The dailies include: *Al Anba* (The News; circ. 10,000; founded 1968), *Globes* (circ. 40,000; founded 1983), *Ha'aretz* (The Land; circ. 65,000-75,000; founded 1918), *Hadashot* (The News), *Al Hamishmar* (The Guardian; founded 1943), *Hamodia* (The Informer; circ. 25,000), *Hatzofeh* (The Watchman; circ. 60,000; founded 1938), *Israel Nachrichten* (News of Israel; circ. 20,000; founded 1974), *Al-Itihad* (Unity; circ. 60,000; founded 1944), *The Jerusalem Post* (circ. 30,000-50,000; founded 1932), *Le Journal d'Israël* (circ. 10,000; founded 1971), *Letzte Nyess* (Late News; circ. 23,000; founded 1949), *Ma'ariv* (Evening Prayer; circ. 160,000-270,000; founded 1948), *Mabat* (circ. 7,000; founded 1971), *Nasha Strana* (Our Country; circ. 35,000; founded 1970), *Al-Quds* (Jerusalem; circ. 55,000; founded 1968), *Ash Shaab* (The People), *Shearim* (The Gates), *Uj Kelet* (circ. 20,000; founded 1918), *Viata Noastra* (circ. 30,000; founded 1950), *Yated Ne'eman* (circ. 25,000; founded 1986), and *Yedioth Aharonoth* (The Latest News; circ. 300,000-600,000; founded 1939).

Weeklies and other Periodicals Israel has a large number of weeklies, fortnightlies, and other periodicals being produced at varying increments of time. These publications are largely niche marketed to a broad variety of special interests. The circulation numbers of these volumes ranges from the hundreds of thousands to just over one thousand.

Some examples of the publications, listed with brief amounts of background information and chosen to offer a sense of the diversity available, include: *Aurora* (circ. 20,000; founded 1963; weekly; for expatriates), *Bama'alah* (journal of the young Histadrut Movement), *Bamahane* (In the Camp; circ. 70,000; founded 1948; military, illustrated publication of the Israel Armed Forces), *Glasul Populurui* (weekly of the Communist Party of Israel), *Al-Hurriya* (Freedom; weekly of the Herut Party), *Jerusalem Report* (circ. 65,000 worldwide; founded 1959), *MB* (Mitteilungsblatt; founded 1932; German journal of the Irgun Olei Merkus Europa [The Association of Immigrants from Central Europe]), *Laisha* (circ. 150,000; founded 1946; women's magazine), *Al Mirsad* (The Telescope; news and current affairs), *Otiot* (founded 1987; for children), *As-Sinnarah* (for Christian and Muslim Arabs in the region), *Ariel* (circ. 30,000; founded 1962; review of all aspects cultural in Israel by the Ministry of Foreign Affairs), *Israel Law Review* (founded 1965), *Lilac* (founded 2000; Israel's first magazine for Arabic women), *Nekuda* (voice of the Jewish settlers of the West Bank and Gaza Strip), *Israel Journal of the Medical Sciences* (founded 1965), and *Sinai* (founded 1937; Torah science and literature).

Economic Framework

With the average annual income being US$18,900, Israel is in a good position compared with its neighbors. Israel's economy is based on exporting computer software, military equipment, chemicals, and agricultural products. The economy has significantly improved during the 1980s and 1990s as Israel has been able to allocate less to defense and more into the civilian sector. In 1973 over forty percent of state funds were being funneled to defense expenditures, whereas today it stands at around 12 percent. Though the economy hit a period of recession in the late 1990s recovery began in 2000 under the Barak Government and was aided by the surge in the peace process during that time.

Also relevant to the economy, Israel continues to receive substantial funding from the United States and various Jewish communities around the world. However, while all of the assistance is extremely beneficial and indeed necessary in helping Israel's economy remain strong, the on-the-ground situation of continuing and often escalating violence, security problems, and a general stalling of the peace process has led to less promising short-term economic returns for the near future.

PRESS LAWS

The Daily Newspaper Publishers' Association of Israel represents publishers in negotiations with official and public agencies. It also negotiates contracts with employees and distributes newsprint. It has members from all daily papers and is affiliated with the International Federation of Newspaper Publishers.

The Israeli Press Council (Chair Itzhak Zamir; founded 1963) deals with drafting codes of professional ethics that are legally applicable to all journalists and other issues of common interest to all the press.

Also concerned with the enactment of legal codes and protection of the press in Israel are the Foreign Press Association, the Israel Association of the Periodical Press, and the Israel Press Association.

In 1986 the government approved the establishment of private radio and television stations to be run in competition with state systems.

CENSORSHIP & STATE-PRESS RELATIONS

Censorship was extremely tight in the beginning years of the state through the early 1970s and the Yom Kippur War.

A huge scandal in the 1980s involved the closing of *Hadashot* for four days by military censors after the paper ran a photograph displaying two Arab terrorists being led away for interrogation by agents of the General Security Service. The scandalous aspect was that the terrorists had already been reported to have ''died of their wounds'' according to an official communiqué.

The major issue with censorship in Israel boils down to this: Anything related to national security or military operations are off-limits to journalists. Of course, most of the news attempting to be reported from Israel deals with issues easily construed as related to national security and/or military operations. Thus, there can be understood to be significant curtailment of freedom of the press in Israel. Material produced by foreign journalists is routinely supposed to be passed by censors before it is broadcast. As well, besides the official channels of censorship, it is commonly recognized that bribery, intimidation, and violence on the part of the government/military plays into the equation of what gets printed/broadcast and what does not.

What must be recognized is that Israel feels that it is a nation-state constantly under siege, being probed for its weaknesses. Its civilians, as well as its military, are constantly being shot at and bombed. On the other side, Israel is holding captive thousands of Palestinians in dismal conditions, including curfews, house arrests, arbitrary detainment, and the like. This creates animosity toward them and attacks are perpetrated by the Palestinians which consequently provokes further and harsher responses by the Israelis. While it needs to be recognized this situation has created a vicious cycle of violence it must be also be recognized that it is absolutely essential that this situation not be allowed to become an excuse for violation of international standards of journalistic practice and/or of human rights by Israel (or by Palestinians). As it currently stands, Israel appears to be abusing its upper-hand of military might and has been accused by multiple human rights agencies, time and again, to be in violation of numerous standards of human rights and journalistic practice.

Considerations of some recent, more specific examples are in order. According to Reporters Without Borders, since the start of the second *Intifada* (uprising) on September 29, 2000, over 45 journalists have been reported injured by gunfire. The Israeli Defense Ministry in mid-December 2001 issued a statement concerning this matter only acknowledging nine of the cases and exonerating *Tsahal* (the Israeli military) in eight of the nine occurrences.

Then, at the end of 2001, the Israel GPO (Government Press Office) said that it would not renewing foreign press passes to Palestinian journalists. Instead, the GPO would give out Orange Assistant Cards that would only be valid in the Territories and not give immediate access to Israel because the Palestinian journalists ''spread propaganda and do not meet journalistic standards for balanced coverage.''

On January 28, 2001, Cameraman Ashraf Kutkut and reporters Mas'adah 'Uthman and Duha Al Shami, all working for Al Wattan TV, were attacked by Tsahal at the entrance of Ein Kenia, a village near Ramallah in the West Bank, although they all had valid press cards. Al Shami was beaten by the soldiers and the crew's equipment confiscated at the checkpoint. Eventually the crew was released, and the next day they retrieved their cameras and video cassettes after they had been searched by Israeli authorities.

On February 11, 2001, Khalid Jahshan, a Palestine Television photographer, Husam Abu-Allan, an AFP photographer and Lu'ay Abu-Haykal, a Reuters photographer, were beaten by Israeli troops in Hebron.

On February 12, 2001, the Israeli army bombed Palestinian residential areas in the West Bank. One of the buildings targeted was the *Al Hayat Al Jadida* newspaper, located in Ramallah. The Palestinian Al Salam Television was also shelled by Israeli forces.

According to a transcript from the International Press Institute, on April 20, Laila Odeh, Abu Dhabi TV bureau chief was shot at by Israeli troops and wounded while she and her crew were filming at the Rafah refugee camp in Gaza. She was hit in the leg by live ammunition after identifying herself as a journalist to Israeli soldiers positioned nearby. By her own account, and that of others at the scene, she left the area immediately when ordered to do so by IDF (Israeli Defense Force) soldiers, and was shot as she was fleeing. The International Press Institute further reported that after significant criticism from various press associations the government blamed the reporter with illegitimate reconstructions of the scene as a riot scene even though the Foreign Press Association in Israel advocated that Odeh was nowhere near a riot when shot.

May 13, 2001, Israeli troops shot and wounded Iman Masarweh as she was driving near East Jerusalem in a car marked ''Press.'' Masarweh, a London-based Quds Press News Agency reporter, was hospitalized and operated on to remove the bullet. She noted that there were ''no confrontations taking place when the soldiers targeted and shot her.''

On May 15, 2001, it is reported that Bertrand Aguirre of French television TF1 was shot by an Israeli sniper who jumped out of a jeep, pointed an M-16 and fired. Aguirre's flak jacket saved his life, but the disturbing aspect of the situation is that this occurred while he was standing among a group of cameramen, being filmed while speaking into a microphone. An Associated Press Television News video captured the whole incident on film. As of July 2001, no statement had been offered by the Israeli government despite promises to investigate the matter.

June 28, 2002, while visiting neighbors with family, Nizar Ramadan, correspondent of the newspaper *Qater*, was arrested in Hebron and taken to the Ofer detention center. Also that day, Israeli soldiers seized and destroyed material in his office. On July 6, Ramadan's detention was extended 18 days without explanation. By July 30, his lawyer had still not been allowed to visit him.

As of July 30, 2002, five Palestinian journalists who have been jailed since April remain incarcerated. Two of these have been accused of aiding terrorists, but no proof has been offered. The other three still have no idea why they are being held. Reporters Without Borders continued to write the government on their behalf. Since May 29, 2002, when Israel began to occupy Palestinian cities and towns, more than 20 Palestinian journalists have been arrested, many being treated violently.

Attitude toward Foreign Media

Recognizing that significant harassment, detainment, and deaths have occurred in the past couple of years, especially since the September 29, 2000, inauguration of the new Intifada sparked by Ariel Sharon's visit to the Al-Aqsa Mosque, still foreign can often find a more welcoming home in Israel than in many of the surrounding Arab countries as far as concerns freedom of movement, ease of transmitting copy, and general access to compatible, even superior technology. Generally, if issues of national security are avoided, Israel is a relatively safe base considering the issues often being covered. Due to the intense output of news originating from the area, even recognizing the substantive dangers, the country boasts of the largest contingents of foreign journalists hunkered in one place compared to anywhere else in the world.

Some of the foreign bureaus based in Israel include: Agence France-Presse (France) Agencia EFE (Spain), Agenzia Nazionale Stampa Associata (ANSA; Italy), Associated Press (AP; USA), Deutsche Presse-Agentur (dpa; Germany), Jiji Tsushin-Sha (Japan), Kyodo News Service (Japan), Reuters (UK), United Press International (UPI; USA), and Informatsionnoye Telegrafnoye Agentstvo Rossii—Telegrafnoye Agentsvo Suverennykh Stran (ITAR-TASS; Russia).

News Agencies

There are three news agencies in Israel (including the Occupied Territories). The Israeli News Agency (ITIM), founded in 1950 by a group of newspapermen is controlled by a board representing the newspaper dailies of the country that hold shares in the agency. It has staff reporters covering various sections of the country that then furnish news to the newspapers and as well to radio stations.

The Jewish Telegraphic Agency (JTA) is the oldest and best-known agency in Israel. Internationally, it has bureaus in New York, Paris, Buenos Aires, Johannesburg and has access to other fields through stringers.

The Palestine Press Service is the only Arab news agency in the Occupied Territories.

BROADCAST MEDIA

In 1986 the Israeli government approved establishment of privatized and commercialized television and radio stations to be run in competition with the state system. However, while this is occurring, a debate, similar to that in the United States, as to how this will affect the content of programming available on these media, especially in relation to educational content. The debate was exacerbated in 1996 when the government declared that they wished to privatize all broadcasting. One of the most prominent skeptics of the current trend in Israeli television is Professor Elihu Katz who was one of the founders of Israeli television. He fears that with the considerable increase of channels television will lose its ''agenda-setting'' function of providing education to society and fostering civic involvement in the democratic process; in essence, he is suggesting that there will be largely no shared experience from which to foster societal dialogue. Of course, this is not the opinion of everyone, but then that is obvious by the progression of the matter.

For the moment, the Israel Broadcasting Authority (IBA), which is modeled closely akin to the BBC, maintains state-ownership and responsibility for Kol Israel (The Voice of Israel) radio and Israel Television (ITV). It derives its funding primarily by license fees on television sets, but also about twenty percent from advertising. IBA's ITV broadcasts began in 1968. It has stations in Jerusalem and additional studios in Tel-Aviv. One color network (VHF and UHF capabilities) and one satellite channel (began in the early 1990s) are run, broadcasting in Hebrew, Arabic, and English. Channel One, is the main channel and provides news, original productions, films, and children's and entertainment programming. One and a half-hour of each evening's broadcasts is offered in Arabic.

IBA's radio broadcasting began in 1948 and, as of 2002, there are stations in Jerusalem, Tel-Aviv, and Haifa. IBA broadcasts six programs that are available both locally and internationally on medium, short-wave, and VHF/FM frequencies. Taking into account the production of all the programming, sixteen languages are utilized: Hebrew, Arabic, English, Yiddish, Ladino, Romanian, Hungarian, Moghrabi, Persian, French, Russian, Buchranian, Georgian, Portuguese, Spanish, and Amharic. Some of the channels and their offerings include: Reshet Alef (first network) broadcasting children's programs and discussions on cultural and general events; Reshet Bet (second network) providing news and discussion of current events; Reshet Gimmel (third network) playing easy listening music; Kol Haderech interspersing traffic reports with music; Reka being designated for new immigrants broadcasting mainly in Russian and Amharic; Kol Hamusica offering classical music; Kol Zion Lagola is beamed to Jewish communities abroad; and Kol Yisrael in Arabic is broadcast for Israeli Arabs and listeners in Arab countries.

Founded in 1991 and established by law in 1993, the government established the Second Channel TV and Radio Administration to supervise the running of the Second Television Channel and sixteen regional radio stations. The administration authorizes and supervises three licensees who are given a four to six-year period to broadcast programming. Each licensee broadcasts two days a week and Saturdays are rotated. General entertainment offerings and films make up the bulk of the programming. The stations on Second Channel receive all of their funding from advertising and though supervised by a government authority Second Channel is a commercial operation that sees itself in competition with the state channel.

Since the late 1980s, cable TV has had a monumental impact on Israeli culture. Today it reaches over 65 percent of all households. By law the government issues one license per designated area with funding to the licensee provided by user fees. Typically, thirty to forty channels are offered with a significant amount of foreign programming picked up by satellite. Channels include: MTV, SKY NEWS, CNN, BBC, and also channels from Egypt, France, Germany, India, Italy, Jordan, Morocco, Spain, Russia and Turkey. Of course, in heavy, and rather unregulated, competition with cable television is the satellite television market.

Television In 1965, Israel became the first country in the world to sanction educational television (known as Israel Educational Television [ETV]) before general-purpose television. The government realized television's importance for educating society (and of course for disseminating their perspectives). Funding for the project was secured from the Rothschild Foundation and they also managed supervisory responsibilities. Later, the Ministry of Education and Culture took over responsibilities for funding and supervision of ETV. Programming largely consists of school programs on a variety of subjects and adult education.

Of the current commercial television stations, it should be noted that the influential newspapers *Yediot Aharonot* and *Ma'ariv* are senior partners in two of the companies. This suggests that the papers are well aware that there will be cuts in advertising revenues for the newspaper industry due to the popularity of television as a medium and so are making sure to grab a stake in the next lucrative market burgeoning in Israel.

In the early 2000s there were seventeen broadcast stations in the country with thirty-six additional low-power repeaters, broadcasting to 1.69 million televisions and according to a finding by IBA, eighty-seven percent of Israelis on a daily weekday basis. As well, May 18, 1996 Israel's Amos 1 satellite was launched and began transmitting local television and radio programming.

Radio The first radio station in the Palestine area came on air March, 30, 1936, as The Palestine Broadcasting Service (PBS) with its Hebrew name being agreed upon as Kol Yerushalyim (The Voice of Jerusalem). It was an organ of the British administration, but did provide news bulletins to the Jewish and Muslim populations however skewed the perspective may have been to these populations. In 1940, the Haganah (Jewish Underground) opened a pirate radio station called Kol Israel (Voice of Israel) on 42 meters (about 7000 kHz). In June of the same year it is ends broadcasting due to potential invasion by Axis powers. Then, with the establishment of Israel as a state in 1948, the radio station Kol Yerushalyim is turned over to the Israelis and they rename it Kol Israel. Two years later, in 1950, the military station Galei Tzahal was added to the foray. Both stations still operate.

Currently, there are roughly 23 AM, 15 FM, and 2 short-wave licensed stations operating in Israel. They broadcast to 3.07 million radios. Radio is utilized as a good medium to disseminate information since it is noted as being able to reach over ninety percent of the population.

As well as the licensed stations, unlicensed stations are also ubiquitous. The government tends to be lenient on these stations even though they are illegal (one can speculate it gives a feeling of leniency to the government that tends come across harshly in its censorship of other aspects of the press). Some of the ''pirate'' stations are even commercial, being funded by advertising. The first unlicensed station was the Voice of Peace started in 1973 and took its cues from similar pirate stations in Europe. It ceased operation October 1, 1993, saying that ''the goal has been achieved.''

Two examples of specific stations are Galei Tzahal and Arutz 7 (Channel 7). Galei Tzahal is Israel Defense Forces (IDF) Radio set up by the military in 1950. It broadcasts twenty-four hours a day with news, music, and talk shows on two channels. News and talk programming comprise the first channel and music and traffic reports make up the second. Though it is still funded by the army, the stations main listeners are now civilians. It remains a popular Israeli channel. Arutz 7, formerly designated Voice of the Gazelle, is a station that promotes the perspectives of ultra-orthodox groups and of Israeli settlers in the occupied territories.

Electronic News Media

Israel actively utilizes the Internet for government, military, public, and private purposes. The country is know for its information technology (IT) industry and is known to possess one of the world's most technologically sophisticated populations. In a country of about six million people there are approximately one million Internet users working from twenty-one Internet Service Providers (ISPs).

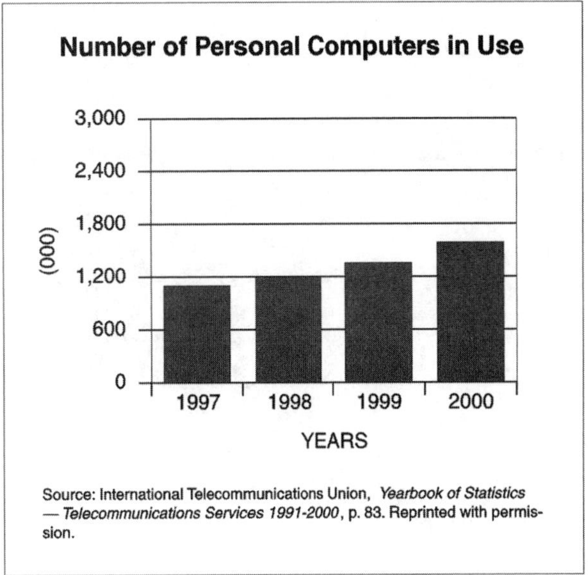

Source: International Telecommunications Union, *Yearbook of Statistics — Telecommunications Services 1991-2000*, p. 83. Reprinted with permission.

Summary

Being one of the younger states in the world, Israel has made a dramatic splash on the world stage. Often, despite significant and numerous lapses, it seems that the country is headed in an appropriate direction concerning press freedoms and use of technology. However, the negative treatment of the press concerning violence and censorship is a glaring mark against the state. Since its birth, it is obvious the state has remained continually encumbered and beset by various factors, but this cannot be allowed to be an excuse for extreme limitations being placed upon journalists and speech in a country that boasts itself a democracy. The press in Israel compared with many of its surrounding Middle Eastern neighbors enjoys comparatively bountiful freedoms.

Bibliography

BBC News. *Israel and the Palestinians: History of the Middle East Conflict.* Available at http://news.bbc.co.uk/2/hi/in_depth/middle_east/2001/israel_palestinians/

Black, Ian, and Benny Morris. *Israel's Secret Wars: History of Israel's Intelligence Services.* New York: Grove Weidenfeld, 1992.

CBS News. *Israel Clamps Down on Foreign Press.* Available at http://www.cbsnews.com/stories/2002/04/02/.

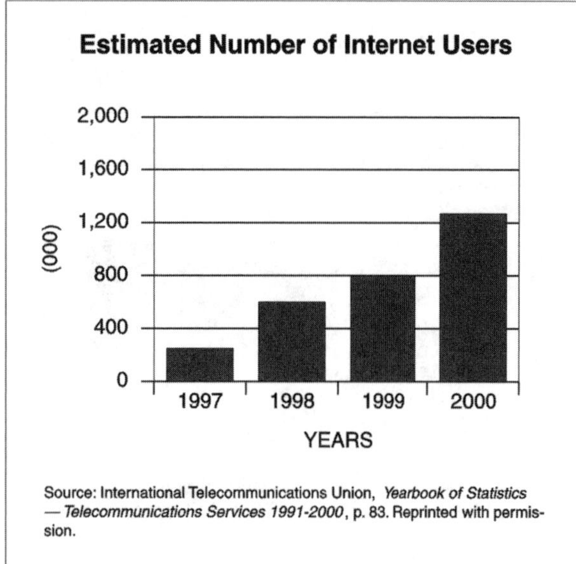

Source: International Telecommunications Union, *Yearbook of Statistics — Telecommunications Services 1991-2000*, p. 83. Reprinted with permission.

CIA. *The World Factbook 2001.* Available at http://www.cia.gov/cia/publications/factbook/.

Cohen, Mark R., and Abraham L. Udovitch. *Jews Among Arabs: Contacts and Boundaries*. Princeton: The Darsin Press, 1994.

Committee to Protect Journalists (CPJ). *Middle East and North Africa 2001: Israel and the Occupied Territories.* Available at http://www.cpj.org/.

Ellis, Mark H. *Beyond Innocence and Redemption: Confronting the Holocaust and Israeli Power.* San Francisco: Harper and Row, 1990.

Hazony, Yoram. The Jewish State: The Struggle for Israel's Soul. New York: Basic Books, 2000.

Kurian, George, ed. *World Press Encyclopedia*. New York: Facts on File, Inc., 1982.

Maher, Joanne, ed. *Regional Surveys of the World: The Middle East and North Africa 2002*, 48th ed. London: Europa Publications, 2001.

Masalha, Nur. *Imperial Israel and the Palestinians: The Politics of Expansion*. London: Pluto Press, 2000.

Redmon, Clare, ed. *Willings Press Guide 2002*, Vol. 2. Chesham Bucks, UK: Waymaker Ltd, 2002.

Reporters Sans Frontières. *Israel Annual Report 2002.* Available at http://www.rsf.fr.

Russell, Malcolm. *The Middle East and South Asia 2001*, 35th ed. Harpers Ferry, WV: United Book Press, Inc., 2001.

Sumner, Jeff, ed. *Gale Directory of Publications and Broadcast Media*, Vol. 5, 136th ed. Farmington Hills, MI: Gale Group, 2002.

The Middle East, 9th ed. Washington, DC: Congressional Quarterly Inc., 2000.

—*Clint B. Thomas Baldwin*

ITALY

BASIC DATA

Official Country Name:	Italian Republic
Region (Map name):	Europe
Population:	57,679,825
Language(s):	Italian, German, French, Slovene
Literacy rate:	98.0%
Area:	301,230 sq km
GDP:	1,073,960 (US$ millions)
Number of Daily Newspapers:	88
Total Circulation:	6,024,000
Circulation per 1,000:	121
Total Newspaper Ad Receipts:	1,828 (Euro millions)
As % of All Ad Expenditures:	23.20
Number of Television Stations:	358
Number of Television Sets:	30,300,000
Television Sets per 1,000:	525.3
Number of Cable Subscribers:	57,700
Cable Subscribers per 1,000:	1.0
Number of Satellite Subscribers:	2,350,000
Satellite Subscribers per 1,000:	40.7
Number of Radio Stations:	4709
Number of Radio Receivers:	50,500,000
Radio Receivers per 1,000:	875.5
Number of Individuals with Computers:	10,300,000

Computers per 1,000:	178.6
Number of Individuals with Internet Access:	13,200,000
Internet Access per 1,000:	228.8

BACKGROUND & GENERAL CHARACTERISTICS

The Italian media system entered the new century with a combination of continued reliance on the traditional printed press and participation in the global shift to new delivery systems, including online journalism, the spread of personal computers, and digital television. Despite increasing reliance on digital technologies in every area of communication in Italy, the term ''press'' still mainly connotes the daily newspapers. Italy's daily newspapers have five distinguishing characteristics that set this medium apart from its counterpart in other west European countries: historically low levels of readership; a predominance of regional over national papers; a notable lack of independence of the press; virtual non-existence of a popular press; and the existence of a group of daily ''news''papers that are devoted solely to either sports, religious news or other specialized topics.

The first characteristic is the one most often stressed by analysts of the Italian press. Compared with other member countries of the European Union (EU), Italy's aggregate daily newspaper circulation (the social indicator used as a proxy to measure readership) ranks just above Greece and Portugal, the two least advanced Mediterranean European Union (EU) members. Paolo Mancini reports that aggregate daily newspaper circulation in Italy stood at 109 per thousand citizens in 1999, and he remarked that this is very low indeed when one considers that the comparable figure is near 600 in Norway (323). Throughout most of the twentieth century, readership of daily newspapers was constant at about five million. There was a small increase in the 1980s, fueled by a turn to commercialization of the press, to a high 6.5 million in the year 1990. Since then, the number has been falling again, to 6 million in 1998 (ISTAT 214). This figure of 6 million was computed by taking the annual circulation of daily periodicals, (2.2 million) and dividing by 365 days. This also means that aggregate daily newspaper circulation has decreased to 105 per thousand persons.

There are several direct and indirect causes of the low-readership phenomenon. A direct cause is related to the logistics of matching the reader with the paper. As is typical in other European nations, newspaper distribution in Italy is conducted almost exclusively via newsstands. However, for a variety of reasons related to permit requirements and attempts by operators to limit competition, the number of newsstands in Italy per 1000 persons is below that in Germany and France. Another technical problem is the fact that prices are determined by a joint committee of government and business, and have inevitably crept up. In addition to pointing to availability of newsstands and price per copy, we can address the obvious question: do Italians simply not read in general? True, Italians are not avid readers, but this statement needs to be qualified.

According to a survey conducted in 1956 (Lumley 4), nearly two thirds of the population reported never reading anything at all. Regional differences are significant, however. Until the fifties, Italy's population outside the major urban centers was mainly rural and poor, and illiteracy was still fairly high in the Mezzogiorno region and in rural areas in general. Almost four fifths of the population spoke a local dialect and were not very familiar with Italian. In some local dialects, the lira was referred to as the franc, while in another it was called a pfennig, which lends testimony to Italy's much more fragmented history. Italian is still in the process of becoming the language that every Italian is comfortable with, and much of the new vocabulary, including technical and specialized language transliterated from other languages, was slow to trickle down to the less educated tier of the population. More often than not, Italian journalists writing for major daily papers did not engage in concerted efforts to translate or explain unfamiliar words to their reading public.

Literacy rates increased in the next two decades, and most Italians were now able to read a newspaper. Yet, they still chose not to do so, for a variety of reasons, including alienation from bureaucracy and journalistic jargon used by the press, the non-availability of popular magazines and dailies, and the fact that a high proportion of the potential readership, women in particular, felt excluded from the mainstream public sphere (Lumley 4). Other types of media have a higher appeal to this population. Since the 1950s, radio and TV were the media of choice. More recently, it is not surprising that newspaper circulation decreased in the last decade, due to increased reliance on the Internet for access to daily news.

The predominance of regional over national newspapers in Italy is striking. One reason for this phenomenon is that the capital, Rome, is not an international center on the order of New York, Paris, or London, while several cities in northern Italy, notably Milan and Turin in the northwest, Bologna and Venice in the northeast, are important urban centers. While some regional newspapers have a high circulation and are nationally distributed, they tend to convey a regional bias that is often linked to the family that owns the paper. This has been the case for

Il Corriere della Sera, whose owners have long imposed their own Milanese bias, and for *La Stampa*, owned by the Agnelli family of Turin, who are the major stockholders of the Fiat Company and who impart a Piedmontese bias to this nationally distributed paper. The lack of a truly national newspaper leaves room for many regional and multi-regional papers, e.g. *Il Mattino*, which is based in Naples and *Il Resto del Carlino*, based in Bologna (Lumley 2). Some party-affiliated daily newspapers, notably *L'Unità*, and other sectarian daily newspapers have a truly national character and nationwide readership, and seem to be filling the void to some extent.

The third characteristic of the Italian daily press, its lack of independence, is intertwined with the previous one. Ownership by rich families, industrial groups and other financial power centers is typical, with often many newspapers published by the same group. A notable non-industrial financial center is the Catholic Church, which supports publication of the widely circulated daily paper of the Vatican, *L'Osservatore Romano*. In past decades, it was also typical to see daily newspapers published by political parties, which used the medium to circulate information to their members. While the Italian reading public is small, it is politically savvy. Italians display high percentages of party membership and voting turnout, and membership is also high in labor unions and in a variety of cultural, professional and political interest groups (Mancini 320-1). Party newspapers could thus derive great political benefit from this method of communicating with their members. While most of the party papers have disappeared in the past decade, *L'Unità*, the traditional publicity arm of the Communist Party (recently reborn as the Democratic Party of the Left) is still circulated nationwide, but has declined in importance.

One origin of Italy's press sectarianism is the genre of journalism that historically developed in Italy. As is the case in several other west European countries, journalism in Italy has grass-root beginnings in literary gazettes. As such, journalism has traditionally specialized in interpretation, intricate commentary and complex analysis rather than direct news reporting and detailed descriptions of events. Italian journalists are experts at the *inchiesta giornalistica*, the investigative in-depth report. Analysts of the Italian daily newspapers often note the irony residing in the fact that this medium of public discourse employs highly skilled journalists who face a public that does not read daily newspapers in significant numbers. Other origins lie in the fact that the press developed at the time of unification of the country, which fostered the founding of the Party newspapers, and the fact that the seat of power of the Catholic Church happens to be in the Italian peninsula. The Vatican is the world's richest nation in terms of income per capita, and it constitutes one of the main power bases, with a political agenda that is definitely not independent.

The final two major characteristics of the Italian press, non-existence of a popular press and the presence of daily newspapers devoted to a single non-news topic, are to some extent overlapping. Instead of producing tabloids, a format that is popular in several other EU member countries, Italian publishers focus on newspapers with specialized topics that tie in with a major passion of all Italians, sport, and in particular soccer. On days following a national soccer match or a World Cup competition, the circulation of sports papers like *La Gazetta dello Sport* and *Il Corriere dello Sport-Stadio* soars into the hundreds of thousands (Grandinetti 29, 40).

Daily, Weekly & Other Periodicals According to the most recent statistics (*Annuario Statistico Italiano* 214), slightly over 10 million distinct periodicals appear in Italy (data for 1998). A relatively small percentage of these are daily printed newspapers. Of these, about two-thirds are listed as providing general daily news coverage, while the others deal with a variety of topics, including topics of interest to members of professional areas, commerce, sports, the arts, and labor unions (*Annuario* 214). A detailed listing of current and out-of-print newspaper titles, together with their place and first date of publication, ownership, editorial board, description of relevant facts, and a short bibliography related to each newspaper is provided by Grandinetti (1992) and readers interested in this detail should consult that publication. For the purpose at hand, a brief description of the major national, regional and party-affiliated papers follows. The nationwide Italian press has two major daily newspapers: *La Republica* and *Il Corriere della Sera*, both of which are published with local sections for each of the major urban areas. There are also a number of large regional and newspapers, notably *Il Mattino* (Naples), *Il Messaggero* (Rome) and *La Stampa* (Turin), which is the third largest daily newspaper. Many of the daily papers covering general news originated in the nineteenth century. Today, the major national and local newspapers are no longer affiliated with political parties, as used to be the rule in the past. The notable exception remains *L'Unità*, the traditional newspaper of the Communist Party (Mancini 323).

In addition to the relatively few daily newspapers, there is a large number of weekly (482), biweekly (384) and monthly (2,148) magazines, with an additional 6,817 periodicals that have a lower frequency of circulation (*Annuario 2000* 214). In the beginning of the twenty-first century, the number of daily newspapers has increased, from a low of 113 in 1995 to 126, while the number of weeklies has declined significantly, from 624 in 1995 to its 2002 total of 482. Weekly magazines play an important role in distributing general news information to the public, with 176 of them devoted solely to news coverage and the remaining to music, sports, religion, and many other topics. The widest circulated weeklies in the general news category are *Panorama* and *L'Espresso*. Considering that these two weeklies are owned, respectively by the *Mediaset-Berlusconi Group* and the *Espresso-La Repubblica Group*, they reflect the main political trends of weekly press coverage and journalism.

New trends in commercial journalism The year 1989 accentuated a new trend in Italian journalism, as the ''soft'' revolutions took their course in central and eastern Europe. Press coverage on events impacting on Italy, in particular increased immigration, revealed the dimensions of an Italian national identity. Immigration from north and central Africa, Asia and the ex-Eastern bloc nations has seen a rise since 1970 and increased sharply after 1989, especially from Albania, Poland, Romania, the Philippines, Sri Lanka and India. Lax immigration policies and an extensive *economia sommersa* (underground economy) have traditionally lured immigrants, the vast majority of whom are illegal, to the peninsula. Anna Triandafyllidou's study published in 1999 documents the concomitant upsurge of ethno-nationalism in Italy. She points out that national community in Italy is not merely based in its territorial boundaries and its culture, but also by the melding of a restoration of Roman historic tradition with the revolutionary elements of the fascist legacy into the so-called *Risorgimento* (resurgence) movement. The development of a xenophobic attitude has been both demonstrated and perhaps even accelerated by public discourse in the press. Articles in the representative weeklies *Panorama* and *L'Espresso* show a discourse that continually differentiates Italians from immigrants. Immigrants are treated ''not as individuals but as members of a given group that is categorized beforehand. . . (83).'' The following titles of articles published in the two weeklies are representative of this public discourse: *L'integrazione impossible* (The impossible integration), *L'Espresso*, Oct. 10, 1990; *L'Immigratio che ci meritamo* (The immigrant we deserve), *L'Espresso*, Oct. 13, 1991; *A ciascuno il suo profugo* (a refugee for everyone), *L'Espresso*, June 23, 1991; *Oggi albanesi, poi. . .* (Today Albanians, tomorrow. . .), *Panorama*, June 30, 1991; and *Immigrati: quanti sono davvero e come fanno a entrare?* (Immigrants: How many are there really, and how do they get in?).

In March 1999, the United Nations Committee for the Elimination of Racial Discrimination issued a strongly worded criticism of Italy's practice of discrimination against Roma people. While it did not single out the Italian press, the Committee made mention of the lack of appropriate knowledge and training of law enforcement and other public officials in regards to the provision of the Convention. In looking at the role the Italian press has played in the public discourse regarding immigration, using the sample of titles of articles listed above, one may conclude that the press has not helped educate the public about the human rights of marginalized people and has instead devoted coverage to their ''otherness.''

Top Ten Daily Newspapers
(2000)

	Circulation
Corriere della Sera	718,000
La Repubblica	646,000
La Gazzetta dello Sport	456,000
Il Sole 24 Ore	410,000
La Stampa	399,000
Il Messaggero	292,000
Corriere dello Sport	285,000
Il Giornale	235,000
Il Resto del Carlino	188,000
La Nazione	155,000

Source: World Association of Newspapers and Zenithmedia, *World Press Trends 2001*, p. 127.

ECONOMIC FRAMEWORK

Prior to the onset of commercialization of the 1980s, expansion of their paper's readership was not a prime economic strategy of newspaper publishers. Enzo Forcella, a well-known analyst of Italian journalism, explained in a 1959 essay entitled *Millecinquecento Lettori* that a journalist should try to reach only the following 1,500 privileged readers (Forcella 451):

> ''. . .a political journalist can count on about one thousand five hundred readers in Italy: ministers and undersecretaries (all), members of parliament (some), party leaders, trade-union representatives, high prelates and some industrialists who want to appear well informed. The rest don't count, even if the newspaper sells three hundred thousand copies. First of all, it is not believed that the common reader reads the first pages of the newspaper and, in any case, his influence is minimal. All of the system is organized for the relationship between journalists and the privileged group of readers.''

Forcella's comments are often quoted because they encapsulate the main goals of newspaper publishers in the period up to the oil crisis and the resulting economic stagflation periods experienced by west European countries, and notably Italy, in the mid-seventies. The mid-seventies were a watershed for European economies, and Italy in particular. Until 1971, the Italian economy enjoyed high growth rates and unemployment rates that were stable, with high unemployment concentrated in the

Mezzogiorno. Wage pressure was becoming evident in the northern industrial region at the end of the sixties, contributing to strikes and fueling wage inflation. Then came the two oil shocks of the 1970s, and economic growth could only be maintained by an accommodating monetary policy adopted by the Banca d'Italia. Accordingly, inflation reached 20 percent per year. Following the second oil shock of 1979-80, unemployment rates started to rise despite the easy monetary policy. High unemployment and inflation are costly for both business and government, because of two mechanisms. The first is the *cassa integrazione* (generally called the *cassa*), a system jointly financed by business (at the rate of one percent of gross salaries) and by government. It pays at least 80 percent of one's salary over a period that may be unlimited. Many of the unemployed continue to work, at near full compensation, in the underground economy, which is estimated to be 20-35 percent of the economy (Neal and Barbezat 232). The underground economy is very diversified and closer to the surface than in other EU members, as many enterprises in Italy sublet their business space during night hours (Dauvergne 31). The second mechanism interacting with inflation, and some arguing that it is the main cause of inflation, is the *scala mobile*, which indexed salary increases to the projected cost of living. Since rising wages were a major factor causing rises in the cost of living, the Italian economy was caught in an inflationary wage-price spiral that contributed to a number of problems, including rising pension costs, balance of payments deficits and government deficits.

On the government side, economic problems contributed to short-lived administrations. On top of being plagued by persistent economic problems, Italy entered the period of the terror of the Red Brigades. The *Brigatte Rosse* (Red Brigades) was founded in 1969, an offshoot of the student protests and social movement of 1968, and vouched to establish a Marxist-Leninist state in a new Italy that would no longer be a member of NATO. The Red Brigades started a spate of terrorist acts in 1973, which included kidnapping and shootings of businessmen and others. Indro Montanelli, the editor of *Il Giornale*, was shot in the legs in 1977. The group lost all political support from the Left when it murdered former prime minister Aldo Moro, who was then the leader of the left wing of the Christian Democratic Party. After many members were arrested, the group disappeared in 1989. The murder of government adviser Marco Biagi in March 2002 has led to fears that the Red Brigades may be staging a comeback, however.

In the private sector, big industry is described (Dauvergne 32) as having found a "second wind" in the 1980s, but this was largely accomplished by means of massive layoffs (Locke Chapter 2) rather than truly innovative strategies. In the communications industry, the second wind was the beginning of a period of crass commercialization, and an end to the period where industrial groups held on to publishing enterprises that were not profitable and were considered useful mainly as a public relations tool.

The rise in commercialization of the media since the 1980s and the development of the Internet, has led to a shift from the printed press to the mass media as the prime vehicle for carrying political messages to the people, and this in an increasingly profit-oriented fashion. Gone are the party newspapers like *Il Popolo*, *L'Avanti* and *La Vocce Repubblicana*, the respective daily newspapers of the Christian Democrat, Socialists and Republican political parties. The new political party of *Forza Italia* relies solely on paid messages carried via commercial media for its advertising.

The market approach, so evident since the 1980s, has also brought with it an end to the era of massive subsidies from political and industrial owners to the media (Mancini 322), and this happened without reliance on money-making infotainment, and fluff entertainment programming. Indeed, TV news programming has increased significantly in the 1990s (it rose 11 percent from 1992 to 1996), and has well kept pace with cultural programming, which itself rose 13 percent during the same period (Mancini 322). However, it must be admitted that political sensationalism and exaggeration of conflicts is more visible in the new commercialized news environment than it was prior to the 1980s. Reporting is done using a simpler, less nuanced, less complex and, hence, less analytical and critical manner in the new media environment. There is an additional hidden social cost to the "sensationalization" of events in an effort to attract readers and viewers in the profit-oriented media. Sensationalization places increased emphasis on escalation of conflicts and de-emphasizes peacemaking and conflict resolution. Accordingly, coverage of the possibility of America waging war on Iraq takes on the quality of a TV program rather than the grim reality of a bloody war.

The Attempt at an Independent Press While private ownership of the press was also typical in Italy before 1980, the owners of the media did not pursue a profit motive as much as they sought to favorably influence public opinion. What has remained unchanged throughout, is the lack of success of independent newspapers. Most attempts at establishing an independent newspaper in Italy fail. A typical example is the appropriately named *L'Indipendente*, founded in November 1991 with financial backing from a group of northern Italian investors (Publikompass) under the leadership of Guido Roberto Vitale, an investment banker, and also brother to Alberto Vitale, the CEO of Random House. The investors adopted the mission to create an objective newspaper in the English tradition. The paper's founding editor-in chief, Riccardo Franco Levi expressed the paper's ambitious editorial goal: "The idea was to found a quality newspaper, which Italy does not really have. . .In Italy, newspapers are aimed simultaneously at university professors and taxi drivers. We wanted to split that target, and we also wanted to separate news from opinion, something not usually done in Italy. And we wanted to be rigorously independent, as the masthead suggested" (Shugaar 16). The Levi interview uses the past tense, because the experiment in independent journalism was short-lived, even though *L'Indipendente* continues to be published to date. Although the paper contained truly independent journalism in its initial months, it was perceived by the reading public as uninspired and sterile. No one read the paper any more after its first few days and the other investors relieved Riccardo Franco Levi as editor-in-chief on February 14, 1992. By then, circulation had plummeted to about 15,000 after an early peak of 200,000. He was replaced by Vittorio Feltri, who represented the paper's financial backers and who adopted the goal of turning the paper into the black, even if this would involve making political alliances. By year-end, circulation recovered to the respectable 100,000 level, and the paper had become another mouthpiece for the northern industrial/political power base (Shugaar 17).

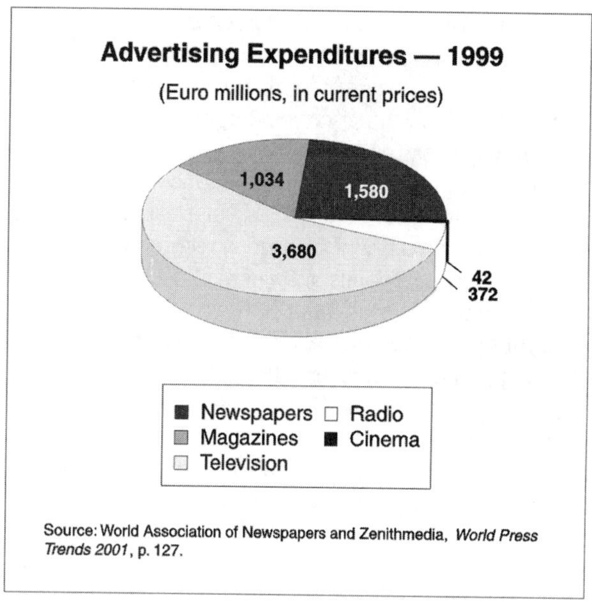

Source: World Association of Newspapers and Zenithmedia, *World Press Trends 2001*, p. 127.

Press Laws & Censorship

The foundation for Italian press law is provided by the constitutional principle of freedom of individual expression, and in additional legislation. Article 21 of the Italian Constitution, approved on December 22, 1947 and effective January 1, 1948. The article sets out by providing that all persons have the right to express their thoughts freely, either verbally, in written form, or in any other form of communication (Pace). It further makes clear that the press will not be subjected to any authorities or to censorship. However, the broad freedom granted to the press in this sentence is immediately curtailed in the following paragraph of Article 21, which was the subject of heated debate during the constitutional assembly. As a rule, expressions in the press that are "counter to morality" are not permitted. Under certain circumstances, judicial authorities may order restraints to the press, provided that they base these orders on existing press laws in the civil and criminal code. In extreme situations and when judicial authorities have not yet been able to apply legal restraints police authorities may enforce a 24-hour sequestration.

A number of specific laws governing the press are also included in the Italian legal code, notably the Albertine Edict of 1848, the Penal Code, Public Security laws, and legislation setting up the Order of Journalists (1963) that lays out the guidelines for the journalism profession. Article 2461 of the Civil Code established the RAI (*Radio televisione italiana*). Additional legislation provides legal penalties for slander against the state's religion, attacks against heads of state of foreign nations, espionage and similar offenses. In reality, however, court-ordered sequestration or legal penalties have seldom been applied to the printed media, despite the publication of sometimes-vicious attacks on the pope, the president, and other government officials. A notable exception took place during the legal court proceedings against members of the Red Brigade terrorist group, when *Il Messagero* published parts of an informant's secret pre-trial testimony, and a prison sentence was imposed on the journalist and a law enforcement officer.

While direct sequestration and penalty are rare, censorship of a more insidious variety has characterized the Italian press since the passage of the Constitution, since editors have been subservient to a political party, groups of industrial owners or the editorial politics of the private owner of a media empire (Berlusconi).

Compared with other advanced industrialized nations, freedom of the Italian press is not highly ranked. In its global survey of 186 countries, Freedom House (2001) assessed each country's system of mass communications. The authors of this study strive to use universal criteria, rooted in the United Nations Declaration of Human Rights, notably freedom of opinion and expression. Rather than studying constitutions and other laws, an attempt is made to observe everyday reality and practice. The following four dimensions are taken into account: government laws on the content of the news media; the degree of political influence on news content;

economic influence on the media, either by government or private parties; and the degree of oppression of the media, either by means of physical threats or harm to journalists, or via direct censorship of the news and its distribution. Data for each dimension are gathered from a number of sources, including judgments of overseas correspondents and findings of international human rights organizations. When a form of restriction is considered to be present, points are recorded. Hence, the more points a nation scores, the less free is its press. While most European countries received low scores and ranked in the "free press" category, Italy received a ranking of 32, placing it in the "partly free" press group. Considering the pattern of ownership, industrial and political control of the major newspaper publishing groups and media networks, this finding is not too surprising.

In a more recent evaluation of the Italian media, the second annual Freedom of Expression awards, handed out by the Index on Censorship group in London in March 2002, the censorship award went to Silvio Berlusconi, for having placed "unprecedented powers of censorship into practice," and for having combined in the person of the prime minister the triad of "media, man and government" (Wells).

State-Press Relations

While Italian newspapers have been tied to politics since the nation's unification, a political party press emerged towards the end of the nineteenth century, with the publication of the Socialist Party's newspaper *Avanti!*, which was followed by the publication of daily newspapers by every political party, from Anarchists to Republicans. This press subculture provided discourse within the parties, while the commercial press reached out to the wider reading public. An obvious result of the strong party affiliation of a group of newspapers over approximately a century has been the move of journalists to high-level politicians and vice versa. Giovanni Spadolini's career path from editor of *Il Corriere della Sera* to leader of the Republican Party and subsequently to prime minister is a typical example (Lumley 6). Silvio Berlusconi's path from a brief term as prime minister to Mediaset media mogul is even more extreme, since he moved back into the prime minister seat in June 2001 and yet retained control over his media empire.

During the Fascist period, government interference in the press and political shaping of newspaper content were common. After the end of World War II and in the middle of the Cold War, government interfered with the press by means of covert funding of some newspapers and spying on the activities of others. During the stagflation period in the mid-1970s, a system of government subsidies to the press and a legal limit on TV advertising were instituted to protect newspapers that were failing financially. Dependence on government assistance and favorable legislation indirectly increased the political subservience of newspaper editors. At the same time, the journalism profession itself was molded by government in the postwar period. Political parties voted in 1944 to keep legislation that restricted access to the journalism profession to those persons admitted to the so-called *albo dei giornalisti* (the journalists' register). Furthermore, a 1963 law defined the profession of journalism, as it also defined the professions of lawyer and physician (Lumley 6-7).

While the period 1946-1974 can certainly be characterized as one where the press was largely beholden to government, many of the wide-circulation newspapers were molded by industrial owners rather than by government, and were used by them to gain access to the public political sphere. A newspaper that is owned by an industrial group will tend to be soft on environmental concerns, and cater to its owners' interests, lest its editor-in-chief be replaced.

The 1980s saw a major transformation of the mass media in Europe, and the Italian media shared in this transformation. It was evidenced in an economic expansion of the media system, persistent replacement of public by private ownership and increasing market competition. The major daily newspapers and periodicals were in 2002 owned by industrial groups.

Three major industrial groups presently have control, directly or indirectly, of daily and weekly publications and their publishers. These three groups are (1) the *Espresso-La Republica* group; (2) *Fiat-Rizzoli* (which owns part of *Il Corriere della Sera*, *La Stampa* and the publishing company *Rizzoli*); and (3) *Mediaset-Berlusconi* group, which controls the daily newspaper *Il Giornale*, the weekly magazine *Panorama* and TV channels Canale 5, Italia 1 and Rete 4 (Triandafyllidou 85). Fiat-Rizzoli is the primary stockholder of *Il Corriere della Sera*, until recently the widest-circulated daily newspaper (Mancini 319-20) When we add *La Stampa*, the number-three paper in terms of circulation, to the portfolio, the power of Fiat-Rizzoli over the daily news is shown to be extensive. *La Republica*, which is the long-standing contender for first place, and has temporarily taken over *Il Corriere della Sera* in sales volume, is part of a large portfolio of newspapers, the Espresso-La Republica Group, owned by De Benedetti, a private entrepreneur. Lastly, Silvio Berlusconi, the one time ex-prime minister who was recently reelected as prime minister under a center-right coalition, owns the Mediaset empire, in addition to a number of other businesses.

ATTITUDE TOWARD FOREIGN MEDIA

Members of foreign media, operating either as foreign correspondents in Italy or in association with offices of foreign press agencies there, are treated with the utmost cordiality by Italians. The foreign press has access to office facilities, receives subsidies for some operating expenses, and its members receive a number of personal perks. It is not unusual for a foreign correspondent stationed in Rome to remain in Italy after retirement.

Expulsions of members of the foreign media are unheard of in Italy today. However, there are instances where cordiality ends. There are occasions when journalists, including foreign correspondents, are simply not allowed to witness certain events, e.g., when law enforcement officers crack down heavy-handedly on immigrants. One such occasion, reported by eyewitnesses to the European Roma Rights Center (2000), was the raid of the Roma camp at Tor de' Cenci near Rome, on March 7, 2000, and the clandestine expulsion of 112 of its occupants. The foreign media are also treated with disdain by leading politicians when they react to their objective coverage of elections, scandals and general political events in Italy. Foreign correspondent for *The Observer*, Rory Carroll (2001) described Berlusconi's accusations of the foreign press as engaging in a communist plot and conducting character assassination. The foreign press did indeed engage in a concerted effort to paint Berlusconi ad a crook who should never have been considered eligible for public office because he heads a media empire. In the words of Giovanni Agnelli, the head of Fiat and a business rival of Berlusconi in the media field, the foreign newspapers ''addressed themselves to our electorate as if it were the electorate of a banana republic.'' However, foreign correspondents do not have to go in hiding after filing their stories critical of Italy's most powerful politicians, showing again that the foreign media are well treated. The concerted feeding frenzy of the foreign media concerning the Berlusconi re-election and corruption scandals may however have led some Italians to lose respect for what they believed to be an objective foreign press.

NEWS AGENCIES

The national Italian news agency is the *Agenzia Nazionale Stampa Associata* (ANSA), the National Associated Press Agency. ANSA is Italy's largest press agency, and was established in Rome on January 13, 1945 as a cooperative company that was committed to maintain standards of independence and objectivity. Its statute declared that ANSA services would be distributed to publishers of Italian newspapers and to third parties, in the spirit of democratic liberty that is guaranteed by the Constitution, and to foster mutual assistance among its partners. The statute went on to state that collection and distribution of information to partners and non-partners would be done under criteria of rigorous impartiality and objectivity. The agency's written promise of rigorous independence was compromised as early as 1949, when ANSA became the recipient of government subsidies and its directors became government appointees.

ANSA presently consists of 43 publishing houses that print 50 daily newspapers. It has employment of 1000, as follows: 400 correspondents (94 of these abroad), 400 technical and administrative staff and 200 other employees. It is headquartered in Rome and maintains 19 regional bureaus in Italy and around the world. ANSA distributes domestic and foreign news, regional news, and international news in non-English languages, by means of satellite and data lines. ANSA no longer plays a pivotal role in providing information to Italy's daily newspapers, since the major international agencies (Associate Press, Reuters, United Press International and Tass) are available at low cost to Italian newspaper editors. ANSA's website can be accessed at http://www.ansa.it.

There are several other active news agencies, all of which are specialized to some extent. AGI Italy distributes daily news and columns on energy, life in Italy, European statistics, and other areas. ADN Kronos (owned by Guiseppe Marra Communications) focuses on daily news and job advertisements from both employers and job seekers. The Zenit news agency, which distributes religious news under the heading ''The World Seen from Rome.''

BROADCAST & ELECTRONIC NEWS MEDIA

Until the 1990s Italy's national media consisted of print and broadcasting, the telephone system was not yet integrated with broadcasting, and the media economy was tied in to the state in a variety of ways. An attempt was made in 1990s to regulate the media and its ownership. Legge Mammì or Law 223, passed in 1990, prohibited cross-ownership between publishing and television companies, while Legge Maccanico or Law 249 capped the number of television channels that could be owned by the same operating company to 20 percent of the market, and prevented Telecom Italia, the nation's largest telecommunications company, from entering the terrestrial television market (Forgacs 131). The attempt at regulation was largely ineffective due to the integration of the various media markets. Analysts Pilati and Poli (199) argue for introduction of pragmatic rules rather than quantitative ceilings as a method to control market share.

In the 1980s and 1990s, the non-print media system was still dominated by television. Recently, however,

Italian audiences have begun to turn away from generalist television, both because of its program content and because of increased use of the Internet for both entertainment and access to news. As mentioned above, TV journalism is more sensationalist and less complex than the traditional written word in the Italian Press. Since the largest audiences for news are TV audiences, TV basically sets the stage for what printed journalism must cover. Mancini (323) points to an important change in the role of the news-consuming public in Italy in the past 20 years. The average citizen in today's public sphere must possess his or her own political point of view and must have a strong emotional response to the sensationalized political events. He speculates whether the new dramatization in TV and press alike will "draw citizens closer to politics or contribute to their progressive withdrawal from it."

There are two major broadcasting networks in Italy: RAI (Radio televisione italiana) and Mediaset. Public service radio and television has been provided solely by the RAI, which operates under a renewable charter granted by the State. Its current charter will expire in 2014. RAI is set up as a limited company of national interest (*società per azioni d'interesse nationale*), outlined in Article 2461 of the Civil Code and headquartered in Rome. (Hibberd 153). Since it began operations in 1945, when liberal democracy had been restored, it was important for Italians to establish an impartial broadcasting network. The president of RAI stated its goal as follows (Hibberd 159):

> In a liberal regime, characterized by the coexistence of different political parties and by the possibility of an alternation of power, the radio cannot be the instrument of government power or of the parties of opposition, but must remain a public service of dispassionate and impartial information which all listeners, whatever their beliefs, can draw upon.

Until September 2000, the state holding company IRI (Istituto per la Ricostruzione Industriale) held 99.5 percent of RAI's shares. After that date, its ownership was turned over to the Treasury. In 1976, the monopoly of RAI was ended by the Italian Constitutional Court, and the broadcasting system was opened to market competition. In the new century, with the application of new technologies and convergence of all forms of communication, it is likely that several parts of public service broadcasting, until today still under the auspices of RAI, will be privatized.

Television subscriptions numbered near 16 million in 1999 (ISTAT 215), or 276 per 1000 persons. Although this number has steadily decreased over the last few years, TV access is still much more widespread than daily newspaper use. There are again significant regional differences. Most of the subscribers to RAI-TV are from the North-Central region (11 million, for 309 subscriptions per 1000 inhabitants), and a much smaller number from the Mezzogiorno region (4.6 million, or 219 per 1000 inhabitants). The extremes are Liguria (357 per 1000 inhabitants) and Campania (175 per 1000 inhabitants).

The number of hours of TV programming broadcast by the two major networks is spread over several channels. RAI-TV's Rai Uno and Rai Due broadcast 8,760 hours in 1999 (27 percent of the total for the network) and Rai Tre broadcast 15,227 hours (47 percent). Mediaset's Canale 5, Italia 1 and Rete 4 each broadcast 8,760 hours. News programming was mostly provided by Canale 5 (3,209 hours) and Rete 4 (1,580 hours).

Similar to the printed press, Italy's broadcasting network also has a large number of companies that provide programming at the local level. A recent study of Italy's local broadcasting network interprets the meaning of the term local on the basis of both geographical location and own-programming. F. Barca (1999) conducted a quantitative count of the number of companies and then distinguished between those who produce at least a limited share of their own programming, on the one hand, and those who simply reproduce programs that were originally broadcast by other companies, on the other. The author found that the local broadcasting network is a crowded and active one. Owning a local TV station does not only yield direct economic advantage, but plays a more indirect role in owners' other economic activities as well (e.g., political participation).

As Italy is entering the digital age, an Internet audience numbering into the millions has emerged among the public. Recent online surveys of Italian Internet audiences (Magistretti 2001) show that they constitute the better educated, more well to do, and more liberal among the Italian population. The Internet audience comprises people who are distrustful of both the daily press and television, and use the Internet to obtain access to objective news (not just Italian), music, various forms of entertainment, merchandise and services.

The Internet also provides services for those who simply seek easier access to their favorite daily newspaper, or who wish to read their paper while away on travel. On-line newspaper delivery has expanded in the last few years. The first electronic editions to appear online were those of *L'Unità* and *L'Unione Sarda*, both in 1995. The following is a list of Italian newspapers, with their URLs, that can be read online. The list is likely to expand.

- *Brescia oggi,* www.bresciaoggi.it
- *Il Corriere del Sud,* www.corrieredelsud.it
- *Il Golfo,* www.ischiaonlin.it/ilgolfo
- *Il Messagero,* www.ilmessagero.it

- *L'Unità,* www.unita.it
- *La Stampa,* www.lastampa.it
- *La Repubblica,* www.repubblica.it
- *La Gazzetta dello Sport,* www.gazzetta.it

Online journalism in Italy is more innovative than its printed paper form, but is constrained by advertising. While the layout of printed newspapers maintains boundaries between articles and advertising, the Internet makes possible the use of links that take readers to a variety of products or to the website of a sponsor where they can read more detailed information about the topic treated in the journal article. This makes the article the hub of a variety of advertisements, and compromises the independence of the journalist and the newspaper (Sorice 206). On the positive side, however, the Internet makes possible the use of advertisements that are that are interactive with the consumer (Pasquali 188). Another problem faced by Italian online journals is their local focus, which to some extent conflicts with the global focus of the Internet. Thus far, printed newspapers have not seen a decline in sales that is directly due to a shift of readership to their online versions. *La Republica* has had remarkable success with the combination of its printed version and a very differently formatted online version, where readers can move to in-depth analyses of stories, participate in dialogues, and access a variety of special services and offers (Sorice 207). Personalization of service is an important marketing tool to attract subscribers to online newspapers.

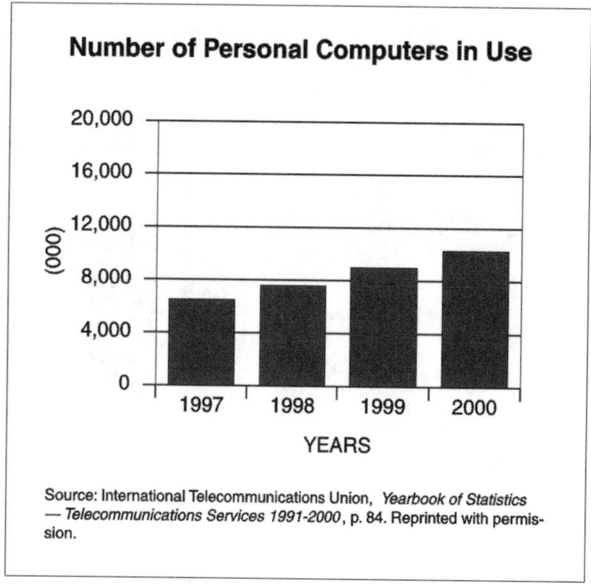

Source: International Telecommunications Union, *Yearbook of Statistics — Telecommunications Services 1991-2000*, p. 84. Reprinted with permission.

The Italian television system is about to enter digital terrestrial television (DTT), which is expected to be widely available and replace analogue television in the next few years. Law 249 of 1997 also set up the *Autorità per le Garanzie nelle Comunicazioni*, a regulatory agency that became operational in 1998. It made a number of recommendations in its white paper on digital terrestrial television, made public in November 2000. AGCOM predicts that DTT will enhance diversification of programs and will bring the public back to their television units. DTT will also be interactive and thus provide a number of flexible user options. Another visual medium, Italian cinema, is lagging behind in technology. To once again become a significant participant in the global market, with films that have more appeal than the mere nostalgia of films like *Il Postino* and *La Vita è Bella*, the Italian film industry must begin to use strategies that rely on digital technology and integration with culture production in other media.

EDUCATION & TRAINING

The journalism profession is outlined in legislation of 1963 that set up the *Ordine dei Giornalisti* (Order of Journalists). The *Ordine* established two basic categories of journalists, *professionisti* (full-time professionals, typically employed by one newspaper), and *pubblicisti* (free-lance journalists). A third category was added in the late 1970s, comprising such professionals as managing editors of professional and academic periodicals. The *Ordine* further establishes the vertical hierarchy from apprenticeship to licensed professional. The *Ordine* has the legal authority to impose penalties for violations of the rules and is accorded a number of other disciplinary powers. In 1968, a provision was added relating to press organization, in particular, the requirement that the *dittore responsabile* be a member of the *Ordine*. The *dittore responsabile* is a designated individual in whose single person resides the responsibility and, hence, liability for the material printed in the publication. This person may not be a member of Parliament, because deputies and senators are immune. For newspapers where the *dittore responsabile* is not an actual editor, the day-to-day operations of the paper are conducted by a managing editor or *editore operante* (Porter ix). The position of *dittore responsabile* existed in Italy more than hundred years prior to the 1968 provision, which only stipulated that the person be registered on the *Ordine*. Historically, Italian printers were often punished for producing materials they did not themselves write and expressing views that they might not even agree with. The Albertine edict of 1848 (named for King Carlo Alberto of Sardinia) separated printers from the responsibility for the content of their productions by stipulating that each piece of publication must have a designated *dittore responsabile*.

To become a professional journalist in Italy, even today, requires that one achieves registration to the *Ordine*. To become registered, aspiring journalists must

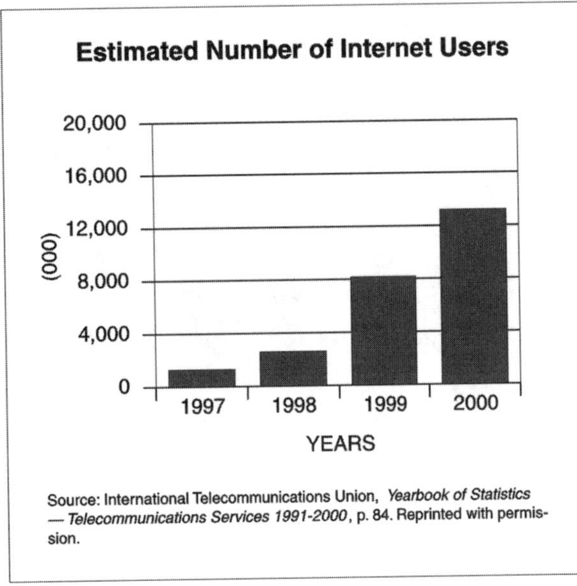

Source: International Telecommunications Union, *Yearbook of Statistics — Telecommunications Services 1991-2000*, p. 84. Reprinted with permission.

pass an examination (the *Esame di cultura generale*) and complete an apprenticeship. The examination is offered in April and October, and contains questions covering law, politics, and general knowledge, and can only be taken if applicants are at least 18 years of age and after they have completed an 18-month apprenticeship as a *practicanto* for low pay or no pay at all. Candidates who pass the written examination must stand for an oral examination held the next day, which covers questions on the following five topics determined by law: elements of the history of journalism; elements of sociology and social psychology; techniques and practices of journalism; judicial standards related to journalism and legislation relevant to the media; and professional ethics. The strict regulation of the journalism profession is reminiscent of the medieval guild system. Since most of the professional journalists have achieved registration via this route, university education and the earning of a degree in journalism is not yet highly valued as a way to enter and be successful in the profession (Holtz). Most professional journalists maintain the belief that the skills needed to become a member of the trade consist of writing skills, intuition, curiosity, and guts, as opposed to an education focusing on the humanities and the social sciences. The powerful journalists' trade association, the FNSI, still lobbies to limit expansion of university programs in journalism and also to directly limit the number of journalists listed on the *Ordine*. An aspiring journalist can theoretically obtain an apprenticeship by walking into the offices of the newspaper and applying for the position. In reality, however (Porter 51), apprenticeships tend to go to those applicants whose path has been prepared by means of a phone call or a letter from ''somebody who knows somebody.''

Once the apprentice is in the door, actual on-the-job training is very limited, since those who know and practice the craft have no time to teach it to a *practicanto*. The main pedagogical tool is trial and error, learning by cues, and the accumulation of skills by watching the more experienced journalists at their desks. This type of learning is not restricted to fresh *practicanti*. It is typical to newsroom operations, and even staff members receiving an assignment to one of the foreign desks do not receive formal training.

Despite the political opposition from the organized profession and its political backers, journalism schools and universities are beginning to be sanctioned by the *Ordine* as an acceptable alternative to the apprenticeship. Students using this education plan still have to pass the examination, however. Four schools (located in Bologna, Milan, Perugia and Urbino) and two universities (Milan and Rome) offer journalism programs that are recognized by the *Ordine*. Many additional journalism programs have been installed in educational institutions in Italy and as extension programs of universities abroad, and universities that have degree programs in Communications also are adding more and more journalism. These programs and courses have yet to be recognized as equivalent by the *Ordine*. Only those programs that have course content approved by the *Ordine* will eventually be approved as equivalent to the apprenticeship.

SUMMARY

The Italian media has been characterized by low degrees of freedom of the press, small numbers of readers and circulation of both newspapers and weekly magazines, lack of presence of both a popular press, and nonexistence of truly national let alone international newspapers. The media have traditionally been subservient to the state and to private owners. Even the profession of journalism is under government control. Since the printed press tends to follow agendas set by its industrial owners, and there is no popular press, television has temporarily captured the attention of the public. However, excessive commercialization and disenchantment with programming content has turned many viewers away from the medium in the 1990s. New technology is making its way into media communication, in the form of mobile telephony, satellite dishes, increased use of personal computers and the Internet, online journalism, and introduction of digital terrestrial television. Several trends can be predicted for the early twenty-first century:

- While dependence of the press on political and industrial powers is not typical for member countries of the EU, this phenomenon is not likely to disappear, since media mogul Silvo Berlusconi was elected prime minister in 2000. Since economic realities have led newspaper owners to expect profits denominated in Lira or Euros, rather than merely political gain, one can expect that government subsidies to the media will rise. This will not decrease the dependence of the press; rather it is tantamount to exchange of one master by another.

- Journalism will become more and more a profession learned by means of higher education at Italian universities, rather than a craft learned in apprenticeships and through experience. The globalization of the press via the Internet and the ease of access to foreign media is likely to contribute to this trend.
- Events in relation to terrorist attacks in the United States, with the help of networks operating in Europe, and the continuing influx of illegal immigrants who are refugees from the Balkans and other parts of the world is likely to continue to fuel anti-immigrant sentiments in Italy, which is likely to color the public discourse for a number of years.
- In view of the concentration of ownership of the non-public media in private hands, it is very unlikely that the Italian people will become avid consumers of domestically produced news and related materials. More likely than not, the foreign press may increase in importance, both in hard copy form, TV programs and access to the Internet. Why read a politically biased domestic paper when one can read the BBC News, *Le Monde*, *The Economist* and a host of well-respected media online?
- Looking beyond the current prime minister's negative stance towards the EU, it seems likely that Italy cannot distance itself significantly from the EU and yet remain one of the participants in the G7 summit meetings of the leaders of the worlds main economic powers. Thus, Romano Prodi's pro-EU stance (Willey) is likely to see a return in future Italian prime ministers, bringing with it the EU directives and a social contract that combat media elitism and seek to encourage use of the media to provide social inclusion rather than exclusion based on politics, region, class and immigrant status. The Italian press would benefit from participation in the public discourse surrounding this trend.
- Convergence of the different segments of the Italian media (print, film, broadcasting, telephony) will continue, with newspapers and magazines having online editions, broadcasting organizations having websites, digital TV transmission, digital editing and online delivery of films. (Forgacs 2001). Technical convergence also will contribute to increased economic convergence, which in Italy is a disturbing trend considering the lack of independence of the press and the media. The concomitant rise in consumer convergence, however, is a positive trend and a possible vehicle to democratize the media, provided that use fees do not lead to exclusion of the economically disadvantaged.

BIBLIOGRAPHY

Barca, F. 1999. ''The Local Television Broadcasting System in Italy.'' *Media, Culture and Society* 21(1): 109-122.

Brancato, Sergio. 2001. ''Italy in the Digital Age: Cinema as New Technology.'' *Modern Italy* 6(2): 215-222.

Carroll, Rory. 2001. ''Berlusconi attacks Foreign 'Plotters.''' *The Observer*, Sunday, May 6, 2001.

Colombo, Fausto. 2001. ''Mobile Telephone Use in Italy in the 1990s: Interpretative Models.'' *Modern Italy* 6(2): 141-151.

Dauvergne, Alain. 1983. ''Italy's Secret Strengths: How the Bumblebee of Western Europe Remains Aloft.'' *World Press Review* 30(5): 30-32.

European Roma Rights Center. 2000. *Letter to the Italian Prime Minister*. (Signed by Executive Director Dimitrina Petrova). Sunday, 12 March.

Forcella, Enzo. 1959, ''Millecinquecento Lettori.'' *Tempo Presente* 6: 112-127.

Forgacs, David. 2001. ''Scenarios for the Digital Age: Convergence, Personalization, Exclusion.'' *Modern Italy* 6(2): 129-139.

Freedom House. 2001. *The World Audit*. New York: Freedom House Publications.

Grandinetti, Mario. 1992. *I Quotidiani in Italia: 1943-1991*. Milan, Italy: FrancoAngeli s.r.l.

Hibberd, Matthew. 2001. ''Public Service Broadcasting in Italy: Historical Trends and Future Prospects.'' *Modern Italy* 6(2): 153-170.

Holtz, Torsten. 1998. ''Widespread Prejudices.'' The New Euroreporter. October.

ISTAT (Istituto Centrale di Statistica). 2000. *Annuario Statistico Italiano*. 2000. Rome, Italy: Istituto Nazionale di Statistica.

Kennedy, Frances. 2002. ''Italy Fears Revival of Red Brigades after Government Aide is Shot Dead.'' *The Independent*. March 21, 2002.

Locke, Richard M. 1995. *Remaking the Italian Economy*. Ithaca and London: Cornell University Press.

Lumley, Robert. 1996. *Italian Journalism: A Critical Anthology*. Manchester and New York: Manchester University Press. Distributed by St. Martin's Press in the USA and Canada.

Magistretti, Stefano. ''Two Online Surveys of Italian Internet Audiences: A Summary of Findings.'' *Modern Italy* 6(2): 171-180.

Mancini, Paolo. 2000. ''How to Combine Media Commercialization and Party Affiliation: The Italian Experience.'' *Political Communication* 17(4): 319-324.

Neal, Larry, and Daniel Barbezat. 1998. *The Economics of the European Union and the Economies of Europe.* New York and Oxford: Oxford University Press.

Pace, Alessandro. 1990. ''Constitutional Protection of Freedom of Expression in Italy.'' *European Review of Public Law* 2: 71-113.

Pasquali, Francesca. 2001. ''Imagining the Web: The Social Construction of the Internet in Italy.'' *Modern Italy* 2001(2): 181-193.

Pilati, Antonio, and Emanuela Poli. 2001. ''Digital Terrestrial Television.'' *Modern Italy* 6(2):195-204.

Porter, William E. 1983. *The Italian Journalist.* Ann Arbor MI: The University of Michigan Press.

Shugaar, Antony. 1995. ''Berlusconi's Untamed Press.'' *Columbia Journalism Review* 33(6): 19.

———. 1993. ''What, No Strings? The Italian Tradition and L'Indipendente.'' *Columbia Journalism Review* 32(4): 16-18.

Sorice, Michele. 2001. ''Online Journalism: Information and Culture in the Italian Technological Imagery.'' *Modern Italy* 6(2): 205-213.

Triandafyllidou, Anna. 1999. ''Nation and Immigration: A Study of the Italian Press Discourse.'' *Social Identities* 5(1): 65-88.

Wells, Matt. 2002. ''Censorship 'Award' for Berlusconi.'' *The Guardian.* Friday, March 22.

Willey, David. 1999. ''Europe Profile: Romano Prodi.'' Interview by David Willey, correspondent for BBC News in Rome. May 10, 1999.

—Brigitte Bechtold

JAMAICA

BASIC DATA

Official Country Name:	Jamaica
Region (Map name):	North & Central America
Population:	2,665,636
Language(s):	English, Creole
Literacy rate:	85.0%
Area:	10,990 sq km
GDP:	7,403 (US$ millions)
Number of Television Stations:	7
Number of Television Sets:	460,000
Television Sets per 1,000:	172.6
Number of Cable Subscribers:	257,140
Cable Subscribers per 1,000:	98.9
Number of Radio Stations:	23
Number of Radio Receivers:	1,215,000
Radio Receivers per 1,000:	455.8
Number of Individuals with Computers:	120,000
Computers per 1,000:	45.0
Number of Individuals with Internet Access:	80,000
Internet Access per 1,000:	30.0

BACKGROUND & GENERAL CHARACTERISTICS

At the beginning of the twenty-first century, Jamaica supported a vast variety of media, ranging from daily newspapers to weekly shoppers, from news and editorial content to publications dedicated to spreading the word about the ample Jamaican culture. Jamaica had three daily newspapers: the *Daily Gleaner*, the *Observer* and the *Star*, an afternoon tabloid put out by the publishers of the *Gleaner*. The *Gleaner*'s coverage of local news, sports and features was regularly of high quality, and the paper knew and was unafraid of expressing its voice. The *Observer* was founded in the early 1990s and was published in a tabloid format with a broadsheet bent. Both the *Gleaner* and *Observer* put out a Sunday paper. In addition to these local publications, some outside media made it to Jamaica; U.S. newsmagazines like *Time* and *Newsweek* were available at news stands, as were some of the major U.S. dailies (though they were frequently a couple of days out of date) and the Sunday broadsheets from the United Kingdom.

Of the papers supported by Jamaica, the *Daily Gleaner* seemed on the soundest footing in 2002. The Gleaner Company published the *Daily Gleaner*, the company's flagship paper. Established in 1834, it was the oldest operating newspaper in the Caribbean. The company added the *Sunday Gleaner* in 1939. It also published the *Afternoon Star*. There was also a *Weekend Star* that contained mostly reviews of Jamaican music, dance, theater, and social culture. It was first published in 1951. The *Gleaner* took no prisoners, particularly in its political coverage. It earned its reputation in its coverage of the Manley administration of the 1970s, and in the early 2000s it took on all parties with its non-partisan coverage. In an effort to promote education, the Gleaner Company also began publishing *The Children's Own*, a weekly put out during school terms to promote creative learning. In 2002, the Gleaner Company had perhaps the strongest presence in Jamaica. The group had offices in Toronto, Ontario, Canada; London; and New York in addition to its headquarters in Kingston. The newspaper group made nearly $1.8 million in 2000, after making just over $1.6 million in 1999.

The *Gleaner* targeted young, male readers. It drew 54 percent of its readers from males. Some 56 percent of its readers were between the ages of 18 and 34, with another 26 percent between 35 and 44. Only 18 percent of the Gleaner's readers were 45 or older. Of the chain's readers, 43 percent made between US$31,000 and US$45,000 a year; some 32 percent make US$30,000 or less. Only 12 percent earn US$46,000 or more.

Many of Jamaica's other, less traditional publications focused on the country's culture, music and entertainment. For instance, *Destination Jamaica* was an annual publication that focused primarily on the hospitality industries. *Track and Pools*, another Gleaner publication, covered the racing industry. Moreover, the *Weekend Star* complemented its daily publication with more information about local music, dance, theater and the social culture.

The *Star*, another Gleaner publication and the island's tabloid, provided the more salacious stories not found in the more-traditional newspapers. A similar publication, *X News*, provided entertainment listings and news from the music world.

Other regional publications helped keep readers in their areas informed. The *Western Mirror* was published in Montego Bay for the western side of the island, while the *North Coast Times*, based in Ocho Rios, was a tourist-oriented publication. The *Observer*, founded by Gordon ''Butch'' Stewart in the early 1990s, rivaled the kind of coverage found in he *Gleaner*. However, most observers appeared to feel the paper sometimes struggled to figure out its target audience.

While Jamaica supported several quality print publications, radio was also popular in the country. Its roots could be traced to a ham radio operator, John Grinan, who in 1939 while operating at the start of World War II, followed wartime regulations and turned his equipment over to the government. Thus, Radio Jamaica was born. Grinan convinced government officials to use his amateur equipment to operate a public broadcasting system, and the government adapted his equipment to match demands. Regular scheduled broadcasts started from Grinan's equipment, the first one coming November 17, 1939. Indeed, the first radio station, VP5PZ, took its name from Grinan's call-sign. At first there was only a single broadcast per week, emanating from Grinan's home. After May 1, 1940, though, the station picked up a small staff. Daily broadcasts started in June 1940.

The broadcasts got better and better, despite the adversity of working in an inadequate facility. The first program manager was appointed and the station started offering more and more options, in addition to news and wartime information. Eventually, broadcasts included live performances of local artists. As of 2002, most of Jamaica's radio was dedicated to this kind of perpetuation of local artists and culture. But back then, running the station became financially prohibitive for the government, and the decision was made to issue a license to a private company to provide the broadcasting services.

The Jamaica Broadcasting Company, a subsidiary of the Re-diffusion Group in London, England, got the first license in 1949. The license allowed Jamaica Broadcasting Company to operate regular broadcasting, and the company took over the operations of the station, known as ZQI since 1940, on May 1, 1950. Commercial broadcasting began on July 9, 1950. Thus was born Radio Jamaica.

The new company was handed the responsibility of covering the entire island with radio broadcasting. Not wanting to limit it to urbanites, the mandate was to have rural residents exposed as well. To make sure that happened, the company distributed wireless sets to about 200 listening posts around the island. They were placed at natural gathering spots, like schools, police stations, and stores around the various villages.

One important mandate was that the radio broadcasting would be commercial, meaning they would have to figure out how much air time was worth, and advertisers for the first time would be forced to pay for the time used for their advertisements. It was decreed the station's only revenue would come from these advertisements and from sponsorships of individual broadcasts. Consequently, listeners for the first time had their programming interrupted with commercials.

In August 1951, the station moved, from its original location to what, at the time, was called a ''modern, air-conditioned and excellently equipped'' studio. Two years later, the station made history, installing frequency-modulated transmitters. Radio Jamaica thus became the first country in the British Commonwealth to broadcast regularly scheduled programming on the FM band.

In February 1951, the station decided it needed to expand the radio's reach. The company started a re-diffusion service, using a division of Jamaica Broadcasting Company Limited, to provide programming transmitted by wire. Carried to homes, retail outlets, bars, hotels, and the like, the service became quite popular, particularly because it offered something that had not been available: total coverage of national events. By 1958, more than 15,000 subscribers had this service.

Non-stop music became a staple of Radio Jamaica in the early 1960s, when *Reditune*, a tape machine system that provided non-stop, but taped, music of various sorts. The tape system eventually gave way to the more sophisticated *Musipage* system, which broadcast the music live from the station. In 1972, Radio Jamaica introduced a second daily radio feed on the FM band. RJR-FM filled a need for soothing, uninterrupted music. Radio Jamaica purchased the television and Radio 2 assets from the Jamaican Broadcasting Corporation, the government-owned system, for about $70 million Jamaican. With all its success, Radio Jamaica Limited evolved. In 2002 it was doing business as the RJR Communications Group, the largest electronic media corporation in the Caribbean. The RJR umbrella sheltered Radio Jamaica Limited, Television Jamaica Limited, and Multi-Media Jamaica Ltd. The goal, apparently realized, was to touch the lives of the majority of Jamaicans through coverage of news and world affairs and the entertainment industry, with some educational and informative programming as well.

ECONOMIC FRAMEWORK

In the early 2000s, agriculture employed more than 20 percent of Jamaica's population. Bauxite, aluminum, sugar, bananas, rum and coffee were key exports from the island, with tourism responsible for an important part of the island's economy. The government's austerity program lowered inflation nearly 20 percent in six years, from 25 percent in 1995 to around 6 percent in 2000 (although it was up to about 7 percent in 2001). A declining gross domestic product, according to some sources, showed signs of recovery. The per-capita GDP was roughly $3,389. The GDP grew by 0.8 percent in 2000.

More and more Jamaicans began to earn a decent living, although the island's unemployment rate in 2000 was around 15 percent nationally and even higher among women. More than a quarter of the island's population lived below the poverty line, and 13 percent lacked health care, education, and economic opportunities. The central bank prevented a drastic decrease in the exchange rate, although the Jamaican dollar has still been dropping. At the end of 2001, the average exchange rate was $47 Jamaican dollars to US$1.

According to information compiled by the U.S. Department of State, weakness in the financial sector, speculation, and low levels of investment erode confidence in the productive sector. The Jamaican government raised US$3.6 billion in new sovereign debt in 2001, which was used to help meet its U.S. dollar debt obligations. Net internal revenues, according to the Department of State, rose from US$969.5 million in the beginning of 2001 to more than US$1.8 billion by the end of the year.

In terms of the newspaper industry, Jamaica's import figure for paper and paperboard stood at just under US$90 million in 1996, whereas it had grown around 20 percent every year between 1992 and 1995. After that, though, the growth stalled due in large part to a recession. However, some areas continued to do well, including newsprint, sanitary napkins, and various types of tissue. The Jamaican government continued a gradual reduction in overall duties, to the point that some import categories had no duty, including paper used in the printing industry, corrugated paper and paperboard, cigarette paper, and dress patterns.

The combination of high interest rates and an increase in the availability of better-quality imported products put some small amount of pressure on local manufacturers. The United States had 60 percent market coverage and was the country's major source for paper and paperboard products. Other countries, among them Canada (newsprint) and Trinidad (sanitary paper items), were also quite competitive.

In 1992, Jamaica imported US$2.3 million in newsprint rolls; by 1996, it had grown to US$7.5 million. Newsprint formed one of the significant import segments for Jamaica. Several newspapers were now printed nationwide: the *Gleaner*, the *Observer*, and the *Herald*. In 1996, importation of newsprint accounted for 8.6 percent of the total paper products imported. The import market share, therefore, had more than doubled in four years. In fact, 1995 showed more import than 1996, but that was almost certainly because the *Herald* quit publishing daily in 1996.

Relatively high interest rates for most commercial enterprises, in addition to the higher quality of imported goods, had a negative effect on the production inside Jamaica in the 1990s. These facts were proven by the import figures for things like paper for printing, toilet tissue, and sanitary towels.

The local printing industry complemented the manufacturing industry, so any stagnation or lack of growth in general manufacturing would be reflected through lack of growth in the total market for printing products (including paper); therefore, a gradual decrease in these imports would be seen.

The United States continued to be the major import source of paper products and paperboard. In 1996, the overall market share for the U.S. was 60 percent. The United States dominated some areas, such as Kraft paperboard, where their market share is 97 percent, and writing and printing paper (80 percent). There was considerable competition in other categories; for instance, Canada was the source for about 80 percent of newsprint.

According to the U.S. Department of Commerce National Trade Data Bank (November 2000), paper and paperboard were very broad groupings which covered three main uses: communication, packaging, and hygiene/sanitary use. Despite growth in the use of computers, e-mail, and other electronic means of corresponding, paper continued to be an important medium for allowing communication. Major-end users are newspapers (newsprint), the printing industry, government agencies, and private offices involved in commercial activities.

Of Jamaican newspapers, the *Gleaner* claimed the highest circulation, boasting 100,000 copies printed on Sundays. Since late 1997, the Gleaner company had a deal to publish a daily international edition of the *Miami Herald.* Moreover, the printing industry in Jamaica in the early 2000s consisted of several companies which worked in tandem with various commercial enterprises and government agencies in the production of various items such as labels, letterheads, business cards, flyers, newsletters, brochures, magazines, annual reports, calendars, posters, computer forms and greeting cards, etc.

The government of Jamaica and its various ministries and agencies are big users of paper for communication, administration, and recording purposes. Significant government organizations which spring to mind in this area include the Jamaica Information Service, the Inland Revenue Department, the Electoral Office, the Statistical Institute of Jamaica and the Ministries of Finance and Health.

Press Laws

The Jamaican Senate in June 2002 passed the country's first Access to Information Bill, the equivalent to the U.S. Freedom of Information Act. The bill did cause consternation, however, because of a clause that allowed the minister of information to exclude any statutory body from the influence of the information law. Minority senators objected on grounds that the clause gave the minister sweeping powers to exclude entire agencies from the purview of the information law, rather than exempting specific documents. The clause did provide for an approval authority; however, the minister had to obtain ''affirmative resolution'' or the consent of both houses of parliament. Nine government senators voted in favor of the clause, while three Opposition and two independent senators objected. At the same time, the Cabinet reviewed detailed proposals for a law to replace the Official Secrets Act, an antiquated law that generally provided for penalties to public officials for disclosing information.

In 2001, the government agreed to amend a new law that made it a crime to report on certain government investigations. The so-called Corruption (Prevention) Act was designed to bring Jamaica into compliance with the 1996 Inter-American Convention against Corruption. Under the bill, journalists could be fined up to US$12,250 or jailed for up to three years, or both, for publishing information about the work of any state anti-corruption commission. After several media and civic groups conducted seminars and published information about the offending clauses, the government passed the bill without them.

Censorship

In the early 2000s, some aspects of the media were under government control. The biggest issues facing the press concerned the limits to its freedom, the responsible use of that freedom, the relationship between the press and the Jamaican government, the influence of imported content, and the role of the press in the development of young, independent countries.

State-Press Relations

Despite some government control over the media, generally speaking the press acts independently. According to Jamaican columnist Martin Henry, the English-speaking commonwealth Caribbean has largely a free press. Still some issues connected to state-press relations were raised at a 2001 conference in Jamaica, which co-occurred with violent protests in the country. The minister of finance had announced a large tax hike on gasoline. After a quiet weekend, some protests began the following Monday, intensified, Henry believed, at least in part by the media.

At noon the first day, a few scattered roadblocks, which are a popular form of protest on the island, were set up. The situation was reported on midday broadcasts. By later that afternoon, Kingston was practically shut down by roadblocks, violence had escalated, and nine people had been killed.

The problem, as many observers saw it, was that the media were allowed to report on the protests, but they were not allowed to report on the inner workings of the government because of the Official Secrets Act. The act, journalists believed, restricted such access, and thus impeded the flow of information to the public. Had the public had more information about why the government felt the need for the tax hike, perhaps the violence could have been avoided. When the government did release more detailed information, protesters withdrew.

Protesters wanted media coverage. According to Henry, roadblocks became a popular form of protest because they often provided a chance for dramatic footage. Protesters frequently refused to disperse until after the cameras arrive. Then, too, the media themselves questioned the government. The *Daily Gleaner* and the *Observer* both frequently and with justification question the politics, practices, policies, and procedures of government and political parties.

One visible forum for political discussion is the talk show, which flourishes in Jamaica and across the Caribbean, for that matter. Some of the talk shows ardently pursued government accountability, pressing particularly about libel laws and the Official Secrets Act. Before the tax protests, the more critical talk show hosts were accused of being negative. After the protests, in which nine people died, they were perceived as more justified.

Many problems were ready topics. High unemployment, underemployment, growing debt, and high interest rates were among the most serious of Jamaica's economic problems. Both major political parties had ties with two large trade unions.

By the end of the 1960s, it was evident that media was going to play a key role in the establishment of nationhood. According to information obtained on the Web site of the Caribbean Institute of Mass Communication (CARIMAC), the problem was that most of the people working in the media were ''outsiders'' lacking in any kind of Caribbean perspective. So, in 1969, the Jamaican government started looking into the idea of putting a regional media-training center on the island, in an effort to correct the problem. Finally CARIMAC was located at the University of the West Indies (UWI) at Mona, and it followed certain principles. The program had a theoretical basis and a foundation in the Caribbean environment; it included courses in social sciences and communications, as well as in Caribbean studies. In addition, it gave practical training in mass media, concentrating on writing, interviewing, and production. The program was also designed to address the needs of media at all levels. With help from a variety of international and national agencies, the one-year degree program in mass communications was established at UWI-Mona in October 1974, with 31 students in the course.

CARIMAC moved four years later. In 1977, three years after the establishment of CARIMAC, a bachelor's degree program was added. Students of the Faculty of Arts and General Studies were able to choose from three different degree programs: Social Sciences with Communications; Languages and Literature with Communications; and Social Sciences, Languages, and Literature with Communications.

The institute continued to evolve. In 1990, the semester system was adopted, and students could choose from a wider curriculum. In 1994 CARIMAC added a master's degree program (in Communications Studies). The program consisted of a combination of formal lectures and seminars, taught by an inter-disciplinary team of instructors. In 1996, CARIMAC changed its name to The Caribbean Institute of Media and Communication. Then, in 1998, the undergraduate degree was revamped. First, the school added two new specialties, multimedia and public relations. Then, improvements were made to existing areas: Print became Text and Graphic Production; and audio-visual became Social Marketing. Television and radio were switched to Broadcasting Skills (Television) and Broadcasting Skills (Radio). Finally, new communications electives were added to reflect industry changes and technological advances. In addition, CARIMAC had an active outreach program, hosted regional seminars in various countries, ran workshops and conferences, and offered in-serves training for members of the media.

As part of the UWI, CARIMAC helped both governmental and non-governmental development agencies in the Caribbean. The institute assisted in communication methods and technology for development purposes in health, agriculture, community development, public education, and other areas. Moreover, as the only regionally recognized tertiary-level training program to media and communication in the Caribbean, CARIMAC was also the Caribbean's representative in the network of Global Journalism Training Institutions (Journet). CARIMAC trained students for work in print, radio, video, multimedia, and public relations.

Another group of great interest in the Caribbean, the Caribbean Environmental Reporters' Network (CERN), developed out of a training workshop in Jamaica in July 1990. In November 1992, at a follow-up workshop in Barbados put on by CARIMAC and the Caribbean Conservation Association, the concept was formally approved, and CERN was born. From the 10 journalists who originally formed the network, the staff grew to more than 35 journalists in 13 Caribbean states. CERN collaborated with media houses across the region, providing these organizations with accurate, up-to-date coverage from a Caribbean perspective.

CERN hoped to host one regional gathering every year on a topic pertaining to environmental journalism so that reporters would learn more about these issues. Too, CERN offered networking and information exchange possibilities between reporters throughout the Caribbean who had similar interests. These professional connections supported the dispatch of reporters to international events around the world, thus achieving broader media coverage of environmental issues.

CERN produced a weekly radio magazine series on community environmental action in the Caribbean, entitled *Island Beat.* The 10-minute program aired on more than 25 stations in 15 countries every week. It was distributed through the CANA Satellite network.

NEWS AGENCIES

The government is served by the Jamaica Information Service (JIS), which, through radio and television programs, video recordings, advertisements, publications, and news releases disseminates information on government policies, programs, and activities.

BIBLIOGRAPHY

Committee for the Protection of Journalism. *Attacks on the Press,* 2001. Available from http://www.cpj.org.

Henry, Martin. *Tax Protests Focus Jamaican Media's Role.* The International Communications Forum, 2001.

Jamaica Gleaner Internet Edition, Feb. 7, 2002. Available from http://www.jamaica-gleaner.com.

Jamaican History, 2002. Available from http://radiojamaica.com.

''Information Bill Gets Rough Passage in Senate.'' *Jamaica Observer Internet Edition,* June 29, 2002. Available from http://www.jamaicaobserver.com.

''Media,'' Jamaica Information Service, 2002. Available from http://jis.gov.jm/information/media.htm.

Thomas, Polly, and Adam Vaitilingam. ''Rough Guide to Jamaica,'' 2001.

U.S. Department of Commerce. *National Trade Data Bank,* November 3, 2000.

—Brad Kadrich

JAPAN

BASIC DATA

Official Country Name:	Japan
Region (Map name):	East & South Asia
Population:	126,771,662
Language(s):	Japanese
Literacy rate:	99.0%
Area:	377,835 sq km
GDP:	4,841,584 (US$ millions)
Number of Daily Newspapers:	110
Total Circulation:	71,896,000
Circulation per 1,000:	669
Newspaper Consumption (minutes per day):	28
Total Newspaper Ad Receipts:	1,247 (Yen billions)
As % of All Ad Expenditures:	27.60
Number of Television Stations:	7108
Number of Television Sets:	86,500,000
Television Sets per 1,000:	682.3
Television Consumption (minutes per day):	185
Number of Cable Subscribers:	18,705,060
Cable Subscribers per 1,000:	147.4
Number of Satellite Subscribers:	10,620,000
Satellite Subscribers per 1,000:	83.8
Number of Radio Stations:	305
Number of Radio Receivers:	120,500,000
Radio Receivers per 1,000:	950.5
Number of Individuals with Computers:	40,000,000
Computers per 1,000:	315.5
Number of Individuals with Internet Access:	47,080,000
Internet Access per 1,000:	371.4

BACKGROUND & GENERAL CHARACTERISTICS

The Japanese media presents some startling differences when compared with the press in other leading industrial countries of the world. At first glance, the condition of the Japanese press seems to be parallel to that found in the United States. There are major national daily newspapers, a prestigious financial newspaper, and many regional and local newspapers. The level of reporting is quite good. There is a vigorous and increasing use not only of television for the dissemination of news, but also of the Internet. The population is highly literate; indeed, Japan has one of the highest literacy rates in the world, at over 90 percent. The vast majority of Japanese people read at least one newspaper every day.

Just five newspapers are ''national'' papers, and their circulation (in both morning and evening editions) accounts for half of the country's total newspaper circulation. These are (with 1996 circulation figures in millions, combining morning and evening editions) the *Asahi Shimbun* (12.7), the *Mainichi Shimbun* (5.8), *Nihon Keizai Shimbun* (4.6), *Sankei Shimbun* (2.9), and the *Yomiuri Shimbun* (14.55).

Daily and Non-Daily Newspaper Titles and Circulation Figures

	1996	1997	1998	1999	2000
Number of Daily Newspapers	109	109	108	109	110
Circulation of Dailies (000)	72,705	72,699	72,410	72,218	71,896
Number of Non-Daily Newspapers	1	1	1	NA	NA
Circulation of Non-Dailies (000)	NA	NA	NA	NA	NA

Source: World Association of Newspapers and Zenithmedia, *World Press Trends 2001*, pp. 8, 10, 17, 19. Note: NA stands for not available.

A closer examination of editorial style and content shows a considerable uniformity among these newspapers. It is almost impossible to characterize one or another of them as predictably and regularly representing a specific political position, as, by way of example, the *New York Times* can be assumed to take a liberal standpoint, while the *Wall Street Journal*'s editorial page usually is conservative. Part of this uniformity in editorial posture is due, of course, to the overwhelming dominance of the Liberal Democratic Party, with its six or so internal political clans but a broad consensus on policy.

To understand this condition, it is useful to take a brief excursion into the history of Japanese journalism. Newspapers as we know them came late to Japan, and were not much present until the very end of the era of feudalism, which was precipitated by the arrival in 1853 of an American armada. Initially, they seem to have been crudely printed gossipy broadsheets (*yomiuri*, literally ''for sale to read''). The Shogunate made many efforts to control the dissemination of information and opinion, although with the proliferation of lending libraries it was not possible to make any tight controls effective. It was not until the modernizing reforms of the Meiji Restoration (1868-1912) that a formal press was permitted.

Historical Stages in the Modern Era (since 1868): An Overview The development of this modern system has gone through several distinct phases, some of which are discussed in more detail below. Even before the early days of that 1868 revolution known as the Meiji Restoration, the transitional period between the arrival of American ships (1853) and the actual removal of the Shogunate (1868) saw the development of a number of news outlets. The first of these was the *Nagasaki Shipping List and Advertiser*, an English paper published in 1861. Since many Japanese products contained satirical comments on the crumbling central government, they were unpopular with the leading officials. But early Japanese travelers to the west, within two years of the arrival of the Americans, immediately saw the utility of accurate and widely available national news and pressed for change in Japan's newspaper policies. In response, the Shogunate reorganized the Office for Studying Barbarian Writings so as to facilitate the acquisition and dissemination of foreign news inside Japan. A further reorganization in 1863 led to the inclusion of domestic news in the mix, also ironically derived from foreign newspapers (since the Tokugawa developments in the popular development and dissemination of news had not matured to any level of reliability).

Once the Meiji Restoration was accomplished in 1868 and solidified in the next several years, the development of a national press became a priority for the national government. In the early years of the twentieth century, the ''people's rights'' movement gave further impetus to the growth of a professional press tradition. These positive developments were even accelerated in the period of so-called ''Taisho Democracy'' (1912-1926) as Japan seemed to be considering the development of a mature and liberal form of social organization. However, the descent into militarism, which accelerated after the later 1920s, put Japanese newspapers into a difficult position relative to the government and national policy from which only the end of the war and the beginning of the American Occupation was able to deliver them.

Clearly a new phase in Japanese press history began with the surrender on August 15, 1945. General MacArthur's policies mandated a free press but paradoxically controlled what could be reported about the Occupation. After a change in direction in Occupation policies caused by the emerging tensions of the Cold War (''the Reverse Course''), left-leaning publications were censored and put out of business by the Americans. By the early 1950s, however, Japan was on its own, and the current party system and press tradition entered into a phase of rapid development. Many of the restrictions put in place during the Occupation period were lifted.

The system of government that emerged after the Occupation seems at first glance to be based on the western model, but major commentators have noted that highest priority is given to consensus and cooperation. In journalism, the most salient example of this tendency is the continued existence and prominence of the press clubs. Consequently, one can look in vain in Japan for a western-style adversarial relationship between the gov-

Top Ten Daily Newspapers
(2000)

	Circulation
Yomiuri Shimbun	14,407,000
Asahi Shimbun	12,393,000
Mainichi Shimbun	5,685,000
Nihon Keizai Shimbun	4,703,000
Chunichi Shimbun	4,635,000
Sankei Shimbun	2,905,000
Hokkaido Shimbun	1,969,000
Shizuoka Shimbun	1,456,000
Nishi-Nippon Shimbun	1,029,000
Kyoto Shimbun	824,000

Source: World Association of Newspapers and Zenithmedia, *World Press Trends 2001*, p. 131.

ernment and the mainstream press, between commentators in the press and corrupt businesses, and even to quite a fair degree between and among the various leading newspapers themselves.

Challenges From the Script System The mechanical challenges of printing a daily newspaper anywhere in the world should not be underestimated. In Japan, as elsewhere, hand set moveable type was one option. Since the runs of Tokugawa broadsheets were limited to as few as dozens or the low hundreds of copies, crude materials such as rice cakes were used for inking the paper with the appropriate marks, and some publishers even resorted to the use of blocks of a hard, taffy-like sweetening material called *mochi*. If the Japanese newspaper world was to come of age in the Meiji period (after 1868), with high volume and multi-page runs issued daily, however, it would need to adopt modern machinery.

However, there are significant complexities in the Japanese script system that precluded the development of linotype machines in Japan until 1920. (Rotary drum presses were beginning to enter Japanese usage as early as about 1900.) The Japanese use a great number of Chinese characters (*kanji*), and to read a newspaper requires knowledge of at least 2,000 of these characters. Obviously, a keyboard is difficult to devise or to operate which would allow for these thousands of *kanji*.

However, since the Japanese language (unlike Chinese) is highly inflected, in order to express Japanese in writing at all a supplementary script is required (*hiragana*). Derived from stylized and simplified elements of the Chinese characters, this is a basic collection of forty-eight characters which, when combined with simple diacritical marks, allows for the representation of all 104 sounds that one can make in Japanese. A second and parallel syllabic system was later also developed, called *katakana*. Although the characters are similar in their essentials, this is a much more angular script in appearance than the rounded *hiragana*, and has been preferred in modern times for the written representation of foreign words and phrases.

Finally, it is possible to take the entire Japanese language and write it down in western style characters (*romaji*). It was briefly proposed after the Second World War that Japan be required to shift to western-style writing (as happened in Vietnam in 1906), but this idea died quickly.

In this most cumbersome of all the world's script systems, all four of these scripts are used in regular daily contexts, including in newspapers. The symbols of three of the four (*hiragana*, *katakana*, and *romaji*) tell the reader how to pronounce the word, but pronunciation of the *kanji* is not self-evident, and must be memorized. It is not uncommon to see a small-print pronunciation clue written above a *kanji* character in *hiragana*, and increasingly, signs in Japan are presented in two or more script systems simultaneously.

Adding additional complexity, the Japanese language is fairly ''sound-poor'' while nonetheless being ''symbol-rich'', which means that there are an extraordinary number of homonyms. For example, out of the 35 characters that can be vocally rendered by the sound *rin*, the meanings vary all the way from ''morals'' to ''a female Chinese unicorn'' to ''luring fish with a bonfire.'' Finally, each character has both a classical Chinese pronunciation and a Japanese language pronunciation.

Therefore, we may come to three conclusions. It is very difficult even for native speakers to become truly and fully literate in their own language. It is a high challenge to achieve exclusive precision of meaning either in speech or in writing. It is also a major undertaking to devise a keyboard that will enable its user efficiently to write the Japanese language in the form that most closely approximates that which Japanese eyes and ears would find comfortable and familiar. As to this last problem, modern computers have helped greatly to mitigate the difficulties of typing in Japanese, since they can fairly easily supply pull-down scrolls and menus, listing options both for meanings and characters.

ECONOMIC FRAMEWORK

The Convoy System Japanese businesses, banks, and other public institutions generally have tended to utilize what has been nicknamed ''the convoy system.'' In this approach, the entire convoy moves at the speed of the slowest ship. The penalty for deviating is vulnerability to opponents; the deficiency in the strategy is that the entire group moves very slowly. Metaphorically, it is very difficult to innovate or take any kind of financial or strategic chance when one is constrained by a strong and subtly enforced need to stick with the other ''ships'' in the convoy.

One effect of the ''convoy approach'' is to diminish forces of raw economic self-interest. Two places in the press world where one might expect that monetary forces and personal ambition would find strong expression are between and among newspapers, and in the competition between and among individual reporters.

Case Study Number One: Newspaper Holidays Despite competition to gain circulation share, until 2002 all major newspapers in Japan cooperated in setting aside twelve days a year when they did not publish. Ostensibly, the newspapers declared these holidays, one per month, in order to give time off to the delivery personnel. Almost all daily newspapers in Japan are home delivered through a network mainly comprised of students, and about 90 percent of homes in Japan are serviced in this way. Two of the largest newspaper conglomerates, the *Asahi* and the *Mainichi*, by tradition have published on January 1 a list of twelve days during the year when they would not produce a newspaper, and other major newspapers would fall into line.

This system began to come unglued in the winter of 2002, when the smallest of the national newspapers (*Sankei Shimbun*) published on February 12, one of those pre-set holidays. The larger national papers then also broke the holiday with ''special editions,'' explaining they were making an exception because they wanted to cover the Winter Olympics. On the following month's pre-designated holiday, the *Sankei Shimbun* published but restricted its distribution to newsstand sales. However, some of the other national dailies not only printed but also activated their home delivery network. In explanation, the *Asahi* spokesperson explained that their breach of the voluntary holiday arrangement was part of ''our customer-satisfaction efforts,'' while *Mainichi* defended its shift in policy by noting that there were too many newspaper holidays (*Wall Street Journal* A21).

This incident suggests that Japanese newspapers may be feeling pressure from at least three sources: (1) Increasing competition arising from inside Japan (especially web-based electronic publication); (2) Mounting broadcast pressure from outside (e.g., CNN, MSNBC, etc.); (3) Widely available print competition from newsstand publications as the *International Herald Tribune* and the *Asian Wall Street Journal*, not to mention nearby international papers of some excellence such as the *South China Post*. Perhaps in combination, these pressures are finally serving to break down one strand of the historically tight financial affiliations among those media conglomerates that, logically, should be at each other's throats.

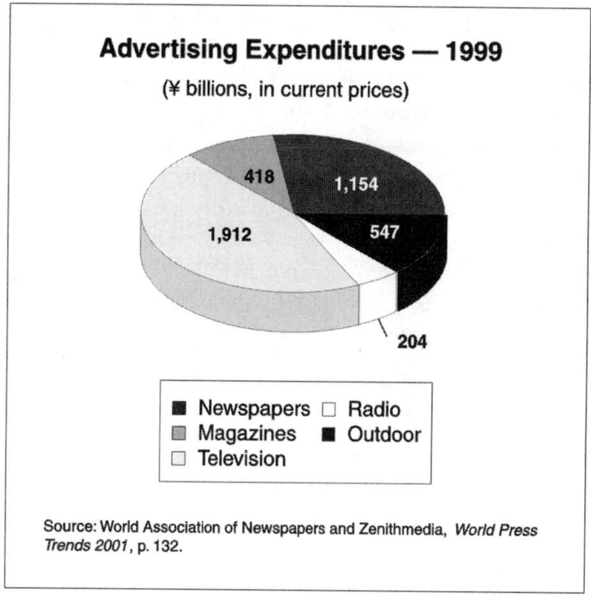

Source: World Association of Newspapers and Zenithmedia, *World Press Trends 2001*, p. 132.

Case Study Number Two: The Press Clubs Although the very first press club was formed in 1890 by newspapermen trying to get clearance to cover the initial meeting of the new Diet, following the Meiji Constitution that was promulgated the year before, most remaining press clubs were originally formed in the waiting rooms of governmental ministries. In the period 1906-1910, two approaches emerged, associated with two prime ministers, for the influence and control of these groups of newsmen. Okuma encouraged journalists to visit his party's headquarters, and brought reporters into the stories early. Obviously, those who were physically proximate were more likely to get the ''scoops.'' Katsura, on the other hand, used money, liquor, and women to try to influence journalists' coverage of his policies. Either of these approaches, whether Okuma's ''softer'' technique or Katsura's virtual bribery, served to reinforce the tendency to pass along reports issued by the government without too much addition or challenge. Journalists either did not want to cut off access, or did not want to dry up the various attractive perquisites.

There are now about one thousand clubs, with about twelve thousand members. Their internal structures privilege a few reporters, who get the hottest tips and leads. Only a foolhardy modern reporter would jeopardize his access. For example, there was highly limited coverage in the Japanese news media of some insensitive 1986 remarks by Prime Minister Nakasone. The howls of protest from America were settled only by a formal and written apology, but the matter received scant attention in the Japanese media.

Furthermore, the ''lecture system'' akin to a daily briefing, but without questions allowed, prevails for passing information from the government to the press. By contrast with ''investigative journalism'' or ''question and answer'' press conferences, this approach gives great control to the government's purveyors of the news. Additionally, the agencies of government establish the rules for transmitting and publishing the news beyond the familiar ''off the record'' approach used worldwide. The penalties for publishing remarks unauthorized for printing are administered by the Japanese Newspaper Association, but in practice reflect the interests of the agencies of government.

One result of the press club environment is that the general public is generally kept in ignorance of any political reality or view that threatens the status quo. Another result is that reporters who might be assumed to be in competition with each other are in actuality all feeding from the same trough. The term ''freedom of the press'' therefore has a very specific and somewhat limited meaning in Japan.

Press Laws & Censorship

Japan's history involving press laws is unusually complex, even considering its long march toward the twenty-first century. It is most coherent to approach the topic somewhat chronologically, noting the cumulative effect from era to era.

Transition to Constitutional Monarchy (1856-1889) In an attempt to gain some familiarity with the news of the world, the struggling Shogunate established the ''Barbarian Literature Research Department'' in 1856. Initially comprising fifteen men, it rather quickly grew into an academic institute, was renamed the ''Development Institute'' in 1863, then progressed into the kernel that finally matured as Japan's great Tokyo University.

In 1868, as the anti-Shogun revolution proceeded, the triumphant ''restorationists,'' who were going to ''restore'' the Emperor to his ''rightful position'' at the head of the government, banned all pro-Shogun newspapers and sent publishers to jail. Newspapers in the future must have a publication license, obviously issued by the restorationists. Consequently, one of the first acts of the new government, in February, 1869, was to issue a Newspaper Publishing Ordinance, encompassing the key provisions that there would be no prepublication censorship, that editors' names and addresses must be carried in the newspapers, and that they would be responsible personally for newspaper contents.

Under this new law, the first true daily newspaper began on December 1, 1870, as the *Yokohama Mainichi Shimbun* (Daily News). However, the early days of the new government were marked by considerable unrest (as many as thirty riots per year), and so in 1873, the fundamental press law was revised as the Newspaper Stipulations. To the original eight articles of the 1869 Ordinance were now added ten additional articles. Their general tendency was to make it harder to publish editorial opinion that could be construed as unsympathetic to the authorities. The very next year, however, saw a major crisis, a revolt of a conservative wing of the 1868 restorationists, and there was a significant amount of political commentary in the newspapers. This opinion could roughly be divided into a pro-government and a pro-rights section; in response, the authorities issued and withdrew the status of ''newspaper by appointment'' quite freely.

The revolt of the conservative samurai having been contained, on June 28, 1875, a new ''Press Ordinance'' was issued, consisting of 16 articles. Its most startling bias was that any form of criticism of the state could lead to fines and imprisonment. Later that same year, on July 6, a Libel Law strengthened this tendency, and a year later, on July 5, 1876, the Home Affairs ministry gained the power to enforce a press ban for disturbance of the national security.

Nonetheless, a people's rights movement continued to emerge, so that there remained a number of relatively liberal newspapers in print. This led the government to issue a new Press Ordinance in 1883. Its forty-two new provisions allowed suppression of a newspaper if its editorial approach threatened ''public peace or morals.'' The enforcement of this ordinance was devastating to independent partisan newspapers. Finally, on December 25, 1887, the Peace Preservation Law further supported tight control of the press.

Constitutionalism and Initial Imperialism (1889-1912) After long discussion and negotiation, the Meiji Constitution was promulgated on February 11, 1889. This fundamental document in Japanese modern history had three articles that directly impacted the press. Article Eight allowed that extraordinary imperial ordinances could override any laws. Article Twenty-nine promised the citizenry that they ''shall within the confines of the law, enjoy the liberty of speech, writing, publication, assembly, and association.'' ''The confines of the law'' was not, however, defined. Article Seventy-six established that all existing press laws as well as the Law on Public Meetings and Associations were to go into effect as part of the new constitution.

What these constitutional guarantees really meant can easily be measured. Between 1892 and 1895, 490 publications were suspended. National unity apparently over-rode all other considerations, as Japan entered an era of increasingly overt expansion. However, the introduction in this period of the rotary press method of printing had the effect of radically increasing the circulation of those newspapers still allowed to print. Circulations during this period of the leading papers were up to the 75,000-90,000 range, with a top figure of 140,000.

In these major newspapers in the 1890s, the nature of imperialism was openly debated, for instance the advisability of war with Russia. However, since Japan won both of its wars in this period (against the Chinese in 1895, and the Russians in 1905), this discussion was somewhat truncated by the passage of events. Nonetheless, the compromising nature of the resolution to the war with Russia led to widespread opposition to government policy, one result of which was that most Tokyo newspapers were shut down by the government, and there was considerable consolidation among the survivors.

Yet another new Press Law dated May 5, 1909, was issued to try to control criticism of the government. Legal responsibility now was extended even to proofreaders. Half of Japan's newspapers were out of business within a year.

Liberalism and Democracy (1912-1926) Historians frequently and energetically debate whether or not there was a period that can properly be called "Taisho Democracy." Far from being a sterile or arcane argument among academics, the debate over the nature of Taisho democracy provides a central touchstone.

Before 1912, most of the institutions of government were in the hands of a collection of non-democratic power groups, including the institution of the Emperor, the remains of the restorationists, a collection of senior statesmen, the upper house of the parliament, the Privy Council, and the military leadership. Among those who felt that there should be more democracy as an abstract goal and those who worried that Japan could never really catch up to the West unless it went beyond superficial imitation, there was much frustration.

The catastrophic personal weakness of the Taisho emperor himself opened the door to a pro-democracy effort. Yoshihito, the Taisho Emperor (1879-1926), had suffered from meningitis as an infant. He was physically frail, hyperactive, and may have had some problems with mental stability. He was never able to exert public authority on behalf of the imperial institution, and had none of his father's genius for public symbolism.

An affiliated ingredient was the continuing concern that Japan had reached a kind of glass ceiling in its efforts to be a player on the world stage. Some felt that Japan had adopted the externals of western culture without buying into its essence of individualism. They saw liberalization as key.

The old Popular Rights movement resurfaced, this time in the form of a movement to encourage the development of political parties. These reformers emphasized that the only available route for the emergence of any true democracy was to control the government and its policies through the lower House of Representatives. Then, they hoped, public opinion, expressed both through the media and through elections, could be brought to bear on policy formation and the control of the various oligarchic factions might be diminished, if not entirely broken. Hence there occurred a long struggle to see if it might be possible to set up disciplined, policy-making political parties which were responsive to the electorate. Freedom of the press had the potential to play a central role in this effort. Debate has continued as to whether the Taisho democracy was a step on the way to true democracy or a tripping point.

Freedom of the Press in the Taisho Period During the first half of the period, the central issue was whether or not cabinets could be made responsible to the Diets. With the restoration oligarchs aging but still struggling to control politics, the editorial policies of the *Osaka Asahi Shimbun* (Morning Sun) emerged as a key focus for the people's rights movement. In 1918 there were major rice riots, leading to martial law and a press blackout. The *Osaka Asahi Shimbun* responded defiantly by publishing with blank spaces where the censored articles originally would have appeared. The government, incensed, threatened to close the paper, whereupon the paper's editorial leadership resigned. Their successors published an apology on October 14, 1918 (as quoted in de Lange, 126-127): "in recent years our arguments have greatly lacked in moderation, and we realize we have been given to favouritism." *Osaka Asahi Shimbun* next announced it would in future be "free from party affiliations," and the movement for constitutional government and universal suffrage thus was damaged. In a highly ironic twist, the new prime minister to emerge in this crisis period was Takashi Hara, who had been president of the rival newspaper the *Osaka Mainichi Shimbun*.

Surpassing even this elaborate shuffle being carried out by the two great Osaka newspapers in 1918, 1923 brought a further element of drama. The great earthquake and fire of September 1, 1923, devastated Tokyo's newspapers, opening the door for the Osaka-based *Asahi* and *Mainichi* to become national newspapers with circulations of over one million per day. But by this time, with the 1918 humiliation of the *Asahi* fresh in mind, neither one was likely to become a partisan opponent of the government, especially since the mildly reformist Hara was assassinated in 1921 by a rightist.

If one of the hallmarks of a free and democratic society is a free and unfettered press, it is clear that the Taisho period, while marking the emergence of *Asahi* and *Mainichi*, hardly saw the parallel development of an uncensored press. Censorship was self-imposed, unless there was a public crisis of any description, at which time the government moved in forcibly.

The Age of Militarism (1931-1945) Although there were minor incidents earlier, most historians would date the rise of militarism from the 1931 Mukden Incident. *Yomiuri Shimbun* had migrated from a small-circulation literate and literary paper, through a period of post-earthquake populism, to nonetheless losing ground to *Asahi* and *Mainichi* as these two papers moved into a commanding position as the nation's serious providers of hard news. Its relative market share dropping steadily from 15 percent down to 5 percent, after the Mukden Incident *Yomiuri* made yet another lurch in style, still seeking to locate a viable marketplace niche. In the early 1930s, it took on an editorial stance favorable to aggressive action on the mainland, notably in Korea, Manchuria, and China. Thereby becoming a leading force for public support of aggressive militarism, it was able to increase its circulation and at the same time immunize itself from hostile government action.

After the assassination of Prime Minister Inukai and an attempted coup by militarists on May 15, 1932, the now openly military government established a formal system of ''thought police,'' supported informally by groups of right wing extremists, and bookstores and newspapers were raided and closed across the country. In February 1936 an even more extreme set of militarists attempted a coup but failed, resulting in a massive purge of the most radical militarists, but this had little impact on freedom of the press, since that liberal entitlement had already been drastically curtailed. However, on July 7, 1937, the Marco Polo Bridge Incident opened the China war, and on April 1, 1938, a National General Mobilization Law included articles giving sweeping powers under Article Sixteen and Twenty to limit newspaper coverage, restrict or confiscate papers, and capture original plates.

By 1940, as the crisis deepened, the government created a single national press agency. A first step was to reduce the number of newspapers nationally from about 1,500 to 300. Later that year, the information departments of all key ministries were merged, further centralizing news flow. Paper was in short supply, with the result that the number of pages per issue was reduced, columns were crowded, and print made smaller. After the formation of ''The Newspaper League'' in May of 1941, the number of papers continued to shrink so that by the time of Pearl Harbor, there were only fifty-four papers remaining. The contents of the surviving papers increasingly were slanted toward the prevailing military ideology, with emphasis on State Shinto, Emperor worship, the way of the warrior, and the divine origins of the Japanese race.

The war did not go well, despite the creation of a ''National Spiritual Mobilization Movement'' which rhapsodized on the beauty of the shattered jewel and the solidarity of one million hearts beating as one. By March 23, 1944, Mainichi Shimbun was emboldened to criticize the war plans (''Of what use are bamboo spears against airplanes?''). However, it seems actually to be the case that most of the Japanese public was uninformed about the negative progression of the war and was genuinely stunned by the surrender.

The Occupation (1945-1952) and Beyond One of the early acts of the Occupation government was to issue a ''Memorandum on Freedom of Speech and Newspapers,'' a Press Code, and an order removing all legal constrictions on the press. The Press Code was the most important. Its ten articles emphasized adherence to the truth, but there were limits on the coverage of the Occupation itself. Not only could the Occupation government carry out pre-publication censorship, but also there could be no reference to such activity. In fact, there was more censorship over the Occupation government than over the old militaristic ideologies.

Under the tutelage of the Occupation, a new constitution was drawn on November 3, 1946, which included an apparently absolute statement about freedom of the press (Article Twenty-one). However, as the Cold War began and then deepened, American policy toward Japan entered into a period of change (''the Reverse Course''), through which Japan increasingly would be built up as an ally against the various socialist and communist forces of the world. This meant that there would be less and finally no tolerance at all for leftist newspapers, such as *Yomiuri* had become, and on June 26, 1950, the day after the invasion of South Korea, a ''red purge'' was carried out. However, the signing of a general peace treaty on April 28, 1952, allowed the Japanese left wing press to re-emerge.

Since that time, Japan has had an ostensibly free press system. However, this openness has been severely restricted by the existence of the press club system.

STATE-PRESS RELATIONS

Relations between the Japanese press and the state have gone through rather dramatic changes since the Occupation. As long as the economy and attendant issues of statecraft were working well, it seemed to matter very little if the Japanese media gave the government a ''free pass.'' But it also meant that underlying difficulties in the system were not publicly debated, alternate arrangements were not explored, and corrupt practices were slow to be exposed. Superficially, this criticism might seem hard to sustain, since leading newspapers have been sharp on occasion in denunciation of a particularly inept politician. However, the underlying national economic and political system remains essentially unchallenged. In other advanced countries, the press might be expected to play a substantive role in the search for new approaches to national problems.

The Era of "The Bubble" In the 1980s, one would have anticipated a highly laudatory attitude by the Japanese press toward the national government. Within the span of a single generation, the Liberal Democratic Party had led Japan from a condition of partial recovery from the war, to a position where Japan seemed to possess the leading economy of the world. Indeed, in the years between 1985 and 1990, Japan was emerging as the world's most dynamic country. Scholarly and popular bookstores in the western world were filled with studies predicting the consequences, presumed to be undesirable, of Japanese domination of most of the leading-edge industries of the world.

This progression from humiliation and profound defeat in 1945 to world prominence by 1985 was widely attributed to the development and implementation of a single national industrial policy. The setting of such a standard was almost universally credited to two agencies of government, the Ministry of Finance (MOF) and the Ministry of International Trade and Industry (MITI). In conjunction, these two bureaucracies set the course for successful collaboration among the Japanese government, industrial giants, and bureaucracy.

Only much later was it observed that those setting industrial and national policy would have to predict with great accuracy what would be the future needs and trends. Especially, this would be the case if market conditions were not allowed easily to correct errors of judgment (e.g., 64K DRAM computer chips, Beta VCRs, and high definition TV). One study completed in the late 1990s concluded that MITI had predicted future business opportunities in its area of expertise with an accuracy rate of barely more than 50 percent. In retrospect, it may very well be true that the lightly regulated marketplace provides efficiencies competitive with any "industrial policy" worked out at the national level by governmental agencies. However, none of this would have been heard from Japan's journalists, even after the "bubble" had burst. One could more easily go to *The Wall Street Journal* to read a leading Japanese thinker such as Kenichi Ohmae, and a minority voice in MITI itself, belonging to Taichi Sakaiya, found his popular audience in the west with books such as *The Knowledge-Value Revolution*.

Journalism and Scandals Little in the way of constructive analysis let alone criticism appeared in Japanese popular journalism at the time, although one could argue that deeper and underlying problems in the Japanese system pointed the way of the biggest story of the period 1985-1995. Foreign journalists long based in Japan wrote such critiques, but were quickly dismissed as "Japan-bashers." In a curious echo of the Tokugawa era, Dutch journalists, led by Karel van Wolferen, provided most of the initial intellectual firepower.

Among the Japanese journalists, what negative attention was given to government once again was lavished on more scandalous breaches of the public trust, similar to coverage of the Lockheed scandal in 1976 that had exposed actual bribery of former Prime Minister Kakuei Tanaka. Even in those instances, however, the initial energy for investigating Tanaka's "money politics" in 1974 and the Lockheed payoff in 1976 had come from American sources. In the first instance, it was a *Los Angeles Times* reporter, and in the second an American Senate investigating committee that asked all the difficult early questions and pressed the issue to the level of public consciousness in Japan.

The Recruit Scandal In the period after 1985, while the Japanese economy still seemed to be ascending, the biggest newspaper story concerned the Recruit Cosmos Company. In a complex affair involving bribery, stock trades, and influence peddling, the first symptom was that this company had tried to corrupt the deputy mayor of Yokohama. By the time the story had ended, the toll could be measured by the resignation of thirty-one leading political and business leaders, thirteen indictments, and one suicide.

Worse, it appeared as if the entire establishment at the top of government and public information services might be involved. *Asahi Shimbun*, whose cub reporter had initially uncovered the Yokohama angle, only tentatively dealt with the story, keeping it off the front page for quite a while and appearing to be willing to suppress the coverage. Then, one of the resignations was by a *Yomiuri Shimbun* vice president, while another involved the president of *Nihon Keizai Shimbun*. Only after careful investigation to be sure that none of its employees was directly involved, did *Asahi Shimbun* actually begin to press ahead with more vigorous coverage and presentation of the story.

Once *Asahi* decided to give prominent play to the scandalous story, its coverage quickly was removed from the original investigative team in Yokohama and turned over to the more senior Tokyo office. In the Tokyo office, *Asahi*'s press club reporters could more effectively manage the coverage, and limit damage to allies among the politicians, businessmen, and publishers. Then, as a fitting coda to the whole matter, the prestigious journalistic award that honored the breaking of this story went to reporters from *Mainichi Shimbun*. The *Mainichi* reporters at best had been tertiary initiators and investigators.

Corruption Involving the MOF? In 1991, another scandal opened up the gap between independent journalism and the government when a story was leaked to the *Yomiuri Shimbun* to the effect that the leading securities trading houses had been manipulating stocks while guaranteeing good results to their major investors. The Ministry of Finance ordered the practice stopped, and, when it continued, someone in the middle ranks of the MOF leaked the story to the *Yomiuri*. Interestingly, when inquiries were made about the leak, MOF sources stated that it was the ''turn'' of *Yomiuri*. Apparently, the comment meant that since *Mainichi* and *Asahi* had benefited from the coverage of earlier scandals, the rotational system this time led to *Yomiuri*.

In such a world, clearly there would strong incentives in place for reporters both to keep their ''leak lines'' open, and also for them to give gentler coverage to miscreants in the governmental bureaucracies in anticipation of future tips. A subsequent article in the weekly magazine *Shukan Themis* tried to expose the collusion of MOF in this scandal. Issues of that magazine were recalled from distributors the day prior to official publication, and the magazine then reported that it was suspending publication due to pressure from a branch of government handling taxation of magazines.

Shin Kanemaru A last example from this ''bubble'' period finally resulted in the ''fall of the Don,'' Shin Kanemaru. Kanemaru was head of several shadow political assemblages, and arguably was the most important back-door politician in Japan by the early 1990s. The accusations in this scandal involved gangland payoffs (in cash) by a delivery company to leading politicians. Although lists of the recipients and their illegal receipts had long circulated within the mainstream newspaper world, the story was broken only in July 1991 by the weekly *Shukan Shincho*, while the major newspapers continued merely to report the press releases of the Tokyo prosecutor's office.

No mainstream reporters investigated who received money or whether it influenced important public policy decisions. As the scandal unfolded and threatened the foundations of the most important branch of the ruling Liberal Democratic Party, newspaper coverage continued to be very restrained. Kanemaru was punished with a fine of $2,000 (about $600,000,000 had been siphoned to various politicians, and he himself was found to be holding a huge quantity of cash and gold in his home, presumably for the purpose of making further unsupervised and unreported bribes). Only with public outcry over the disparity between the penalty and the violation did the mainstream newspapers begin to criticize the outcome, forcing Kanemaru to resign from the Diet.

''Revisionism'' and ''Japan-bashing'' These incidents show that the Japanese newspapers were not likely to be vigorous in keeping the government honest, and that their deeply ingrained system of caution and restraint served to protect the ruling factions of the government from independent scrutiny. Indeed, Japanese journalists essentially missed the biggest story of these decades. That story should have been an attempt to disclose to the Japanese public that their vaunted policy-making machinery was failing to keep pace with the incredible advances in information technology and with the emergence of a global economy.

American and European fans of Japanese industrial policy were also slow to catch on to the limitations of the Japanese economic practice and tradition. For a number of years, they continued to hold up Japan as a model for the other advanced industrial societies of the world. The name given to supporters of the Japanese approach was ''revisionists,'' and most of them came from the world of foreign journalists observing Japan.

Revisionism got its name originally because its proponents were thought to be advocating a change in United States domestic economic and labor policy, namely toward the more managed model associated with MOF and MITI. The trouble in the United States, they seemed to be saying especially in the middle and later parts of the 1980s, was due to the laissez-faire approach associated with the policies of President Ronald Reagan. The United States needed an ''industrial policy'' like other grown-up nations. Revisionism furthermore depended on a view that Japan's various institutions were unique and therefore differed fundamentally from institutions in the United States. Even prevailing macro-economic theories, derived as they were from western history, would not be applicable. Consequently, as a kind of perverse byproduct, Japan's exceptional quality could be held significantly responsible for US-Japan trade friction.

In reaction, the Japanese journalistic world interpreted revisionism as if it were just another way of blaming Japan for disagreements with the United States over trade issues (''Japan bashing''). By this curious alchemy, the ''big three'' among the revisionists, Karel van Wolferen, Clyde Prestowitz, and James Fallows, quickly became labeled in Japan as ''Japan bashers.'' All of them were well-informed and essentially friendly admirers of Japan. However, the counter-reaction in Japan even to their carefully researched and reasoned commentary in the days of Japan's ''bubble economy'' was strident as well as condescending. They were not eager to be criticized by writers they perceived as hostile observers most of whom lived in a country whose golden age they believed was in the 1950s and that now was in decline. Unfortunately, the thoughtful commentary by ''the big three,'' supplemented by Robert Reich in many essays arguing for imitation of Japan's approach to the formulation of industrial policy, was soon pushed aside by cruder works such as Meredith Lebard's *The Coming War with Japan*, Bill Emmot's *Japanophobia*, Pat Choate's *Agents of Influence*, and Michael Crichton's novel *Rising Sun*. Thus, initial Japanese sensitivity toward the original revisionist arguments could quite easily be demonstrated to be valid, as American journalists and popular writers poured out material that many thoughtful readers in America legitimately could call racist, ''Japan bashing'' yellow journalism.

By retreating early into victimology, the Japanese press had immunized itself against consideration of moderate reform. One cost for Japan was not that the bubble burst (as all do), but that Japan was not able to make adjustments in its political and economic system. Japan's hopes of being the leading economy of the world were lost in a full decade of off-and-on recession, in a progressive ''hollowing-out'' of its industries as leading corporations moved manufacturing overseas, and in the paralysis of a banking and financial structure that seems to have concealed many trillion dollars worth of bad loans. Revisionism died a fairly quiet death, increasingly ignored in the west and hated in Japan.

The Japanese Media and Its Role in Setting the National Agenda Therefore, finally, how should we characterize the relationship between the media and the state in Japan? Harvard's Susan J. Pharr has offered an exceptionally interesting and powerful metaphor in an essay published in 1996: ''Media as Trickster in Japan: A Comparative Perspective'' in the book edited by she and Ellis Krauss. In this essay, and in others that fellow scholars have written for her book, evidence and argument are provided both from theoretical assessments and from case studies, leading to a mildly more hopeful view of the Japanese media.

In addition to the many occasions on which the press has over-focused on scandal and avoided alienating government ''handlers,'' there have also been moments of achievement. Environmental pollution, a surprisingly severe problem in Japan, is on the national agenda thanks to journalistic coverage. Twice at least a ten-year period, something resembling a moment of potential political reform has surfaced (in 1993, and again with the emergence of Prime Minister Koizumi in 2001), both significantly helped along by the media. The government's weak handling of the crisis presented by the 1995 Kobe earthquake certainly also was highlighted in news coverage. Furthermore, Pharr points out that the media in Japan should not be confined to the five national papers. The weekly publications as well as anti-mainstream papers seem freer to deviate from the ''press club'' and ''lecture'' systems of gathering news. Finally, it is probable that Japanese public opinion, informed and encouraged by newspapers and other forms of media, is much more sophisticated than the national political leadership in understanding what needs to be done. This certainly is the view of a leading American observer who has lived in Japan for decades (Alex Kerr, in his two important books *Lost Japan* and *Dogs and Demons*).

After reviewing the standard social-utility positions traditionally assigned to the media in Japan (spectator, watchdog, and servant of the state), Pharr concludes that none of these are fully satisfactory in explaining the relationship. She borrows from symbolic anthropology the notion of ''stranger-outsiders'' living in an ''unfixed social position.'' Pharr approvingly cites the work of Barbara Babcock-Abrahams in interpreting the tricksters as ''active mediators who are independent and both creative and destructive simultaneously, and who ultimately alter or stretch social and political boundaries and prevailing arrangements of authority'' (25).

What does a ''trickster'' actually do? The trickster ''provides release'' by bringing ridicule and defiance to bear on the structures and institutions of public life. It also ''evaluates,'' often rather harshly, with the result that the national community must confront some of its own mythologies. Third, the trickster ''horrifies'' by making sure that the public must look at the outlandish aspects of modern society. Additionally, the trickster ''induces reflection,'' and finally it forces the wider community to ''bond.''

This application of anthropological theory to mass communications reality provides a tool for deeper understanding of the potential role of the Japanese media, and goes far beyond the surface issues raised by such terms as ''liberal,'' ''conservative,'' ''national,'' ''regional,'' ''self-censorship'' and ''free democratic press.'' When studied closely in Pharr's article and accompanying essays, the notion leads toward an approach with improved texture and nuance. It also requires that we distinguish (at the very least) between the media conglomerates and their front-line practitioners, a few of whom are able and willing to ''secure a measure of autonomy and space.'' In such a view, without denying the problems that exist, Pharr and her fellow authors find good hope that Japanese conformism will not entirely overwhelm clear and free thinking in the media about the future needs of the land and its people.

ATTITUDE TOWARD FOREIGN MEDIA

Given the high level of readership of newspapers in Japan, the main utility of foreign and foreign-language

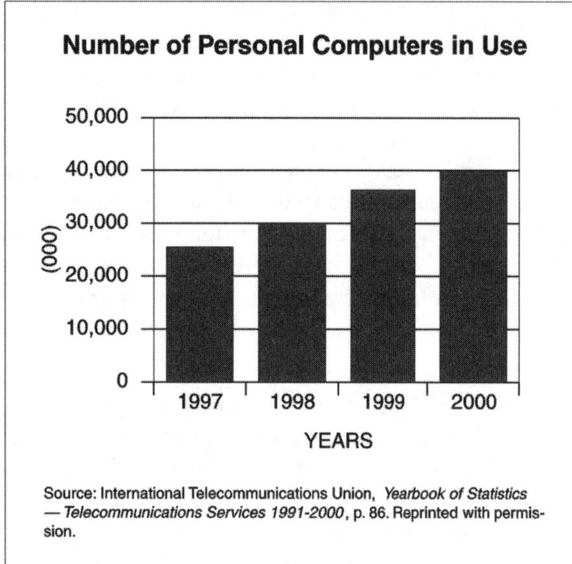

Source: International Telecommunications Union, *Yearbook of Statistics — Telecommunications Services 1991-2000*, p. 86. Reprinted with permission.

media is to serve the international community. Many Japanese who are involved professionally with the wider world, however, can read English well. Consequently, it is not at all unusual when using the bullet trains to see Japanese individuals reading *The International Herald Tribune* or *The Japan Times* either to the exclusion of or in preference to Japanese language newspapers. English language versions of *Asahi*, *Mainichi*, *Yomiuri*, and *The Asian Wall Street Journal* are also widely available.

The Japan Times mines the major international news services for articles and often reprints them whole and unedited. In this way, it serves somewhat as an anthology of world reporting, easily available inside Japan to those who can read English.

However, those five national Japanese newspapers publishing in the Japanese language and producing half of the daily copies available in the whole country rely much more heavily on their own reportage system for their information and texts. Perhaps this is why the business and intellectual leadership in Japan turns to the English-language press to the degree that it does. Just as in the 1850s, if one really wants to know what is going on in the outside world, one needs to seek information and interpretation from that world, and not rely solely on sources internal to Japan.

News Agencies

As in other areas of media history, Japan's first news agency (1871) was associated with an external power, Denmark. Mitsui established its first native agency in 1888, with the active support of the Japanese government. By 1926, there were thirty-three news agencies based in Tokyo alone. However, as the age of militarism set in, centralization took place rapidly, and by 1936, the government permitted only the Domei News Agency to exist. After the war, Domei broke into two units (Kyodo and Jiji), still the largest in Japan.

Kyodo is a cooperative, comprising sixty-three newspapers and Nippon Hoso Kyokai's radio and TV. It is linked to international news agencies, and maintains thirty foreign bureaus. Daily, it provides about 150-200 articles, of which about 75 percent originate with its own writers.

Jiji in its earlier years emphasized the delivery of news to corporations, businesses, and government agencies, but after 1959 broadened its scope to compete with Kyodo in providing general news coverage.

The Radio Press specializes in translating foreign short wave broadcast information.

The major trading conglomerates maintain their own internal news agencies. Mitsui, for example, has about 1,600 agents in over 500 overseas locations, transmitting about 65,000 bulletins of information daily. The leading foreign news agencies have also made considerable penetration in Japan, usually operating through annual contracts and set fee structures.

Broadcast Media

NHK (Nippon Hoso Kyokai) is the public broadcasting system of the country. TV users pay reception fees which produce 98 percent of NHK's revenues. In the mid-twenties, NHK was founded as the sole radio broadcaster, and remained so until 1945. The Broadcasting Law of 1950 allowed commercial competition, which began in the following year on radio and in 1953 on TV.

Early in the twenty-first century, NHK used two television channels, and for radio employed one FM and two AM channels. In 1987, NHK introduced twenty-four-hour satellite broadcasting, and as of 2002 was using twenty-two languages to send broadcasts around the world.

Commercial broadcasting dates from 1951, first of course on radio and after 1953 on TV as well. By 1990, there were 83 radio stations of all varieties, and 109 TV stations. Radio stations collaborate in cooperatives led by Nippon Cultural Broadcasting, Nippon Broadcasting System, and the Japan Radio Network. Prominent television networks are the Japan News Network, the Nippon News Network, the All Nippon News Network, and the Fuji News Network. One prominent station leads each of these networks.

The central enabling legislation, nicknamed ''The Three Radio Wave Laws,'' passed in 1950, requires that broadcast media be independent of the government, but also that it maintains neutrality in politics. The same dynamic seen in other industrialized countries operates in Japan. Commercial TV news, heavy budgets for advertising, and continuous broadcasting all have given televised programming more weight in Japanese society than can now be assigned to the print media. Approximately 95 percent of Japanese people watch television daily for an average of three and one half-hours. In a country of 127 million people, there were 87 million TV sets (1997), and 121 million radios. Counting every station, Japan had 7,108 broadcasters in 1999 (CIA World Factbook).

Electronic News Media

Internet communications have surged in Japan, with about 47 million people using the Internet in 2000. There are more than seventy Internet service providers, almost all having the potential to connect with customers through telephone lines. However, wireless Internet services are growing explosively, so that at least one third of the users opt for that form of connection.

A number of the leading newspapers have now developed web capability both in English and in Japanese. English-language versions of papers such as *Asahi Shimbun*, *Chubu Weekly*, *Chunichi Shimbun* (Nagoya) and twenty-eight other papers ranging from the national to the local are all available online. Additionally, the Nippon Television network, a leading commercial TV organization, maintains its own web site, as does a site associated with the Nikkei stock market. A simple web search, using intuitive categories, reveals a rich world of electronic media. The full impact of this new form of news dissemination remains to be seen, but it is safe to assume that over the next few years, the entire information industry will be transformed.

Education & Training

In the early days of Japanese news history, the status of reporters was generally without much glamour or prestige, and lower middle class citizens filled most of the positions. Until 1950, the census grouped reporters together with dancers, clerical workers, teachers, and medical technicians. However, since the Occupation, the educational level of reporters has improved considerably, reflected since 1950 in their census classification with physicians, professors, and other professional workers.

However, perhaps because of the limited use of the Japanese language in the world as well as limits on the nature of Japanese reporting, there are no international press superstars of the sort the world has found in some other countries. The work is not particularly glamorous, the hours are long and late, the pay unspectacular, and the chances are very low for a major breakthrough story.

On television, as in many other countries, stations display newsreaders with generically attractive facial features, often nearly Caucasian in appearance. Newsreaders on TV fairly strictly follow Japanese gender stereotypes, with the males always senior and serious, and the women submissive and assigned to handling softer topics.

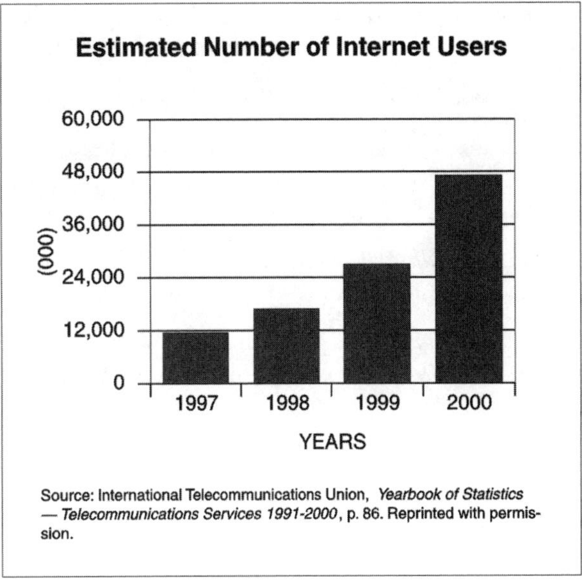

Source: International Telecommunications Union, *Yearbook of Statistics — Telecommunications Services 1991-2000*, p. 86. Reprinted with permission.

Summary

Japan indeed has a complex news media industry and history. Although Japan has almost all the elements of a world-leading press, both its media history and its customs have combined to create a situation wherein its greater potential seems unlikely to be realized. In this view, Japan's media reflects most simplistic assessments of the prospects for the country as a whole.

On the other hand, Japan is open to almost all the forces lumped together under the rubric ''globalization.'' Further, Japan has shown remarkable resilience in the past 150 years. It has a highly educated and energetic population, one of the most literate in the world despite the challenges of its language, and a long tradition of innovation and adaptation. Only the most foolhardy or willfully pessimistic would suggest that Japan has anything but a bright future, led by its public opinion and its news media. Japan will develop in its own way and on its own schedule.

Bibliography

The Central Intelligence Agency (CIA). *World Factbook 2001*. Available from www.cia.gov.

de Lange, William. *A History of Japanese Journalism: Japan's Press Club as the Last Obstacle to a Mature Press*. Richmond, England: Japan Library, 1998.

Frederic, Louis. *Japan Encyclopedia*. Cambridge: Harvard, 2002.

Huffman, James. *Creating a Public: People and Press in Meiji Japan.* Honolulu: University of Hawaii, 1997.

———. *Politics of the Meiji Press: The Life of Fukuchi Gen'ichiro.* Honolulu: University of Hawaii, 1980.

Japan: Profile of a Nation. Revised Edition. Tokyo: Kodansha, 1999.

Japan: An Illustrated Encyclopedia. Two volumes. Tokyo: Kodansha, 1993.

Kasza, Gregory J. *The State and the Mass Media in Japan, 1918-1945.* Berkeley: University of California, 1988.

Kerr, Alex. *Lost Japan.* Oakland, CA: Lonely Planet, 1996.

———. *Dogs and Demons: Tales from the Dark Side of Japan.* New York: Hill and Wang, 2001.

Landers, Peter. ''Read All About It-and More Often: Japanese Newspapers Spike a Tradition.'' *The Wall Street Journal,* March 12, 2002.

Pharr, Susan J. and Ellis S. Krauss, editors. *Media and Politics in Japan.* Honolulu: The University of Hawaii, 1996.

van Wolferen, Karel. *The Enigma of Japanese Power.* New York: Vintage, 1990.

—Richard B. Lyman, Jr.

JERSEY

BASIC DATA

Official Country Name:	Jersey
Region (Map name):	Europe
Population:	88,915
Language(s):	English, French, Norman-French
Literacy rate:	N/A

Jersey is the largest and southernmost of the Channel Islands, which lie northwest of France in the English Channel. Along with the other Channel Islands, it once belonged to the medieval Dukedom of Normandy and was the only British soil occupied by Nazi troops. Because Jersey is a British crown dependency, the chief of state is the British Monarch. A London-appointed Lieutenant Governor heads the government and presides over a unicameral Assembly of the States. The population of Jersey is nearly 89,000. The official languages are English and French, but a Norman-French dialect is widely spoken in rural districts. Jersey is most widely known for its signature breed of dairy cattle that contribute to the export of milk products, but financial services in fact comprise the greatest contributor to the island's economy. Tourism also plays an important role, as does agriculture, especially flowers.

Citizens of Jersey enjoy the press and speech freedoms of England. The *Jersey Evening Post* is the only newspaper published in Jersey. Founded in 1890 as the *Evening Post,* the English-language publication is now part of the Guiton Group, a media company with interests throughout the Channel Islands. The *Jersey Evening Post* publishes Monday through Saturday; daily circulation is approximately 23,000 and it is available online.

There is one FM radio station and one television station.

BIBLIOGRAPHY

''Jersey,'' *CIA World Fact Book (2001).* Available from http://www.cia.gov.

''History of the JEP,'' *Jersey Evening Post (2002).* Available from http://www.jerseyeveningpost.com.

—Jenny B. Davis

JORDAN

BASIC DATA

Official Country Name:	Hashemite Kingdom of Jordan
Region (Map name):	Middle East
Population:	5,153,378
Language(s):	Arabic, English
Literacy rate:	86.0%
Area:	92,300 sq km
GDP:	8,340 (US$ millions)
Number of Television Stations:	20
Number of Television Sets:	500,000
Television Sets per 1,000:	97.0

Number of Cable Subscribers:	980
Cable Subscribers per 1,000:	0.2
Number of Satellite Subscribers:	109,000
Satellite Subscribers per 1,000:	21.2
Number of Radio Stations:	12
Number of Radio Receivers:	1,660,000
Radio Receivers per 1,000:	322.1
Number of Individuals with Computers:	150,000
Computers per 1,000:	29.1
Number of Individuals with Internet Access:	127,317
Internet Access per 1,000:	24.7

The desert kingdom of the Hashemite dynasty/family, Jordan lies east of Israel and south of Syria. A product of the collapse of the Ottoman Empire, Jordan has been a victim of the creation of Israel. One of the main trade routes once flowed through Haifa, which is currently an Israeli port, forcing Jordan to look elsewhere, primarily to Lebanon's destabilized harbors. Otherwise Jordan must use more difficult trade route strategies. In 1946, Jordan's population at independence was approximately 400,000. That figure included nomads, peasants, villagers and a modest number of urban dwellers (De Blij 310). However, the configuration of Israel and partition of Palestine have impacted the country greatly, pumping up the numbers of refugees, incorporating peoples who lived along geographic lines of demarcation and finding themselves faced with the idea of beginning a national independent life as a poor country. Jordan in 2002 was still a poor country with little to sustain an impoverished population. Regional war and political and religious conflicts have left Jordan with persistent problems facing a hard-pressed monarchy that is unpopular with a large portion of the citizens. Many people in Jordan do not even consider themselves citizens of the country and support for the government is minimal at best.

Geographic location plunges Jordan into a larger than expected role in regional Middle Eastern politics and economics. During his 46-year reign, King Hussein of Jordan created an image of peacemaker in the region. The press in Jordan and internationally looked favorably on Hussein, especially since he had a beautiful American-born queen as his last wife. Americans were fascinated by the positive image generated by the semi-free press in Jordan and in Europe, often showing images of the queen. What was not so readily observed was the poverty of the country and the various groups whose dissent threatened to bring Jordan into conflict with Israel—the war in 1967 had been so disastrous for the country that another could not be entered into lightly. War had to be avoided, but geographic location left Jordan vulnerable on all sides to political unrest and regional difficulties of the Middle East. American, British and some French aid kept Jordan afloat, and kept the semi-free press supportive of America and its allies. The death of King Hussein in 1999 abruptly ended the positive image of leadership and "peaceful" efforts in a politically unstable region, leaving his son, King Abdullah II, the difficult task of having to stabilize a country and a monarchy vulnerable to the dangers of the region and the poverty and dissatisfaction of its own inhabitants. King Abdullah II traveled in 2002 to England and to the USA in an effort to prevent an attack on Iraq and in order to seek the creation of a Palestinian State. Combined with the lack of oil, poor soil and agricultural production (though they still produce melons, tomatoes, sheep, and goats), regional dangers and a controversial queen—Abdullah's wife Rania is a Palestinian and proud of it, to the point of walking in peaceful marches in support of a Palestinian State, and the youngest reigning consort in the world—Jordan's press could be expected to be more critical were the King's government not capable of interference in the press and media.

There are mixed signals on the "freedom of the press" ideals in Jordan. King Abdullah II says that he advocates a transparency in the press, indicating that there is nothing to hide and that Jordan has nothing to fear. However, there is only one press association in Jordan and all journalists are expected to belong to the Jordan Press Association. Jordan recently punished a journalist who was critical of government corruption in an article published on a US website. Reporters Without Borders has protested the imprisonment of Toujan Faisal, 53, who was accused of slandering state institutions in *Arab Times*, published out of Houston, Texas. Faisal was the first Jordanian female legislator. She was recently released on "humanitarian grounds" by the King, due to her failing health. Human rights activists and watch groups target Jordan's King Abdullah for using tribal chiefs and tribal based law codes and secret police to catch "offenders" who use the press to expose violations.

One very controversial topic in the country of Jordan concerns the killing of women by male family members who deem that the woman has somehow brought shame to the family name. The laws in Jordan favor the males and women have been secretly smuggled into the USA

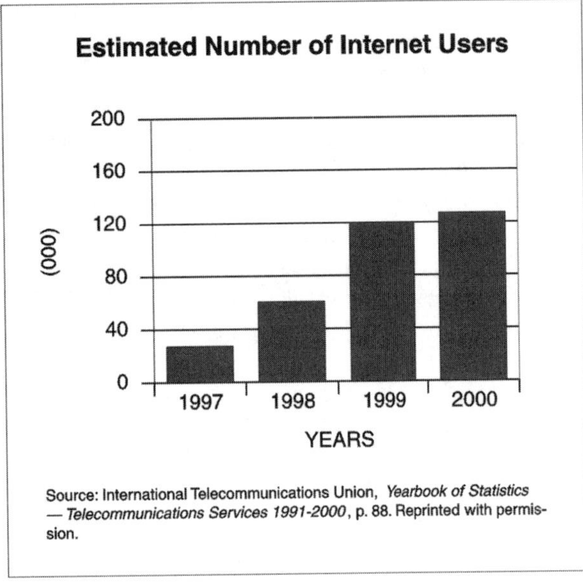

Source: International Telecommunications Union, *Yearbook of Statistics — Telecommunications Services 1991-2000*, p. 88. Reprinted with permission.

to ''safe houses'' from and to which they must constantly move around in order to escape assassins hired by their families to kill them. In Jordan stoning or burning alive are most common methods used to kill women. While the American Queen Noor reigned in Jordan, Barbara Walters interviewed her and asked why she as a woman and queen could not do something to stop the growing number of female killings. Queen Noor indicated that it was not her place to discuss the matter or take action. After the death of her husband Hussein, though, she returned to America and now works to stop female killing—from her office in Washington, DC, where she is protected against retaliation. Considering the geographic location of Jordan and the political atmosphere of the region and the basic Arab culture that permeates the area, it is highly unlikely that there will be a change in the laws any time soon, but the press is reluctant to highlight the issue as it is only semi-free.

The King and his government use the Internet extensively to combat ''bad press'' and promote a positive image on the Hashemite dynasty. New websites about King Abdullah and his family promote a positive image of the king while providing access to information about the family dynasty, the country and the government. Of course, these are ''controlled'' sites so that ''accuracy'' can be maintained. Most of the ''official sites'' have been available since 1999, when the Internet began to take hold and expand in Jordan. *Majesty* magazine from London has done some extensive profiles of the King and his family, but these are carefully screened monarchy-supportive pieces, indicating the promise of a strong potential of the young king and his wife for the future. Most state controlled websites exhibit the image of the strength of Jordan militarily, governmentally, economically and potentially in all areas. The Queen is represented as the image of the good wife and mother, supportive of her royal husband and sons, producing and protecting a good family life for her husband to return to after a day in the work of the monarchy. Some of the same images and text can be found on the various websites.

King Abdullah would like to be known for his democratic ideals but sites like *Middle East Report*, *Arab Times*, and the Human Rights Watch are less than enthusiastic about the ''democratic'' image of the Jordanian king and his government. A press report suggesting that the events following the September 11, 2001, terrorist attacks on the United States allowed Arab countries to put a hold on ''democratic experiments'' in their nations questions any hope for Jordanian democracy and a truly free press in the near future.

King Abdullah II wishes to further expand some positive developments for the press in Jordan, primarily a relaxation of the Press and Publications Law (PPL). The Jordanian King sits geographically vulnerable in the Arab world, needing to fully cooperate with strong allies in the west to protect his own Hashemite Kingdom from the turmoil of the region surrounding him and retaliations possible from ''neighbors'' less favorable to western powers. In 1999 certain PPL provisions, which had permitted censorship of newspapers and imprisonments imposed arbitrarily for ''seditious'' articles and other writings determined to be unacceptable, were annulled. However, the changes left intact other provisions that restrict press freedoms; therefore the press in Jordan is today less than a free press. It is semi-free at best and suffering from the strain of the effects imposed by the government to satisfy a pro-western foreign policy it needs to keep in place to protect the country from problems in surrounding regions plagued with political turmoil. However, security services control the media and the press, therefore arrests are reduced as what is published has been reviewed, and the lower arrest rate for journalists looks better internationally.

According to the *Middle East and North Africa Country Report,* The Jordanian Penal Code still contains a number of statutes that can impose lengthy prison terms and harsh fines for offenses such as inciting sedition, defamation and publishing false news. Article 195, which prohibits *lese-majeste* (insult to the dignity of the king), remains intact on the legal code and carries a sentence of up to three years in prison; it is invoked to trap and prosecute journalists who are critical of the government. While it was more harshly used during the reign of King Hussein, his son King Abdullah has used the code sparingly but still maintains the right to invoke it. He has tried to be, at least publicly, less harsh on the issue than his father was, and his speech regarding being transparent to the world as they have nothing to fear would necessarily dictate that he maintain this ideal.

Some of Jordan's main newspapers are *Ad Dustour*—an Arabic-language daily; *Jordan Times*—an English-language political daily; and *The Star*—an English-language weekly. These are also available online as well.

BIBLIOGRAPHY

The Central Intelligence Agency (CIA). *World Factbook 2001*. Directorate of Intelligence, 2002. Available from www.cia.gov.

Committee to Protect Journalists. *Middle East and North Africa Country Report: Jordan*. 2001. Available from www.cpj.org/attacks01/mideast01/jordan.html.

De Blij, H.J., and Peter O. Muller. *Geography: Realms, Regions and Concepts*. Tenth edition. New York: John Wiley and Sons, 2002.

''Don't Blink: Jordan's Democratic Opening and Closing,'' 1998. Available from www.merip.org./pins/pin98.html.

Human Rights Watch Press Release, 1999. Available from www.hrw.org/press 1999/oct/jor1029.html.

Sussman, Leonard. *Freedom House Press Freedom Survey,* 1999. Available from www.freedomhouse.org.

—Pamela M. Gross

KAZAKHSTAN

BASIC DATA

Official Country Name:	Republic of Kazakhstan
Region (Map name):	East & South Asia
Population:	16,731,303
Language(s):	Kazakh (Qazaq), Russian
Literacy rate:	98.0%
Area:	2,717,300 sq km
GDP:	18,230 (US$ millions)
Number of Television Stations:	12
Number of Television Sets:	3,880,000
Television Sets per 1,000:	231.9
Number of Radio Stations:	86
Number of Radio Receivers:	6,470,000
Radio Receivers per 1,000:	386.7
Number of Individuals with Internet Access:	100,000
Internet Access per 1,000:	6.0

BACKGROUND & GENERAL CHARACTERISTICS

General Description The Republic of Kazakhstan (*Qazaqstan Respublikasy*) is the largest Central Asian republic of the former Soviet Union. Four times the size of Texas and covering a greater geographic expanse than all of Western Europe, Kazakhstan was settled by nomadic tribes who migrated into the region five hundred years ago. The country's name comes from the Russian version of *qazaq,* meaning ''renegades,'' from the country's tribal history. During the early eighteenth century, Russian tsars gradually took over in ruling the original peoples of the khanate—a blend of Turkic and Mongol (Moghol) ethnic groups. By the mid-19th century, Russian rulers dominated Kazakhstan, though the Kazaks themselves continued to be the largest nomadic group and included about two million people at that time.

As of July 2001 Kazakhstan's population numbered 16.7 million, composed of a diverse array of ethnic groups in the following proportions, according to the 1999 census: 53.4 percent Kazakh, 30 percent Russian, 3.7 percent Ukrainian, 2.5 percent Uzbek, 2.4 percent German, and 1.4 percent Uighur, with the other 6.6 percent consisting of such peoples as Chechens, Koreans, Kurds, and other Central Asian ethnic groups. About 20,000 refugees from other parts of the former Soviet Union reportedly were living in Kazakhstan as of June 2002, according to the office of the UN High Commissioner for Refugees. Members of most ethnic groups reportedly were getting along relatively peaceably together in 2001, although the Uighurs have been the targets of harsh discrimination, ill-treatment, and violence in recent years. Additionally, many ethnic Russians purportedly dislike their inability to claim dual citizenship and the requirement that they must pass a Kazakh language test to qualify for government employment.

Coming from a patriarchal tradition, Kazakhstan continues to struggle with authoritarian rule, even in the post-Soviet period. In early August 2002, Kazakhstan's political future as a viable, multi-party democracy was seriously being called into question. President Nursultan Nazarbayev has been head of state since 1990 when he was elected president and has dubiously been chosen twice again by the people since then—in 1995, by a referendum to extend his mandate and in 1999, through an election where the main opposition candidate was outlawed from participation.

Allegations of government corruption involving the president and other political figures and of a secret Swiss bank account opened in 1996 or 1997 containing US$1 billion in public monies from Kazakhstan's sale of a large share of its lucrative oil fields to the Mobil Corporation, coupled with the ruling party's domination of politics and the media, threatened the country's political stability and prompted the government to wield increasing pressure selectively against the media. As Peter Baker of the Washington Post Foreign Service stated in June 2002 regarding Nazarbayev, ''His relationship with oil companies has prompted investigations in Switzerland and the United States as prosecutors in both countries probe whether an American lobbyist helped steer millions of dollars in oil commissions to him and other Kazakh leaders.''

The former prime minister, Akezhan Kazhegeldin, leader of the Republican Popular Party of Kazakhstan (RPPK), one of the main opposition parties, currently lives in exile, convicted of corruption and abuse of power and sentenced in absentia by the Nazarbayev regime to ten years' imprisonment. He continues to remain politically active, hoping to return one day to Kazakhstan and to reassume his leadership role. Another key opposition leader, Muktar Ablyazov, the former energy minister and leader of the Democratic Choice of Kazakhstan (DCK) party, which was established by liberal politicians and registered in January 2001, was arrested in March 2002. Galymzhan Zhakiyanov, the former governor of the Paladar region, was arrested in Almaty the following month, charged with corruption and abuse of power. Despite a great international outcry against the arrests of these two persons, Zhakiyanov was judged guilty in August 2002 and was sentenced to ten years' imprisonment, provoking an even larger international protest against the Nazarbayev regime.

Kazakhstan's government reported 950 privately owned newspapers and 342 privately owned magazines, according to the U.S. Department of State's annual country report covering the state of human rights in Kazakhstan in 2001. A reported 1,431 mass media outlets and information agencies operated in the country as of August 1, 2001, and about four-fifths of these were privately owned. However, the specific owners of media outlets are not always easy to identify. As IREX noted in their report on the panel research they conducted in Kazakhstan in 2001, ''Media ownership is not transparent at all, yet most people know the owners from rumors. . . .As some panelists mentioned, 'the main thing media owners are non-transparent about is the fact that people close to the presidential family own media outlets.'''

A wide range of critics and commentators, coming from the U.S. Department of State, domestic and international media organizations and human rights advocacy groups, Kazakhstan's political opposition in Kazakhstan and in exile, the country's own journalists and opposition politicians, and the foreign press all echo the same views regarding the increasingly dismal state of affairs and of the press in Kazakhstan. The situation seemed to be reaching a breaking point by August 2002. Nazarbayev's rapidly escalating efforts to suppress or eliminate all criticism of himself, his family, the ruling party, and the government, coupled with his attempts to eliminate perceived or actual political opponents by whatever means he deemed were necessary, did not bode well for the political stability and democratic future of Kazakhstan.

Citing the Freedom House human rights survey released in mid-2002, the Kazakhstan 21st Century Foundation noted that Kazakhstan received a failing grade from Freedom House for press freedom. The survey reportedly showed that the Nazarbayev regime ''ignores constitutional provisions for freedom of the press by dominating most newspapers as well as printing, distribution and broadcast facilities, and controlling Internet access,'' in the words of the Foundation. Noting that the president's oldest daughter directly controlled printing and broadcasting outlets, that offending Nazarbayev can be considered criminal behavior, that publishing truthful articles that upset the president can result in imprisonment, and that the country's ''tax police'' have been used to stifle journalistic expression, Freedom House summarized that ''the government has repeatedly harassed or shut down independent news media.''

Nature of the Newspaper Audience About 98 percent of the adult population of Kazakhstan reportedly is literate. The average per capita annual income is US$1,190. The population is distributed across several urban areas, including the cities of Astana (meaning ''capital city,'' previously known as Akmola until renamed by President Nazarbayev, who moved the capital in December 1998 to his home territory); Almaty in the east; and Karaganda, and across the rural areas of the country known as ''the regions.'' The country is composed of fourteen administrative divisions and three cities.

Russian is the language used by about 75 percent of the people, including those belonging to other ethnic groups, including Kazakhs. However, in an apparent effort to gain linguistic and ethnic control of the country—perhaps to align the press with his own ethnic group's views and interests as he seeks to knit the various ethnic groups in Kazakhstan into a new national identity—President Azarbayev issued a decree that was enacted into law and came into effect on January 1, 2002, that all broadcasting outlets—television and radio—must broadcast at least 50 percent of their programming in the Kazakh language.

Quality of Journalism: General Comments The quality of the press is variable, the basic impediment being the high cost of production and publishing and the lack of sufficient means to ensure that editors and journalists will not face exorbitant tax burdens and fines imposed by a government interested in squelching any opposition or criticism. Additionally, an older, Soviet style of journalism, dominated by analysis rather than by investigative reporting, continues to hold sway in the country. This impairs the ability of readers to obtain clear, concise, and accurate accounts of current events and the story behind the story.

Financial problems also impair the quality of journalistic reporting. As IREX reported in their *Media Sustainability Index Report* based on research conducted in May and June 2001 with a panel of journalists in Kazakhstan, "Aside from professional standards or educational background, the Kazakh press is faced with technical and equipment dilemmas." With shortages of adequate video equipment for television production and computers for the print media, the technical quality of journalistic production is impaired. Additionally, because most journalists are underpaid, the practice of taking money for more-positive reporting is common, compromising the accuracy of reporting.

Historical News Traditions As noted above, the two types of journalism in Kazakhstan today are investigative—still rather rudimentary in its development—and analytic. The analytic style is a carry-over from the Soviet period, when virtually all media were obliged to produce government-approved propaganda, limiting the possible contributions of journalists to the analysis of then-current Communist party politics, tactics, and actions.

Distribution of Newspapers by Language Most of the readership in Kazakhstan prefers newspapers in the Russian language, despite the fact that only a third of the country's population is ethnic Russian. Accessibility to news via the broadcast media thus will likely become more complicated as the new language law that took effect in 2002 is implemented. The law requires at least 50 percent of all programming on television and radio to be in the Kazakh language, but not all stations are observing this requirement, since the cost of producing programs in the local language is too high for many media outlets.

Ethnic & Religious Orientation A large sector of the population in Kazakhstan—about percent 47 percent—is Muslim, primarily Sunni Muslim, with another 44 percent being Russian Orthodox Christian. Two percent are Protestant and another 7 percent adhere to other religions or have no particular religious affiliation. The Muslim Uighur minority in the country has faced severe persecution and discrimination and occasionally even death, as have the activists who defend them. The Uighur ethnic minority, traditionally a more conservative group of Muslims, has been persecuted not only by the Nazarbayev government but also by the governments of other Central Asian republics since the break-up of the Soviet Union in 1991.

The minority press, in terms of ethnic minorities, can basically be labeled a secular and essentially Russian ethnic press. The religious minorities do not appear to have a strong presence in the media; nor does the religious majority, for that matter. The basic orientation of the press is inclined more toward expressing divergent political views, particularly concerning the quality and degree of democracy to which Kazakhstan's peoples should aspire, than toward expressing specific religious perspectives. The ethnic quality of the press is reflected more in the efforts of the Russian minority to continue to exert some influence on political affairs in the wake of a growing interest and effort by Nazarbayev and his ruling party in extending the benefits of government to the Kazakh people ahead of other ethnic groups. Additionally, Korean, Uighur, Ukrainian, Kurd, and German newspapers are published in Kazakhstan, though the volume of their sales has dropped in recent years due to insufficient financing and perhaps to inadequate coverage of issues of interest to the ethnic minorities involved.

Political Ideology The press in Kazakhstan is heavily biased in favor of the ruling party, President Nursultan Nazarbayev's People's Unity Party (PUP). Most private newspapers also are biased in favor of the ruling party, since they in fact are not entirely "private." Government supporters very often provide some of the financing for the "private" press, making news tipped in favor of the president and the key government positions and views. The opposition press is likewise political, in that the newspapers associated with opposition party candidates present their party perspectives and criticize the president and his party.

Geography of Readership and Newspaper Publishing and Distribution Those living in large cities such as Astana and Almaty have much greater access to newspapers than those living in "the regions," as the more sparsely populated, rural areas of the country are known. Outside of the major cities, it is much more difficult for newspapers to find printing facilities and to publish regularly.

Daily, Weekly, and Bi-Weekly Newspapers Of the government-supported papers, *Kazakhstanskaya Pravda* (also on the Internet at http://www.kazpravda.kz/) is one of the most influential, published five times a week in the Russian language. *Yegemen Qazaqstan* also is a government-supported paper published five times weekly, though in Kazakh. Two newspapers that are privately owned but favor the government are *Ekspress-K,* published in Russian five times weekly, and *Zhas Alash* (http://www.zhasalash.kz/), published in Kazakh four times each week. The *Almaty Herald* (http://www.herald.kz/) is Kazakhstan's main newspaper published in English.

SolDat and *XXI Vek* (21st Century) are two independent weekly newspapers that have faced frequent harassment from the Nazarbayev regime. One private, biweekly newspaper, *Vremya Po* (The Globe), includes an English page in its issues. Like *SolDat* and *XXI Vek,* this paper also was singled out for negative government attention in 2001. *Nachnem s ponedelnika* is a private opposition weekly published in Russian.

Foreign Language Press The May 2002 amendments to the Mass Media Law made it more difficult for foreign-produced programs to be aired on Kazak television and radio. This was anticipated to have a negative effect on small independent broadcasters, who cannot afford to produce all of their own programs and must now substitute for some of the foreign programs they previously transmitted on their airwaves, according to the Committee to Protect Journalists.

Minority-owned Press In Kazakhstan today, the Russian minority has a strong presence in the media. Russian-language newspapers are readily produced, although the Russian community has felt increasingly pressured to restrict its reporting to government-approved material. Although a new language law for the media came into effect on January 1, 2002, that requires broadcasting media to provide at least half of their output in the Kazakh language, Russian media producers have continued to operate in the country.

ECONOMIC FRAMEWORK

Economic Climate and Its Influence on Media Kazakhstan has a vast, undeveloped potential for economic development, based on its large oil reserves and valuable minerals. In addition, the agricultural potential of the fertile southern part of the country has yet to be fully developed. Because construction of the oil pipelines needed to transport crude oil out of the Tengiz oil field was only begun in March 2001, the country is not yet profiting from its rich oil resources as significantly as it will in the future.Additionally, political corruption involving the oil deals is likely to be consuming a share of the monies that could be going to rebuild dilapidated infrastructure and meet the basic social needs of Kazakhstan's people. The main exports are oil, ferrous and nonferrous metals, machinery, chemicals, grain, wool, meat, and coal. Half of Kazakhstan's working population is employed in the services sector, with just over a quarter (27 percent) employed in industry and just under a quarter (23 percent) employed in agriculture in the mid-1990s. Life expectancy in 2001 was an estimated 58 years for men and 69 years for women.

As of mid-2002, repercussions from an ever-growing scandal involving high government figures, including the president of Kazakhstan, were threatening to erase the remaining vestiges of democracy in the country. The $1 billion from the public treasury allegedly placed by Nazarbayev in a Swiss bank account in 1997 apparently stemmed from a deal worked out by the government to sell a major share of Kazakhstan's Tengiz oil fields to the Mobil Corporation. Very few—apparently, only Nazarbayev himself, the prime minister, and the national bank's chairman—were aware of this account before Kazakhstan's prime minister, Imangali Tasmagambetov, informed the parliament in April 2002 of its existence. The general political climate in the country began heating up still further in the first half of 2002 as key opposition figures were increasingly accused of corruption and illegal behavior and met with legal cases and sanctions against them.

Print Media versus Electronic Media The electronic media have had much greater success in dispersing a range of perspectives, information, and commentary in Kazakhstan, due to the general government imposition of restrictions on the print media. However, starting in 2001, even Internet news sources found themselves limited increasingly by Nazarbayev and his government, which reclassified the Internet as a form of "mass media" and thus subject to government scrutiny and electronic eavesdropping.

Types and Concentration of Ownership: Government, "Private," and Opposition Newspapers The press is basically divided into three types: government, opposition, and "private." Little by way of a truly independent press exists in Kazakhstan today, owing to the fact that some newspapers are directly owned and controlled by government figures, others are produced by opposition parties and candidates—some of them currently living outside of Kazakhstan to avoid persecution or prosecution inside Kazakhstan—and still others are nominally "private." A number of private and independent newspapers reportedly receive financial backing from pro-government sponsors and thus are influenced in their content by the source of their financial support. For example, the president's daughter and son-in-law controlled two private newspapers—*Karavan* and *Novoye Pokolenie*—as well as the Franklin Press printing house.

Advertisers' Influence on Editorial Policies An estimated 90 percent of revenue for the private and opposition press comes from advertising. Only a small proportion of the funds required by publications comes from subscriptions or sales of issues. Advertisers try to limit publication of information on their competitors.

PRESS LAWS

Constitutional Provisions and Media Guarantees The Constitution officially protects free expression to a degree. With the Constitution requiring that persons respect the president's dignity, the president and other government officials are protected from what Kazakhstan's politically charged courts decide is insulting. Similarly, owing to amendments passed in March 2001 that strengthened the media law on libel and to widespread government attempts to limit reporting on certain topics and to subdue criticism of the president, his party, and the government, the apparent legal guarantees of free expression hardly play out in reality. Journalists must practice diligent self-censorship in order to avoid coming up against the law, and even cautious efforts at restraint and publishing factual accounts can bring penalties if the courts choose to broadly interpret the Constitution and the media laws. Topics that journalists are not permitted to freely cover include ''the president and his family, corruption at the government level, oil revenue distribution, and ethnic relations,'' according to a research report by IREX.

Press Laws in Force The press laws in force in Kazakhstan in 2002 served primarily to protect the interests of the president and his government. As the U.S. Department of State's Bureau of Democracy, Human Rights, and Labor stated in their Country Report for Kazakhstan covering events in 2001, ''Amendments to the media law, passed in March, strengthened libel laws, limited the rebroadcast of foreign-produced programming, classified Web sites as mass media, and introduced a requirement that journalists receive permission prior to taping interviews.''

Particularly detrimental is a newly passed law, ''On Political Parties,'' proposed early in 2002 by the pro-Narbayev *Otan* (Fatherland) party, approved by the legislature, and signed by the president in July 2002. The law ''sets a prohibitively high threshold for registering political parties, effectively disqualifying opposition groups and steering the country further away from democracy,'' according to a news report distributed by the Washington-based Kazakhstan 21st Century Foundation. The Organization for Security and Cooperation in Europe as well as human rights advocacy groups in Kazakhstan are reported to have stated that the law can be used as a weapon against opposition groups and thus endangers political pluralism.

Media laws also include prohibition of television advertising of alcohol and tobacco products, of violence, and of ''pornography.''

Registration and Licensing of Newspapers and Journalists State law requires that all media outlets—the press, broadcasting services, and Internet sites—register with the government. In 1996 the government, under the authority of the Ministry of Transportation and Communication, began granting private broadcasters licenses. The initial costs of licensing for radio and television frequencies were excessively high, and more than 200 outlets were closed down. Afterwards, the Ministry of Information reduced licensing fees and gave more favorable treatment to regional media, which nonetheless failed to remedy the fact that many stations by that time had simply permanently closed their doors. Obtaining licenses depends on government loyalty and often on the ability and willingness to pay bribes to the government officials who distribute them. As one respondent on an IREX panel in 2001 expressed it, ''in licensing we have the complete tyranny of the state; bribes and blackmail accompany the procedure.''

Press-related Laws As the U.S. State Department reported concerning media status in 2001, the Prosecutor General has ''the authority to suspend the activity of news media that undermine national security; however, this authority has never been invoked.'' On the other hand, by 2002 this appeared to be changing. With government officials seeking to limit the publication of information on the political scandal involving the Swiss bank account containing substantial public funds from Kazakhstan, it appeared likely that supposed breaches of national security by the press would meet with government-imposed penalties.

In 1999 a law was passed that listed types of government secrets whose publication is criminally prohibited. Included among the items on the list of secrets about which the press must remain silent are statements on the president and his family's health and financial affairs, economic information such as the extent of and details on the country's mineral reserves, and how much the government owes foreign creditors.

Independence of the Judiciary The courts in Kazakhstan are currently very tied into the presidency and the executive branch of government. An independent judiciary does not exist. Members of opposition parties who report their perspectives on government affairs or the president have little judicial protection. Additionally, those judged guilty of defamation or of threatening national security through their work as reporters, editors, and publishers have little hope of winning an appeal; the cards are already stacked against them. As members of the Executive Committee of the leading RPPK opposition party wrote in late July 2002 after the passage of a new law entitled ''On Political Parties'' that would likely severely curtail the number and viability of opposition parties, ''In a country where the entire judiciary reports to just one individual it is not going to be particularly difficult to find a reason to first suspend and then liquidate a party.''

CENSORSHIP

BBC Monitoring states, ''In May 2000 the US-based Committee to Protect Journalists placed Nazarbayev on its annual list of the 'Ten worst enemies of the press.''' Although Nazarbayev was not on the top-ten list for 2001, his actions toward the press in fact have worsened over time. The U.S. State Department remarked in its human rights report on Kazakhstan for events occurring in 2001, ''Although the media expressed views that were independent and occasionally highly critical of the Government, the Government used its influence to limit the media's content.''

Censorship has been a growing problem for the media, especially surrounding news of secret government shifts in public funds to Swiss bank accounts. Starting in late 2001, when news of the government's involvement in corrupt or questionable practices burgeoned, censorship was more actively practiced by government authorities against the print and broadcast media. As IREX reported from its 2001 research on the status of journalism in Kazakhstan, ''journalists feel constrained by their editors and owners to the extent that they not only abstain from writing the truth, but also survive on articles praising officials and business people, and on favorable reporting about sponsors.''

In May 2002 journalist Sergey Duvanov posted on the Internet a bold, lengthy statement accusing the president of criminal violation and Kazakhstan's people of failing to stand up to government misrule and corruption. Entitled ''Silence of the Lambs,'' Duvanov's Internet posting was expected to result in Dubanov's imprisonment. By July 2002 the president was accusing Duvanov of libel, following the June opening of a criminal defamation case against Duvanov by the Prosecutor-General's office. Duvanov allegedly had insulted the honor and dignity of the president, a criminal offense in Kazakhstan.

STATE-PRESS RELATIONS

The Right to Criticize Government: Theory & Practice According to the Constitution, freedom of speech and freedom of the press are guaranteed in Kazakhstan. However, the opposite situation is true in practice. As BBC Monitoring noted, ''During the president's 1999 re-election campaign, government authorities brought criminal cases against several independent media outlets, charging them with 'freedom of speech abuses.' After the election, a number of private newspapers were fined, subjected to tax audits and shut down.'' The situation for the opposition press is even worse. Government ownership and intimidation of printing houses has discouraged many printers from publishing opposition newspapers.

A heightening climate of threats toward the physical safety of journalists has been prevalent in Kazakhstan under the Nazarbayev regime. In February 2001 a television journalist and commentator, Gulzhan Yergaliyeva, and her husband and son were brutally attacked in a robbery attempt after the journalist aired a program ''Social Agreement'' that criticized government policies. The office of *SolDat,* a leading independent newspaper, was burned, and computer equipment was stolen. By October 2001 *SolDat,* financially unable to continue its operations six months after its last issue was published, was forced to close and consequently lost its license.

A leading independent newspaper, *Delovoe-Obozrenie Respublika* (*Respublika* Business Review) received a decapitated dog at its door in May 2002 with an attached note reading, ''There will be no next time,'' apparently in return for covering the presidential scandal involving Swiss bank accounts. The head of the dog appeared two days later at the door of Irina Petrushova, a Russian citizen and the paper's editor-in-chief, who also found two funeral wreaths at her home during May.

In early July 2002 Petrushova was sentenced to one and a half years in prison for supposedly working in the country without permission. However, she was released by a judge who saw her case as falling under an amnesty granted the previous year. Petrushova's lawyer claimed her case was one of government intimidation, since the newspaper where she worked was suspended in April for two months, purportedly due to technical violations, but had frequently published articles on cases of government corruption and of opposition activists targeted by the government.

In another case, Lira Baisetova, a journalist for the same independent paper, published an article on the Swiss bank account scandal in *SolDat,* since *Respublika* already had been shut down. Her article reported an interview she had conducted with Bernard Bertossa, the former Prosecutor of Geneva, Switzerland, who confirmed that Swiss authorities had frozen bank accounts owned by Nazarbayev and two former prime ministers of Kazakhstan; the Prosecutor could not say whether the accounts were funded illegally, since Kazakh judicial authorities reportedly were being uncooperative in the investigation. The news confirmed what many in Kazakhstan and elsewhere previously had heard of the scandal.

By July, Baisetova was in hiding in a rural part of Kazakhstan after her 25-year-old daughter, Leila, who was reported on May 23 as having disappeared, died in a government hospital in June. Leila reportedly had been in a coma after her arrest on alleged heroin charges, and the journalist was unable to see her before the daughter died. Suspicions were that the daughter, whose body reportedly showed signs of torture based on photographic evidence, was murdered in retaliation for Baisetova's role in placing increased media attention on the Nazarbayev Swiss bank account scandal. Baisetova previously had been physically attacked herself in 2000 and 2001 as well as monitored and harassed by anonymous phone calls. The same day Leila disappeared, the offices of the newspaper where Baisetova worked were fire-bombed.

In a Radio Free Europe/Radio Liberty report, journalist Bruce Pannier noted that *SolDat*'s offices also were attacked two days before Leila Baisetova disappeared, with unknown persons entering the building, beating two journalists, and destroying equipment. Pannier added, ''Other media outlets in Kazakhstan have reported crimes against their personnel and property.''

Managed News Interestingly, government suppression and harassment of journalists and the media was somewhat selective, at least through 2001. In May 2001 the results of a survey of journalists were published that indicated that most of those interviewed saw the media in Kazakhstan as controlled by the president's eldest daughter and her husband; by Timur Kulibayev, another son-in-law of President Nazarbayev; and by other ''oligarchs.'' However, no negative repercussions reportedly were felt by Andrey Sviridov, the journalist who had reported the poll's findings.

For the private press, which depends on outside sources of financial support and some government subsidies in order to remain viable, contributors often are pro-government and thus influence the content published. Whether employed by the state press or the private press, journalists must practice self-censorship to avoid negative repercussions. Opposition papers are less inclined to exercise this sort of self-monitoring and self-control and thus are more likely to face closures or other negative action by the government.

At least twenty newspapers and twenty television broadcasting stations, including the popular TAN-TV company based in Almaty, reportedly faced temporary or permanent suspensions in the opening years of the new millennium due to government repression. Because Nazarbayev's government also either directly or indirectly has threatened damages to publishing houses that print newspapers critical of government interests, certain newspapers also have had difficulty publishing on a regular schedule. For example, *SolDat,* a key independent paper, repeatedly has been obstructed from publishing for a number of reasons, including problems with finding a willing printer. Eurasia Internet cited the Committee to Protect Journalists in reporting that in 2001, ''at least five printers in the city of Almaty had refused to produce the paper.''

Editorial Influence on Government Policies Little influence by editors on government policies can realistically be achieved in Kazakhstan's present climate of government intimidation, harassment, and control of the media. However, a large social protest movement directed against environmental and health degradation from decades of nuclear testing and its ramifications in the Semipalatinsk region of Kazakhstan has had some effect on government decision-making. A law was passed to guarantee health services to those most adversely affected by the years of nuclear testing in the region, but funds have not been sufficiently allocated to back up government promises of health assistance. Countless persons now suffer from severe birth defects, cancer, and other deformities and diseases as a result of the testing program begun in the Soviet era and continued into the 1990s.

Attitude toward Foreign Media

A growing number of journalists of the political opposition are living outside of Kazakhstan, and many of them continue to promote the ideas of the opposition that cannot be publicized from within the country. Commenting on amendments passed in March 2001 that altered Kazakhstan's media law, the U.S. Department of State noted, ''Specifically, the amendments expanded the concept of libel to make media outlets responsible for the content of reprints or rebroadcast of foreign information, including international press services.'' Consequently, domestic journalists, editors, publishers, and broadcasters can come under fire for publishing or broadcasting news the government deems deleterious to its interests. The March 2001 amendments also reduced the percentage of foreign programs permissible to be broadcast in Kazakhstan, where rebroadcasts of programs produced overseas will account for only 20 percent of broadcasts by 2003.

News Agencies

The Kazakhstan Today agency (with a companion Internet site at http://www.hotline.kz/), the Kazakhstan

Press agency (http://www.kazpress.kz/news/), the Koda news agency (http://news.site.kz/), and Interfax Kazakhstan all operate inside the country. However, they are not generally viewed as independent news sources, due to the fact that subscription costs are usually high and most media outlets thus cannot afford to access the information the agencies provide. International news agencies like Reuters, the Associated Press, and l'Agence France-Presse focus mainly on oil industry-related or other economic news, and their services are equally unaffordable to the majority of journalists.

BROADCAST MEDIA

In 2001 a reported 45 independent television and radio stations operated in Kazakhstan. These included 17 television stations, 15 radio stations, and 13 television-radio combinations. Eleven of the broadcasting stations were located in Almaty, the former capital city. A reported 37 television and radio stations were granted new licenses in 2000, in addition to the licenses held by existing radio and television broadcasting stations.

By 2002 the president's eldest daughter, Dariga Nazarbayeva, was reported to virtually control the sphere of radio and television broadcasting in Kazakhstan. Although a 1991 law stated that competition among broadcasting outlets was to be encouraged, Nazarbayev amended that law in 1999 to achieve just the opposite effect. The newer law essentially undid the anti-monopolistic legislation passed earlier in the decade, making it possible and legal for a government monopoly on the media to gradually take shape.

As BBC Monitoring observed, Nazarbayeva and her husband ''have been the main beneficiaries of the privatization of formerly state-run media.'' Head of the Khabar information agency (Internet site: http://www.khabar.kz) until 2001, the president's daughter controlled several television stations within the national television broadcasting network. As of mid-2002 two private television stations in the country—NTK and KTK—were owned by Dariga Nazarbayeva. And until Nazarbayeva's husband, Rakhat Aliyev, became embroiled in a political scandal in late 2001 involving allegations of efforts to replace Nazarbayev, the president's son-in-law owned a principal media holding company in Kazakhstan. By mid-2002 Aliyev was living in Vienna as Kazakhstan's ambassador to Austria. His wife continued to live and work in Kazakhstan.

The privately owned television stations Khabar and Khabar 2, broadcasting in both Kazakh and Russian, and ORT Kazakhstan, are included among the holdings of the president's daughter and son-in-law and receive public funding. As to radio in the country, radio stations Europa Plus, Russkoye Radio, Radio Hit FM, and Radio Karavan all are privately owned by the same couple. Kazakh Radio is government-owned and broadcasts in both Kazakh and Russian. Kazakh Commercial TV is privately owned and broadcasts in Kazakh and Russian as well.

Besides Kazakhstan's domestic broadcasting networks and stations, the British Broadcasting Corporation and Radio Free Europe/Radio Liberty broadcast programs accessible to Kazakhstan's audiences.

ELECTRONIC NEWS MEDIA

The two principal Internet service providers (ISPs) are government-controlled: Kaztelecom and Nursat. The opposition website Eurasia has faced repeated blockage of its content, although proxy servers have continued to provide viewers with access to the Eurasia site. According to the U.S. State Department, ''In September [2001] human rights monitors alleged that Kaztelecom and Nursat users were unwittingly viewing a 'mirror site' of the opposition Eurasia page. On the 'mirror site' users view a page that mimics the original, but without material highly critical of the Government.'' Another opposition website, Aziopa, was blocked by the government ISPs in 2002.

The Internet had provided unprecedented publishing access to the opposition press, and many independent journalists used the Internet to convey their views and critiques of politics and society in Kazakhstan. However, amendments were added in May 2002 to the Law on Mass Media to make free expression via the Internet considerably less free.

The National Kazakh Security Committee, the successor to the famed Soviet KGB, has been empowered by the ruling regime to ''monitor e-mail traffic, access to the internet, faxes and phone calls by any organization, company or person it deemed suspicious,'' according to BBC Monitoring. In May 2002 the president approved amendments to the Mass Media Law, already a restrictive piece of legislation. The amendments essentially labeled web sites as ''mass media,'' shifting them to a new category and making them subject to state monitoring and censorship.

EDUCATION & TRAINING

The education of journalists takes place primarily in seven departments of journalism located at state universities throughout Kazakhstan. Prospective journalists receive four years of training, costing them about US$600 per year, a fee which many reportedly find affordable. However, improvements in the training of journalists are clearly needed, in order to develop a more fact-oriented, investigative style of reporting that would represent an advancement over the more commonly used Soviet style of journalistic practice emphasizing ''analytic'' writing. As IREX's 2001 report noted, ''The need for reform in journalism education is long overdue. But lack of resources, qualified staff, donor interest, and investment, together with authoritarian rule and the practice of journalism to promote interests rather than present objective news and events to the public, still plague this unreformed society.''

The principal school of journalism is the Department of Journalism at the Kazakh State University, where students planning careers as television and print journalists, public relations professionals, and international affairs journalists receive training. Private training facilities also exist, but the majority are state funded.

Short-term and international training opportunities also are available to some journalists through international donor organizations such as the U.S. Information Agency, the U.S. Agency for International Development, the UN Development Program, UNESCO, the Soros Foundation, the Eurasia Foundation, and the British Council, according to IREX. Better opportunities for training journalists in the areas of reporting, legal issues, marketing, and media management would be beneficial, based on the comments of the panelists IREX interviewed in 2001.

Journalists are generally very underpaid in Kazakhstan, which leads many to leave the journalistic profession and seek higher-paying government jobs. A few rather well-financed private media outlets do offer more lucrative work for journalists. Nonetheless, journalists in the rural areas earned about US$50 monthly in 2001, while those working in Almaty made about US$200-250 each month.

Several active media associations operate in Kazakhstan. According to IREX, in 2001 the following six organizations represented journalists' interests: ''the Association of Independent Mass Media of Kazakhstan and Central Asia (ANESMICA); the National Association of TV Broadcasters; the Association of Kazakh Broadcasters; the Journalists in Trouble Foundation; the International Foundation for the Protection of Glasnost (*Adil Sez*); and the Kazakh Branch of the Internews International Network.'' The most effective of these appeared to be ANESMICA, established in 1995, and *Adil Sez*, set up in 2000 in connection with the Russian Glasnost Defense Foundation. To a certain extent, at least some of the associations help journalists in legal difficulty, providing them with legal defense and monitoring government treatment of journalists and the media.

Besides the above associations, two press clubs were operating in 2001: the Kazakh Press Club and the National Press Club. Rather than being effective tools for introducing journalists' interests into legislative decision-making or for protecting the rights of journalists, the press clubs have operated in more commercial directions such as organizing public relations events and press conferences and sometimes running training seminars with the support of international donor organizations.

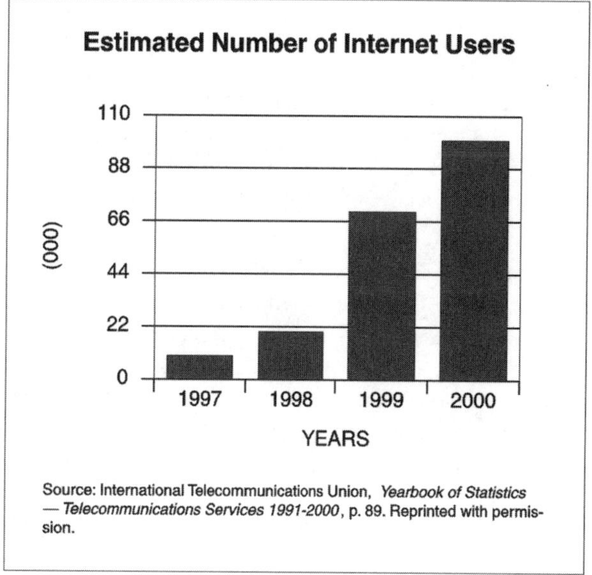

Source: International Telecommunications Union, *Yearbook of Statistics — Telecommunications Services 1991-2000*, p. 89. Reprinted with permission.

The Union of Journalists is the direct descendent of the earlier press union that operated during Soviet days. Media professionals in Kazakhstan appear to view the current Union as doing little to represent their interests before the legislature. As IREX observed, ''Media professionals in Kazakhstan do not have a single trade union, because of the conflicting interests between different media outlets.''

SUMMARY

Conclusions President Nazarbayev met with President George W. Bush in December 2001 and pledged to support human rights and further efforts to democratize Kazakhstan. However, recent confirmation of the existence of Swiss bank accounts holding significant public monies from Kazakhstan and the strong likelihood that government officials have been involved in an oil scandal make it increasingly unlikely that Kazakhstan will follow an unbroken path toward economic development and greater democracy unless international pressure is applied or a widespread domestic movement prompts significant change in government leadership.

Among the numerous international critics of Nazarbayev and his non-democratic, authoritarian practices is U.S. Congressman Norman Dicks, who in a statement before the House of Representatives on July 18, 2002 observed that Nazarbayev ''has shut down many newspapers and television stations in Kazakhstan, preventing its citizens from having a free press.'' Congressman Dicks requested that the international community place special attention on the problematic behavior of President Nazarbayev and not allow the president to continue to act in repressive ways against the media in his country.

Congressman Dicks also asked that a July 12, 2002, letter from the Editorial Board of *The Washington Post* be included in the Congressional Record. In that letter (''New Allies, Old Formula''), the Washington Post's editors observed that in Kazakhstan, ''A score of newspapers and an equal number of television stations have been forced to shut down in recent months, and a number of journalists have been attacked or threatened.'' The Editorial Board questioned in their letter of July 12 whether recent overtures by the U.S. Government to Kazakhstan, including a July 2002 agreement between the Nazarbayev regime and the Bush administration granting Kazakhstan's permission for U.S. military planes to stop and refuel in emergencies at the international airport in Almaty, might not be perceived by Kazakhstan officials as giving the green light to Nazarbayev's repressive tactics in trying to silence his critics.

The editors of *The Washington Post* raised the issue of whether the ''War on Terrorism'' being waged by the United States following the September 11, 2001, attacks was extending too broadly the U.S. tendency to condone government repression in certain countries in the name of fighting terrorism. As they succinctly put it, ''Does the Pentagon really need another landing arrangement in Central Asia? If such agreements were withheld—or frozen—Mr. Nazarbayev and other Central Asian dictators would be quick to get the message.''

Trends and Prospects for the Media: Outlook for the Twenty-first Century In the existing climate of government-imposed media restrictions, coupled with hostile government attitudes and practices toward the press, life in Kazakhstan is coming to resemble what seventeenth-century English political philosopher Thomas Hobbes once described as the conditions of life where no government exists at all. In Hobbes's words, in a ''state of nature'' where people are left to their own devices and no government regulates their selfish pursuits, life is ''a war of all against all'' and is ''solitary, poor, nasty, brutish, and short.'' In Kazakhstan's case, it seems that life for journalists under the Nazarbayev regime ironically parallels Hobbes's depiction of life without government. The outlook appears similarly bleak for the readership of Kazakhstan's newspapers, considering their currently limited ability to access news representing a broad political spectrum where issues are debated in a journalistic style more typical of that in democratic countries.

Unless the international diplomatic community, foreign governments, and a wide-ranging, solidaristic, grassroots movement begins to exert pressure more concertedly on Nazarbayev and his ruling party to democratize the country and allow free expression, the future of objective journalism in Kazakhstan may be in dire jeopardy. Hashhuu Naranjargal, the author of a November 1998 report by the International Federation of Journalists on the rights of the media and of journalists in Central Asia, observed that in Kazakhstan, ''supporters of democracy and most of the journalists stated they are in need of international support. International human rights organizations and international organizations and trade unions protecting media freedom must take urgent actions against the anti-democratic processes they currently see developing in the country.'' The message Naranjargal carried from journalists in Kazakhstan in 1998 to the rest of the world implores even greater attention in 2002 as the rule of law breaks down under Nazarbayev and as media professionals face ever-graver dangers and threats to their professional and personal lives.

SIGNIFICANT DATES

- 1996 or 1997: Swiss bank account allegedly is opened by President Nursaltan Nazarbayev with US$1 billion in public funds from Kazakhstan's sale of oil shares to the Mobil Corporation.
- 1999: Nazarbayev is reelected president in an election where leading opposition candidate Akezhan Kazhegeldin is barred from participating.
- May 2000: Nazarbayev is placed on the annual list of the ''Ten worst enemies of the press'' published by the New York-based Committee to Protect Journalists.
- February 2001: Television journalist and commentator, Gulzhan Yergaliyeva, and her husband and son are targeted in a robbery and beatings after the journalist airs her program, ''Social Agreement,'' on which government policies are criticized.
- May 2002: A decapitated dog is found outside the offices of a leading independent newspaper, *Delovoe-Obozrenie Respublika* (*Respublika* Business Review) with a note attached stating, ''There will be no next time.'' Two days later, the head of the dog is found at the door of the paper's editor-in-chief, an open critic of the Nazarbayev regime who has suffered repeated harassment.
- May and June 2002: Journalist Lira Baisetova's daughter, Leila, disappears after her mother publishes a story on the Nazarbayev corruption scandal in the independent newspaper *SolDat.* The daughter later is reported to be in a government hospital, reportedly in a coma, and dies five days later.

- August 2002: Former governor of the Paladar region, Galymzhan Zhakiyanov, is convicted on charges of corruption and abuse of power and sentenced to 10 years in prison, amid international outcries and protests.

BIBLIOGRAPHY

Abyz News Links. ''Kazakhstan: Newspapers and News Sources,'' 2001. Available at http://www.abyznewslinks.com/kazak.htm.

Akiner, Shirin. *The Formation of Kazakh Identity: From Tribe to Nation-State.* London: The Royal Institute of International Affairs, Russian and CIS Programme, 1995.

Alaolmolki, Nozar. *Life After the Soviet Union: The Newly Independent Republics of the Transcaucasus and Central Asia.* Albany, NY: State University of New York Press, 2001.

Almaty Herald. ''About Us,'' 2001. Available at http://www.herald.kz.

BBC Monitoring. ''Country profile: Kazakhstan.'' The British Broadcasting Corporation, June 13, 2002. Available at http://news.bbc.co.uk.

BBC Monitoring. ''Journalist's daughter dies in Kazakhstan after Swiss corruption probe.'' The British Broadcasting Corporation, July 11, 2002.

Baker, Peter. ''New Repression in Kazakhstan: Journalists Targeted After President Implicated in Scandal.'' Washington Post Foreign Service, June 10, 2002, A12. Available at http://www.washingtonpost.com.

Bisenova, Alima. ''Nazarbayev Media Maneuver Indicative of More Conciliatory Stance towards Opposition.'' Eurasia Insight article, March 20, 2002.

Blua, Antoine. ''Kazakh Government Clamps Down on Independent Media.'' EurasiaNet Partner Post from Radio Free Europe/Radio Liberty, EurasiaNet Human Rights article, March 9, 2002.

Bureau of Democracy, Human Rights, and Labor, U.S. Department of State. ''Kazakhstan.'' *Country Reports on Human Rights Practices 2001.* Washington, DC: Bureau of Public Affairs, U.S. Department of State, March 4, 2002. Available at http://www.state.gov.

Central Intelligence Agency. ''Kazakhstan.'' *The World Factbook 2001.* Washington, DC: CIA. Available at http://www.odci.gov/cia/.

Committee to Protect Journalists. ''Kazakhstan: Two opposition newspapers attacked.'' CPJ 2002 news alert. New York, May 22, 2002. Available at http://www.cpj.org.

Dailey, Erika. ''The Internet a High-Tech Venue for Human Rights Violations in Central Asia and the Caucasus.'' EurasiaNet Human Rights article, February 16, 2000.

Dawisha, Karen, and Bruce Parrott, eds. *Conflict, cleavage, and change in Central Asia and the Caucasus,* Democratization and Authoritarianism in Postcommunist Societies: 4. Cambridge, UK, New York, NY, and Oakleigh, Melbourne, Australia: Cambridge University Press, 1997.

Dicks, Norman D. ''Statement of Hon. Norman D. Dicks of the U.S. House of Representatives, July 18, 2002.'' Washington, DC: Congressional Record, July 18, 2002.

Dombrovsky, Nicolay. ''Democratic Choice of Kazakhstan members anxious for ailing leader.'' *The Almaty Herald,* June 2002. Available at http://www.herald.kz/wn/1.htm.

Dunphy, Harry. ''State Department reveals concerns about legislation in Kazakhstan.'' The Associated Press, July 22, 2002.

Duvanov, Sergei. ''Kazakhstan's Security Services Attempt To Establish Control Over Internet.'' EurasiaNet Business and Economics article, May 11, 2000.

Eurasia Internet. ''Kazakhstan: Parliamentary Briefing.'' July 15, 2002. Available at http://eurasia.org.ru/.

EurasiaNet. ''Kazakhstan Becoming A Key To Russia's Central Asia Strategy.'' Eurasia Insight article, February 1, 2001.

George, Alexandra. *Journey into Kazakhstan: The True Face of the Nazarbayev Regime.* Lanham, MD, New York, NY, and Oxford, UK: University Press of America, Inc., 2001.

Human Rights Watch. ''Kazakhstan.'' *Human Rights Watch World Report 2002.* Available at http://www.hrw.org.

IAC Eurasia. ''21st Century Pirates: Companies Kaztelecom and Nursat.'' London: IAC EURASIA-Internet, March 5, 2002.

Integrated Regional Information Networks (IRIN). ''Independent press stifled in Kazakhstan.'' August 1, 2002. Available at http://www.dfn.org.

Interfax-Kazakhstan news agency. ''Kazakh journalist suspected of libelling president'' (report excerpt). Almaty, July 15, 2002. Transmitted by BBC Monitoring Service, July 16, 2002.

International Research and Exchanges Board (IREX). ''IREX Publishes Its First Media Sustainability Index,'' 2001. Available at http://www.irex.org.

IREX. ''Kazakhstan.'' *2001 Media Sustainability Index Report.* Available at http://www.irex.org/msi.

Internet Encyclopedia of Philosophy, The. ''Thomas Hobbes (1588-1679).'' 2001. Available at http://www.utm.edu/research/iep/h/hobbes.htm.

Kaiser, Robert G. ''Kazakhs' Season of Repression: President of Key U.S. Ally Puts Critics on Trial, in Jail.'' *The Washington Post,* Washington, DC, July 22, 2002, A01. Available at http://www.washingtonpost.com.

Kazakhstan Press Club. ''What is the Kazakhstan Press Club (KPC)?'' 2002. Available at http://www.pressclub.kz.

Kazhegeldin, Akezhan. *Kazakhstan: Meeting the Challenges Ahead.* Printed in the United States, 1998.

Kusainov, Aldar. ''Nazarbayev Presses against Political Opponents.'' EurasiaNet Human Rights article, April 2, 2002.

Kusainov, Aldar. ''Opposition in Kazakhstan Press Campaign To Dilute President's Authority.'' EurasiaNet Human Rights article, March 19, 2002.

Landau, Jacob M., and Barbara Kellner-Heinkele. *Politics of Language in the ex-Soviet Muslim States: Azerbaijan, Uzbekistan, Kazakhstan, Kyrgyzstan, Turkmenistan and Tajikistan.* Ann Arbor: The University of Michigan Press, 2001.

Meehan, Martin T. ''Erosion of Human Rights and Fundamental Freedoms in Kazakhstan.'' Statement of the Hon. Martin T. Meehan of the U.S. House of Representatives, May 23, 2002. Washington, DC: Congressional Record, May 24, 2002, page E918.

Naranjargal, Hashhuu. ''On the Road to Freedom?'' Brussels: International Federation of Journalists, November 1998. Available at http://www.ifj.org.

One World—Nations Online. ''Countries and Nations: Kazakhstan,'' 2002. Available at http://www.nationsonline.org/oneworld/kazakhstan.htm.

Paksoy, H.B., ed. *Central Asia Reader: The Rediscovery of History.* Armonk, NY and London: M.E. Sharpe, 1994.

Pannier, Bruce. ''Kazakhstan: Independent Media Feeling Under the Gun.'' Radio Free Europe/Radio Liberty, Prague, July 10, 2002. Available at http://www.rferl.org.

Pannier, Bruce. ''Kazakhstan: Opposition, Independent Media Pressured ahead of Ablyazov Trial.'' EurasiaNet Human Rights article, June 22, 2002.

Philadelphia Inquirer, The. ''Former Kazak governor gets 7 years.'' *The Philadelphia Inquirer,* Philadelphia, Pennsylvania: August 3, 2002, A-2.

Radio Free Europe/Radio Liberty. ''Kazakhstan: Journalist Sentenced to Jail Released on Amnesty.'' Almaty, July 4, 2002. Available at http://www.rferl.org.

Radio Free Europe/Radio Liberty. ''Kazakhstan: Press Freedom.'' Source: *Freedom House Survey of Press Freedom 1999.* Available at http://www.rferl.org.

Rashid, Ahmed. *The Resurgence of Central Asia: Islam or Nationalism?* Karachi: Oxford University Press, and London and New Jersey: Zed Books, 1994.

Reeker, Philip T. ''Harassment of Political Opposition and Independent Media in Kazakhstan.'' Statement by Philip T. Reeker, Deputy Spokesman, Office of the Spokesman, U.S. Department of State, 2002/449. May 23, 2002.

Reporters without Borders. ''Kazakhstan.'' *Annual Report 2002.* Paris, France: Reporters sans frontières, April 30, 2002. Available at http://www.rsf.org.

Republican People's Party of Kazakhstan (RPPK), Executive Committee. ''The law 'on political parties' delivers a precision strike at RPPK,'' July 24, 2002.

Richmond, Simon. ''Kazakstan.'' *Central Asia,* 2d ed. Melbourne, Australia: Lonely Planet Publications, April 2000.

Sayid, Karim. ''Journalists in Kazakhstan Press for More Freedom of Speech.'' Biweekly Briefing. *The Analyst,* November 21, 2001. Available at http://www.cacianalyst.org/November_21_2001/.

Serikbaeva, Klara, text, and Dragoljub Zamurovic, photographs. *Kazakhstan.* London: Flint River Press Ltd, 1995.

Svanberg, Ingvar, ed. *Contemporary Kazaks: Cultural and Social Perspectives.* New York: St. Martin's Press, 1999.

Transitions Online. ''Kazakh Scandals Throw Spotlight on Democracy.'' EurasiaNet Partner Post, Eurasia Insight article, April 28, 2002.

Transitions Online. ''Kazakhstan: New Government, New Ideas?'' EurasiaNet Partner Post, Eurasia Insight article, February 8, 2002.

Vassiliev, Alexei, ed. *Central Asia: Political and Economic Challenges in the Post-Soviet Era.* London: Saqi Books, 2001.

Voice of Democracy. ''Democracy Adieu.'' Washington, DC: Kazakhstan 21st Century Foundation, July 12, 2002.

Washington Post Company. ''Kazakhs' season of repression.'' *The Washington Post Online,* July 23, 2002.

Washington Post Editorial Board, The. ''New Allies, Old Formula.'' Washington, DC: *The Washington Post,* July 12, 2002.

Weinthal, Erika. *State Making and Environmental Cooperation: Linking Domestic and International Politics in Central Asia.* Cambridge, MA: The MIT Press, 2002.

World Bank Group, The. ''Country Brief: Kazakhstan,'' September 2001. Available at http://lnweb18.worldbank.org/ECAeca.nsf/.

world-newspapers.com. ''Kazakhstan News Sites,'' 2002. Available at http://www.world-newspapers.com/kazakhstan.html.

—Barbara A. Lakeberg Dridi, Ph.D.

KENYA

BASIC DATA

Official Country Name:	Republic of Kenya
Region (Map name):	Africa
Population:	30,765,916
Language(s):	English, Kiswahili
Literacy rate:	78.1%
Area:	582,650 sq km
GDP:	10,357 (US$ millions)
Number of Daily Newspapers:	4
Total Circulation:	250,000
Circulation per 1,000:	13
Number of Nondaily Newspapers:	10
Total Circulation:	110,000
Circulation per 1,000:	6
Total Newspaper Ad Receipts:	1,280 (Kenyan Shilling millions)
As % of All Ad Expenditures:	40.30
Number of Television Stations:	8
Number of Television Sets:	730,000
Television Sets per 1,000:	23.7
Number of Radio Stations:	38
Number of Radio Receivers:	3,070,000
Radio Receivers per 1,000:	99.8
Number of Individuals with Computers:	150,000
Computers per 1,000:	4.9
Number of Individuals with Internet Access:	200,000
Internet Access per 1,000:	6.5

BACKGROUND & GENERAL CHARACTERISTICS

Introduction Kenya's media is noteworthy given the continent's history that has had a devastating effect on the industry. At independence most African states had media that could have been developed into vibrant institutions (de Beer, Kasoma, Megwa & Steyn, 1995). In most cases, however, African nations engineered systematic schemes that decimated the industry as G.B.N. Ayittey (1992, 1999) chronicles. What sets Kenya apart is her ability to travel this tortured path behaving like every other African media bullying nation, yet maintain one of the few, by African standards, vibrant media outlets

But circumstances are changing. Kenya emerged as a state a little over a century ago, suffered colonialism, then experimented with hardly defined ideologies for a generation, but is now set to enter another epoch—since the constitution barred Danielarap Moi from standing for another electoral term when his last one ended in 2002. In Africa where government policies are subject to the whims of the leader, this new shift will be fundamental.

Kenya lies on Africa's eastern seaboard neighboring Somalia, Ethiopia, Sudan, Uganda, and Tanzania. With a population of about thirty million, the parchment of 45 tribal groupings, that Peter Mwaura (11) calls ''separate mini-states,'' came under British colonial control in 1884 following the Berlin conference to partition Africa (Maloba; Hachten). In 1963, the country gained independence from Britain under the Kenya African National Union (KANU) government. The then opposition party, Kenya African Democratic Union (KADU) maintained a token presence in parliament for a while, then dissolved to merge with KANU. KANU has been in power initially under the nation's founding father, Jomo Kenyatta, until his death in 1978, when Moi took power in a constitutional succession. He was president until 2002.

Both towards the end of Kenyatta's reign and especially during the Presidency of Moi, the executive branch progressively excluded competitors from the government. In the late 1980s people excluded from mainstream politics began to demand participation through alternative political parties. Kenya had, until 1982, been a *de facto* one party state, but in that year Parliament enacted a law making the country a *de jure* one party state. KANU assumed greater influence in setting national policies and at one time considered itself superior to parliament. By the end of the decade, civil unrest in the country forced the party, in 1990, to repeal the law criminalizing multi-partism. Today there is just a little under fifty political parties in the country. About ten of them are represented in parliament but there are only a handful of serious parliamentary parties.

While Kenyatta's reign from 1963 to 1978 had been characterized by less stringent control of the media, at least from the President himself, the press in Kenya, under Moi, was very different. This is not to say that there were no efforts to control the press under Kenyatta's regime. Those around the President, as P. Ochieng, Frank Barton and Gunilla Faringer demonstrate, frequently called newsrooms ostensibly on behalf of the President to demand the spiking of a story. But such control may have emanated from government functionaries than from, or through, the sanctioning of Kenyatta himself. Barton (86) tells of an encounter between Kenyatta and Kenya's then three leading Editors-in-Chief: Githii, Young, and Singh:

> The three men sat together in a room waiting for Kenyatta to call them in. When at last he did so he told them: "I have Uganda's President Amin here, and I am very angry with him because he has banned your newspapers. And when I say your newspapers, I mean Kenyan newspapers, and although they are privately owned, they are still Kenyan newspapers and if they are Kenyan newspapers they are my newspapers". . . "So,' he went on, "that means that if he has banned my newspapers, he has banned me—and I don't like it." (86)

George Githii tells of another encounter with Kenyatta. The *Nation* had been running editorials that contradicted the debate on detentions without trial then taking place in the country—which were supported by the executive branch. As a consequence a reporter with the paper was deported. Githii went to see Kenyatta on the matter. He writes:

> Personally, I found President Kenyatta very, very tolerant. Once my newspaper printed editorials against preventive detention, which angered some members of the executive. . . . Eventually, I made an appointment to see the President. His reaction was: "Those were your views; *now remember* to print ours." (63)

Moi, on the other hand, even while Vice President, had pesky relationships with the editors. Barton notes that:

> Vice-President Arap Moi began to make regular phone calls to Young complaining about things in the *Standard*. Young found that the servility which was needed in some African quarters was not the best line with the Vice-President, and so he replied to Moi with as much vigour as Moi used to him. Things often ended up virtually a shouting match between the two. (87)

Kenyatta had assured the media that "Kenya's press need have no fears regarding curtailment of its freedom. . ." (Faringer 60) as long as the media exercised responsibility. While the media in Kenya was then foreign owned they generally supported the government. Probably as a result the government saw no need of owning a medium of their own. But those around Kenyatta, Barton notes, were very keen on owning a newspaper (82). When Moi came to power his government purchased then *Nairobi Times* and christened it *Kenya Times*. It was managed by Kenya Times Media Trust (KTMT).

Print Media The print media can be divided into four sectors: the regular daily newspapers, the magazines, the regional newspapers, and the printed sheets that also seek to pass for newspapers in the urban centre streets.

Kenya has four daily national newspapers in English and one in Kiswahili all published in Nairobi with a combined daily circulation of almost 400,000. Relative to other nations, even those of Africa, the history of the press in Kenya is rather recent. Literacy started in Kenya following the arrival of Protestant missionaries nearly a century and a half ago (Church of the Province of Kenya). The missionaries embarked on teaching new converts how to read and write primarily so that the new converts could read biblical literature for themselves. The initial publications carried religious materials. To date, the church is still involved in some magazine publishing.

The oldest mass circulating newspaper is the *Standard* founded in 1902 by a Parsee migrant, A. M. Jeevanjee. The British settlers who came to Kenya had brought in Indians to work on the construction of the railway line from the coast to the interior to open up the countryside for settlement. Most of the Indians settled in Mombasa and engaged in commerce. *Standard* catered for these civil servants and business community. But two years later, Jeevanjee sold his interests to the partnership of Mayer and Anderson who renamed it *East African Standard* marking the beginnings of the European press. The *Standard* became the largest and most influential publication in colonial East Africa (Hachten). In the hands of Mayer and Anderson, it was a typical European people's paper concerned with the happenings in Britain and urging subservience to the settlers, a tune that for a long time remained the tone of other settler controlled media including *Mombasa Mail* and *Nairobi News* (Abuoga & Mutere, 1988; Maloba, 1992). Change in the *Standard* to identify with the aspirations of Africans was painstakingly slow even after independence. Over the years the *Standard* changed hands until Lonrho acquired it in 1967 (Faringer 35).

Lonrho had a lot of business interests in Africa and the paper served more of a safeguard of these interests. Barton (88) notes that for Lonrho "newspapers were only a means to an end, the end being the much more profitable business of packaging, breweries, transport, mining and other ventures in different parts of the Continent." Following Tiny Rowland's death in the mid-1990s and the reorganization at the Lonrho headquarters in London, it is understood that the *Standard* may once again have been sold, this time to a group of Kenyan political businessmen who then gained control also of the television channel KTN. It is not clear who owns this media establishment, whether Lonrho East Africa or these Kenyan businessmen. The *Standard* today, with a daily circulation of 54,000, has outlasted other competitors. At one time this media house published a Kiswahili paper called *Baraza*. Besides the *Standard* and KTN, this media house also operates Capital FM currently licensed to broadcast in Nairobi. The Capital FM launched operations in September 1996.

Prior to the founding of the *Nation* published by Nation Media Group (NMG) Kenya had a very vibrant nationalist press. Faringer (10) categorizes media in Kenya at independence into a three tier system with the European press at the top, the Indian in the middle, and African at the bottom. Although Rosalynde Ainslie (99) says that the press in Africa was a European creation, which is true, African nationalists adapted the press very much to their struggle. By 1952 Ainslie (109) reports that Kenya had nearly 50 newspapers. However, the speciality of these publications was not news as much as it was essays that agitated for freedom. Most of the contributors were nationalists, with no journalistic experience, who later became post independence leaders. All these papers folded up with the coming of independence.

The *Nation,* with a circulation of 184,000, is Kenya's most widely circulated newspaper today according to Lukalo and Wanyeki. It was first registered in 1959 by Michael Curtis and Charles Hayes (Ainslie 104) both newspapermen in London and Nairobi, respectively. The spiritual leader of the Ismaili community Aga Khan purchased the *Nation* a year later. The paper was the first to adopt a policy of Africanization (Hachten; Abuoga & Mutere; Faringer). Besides the English language *Nation* the NMG also publishes a Kiswahili edition *Taifa Leo. Taifa,* with a 35,000 daily circulation, is an abridged version of the *Nation. Taifa* does not have a separate group of reporters. It uses the same pool of reporters as the *Nation.* While the Aga Khan is still the majority shareholder in the NMG, the firm is currently traded at the Nairobi Stock Market.

Kenya's press has always been private and foreign owned. The NMG publishes the *Daily Nation* and *Taifa Leo* on week days, and *Sunday Nation* and *Taifa Jumapili* on Sunday. Both the Saturday and Sunday editions have pullouts including a children's magazine. On the other days of the week they carry special sections: education on Monday, business on Tuesday, society on Wednesday, real estate on Thursday, and entertainment on Friday. The *Nation*, although targeting the Kenyan market, is also distributed throughout the East African region. NMG also publishes the *EastAfrican*, a conservatively designed weekly newspaper focusing on economic news in East Africa. They also own Nation TV, and Nation FM Radio both which for the moment do not have a license to operate throughout the country. They were licensed in 1998 and went on air a year later, only to broadcast in the capital Nairobi as are other radio and television stations.

The *People*, owned by Kenneth Matiba, started as a weekly, but turned daily with a Sunday edition in December 1998. In 2002 it had a daily circulation of 60,000. Initially founded to serve as the voice of the opposition politics and to report materials that *Nation* and *Standard* feared to touch, the *People* has since landed on lean times. How long it survives may depend on the outcome of its appeal against multimillion-shilling judgments that courts have returned against the paper in libel cases. But other challenges the paper faces may relate partly to the difficulty in attracting sufficient advertising revenue and partly because it has never really shed its image as a partisan newspaper trumpeting the opposition point of view.

In 1983 KANU bought Hilary Ng'weno's *Nairobi Times* and named it *The Kenya Times* (Abuoga & Mutere; Ochieng). Ng'weno, the first African editor of the *Nation*, founded *Nairobi Times* intending it to be a quality afternoon paper. He was, at the same time, publishing *Weekly Review*, a quality news weekly that in the late 1970s used to be known for its incisive commentaries and two children's magazines. With diminishing revenue from advertising Ng'weno sold the *Times*. As *Kenya Times* the paper has suffered an identity crisis, and not without a cause, often seen as the mouthpiece of the ruling party and government. While there is no independent verification of its circulation, its internal figures say that it has a 50,000 daily circulation. The *Kenya Times* until recently was not a member of the ABC but even after joining the bureau seldom discloses their circulation figures. This makes it difficult to independently establish its market performance.

A.S. Kasoma De Beer et al notes that the *Kenya Times* ''often reflected official government policy'' (238). But a former Editor-in-chief of the paper, Philip Ochieng, submits that the ''only thing which stands in the way of The *Kenya Times* is its false identification in the public's mind with the ruling party, a fact which weighs very heavily upon it, many people claiming, despite absence of evidence, that it publishes only what the party and the government want it to publish'' (154). But Ochieng's is a lone voice. Hachten (24) notes that in a one party state a party newspaper is often indistinguishable from a government paper. Kenyan newspapers do not have any ideological leanings that would differentiate them. Even in the case of the *People* the distinguishing factor is not so much ideology as the stories they choose to print possibly with the intention that such stories may embarrass those in the government. These often expose some of the corruption deals government functionaries may be involved in. And not too infrequently these stories have landed the people in legal trouble. One government minister has been awarded a total of Ksh. 60 million in court rulings. If these fines are executed then some of the newspapers may be forced to close shop. Possibly because of this *Kenya Times* has remained at the bottom of the ladder in terms of circulation figures, advertising revenue, operating capital base, trained personnel and influence amongst the major newspapers in the country. KTMT also used to publish a Kiswahili edition *Kenya Leo. Kenya Leo* was in many ways similar to *Taifa Leo* carrying a summary of stories in the *Times*.

Besides the national daily newspapers there are several weekly publications circulating in the Coastal town of Mombassa. Because they only focus on issues of the coast their readership is confined to the coast and they are hardly of any national influence.

An emerging trend in the Kenya media scene is the publication of what, in Kenyan terminology, is called the gutter press but would be best described as ''now-you-see-them-now-you-don't'' press. The sheets are sold on news-stands and often on street corners for less than half the price of the daily newspapers. They are poorly written, poorly edited, poorly laid out, poorly printed, and contain poor pictures. Generally they have no fixed address, no known publisher, and tend to focus on rumour sometimes making very spectacular claims. They have no clear frequency, will appear out of the blue, make some spectacular claim that regards either sexual or corruption scandal involving a prominent personality, then disappear. They may only occasionally write on current affairs. These are likely to be found in most major towns and in mainly the major languages besides English and Kiswahili. It is said that sometimes they are sponsored by politicians who use them to launch a smear campaign against their opponents. But there is no way of proving this. These papers have drawn the anger of the Kenyan government in no small way. As a consequence the government is moving to pass a Statute Law (Miscellaneous Amendments) Bill 2001.

There has been a proliferation of other media in the country. The magazine industry has been vibrant not so much in its longevity as much as the frequency of magazines that have come up and gone under. *The Weekly Review*, probably the region's premier newsmagazine with a distinguished style of journalism during its lifespan was founded in 1975 (Abuoga & Mutere; Hachten). Published by Hilary Ng'weno's Stellascope, the weekly in the late 1970s and early 1980s had the best analytical and investigative journalism in the region (Faringer). As a consequence of its analytical reporting the government instructed firms in which the state had interest to cease advertising in the paper. This eroded the papers ability to survive economically. Later it toned down its critical reportage and, in 1998 before it folded up, had become a mere shadow of its former self. Ng'weno chose to retire the title and focus on his other business interests including television. *Financial Review* and *Economic Review*, both now defunct, made a major impact in business journalism in the country until the former was proscribed and the latter disappeared from the news-stands in the latter part of 1998. Today, however, there is no towering newsmagazine that would offer compelling reading like the *Weekly Review* did.

An interesting phenomenon is that in spite of the poor economy there has been quite an increase with diversity of media outlets in the 1990s that had not existed before. The changing political environment in the country with increased civil activism could be a contributing factor. Whereas previously the government could simply ban a publication with a single edict from the minister in charge, and this happened many times, the potential that such a ban would now be vigorously argued in court is much higher. A Nairobi businessman S. K. Macharia was, in the mid-1990s, through his firm Royal Media, licensed to operate Citizen radio and Television station. But he seems to have fallen foul of the government and his license to operate was temporarily withdrawn. He has got it back after a court petition, however, both his FM and TV stations are still off the air at the time of writing.

The church, through the National Council of Churches of Kenya (NCCK), at one time had its own publications *Target* and *Lengo* publishing in English and Kiswahili respectively. *Target*, especially in the later part of 1960s and early 1970s was very analytical, an approach that often put it at odds with the Kenyatta government, but more specifically with the then Attorney General who accused the paper of having sympathies for communism. The paper, following an internal reorganization, seemed to lose its objectives and funding and finally in 1997 folded up. NCCK's verbal exchanges with Kenyan government have a long history. When they published *Beyond* again they ran into trouble with the government, when in its analysis of the 1988 general elections, the paper said that the elections were a ''mockery of democracy'' (Faringer 66). The government proscribed the magazine and imprisoned its editor. Most of the other publications that the church has been identified with published social issues and not news.

ECONOMIC FRAMEWORK

De Beer et al (209) observe that ''Africa's economic situation has declined significantly in the three decades of post-colonialism.'' While Kenya's economy grew steadily in the years following independence, the 1990s have been truly economically lost decade for Kenya. According to the Central Bank of Kenya after the economy contracted in the early 1990s it grew by 5 percent in 1995, by 4.6 percent in 1996 and recorded only a 2.7 percent growth rate in 1997. This fell further in 1998 to 1.6 percent before recovering minimally to 2 percent in 1999. In 2001 the economy grew by 0.8 percent.

Investment in Kenya fell 10 times between 1978 and 1998 from nearly (Kenyan Shilling) (Ksh.) 250 billion to a low of just over Ksh. 24 billion. In 1993 the country attracted a mere $2 million in investment. Although in 1999 over $42 million was invested in Kenya that pales in comparison to $183 million and $222 million invested in neighbors Tanzania and Uganda, respectively—countries that a decade and a half earlier found it nearly impossible to attract a fraction of what was being invested in Kenya. Today, Uganda produces nearly all the products that, less than a decade ago, it imported from Kenya.

There are several factors that account for Kenya's poor economic performance. Since the late 1980s, the country's political leadership took to rather rambunctious exchanges with diplomats accredited to Nairobi and officials on international financial bodies. It is at times difficult to understand who enunciates government policy on international relations. When it is to their convenience KANU leaders compete in making uncoordinated, often bellicose, statements on all manner of policy. The result is a public relations disaster. The abortive military coup against the Moi government in 1982 did not help either. But rather than address the eventual public relations damage the government sat on its hands. In the early 1990s, the country was ravaged by internal ethnic clashes and increased insecurity countrywide impacting tourism and agricultural sectors, Kenya's cash cows, negatively. The agricultural sector has performed dismally from a combination of factors including falling prices in the world market and neglect from the government. With less money in the economy domestic savings fell from Ksh. 106 billion in 1996 to Ksh. 61 billion in 2001.

The single biggest factor that has affected the Kenyan economy is corruption. In the 1992 general election the ruling party is accused of having printed money to finance the elections thus worsening the rate of inflation by nearly 60 percent. The involvement of the state in the business enterprise has not been helpful. It has especially been hurtful to the extent that it has eroded investor confidence in the economy. Some of the specific actions have been the government's sponsorship of politically correct banks, which were founded and run without reference to the appropriate banking regulations. Some of these banks collapsed with people's savings.

As a consequence the volume of trade at the Nairobi Stock Exchange has fallen. Between 1999 and 2001 about 140 investors pulled out of Kenya, 106 shut down their investments, 15 sold their investment, and nearly 20 were put in receivership. Over the same period, while the number of job seekers entering the market increased by one and a half million people, the economy only generated 30,000 jobs. Still the economic sector has been impacted negatively by government corruption, by the wear

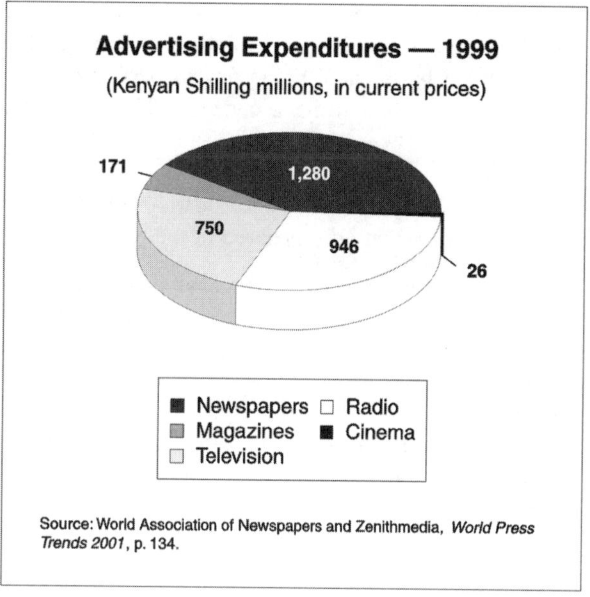

Source: World Association of Newspapers and Zenithmedia, *World Press Trends 2001*, p. 134.

and tear of infrastructure, and by the cessation of aid to the country by the donor community limiting the available hard currency for imports. The advertising revenue fell, in a country where over 60 percent of the economy is service based, the remaining 40 percent distributed between, industry, manufacturing, and agriculture.

More than 70 percent of Kenya's population 15 years and above is literate. Increasingly though more children are not completing primary education. Several factors account for this: high fees, inflation, lack of learning materials, labor disputes, poor pay for teachers and falling educational standards. The AIDS scourge is another factor. As many as 700 people die in a day as a consequence of AIDS related infections.

Kenya's is an oral society and the reading culture is yet to take hold. This is complicated by the high cost of books. The nation has a national library but it only operates in the eight provincial headquarters, some located more than a day's journey away. But they are also poorly equipped.

One out of every other Kenyan lives on just a dollar a day. With a newspaper costing about half a dollar few can afford it. Then with 45 different languages and papers published only in English and Kiswahili, language becomes yet another hindrance. The other challenge is infrastructure. The teledensity is only eight telephone lines per one thousand people (Lukalo and Wanyeki) although mobile phone systems are catching on fast. The road network is equally poor. Many of Kenya's far-flung districts are inaccessible at the best of times and impossible to reach during the rainy season. It is a near impossible task to distribute newspapers throughout the country. The postal system is another hindrance in the circulation of newspapers and magazines. Kenya does not have a home mail delivery system. This makes it difficult to develop a subscription base thus denying newspapers and magazines the opportunity to have a dependable readership and a pool of cash to draw from. The few subscribers often end up receiving their magazines long after the issue is already on the newsstands or may not receive it at all, the issue having disappeared in the postal system.

Kenya's newspaper publishers have their own distribution networks. The country has a paper-manufacturing firm, however, the Kenyan produced paper is expensive relative to imported paper. While the big advertisers may seek to influence the coverage of news that affect them the major influence on editorial policies usually come from politicians. Senior politicians seldom let pass an opportunity to cultivate a symbiotic clientele relationship with journalists especially those from their own ethnic communities. It is not uncommon for politicians to call journalists from their own tribe when they have a story to break.

Unions Most reporters in Kenya are members of the Kenya Union of Journalists. Reporters with the government associated media (*Kenya Times*, KBC, and the Kenya News Agency) are not allowed to join the union. The union has occasionally succeeded in negotiating better terms for its members. There are several organizations in the country that seek to bring journalists with common interests together. These would include the Kenya Education Writers' Association, the Kenya Professional Journalists' Association, the Association of Media Women in Kenya, the Network for the Defence of Independent Media in Africa, the Media Institute, the Association of Food and Agriculture Journalists, the Media Development Association, and the Kenya Correspondents' Association and Foreign Correspondence's Association. However, their effectiveness remains in question.

Journalism as a Career Most journalists tend to negotiate their pay on an individual basis. While the annual gross national per capita income in Kenya is around $360, most journalists earn well above that per month. However, there is quite a disparity between journalists employed by the government and those working in the private media. Those working in private media earn far better that of journalists in the government controlled media.

PRESS LAWS

Strictly speaking Kenya does not have a press law. Even what passes for press law is a carry over from the colonial governments' regulations in respect of press freedom. Critics have argued that the law, even if it was not good for the operation of the media, served the new rulers well by giving them a tool with which to control the media. What passes for media law in Kenya is a general section 79 of the constitution that states:

> Except with his own consent, no person shall be hindered in the enjoyment of his freedom of expression, that is to say, freedom to hold opinions without interference, freedom to receive ideas and information without interference, freedom to communicate ideas without interference (whether the communication be to the public generally or to any person or class of persons) and freedom from interference with his correspondence.

There is nothing in the constitution that refers explicitly to the media. The section that seems relevant to journalism would be the clause referring to ''freedom to communicate ideas without interference.'' However, such freedom could be withdrawn ''in the interests of defence, public safety, public order, public morality or public health'' according to Section 79 subsection (2) paragraph (a) of the constitution.

Parliament has just passed a Statutes Law (Miscellaneous Amendments) Bill 2001, which is awaiting presidential accent. President Moi has already signalled that he will sign the new bill into law. Briefly, the new bill will require any newspaper publisher to increase their bond from the present Ksh. 10,000 ($125) to Ksh. 1,000,000 ($12,500). A publisher who fails to comply with the requirement will be liable to one million shillings fine and up to three years jail term. A second time offender will be liable for up to five years' jail term and will be barred from printing or publishing a newspaper. The bill also criminalizes selling a book, a magazine or a newspaper whose publisher has not deposited the bond, has failed to file returns, or has failed to comply with the law in any form. The section of the law that the bill is amending is a carry over from the colonial laws, and it is interesting that the Kenyan legislators have chosen to make it more punitive that the colonial government did.

Kenya's judiciary is supposedly very independent. The President appoints all the senior members of the bench including the Chief Justice. They enjoy security of tenure and can only be relieved of their duties on incapacitation, on achieving retirement age, or on advice of a committee appointed to review a member's performance. However, Kenya's judiciary has lately come under severe criticism. Besides being seen as lacking independence from the executive, the general public tends to view the bench as corrupt. In a recent survey by Transparency International Kenyan Chapter, the public perceived the judiciary to be among the most corrupt institutions in the country, only a little better than the worst, the Police department. Members of the bench from the Commonwealth countries who recently visited Kenya told the judiciary to clean its act so as to restore public confidence.

CENSORSHIP

The Ministry of Information and Broadcasting is charged with the task of censoring the media. But in reality media in Kenya have to deal with different departments, among them the Attorney General's Office, where newspaper returns are filed, and the Ministry of Information, which accredits journalists. But it is the sleuths in the Office of the President who scare the press most. While publishers are required to register a publication and file returns with the AG, most publishers often ignore the requirement either out of ignorance or for whatever other reason, at no cost. The AG will only follow up an offending publisher for reasons that may not be strictly related to the offence. For example in 1989 the editor of the magazine *Beyond*, Bedan Mbugua had published the magazine for a while without filing the returns and nobody bothered him. However, it was only when the magazine ran a commentary on the 1988 elections and said that the elections had been rigged that the government charged it with the violation. Obviously there were other magazines that were not following the regulation but since they had not rubbed the government the wrong way, the government chose to look the other side.

Although the Ministry of Information and Broadcasting licences journalists, many journalists operate without accreditation. However, the sleuths in the Office of the President can arrest or detain, without providing any reason, any journalist who publishes a story that they do not fancy. The Ministry of Information censors films and movies to ensure that they are keeping within the cultural norms of the country. But Kenya's biggest censors are the editors themselves seeking to be careful to avoid problems (Ochieng).

Kenyan journalists have not been proactive in putting in place a media council that would serve to receive and arbitrate complaints against the media. In mid-2002, the formation of such a council is in place, but given the Bill awaiting the President's approval, this council may not find much to do.

It is hard for a Kenyan journalist to walk to any official and get information that may be useful. It is often a frustrating experience for a reporter at an accident scene whose need may only be to confirm the number of victims injured. But the police would not speak, constantly referring the inquirer to the headquarters. While at the moment there is a Police Spokesperson, other government departments do not have similar positions and as such it is not easy to get information from them.

STATE-PRESS RELATIONS

Kenya subscribes to the development communication paradigm based on the notion that given that the nation is a developing one then every agency in the country, the media included, should focus on development activity and not criticise those in power. Government officials would insist that the government welcomed positive and constructive criticism. But of course it is left to the government to define what is positive and constructive criticism. Over the years the freedom to criticize the Kenya government has greatly improved. In a recent cartoon published coinciding with the 2002 Oscar awards, the cartoonists gave several government functionaries awards. President Moi was awarded Best Director Award, but then the cartoonist changed his mind, crossed off the word Director and replaced it with Dictator with all the letters in upper case. The *Nation* carried the cartoon. It was quite a statement of how far the country has come.

The Kenyan government has not, however, always been tolerant. Publications that did not in the past please government functionaries were simply proscribed and sometimes this included past issues as was the case with *Beyond*, *Development Agenda*, and *Nairobi Law Monthly* Magazines. The *Nation* was, in 1989, suspended from covering Parliament, ostensibly for the claim of having been disloyal to the country.

Kenya has a news agency, Kenya News Agency (KNA), founded soon after independence and has, over the years, had offices and field reporters throughout the country. Graduates of government owned Kenya Institute of Mass Communication have almost automatically ended up in this outfit as field information offices where they effectively became the reporters in the field for the agency. Their assignment has been to file at least a story a week from their beat. This has provided an easy way to cover the entire country as newspapers and KBC could rely on KNA to cover the rural areas for them. But it has also served another purpose in that KNA reporters are trained to see news in the way that the government wants them to. So the stories are uniform. In the same way, for a long time, reporters from the newspapers were not allowed to cover presidential functions. Both the President and the Vice President have press units detailed to cover their activities. The press unit staffs have been KIMC trained and schooled in the government's way of presenting news. As Ochieng (43) puts it "We in the newspapers received only one interpretation of what the President was supposed to have said or done on any particular occasion: that of the Presidential Press Unit, relayed to us through the Kenya News Agency (KNA)."

ATTITUDE TOWARD FOREIGN MEDIA

Kenya requires foreigners to have work permits. This does apply to international correspondents working in the country. The government issues accreditation to foreign correspondents whether they are working for international media or local media houses. An international correspondent would have little difficulty working in Kenya as long as they do not begin reporting on Kenyan politics in a manner that displeases those in the executive. That means always praising the executive. Both foreign correspondents and foreign reporters working for local media have been deported whenever they have written stories that did not please the executive. For instance in 1987, the government barred journalists from Sweden and Norway from visiting Kenya after papers in their countries had carried critical stories on Kenya's human rights record. Three years' later international journalists covering civil unrest in Nairobi's Eastlands district were detained and, after release, received threatening calls most probably from state security (Faringer 67). This is a fate that has fallen even on Kenyan reporters working for international press. A Kenyan Reuters correspondent was once picked up and held for nearly 13 hours for having filed a story to the effect that members of the public had thrown stones at the presidential motorcade. Local media reporters had been scared to cover the incident when the Reuters story began to print in the newsrooms. Philip Ochieng recalls how several editors from the *Nation*, including himself (he was a sub-editor then), were once detained for having attributed a story to an ''anonymous'' source.

Due to government repression of coverage of local issues Kenyans have, during moments of sensitive developments in the country tended to rely mainly on international news outlets especially BBC which broadcasts both in English and Kiswahili. Other channels include radio Deutsch Welle, Radio South Africa and Voice of America. Often people, even in rural Kenya, would tune to BBC *Network Africa* and *Focus on Africa* news programs for breaking news. There is a general feeling that the only trustworthy news items from KBC radio and television stations are death and time announcements; everything else is KANU propaganda. Conversely, there is a tendency to believe that everything on Kenya in international media is true. This is a consequence of the government's own control of the media. It would not allow dissenting views to be carried in the local press, would not allow opposition activities to be covered over KBC and would not allow civil unrest to be covered in the local media even when people are aware that something is happening in a part of the country. A reporter who broke the news in a KTN report that the then Health Minister, Mwai Kibaki, had defected from KANU to launch an opposition party lost her job.

While government has had little control of electronic media it has at times sought to control international print media by confiscating the issues that are shipped to be sold in the country. These would be when such media have stories written on Kenya that the government did not like. All Kenyan media houses subscribe to international news agencies mainly Reuters, AFP, AP and Gemini. Prior to the end of the cold war Kenya was a member of the non-aligned nations and subscribed to news agencies associated with the movement. Through arrangements with the then USSR's TASS it made it possible to access a pool of stories from other third world capitals.

Television stations in Kenya also relay international news programs from western stations. KTN for example relays CNN international news while KBC sometimes relays BBC news bulletin and Deutsch Welle television news. However, when these stations carry a story critical of Kenya then the relays of that day may be left out. Kenya does not have restriction on foreign ownership of the local media. Until the launching of *Kenya Times* the print news media in Kenya were foreign owned with the exception of the Stellascope publications owned by Hilary Ng'weno. Even the *Kenya Times* at one time was co-owned by British media mogul Robert Maxwell.

BROADCAST MEDIA

For a long time the Kenya Broadcasting Corporation (KBC) dominated Kenya's electronic media scene. Formerly the Voice of Kenya, the station, founded in 1927, runs a nation-wide television service, two radio channels broadcasting throughout the country, in English and Kiswahili, and 16 regional ethnic language stations (Abuoga & Mutere 100). Today, it also has FM station covering the city and is planning another FM station for the Central Province, home to the populous Kikuyu community. KBCTV's news presentation format has always been predictable especially in the last decade and a half beginning with the 1982 attempted coup. The lead story has been on the president's activities including Sunday church attendance. The radio has not been any different.

Although KBC is publicly owned in the same format as the BBC with its budget drawn from the Treasury, the government exercises control in the appointment of management to ensure that KANU receives favorable coverage. KBC's television station broadcasts throughout the country in both English and Kiswahili. Its 7:00 p.m. and 9:00 p.m. news bulletins are in Kiswahili and English respectively. It has two parallel radio stations: the general and national service broadcasting in English and Kiswahili respectively. KBC, through its other regional stations, broadcasts in 12 other regional languages.

However, this reporting style has been nominally challenged by the launching of other stations. These stations, six in all, have not challenged KBC's dominance significantly. Other stations launched recently include KBC Channel II a subscriptions only cable network whose main shareholder is a South African firm, MultiChoice; Citizen TV, *Nation*, Family, and Stellavision. These stations, except the Nation TV, due to constitutional, financial and logistical limitations, have not been able to compete appropriately in news coverage. While Nation TV, with its financial muscle, could offer the biggest challenge to the two stations it is licensed to broadcast only in Nairobi. Its application for a nation-wide broadcast has been pending government approval for nearly a dozen years now. While it is not clear who the main shareholder in KTN is, it is understood that it is owned by the publishers of the *Standard* who are part of the Kenyan political establishment (De Beer et al 229).

Television has not made an impact in Kenya's countryside (Mytton; Ochieng; Bourgault; De Beer et al). To start with, the cost of a television set is prohibitive for rural people. A 21-inch colour television plus a VCR, for example, would cost at least five to 10 times the official average income of a primary school teacher. As a result television is a low priority for rural population that can ill afford it.

Owning television is complicated by another factor: the rural electrification programme. Most of the rural areas have little access to electricity. Rural folk run their televisions on batteries and solar systems. They can only receive KBC and even then the reception is often poor. Television is sadly still an elite media. Even in terms of content they tend to cover only urban events. Ochieng dismisses television as being of little communication significance to Kenyans for two reasons. He says, "Television, is out of reach for the majority of the people because it is urban-oriented and urban-based and because TV receivers are too expensive. Secondly, both television and radio deal with selected ideas which have to do with the strengthening of the security and integrity of the state, and not necessarily with social enlightenment as such" (108).

Most Kenyans have greater access to transistor radio receivers. Transistor radios today are cheap and available at nearly every street corner from hawkers. J.B. Abuoga and A.A. Mutere and G. Mytton suggest several reasons that make the medium popular. These include the low rate of functional literacy, the poor economy, the poor communication network, transport system and the people's lifestyles. Experience indicates that the largest single groups of media consumers in the rural are the teachers and agricultural extension workers (Wilcox; Quist). They are comparatively well educated, have a regular monthly income, are more interested in current affairs and are often opinion leaders. However, most schools are located in far-flung regions that are inaccessible so that this one single large market does not have an opportunity to buy newspapers. The alternative is mainly the radio.

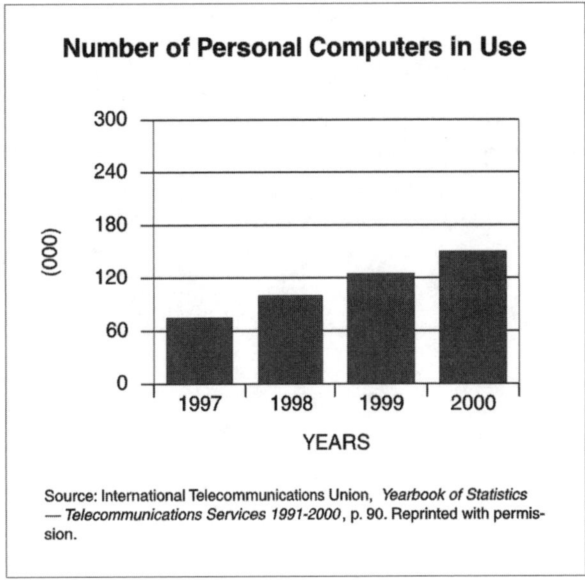

Source: International Telecommunications Union, *Yearbook of Statistics — Telecommunications Services 1991-2000*, p. 90. Reprinted with permission.

The government knows only too well the strength of this medium and used it for political expediency. The government is familiar with the daunting task anybody who wanted to reach the entire country has. Only radio can reach all these people. Unconcerned with the language and distance barrier of the newspapers, the radio reaches the Maasai in his manyatta, the Somali herdsman in the outback in the north and the expatriate in his air-conditioned Nairobi home, all at once. To monopolize access to these people the government controls the radio. The initial FM radio stations to be licensed were allowed to broadcast only in the capital, Nairobi.

Overall there are at least six radio stations licensed to operate only within Nairobi. Apart from this there is the Family FM radio and Television station in Nairobi, but this is a religious broadcast relaying primarily religious content. Another station worth note is Kameme in Central Province that broadcasts in Kikuyu. However, its broadcast does not include news. Recently in an answer to a question in Parliament the Information Minister said that over 30 licenses for FM stations had been issued. But generally they would be given to politically correct individuals some of who would be holding them only for commercial speculative gain.

ELECTRONIC NEWS MEDIA

All the major news houses are available on the Internet. The *Nation* newspapers, the *Standard* newspapers, and KBC web pages are updated daily. The *Nation* website has searchable back editions going to 2000 while the *Standard* has only up to a week. They are, however, not indexed. The *EastAfrican* is also available online. Although *Kenya Times* is online it is seldom current. Both

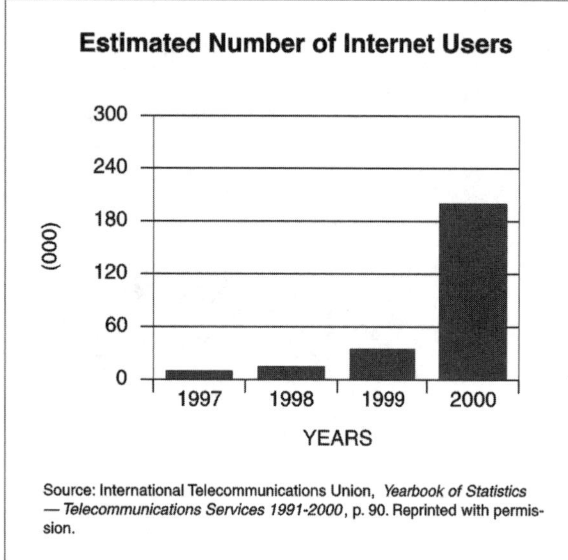

Source: International Telecommunications Union, *Yearbook of Statistics — Telecommunications Services 1991-2000*, p. 90. Reprinted with permission.

the *Nation* and KBC websites are much easier to navigate. The KTN website had not been updated for the first six months of 2002.

EDUCATION & TRAINING

There has been, in the last couple of years, an increase in the number of universities starting departments of communication and journalism education. Besides the School of Journalism at the University of Nairobi, that has been in existence for the last two decades, other public universities such as Kenyatta, Jomo Kenyatta University of Agriculture and Technology, Moi, and Maseno all have either courses or departments of communication or journalism being developed. The same is true for private universities. Probably the oldest department in the private universities is at Daystar University, which began, in the late 1970s, offering graduate degrees in communication theory. The department expanded beginning in 1984 when it launched undergraduate communication courses with tracks in print and electronic media, public relations, and communication theory. But now there are departments of communication or journalism at United States International University-Nairobi and at the Nazarene University. There are also smaller colleges and institutes that offer training in media and other associated areas of interest. For example there is a school recently launched in Kenya in memory of the late award-winning photographer Mohamed Amin in Nairobi specialising in television journalism.

The Kenya Institute of Mass Communication for a long time was the main training institution for Kenyan journalists. It offers nine to 12 month courses in print and electronic media leading to certificates and diplomas in journalism. Philip Ochieng, one of Kenya's brightest journalists, complains of the calibre of Kenyan journalists lamenting their training. While Ochieng's comments may be true as far as they apply to the period he was writing about, a case can be made that the situation is greatly changing so much so that the problem now is getting employment for many Kenyans trained in journalism and mass media.

While the number of the institutions and courses being offered continue to rise, the same can not be said of the faculty, the literature, and academic journals. In many instances it is difficult to find teachers for the courses that are being offered leave alone finding people who are going to conduct research in mass media.

SUMMARY

Moi has towered Kenya's political scene since the late 1970s and greatly impacted the direction the media took both through his relations with the media and the policies that his government put in place. His legacy will continue to influence the direction the media take. During Moi's presidency the executive reigned supreme, but there is just a glimmer of hope that some of the powers the office enjoyed will be trimmed in the new government. However since some of those poised to take over are a carry on from Moi's system, the question looms regarding what direction the system will take. Kenya's media has, through the last decade, developed muscles that may come useful in a new dispensation. The personnel are at the moment more educated that at any other time. The civil society has greatly become more active, more critical of the judiciary, and more demanding of the legislative.

BIBLIOGRAPHY

Abuoga, J. B. and Mutere, A. A. *The history of the press in Kenya*. Nairobi: ACCE, 1988.

Ainslie, Rosalynde. *The Press in Africa: Communications Past and Present*. London: Victor Gollancz Ltd., 1966.

Ayittey, G.B.N. *Africa Betrayed*. New York: St. Martin's Press, 1992.

———. *Africa in Chaos*. New York: St. Martin's Press, 1999.

Barton, Frank. *The Press of Africa: Persecution and Perseverance*. New York: Africana Publishing Company, 1979.

Bourgault, L. M. *Mass media in Sub-Saharan Africa*. Bloomington, Indiana: Indiana University Press, 1995.

Boyce, G. ''The Fourth Estate: The Reappraisal of a concept.'' In George Boyce, James Curran and Pauline Wingate (Eds.) *Newspaper History from the 17th Century to the Present Day*. London: Sage, 1978.

Church of the Province of Kenya. *Rabai to Mumias*. Nairobi: Uzima, 1994.

De Beer, A. S. Kasoma, F.P. Megwa, and E. Steyn. ''Sub-Saharan Africa''. In John C. Merrill (Ed). *Global journalism: Survey of international communication* 3rd Ed. New York: Longman, 1995.

Faringer, Gunilla L. *Press Freedom in Africa*. New York: Praeger, 1991.

Githii, George. ''Press Freedom in Kenya.'' In Olav Stokke (Ed.) *Reporting Africa*. New York: African Publishing Corporation, 1971.

Hachten, W. *Muffled drums: The news media in Africa*. Ames: Iowa State University Press, 1971.

Hachten W. ''African censorship and American correspondents''. In Beverly G. Hawk (Ed.) *Africa's media image*. New York: Praeger, 1992.

Maloba, W. ''The media and Mau Mau: Kenyan nationalism and colonial propaganda''. In Beverly G. Hawk (Ed.) *Africa's media image*. New York: Praeger, 1992.

Mwaura, Peter. *Communication Policies in Kenya*. Paris: UNESCO, 1980.

Mytton, G. *Mass Communication in Africa*. London: Edward Anorld, 1983.

Karimi, J. and Ochieng, P. *The Kenyatta Succession*. Nairobi: Transafrica Book Distributors, 1980.

Ochieng, P. *I Accuse the Press: An insider's view of the media and politics in Africa*. Nairobi: Initiatives Publishers, 1992.

Quist, M. *Step Magazine Readership Survey or Are We Really in Step?* Nairobi: Daystar Communications, 1982.

Wilcox, D. *Mass media in Black Africa*. New York: Frederick Praeger, 1975.

—Levi Obonyo

KIRIBATI

BASIC DATA

Official Country Name:	Kiribati
Region (Map name):	Oceania
Population:	91,985
Language(s):	English, Gilbertese
Literacy rate:	N/A

Kiribati (pronounced ''Kiribass'') is one of the smallest countries in the world. Although it includes some 33 atolls—only twenty of which are inhabited—its total land area is only 264 square miles. The island group, located in Oceania between Australia and Hawaii, was once called the Gilbert Islands and was controlled by Britain. It achieved self-rule in 1971 and, when it declared independence in 1979, it did so under its new name. Kiribati is governed by a President, and the legislative branch consists of a 41-seat unicameral House of Assembly, or *Maneaba Ni Maungatabu.* The approximate population is 92,000. Natural resources are scarce in Kiribati, as is skilled labor. The most important exports are copra (the white meat of the coconut) and fish. Financial aid from Britain and Japan also supplement the gross national product.

Freedom of speech and of the press is generally respected. There are two main papers in Kiribati, and both are weekly. *Te Uekera* is a government-owned paper managed and owned by a board that is overseen by a government minister. Its approximate circulation is 1,800. Its competition comes from the country's independent newspaper, *The Kiribati Newstar,* which debuted in May 2000. It appears on Friday and publishes in the native language with some English content. It is available online. The Catholic Church publishes a monthly newspaper called *Te Itoi ni Kiribati,* and the Protestant Church produces a weekly newspaper called *Kaotan te Ota,* but publication is irregular. There are two radio stations, one AM and one FM, for 17,000 radios. There is one television station broadcasting to 1,000 televisions, and TSKL is the island's sole Internet service provider.

BIBLIOGRAPHY

''Country Profile.'' *Worldinformation.com,* 2002. Available from http://www.worldinformation.com.

''Country Report—Kiribati.'' *Australian Press Council,* 2002. Available from http://www.presscouncil.org.

''Kiribati.'' *CIA World Fact Book,* 2001. Available from http://www.cia.gov.

''Political Rights and Civil Liberties.'' *Freedom House,* 2000. Available from http://www.freedomhouse.org.

—Jenny B. Davis

KUWAIT

BASIC DATA

Official Country Name:	State of Kuwait

Region (Map name):	Middle East
Population:	2,041,961
Language(s):	Arabic, English
Literacy rate:	78.6%
Area:	17,820 sq km
GDP:	37,783 (US$ millions)
Number of Television Stations:	13
Number of Television Sets:	875,000
Television Sets per 1,000:	428.5
Number of Satellite Subscribers:	498,000
Satellite Subscribers per 1,000:	243.9
Number of Radio Stations:	18
Number of Radio Receivers:	1,175,000
Radio Receivers per 1,000:	575.4
Number of Individuals with Computers:	250,000
Computers per 1,000:	122.4
Number of Individuals with Internet Access:	150,000
Internet Access per 1,000:	73.5

BACKGROUND & GENERAL CHARACTERISTICS

Kuwait is a Middle Eastern country strategically bordered on the east by the Persian Gulf and precariously sandwiched between Iraq on the north and west, and Saudi Arabia on the south and west. Hosting a land area of 6,877 square miles, a desert-like climate, and a population of 2,500,000 Kuwait has provided a theater for ongoing territorial disputes, disputes which have impacted the free flow of information in that and surrounding countries.

Although English is widely spoken, the official language of Kuwait is Arabic. The population is 85 percent Muslim, with Protestant and Catholic Christianity, Hindu, Parsi and other religions combined accounting for the remaining 15 percent. The literacy rate for Kuwaitis is approximately 79 percent.

History Kuwait is classified as a constitutional monarchy and has been a fully independent country since June 19, 1961. No political parties are allowed and voting is restricted to qualifying Kuwaiti males over age 21. Although the state of Kuwait's civil legal system is significantly related to Islamic law, compulsory Islamic law for criminal justice has not been formally adopted.

Significant historical developmental periods of Kuwait demonstrate a diversity of political, financial, ethnic and religious influences. These eras include: early civilizations when the land now known as Kuwait was part of the B.C., West Asian Sumer Kingdom; the middle 18th century settlement by the Utub, an Arab group splintered from the Anizah tribe; 1756 when Sheikh Sabah bin Jaber I was chosen ruler; 1899 when Britain joined with Kuwait to help protect Kuwait's sovereignty which was threatened by Turkey; and 1961 which marked Kuwait's separation from Britain, although Britain continued to provide protection when Kuwait was threatened by Iraq. During the 1980s, Kuwait supported Iraq in its conflict with Iran, but Iraqi-Kuwaiti relations worsened and Iraq invaded Kuwait on August 2, 1990. Iraq's invasion impacted almost all aspects of Kuwaiti cultural, physical and political lifestyles, resulting in temporary media shut downs. After Iraq's occupation ended, the Kuwaiti government took steps to restore law and order and to move toward a population consisting of a majority of Kuwaitis, to be in part achieved by reducing the number of foreign persons allowed in Kuwait. In 2002, Kuwaitis constituted about 35 percent of the population. Issues of national security, immigration restrictions, and the influence of Islam in Kuwait, are among factors impacting the rebuilding of the modern press in Kuwait.

Newspapers and Other Publications Modern Kuwait's print media had its beginning in the 1920s, expanding in the 1960s (Kamaliour & Mowlana) with the emergence of a number of publications. Most newspapers in Kuwait are individually owned, allowing for a wide range of expressions of opinion, but are limited to some degree in that speaking against the government or Islam is not allowed. Independent newspapers were somewhat challenged after Iraq's invasion, when the Kuwaiti government became involved in publishing news. However, government newspapers were discontinued because they could not compete with privately owned publications.

Arabic daily newspapers from Kuwait include: *Al-Rai Ala-Am* (*Public Opinion*) which started publication in 1961 and hosted a 2001 circulation of about 87,000; *Al-Seyassah* (*Policy*), founded in 1965, with a circulation of 70,000; and *Al-Qabas* (*Starbrand*), a somewhat liberal publication founded in 1972. Before the Iraqi invasion in 1990, *Al-Qabas* reportedly had a circulation of about 120,000, compared to its 2001 circulation of 79,000. In 2002, its online Arabic *Al-Qabas* site reported 30,000 weekly hits.

Another Arabic newspaper, *Al-Watan* (*The Homeland*), started publication in 1974 and had a 2001 circulation of 60,000. *Al-Anbas* (*The News*) was founded in 1976 and had a 2001 circulation of about 107,000. Other newspapers include *Al Dostoor*, a general interest publication; and *Al Iklisadia*, a business publication.

Newspapers published in English include the *Kuwait Times*, founded in 1961, with a 2001 circulation of 28,000; *Kuwait Today*; and the *Arab Times*, founded in 1977 reporting a circulation of 42,000. *The Washington Post* is also received in Kuwait.

Weekly publications include *Al-Mousaher*, an economic publication; *Murat al-Umma* (*Mirror of the Nations*) with a circulation of 80,000; and *Al Yaqza* (*The Awakening*), a general and political publication founded in 1966, reporting in 2001 a circulation of 91,000. *Al-Mujtamaa* is a weekly Islamic magazine.

Other magazines include *Al-Arabia* (*Pioneer*), founded in 1958 reporting in 1994 a circulation of 360,000. The widely read educational journal which was halted because of the Iraqi invasion but restarted publication in 1991. Other publications include general interest magazines *Al Forgan*, *Anhaar* and *Mishkat Al Rai*; *Al-Nahda, Al-Moukhtalef*, *Ousraty*, *Annas*, *Hayatania*, *Al-Majales*, and *Al-Balagh*, a general and Islamic publication with a 2002 circulation of 29,000.

Other sources of information in Kuwait include the *State of Kuwait Official Gazette*, a Sunday weekly journal published since 1954 by the Ministry of Information (2002 circulation of 5,000), and *Kuwait Magazine*, published monthly since 1961. The Ministry of Defense publishes a monthly magazine, *Homat Alwatan*.

Economic Framework

The economy of Kuwait has moved from a poor nomadic lifestyle resulting from the desert-like condition of its land, to a somewhat thriving sea port based on its location on the Persian Gulf, to a somewhat diminished level after WWII, to one of the wealthiest nations in the world based on the discovery of oil in the 1930s. According to F.E. Kazan (Kamaliour & Mowlana), Oil is the prime mover that led to the economic prosperity of Kuwaiti society, attracted a diversified population to Kuwait, led to the increase in the literacy and urbanization rates, and finally led to progress in the levels of socioeconomic and political development. All these factors, in turn, ushered in the progress of Kuwaiti mass media. Further, by maintaining its ties with the East and with the West, Kuwait has been able to provide economic security and a high standard of living for its citizens.

Press Laws and Censorship

As a primary regulator of the media, the 1991 Kuwaiti constitution guaranteed freedom of press, but only within the limits of the law. Although freedom of the press is a concept associated with Kuwait, and in spite of the fact that the Kuwait News Agency (KUNA) is considered to be independent, certain agency structures and national laws limit free exercise. For instance, KUNA as a part of the Ministry of Information has historically controlled Radio Kuwait and the Kuwait Television stations.

In 1956 the first press law was passed. Then the 1961 Press and Publishing Law provided for such sanctions as fines and imprisonment for publishing materials critical of the government, rulers, other Arab states, allies of Kuwait or religious figures.

Another press law passed in 1976 provided for suspending the licenses of media sources who broke press laws, but later these restrictions were softened and the media began to monitor itself to some degree. However, beginning in 1986, the Ministry of Information required all publications to submit copy to the ministry in advance for approval and forbade criticism of the ruler and his family, other Arab leaders, and Islam, as well as the acceptance of foreign funding.

Censorship

Kuwaiti press laws have been enforced in a number of cases. For instance, the *World Press Freedom Review* reported an incident in which a publication which might be viewed as lending support to Iraq was banned from Kuwait; an incident in which a university professor was sentenced to prison for allegedly defaming Islam and others were fined for allegedly writing immoral poetry (2000); incidents in which a television station was banned for insulting the Emir, an offense against the Kuwaiti Constitution (1999); and an incident in which the editor-in-chief of a leading daily newspaper was sentenced to prison for allegedly insulting the Divine Being (1998).

State-Press Relations

Private media enjoys a great deal of freedom in Kuwait, yet is subject to governmental sanctions for violating news and publication laws. The press is economically dependent on state financial subsidies.

Attitude Toward Foreign Media

Kuwait depends to a large degree on its Western allies for defense. For instance, in 2002, The Associated Press reported that the United States planned to sell Kuwait missiles to help Kuwait protect itself against hostile neighbors. Such factors as Kuwait's continuing ties with both the East and the West present a sometime complex and incongruent situation for the media. Although foreign media is welcome in Kuwait, evidenced by Broadcasts from the BBC World Service, Voice of America, All India Radio and Pakistan Radio being received in Kuwait, sanctions for violation of Kuwait's publication laws apply. Kuwait extends accreditation to foreign correspondents, but there are instances in which publications and journalists have been banned from entering Kuwait.

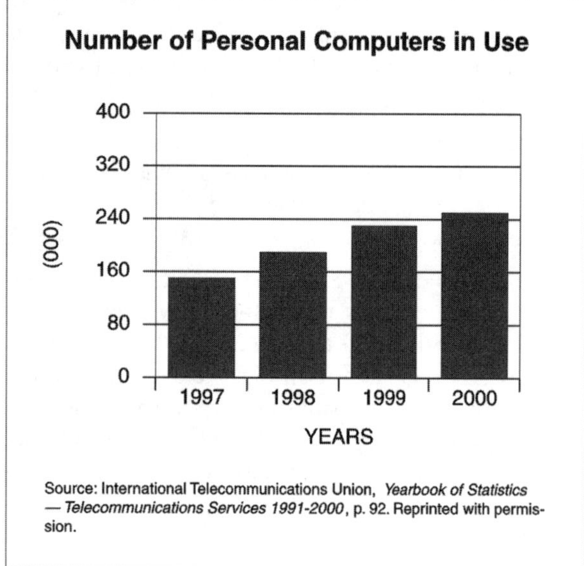

Source: International Telecommunications Union, *Yearbook of Statistics — Telecommunications Services 1991-2000*, p. 92. Reprinted with permission.

Foreign bureaus include the Middle East News Agency, Egypt; New China News Agency; AFP, France; and the Associated Press, USA. Russia, Turkey, Libya and Germany are also represented. Online foreign news sources include *Al Bawaba* (Arabic/English) and *Arabia* (Arabic/English), as well as English sites: *Kuwait Daily*, *Middle East News Online*, *Moreover*, *One World*, the *Washington Post*, and *Zawya*.

News Agencies and Associations

The Kuwait News Agency (KUNA) was established in 1976 as an independent institution, but functions as an arm of the Ministry of Information. The agency conducts research and provides information on general and special political and socioeconomic issues. In 1986, KUNA provided about 50,000 information releases, and was to become the leading Middle Eastern news agency. There is also an independent Kuwait Journalist Association.

Broadcast Media

The broadcast media in Kuwait does not have a history of independence. The Ministry of Information in Kuwait Aowns, finances, controls and manages radio and television media in Kuwait (Kamaliour & Mowlana).

Radio The first radio broadcasts in Kuwait originated in 1951, and after Kuwait's liberation from Britain in 1961, the radio medium grew. After the Iraqi invasion in 1990, Kuwait radio continued to broadcast from other countries in efforts to encourage Kuwaiti citizens to remain loyal and reject Iraq's occupation of their country.

In 2002, Kuwaiti radio stations provide public programs 24 hours a day. There are various Arabic radio stations such as Radio Kuwait which broadcasts news, music and talk radio; a Super Station FM 99.7 which began in 1994; Radio Kuwait (English); two English FM stations; plus the American Armed Forces Radio.

Television Kuwaiti television originally started in 1957 as a private enterprise, but after Kuwait gained its independence from Britain, control was given to the government. Iraq destroyed television facilities during the 1990 invasion, but after Iraqi occupation ended, Kuwait's links with the West again proved beneficial as it received financial support in rebuilding efforts. In 1998, efforts were made within Kuwait to allow television to be a private industry by the year 2000, but these efforts were subject to governmental approval.

There are 13 Kuwait Television broadcast stations, plus several satellite channels. Programs in Arabic and English are provided, including a sports station and the Kuwait Satellite Channel which started transmission in 1992.

Electronic News Media

In addition to television and radio, the development of movies and VCRs provided additional avenues for electronically communicating information. However, the introduction of the Internet provided unprecedented opportunities for freedom of the press throughout the world. In 2000, there were three Internet service providers and some 100,000 users in Kuwait.

The Palestinian/Israeli conflict has impacted the media in the Middle East, resulting in news releases which demonstrate the overlapping connections between the Kuwaiti government, the West, other Arab states and the press. For instance, in 2002, KUNA reported that Kuwaiti officials opposed using oil as a weapon to force Israel to withdraw from Palestinian territories.

Electronic News Media

The State of Kuwait provides information and images about history and culture. An English window for *KuwaitOnline* provides information on a variety of online resources. These include: *Al-Forgan Magazine*, the first online Islamic Magazine at the State of Kuwait; *Online First Aid*; *Al-Qadisia Club*, an online sports club; and an interactive site *KOL Corner* for expressions of opinion.

Education & Training

The University of Kuwait offers a Bachelor of Arts degree in the Department of Mass Communication. In addition, a graduate program in mass media was being prepared for addition to the curriculum. Students are taught how to translate news from Arabic to English and English to Arabic, and an internship program is required. A state of the arts computer lab is equipped for teaching electronic publishing, image processing and multimedia applications using Macintosh and Pentium formats. Undergraduate courses in advertising, radio, television, public relations and propaganda, research methodology, theory, Kuwaiti mass media history, ethics, law, and mass communication technology are taught. The Media Law emphasis provides information regarding Kuwaiti governmental regulation of print and broadcast media, including sanctions for violating publication laws.

SUMMARY

Just as the country of Kuwait is geographically triangularly sandwiched between Iraq, Saudia Arabia and the freedom of the sea, Kuwaiti mass media seems to be sociologically triangularly sandwiched between Kuwait's political and economic loyalty to its citizens; its religious loyalty to Islam and other Arab nations; and its dedication to the concept of freedom of speech fundamental to democracy and Kuwait's ties with the West. In 2002, the ongoing tension between these competing ideological perspectives required Kuwaiti media to perform unique three ring, journalistic balancing acts.

BIBLIOGRAPHY

The American School of Kuwait. *Life in Kuwait,* 2002. Available from http://www.ask.edu.kw/.

Amman, J. *Latest Internet content and technology group in the middle east formed by Arab, American and European investors,* 2000. Available from http://www.middleeastevents.com/.

ArabNet. *Kuwait Culture, Media*, 2002. Available from http://www.arab.net/.

Central Intelligence Agency. *The World Fact Book 2001*, Directorate of Intelligence, 2002. Available from http://www.odci.gov/cia/.

Kamalipour, V.R., and H. Mowlana, eds. *Mass Media in the Middle East: A comprehensive handbook by F.E. Kazan.* Westport, CT: Greenword Press, 1994.

Kuwait Information Office. *Kuwait at a Glance,* 2002. Available from http://www.kuwait-info.org.

''News and Media from Kuwait,'' 2002. Available from http://www.kuwaitmission.com.

A Review of the Events of 2001: Facts in brief on Middle Eastern countries. Chicago: World Book, Inc, 2002.

World Press Freedom Review, 2002. Available from http://www.freemedia.at/wpfr/kuwait.html.

—Duffy Wilks

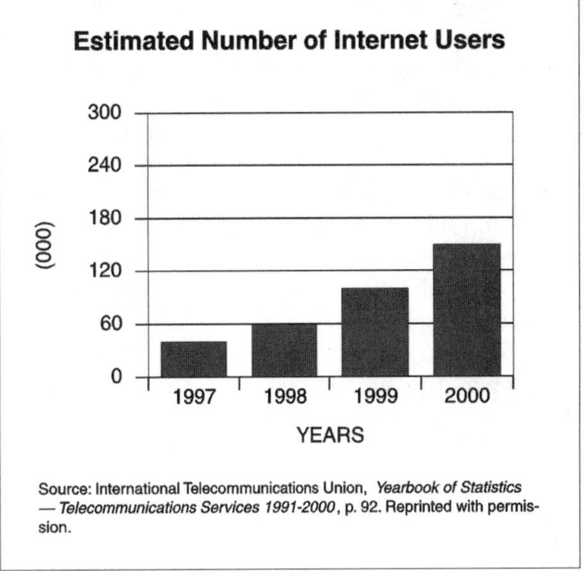

Source: International Telecommunications Union, *Yearbook of Statistics — Telecommunications Services 1991-2000*, p. 92. Reprinted with permission.

KYRGYZSTAN

BASIC DATA

Official Country Name:	Kyrgyz Republic
Region (Map name):	East & South Asia
Population:	4,753,003
Language(s):	Kirghiz, Russian
Literacy rate:	97.0%
Area:	198,500 sq km
GDP:	1,304 (US$ millions)
Number of Television Sets:	210,000
Television Sets per 1,000:	44.2
Number of Radio Stations:	28
Number of Radio Receivers:	520,000
Radio Receivers per 1,000:	109.4
Number of Individuals with Internet Access:	51,600
Internet Access per 1,000:	10.9

BACKGROUND & GENERAL CHARACTERISTICS

Kyrgyzstan was one of 15 constituent republics of the former Soviet Union that upon the devolution of the

Soviet Union became a separate nation. It declared its independence in 1992 and since that time has been pursuing policies aimed at democratic government, decollectivization, privatization, and the change to a market economy. The policies enacted since independence and the relative success of these policies in achieving these goals have been cause for economists and political scientists to judge that the transition in Kyrgyzstan has been among the most successful of all the former republics. However, it is generally agreed that the transition to and relationship with a free and independent media has been the least successful of all its policies. In addition, since the start of the new millennium an even more adversarial relationship with the government has become apparent, to the extent that media relations are now seen by external observers as the most serious impediment to true progress, and indeed is cause for suggesting that many of the gains of the first 10 years of independence are now being seriously eroded. Some observers have suggested that the need for the United States to have a significant presence in the Muslim world following the terrorist attacks of September 11, 2001, and in particular the predominantly Muslim Kyrgyzstan, has muted U.S. criticism of Kyrgyzstan government policies toward the media and perhaps encouraged Kyrgyz government attacks on the fledgling independent media.

The legacy of the 70 years of Soviet influence has created a highly educated, highly literate population. In a nation of 4.7 million people there is almost 100 percent literacy (99 percent males, 96 percent females). Most of the population is concentrated in the two large cities of Bishkek (the capital) and Osh, but a significant part of the population resides in smaller urban centers: 38 percent of the population is urban and 62 percent rural. Most of the urban centers have newspapers, and all have television coverage. In the rural areas radio and TV coverage is spotty, in large part due to the mountainous terrain, for much of Kyrgyzstan lies in the northern ranges of the Himalayas. Within the country there are significant ethnic concentrations geographically. The north and rural interior mountain valleys are predominantly populated by ethnic Kyrgyz with concentrations of ethnic Russians in the cities and larger communities. In the south, ethnic Uzbeks are a significant majority, and the media reflect their differing cultural attributes, particularly their Uzbek language. Small concentrations of ethnic Germans, Tatars, Jews, Tadjiks, who are often refugees from war in Afghanistan and Tadkjikistan, are present but are served by the mass media. All ethnic groups except Russians, Germans, and Jews are Muslim.

It is difficult to assess the quality of journalism in Kyrgyzstan for the turmoil over the past 10 years since independence has meant that there has been little history of a consistent regular press, and the turmoil caused by the constant animosity between the press and the government has provided little impartial basis on which to judge. Local westerners rate it a 3 out of 10 and getting worse as a result of the terrible economy, making it difficult for the media outlets to fund quality coverage. Moreover there is a complete lack of historical tradition in journalism, for up to 1990 the Communist government rigidly controlled the press in content and orientation. What can be said was that upon the fall of the Soviet Union there was an immediate and vociferous expression of dissatisfaction that was given voice by the media, and this dissatisfaction has not abated, notwithstanding persistent and punitive actions against the media by the government. In short, 10 years of a free press has been characterized by the voices of dissatisfaction accusing the government of seeking to curtail and control public opinion. The result has been a print media that has focused on providing political commentary to the detriment of providing solid factual news.

Following are the data on newspapers and electronic media in Kyrgyzstan, but what it does not show is the irregular appearance of many of the newspapers on the streets, the complete lack of audited sales (hence the circulation figures are generally unreliable), and the number of newspapers that come into circulation, publish for a short amount of time, and then cease publication without explanation. Most Kyrgyz newspapers are tabloids with 8 to 16 pages per issue. Twelve pages are average. Most are printed overnight and hence are morning editions. Later editions are unknown, and Sunday newspapers are rare. The Friday editions are the largest in volume with 32 pages and also contain the most advertisements, often up to 50 percent, and commanding the highest prices for ads. Otherwise advertising rarely exceeds 20 percent of the content and particularly in those newspapers out of favor with the government, this percentage may be as low as one percent.

Popular magazines (the most popular journal being the *AKI Press* journal) are available weekly and are dedicated to sports, fashion, film, or automobiles. There are three English language newspapers that come out sporadically and usually cover a week's news. They are the *Kyrgyzstan Chronicle*, *The Times of Central Asia*, and the *Bishkek Observer*. Other language newspapers can occasionally be found in specialized bookstores and kiosks, though invariably the news is dated.

Of the urban centers in Kyrgyzstan, 10 have some form of electronic or print media. The largest and most competitive market is in Bishkek with 18 newspapers, 11 radio stations, and 4 TV stations. The most popular newspaper is *Delo Nomar* (50,000), followed by *Slovo Kyrgyzstana* (24,000), *Moya Stolitsa* (25,000), *Aalam* (18,000), *Res Publica* (7,000), *Ordo* (10,000), *Kyrgyz*

Tuusu (10,000), and *Kyrgyz Rukhu* (7,000). *Vechernyi Bishkek* is the largest circulation newspaper with anywhere between 20,000 and 60,000 copies depending on press run, but in view of its government ownership has a dubious claim to being the most popular newspaper. Many other newspapers appear but have limited circulation. For instance *Obshestvenniye Rating*, *Tribuna*, and *Erkin Too* all have circulations of less than 10,000 copies. The cost of a newspaper in 2002 was 3 soms or 0.10 cents U.S. on weekdays and 6 soms on Fridays. The high circulation newspaper *Moya Stolitsa* has been at the forefront of legal pressure, usually from government ministers for alleged libel. Publication ceased in 2001 as a result of the refusal of the government printing house to print the newspaper, but it has since resumed publication.

Twenty-four other smaller urban centers claim to have newspapers, but it is usually only one local newspaper (though Bishkek newspapers are circulated in these cities). For example the city of Jalalabad, the fourth largest city, has four local newspapers, but they only publish once per week. Similarly a city like Karakol in the mountains of Eastern Kyrgyzstan boasts seven newspapers, but circulation is significantly less than 5,000, and the papers only publish once per week. The exception to this pattern is the city of Osh with 12 newspapers, but none have a circulation larger than 5,000. Similar to Bishkek, Friday and Saturday are the most popular days of publication. In total with a circulation of only 15 per 1,000 people, Kyrgyzstan exhibits one of the lowest newspaper readership levels in the world.

Economic Framework

The economic performance of Kyrgyzstan over the first years of its existence has been rated possibly the best of all former Soviet Central Asian republics. However, while this is cause for optimism in the long term, the performance has been dismal by world standards. Growth rates have been negative or very low; inflation has been as high as 300 percent and in 2002 was still at an unacceptable 37 percent. The result has been low wages, limited foreign investment, and a general moribund economy. Criticism of such a poor economic performance has been limited in the media; rather they have concentrated on the perceived practices of nepotism, cronyism, and corruption that are seen as underlying cases of the poor economic performance. Furthermore the media has spent much time reacting to the autocratic rule of the one man who has held the presidency in the 10 years since the Soviet Union disbanded, President Askar Akaev. Certainly low per capita incomes have limited newspaper purchases, but it would not appear to be a major factor in media success.

The irregular appearance of newspapers on the street and the popularity of television as a medium make television the preferred news source. Newspapers are either government owned (*Vechernyi Bishkek* has the government as a majority owner) or privately owned. There are approximately 14 private TV stations and 11 radio stations. In Osh two television stations (Osh Television and Mezon) broadcast in the Uzbek language, and there have been instances when the government has accused the station of both televising too much Uzbek programming and also inciting ethnic hate during elections. It is difficult to classify the types of Kyrgyz newspapers. They are generally popular, but the incessant criticism of government and other entities would suggest that some might be yellow. However, the vicious backlash that has been waged against such journalism is not in keeping with traditions of yellow journalism elsewhere in the world. The small circulations and small staffs have militated against any concentration of ownership in newspaper chains. Competition is ostensibly present, and hence there are no monopolies or the need for antitrust legislation.

The government, through the publishing house Uchkun, owns the distribution network in Kyrgyzstan. Being government-owned, they have few problems obtaining newsprint. The government recently passed a decree (Decree 20) that gives Uchkun and, by default the government, a monopoly on newsprint allocation, a potentially serious threat to a free press. In addition the government controls the small advertising market and hence has a considerable control over editorial and news content. The average cost of newspaper printing was US$10,500 for 35,000 copies in 2002.

Press Laws

The relationship between the government and the media since the fall of the Soviet Union is the one area that has dominated the emergence and functioning of the press and currently appears to be getting worse rather than better.

The Constitution of the Kyrgyz Republic, adopted in 1993, provides, under Article 16, the rights of all citizens ". . .to free expression and dissemination of one's thoughts, ideas, opinions, freedom of literary, artistic, scientific and technical creative work, freedom of the press, transmission and dissemination of information." Two supplementary laws that govern the media were passed in 1997: "On guarantees and free access to information" and "On the protection of professional activities of Journalists." "The Law of the Kyrgyz Republic on Mass Media" was originally passed in 1992, and despite pressure to amend this law, it remains in place as the most important law governing the media. There are no freedom of information laws in Kyrgyzstan.

As a requirement of that statute all of the country's mass media, including media owners and journalists, must register with the Ministry of Justice in the case of print, or the National Agency for Communications in the case of electronic media and cannot work or publish until permission has been granted by the Ministry. Permission is usually forthcoming in the one-month period required for a decision. The National Agency for Communications also reviews program schedules and issues electronic frequencies for broadcasting. In some cases the agency has unilaterally required stations to change frequencies thus incurring significant disruption and cost to the station. As a result of these restrictions Radio Free Europe estimates only two radio stations in the country are broadcasting legally. There is a fee for registration, but posted bonds are not required.

The press laws establish quite clearly what is prohibited material, namely official state secrets, intolerance toward ethnic minorities, pornography, and desecration of Kyrgyz national symbols like the national seal, anthem, or flag. The statute also identifies ''encroachment on the honor and dignity of the person'' as an offense. The statute (Articles 24-28) takes great care to identify indemnity of moral damage and other offences of this kind, and it is these provisions in the law that have been extensively used to stymie and restrict the media. Furthermore libel is a criminal, not a civil, action, and attempts to change this have been overwhelmingly defeated in the national Parliament with little hope given for this status to change. The result has been imprisonment of journalists, heavy fines, and ultimately media cessation of publication. It is this situation and the lack of an incentive to change that suggests an unfavorable prognosis for improvement. In the application of these press laws the judiciary has generally been favorable to the plaintiff in the case of honor and dignity suits launched against the media. This might be expected insomuch as the president and Parliament appoint the judiciary.

STATE-PRESS RELATIONS

The right to free speech and freedom of the press, while enshrined in the Constitution and the media laws, is in practice generally not respected. Moreover, legislation that would further restrict the media seems to be an ongoing threat.

The state controls the television and much of the radio, and these outlets receive significant subsidies, which permit the government to influence the media. While the power of the government to affect and in some cases silence media agents has been clearly shown (many of whom were imprisoned, fled, or faced trial on flimsy charges), it might be suggested that in lieu of a strong vocal opposition to the president, the fact that there is independent media who still voice opposition and protest suggests that there may be hope for some form of editorial influence on government policies.

In an attempt to break the stranglehold on the printing and distribution of the print media by Uchkun, the European Union attempted in 2002 to sponsor the import of new printing presses. To date the government has withheld an import license for the equipment, and hence alternative presses for newspaper publishing are not available. Ironically, while the former Soviet Union promoted a strong and vociferous trade union movement, in the years since independence no form of worker protest against media manipulation has occurred.

CENSORSHIP

There is no single agency in Kyrgyzstan concerned with monitoring the press, but the fact that Uchkun is the only newspaper-publishing house in the country and that it is government owned creates a de facto censorship. For example, Uchkun refused to publish *Res Publica* (pending payment of a fine to the president of the state TV and corporation) in 2000, and in 2002 it was refusing to print both *Res Publica* and *Moya Stolitsa-Novosti* (notwithstanding court orders to publish the newspapers) over alleged ''moral damage'' to the president of Uchkun. In view of the possibility of jail and the heavy fines that have been levied against journalists and independent newspaper owners, it is generally agreed that self-censorship is a significant occurrence in Kyrgyzstan. For example, one journalist in Jalalabad was sentenced to two years in prison and a fine equivalent to US$2,250—both penalties were subsequently reduced on appeal. In 2001 *Res Publica* was fined an equivalent of US$5,000 for criticizing the justice department, and the independent newspaper *Asaba* was required to pay the equivalent of US$105,000 to a parliamentary deputy for repeated insults over an eight-year period. The challenge, as one observer put it, is ''to stay out of jail but publish something that has some relation to the truth.'' In what may be seen as a response to the increasing pressure on the media from government, there has been a significant increase in the number of agencies, foundations, and associations both internally and externally created. Most important is the Public Association of Journalists, a media non-government organization or NGO, ''Glasnost (openness) Defense'' Public Foundation to defend journalists in court (established in 1999); the public association ''Journalists'' representing 160 media professionals in the republic (founded in 1998); the Public Foundation of Media Development and the Protection of Journalists' Rights (founded in 1998); and the ''Press Club'' founded in 2000. The Association of Independent Electronic Mass Media of Central Asia, ''Anesmi,'' (founded in 1995) represents the electronic media but is for all practical purposes defunct. There is also a Center of Women Journalists of Central Asia, as there are a large number of female journalists in Kyrgyzstan, where gender issues are increasingly coming to the fore in this predominantly Islamic country. Journalists can also be part of the Union of Journalists of the Kyrgyz Republic. In Osh the Resource Media Center has been active in the fight for journalists' rights. Sadly there is no Press Council that mediates disputes between plaintiffs and the media in the event of perceived slights; rather litigation is the preferred means of dispute resolution.

ATTITUDE TOWARD FOREIGN MEDIA

Article 30 of the state media law guarantees the right of foreign mass media to operate in Kyrgyzstan without opposition. Generally the government's attitude toward foreign media has been one of dislike as a result of the criticism that has been directed toward Kyrgyzstan's record on media freedoms. There have been instances of foreign journalists being assaulted—in 2002 a journalist from the Kyrgyz-Turkish newspaper *Zaman Kyrgyzstan* was assaulted, but whether this was directed against him as a representative of the media or just unrelated street crime cannot be ascertained. More significantly western governments, particularly the United States and UNESCO, have played a major role in the protection and education of journalists in order to stimulate an independent media. UNESCO has established a Media Resource Center in Bishkek to which journalists from Europe and the America's come to instruct others in the best practices for journalists. English language classes and computer literacy classes have also been taught. In the future management courses will be taught. Of more direct impact has been the establishment, as a result of U.S. State Department funding, of Internews. Internews is a non-governmental organization (NGO) that operates ''based on the conviction that vigorous and diverse mass media form an essential cornerstone to an open society.'' To that end it produces TV news programs and youth radio stations but more recently has become involved in the defense of TV stations, radio stations, and journalists who have been sued under the nation's media laws. Internews is also active in the proposed amendment of current media laws. Foreign correspondents do not have to be accredited, nor do they require special visas. Cables are not approved, nor have there been any instances of foreign correspondents being prevented from doing their job. Domestic journalists have free access to international press organizations. The Kyrgyz government tacitly supports the UNESCO Declaration of 1979 by its support of the OSCE office in Bishkek that monitors this declaration.

NEWS AGENCIES

The official government news agency is named Kabar. It is responsible for all government pronouncements and is the best source for local news but is generally considered untrustworthy. Western NGOs and other

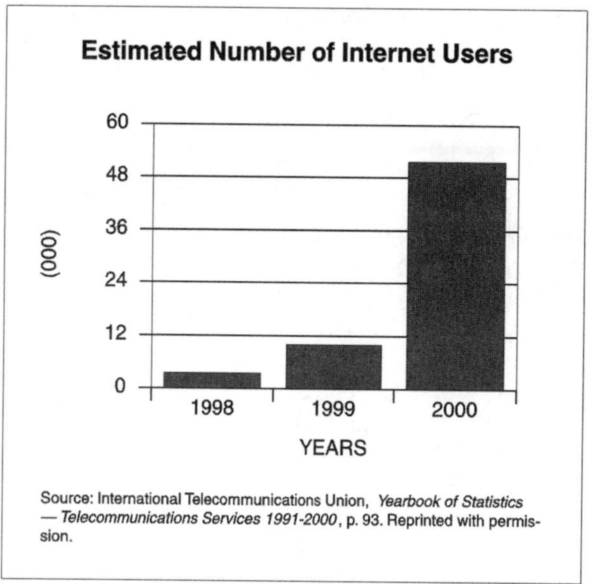

Source: International Telecommunications Union, *Yearbook of Statistics — Telecommunications Services 1991-2000*, p. 93. Reprinted with permission.

interested parties have incontrovertible proof of Kabar supplying patently false and misleading information in the past. There are a number of independent news agencies: Belyi Parokhod, Jihan, and Internews, all of which provide both national and international coverage as well as local politics and commentary. Most major international news bureaus cover Kyrgyzstan out of Moscow (AP) or Karachi (Reuters). Thus detailed, ongoing international pressure on the government to recognize and respect media freedoms is less than in other, larger countries.

BROADCAST MEDIA

The state owns and controls the TV station transmitters and therefore is in a position to control electronic news broadcasts. There are five TV channels in the capital city of Bishkek. Channel one is Kyrgyz programming, channels two and three are feeds from Moscow, channel four is a Turkish feed, and channel five is the independent channel showing mostly soap operas and pirated western movies.

ELECTRONIC NEWS MEDIA

The importance of the Internet as a source of information is limited owing to the lack of computers and the poor telecommunications network in the country. In an attempt to expand the Internet as a news source, the U.S. State Department opened seven information centers in seven cities and towns with free access to the Internet to enable citizens to access various press sites. In 2003 it will open five more urban centers. In yet another example of a contradiction between theory and practice, the government has undertaken to increase electronic access and communication, while shutting down the online news site ''Politica KG'' in 2000 during the presidential election.

EDUCATION & TRAINING

There are a number of schools of journalism in Kyrgyzstan institutes of higher education. The primary institutions teaching journalism are the American University in Kyrgyzstan (AUK), Slavic University, and Bishkek Humanities University. Many Kyrgyz students in standard literature classes also see journalism as a viable and attractive career. The numbers graduating from these institutions are small. For example, AUK graduated 10 journalism students in 2001.

SUMMARY

The most serious problem facing the provision of an independent media in Kyrgyzstan is the attitude and policies of the government. In the earliest years of independence there was cause for hope that the media would grow to become a solid acceptable force in the progress of the nation. By the late 1990s the situation had begun to deteriorate with a significant growth in the number of lawsuits, harassment of journalists by means of intimidation, and use of the taxation system to challenge the existence of an independent media. Matters came to a head in 2000 when the president, Askar Akaev, sought a third term in office, normally prohibited under the Constitution but permitted by the Supreme Court on the basis that he became president under the old Soviet regime and hence technically had not served two terms. The media outcry was met by a series of punitive measures against any of the media that opposed his campaign for a third term. Thus the situation exists in the early twenty-first century where, on a scale of one to one hundred (Free= 0-30, partly free= 31-60, and Not free 61-100), the 1999 Freedom House Survey of Press Freedom rated Kyrgyzstan 64 and is considered without a free press, a situation reminiscent of the press under the Soviet regime only 10 years earlier.

The prospects and prognosis for the media in the twenty-first century is dependent on the state of relations with the government. Certainly the government in its official statements espouses the need for a free and independent media, but in practice it is a long way from that reality. From here the government can go even further in its challenge to the independence of the media, secure in the knowledge that for the foreseeable future western governments need to be on good terms with Islamic governments. Or it can address the concerns voiced by both the OSCE and the U.S. government that human rights and the state of the mass media are areas of immediate and serious concern and can address these issues to the satisfaction of Kyrgyz journalists, media, and outside observers.

BIBLIOGRAPHY

Freedom House Media Ratings, 2002. Available from http://freedomhouse.org.

Kyrgyzstan 2001 World Press Freedom Review. Available from http://freemedia.at.

U.S. Agency for International Development (USAID). ''Report on Independent Media,'' 2002. Available from http://www.usaid.gov.

U.S. Department of State. ''Country Reports on Human Rights Practices 2001.'' Available from http://www.state.gov.

—Richard W. Benfield

Laos

Basic Data

Official Country Name:	Lao People's Democratic Republic
Region (Map name):	Southeast Asia
Population:	5,497,459
Language(s):	Lao, French, English,
Literacy rate:	57%

Laos, located in Southeast Asia northeast of Thailand and west of Vietnam, was settled between the fourth and eighth centuries and was known as the Lane Xang, or Million Elephants Kingdom. The French took control of the government in 1893—Europeans had been trading with Laos for more than 200 years—but the monarchy continued until Communists took control of the government and deposed the monarch in 1975. The state is headed by a President, who appoints a Prime Minister to preside over the unicameral, 99-seat National Assembly. The official language is Lao, but French is used in diplomacy and English and ethnic languages are also spoken. The approximate population is approximately 5.6 million, and the literacy rate is only 57 percent. Laos is a land-locked country with a primitive infrastructure. Its economy is dominated by fishing, forestry, and agriculture.

Because Laos is a Communist country, the government owns and supervises all media outlets, and it considers the role of the media to be furthering the national political agenda. Laos supports two daily newspapers, both of which are written in Lao. *Pasason* (''The People'') is the national newspaper. Its approximate circulation is 10,000. The country's second daily, *Vientiane Mai* (''Vientiane Message''), predominantly serves the capital, Vientiane, and its circulation is approximately 5,000. Enjoying much smaller circulations are the *Vientiane Times,* a bi-weekly English-language newspaper, *Vientiane Business-Social,* a weekly English-language newspaper, and *Le Rénovateur,* a weekly newspaper published in French. *Pasason Van Athit* publishes every Sunday. The government also issues weekly and monthly publications sponsored by various government branches like the army and the Education Ministry.

There are 13 radio stations, 12 AM and one FM, for 730,000 radios. Two national television stations broadcast to 52,000 televisions. There is one Internet service provider.

Bibliography

''Country Profile.'' *Worldinformation.com, 2002.* Available from http://www.worldinformation.com.

''Laos.'' *CIA World Fact Book.* Directorate of Intelligence, 2001. Available from http://www.cia.gov.

''Mass Media News Organization,'' *Lao News Agency, n.d.* Available from http://asean.kplnet.net.

—*Jenny B. Davis*

Latvia

Basic Data

Official Country Name:	Republic of Latvia
Region (Map name):	Europe
Population:	2,385,231
Language(s):	Latvian or Lettish, Luithuanian, Russian

Literacy rate:	100.0%
Area:	64,589 sq km
GDP:	7,150 (US$ millions)
Number of Daily Newspapers:	21
Total Circulation:	322,000
Circulation per 1,000:	165
Number of Nondaily Newspapers:	59
Total Circulation:	596,000
Circulation per 1,000:	305
Total Newspaper Ad Receipts:	11.3 (Lats millions)
As % of All Ad Expenditures:	37.20
Number of Television Stations:	44
Number of Television Sets:	1,220,000
Television Sets per 1,000:	511.5
Number of Cable Subscribers:	184,080
Cable Subscribers per 1,000:	76.7
Number of Satellite Subscribers:	90,000
Satellite Subscribers per 1,000:	37.7
Number of Radio Stations:	65
Number of Radio Receivers:	1,760,000
Radio Receivers per 1,000:	737.9
Number of Individuals with Computers:	340,000
Computers per 1,000:	142.5
Number of Individuals with Internet Access:	150,000
Internet Access per 1,000:	62.9

BACKGROUND & GENERAL CHARACTERISTICS

Most newspapers in Latvia are less than a decade old, although the first newspaper in Latvian appeared in 1822. Since becoming an independent country, Latvian media enjoys greater freedom than ever before in its history. The government generally respects freedom of speech and expression. As Latvia works to transform its economic and political systems, the major barriers to a free society and independent media are largely of a financial nature. Although newspaper circulation figures are typically small in Latvia, the industry can be characterized as an active one that enjoys a large measure of constitutionally guaranteed freedom. Most press activity occurs in the more populous western region of the country, particularly in the capital of Riga.

The Latvian newspaper market has only existed in its present state for the last decade, since independence in 1991. Until the end of the Soviet period, it was not possible to speak of free, democratic media in Latvia. Beginning in 1985, Gorbachev's policy of glasnost gave newspaper and magazine editors in Latvia and other republics of the Soviet Union some opportunities to publish information on a wider range of formerly proscribed subjects, including crime, illegal drugs, occupational injuries, and environmental issues. An article published in October 1986 in the Latvian literary journal *Literatura un Maksla,* discussing the environmental impact of a new hydroelectric station that was to be built on the Daugava River, helped to arouse so much public opposition that a decision was made by the Soviet government in 1987 to abandon the project. Subsequently, after the pivotal June 1988 plenum of the Latvian Writers Union, the speeches delivered at this plenum denouncing the Soviet Latvian status quo and demanding greater autonomy for the Latvian republic received nationwide attention when they were published in four successive issues of *Literatura un Maksla.*

After a brief period of independence between the two World Wars, Latvia was annexed by the USSR in 1940. It reestablished its independence in 1991 following the breakup of the Soviet Union. Although the last Russian troops left in 1994, the status of the Russian minority (some 30 percent of the population) remains of concern to Moscow. Latvia continues to revamp its economy for eventual integration into various Western European political and economic institutions.

Latvian is the official language, however, Russian is spoken by a large number of individuals. The main ethnic groups are Latvian, 56.5 percent; Russian, 30.4 percent; Belarusian, 4.3 percent; Ukrainian, 2.8 percent; Polish, 2.6 percent; and others, 3.4 percent. Ethnic tensions between the non-Slavic majority and the large Russian minority are clearly reflected in the media. The conflict between the two languages stems from more than 50 years of ethnic tension between the republic's Russian and Latvian populations. In 1940, Soviet leader Joseph Stalin moved thousands of Russians into Latvia to gain ethnic control over the region. Although ethnic Latvians

Daily and Non-Daily Newspaper Titles and Circulation Figures

	1996	1997	1998	1999	2000
Number of Daily Newspapers	NA	24	21	20	21
Circulation of Dailies (000)	NA	284	260	321	322
Number of Non-Daily Newspapers	101	117	72	61	59
Circulation of Non-Dailies (000)	NA	509	525	655	596

Source: World Association of Newspapers and Zenithmedia, *World Press Trends 2001*, pp. 8, 10, 17, 19. Note: NA stands for not available.

made up more than 75 percent of the population in 1939, by 1990 Russians, Ukrainians, and Belarusians comprised more than 44 percent of the country's population.

Latvia is located in Eastern Europe, bordering the Baltic Sea, between Estonia and Lithuania. On the east it borders Belarus and Russia. The country is slightly larger than West Virginia, and has a population of 2.4 million. Riga is the capital and by far largest city with approximately 795,000 residents.

In 1997 Latvia was the home of 229 newspapers, with total newspaper circulation close to three million. Seventy-two of the papers were published at least three times a week, though only a few of these claimed high circulation. There are no Sunday papers in Latvia. On Saturday a weekend edition is published. Papers published six days a week represent about 60 percent of total daily newspaper circulation. *Diena,* which is published six times weekly, is the largest daily newspaper in Latvia. In 1999 it had 21.1 percent of Latvia's readership. *Diena* is an independent newspaper based in Riga with over 352,000 readers, printing approximately 73,000 papers daily. In 1999, *Diena* began producing a Russian-language spin-off, with content drawn from its own pages. In comparison to Latvian newspapers, it is believed that Russian language publications tend to propagandize to a greater extent. While *Diena* began in 1990 as a government-funded effort to provide objective information to the public, it is now an independent newspaper that has consistently upped the level of competition in the Latvian market. Rather than rely on the Latvian postal service to deliver newspapers around Riga, it developed it own delivery system.

The second largest newspaper in 1999 was *Lauku Avîze* with 19.2 percent of the readership and slightly over 72,000 copies circulated. Unlike *Diena, Lauku Avîze* is only printed three times a week on Tuesday, Thursday and Saturday. Founded in 1988, it is published in Riga but is directed toward predominantly rural readers. It is a combination of political news coverage and commentary as well as advice about agricultural and horticultural activities. After these two papers, news circulation figures drop off significantly. The third largest paper is *Panorama Latvil* with 6.2 percent of the readership in Latvia. *Panorama Latvil,* established in 1991, is a Russian daily with a readership of 125,000 and a circulation of 24,000. *Cas* is another Russian paper with a circulation of about 20,000 copies.

There are three national evening newspapers: *Rigas Balss* (35,000 copies in Latvian and Russian), *Vakara Zinas* (13,000 copies in Latvian), and *Spogulis* (12,000 copies in Latvian). These papers are published six days a week, representing about 20 percent of total daily newspaper circulation. The major regional papers published at least three times a week are: *Kurzemes Vards* (11,000 copies in Latvian), *Zemgales Zinas* (10,000 copies in Latvian), and *Liesma* (9,000 copies in Latvian). The regional papers comprise about 30 percent of the daily audience. In addition to Latvian and Russian newspapers, the *Baltic Times* is an English language weekly published in Riga.

Most newspapers and magazines in Latvia are privately owned. All major cities publish their own newspapers. There are 14 national and 10 regional dailies. Average circulation per issue for all dailies is 284,000 copies; non-dailies total 509,000 copies. Many of the small towns and rural areas have newspapers that are published between three and six times weekly with circulations between 5 and 25 thousand. Private companies, such as Latvijas Presses Apvieniba, and the joint stock company Diena, control the newspaper distribution system. The state publishes the weekly *Likuma Varda* and *Latvijas Vestnesis,* which appear four times a week.

The magazine market is very fragmented. The most popular are women's magazines, while traditional magazine circulation has declined. The specialized magazine sector is not well developed in Latvia. The biggest publishers are Izdevnieciba Santa and Izdevnieciba Baltika, which control 60 percent of the magazine market.

The Latvian newspaper audience is generally well educated and values freedom of expression and a responsible press. With the quickened pace of change in the last decade stemming from the country's move from a Soviet dependency to a free market economy, the desire for news has increased. Between 1990 and 1995, circulation

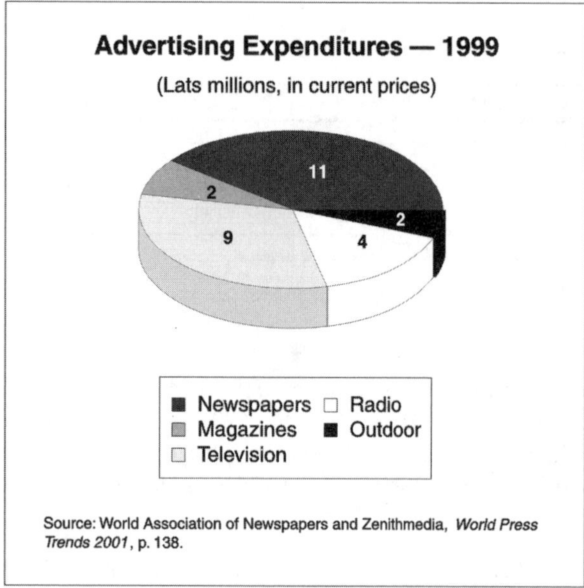

Source: World Association of Newspapers and Zenithmedia, *World Press Trends 2001*, p. 138.

growth was 26 percent, among the highest rate of growth for recorded nations. In Riga, which contains almost 32 percent of Latvia's 2.34 million residents, three Latvian-language morning dailies, two afternoon dailies and a host of specialty publications compete for the attention of readers. Illiteracy is very low in Latvia, in part because all children between 6 and 16 must attend school, and many choose technical and higher education.

Journalists in Latvia are struggling to cast off a half century of Soviet coercion and censorship. Understandably journalism is still in its infancy, with a mixed result. The press corps is estimated to be among the world's youngest and perhaps most inexperienced in the three Baltic nations of Latvia, Estonia and Lithuania. The press suffers from too few journalists and reporters who are able to put information in context. There have been some reported instances in which owners and editors took payoffs for favorable stories. Tough investigative reporting, which was forbidden under the Soviets, is still difficult to find in Latvian papers.

ECONOMIC FRAMEWORK

Economic difficulties greatly affect media outlets in Latvia. For example, the 1995 banking crisis, in which a number of the country's banks went bankrupt, directly affected the financial viability of many media outlets and sharply diminished the advertising market. In 1996, 43 percent of media advertising was in television, followed by newspapers at 35 percent, radio at six percent, magazines at four percent, and outdoor venues and other categories comprising the remaining 10 percent. Although new publications continue to appear, economic difficulties have forced others to close.

Latvia's major industries are buses, vans, street and railroad cars, synthetic fibers, agricultural machinery, fertilizers, washing machines, radios, electronics, pharmaceuticals, processed foods, and textiles.

In the early 1990s, as the transition to a market-oriented economy began and competition intensified, both the circulation and the content of newspapers and magazines changed. Rising production costs caused subscription rates and newsstand prices to increase, and sales declined steadily. Nevertheless, in 1995 Latvia had a daily newspaper circulation rate of 1,377 per 1,000 people, compared with 524 per 1,000 people in Finland, 402 per 1,000 people in Germany, and 250 per 1,000 people in the United States. Though more than 200 newspapers and 180 magazines were in circulation in the late 1990s, the number of newspapers and magazines declined.

The top publishing company is AS Diena, which publishes *Diena* and *Spogulis,* as well as five regional newspapers. It is a joint stock company in which 49 percent belongs to Swedish shareholders the Bonnier Group, and 51 percent belongs to local private shareholders. The company has its own printing plant and independent home delivery distribution system in Riga and newsstand retail chain. The national distribution is carried out by the national post office.

The second largest publishing company is AS Preses Nams (publishing *Neatkariga RA, Rigas Balss,* and *Vakara Zinas*). It is also a joint stock company. One hundred percent of the company belongs to local private shareholders. The company was established in 1998 through the privatization process of the largest state owned printing plant, which now belongs to the company. This group does not have its own distribution system.

There are no cases of cross ownership. In Latvia there are no government subsidies in the newspaper market, national or local. There are only indirect benefits like 0 percent value added tax (VAT) for newspaper sales, though advertising income is VAT applicable.

PRESS LAWS

The Latvian Constitution provides for freedom of speech and of the press. According to Article 100, ''Everyone has the right to freedom of expression, which includes the right to freely receive, keep and distribute information and to express their views. Censorship is prohibited.'' The government generally respects this right in practice. The 1990 Press Law prohibits censorship of the press or other mass media. But the Law on the Media, revised in October 1998, contains a number of restrictive provisions regulating the content and language of broadcasts. This law states that no less than 51 percent of television broadcasts must be of European origin, of which 40 percent should be in the Latvian language. These provisions, however, are not always implemented.

The Law on Press and other Mass Media prohibits publishing of information that belittles honor and dignity of natural and legal persons and contains libel. A new criminal law allows penalties of up to three years' imprisonment for libel and incitement of racial hatred. Penalties for libel and for incitement to ethnic violence, while intended to reduce ethnic tensions, can have a chilling effect on journalists.

Latvia's Saeima (parliament) ratified the Convention for the Protection of Human Rights and Fundamental Freedoms on June 4, 1997.

CENSORSHIP

There were several occasions when officials have brought journalists and media organizations to court for libel. In 1998, the former Minister of Economy, Laimonis Strujevics, sued the daily newspaper *Diena* for alleged defamation. The newspaper had sharply criticized particular decisions of the minister and claimed that, through these decisions, he favored certain economic groups to the detriment of the state's financial interests. The newspaper lost the case in the lower court, but at the beginning of 2002 was appealing the ruling. In general the newspapers serve as watchdogs over government. One problem is that there is no Freedom of Information law to help reporters with access to official documents.

Journalists may legally conceal their sources, but in case of trials, they may be subject to imprisonment if they refuse to disclose such information. Since 1951, a law has permitted editors and publishers to refuse to tell where they received information. Cases of editors being imprisoned for failing to reveal their sources at trials are very rare.

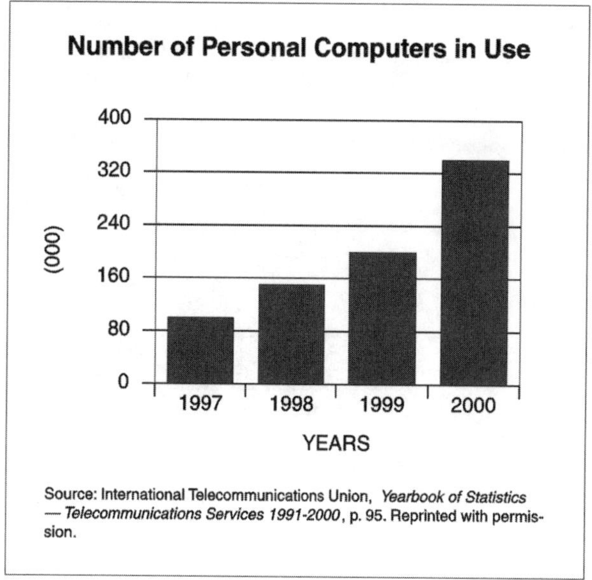

Source: International Telecommunications Union, *Yearbook of Statistics — Telecommunications Services 1991-2000*, p. 95. Reprinted with permission.

STATE-PRESS RELATIONS

Latvia is a parliamentary democracy. The key indicators of a democratic state have been put in place after 50 years of Soviet domination. One of the key elements of a working democracy is a free press. The media in Latvia are owned by different sources and cover a broad spectrum of opinion and support a wide range of philosophies.

All mass media are subject to preliminary registration at the Ministry of Justice as provided by the Law on Press and other Mass Media. Activities of electronic mass media are subject to licensing. Newspapers do not receive state subsidies. National radio and television, on the other hand, receives a state subsidy equal to 80 percent of its annual budget. The fact that there is no support from government to newspapers has created a significant amount of competition. This competition may act as a driving force to improve, but also forces newspapers to rely more and more on entertainment at the expense of quality journalism.

In general the media is editorially independent and the media's newsgathering function is not affected by government or private owners. Attempts by organized crime to receive special treatment in publications have been publicized in spite of potential threats to personal safety. On a few occasions this has not been the case. When an influential economic group in the port city of Ventspils purchased a media group including the Preses Nams publishing house and several daily newspapers, the political and economic interests of the owners apparently affected news coverage. This situation may produce self-censorship.

ATTITUDE TOWARD FOREIGN MEDIA

Foreign correspondents have free access to Latvian affairs. However, foreign investment may not exceed 20 percent of the capital in electronic media organizations. A 1994 city ordinance prohibits the sale of ultra-nationalist Russian-language newspapers in Riga.

There are several partnerships between Scandinavian and Baltic countries, including Latvian financial interests. The Baltic News Service (BSN) produces between 500 and 700 news items daily in five languages, including Estonian, Latvian, Lithuanian, Russian, and English. BSN is owned by the leading Finnish and Swedish dailies Kauppalehti and Dagens Industri as well as the Direkt news agency of Sweden and Bridge Telerate of the United States. BSN was founded by a group of Baltic students in Moscow in April 1990 at the height of the Baltic states' struggle for freedom to bring news direct from the three countries to Moscow-based foreign correspondents.

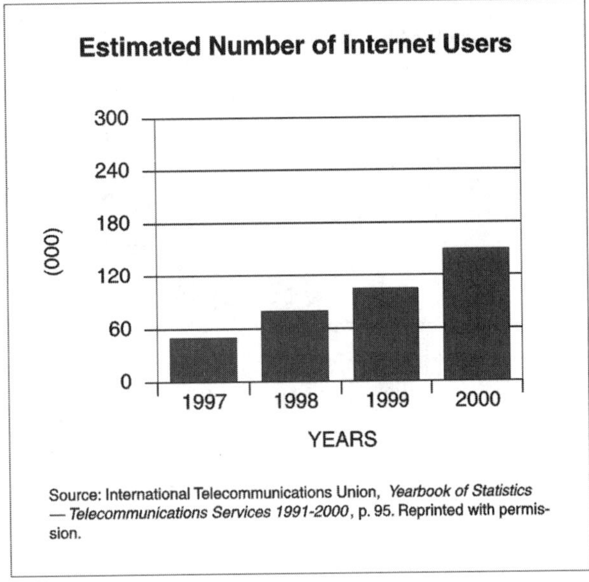

Source: International Telecommunications Union, *Yearbook of Statistics — Telecommunications Services 1991-2000*, p. 95. Reprinted with permission.

NEWS AGENCIES

The only press and journalists' organization in Latvia media is the Latvian Journalists Union and Latvian Press Publishers Associations. The union has 500 registered members, 350 of which are considered active members. Women make up approximately 50 percent of the membership of the Journalists Union.

BROADCAST MEDIA

Latvian Radio and Latvian Television are non-profit state enterprises with limited liability. Licenses for broadcasting activities are issued by the National Council of Radio and Television. In the broadcasting sector, the regulation of activities of all radio and TV stations in Latvia, public and private, is within the competence of the National Council of Radio and Television. The Council consists of nine members who are appointed by the Saeima.

Broadcasting is the primary source of information for most Latvians. The country has two state-owned television networks, LTV-1 and LTV-2, and nine major privately owned stations. The private Latvian Independent Television has almost twice as many viewers as LTV-1, its nearest competitor. Satellite television enjoys approximately 10 percent of the total Latvian viewership each week and there are numerous independently owned cable channels.

A large number of independent radio outlets broadcast in both Russian and Latvian. Approximately 10 privately owned radio stations operate in Riga. The major public radio stations are Latvijas Radio 1, with the greatest number of listeners each week; Latvijas Radio 2; and Latvijas Radio 3.

In an effort to improve its quality and ability to compete, Latvian television has introduced a method of budget allocation based partly on a system used at the British Broadcasting Corporation. Managers hope that staff members will respond with greater motivation and creativity.

ELECTRONIC NEWS MEDIA

The government does not restrict access to the Internet. Even as computer use and Internet usage increases, online journalism for many newspapers seems only an afterthought. Except for the largest dailies, newspapers in Latvia have been slow to embrace the Internet as a vehicle for communicating with readers. This may improve as the percentage of the population connected to the Internet increases.

EDUCATION & TRAINING

Latvian universities have accredited journalism and mass media programs. In addition, the Nordic Journalist Center (NJC) has trained close to 4,500 Russian and Baltic journalists between January 1992 and January 2002 since the demise of the Soviet Union. NJC specialists estimated that activities in the Baltics will soon no longer be necessary. Estonia, Latvia and Lithuania will be able to undertake the basic and further education of journalists without foreign assistance.

SUMMARY

Since the late 1980s when the first independent newspapers appeared, the Latvian press has enjoyed a freer press than at any time in its history. According to Freedom House's annual Survey of Press Freedom, Latvia was rated "Free" in 1991, "Partly Free" in 1992 and 1993, and "Free" in 1994 through 1999. In general, the government has respected freedom of speech and the press. Newspapers published in both Latvian and Russian feature a wide range of criticism and political viewpoints.

By 2000, two major publishing companies owned about 65 percent of the newspaper market. With respect to electronic media the main tendency is towards the acquisition of Latvian broadcasting companies by foreign investors. Scandinavian media groups are taking the lead in this area.

On the whole, the Latvian press appears to have a bright future. The problem of economic viability will continue to be an issue in the twenty-first century. Investigative and more professional reporting will also be likely as the Latvian universities train a new generation of journalists, and journalists gain experience and a firmer understanding of a free and democratic press.

SIGNIFICANT DATES

- 1990: Law on Press and other Mass Media passed by parliament, which prohibits censorship of the press or other mass media.
- 1992: Code of Journalism Ethics adopted by Latvian Union of Journalists, presenting media ethics for journalism students and teachers as well as scholars and practitioners.
- 1995: Law on Radio and Television passed by parliament, which requires that no more than 30 percent of private broadcasts may be in languages other than Latvian; in prime time, 40 percent of television broadcasts must be of Latvian and 80 percent of European origin. Moreover, foreign investment may not exceed 20 percent of the capital in electronic media organizations.
- 1997: Ratification of the European Convention for the Protection of Human Rights and Fundamental Freedoms, which includes freedom of expression, and the right to hold opinions and to receive and impart information and ideas without interference by public authority and regardless of frontiers.

BIBLIOGRAPHY

Dreifelds, Juris. *Latvia in Transition*. Cambridge: Cambridge University Press, 1996.

European Codes of Journalism Ethics. Latvia. Adopted at the Conference of the Latvian Union of Journalists on 28 April 1992. Available from www.uta.fi/ethicnet/latvia.html.

European Journalism Center. ''The Latvian Media Landscape,'' 2000. Available from www.ejc.nl/jr/emland/latvia.html.

Garneau, George. ''Circulation woes reach beyond U.S.'' *Editor and Publisher*. 128 (June 17, 1995): 20-22.

Hickey, Neil. ''A Young Press Corps.'' *Columbia Journalism Review*. 38 (May 1999): 18-19.

Jarvis, Howard. ''Latvia.'' *World Press Freedom Review*, 2001. Available from www.freemedia.at/wpfr/latvia.htm.

Karatnycky, Adrian, Alexander Motyl, and Aili Piano. ''Nations in Transit 1999-2000: Civil Society, Democracy, and Markets in East Central Europe and Newly Independent States.'' Freedom House. March 10, 2001. Available from www.freedomhouse.org/research/nitransit/2000/latvia/latvia.htm.

Kerwin, Marie. ''Goss press salvaged for Latvia: Newspaper As Bureau's Uldis Grava leads drive to have Indianapolis Newspapers' 1958 Press dismantled and shipped abroad.'' Editor and Publisher. 125 (January 18, 1992): 16.

Kruminya, Mara. ''Economic Reform at Latvian TV: Motivation Is the Key to Quality,'' Baltic Media Center. Update No. 21. January 1997. Available from www.dk-web.com/bmc/update21/motivati.htm.

''Latvia: County Profile''. British Broadcasting Corporation News. March 8, 2002. Available from news2.thdo.bbc.co.uk.

''Latvia—A Country Study''. Federal Research Division. Library of Congress, 2000. Available from lcweb2.loc.gov/frd/cs/lvtoc.html.

''Latvia: Press Overview.'' International Journalists' Network. International Center for Journalists, 2000. Available from www.ijnet.org/Profile/CEENIS/Latvia/media.html.

Mack, Silvija Brizga. ''My Sojourn in Lithuania, Latvia and Estonia: A Knight International Press Fellowship Report.'' International Center for Journalists. Washington, D.C., June 15, 1997.

Mass Media Law and Practice (Baltic Edition). ''Twenty-two Categories on Mass Media Regulation in Lithuania, Latvia, and Estonia.'' 6 (July 1998).

Straumans, Andris. ''Latvian Newspapers vie for Web Readers.'' Latvians Online. June 4, 2001. Available from latviansonline.com//features/feature-prese.shtml.

Sulmane, Ilze. ''Ethnic and Political Stereotypes in Latvian and Russian Language Press in Latvia.'' 15th Nordic Conference on Media and Communication Research. Reykjavik, Iceland, August 11-13, 2001.

UNESCO. ''Cultural Activities: Newspapers, Books and Libraries,'' 1995. Available from www.unesco.org/culture/worldreport/html_eng/table1.htm.

—Carol L. Schmid

LEBANON

BASIC DATA

Official Country Name:	Lebanese Republic
Region (Map name):	Middle East
Population:	3,627,774
Language(s):	Arabic, French, English, Armenian
Literacy rate:	86.4%
Area:	10,400 sq km
GDP:	16,488 (US$ millions)

Number of Daily Newspapers:	13
Total Circulation:	220,000
Circulation per 1,000:	96
Number of Nondaily Newspapers:	2
Total Newspaper Ad Receipts:	60.2 (US$ millions)
As % of All Ad Expenditures:	24.80
Number of Television Stations:	15
Number of Television Sets:	1,180,000
Television Sets per 1,000:	325.3
Number of Cable Subscribers:	25,370
Cable Subscribers per 1,000:	5.9
Number of Radio Stations:	46
Number of Radio Receivers:	2,850,000
Radio Receivers per 1,000:	785.6
Number of Individuals with Computers:	175,000
Computers per 1,000:	48.2
Number of Individuals with Internet Access:	300,000
Internet Access per 1,000:	82.7

BACKGROUND & GENERAL CHARACTERISTICS

Lebanon (*Lubnan*) or the Lebanese Republic (*Al Jumhuriyah al Lubnaniyah*) can be thought of as, ''a land in-between.'' This definition well describes its geographical positioning, political situation, religious compilation, and communication and press orientation. Noting increasing connections with international bodies and an increasing respect for international norms, it is expected that these factors will increase the stability of the country's politics and infrastructure, facilitating development through all levels of society and engendering a better place to live for its citizens.

Country Geography Geographically, Lebanon can be found bordering the eastern coast of the Mediterranean Sea. It is also bordered by Israel (south) and Syria (north and west). Lebanon has felt intense political pressures from these two neighbors throughout its history. The outside political pressure has been intensified because many Lebanese identify themselves far more readily by their local, tribal/ethnic, and religious affiliations than by their national association.

Lebanon (population between 3.6 and 4.3 million) is normally divided into four roughly parallel topographical zones that run the length of the country. One region is the Mediterranean coastal plain located primarily in the north, which is home to the major cities of Lebanon including Tripoli, Jubail (Byblos), Beirut, Saida (Sidon), and Sur (Tyre). The mountain ranges of Lebanon receive significant snowfall during the year and provide a beautiful panorama for surrounding areas. The presence of snow seems to have been deemed important enough to have played an integral role in the very naming of the country; Lebanon means white (*laban*) in Aramaic. And as well as having the rarity of snow, Lebanon has one other rarity in the Middle East—no desert.

Country History Lebanon has been active as an entity since the ancient world; however, for much of its history, it has been a war zone for would be conquerors, usurpers, and overlords. It was the homeland for the Phoenicians/Canaanites (c.2700-450 B.C.) and also served as host to the Babylonians, Egyptians, Romans, and others. Yet, despite the desires of its nemeses, Lebanon remained free of total subjugation from would-be conquerors and provided perennial refuge to persecuted racial and religious minorities from all over the region due to its mountainous, rugged terrain. Thus, early on in its history from the influx of both conquerors and persecuted Lebanon gained a type of cosmopolitanism, becoming composed of multiple ethnic backgrounds and religious orientations.

In the ninth and tenth centuries, besides settled Sunni populations along the coasts, *Mitwali* (Shi'a) began to establish communities in the mountain area just off Lebanon's coast. Then in the eleventh century, the Druze also established enclaves as well. The years 1291 through 1516 saw the Mamluk—a warrior caste made up of Turks, Mongols, and Circassians—period of rule. While the Mamluk's ruled over Egypt, Syria, and other Arabian holy areas, the Lebanese, through persistent political maneuvering, continued to maintain autonomous functioning. The Maronites of the province fared especially well during this period due to their contacts with Italy and the Roman Curia. The Druze and Mitwali, who had not established the same contacts, were not privy to the same favoritism. This created discontent against the Maronites. So, in the thirteenth century, taking advantage of Mamluk preoccupation with the Mongol threat from Persia, the Druze and Shi'a revolted against the Maronites creating havoc in central Lebanon.

The year 1516 began the rule of the Ottomans. It was in this year that they conquered Syria from the Mamluks and incorporated Lebanon into their empire. Yet, even with the Ottomans, Lebanon was allowed to function relatively autonomously. During a weak point in Ottoman rule, Fakir ad-Din II (1586-1635) of the Druze House of Ma'an attempted complete independence from the Ottomans and succeeded for a number of years, but it did not last and he was eventually executed in 1635 in Constantinople. After this, the House of Ma'an was succeeded by the House of Shihab. This dynasty enjoyed a two-hundred-year rule, ending with the exile of Bashir II in 1840.

The Ottomans then set up a system of Kaimakams—one Druze and one Maronite—to rule under the Turkish pashas of Beirut and Sidon. This began the reemergence of Maronites to power, which led to years of sectarian violence, which the Ottomans did little to curtail. The Ottomans lack of interest in Lebanon turned out to be the Europeans gain.

The European powers, sensing an opportunity, began to move beyond the traditional trading activities that they had engaged in for centuries with Lebanon and began to establish political/military alliances with particular ethnic factions. The French formed with the Maronite Christians, the Russians with the Orthodox Christians, and the British with the Druze and the Sunnis. Thus, after 1860, the Europeans were able to externally control some of the Lebanese.

European influence proved strong enough to set up an international committee consisting of Austria, France, Great Britain, Prussia, Russia, and the Ottomans to facilitate the restoration of order inside Mount Lebanon. Violence was curtailed through the policies arising from this conference, and the period of 1860-1914 became known as a renaissance for Lebanese culture. Roads and railroads were built, Arab literature and learning blossomed, and overall the culture simply flourished. Beirut transformed from a Sunni town into a coastal cosmopolitan commercial center. Increasing prosperity was experienced by many and, very importantly, this period led to exceptionally strong feelings of Lebanese identity and Lebanese leadership for the Arab nationalist movement among the people of Mount Lebanon.

After World War I the League of Nations mandated the five provinces of the Ottoman Empire to France—this mandated area today makes up modern Lebanon. This newly formed area, bequeathed to France in 1920, was called "Grand Liban." At its outset the territory was evenly divided between Christian and Muslim populations. However, due to French ties with Maronite Christians, the tables of favoritism flipped once again and the Maronites became the new ruling power of the area. The Druze and Shi'ites detested this turn-of-events. To combat opposition and consolidate their authority, the Maronites established associations with the Sunnis and other factions of reasonably placid orientation. Though there were periodic outbursts of violence over French rule and Maronite governing up to the beginning of World War II, these proved inconsequential due to the large showing of French military that remained stationed in the area. Yet once again, despite overarching rule by an outside power, Lebanon remained an autonomously governed area, only subject to veto on its ruling decisions.

On May 26, 1926, French Lebanon became the Republic of Lebanon (*Al Jumhuriyah al Lubnaniyah*). The initial constitution of the Republic proved an unsuccessful document by which to govern, but through all of its numerous revisions, up to current times, it has remained the principle document organizing the Lebanese government. Importantly, in November 1941, France formally declared Lebanon a sovereign independent state, although France continued to maintain a strong military presence in the state. Then, in 1943 due to constitutional reform measures being taken in Lebanon, the French arrested the President of Lebanon. This nefarious act united the various factions of Lebanese politicians, as well as British and Americans who took the side of the Lebanese. France was forced to acquiesce to Lebanese demands for complete independence and all of its troops completely withdrew on December 31, 1946 (Evacuation Day).

Lebanon has continued to see hard times since its independence. However, up until 1975 a modicum of solid national consistency was maintained in the country. Its position on the Mediterranean coast with a number of seaports has made it an important economic player in the area, which has also helped to increase outside interest in its stability and helped to attract foreign aid for development.

Lebanon's long and devastating civil war (1975-1991) consisted of numerous factions vying for often weakly defined and definitely elusive goals. The factions included: The Palestinian Liberation Organization (PLO), Shi'ites (Amal and Hezbollah/Hizbullah), Maronite, Phalangist, Lebanese National Movement (LNM), and Lebanese Forces (LF). In addition to Lebanon's internal fighting, concurrent Israeli and Syrian incursions in the country further exacerbated the destructive and chaotic nature of the time. Its people and infrastructure bore heavy losses. Lebanon is recovering from these losses, but it is doing so slowly. The future is open and looks promising but could hold either promise or peril for this country.

State of the Press With all of its historical difficulties, Lebanon has managed to produce a highly literate, educated, and critical populace. As reported by the U.S. Central Intelligence Agency in 2002 using a 1997 estimate, an average of 86.4 percent of the Lebanese population is considered literate (males, 90.8 percent; females, 82.2 percent). A significant factor driving this educational process is the presence of relatively diverse and sophisticated press and media systems that facilitate continuing education of the Lebanese populace above and beyond traditional schooling. As well, Lebanon has had a positive relationship with the press due to its ethnically diverse population base—each segment requiring papers focused to its particular interests. This niche marketing of papers has allowed for a vibrant dialogue to occur in the Lebanese political and social scene, enough so that one historian has designated Lebanon as the ''true cradle of Arab journalism.'' With multiple opinions available to them, the Lebanese have typically become savvy enough readers/listeners/viewers to gravitate back and forth between papers/channels depending upon which political or social slant they want to read/hear/view. Often, they can tune into a random station generating a broadcast with news content and, within a small portion of time, can suggest the political orientation of the message, some of the history driving the issue being discussed, and some of the key figures related to the topic.

Lebanese traditions with the press and the media date back more than 150 years. The first newspaper, *Hadikat Al-Akhbar* (*The Garden of News*), was published in Lebanon in 1858 through the direction of Khalil El-Khouri and was followed two years later in 1960 by three other papers: *Nafeer Souria* (*The Call of Syria*) published by Butrus Al-Bustani in Lebanon, *Aj-Jawa'ib* (*The Traveling News*) published in Istanbul, and *Barid Paris* (*Paris Mail*) published in France. The time of the Ottoman Empire was an era of significant persecution for journalists in Lebanon. Some of the journalists ended up fleeing to Egypt and founding some of the country's major papers like *Al-Ahram* and *Al-Musawar*. After the Ottomans, the French enacted even harsher press laws. Yet, the Lebanese press was resilient and, by 1929, there were 271 papers with a majority calling for national independence from external oppressive regimes.

At the end of World War II, Lebanon finally gained full independence but, fascinatingly, the first indigenous ruling regime enacted even harsher press laws than the French. However, again the press refused to bow to pressure and, by 1952, a popular revolt was fomented against the government that led to relaxed press laws. In 1962 laws were enacted that guaranteed freedom of the press in Lebanon. Civil war was the next trial that the Lebanese press had to endure during the period 1975-1991. Yet, emerging from the bloody chaos of the war in 1991, the Lebanese press had 105 licensed political publications comprised of 53 dailies, 48 weeklies, and 4 monthly magazines. As well, more than 300 non-political publications were being published. The Lebanese press is tenacious and stalwart, and it continually grows.

In the 2000s, *An-Nahar* or *Al-Nahar* and *Al-Diyar* are arguably the most influential daily papers in terms of raw circulation numbers. *Al-Nahar* is more of a prestigious publication, and *Al-Diyar* is more populist in orientation. *Al-Safir* and *Al-Anwar* are second runner-ups. For all of these papers, the readership ratio is roughly two to one favoring men over women; this is, however, reversed for one paper, *L'Orient le Jour*, where more women than men compose its reader base.

Dailies Almost every publication from Lebanon is published in the capital city of Beirut. Lebanese news is published in four languages: Arabic, French, Armenian, and English. The leading Arabic dailies include: *An-Nahar* (*The Day*), *Al-Safir* (*The Ambassador*), *Al-Diyar* or *Ad-Diyar* (*The Homeland*), *Al-Amal* (*The Hope*), *Lisan ul-Hal* (*The Organ*), *Sada Lubnan* (*Echo of Lebanon*), *Al-Hayat* (*The Life*), and *Al-Anwar* (*The Lights*).

An-Nahar has a circulation of 45,000. It was founded in 1933 as an independent, moderate right-of-center paper, attempting to speak on behalf of the Greek Orthodox community and appeal to a broader audience as well. It has been noted as being a watchdog for public rights and an excellent source for reporting diverse and divergent views in a professional manner. *Al-Safir*, founded in 1974, has a circulation of 50,000. As a political paper, it represents Muslim interests with strong news coverage and background articles, strongly promotes Arab nationalism, and is pro-Syrian. *Al-Diyar* or *Ad-Diyar* is unlike most of the competition because it comes out on Sundays. The paper is strong in classified advertising and is widely read, but its sensationalist style has often lacked professional ethics. *Al-Amal*, founded in 1939, and with a circulation of 35,000, is the voice of the Phalangist party. *Lisan ul-Hal* has a circulation of 33,000 and was founded in 1877; *Sada Lubnan* has a circulation of 25,000 and was founded in 1951; and *Al-Hayat* has a circulation of 31,034 and was founded in 1946 as an independent. *Al-Anwar*, founded in 1959, has a circulation of 25,000. It is published by the famous publishing house of Dar al-Sayyad owned by the Freiha family; the paper typically attempts to appeal to wide readership and is noted for stressing production quality and professional journalism.

Other Arabic papers include: *Al-Harar, Al-Bairaq (The Banner), Bairut (Beirut), Ach-Chaab (The People), Ach-Charq or Al-Sharq (The East), Ach-Chams (The Sun), Ad-Dunya (The World), Al-Hakika (The Truth), Al-Jarida (The [News] Paper), Al-Jumhuriya (The Republic), Journal Al-Haddis, Al-Khatib (The Speaker), Al-Kifah al-Arabi (The Arab Struggle), Al-Liwa (The Stan-*

dard), Al-Mustuqbal, An-Nass (The People), An-Nida (The Appeal), Nida' al-Watan (The Call of the Homeland), An-Nidal (The Struggle), Raqib al-Ahwal (The Observer), Rayah (Banner), Ar-Ruwwad, Sawt al-Uruba (The Voice of Europe), Telegraf-Bairut, Al-Yaum (Today), and *Az-Zamane* or *Al-Zaman.*

With Lebanese Arabs making up 95 percent of the population and with a Muslim religious orientation of various persuasions (including Shi'a, Sunni, Druze, Isma'ilite, Alawite or Nusaryi) making up roughly 70 percent of the faith perspective, it should be apparent why there is a plethora of Arabic newspapers compared to a small minority of other dailies. The other dailies include three Armenian, two French, and one English. The Armenian papers are: *Ararat, Aztag,* and *Zartonk.* The French papers are *L'Orient-Le Jour* (from the publishers of *Al-Nahar* and noted for well-researched background information, intelligent feature stories, and thoughtful editorials) and *Le Soir.* Since a significant number of the country's elite speak French, the French-language newspapers have a higher degree of influence than one might expect. The English paper is the *Daily Star.*

Weeklies and other Periodicals Along with a rich and robust plate of dailies, there is also a burgeoning repertoire of Lebanese weeklies. The weeklies include: *Al-Alam al-Lubnani* (*The Lebanese World*), *Achabaka* (*The Net*), *Al-Ahad* (*Sunday*), *Al-Akhbar* (*The News*), *Al-Anwar Supplement, Dabbour, Ad-Dyar, Al-Hadaf* (*The Target*), *Al-Hawadess* (*Events*), *Al-Hiwar* (*Dialogue*), *Al-Hurriya* (*Freedom*), *Al-Moharrir* (*The Liberator*), *Al-Ousbou' al-Arabi* (*Arab Week*), *Sabih al-Khair* (*Good Morning*), and *Samar.*

Al-Alam al-Lubnani, founded in 1964, has a circulation of 45,000; it is published in Arabic, English, French, and Spanish, and contains matters of politics, literature, and social economy. *Achabaka*, founded in 1956, has a circulation of 108,000, while *Al-Ahad*, a political paper, has a circulation of 32,000. *Al-Akhbar*, the voice of the Lebanese Communist Party, has a circulation of 21,000. The *Al-Anwar Supplement*, a cultural-social paper, has a circulation of 90,000, while the *Ad-Dyar*, a political paper, has a circulation of 46,000. *Al-Hadaf*, founded in 1969, is the voice for the Popular Front for the Liberation of Palestine (PFLP). *Al-Hawadess* has a circulation of 120,000; *Al-Hurriya* has a circulation of 30,000 and is the voice of the Democratic Front for the Liberation of Palestine). *Al-Ousbou'al-Arabi*, a political and social paper, has a circulation of 87,000 throughout the Arab world, while *Samar* is published for the teenage audience.

Some selected examples of periodicals other than weeklies include: *Alam at-Tijarat* (*Business World*), *Arab Construction World, Arab Defense Journal, Arab Economist, Al-Intilak* (*Outbreak*), *Fairuz Lebanon, Al Computer, Communications, and Electronics, Fann at-Tasswir, Al-Mukhtar* (*Reader's Digest*), *Rijal al-Amal* (*The Businessman*), *Tabibok* (*Your Doctor*), and *At-Tarik* (*The Road*).

ECONOMIC FRAMEWORK

As noted above, at least 86.4 percent of the Lebanese population older than fifteen years of age is estimated as literate; thus, illiteracy is not an impediment to newspaper readership. Due to a large proportion of urbanization (83.7 percent), distribution is also not a typical impediment. However, price and time can be significant obstacles. The most respected newspapers can cost up to US$1.32. In a country where the average GDP is US$5,000 and unemployment is at 18 percent, costs can tend to add up quickly. Placed comparatively next to the monthly costs of television subscription, the expense of newsprint becomes more obvious. On a monthly basis, purchasing a newspaper 6 days a week costs about US$29 a month while linking up to satellite television costs between US$10-12. And then even beyond the concern of cost is the concern of time. Those who have been able to find employment are more concerned with getting there and getting home than with picking up a paper. Jamil Mroue of the *Daily Star* has suggested that to combat this dilemma of cost and time, home delivery of papers should be increased, upping readership (which currently hovers at only 50 percent of the population according to the British Broadcasting Service) and at the same time lowering cost by increasing distribution.

Of course, a significant aspect creating the economic woes facing Lebanon was the civil war that raged from the 1970s until the early 1990s, which devastated much of the infrastructure of Beirut and also took its toll through civilian death. The war also caused what has come to be known as ''brain-drain'' or the mass migration of educated intelligentsia to other countries offering better rates of pay and social benefits. Specifically with the press/media, numbers of journalists were killed during the fighting and numerous offices/studios/printing plants were bombed, looted, and/or otherwise sabotaged.

During the beginning years of the war, when fighting was extremely intense, many publications were forced to shut down. However, even in the darkest hours about 24 newspapers and other periodicals were still being regularly published. Also, as soon as the fighting lessened, some of the other publications almost immediately resumed schedule. Papers were able to so easily resume because so many of them were privately owned by either individual proprietors or by publishing houses. All of the typical bureaucracy of government was avoided in getting everything back up and running. Still due to lack of external

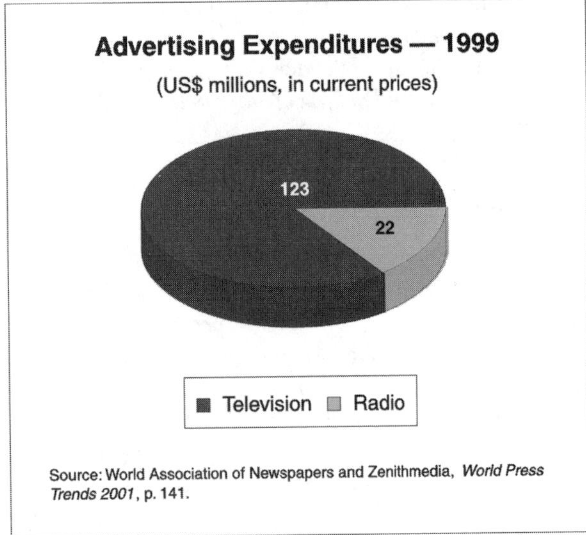

Source: World Association of Newspapers and Zenithmedia, *World Press Trends 2001*, p. 141.

investment in the country, internal unemployment, and the need to cope with immigrant worker populations, physical and economic reconstruction has been slow overall.

While it has been a positive experience for Lebanese press to be privatized, due to the niche marketing of much of the industry to specific ethnic-religious enclaves there has also been a narrow margin of profit. As it has been said, while the Lebanese press may be healthy, they certainly are not wealthy. This would normally be something that could be dealt with, but there are extenuating circumstances in the case of Lebanon. There is a legal requirement that any aspiring publisher must be licensed by purchasing an existing title. The government is refusing to issue any new licenses. Thus, there has become a huge market in newspaper publishing licenses, exorbitantly driving up the price to amounts that make it virtually impossible for anyone but a publishing house to undertake starting a new publication—especially since the profit margin is small. For instance, it could easily cost in the realm of US$300,000-400,000 to acquire the license for a weekly. (The price to acquire a daily could easily double that amount.) This creates an economic hurdle brought about by a government decision that is inhibiting press freedom in Lebanon.

As well, due to the small margin of realized profit available to newspapers, many of them are open to bribery or ''subsidies with strings attached'' from foreign sources. It comes down to being willing to slant the news in someone's favor in order to stay in business. And it is not only corporations or ''rogue'' nations that have been implicated in this practice—Russian and American sources have been named as well. The same can be said for advertising. Again, because of small margins of profit, newspapers actively seek out advertising dollars. However, it is typically not local merchants buying ad space. The advertising dollars seem to come from outside foreign corporations who often have more than simply a product to sell.

As it currently stands, there are about 23 publishing houses operating in Lebanon producing a significant amount of the print that is sold in the country. One of the larger and more well-known houses is Dar Assayad Group (SAL and International). Dar Assayad, owned by the Freiha family, publishes *Al-Anwar; Assayad; Achabaka; Arab Defense Journal; Fairuz Lebanon; Al-Idair; Al Computer, Communications, and Electronics;* and *Al-Fares*. There are also numerous private owners of publications who have held the licenses to such publications for many years, but it has become far less plausible for such private procurement of publishing licenses to continue occurring as the situation stands.

Press Laws

The major laws concerning press and media are the 1962 Press Law and the Audiovisual Media Law (Law 382/94) passed by the parliament in October 1994 and finally applied on September 18, 1996. The 1962 Press Law, which has significant similarities with many other Arab states' press laws, states that nothing my be published that endangers national security, national unity, or state frontiers, or that insults high-ranking Lebanese officials or a foreign head of state. More positive portions of the law, such as Article Nine, state that journalism is ''the free profession of publishing news publications.'' It defines a journalist as anyone whose main profession and income are from journalistic aspects. The 1962 law also set the standard for Lebanese journalists as being at least 21 years of age, having a baccalaureate degree, and having apprenticed for at least four years in journalism. The 1962 Press Law also organized journalists into two syndicates: the Lebanese Press Syndicate (owners) and the Lebanese Press Writers (reporters) Syndicate. As well, a Higher Press Council was created, along with other committees, to consider other issues pertinent to journalists—including devising a retirement plan.

Before and during the civil war of 1975-1991, the 1962 Press Law was rarely enforced, and this was taken advantage of by the press. Upon emerging from the conflict, the government has attempted to become more stringent. In 1994 the government attempted to enforce penalties of detention and fines upon various press establishments but met with significant opposition and gave way under pressure. However, fines and other forms of sanctions remain a significant and ever present threat to press freedom.

Press freedom and media freedom issues often run closely parallel courses. Early in January 1992, the government proposed that any television station wishing to continue its broadcasting not include any "information" programming as that was the purview of the government. The media immediately assailed the government, and the proposal was withdrawn a few days later. Then the government proposed the Audiovisual Media Law of 1994, which did get enacted. It divided television and radio stations into categories related to whether or not they were licensed for broadcasting news and/or political coverage or only entertainment or general concern content. Fascinatingly, this law abolished Lebanon's state broadcasting monopoly. Thus, Lebanon became the first Arab State to authorize private radio and television stations to operate within its borders. However, even though this seems to be a monumental achievement, the downside to this equation is that many of the small operators of illegal stations were closed and influential politicians and corporate conglomerates were the ones who received the bulk of the private licenses. The initial idea with the Audiovisual Media Law was to offer a one-year provisional permit to license applicants and then, if all requirements were met, to bestow a 16-year license. In actuality, licenses were typically immediately granted or denied.

No individual or family is allowed to own more than 10 percent in a television company. Television stations themselves are required to broadcast to the entire country for at least 4,000 hours per year with at least 40 percent of the programming being locally produced. Nothing is allowed that is in the least bit favorable to the establishment of relations with "the Zionist entity." The Audiovisual Media Law is supposedly based upon a premise of seeking to promote balanced news coverage; thus, in any given program there is supposed to be an equal airing of political perspectives ideally providing a balanced orientation. The reality of the situation is of course far from the ideal. In order to monitor and assess whether or not the law is being followed the National Council for Audiovisual Media has been created (CNA). A portion of the controversial aspect of the council's task comes from a portion of the mandate that they have been given. In Arabic a part of their task has been specified as *riqaba*, which can be translated as either censorship or monitoring/supervision. It has been suggested that since prohibitions related to content are dealt with in the Lebanese Penal Code, the CAN's task is more closely related to the second understanding of *riqaba*.

CENSORSHIP

The Ministry of Information always maintains the "right" or at least the ability to control and censor press and media materials. Even though the press got foreign publication censorship abolished in 1967 and persuaded the Ministry of Information to withdraw censors from television stations in 1970, many changes and even the establishment of laws are seemingly no guarantee that they will be followed. The establishment of the CNA is a case in point—such an organization can one day be a promoter of accuracy in media and another day become its very antithesis.

In fact, on August 8, 2001, the CNA issued a document to the Council of Ministers relating to coverage of events. On August 9, Minister of Information Ghazi Aridi suggested an ominous warning to media saying that he would utilize the law to end "mistakes by media outlets, which threaten state security." Correspondingly, the *An Nahar* was charged with defaming the army, and lawsuits were brought against the author of the article, Raphi Madoyan, as well Joseph Nasr, the Editor-in-Chief of *An Nahar*. On August 16, journalist Antione Bassil, and on August 19, journalist Habib Younis, were arrested without warrants and interrogated without lawyers present. On April 8, 2002, journalist Saada Allao had to face the press court of Lebanon for writing articles in November 2001 that were critical of the judicial handling of a case concerning the disappearance of a little girl. Allao had quoted the little girl's mother relating how nothing had been done since she filed a complaint years earlier and had been told by the courts that the documents had been lost. For this article, Allao was on trial and facing three years of imprisonment or a fine of 20 million Lebanese pounds or about 13,500 euros. These are but a small example of how censorship continues to be utilized in Lebanon. As well, it can easily be imagined how self-censorship is practiced by journalists due to concerns for their own and their family's physical and psychological safety.

The problem remains that a country with a ruling on the books that deems it illegal to legitimately criticize the state or emissaries of the state, whether or not such criticism can lead to national instability or interstate instability, essentially retains the "right" for itself to arbitrarily prosecute journalists. In instances such as these, it is the state that defines what constitutes criticism and what the punishment should be given, which is antithetical to freedom of the press.

ATTITUDE TOWARD FOREIGN MEDIA

Foreign media are typically welcome in Lebanon, but there are continuing instances of censorship and intimidation being propagated by the government. Other than case examples already presented, on August 9, 2001, Yehia Houjairi, cameraman of the Kuwaiti state television channel was arrested outside the courts of law for filming a demonstration against a recent raid on anti-Syrian circles called the CPL (Free Patriotic Movement). The chairman of the photographers union intervened on his behalf, and he was subsequently released. On the

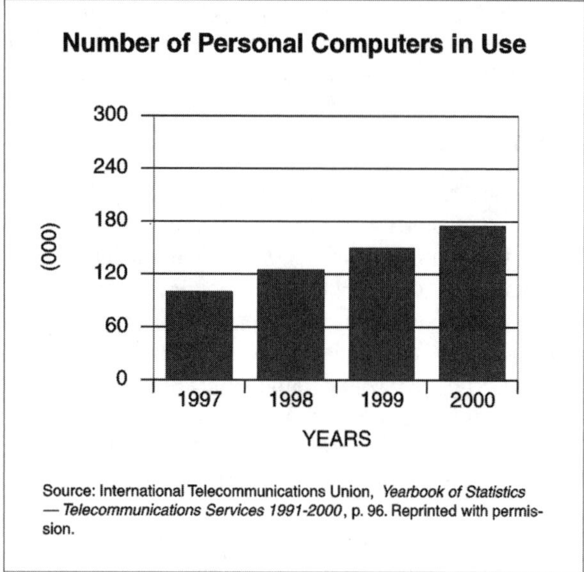

Source: International Telecommunications Union, *Yearbook of Statistics — Telecommunications Services 1991-2000*, p. 96. Reprinted with permission.

same day, Hussein el Moulla was assaulted by a plain-clothes intelligence officer in front of the law courts while photographing the same demonstrations and then was also arrested. On November 3, 2001, Tunisian journalist Taoufik Ben Brik was not allowed to board a plane to fly to an anti-globalization summit he had been invited to attend in Beirut. The employee told him, "Your security cannot be guaranteed."

The foreign press is welcome in Lebanon. However, it remains a significant concern that, even if somewhat limited, seemingly random acts of not only censorship, but violent censorship continue to occur.

NEWS AGENCIES

The Lebanese domestic news agency is the National News Agency (NNA). It can be accessed on the Internet at http://www.nna-leb.gov.lb. It remains state-owned. There is also a single press association, the Lebanese Press Syndicate or Lebanese Press Order. It was founded in 1911 and has 18 members. It is available on the Internet at http://www.pressorder.org.

Currently, there are around 16 foreign bureaus in Lebanon, all of them essentially in Beirut. The bureaus include: Agence France-Presse (AFP), Agenzia Nazionale Stampa Associata (ANSA [Italy]), Allgemeiner Deutscher Nachrichtendienst (ADN [Germany]), Associated Press (AP [USA]), Kuwait News Agency (KUNA), Kyodo Tsushin (Japan), Middle East News Agency (MENA [Egypt]), Reuters (United Kingdom), Rossiiskoye Informatsionnoye Agentstvo Novosti (RIA Novosti [Russia]), United Press International (UPI [USA]), Xinhua (New China) News Agency (People's Republic of China), BTA (Bulgaria), Iraqi News Agency (INA [Iraq]), Jamahiriya News Agency (JANA [Libya]), Prensa Latina (Cuba), and Saudi Press Agency (SPA).

BROADCAST MEDIA

Television Before the licensing requirement brought about by the Audiovisual Media Law in 1994, a multitude of stations dotted the electronic landscape. This has been curtailed. There are now seven television stations that can legally broadcast news information—the seventh just gained licensing in 2001. Télé-Liban began in 1959 but really came into its own in late 1977 as a merger between La Compagnie Libanaise de Télévision (CLT) and Télé-Orient and their subsidiaries of Advision and Télé-Management; in 2002 it faces significant financial hurdles and has suffered neglect in the hands of the government. The Lebanese Broadcasting Company International (LBCI), founded in 1985 by Christian businessmen, is the most universally watched in all regions. National Broadcasting Network (NBN) had a license initially granted before the station even existed; the major single stockholder is speaker of the Lebanese House, Nabih Berri. Murr TV (MTV), founded in 1992, and Future Television or Future TV (FTV), *Al-Manar* (Lighthouse) Television, and NTV are the remaining stations.

Another television station in operation that is not licensed to broadcast news is Télé-Lumiere, an educationally-based station owned by the Catholic Church.

Satellite television is accessible from Arabsat, Eutelsat, Intelsat, Polsat, as well as others. LBC-Sat, Future TV, Middle East Broadcasting Centre (MBC), Syrian TV, CNN, BBC, French TV5, French Arte, and French La Cinquieme are popular channels. Showtime and Orbit packages are available. Euronews and Al-Jazeera are available on Arabsat C-band.

Television broadcasting is said to be able to reach more than 97 percent of the Lebanese adult audience. All told, there are around 15 total stations (with five repeaters) broadcasting to 1.18 million sets.

Radio Following the example of television, only a small number of radio stations have been allowed to broadcast news: Voice of Lebanon, Voice of the People, Radio Lebanese Liberty, Radio Lebanon (government owned), Voice of Tomorrow, and Voice of Light.

As well, local broadcasting is disallowed, and licenses are only provided for stations that can cover the entire country with their programming. The reasoning for this is to attempt to cause people to look beyond their local confines to the greater national area in order to engender feelings of national unity. A few small stations are avoiding closure, including a station broadcasting the Holy Quran, *Sawt al-Mahabba*, and Voice of the South.

Radio broadcasting reaches 85 percent of the Lebanese adult audience. However, while relatively ubiquitous in nature, it is a medium that is still trying to shake off images of wartime use for sending flash bulletins. If radio is utilized, it tends to be less for news than for music. Of those broadcasting news, the favorites seem to be Voice of Lebanon (*Sawt Libnan*) and Radio One (105.5 FM), which relays news neutrally interspersed with music.

Currently there are around 20 AM, 22 FM, and 4 shortwave stations in Lebanon broadcasting to around 2.85 million radios.

Internet Lebanon's government has established its own site on the Internet. As well, there are a numerous other sites that are available originating from Lebanon. The country code is.lb and as of 2000, there were 22 Internet Service Providers (ISPs) in the country and 227,500 Internet users according to the U.S. Central Intelligence Agency.

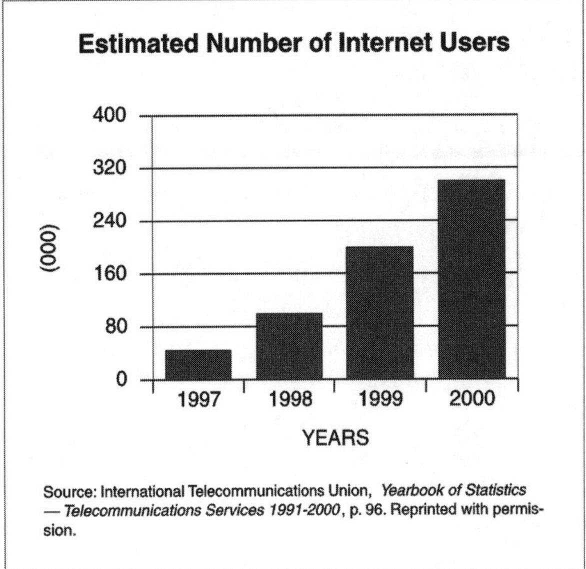

Source: International Telecommunications Union, *Yearbook of Statistics — Telecommunications Services 1991-2000*, p. 96. Reprinted with permission.

EDUCATION & TRAINING

Journalists can gain their necessary baccalaureate education and further graduate education in the country from the Lebanese University, the American University of Beirut, or another acceptable institution.

SUMMARY

The strength and weakness of Lebanon lies in its diversity. The people of Lebanon's commitment to locality has kept them from ever being entirely subjugated, but it has also kept them from ever being completely united. Hopefully, the Lebanese have had their fill of war. Connections are being established and reestablished. Buildings and lives are being built and rebuilt. The fact that Lebanon has always been relatively open to media and opinions, and the fact that media and opinions are more readily available today than ever before, is suggestive of great potential for the people and the country of Lebanon. They only have to take advantage of the opportunities.

BIBLIOGRAPHY

All the World's Newspapers, 2002. Available from http://www.webwombat.com.au/intercom/newsprs/index.htm.

Atalpedia Online. *Country Index*, 2002. Available from http://www.atlapedia.com/online/country_index.

BBC News Country Profiles, 2002. Available from http://news.bbc.co.uk/hi/english/world/middle_east/country_profiles.

Boyd, Douglas. *Broadcasting in the Arab World: A Survey of the Electronic Media in the Middle East*, 3rd ed. Ames, IA: Iowa State University Press, 1999.

Central Intelligence Agency. *The World Factbook 2001*, 2002. Available from http://www.cia.gov/cia/publications/factbook/.

Centre for Media Freedom—Middle East and North Africa (CMF MENA). *Lebanon Code of Ethics*, 2002. Available from http://www.cmfmena.org/publications/Lebanon_Media_Environment.rtf.

———. *The Media Environment in Lebanon: Public Access and Choice*, 2002. Available from http://www.cmfmena.org/publications/Lebanon_Media_Environment.rtf.

Committee to Protect Journalists (CPJ). *Middle East and North Africa 2001: Lebanon*, 2002. Available from http://www.cpj.org/attacks01/mideast01/lebanon.html.

Freedom House. *Freedom in the World: Lebanon*, 2002. Available from http://www.freedomhouse.org/research/freeworld/2002/countryratings/lebanon.html.

International Press Institute. *World Press Freedom Review*, 2002. Available from http://www.freemedia.at/wpfr/world.html.

Kalawoun, Nasser M. *The Struggle for Lebanon: A Modern History of Lebanese-Egyptian Relations*. London: I.B. Tauris, 2000.

Kraidy, Marwan. ''Transnational Television and Asymmetrical Interdependence in the Arab World: The Growing Influence of the Lebanese Satellite Broadcasters.'' *Transnational Broadcasting Studies Journal (TBS)*, Fall/Winter 2000, No. 5. Available from http://www.tbsjournal.com/Archives/Fall00/Kraidy.htm.

Lebanese Broadcasting Corporation International (LBC). *Profile and History*, 2002. Available from http://www.lbci.com.lb/history/index.htm.

Maher, Joanne, ed. *Regional Surveys of the World: The Middle East and North Africa 2002*, 48th ed. London: Europa Publications, 2001.

Redmon, Clare, ed. *Willings Press Guide 2002*, Vol. 2. Chesham Bucks, UK: Waymaker Ltd, 2002.

Reporters Sans Frontieres. *Lebanon Annual Report 2002*. Available from http://www.rsf.fr.

———. *Middle East Archives 2002*. Available from http://www.rsf.fr.

Russell, Malcom. *The Middle East and South Asia 2001*, 35th ed. Harpers Ferry, WV: United Book Press, Inc., 2001.

Stat-USA International Trade Library: Country Background Notes, 2002. Available from http://www.stat-usa.gov.

Sullivan, Sarah. ''Roundtable Examines Ethics, Media Freedom in Lebanon.'' *Transnational Broadcasting Studies Journal (TBS)*, Spring/Summer 2002, No. 8. Available from http://www.tbsjournal.com/beirut.html.

Sumner, Jeff, ed. *Gale Directory of Publications and Broadcast Media,* Vol. 5, 136th ed. Farmington Hills, MI: Gale Group, 2002.

UNESCO Institute for Statistics, 2002. Available from http://www.uis.unesco.org.

World Bank. *Data and Statistics*, 2002. Available from http://www.worldbank.org/data/countrydata/countrydata.html.

World Desk Reference, 2002. Available from http://www.travel.dk.com/wdr/.

Zisser, Eyal. *Lebanon: The Challenge of Independence*. London: I.B. Tauris, 2000.

—Clint B. Thomas Baldwin

LESOTHO

BASIC DATA

Official Country Name:	Kingdom of Lesotho
Region (Map name):	Africa
Population:	2,143,141
Language(s):	Sesotho, English, Zulu, Xhosa
Literacy rate:	71.3%

BACKGROUND & GENERAL CHARACTERISTICS

Lesotho is landlocked and completely encircled by South Africa, with approximately 2.14 million people of which 99.7 percent speak Sesotho, with English used as the business language. The kingdom is a fragile democracy—a hereditary constitutional monarchy having a king as head of state without executive or legislative powers. Executive power is vested in the cabinet headed by a prime minister. Predominantly mountainous with a literacy rate of 83 percent, the kingdom's population is concentrated wherever arable land is found, primarily in the lower veld, along rivers and the capital of Maseru.

The press's growth and size are inhibited by Lesotho's weakened infrastructure, dependence on South Africa (35 percent of male wage-earners work as miners), and a mostly rural population (agriculture caters for 57 percent of the domestic labor force, with 86 percent of the population as subsistence farmers) with a low per-capita income—factors relegating the purchase of newspapers, radios, television and the Internet as unaffordable luxuries. The HIV/AIDS prevalence of 23 percent threatens life expectancy, population size and socioeconomic productivity, including media patronage.

Since attaining its independence from Britain in 1966, Lesotho has undergone more than one coup, and has been engulfed in several political mayhems resulting in killings, looting and property destruction involving the press, which is caught in a quagmire adversely affecting its quality and existence.

Lesotho's economic and press sustainability is dominated by its geography and dependence on South Africa, the main buyer of water, Lesotho's primary resource. The economy is based on a declining Gross Domestic Product that in 1990 was 67 percent; in 1997, 33 percent; and in 2000, 11.5 percent, as well as from mineworkers employed in South Africa, erratic subsistence agriculture (wheat, corn and sorghum) and livestock production. Growing privatization emanating from the IMF-driven restructuring has led to the need for a poverty reduction and growth package to deal with escalating unemployment precipitated by subsequent retrenchments intended to reduce the size of the government, the largest single employer. There is a small manufacturing industry that depends on farm products supporting canning, milling, leather and jute initiatives.

Civil disorder in 1998 destroyed 80 percent of the commercial infrastructure in major cities, many of them lacking in insurance coverage. Political turmoil has adversely affected the media, especially the independent press, which lost buildings, equipment, the ability to cover events, personnel through retrenchment, sales and advertising. This was compounded by government directives discouraging advertising in papers considered critical of the ruling party. The resulting shoestring budget impedes the press' long-term development. Even with reconstruction efforts underway, progress in advertising and circulation are limited by the drop in readership due to lost jobs and an increase in the cost of printing and premiums. Economic development is impeded by a lack of natural resources, serious land shortages, a fragile ecology, and vulnerability to cyclic adverse climatic conditions, leaving the country a net importer of foodstuffs.

Although there are various small publications, periodicals and newsletters, most of Lesotho's media are sate-owned. The Lesotho News Agency (LENA), the only news agency, controls a widely disseminated newspaper. The Inter Press Service (IPS) of Italy operates under the auspices of LENA, a foreign bureau and a national radio broadcasting station. Prohibitive printing costs, poor technology and unavailability of newsprint make it difficult for Lesotho's small publications. Generally, low investment in this sector has adversely impacted the growth of the printing and publishing industry. Most of the country's printing jobs, including major works from the government, are being done outside the country. Government operated weekly papers are *Lenstoe la Basotho, Lesotho Today, Lesotho Weekly, Makatolle, The Mirror, MoAfrica, Public Eye, Mopheme (The Survivor), The Sun, The Southern Star and Shoeshoe* (a quarterly). The *Leselinyana la Lesotho* (Light of Lesotho) is published fortnightly, and *Moeletsi oa Basotho,* a weekly, are published by Lesotho Evangelical and Roman Catholic churches, respectively.

The Lesotho National Broadcasting Service is government-owned and broadcasts in Sesotho and English. Its radio and television transmissions began in 1964 and 1988, respectively.

The are six publishers: Longman Lesotho (Pty) Ltd; Macmillan Boleswa Publishers of Lesotho (Pty) Ltd; Mazenod Institute; Morija sesuto Book Depot; St Michael's Mission and Government Printer.

PRESS LAW

The government, which controls mass media, has paid lip service to the adoption of a national media policy for many years. Despite its suspension from 1970-1986 and being rewritten in 1990, there has been very little change in the key elements of the constitution. While freedoms of expression, peaceful assembly and association are proclaimed, Lesotho's successions of governments have failed to articulate and adopt a national media policy, with one proposal shelved by the Ministry of Communication for years. Changes of governments also meant that new governments ignore or reverse promises made by their predecessors.

Government's control of media's purpose is not only to ensure timely dissemination of government policy, but also censorship. Government and independent journalists have been attacked for reporting certain matters or for being in the wrong place. Government and security forces have successively suppressed free press, and shot, maimed, defamed and fired journalists for reporting anything other than official statements from the government. The media has not been cowed into silence and continues to publish amidst many obstacles and is enjoying some degree of press freedom. But overall, there is a great deal of self-censorship and restraint by government-owned media.

STATE-PRESS RELATIONS

State-press relations are defined by draconian internal security legislation giving considerable power to the military and police, and restricting the right of assembly including certain forms of industrial activity. Independent press and its staff suffered the worst atrocities in September 1998 due to looting and burning of buildings compounded by security forces' arbitrary arrests, incommunicado detentions and ill-treatment of detainees. The persisting political climate has proven harsh, where journalists are often faced with intimidation from the government, and attacks and accusations for supporting the government's opposing political parties.

ATTITUDE TOWARD FOREIGN MEDIA

The attitude toward foreign media is a mixed bag with media associations having international links operating in Lesotho. They are: The National Union of Journalists and the Media Institute of South Africa (MISA, the local chapter being called Media Institute of Lesotho-MILES), News Share Foundation (a journalist cooperative), the Commonwealth Journalists Association, and the Adopt-A-Media Network.

ELECTRONIC NEWS MEDIA

Regarding electronic News Media, Lesotho lacks resources to develop a film industry, but the Lesotho Council of Churches owns a mobile video outfit that produces videos for the international and local market. MILES also is funding the development of the Lesotho video industry, and it operates a video production unit for assisting members with technical support and training skills. Lesotho is rapidly becoming computerized with the government controlling most facets of information technology.

In 2000, government-run Lesotho Telecommunications Authority (LTC) was providing telephones and fax service in a joint venture with South Africa's Vodacom. The project will include a cellular telephone service, with the government relinquishing ownership in June 2001.

The Internet has made slow inroads reflecting low incomes and a small potential market. Before localizing the service, Lesotho's Office Equipment's Internet connectivity was through service providers in South Africa. The University of Lesotho's Institute of Extra-Mural Studies owns its own Internet service and runs an Internet café for students and the public. South Africa's electronic and print media of varying reliability and quality is widely available in Lesotho. Independent newspapers, including the *Mirror, MoAfrica,* and *Mopheme* (The Survivor), tend to be critical of the government and can be found on the Internet.

Education & Training

Christian missions under the Ministry of Education's direction provides a free, compulsory, seven-year elementary education. Provisions for secondary, technical, vocational and post secondary education have increased. Lesotho's background in media training is poor with the National University of Lesotho offering a diploma certificate in mass communications with most of the training done in-house or as short courses organized by groups such as MILES and CM Media.

Summary

Considering a history of government suppression, shootings and maiming of journalists, the media has not been silenced and continues to publish and enjoy some degree of freedom. However, there exists a persistent threat of an armed conflict with a Lesotho Defense Force historically involved in domestic politics, and factional infighting in addition to the government feverishly suppressing a free press. Opposition in parliament may strengthen democracy's weak roots in Lesotho by promoting a favorable press environment. MILES' steadfast advocacy for constitutional reforms and a self-regulating media-driven body in opposition to government's media-control legislation holds further promise for an improved free press.

Bibliography

''Foreign Journalists Expelled, Harassed.'' Africa News Service. November 16, 2000.

Gamble, Paul. ''Lesotho.'' In *Economist Intelligence Unit Country Profile: Botswana and Lesoto* (May 2002): 51-95.

Gay, J., D. Gill, and D. Hall, eds. Lesotho's Long Journey: Hard choices at the Crossroads.'' Maseru, Lesotho: Sechaba Consustants, 1995.

IMF. Lesotho Statistical Annex, June 2001.

Windhoek, Namibia. ''Editor Loses Defamation Case.'' In *Lesotho Alert.* Media Institute of Southern Africa, October 23, 2000. Available from http://www.misanet.org/.

———. ''Minister Threatens to Fire Journalists.'' In *Lesotho Alert.* October 12, 1998. Available from http://www.misanet.org/.

———. ''Speaker Lifts Ban Against Media.'' In *Lesotho Alert.* September 16, 1997. Available from http://www.misanet.org/.

———. ''Speaker of Parliament Shuns Discussion on Ban.'' In *Lesotho Alert.* September 16, 1997. Available from http://www.misanet.org/.

''World Development Indicators.'' World Bank. Washington, DC, 2002.

—Saliwe M. Kawewe, Ph.D.

Liberia

Basic Data

Official Country Name:	Republic of Liberia
Region (Map name):	Africa
Population:	3,225,837
Language(s):	English, ethnic group languages
Literacy rate:	38.3%
Area:	111,370 sq km
Number of Television Stations:	2
Number of Television Sets:	70,000
Television Sets per 1,000:	21.7
Number of Radio Stations:	10
Number of Radio Receivers:	790,000
Radio Receivers per 1,000:	244.9

Background & General Characteristics

The Republic of Liberia is slightly larger than the state of Tennessee in the United States. Liberia is a democratic country situated on the western African coast and borders the Atlantic Ocean along its entire southwest coastline of 579 kilometers. Much of Liberia is covered with tropical rain forest while 10 percent is water and the country's terrain ranges from coastal plains to plateau to low mountains. Liberia's climate is tropical.

A low literacy rate of 38.3 percent (male 53.9 percent and women 22.4 percent) makes radio the preferred medium of communication, with about 800,000 radio receivers nationwide.

The legal and constitutional frameworks exist for a free and independent press in Liberia, but the reality is that government routinely shuts down independent media houses. Journalists who are critical of the government are frequently jailed without due process. Most press activities are concentrated around Monrovia, the capital. The press exercises self censorship and continues to criticize the government at their own risk.

In 2002, Liberia was home to two independent daily newspapers, the *Inquirer* and the *News*. Another independent newspaper, *New National*, publishes biweekly. A fourth independent newspaper, *The Analyst*, published sporadically until police closed it down on April 25, 2002. The government's Ministry of Information publishes the *New Liberian bi-weekly*. The ruling National Patriotic Party publishes the *Pepperbird* sporadically. Two government ministers own the *Monrovia Guardian* and *Poll Watch*, respectively; both are bi-weekly. Three other independent newspapers, *The Journalist*, the *Concord Times*, and the *Daily Times* remain closed.

Economic Framework

A seven-year civil war which began on Christmas Eve 1989 ended with elections in July 1997 and brought President Charles Taylor to power. The years of fighting coupled with an unsettled domestic security situation has led to the flight of most businesses and has disrupted formal economic activity. The rebuilding of the social and economic structure of Liberia is stagnant. An United Nations-imposed sanction is in place until May 2003. The government relies on revenue from its maritime registry and lumber exports to provide the bulk of its foreign exchange earnings. Eighty percent of Liberia's 3.2 million people live below the poverty line and unemployment is 70 percent.

Most newspapers print a maximum of 1,000 copies and the advertising rates are abysmally low. A full-page ad costs about $100 (U.S.) in a daily newspaper with 1,000 circulation. All newspapers are printed in English, the official language. Beside English, Liberia has sixteen ethnic groups and four language families.

The currency exchange rate between the American dollar and Liberian dollar is about 1:50. Newspapers pay approximately $200 (U.S.) or $10,000 (L) to print 1,000 copies of an 8-page paper. Newspapers typically retail for $20 (40 cents U.S.), the same price of a pint of rice, Liberia's food staple.

Sabannoh Printing Press had a monopoly on newspaper printing until March 2002 when the government granted a permit to the Press Union of Liberia to operate Liberia Printing Incorporated.

Press Laws

The Liberian Constitution guarantees press freedom. Article 15(a-e) states:

a) Every person shall have the right to freedom of expression being fully responsible for the abuse thereof;

b) The right includes freedom of speech and of the press;

c) There shall be no limitation on the public right to be informed about the government and its functionaries;

d) Access to state-owned media shall not be denied because of any disagreement with or dislike of the ideas expressed;

e) This freedom may be limited only by judicial action in proceedings grounded in defamation or invasion of the rights to privacy.

Liberia, in theory, has an independent judiciary but the president exercises strong executive powers that frequently cross the lines that separate it from the legislative and judicial branches.

Censorship

Self-censorship is very common. A Communication Act promulgated by government on August 28, 1989, empowers a National Communications and Regulation Commission to "devise policies and/or regulations to govern the creation, establishment and operation of all electronic and print media within the territorial confines of the Republic of Liberia."

State-Press Relations

There is mutual suspicion between government and the independent press. The Press Union of Liberia, established in 1964, is dynamic and defends the rights of journalists.

Attitude toward Foreign Media

Foreign journalists need a clearance from the Ministry of Information. There are documented cases of foreign journalists who were charged with espionage, detained and had their equipment and tapes confiscated. All were released after appeals from the international community.

Broadcast & Electronic News Media

The Liberia Communications Network (LCN), owned by Liberia's president Charles Taylor, has a nationwide reach and broadcasts on FM and short wave frequencies. There are three other stations with short wave frequency capability; two of which are religious stations. The first of these, Eternal Love Winning Africa (ELWA) has broadcast in Liberia off and on since 1954. The second, Radio Veritas, owned by the Catholic Diocese of Liberia, has been shut down frequently because of Veritas's stance on human rights and social justice issues. STAR Radio, another independent radio station with short wave transmittals remains closed.

The government-owned Liberia Broadcasting System (LBS) is heard only around Monrovia as are the privately owned FM radio stations DC-101, Liberia Christian Radio, and LOVE-FM. Stone FM is heard mostly around Harbel, near the Firestone rubber company. There are two television broadcast stations plus four low-power repeaters. Private video clubs proliferate. The Liberia News Agency (LINA) rarely sends out wire stories.

The only public Internet service, Data Tech, launched in early 1999 is controlled by a family with close personal ties to the president (World Reporter).

EDUCATION & TRAINING

The University of Liberia awards a bachelor of arts in mass communications. Civil strife has led to frequent closures of the University. A brain drain has mitigated the quality of trained journalists in the country. The Liberian Institute of Journalism, the Press Union of Liberia, and some diplomatic missions offer occasional in-service training. Many journalists acquire skills through apprenticeship.

The Press Union of Liberia gives annual merit awards to individuals and media institutions.

SUMMARY

Liberia's current president, Charles Taylor, tolerates minimal criticism yet the independent press remains strong partly because it is unified by the dynamic Press Union of Liberia. Press freedom is protected by the constitution, but like most developing nations, the press laws in Liberia are only as good as the government that enacts, enforces, and interpret such laws.

BIBLIOGRAPHY

Allen, William C. ''Soaring Above the Clouds of Mediocrity: The Challenges of the Liberian Press in the '90s.'' Liberian Studies Journal (XV:1, 1990):74-84.

Best, Kenneth Y. ''The Liberian Press: Quo Vadis?'' Liberian Studies Journal (XXII:1, 1997): 45-67.

Burrowes, Carl Patrick. ''Modernization and the Decline of Press Freedom: Liberia 1847 to 1970.'' Journalism & Mass Communication Monographs 160 (Dec. 1996).

Central Intelligence Agency. ''Liberia.'' *The World Factbook.* Available from www.cia.gov.

Constitutional Advisory Assembly. Constitution of the Republic of Liberia. Monrovia, Liberia: Sabannoh Press Ltd., 1983.

Freedom Forum. ''Liberian battle for control of shortwave radio heats up.'' September 5, 2001. Available from www.freedomforum.org.

———. ''Liberian journalists freed after more than a month in jail on espionage charges.'' April 2, 2001. Available from www.freedomforum.org.

Nelson, Estella. ''PUL Regrets Action Against Press Freedom.'' The News [Monrovia]. May 6, 2002. Available from http://allafrica.com.

———. ''Journalists Seek Close Collaboration With Government.'' April 21, 2002. Available from http://allafrica.com.

Rogers, Momo K. ''The Liberian Press: An Analysis.'' Journalism Quarterly (No. 63, 1986): 273-281.

———. ''The Press in Liberia, 1826-1996: A Select Chronology.'' Liberian Studies Journal (XXII:1, 1997): 95-120.

———. ''Liberian Journalism, 1826-1980: A Descriptive History.'' Ph.D. diss., Southern Illinois University at Carbondale, 1987.

World Reporter. ''Liberia's naked ambition?'' October 30, 2001. Available from www.worldreporter.org.

—Dr. William C. Allen

THE LIBYAN ARAB JAMAHIRIYA

BASIC DATA

Official Country Name:	Socialist People's Libyan Arab Jamahiriya
Region (Map name):	Africa
Population:	5,240,599
Language(s):	Arabic, Italian, English
Literacy rate:	76.2%
Area:	1,759,540 sq km
Number of Television Stations:	12
Number of Television Sets:	730,000

Television Sets per 1,000:	139.3
Number of Radio Stations:	24
Number of Radio Receivers:	1,350,000
Radio Receivers per 1,000:	257.6

BACKGROUND & GENERAL CHARACTERISTICS

Libyan Arab Jamahiriya is a country in northern Africa that is slightly larger than the state of Alaska. It shares borders with Tunisia, Algeria, Niger, Chad, Sudan, Egypt, and the Mediterranean Sea. Its terrain is mostly barren, flat, or plains- and plateaus-endowed. The climate is Mediterranean on the coast, but hot, dry, and radically desert-laden (90 percent of the Libyan territory) at the interior. There are about 5.3 million Libyan residents; 625,000 are African majority workers (500,000) and the remainder are workers from the Maghreb, Egypt, Italy, Malta, Pakistan, Turkey, and Eastern Europe. Ninety-seven percent are Sunni-Muslims, of Berber and Arab descent, and the remaining three percent are from other Arab neighbors such as Italy, Greece, Malta, India, Turkey, and Pakistan. Arabic is the official language, but Italian and English are widely spoken and understood in metropolitan/harbor areas. Since the coup of 1969 against the Idriss al Swnissi monarchy, Col. Muammar Abu Minyar al-Qadhafi (hereafter, Qadhafi) has ruled this oil-rich country, embracing what he baptized "The Third International Theory," an alleged mixture of socialism and Islam. In 1987, Libyan expansionism was stopped as military troops were ejected from Northern Chad (Aozou Strip). During the period 1992 through 1999, UN sanctions were imposed on the Qadhafi regime, particularly in view of the alleged worldwide terroristic activities at the wake of the 1988 Lockerbie bombing.

Government & Political Framework The official name of Libya is Al Jumahiriyah al Arabiyah ash Shabiyah al Ishtirikiyah al Uzma (Arabic) or The Great Socialist People's Libyan Arab Jamahiriya. The term *Jamahiriya* means roughly "state of the masses." Libya is a military dictatorship. There are 25 *baladiyats* (municipalities) or 13 *aqalims* (regions). The country gained its independence from Italy in December 24, 1951, and after the Qadhafi coup a Constitution was introduced which was amended in 1977. Its basic tenets are a legislative unicameral branch or the General People's Congress, whose members are elected via universal and mandatory suffrage across a pyramid of people's committees, local councils, and such. There is one Supreme Court, with the whole legal regime variously predicated both upon civil law and Islamic law (*Shari'a*). At the executive level, Qadhafi is the head of state, with no official title, and Mr. al-Shamekh is the premier or head of government. The opposition is weak, and is based on nationalistic and/or Libyan Islamic tendencies. Libya is a member of a number of international organizations, including the Arab Fund for Economic and Social Development (AFESD), the Council for Arab Economic Unity (CAEU), G-77, IMF, INTERPOL, MONUC, the Organization of Arab Petroleum Exporting Countries (OAPEC), OPEC, the UN, and UNESCO.

ECONOMIC FRAMEWORK

The Libyan economy is mainly based upon oil exports. In fact, crude oil and refined petroleum goods represent the quasi-totality of exports (US $14 billion), 25 percent of the GDP, and all public revenues ($7 billion). The total real GDP amounts to about $46 billion, and external debt is about 10 percent of this figure. Libya has the highest per capita GDP, about US $9000, but in reality income is very unevenly distributed, as unemployment remains extremely high at 30 percent. The country imports 75 percent of its food and consumer goods, although textiles, food processing, petroleum products, cement, and handicrafts are growing production branches. Some of Libya's trade partners include Italy, Germany, Spain, Turkey, Tunisia, Great Britain, France, and South Korea.

PRESS LAWS

The daily newspaper circulation in Libya is very low at 13 per 1,000 people. There are very few laws to protect, promote, and foster a spirit and a practice of open and free press in Libya, despite the constitutional rhetoric and Qadhafi's "state of the masses" or Jamahiriya polemics. In truth, there are only four daily, legislated newspapers in Libya, including the Arabic *Al Fajr al Jadid* (The New Dawn), published by the Jamahiriya News Agency (JANA). The Libyan state owns and controls the country's media and press systems. No opinions against the military rule are permitted. There is, by law, only one Great Socialist People's Libyan Arab Jamahiriya Broadcasting system as the national television broadcast medium. No privately owned televisions stations are allowed. Prior to October 1998, the national radio system was named the Voice of the Greater Arab Homeland. When Qadhafi changed his ideological and geopolitical orientations and partnership to Africa, away from the Arab world and the Middle East, the radio system took on a different name, The Voice of Africa.

CENSORSHIP

Some political divergence of contentions and opinions may be allowed within the *Majlis* or the Libyan

Chamber. When it comes to the media and press, however, the rules are strictly censorship-focused. Even self-censorship is imposed upon the Libyan media and press via the use of clandestine informants or spies. For example, on October 1, 2000, media and press matters became ''so disturbing'' that the Ministry of Information, Culture, and Tourism was disbanded.

State-Press Relations

There are no democratic or competitive media and press relations with the Libyan regime. JANA is under the strict iron hold of the Libyan leader. Qadhafi is notorious for eliminating opponents, particularly in Europe, Egypt, and the Sudan. Qadhafi relies mostly on his family, in particular his second son Saif al-Islam.

Attitudes Toward Foreign Media

The foreign media and press, Arab, Western, and Eastern are strictly under the supervision of the military regime. For instance, while Qadhafi stated that all foreign media are welcome to attend the trial of six Bulgarian medics accused of infecting people with the HIV virus, in actuality only a few Bulgarian media representatives were issued visas, while others were blatantly refused. Many media from other countries were also thus unable to attend. No foreign media and press can enter the country without Qadhafi's permission.

News Agencies

JANA, Jamahiriya Broadcasting, and Voice of Africa are closely monitored and used for the regime's propaganda. Any journalist, media, press, or newscasting system that criticizes Qadahfi's Jamahirya may be immediately suspended, arrested, or even disappear. According to World Press Freedom Review, Mr. Abdullah Ali al-Sanussi al-Darrat, journalist of the Benghazi's *Al-Zahf Al-Akhdar* (The Green March), was suspended in March 1998 due to ''his articles attacking fraternal Arab states and friendly countries.'' Other members of the same publication were later suspended. Mr. Al-Darrat disappeared.

Broadcast Media

All Libyan media broadcast systems are solely under Qadhafi's control. In late October 2000, it seemed that Qadhafi agreed with the French government on a ''program to assist employees in the media sector [that] will allow Libya to benefit from cutting edge media and telecommunication technology'' (World Press Freedom Review).

Electronic News Media

There are about 8,000 Internet users, with only one Internet Service Provider (ISP). Internet use is closely monitored. There are numerous sites related to Libya but few of them are run from within the country itself.

Education & Training

Primary and secondary education is compulsory in Libya between the ages of 6 and fifteen. Only about one-fifth of college-age people in Libya attend a university. There are many universities, colleges, and institutes in Libya, particularly in Tripoli, Benghazi, and Sabha. Education output has grown remarkably since the beginning of the Qadhafi regime, climbing up from about 35 percent to 80 percent in 2002. In the field of journalism, media, and press there are a few programs, especially in Tripoli and Benghazi. Many journalists possess media and journalism degrees from Italy, England, the USA, or the Arab world.

Summary

Despite a few recent measures to liberate the press and media in Libya, the information and press systems in that country are clearly controlled by the Qadhafi regime. The removal of the sanctions and the media globalization are major potential emancipators of this sector of the Libyan society and economy. The press also has the opportunity to play a role in leading the way to this change, but it has not yet become involved in this conflict.

Bibliography

Afrol News, 2002. Available from www.afrol.com.

American Political Science Review. Washington, DC: American Political Science Association, 1998.

The Central Intelligence Agency (CIA). *World Factbook 2001*. Directorate of Intelligence, 2002. Available from www.cia.gov/.

International Press Institute, 2002. Available from www.freemedia.at/.

Sarri, Samuel. *Ethics of the International Monetary Systems*. Philadelphia: University of Pennsylvania Press, 1998.

World Almanac and Books of Facts. New York: K-III Reference Co., 2002.

—Samuel Sarri

LIECHTENSTEIN

Basic Data

Official Country Name:	Principality of Liechtenstein

Region (Map name):	Europe
Population:	32,207
Language(s):	German, Alemannic
Literacy rate:	100%

The Imperial Free Territory of Schellenberg (1699) and the County of Vaduz (1712), purchased by the German princely family of Liechtenstein, were merged to form modern Liechtenstein in 1719. Liechtenstein was, successively, a member state of the Holy Roman Empire until its dissolution in 1806, Napoleon's Confederation of the Rhine from 1807 to 1815, and the German Confederation until 1866. Geographically separated from a united Germany by Austria and Switzerland, Liechtenstein opted for a custom's union, first with Austria and since 1923 with Switzerland. The first Liechtenstein Prince to take up permanent residence in the principality was Francis Joseph II, who reigned from 1938 to 1989.

Liechtenstein is a constitutional monarchy with a reigning prince; since 1989 this has been Hans Adam II. The government is centered in the capital, Vaduz, where a 25-member Diet, or legislature, represents the principality's population of over 32,000 residents. Article 40 of the Constitution of Liechtenstein guarantees each person the right to freely express his opinions and to communicate his ideas verbally, in writing, and in print, or by picture, within the limits of the laws and of morality. The same Article 40 rejects censorship except in public performances and exhibitions.

Although a small nation, Liechtenstein has a highly developed industrialized economy based on the free-enterprise system. Low business taxes and easy incorporation rules have enabled almost 74,000 companies to establish offices within the principality. Liechtenstein's workforce is divided among the service industry, agriculture, fishing, foresting, horticulture, and industry, trade, and building, and the country's workers are among Europe's highest wage earners.

Newspapers and periodicals and radio and television represent the media in Liechtenstein. Liechtenstein's two daily newspapers are *Zeitungen* (www.vaterland.li), with a 1995 circulation of 8,920, and the *Liechtensteiner Volksblatt* (www.lol.li/Volksblatt), with 8,700 readers in 1995. The *Liechtensteiner Woche* is a weekly newspaper with a 1998 circulation of 13,900. Liechtenstein prints two weekly periodicals of general interest, *Liechtensteiner Anzeigere,* which had a 1995 circulation of 29,000, and the *Liechtensteiner Wochenzeitung,* with 13,880 readers in 1995. Liechtenstein has only one radio station, Radio Liechtenstein (Radio L, www.radio.li), and only one television station, XML Television. The three press bureaus in Liechtenstein are L-Press, Mediateam, and Pressburo Vaduz. The population of Liechtenstein also has ready access to newspapers, periodicals, radio stations, and television stations published and/or broadcast from outside the borders of the principality. Liechtenstein citizens considering a career in the media usually attend universities in neighboring Switzerland, Austria, or Germany.

BIBLIOGRAPHY

Constitution of the Principality of Liechtenstein. Vaduz: Gutenberg, 1982.

Kranz, Walter, ed. *The Principality of Liechtenstein.* Vaduz: Government Printing Office, n.d.

Seger, Otto. *A Survey of Liechtenstein History.* Vaduz: Government Printing Office, n.d.

World Mass Media Handbook, 1995 ed. New York: United Nations Department of Public Information, 1995.

—William A. Paquette

LITHUANIA

BASIC DATA

Official Country Name:	Republic of Lithuania
Region (Map name):	Europe
Population:	3,610,535
Language(s):	Lithuanian, Polish, Russian
Literacy rate:	98.0%
Area:	65,200 sq km
GDP:	11,314 (US$ millions)
Number of Daily Newspapers:	99
Total Circulation:	124,700,000
Total Newspaper Ad Receipts:	73 (Litai millions)
As % of All Ad Expenditures:	39.60
Number of Television Stations:	20
Number of Television Sets:	170,000
Television Sets per 1,000:	47.1
Number of Cable Subscribers:	330,040

Cable Subscribers per 1,000:	89.2
Number of Satellite Subscribers:	50,000
Satellite Subscribers per 1,000:	13.8
Number of Radio Stations:	116
Number of Radio Receivers:	1,900,000
Radio Receivers per 1,000:	526.2
Number of Individuals with Computers:	240,000
Computers per 1,000:	66.5
Number of Individuals with Internet Access:	225,000
Internet Access per 1,000:	62.3

BACKGROUND & GENERAL CHARACTERISTICS

Historical Traditions Lithuania, the largest of the Baltic nations, has experienced and been influenced by numerous foreign occupations. The name Lithuania was first mentioned in the Latin chronicle *Annales Quedlinburgenses* in AD 1009, and it was thought that the Lithuanian peoples were descendants of ancient Roman settlers. However, it is more likely that the original people came from Asia about 4,000 to 10,000 years ago. Lithuania's development as a nation was not linear: it has existed as an independent state only intermittently throughout its history of invasions and occupations. However, even when the national language, Lithuanian, was banned and reading or writing books in the native tongue was forbidden, the people were determined to preserve their heritage and traditions for future generations. This strong attachment to their culture remains a characteristic of Lithuanians in the twenty-first century.

Lithuania adopted Christianity at the end of the fourteenth century and has remained predominantly Roman Catholic. During the Soviet domination and ban on religion, Catholicism was never totally suppressed. It was ready for a revival when independence was achieved. Religion always played a significant role in Lithuanian publications and the initial books to be published in Lithuanian were religious ones. The first book, *Catechism*, was written by Mazvydas and published in 1547 in the town of Karaliaucius. The first publishing house was founded in Vilnius.

In the fourteenth century, Lithuania and Poland formed a confederation that lasted almost two hundred years and became one of medieval Europe's largest empires. In the eighteenth century Lithuania came under Russian rule and Russia attempted unsuccessfully to eradicate the Lithuanian culture and language. The religious emphasis of the publications changed, and secular literature became more widespread. By the early twentieth century, most writing was linked to the independence movement.

The occupation of Lithuania by imperial Russia lasted until 1915, and from 1864 to 1904, the Russian alphabet was introduced, and the press in Latin was banned. Nonetheless, the people of Lithuania protected their identity and rights and successfully rallied against the larger country of Russia. The ban on the press was lifted in 1904. In 1905, the *Vilnius Seimas* (legislative body) urged the people to stop paying taxes and to refuse to send their children to Russian schools. After World War I, on February 16, 1918, the country proclaimed its independence; it adopted its first permanent constitution on August 1, 1922. The second permanent constitution was adopted on May 12, 1938.

Lithuania was an independent nation between World War I and II and maintained its religious affiliation to Catholicism. From this religious group emerged a cadre of progressive individuals who played an important role in the intellectual life of the country, including the press. However, in 1940 Lithuania was once again annexed to the USSR and the Soviets undermined the creativity of the writers. With the arrival of the occupying Soviet troops, the intellectuals were arrested, or if they were able, they migrated to the West. Those who remained continued to write in secret. On July 21, 1940, the national Seimas proclaimed the country a Soviet Socialist Republic, and on August 3, 1940, Lithuania became the fourteenth member of the Soviet Union. This event minimized the country's ties to the West and the influence of its media, thus essentially leaving Lithuania in a news vacuum.

The Soviet regime decimated the entire economy of the country; all financial establishments were nationalized. Local culture became sovietized. The only respite came at the end of 1941 when the Soviets became more involved in their war with Germany and withdrew their troops. With the withdrawal of the Communists, there was a resurgence of hope for freedom, and the Lithuanians strove to regain their independence by proclaiming a provisional government. However, the Germans did not recognize this administration and it was abolished. Nonetheless, major resistance newspapers were published, the anti-Nazi movement flourished, and consequently the Germans failed to organize a local SS legion.

On July 13, 1944, the Soviets re-entered Vilnius, and the entire country was once again under Soviet domination. Although Lithuania attempted to resist the occupation, the Soviets destroyed the economy, and the rights that had been established by the Republic of Lithuania were eroded. Any signs of independence and national identity were extinguished. For the next 40 years Lithuania was subjugated to the political, economical, and cultural goals of the Soviet Union, including press censorship. This strict control continued until the 1980s when the Soviet policy changed and people were given more freedom to speak out against the government without fear of reprisals. By the end of the 1980s, economic chaos in the Soviet Union forced the Soviet president, Mikhail Gorbachev, to institute reforms: *glasnost* was declared. Also during this period, Lithuania established many democratic changes, and the press became more and more independent. In 1988 the Lithuanian Communist Party (LCP) was forced to relinquish its monopoly on the press and by 1989 censorship ceased. This angered Gorbachev who then tried to curb the media. In January 1991, Soviet forces occupied the LCP in Vilnius and took control of the newspaper presses. The troops also occupied the Committee of Radio and Television and the TV tower. This move revealed the magnitude of Gorbachev's fear of the influence of the press and the extent to which he would go to curb its power. However, although he had considerable success against the broadcast media, he could not control the print press. The final collapse of the Soviet Union gave Lithuania the freedom to govern itself for the first time since 1940. On March 11, 1990, it became the first of the Soviet republics to declare its independence. This proclamation was officially recognized in September of 1991.

The arrival of independence and the end of censorship presented newspapers with very different but nonetheless difficult problems. Lithuania was faced with enormous economic, political, and social challenges. The economic crisis that confronted this newly independent country included increasing inflation: the once plentiful and subsidized Soviet newsprint became ten times more expensive. The once state-owned centrally located printing plants were outmoded, and there were problems with distribution. Editors were forced to move deadlines back and often morning papers were not delivered until the next day. In February, 1992, in the lobby of a hotel in Vilnius, more than 30 dailies and weeklies were stacked on the counter and remained unsold for the rest of the day as did thousands of others in the kiosks throughout the city. Inflation forced the public to choose between a newspaper or bread and milk. Also owing to a lack of funds, Lithuanian television and radio failed to produce programs of interest to the public. Yet some dailies survived this crisis, namely, the *Respublika* (Republic) and *Lieutuvos Rytas* (Lithuania's Morning), which were published in Vilnius and remained in circulation as of 2002.

In addition, competent, objective journalists were scarce. Most journalists were educated under the Soviet system; instructed that the function of journalist is to interpret determined events, they did not strive to present accurate and unbiased articles that encouraged readers to form their own opinions. Lack of training and experience in the newer philosophy caused these people to replace the Soviet papers with hundreds of new papers that were equally opinionated and short on facts.

Lithuania, like other countries of post-communist Europe, was also plagued with weak and questionable government officials. The unstable infrastructure created a void that was quickly filled by a criminal element. The crime rate in the 1990s in Lithuania tripled from the rate in 1988. Organized crime posed a serious threat to journalists and investigative reporters. The sophisticated crime rings exceeded police effectiveness, thus leaving little insurance of protection for journalists. At the end of 1995, a bomb explosion in the offices of the *Lieutuvos Rytas* newspaper was connected to the Kaunas Mafia, who were thought to have swindled the state of its property during the privatization process.

Given the prevalence of crime in the late 1990s, the Lithuanian media obliged with an anti-crime and corruption effort. However, apparently crime had begun to actually infiltrate the very newspapers that were reporting and campaigning against it. Allegations were made that money was being exchanged between the journalists and police for news and information; on October 21, 1997, Saulius Stoma, the former editor-in-chief of the *Lietuvos Aidas* (Echo of Lithuania) daily newspaper was convicted of stealing money from the publication's account. He was convicted and sentenced to five years imprisonment.

Another serious defect of the press during the late 1990s was the lack of any serious and accurate international coverage. Only ten percent of both state and private prime time television newscasts was devoted to international affairs.

Nature of Audience The estimated 2002 population of Lithuania is approximately 3.6 million, which is composed of the following ethnic groups: Lithuanian (80.6 percent); Russian (8.7 percent); Polish (7 percent); Byelorussian (1.6 percent); and other (2.1 percent). The literacy rate of the country, defined as the ability to read at 15 years of age, is high with a total of 98 percent (99 percent for males and 98 percent for females). While the official language is Lithuanian, Polish and Russian are also spoken. Newspapers are printed in Lithuanian, but some of them produce editions in Russian.

Newspapers The three most popular newspapers, with circulations between 50,000 to 100,000, and considered

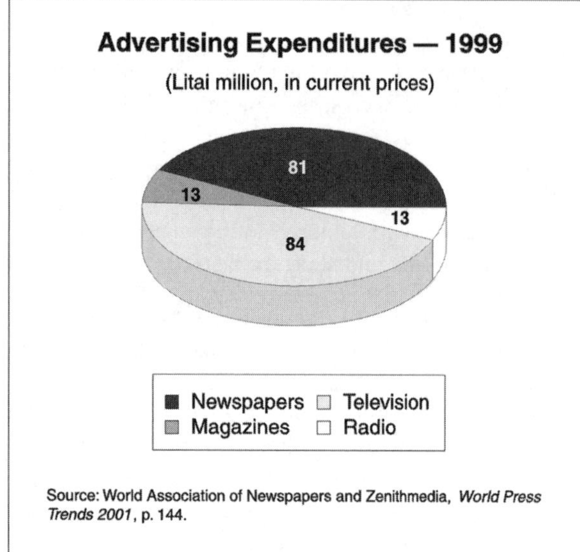

Source: World Association of Newspapers and Zenithmedia, *World Press Trends 2001*, p. 144.

the most influential are *Kauno Diena* (Kaunas Daily), *Respublika* (Republic), and *Lietuvos Rytas* (Lithuania's Morning). *Kauno Diena*, founded in 1945, has a circulation of 50,000 and is available in Lithuanian six times a week. *Respublika*, established in 1988, was the first independent Lithuanian daily newspaper. It has a circulation of 55,000 and is available six times a week in Lithuanian, with five Russian editions per week. *Lietuvos Rytas*, founded in 1990, reports on news and investigations of events in Lithuania and worldwide. It has a circulation of 85,000 copies on weekdays and 135,000 copies on Saturdays, and is available six times a week in Lithuanian, with two weekly Russian editions. Smaller newspapers with a circulation between 10,000-25,000 include: *Lietuvos Aidas* (Echo of Lithuania), 20,000, in Vilnius, available five times a week in Lithuanian only; *Vakarines Naujienos* (Evening News), 15,000, in Vilnius, available five times a week in Lithuanian and Russian; and *Vakaru Ekspresas* (Western Express), 15,000, in Klaipeda, available six times a week in Lithuanian only. The *Kurier Wilenski* (Vilnius Express) is a Polish language newspaper available five times a week with a circulation of 8,000. There are also several periodicals available. *Lietuvos Spauda* (Lithuanian press) is the largest commercial periodical publisher in Lithuania.

ECONOMIC FRAMEWORK

Overview Lithuania has few natural resources and was primarily an agricultural country prior to 1940. During the period of Soviet domination, 1940 to 1990, a large but inefficient industrial sector was established. After independence in the 1990s, Lithuania began a comprehensive economic reform toward a market-driven economy, including price reforms, privatization of enterprises, and encouragement of foreign investments. However, 50 years of Soviet occupation had had a devastating economic impact on the country and it was slow to rebound. There was high unemployment, estimated at 10.8 percent, coupled with a slow rate at which new jobs were created. The cost of living increased but salaries and pensions were not commensurate with the escalation. People had trouble maintaining even a minimal standard of living. Lithuania saw a growth in soup kitchens and charitable organizations. Lithuanians spent about 50 percent of their income on utilities and the rest for rent and other necessities. Crime increased and was increasingly emphasized in the press throughout the 1990s.

Advertising An important factor that has a direct financial effect on the status of the media is advertising or the lack of it. This aspect of the economic system remained undeveloped at the end of the twentieth century. The total advertising expenditure was estimated at 0.2 percent of gross domestic product (GDP). The print media accounted for 50 percent of this expenditure with the daily *Lietuvos Rytas*, the dominant newspaper. Television accounted for 30 percent of the expenditure, radio 10 percent, and outdoor media the remainder. Western brand goods dominated television airtime, but local advertisers expanded their presence and hoped to steadily increase their presence.

PRESS LAWS

The Lithuanian Constitution, adopted on October 25, 1992, guarantees the freedom of speech, information, and the press as stated in the following articles. Chapter 1 Article 25 specifically states:

(1) Individuals shall have the right to have their own convictions and freely express them.

(2) Individuals must not be hindered from seeking, obtaining, or disseminating information or ideas.

(3) Freedom to express convictions, as well as to obtain and disseminate information, may not be restricted in any way other than established by law. when it is necessary for the safeguard of the health, honor and dignity, private life, or morals of a person, or for the protection of constitutional order.

(4) Freedom to express convictions or impart information shall be incompatible with criminal actions—the instigation of national, racial, religious, or social hatred, or violence, or discrimination of slander, or misinformation.

(5) Citizens shall have the right to obtain any available information which concerns them from State agencies in the manner established by law.

Article 44 states:

(1) Censorship of mass media shall be prohibited.

(2) The State, political parties, political and public organizations, and other institutions or persons may not monopolize means of mass media.

CENSORSHIP

Censorship was enforced during the fifty years of Soviet occupation but the press in Lithuania, since independence, has been heralded as among the most free in the former Soviet states. The constitution provides for free speech and a free press and is essentially free from any overt governmental influence. However, the same article that guarantees this freedom also states that it can be limited if it is necessary to protect the ''health, honor and dignity, private life, or morals of a person, or for the protection of constitutional order.''

There is another apparent contradiction between the Lithuanian legal code and the Constitution. Article 33 of the Constitution states that ''Each citizen shall be guaranteed the right to criticize the work of State Institutions and their officers, and to appeal their decisions. It shall be prohibited to persecute people for criticism.'' Yet, the Penal Code provides for punishment of up to six months imprisonment or a fine for a public insult, in print or other means of dissemination of information, of a State officer in connection with the duties fulfilled by this person. Precedence was established for this law in 1998 with case against the publishers of *Europa*. In addition to these constitutional discrepancies intimidation by organized crime groups resulted in increased fear among journalists and even incidents of murder.

STATE-PRESS RELATIONS

The press is no longer subsidized as it was under the Soviet occupation, and most newspapers and distributors are privately owned. However, because of the serious problems that faced the nation after independence, the relationship between the media and the government was not always friendly. The newspapers staged a strike in 1991 when the government decided to confiscate media property formerly owned by the Communists. In addition, the government banned foreign investments.

In 1997, Lithuania was the only country in the Baltic region that was self-regulating. It had no state commission for press control. Also at the end of the 1990s, the Lithuanian Parliament amended the law on the media and removed the ceiling for compensation for libel and slander. This change caused journalists to fear an increase in unwarranted and frivolous lawsuits and limitations in their press freedoms. On November 22, 2001, the Lithuanian parliament passed a bill that placed a nine percent value-added tax on mass media.

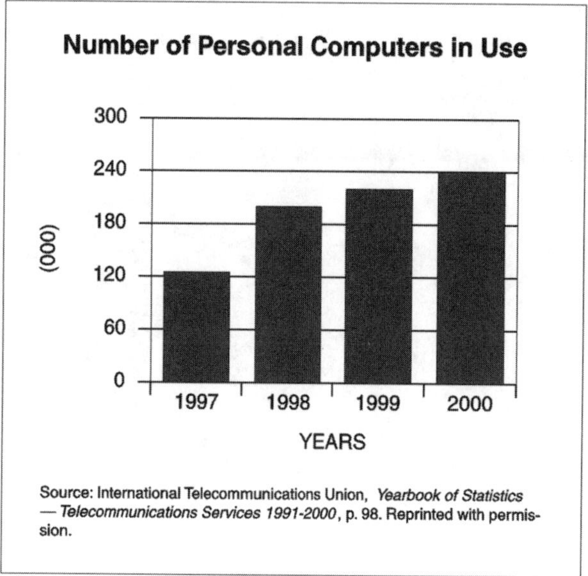

Source: International Telecommunications Union, *Yearbook of Statistics — Telecommunications Services 1991-2000*, p. 98. Reprinted with permission.

ATTITUDE TOWARD FOREIGN PRESS

Lithuanian reporters criticized the western media for using what they considered to be a double standard. The incident that provoked this outcry involved the kidnapping and murder of a photographer from *Itar-Tass* in 1999 and the failure of the western press to consider the event newsworthy. The arrest, at the same time, of Andrei Babitsky of Radio Liberty was given extensive coverage by the western press.

NEWS AGENCIES

There are two News Agencies in Lithuania: Lithuanian News Agency (ELTA) which is available online in Lithuanian and English, and the Baltic News Agency (BNS). The BNS is the largest and only news agency that covers all the Baltic States. It employs 140 people and provides news six to seven hundred times per day in five different languages. It has its headquarters in Tallinn, Estonia, but has larger regional office in Vilnius, Lithuania, and Riga, Latvia.

BROADCAST MEDIA

The state owns part of the National Radio and Television public broadcasting company but the majority of the mass media is privately owned. The top television station is LNK, whereas the national broadcasting station ranks fourth and last. However, the national radio broadcasting station ranks at the top for listeners. There are approximately 1.9 million radios in Lithuania with three AM stations and one hundred and twelve FM. There are twenty television broadcast stations with thirty repeaters and 1.7 million televisions. The leading private media are financially viable, but the National Radio and Television

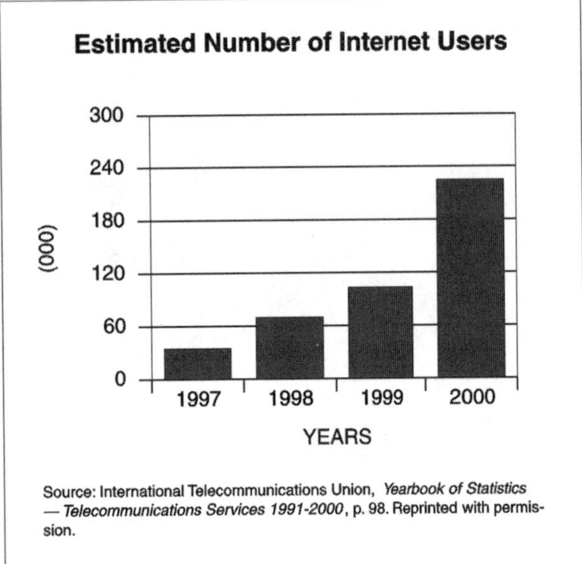

Source: International Telecommunications Union, *Yearbook of Statistics — Telecommunications Services 1991-2000*, p. 98. Reprinted with permission.

owed its creditors 15 million *litas* in 2001. The majority of Lithuanians receive their news from radio and television.

ELECTRONIC NEWS MEDIA

In 1996, there were more than 240,000 personal computers, and in 1998 there were 24 Internet hosts per 1,000 population in Lithuania. In 2000, Internet users rose to 225,000; in 2001 there were approximately 25 Internet Service Providers (ISPs). In 2001 an estimated 2 percent of the population was connected to the Internet. There are no restrictions or regulations on the use of the Internet and the law affecting the market, the one granting Lithuanian Telecom a monopoly, expires in 2003.

EDUCATION & TRAINING

The press in Lithuania, similar to the other Baltic States, is probably among the world's youngest. Newsroom and magazine offices find eager but miscast persons in their twenties. Those few journalists who worked during the Soviet period when all publications were owned by the state and controlled by the Communist Party have not been asked to continue with news agencies, leaving few experienced and qualified journalists. Education and training remains a high priority for upgrading and improving the media.

SUMMARY

The press in Lithuania has emerged from its censorship under Soviet domination and has expanded and made many improvements. Nonetheless, at the beginning of the twenty-first century it was encountering problems that detracted from its competency. By contrast to the Latvian and Estonian press, there is an increasing sensationalism in the news that mars the Lithuanian media and journalists continue their role of scandal-hunters. In 2001 scholars and intellectuals complained publicly and wrote to the president about the ten-year decline of moral principles that was widespread in the media. This trend was especially disturbing since the news media ranks among the most trusted institutions, despite its generally low level of talented journalists. In 2001 the media in Lithuania had a 70 percent public confidence rating, the highest of all institutions.

As of 2002, the majority of mass media was privately owned and the leading private media were financially stable. The newspaper distribution system was privately owned, and the media were editorially independent. A number of the privately owned newspapers and some of the independent television stations were editorially diverse. These were progressive steps. However, there were signs that also threatened to limit the freedom of the media and were causing great concern among journalists. Assessing both the positive and negative aspects of the media in Lithuania may extend through the first decade of the twenty-first century during which time the Lithuanian media may well establish a strong new journalistic tradition.

SIGNIFICANT DATES

- 1997: A Conference for East European journalists held in Vilnius concluded that the Lithuanian media is freer than elsewhere in the former Soviet Union.
- 1998: The Swedish media concern, Marieberg, acquired the majority shareholding in the independent LNK television in September. They purchased a forty-four percent shareholding. On April 13, 1998, for the first time in Lithuanian media history, the publishers of the newspaper, Europa, were sentenced for defamation and insult.
- 1999: Polls in Lithuania indicated that the public's trust in the media was at 60 percent whereas their trust in the parliament was only 20 percent.
- 2000: In January, the state-run Lithuanian Radio and Television (LRTV) suspended broadcasts from Radio 2 (culture and education) and Radio 3 (classical and jazz) because of funding problems. On July 27, 2000, President Valdas Adamkus vetoed a new Law on Mass Media that proposed the establishment of a Mass Media Controller financed by the state budget. Journalists were opposed to the idea. In December, the pan-Baltic IT company Tilde Group launched Internet TV portals in all three Baltic States with the Lithuanian TV considered the best.
- 2001: Reuters announced that it would reduce its coverage of the Baltic States in April 2002 because

of decreasing interest in the area. Finnish business daily Kauppalehti bought Baltic News Service (BNS).

BIBLIOGRAPHY

Adamkus, Valdus. ''Lithuania: Negative Media Trends Critiqued.'' In *IPR Strategic Business Information Database* (May 29, 2001).

Fenton, Tom. ''Mafia targets journalists abroad.'' *Editor & Publisher* vol. 127, no. 27 (July 2, 1994): 15-16.

Girnius, Saulus. ''The Economies of the Baltic States in 1993.'' *RFE/RL Research Report* vol. 3, no. 20 (20 May 1994): 1-14.

——— ''Lithuania.'' *RFE/RL Research Report* vol. 1, no. 39 (2 October 1992): 70-74.

Hickey, Neil. ''A Young Press Corps.'' *Columbia Journalism Review* 38 (May 1999): 18.

Jarvis, Howard. ''Lithuania.'' *World Press Review, 1997-2001*. Available from http://www.freemedia.at/wpfr/.

Lieven, Anatol. *The Baltic Revolution Estonia, Latvia, Lithuania and the Path to Independence*. New Haven: Yale University Press, 1999.

''Lithuania,'' *Europa World Year Book 2001*, 42nd ed., vol. 2, 2504-22.

''Lithuania Online News.'' *News On-Line,* 17 April 2002. Available from http://www.only/news.htm.

Navazelskis, Ina. ''Lithuania: a killing and a crusade.'' *Columbia Journalism Review* vol. 34, no. 2 (July-August 1995): 13-14.

Nichols, Ana. ''Channel hopping: the advertising landscape in Lithuania is confused and fast changing. But Western interest in growing.'' *Business Eastern Europe* vol. 24, no. 39 (25 September 1995): 4.

RFE/RL Research Institute Staff. ''The Media in the Countries of the Former Soviet Union.'' *RFE/RL Research Report* vol. 2, no. 27 (2 July 1993): 1-15.

Rose, Richard, and William Maley. ''Conflict or Compromise in the Baltic States?'' *RFE/RL Research Report* vol. 3, no. 28 (15 July 1994): 26-35.

—Jean Boris Wynn

LUXEMBOURG

BASIC DATA

Official Country Name:	Grand Duchy of Luxembourg
Region (Map name):	Europe
Population:	437,389
Language(s):	Luxembourgian, German, French, English
Literacy rate:	100%

The Grand Duchy of Luxembourg, bordered by France, Germany, and Belgium, became an independent nation in 1890. Although a relatively new state, Luxembourg has a long history dating back to the region's incorporation into, first, the Ancient Roman Republic and Empire, and successively, the Holy Roman Empire, Republican and Napoleonic France, and the United Kingdom of the Netherlands. Today, modern Luxembourg is a constitutional monarchy with executive authority invested in the Grand Duke, Henri since 2000. Legislative authority is shared between the Grand Duke and the elected Chamber of Deputies. All legislation becomes law with the Grand Duke's signature. Judicial authority is invested in the courts of law. During World War II, Luxembourg joined a custom's union with neighboring Belgium and was one of the signatory nations that created the European Coal and Steel Union and the European Union. Luxembourg's industrial base is steel, chemicals, and rubber production. The banking industry accounts for a substantial portion of the nation's economic base. Family-owned farms represent the smallest sector of Luxembourg's economic sector.

Article 24 of the Constitution of the Grand Duchy of Luxembourg guarantees freedom of speech in all matters. Freedom of the press is guaranteed, subject to the repression of offences committed in the exercise of these freedoms. Censorship is strictly forbidden. No publisher, printer, or distributor can be prosecuted if the author is known, is a native-born citizen of Luxembourg, or is a resident of the Grand Duchy. The Law of 27 July 1991 governs electronic media in Luxembourg and guarantees the right of free audiovisual communication from a variety of sources, assures the independent flow of information, respects the human rights and dignity of each individual to receive information, and promotes intercultural exchanges. The proposed Law of 5 February 2002, under consideration by the Chamber of Deputies, seeks further safeguards in an electronic information age for journalists' sources, the right of journalists to freedom of expression, and the freedom of journalists to establish their own professional standards of journalism.

Le Service Information et Press (SIP) of the Luxembourg government, created by the Law of 27 July 1991, replaced the older Office of Information. The SIP guarantees communication between the government, the media, and the people of Luxembourg, promotes good relations between the Luxembourg government and foreign countries, assures the right to public information, publishes public documents, and facilitates the right of the national and foreign media to access information within the country. The Law of 27 July 1991 created Le Service des Medias et des Communications for electronic media to assist the prime minister in the definition and enforcement of the media's rights, regulate satellite programming in Luxembourg, oversee foreign investment in media ownership, and represent Luxembourg in media discussions within the European Union.

Because Luxembourg is situated at the crossroads of Europe and represents both French and German culture, a variety of media exist. Luxembourg's major newspapers are the *Luxembourger Wort* (www.wort.lu) with a 1995 circulation of 81,500; *La Voix du Luxembourg* (www.lavoix.lu); *Tageblatt* (www.tageblatt.lu), which had a 1995 circulation of 25,000; *Le Quotidien, Editions Letzeburger Journal SA* (www.journal.lu), with a circulation of 12,000 in 1995; and *Zeitung vum Letzebuerger Vollek,* which had a circulation of 3,000 in 1995. Twelve local, regional, or weekly newspapers are also printed in Luxembourg. Twenty-seven periodicals are published in Luxembourg and include the weekly general-interest magazines *Letzeburger Land,* which had a circulation of 3,000 in 1995, and the *Revue D'Letzebuerger Illustreiert,* with a circulation of 16,000 in 1995. A special interest consumer periodical, *De Konsument,* had a bimonthly readership of 34,000 in 1995.

Luxembourg has 2 national radio stations, 4 regional radio stations, and 20 local radio stations. Radio-Tele Luxembourg is the nation's principal radio station. Television is the most used media in Luxembourg; 95 percent of the population watches cable television, and only 1 percent of the population does not own a television set. Luxembourg's four national television stations are RTL Tele Letzebuerg, Nordliicht TV, Uelzechtkanal, and De Kueb TV. More than 40 foreign television stations are received by Luxembourg television sets. Two new and specialized television stations were added in 2002, Tango TV and Parlament TV. RTL Letzeburg is Luxembourg's principal television station, with more than 130,000 viewers. The language of transmission is Luxembourgeois (the local dialect), but the programming is simultaneously broadcast in French.

All television and radio broadcasting in Luxembourg is done through Compagnie Luxembourgeoise de Telediffusion (CLT). CLT was established in 1929 and began broadcasting multilingual programs in 1932. In 1954, CLT received an exclusive license for broadcasting radio and television within the Grand Duchy. CLT's broadcasting license was extended in 1995 to the end of 2010. In 1995, 12 television channels and 12 radio stations belonged to the CLT group. CLT broadcasts four television and three radio stations via the Astra satellite system, which began service in 1985. The 1991 Law on Electronic Media allowed the creation of 4 new radio networks and 15 local radio stations, thus ending the CLT monopoly of radio. Commercial and religious programs are broadcast in French, German, English, Italian, Portuguese, and Spanish. More than 40 international television programs are broadcast by cable and satellite.

Press agencies operating within Luxembourg are AFP Agence France-Presse, Agence de Presse Luxpress, Agence Reuters, and Agence DPA. The acquisition of GE American Communications, Incorporated, in 2001, allows Luxembourg the transmission capability to reach North and South America. Mediaport Luxembourg (www.mediaport.lu) is the principle Internet site for information about Luxembourg and the government of the Grand Duchy.

Le Conseil de Presse, created by the Law of 20 December 1979, recognizes and protects the rights of journalists in Luxembourg, establishes credentialing criteria for journalists, and represents the editors and newspaper reporters of the Association Luxembourgeoise des Journalistes (AJL) and the Union of Journalistes Luxembourg (UJL). Le Conseil de Presse has 40 members, 20 from among Luxembourg's editors and 20 from the nation's newspaper reporters. Membership changes every two years. Decisions made by the Conseil de Presse can be appealed to the Commission d'Appel. Luxembourg citizens seeking a career in the media attend universities in the neighboring countries of France, Belgium, Germany, and Switzerland.

BIBLIOGRAPHY

Majerus, Pierre. *The Institutions of the Grand Duchy of Luxembourg.* Luxembourg: Press and Information Service, 1973.

Margue, Paul. *A Short History of Luxembourg.* Luxembourg: Information and Press Department, 1974.

Turner, Barry, ed. *Statesman's Yearbook 2002.* New York: Palgrave, 2001.

World Mass Media Handbook, 1995 ed. New York: United Nations Department of Public Information, 1995.

—William A. Paquette

Macau

Basic Data

Official Country Name:	Macau
Region (Map name):	East & South Asia
Population:	445,594
Language(s):	Portuguese, Chinese (Cantonese)
Literacy rate:	90%

Macau, a peninsula bordering China and the South China Sea, was colonized by the Portuguese in the sixteenth century, becoming the first European settlement in the Far East. In 1987 through an agreement with Portugal and China, Macau became a special administrative region of China. Despite China's socialist system, Macau enjoys a high degree of autonomy. The president of China serves as the chief of state, but the local government is run by a chief executive who presides over a 23-seat, unicameral Legislative Council. The population of Macau is approximately 445,000, and the literacy rate is 90 percent. National languages are Portuguese and Cantonese, but the majority of the population speaks Cantonese. Mainstays of the economy are tourism—especially gambling—textiles and fireworks.

Although the press in Macau is private, it is not outspoken, especially concerning the Chinese capital of Beijing, crime syndicates, and activities that challenge the political and business status quo. The government owns controlling interests in radio and television stations. The largest newspaper is the Chinese-language daily *Macao Daily News,* which boasts an average circulation of 50,000 and appears online. Other dailies printing in Chinese are *Ou Mun lat Pou, Journal Si Man, Jornal Va Kio, Tai Chung, Journal Cheng Pou,* and *Seng Pou.* Only *Va Kio* is available online. There are five main Chinese-language weeklies. *Son Pro* and *Jornal Si-Si* appear on Saturday, *Jornal O Puso de Macau* and *Observato'rio de Macau* publish on Friday, and *Semanario Recreativo de Macau* prints on Wednesday. The two Portuguese-language dailies are *Jornal Tribuna de Macau* and *Macau Hoje.* Both print Monday through Saturday only and are available online. Portuguese weeklies include *O Clarim* and *Ponto Final,* both of which appear on Friday. *Ponto Final* is available online.

There are two FM stations in Macau broadcasting to 160,000 radios. There are 49,000 televisions and one television station. There is one Internet service provider.

Bibliography

The Central Intelligence Agency (CIA). ''Macau.'' *World Fact Book 2001.* Available from http://www.cia.gov/.

''Country Profile.'' Worldinformation.com, 2002. Available from http://www.worldinformation.com/.

''Macau.'' Freedom House, 2000. Available from http://www.freedomhouse.org/.

Macau Daily News, (1998). Available from http://www.macaodaily.com/.

—Jenny B. Davis

Macedonia

Basic Data

Official Country Name:	The Former Yugoslav Republic of Macedonia

Region (Map name):	Europe
Population:	2,046,209
Language(s):	Macedonian Orthodo, Muslim, other
Literacy rate:	NA
Area:	25,333 sq km
GDP:	3,573 (US$ millions)
Number of Television Stations:	31
Number of Television Sets:	510,000
Television Sets per 1,000:	249.2
Number of Radio Stations:	49
Number of Radio Receivers:	410,000
Radio Receivers per 1,000:	200.4
Number of Individuals with Internet Access:	50,000
Internet Access per 1,000:	24.4

The media scene in Macedonia livened up within a few years after the country declared its independence from Yugoslavia in 1991 and commenced a double transition toward democracy and capitalism. Media outlets started to compete for the attention of a literate (94 percent) and multi-ethnic audience, hungry for respite from the propaganda humdrum in the communist-ruled Yugoslavia. Hundreds of private newspapers and magazines emerged, and some 250 private broadcasters took to the air.

The promise for a quick transition to Western-style free press in Macedonia has been since dampened. The media scene is still much livelier than during the Yugoslav period, but it has suffered from government interference, political and ethnic biases of publications, a malfunctioning economy, and uneven and often poor quality of journalism. Plagued by high unemployment and decline in living standards, Macedonia endured series of economic, political and social crises during the 1990s. It is hardly surprising that media have been preoccupied with issues of security and politics.

The Ministry of Information listed 818 officially registered newspapers and magazines as of June 2000, but the actual number is considerably smaller. Of those, 51 are published in Albanian language, 6 in Turkish, 4 in Vlachian, 3 in Romany (Roma), 2 in Bosnian, and 5 in English. More than 600 publications are based in Skopje.

In March 2000 Macedonia had 11 dailies, 2 in Albanian and 1 in Turkish. Most popular by circulation are: *Dnevnik* (daily 60,000; weekend 70,000), *Večer* (50,000), *Utrinski Vesnik* (30,000), *Vest* (25,000), *Nova Makedonija* (20,000), *Denes* (15,000), *Sport* (15,000), *Fakti* (10,000), and *Flaka* (3,000). The independent *Dnevnik* is considered to be the most influential newspaper, and *Nova Makedonija* has traditionally been the voice of the government. Most newspapers are losing money.

The government owns one third of NIP Nova Makedonija, publisher of *Nova Makedonija* and *Večer*, as well as the weekly *Puls*, the Albanian-language daily *Flaka*, and the Turkish-language *Birlik*, which comes out three times a week. All other print media in Macedonia are private.

Fokus (12,000), *Start* (10,000), and *Denes* (7,500) are the most important weekly political magazines. Macedonia has a lucrative but limited market for entertainment weeklies, such as *Kotelec* (15,000), *Ekran* (9,500), and *TEA* (7,500). The biweekly political magazine *Forum* (6,000) is also influential and profitable and, along with *Fokus*, charges the highest rates for advertising in print media.

Three television channels—the state-owned Macedonian Television (MTV) and private A1 TV and Sitel TV—provide national coverage. Only MTV, broadcasting since 1966, has full 24-hour programming. A1 TV has a program split similar to MTV with about one fifth of its programming devoted to news, whereas Sitel TV is more entertainment- and sports-oriented.

The state-owned Macedonian Radio and private Kanal 77 have national radio coverage. There is a large number of local private stations, so many towns have at least one station; most are entertainment-oriented.

The multiethnic populace requires special program considerations, and MTV first broadcast in Albanian in 1967 and in Turkish in 1969. MTV maintains three hours of daily programming in Albanian (MTV-PA) and 90 minute of programming in Turkish. Similarly, Macedonian Radio has eight hours of daily programming in Albanian and five hours in Turkish.

Dozens of unlicensed, pirate radio and television stations operate locally without paying any fees and violating copyright laws. The government's efforts to enforce the regulations have been inconsistent.

Macedonia's principal information agencies are the government-owned Macedonian Information Agency and private Makfaks.

Article 16 of the Constitution guarantees freedom of speech and access to information and forbids censorship. Instances of media suppression are still reported, although direct government involvement seems to be limited to crisis situations. For example, the 2001 ethnic

Albanian insurgency precipitated a government crackdown on Albanian-language TV and radio programs, including the suspension of broadcasts for several days. Police also limited journalists' access to conflict areas, and ethnic-Albanian journalists complained of harassment.

Newspapers and magazines must register with the Ministry of Information according to a 1976 statute. Broadcast media are regulated by the Law on Broadcast Activity, adopted in 1997. The Broadcasting Council, whose members are selected by the parliament, disburses broadcast licenses. The government, however, gives the final approval and thus exerts a measure of control. A proposed draft law on public information in 2001 caused outcry from media organizations, as it intended to introduce licensing for local journalists and registration for foreign correspondents.

Political parties in power can manipulate the media by allocating advertising and ensuring income for some media and none for others. Political and business affiliations of owners also greatly influence the coverage and staffing decisions.

Although primarily a formality, distributors of foreign newspapers and magazines must obtain permits from the Ministry of Interior. Foreign media are readily available, especially in Skopje, but prices of Western print media are usually prohibitive for most Macedonians.

Broadcast programs from neighboring countries can be received in the border areas. Macedonia does not restrict individual Internet users, although the computer ownership is not particularly high because of its costs. Internet cafes are quickly becoming the alternative to home-based Internet. Most major media outlets maintain Web sites.

The Macedonian media has been polarized along ethnic lines, which has hurt the objectivity of reporting. With the allayment of ethnic tensions the quality of journalism can be expected to improve. Yet Macedonia's media faces a credibility problem. The public's trust in the media is generally low, especially among ethnic Albanians, and surveys indicate that a majority of the population believes news media serve the interests of powerful people and organizations.

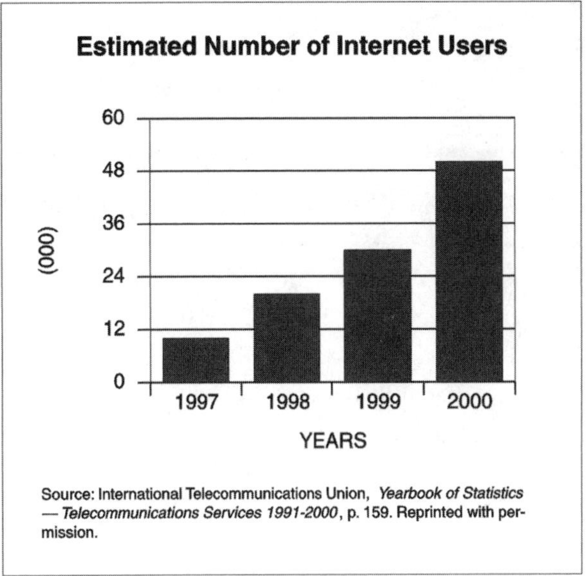

Source: International Telecommunications Union, *Yearbook of Statistics — Telecommunications Services 1991-2000*, p. 159. Reprinted with permission.

BIBLIOGRAPHY

Country Reports on Human Rights Practices 2001: Macedonia. Washington, DC: U.S. Department of State, 2002.

Human Development Report 2001. New York: United Nations Development Program, 2002.

Macedonia: Press Overview. International Journalists Network, 2002. Available from http://www.ijnet.org.

The Mass Media in the Republic of Macedonia. Skopje: Agency of Information, Ministry of Information, 2001.

Media Overview: Macedonia, 2000. Vienna, Austria: GfK, Austria, 2001.

Media Monitoring in Macedonia, 2002. Düsseldorf: European Institute for Media. Available from www.eim.org.

Naegele, Jolyon. ''Macedonia: News Media Under Fire for Poor Reporting, Government Manipulation.'' RFE-RL Newsline, May 3, 2002. Available from www.rferl.org.

Nations in Transit: 1999/2000. Washington, DC: Freedom House, 2000.

Republic of Macedonia Statistical Yearbook 2000. Skopje: National Statistical Office, 2001.

Sopar, Vesna, and Emilija Jovanova. ''The Media System in the Republic of Macedonia: Broadcasting between the Normative and the Real.'' Media Online/Media Plan, June 12, 2000. Available from www.mediaonline.ba.

Turner, Barry, ed. *The Statesman's Yearbook 2002*. New York: Palgrave, 2001.

—*Christopher D. Karadjov*

MADAGASCAR

BASIC DATA

Official Country Name: Republic of Madagascar

Region (Map name):	Africa
Population:	15,982,563
Language(s):	French, Malayasy
Literacy rate:	80.0%
Area:	587,040 sq km
GDP:	3,878 (US$ millions)
Number of Television Stations:	1
Number of Television Sets:	325,000
Television Sets per 1,000:	20.3
Number of Radio Stations:	14
Number of Radio Receivers:	3,050,000
Radio Receivers per 1,000:	190.8
Number of Individuals with Computers:	35,000
Computers per 1,000:	2.2
Number of Individuals with Internet Access:	30,000
Internet Access per 1,000:	1.9

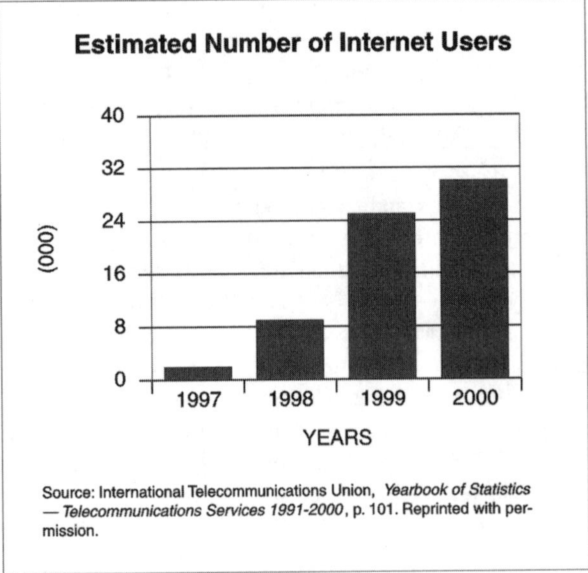

Source: International Telecommunications Union, *Yearbook of Statistics — Telecommunications Services 1991-2000*, p. 101. Reprinted with permission.

Located in the Indian Ocean east of southern Africa, Madagascar, the fourth largest island on earth, is known for its unique mammals, birds, and plants. Many of the 15 million Malagasy people are descendants of Africans and Indonesians.

An astonishing and little known fact of Madagascar's history involves the pre-Holocaust suggestion by Hitler's henchmen Hermann Goring in 1938 and Heinrich Himmler in 1940, that 4 million European Jews be forcibly emigrated to this distant and remote island. After the war, Madagascar gained independence from French colonialism (1960) and since then has had a checkered political situation with a series of military and civilian rulers.

Although Malagasy is the official language, French is most often spoken and written. An average of 88 percent of Madagascar's males and 73 percent of its females over the age of 15 can read and write. The major religions of Madagascar are indigenous beliefs (52 percent), Christianity (41 percent), and Muslim (7 percent). Widespread poverty in Madagascar reduces life expectancy to the mid-50s.

The major daily newspapers in Madagascar include *Midi-Madagasikara, The Madagascar Tribune,* and *L'Express,* all privately owned, written mainly in French and circulated from the capital, Antananarivo. *Gazetiko,* written in Malagasy, is also printed in Antananarivo. *Maresaka, Basy-Vava, Imongo,* and *Vaovao* are also published daily.

Weekly newspapers include the French *Dans Les Medias Domains* (In the Media Tomorrow), which has a large circulation in outlying areas while *Lakroa N'Y Madagasikara,* written mostly in Malagasy, is a Roman Catholic weekly which also reaches remote areas. *Feon'ny Merina* (Voice of the Merina) is a weekly newspaper in Malagasy and is directed at Merina people of Malay origin.

Monthly newsmagazines include the French *Revue de l'Ocean Indien,* which contains information and analysis relevant to the people of the Indian Ocean area. Political, legal and economic issues are covered monthly in the mostly French *Jureco* while every three months, *Madagascar Magazine,* entirely in French, deals with economic, commercial and cultural issues. Appearing every three months, *Vintsy Magazine* (two-thirds in Malagasy, one-third in French) deals with ecological issues while *Antsa* (half in Malagasy, half in French) is dedicated to artists and culture.

Madagascar's economy is primarily agricultural with some textile manufacturing and agricultural products processing. Economic growth and per capita incomes have sharply declined since the 1970s partly due to the government's lack of commitment. Persistent malnutrition and poorly funded education and health care are ongoing concerns.

Theoretically, press law is founded upon Article Ten of Madagascar's Constitution: ''Freedom of opinion and expression, communication. . .and conscience shall be guaranteed to all and may be limited only in respect of the rights and liberties of others and. . .to safeguard public order.'' More specifically, Article Eleven assures, ''Information in all forms shall be subject to no prior restraint. . .[however] conditions of freedom of information and its responsibility shall be determined by law and by codes of professional ethics.''

In practice, human rights organizations point out that Madagascar's government has been known sometimes to pressure media personnel to avoid coverage of issues contrary to the government's interests. Likewise, politicians opposed to the ruling regime are denied access to state-run media. Journalists are strongly encouraged to practice ''self-censorship.''

In the late 1990s, the frequency and seriousness of censorship incidents increased in Madagascar. In 1998 the editor-in-chief of *L'Express* and a reporter were sentenced to three months in prison for contempt of court.

In 2000 a journalist was threatened with dismissal for his reports about government censorship of opposition politicians. Another journalist publicly disagreed with a local government official and was physically attacked by him. A radio reporter, beaten by a government official, was sentenced to prison for broadcasting negative information about the official. One journalist asserted that politicians use physical violence and intimidation rather than the courts to redress their grievances against journalists.

In 2001 journalists insisted that a member of the legislature's opposition party who was imprisoned for six months on an allegedly trumped up charge was really punished for criticizing the President. While reporting on government opposition rallies in early 2002, an editorial in the *Midi Madagasikara* urged the government not to ''shoot the messenger'' that reports the news and implored the public to fight for free media.

In the area of broadcast media, Madagascar has three main TV stations: RTM, Radio-Television Malagasy, state owned; RTA, Radio-Television Analamanga, privately owned; and MATV, Madagascar TV, privately owned. RTA and MATV broadcast mostly to Antananarivo and its nearby areas.

Radio news is broadcast from privately owned FM stations such as Radio Lazan Iarivo (Glory of Iarivo), Radio Korail, and Radio Antsiva; all three are based in Antananarivo. RNM (Malagasy National Radio) is state owned. Radio Don Bosco, a Catholic FM station, operates only in the capital area. Radio Feon'ny Merina, privately owned, targets Merina people of Malay origin, while Radio Tsioka Vao, privately owned, is known to be pro-government. In total the government owns 17 AM and three FM stations. In 2002 the news media exhorted the public to be aware that many radio journalists are forced to articulate a pro-government point of view.

The electronic media in Madagascar is disproportionately sophisticated in that each daily newspaper is available on the Internet, yet there are only two Internet service providers.

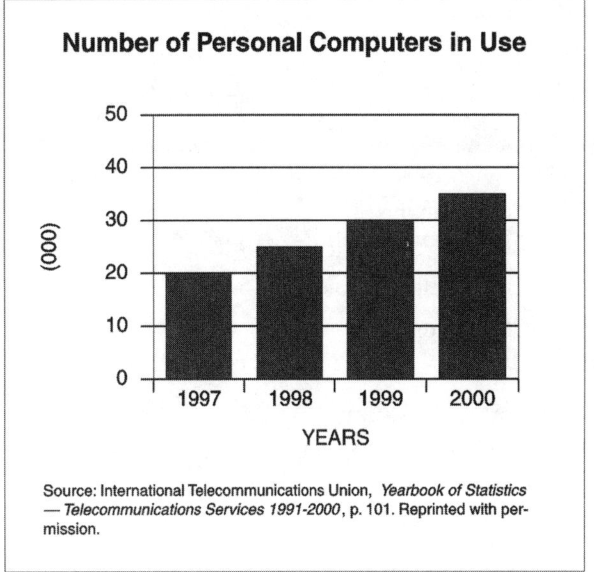

Source: International Telecommunications Union, *Yearbook of Statistics — Telecommunications Services 1991-2000*, p. 101. Reprinted with permission.

In the years to come, the uncomfortable relationship between Madagascar's unstable and volatile political situation and its independent journalists will define the extent to which vibrancy, openness, and fairness will characterize Madagascar's print, electronic, and broadcast media.

Bibliography

''Africa Countries: Madagascar,'' 2002. Available from http://www-sul.stanford.edu/depts/ssrg/africa/madag.html.

''Madagascar.'' *CIA: The World Factbook,* 2002. Available from http://www.cia.gov.

''Madagascar.'' *World Press Freedom Review,* 2002. Available from http://freemedia.at/wpfr/madagas.htm.

—Howard A. Kerner

Malawi

Basic Data

Official Country Name:	Republic of Malawi
Region (Map name):	Africa
Population:	10,548,250
Language(s):	English, Chichewa

Literacy rate:	58.0%
Area:	118,480 sq km
GDP:	1,697 (US$ millions)
Number of Television Stations:	1
Number of Satellite Subscribers:	100
Number of Radio Stations:	16
Number of Radio Receivers:	2,600,000
Radio Receivers per 1,000:	246.5
Number of Individuals with Computers:	12,000
Computers per 1,000:	1.1
Number of Individuals with Internet Access:	15,000
Internet Access per 1,000:	1.4

BACKGROUND & GENERAL CHARACTERISTICS

Malawi is a landlocked country in Southern Africa. The main towns are Blantyre (pop. 350,000), Lilongwe (250,000), Mzuzu (80,000) and Zomba (70,000). Malawi's economy is based on its agriculture, which accounts for 40 percent of the gross domestic product (GDP), 90 percent of export revenues and 90 percent of rural employment. Malawi gained its independence in 1964 from Great Britain and until 1993 the country remained under the authoritarian rule of Dr. Kamuzu Banda. In May 1994, President Banda lost the presidential election to the United Democratic Front (UDF) led by Bakili Muluzi. Muluzi was re-elected in 1999 to serve another five-year term as president in the country's new democracy. Malawi has eleven ethnic groups, namely Chewa, Nyanja, Tumbuka, Yao, Lomwe, Sena, Tonga, Ngoni, Ngonde, Asian, and European. The official languages are English and Chichewa, but there are other regional dialects. The World Bank estimated that Malawi is one of the poorest countries in the world.

From independence in 1964 to 1992, the only sources of news in Malawi were two newspapers (*Daily Times* and the weekly *Malawi News*), put out by the Malawi Broadcasting Corporation and the Malawi News Agency. During that time, there was no constitutional provision for freedom of expression or of the press. The news media was pro-government and pro-Malawi Congress Party (MCP), the ruling party. Since 1994, the situation has changed. As of 2002, Malawi had 11 independent newspapers: two dailies—*The Nation* and *Daily Times*; seven weeklies—*New Vision*, *Weekly Chronicle*, *Statesman*, *Malawi News*, *Weekend Nation*, *Enquirer*, and *UDF News*; one government-owned biweekly—*Weekly News*; one privately owned weekly paper, *The People's Eye*; and finally, *The Mirror*, published four times a week. There is no Audit Bureau of Circulation (ABC) in Malawi to certify the sizes of circulation for newspapers and magazines (Fumulani). Newspapers circulate in urban areas, which have about 10 percent of the country's population, while only a few trickle to the rural areas. The World Bank reports that daily newspaper circulation in Malawi is 3 per 1,000 people.

ECONOMIC FRAMEWORK

After 30 years of one-party rule, Malawi became a multi-party democracy. The political transition was smooth in 1994, but the results of the presidential elections of July 1999, which returned Muluzi as president, have been continually contested, and genuine democratic processes have not yet fully taken root. The mass media is still government-controlled and trade unions have limited power.

Malawian economy prospered in the 1970s with the assistance of foreign aid and investment and grew at an annual rate of 6 percent. This growth did not, however, spur broad-based economic development. In 2002, agriculture remained the basis of Malawi's economy, contributing 40 percent of GDP and 90 percent of rural employment, while tobacco, the main cash crop, accounted for more than two-thirds of exports. Malawi's limited natural-resource base, combined with poor physical and financial infrastructure, a slow-moving bureaucracy and rising crime, has made it less able to attract foreign investment. Thus, Malawi remains one of the poorest countries in the world, ranking 159 out of 162 countries on the United Nations' *UNDP Human Development Index (HDI)*. Malawi's poverty headcount (percent below poverty line) was 66 percent in 1998 (World Bank).

There is a willingness on the part of many journalists to disseminate information and offer the Malawian public an alternative but the media face a number of constraints such as the practical problems of sourcing newsprint; the costs of printing; the weak production infrastructure; unfavorable finance and tax arrangements; indifference or hostility to emerging media; lack of spare parts, supplies and advertising; and high taxes on equipment (Banda).

The economy itself is not stable: the inflation rate grew from 9 percent in 1997 to 30 percent in 2000, increasing printing costs. Newspapers were priced higher in order to recover these costs, ultimately two or even three times the original cost. The adverse effect was that many readers ended up not buying any newspaper. Another problem that affects media owners is the ever-increasing costs of newsprint. One newspaper owner explained that it was difficult for many newspapers to survive economically, but they managed probably because they had committed teams who made great sacrifices. At one time they relied on family members to assist with loans since local banks saw media as bad business. Only newspaper companies that have political backing and have enough financial resources remain in the media market.

Radio in Malawi, the most effective form of media, reaches nearly 90 percent of the population of 11.3 million. However the state-owned Malawi Broadcasting Corporation (MBC) dominates radio broadcasting. Newspapers only circulate in towns while a few trickle to the rural areas.

PRESS LAWS

In 1994, Malawi said goodbye to dictator Hastings Kamuzu Banda when Bakili Muluzi defeated Banda in the country's first democratic elections since its gaining independence from Britain in 1964. When Malawi became a multi-party democracy in 1994, the government guaranteed freedom of the press in the new constitution that superseded old laws restricting the press and now provided for freedom of speech and press. Although the new Malawian law maintained that ''the press shall have the right to report and publish freely within Malawi and abroad, and to be accorded the fullest possible facilities for access to public information,'' practice did not always correspond to principle. Some restrictive laws have remained in place. The Official Secrets Act, for instance, makes it an offense to publish or communicate ''any secret official code, work, sketch, plan, article or other document that could be useful to the enemy.'' Thus any journalist reporting on security issues runs the risk of committing offense. Further, it is an offense to write with the intent of wounding the religious feelings of others or to produce, print, publish, import, possess, or circulate matter that is considered obscene. Libel is also a crime in Malawi, and according to one Malawi Broadcasting Company worker, ''A mere negative joke about the ruling party can cost someone a job here.'' Under the 1994 Communications Act, MBC was subject to the discretion of the controlling government minister regarding its content, and the minister was empowered to require MBC—or any private broadcaster—to broadcast certain materials or prohibit broadcasts that would be contrary to public interest.

In November, 1998, Parliament passed a new Communications Act, which for the first time established an independent regulatory body for broadcasting and telecommunications: the Malawi Communications Regulatory Authority (MACRA). This Act replaced the Malawi Broadcasting Corporation Act and the Radiocommunications Act of 1994. The newly established MACRA, an independent body, was charged with ensuring ''reliable and affordable communication services'' throughout the country. Under the bill, MACRA is responsible for protecting the interests of consumers, promoting open access to information, promoting competition, and providing training in communication services. It is also required to be independent and impartial while doing so. In regards to broadcast media, MACRA is also responsible for ensuring regular news programming on issues of public interest, supporting the democratic process through civic education, promoting a diverse range of national and local broadcasting and ensuring equal treatment in elections. The passing of a new communications bill gave a ray of hope to Malawian journalists.

Whether the bill has had any positive impact on the environment is still unknown, especially in regards to ensuring equal access and treatment among the political opposition. In March 2000, the UK-based organization Article 19 unveiled evidence of media manipulation during the 1999 presidential election campaign, identifying two misinformation teams that helped the ruling United Democratic Front (UDF) party use illegal advertisements and fabricate news reports to ensure re-election. The report also contended that during the 1999 election campaign, the state-owned Malawi Broadcasting Corporation ran live coverage of only President Muluzi's political rallies.

CENSORSHIP

During the Banda regime there was no such thing as press freedom; journalists lived in fear and constantly had to self-monitoring their writing. The government maintained control of the press with the Prohibited Publications Act. This Act allowed the government to ban any publication that it considered false or critical of Malawi (Banda). No outside journalists were allowed into the country at this time.

President Bakili Muluzi's government came into power promising an end to censorship and other human rights abuses. In 1995 a new constitution was put together after Banda was voted out of power by the United Democratic Front. The constitution had articles covering the following topics: 1) The protection of free expression; 2) The protection of free opinion; 3) The right to have access to information and 4) The freedom of the press. However, Muluzi's new democracy failed to ensure full press freedom. A 30-year legacy of self-censorship among journalists remained strong, and many preexisting laws remained in conflict with the new democratic provisions (Cooney). Government officials continued to issue negative statements against the media. Muluzi threatened through the overzealous offices of his press assistants to take several journalists to court on civil defamation charges.

Just before the 1999 elections and soon after that, there were incidents of open threats by politicians to dismiss from the civil service and statutory organizations any media practitioner deemed to be supporting the opposition or leaking information to the press. Journalists had been detained for short periods of time since the 1994 election. The editor of the main opposition newspaper, the *Daily Times*, was suspended in 2000 by the editor-in-chief and subsequently replaced by an acting editor more inclined to refrain from publishing articles critical of the government. The government continued to threaten and harass members of the media. The *Daily News* offices were raided by the army because of an article they published stating that AIDS percentages were higher in the army than the civilian population. On several occasions, politicians have threatened to take newspapers and their reporters to court. In late 2001, the *Chronicle* was fined a total of over US$37,000 by the courts in lawsuits, one involving a case in which the newspaper speculated on possible misconduct by a minister in his work.

State-owned Malawi Broadcasting Corporation (MBC) is the most important medium for reaching the public. MBC programming was dominated by reporting on the activities of senior government figures and official government positions. Parties and groups opposed to the government largely were denied access to the broadcast media. MBC reporters were disciplined or fired for their reporting on opposition parties. News stories were pulled in midbroadcast and press conferences heavily edited to avoid dispersing politically sensitive material. MBC refused to air paid public announcements of labor union events.

State-Press Relations

There are now a number of private newspapers in Malawi, including some owned by political parties or openly affiliated with them. Publishers are not required to register with the state, although the Minister of Information does give accreditation to journalists. After 1994, for the first time, there were more than 20 newspapers in Malawi. Many independent newspapers that were established did not survive for more than two years. Major reasons cited by most publishers were poor financing, high newsprint and printing costs, poor skills in managing a newspaper business, and lack of trained newsroom staff. The following newspapers were short-lived: *The New Voice*, *The Watchers*, *The Malawian*, *Michiru Sun*, *City Star*, *Financial Observer*, *Weekly Mail*, *News Today*, *The Herald*, *New Express*, *Daily Monitor*, and *The Democrat*, which collapsed in 1996. *The Independent* and *The Star* were phased out in 1999 because of lack of support from influential politicians. Four of the newspapers, *The Malawi News* and *The Daily Times* (both owned by the late president Banda's business empire), and the *Nation* and *Weekend Nation* (owned by Aleke Banda, the country's agriculture minister and first vice president of the ruling UDF) have remained the strongest players with a reasonable impact on the market. *The Mirror* (owned by Brown Mpinganjira, the country's foreign minister and prominent personality in Muluzi's UDF) has survived the turbulent times in the newspaper publishing industry.

Government has also stretched its arm to suffocate the private media by banning government advertising in the *Daily Times* and the *Malawi News*, Malawi's strongest opposition newspapers. Government is the biggest advertiser in the country, and advertising is the major source of revenue for all newspapers in the country. The ban occurred after the independents *The Daily Times* and *Malawi News* published critical coverage of government mismanagement and corruption. Journalists for private publications are said to face ''constant harassment'' from the state, and many journalists use pseudonyms (Banda).

Attitude toward Foreign Media

Under the dictatorship government of President Banda, no foreign journalists were allowed into the country at all. After the first democratic government in Malawi, foreign correspondents had free access to Malawian affairs. However, it would appear that supporters of the government are extremely sensitive to foreign reports about Malawi. Banning or jailing of foreign correspondents by the Malawian government has not been an issue. Visitors from the following countries are not required to have visas: United States, Germany, Holland, Sweden, Norway, Finland, Switzerland, Portugal, Luxembourg, Belgium. Visitors from the following countries are required to carry visas that expire after three months: Algeria, Angola, Brazil, Burundi, Cameroon, Egypt, Ethiopia, France, Libya, Mexico, Morocco, Russia and other Eastern European Countries, Rwanda, Senegal, Somalia, Spain, Sudan, and Zaire.

Foreign ownership of Malawian press is discouraged. Business may be conducted by individuals, partnerships, trusts, Malawian companies, branches of foreign companies, or through joint ventures, i.e., foreign and Malawi owned. A branch of a foreign company must have at least one Malawian resident as its director.

News Agencies

The oldest news agency, the Malawi News Agency (Mana), has its head office in Blantyre and offices in

Mwanza and Mzuzu. The other news agencies, *Daily Times* and *Weekly Malawi News*, are both located in Blantyre. One foreign news bureau is located in Blantyre, Agence France-Presse (France).

The biggest printing press, Blantyre Print and Publishing, belongs to the business empire of the late president Kamuzu Banda. It prints both newspapers and books. This press has been in existence since 1962 when Banda bought it from the Paver brothers who sold Banda both the press and the *Nyasaland Times* (forerunner to the *Daily Times*). The other major printing press in the newspaper sector is owned by Aleke Banda's Nation Publications, Ltd. Besides these, there is a chain of small printers dotted around the country, most of them owned by Indian business tycoons.

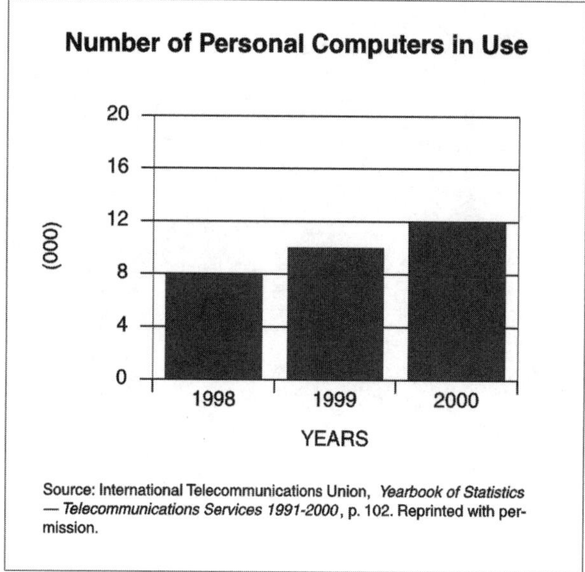

Source: International Telecommunications Union, *Yearbook of Statistics — Telecommunications Services 1991-2000*, p. 102. Reprinted with permission.

BROADCAST MEDIA

As part of the previous regime's control of the airwaves, television broadcasting was banned until 1994. Prior to 1994, Malawi had a single state-controlled Malawi Broadcasting Corporation (MBC) radio station, which covered the whole country, and a small private religious broadcaster that had a radius of 20 kilometers (km) from the capital, Lilongwe. Today Malawi has two government controlled Malawi Broadcasting Corporation (MBC) radio stations, two commercial stations broadcasting in Blantyre, a community radio station in Monkey Bay, a private training-commercial radio station, three religious stations, and seven private radio stations. As of 1999, there were 2.6 million radios in Malawi. The state-owned Malawi Broadcasting Corporation (MBC) dominates the radio market with its two stations, transmitting in major population centers throughout the country. News coverage and editorial content clearly are pro-government. Radio in Malawi reaches nearly 90 percent of the 11.3 million people living there. Only one television station exists in the country, the state-controlled Television Malawi (TVM), which was established in 1998. Fewer than 100,000 of Malawi's 11.3 million people own television sets.

Malawi Broadcasting Corporation has a two-channel radio network currently broadcasting for 19 hours for Radio 1 and 24 hours for Radio 2 each day. Radio 1 broadcasts in English, Chichewa, Tumbuka, Yao, Lomwe, Sena, and Tonga. Broadcasts are available on medium wave, short wave, and FM frequencies. Radio 2 broadcasts in English and Chichewa on FM stereo. The news coverage of these two stations is basically the same. The first private station, FM101, broadcasting to a radius of about 70 km from Blantyre, began operating in 1998. The second privately run station, Capital Radio 102.5, also based in Blantyre and reaching an area of 60 km around the city, took to the airwaves in 1999. The two stations concentrate mostly on musical and entertainment programs.

The government-controlled Malawi Broadcasting Corporation still dominates radio broadcasting in Malawi. All new stations that wish to establish a radio station have to get a license from MACRA, which is responsible for regulating the provision of broadcasting, licensing of broadcasting providers and planning and allocating the use of the frequency spectrum. MACRA has the discretion to limit foreign ownership of companies receiving licenses and to limit the proportion of airtime devoted to advertising, provided that such limitations are applied equitably.

According to the new Communications Act of 1998, the MBC must operate without political bias and independent of any political party. It must support the democratic process, refrain from broadcasting any matter expressing its own opinion on current affairs, provide balanced election coverage, and have regard for the public interest. Licensing of private broadcasting before 1998 was the responsibility of the postmaster-general, who was a senior civil servant within the Ministry of Information, Broadcasting, Posts and Telecommunications. Since no criteria or procedure existed for licensing in broadcasting, in practice the minister had all the power. The new bill, by contrast, established clear criteria and a formal procedure for issuing licenses in all areas, as well as establishing an independent body to oversee them.

The single television station in the country, the state-controlled Television Malawi (TVM), is a public broadcaster, its goal to ''foster unity and development [and to] provide civic education and information.'' The station

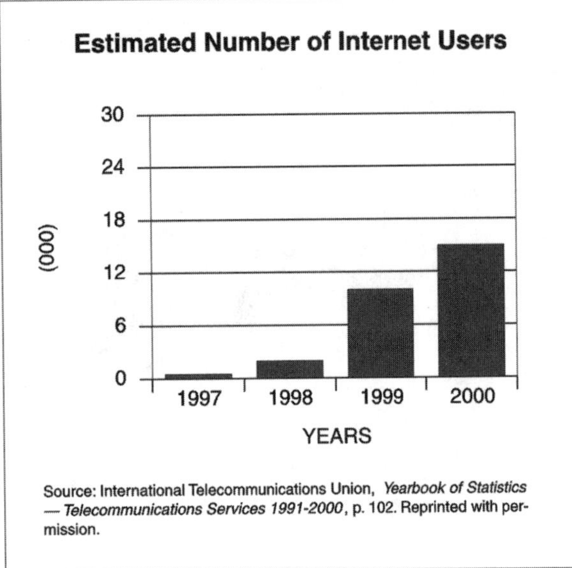

Source: International Telecommunications Union, *Yearbook of Statistics — Telecommunications Services 1991-2000*, p. 102. Reprinted with permission.

broadcasts about 55 hours per week, with about 10 hours of local content. Because TVM has a limited number of cameras, local broadcasting is extremely difficult, and much of the station's material is obtained through relay (rebroadcasting) agreements with outside stations such as Deutsche Welle, BBC and TV Africa. Satellite TV, carrying such stations as CNN, BBC, and South Africa's Mnet, is available to those who can afford sets, decoders, and satellite dishes. Fewer than 100,000 of Malawi's 11 million people own television sets.

With no private companies to make commercials and only a small TV market, TVM has had many financial problems. In spite of that, however, TVM announced in March 2000 its plans to extend coverage to 100 percent of the country by year's end. As of 2002, however, the station reached only about 70 percent of the country.

ELECTRONIC NEWS MEDIA

MalawiNet, the main Internet Service Provider (ISP), was established in 1997 as the only commercial Internet Service Provider. MalawiNet is jointly owned by ComNet of USA (42 percent), Malawi Posts and Telecommunications Corporation (MPTC) (38 percent), and Bj Trust of Malawi (20 percent). The MPTC later liberalized the market, allowing private ISPs to obtain their own connections, either via MalawiNet's POPs in Lilongwe or Blantyre or via a direct international link from MPTC. At the end of 2001, Malawi had 8 ISPs. News organizations in Malawi cannot afford publishing through the Internet because of limited resources. Only *The Nation* has an Internet site that publishes their news: http://www.nationmalawi.com/.

EDUCATION & TRAINING

The Malawi Polytechnic, a constituent college of the University of Malawi, offers undergraduate studies in journalism. The Malawi Institute of Journalism, an affiliate of the University of Malawi, was established in 1996. The institute offers diploma and certificate courses in journalism. A number of private schools run by professional journalists were also opened in the late 1990s. Among these are Pen Point School of Journalism, Norman Communications Centre, and Grefa Communications.

Major media organizations and associations are the Journalists' Association of Malawi, the Malawi Media Women's Association, the Media Council of Malawi and a chapter of the Media Institute of Southern Africa (MISA). The MAMWA has played a major role in attracting a female audience to radio. One of MAMWA's significant achievements is the Dzimwe Community Radio Station in Monkey-Bay District, which was licensed in 1997. The station covers a radius of 95 kms and reaches 3.2 million listeners. Mindful of the fact that most people within this community live below the poverty line and cannot afford radios and batteries, MAMWA asked them to form listening clubs in order to increase access to radio sets. Radio listeners clubs are set by women media professionals who organize rural women into groups that meet once a week to debate a theme that directly affects their lives. The discussions are recorded and presented to government officials, community authorities, and representatives of non-governmental organizations for replies that are also recorded. Discussions and replies are broadcasted by the Dzimwe Community Radio Station.

In May 2002, Malawi's largest daily newspaper, *The Nation*, underwrote a new national Young Sports Journalism Award as part of an initiative to identify and develop new sports writers. The competition is designed for practicing junior journalists but is also open to anyone who aspires to the field.

SUMMARY

The autocratic, repressive Banda regime prior to 1994 crippled Malawi's media. The country's democratic government, voted into power in 1994, caused some exciting developments in the media industry between 1994 and the close of the century. From the single state-controlled Malawi Broadcasting Corporation (MBC), which covered the whole country, and a small private religious broadcaster with a radius of 20 km from the capital, Lilongwe, Malawi had as of 2002 two private stations based in Blantyre, a community radio station in Monkey Bay, and a second FM channel on MBC, called Radio 2. From two state owned newspapers in 1994, the country has experienced a bloom of new independent newspapers. The poor state of the Malawian economy and the deplorable attitude of most reporters and editors who refuse to stick to the ethics of the profession remain serious problems facing media development in Malawi. These are aggravated by the fact that most of the newspapers in the country, including the two dailies, are owned by politicians and lack independent editorial judgment and policies. Bakili Muluzi has improved things in the media, but there is still a hint of the autocratic system in the air especially in the manner with which the media are dealt. It is hoped that Malawi will move to a more independent broadcast media and greater autonomy for the MBC as a public broadcaster.

SIGNIFICANT DATES

- 1994: Malawi became a multi-party democracy, the first government guaranteed freedom of the press in the new democratic constitution.
- 1998: The state-controlled Television Malawi (TVM) was established.
- 1998: Parliament passed a new Communications Act, which for the first time established an independent regulatory body for broadcasting and telecommunications: the Malawi Communications Regulatory Authority (MACRA).

BIBLIOGRAPHY

Banda, Zeria. ''The Malawi News Media,'' Master's thesis, Ball State University, Indiana, 1998.

Cooney Brendan. *Malawi Media Report*. Grahamstown, South Africa: Rhodes University, 2001.

Reporters Without Borders. *Malawi: Annual report 2002*. Available from http://www.rsf.fr/.

USAID. *USAID's Program in Malawi*, 2002. Available from http://www.usaid.gov/country/afr/mw/.

World Bank. *World Development Indicators*, 2000. CD-Rom, World Bank, Washington, DC.

—Gladys Mutangadura

MALAYSIA

BASIC DATA

Official Country Name:	Malaysia
Region (Map name):	Southeast Asia
Population:	22,229,040
Language(s):	Bahasa Melayu, English, Chinese dialects, Tamil, Telugu
Literacy rate:	83.5%
Area:	329,750 sq km
GDP:	89,659 (US$ millions)
Number of Daily Newspapers:	31
Total Circulation:	2,191,000
Circulation per 1,000:	130
Number of Nondaily Newspapers:	1
Total Circulation:	17,000
Circulation per 1,000:	1
Total Newspaper Ad Receipts:	1,765 (Ringgit millions)
As % of All Ad Expenditures:	58.60
Number of Television Stations:	27
Number of Television Sets:	10,800,000
Television Sets per 1,000:	485.9
Number of Satellite Subscribers:	525,000
Satellite Subscribers per 1,000:	23.6
Number of Radio Stations:	92
Number of Radio Receivers:	10,900,000
Radio Receivers per 1,000:	490.3
Number of Individuals with Computers:	2,400,000
Computers per 1,000:	108.0
Number of Individuals with Internet Access:	3,700,000
Internet Access per 1,000:	166.4

BACKGROUND & GENERAL CHARACTERISTICS

The southeast Asian country of Malaysia includes people from many other Asian and western countries and numerous ethnic groups. This diversity is reflected in its economy, politics, social systems, and culture. The first people to inhabit the Malaysia peninsula, the Malays, came down from South China around 2000 B.C. Around 600 A.D. Sri Vijaya headed a strong empire in southern Sumatra that dominated both sides of the Straits of Malacca. In the 1300s, Sri Vijjaya fell and the Majapahit Empire controlled Malaysia. The Muslims began to dominate the peninsula around 1400 when a fugitive slave from Singapore founded a principality at Malacca. This Muslim principality fell to Portugal in 1511, and in 1641, the Dutch took control from the Portuguese. The British East India Company entered the peninsula in 1786, and in 1819, the British established a settlement at Singapore. In 1784, British treaties protected some areas. In 1895 four states became the Federated Malay States. Thailand in 1909 ceded four northern states (Kedah, Kelantan, Trengganu, and Perlis) to the British, together with Johor in 1914, and this whole area became known as the Unfederated Malay States. In 1892, separate British control was extended to North Borneo, and in 1898 Sarawak became a separate British protectorate.

In December 1941, during World War II, the Japanese conquered Malaya and Borneo, and they held it throughout the war. After World War II, the British formed the Malayan Union that included the nine peninsular states along with Pinang and Malacca. In 1946, Singapore and the two Borneo protectorates became separate British protectorates. On February 1, 1948, the Federation of Malay succeeded the Malayan Union. In 1957, the Federation of Malay became an independent member of the British Commonwealth. In 1962, Malaya and Great Britain agreed to from the new state of Malaysia that would include Singapore, and the British Borneo territories of Sarawak, Brunei, and North Borneo, but Singapore voted not to join. However, for two years Singapore was part of the Federation of Malay states until 1965 when Singapore became independent. The ''Federation'' was dropped that same year, and Malaysia became the official name of the newly independent British colonies. Malaysia has a combined land area of 329, 760 square kilometers and is similar in size to New Mexico in the United States.

Nature of Audience As of 2001, the multiracial population of peninsular Malaysia was estimated at 22,229,040. There are three main ethnic groups: the Malays, called *Bumiputera* (''sons of the soil,'' 58 percent); Chinese (30 percent); the Indians (10 percent), and others (10 percent). More than 50 percent of Malaysians live in urban areas. Most of the Chinese live in urban and tin mining areas, while many Malays live in rural areas. The Chinese who live in urban areas are wealthier, and over the years spurts of ethnic violence have erupted between them and the Malays. The indigenous *Orang Asli* aborigines number about 50,000. The *kampung* forms the basic unit of Malay society, a tightly knit community consisting of kinship, marriage ties, and neighbor relationships which are regulated by traditional Malaysian values. In 1999, the four major languages were Malaya, Tamil (an Indian dialect), Chinese, and English.

The 1990s brought economic prosperity to Malaysia, which is rated as an upper middle-class country. The unemployment rate in the 1990s remained at nearly 4 percent. The literacy rate is 92 percent, and all Malaysians are required to attend school at least until age 15. Many Malaysians obtain degrees from local and foreign universities. With government loans some study in the United States, New Zealand, Australia, or the United Kingdom.

Written literature in Malaysia goes back to the sixteenth century and describes old Malaya society, for example, *Hikayat Hang Tuah* (Hang Tuah's Life Story) and *Sejarah Melayum*, a history of the Malaysian peninsula. The first newspaper in Malaysia, begun by the British in Panang in 1805, was the *Prince of Wales Island Gazette*.

The Malay government has continuously censored the press in response to political instability which characterized the peninsula for much of the twentieth century. In 1968, the Malaysia National News Agency, Bernama began operating. In 1984, the Printing and Publications Act enabled the Minister of Home Affairs to revoke any publications licensees deemed dangerous to the state. Malaysia is one of the most authoritarian and repressive countries regarding the press.

In the 1930s under British control, the country developed restrictive policies toward the press because it feared the spread of communism. In April 1930, the Malayan Communist Party was founded in Singapore. Mainly urban Chinese were members of the party, and as a result many were arrested. This group later became involved in the local labor movement. In 1990, the Communist Party in Malaysia collapsed.

Despite the threat of communism in the 1930s, the Malay vernacular press flourished in that decade. Between 1900 and 1918 of the 13 newspapers and periodicals started, Singapore published eight, Pennang published three, the federated states had two, and Kelantan had one. During the first two decades, the Singapore press produced *Al-Iman* (1906-1908) and *Neracha* (1911-1915), Islamic religious reform journals. The secular newspapers included *Utusan Melaya* (1907-1921) and *Lembaga Melaya* (1914-1931).

Early Publications & Two Early Editors *Utusan Melayu* and *Lembaga Melaya* were modeled on the English press and sought to provide a more balanced view of the news. However, both newspapers reflected the views of the man who edited them, Mohd Eunos b. Abdullah, the so-called father of Malay journalism. Born in Singapore in 1876, the son of a prominent merchant from Sumatra, Abdullah was educated in the Malay School in Kampong Glam and graduated in English from the Raffles Institute in 1894. At thirty-one, after working several years as a master attendant in the ports of Singapore and Muar in Jahore, he took a job with the *Free Press,* Singapore's oldest newspaper. For the *Free Press*, he edited the Malay edition, and he witnessed a growing demand for a vernacular press. Abdullah with the help of William Makepeace, the owner of the *Free Press* founded the *Utusan Melaya* in 1907.

Published three times weekly in the vernacular Malaya language, the *Utusan Melaya* presented the cable and local news that appealed to an urban Singapore audience. This newspaper also commented on a wide range of public issues. Moreover, the paper was used as a language teaching medium in the schools.

In 1914, Abdullah also served as editor of the moderately progressive *Lembaga Melayu*, which mirrored the *Malaya Trinbure*. It did not publish editorials until 1929 but did publish accounts from the overseas wire service. This newspaper was the only daily published in Malaysia until it stopped publication in 1931.

In 1931, Onn b. Ja'afar founded the *Warta Malaya*, which became successful after the *Lembaga Melayu* folded. The *Wasta Malaya* became an important voice for the Malay readers because it shifted focus from Singapore to the Malaya peninsula. *Warta Malaya* influenced the start-up of thirty-four other newspapers and periodicals between 1920 and 1930. *Warta Malaya* discussed wide-ranging issues that included controversial topics regarding non-Malay demands for increased rights and higher education and the development of the Malay economy for the Malays. It was also critical of the British occupation of Malaysia. Onn b. Ja'afar became an outspoken critic of colonial authority and the Malaya relationship with Great Britain.

By the mid 1930s there were over eighty-four periodicals published in Singapore and throughout the Malay Peninsula. During the years 1935 and 1936 there were twenty-five new Malaysia newspapers published in the Malay language. Increasing commercialization and professionalism in journalism, coupled with the affordable price, caused newspapers to flourish. By 1931, with over one-third of the males literate, these newspapers and magazines were widely popular, especially among schoolteachers and government workers. In addition to *Warta Malaya* (1931-1941), prominent Malaysian newspapers in circulation before World War II include *Majils* (1931-1941), *Lembaga* (1935-1941) and *Utusan Malayu* (1939-1941).

Political Unrest In January 1941, Japanese troops invaded northern Malaysia, and the Japanese took over Sarawak in 1942. The British surrendered Singapore to the Japanese the same year, and the Japanese killed many Chinese residents, while others fled from the cities to the jungles. Many newspapers were suspended during the war. Then the British returned in 1945. The decade that followed included episodes of ethnic unrest and a resurgence of the Malaysia Communist Party in 1946, and in 1948, the British expanded their control over the media during what was called the Emergency, when communists tried to gain control over the government. During this twelve-year period, the government initiated aggressive media campaigns to control the terrorists. It. was not until 1960, however, that the communist insurgency was suppressed.

Inter-ethnic violence shook Malaysia in 1969 when the Malaysian Chinese Association withdrew from the government. Its removal destroyed the alliance of ethnic political parties. There were demonstrations, parades, and rumors of ethnic violence. At least 178 people died in rioting. The government declared a state of emergency, and Tn Abdul Razak (1922-1976), the prime minister, and the National Council temporally replaced the government.

On August 13, 1970, Malaysia proclaimed a national ideology, while the sultan served as the supreme ruler. The government proclaimed a five-point ideology, *Rukunegara*, for Malaysia. These principles included loyalty to the supreme ruler; the belief in God; respect for the Constitution, especially the special rights of Malays and the rule of law; and respectful behavior towards one another.

Social unrest, government censorship, and the 1967 Publications Act that was amended in 1984 put further restrictions on a free press in Malaysia. In 2002, Malaysian newspapers are primarily government controlled and censored. These newspapers contain about 60 percent of local and national news; the remaining space covers topics related to other parts of the world.

Newspapers & Their Circulation The oldest English daily, *New Straits Times* (formerly the *Straits Times*), founded in 1845 in Kuala Lumpur, is a business and shipping information paper with a circulation of 190,000. *The Star*, modeled on its Hong Kong cousin and on popular British tabloids, was founded in 1971 in Selangor. It has an average circulation of 192,059. The afternoon *Malay Mail* began circulation in Kuala Lumpur in 1896. It emphasizes lighter news and features and has a circulation of 75,000. Also, *The Business Times* was founded in Kuala Lumpur in 1976, by splitting the shipping and financial sections of the *New Straits Times*. It has a circulation of 15,000.

Post World War II Newspapers and Their Circulation The Malay language newspapers after World War II attempted to carve out a separate Malay culture and identity. Of the five Malay language newspapers, the largest is the morning daily *Berita Harian* founded in 1957 in Kuala Lumpur with a circulation of 350,000. The *Metro Ahad*, also in Kuala Lumpur, has a daily circulation of 132,195. The *Watan* has a circulation of 80,000.

The four Tamil language newspapers are also published in Malaysia's capital, Kuala Lumpur. These newspapers are the *Malaysia Nmban* with a circulation of 45,000; the *Tamil Nessan* founded in 1924 with a daily circulation of 35,000 and a Sunday of 60,000; *Tamil Osai* with a daily circulation of 21,000 and a Sunday circulation of 40,000; and the *Tamil Thinamani* with a daily circulation of 18,000 and Sunday circulation of 39,000.

The seven Chinese language newspapers primarily cater to urban Malaysian Chinese. The *China Press* in Kuala Lumpur has a circulation of 206,000. The *Chung Kuo Pao*, also in Kuala Lumpur, has a circulation of 210,000. The *Guang Ming*, a daily in Selangor, has a circulation of 87,144. The *Kwong Wah Yit Poh*, founded in 1910 in Panang, has a circulation of 65,939 daily, and on Sunday 76,958. The *Nanayang Siang Pau* founded in 1923 in Selangor has a daily circulation of 183,801 and a Sunday edition circulation of 220,000. The *Shin Min Daily News*, established in Kuala Lumpur in 1966, is a daily morning paper with a circulation of 82,000. The *Sin Chen Jit Poh*, founded in 1929 in Petaling, Selangor, has a daily circulation of 227,067 and a Sunday circulation of 230,000.

There are four daily newspapers in English and Chinese in Sabah. The largest is the *Sabah Times* with a circulation of 30,000. It is followed by the *Daily Express* (25,520), *Syarikat Sabah Times* (25,000), and the *Borneo Mail* (14,000). The largest Chinese newspaper in Sabah is the *Hwa Chiaw Jit Pao* (circulation 28,000), *Merdeka Daily News* (6,948), *Api Siang Pau* (3,000), and *Tawau Jih Pao* (circulation not known).

There are five Chinese and three English newspapers in Sarawak. The Chinese newspaper with the largest circulation is the *See Hua Daily News* (80,000). The others are *International Times* (37,000), *Malaysia Daily News* (22,735), *Miri Daily News* (22,431), and the *Berita Petang Sarawak* (12,000). The English newspaper in Sarawak with the largest circulation is the *Borneo Post* with 60,000 subscribers. The others include *The People's Mirror* (24,990) and the *Sarawak Tribune and Sunday Tribune* (29,598).

On Peninsular Malaysia the Sunday papers in English include the *New Sunday Times*, established in Kuala Lumpur in 1932, with a circulation of 191,562. A competing Sunday paper in the English language founded in Kuala Lumpur in 1896 is the *Sunday Mail* with a circulation of 75,641. The *Sunday Star* in Selangor has a circulation of 232,790.

Sunday newspapers in the Malay language include *Berita Minggu* printed in Kuala Lumpur (421,127), the *Mingguan Malaysia* founded in 1964 in Petaling Jaya (493,523), and the *Utuan Zaman* also in Petaling Jaya and founded in 1964 (11,782).

The one Sunday paper in the Tamil language, the *Makkal Osai*, is printed in Kuala Lumpur and has a circulation of 28,000. As of 1999, there was no Chinese language Sunday paper in Malaysia.

The newspapers with the largest readerships in Malaysia in 2002 are *The Star* and *The Sunday Star*. First published in 1971, as a regional newspaper in George Town, Penang, *The Star* was the first tabloid newspaper published in Malaysia and the first English newspaper printed with the web offset process. It became Penang's premier newspaper in 1976, outselling *The New Strait Times*, a newspaper that was 139 years old. Also, Tunku Abdul Rahman retired in 1970 as Malaysia's first prime minister, and in 1976, he became chairman of the board. The same year, *The Star* went national by moving its headquarters from Penang to Kuala Lumpur. In 1981 it moved its headquarters to Petaling Jaya to accommodate a growing staff, as well as to improve with the latest technology in publishing. In 1995, *The Star* became the first Malaysian newspaper to launch an edition on the World Wide Web.

In June 2001 the daily circulation of *The Star* reached 279,647 and *The Sunday Star* reached 292,408. *The New Strait Times* had a circulation of 136,273, and *New Sunday Times* had 155,565. *Malay Mail* had a circulation of 34,206, and the *Sunday Mail* had one of 50,215. That same year 5,843 titles were published in Malaysia, amounting to over 29 million copies. There were 42 daily newspapers in 1996 compared to 44 in 1995. The average circulation of newspapers in 1996 was 3.3 million.

There are numerous magazines published each year in Malaysia, but many go out of print because of the difficulty in getting sufficient numbers of advertisers to support them. The top ten magazines in 2000 published in the Malay language are *Al Islam*, *Anjung Seri*, *Bola Sepak*, *Dewan Ekonomi*, *Dewan Kosmik*, *Dewan Masyarakat*, *Dewan Pelajar*, *Dewan Siswa*, *Ibu*, and *Jelita*. The most popular English language magazine is *Aliran Monthly*, a reform movement magazine working towards establishing freedom, justice and solidarity for all Malaysians. Aliran Kesedaran Negara (ALIRAN), established in 1977, Malaysia's first multiethnic reform movement and the nation's oldest human rights group, publishes it.

Daily and Non-Daily Newspaper Titles and Circulation Figures

	1996	1997	1998	1999	2000
Number of Daily Newspapers	40	33	33	NA	31
Circulation of Dailies (000)	2,408	2,257	2,487	NA	2,191
Number of Non-Daily Newspapers	2	3	1	NA	1
Circulation of Non-Dailies (000)	32	312	11	NA	17

Source: World Association of Newspapers and Zenithmedia, *World Press Trends 2001*, pp. 8, 10, 17, 19. Note: NA stands for not available.

Other popular English language magazines include *Far Eastern Economic Review*, *Female*, *Fortune*, *Life*, *Men's Review*, *National Geographic*, *New Idea*, *Newsweek*, and *The Planter*. The top Chinese-language magazines published in Malaysia as of 2000 are *Business World*, *Feminine*, *Photo Pictorial*, *Reader's Digest*, *Utusan Pegguna*, *Women*, and *Modern Home*.

ECONOMIC FRAMEWORK

The economy in Malaysia recovered after a slow down in 1997. Prime Minister Mahathir blamed international speculators, especially U.S. billionaire George Soros, whom Mahathir believed was responsible for manipulating the currency market in Asia in 1997. In response to the declining economy Mahathir cut government spending by 18 percent and delayed huge development projects. By 2000, the Malaysian economy had improved, and the annual gross domestic product (GDP) had increased. The sixth Malaysia plan was successful because of continued governmental fiscal restraints and double-digit export growth. This plan encouraged trends toward privatization and increased industrialization.

While privatization is a goal in the business sector, a free press without government restrictions is hardly a priority. The government controls the presses and the publishing enterprises throughout Malaysia. There are strong political and economic ties between the government and the media. In 2002, for example, the Ministry of Finance owned 30 percent of the consortium that operates Mega TV. A subsidiary firm, Sri Utara, of the investment arm of the Malaysian Indian Congress, a political party in the coalition government, owns 5 percent of Mega TV.

Political Ownership of Media The political parties and their investment companies control the major newspapers in Malaysia. The Utusan Melayu Group publishes three Malay language dailies and has strong ties to Prime Minister Mahathir's party. In addition, the *Star* is owned by the Malaysian Chinese Association, a party affiliated with the ruling coalition. Private interests aligned with the Malaysian Indian Congress control all the Tamil newspapers. The investment arm of Mahathir's party, the Fleet Investment Group, has controlling interest in TV 3 and the *New Straits Times*.

According to *Aliran*, the journal of social reform, these connections reveal the biases of the Malaysian media. During the 1995 general elections, the daily newspapers carried government advertisements in full but accepted only partial advertisements from oppositional parties. Some believe that newspaper owners do not allow new entrants into industry despite the fact that they may add to the public good. What the imprisoned Assistant Prime Minister Anwar called an ''informed citizenry through a contest of ideas,'' is as of 2002 as elusive as ever in Malaysia.

Distribution Issues Due to the various geographic features especially the straits that separate Peninsular Malaysia from Malaysia on the island of Borneo, there are problems connected to newspaper distribution, as well as the desire for some papers to go national or have sites on the Internet. Newspaper circulation reflects ethnic and geographic divisions. English papers are popular in large urban areas. The rural areas are conservative and read more Malay newspapers that catered to Muslims. Still there are few East Malaysian papers on the peninsula and still fewer peninsular papers can be found in circulation in East Malaysia. Singapore with a 90 percent Chinese population does not allow the circulation of papers from Malaysia, nor does Malaysia allow circulation of newspapers from Singapore.

The *Star* was the first Malaysian newspaper to be launched on the World Wide Web on June 23, 1995. The *Star* and *Sunday Star* also publish four magazines. *Kuntum*, an educational monthly in Bahasa Malaysia is for children ages six to twelve. Though not particularly popular, *Shang Hai*, is regarded as the most authoritative Chinese magazine in the country. *Galaxie*, is a light reading English entertainment magazine published fortnightly, claimed to be popular with teenagers and working adults. In addition, *Flavours* is a magazine devoted to good food and dining in Malaysia.

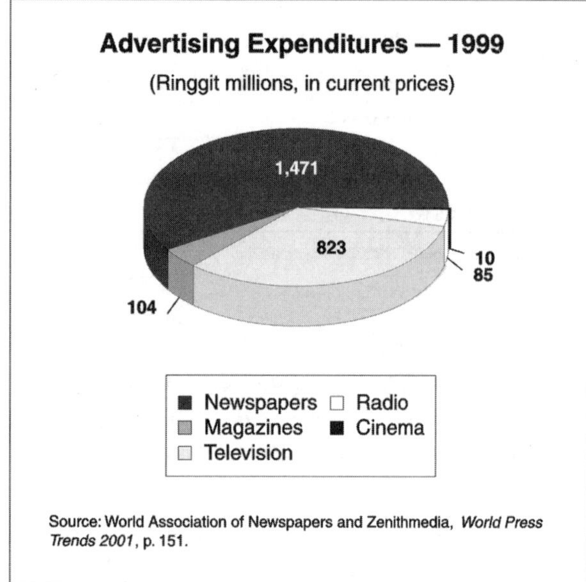

Source: World Association of Newspapers and Zenithmedia, *World Press Trends 2001*, p. 151.

In 2002, in addition to the Star, quite a few papers had Internet sites. The English ones include *New Straits Times*, *HarakahDaily.com*, *Sarawak*, *Bansar.com*, *Malasiakini.com*, and *Bernama*, the Malaysian National News Agency. Malay-language newspapers with Web sites are *Dinmani.com* in Tamil characters, *Sinchew-i.com*, and *Utusan Malaysia*. Internet links to Malaysian Chinese newspapers are *Kwong Wah Yit Poh* and *Nanyang Siang Pau*.

Newspaper Cost and Prices The paper pulp prices have remained stable since the 1980s in Malaysia. In late 1980, the price for pulp was US$445 per ton; in 2002, the price was US$450 per ton. Malaysia purchases most of its newsprint from Canada. In the 1990s, Malaysia began recycling newsprint when Theen Seng Paper Manufacturing Sbn. Bhd started operating in Selangor darul Ehsan, Malaysia. This firm is the long established leading manufacturer of recycled paper in that country.

The average daily price for a newspaper in Malaysia has increased from 17 cents per copy in 1980 to 40 cents per copy in 2002. Sunday papers run about 60 cents for each edition.

Unions The National Union of Journalists represents journalists in Malaysia. Labor strikes among journalists in Malaysia are rare, but disagreements with the government's strict policies have increased especially after the conviction of Anwar in 1998. In December 2001 about 40 journalists at the *Sun* staged demonstrations outside their office in Kuala Lumpur protesting the government's suspension of two editors. Altogether in 2002 there were nearly 7,000 people employed as journalists, photographers, and editors in the country.

PRESS LAWS

In Malaysia two opposing positions define the newspapers. The Barisan National, the ruling coalition, contrasts directly with its opposition. Press accounts suggest the Barisan is moderate and its opposition is extreme. Barisan promotes harmony among ethnic groups while the opposition creates ethnic conflict. The press in Malaysia fluctuates between ideas about democracy as ideal and the elitism that is the fact in this classist society.

As of the early 2000s, the restrictions on the press laws in Malaysia have been associated with Mahathir Mohamad, who became prime minister in 1981 and in 1982 joined Malaysia's ruling party, the United Malay National Organization (UMNO). Dr. Mahathir Mohamad was responsible for the Printing Presses and Publications Act of 1984, which mandates all publications to have a license that can be revoked by the Minister for Home Affairs. There is no judicial review, and the ministers' decisions are final. These press laws constitute a holdover from British rule when the British successfully curtailed the spread of communism in Malaysia by censoring the press.

In 2002, the press restrictions are used by the UNMO to suppress any views that put the government or the Malaysian people in an unfavorable light. Most Malaysians read information that has been censored by the government. The UMNO and the Barisan National coalition are both allied in a national coalition that controls radio and television stations, as well as newspapers.

These coalitions put more restrictions on the press following the November 1997 election, when the Pan Malaysian Islamic Party (PAS) gained significantly against (UMNO). This election caused the UMNO-controlled government to ban the *Harakak*, the press-controlled newspaper that could only be sold to PAS party members. In 1998, this newspaper also increased in circulation following the prosecution of former Deputy Prime Minister Anwar Ibrahim.

In 1987, three national newspapers closed under the Internal Security Act, the Printing Presses and Publications Act, and the Judicial Act. These newspapers, the English-language *Star*, the Chinese-language *Sin Chew Jit Poh*, and the Malay-language *Waton*, reported on the racial aspects of a political conflict between two government parties. In 1988, the government allowed these papers to reopen after they made substantial changes in their editorial management.

Although the government does not directly censor what is published in the print media, the ISA has affected the print media in Malaysia. In May 2001 the publisher of two major dailies controlled by Nanyang Press Sdn Bhd, *Nanyang Siang Pau* and *China Press* were sold to the Malaysian Chinese Association (MCA), a political party that is the second largest of the ruling coalition in Malaysia. The MCA gained control over these dailies, in addition to the seventeen other Chinese publications and magazines it owns. The Chinese Malaysian community opposed this action, but MCA purchased Nayang Press holdings after a rarely held government assembly meeting, Extraordinary General Meeting (EGM), approved the purchase. The effect of this purchase was to further curb the freedom of the Malaysian Press because the government directly controls all Malay and English presses.

The control shows up in various ways. In June 2001, the director of *Utusan Melayu*, Raja Ahmad Aminilah was forced to resign from the government controlled media group because he wrote a letter of appeal advocating that the jailed politician, Anwar Ibrahim, be allowed to choose his own medical treatment. Under the Sedition Act in May 2001, a party youth leader for Teluk Intan Branch, named Azman Majohan, was arrested by the police and held for ten days for uttering seditious words at a political rally in Taiping town. On May 2, 2001, the Hulu Klang state assemblyman Mohamed Azmin Ali was sentenced to jail for 18 months by a sessions court in Kuala Lumpur, after he was found guilty of providing false information in Datuk Seri Ibrahim's corruption trial that took place in March 1999.

On that same date, Anwar Ibrahim was not allowed to appeal his case in court to deny allegations (four on sodomy, and one corrupt practice) against him, although these charges were dropped by a High Court. Dr. Rais Yatin the de facto law minister said the charges were dropped because Anwar was already serving a fifteen year jail term. However, the defense team noted that Anwar was innocent, and there was no evidence to support the charges brought against him. Anwar was an advocate of freedom of the press in Malaysia and this caused the rift between him and Prime Minister Mahathir. It began in March 1996 at an Asian journalists' meeting when Anwar said that journalists should be a vehicle for ''the contest of ideas and cultivate good taste.'' Shortly after that speech, Anwar told *Time* magazine that his views about a free press were in the minority: ''My principle is an informed citizenry, is responsible citizenry, so there must be respect for freedom of the press.''

In March 2001, the Home Affairs Ministry held up the distribution of *Far Eastern Economic Review* and *Asia Week* because of a photograph that made Prime Minister Mahathir look bad.

A libel award in July 2000 by Malaysia's highest court sent chills down the spines of timid journalists in Malaysia.. The high court upheld a 7 million ringgit (US$1.8 million) libel award to a Malaysian business tycoon, Vincent Tan. The court believed Tan had been damaged by four Malaysian industry magazine articles published in 1994. The journalist who was fined 2 million ringgit in the case, the 40-year veteran M. G. G. Pillai noted that during his whole career he had not earned enough money to pay the court costs or damages awarded against him. Pillai believed the decision by the high court reduces journalists to being public relations officers. This high court decision even prompted prominent international bodies to issue a report titled ''Malaysia 2000: Justice in Jeopardy,'' which expressed deep concern about the judicial system in Malaysia.

Fallout from this high court decision caused several independent publications to have their annual permits rejected. The Home Ministry also put limits on the publication of the very popular *Harakah*, making it go from being bi-weekly to being bi-monthly. One columnist James Wong Wong concluded that all the acts that restrict freedom of the media, like the Internal Security Act, the Sedition Act, and the Official Secrets Act, have instilled fear among journalists and senior editors throughout Malaysia.

CENSORSHIP

All the media and press acts, the Printing Presses Acts, the Internal Security Act, and the Control and Import Acts give the Ministry of Information and the censors authority to ban imported and domestic material in Malaysia. In June 2001, the government confiscated more than 1,000 political books after conducting a raid by the Home Ministry Office in Jahor Bari. It was believed that the books confiscated by the government contained material alleged to be dangerous to racial harmony.

In another incident in May 2001 the Home Minister banned a book titled *Pengakuan Paderi Melayu Kristankan Beribu-ribu Orang Melayu* (Malay Priest Confesses to Having Converted Thousands of Malays to Christianity) because the book was believed to be detrimental to public order. Moreover, the Home Ministry in June 2001 held back three issues of the international news magazine *Asia Week* cover dates May 25 and June 8 contained criticism of the Malaysian Prime Minister, Dr. Mahathir.

There are few federal laws that restrict officials from providing journalists with information, unless the information has an effect on national security or the military. Government official can order the press not to talk with journalists or corespondents, if they deem the information sensitive.

STATE-PRESS RELATIONS

Deputy Prime Minister Abdullah Ahrmad Badari, who took office following the sentencing of Anwar in

1999, is the Minister of Information. He has the responsibility for carrying out the communication activities through three departments: Department of Information, the Department of Broadcasting, and Film Negra Malaysia (National Film Unit).

Through the departments of Information, Broadcasting, and the National Film Unit, the Ministry of Information directs all the channels of news information in the country. This includes billboards and special television documentaries and films related to Malaysia, as well as codes and standards for radio and television.

By 2000 the relationship between journalists and the government had grown increasingly strained. Journalists and reporters have very little rights when it comes to criticizing the government. Evidence of this contentious relationship between the press and the government has caused several editors to be removed, as well as newspapers and magazines to be indefinitely suspended or completely shut down.

In January 2000, A. Kadir Jasin, the chief editor of *New Straits Times* Press Bhd lost his position after a disagreement with the government. Kadir published a series of articles that angered some of the top government officials and led to his removal.

Following the trial of Anwar Ibrahim in 1998, the government took a hard line and threatened that it would place more restrictions on the local and foreign press. In July 1998, the Deputy of Information Minister Suleiman Mohamad stated, ''If the media indulge in activities that threaten political stability or national unity, we will come down hard regardless of whether they are locals or foreign.''

Johan Jaafar, the editor of the leading Malay-language daily, the *Utusan Malaysia*, was forced under government pressure to resign in July 1998. The government disliked his paper's coverage of the operational problems regarding a new airport under construction. The stories were embarrassing to the UMNO party which is a major stockholder of the paper.

Magazines have also fallen under the government's scrutiny. In March 1999, the government notified the editor of *Detich*, a bi-monthly magazine, that its publishing license would not be renewed. Forced to suspend publication by the government, the *Detich* suffered major financial losses. The editor Ahmad Lutfi Othman told reporters after the government suspended the license: ''We hope the ministry will be more rational in the future. We may have criticized the government occasionally but we never intended to break the law.''

In August 2000 the government revoked the license of another magazine, this one edited by Ahmad Lutfi Othman. The decision to revoke the *Wasilah* license was politically motivated: Lutfi is a member of the Pan-Malaysian Islamic Party, one of the opposition parties to the UMNO.

Several individuals in January 2000 were arrested by the Malaysian government for alleged criticisms made toward the government. Some of those arrested were prominent party members, defense lawyers, and media professionals, for example, Zulkifi Suong, editor of *Harakah*, and Chia Lim Thye, the owner of *Harakah*'s printing company. Both Suong and Thye were charged with sedition relating to an article *Harakah* published in 1999 about the sacking of Anwar Ibrahim. In court, Thye and Suong pleaded not guilty to the charges, yet restrictions and limits were placed on the newspaper.

In April 2000, in order to smooth relations with the Malaysian media, the government announced plans to review the colonial era publishing laws. This pressure came from the press freedom community in Malaysia. The laws to muzzle the press and human rights groups began under British rule in 1948 and were tightened under Prime Minister Mahathir in 1984. Some 581 journalists signed a petition stating that opposition to these laws was growing, and they advocated that the government create a national press council to regulate the industry. Apparently, their petition fell on deaf ears because as of 2002, no council has been created to review the press laws.

The government has learned to pressure local media in various ways. Apparently upset with what the Malaysian press published from the international wire services (about 20 percent of Malaysia's news comes from that service), Prime Minister Mahathir announced that Moslem nations should set up their own international news agency to counter what he called the distorted views of the Islamic world. According to Mahathir, ''If we don't have any faith in our own news agencies, we tend to publish what is distributed by the Western wire services.'' He continued: ''As a result, we don't get at least an alternative view.'' He was also critical of the media's portrayal of terrorism as a solely a Muslim invention.

ATTITUDE TOWARD THE FOREIGN MEDIA

The government continues to have a very suspicious view of the foreign media. In August 1998, Information Minister Mohamad Rahmat announced the government's plans to put more restrictions on foreign journalists in the country. Foreign journalists in Malaysia are required to register with the Home Minisitry, and they have to obtain a work permit. They are also required to furnish the Ministry of Information with details about their professional and personal background and provide information about their employers before they can receive a government issued pass. While Rahanat did not announce what the new rules or restrictions would be for the foreign press, he made it clear that foreign journalists may not produce in ''negative and bad news.''

While no foreign journalist was jailed in the 1970s, this was not the case in the 1990s. A veteran Canadian journalist Murray Hiebert in September 1999 got a six weeks jail sentence for ''scandalizing the court,'' a ruling from an antiquated piece of colonial legislation. His sentence originated from his 1997 article in *Far Eastern Economic Review* titled ''See You in Court'' that addressed the growing number of law suits being filed in Malaysia. The article centered on a suit brought by the wife of a distinguished judge who sued an International School for dropping her son from a debate team. Heibert noted that this case moved suspiciously quickly thorough the court system. The judge's wife sued Heibert because she believed his article undermined the Malaysian judiciary. The court held Heibert's passport and set his bail at US$66,000. Heibert accepted the six-weeks jail term because had he appealed he would have had to wait a longer period of time before the case was resolved in court. According to his lawyers, Heibert was the first foreign journalist in over fifty year to be jailed for contempt in Malaysia.

U.S. President Bill Clinton and Canadian Prime Minister Lloyd Foxworthy spoke out against Heibert's incarceration. Prime Minister Mahathir in an address to the UN General Assembly responded by going on the offensive, by talking about the double standards in the West regarding human rights issues: ''I think American habits of arresting other citizens in other countries and bringing them back to trail in America is contrary to international law.'' Mahathir accused Canada of violating human rights in the treatment of its own indigenous groups. Later at an assembly of 1,400 Commonwealth jurists in Kuala Lumpur, he lashed out at the Western media, the United Nations, currency traders, and human rights groups who have a distorted view of right and wrong.

Prime Minister Mahathir frequently gives advice on how the media should behave. The 1999 *World Press Freedom Review* summed up Mahathir's style for handling foreign media. ''Free reporting and fair comment on sensitive topics will most likely be greatly curtailed given the potential consequences. 'Advice' on how the media should behave emanates regularly from the Prime Minister's Office, setting a clear official tone.'' The review continued: ''In his typical diatribes against the media, Mahathir calls for what he interprets as 'responsible' journalism and feels Western media should be held responsible for their 'misreporting' In practice, his view is that regardless of a story's accuracy or an overwhelming public interest, nothing should be published if it undermines the position of those in authority creates tension or unrest.'' The review concluded: ''The prime minister claims that freedom is dangerous, and in less developed countries like Malaysia, the government has to curtail freedom of speech for the good of the people.''

The government continues to restrict material it deems to be sensitive. For example, in February 1999, the Malaysian government banned its own agencies from subscribing to foreign publications found to be critical of Malaysia. Those publications banned from government agencies were *Asiaweek*, *The Far Eastern Economic Review*, and the *International Herald Review*. Sine the 1970s, the government has been extremely suspicious of these publications.

NEWS AGENCIES

A statutory body that the Malaysian Parliament authorized in 1967 to be Malaysia's national news agency, Pertubohan Berita Nasional Malaysia (Bernama), began operations in 1968. Bernama has an appointed five-member supervisory council and a board made up of six representatives each from the newspapers and the federal government all subscribers of Bernama. They also have alternate members appointed by the government. Bernama offices are located in all the states of Malaysia. They are also located in Washington, D.C., London, New Delhi, Dhaka, and Melbourne. In 2000, Bernama was equipped with fully computerized technology. Its purpose is to provide news services, general and economic, to subscribers in Malaysia and Singapore. Moreover, most of the Malaysian newspapers are subscribers to Bernama, as well as the electronic media, including radio, television, and the Internet. Before 1998, nearly all Bernama news and information was in the form of still photographs and text, but that year the agency launched BERNAMA TV. Bernama also disseminates its news on the Internet.

Bernama was given the official right in June 1990 to distribute news throughout Malaysia, and it does so in Malay and in English. Bernama also has an exchange agreement with other agencies, including Antara (Indonesia), Organization of Asian News Agencies (OANA), Association of South East Asian Nations (ASEAN), and the Middle East News Agency.

In late 1999, there were several foreign news bureaus with offices in Malaysia, all located in Kuala Lumpur: Agence France Presse (AFP), the U.S. Associated Press (AP), Italy's Inter Press Service (IPS), Press Trust of India, Thai News Agency, the U.S. United Press International (UPI), the U.K. Reuters, and the People's Republic of China.

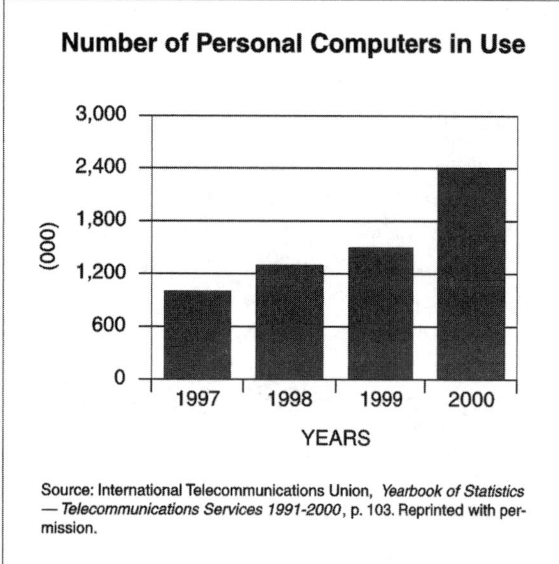

Source: International Telecommunications Union, *Yearbook of Statistics — Telecommunications Services 1991-2000*, p. 103. Reprinted with permission.

BROADCAST & ELECTRONIC NEWS MEDIA

Similar to the print media, the electronic news media also fall under government control. The Malaysian Parliament, approved by the Broadcasting Act in December 1987, gives the Minister of Information the authority to monitor and control all radio and television broadcasting. The minister can likewise revoke any license held by a private company deemed to have violated the provisions of this act.

The government also has strict codes that the radio and television media must follow. The May 2002 version of the Malaysian Advertising Code of Ethics for Television and Radio protects the television industry as well as the government's social pollicies. This code controls the content of commercials and advertisements. The code restricts programs or advertisements that promote an excessively materialistic lifestyle. Using sex to sell products is restricted. In addition, scenes involving models undressing are not allowed. Women have a strict dress code: they must be covered from the neckline to below the knees. Swimming trunks for men and women can only be shown in scenes involving sporting or athletic events. All scenes or shots must be filmed in Malaysia, and only 20 percent of foreign footage is allowed and then only after it is approved by the minister. Moreover, all musicals and songs must be produced in Malaysia.

Unacceptable products, services, and scenes include alcoholic beverages. Blue denims are restricted; however, certain jeans made of other materials can be advertised. Dramatizations that show the applications of products to certain parts of the body, such as the armpits, is restricted. Clothes with imported words or symbols are restricted because they may convey undesired messages. Other restrictions include scenes which suggest intimacy, disco scenes, feminine napkins, and kissing between adults.

Radio Malaysia broadcasts over six networks in various languages and dialects. Besides Radio Malaysia, Suara Islam (Voice of Islam) and Suara Malaysia (Voice of Malaysia) broadcast regularly in Peninsular Malaysia. Radio Television Malaysia broadcasts in Sabah and Sarawak. There is also Rediffusion Cable Network Sbn Bhd and Time Highway Radio, both of which have offices in Kuala Lumpur and primarily serve East Malaysia.

Other television networks besides Radio Television Malaysia in Sabah and Sarawak are situated on Peninsular Malaysia. Television Malaysia, founded in 1963, controls programming from its main office in Kuala Lumpur. TV 3 (Sistem Televisyen Malaysia Bhd) is Malaysia's first private television station that began broadcasting in 1984. Meast Broadcast Network systems began operating when Malaysia's first satellite was launched in January 1996. Malaysia launched a second satellite in October of that year. Mega TV, which started broadcasting in 1995, has five foreign channels, and the government owns 40 percent of Mega TV. The commercial station, MetroVison began broadcasting in July 1995. It is 44 percent owned by Sendandang Sesuria Sbn Bhd and 56 percent owned by Metropolitan Media Sbn Bhd. In addition, as of 1996, when the government ended the ban on private satellite dish ownership, Malaysians can own dishes.

Malaysia's wealthiest media baron is Ananda Kirshnan, who owns the direct satellite and broadcast company, Astro. Kirshman is a powerful ally of the Malaysian government, and his financial ventures are directed to helping Prime Minister Mahathir achieved a fully developed Malaysia by 2020. Khazanah Nasional, a government-owned investment company, bought a 15 percent stake in Astro in 1996 for US$260 million. Regulators in the government have steadily supported Krishman's companies by providing him with essential licenses in telecommunications, satellites, and gambling. Kirshman, a graduate of Harvard University's Business School, wants to "provide Asian alternatives to the Western media offensive." In 1997, his studios were working overtime to produce shows that would be morally accepted to the conservative Asian audiences not only in Malaysia but also to the Philippines and Vietnam.

The growth of the Internet in Malaysia has created problems for the Malaysian government. One government project begun by Mahathir in the late 1990s was Cyberjava, the multi-media Super Corridor designed to attract high tech industry and serve as a community totally wired to the Internet similar to the Silicone Valley in California. It covers the same area as Singapore and is located on the tip of Peninsular Malaysia. In keeping with his promise Mahathir has pledged not to censor the Internet, and to promote Cyberjava, he has been forced to have a hands-off policy regarding the Internet. In 1998, the Malaysian government allowed Malaysia's first commercial non-government controlled online newspaper, *MalaysiaKini* to begin operations.

In March 2001, the government-operated press instituted a campaign to undermine the credibility of *Malaysiakini*, the only non-government controlled online newspaper that began in 1999. The most credible media voice in Malaysia, this paper took advantage of Mahathir's promise not to ever censor the Internet. Mahathir, however, became upset with *Malaysiakini* when the *Far Eastern Economic Review* reported that it received funding from George Soros' Open Society Institute. The prime minister was quoted to have said that loyal Malaysians should stop reading *Malaysiakini* because of the possible link to Soros. Mahathir has often attacked Soros in his speeches probably because Soros is a Jew, and Mahathir is a Muslim. Steven Gan, the editor of *Malaysiakini*, refuted the charges and even produced financial records that showed that the paper had never received any money from Soros. Gan received the International Pioneer Press Freedom Award in 2000.

In the early 2000s, the debate about trying to censor the Internet in Malaysia continues. In March 2002 both the public and Parliament are split on the issue; half want to see tighter controls and censorship, and the remaining half wants the Printing Press laws to be discontinued and the Internet to be free from government censorship.

Education & Training

Some of the first courses for journalists in Malaysia were conducted by the South East Asia Press Center (SEAPC), formed in 1966 and supported by the Ministry of Information, local newspapers, and the Press Foundation of Asia. Its purpose was to provide something on the order of inservice education for people already employed as journalists in the country. Graduated courses in journalism are offered by the Universiti Sains Malaysia. Programs in journalism began in 1971 in the School of Humanities at that institution. In 2000, one of the major criticisms among journalists' in academia is the lack of enivronmental journalism in the Malaysian curriculum.

Courses in mass communications were first offered at Institut Teknololji Mara (ITM). Mostly the Malaysian government finances this institution and students must be *bumiputras* in order to attend. The school is situated in the suburbs of Kuala Lumpur. Universsiti Kebagsaan Malaysia (the National University of Malaysia) also has courses and offers degrees in mass communication and journalism. The school is located in Bangi, south of the capital. Through the Department of English, the University of Malaya offers courses specializing in theory and research in mass communications. The Institute ACT in Petaling Jaya has a center for continuing education and focuses on media technology and journalism. Tanku Abdul Rahman College, in Kuala Lumpur (TARC), also offers bachelor degree programs in mass communications and journalism.

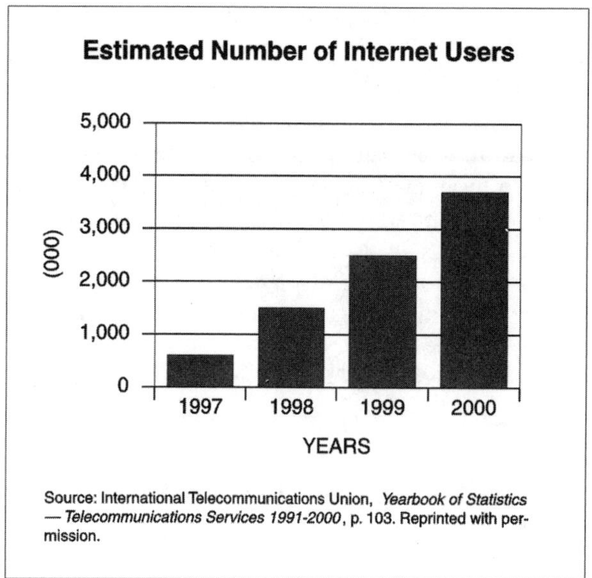

Source: International Telecommunications Union, *Yearbook of Statistics — Telecommunications Services 1991-2000*, p. 103. Reprinted with permission.

The headquarters of the Asian Institute for Broadcasting, affiliated with the Ministry of Information is the Institut Penyiarn Tun Abdul Razak (IPTAR) at Angkaspuri. There are courses at that institution through the Asian Institute for Broadcasting (AIBD). This institution receives partial support from UNESCO and the Malaysian government.

The National Union of Journalists (NUJ) is the major journalistic association in Malaysia, and it is affiliated with the Confederation of ASEAN Journalists. The other association is the Newspaper Publishers Association.

Steven Gang, the editor of *MaylasiaKini* received the International Pioneer Press Freedom Award in 2000 for his efforts at keeping his online newspaper free from government intrusion. In May 2001, on "World Press Freedom Day," the Committee to Protect Journalists meeting in New York City put Mahathir Mahamad on the "Top Ten Enemies of the Press" list.

Summary

While Malaysia has kept up with the rest of the world in technology and a prosperous economy, a truly free press in 2002 does not exist in this Southeast Asian country. Little has changed. The government still views the media as a means for promoting the government. It believes the press should not be sensational but should be a watchdog for society.

Journalists in Malaysia have to contend with many obstacles that journalists who live in other countries do not. The local and foreign journalists in Malaysia have to contend with various press laws and publications acts, as well as libel suits. It seems little change can be expected in the years to come so long as the government associates gains with a press controlled by the authorities.

SIGNIFICANT DATES

- 1984: The Printing Presses and Publications Act is revised.
- 1994: The Communist Party is no longer active in Malaysia.
- 1998: Deputy Prime Minister Anwar is charged with corruption and jailed.
- 1998: *MaylasiasKini*, the first on-line commercial newspaper, is established.
- 1998: Murray Heibert is the first foreign journalist jailed in Malaysia in over fifty years.
- 1998: A. Kadir Jasin, editor of *New Straits Times,* is forced by authorities to resign.
- 1998: Authorities cancel the publication of two magazines, *Esklusif* and *Wasilah.*
- 1999: The National Union of Journalists (NUJ) urges the government to provide a more favorable environment for the press industry.
- 1999: Five hundred and eighty-one journalists call for an appeal of Printing Presses and Publications Act.
- 2001: The debate over the licensing of publications escalates.

BIBLIOGRAPHY

Asher, R. E., ed. *The Encyclopedia of Language and Linguistics,* vol. 5. New York: Pergamon Press, 1994.

Barr, Cameron W. ''Combative Leader Challenges Both His People and Foreign Press,'' *Christian Science Monitor*, vol. 90, issue 212 (28 September 1998): 8.

''Detention Without Trial: Internal Security Act, ISA,'' *Malaysian Civil and Political Rights*, 2nd Quarter 2001 (April-July 2001), Suram, Selangor, Malaysia.

The Europa World Year Book, vol. II. London: Europa Publications Limited, 1999.

''Foreign Labor Trends, Malaysia, 1994-1995,'' U.S. Department of Labor Bureau of International Labor Affairs, prepared by the American Embassy, Kuala Lumpur, Malaysia, 1995.

Gullick, John. *Malaysia: Economic Expansion and National Unity.* Boulder, Col.: Westview Press, 1981.

Ingram, Derek. ''Commonwealth Press Union,'' *Round Table*, vol. 349, issue 1 (January 1999): 28.

Kurian, George Thomas, ed. *World Press Encyclopedia.* New York: Facts on File, Inc., 1982.

Loo, Eric. ''Media Tightly Prescribed,'' *Neiman Reports*, vol. 50, issue 3 (Fall 1996): 79.

''Mahathir's Dividend,'' *The Economist*, vol. 330 (12 March 1994).

''Malaysia's Rough Justice,'' *The Economist*, vol. 348 (28 August 1998).

Martin, Stella, and Denis Walls. *In Malaysia.* London: Brandt Publications, 1986.

Murphy, Dan. ''Malaysia's Strike on Freedoms,'' *Christian Science Monitor*, vol. 93, issue 74 (13 March 2001): 3.

Neto Anil. ''Libel Award Chill Malaysia's Journalists,'' *Asia Times*, July 15, 2000. Available at http://www.atimes.comINTERNET.

Osman, Mohd Taib. *Malaysian World-View.* Singapore: Institute of Southeast Asian Studies, 1985.

''Publish and be Chastised,'' *The Economist*, vol. 358 (3 March 2001).

Roff, William R. *The Origins of Malay Nationalism.* New Haven, CN.: Yale University Press, 1967.

Ross-Larson, Bruce, ed. *Malaysia 2001: A Preliminary Inquiry.* Kuala Lumpur, Malaysia: Syed Kechik Foundation, 1978.

''The Shaming of Malaysia,'' *The Economist*, vol. 349 (7 November 1998).

Sumner, Jeff, ed. *Gale Directory of Publications and Broadcast Media*, 136th ed., vol. 5. Farmington Hills, MI.: Gale, 2002.

Van Wolferen, Karel, ''The Limits of Mass Media,'' *NIRA Review* (Winter 1995).

—Lloyd Johnson

MALDIVES

BASIC DATA

Official Country Name:	Republic of Maldives

Region (Map name):	East & South Asia
Population:	301,475
Language(s):	Maldivian Dhivehi, English
Literacy rate:	93.2%

The Maldives is a nation of coral atolls scattered off the southwest coast of India in the Indian Ocean. Originally a sultanate, Maldivians fought for more than a century to stave off Western colonization, but eventually agreed to become a British protectorate in exchange for relative independence. The country declared independence in 1965 and is now a republic. Its estimated population is 301,475, and the literacy rate is approximately 93 percent. The official language is Dhivehi, a dialect of Sinhala that derives its script from Arabic. English also is widely spoken, especially in business and government. The president acts as both head of state and government, presiding over the 50-seat, unicameral People's Council. Tourism is by far the largest industry in the Maldives—more than 90 percent of the government's tax revenues come from import duties and taxes on tourism. Fishing and boat building also contribute to the economy.

Maldivians do not have freedom of press or expression. Maldives' laws prohibit all speech and action that could incite citizens against the government or that could be construed as libelous, a national security threat, or critical of Islam. Authorities can shut down newspapers and sanction editors, leading most journalists to practice self-censorship. The situation is improving, however, and the media has begun to criticize specific government policies, though not the political system as a whole.

Haveeru is the leading daily newspaper. It began publishing in January 1979 and prints in Divehia and English, and is available online. Other dailies include *Aafathis* and the *Miadhu News;* both print in Divehia with a much smaller sections in English, and both appear online. The *Monday Times* is a popular, magazine-style newspaper that prints weekly in English and appears online. The *Maldives News* also prints in English, but appears bi-weekly. *Dheenuge Magu,* a Divehi-language religious publication, appears weekly.

There is one state-run radio station, and one television station, also state-run. There are 35,000 radios, 10,000 televisions, and one Internet service provider.

Bibliography

''About Haveeru.'' In *Haveeru.* 2002. Available from http://www.haveeru.com.mv/haveeru/.

''About us.'' In *Aafathis.* 2002. Available from http://www.aafathisnews.com.mv/.

''Maldives.'' *Central Intelligence Agency. World Fact Book 2001,* 2002. Available from http://www.cia.gov.

''Maldives.'' Freedom House, 2001. Available from http://www.freedomhouse.org.

—Jenny B. Davis

Mali

Basic Data

Official Country Name:	Republic of Mali
Region (Map name):	Africa
Population:	10,685,948
Language(s):	French, Bambara
Literacy rate:	31%

In 1991, student riots led to an end of one-party rule in Mali. The establishment of mainstream constitutional politics was followed by laws establishing freedom of the press. Mali has about 10 daily newspapers, more than 15 weekly or twice-weekly newspapers, and about six monthly or twice-monthly publications.

There is a government-owned newspaper, *L'Essor,* a daily founded in 1949 that has a circulation of about 3,500. Another daily, *Les Echoes,* founded in 1989, is allied with the ruling party and has a circulation of about 30,000. The lone news agency, Agence Malienne de Presse et Publicite (AMAPP), is controlled by the Ministry of Culture. Independent daily newspapers include *Le Malien, Nouvel Horizon* and *La Republicain,* founded in 1992. Weeklies include *26 Mars,* founded in 1998, and *Concord.*

An important factor in the growth of independent newspapers in Mali was the creation by Malian journalists of independent associations such as The Network of Economic Journalists of Mali, and an association of press editors as well as the establishment of a national commission for issuing press cards. Moreover, the *Union Nationale des Journalistes du Mali* (National Journalists Union of Mali) is an active sentinel and advocate for Malian journalists that constantly speaks out on behalf of harassed colleagues.

Most newspapers are published in French, Mali's official language, though some publish in Arabic and Bambura—the language spoken by more than 80 percent of the population. Literacy is low, about 31 percent for Mali's more than 10.5 million citizens.

Libel laws remain on the books in Mali, although the government has abolished prison terms for ''ordinary libel.'' However so-called ''offences'' against the head of state, ministers and public institutions are punishable by a three- to 12-month prison sentence.

Despite this, and because of a flourishing and diverse independent press, Mali remains one of Africa's vanguard states for press freedom.

BIBLIOGRAPHY

Central Intelligence Agency (CIA). ''Mali.'' *The World Factbook 2001,* 2002. Available from http://www.cia.gov.

The Europa World Yearbook 2001. London: Europa Publications, 2001.

International Journalists' Federation, ''Mali Press: Overview,'' 2001. Available from http://www.ijnet.org/Profile/Africa/Mali/media.html.

Nyamnjoh, Francis B., ''West Africa: Unprofessional and unethical journalism,'' Friedrich-Ebert-Stiftung, 2000. Available from http://www.fes.de/fulltext/iez/00710a01.htm.

Reporters Sans Frontières. ''Mali: Annual Report 2002.'' Available from http://www.rsf.fr.

World Press Freedom Review. ''Mali.'' International Press Institute, 2001. Available from http://www.freemedia.at/wpfr/mali.htm.

—Denis Fitzgerald

MALTA

BASIC DATA

Official Country Name:	Republic of Malta
Region (Map name):	Europe
Population:	391,670
Language(s):	Maltese, English
Literacy rate:	88%

The Republic of Malta is an independent island state in the center of the Mediterranean Sea, with a generally literate population. A member of the Commonwealth since 1814, Malta received independence from the United Kingdom in 1964. Since then, the island has become a center for finances and freight shipment. Major resources include its large supply of limestone, its location in the sea, and its productive labor force. However, Malta imports 80 percent of its food stores, has limited water resources, and has no domestic island energy sources. The country's economy depends on foreign trade, tourism, and manufacturing (electronics and textiles, particularly). Tourism is growing; one element that encourages the growth is a population that speaks Maltese, English, and Italian. As of 2002, Malta is a candidate for membership in the European Union; in preparation many of its industries were being privatized.

The Maltese constitution and the general culture provide for freedom of the press; since 1992 the government has actively encouraged programs leading to diversification in the media.

Independent press organizations include The Press Club and Institute of Broadcasters, whose Code of Ethics requires ''balance, accuracy and fairness,'' confidentiality of sources, fact verification, respect for individuals, and human rights shielding.

International agencies and organizations regard Malta as having a free press. For example, *Press Freedom Survey 2000* by Freedom House designated Maltese press as free. The International Press Institute (IPI), based in Vienna, stated in 2000 that no violence against journalists had occurred in Malta. In 2002 World Audit awarded Malta 14/100 points. (Lower numbers are preferred: for example, the US is 11/100 and UK is 16/100.)

Media, in English, Italian, and Maltese, include newspapers, radio, and television. The two main political parties own newspapers and television and radio stations that disseminate their opposing views. Independent media are also available to the public.

The broadcast media is supervised by the governmental body, the Broadcasting Authority. Various numbers of radio stations (13-19) are reported. Approximately 255,000 households have radios. In 2002, Malta had six broadcast television stations: three government stations, one station belonging to the governing party, one station belonging to the opposition party, and one commercial station. In addition, one commercial cable network was in operation. The approximately 280,000 households with television sets receive approximately 20 stations, including not only do Maltese stations but also many stations from Italy.

In 2001, various newspapers were available: four daily newspapers, according to the *Europa Yearbook* (approximate combined circulation 54,000 copies per issue), six weekly newspapers, and five Sunday editions. Total newspaper circulation is approximately 145/1,000 persons.

Newspapers include *The Malta Independent* (English); *In-Nazzjon* (Maltese), reported circulation 20,000;

L'Orizzont (Maltese), reported circulation 23,000; *The People* (English); *The Times* (English), reported circulation 23,000. Weekly newspapers and Sunday editions include *Business Times*; *Il-Gens* (Maltese), reported circulation 13,000; *Il-Gwida* (Maltese and English), reported circulation 12,000; *Kulhadd* (Maltese); *Lehen Is-Sewwa* (Roman Catholic press), reported circulation 10,000; *The Maltese Business Weekly* (English); *The Malta Independent* on Sunday (English); *Il-Mument* (Maltese), reported circulation 25,000; *The People* on Sunday (English); *The Sunday Times* (English), reported a circulation of 35,000; and It-Tórca (Maltese), reported a circulation of 30,000.

Bibliography

Central Intelligence Agency (CIA). *The World Factbook 2001*, 2002. Available from http://www.cia.gov/.

Freedom House. *Political Rights and Civil Liberties*, 2001. Available from http://www.freedomhouse.org/.

———. *Press Freedom Survey 2000*, 2000. Available from http://freedomhouse.org/.

IPI: Violations of Press Freedom Commonplace in Europe. In Lexis-Nexis Academic Universe. Vienna: Deutsche Presse-Agentur, 2000.

Malta Press Club and Institute of Broadcasters International Journalists' Network. *Code of Ethics*, 2002. Available from http://www.ijnet.org/.

U.S. Department of State. *Human Rights Reports: Malta, 1999 Country Reports on Human Rights Practices*, 25 February 2000. Available from http://www.state.gov/.

World Audit. *Democratic Profile*, 2002. Available from http://www.worldaudit.org/.

World Almanac and Book of Facts. *Republic of Malta,* 2002.

—Emily Dial-Driver

Marshall Islands

Basic Data

Official Country Name:	Republic of the Marshall Islands
Region (Map name):	Oceania
Population:	68,126
Language(s):	English, Marshallese, Japanese
Literacy rate:	93%

The Marshall Islands is perhaps best known for its impact on American swimwear—the bikini takes its name from one of the country's more than a thousand islands. Located in the North Pacific Ocean between Hawaii and Papua New Guinea, the country became a battleground in the Pacific Theater during World War II. The United States took over the country's administration after the war, but the islands remained under siege as the United States conducted nuclear tests on several islands between 1947 and 1962. The U.S. government has since paid out more than $100 million in damages, but many areas remain contaminated. Bikini Island, for example, is uninhabitable as a result of this testing.

The Marshall Islands received its independence in 1986 under a Compact of Free Association, but still retains close ties to America. The estimated population is 68,000. The official language is Marshallese, but English also is spoken. The literacy rate is approximately 93 percent. The government and the state are headed by a president, who also presides over a 33-seat, unicameral parliament. U.S. governmental assistance is the mainstay of the Marshallese economy, but agriculture also is important, especially coconuts, tomatoes, melons and breadfruit. The tourism industry is a small but growing economic sector.

Press and speech freedoms generally are respected, but journalists sometimes avoid sensitive political issues. There is no daily newspaper. The *Marshall Islands Journal* is a privately owned weekly newspaper that provides national and international coverage of news, politics, and events in English and Marshallese. The *Marshall Islands Gazette* appears monthly. It is owned by the government and avoids political coverage.

There are seven radio stations, three AM and four FM. There are three television stations, two of which are associated with the U.S. military, and one Internet service provider.

Bibliography

Central Intelligence Agency (CIA). ''Marshall Islands.'' *World Fact Book,* 2001. Available from http://www.cia.gov/.

''Country Profile: Marshall Islands.'' BBC News, 2002. Available from http://news.bbc.co.uk/.

—Jenny B. Davis

MARTINIQUE

BASIC DATA

Official Country Name:	Department of Martinique
Region (Map name):	Caribbean
Population:	414,516
Language(s):	French, Creole patois
Literacy rate:	93%

Martinique is a part of the Windward Islands chain in the Caribbean Sea, north of Trinidad and Tobago. Christopher Columbus was the first European to visit the island, landing in 1493. The French colonized the island in 1635 despite opposition from the indigenous Carib Indian population, and it has remained connected to France ever since. In 1974 its association with France was upgraded from an overseas department to a region. There are rumblings among the population for increased autonomy, but its status so far remains unaffected. The French president is the chief of state and is represented locally by a Paris-appointed prefect.

The country is governed by a unicameral, 45-seat General Council and a unicameral, 41-seat Regional Assembly. Both bodies are led by a president. The official language is French, but many speak Creole Patois. The population is approximately 415,000; the literacy rate is 93 percent. Mainstays of the economy are: sugarcane, bananas, tourism and light industry. Most of the sugar produced on the island is used in the production of rum.

Freedom of the press is guaranteed under the French law. Martinique's daily newspaper is the French-language *France Antilles.* It appears Monday through Saturday; its approximate circulation is 65,000. Other weekly publications include: *Le Progressiste, Aujourd'hui Dimanche, Justice, Le Naif,* and *Antilla.*

Martinique does not have an AM radio station, but there are 14 FM stations for 82,000 radios. There are 11 television stations broadcasting to 66,000 televisions. There are two Internet service providers.

BIBLIOGRAPHY

Central Intelligence Agency (CIA). ''Martinique.'' *World Fact Book, 2001.* Available from http://www.cia.gov/.

''Country Profile.'' Worldinformation.com, 2002. Available from http://www.worldinformation.com/.

''Media: Newspapers.'' MediaCourier.net, 2001. Available from www.mediacourier.net/.

—*Jenny B. Davis*

MAURITANIA

BASIC DATA

Official Country Name:	Islamic Republic of Mauritania
Region (Map name):	Africa
Population:	2,667,859
Language(s):	Hasaniya Arabic, Pular, Soninke, Wolof, French
Literacy rate:	37.7%

BACKGROUND & GENERAL CHARACTERISTICS

Mauritania is a primarily desert country in northwest Africa, situated south of the Western Sahara, southwest of Algeria, west and north of Mali, and north of Senegal. The country's western border is the Atlantic Ocean. The capital of Mauritania is Noakchott. A country of 2.5 million people, Mauritania's population is composed of Arab Berbers in the north and darker-skinned Africans in the south. Many of the people are nomads. The language groups in the country include Arabic (the official language), French, and local languages. Most Mauritanians practice Islam.

Maaouiya Ould Sid Ahmed Taya is the president of Mauritania, a highly centralized, constitutional Islamic republic with a strong presidency. Although the 1991 constitution provided for a civilian government with an executive branch, senate, and national assembly, President Taya exerts considerable political power over the rest of the government. He came to power in 1984 as the leader of a military junta and was officially elected president of the republic in 1992 during the country's first multi-party election under the new constitution. Taya was reelected in 1997 by 90 percent of the vote, winning out over four other candidates in an election boycotted by a five-party coalition, the Opposition Front. General and local elections held in October 2001 were won by the president's Republican Democratic Party, enabling President Taya to keep firm control over Mauritanian politics and governance.

Newspapers in Mauritania are tightly controlled by the state, which reviews all copy to be published two or three days in advance of the publication date. Five copies of all newspaper issues must be presented to the Ministries of Justice and of the Interior for this pre-publication review. Material deemed insulting to Islam or a risk to national security cannot be published. All newspapers must be registered with the Ministry of the Interior.

The principal newspapers in the country are in French and Arabic, and a wide variety of newspapers exists. Over three hundred newspapers and journals are registered with the government but only about a third of these publish on a regular basis; some have never published an issue. Only about twenty-five private newspapers publish regularly, most of them weeklies printing a maximum of three thousand copies for any one edition.

Key newspapers include *Al'Sha'b*, a government-owned paper published in Arabic; *Horizon*, also government owned, but published in French; *Journal Officiel*, the official gazette published in French; *Le Calame*, appearing in both Arabic and French; *l'Eveil-Hebdo*, a French bi-weekly; and *Rajoul Echaree*, published in Arabic and French.

Those campaigning to end the practice of slavery in Mauritania, which was officially stopped in 1981 but purported to still exist, despite government denials, have sometimes found it difficult to publicize their cause and their campaign activities via the media. As Amnesty International stated in their 2002 annual report, ''Human rights organizations, including those campaigning against slavery, remained illegal, and freedom of expression remained limited.'' In September 2001 the European Parliament passed a resolution calling for improvements in specific human rights situations in Mauritania, including an end to slavery and greater guarantees for freedom of expression. In November 2001 independent journalist Gilles Ammar and his cameraman were expelled from Mauritania, allegedly for attempting to produce a report on slavery.

Economic Framework

Mauritania's economy is based on fishing and mining. The principal exports are fish and fish products, iron ore, and gold. The average per capita annual income is only about US$370.

Certain financial benefits apply to those who publish mass media. Publishers and printers of newspapers, journals, and privately printed books do not have to pay government taxes on the materials they use to produce their publications.

Press Laws

The Constitution guarantees freedom of speech and of the press. However, government control of the media involves pre-publication censorship made possible by Article 11 of the Constitution, which states that content and media can be banned if they threaten national sovereignty, security, or unity or the territorial integrity of Mauritania or if they insult Islam or foreign heads of state.

Censorship

Censorship is a problem for journalists in Mauritania, though conditions for the press appeared somewhat better in 2001 than in the previous year, based on the annual report of Reporters Without Borders. Papers produced by non-governmental organizations and by the private press are more open in their criticism of government officials and policies and of the opposition parties than are the state-owned papers. As the U.S. Department of State's Bureau of Democracy, Human Rights, and Labor expressed it in their annual report for January through December 2001, ''Antigovernment tracts, newsletters, and petitions circulated widely in Nouakchott and other towns.''

The U.S. State Department reported that in December 2000 one weekly newspaper, *Al Alam*, was banned. In 2001 seven issues of various journals were seized by the authorities as objectionable material under the censorship laws. In July 2002 an issue of *Le Renovateur*, one of the country's bi-monthly newspapers, was seized by the Ministry of the Interior, Posts and Telecommunications despite the fact that the issue had been properly registered. The seizure was likely related to an article it contained on rising prices of essential goods and on foreign exchange, according to the Media Foundation for West Africa (MFWA) in Accra, Ghana. MFWA issued an alert on August 9, 2002, requesting that letters be sent to Mauritania's president and the Minister of the Interior to protest frequent seizures of newspapers in the country.

State-Press Relations

Besides the requirement that newspapers must all register with the government, all journalists must carry government-issued press cards to participate in official press events.

The general atmosphere surrounding the press in Mauritania appears to be cautiously positive but restrictive, particularly in terms of the continuing prohibition of private radio broadcasting licenses. Moreover, state-controlled media voice views that favor the government, so it cannot be said that Mauritania enjoys a very large measure of press freedom.

One example of government interference with journalistic reporting was the detention and questioning in July 2001 of reporter Mohammed Lemine Ould Mahmoudi, a contributor to the weekly *Le Calame* and managing editor of the weekly *Hasad Al-Ousbou'é*. Mahmoudi was arrested due to suspicions that he knew something about who had produced anti-government graffiti and who had committed acts of sabotage during an official visit to one of the country's regions. After a few hours of questioning, Mahmoudi was released.

ATTITUDE TOWARD FOREIGN MEDIA

Mauritanian correspondents for foreign broadcasters have occasionally had problems with government repression. For example, in April 2001 the Minister of Communications temporarily banned journalist Mohammed Lemine Ould Bah, Mauritania's correspondent for Radio France International and Radio Monte Carlo, from practicing journalism and working with these broadcasters after Bah reported on conflict between Mauritania and its southwestern neighbor, Senegal.

Mauritanians can access foreign television programs from France and Arab countries through satellite receivers and dish antennae. Although the government had interfered with certain broadcasts of Radio France International and the Qatar-based Arabic television station, Al-Jazeera, due to programs of theirs that had been critical of the Mauritanian government, no such interference reportedly occurred in 2001, according to the U.S. State Department's report on human rights practices.

NEWS AGENCIES

Mauritania's official news agency is the Mauritanian News Agency.

BROADCAST MEDIA

The state owns all domestic television and radio broadcasting services, whose coverage typically provides a favorable picture of the government. The political opposition has limited access to radio broadcasting, although during the last election the opposition candidates were allowed much greater access to the media than at other times. Foreign broadcasts from France, Arab countries, and other locations, such as Africa No. 1 from Gabon can be received via FM in the country. However, private radio stations within Mauritania are unable to obtain broadcast licenses. Domestic rebroadcasting on FM stations of Radio France International programs is permitted, enabling listeners in Mauritania to hear news of the opposition parties.

The national broadcasting network is the Office de Radiodiffusion-Television de Mauritanie (ORTM). Mauritanian TV broadcasts throughout the country on one channel but can be picked up by satellite in eleven regional capitals. Its programs are produced in Arabic, French, and various local languages. Radio programs by the national broadcaster are transmitted on FM and short wave and by Arabsat 2B satellite. Radio France International is transmitted on FM in Nouakchott, the capital city. No domestic radio stations exist, due to government refusal to grant licenses to private radio broadcasters within the country. However, radio is the most popular form of media in the country.

ELECTRONIC NEWS MEDIA

About 300 persons accessed the Internet regularly in 1999. Five domestic Internet service providers operate in Mauritania, unrestricted by the government. Internet connections were improved in 1999 to make Internet access available in Nouadhibou, the country's principal commercial city. The Internet is now available there and in five regional capitals. Internet sites are maintained by some of the privately owned newspapers in the country, and in 2001 these sites were able to operate without government censorship.

SUMMARY

Although Mauritania has a ways to come before its press can be called free, some positive conditions appear to exist in the relations between the press and the state, such as permissiveness regarding Internet service provision and the reception of foreign television and radio broadcasts in the country. However, the amount of media control exerted by the government, particularly in terms of government bans on private radio broadcasting and the required government pre-publication reviews of press materials, is restrictive compared with basic international standards for free expression and public debate and dissent. Hopefully, a reduction in government tensions over border disputes with Senegal involving the use of the Senegal River, mixed with domestic and international efforts to promote more multi-party democratic political activity, will eventually change this situation and make Mauritania a more positive environment for journalistic practice.

SIGNIFICANT DATES

- 1997: President Taya reelected with 90 percent of the vote.
- 1999: Internet access made available in Nouadhibou, the country's principal commercial city.
- December 2000: *Al Alam*, a weekly newspaper, is banned and stops publishing.
- April 2001: The Minister of Communications temporarily bans journalist Mohammed Lemine Ould Bah, Mauritania's correspondent for Radio France International and Radio Monte Carlo, from practicing journalism in the country.

- September 2001: The European Parliament passes a resolution calling for improved human rights in Mauritania, including an end to slavery and better guarantees for freedom of expression.
- October 2001: General and local elections won by Republican Democratic Party, President Taya's party, allowing him to stay in firm control of politics and the government in Mauritania.
- November 2001: Independent journalist Gilles Ammar and his cameraman are expelled from Mauritania, allegedly for attempting to produce a report on slavery.
- August 2002: The Media Foundation for West Africa issues an alert on August 9, 2002, requesting that letters be sent to Mauritania's president and the Minister of the Interior to protest frequent seizures of newspapers.

BIBLIOGRAPHY

Amnesty International. ''Mauritania.'' *Amnesty International Report 2002*. London: Amnesty International, 2002. Available from web.amnesty.org/.

BBC Monitoring. ''Country profile: Mauritania.'' Reading, UK: British Broadcasting Corporation, 2002. Available from www.news.bbc.co.uk.

Bureau of Democracy, Human Rights, and Labor, U.S. Department of State. ''Mauritania.'' *Country Reports on Human Rights Practices 2001*. Washington, DC: Bureau of Public Affairs, U.S. Department of State, 2002. Available from www.state.gov/.

Committee to Protect Journalists. ''Mauritania.'' *Attacks on the Press in 2001: Africa 2001*. New York, NY: CPJ, 2002. Available from www.cpj.org/attacks01/mideast01/mauritania.html.

Media Foundation for West Africa. ''Another Newspaper Publication Seized.'' Press release. Accra, Ghana, August 9, 2002. Available from www.allafrica.com/stories/.

Reporters Without Borders. ''Mauritania.'' *Africa Annual Report 2002*. Paris, France: Reporters sans frontières, 2002. Available from www.rsf.org/.

—Barbara A. Lakeberg-Dridi

MAURITIUS

BASIC DATA

Official Country Name:	Republic of Mauritius
Region (Map name):	Africa
Population:	1,179,368
Language(s):	English, Creole, French, Hindi, Urdu, Hakka, Bojpoori
Literacy rate:	82.9%

BACKGROUND & GENERAL CHARACTERISTICS

A small island nation, located east of Madagascar in the Indian Ocean, having a population of slightly more than 1.1 million, Mauritius is a stable democracy based on a plural society of several ethnic communities, including three main ones: Indians (Hindus and Muslims), Chinese, and Creoles. Citizens of Indian origin are divided among Hindus (52 percent) and Muslims (16 percent); Christians total about 28 percent, and Buddhists and others about 2 percent. Chinese residents are usually either Buddhist or Catholic. Creoles are mostly of French mixed descent and follow the Catholic faith.

Because of its history, English and French influences are evident, with French preferred over English. This is seen also in the circulation of newspapers in the two languages.

Mauritius is internationally regarded as a functioning democracy with a commendable record of regular fair and free elections and a fairly good human rights record as well. It boasts the highest per capita income in Africa.

Historical Traditions Mauritius was a British colony before it attained independence on March 12, 1968. The island was first discovered by Arab explorers in 975 A.D. Among the European powers, it first came under Portuguese control in 1505. By the end of the sixteenth century, Mauritius fell under Dutch authority when, in 1598, the Dutch Admiral Van Warwyck landed his fleet in a bay on the southeast end of the island and named it after himself; Warwick Bay was later renamed Grand Port. Van Warwyck named the island Mauritius after Prince Mauritius Van Nassau, the stadhouder of the Netherlands at that time. Although Dutch ships on the way to the Dutch East Indies (modern Indonesia) occasionally stopped in Warwick Bay for shelter, food, and fresh water, there was no serious effort to develop the island.

In September 1715, Guillaume Dufresne d'Arsel occupied Mauritius in the name of French King Louis XV, naming it Ile de France. Warwyck Bay was renamed Port Bourbon and a little used dock in the northwest was named Port Louis.

The transformation of Port Louis into a thriving sea port was the work of Bertrand Mahe de Labourdonnais, who, in the 1740s, built forts, barracks, warehouses, hospitals, and houses. Roads were built throughout the island, and a shipbuilding industry was founded. The French period also marked the beginning of the island's sugar industry and the importation of African slaves.

In 1785, Ile de France became the headquarters of all the French possessions east of Cape Horn. During the Napoleonic wars, the British occupied Mauritius in 1810. The Treaty of Paris restored most of the former French possessions to the Bourbon King of France, but not Mauritius, which remained a British possession.

Under the British, the sugar industry experienced rapid growth as an export crop. In addition, although the slave trade was abolished in 1807 and slavery itself in 1833, plantation owners in Mauritius kept both practices alive until 1835. Even then, it took a payment of 2 million pounds to the owners to get them to abide by abolition. In the following years, the British encouraged thousands of Indians, both Hindus and Muslims, to migrate to Mauritius as indentured laborers. That process continued until 1907 when indentured labor was also abolished.

During World War II, Mauritius became important to the war effort because of its strategic location. The British based their fleet at Port Louis and Grand Port and built an airport at Plaisance and a sea plane base at Baie du Tombeau. During the war, a large telecommunications facility was built at Vacoas.

The Republic of Mauritius is a parliamentary democracy, governed by a prime minister, a council of ministers, and a National Assembly with 62 elected members and 4 others nominated by the election commission from the losing political parties to give representation to ethnic minorities. Assembly members serve five-year terms. The president and vice-president are elected by the National Assembly, also for five years. National and local elections, supervised by an independent commission, take place at regular intervals.

Politics did not become an important part of island life until 1936, when the Labour Party was founded. After World War II, the Mauritius Labour Party (MLP) won the majority of seats in the Legislative Council established under the 1948 constitution. By 1959, the party had gained wide acceptance, and that year, MLP leader Dr. (later Sir) Seewoosagur Ramgoolam was elected Chief Minister. In 1965 he became Prime Minister, a post he held until 1982. During Ramgoolam's administration, Mauritius became an independent country within the Commonwealth of Nations in 1968; in 1992, it became a republic.

The island's politics were marred by violence when the Mouvement Militant Mauricien (MMM), under the leadership of Franco-Mauritian Paul Berenger, gained power in the elections of 1982. With Berenger as the MMM's General Secretary, and Hindu British-trained lawyer Anerood Jugnauth serving as President, the MMM captured all 62 seats in the legislature. Jagnauth became Prime Minister and Berenger his Finance Minister. In elections held September 17, 2000, Jugnauth retained his post as Prime Minister, with Berenger as his Deputy Prime Minister.

Print Media The oldest newspaper published in Africa was in Mauritius: *Le Cerneen,* which was a French-language organ of the sugar industry. The second oldest daily in Mauritius, also in French, was first published in 1908 to represent the interests of the Creole community.

The growing numbers of immigrant Chinese and Indian laborers and their descendants produced the first Chinese paper, *Chinese Daily News,* in 1932, and the first Indian daily, *Advance,* in 1939. Improved literacy and the people's growing interest in politics led to more dailies: *China Times* (1953), *New Chinese Commercial Paper* (1956), *Star* (1963), *L'Express* (1963), *Le Militant* (1969), *Liberation* (1971), *The Nation* (1971) and *Le Populaire* (1973).

As of 2002, there were a dozen privately-owned newspapers published in Mauritius and one on nearby Rodrigues Island. Most of them freely express their views in opposition to reigning government, and although sometimes they seemingly overstep their limits, the government has yet to invoke the libel laws available to it. With the exception of the Chinese dailies, all daily newspapers are published in both French and English. Additionally, the *Mauritius News,* a bilingual newspaper that is published monthly in London, England, has a wide circulation in Mauritius as well as in the Mauritian community in the United Kingdom. The newspapers extensively use two wire services: the All Africa Newswire available in English and French, and the Pan African News Agency, which provides its news stream in English, French, and Arabic. Copies of the larger Mauritian newspapers and magazines, such as *ImpactNews, Le Quotidien, News on Sunday, 5-Plus Dimanche, The Sun, Sunday* and *Week-End* are all available on microfilm at the U.S. Library of Congress facility in New Delhi.

ECONOMIC FRAMEWORK

After its independence from Britain, Mauritius drastically revolutionized its low-income, agricultural-based economy that largely relied on sugar production to a labor intensive, export oriented industrialized economy that also features a thriving tourist sector. The tourist department advertises Mauritius as "the most cosmopolitan island in the sun" with a "charming population, always wearing a smile." The island nation does offer excellent hotel accommodation, a full range of water and land sports, beautiful beaches, and deep blue lagoons, all of which have combined to make the island a popular tourist destination, which contributes to the economy and well-being of its slightly more than one million inhabitants. Despite the recent industrialization, sugar exports still account for 25 percent of the country's export earnings. Mauritius has also developed into an off-shore finance and investment center, attracting more than 9,000 off-shore ''entities,'' mostly interested in conducting trade with India and South Africa, as well as an investment in the banking sector. The island's annual economic growth rate has averaged 5 to 6 percent, which in turn has led to increased life expectancy rates, lower infant mortality, and the creation of a sophisticated infrastructure. In 1999, Mauritian exports were estimated at $1.6 billion and its largest export clients were the United Kingdom (32 percent), France (19 percent), and Germany (6 percent). That same year, its imports were valued at $2.3 billion, with most goods coming from France (14 percent), South Africa (11 percent), India (8 percent), and the United Kingdom (5 percent). The country's external debt stood at $1.9 billion in 2001.

PRESS LAWS

The Constitution, adopted on March 12, 1968, and amended on March 12, 1992, recognizes freedom of speech and of the press. By all accounts, the government of Mauritius respects these freedoms. The Constitution prohibits arbitrary arrest and detention, but because there were reports of several prisoners dying while in police custody in 1998 and early 1999, the Commissioner of Police established a Complaint Investigation Bureau (CIB) in October 1999 to investigate complaints against the police. The national Human Rights Commission established in April 2001 supervises the CIB. The government has permitted prison visits by foreign diplomats, the national ombudsman, the United Nations Human Rights Commission (UNHRC), and the press. In fact, the press has taken an active role in making prison visits and in reporting the living conditions in the media. The government recognizes the fact that many of its citizens greatly respect what it considers to be the fundamental freedoms. For example, although the Public Security Act of 2000 allows police officers of the rank of assistant superintendent and above to search a premises without a warrant in any situation where the delay in obtaining a warrant may be prejudicial to public safety, the government had not implemented the law as of 2002 because of strong public pressures against it.

However, in March 2001, the police briefly detained the editor of the newspaper on Rodrigues island on a charge of publishing false information. The article in question, alleged that a Rodrigues man died as a result of injuries received in police custody. A hearing originally scheduled for November 2001 was postponed to 2002. The Constitution provides for an independent judiciary, which consists of the Supreme Court with appellate powers, and a series of lower courts. The government respects the independence and integrity of the judiciary.

BROADCAST & ELECTRONIC NEWS MEDIA

Since 1999 there has been considerable debate about and subsequent changes to the government's control over radio and television broadcasting. In the campaign preceeding the September 2000 elections, the issue of the government's control and misuse of the state-owned Mauritius Broadcasting Corporation (MBC) held center-stage. After the elections, the new government vowed to depoliticize the MBC. By the end of that year, the Mauritian Journalists Association noted in its report that the government was placing far less pressure on it than it had before the election.

Meanwhile, in August 2000, the National Assembly passed the Independent Broadcasting Authority Act, which created the Independent Broadcasting Authority (IBA) with a mandate to regulate and license all radio and television broadcasting. The law provided for the private ownership of broadcast stations and reemphasized the independence of the IBA. However, the IBA is composed of representatives of several ministries and is chaired by Ashok Radhakissoon, an appointee of the Prime Minister, It also is answers to the Prime Minister on matters of national security and public order. The following July and August, the IBA began formulating licensing rules and hearing applications for broadcast licenses. In December 2001, it authorized two private radio stations and announced that a third radio station would be authorized to broadcast. However, the stations were not able to broadcast at the time the they were authorized because they had not yet received ''multicarrier'' service. Thus the implementation of the law has been slow and the government's monopoly in broadcasting local news and programming continued in early 2002. Some government observers felt that the government was intentionally causing the delays because it did not want to let go of its control over broadcasting. However, while the new stations were waiting to provide service, a private news organization opened up on the Internet that broadcast local news out over the Internet, thereby circumventing the ban on private party television or radio local news broadcasts. Also, foreign international news services such as the British Sky News, French Canal Plus, and CNN were already available to anyone by subscription. Additionally, almost all major Australian cities carry news from Mauritius by broadcasting programs in French. Two popular community radio programs are: the Melbourne South Eastern Community—Mauritian Community Program on 3 SER 97.7 FM (stereo) and the Mauritian, Rodriguan, and Seychelles Community Program, which is run by volunteers, on 3 ZZZ 92.3 FM. The stations broadcast music, news, quiz programs, interviews, and "radiothons" in French and Mauritian Creole.

BIBLIOGRAPHY

Editor & Publisher International Yearbook. New York: Editor and Publisher Co., 1999.

Statistical Yearbook, Paris: UNESCO, 2000.

World Press Trends. Paris: World Association of Newspapers, 2000.

World Radio and TV Handbook. Amsterdam: Billboard Publications, 2001.

World-newspapers.com. Available on the Internet at http://www.world-Newspapers.com.

—Damodar R. SarDesai

MAYOTTE

BASIC DATA

Official Country Name:	Territorial Collectivity of Mayotte
Region (Map name):	Africa
Population:	155,911
Language(s):	Mahorian, French
Literacy rate:	N/A

BACKGROUND & GENERAL CHARACTERISTICS

The French constitution and language establish parameters for media activities in Mayotte, an island locale that has doggedly refused to cast aside its colonial heritage and Creole character. In 2002, Mayotte was still French despite France's efforts to wean it from dependency and push it toward union with its Comoran neighbors.

Both geography and language patterns work against coherency in the media. Situated northwest of Madagascar in the Mozambique Channel, Mayotte (Mahoré) is an Overseas Territorial Collectivity of France and is the only segment of the scattered Comoros archipelago whose citizens, in the referenda of 1974 and 1976, opted not to be part of the independent Republic of the Comoros. Mayotte comprises two main islands with a total area of 144 square miles. In 2001 it had a population of about 163,000; its chief town, Mamoutzou, had 20,000 residents, while its old capital, Dzaoudzi, had about 10,000.

Though French is the official and commercial language and thus the language of the media, only thirty-five percent of Mahorais speak it. The native language in daily use is Shimaoré (Mahorian), a Swahili dialect influenced by Arabic.

Media Activity Mayotte's one newspaper in 1997 was a French-language weekly.

In charge of territorial broadcasting is *Radio-Télévision Française d'Outre-Mer* (RFO-Mayotte). For one hour a day, it conducts its broadcasts in Shimaoré.

In 1997 three television stations served Mayotte, and in 1998 one AM and four FM radio stations were operating. Mahorais owned some 30,000 radios and 3,500 TVs in the mid-1990s.

BIBLIOGRAPHY

Political Handbook of the World, 1999. Ed. Arthur S. Banks and Thomas C. Muller. Binghamton, NY: CSA Publications, 1999.

The Statesman's Yearbook: The Politics, Cultures, and Economies of the World, 2000. Ed. Barry Turner. 136th ed. New York: St. Martin's Press, 1999.

World Almanac and Book of Facts, 2002. New York: World Almanac Books, 2002.

—Roy Neil Graves

MEXICO

BASIC DATA

Official Country Name:	United Mexican States
Region (Map name):	North & Central America
Population:	101,879,171
Language(s):	Spanish, various Mayan, Nahuatl
Literacy rate:	89.6%

Area:	1,972,550 sq km
GDP:	574,512 (US$ millions)
As % of All Ad Expenditures:	13.80
Number of Television Stations:	236
Number of Television Sets:	25,600,000
Television Sets per 1,000:	251.3
Number of Cable Subscribers:	2,263,800
Cable Subscribers per 1,000:	23.1
Number of Satellite Subscribers:	668,000
Satellite Subscribers per 1,000:	6.6
Number of Radio Stations:	1378
Number of Radio Receivers:	31,000,000
Radio Receivers per 1,000:	304.3
Number of Individuals with Computers:	5,000,000
Computers per 1,000:	49.1
Number of Individuals with Internet Access:	2,712,000
Internet Access per 1,000:	26.6

BACKGROUND & GENERAL CHARACTERISTICS

General Description Mexico is located in Middle America, bordering the Caribbean Sea and the Gulf of Mexico, with the United States to its north and Belize and Guatemala to the south. The climate varies from tropical to desert, and its terrain consists of high, rugged mountains, low coastal plains, and high plateaus (desert). The site of advanced Amerindian civilizations, Mexico was under Spanish rule for three centuries before achieving independence early in the nineteenth century. The language across the country is Spanish.

Economically, the country was affected by a devaluation of the peso in late 1994, which triggered the worst recession in over half a century. As of the early 2000s, however, the nation was making an impressive recovery. Ongoing economic and social concerns include low wages, underemployment for a large segment of the population, and inequitable income distribution, with the top 20 percent of income earners accounting for 55 percent of income. Moreover, few advancement opportunities existed at the turn of the millennium for the largely Amerindian population in the impoverished southern states, one of which, the Chiapas, had been in open rebellion since 1994.

The literacy rate in Mexico is high with about 92 percent of the population (as of the early 2000s) over the age of 15 able to read and write. The Mexican population speaks Spanish, with a small percent speaking various Mayan, Nahautl, and other regional indigenous languages. The ethnic breakdown was as follows: mestizo (Amerindian-Spanish) 60 percent, Amerindian or predominantly Amerindian 30 percent, white 9 percent, other 1 percent. About 89 percent were Roman Catholic, 6 percent Protestant, and 5 percent other.

In July, 2000, when Vicente Fox won the presidential election, a new federal political party, National Action Party (PAN), came into power after 71 years of another dominant party, Institutional Revolutionary Party (PRI). The government incorporates a mixture of U.S. constitutional theory and civil law system; it also has judicial review of legislative acts. Economically, the country is now a federal republic and favors a free market economy, with a mixture of modern and outmoded industry.

Quality of Journalism & its History For most of the second half of the twentieth century, journalism was dominated by government officials and directives, often involving bribes. PRI routinely spied on journalists using the national intelligence agency, then the Center for Information and National Security. To make matters worse, journalists themselves had little professionalism and lacked higher education. The profession was a dangerous one, since police, the military, and drug lords routinely threatened and even assassinated journalists and their editors. Fortunately, the 2000 election gave the prospect of openness among the government departments and officials. In addition, attempts by privatized media outlets to engage in more objective journalism offered hope of journalism's evolution in the twenty-first century.

Before journalism existed as it does in the modern world, Spain ruled Mexico for three centuries with an autocratic system opposed to any type of free press. A small elite class and a powerful Catholic clergy dominated Mexico. Nonetheless, printing presses existed in Mexico as early as 1536, and small circulation newspapers, such as the *Gacetade* in Mexico City, began to appear about 1660. These publications used political cartoons as a medium for attacking the authorities of both the state and church. General education was not available, and so illiteracy was high. In 1819, the Spanish were removed as colonial overlords, and Mexico declared its independence from Spain.

Throughout the nineteenth century, amid political instability, journalists pleaded for a free press and frequently cited U.S. newspapers and U.S. constitutional guarantees as models worth emulating. Yet the 1850s laws checked newspaper criticism of the government. Many Mexican presidents resorted to closing newspapers and imprisoning their employees. Prior to the Mexican Revolution of 1910, powerful individuals in the government and the church successfully bribed journalists. This practice of providing cash for coverage took hold quite easily throughout Mexico because journalists were so poorly paid. These bribes became known as *embutes*.

Following the revolution in 1910, a number of new papers started, particularly in Mexico City, for example, *El Universal* in 1916 and the *Exelsior* in 1917. During the 1920s and 1930s an alternative medium, radio, spread across Mexico. The ruling president awarded these licensed stations to his wealthy friends; therefore, criticism was non-existent. Then, too, the PRI party sustained its control for seven decades; it used broadcast media including television, particularly with Televisa, as a series of quasi-public relation stations. It makes sense then that Mexican electronic media did not confront official censorship: its owners were close friends of those who ruled. Extremely wealthy themselves, these owners had no reason to promote change that threatened to lead to a redistribution of wealth. To seal the arrangement, the Mexican media were characterized by *gracetillas* (advertisements paid for by the government), essentially propaganda pieces, which brought considerable revenue to radio and television stations.

Numbers of Newspapers The most popular newspaper format seems to be daily, yet there are a number of weekly newspapers. Mexico's national English newspaper is *The News*. It is part of *Novedades Editores* which publishes two papers and 15 magazines and has an online publication, TheNewsMexico.com. Another paper, *Express*, is mainly distributed in hotels and resorts. The average price of these papers ranges from 4 to 10 pesos.

The largest newspaper by circulation in Mexico, the tabloid *Esto*, had at 2002 a circulation of 385,000. The second largest, a scandal driven newspaper with a circulation of 330,000, was *La Prensa*. Next was *El Universal*, a widely respected paper with growing influence, with a circulation of 170,000. The fourth was *El Financiero*, a tabloid with a circulation of 147,000. Some of the smaller papers were: *Reform* (125,000); *El Norte* (119,000); *El M* (100,000); *La Jornada* (100,924).

The Most Influential Newspaper The most influential paper, *El Universal* from Mexico City, began in 1916. Felix Fulgencio Palavicini started this paper to promote the ideas of the Mexican Revolution. Through a sequence of owners, the newspaper grew steadily. It implemented the latest technology and led the fight between press and government. During the 1980s *El Universal* fought to end the governmental monopoly on newsprint. In 2001 it initiated *El Universal Online*. In addition to this paper, the second and third most influential ones are *Reform* and *La Jornada*. In 2002, the *Milenio* and the *La Presena* still had the largest circulation, but their contents are based upon yellow (sensational) press. The three most influential magazines in Mexico are the *Proceso* (Politics), the *Contenido*, and the *Siempre*.

ECONOMIC FRAMEWORK

Mexico's free market economy with its mixture of modern and outmoded industry and agriculture was throughout the last quarter of the twentieth century increasingly dominated by the private sector. The number of state-owned enterprises in Mexico fell from more than 1,000 in 1982 to fewer than 200 in 2000. The Zedillo administration (1994-2000) privatized and expanded competition in seaports, railroads, telecommunications, electricity, natural gas distribution, and airports.

A strong export sector helped to cushion the economy's decline in 1995 and led the recovery in 1996-2000. Private consumption became the leading driver of growth in 2000, accompanied by increased employment and higher real wages. Entering the twenty-first century, Mexico still needed to modernize its economy and raise living standards. Trade with the United States and Canada had tripled since NAFTA was implemented in 1994. Moreover, in 2000, Mexico completed free trade agreements with the European Union (EU), Israel, El Salvador, Honduras, and Guatemala, and it sought additional trade agreements with other countries in Latin America and Asia to lessen its dependence on the United States.

Types of Newspapers As of the early 2000s, Mexico had about 340 dailies, most of which were morning editions. Most major cities had at least two competing dailies, with the exception of Mexico City, which had 25 to 30 dailies. Despite a population in Mexico City of about 2 million, the total circulation of all papers was only about 700,000 copies per day.

Newsprint Availability Newsprint was in 1935 handled by the government owned *Productora Y Importadora de Papel* (PIPSA). Its monopoly was created to provide low cost newsprint material for the newspapers, but over time it became a political weapon to be used against newspapers that carried negative stories about the PRI ruling federal party. PIPSA would punish newspapers that did not totally support the government by delaying deliveries of newsprint or it would send inferior newsprint. However, the 62-year old paper company lost its monopoly in 1990, and the new free market created much competition. PIPSA in the 1990s had uneven productivity and then slow growth. With some internal changes and by expanding facilities and product lines, PIPSA was able to claim 79 percent of the market. The average consumption of newsprint as of 2002 was about 378,000 metric tons, most of which supported daily newspaper production.

PRESS LAWS

Of the following press laws, some applied to newspapers and others to the electronic media. The application of these laws, however, has been inconsistent at best. In general, friends of the ruling national party were able to avoid close monitoring or prosecution whereas critics of the government inevitably faced legal difficulties. However, under President Fox this historical trend seemed less prevalent and less likely to continue.

Constitutional Guarantees for the Press Article 6 of the 1917 Constitution stipulates that the expression of ideas shall not be subject to any judicial or administrative investigation, unless it offends good morals, infringes the rights of others, incites to crime, or disturbs the public order.

Article 7 of the Constitution stipulates that freedom of writing and publishing writings is inviolable. The law specifies that no law or authority may establish censorship, require bonds from authors or printers, or restrict the freedom of printing, which is limited only by the respect due to private life, morals, and public peace. The law protects the publishing company, printing press, and employees such as vendors, newsboys, and workmen.

Constitutional Guarantees for Radio and Television Article 4 stipulates that radio and television are activities of public interest; therefore, the state should supervise their carrying out of their specific social function. Moreover, Article 5 specifies that radio and television must contribute to strengthening national integration and the improvement of forms of human co-existence. Through their transmissions they should affirm the principles of social morals, human dignity, and family connection; avoid vicious or disturbing influences on children and young adults; contribute to raising the cultural level; preserve national customs, correct language, and the Mexican nationality; and strengthen democratic convictions, national unity, and international friendship and cooperation.

CENSORSHIP

Senior governmental officials closely monitor daily newspaper coverage of the government. This scrutiny existed in the early 2000s despite the fact that the newspapers were mostly bought and read by educated urban people, the elite of whom tended to favor the government. Although the two major television-broadcasting outlets, Televisa and Aztec TV, are privately owned, they operate, as do newspapers, in accord with an unwritten rule that they do not criticize the president. However, in practice, media giants have little to fear because they are part of the ruling class that governs them. Journalists attend prestigious events including foreign trips with President Fox. Moreover, federal departments and agencies purchase considerable advertising.

Federal Radio and Television Law Article 3 specifies that radio and television support mass education, disseminate knowledge, extend ideas that strengthen Mexican principles and traditions, and stimulate the capacity for progress, the creative faculty, and the objective analysis of the country's affairs. Then Article 4 assures that this activity be conducted truthfully, within a framework of respect for private life and morals, without affecting the rights of third persons or disturbing public peace and order. In Article 5 recreational programs are given the mission of providing healthy entertainment that affirms national values, does not go against good customs, avoids corruption of language and vulgarity, and serves the purpose of ennobling the tastes of the audience. Article 6 states that radio and TV programming should contribute to the country's economic growth, and Article 7 states that advertising should be responsible and in the national interest with an eye to balance in family spending.

In 2002 President Fox signed Mexico's first freedom of information bill, which allows government documents to be review by the press as well as members of the public. The new law calls for all federal agencies, the federal courts, as well as the Bank of Mexico, to post their public information on the Internet within a year. Certain information, such as that pertaining to national security or foreign relations, has a 12-year waiting period. Finally, officials who hide, destroy, or fail to provide information may be fined, dismissed, or face criminal charges.

STATE-PRESS RELATIONS

While the Mexican press purports to be free, it is a fact that dozens of journalists and editors were murdered in the 1980s and 1990s, among them Hector Felix Miranda (1988); coeditor of *Tijuana Weekly* (ZETA), Victor Manuel Oropeza (1991); and political columnist for *Diario De Chihuahua*, Jorge Martin Dorantes (1994). That this criminal activity continued was the result of corrupt officials, including police and military, and widespread failure to solve and successfully prosecute those responsible. With the Fox administration, hope increased that state-press relations in the early 2000s would substantially improve.

PRESS ASSOCIATIONS

One of the Foreign News Bureaus represented in Mexico is the World Association of Newspapers (WAN). Consisting of a group of 71 national newspaper associations, with individual newspaper executives in 100 nations, 13 national and international news agencies, a media foundation, and 7 affiliated regional and worldwide press organizations, WAN represents more than 18,000 publications on five continents. It has three goals: to defend and promote press freedom and the economic independence of newspapers; to contribute to the development of newspaper publishing by fostering communications and contacts between newspaper executives from different regions and cultures; and to promote cooperation between WAN's member organizations, whether national, regional or worldwide.

Also represented is the Inter American Press Association (IAPA), which includes all major papers and many smaller rural papers in the United States, Mexico, and Latin America. A number of its executives are Mexican newspaper owners, publishers, or editors. The IAPA is dedicated toward promoting a free press. In addition, Grupo de Diarios-America (GDA), a consortium of the 12 most influential newspapers in Latin America, is present. In each country these newspapers are the public opinion leaders with maximum creditability. Each of the newspapers also has a dominant circulation and an upscale readership in its market. Members of GDA include: *El Nacional* and *El Universal* (Mexico City) and *El Tiempo* (Monclova).

NEWS AGENCIES

As of 2002, four news agencies were operating in Mexico. *Association de Editores de los Estados* (AEE), domestic news association, subscribed to the foreign news association WAN. Also represented were *Multimedios Estrellas de Oro* (MEO); the governmental organization, *Agencia Mexicana de Noticias* (Notimex); and Reuters Mexico, the worldwide leader in financial information and services.

BROADCAST MEDIA

Radio In 1997 there were 31 million radios in Mexico receiving broadcast from 865 AM stations, about 500 FM stations, and about 13 short-wave stations. Grupo Radio Centro, Mexico's leading radio broadcaster, produced the most popular stations, most of which were located in Mexico City. Radio Centro had 20 production studios and produced virtually all of its own programming. A subsidiary, Organización Impulsora de Radio, served as a national sales representative and provided programming to more than 100 affiliate radio stations across Mexico.

Television In 1997 there were almost 30 million television sets owned across Mexico receiving 236 television broadcasting stations. As of 2002, Grupo Televisa was the largest Spanish speaking communication conglomerate in the world. It began with radio under the leadership of Emilio Azcarraga. The company expanded into television in the 1970s, and afterward it became a multi-media corporation. In the early 2000s, it was Mexico's largest television network controlling over 300 stations across four networks. Almost 60 percent of the corporation's revenues came from television, particularly the successful export of Spanish soap operas, known as *telenovelas*. Moreover, with the expansion of the Spanish speaking population in the United States, the U.S. market for Grupo Televisa products of all types increased substantially. Televisa owned 17 radio stations along with music labels, mobile phones, satellite interests, and other businesses. On the print side, Televisa controlled Edivisa, S.A. de C.V, a publishing giant with over 40 Spanish magazines, including a weekly television guide and other popular products. Edivisa also published Spanish versions of *Elle*, *Cosmopolitan*, and *Harper's Bazaar*.

The television-broadcasting segment included the production of television programming and nationwide broadcasting of Channels 2, 4, 5, and 9 (television networks), and the production of television programming and broadcasting for local television stations in Mexico and the United States. The broadcasting of television networks was performed by television repeater stations in Mexico that were as of 2002 wholly-owned, majority-owned, or minority-owned by the Group or otherwise affiliated with the Group's television network station broadcasts.

The programming for the pay television segment included programming services to cable and pay-per-view television companies in Mexico, other countries in Latin America, the United States, and Europe. The programming services consisted of both programming produced by the Group and programming produced by others. Programming for pay television revenues were derived from domestic and international programming services provided to the independent cable television systems in Mexico and the Group's DTH satellite businesses and formed the sale of advertising time on programs provided to pay television companies in Mexico.

The programming licensing segment consisted of the domestic and international licensing of television programming. Programming licensing revenues were derived from domestic and international program licensing fees. The cable television segment included the operation of a cable television system in the Mexico City metropolitan area and derived revenues principally from basic and premium service subscription and installation fees from cable subscribers, pay-per-view fees, and local and national advertising sales. The radio segment included the operation of six radio stations in Mexico City and eleven other domestic stations owned by the Group. Revenues were derived by advertising and by the distribution of programs to nonaffiliated radio stations. The other business segments included the Group's domestic operations in sports and show business promotion, soccer, nationwide paging, feature film production and distribution, Internet, and dubbing services for Mexican and multinational companies.

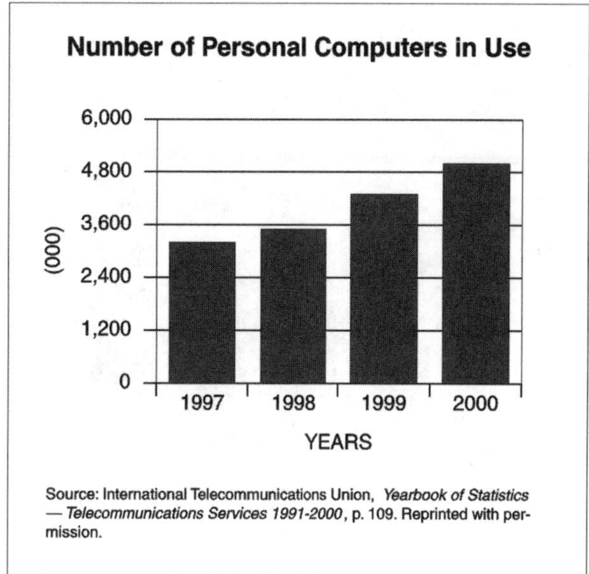

Source: International Telecommunications Union, *Yearbook of Statistics — Telecommunications Services 1991-2000*, p. 109. Reprinted with permission.

ELECTRONIC NEWS MEDIA

As of 2002, only 5 percent of Mexicans had web access, but places such as Internet Cafes were becoming popular after school destinations. Expanding access was a major government priority. The Internet growth rate in Mexico given its lower base is the second highest in Latin America, only exceeded by that of Brazil. Mexico is a newly industrialized country with a growing economy largely due to the success of NAFTA. But the economic development has not seen equally successful movement to Internet and e-commerce business. Across Mexico Internet access in the early 2000s was still not sufficient to supply the necessary critical mass to customers. In addition many Mexican customers simply lacked the money to purchase online. The Mexican federal government wanted to upgrade the country's telecommunication system so that Internet access would be available in rural as well as urban areas by 2010. Collectively a number of forces in Mexico were converging to promote electronic news, and information services.

The early 2000s saw a number of online newspaper websites in Spanish: from Mexico City, *El Universal*, *El Financiero*, *Reforma*, *La Jornada*, *Mexico Hoy*, and *Crónica*; in addition, 11 other newspaper websites in various regions across the country. Finally, two U.S. newspapers, *San Antonio Express News* and *San Diego Union Tribune-Mexico*, had special Mexican news sites.

Access Mexico Connect, popularly known as MexConnect, was in the early 2000s a very successful free monthly electronic magazine focusing on information about Mexico and promoting Mexico to the world. The electronic magazine was supported by a searchable database of over 10,000 Mexican related articles. It received over a half million hits per month, and 80 percent of its users were located in one of three countries, the United States, Mexico, and Canada. As of 2002 it was Mexico's most read English site and ranked in the top 5 percent of all Internet sites in the world. In addition it offered a resource center with a variety of Mexican activities such as classified aids, tourism, employment, email, and other e-commerce activities. MexConnect sought to promote Mexican trade, advertising, and commerce around the world.

EDUCATION & TRAINING

In the early 2000s, the education and training of journalists was a joint effort. One international organization, Investigative Reporters and Editors (IRE), is headquartered at the Missouri School of Journalism in Columbia, Missouri. The not-for-profit institute, made up of 4,000 reporters, editors, and academics, intends to work with Mexican journalists to launch a Mexican Reporting Institute. The primary objectives of the institute are to train Mexican reporters, broadcasters, and editors in advanced reporting skills; to develop a cooperative network of journalists throughout Mexico; and to support efforts of Mexican journalists to improve public access to information.

Six institutions in Canada, the United States, and Mexico participate in a Journalism and Globalization Program (JAG) that provides selected students with journal experience in an international setting. Besides offering students the opportunity to expand their cultural and global perspectives, JAG challenges them to think about alternative methods of reporting. The participating schools in Canada are Mount Royal College in Calgary and Humber College in Toronto. In the United States the participating schools are the University of Iowa and University of Georgia, and in Mexico the participating institutions are Universidad de Colima and Universidad Autonoma de Guadalajara.

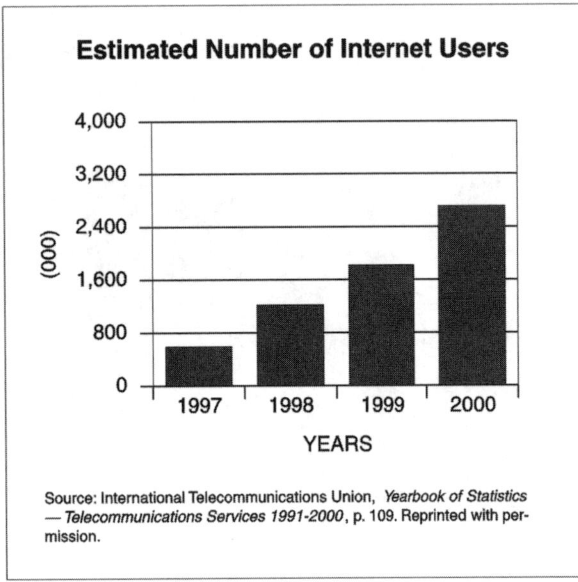

Source: International Telecommunications Union, *Yearbook of Statistics — Telecommunications Services 1991-2000*, p. 109. Reprinted with permission.

SUMMARY

Historically, the Mexican press has been compromised by violence and criminal activity. Yet press laws in the twentieth century and governmental changes in the early 2000s suggested reasons to hope for the continued evolution of an increasingly professional press. With the additional help of NAFTA, these changes bode well for the future of the Mexican media. The passage in 2002 of a freedom of information act indicated that journalists and others would in the early twenty-first century be able to obtain government documents denied to them for generations. Then, too, increasing numbers of well-educated, professional journalists entering the profession would improve it. As traditional print sources in Mexico migrate to electronic services along with new entrants such as MexConnect, media in Mexico are bound to find their place in the global market.

SIGNIFICANT DATES

- 1994: NAFTA agreement is signed by Mexico, the United States, and Canada.
- 1994: Chiapas revolt begins.
- 2000: President Fox is elected.
- 2002: Freedom of Information Act is signed into law.

BIBLIOGRAPHY

Adler, Ilya. ''Press-Government Relations in Mexico: A Study of Freedom of the Mexican Press and Press Criticism of Government Institutions.'' *Studies in Latin American Popular Culture,* vol.12 (1993): 1-30.

Barrera, Vivian and Denise Bielby. ''Places, Faces, and Other Familiar Things: The Cultural Experience of Telenovela Viewing Among Latinos in the United States.'' *Journal of Popular Culture* vol. 34, 4 (2001): 1-19.

McAnany, Emile and Antonio La Pastina. ''Telenovela Audiences.'' *Communication Research,* vol. 21, 6 (Dec 1994): 828-847.

McPhail, Thomas. *Global Communication: Theories, Stakeholders, and Trends.* Boston: Allyn & Bacon, 2002.

Perkins, Michael. ''Freedom(s) of the Press in Latin America.'' *Gazette* 64 (2002): 5-19.

Vargas, Jocelyn. ''Expanding the Popular Culture Debates: Puertorriqueñas, Hollywood, and Cultural Identity.'' *Studies in Latin American Popular Culture,* 15 (1996): 155-174.

—Thomas McPhail

MICRONESIA

BASIC DATA

Official Country Name:	Federated States of Micronesia
Region (Map name):	Oceania
Population:	133,144
Language(s):	English, Trukese, Pohnpeian, Yapese, Kosrean
Literacy rate:	89%

Micronesia, a group of 600 islands in the North Pacific Ocean, is an independent country made up of four districts: Pohnpei, Chuuk, Yap, and Kosrae. Prior to establishing its sovereignty in 1978, Micronesia was part of a trust territory created by the United Nations following World War II (the United States was trustee). Democratic elections were held the following year, and Micronesia joined the United Nations in 1991. The estimated population is 135,000. English is the official and most common language, but local dialects like Trukese, Pohnpeian, Yapese, and Kosrean are also spoken. The literacy rate is 89 percent. Micronesia's President leads both the state and the government, and heads a 14-seat unicameral Congress. In 1986, Micronesia and the United States entered a Compact of Free Association, meaning the U.S. would provide more than $1 billion in financial and technical assistance to the island nation. This agreement expired in 2001, leaving the Micronesian economy extremely fragile. Other than foreign aid, the economy relies on farming and fishing. The potential to develop tourism exists, but it is hindered by lack of adequate facilities, the country's underdeveloped infrastructure and its remote location.

Since 1998, Micronesia is experiencing increased media freedom. There is no daily newspaper. The Pohnpei district boasts three English-language publications. A bi-weekly publication called *Micronesia Focus* has published since 1993, *The FSM News,* a newspaper founded in 1994, which appears monthly, and the *National Union,* begun in 1979, which prints every two weeks. The *National Union,* a free publication, focuses on national government news and accepts no advertising. The Yap shirt also produces a newspaper called the *Yap State Bulletin.* Like the *National Union,* this free publication appears every two weeks, highlights government news, and contains no advertisements.

There are six radio stations, one FM and five AM, and three television stations. There is one Internet service provider.

BIBLIOGRAPHY

''Country Profile: Micronesia,'' *BBC News. (n.d.).* Available from http://news.bbc.co.uk/hi/english/world/asia-pacific.

''Federated States of Micronesia,'' *University of Queensland, Australia's CocoNET Wireless (1995).* Available from http://www.uq.edu.au.

''History,'' *Government of the Federated States of Micronesia (2002).* Available from http://www.fsmgov.org/info/hist.html.

''Micronesia,'' *CIA World Fact Book (2001).* Available from http://www.cia.gov.

—*Jenny B. Davis*

MOLDOVA

BASIC DATA

Official Country Name:	Republic of Moldova
Region (Map name):	Europe
Population:	4,431,570
Language(s):	Moldovan (official), Russian, Gagauz
Literacy rate:	96.0%
Area:	33,843 sq km
GDP:	1,286 (US$ millions)
Number of Television Stations:	1
Number of Television Sets:	126,000
Television Sets per 1,000:	28.4
Number of Cable Subscribers:	50,740
Cable Subscribers per 1,000:	11.8
Number of Satellite Subscribers:	3,000
Satellite Subscribers per 1,000:	0.7
Number of Radio Stations:	60
Number of Radio Receivers:	3,220,000
Radio Receivers per 1,000:	726.6
Number of Individuals with Computers:	63,500
Computers per 1,000:	14.3
Number of Individuals with Internet Access:	52,600
Internet Access per 1,000:	11.9

BACKGROUND & GENERAL CHARACTERISTICS

In 2002, 180 newspapers and magazines were published in the Republic of Moldova. Printed media, as well as TV and radio programs appear in Romanian, Russian, Gagauzi, Bulgarian, Ukrainian, and Yiddish languages. Although the Constitution defines Moldavian as an official language, it is a regular practice among many people, including the intellectual elite and officials to refer to Moldavian as Romanian to emphasize once common history and culture of Moldova and Romania.

The Moldavian population is, in general, well educated and overall is interested in mass media. According to the census taken in 1989, 96.4 percent of the adult population were literate. About 70 percent of them had secondary or higher education. Moldova has a mandatory 9-grade school education for young people.

Press History The history of the Moldavian press begins in 1790 when the first official periodical *Curier de*

Moldavie (Moldavian Herald), in the French language, was initiated in the city of Yassy near the Russian Army Headquarters. The periodical was dislocated to the territory of the Moldavian Knighthood after the Russo-Turkish war of 1787-1791. In 1829, famous writer Georgi Asaki introduced to the public the first newspaper (*Albina Romanesca,* or Romanian Bee) in the native Romanian language. It was published in Yassy every two days on four pages. In July 1854, Moldova, which was then called Bessarabia and was a province in the Russian Empire, commenced the publication of the official newspaper *Bessarabskie Oblastnye Vedomosti* (Bessarabian Official Reports) under the auspices of the local governor authorities. The first magazine *Kishinevskie Eparkhial'nye Vedomosti* (Official Reports of Kishineu Parish) which appeared in 1867, both in Russian and Romanian languages had religious orientations. In 1917, it changed its name to *Golos Pravoslavnoi Bessarabskoi Tserkvi* (Voice of Bessarabian Orthodox Church).

The history of private press begins with the *Bessarabski Vestnik* (Bessarabian Herald) which was published on a weekly basis in the city of Chisinau in 1889 by Elizabeth Sokolova, the wife of the local high official. Along with the official reports, it placed articles reflecting the social, political, and economic life of the province; literary essays; and humor stories. The weekly leaned toward democratic circles of the Bessarabian society.

In 1854-1899, Bessarabia had 28 printed publications, including 9 newspapers, 2 magazines, 14 publications by various institutions, and 3 address-calendars. Their number had increased dramatically to 254 by the beginning of the twentieth century. It included both official and non-official newspapers and magazines such as *Literary Almanac*, *Bessarabian Agriculture*, *Wine and Gardening*, *Wine and Winery*, among them. Sixteen publications were in Romanian.

In 1918-1940, the larger western part of Bessarabia became occupied by Romania, while the smaller one attained a status of Moldavian Autonomous Socialist Republic within the Soviet Ukraine. The Moldavian press in Romania developed under the great influence of local nationalism and Romanian culture, while in Socialist Moldavia (until 1991), all state-owned media promoted the ideas and practices of the Communist party and its ideology. No independent mass media existed in the Socialist Moldavia. Though mass media achieved significant accomplishments during the Soviet times, such as the publication of ninety printed editions in various ethnic languages, and the development of the huge radio and TV broadcasting networks, to name a few, they had a strict state and party censorship.

Mass Media under Democracy In 1991, Moldova was proclaimed a sovereign state. As a democratic, free market-oriented country, Moldova eliminated the state and Communist party monopoly and the censorship in media production: state publishing houses, radio stations, and printed media became privatized. The emergence of independent media, news agencies, TV channels, and radio stations became a reality. Religious press grew fast. Demand, supply, and competition started ruling the mass media market. However, the first results were not quite encouraging for many media employees. The process of privatization did not proceed in a just, fair way for them, because journalists, reporters, and other media professionals were deprived of the right to purchase any publishing, broadcasting, and photographic facilities. Many media that were purchased, furthermore, could not find financial resources and consequently failed. In the mid-1990s, the government began to nationalize some of them. As a result, 50 percent of all printed and electronic media returned to state control. This, of course, did not promote the freedom of press in the country. The journalists faced a dilemma: to fight for a real independence, including a financial one, or serve the interests of the government which guaranteed salary and means for existence in exchange for surrendering certain freedoms. Due to the economic difficulties, many journalists chose a third way: to serve the political interests of the parties that mushroomed (over fifty at the beginning of 1990s) since the sovereignty was proclaimed. This decision led them, to a great extent, to lose their professionalism and objectivity. The political parties' press dominated the market in the first half of the 1990s. A decade later, when the citizenry realized that the press media was not objective, the number of parties and party press significantly dwindled. Though 40 percent of the press still belonged to the parties in 2002, their circulation did not reach the circulation of the independent press.

Most Popular Newspapers and Magazines Two newspapers stand out on the media scene; *Moldova Suverena* (Sovereign Moldova), with a circulation of 7,000 copies, in Romanian, and *Nezavisimaya Moldova* (Independent Moldova), with a circulation of 10,500 copies in Russian. Both support the party in power and the political forces associated with it. This was borne out in 2001 parliamentary elections, when they both upheld the political alliance headed by the Prime Minister Dmitry Bragish.

The nationalistic resurgence movements of Moldova promote their agenda through a variety of newspapers. One of them, *Literature si Arta* (Literature and Art, with 18,200 copies), a weekly published in Romanian, belongs to the Union of Writers of Moldova. Traditionally, it leans toward the right and disseminates the national-patriotic sentiments. In 2001 parliamentary elections, it backed up the Party of Democratic Forces since its editor-in-chief Nikolai Dabizha could be found among the candidates of this party.

The right spectrum of the Moldavian press is represented by the daily *Flux,* which is considered the most influential newspaper in the Romanian language (36,000 copies). It expresses the outlook of the pro-Romanian circles in the country under the leadership of Yuri Poshka, the Chairperson of Christian-Democratic People Party. The independent *Jurnal de Chisinau* at 11,000 copies, and *Tara* (Country) at 7,500 copies, both in Romanian, and *Novoe Vremya* (New Time) at 10,000 copies, published in Russian by the Democratic Party, can also be numbered among this spectrum.

In 1995, the Party of Resurgence and Accord (PRA) headed by the ex-President Mircea Snegur launched the Russian-language newspaper *Moldavskie Vedomosti* (Moldavian Official Reports), at 6,000 copies. It gradually lost its party affiliation, though still remains between the right and the center media in the political arena. The former official newspaper, *Luceafurul* (Morning Star), with a circulation of 10,000 copies, claims to be independent from the PRA since 2001, however, it still adheres to a great extent to the politics of this party.

The Romanian-language weekly *Saptamina* (Week), 17,400 copies, represents the political views of the centrist movements and adheres to the party in power. It was founded in 1992.

Kishinevskie Novosti (Chisinau News), 8,400 copies, adheres to the left. Since its foundation in 1991, it remains one of three most popular newspapers published in Russian. It successfully combines information with advertisements, allocating balanced space to classified ads and to information on serious and light aspects of life in the capital.

The Communist Party of Moldova disseminates 25,000 copies of the newspaper *Communist*, both in Romanian and Russian, which was published once a week until 2001 and twice a week since then. The publication enjoys popularity predominantly among the Party supporters and elderly generation. Over time, it has become less orthodox in expressing Communist views and ideology.

The extreme political orientation of many national newspapers makes it difficult for the readers to form an objective opinion on the events in the country, since very few individuals, due to the present severe financial constraints, can afford to buy a diverse array of publications. The population is equally as swayed in the remote rural areas where they predominantly read press materials, listen to radio programs, and watch TV shows produced by local companies.

There are also periodicals for various sub-groups of the population. Some of them target children and teenagers, *Noi* (We), in Romanian; *Drug* (Friend), in Russian and a private magazine *Welcome Moldova*, in English; or youth *Tineretul Moldovei* (Young Moldavian), in Romanian and *Otechestvo* (Fatherland), in Russian; and others are designed for women. Most of the press comes from Romania, Russia, and Ukraine. There are also a variety of periodicals devoted to sports, hobbies, and recreation. Among the sports periodicals are *Rest with Soccer*, *Sport Plus*, and *Sport-Curier*.

On the territory of self-proclaimed Pri-Dnestr Moldavian Republic, the mass media work under strict state censorship. Most of them keep to pro-government orientation. *Pridnestrovskaya Pravda* (Pri-Dnestr Truth) and *Pridnestrovie* (Pri-Dnestr) are the most known in that area.

The democratic processes in Moldova created opportunities for the development of new information agencies. The monopolist of the one state agency, ATEM, dissolved. Among more than a dozen new agencies, there is the government agency Moldpres (1940), the Chisinau municipal council agency Info-prim (1998), and the independent agencies Basa-pres (1992), NICA-pres (1993), Interlic (1995), AP ''FLUX'' (1995), and ''DECA''-pres (1996).

PRESS LAWS

Freedom of expression, speech, and access to information are basic rights guaranteed by the Constitution of Moldova, which was adopted in 1994. According to Article 32, every citizen is guaranteed ''the freedom of thought, opinion, and their public expression in words, paintings, or by other means.'' Article 34 guarantees the right to have access to any information concerning governance and the functioning of state bodies. Article 5 forbids censorship.

The Constitution's articles of the press are supported by three major laws, the Law on Press (1994), the Law on TV and Radio (1995), and the Law on Access to Information (2000). The Law on TV and Radio is considered by legal experts a major step forward for it envisions the transformation of state broadcasting in public and private sectors. It also stipulates the procedures for the establishment of independent broadcasting companies.

The Law on Press guarantees political pluralism (Article 1, paragraph 1). Any legal organization or any citizen of the country over eighteen years of age has the right to open a news agency or launch a periodical (Article 5, paragraph 1). All media must be registered in the Ministry of Justice. The state pledges to defend the honor and dignity of journalists, their life, and property (Article 20, paragraph 3). The media must not inflict harm upon the honor and dignity of any citizen or to his/her private life, his/her right to have an opinion; to the national security, territorial integrity, public calm and law. They are not to disclose confidential information.

The Criminal Code of the Republic of Moldova, Article 7, guarantees citizens the right to file law suits against those media which publish false information about them. The Code stipulates significant fines (up to 200 minimum monthly salaries) for publishing false information in the press. Defamation in any print form can be punished by up to three years imprisonment or up to 50 minimum monthly salaries.

The Coordination Council on TV and Radio Broadcasting grants and revokes licenses for TV broadcasting and allocates radio frequencies on a competitive bid basis, sponsored by the Ministry of Transport and Communications.

The professional journalist organizations consider some articles of the laws inaccurate, incomplete, or contradictory, which interferes with the free functioning of the press. For example, they expressed concern about Article 7, paragraph 4 of the Law on Press, which does not specify in which cases the court has the right to terminate a license. It does not specify the words ''misuse of the media'' which can have multiple interpretations. The concerns were also expressed by journalists about the possibility of abuse of Article 7, paragraph 1 of the Legal Code for moral damage in cases of criticizing the activities of government officials.

STATE-PRESS RELATIONS

Although the existing laws of the Republic of Moldova guarantee mass media the freedom of expression, from time to time many of them come across serious problems. The ban on censorship does not imply its total elimination. An unofficial, covert censorship often takes its place in many mass media. This perspective is supported by the survey of journalists conducted by the Center for the Support of Freedom of Expression and Access to Information in November, 2001. The presence of direct or indirect censorship was acknowledged by 95.6 percent of journalists.

The party and political censorship grossly prevail. The government efficiently uses the imperfect laws and economic leverages in exercising its pressure on media. The laws are often used to defend not the freedom of expression and speech, but the reputation of corrupt individuals. About 800 lawsuits were filed by government officials against journalists since 1995. There are grave obstacles in implementing the Law on Access to Information. Since its adoption, not a single lawsuit was filed against any state official for hiding any publicly significant information. The press services of the government and governmental bodies appear to serve as filters, not suppliers, of information.

The licensing of electronic mass media serves as another powerful tool of intrusion and direct control of the state over the content of the press materials. The Coordination Council on Radio and TV Broadcasting includes only the representatives of the power; lay people are not among them.

The critical coverage of the government and governmental bodies can be found mainly in the opposition party media. Shutting down the *Commersant Moldovi* (Moldavian Salesman) in 2001 serves as an outstanding example of persecution of media for critical coverage of some events. The newspaper was accused of promoting separatism of the country when it published interviews with the leaders of the unrecognized Pre-Dnestr Moldavian Republic, which fought for secession from Moldova.

The state and independent mass media find themselves in unequal economic conditions. The low quality of life of the population (in 2002, 75 percent of the population lived below the poverty line) deprived independent mass media of their major financial support from their readers. The newspapers and magazines that had circulation of 200,000 and more during the Soviet times dropped their circulation to between 10 and 15 thousand copies. The high cost of paper imported by Moldova, constantly increasing tariffs for photographic services, and taxes which are as high as in other businesses put many publications on the brink of bankruptcy. In these conditions, the government uses sales tax as one of the forms of manipulation with mass media. The introduction or elimination of the tax depends upon every new government. Growing tariffs on subscription and delivery of media worsen the situation.

Foreign capital's ownership of stock in Moldavian print-media companies is restricted by law to no more than 49 percent; for electronic media the percentage cap is 85 percent.

The deepening economic crisis in the country does not allow private businesses to place their commercial advertisements in media to increase their income. Additional taxation of advertisement does not encourage media hunts for potential customers. Many companies spend tiny amounts of money on advertising.

The journalists encounter many problems because they do not have a trade union of their own. They are members of the Union of the Workers of Culture, a part of the independent trade union of Moldova Solidaritatea (Solidarity), which does not effectively defend its members. As a result, in 2002, a group of concerned journalists created a steering committee to establish a professional union of their own.

The journalists of Moldova can join various creative organizations, such as the Union of Journalists of Moldova. The newly created League of Journalists of Moldova acts as an alternative association to support and defend their rights and to promote professionalism. The journalists exercise their rights and actualize interests and needs through other alliances, such as the Association of Electronic Press or APEL, the Committee for the Freedom of Press in Moldova, Independent Journalism Center, and Center for the Support of Freedom of Expression and Access to Information.

Attitude toward Foreign Media

The Republic of Moldova is a democratic society. In 2002, over 70 foreign publishing houses, information agencies, radio and TV companies received accreditation with ITAR-TASS, RIA Novosti, Radio Free Europe, BBC, Editing-Frans, Deutsche Press, ARD, International Media Corporation, Journalism 2, and PRO-TV among them. The accreditation of foreign journalists is carried out by the Ministry of Foreign Affairs in accordance with the Procedures for Accreditation and Activity of Foreign Journalists, approved by the government in 1995.

The Western press is distributed mainly by subscription. It is not available for retail sale. One can purchase Western newspapers and magazines only in the governmental institutions, elite hotels, and restaurants. Private companies deliver *The Wall Street Journal Europe*, *The Guardian Europe*, *Financial Times*, *Bild*, *Le Monde*, *Newsweek*, and others.

The press from Russia prevails in retail sale due to high demand. Three Russian publications *Argumenty I Fakty* (Arguments and Facts), *Komsomol'skaya Pravda* (Komsomol Truth), and *Trud* (Labor) have supplements with an overview of major political, economic, and cultural events in the Republic of Moldova.

Broadcast Media

While prior to 1991 Moldova had only one state-run TV company, in 2002 there were 39 non-cable TV studios and 47 cable TV studios. Only four of them belong to the state. These stations are, Teleradio-Moldova, Gagauzia, Euro TV-Chisinau, TV-Balti. The most popular private TV studios are NIT, ORT Moldova, PRO-TV, TV6-Balti, and TV26-Chisinau. The biggest cable TV studio, SunTV, is a joint venture of USA and Moldova with 70 percent of the stock belonging to the American side. The cable TV network develops rapidly not only in the capital Chisinau, but all over the Republic, with Balti-6 and TV-SAD in Beltsy; Centru-TV, SATELIT-TV, and Alternative-TV in Chisinau; and Inter-TV in Faleshty. Practically every district, capital, and big city has cable TV. Though censorship is outlawed in radio and TV, the hidden censorship influences the work of some companies. It relates to the greatest extent to the state company Teleradio Moldova. Its chair is elected by the Parliament and often exercises subtle pressure on the journalists in the interests of the Parliament majority and blocks the opposition from access to the listeners. In one case, the head of the company repeatedly dismissed two journalists. Yet in each case they appealed in court and were reinstated.

In March and April, 2002, the bigger part of the journalist core of the Teleradio-Moldova company went on ''passive'' strike to protest against the subtle censorship. The journalists also demanded the adoption of the Law on Public TV and to turn the state TV company into a public one to reflect the interests of all layers of Moldavian society.

The international TV companies must get a license to operate in the country. Among those that were granted licenses are Romanian Public Television TVR-1 and TV company TV-5 (Francofonia, a Belgium-France Switzerland conglomerate). Broadcasting of Russian TV channels is regulated by the Agreement, signed in 1997 by the governments of the Moldavian Republic and the Russian Federation. Some other international channels are aired by local companies on the basis of bilateral agreements, which are registered by the Coordination Council on TV, and Radio Broadcasting. Russian ORT, RTR, NTV, Ren-tTV, and Romanian PRO TV enjoy the most popularity among the Moldavian audience.

As Moldova received independence, the number of radio stations significantly grew in the country. There were 28 stations in 2002, with 21 of them in the capital city of Chisinau. Radio-Polidisc (Chisinau), Radio-Nova (Chisinau), HIT-EM (Chisinau), BlueStar (Beltsy), Radio-Sanatate (Edintsy), and the State Radio Station are known to be the most popular.

The following foreign radio stations acquired licenses to broadcast in the Republic: France-International, Free Europe, and the BBC. Radio stations of Russia and Romania are very popular too.

The Coordination Council on TV and Radio Broadcasting issues licenses. The Council also controls the implementation of laws by TV and radio companies. Its nine members represent each branch of power on an equal basis. The Council is re-elected every five years and the chair is elected by its members.

In the late 1990s, the country witnessed the growth of electronic online press. Reporter.md, MoldNet, MoldovaOnline, Infomarket.md, Integrare Europeana,

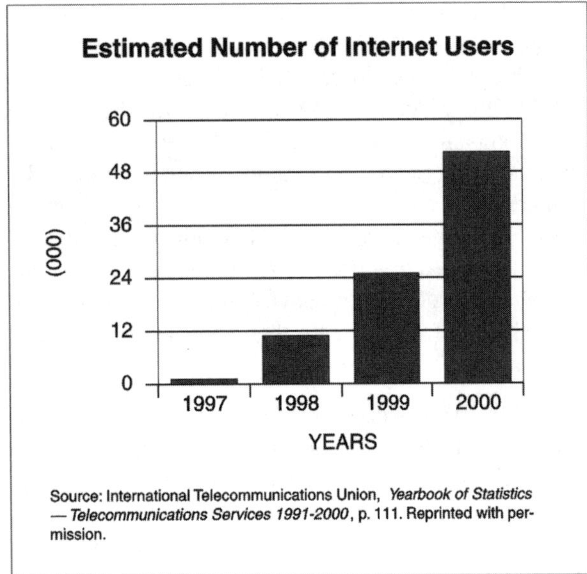

Source: International Telecommunications Union, *Yearbook of Statistics — Telecommunications Services 1991-2000*, p. 111. Reprinted with permission.

YAM.ro, Moldova-Azi, and Press Box.md are among the most popular electronic information agencies. In general, access to electronic media among the population is still insignificant because of its high cost. Only the few wealthy individuals, big companies, and some universities can afford subscriptions to the Internet. The Internet is more accessible in the capital Chisinau and in big cities; less so in rural areas where the majority of the population lives.

EDUCATION & TRAINING

Until 2001, Moldova State University had been the only educational institution that prepared the journalist cadres for the country in both Romanian and Russian languages. Between 1966 and 2002, 1,500 journalists graduated from the University. In 2001, departments of journalism were launched in two private institutions, the International Independent University and Slavic University.

BIBLIOGRAPHY

Corlat, S. *Editii Electronice in Format HTML.* Chisinau: Centrul Editorial al FJSC a USM, Moldova, 2002.

Coval, D. *Jurnalism de Investigatie*. Chisinau: Centrul Editorial al FJSC a USM, 2001.

———. *Problematica Presei Scrise*. Chisinau: Centrul Editorial al FJSC a USM, 1997.

Dreptul Tau: Accessul la Informatie. Chisinau: Universul, 2001.

King, Ch. *The Moldovans : Romania, Russia, and the politics of culture*. Stanford, Calif.: Hoover Institution Press, 2000.

Koval, D. *Pervaya Chastnya Gazeta v Bessarabii v XX Veke*. Chisinau: Centrul Editorial al FJSC a USM, 1996.

Marin, K. *Comunicare Institutionala*. Chisinau: Centrul Editorial al FJSC a USM, 1998.

MASS-MEDIA in Societatile in Transitie: Realitati si Perspective. Chisinau: Central Editoria al FJSC a USM, 2001.

Moraru, V. *Mass Media Versus Politica*. Chisinau: Centrul editorial al FJSC a USM, 2001.

—Grigory Dmitriyev and Viktor Kostetsky

MONACO

BASIC DATA

Official Country Name:	Principality of Monaco
Region (Map name):	Europe
Population:	31,693
Language(s):	French, English, Italian, Monegasque
Literacy rate:	99%

When infighting forced the Grimaldi family to leave the Holy Roman Empire in the late thirteenth century, they fled to a tiny patch of land along the French Mediterranean coast called Monaco. Francois Grimaldi became the first monarch, and his descendants have ruled the country ever since. Now a constitutional monarchy, the government is headed by a Minister of State, who presides over a unicameral, 18-seat National Council. The official language is French, but English and Italian are also widely spoken. Some older residents speak the native language, Montegasque, which is a mixture of French Provençal and Italian Ligurian. Approximately 35,000 people live within the country's single square mile. The famous casinos of capital Monte Carlo, combined with beautiful scenery and a mild climate, have made Monaco a popular destination, and tourism accounts for about 25 percent of its gross national product. Banking is also an important sector of the economy, employing approximately 5 percent of the workforce. Monaco levies no income tax and business taxes are low, making it a haven for individuals and companies, but also a magnet for money laundering and organized crime. English writer Somerset Maugham once called it ''a sunny place for shady people.''

Freedom of expression is guaranteed by the Montagasque constitution, but its penal code prohibits denunciations of the Grimaldi family. The Centre de Presse is the official, state-run distribution point for information and photographs. It also handles press credentials for journalists. Monaco's daily newspaper is the *Nice-Matin.* Although it is published in Nice, France, it dedicates two pages to news coverage in Monaco. It is available online. The Ministry of State publishes a weekly government journal called the *Journal de Monaco.* It was founded in 1898 and provides information about legislation.

There are no FM radio stations in Monaco, but there is one AM station serving the country's 34,000 radios. There are five television stations, 25,000 televisions and two Internet service providers.

BIBLIOGRAPHY

"Country Profile," *Worldinformation.com (2002).* Available from http://www.worldinformation.com.

"Monaco," *CIA World Fact Book (2001).* Available from http://www.cia.gov.

"Monaco," *Freedom House (2000).* Available from http://www.freedomhouse.org.

Nice-Matin. (n.d.). Home Page. Available from http://www.nicematin.fr.

"Travel Guide-Europe-Monaco," *Americanexpress.ca (2001).* Available from www.americanexpress.canada.travel-guides.com.

—Jenny B. Davis

MONGOLIA

BASIC DATA

Official Country Name:	Mongolia
Region (Map name):	East & South Asia
Population:	2,650,952
Language(s):	Khalkha Mongol, Turkic, Russian
Literacy rate:	82.9%

Mongolia (Mongol Uls) has moved from being a largely agricultural and nomadic society, to being split between a nomadic and an urban population. One-third of all Mongolians reside in the capital city of Ulan Bator (Ulaanbaatar). Just larger than Alaska in size, 90 percent of its land is pasture or desert wasteland; 9 percent is forested; and 1 percent is arable. There is scant rain and large seasonal climate fluctuations occur.

Mongolia, with Soviet backing, gained its independence from China in 1921, but as of 1990 dropped its Soviet styled single-party state and began movements toward democratically oriented governance. Currently, 18 parties are active in the Mongolian political system. However, the Mongolian People's Revolutionary Party (MPRP)—the former party of Soviet rule—still has significant influence, including the support of current president Natsagiyin Bagabandi and a strong showing of 72 out of 76 seats in the 2000 parliamentary elections.

This has created some directional uncertainty concerning the political future of Mongolia. As with many countries experimenting with new systems of political governance, Mongolia's economic situation has been a struggle. While new avenues are being sought, there continues to be an inability to create and sustain a viable economy. Being landlocked and losing significant trading prospects with the collapse of the Soviet Union, they have been aggressively pursuing relationships with all countries, but have yet to find an economic niche that can provide any consistency and growth. Mongolia's precarious economic and still new political activities have lent themselves both positively and negatively to press and broadcast media situations.

Mongolian press began in 1920 under the Mongolian Communist Party (equivalent with the MPRP at the time) with *Unen* (*Truth*)—similar to Soviet *Pravda*—being the oldest newspaper published in the country; and *Dzaluuchuudyn Unen* (*Young People's Truth*), founded by the Central Committee of the Revolutionary Youth League; and *Ulaan Od* (*Red Star*) founded by the Ministries of Defense and Public Security following respectively in 1924 and 1930.

During those years the government directly oversaw all publishing. However much has changed since then. In a May 22, 2001, press conference newly elected Bagabandi iterated that he would seek to ensure press freedom through legal guarantees. However, while a Law of Press Freedom passed August 28, 1998, and enacted January 1, 1999, exists it has yet to obtain the necessary guarantees to assure its full implementation. In fact, soon after the MPRP regained power, the Ministry of Justice and Home Affairs closed three newspapers without legal authority. Further, while the 1998 law forbids state ownership or financing of media or of their organizations, the majority of radio and television stations are still state-owned and there continue to be problems in transferring this state-owned material to private hands. Government reticence also extends to allowing access to information.

The government, while taking no official actions against the media except in a couple of fairly justifiable cases, continues investigations into local media and press operations that—whether accurate or not—seem to these organizations negative and threatening.

As of a 1991 decree, The Ministry for Justice and Home Affairs is in charge of issuing licenses for all newspapers and can also confiscate them if newspapers break any ordinances. Additionally, the government has attempted to use moral rules and tax laws to keep tight rein on the ''free'' media. In many senses this has led to much self-censorship by the press. Even with these legal hurdles existing 1,150 newspapers were reported registered in 2001. With newspaper circulation essentially limited to Ulan Bator and only one-third of the country's 2.4 million people living there, this is a large figure. One factor in the high number of registered papers has to do with the fact that many of the papers are small circulation presses, some being literally one-person operations. There are only four dailies in Mongolian. Still, overall newspaper circulation stands on average at about 27 per 1,000 people.

Government has relinquished control of newsprint, but costs fluctuate dramatically due to shortages of paper and fuel supplies. Thus, the process of buying privately is prohibitive for many of the small presses. Also hindering newspapers is the fact that 90 percent of the advertising market is obtained by government television and radio leaving the press with little to exploit for income. Therefore, they are primarily dependent on circulation sales for income, but this presents an extra challenge in a country with per capita income of about $400 U.S. dollars per year. While there is lack of capital working against the press, one favorable aspect of the population is an average 97 percent literacy rate for both males and females. According to a 1998 poll more than 68 percent of Mongolians favor newspapers as their favorite form of media—one of the highest percentages in the world.

Dailies include: *Odiriyn Sonin* (*Daily News*; independent; succeeded state paper *Ardyn Erh*; founded 1990), *Onoodor* (independent; largest newspaper with regular 12-page issues and advertisements; founded 1996), *Zuuny Medee* (independent; succeeded state paper *Zasigyn Gazryn Medee*), *Mongolia This Week* (independent; first and only daily in English), and *Unen* (*Truth*; organ of the MPRP). Circulation figures are still generally not reported and at least one editor suggested this is one major problem that needs to be resolved in order to begin facilitating a freer press. However, before their name transition *Onoodor* and *Zuuny Medee* were among the largest circulations. An interesting variation from some of the other publications available is *Ger Magazine* (published online with guidance from the United Nations Development Program, UNDP), which is concerned with Mongolian youth in cultural transition. The name of the magazine is meant to be ironic because a *ger* is the Mongolian word for yurt—a yurt being traditional nomadic housing—but the magazine is about urbanization and globalization of Mongolian youth.

Broadcast media runs in a similar vein with the press. Private radio and television stations exist alongside state-owned operations, but lack of funding and lack of general infrastructure tend to limit the capacity for private ventures (this is the downside of the media law not allowing the government to fund media). What privatization has occurred is primarily limited to Ulan Bator with others only having access to state television and radio for news and a few private stations that primarily play music (music is cheaper than live programming). However, according to the International Journalists' Network, even state-owned television and radio stations are now required to be run as a ''self-funding national public broadcasting system.'' This is still much more the ideal than the actual.

One state-owned radio broadcast station, The Voice of Mongolia, began in 1965, is operated by Mongolian Radio and Television. It broadcasts eight hours a day in Mongolian, English, Chinese and Russian, and remains the sole international radio broadcasting station for the government of Mongolia. Overall, 2001 estimates suggest there are seven AM, nine FM, and four short-wave radio broadcast stations in the country. They broadcast to 155,900 radios (according to 1999 estimates).

Mongolteleviz is the state-owned television station under Mongolian Radio and Television and broadcasts nationwide. Other private stations include Eagle (Bürged) TV, MN Channel 25, and UBSTV. As of 1999, there were four television broadcast stations with 18 provincial repeaters and numerous low power repeaters. They broadcast to 168,800 televisions—approximately 50 to 60 percent of households possessing a television. Montsame is Mongolia's state-owned news agency.

The Internet is a relatively new medium for Mongolia with its first connection established in 1995, but it is up and coming. There is no direct infringement by the government concerning private Internet use by citizens. As of 2001 there were five Internet service providers in the country and between 10,000 and 15,000 subscribers. The United Nations Volunteers and United Nations Development Programme are currently running a major program in partnership with the Open Society Institute-Mongolia and with funding from the government of Japan to increase ICT access and utilization.

There is respect for the academy in Mongolia and journalistic training can be gained there. Perhaps one of the most prescient statements offered about Mongolia in recent years comes from the head of DataCom and board member of the Open Society Institute-Mongolia. D. Enkhbat says, ''Mongolia cannot solve the task of creating [an] open society without creating mechanisms for the free flow of information.''

BIBLIOGRAPHY

All the World's Newspapers. Available from http://www.webwombat.com.au.

Arignews: Daily Frontier News Bulletin. Available from http://www.eurasianet.org.

Atalpedia Online. *Country Index*. Available from http://www.atlapedia.com.

Boyd, Douglas. *Broadcasting in the Arab World: A Survey of the Electronic Media in the Middle East*, 3rd ed. Iowa State University Press, Ames, IA: 1999.

British Broadcast Company. *BBC News Country Profiles*. Available from http://news.bbc.co.uk.

Central Intelligence Agecy. *The World Factbook 2001*. (2002) Available from http://www.cia.gov.

Eurasianet. *Initial Analysis of State Media Law and Resolution Passed Friday, August 28, 1998*. Available: http://www.eurasianet.org.

Eurasianet: Mongolia Media Links. Available from http://www.eurasianet.org.

Government of Mongolia. Available from http://www.pmis.gov.mn.

International Journalists' Network (IJNet). *Mongolia: Press Overview*. Available from http://www.ijnet.org.

International Press Institute. *World Press Review*. Available from http://www.freemedia.at.

Kurian, George, ed. *World Press Encyclopedia*. Facts on File Inc. New York: 1982.

The Library of Congress. *Country Studies*. Available from http://lcweb2.loc.gov/frd/cs.

Maher, Joanne, ed. *Regional Surveys of the World: The Middle East and North Africa 2002*, 48th ed. Europa Publications. London: 2001.

The Middle East, 9th ed. Congressional Quarterly Inc. Washington, DC: 2000.

Mongolian Radio and Television. Available from http://web.mol.mn.

Redmon, Clare, ed. *Willings Press Guide 2002*, Vol. 2. Waymaker Ltd. Chesham Bucks, UK: 2002.

Reporters Sans Frontieres. *Bahrain Annual Report 2002*. Available from http://www.rsf.fr.

Reporters Sans Frontieres. *Middle East Archives 2002*. Available: http://www.rsf.fr.

Russell, Malcom. *The Middle East and South Asia 2001*, 35th ed. United Book Press, Inc. Harpers Ferry, WV: 2001.

Stat-USA. *International Trade Library: Country Background Notes*. Available from http://www.stat-usa.gov.

Sumner, Jeff, ed. *Gale Directory of Publications and Broadcast Media*, Vol. 5 136th ed. Gale Group. Farmington Hills, MI: 2002.

UNESCO Institute for Statistics. Available from http://www.uis.unesco.org.

United Nations. *Ger Online Magazine*. Available from http://www.un-mongolia.mn/ger-mag.

United Nations in Mongolia. Available from http://www.un-mongolia.mn.

United Nations Volunteer Programme. *Freedom Of Expression: Introducing investigative journalism to local media in Mongolia*. Available from http://www.unvolunteers.org.

U.S. Department of State. *Country Reports on Human Rights Practices-Mongolia*. Available: http://www.state.gov.

World Bank. *Data and Statistics*. Available from http://www.worldbank.org.

World Desk Reference. Available: http://www.travel.dk.com.

—Clint B. Thomas Baldwin

MONTSERRAT

BASIC DATA

Official Country Name:	Montserrat
Region (Map name):	Caribbean
Population:	6,409
Language(s):	English
Literacy rate:	97%

Montserrat, a Caribbean island southeast of Puerto Rico, is in the process of rebuilding after volcanic eruptions began in 1995 and culminated in a catastrophic eruption in 1997. The Soufriere Hills volcano destroyed the southern half of the island, wiping out the airport and seaport and prompting as much as two-thirds of the population to flee to neighboring islands. The capital, Plymouth, was evacuated and, after being blanketed by volcanic ash, remains abandoned. Reconstruction efforts began in 1998, and slowly residents are returning to the area of the island called the ''Safe North.'' The population in 2001 was approximately 7,600 and growing. The official language is English, and the estimated literacy rate is 97 percent. Montserrat is a British dependency, and the chief of state is the British Monarch, who appoints a local Governor. Heading the government is a Chief Minister, who presides over a unicameral, 11-seat Legislative Council. Rice milling, electronic component assembly, and tourism were once the island's economic mainstays, but they were largely wiped out by the volcano. The economy is beginning to bounce back thanks to millions of dollars in British aid. Not surprisingly, one of the biggest economic growth areas is construction.

As a British dependency, Montserrat enjoys the same press freedoms. There is currently no daily newspaper. Before the volcanic crisis, the island boasted a number of weekly newspapers but currently only *The Montserrat Reporter* remains. Founded in 1985, the *The Montserrat Reporter* began as an instrument of the National Development Party but is considered politically independent today. It appears every Friday, and its circulation is approximately 750. It is available online.

There are three radio stations on the island, one AM and two FM, serving 7,000 radios. A single television station broadcasts to 3,000 televisions. There are 17 Internet service providers.

BIBLIOGRAPHY

''Country Profile,'' *Worldinformation.com (2002).* Available from http://www.worldinformation.com.

e-Mail correspondence, Merrick Andrews, *Montserrat Reporter* journalist, merrickandrews@hotmail.com.

''Media,'' *Media Courier (1999).* Available from http://www.mediacourier.net.

''Montserrat,'' *CIA World Fact Book (2001).* Available from http://www.cia.gov.

The Montserrat Reporter, (2002.) Home Page. Available from http://www.montserratreporter.org/.

—Jenny B. Davis

MOROCCO

BASIC DATA

Official Country Name:	Kingdom of Morocco
Region (Map name):	Africa
Population:	30,645,305
Language(s):	Arabic (official), Berber dialects, French
Literacy rate:	43.7%
Area:	446,550 sq km
Number of Television Stations:	35
Number of Television Sets:	3,100,000
Television Sets per 1,000:	101.2
Number of Satellite Subscribers:	957,000
Satellite Subscribers per 1,000:	31.2
Number of Radio Stations:	58
Number of Radio Receivers:	6,640,000
Radio Receivers per 1,000:	216.7
Number of Individuals with Computers:	350,000
Computers per 1,000:	11.4
Number of Individuals with Internet Access:	200,000
Internet Access per 1,000:	6.5

BACKGROUND & GENERAL CHARACTERISTICS

Between 1912 and 1956 Morocco was a protectorate within the French colonial empire of North Africa. After it won its independence, the kingdom of Morocco was left with a deeply rooted French cultural influence that went on to provide much of the framework for its judicial, political, and educational systems. Morocco also inherited a press formed and nurtured by French journalistic traditions. Historically, French newspapers reflect particular political viewpoints and social agendas. Rather than striving for factual and unbiased news reporting, they are essentially the journalistic expression of a given political ideology. Moroccan newspapers have continued this tradition and today provide their readers a steady flow of editorialized news. Each newspaper, whether nationally prominent or printing only a few thousand copies, reflects a given political tendency, encompassing varied political viewpoints from monarchist to communist. Morocco has also perpetuated a French concept of the freedom of the press, born out of the authoritarian regimes of the nineteenth century. Thus, the Moroccan government accepts mild forms of political criticism but tolerates no attack on the monarchy or Islam. Journalists and newspaper editors are considered professionals who must report the news, but they are also considered educated, patriotic citizens who should be mindful of their social responsibilities to the public. If newspapers in Morocco expect to remain in business, they must agree to exercise some form of restraint and to practice self-censorship. To guarantee that criticism of official policies remains within appropriate boundaries, the government grants a subsidy of 50 million dirhams to the press (approximately US$6 million) each year. Since advertising revenues and newsstand sales represent only a slim portion of the operating budget of most Moroccan newspapers, the yearly government subsidy provides an effective means to prevent the Moroccan press from operating with full autonomy.

Like other former French colonies of North Africa, Morocco enjoys the diversity of a bilingual press. Newspapers are published either in French or Arabic. Even after the country gained its independence in 1956, French was still used by the upper echelon of Moroccan society, while Arabic remained the spoken language of the masses. Since the 1970s, however, Arabic has gained a considerable popularity and Arabic-language newspapers have flourished, as Morocco underwent a process of reclaiming its cultural heritage. Today, French is still the language of the cultural elite in Morocco. It is the language of private schools, diplomats, and educated professionals, but Arabic newspapers now represent the majority of the Moroccan press. In 1983 the French-language newspaper *Le Matin* enjoyed the largest circulation of all Moroccan dailies, with 50,000 copies. That privilege belonged in 2002 to the Arabic-language newspaper *Al Ittahid Al Ichtiraki*, with a daily circulation of 110,000. In that year, Arabic dailies attracted a readership in excess of 260,000, while French-language newspapers reached about 200,000 people.

With a population of 30,645,395 (2002), a GDP of $108 billion, and a literacy rate of only 44 percent, Morocco publishes 22 major daily newspapers, with an aggregate circulation of 704,000 (circulation per thousand: 27.) The press consumes 19,000 metric tons of newsprint annually. Many new dailies have appeared since 1990, and their number continues to increase. Old vanguards of the past, such as the longest-running French language daily *Maroc-Soir* (established in 1908) and the pro-monarchist Arabic language newspaper *Al Mithaq Al Watani* (established in 1977), have disappeared. The most influential newspapers are published either in Rabat (the capital) or in Casablanca. In addition to the major national newspapers, Morocco also published a total of 644 dailies and weekly papers in 2001 (430 in Arabic, 199 in French, 8 in the Berber dialect, 6 in English, and 1 in Spanish) and over 700 periodicals with an aggregate circulation of 3,671,000.

In terms of circulation, the largest Moroccan daily newspapers were in 2001:

- *Al Ittihad Al Ichtiraki* (1983), socialist, published in Arabic, circulation: 110,000.
- *Le Matin du Sahara et du Maghreb* (1972), royalist, in French, circulation: 100,000.
- *Al Alam* (1946), published by the pro-government Istiqlal party, in Arabic, circulation: 100,000.
- *L'Opinion* (1965), published by the pro-government Istiqlal party, in French, circulation: 60,000.
- *Libé ration* (1964), democratic left, in French, circulation: 20,000.
- *Al Anbaa* (1963), official publication of the Moroccan Ministry of Information, in Arabic, circulation: 15,000.
- *Al Bayane* (1971), communist, in French, circulation: 5,000.

Among the most popular periodicals are *Maroc Hebdo International* (French), *Al Mouatine Assiyassi* (Arabic), *l'Economiste* (French), *Al Ayam* (Arabic), and *Jeune Afrique* (published in France).

ECONOMIC FRAMEWORK

In the past the majority of Moroccan newspapers did not represent actual commercial ventures or profit-making corporations, since they were essentially the written public outlet of political parties. As such they were owned by political interests and survived on contributions and government subsidies. In the last 10 years an influx of new capital has led to the creation of newspapers and periodicals that aspire to become commercially profitable. It should be noted, however, that the new publications are still heavily dependent on the government's budgetary allocations and that this reliance is inversely proportional to the professional autonomy of the younger generation of journalists. Out of the seven major Moroccan daily newspapers, four are pro-government (including one overtly royalist), two are issued by the Istiqlal coalition party, and another is published by the Moroccan Ministry of Information. The other three are in the opposition (center-left, socialist, and communist), but even that definition does not fully represent an independent political alternative. The new Moroccan prime minister is Abderrahamane Youssefi, who was once a left-wing activist, and a coalition of liberal royalist ideas and socialist tendencies seems to be the new political reality. The openly communist daily *Al Bayane*, a few far-left weeklies, and hard-line Islamic fundamentalist periodicals are the only means of true criticism in the Moroccan press. However, they are regularly harassed by the authorities, and their readership is quite limited. In terms of circulation, the pro-government dailies represent 75 percent of all major Moroccan newspapers, while the socialist, Arabic-language daily *Al Ittihad Al Ichtiraki* remains the most widely read paper in Morocco, with a circulation of 110,000.

Press Laws

The Moroccan press faces a double challenge when it seeks to operate within contemporary western standards of the freedom of the press. Political traditions inherited from the French and the authoritarianism of the monarchy have created a legal framework that allows the government to restrict the flow of information. Newspapers can be fined, suspended, or banned, and a journalist's freedom of expression limited for the purpose of guaranteeing social order or insuring national security. Morocco is a monarchy with a king possessing real and unchecked executive powers, and such a political construct is not easily compatible with the criticism and scrutiny of a free press. King Mohammed V instituted the first national press code in 1963 on the framework of the previous laws that had been in force under the French protectorate between 1912 and 1956. The code was later strengthened under his successor, King Hassan II. In 1999 the accession to the throne of his liberal-minded son, King Mohammed VI, had raised the hope of a radical reform of Moroccan press laws, but such aspirations have not been fully realized. The Parliamentary Commission for Foreign Affairs and National Defense adopted a new national press code on February 8, 2002. Somewhat more lenient than its predecessor (it contains fewer criminal penalties for libel), the code still maintains sentences of three to five years imprisonment for defaming the king or the royal family (as compared with five to twenty years imprisonment in the previous code.) Article 29 also gives the government the right to shut down any publication ''prejudicial to Islam, the monarchy, territorial integrity, or public order.'' Moroccan officials maintain that the kingdom enjoys a freedom of the press unparalleled in other Arab nations in the region. It is a fact that Morocco has never silenced political criticism in the press with the ruthlessness and violence evidenced in Algeria or the Sudan. King Mohammed VI and his ministers find themselves in the awkward position of moving Morocco into the twenty-first century, of being politically pro-western while exemplifying the values of a moderate Islamic nation. As the king declared in an interview he granted to *Al Sharq Al Awsat* in July 2001: ''Of course I am for press freedom, but I would like that freedom to be responsible. . . .I personally appreciate the critical role that the press and Moroccan journalists play in public debate, but we need to be careful not to give in to the temptation of the imported model. The risk is seeing our own values alienated. . . . There are limits set by the law.''

Censorship

Mindful of the increasing popularity of Islamic fundamentalism in the poorer sectors of the country (20 percent of the population lives under the poverty level), Morocco is trying to build a modern economy that could lift it out of chronic stagnation. It must also avoid the risk of antagonizing conservative clerics and activists who do not share the elite's predilection for western values. The press is expected to exercise restraint and self-control when dealing with criticism of official government policies. According to Reporters Without Borders and the Committee to Protect Journalists (CPJ), two international organizations dedicated to the protection of journalists' freedom of expression throughout the world, the actions of Moroccan officials against freedom of the press have increased in their severity since 2000. In its ''Middle East and North Africa Report,'' the CPJ indicates that three Moroccan weekly newspapers, *Le Journal, Al Sahiffa*, and *Demain* were permanently banned by the government in December 2000. They had published articles questioning Morocco's military activities in a disputed part of the Western Sahara and had investigated the possible involvement of Prime Minister Youssefi in a plot to assassinate the late King Hassan II in 1972. In April 2000 the editors of *Al Ousbou* and *Al Shamal* were sentenced to jail, ordered to pay fines, and banned from journalism for three years for investigative articles published on Moroccan Foreign Minister Muhammed Ben Aissa. Reporters Without Borders also reports than in 2001 the managing editor of *Le Journal Hebdomadaire* was sentenced to three months in jail and ordered to pay a fine of $200,000 for publishing a series of articles on the same foreign minister. These articles investigated allegations that the foreign minister misappropriated public funds while serving as ambassador to the United States.

State-Press Relations

In Morocco, state-press relations constitute a mutually grating and benefiting tug of war. The government supports the press with generous yearly subsidies, but it expects all journalists and editors to exercise restraint and to refrain from any negative criticism of the royal family, official state policies, or Islam. Investigative reporting is discouraged and most newspapers comply with the state's wishes by not addressing sensitive issues. In 2001 the Moroccan Ministry of Information allotted 20 million dirhams to be distributed among the major national newspapers. It also contributed ten million dirhams for the purchase of printing paper and international phone and fax bills. It paid another 10 million dirhams for the publication of legal and official announcements and an additional 10 million for various press-related expenses. The total budgeted amount for 2001 exceeded 50 million dirhams (US$6 million). Traditionally, that money is given for the encouragement and promotion of an independent press with high professional standards. By western standards, however, the very existence of such subsidies is difficult to reconcile with the establishment of an autonomous press. The Moroccan government also exerts another measure of control on the press by requiring every journalist, editor, or foreign correspondent to qualify for an official press card. The number of these cards has increased from 921 in 1992 to 1,097 in 1999.

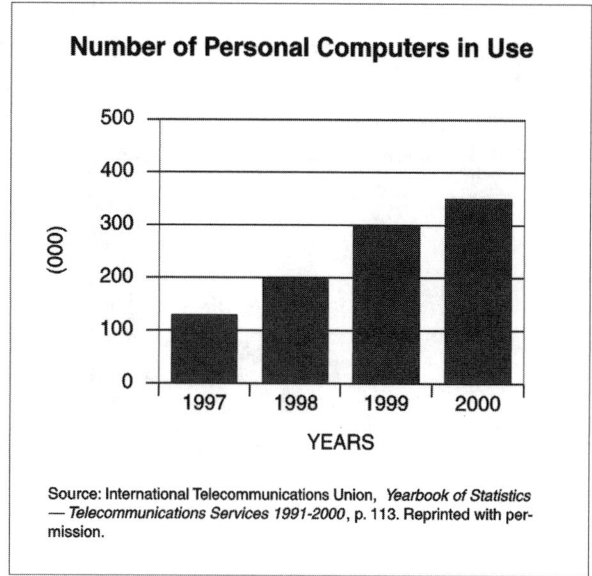

Source: International Telecommunications Union, *Yearbook of Statistics — Telecommunications Services 1991-2000*, p. 113. Reprinted with permission.

Attitude toward Foreign Media

French newspapers and periodicals still attract a large number of readers in Morocco. Major Parisian newspapers, such as *Le Figaro* and *Le Monde*, are widely read among Moroccan professionals. English, Spanish, and American publications are also available, and they provide a welcome (if at times censored) source of alternate information, especially for sensitive or potentially damaging information dealing with Moroccan foreign policy or the royal family. The U.S. press, however, is largely seen among younger professionals and English-speaking students as presenting a unilateral, capitalistic, and pro-Israeli point of view. When searching foreign media for news dealing with the Arab world, Moroccan intellectuals are more likely to turn to French newspapers and periodicals, since the majority of French media is traditionally pro-Palestinian. American newspapers are often distrusted and suspected of being controlled by Jewish interests.

The success of the foreign press in offering Moroccan readers stimulating investigative reporting is illustrated by the vehemence of censorship and harassment it endures on a regular basis. In 2001 alone, the Spanish newspapers *El País* (7/22) and *El Mundo* (9/6), the Spanish weeklies *Cambio* (3/19) and *Hola* (11/23), the French daily *Le Figaro* (3/4) (7/5), and the French weeklies *Le Canard Enchainé* (10/31), *VDS* (3/7), *Jeune Afrique* (3/15), and *Courrier International* (5/17) were intercepted, blocked, seized, or otherwise removed from the newsstands by the Moroccan police. On November 4, 2001, Claude Juvénal, the Rabat bureau chief of Agence France-Presse (AFP), was ordered to leave the country because of his investigative reports on alleged corruption in the armed forces.

News Agencies

The Associated Press (AP) and Agence France-Presse (AFP) maintain active accredited bureaus throughout Morocco. The Maghreb Arab Press Agency (MAP), inaugurated in 1977, has become one of the largest news agencies in the Arab world. A state-owned corporation, it is headquartered in Rabat and has 10 regional and 17 international offices.

Electronic News Media

The development of the Internet has brought a new dimension to news reporting in Morocco. Many of the major dailies and weeklies can now be accessed on their own Web sites. The number of Internet users has dramatically increased to over 120,000 in 2002, with eight Internet Service Providers (ISP) in operation. In 1996 the government created *Mincom Ilaycom*, a large official Web site with a search engine, for the purpose of disseminating official information about Morocco (www.mincom.gov.ma). It was followed by the launching of Marweb.com, another search engine and reference data bank particularly useful for its weekly review of the Moroccan press. In 2001 Morocco had 1,425,000 telephones (including 116,645 cell phones,) 27 AM and 25 FM radio stations (with 6.65 million sets), and 35 TV stations with 3.1 million TV sets. Satellite relays, optical cables, dish systems, and digital equipment now bring Arab, European, and American television programming into every region of the country.

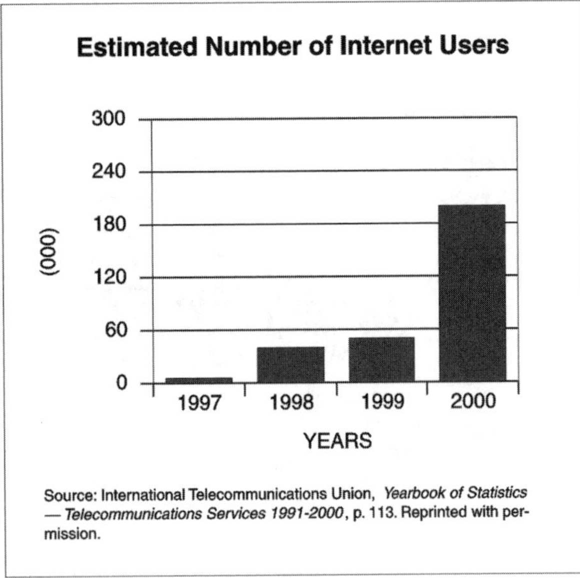

Source: International Telecommunications Union, *Yearbook of Statistics — Telecommunications Services 1991-2000*, p. 113. Reprinted with permission.

EDUCATION & TRAINING

Moroccan journalists are trained at the Higher Institute of Journalism, established in 1980, which operates an influential alumni association (the ALISJ), and at the Higher Institute of Information and Communication (ISIC), established in 1996. Several professional press organizations also play an important role in setting standards and defending their members' rights: the National Union of the Moroccan Press (SNPM), established in 1963, which receives an annual government subsidy of 200,000 dirhams, the Moroccan branch of the International Union of French-Speaking Journalists (UJIPLF) and the Press Club, established in 1992, which also receives an official yearly subsidy of 200,000 dirhams.

SUMMARY

The Moroccan press faces the challenges and the hopes that are common to developing North African nations. The press and the government are locked in a mutually dependent relationship that creates both encouraging opportunities and disturbing issues involving a journalist's need to report the news in an impartial and unhindered manner. The Moroccan press is growing and has made great strides since the 1960s toward achieving its autonomy. The government keeps controlling the press via generous subsidies and repeated censorship. It fosters a climate of subtle intimidation that seriously impairs Moroccan newspapers and periodicals from openly questioning government policies and established societal traditions. Morocco justifies this attitude by maintaining that it must moderately muzzle the press if it ever hopes to succeed as a pro-western, moderate Islamic nation in a region of the world where fanaticism is a constant menace to civil liberties.

BIBLIOGRAPHY

The Central Intelligence Agency (CIA). *2001 World Factbook.* Directorate of Intelligence, 2002. Available from http://www.cia.gov/.

Committee to Protect Journalists. Available from http://www.cpj.org/.

The Editor and Publisher International Yearbook. 81st edition. 2001.

Kingdom of Morocco. Available from http://www.mincom.gov.ma

Marweb.com. Available from http://www.marweb.com/.

Mohamed El Kobbi, *L'Etat et la Presse au Maroc.* Paris: L'auteur, 1992.

Mohammed Rhazi, *Introduction à l'Etude de la Presse au Maroc,* Dissertation: Université de Paris II. 1981.

Organisation Marocaine des Droits de l'Homme, *Liberté de la Presse et de l'Information au Maroc: Limites et Perspectives.* Rabat: OMDH, 1995.

Reporters without Borders. Available from http://www.rsf.org

UNESCO Statistical Yearbook, 1999

—Eric H. du Plessis

MOZAMBIQUE

BASIC DATA

Official Country Name:	Republic of Mozambique
Region (Map name):	Africa
Population:	19,371,057
Language(s):	Portuguese (official), indigenous dialects
Literacy rate:	42.3%
Area:	801,590 sq km
GDP:	3,754 (US$ millions)
Number of Television Stations:	1
Number of Television Sets:	67,600
Television Sets per 1,000:	3.5
Number of Radio Stations:	41
Number of Radio Receivers:	730,000

Radio Receivers per 1,000:	37.7
Number of Individuals with Computers:	60,000
Computers per 1,000:	3.1
Number of Individuals with Internet Access:	30,000
Internet Access per 1,000:	1.5

BACKGROUND & GENERAL CHARACTERISTICS

Mozambique, formerly Portuguese East Africa, is located in East Africa, just across from the island of Madagascar. Mozambique is bordered by South Africa (south); Zimbabwe, Swaziland, and South Africa (west); Tanzania (north); Malawi and Zambia (northwest); and the Indian Ocean (east). Its capital is Maputo, which was called Lourenco Marques during the days of Portuguese colonial rule.

In 2002 Mozambique's population was almost 20 million people. It is expected to reach 33.3 by 2025 and soar to 47.8 million by 2050. More than 96 percent of the population is made up of black Africans, with smaller groups of Portuguese, Asians, and mulattos (mixed racial descent). Although Portuguese is the official language, there are also many African languages spoken throughout the country.

The Portuguese started coming to East Africa in the sixteenth century. By the next century, the Portuguese were competing with Arabs for trade in gold, slaves, and ivory. Despite strong African resistance, Portuguese colonials slowly extended their control from the coast toward the interior where many of the indigenous people lived. By the end of the nineteenth century, when Europe held its "Scramble for Africa," what is now Mozambique was ceded to Portuguese control.

Although in some of the British-controlled colonies in Africa it was expected that indigenous Africans would ultimately get a chance to run their own affairs, there were no such illusions by the Portuguese, who regarded their colonies as permanent "overseas provinces." The Portuguese said that the colonies could send representatives to sit in the Portuguese legislature, and they also followed an "assimilado" policy, which meant that Africans who had the proper education and backgrounds could aspire to be assimilated into Portuguese culture. In other words, they would become Portuguese, instead of Mozambicans. Initially, the Mozambique Company took over control of the country and used its authority to force the Africans to pay taxes and work on plantations, but this ended in 1926 as the Portuguese government decided to reassert itself. By 1951 Portugal had transformed Mozambique into an overseas province, as distinct from a colony.

As other European colonies in Africa and Asia achieved independence, Mozambique's Africans began to organize to resist Portuguese rule. These efforts eventually resulted in various black groups coming together, on June 25, 1962, to form the Mozambique Liberation Front (FRELIMO). In September 1964, FRELIMO launched guerrilla warfare against the Portuguese, who responded by sending in reinforcements to try and contain the spreading conflict. Soon after that, the new Portuguese government initiated negotiations with FRELIMO and also with other guerrilla groups in Angola and Portuguese Guinea. The talks, in neighboring Lusaka, Zambia, between FRELIMO and Portuguese representatives resulted in Mozambican gaining its independence from Portugal at midnight on June 24, 1975. The FRELIMO party, during its liberation days and its headquarters in neighboring Tanzania, had developed strong ties with the Soviet Union, which had armed and trained some of its guerrillas. At independence, Mozambique continued its close ties with the Soviet Union and took some steps to implement socialism. FRELIMO regarded itself as a vanguard movement, similar to the communist parties of the Soviet Union, Cuba, China and Eastern European countries, whose mission was to transform society. Under the revised November 1990 constitution, Mozambique became a parliamentary multiparty democracy. Mozambique's history of struggle helped shape the media system that the country inherited from its Portuguese colonial masters.

Media History Portuguese is the Mozambique's official language. Other languages are Makua-Lomwe, Tsonga, Shona, and Swahili. Life expectancy is 47 years for men and 50 for women, although this is likely to drop as the HIV/AIDS epidemic continues to ravage the country.

Literacy is low; an estimated two-thirds of the population is illiterate. In 2002 education was compulsory for those aged 7 to 14. Under Portuguese rule, educational opportunities for blacks were almost non-existent; only a few of the elite got a chance to study in Portugal. As of 1997, there were 1.74 million children in 5,689 preprimary school institutions; 1.89 million children in 6,025 primary schools; 51,554 students in 75 high schools; 12,001 students in 25 technical institutions; and 7,156 students in 3 colleges/universities.

The road for the media in Mozambique has been a rocky one. Under Portuguese rule, there were no independent media outlets. Illiteracy was so high among the Africans that indigenous newspapers were not feasible. The first newspaper in Mozambique was the *Lourenco Marques Guardian*, which started publishing in 1905. It was published in the country's capital city, and its target audience was the British community within the city. The Roman Catholic Church acquired the *Guardian* in 1956, changed its name to *Diario*, and began publishing it biweekly in English and Portuguese. After continuing policy conflicts between the archbishop of Lourenco Marques and the more liberal bishop in Beira, *Noticias da Beira* became the country's second newspaper in 1918. *Noticias da Beira* was a biweekly newspaper, also published in English and Portuguese. Fourteen years later, in 1932, the bishop was supported in the launching of *A Vox Africana*, by local Africans.

In 1950 the bishop was at it again, this time with the launch of *Diario de Mocambique*, a daily Beira newspaper. His move was matched by the Lourenco Marques archbishop who turned *Diario* into a daily newspaper. Another newspaper appeared in 1926, started by a retired Portuguese military officer. It was called *Noticias* and was a Portuguese language publication based in Lourenco Marques. *Noticias* became the country's official Portuguese newspaper. In 1975 the FRELIMO government took over *Noticias*, which became a government-controlled publication. *Noticias da Beira* remained the country's second newspaper, but all other daily newspapers disappeared as the country embarked on its Marxist-Leninist path under Machel. Agencia de Informacao de Mocambique (AIM) is the country's domestic news agency, a government-run institution charged with collecting and distributing news about Mozambique and cooperating with other news agencies, including the Pan African News Agency. Reuters, Novosti, and German, Italian, and Portuguese news organizations have also been allowed to operate in Mozambique.

The 1990 constitution opened up the political process to competition, but it also gave the media more freedom from government control and interference. Mozambique has moved away from its post-independence rigid Marxist-Leninist tendencies, where the media was seen as nothing more than a propaganda organ. State-controlled Radio Mozambique remains the country's main source of news and information. Private and commercial radio stations are also allowed to operate, unlike in neighboring Zimbabwe. An estimated 40 community radio and television stations, supported by UNESCO and the government, exist around the country. Parts of the country also get BBC World Service and RTP, the Portuguese television's African service. In 1995 there were 660,000 radio receivers; by 1997 this had increased to 730,000. During the same period, the number of television receivers went from 60,000 to 90,000. The number of listeners and viewers is much higher because radios and televisions are shared among family members, friends, neighbors, and communities, with a resultant multiplier effect in total audiences. The new constitution protects freedom of the media and has resulted in a number of radio stations, including those linked to the RENAMO opposition group, the Roman Catholic Church, and even one that is youth-oriented.

Circulation of the print media is limited because of the high illiteracy levels in the country. However, in 1995 it was estimated that there were three daily newspapers with a circulation of 130,000. By 1996 the number of daily papers had dropped to two, and the circulation had plummeted. The major newspapers are *Diario de Mozambique* (*Mozambique Daily*), established in 1981 and published in Beira; *Demos Portuguese*, published in Maputo; *Noticias* (*News*), established in 1926 and published in Maputo; *Savana*, a Portuguese weekly that was established in 1994 and published in Maputo; and *Domingo*, another Portuguese weekly that was established in 1981 and published in Maputo. Other newspapers include *O'Popular*, a privately owned daily, and *Fim de Semana*, a privately owned weekly tabloid.

The only newspaper with a circulation in the 25,000 to 50,000 range is the Portuguese language *Noticias*, which is also the country's largest newspaper. *Diario de Mozambique*, the country's other daily, falls in the 10,000 to 25,000 circulation category. These two are also the most influential newspapers in the country. There are four non-daily newspapers, with an estimated total circulation of 160,000.

Economic Framework

Although Mozambique averages 55 inches of rainfall per year, it usually imports food. Its agricultural products include shrimp, fish, tea, sisal, coconuts, corn, millet, cassava, and peanuts. Tantalite, gold, iron ore, titanium, oil, and natural gas are among some of the minerals found in Mozambique. Although Mozambique was still desperately poor in 2002, with an average annual income of U.S. $210, the economy was improving, unemployment was dropping, and there was positive economic growth over the past few years.

Censorship

There is no overt censorship in Mozambique, but there is a certain level of self-censorship. The new Mozambique constitution protects press freedom, which has allowed Mozambican journalists to write stories critical of the government, without fear of victimization. Journalists have also been critical of official corruption and mismanagement. Although the media is free to write, publish, and broadcast what they want, they face criminal libel laws, which may have a chilling effect on their ability to gather and disseminate news and information. The private sector has not been spared from scrutiny. A crusading editor was, however, killed, and there was widespread speculation that his assassination was because of the dirt he had uncovered on certain people in public life.

ATTITUDE TOWARD FOREIGN MEDIA

The government owns *Noticias* and also runs Agencia Informacao Mocambique (AIM), the country's domestic news agency. In the past, only Cuban, communist, and African journalists and news agencies were welcome. At that time, Mozambique espoused a Marxist-Leninist philosophy, which regarded the media as appendages of the ruling party, whose role was to propagate the policies and philosophies of FRELIMO. Western journalists and media were not welcome. Western journalists and media now are welcome in Mozambique. Portuguese newspapers and magazines are now available. Portuguese journalists and others from the Western countries operate freely. Although the opposition complains that it does not get enough coverage in the media, that claim is less valid in the 2000s than in the past. Even the government media gives coverage to the opposition party.

EDUCATION & TRAINING

There is a great need to recruit and train talented journalists. The British and Canadians have provided some training and skills courses for Mozambican media personnel. There have also been short courses and seminars held in Mozambique, Zimbabwe, Zambia, Namibia, and South Africa, which have given the Mozambicans some hands-on training, as well as opportunities to meet and work with fellow Southern African media practitioners. But, the need for media personnel in Mozambique is great.

SUMMARY

Mozambique's political process was opened up to multi-party competition and a new constitution guaranteed press freedom and opened up the country to multiple voices. The future of the media is much brighter in Mozambique in 2002 than it was 15 years ago. Mozambique seems to have adopted many democratic trappings, including acceptance of the often adversarial relationship between the government and the media. Media workers operate in an environment where the government has become less intrusive and less threatening. Improved opportunities in education, an economy that is improving, and the availability of more consumer goods to more people are among other factors making Mozambicans more optimistic about their future.

BIBLIOGRAPHY

Africa, 7th edition. Worldmark Press Ltd., 1988.

British Broadcasting Corporation. *Country Profile: Mozambique*, 2002.

Merrill, John C., ed. *Global Journalism: Survey of International Communication*, second edition. New York: Longman, 1993.

''Newspapers of Africa.'' *International Editor and Publisher Yearbook*, 2002.

World Almanac and Book of Facts 2002. PRIMEDIA Reference Inc., 2002.

—*Tendayi S. Kumbula*

MYANMAR

BASIC DATA

Official Country Name:	Union of Myanmar
Region (Map name):	Southeast Asia
Population:	41,994,678
Language(s):	Burmese, minority ethnic groups have their own languages
Literacy rate:	83.0%
Area:	678,500 sq km
Number of Television Stations:	2
Number of Television Sets:	320,000
Television Sets per 1,000:	7.6
Number of Satellite Subscribers:	1,758
Number of Radio Stations:	8
Number of Radio Receivers:	4,200,000
Radio Receivers per 1,000:	100.0
Number of Individuals with Computers:	52,000
Computers per 1,000:	1.2
Number of Individuals with Internet Access:	7,000
Internet Access per 1,000:	0.2

BACKGROUND & GENERAL CHARACTERISTICS

Censorship characterizes Myanmar media. The Union of Myanmar, as Burma was renamed in 1989 after a military junta established the State Law and Order Restoration Council (SLORC), is controlled by a rigid socialist government directed by the armed forces. Media can only report news sanctioned by the government. Minimal international news is reported. Aung Zaw, editor of *Irrawaddy* magazine, described journalism in Myanmar as ''comatose.''

At least four Burmese-language and two English daily newspapers circulate. Myanmar newspapers print official decrees such as the 1982 citizenship law. *Myanma Alin* (New Light of Myanmar), published since 1914, is distributed in four languages and contains daily government press releases and negative international wire articles about countries critical of Myanmar. Editorial cartoons denounce the opposition's National League for Democracy. In summer 1988, Burmese media briefly experienced relaxation of rigid rules. Millions of democratic protestors peacefully demonstrated. Government newspapers reported factually about this democratic movement, and newspapers and periodicals were created to chronicle events. On September 18, the military led by Lieutenant General Khin Nyunt violently subdued the protestors. The junta stopped all but two newspapers, and they reverted to printing warnings, military slogans, and martial laws for Burmese citizens. Khin Nyunt blamed the media for provoking the demonstrations and accused reporters of falsifying stories.

Conditions for Burmese journalists have worsened. Monitored by the Military Intelligence Service, imprisonment, or hard labor sentences, reporters cautiously prepare media that the government cannot interpret as offensive. Myanmar officials are especially angered by media they think might cause people to regard the government disrespectfully. Most Burmese realize that news is for the most part manufactured to portray the junta as Myanmar's best rulers.

Imprisoned Burmese editors San San Nweh and U Win Tin received the 2001 Golden Pen of Freedom from the World Association of Newspapers. Charged with supporting freedom of expression and democracy, the editors refused to denounce those beliefs in order to be released. Like many jailed Burmese journalists, they suffered poor health due to their captivity and beatings by prison guards. San San Nweh was specifically arrested for giving human rights reports to European journalists. Editor of the daily *Hanthawati* newspaper, U Win Tin was tried and convicted by a military court for allegations of belonging to the Communist Party of Burma. His incarceration was lengthened because writing materials were found in his cell.

Burmese media professionals have persevered. Exiled Burmese journalists can write factually about their homeland for international media use. Many Burmese journalists live in Thailand so they can clandestinely distribute publications into neighboring Myanmar. In Norway, the Democratic Voice of Burma is a dissident news service.

STATE-PRESS RELATIONS

Prior to military rule in the late twentieth century, Burma had an active media. Burma's first newspaper, *The Maulmain Chronicle*, was published in 1836 as an English weekly while Burma was a British colony. The Burmese monarch, King Mindon, encouraged newspaper publication and entertained editors at his palace. He supported the creation of *Yadanaopon*, the first newspaper printed entirely in Burmese. The media was essential in resisting colonial rulers. Burma gained independence from Great Britain in 1948. At least thirty Burmese, English, and Chinese language newspapers were permitted to report domestic and international news, interview prime ministers, and interact with journalists worldwide. U Thaung founded *Kyemon* (The Mirror Daily) in 1957, and its 90,000 circulation was Burma's largest. Although most southeastern Asian governments promoted state-regulated censorship, Burma supported freedom of the press.

A 1962 military coup which resulted in General Ne Win declaring himself dictator of Burma altered the country's media. Wanting to isolate Burma to achieve his socialist agenda, the general decided which newspapers could be nationalized and remain in circulation and which publications would be halted. He formed the Press Scrutiny Board, which still existed in the early twenty-first century, to regulate censorship. All journalism organizations were disbanded. Ne Win demanded the arrest of media professionals he considered hostile to his policies. Foreign journalists were ordered to depart Burma, and many Burmese reporters either quit their jobs or went into exile.

Political parties were united into the Burma Socialist Program Party, which further tightened control of the press. The 1962 Printers' and Publishers' Registration Act stated that only government-approved media could apply for the annual licenses that were mandatory for operation. Media was ordered to focus on topics supportive of Burma's socialist revolution. By December 1965, private newspapers were forbidden. Military leaders established The Working People's Daily as the official distributor of government news. The bureaucracy controlled access to limited supplies of newsprint and paper. The traditional Burmese media was effectively paralyzed.

CENSORSHIP

Censorship involves inking over passages, tearing out pages, and preventing material from being printed by reviewing material before approving it for publication. Many magazines and books in Myanmar are missing thick sections and covered with black ink. Some censors can be bribed to assure publication.

The government tries to block news regarding any negative events in Burma, with the end of keeping the current government in power. Because reporters cannot prepare factual accounts about topics that the government considers taboo, news is unreliable. Political enemies such as opposition leaders are described unfavorably, and all state-owned media is required to present these opinions. Events that are covered internationally, such as opposition leader and Nobel Peace Prize laureate Aung San Suu Kyi's release in 1995, are restricted from Myanmar media. The Ministry of Information indoctrinates government journalists at journalism courses. Reporters are expected to write pro-government propaganda and never criticize leaders or their political actions. Articles are not to mention political corruption, reform, education, and HIV/AIDS. Even stories telling about losing Myanmar sports teams and torrential rainstorms are forbidden. The press is not welcome at government meetings.

In 1998, the Committee to Protect Journalists (CPJ) identified Myanmar and Indonesia as the most hostile Asian environments for media. Rumors circulated that Myanmar military police had tortured and killed two journalists because their newspaper, *The Mirror*, had accidentally published a photograph of Khin Nyunt next to a headline describing criminals. Such placement of photographs and headlines has occasionally occurred, and readers realize it might be a subversive reaction to enduring censorship laws and political conditions. Journalists often try to hide information and criticisms in media through careful wording or images.

Unlike other newspapers in Myanmar, *The Myanmar Times* is not forced to comply with junta press regulations. Published weekly in Burmese and English at Rangoon since 2000, *The Myanmar Times*, with a total circulation of 30,000, is edited by an Australian journalist, Ross Dunkley. He has been permitted to print exclusive articles about discussions between the Myanmar junta and Suu Kyi. Media professionals speculate that Dunkley is allowed more press freedom because Khin Nyunt and Office of Strategic Studies (OSS) representatives are using *The Myanmar Times* to convince international readers to accept the junta. Other publications are also designed to attract foreign approval, especially in the form of investments. For example, in the 1990s, the monthly business magazines *Dana* (Prosperity) and *Myanmar Dana* were issued in a superior quality compared to other Burmese media in order to impress readers.

ATTITUDE TOWARD FOREIGN MEDIA

Any international news included in Myanmar media is censored. Events such as political strife, deposed leaders, human rights trials, and student protests in other countries, especially in Asia, are either omitted or described briefly with no details. Foreign reporters are discouraged from visiting Myanmar and sometimes can only enter the country by concealing their profession and securing a tourist visa. The junta deports and blacklists foreign correspondents who attempt to report on the opposition movement. Any reporters that the Myanmar authorities allow in the country are closely monitored.

BROADCAST MEDIA

Because Myanmar is impoverished, isolated, and only has electrical services in approximately 10 percent of its territory, people have limited use of radios and televisions. Sources estimated that there were 3.3 million radios and 80,000 televisions in Myanmar in 2001. The Myanmar government radio station, Burma Broadcasting Service, airs broadcasts that primarily reach urban populations. The government-monitored transmissions play only approved programs, which do not include Western songs or other broadcasts considered contrary to government policies. Shortwave radios are the only means for Burmese residents to gain access to foreign news reports. Some Burmese can receive Voice of America and British Broadcasting Corporation (BBC) programming. They can also secretly broadcast reports to listeners who can pick up their signal.

Initiated in 1980, the government-owned television station has color transmission capabilities but only broadcasts a few shows on evenings and weekends. The Video Act of 1985 outlined what media could tape. Internet access in Burma is rare, and computer laws require government approval for use or ownership of computers, modems, and fax machines which can connect Myanmar with international resources and influences.

BIBLIOGRAPHY

Bunge, Frederica M., ed. *Burma: A Country Study*. 3rd ed. Washington, DC: Federal Research Division Library of Congress, 1983.

Luzoe. *Myanmar Newspaper Reader*. Kensington, MD: Dunwoody Press, 1996.

Neumann, A. Lin. ''The Survival of Burmese Journalism.'' *Harvard Asia Quarterly* 6 (Winter 2002). Available from www.fas.harvard.edu.

Nunn, Godfrey R., compiler. *Burmese and Thai Newspapers: An International Union List*. Taipei: Ch'eng-wen Pub. Co., 1972.

Thaung, U. *A Journalist, a General, and an Army in Burma*. Bangkok: White Lotus, 1995.

—*Elizabeth D. Schafer*